The Cambridge Wagner Encyclopedia

Richard Wagner is one of the most controversial figures in Western cultural history. He revolutionized not only opera but the very concept of art, and his works and ideas have had an immeasurable impact on both the cultural and political landscapes of the late nineteenth and twentieth centuries. From "absolute music" to "Zurich" and from "Theodor Adorno" to "Hermann Zumpe," the vividly written entries of *The Cambridge Wagner Encyclopedia* have been contributed by recognized authorities and cover a comprehensive range of topics. More than eighty scholars from around the world, representing disciplines from history and philosophy to film studies and medicine, provide fascinating insights into Wagner's life, career, and influence. Multiple appendices include listings of Wagner's works, historic productions, recordings, and addresses where he lived, to round out a volume that will be an essential and reliable resource for enthusiasts and academics alike.

NICHOLAS VAZSONYI is Jesse Chapman Alcorn Memorial Professor of Foreign Languages and Professor of German and Comparative Literature, Department of Languages, Literatures & Cultures at the University of South Carolina. His first book *Lukács Reads Goethe* (1997) was followed by two edited volumes, one on German national identity formation between 1750 and 1871 (2000) and the other entitled *Wagner's "Meistersinger": Performance, History, Representation* (2003). His latest book *Richard Wagner: Self-Promotion and the Making of a Brand* (2010) recently appeared in German translation as *Richard Wagner: Entstehung einer Marke* (2012). He is co-organizer with Anno Mungen (University of Bayreuth) of the WagnerWorldWide 2013 project, a series of linked lectures and conferences around the world, to be capped by an edited volume. In 2013, he joined the editorial team of the German journal *wagnerspectrum*.

The Cambridge
Wagner Encyclopedia

Edited by
NICHOLAS VAZSONYI

CAMBRIDGE
UNIVERSITY PRESS

CAMBRIDGE
UNIVERSITY PRESS

University Printing House, Cambridge CB2 8BS, United Kingdom

Published in the United States of America by Cambridge University Press, New York

Cambridge University Press is part of the University of Cambridge.

It furthers the University's mission by disseminating knowledge in the pursuit of education, learning and research at the highest international levels of excellence.

www.cambridge.org
Information on this title: www.cambridge.org/9781107004252

© Cambridge University Press 2013

First published 2013

Printed in the United Kingdom by TJ International Ltd. Padstow Cornwall

A catalogue record for this publication is available from the British Library

Library of Congress Cataloguing in Publication data
The Cambridge Wagner encyclopedia / Edited by Nicholas Vazsonyi.
       pages   cm
Includes bibliographical references and index.
ISBN 978-1-107-00425-2 (Hardback)
1. Wagner, Richard, 1813–1883–Encyclopedias.   I. Vazsonyi, Nicholas, 1963–
ML410.W1C36 2013
782.1092–dc23   2012051615

ISBN 978-1-107-00425-2 Hardback

Contents

Music examples

Examples are numbered consecutively throughout the volume, and listed here in order of appearance, starting with the entry name. The *LEITMOTIVE* of the *RING* listed in Appendix 4 are numbered separately, and are identified with a CWE prefix.

Contributors

ROGER ALLEN
Fellow and Tutor in Music, Dean
St. Peter's College, Oxford University

CELIA APPLEGATE
Professor of History
Vanderbilt University, Nashville

NICHOLAS ATTFIELD
Lecturer of Music
Oxford University

MATTHEW BAILEYSHEA
Associate Professor of Music Theory
Eastman School of Music,
    Rochester

EVAN BAKER
Independent scholar
Los Angeles

DAVID E. BARCLAY
Margaret and Roger Scholten Professor of
    International Studies
Kalamazoo College, Michigan

JOHN W. BARKER
Professor Emeritus of History
University of Wisconsin, Madison

MARK BERRY
Lecturer in Music, Royal Holloway
University of London

PETER BLOOM
Grace Jarco Ross 1933 Professor of
    Humanities
Smith College, Northampton

DIETER BORCHMEYER
Professor Emeritus of German Literature /
    Heidelberg University

DAVID BRECKBILL
Adjunct Professor of Music
Doane College, Nebraska

WERNER BREIG
Professor Emeritus of Music History
University of Erlangen

MATT BRIBITZER-STULL
Associate Professor of Music Theory
    and Composition
University of Minnesota,
    Minneapolis

STEPHEN BROCKMANN
Professor of German
Carnegie Mellon University,
    Pittsburgh

JEREMY COLEMAN
Doctoral Candidate in Music History
King's College, London

DAVID CORMACK
Independent scholar
London

ADRIAN DAUB
Assistant Professor of German
Stanford University

JOHN DEATHRIDGE
King Edward Professor of Music
King's College, London

JAMES DEAVILLE
Professor of Music
Carleton University, Ottawa

DAVID B. DENNIS
Professor of History
Loyola University, Chicago

JOHANNA DOMBOIS
Opera stage director and author
Cologne

MÁRTON DORNBACH
Assistant Professor of German Studies
Stanford University

STEPHEN C. DOWNES
Head of Music, Director of Music Research
University of Surrey, Guildford

ULRICH DRÜNER
Independent scholar
Stuttgart

GLENN EHRSTINE
Associate Professor German and
* International Studies*
University of Iowa

BARBARA EICHNER
Lecturer in Musicology
Oxford Brookes University

BARRY EMSLIE
Cultural Critic
Berlin

JASON GEARY
Assistant Professor of Musicology
University of Michigan, Ann Arbor

WILLIAM GIBBONS
Assistant Professor of Musicology
Texas Christian University, Fort Worth

SANDER L. GILMAN
Distinguished Professor of the Liberal Arts
* and Sciences*
Emory University, Atlanta

HERMANN GRAMPP
Doctoral Candidate in Music History
Freie Universität, Berlin

THOMAS S. GREY
Professor of Music
Stanford University

KAAREN GRIMSTAD
Associate Professor of Scandinavian Studies
University of Minnesota, Minneapolis

ERLING E. GULDBRANDSEN
Professor, Department of Musicology
University of Oslo

JOSEPH HOROWITZ
Independent scholar
New York

DAVID HUCKVALE
Independent scholar
Bedfordshire

MARION KANT
Director of Studies in German
Pembroke College, University of Cambridge

KEVIN KARNES
Associate Professor of Music History
Emory University, Atlanta

ULRIKE KIENZLE
Independent scholar
Germany

WILLIAM KINDERMAN
Professor of Musicology
University of Illinois, Urbana-Champaign

HELMUT KIRCHMEYER
Professor Emeritus of Music History
University of Düsseldorf

LUTZ KOEPNICK
Gertrude Conaway Vanderbilt Professor of
* German and Film Studies*
Vanderbilt University, Nashville, Tennessee

JULIET KOSS
Associate Professor of Art History
Scripps College, Claremont

GUNDULA KREUZER
Associate Professor of Music History
Yale University, New Haven

ALEXIS LUKO
Assistant Professor of Musicology
Carleton University, Ottawa

ROBERTA MONTEMORRA MARVIN
Professor of Music, Director International
* Programs*
University of Iowa

LYDIA MAYNE
Ph.D. Candidate in Music History
Stanford University

STEPHEN MCCLATCHIE
Professor of Music and Principal
Huron University College, London, ON

PATRICK MCCRELESS
Professor of Music Theory
Yale University, New Haven

WILLIAM MELTON
Independent scholar
Hauset, Belgium

MARGARET ELEANOR MENNINGER
Associate Professor of History
Texas State University, San Marcos

STEPHEN MEYER
Associate Professor of Music History & Cultures
Syracuse University

MARGARET MINER
Associate Professor of French
University of Illinois, Chicago

RYAN MINOR
Associate Professor of Music Hisotry
and Theory
State University of New York, Stony Brook

YVONNE NILGES
Privat-Dozent in German Literature
Heidelberg University

JAMES PARSONS
Professor of Music History
Missouri State University

SANNA PEDERSON
Mavis C. Pitman Professor of Music
University of Oklahoma, Norman

PAMELA M. POTTER
Professor of Musicology
University of Wisconsin, Madison

EVA RIEGER
Emeritus Professor of Liberal Arts and Human
Sciences
University of Bremen

MICHAEL SAFFLE
Professor, College of Liberal Arts and Human
Sciences
Virginia Polytechnic Institute and State
University, Blacksburg

HANNU SALMI
Professor of Cultural History
University of Turku, Finland

DANIEL SHERIDAN
Ph.D. Candidate in Cultural Mediations
(Musical Culture)
Carleton University, Ottawa

ERIC SCHNEEMAN
Ph.D. Candidate in Musicology
University of Southern California, Los Angeles

NA'AMA SHEFFI
Professor of History, School of Communication
Sapir College, Negev

MATTHEW WILSON SMITH
Associate Professor of Comparative Literature
Cornell University, Ithaca

SEBASTIAN STAUSS
Wiss. Mitarbeiter, Institut für
Theaterwissenschaft
Ludwig-Maximilians-Universität, Munich

ANTHONY J. STEINHOFF
Professeur régulier d'histoire
Université de Québec à Montréal

EMMA SUTTON
Lecturer, School of English
University of St Andrews

KATHERINE SYER
Assistant Professor of Musicology
and Theatre
University of Illinois, Urbana-Champaign

CHRISTIAN THORAU
Professor of Musicology
Universität Potsdam

CORINNA TREITEL
Associate Professor of History
Washington University in St. Louis

DAVID TRIPPETT
Junior Research Fellow in Musicology
Christ's College, University of Cambridge

ULRICH TRÖHLER
Professor Emeritus of the History of Medicine
Institute of Social and Preventive Medicine,
  University of Berne

LAURA TUNBRIDGE
Senior Lecturer in Music
University of Manchester

HANS RUDOLF VAGET
Helen and Laura Shedd Professor Emeritus of
  German Studies
Smith College, Northampton

STEVEN G. VANDE MOORTELE
Assistant Professor of Music Theory
University of Toronto

NICHOLAS VAZSONYI
Jesse Chapman Alcorn Memorial Professor of
  German and Comparative Literature
University of South Carolina, Columbia

RAY M. WAKEFIELD
Associate Professor of German and Dutch
University of Minnesota, Minneapolis

CHRIS WALTON
Lecturer in Music History
Musikhochschule, Basel

HILAN WARSHAW
Independent filmmaker
New York

HOLLY WATKINS
Associate Professor of Musicology
Eastman School of Music, Rochester

DEREK WATSON
Independent scholar
Peeblesshire

WILLIAM WEBER
Professor Emeritus of History
California State University, Long Beach

ARNOLD WHITTALL
Professor Emeritus of Music
  Theory & Analysis
King's College, London

SIMON WILLIAMS
Professor and Chair of Theater Studies
University of California, Santa Barbara

CHARLES YOUMANS
Associate Professor of Musicology
Pennsylvania State University,
  University Park

JULIAN YOUNG
W. R. Kenan Jr. Professor of
  Humanities
Wake Forest University, Winston-Salem

Editor's preface

The *Cambridge Wagner Encyclopedia* is the first of its kind in English. Nonetheless, two outstanding single-volume reference books on Wagner have stood the test of time: *The Wagner Compendium: A Guide to Wagner's Life and Music* (ed. Barry Millington, 1992), and the *Wagner Handbook* (ed. Ulrich Müller and Peter Wapnewski, trans. John Deathridge, 1992). More recently, *The Cambridge Companion to Wagner* (ed. Thomas S. Grey, 2008) has been added to that list. It is telling that although all of these are comprehensive, albeit differently structured, none claims to be an "encyclopedia," nor are they organized as such. Indeed, how can a single volume possibly cover encyclopedically a life so richly documented (both factually and fictitiously), a body of work so enormously influential, so attentively pondered and interpreted well beyond the spheres of opera and music, and a personality whose reach cannot be measured or captured? Richard Wagner was not just another great composer.

From the start, therefore, this project has been an exercise in compromise. What is essential to know about Wagner, 200 years after his birth, and what is not? Which is more important, the number of topics or the depth with which they are treated?

My guiding principle was to make the encyclopedia a useful and effective starting place for all the kinds of readers this volume has the potential to attract. Who are these anticipated readers? Wagner enthusiasts, those new to Wagner, performers, students of all ages, teachers, even the Wagner expert, who needs to check a fact or wants to explore unfamiliar territory. This book might not give the answer to every question one might have on Wagner, but it will provide the background and basics, as well as some ideas about where to go to find additional, reliable information. Readers will find that not everyone or every work or every issue connected with Wagner has its own entry. However, most everything does appear somewhere in the encyclopedia. There are approximately 550 entries followed by twelve appendices usually in tabular form, offering some basic data on a range of subjects. To find their way around most efficiently, readers should consult the comprehensive index, which contains the titles of works and writings in both German and English, for ease of reference.

I have not made it an editorial policy to refer to works exclusively in one language or another. The default language for this edition is English, and Wagner's works are often referred to in the course of the entries using the English translation. (However, the German titles of some of his works are so readily understandable in their original that they used consistently: e.g., *Tristan und Isolde, Die Meistersinger von Nürnberg*, etc.) Even if in the body of the discussion the English version is used, the headings of the entries themselves are in German. Hence, though it is often *The Flying Dutchman* in the narrative, the entry is under *Fliegende Holländer, Der*. Whether one looks up the title in German or in English, however, things are organized in such a way that there should be no difficulty finding the entry. All translations are by the contributors unless otherwise noted.

My main aim at all times was to try to make the reading experience a pleasantly informative one, while also preserving the individual style of the authors. Hence readers will find that some entries are more conversational, some more essayistic, some more formal and academic. Many authors have gone beyond the basics and offer thoughtful reflections on some of the pressing and even troubling issues that seem to be perennial facets of the Wagnerian universe. I did not realize until this project how enormously difficult it is to write a good encyclopedia entry. It is an art form unto itself.

Editorial conventions

In order to facilitate locating the full original texts of letters and diary entries, the convention followed here is to list the dates only, with no reference to specific editions. Thus readers can easily locate and look up either the German or translated versions.

Cross-references to other entries are marked by the use of SMALL CAPS. Such cross-references are usually marked only on their first appearance per entry. Additionally, when entries relate to others, but no cross-reference appears in the main text, a "see also" section is added at the end for further reading within the encyclopedia. This is then followed by a bibliography which gives full publication information of works cited in the entry, as well as suggested sources for further reading. In the event that the book in question is cited frequently, an abbreviated title is given at the end of the entry with full details in the select bibliography at the end of the encyclopedia.

NICHOLAS VAZSONYI
Columbia, USA, 2012

Acknowledgments

There are many people to recognize and thank, without whom this project would not have come to fruition at all, and certainly not as quickly as it did. In the first place, Vicki Cooper, senior commissioning editor at Cambridge University Press, showed amazing faith and confidence for inviting me to take on this daunting, exciting, fascinating, draining, occasionally frustrating, and ultimately highly rewarding project, even if it did sometimes rob me of my sleep and sanity.

I would also like to recognize and thank the editorial advisory board: Celia Applegate, Thomas Grey, Barry Millington, Sanna Pederson, and Eva Rieger. Both individually and collectively, they helped me with the conception and design, and thereafter stood at the ready with whatever was needed at the time to keep this project running smoothly. In the end, eighty-seven scholars – representing eleven academic disciplines and residing in nine countries around the world – contributed entries for the encyclopedia. Despite the inevitable bumps and missed deadlines along the way, it was the highlight of my task as editor of this project to work with these dedicated, knowledgeable, eloquent people I am honored to be able to call colleagues.

A few of the contributors helped additionally with specific entries and with larger issues. John Deathridge was there from the very start with suggestions for entries, solutions to problems, and as a resource with his seemingly limitless knowledge of all things Wagner; Mike Ashman, who ended up not being able to write an entry of his own, provided important and timely information concerning video recordings; David Cormack, whose article on Jessie Laussot appeared after the entry on her had been written; Ulrich Drüner, who provided additional information on publications and sources. Roberta Marvin, editor of the *Cambridge Verdi Encyclopedia*, and author of the VERDI entry in this volume, was enormously helpful with advice, hints, and support, especially at the beginning of this project, when I was struggling with its enormity. Verdi and Wagner may have been polar figures of nineteenth-century music, but in the case of the Cambridge Encyclopedia projects there was only harmony and collegiality.

My thanks go also to Anno Mungen, director of the Forschungsinstitut für Musiktheater at the University of Bayreuth. For two years in a row, he made sure I got tickets to the Bayreuth Festival, keeping my connection to the ongoing tradition and its many ramifications current. This exposure in turn was enormously helpful as I worked through the entries for this volume.

I was fortunate to have graduate students who assisted with much of the work gathering raw data. Leigh Buches, a graduate student at the University of

South Carolina, was diligent, dependable, and always cheerful, even if the work was sometimes less than thrilling. Later, I was helped enormously by Kyle Miller, a graduate student at the University of Oklahoma, whose assistance was made possible by Sanna Pederson with funds from her Mavis C. Pitman endowed chair. You will see the names of these students credited at various points in the volume. Peter Kay, who had already set the music examples for my own book on Wagner's self-promotion, once again did a spectacular job. My thanks to him also for the speed and accuracy of his work. The preparation of this book would not have been possible without the production team at Cambridge University Press, in particular the careful and exacting eye of the copy editor, Sara Peacock.

Last I would like to thank my own institution's help in facilitating this project, first and foremost the Dean of the College of Arts & Sciences at the University of South Carolina, Mary Ann Fitzpatrick, who at a time of budgetary crisis nevertheless gave me an extra travel stipend which enabled me to conduct research and also meet in person with some of the authors. I also received a Provost's Humanities Grant from the University of South Carolina which gave me some much needed extra time to work on this project.

NICHOLAS VAZSONYI
Columbia, South Carolina, September 2012

Abbreviations

BB/E	Wagner, Richard. *The Diary of Richard Wagner 1865–1882: The Brown Book*. Ed. Joachim Bergfeld, trans. George Bird. Cambridge University Press, 1980.
CWD	Wagner, Cosima. *Cosima Wagner's Diaries*. Ed. Martin and Dietrich Mack, trans. Geoffrey Skelton. 2 vols. New York: Harcourt Brace Jovanovich, 1978–80. [References to entries are by date only.]
ML	Wagner, Richard. *Mein Leben*. Ed. Martin Gregor-Dellin. Munich: List, 1963.
ML/E	Wagner, Richard. *My Life*. Ed. Mary Whittall, trans. Andrew Gray. New York: Da Capo Press, 1992.
NZfM	*Neue Zeitschrift für Musik*.
PW	Wagner, Richard. *Prose Works*. Trans. in 8 volumes by William Ashton Ellis. London: Kegan Paul, Trench, Trübner, 1892–9. Paperback reprint, Lincoln: University of Nebraska Press, 1995.
SB	Wagner, Richard. *Sämtliche Briefe*. Ed. Gertrud Strobel, Werner Wolf, et al. Leipzig: Deutscher Verlag für Musik, 1967–2000; Wiesbaden: Breitkopf & Härtel, 1999–. (see CORRESPONDENCE, EDITIONS).
SSD	Wagner, Richard. *Sämtliche Schriften und Dichtungen*. 16 vols. Leipzig: Breitkopf & Härtel, n.d. [1911].
SW	*Richard Wagner Sämtliche Werke*. Ed. Egon Voss, Gesellschaft zur Förderung der Richard Wagner-Gesamtausgabe and the Bayerische Akademie der Schönen Künste, München. Mainz: Schott, 1970– (see SÄMTLICHE WERKE).
WWV	John Deathridge, Martin Geck, Egon Voss, eds. *Wagner Werk-Verzeichnis* (WWV). Verzeichnis der musikalischen Werke Richard Wagners und ihrer Quellen, erarbeitet im Rahmen der Richard Wagner-Gesamtausgabe, redaktionelle Mitarbeit Isolde Vetter. Mainz: Schott, 1986.

Abgesang. See CANZONA

Absolute music. An aesthetic term typically used to characterize a musical work lacking extra-musical signifiers, such as text or visual images. Broadly conceived, it goes back to the beginning of music aesthetics, but it was Wagner who coined the term.
1. Wagner's negative definition
2. Wagner's change of attitude toward (absolute) music
3. Absolute music as a positive concept

1. Wagner's negative definition

The phrase "absolute music" first appeared as a negative term in Wagner's 1846 *Faust*-inspired PROGRAM NOTES to BEETHOVEN's Ninth Symphony. He described the fourth movement as "almost leaving the confines of absolute music" (die Schranken der absoluten Musik fast schon verlassend, SSD 2:61) with the opening recitative that prepares for the later introduction of words. Because it occurs just once, and without any explanation, there is little evidence to contradict the impression that Wagner used the phrase without intending to coin a term or to refer to anything beyond the immediate context of the instrumental, as opposed to the choral, movements of the symphony.

Three years later, Wagner used the term again in the series of writings from ZURICH. Here, he used it in an emphatically negative way. It seems that Wagner consciously borrowed the term "Absolute" from philosophy, specifically from FEUERBACH's critique of HEGEL. As a philosophical term, Absolute indicates the highest and most abstract value. It is central to the idealist philosophy of Kant, Fichte, SCHELLING, and, above all, Hegel. Absolute-oriented thought dominated philosophy well after Hegel's death. However, with the publication of *Towards a Critique of Hegelian Philosophy* (1839), Feuerbach declared that metaphysical speculation, focused on the Absolute, denied the sensuous materiality of life. Proposing an alternative to Absolute Spirit as a creation of philosophical thought, Feuerbach advocated a more anthropological approach based on the immediacy of sensuous experience. He suggested a radical reordering of being over thinking, the sensuous over the spiritual.

In the wake of Feuerbach's critique, the Absolute became an easy target in the second half of the century. SCHOPENHAUER, who considered himself the archenemy of Hegel, finally became famous when his attack on the Absolute as a metaphysical swindle found resonance.

When Wagner began using the term, then, it had recently received a bold reversal in value, plunging from the unassailable limit of thought to the problematic basis of idealist philosophy. Wagner may have appropriated it in the broadest sense to make the parallel between Feuerbach's radical critique of the venerable Hegelian tradition and his own critique of the Beethovenian heritage. The term further seems to fit Wagner's use in its standing for an abstract system out of touch with reality.

Wagner used the adjective "absolute" pejoratively in KUNST UND REVO- LUTION (1849) but did not refer to "absolute Musik" until his next publication from the same year, *Das KUNSTWERK DER ZUKUNFT*, where it appeared always in relation to Beethoven, "the hero who explored the broad, shoreless sea of absolute music [uferlose[s] Meer der absoluten Musik] to its end and won the new undreamed-of coasts, so that this sea no longer divides contin- ents but rather connects them" (SSD 3:85; PW 1:115). As in Wagner's 1846 essay, Beethoven is portrayed as the composer who finished off absolute music in his Ninth Symphony by introducing words and voices. In a manner some- what like Feuerbach, Wagner argued that the dialectic of history had made absolute music a thing of the past, and that the time had come to envision an "artwork of the future," a phrase that echoed Feuerbach's call for a "philoso- phy of the future."

Wagner initially used the term solely in relation to Beethoven's Ninth in order to designate a type of instrumental music that had ended with Beethoven, but his use changed in *OPER UND DRAMA* (Opera and Drama, 1851), where he used "absolute" to characterize not only music, but also other alienated and limited things. Absolute music appears frequently in Parts I and III along with, most often, "absolute Melodie," and "absolute[r] Musiker," but also "absolute Dichtkunst" (poetry), "absolute Glaube" (faith), "absolute Monarchie," and many others. After this excess of absolutes, Wagner seems to have exhausted his contempt for the concept. The only other person who expounded on absolute music at this time was his disciple Theodor UHLIG, who took up the term in his articles for the *NEUE ZEITSCHRIFT FÜR MUSIK* from 1850 to 1852. Wagner did not use the term again, except in one ambiguous context in his 1857 essay *ÜBER FRANZ LISZTS SYMPHONISCHE DICHTUNGEN* (On Franz Liszt's Symphonic Poems).

2. Wagner's change of attitude toward (absolute) music

This 1857 essay, published as an open letter in the *Neue Zeitschrift für Musik*, is ambiguous because it is not clear how much it evidences a move toward Schopenhauer's view of music. There are certainly passages that praise music in a way that seems to indicate a different mindset than that of *Oper und Drama*, for instance:

> For music is so chaste, sincere, and inspiring by nature that everything it touches is transformed. But just as certain is the fact that music can only be perceived in forms which were originally foreign to it, forms derived from external aspects of human experience. Such forms achieve their latent and truest significance when applied to music in this way. Nothing (NB: as it is revealed to human experience) is less absolute than music, and the champions of an absolute music [die Verfechter einer absoluten Musik]

obviously don't realize what they are saying. To point out their confusion it would suffice to have them name, if they could, any music whose form is not derived from corporeal motion or from verse (according to the causal circumstances).

(SSD 5:191; TRANS. GREY 425)

Here, Wagner offers a dualistic understanding of music in which there is music itself, its essence, and the music accessed by humans through form; absolute music exists but humans cannot access it; therefore music as we know it is not absolute because all of it comes to us through form-giving dance or poetry. Whereas before Wagner had condemned absolute music, here he denies it ever could even exist as music – which in turn creates an unacknowledged contradiction. In his later writings, Wagner continued to avoid renouncing what he had written earlier, leading to infinite confusion.

Most accounts of Wagner's changing AESTHETICS describe a move from the early 1850s, in which he insisted music must serve the drama, to a belief in the primacy of music: in short, he switched from the philosophy of Feuerbach to that of Schopenhauer, from anti-Romanticism to Romanticism, from anti-metaphysics to metaphysics. However, Carl DAHLHAUS has presented a different account of Wagner and absolute music. He argues that although Wagner only used the *term* absolute music in a negative way, his *idea* of absolute music was a positive part of his aesthetic views throughout his life, even in the Zurich writings. For Dahlhaus, the idea of absolute music was that instrumental music, previously maligned for its lack of representational capabilities, was discovered to convey an alternative world by virtue of its very lack. This was first articulated by the early Romantics (Wackenroder and Tieck), shared by HANSLICK, and pushed to its extreme (music would exist even if the real world didn't) by Schopenhauer. Dahlhaus claims that this idea of absolute music was so strong throughout the nineteenth century that it even underlay attacks, such as Wagner's in the 1850s.

3. Absolute music as a positive concept

In 1857, Wagner referred to the "champions of absolute music," presumably Hanslick and supporters of Hanslick, especially in the *Niederrheinische Musikzeitung*. However, this was Wagner's phrase. Hanslick did not call himself a "champion of absolute music" and did not use the term. After the early part of the 1850s, the term is scarcely to be found in either a positive or negative sense for decades. It was only around 1880 that the opposition "program music and absolute music" became the burning aesthetic debate of the later nineteenth century, with Hanslick, BRAHMS, and Dvořák most often associated with the absolute music camp.

After Wagner's death, a few of his supporters tried to retake the term. Using some very twisted reasoning, Rudolf Louis described Bruckner's symphonies as absolute music and claimed these instrumental works were consistent with Wagner's aesthetic beliefs. After the massive upheaval of World War I, however, Romantic metaphysical music became anathema; absolute music took on a new meaning, and lost its historical beginnings with Wagner.

SANNA PEDERSON

Carl Dahlhaus, *The Idea of Absolute Music*, trans. R. Lustig (University of Chicago Press, 1989).
Thomas S. Grey, "Richard Wagner and the Aesthetics of Musical Form in the Mid-19th
    Century (1840–1860)," Ph.D. dissertation, University of California, 1988.
Sanna Pederson, "Defining the Term 'Absolute Music' Historically," *Music & Letters* 90.2
    (2009): 240–62.

Actors and Singers. See *Über Schauspieler und Sänger* (1872)

Adorno, Theodor Wiesengrund (b. Frankfurt am Main, 11 Sep. 1903; d. Visp,
Switzerland, 6 Aug. 1969), sociologist, musicologist, philosopher, founding
member of influential Frankfurt School. Studied philosophy, music and soci-
ology in Frankfurt, and music in Vienna with Alban Berg. Appointment at
Frankfurt University (1930), left Germany in 1933, exile in United States
1938–49 (primarily New York and Los Angeles), returned to Frankfurt after
the war. A product of German idealism (especially HEGEL and NIETZSCHE)
tempered by the Weimar years, Adorno developed a Marxist-based theory of
mass culture influenced by the sociologist Max Weber. Idealism and Marxism
thus formed the twin poles of his dialectical approach to Wagner.

1. *In Search of Wagner* (1937–1938)
2. "Wagner's Relevance for Today" (1963)
3. "On the Score of *Parsifal*" (1956)

1. *In Search of Wagner* (Versuch über Wagner) (1937–1938)

Adorno's most substantial contribution to Wagner criticism, written between
autumn 1937 and spring 1938, and partially revised before publication in book
form in 1952. It is intimately bound up with Frankfurt School co-founder Max
Horkheimer's essay "Egoism and the Movement for Emancipation: Toward an
Anthropology of the Bourgeois Era" (1936), and is essentially a Marxist critique of
Wagner the great bourgeois. For Adorno, Wagner is a paradigmatic figure in the
post-1848, early industrial period during which the bourgeoisie emerged as a
political force. His works, as products of this age, "provide eloquent evidence of
the early phase of bourgeois decadence" (153). But, in the course of ten densely
argued chapters, Adorno goes well beyond a simple Marxist critique by homing
in on the ambiguities and contradictions in Wagner, especially the central
paradox that the "qualities that prompted his contemporaries to speak of 'decadence' is also the path to artistic success" (44). This provides the critical agenda
for a complex interweaving of philosophy, ideology, and a penetrating music
criticism honed by his studies with Berg. Adorno manages to touch on something approaching a comprehensive discussion of the composer and his work.

    Just to mention a few topics: he identifies the "allegorical rigidity of
leitmotif" (46), critiquing the inherent tension between the static nature of
the LEITMOTIV as "miniature pictures" (45) and the dynamic requirements
of musical development over an extended period: "Allegorical rigidity has
infected the motive like a disease. The gesture becomes frozen as a picture
of what it expresses" (46). In Wagner's harmony, he sees an ambiguity which
becomes in itself a means of expression: "In Beethoven and well into high
Romanticism the expressive values of harmony are fixed: dissonance stands
for negation and suffering, consonance for fulfillment and the positive" (67).
He praises Wagner's "art of ORCHESTRATION" as "the productive share of

color in the musical process 'in such a way that color itself becomes action' . . . something that did not exist before Wagner" (71). LOHENGRIN marks the point at which the principle of instrumental combination becomes structurally significant. Adorno's concept of phantasmagoria is an important critical tool in understanding illusion in Wagner's works and, from a Marxist perspective, is a device by which "Wagner's operas tend to become commodities. Their tableaux assume the character of wares on display" (90). In one of the most quoted passages, Adorno suggests that "all the rejects of Wagner's works are caricatures of JEWS" (23).

In Search of Wagner pulls no critical punches. Nevertheless, Adorno's subtlety of argument and criticism, rooted in a profound knowledge of Wagner's scores, is offset by the difficulty of extracting that which is of lasting critical value from the time-specific ideology driven by his Marxist agenda.

2. "Wagner's Relevance for Today" (1963)

In September 1963, Adorno gave a lecture in Berlin, "Wagner's Relevance for Today," in which he revisits his earlier work in a critique of its underlying thesis, "that of the relation between societal aspects on the one hand and compositional/aesthetic aspects on the other" (584). The musical criticism also expands on some earlier points, such as Wagner's use of sequence, which throws new light on the problem of allegorical rigidity as antithetical to musical development. Reviewing Wagner from a post-1945 perspective, Adorno "comments about the historical changes in the attitude towards Wagner's art," declaring "I cannot ignore the political aspect. Too much catastrophe has been visited on living beings for a consideration that purports to be purely aesthetic to close its eyes to it" (585). To the later Adorno, it is not possible "to separate out the ideological and hold on to pure art" (587). The motor of his critical agenda is the paradox that "what is magnificent in his [Wagner's] work cannot be separated from what is questionable" (596).

3. "On the Score of *Parsifal*" (1956)

In 1956 Adorno wrote a short essay "On the Score of PARSIFAL" which, for those who find In Search of Wagner and its sequel forbidding and convoluted, contains the essence of his thought. Its subtle probing of the elusive musical character of Parsifal as aural experience goes some way towards explaining the cultic, elliptical character of the work. "It is as if the style of Parsifal attempts not only to present the musical ideas, but also to compose their own aura to accompany them; this aura forms not in the moment of the event, but in its aftermath. One can only follow the intention by submitting even more to the music's echo than to the music itself" (73).

Adorno's Wagner criticism is comparable only with NIETZSCHE's later Wagner polemics and Thomas MANN's The Sorrows and Grandeur of Richard Wagner as a response to the excesses and distortions of the cult of Wagner worship. The cultural issues he identifies in Wagner's works (ANTI-SEMITIC caricature, eroticism, political significance, etc.) have to a greater or lesser extent driven Wagner debate since the middle of the twentieth century; his criticism of Wagner's music raises many important challenges which have yet to be met. ROGER ALLEN

Theodor Adorno, *In Search of Wagner* (see bibliography).
  "Wagner's Relevance for Today," *Essays on Music* (see bibliography): 584–602.
  "On the Score of *Parsifal*," trans. and commentary by Anthony Barone, *Music & Letters* 76.3
    (1995): 384–97.
Max Paddison, *Adorno's Aesthetics of Music* (Cambridge University Press, 1993).

See also SEXUALITY AND EROTICISM

Aesthetics.

Wagner's aesthetics may seem a formidable topic yet, despite the labyrinthine complexities of some of his major theoretical statements and the convoluted prose in which he habitually expressed himself, his artistic agenda is readily defined: to realize an ideal fusion of poetry and music as a means of dramatic expression. There is no general agreement as to the extent to which Wagner's aesthetics remained consistent; it is certainly true that his view of the comparative importance of music and poetry underwent several changes during his career. Yet this underlying aesthetic trajectory of realizing to the full the expressive potential of dramatic poetry through music remained constant from his earliest writings to the essays of his last years and, in spite of numerous diversions along the way, provides a fundamental cohesion to his creative project. Preoccupation with the relationship between poetry and music is apparent in one of the earliest articles attributed to him, *Pasticcio* (1834), in which he compares the current state of German opera unfavorably with the expressive qualities of the Italian style; he looks forward to the day when "a man will come who in this good style will re-establish the shattered unity between poetry and song" (SSD 12:9; PW 8:64).

1. The writings of the Paris years (1839–1842)
2. The Zurich essays (1849–1852)
3. Schopenhauer
4. *Beethoven* (1870)
5. Last years

1. The writings of the Paris years (1839–1842)

The journeyman Wagner's writings from PARIS are significant in charting both his aesthetic development during his formative years, and the evolving connection between his artistic program and a political agenda bound up with wider societal concerns. In 1840 and 1841 he produced three writings which first appeared in French translation in the REVUE ET GAZETTE MUSICALE DE PARIS and subsequently in the *Abend-Zeitung* (DRESDEN). They are cast in narrative form and are amongst the most directly accessible of his prose works. In the first of these, *Eine PILGERFAHRT ZU BEETHOVEN* (A Pilgrimage to Beethoven, 1840), Wagner articulates his own ideas on the development of opera in the form of statements attributed to the older composer which strikingly anticipate his own later thought: for example, that instruments represent rudimentary organs of creation and nature. "What they express can never be clearly defined or put into words . . . It is quite otherwise with the genius of the human voice. The voice represents the heart of man and its well-defined individual emotion" (SSD 1:110; Wagner/Osborne 76). *Ein glücklicher Abend* (A Happy Evening, 1841) is cast in the form of a fictional dialogue in which Wagner expounds his ideas on the expressive powers of poetry and music: "It is an eternal truth that where the speech of man stops short, there the art of music begins" (SSD 1:140; Wagner/Osborne 83). In this concentrated discourse, there is even a direct anticipation of Wagner's much vaunted "discovery" of SCHOPENHAUER in 1854: "What music expresses is eternal, infinite and ideal. It speaks not of the passion, love and longing of this or that individual, but of passion, love and longing in themselves" (SSD 1:148–9; Wagner/Osborne 90). A further important article defining Wagner's evolving theory of opera dating from the Paris years is *Über die Ouvertüre* (On the OVERTURE, 1841) in which Wagner praises the overture to *Don Giovanni* as distilling the essence of the drama that is to follow. "Here we found the drama's leading thought delineated in a purely musical way but not in a dramatic shape ... Moreover, the musician most surely attains the Overture's artistic end, to act as nothing but an ideal prologue, translating us to that higher sphere in which to prepare our minds for Drama" (SSD 1:201–2; PW 7:161).

These years in Paris were not only a time of considerable intellectual ferment for Wagner, but also a period in which the foundations of his later development were laid; by the time he left for Dresden in 1842, the elements of the aesthetic program which were to nourish his later works were largely in place. These ideas also fed into the period of intense creative activity which saw the composition of the so-called "Romantic operas," TANN-HÄUSER (1845), LOHENGRIN (1848), and the first stirrings of the RING project before his involvement in the DRESDEN UPRISING of 1849 forced him into exile and precipitated a further period of intense theoretical activity.

2. The ZURICH essays (1849–1852)

The three extended theoretical tracts written in the early years of Wagner's exile in Switzerland represent the aesthetic fulcrum of his creative project. It is also true to say that from this point onwards it becomes impossible to separate his artistic agenda from his post-revolutionary political idealism. In *Die KUNST UND DIE REVOLUTION* (Art and Revolution), he claims to rediscover the ANCIENT GREEK idea of Art as the expression of community. "With the Greeks the perfect work of art, the Drama, was the abstract and epitome of all that was expressible in the Grecian nature. It was the nation itself – in intimate connection with its own history – that stood mirrored in its art work, which communed with itself and within the span of a few hours, feasted its eyes with its own noblest essence" (SSD 3:28; PW 1:52). In *Das KUNSTWERK DER ZUKUNFT* (*The Artwork of the Future*, 1849/50) this expression of an ideal community comes to be elided with and politicized as the German "VOLK." HEGEL's influence is also discernible in Wagner's discussion of the arts as belonging to a hierarchical system. Hegel's aesthetic formulation is applied to dance, music, and poetry as the three "sister arts" most necessary for an operatic composer. "The ocean binds and separates the land: so does Music bind and separate the two opposite poles of human Art, the arts of Dance and Poetry" (SSD 3:81; PW 1:110). The fusion of the arts into a total work of art or GESAMTKUNSTWERK is further developed in what is arguably Wagner's most important theoretical tract: *OPER UND DRAMA* (Opera and Drama, 1851). This book-length treatise covers a vast agenda. Most important for the understanding of Wagner's aesthetic development is Part III, in which he develops a theory of opera whereby the means of dramatic expression is a synthesis of speech and tone (the composer as "Tondichter"), with the orchestra adopting the expressive role of the chorus in a Greek tragedy. "That which could not be expressed by gesture in the language of vocal music found expression in a language totally divorced from words, namely that of the orchestra, capable of communicating to the ear what gesture communicated to the eye" (SSD 4:176; Bujić 61).

Wagner's Zurich essays occupy a pivotal place in his creative program and are crucial to an understanding of his developing conception of musical drama, or MUSIC DRAMA, for want of a better term. It is tempting but misleading to read them as theoretical templates for the composition of his later works from *Das RHEINGOLD* onwards. They certainly articulate the ideas that were to provide the impulse for subsequent creative work, but in so doing Wagner was rationalizing the advances he made in the composition of the Romantic operas and in the process of forging a musical language suitable for the composition of the *Ring* tetralogy, rather than providing a blueprint for future creation. Wagner's ideas are therefore a function of the dramatic works rather than the works a realization of theoretical principles. At no point did Wagner ever set words to music in the literal sense, even when in the case of *GÖTTERDÄMMERUNG* he was composing a text set down over twenty years previously. He wrote his own libretti in order to realize an already conceived musical mood into speech. When Wagner "composed" a previously written poem, he was expressing in musical terms the dramatic essence of that poem rather than setting it to music. In this rather simplistic, even banal, statement is contained not only the essence of Wagner's aesthetic ideal but also the reason why his music has such expressive force: the drama is contained within the music.

For those who are perplexed by the often opaque style of the Zurich writings, two subsequent essays, the autobiographical *Eine MITTEILUNG AN MEINE FREUNDE* (A Communication to my Friends, 1851) and *ZUKUNFTSMUSIK* (Music of the Future, 1860) can be read as supplements that clarify many of the more obscure passages in the earlier tracts. In *Zukunftsmusik*, Wagner critiques his earlier Zurich essays, freely acknowledging their difficulties, in an attempt to elucidate more clearly his ideas in an explanatory foreword to a French prose translation of *Der FLIEGENDE HOLLÄNDER*, *Tannhäuser*, *Lohengrin*, and *TRISTAN*, cast in the form of an open letter to his French friend Frédéric Villot. This latter essay contains Wagner's most direct and incisive statement of his artistic ideas, formulated at that crucial point in his development immediately following the completion of *Tristan*. "Here, rapidly outlined, you have the basis of that artistic ideal which became ever clearer to me and which I once felt compelled to describe fully in theoretical terms" (SSD 7:95; Wagner/Jacobs 18). Wagner leaves his readers in no doubt that his theories are a reflection of his artistic impulses rather than a template for future creative work: "My theories were virtually little more than an abstract expression of the artistic process then at work within me" (SSD 7:118; Wagner/Jacobs 32).

3. Schopenhauer

It is well known that Wagner read Schopenhauer's *Die Welt als Wille und Vorstellung* (The World as Will and Representation) in 1854, and that the philosopher's influence on him was profound (see Wagner's letter to Liszt 16[?] Dec. 1854). This event, whilst undoubtedly significant, should not be taken at face value and is to be interrogated. We have already seen how in *Ein glücklicher Abend* (1841), Wagner was moving close to Schopenhauer's view of music, although this essay was written some thirteen years before Wagner's supposed epiphany experience. Compare the passage quoted above with the following from Schopenhauer: "Music does not express this or that particular or definite pleasure, this or that affliction, pain, sorrow … but joy, pain, sorrow themselves, to a certain extent in the abstract, their essential nature" (Schopenhauer 261). Schopenhauer's influence on Wagner's aesthetic program was clearly strong but should not be exaggerated by taking Wagnerian hyperbole at face value. From the outset, Wagner shared much of the same aesthetic ground as Schopenhauer. This is evident in that the eponymous character in *Der fliegende Holländer* (written over a decade before Wagner's first documented encounter with Schopenhauer), in his world weariness and longing for death exhibits all the characteristics of a good Schopenhauerian. Wagner was attracted by the strong element of fantasy in Schopenhauer's philosophy, which resonated with his creative temperament. Wagner's so-called "discovery" of Schopenhauer in 1854 gave his developing concept of musical drama the philosophical and intellectual legitimacy he sought, yet as a creative artist he remained autonomous and answerable only to his own artistic vision. The Schopenhauerian elements in the *Ring*, *Tristan*, *Die Meistersinger*, and *Parsifal* are there and cannot be denied; yet exaggerated claims that Wagner's later creative output was entirely driven by Schopenhauer are misleading.

4. *BEETHOVEN* (1870)

This seminal essay, written to mark the centenary of Beethoven's birth, is the major aesthetic statement of Wagner's later years. It represents not only a partial revision of his earlier theories informed by his ongoing assimilation of Schopenhauer but, more significantly, a reflection on and reassessment of his aesthetic position at this critical point in his career, driven by the cathartic creative experience of *Tristan und Isolde* and *Die Meistersinger*. The central thesis, embedded within a heady mix of historical and literary observations shot through with a good deal of strident anti-French rhetoric, is that music contains the essence of the drama within itself: "Music does not present ideas taken from everyday phenomena, but is rather itself a comprehensive idea of the world, automatically including drama, since drama again expresses the only idea of the world on the same level as that of music" (SSD 9:105; Bujić 70). This, together with Wagner's statement that his works are "deeds of music made visible" ("ersichtlich gewordene Taten der Musik," SSD 9:306) from his essay *ÜBER DIE BENENNUNG "MUSIKDRAMA"* (On the Term "Music Drama," 1872), is often taken to mean that Wagner in his later years reversed his position on the respective importance of music and poetry. Such an assumption represents not only a partial understanding of one of the central theses of *Opera and Drama* – that a means of expression (music) has been made the object while the object of expression (the drama) has been made the means – but is far too blunt a critical tool in the interrogation of Wagner's ever-fluctuating ideas on the relationship between poetry and music.

5. Last years

As is well known, during his last years Wagner's thought turned to disturbing issues of ideology and race which found expression in his so-called *Regenerationsschriften* (REGENERATION essays) and, through the writings of the so-called BAYREUTH CIRCLE, flowed inexorably into the turbulent racial politics of extreme NATIONALISM. This represents the troubling face of Wagner's progressive politicization of his aesthetic project. In striking and welcome contrast to these problematic texts, he penned a series of short articles for the *BAYREUTHER BLÄTTER* on the craft of operatic composition, which are remarkable for their clarity of expression and contain the accumulated wisdom of a lifetime's practical experience. Of particular importance is *ÜBER DIE ANWENDUNG DER MUSIK AUF DAS DRAMA* (On the Application of Music to Drama, 1879), in which Wagner explains with a clarity rare in his earlier theoretical writings his conception of dramatic music: "it is here, in what we may call for short the 'musical' Drama, that we reach sure ground for calmly reckoning the application of Music's new-won faculties to the evolution of noble, inexhaustible art forms" (SSD 10:184; PW 6:182).

Wagner's aesthetic journey thus ended where it began: with reflections on the nature of the relationship of music and poetry in musical drama. Throughout his life he relentlessly pursued this question not so much with the systematic rigor of the philosopher, but with the single-minded zeal of the artist. Wagner's aesthetic ideas were images of the creative imagination that drove the artistic project so memorably and succinctly described in *Zukunftsmusik* as a "channeling into the bed of musical drama the great stream that Beethoven sent pouring into German music" (SSD 7:97; Wagner/Jacobs 19).   ROGER ALLEN

Bojan Bujić, ed., *Music in European Thought, 1851–1912* (Cambridge University Press, 1988).
Dahlhaus and Deathridge, *The New Grove Wagner* (see bibliography): esp. Chapter 4.
Artur Schopenhauer, *The World as Will and Representation*, 2 vols., trans. E. J. F. Payne (New York: Dover, 1969).
Richard Wagner, *Richard Wagner Stories and Essays*, ed. and intro. Charles Osborne (London: Peter Owen, 1973).
    Three Wagner Essays, trans. Robert L. Jacobs (Eulenberg: London, 1979).

Aktionskreis für das Werk Richard Wagners (currently Deutsche Richard-Wagner-Gesellschaft e. V.). This conservative group of Wagner fans, whose president in 2012 was Rüdiger Pohl (Berlin), was founded in 1977, in response to the 1976 centenary production of *Der RING DES NIBELUNGEN*, staged in Bayreuth by Patrice CHÉREAU. The Aktionskreis pleaded for *Werktreue* (fidelity to the work), meaning productions that adhered to the staging instructions as written by Wagner in the score, as opposed to *Regietheater* (director's theater) which they rejected wholesale as an illegitimate and wrong-headed directorial intervention that misrepresents (Ger. *entstellt*) the work as intended by the author/composer. The organization published the *RICHARD-WAGNER-BLÄTTER*, replaced in 1991 with *Mitteilungen der Deutschen Richard-Wagner-Gesellschaft e.V.* The organization is closely associated with the Richard Wagner Festival Wels (Upper Austria), which began in 1983 as the result of an idea from the Just-Doppler family, and has been running annually since 1989. Productions follow the ideology that "nothing can appear on stage that is not indicated in the work." NICHOLAS VAZSONYI

www.wagner-gesellschaft.de

See also PERFORMANCE PRACTICE; PRODUCTION HISTORY; WAGNER SOCIETIES

Alberich (bass-baritone; character in *Der RING DES NIBELUNGEN* with appearances in *Das RHEINGOLD*, *SIEGFRIED* and *GÖTTERDÄMMERUNG*). In the *Nibelungenlied*, the dwarf Alberich guards the Nibelung treasure by means of his magical *Tarnhelm*. The story of Alberich, and of how Siegfried manages to wrest the gold from him, is relayed by Hagen – neither the dwarf nor his hoard plays a role in the main plot of the *Nibelungenlied*. The *Prose EDDA* of Snorri Sturluson presents the story of the dwarf Andvari (which is briefly referenced in the *VÖLSUNGA SAGA* as well). In the *Prose Edda*, the god Loki (Loge) is sent to Nibelheim to steal the dwarf Andvari's gold, including a magic ring. Andvari curses the ring (in the *Poetic Edda*, he curses his entire hoard), "that the ring should bring death to whoever owned it." While Wagner centrally drew on these and other motives in plotting his own *Ring* cycle, he gives Alberich a much more sustained and active trajectory than either the *Nibelungenlied* or the Eddic texts: in the process he turns Andvari into the anti-Wotan, and the pair are even identified as "Schwarz-Alberich" and "Licht-Alberich" (Black-Alberich and Light-Alberich; e.g., *Siegfried* Act I).

Alberich is one of the *Ring* cycle's great Others, which has in part led commentators to read him, like his brother MIME, as a character portraying ANTI-SEMITIC traits. He begins the cycle in a social (and erotic) position entirely opposite from WOTAN and his gods, and he deepens that opposition in making a kind of choice entirely alien to Wotan and his offspring: he foreswears love in exchange for gold and power. Wagner thus sets up Alberich as a funhouse mirror-image of Wotan: Where Wotan has sacrificed his eye for wisdom, Alberich sacrifices the ability to love for another kind of intelligence. In Wotan and Alberich, Wagner opposes two forms of knowledge whose relationship obsessed much of nineteenth-century German thought: what anachronistically we might call reason and instrumental reason. Through his possession of the Rhinegold, Alberich becomes a canny manipulator, but his schemes seem to unravel in sometimes comical, sometimes tragic ways.

Alberich's music, in keeping with his character, is uniformly dark and chromatic, and virtually always harmonically, and even rhythmically, unstable. His most prominent *Leitmotiv* in the cycle is his Curse of the Ring, which he himself sings when it is first heard in *Das RHEINGOLD*, Scene 4 (mm. 3126–30, see Appendix 4: *Leitmotive in Der Ring des Nibelungen*; CWE 9). The Curse returns later in the same scene, in the trombone, immediately after Fafner kills Fasolt, and many more times in the other operas, including a statement at the moment of Siegfried's murder in Act III of *Götterdämmerung*. The motive, used consistently to portray the power of evil, is most frequently played by the trombone, and almost always at the same pitch-level – beginning E–A–C–E, over an F♯ pedal.

Of Alberich's other music, much (such as that in his scenes with the Rhinemaidens; and with Mime, the Nibelungs, and Loge and Wotan, in *Das Rheingold*) – is darkly comic; some, such as the motive of the *Tarnhelm* (CWE 8), is mysterious and magical; and some, such as that immediately preceding the first statement of the Curse, is brooding and sinister. Although Alberich appears only in a few scenes after *Rheingold* – *Siegfried*, Act II, Scenes 1 and 3; and *Götterdämmerung*, Act II, Scene 1 – and though there are no new motivic ideas to be associated with him, he retains a grim presence, through the Curse and a few other motives, virtually to the end of the cycle.

ADRIAN DAUB AND PATRICK MCCRELESS

See also LOVE

Allgemeiner Richard-Wagner-Verein. See WAGNER SOCIETIES

Ambros, August Wilhelm (b. Mauth [now Vyoské Myto, Czech Republic], 17 Nov. 1816; d. Vienna, 28 June 1876), Austrian critic, scholar, and historian of music. Ambros was educated in the same milieu as Eduard HANSLICK, in the German-speaking intellectual and musical community of Prague. While Hanslick became the notorious critical nemesis of Wagner, Ambros remained cautiously supportive of Wagner's progressive AESTHETICS, ideals that appealed to Ambros's enthusiasm for comparative cultural history and a loosely Hegelian notion of historical progress in the arts. His first major publication, *Die Grenzen der Musik und Poesie* (The Boundaries of Music and Poetry, 1856), was written as a response, of sorts, to Hanslick's *Vom Musikalisch-Schönen* (On the Musically Beautiful, 1854), emphasizing parallels between the arts in modern culture as opposed to the autonomy of different mediums. In a lengthy essay on *The NEW GERMAN SCHOOL* published in the collection *Culturhistorische Bilder aus dem Musikleben der Gegenwart* (Cultural-Historical Pictures from Contemporary Musical Life, 1860) Ambros twice speaks of the role of the musical LEITMOTIV in Wagner's operas, apparently the first appearance of this term in print. In the first instance, he is enumerating parallels between Wagner's operas and Liszt's symphonic poems (both said to deploy consistent *Leitmotive* in an effort to guarantee a higher unity of structure). Towards the end of the essay, he points out various precedents for the use of recurring, dramatically signifying melodic tags in MOZART, WEBER, and MEYERBEER, but reserves the term *Leitmotiv* for the example of Wagner's LOHENGRIN (citing the *Frageverbot* or "forbidden question" formula). In later years, after Hanslick had developed a programmatic antagonism to the Wagnerian project, Ambros turned his attention to the historical scholarship for which he is best known. His multi-volume *Geschichte der Musik* (History of Music, begun 1862) covered only music in ancient cultures up through the Renaissance. A later essay ("Wagneriana," pub. 1872) reviews the claims of Wagner and his party in anticipation of recently announced plans for the BAYREUTH FESTIVAL.

THOMAS S. GREY

Amfortas (bass; character in PARSIFAL). In the 1850s, during his work on TRISTAN UND ISOLDE, Wagner first gave detailed attention to WOLFRAM

VON ESCHENBACH'S *Parzival* as the basis for a drama. In his letter of 29/30 May 1859 to Mathilde WESENDONCK, Wagner described "Anfortas" (as the name is spelled in Wolfram) as "the center and crux" (*der Mittelpunkt und Hauptgegenstand*) of the action, as "Tristan of the third act with an inconceivable intensification" (*Tristan des dritten Aktes mit einer undenklichen Steigerung*). Wagner was fascinated by the tragic dilemma of the wounded Grail-King, renamed Amfortas in *Parsifal* (1882). While obliged to reveal the Grail at the Communion Service, not least in order to preserve the life of his father (the aged Titurel), Amfortas suffers unbearable torment when performing his office. His wound opens afresh as he confronts the Grail, whose uncanny power deepens his agony, binding him to life while he longs for death.

In his letter from 1859, Wagner referred to Amfortas's "spear wound, and presumably another one – in his heart." Before the action of the music drama begins, Amfortas had recklessly carried the Holy Spear into combat against his rival, the evil magician KLINGSOR. While at the sorcerer's castle, Amfortas was seduced by Klingsor's agent, the temptress KUNDRY, and wounded by Klingsor, who had seized the spear. Amfortas's spear wound then becomes the symbol of his spiritual impurity, placing him in irreconcilable conflict with the purity of the Grail. The only possible solution is his replacement as predicted in the Grail's prophecy, by someone "knowing through compassion, the pure fool": PARSIFAL.

While devising the opening Communion or "Last Supper" theme as heard at the outset of the Prelude and at the revelation of the Grail in Act I, Wagner commented that "the pains of Amfortas are contained in it" (CWD 11 August 1877). This inflection involves the drop of a semitone (contradicting the rising contour of the Communion theme) unfolding as A♭–G and leading into a darkening harmonic shift from A♭ major to C minor (see Example 11 in *PARSIFAL*). This inflection has often been described as the *Schmerzensfigur* (pain motive). In many parts of the drama, Wagner richly develops this basic musical idea in connection with Amfortas. At two crucial points, we can perceive how this chromatic contamination found its way into the heart of the Communion theme. In his narrative in Act I, when GURNEMANZ describes how Amfortas fell into the arms of an irresistible woman (the transformed Kundry), we hear how her chromatic motive of seduction generates the dissonant inflection within the Communion theme. That seduction is replayed in Act II, with Parsifal taking the place of Amfortas. As she delivers the poisoned kiss, her chromatic motive once more implants the dissonant semitone tension into the Communion theme, while Parsifal recoils, exclaiming "Amfortas" to the falling half-step F–E. This two-note figure or "dyad" has far-reaching significance in the drama (McCreless).

Amfortas's two main passages are his extended lament in the Act I Temple Scene, which delays the Grail Service, and his despairing prayer before Titurel's coffin in Act III. To Titurel's admonition to reveal the Grail in Act I, Amfortas initially resists, providing a moving description of his tormented experience that is at once retrospective and anticipatory. His music contains a poignant theme featuring chromatic descending thirds that is set earlier to the choral text "sinful worlds, with a thousand pains" as well as motivic inflections associated with Klingsor. In Act III, Amfortas yearns more than ever for death, but is instead healed and relieved of his office through Parsifal's arrival at the Grail Temple with the Holy Spear.

WILLIAM KINDERMAN

Patrick McCreless, "Motive and Magic: A Referential Dyad in *Parsifal*," *Music Analysis* 9.3 (1990): 227–65.

Ancient Greece. Like so many of his contemporaries, Wagner was drawn to ancient Greece as a model for cultural, political, and artistic renewal. The German ideal of Greece dates back to the late eighteenth century and to the pioneering art historian Johann Joachim Winckelmann, who in 1755 claimed that the only way to achieve true greatness was to imitate the ancients. Rejecting the Roman-inspired classicism associated with France, Winckelmann extolled the ideal beauty of Greek art while drawing a sharp contrast between the harmonious nature of Greek society and a MODERNITY plagued by division and disunity. This view of Greece strongly influenced prominent German intellectuals of subsequent generations, including HERDER, GOETHE, SCHILLER, and HEGEL. It was against this larger cultural backdrop that Wagner was exposed to ancient Greek history, language, and literature through his schooling in DRESDEN and LEIPZIG, as well as through his uncle ADOLF WAGNER, a noted philologist and translator. Wagner was clearly fascinated by these subjects, and despite his own claim to have neglected Latin in favor of learning Greek, he never mastered the language. While living in PARIS (1839–42), Wagner rekindled his study of classical antiquity with the expert help of a friend, philologist Samuel LEHRS, but again his attempt to learn Greek ended unsuccessfully.

Wagner's most meaningful and lasting engagement with the Greeks came after his appointment as Kapellmeister in Dresden, at which time he began amassing a library filled with several volumes of works by classical authors (DRESDEN LIBRARY). A pivotal moment occurred in the summer of 1847, when he read translations of Aeschylus, Aristophanes, and Plato, along with several scholarly works on classical antiquity. This experience – and in particular that of reading Aeschylus' *Oresteia* – appears to have brought into focus Wagner's existing dissatisfaction with modern theater (including opera) and to have colored his views on the role that he might play in reshaping it. Not only did Wagner's enthusiasm for ancient Greece inform his key theoretical writings of the late 1840s and 1850s but it also influenced aspects of his musical works and thus ultimately formed a vital part of his ambitious aesthetic project aimed at OPERATIC REFORM.

In Die KUNST UND DIE REVOLUTION (*Art and Revolution*, 1849), the first of his three major ZURICH essays, Wagner identifies Greece as the wellspring of all European art, placing Athenian tragedy at the pinnacle of a tradition that had steadily declined from antiquity to the present age. For, whereas Greek art was the public expression of a free, communal spirit, modern art was a commodity that embodied an individual consciousness and was geared primarily toward a wealthy leisure class. Greek tragedy was for Wagner the highest manifestation of this ancient aesthetic, combining music, poetry, and DANCE in a *GESAMTKUNSTWERK* that had mass appeal and was performed free of charge as part of a religious FESTIVAL. Yet with the downfall of ancient Greece came the concomitant demise of Greek tragedy, marked by a splintering of this once-unified artwork into various component parts that went on to develop in unnatural isolation from one another. With his own operatic ambitions in mind, Wagner envisions a return of the total artwork that will come on the heels of a "great revolution of mankind," the successful completion of which will signify the overthrow of existing political and economic structures, and the advent of a free, utopian society. Wagner elaborates on this idea in Der KUNSTWERK DER ZUKUNFT (The Artwork of the Future, 1849/50), heralding the arrival of a modern-day *Gesamtkunstwerk* that will assume the guise of a musical drama and, like the Attic tragedy from which it draws inspiration, will be rooted firmly in the spirit of the VOLK. Acknowledging the impossibility of a return to antiquity, Wagner is careful to note that his objective involves something other than a mere revival or imitation of Greek drama. In reality, the unified artwork that Wagner has in mind is none other than his own MUSIC DRAMA, the blueprint for which is provided in OPER UND DRAMA (Opera and Drama, 1851). Again taking his cue from Greek tragedy, Wagner outlines a work whose plot and characters are drawn from MYTH (albeit Germanic) and in which the orchestra, conceived in symphonic terms, assumes the role of a Greek CHORUS by commenting on and elucidating the action through, among other things, a rich and dynamic network of LEITMOTIVE.

Wagner's essays were aimed partly at creating a theoretical framework for an operatic project that began in 1848 and would eventually become Der RING DES NIBELUNGEN. This work best reflects his AESTHETICS and, for that reason, is most indebted to Greek tragedy. The idea of a tetralogy itself recalls the Attic festivals that featured the performance of three tragedies followed by a lighter satyr-play. The only surviving trilogy, Aeschylus' *Oresteia*, appears to have strongly influenced the conception of the *Ring*, especially insofar as Wagner invested his cycle with a cosmic import that is Aeschylean in nature. Of even greater significance, it seems, was Aeschylus' partially extant Prometheus trilogy, which Wagner knew in a reconstruction by Johann Gustav Droysen. Perhaps most notably, BRÜNNHILDE bears a striking similarity to Prometheus in that both are confined to a remote place for disobeying the rule of the gods, and are ultimately freed by the descendant of a woman they once consoled. Still other aspects of the cycle may owe something to the Oedipus saga, which Wagner discusses at length in *Oper und Drama*. Thus Brünnhilde's self-sacrifice at the end of *Götterdammerung*, which brings about the destruction of Valhalla, is akin to the symbolic destruction of the Theban state that Wagner ascribes to Antigone's act of love in Sophocles' celebrated tragedy.

The parallels that have been drawn between Greek literature and Wagner's other operas are generally less compelling than those pertaining to the *Ring*. Wagner himself claimed that Der FLIEGENDE HOLLÄNDER and TANNHÄUSER were influenced by Homer's *Odyssey*, and he likewise pointed to elements of LOHENGRIN and Die MEISTERSINGER that were inspired by Greek works. Such connections are of little consequence, however, and it seems doubtful that Wagner had classical models in mind as he worked on these operas. Yet the mere fact that he later made such claims attests to the intensity with which the Greeks had captured his artistic imagination.

Wagner's fascination with Greece persisted throughout his life, as evidenced by his friendship with the young NIETZSCHE and the creation of the Bayreuth FESTIVAL THEATER. The latter endeavor, which arose from Wagner's desire to restore the public, dignified character of Greek art, represented his attempt at re-creating the ancient amphitheater in a modern context. Together, the Festival Theater and the operatic tetralogy for which it was ostensibly built stand as a lasting testament to the extraordinary richness of Wagner's lifelong engagement with ancient Greece.   JASON GEARY

Anders, Gottfried Engelbert (b. 1795; d. 1866), pseudonym of German aristocrat who belonged to the triumvirate of Wagner's closest friends during his stay in Paris 1839–42, the other two being Samuel LEHRS and Ernst Benedikt KIETZ. Anders was a music librarian at the Bibliothèque Royale, a contributor to Maurice SCHLESINGER's *REVUE ET GAZETTE MUSICALE*, and author of *Détails biographiques sur Beethoven* (1839), which Wagner even thought to use for his own planned Beethoven biography.   NICHOLAS VAZSONYI

Anti-Semitism. Wagner's hostile views of JEWS and their role in German culture have been controversial ever since he went public with them in 1850. If his position on the "Jewish question" caused a certain amount of debate at the time, it did not move to the forefront of the various controversies that dogged him throughout his career. This changed dramatically as a consequence of the intense examination of the Holocaust, when, in the late 1960s, the larger question of Wagner's anti-Semitism became the focus of heated international debate. The fact that HITLER was an ardent Wagnerian fueled the controversy and problematized the historical role of Wagner as the towering cultural icon of the epoch that witnessed the incubation period of NATIONAL SOCIALISM, the fifty years from the death of the composer to the beginning of Hitler's dictatorship.

Today there is broad consensus regarding Wagner's obsessive Judeophobia as revealed in his essayistic writings, CORRESPONDENCE, and conversations. The question of the anti-Semitic import of the operatic works, however, has become the most contested issue of Wagner studies.

Das JUDENTUM IN DER MUSIK (Jewishness in Music) appeared in the *NEUE ZEITSCHRIFT FÜR MUSIK* on 3 and 6 September 1850, under the pseudonym of K. [Karl] Freigedank ("K., the free thinker") – a pseudonym that apparently fooled no one. The text suggests that Wagner was merely joining an ongoing debate, launched earlier that year by the journal's editor, Franz Brendel. But one document points to an earlier preoccupation with the matter, namely a letter to Wagner of 8 May 1850 in which his wife MINNA recalls a marital altercation *"two years"* ago" when she refused to sit through a reading of an "essay in which you slander whole races, which have been fundamentally helpful to you." This suggests that the origin of the *Judentum* essay was at least sketched in 1848, when Wagner still lived in DRESDEN.

The *Neue Zeitschrift* had been hostile to Giacomo MEYERBEER, the Jewish composer from Berlin who was all the rage at the Paris Opéra, from the publication of Robert SCHUMANN's critical review of *Les Huguenots* in 1837. Meyerbeer's *Le Prophète* (1849) reached Dresden in January of 1850. Wagner saw it at the Paris Opéra in February of that year, and it is likely that what triggered the publication of *Das Judentum in der Musik* was indeed the triumph of *Le Prophète*.

Referring in the essay to the ongoing debate mentioned above about "Hebraic artistic taste," Wagner begins by declaring his intention to explain why Germans instinctively dislike Jews. Now emancipated and, on account of their wealth, exercising inordinate influence in the cultural realm, particularly in music, a clear understanding of the reasons for their rejection, he claims, is called for. Jews speak the languages of their host culture like foreigners, because that is what in fact they are. As such, they are capable of grasping neither the mind nor the art of the "VOLK." If the sound of their speech is repugnant, he writes, their singing is simply unbearable. Jewish music, represented by the "gurgling, yodeling and babbling" of synagogue chant, lacks the proud historical development of German music. Jewish composers can only mimic "our" music; unable to tap into the "Volksgeist," the true source of great art, they produce superficial and idiosyncratic imitations.

Wagner's first exhibit is MENDELSSOHN who, despite prodigious talent, is said to have been incapable of writing truly affecting, passionate music. The second, unnamed but obvious, is Meyerbeer, the "universally famous Jewish musician of our own day," whose operas are characterized as trivial, absurd, and worthless. Wagner views Mendelssohn as a tragic figure; he views Meyerbeer as both tragicomical and contemptible.

Finally, Wagner considers two prominent Jewish writers, Ludwig Börne and Heinrich HEINE, who converted to Christianity in a vain effort to find REDEMPTION. But, he claims, true redemption for Jews – the lifting of the curse upon Ahasverus, the Wandering Jew of medieval Christian legend – is achieved through their "Untergang," a painful and bloody act of self-annihilation, a shedding of their Jewishness. This would be part of a universal utopian project of redeeming Jews and non-Jews alike in the effort to attain a new state of true humanity.

The article was immediately translated into French, published later that year in *Le Diapason. Revue musicale de Bruxelles*, and reprinted in *La France musicale*. The first English translation by William Ashton Ellis appeared in 1892. Since then three further translations have appeared by Evans (1910), Osborne (1973), and Spencer (1988).

The hostility of Wagner's essay, shared by his associates UHLIG, LAUBE, and GUTZKOW, among others, highlights the growth of anti-Jewish sentiment in the aftermath of the emancipation of the Jews in German lands. What in all likelihood activated his enmity was his painfully unsuccessful sojourn in PARIS (1839–42), when Meyerbeer dominated the Opéra of the French capital and the German-Jewish publisher Maurice SCHLESINGER dominated the musical press. The debt of gratitude that Wagner owed to Meyerbeer for the generous support he had received from his celebrated colleague had turned into resentment.

In this regard Wagner could not have failed to notice that a part of the Paris press was hostile to Meyerbeer (Murphy). His *Judentum* article of 1850 echoes and amplifies earlier Parisian criticism of Meyerbeer, including charges of a lack of originality, of a penchant for spectacle and effects for their own sake, and of rootlessness – the mark of a musical Wandering Jew, or *Juif errant*.

Wagner's judgment is based upon an unmistakably racial criterion. He ignores Mendelssohn's conversion and avoids mention of Bartholdy, thus deducing the "Jewishness" of the music from the composer's racial, rather than religious, identity. The fundamental impulses of Wagner's article are delivered through a variety of rhetorical gestures of exclusion: the insistence on the foreign origin of the Jews; the implied concern with purity; and the pervasive language of discrimination, pitting "us" against "them," and "our musical heroes" – BACH, MOZART, BEETHOVEN – against Jewish music. And yet, despite obsessive resentment of Jews, Wagner did not hesitate to work with Jewish artists, provided they dedicated themselves to his cause (see JEWS).

For reasons that are not obvious, Wagner republished the 1850 article in 1869, now as a brochure (brought out by J. J. Weber in Leipzig) with his own name attached. The essay is slightly revised and greatly augmented by an introductory open letter addressed to Marie von MUCHANOFF-KALERGIS (dated New Year, 1869). As in 1850, a variety of factors seem to have moved Wagner again to vent his resentment and hatred. The immediate trigger may have been the negative review of Die MEISTERSINGER (1868) by the Viennese critic Eduard HANSLICK, whom Wagner took to be Jewish and whom he had targeted for satirical treatment in an earlier draft of the opera, by giving the "Marker" of the Mastersingers' Guild the transparent name of "Hanslich." In the letter to Muchanoff, Wagner presents "Dr. Hanslick," the author of an aesthetics of music (Vom Musikalisch-Schönen [On the Beautiful in Music], 1854), as the intellectual spearhead of a far-flung anti-Wagner conspiracy. Other frustrations and humiliations, mostly imagined, lingered under the surface, including recollections of the Paris TANNHÄUSER SCANDAL in 1861, whose failure he blamed on a French press, bribed by Meyerbeer.

More deep-seated was Wagner's frustration with the advance of Jewish emancipation. He was convinced that his opponents in the Bavarian cabinet, von der PFORDTEN and von PFISTERMEISTER, had been influenced by Jews in their opposition to him. And he was especially disappointed that LUDWIG II remained unresponsive to his repeated warnings and entreaties to stem the influence of Jews. As Wagner later wrote to the king, he considered "the Jewish race the born enemy of pure humanity and all that is noble in man: there is no doubt that we Germans especially will be destroyed by them, and I may well be the last remaining German who, as an artist, has known how to hold his ground in the face of a Judaism which is now all-powerful" (letter to Ludwig II, 22 November 1881).

Compared to the article of 1850, the letter to Muchanoff represents an escalation of Wagner's anti-Jewish agitation in at least two significant regards. Drawing on his own chimerical sense of a Jewish conspiracy against him, Wagner here refers to German culture as doomed and decayed by the Jewish parasites feeding on it. The rhetorical ploy of presenting the "victory of Jewry" as not a threat but a fait accompli foreshadows the demagoguery of Wilhelm Marr, Édouard Drumont, and other notorious anti-Semites. More ominous is Wagner's mention, at the conclusion of the letter, of the possibility of the "removal by force [gewaltsame Auswerfung] of the corrosive foreign element" as the sole means of reversing the decline of German culture. He contemplates no specific measures, but he does return to this thought in Erkenne dich selbst

(Know Thyself, 1881), where he speaks of a "grand solution" (*große Lösung*, SSD 10:274), of the Jewish problem.

Expressions of Wagner's hostility to Jews are by no means restricted to the two editions of *Das Judentum in der Musik*. Anti-Semitism – the term became current in the wake of W. Marr's founding of the League of Anti-Semites in 1879 – also informs the essay WAS IST DEUTSCH? (What is German?, 1865/78) as well as the entire set of so-called *Regenerationsschriften* (REGENERATION essays), in one of which, *Erkenne dich selbst*, Wagner coined the label "the embodiment of the demon of the degeneration of mankind" (*plastischer Dämon des Verfalls der Menschheit*, SSD 10:272). On several occasions Joseph Goebbels took up this formulation, and it figures prominently in *Der ewige Jude* (1940), the notorious Nazi film that served as the propagandistic curtain-raiser to the Holocaust.

Although some of Wagner's thinking was grounded in the widespread Judeophobic anti-capitalism of Proudhon, Marx, and Bauer, its deepest roots were psychological and racial. This is evident, among others, from COSIMA WAGNER'S DIARIES, which offer abundant evidence of the composer's obsession with Jews and the "Jewish question," and from a revealing letter to LISZT (18 April 1851), in which he confesses that his "resentment" of Jews is "as necessary to my nature as gall is to the blood."

Anti-Semitism in Wagner's stage works

On the question of the anti-Semitic content of the operas, two distinct, mutually exclusive positions have emerged. Those who argue that the operas must be interpreted in light of Wagner's hatred of Jews tend to cite T. W. ADORNO's authoritative dictum, published in 1938 and later included in his *In Search of Wagner* (German ed. 1952), that "all the rejects of Wagner's works are caricatures of Jews" (23). Adorno had very few precursors, among them P. Bekker (1924) and J. E. de Sinoja (1933), but numerous followers, among them R. Gutman (1968), H. Zelinsky (1978), B. Millington (1984), P. L. Rose (1992), and M. A. Weiner (1995), who fleshed out his seminal observation.

Those who argue that on the contrary there is no basis for viewing SIXTUS BECKMESSER, ALBERICH, or MIME as caricatures of Jews include B. Magee (1968), D. Borchmeyer (1986, 1992), and M. Tanner (1996). Borchmeyer takes what he considers the "philologically unassailable" position that, of Wagner's "violently anti-Semitic polemical writings, there is not a single trace in [the] music dramas" (184).

Neither position is entirely convincing; both lack a clinching point. Given the multi-layered character of the music dramas and their multi-channeled mode of communication, it seems inappropriate to bring to bear a narrowly conceived notion of evidence. The fact that Beckmesser is nowhere called a Jew does not preclude subtextual and coded allusions to Jewish character traits. Likewise the absence of an overt political agenda does not preclude the propagation of a set of inherently discriminatory cultural and moral values – in the sense of "metapolitics" (C. Frantz). Furthermore, it strains credulity that Wagner should have been able to keep his most accomplished creations entirely free of so obsessive a concern as his hostility towards Jews.

On the other hand, it is far too simplistic to diagnose complex characters, such as Alberich or Beckmesser, as mere Jewish caricatures. It is equally shortsighted to conclude that Wagner's ultimate operatic agenda was the propagation of Jew-hatred or, for that matter, that any interpretation not anchored in his anti-Semitism is invalid. Indeed, given Wagner's loquaciousness about his own work, it is worth noting that he never drew attention to any anti-Jewish intent in his works for the stage, and that he always intended them to have universal appeal.

In the end, there is no point in denying that a significant part of the operatic work – Der RING DES NIBELUNGEN, Die Meistersinger, PARSIFAL – is at least imbued with the spirit of anti-Semitism. That spirit is communicated only indirectly, over the heads of the protagonists, as it were, through coded characterizations and allusions. Beckmesser, for example, is nowhere referred to as Jewish, but the accumulated weight of his defining traits probably suggested, and can still suggest, a stereotypical Jewishness, for he lacks creativity and originality; he opposes the "new" music; he is subtly associated with the cruel fairy tale of "The Jew in the Brambles," and he covets the dowry of the daughter of the wealthiest man in Nuremberg. Wagner himself does not connect the dots, but those in the know, those familiar with his views about Jews and with the Grimm Brothers' tale, are free to do so.

Likewise, the historical impact of the Hitler-Wagner nexus cannot be set aside. Hitler, whose cult of Wagner was ignited not by a study of the anti-Semitic writings but by the aesthetic experience of the operas, never invoked *Jewishness in Music* to justify his own hatred or the racial laws of the Third Reich. He rather practiced an ostentatiously and deceptively nonpolitical cult of Wagner, glorifying him as an exemplar of German greatness. By doing so, he nonetheless signaled his agreement with the composer's convictions about Jews and Jewish influence, and by his example, he encouraged legions of so-called nonpolitical music lovers to do likewise.   HANS RUDOLF VAGET

Theodor W. Adorno, *In Search of Wagner* (see bibliography).

Dieter Borchmeyer, "The Question of Anti-Semitism," in *The Wagner Handbook*, ed. U. Müller and P. Wapnewski, trans. and ed. J. Deathridge (see bibliography): 166–85.

Bryan Jens Malte Fischer, *Richard Wagners "Das Judentum in der Musik": Eine kritische Dokumentation als Beitrag zur Geschichte des Antisemitismus* (Frankfurt am Main: Insel, 2000).

Thomas S. Grey, "The Jewish Question," *The Cambridge Companion to Wagner*, ed. T. S. Grey (see bibliography): 203–18.

Bryan Magee, *The Tristan Chord: Wagner and Philosophy* (New York: Metropolitan, 2001): 344–8.

Kerry R. Murphy, "Berlioz, Meyerbeer, and the Place of Jewishness in Criticism," in *Berlioz. Past, Present, Future*, ed. P. Bloom (University of Rochester Press, 2003): 90–104.

Paul L. Rose, *Wagner: Race and Revolution* (New Haven, CT: Yale University Press, 1992).

Hans R. Vaget, "'Du warst mein Feind von je': The Beckmesser Controversy Revisited," *Wagner's "Meistersinger": Performance, History, Representation*, ed. N. Vazsonyi (see bibliography): 190–208.

Marc A. Weiner, *Wagner and the Anti-Semitic Imagination* (see bibliography).

Hartmut Zelinsky, "Die 'Feuerkur' des Richard Wagner oder die 'neue Religion' der 'Erlösung' durch 'Vernichtung,'" in *Richard Wagner: Wie antisemitisch darf ein Künstler sein?*, ed. H.-K. Metzger and R. Riehn (Munich: text + kritik, 1978): 79–112.

Apel, (Guido) Theodor (b. Leipzig, 11 May 1811; d. Leipzig, 20 Nov. 1867), German author and philanthropist. Studied at the Nikolaischule, where he met and befriended Wagner. Studied law at the universities of Leipzig and Heidelberg.

Son of a wealthy landowner, Apel suffered a crippling riding accident which left him blind after 1836. Their frequent and close CORRESPONDENCE from the early 1830s similarly breaks off in mid-1836, only to recommence briefly in 1840 when Wagner, and also MINNA, wrote asking for money to help sustain them during their stay in Paris. Though Apel apparently answered, he does not seem to have sent them the requested money. Again the correspondence breaks off, this time permanently.

During winter 1834–5, Wagner wrote an overture (WWV 37a, now LOST) to Apel's play *Columbus*. Two years earlier, Wagner composed *Glockentöne* (WWV 30, now lost), setting Apel's poem "Abendglocken" (Evening bells) for voice and piano (letter to Apel, 12 Oct 1832).   NICHOLAS VAZSONYI

Appia, Adolphe (b. Geneva, 1 Sep. 1862; d. Nyon, 29 Feb. 1928), Swiss designer and theorist, who revolutionized scenic design. His reforms originated from his contention that Wagner's "scenic concepts were in conflict with his dramatic purpose." Whereas Wagner's achievement had been the creation of a drama where music directly expressed inner action in ways not possible with the spoken word alone, the scenic means he used in staging his music dramas contradicted his dramatic achievement. Realistic spectacle, which was universally employed in late nineteenth-century theater, drew attention away from the action of the drama rather than expressing it. Appia advocated the abandonment of realistic scene-painting and the adoption of light as the primary scenic element, because of its suggestiveness and flexibility. He thought Wagnerian music drama should be played on minimalist or abstract sets where the careful combination of staging and lighting would allow for a direct realization of all aspects of the drama, from its broadest confrontations to its slightest nuances. The lines of the actor's body would be seen with complete clarity on Appia's stage rather than being hidden among the details of realistic stage design.

Wagner was the central inspiration for Appia's career, though he expanded his vision to include other operas and much spoken drama. His ideas proved seminal to much progressive scene design in modern theater. In his time, however, he found it difficult to win acceptance for his ideas. Despite the intervention of his friend Houston Stewart CHAMBERLAIN, COSIMA WAGNER decisively rejected any idea of Appia working at BAYREUTH, so his ideas first came to light through publications, notably *La Mise en scène du drame wagnérien* (Paris, 1895) and *La Musique et la mise en scène* (first published in Munich in German, 1899). He did not have an opportunity to be involved in the staging of a Wagnerian music drama until December 1923 when, on Arturo TOSCANINI's invitation, he designed *TRISTAN UND ISOLDE* at the Teatro alla Scala, Milan. Although Appia was satisfied with the designs and lighting, which attempted to realize the interior world of the lovers to the exclusion of the exterior, the production encountered several technical problems, a mixed critical response, and a confused, even hostile audience response. It was given five performances. In 1924, he began to direct the *RING* for the Basel Municipal Theater, in cubist settings that lacked the symbolist suggestiveness of the designs published in his earlier books. While performances of *Das RHEINGOLD* and *Die WALKÜRE* were well received by the public, the protests of a reactionary faction led to the cancellation of the remainder of the cycle.

Appia was an intensely private and retiring man and was not suited to the public life of the theater and its controversies. Consequently, his ideas were not widely known in his lifetime. However, when the BAYREUTH FESTIVAL reopened in 1951, for economic as well as artistic reasons, WIELAND and WOLFGANG WAGNER adopted the minimalist style that Appia pioneered and, through their productions, his work became more widely known and influential. SIMON WILLIAMS

See also PRODUCTION HISTORY

Archives. See MUSEUMS

Art and Climate. See KUNST UND KLIMA

Art and Revolution. See *Die KUNST UND DIE REVOLUTION*

Art for art's sake. See L'ART POUR L'ART

Art of transition (*Kunst des Übergangs*). Soon after completing the composition of TRISTAN UND ISOLDE, Wagner concluded in a letter to Mathilde WESENDONCK that his best music embodied "the art of transition" of the "finest and most gradual kind" (29 October 1859). Citing the second scene of *Tristan* Act II as his "greatest masterpiece" in this regard, he added that "the beginning of the scene offers life" and "the ending the most solemn, intensely felt longing for death: just take a look at how I've connected these corner-posts, how the scene leads from one to the other!"

Two German musicologists, Carl DAHLHAUS and Ulrich Siegele, have tried to get to the bottom of what Wagner meant by "the art of transition" in technical, musical, and dramatic terms. In his book *Richard Wagner's Music Dramas* (1979), Dahlhaus took an excerpt from *Tristan* Act I, scene 5 (ISOLDE's meeting with TRISTAN) and pointed to a deliberately uncoordinated network of caesuras in the handling of motive and text. His point was that the different levels in Wagner's concept of MUSIC DRAMA enabled him to create subtle senses of change with divergent nodal points in simultaneously sounding structures that avoid sharp formal divisions as a result. Siegele basically made the same point with a larger span of music from the opening of *Tristan* Act I, highlighting four levels – dramaturgy, text, cadences, and motives – in which the caesuras contained in each are set against each other in constant tension.

It was perhaps slightly perverse to choose Act I of *Tristan* to exemplify the "art of transition" when Wagner had made it abundantly clear that he had Act II in mind. Siegele suggests that any analysis carrying on from his own should include dynamics and ORCHESTRATION. Indeed, it is precisely the striking predominance of these features in the second scene of *Tristan* Act II – supposedly surface aspects of composers' scores usually low on scholars' agendas – that persuaded Wagner to choose it in the first place. To cite one example: BRANGÄNE watches over Tristan and Isolde as her anxious song warning of possible danger blends into their intimate duet, a differentiated orchestral tour de force twice shifting to the outer edge of the lovers' enclave where she stands.

Marvelous moments like these in *Tristan* are like cinema tracking shots that seamlessly traverse distances between subtly different emotional situations without cuts. Indeed, Wagner's "art of transition" is no triviality about his music simply moving smoothly from one point to another (MOZART's does it just as well, not to mention other examples) but a notable insight into his cinematic view of theater before the fact. "[N]obody has ever dreamt of anything with every part so well coordinated and clearly extended in every detail over such a large span," he told Mathilde Wesendonck, meaning not just antithetical structures of text and music, but acoustic and visual stimuli integrated on a much wider scale to create the illusion of life. No other remarks by Wagner better illustrate his anticipation of NEW MEDIA technology.   JOHN DEATHRIDGE

Carl Dahlhaus, *Richard Wagner's Music Dramas*, trans. Mary Whittall (Cambridge University Press, 1979): 57–61.

Ulrich Siegele, "'Kunst des Übergangs' und formale Artikulation: Beispiele aus Richard Wagners *Tristan und Isolde*," *Der "Komponist" Richard Wagner im Blick der aktuellen Musikwissenschaft: Symposion Würzburg 2000*, ed. U. Konrad and E. Voss (Wiesbaden: Breitkopf & Härtel, 2003): 25–32.

Artwork of the Future, The. See KUNSTWERK DER ZUKUNFT, DAS

Auber, Daniel-François-Esprit (b. Caen, 29 Jan. 1782; d. Paris, 12 May 1871), French opera composer. Wagner knew Auber's music well, having conducted some of his operas in the 1830s (*Le Maçon, Le Philtre, Lestocq*, and *Fra Diavolo*). In particular, he cherished *La Muette de Portici*, in which he saw both the culmination of French GRAND OPERA and the seeds of its demise. He met Auber occasionally in 1860 at the Café Tortoni (Paris) and wrote an article about the French composer on the occasion of the latter's death ("Reminiscences of Auber," PW 5:35–55).   HERMANN GRAMPP

Autobiographische Skizze (Autobiographical Sketch). Following the signal success of the sprawling grand opera RIENZI (1842), Wagner's longtime literary acquaintance Heinrich LAUBE asked the young composer to contribute an autobiographical essay to the popular weekly magazine he edited, *Zeitung für die elegante Welt*. It appeared in the issues of 1 and 8 February 1843. Wagner apparently understood that he was to give Laube a simple outline (or "sketch") which the experienced author and editor would elaborate into a longer biographical feature. Laube published Wagner's text largely as he received it, however, and this accounts in part for the uncustomary lucidity of Wagner's prose in this piece, much more direct and unadorned than most of his other writing. The text is also of considerable interest as the earliest among Wagner's several autobiographical texts: written ten years into his professional career, its account of the early operas, conducting positions, and the Paris sojourn of 1839–42 benefits from relative proximity to those events. Even here, however, some of the later tendency towards self-mythologization is already at work. Notably lacking from the narrative is any mention of an 1829 Leipzig guest appearance of Wilhelmine SCHRÖDER-DEVRIENT in BEETHOVEN's *Fidelio*, an event described later in MEIN LEBEN (My Life, 1865–81) as the decisive influence on Wagner's turn toward a career in opera. On the evidence of this memoir, he did not take particular notice of the singer until an 1834 performance of Bellini's *I Capuleti e i Montecchi*.   THOMAS S. GREY

Joseph Kürschner, "Varianten und Ergänzungen zu Richard Wagners 'Autobiographischer Skizze,'" *Richard-Wagner-Jahrbuch* (Stuttgart 1886): 286–92.

Richard Wagner, "Autobiographical Sketch," trans. Thomas S. Grey (see Appendix 5: Prose works).

Autograph manuscripts. As for all composers, especially those involved in theater, manuscripts going to and fro inside a complex of diverse human activities that have to do with performance always have elusive afterlives. The early Wagner was no different from other opera composers in the sense that the manuscripts he created as the basis for performance underwent a process of alteration during rehearsal that was regarded as normal at the time. After the work had undergone many alterations in rehearsal, the publication of the score inevitably had to be a compromise between the original autograph manuscript and the reality of its performance. Later on, even when the mature Wagner became more bullish – not to say utopian – about fixing notation in such a way that it left little room for cuts and alterations to the score in rehearsal, the same tension never entirely disappeared. Wagner even had to extend the transformation music in the first act of his final work PARSIFAL – with respect to its music and scenic disposition his most radically predetermined score – when it dawned on him that the scene change would take longer than anticipated.

Wagner's autograph manuscripts have always been about compromise in multiple senses of the word. Generosity – the feeling that he would never have use for a manuscript again – often gave way in time to the realization that he badly needed the autograph for another performance or authoritative edition. Indeed, the madcap nature of his creative life – huge ambition, quick moves from one gargantuan project to the next – seems to have given rise to a classic contradictory Wagnerian combination of insouciant carelessness, as if he were to say "now it's done, my friend: you are quite welcome to the residue," and painstaking care, even sometimes remorse, in the attempts at getting the lucky recipient of the manuscript to return it.

TANNHÄUSER went through no fewer than four stages of alteration after its first performance in 1845 (see WWV 70), among other things involving an interesting stand-off with Johannes BRAHMS about the return of the manuscript of the Venus scene in Act 1. Wagner had re-composed it for the 1861 Paris production and given it to Peter CORNELIUS, only to discover that it had landed in the possession of an arch-rival, who was reluctant to give it back. A first edition of *Die MEISTERSINGER VON NÜRNBERG*, a work that clearly interested Brahms, was demanded in exchange. In a letter dated 26 June 1875, however, Wagner asked him to accept a first edition of *Das RHEINGOLD* instead, as he had "run out" of copies of *Die Meistersinger*, arguing that it was precisely in the first work of the *RING* cycle that the setting-up of the "thematic musical material" would receive Brahms's "friendly attention."

The case is only one of many. In other instances, the manuscripts were frequently given away to settle debts (see MONEY), or went missing by sheer chance. Wagner's peripatetic existence as conductor and manager of concerts of his own works is certainly why such a small number of concert versions of EXCERPTS from works such as *LOHENGRIN* and the *Ring* have survived. The missing links can also be explained by the unthinking generosity of Wagner's heirs. The partial survival of the first complete draft of *Lohengrin*, for example, is mainly due to the habit of the Wagner family in the first part of the twentieth century of making gifts of autographs to prominent personalities and institutions without retaining copies (Deathridge 1989: 57). Some indeed have resulted in permanent loss, including the fourth sheet of the first complete draft of *Lohengrin* beginning with King Henry's words to the protagonist: "Do I properly recognize the power that brought you to this country?" The recipient was Adolf HITLER on his 43rd birthday, just nine months before his seizure of power in 1933.

The Wagner autographs given to Hitler on his 50th birthday by the German Chamber of Industry and Commerce in 1939 constitute the most serious loss of all. They include the full scores of *Die FEEN*, *Das LIEBESVERBOT*, *RIENZI*, *Das Rheingold*, and *Die WALKÜRE*, as well as a complete draft of the music of *Der FLIEGENDE HOLLÄNDER* and a copy of a short score of *GÖTTERDÄMMERUNG* in a variety of hands. (The story put about after World War II that Hitler had the autograph score of *Götterdämmerung* in his possession when he died is a myth.) Wagner had originally presented the autographs to King LUDWIG II of Bavaria in the 1860s and 1870s, and it was from Ludwig's estate that they passed into the possession of the Wittelsbacher Ausgleichsfonds. They have been missing since 1945. Their loss is particularly significant with respect to the first three of the early operas, as no other complete autograph scores of these works have ever existed, and in the case of *Rienzi* no complete printed scores either (Deathridge 1977: 147–54).

The vast bulk of Wagner's surviving autographs, on the other hand, are the simple outcome of what Brahms accurately called his "gigantic capacity for work, colossal industry and horrendous energy." From the very beginning, including the sprawling five-act play *Leubald* (WWV 1) written in his teens, Wagner was prone to highly detailed, calligraphically perfectionist autographs mirroring a systematic filling-out of vast theatrical spaces. ADORNO called them "giant cardboard boxes" (Adorno 32, translation modified). And according to COSIMA WAGNER'S DIARIES, even Wagner himself, while working on the magnificent score of *Götterdämmerung*, sounded skeptical: "I am no composer. I only wanted to learn enough to compose *Leubald* . . . and that is how things have remained – it is only the subjects which are different" (29 January 1870).

Wagner's extant autograph manuscripts are in fact the best proof imaginable of the daring actuality of his works. The sheer rationality of production they present may alienate those sentimentally attached to his music. But the discrete stages in that production (Deathridge 1974/5 and WWV), starting from short outlines in words, progressing through continuous drafts of the libretto, and then carefully calculated levels of composition that normally embraced a consequentially rational transition from a fundamental harmonic setting of the vocal line to ever more elaborate intensifications of a basic grid of music and extra-musical data into the miraculous scores everyone knows, are actually a complete rejection of classical, even operatic, method. No operatic or purely musical work had experienced this level of integration and systematization before. In each of his major theatrical enterprises, Wagner progressed from self-authored prose outline to prose draft, from verse draft to a virtually complete outline musical draft, normally to a musical draft in detail, to a full score sketch in most cases, and then to a final, usually exquisitely written final score that was in essence a virtuosic amalgamation of what Friedrich Kittler has defined as the three levels of a "machine" working in the three "data fields" of verbal, musical (orchestral), and scenic information (232–3). Time and again, Wagner's autograph manuscripts demonstrate a rethinking of text, music, theater, and new possibilities of technical precision that rank their author among the pioneers of modern mass media.

Wagner's letters and writings, and the enormous amount of paper and ink that went into their creation, are in some ways an ironic counterpart to their equivalents in the musical and dramatic realm in the sense that their purpose appears in comparison to be devoted more to special-pleading and the legitimacy of a totally new way of thinking about music and theater than a truly creative tour de force in their own right. In these documents there is a sense that Wagner is writing off the cuff as he actually spoke, still with the startlingly clear handwriting characteristic of his prose, verse, and musical drafts to be sure, but for the most part without the same sweep and innovative gusto. The reason may be simply that writing an essay or a letter for Wagner meant writing it just once – even the longest of his prose works seem to have been written gradually day by day without any apparent need for revision – rather than spending time on the kind of changes we often find in the layers of systematic reprocessing in the autograph manuscripts for his stage works. The same *laissez-faire* attitude noted earlier toward the retention of the latter, however, is true of the autographs of the writings and letters as well, which is why it caused the mature Wagner considerable trouble in tracking them down when he eventually saw the opportunity of collecting the writings into a single edition, or indeed, in the case of the Mathilde WESENDONCK letters, of wanting to destroy the autographs in case they should fall into the wrong hands (Deathridge, *Beyond Good and Evil*: 130, see also CORRESPONDENCE).

Inventories of Wagner's autograph manuscripts for his musical works and letters are to be found in WWV and the WAGNER-BRIEFE-VERZEICHNIS. An inventory of autograph manuscripts for the writings has yet to appear.

JOHN DEATHRIDGE

Theodor W. Adorno, *In Search of Wagner* (see bibliography).
John Deathridge, "The Nomenclature of Wagner's Sketches," *Proceedings of the Royal Musical Association* 101 (1974/5): 75–83.
  "Through the Looking-Glass: Some Remarks on the First Complete Draft of *Lohengrin*," *Analyzing Opera: Verdi and Wagner* (Berkeley: University of California Press, 1989): 56–91.
  Wagner Beyond Good and Evil (see bibliography).
  Wagner's "Rienzi": A Reappraisal Based on a Study of the Sketches and Drafts (Oxford: Clarendon, 1977).
Friedrich Kittler, "World-Breath: On Wagner's Media Technology," *Opera Through Other Eyes*, ed. David J. Levin (Stanford University Press, 1993): 215–35.

Avant-garde. Originally a military term to denote that part of the army which ventured first into harm's way, often at great personal cost, the term "avant-garde" as used in the aesthetic sphere continues to elude conclusive definition. Applied narrowly, it refers to the post-expressionist and Dada movements of the 1920s and 1930s (Bürger). However, this definition fails to acknowledge the existence of the "avant-garde" as an ongoing set of artistic attitudes and practices with roots substantially pre-dating the early twentieth century. Understood more broadly as an idea rather than as a distinct period, "avant-garde" denotes a position claimed by artists since the 1840s (Bourdieu), or a concept based in the radical politics of post-revolutionary France of the 1790s (Calinescu), or an offspring of ROMANTICISM (Poggioli). The problem with broader approaches is that they fail to discern often significant differences between distinct avant-gardist movements. Nevertheless, common to all these definitions is the idea of avant-garde as a mode of opposition to the numerous transformations – social, political, economic, philosophical, technological – following the French Revolution and characteristic of MODERNITY.

The military connotation of "avant-garde" is preserved in the notion of resistance, in the practice of aesthetic risk-taking, as well as in the locational sense of being at the forefront. The self-appointed role of the avant-garde to suggest new directions is evident in the explicit future-orientedness of its practitioners. Claiming the future became a beloved rhetorical position in the first half of the nineteenth century, evident in countless invocations: "new wine demands new bottles" (Franz LISZT); Liszt is "pianist of the future" (BERLIOZ); "l'art d'avenir" (art of the future – Joseph d'Ortigue); "Neue Bahnen" (New Paths – SCHUMANN's 1853 review of Johannes BRAHMS); "the philosophy of the future" (Ludwig FEUERBACH, 1843), not to mention Wagner's own *Artwork of the Future* (*Das KUNSTWERK DER ZUKUNFT*, 1849/50) a concept which earned his works the misnomer "ZUKUNFTSMUSIK."

Politically, the avant-garde is often misunderstood as an anti-modern (not to be confused with anti-modernist) movement, but instead avant-garde regards modernity as an incomplete project, imperfectly executed. Permanently dissatisfied with the status quo, the political wing of the avant-garde, aligned with so-called progressive ideologies and social movements, produces art in service of a political agenda rather than for profit. While indifference to money is a pose adopted almost uniformly by the avant-garde, the art for art's sake movement within the avant-garde distinguishes itself by renouncing all other agendas – political, philosophical, sociological – save for the artwork itself. Like "avant-garde," art for art's sake can be understood historically as *L'ART POUR L'ART* – a French literary movement of the late nineteenth century – or as an idea common to several generations of artists, including composers, beginning in the late eighteenth and continuing into the twentieth century.

From about 1840, Richard Wagner's newly defined artistic persona takes up its rhetorical position at the nexus of ideas permeating the avant-garde and "art for art's sake" movements – nationalized – where disavowal of the market and money become markers for both GERMANNESS and a broad rejection of industrial modernity. Given Wagner's investment in the Germanization of his position, it is paradoxical that French artists of the historical *l'art pour l'art* were among the most significant Wagner enthusiasts, or *Wagnériens*.

NICHOLAS VAZSONYI

Pierre Bourdieu, *The Rules of Art: Genesis and Structure of the Literary Field*, trans. Susan Emanuel (Stanford University Press, 1995).
Peter Bürger, *Theory of the Avant-Garde* (Minneapolis: University of Minnesota Press, 1984).

Matei Calinescu, *Faces of Modernity: Avant-Garde, Decadence, Kitsch* (Bloomington: Indiana University Press, 1977).

Renato Poggioli, *The Theory of the Avant-Garde*, trans. Gerald Fitzgerald (Cambridge, MA: Harvard University Press, 1968).

Avenarius, Eduard (b. Halberstadt, 1809; d. Dresden, 1885) **and Cäcilie.** German publisher who cofounded the book dealership Brockhaus and Avenarius with Fritz and Heinrich BROCKHAUS with stores in Leipzig and Paris. Eduard, who was married to Wagner's half-sister, Cäcilie (daughter of Ludwig GEYER and JOHANNA WAGNER, née Pätz), ran the Paris store until it was sold in 1844 and was thus in that town during Wagner's ill-fated stay between 1839 and 1842. Wagner wrote to Avenarius already before arrival in Paris, asking for help finding lodging. During his stay, there were frequent appeals for money. Correspondence continued, though sporadically, especially letters to Cäcilie. In 1853, Avenarius founded a publishing house with Hermann Mendelssohn in Leipzig, taking over works published by J. J. Weber and a catalog from Georg Wigand, whose brother Otto WIGAND had published works by Wagner. NICHOLAS VAZSONYI

Bach, Johann Sebastian (b. Eisenach, 21 March 1685; d. Leipzig, 28 July 1750), composer and organist. Bach lived within a geographic area of 100 kilometers in radius, moving from one musical post to another. His contemporaries reckoned him one of the great keyboard masters of the time, as well as an accomplished composer of church and chamber music. Richard Wagner, contemplating his life more than a century later, described it otherwise. This "wondrous man of music" embodied the sufferings of Germany in its darkest time: "behold the master, a wretched organist and cantor, slinking from one Thuringian parish to another, puny places scarcely known to us by name; see him so unheeded, that it required a whole century to drag his works from oblivion" (PW 4:162).

As Wagner's observations of an "unfathomably great" man "imprisoned" in his age suggest, Bach's reputation during his lifetime bore little relation to the veneration he achieved after his death (PW 4:162). The apotheosis of Bach as the "the greatest musical poet and musical orator who has ever lived or will ever live" had its first expression in Johann Nikolas Forkel's landmark 1802 biography (Forkel viii), and thereafter Bach's influence entered German and European cultural life by a variety of means. With Felix MENDELSSOHN's revival of Bach's *St. Matthew Passion* in Berlin (1829), the genius of the keyboard became also known as the profound dramatist of Christianity's story of human suffering and faith. Bach's growing reputation paralleled the rise of German national consciousness, and by the 1870s he was regarded as the point to which "all the music of Germany tended" and from which it developed (Spitta 1.i).

The publication of Bach's works under the auspices of the *Bach Gesellschaft* between 1851 and 1900 forms the background to Wagner's veneration of Bach. Early Wagner biographers suggested that Wagner came to appreciate Bach in the early 1830s, when he studied composition with the St. Thomas Church cantor Christian Theodor WEINLIG. Subsequent research indicates that Weinlig himself neither admired nor extensively taught Bach's compositions. Wagner's deepest engagement with Bach probably came during his ZURICH and BAYREUTH periods, when he studied and played Bach with family and visitors. A number of Wagner's essays written in PARIS expressed admiration for Bach's "inexhaustible creative force." In subsequent essays, most importantly *WAS IST DEUTSCH?* (What is German?, 1865/78), Bach embodies the greatness of German art, carried forward by musical geniuses from MOZART and BEETHOVEN to Wagner himself. Bach's presence is also felt in Wagner's music dramas, most obviously in Die *MEISTERSINGER VON NÜRNBERG*, with its evocation of a world like Bach's and with its critique of musical rules, which Bach both honored and transcended (though not, Wagner suggests, in the way that he himself did). Bach's influence is also present whenever Wagner deployed counterpoint. In the final analysis, Wagner must be regarded as more beneficiary than leader of the Bach revival, contributing in his writings to the Bach cult but using Bach's legacy principally as a foil to his own revolutionary art.   CELIA APPLEGATE

J. N. Forkel, *Über Johann Sebastian Bachs Leben, Kunst und Kunstwerke* (Leipzig, 1802).
Phillip Spitta, *Johann Sebastian Bach*, 3 vols., 1873 (repr. New York: Dover, 1952).

Bakunin, Mikhail (b. Priamukhino, Russia, 30 May [Old Style: 18 May] 1814; d. Berne, 1 July 1876), Russian anarchist. A nobleman's heir, Bakunin resigned his army commission to study philosophy in Moscow. Part of the "Stankevich Circle," he translated FICHTE and HEGEL and fell under Alexander Herzen's influence. There followed from 1840 an itinerant revolutionary existence. In Berlin, he shared an apartment with Ivan Turgenev, joined the Young Hegelian party, and penned *The Reaction in Germany* (1842). In Zurich, he travelled with Georg HERWEGH, meeting Wilhelm Weitling and other "German communists." In Paris, he met fellow anarchist and later friend, Pierre-Joseph Proudhon, and his eventual nemesis, Karl Marx. Sympathy for the Polish cause distinguished him from many Russians *and* Germans, and got him expelled from Paris. In 1848, he attended the First Slav Congress in Prague and made his *Appeal to the Slavs*, demanding continental revolutionary unity to overthrow Russian, Austrian, and Prussian autocracy.

Following Wagner's 1849 Palm Sunday performance of Beethoven's Ninth Symphony, Bakunin approached the conductor, announcing: "if all music were to be lost in the coming world conflagration, we should risk our own lives to preserve this symphony" (ML/E 384). Wagner writes a little of their ensuing discussions, generally of a political nature, Bakunin rejoicing in his "creative passion" for destruction (Lehning 58). Had Wagner not yet heard of Marx, he most likely would have done so during these talks. Upon Bakunin's next return from revolutionary Prague, he threw himself into the DRESDEN UPRISING, despite disapproving of its amateurism. He proposed centralizing gunpowder reserves in the Rathaus (town hall) to blow up approaching Prussian troops.

Captured and arrested in Chemnitz with other revolutionaries, including August RÖCKEL but not Wagner, Bakunin received commuted death sentences in Saxony and Austria, before extradition to Russia, where he was held in solitary confinement in St. Petersburg's Peter and Paul Fortress from 1851 to 1857. Released into Siberian exile, he escaped via Japan to San Francisco, whence he resumed his itinerant activities, through London, Lithuania, Stockholm, Switzerland, Lyons, Bologna, and so on. As he disdained participation in the corruption of "bourgeois" political life, his anarchistic conflict with Marx's "scientific socialism" intensified, culminating in expulsion from the First International in 1872. In the wake of this and the FRANCO-PRUSSIAN WAR (1871), Bakunin wrote *Statism and Anarchy*, perhaps the most complete statement of his beliefs.

Though this is as coherent a tract as we have from Bakunin, arguably more powerful were: his insistence upon revolutionary activity; his twin passions for destruction (cf. *GÖTTERDÄMMERUNG*'s Immolation Scene) and revolution-ary fraternity; and his provision of memorable dicta, such as inverting Voltaire to say that, if God existed, it would be necessary to abolish Him (Lehning 128). Bakunin's charisma impressed Wagner greatly; references persist in COSIMA WAGNER'S DIARIES. During his final year, 1876, Bakunin seems, in startlingly later-Wagnerian fashion, to have lost some of the Rousseauvian faith he had held since childhood in man's natural goodness, remarking from Lugano: "If there were in the whole world three people, two of them would unite to oppress the third" (Carr 478). As rehearsals for the first Bayreuth festival began, Bakunin – on his deathbed – requested the works of SCHOPENHAUER.   MARK BERRY

E. H. Carr, *Michael Bakunin* (London: Macmillan, 1937).
Arthur Lehning, ed., *Michael Bakunin: Selected Writings*, trans. Steven Cox and Olive Stevens (London: Jonathan Cape, 1973).

Ballenstedt, Festival in. Ballenstedt is a small town in the Harz district of Germany, seat of power for the princes of Bernburg in Saxony-Anhalt. On 22 and 23 June 1852, it became the venue for a music festival under the direction of Franz LISZT. It was the first time in Germany that a music festival was dedicated to contem-porary music. Despite off-putting and conflicting announcements in the news-papers, more than 1,000 people from all parts of Germany attended. The planned program was changed on the first day because interest became increasingly focused on Wagner, whose then little-known *TANNHÄUSER* OVERTURE opened the festival. It left such an impression that it had to be repeated at the end of the second day. The consequences of the music festival, together with Wagner's writings, and the reaction to the performance of *LOHENGRIN* in Weimar, fundamentally changed Wagner's exposure and situation. Before Ballenstedt, Wagner had only been performed in Weimar; two years later, his work was being performed on more than thirty stages.   HELMUT KIRCHMEYER
TRANS. HOLLY WERMTER

Helmut Kirchmeyer, *Robert Schumanns Düsseldorfer Brahms-Aufsatz "Neue Bahnen" und die Ausbreitung der Wagnerschen Opern bis 1856: Psychogramm eines "letzten" Artikels*, Abhandlungen der Sächsischen Akademie der Wissenschaften, Philologisch-historische Klasse 73.6 (Berlin: Akademie-Verlag, 1993).

Ballet. See DANCE

Barenboim, Daniel (b. Buenos Aires, 15 Nov. 1942), Israeli pianist and conductor. Barenboim made his BAYREUTH debut with *TRISTAN UND ISOLDE* in 1981. *PARSIFAL* followed in 1987, then the *RING* in Harry Kupfer's production (1988). He has argued for the informal ban on Wagner's music in ISRAEL to be lifted, and caused controversy by conducting the Prelude to *Tristan* there in 2001.   CHRIS WALTON

Daniel Barenboim, *Everything Is Connected: The Power of Music* (London: Phoenix, 2009).

Baudelaire, Charles (b. Paris, 9 April 1821; d. Paris, 31 Aug. 1867), innovative French poet, critic, and translator. Baudelaire lived in PARIS for most of his forty-six years, both fascinated and unnerved by the city's rapid transformation into a modern urban center during his lifetime. He composed poetry from adolescence onward, but his first notable publications were extended pieces of art criticism written in response to the Salons of 1845 and 1846. Shortly thereafter, he began to translate works by Edgar Allan Poe into French, eventually producing five volumes of Poe translations as well as a free rendering of Thomas De Quincey's *Confessions of an English Opium Eater*. Baudelaire also continued to write art criticism, to which he added literary criticism, a variety of unfinished autobiographical projects, and a series of prose poems. Most importantly, in June 1857, Baudelaire published *Les Fleurs du mal* (The Flowers of Evil), the collection of verse poems he had been planning since the early 1840s. The first edition of this book was surrounded by scandal: French government censors condemned it as an assault on public decency, ordering Baudelaire to pay a fine and excise six poems from the volume. In 1861, however, Baudelaire succeeded in publishing a second edition, considerably expanded and reorganized. Three years later, in poor health and in financial distress, he traveled to Belgium in the hope of earning money from public lectures and arranging for the publication of his collected works. While still fruitlessly pursuing these ventures in 1866, Baudelaire suffered a paralyzing stroke brought on by syphilis, and died the following year.

Even though allusions to music abound in Baudelaire's other writings, he tried his hand at music criticism only once. Though not formally educated in music, Baudelaire claimed nonetheless to have been transformatively moved by three promotional ORCHESTRAL CONCERTS – consisting of choral and instrumental excerpts from *TANNHÄUSER* and *LOHENGRIN*, plus the overture to *Der FLIEGENDE HÖLLANDER* and the PRELUDE to *TRISTAN UND ISOLDE* – which Wagner conducted in Paris at the Théâtre-Italien early in 1860. Joining the critical controversy provoked by these concerts, Baudelaire expressed his admiration in a letter to Wagner on 17 February 1860, and he subsequently studied a French translation of the four libretti, together with Wagner's prefatory summary of his major prose works. When Wagner was forced to withdraw *Tannhäuser* after three disastrous performances at the Paris Opéra in March 1861, Baudelaire once again reacted sympathetically, this time with an essay on "Richard Wagner" that appeared on 1 April in the *Revue européenne*. Augmented by a supplement critiquing the social and political reasons for *Tannhäuser*'s failure in the French capital, a second edition of Baudelaire's essay, now entitled *Richard Wagner et "Tannhäuser" à Paris*, was released soon afterward in brochure form by the publisher E. Dentu. As a result, Baudelaire was among the earliest and most persuasively articulate of Wagner's proponents in France.

MARGARET MINER

See also *L'ART POUR L'ART*; *TANNHÄUSER*, PARIS SCANDAL OF 1861; WAGNERISM

Baumgartner, Wilhelm (b. Rorschach, 15 Nov. 1820; d. Zurich, 17 March 1867), choral conductor, and composer of songs and piano salon pieces. Baumgartner studied with Alexander Müller in ZURICH, and first met Wagner in DRESDEN in 1847. After Wagner settled in Zurich, he and "Boom" (Wagner's nickname for him) became close. Baumgartner introduced Wagner to FEUERBACH's writings, and Wagner reviewed Baumgartner's songs favorably in 1852. Baumgartner helped prepare the chorus for Wagner's festival concerts (Zurich, 1853).   CHRIS WALTON

Chris Walton, *Richard Wagner's Zurich* (see bibliography).

Bayreuth. Located in upper Franconia on the Red Main River, Bayreuth was first mentioned in local records in 1194 and was recognized as a town by 1231. In 1260, it came into the possession of the Franconian Hohenzollerns; however, only in 1603 did the Margraves make it their principal residence. Ravaged by the Hussites in 1430 and again during the Thirty Years War (1618–48), Bayreuth later enjoyed a golden age under Margrave Frederick and Margravine Wilhelmina, the eldest and favorite sister of Prussian King Frederick the Great. During their rule (1735–63), the court architects erected such baroque jewels as the MARKGRÄFLICHES OPERNHAUS (Margravial Opera House), the New Palace with its courtyard garden, and the row of buildings on the present Friedrichstraße. Napoleon's defeat of Prussia in 1806 put an end to Hohenzollern rule; four years later, the town was incorporated into the new Kingdom of Bavaria. Since 1817, Bayreuth has served as an administrative capital for the Bavarian district that received its current name, Upper Franconia, in 1838.

Bayreuth had only 13,000 residents when Wagner first visited in 1835. On his return in 1871, with visions of staging the RING at the Margravial Opera House, the town was scarcely larger, despite its connection to the Bavarian train network in 1853. Under its long-serving mayor, Theodor MUNCKER, the town's population doubled, its urban infrastructure was modernized, and Bayreuth became the epicenter of the Wagnerian enterprise. The family home, WAHNFRIED, was completed there in 1874. Two years later, the first complete *Ring* cycles were staged at the new FESTIVAL THEATER in Bayreuth, which was formally dedicated in 1882 with performances of Wagner's final work, *PARSIFAL*. After the composer's death in 1883, Wahnfried – and by extension Bayreuth – became the seat of a Wagner cult, with widow COSIMA as high priestess, which became notorious for its extreme German NATIONALISM and its ANTI-SEMITISM. In the 1920s, Bayreuth proved extremely hospitable to Adolf HITLER's National Socialist movement. Later it was named the capital of a regional party – and later governmental – district or *Gau*. Hitler himself was frequently a guest of the Wagner family at Wahnfried and the festival.

Hitler had hoped to turn Bayreuth into a model Nazi town, and this connection made Bayreuth into an important target of Allied planes. Bombing raids destroyed roughly one-third of the town between 4 and 11 April 1945, damaging both the Festival Theater and Wahnfried. American forces entered on 14 April. After the war, Bayreuth resumed its role as an administrative and cultural hub for northern Bavaria. In 1947, a Mozart festival was organized in the Opera House, the forerunner of the present Franconian Festival Weeks. Two years later, Bayreuth was restored as the governmental seat of Upper Franconia. Then, in 1951, Wagner's grandsons, WIELAND and WOLFGANG, reopened the Bayreuth festival. Twenty years later, the Bavarian legislature resolved to establish a university at Bayreuth, which opened in 1975. Now part of the metropolitan region of Nuremberg, Bayreuth had some 72,500 inhabitants in 2009.   ANTHONY J. STEINHOFF

Bayreuth bark. A derogatory term that pithily caricatures the widely influential singing style encouraged at BAYREUTH by COSIMA WAGNER during her tenure as festival director (1886–1906), in which clear enunciation of the text was thought to require hard tone, declamatory utterance of individual words, and explosive treatment of consonants.   DAVID BRECKBILL

See also PERFORMANCE, SINGERS

Bayreuth Circle.
1. Constitution
2. Legacy and influence

1. Constitution

The Bayreuth Circle (*Der Bayreuther Kreis*) is the name given by historians to the group of ideologues who gathered around WAHNFRIED in the last years of Wagner's life, and in the years following his death. This group stood at the center of the growing Wagner cult which dominated the dissemination of Wagner's works and his ideas of cultural and social reform. COSIMA herself presided, and the prime movers were her faithful acolytes Hans von WOLZOGEN and Carl Friedrich GLASENAPP. Wolzogen served as editor of the BAYREUTHER BLÄTTER from its inception in 1878 until his death in 1938. Thoroughly rooted in the traditions of Wilhelmine conservatism, he did much to shape the prevailing style of Wahnfried orthodoxy. Glasenapp produced a portentous, multi-volume and unwieldy biography of Wagner in which scholarly research was subordinated to the manipulation of historical fact in a hagiography which created an idealized image of the composer untainted by revolution and compliant with bourgeois Wilhelmine conservatism.

Heinrich von Stein (1857–87), Henry THODE, Ludwig SCHEMANN, and Houston Stewart CHAMBERLAIN were of greater intellectual prowess than either Wolzogen or Glasenapp, and enjoyed considerable acclaim in their respective fields beyond the limited orbit of Wahnfried. Stein, originally invited to Wahnfried in October 1879 as tutor to the young SIEGFRIED WAGNER, was an important voice in contemporaneous German scholarship and highly regarded by the academic establishment. His writings on aesthetics were widely acclaimed and praised by no less a figure than the philosopher Wilhelm Dilthey. Stein was an intellectual elitist, intolerant of dissent and dismissive of those who did not see art as a means of cultural REGENERATION. His early death at the age of thirty bestowed on his writings an almost mythical status. Henry Thode, who married Cosima's eldest daughter Daniela von Bülow, was an influential though ideologically skewed art historian of the Italian Renaissance who identified Wagner's work with anti-modernism without acknowledging its radical elements. Ludwig Schemann was in many ways the most independent-minded of all. He disliked excessive, uncritical Wagner worship and maintained a healthy distance from Wahnfried orthodoxy. It was Schemann who first drew attention to the similarities between Wagnerian thought as evident in the REGENERATION essays and the writings of Count GOBINEAU. He was an important figure in linking the ideology of Bayreuth with conservative right-wing thinking. Most complex of all was the English-born Houston Stewart Chamberlain. Chamberlain came to the attention of

Wahnfried following his introduction to Cosima in 1888 and can be considered a member of the inner circle from that point, although he did not move permanently to Bayreuth until after his marriage to Wagner's daughter Eva in 1908. He, too, showed a strong independence of mind and trod a difficult path in keeping his intellectual distance from Bayreuth orthodoxy, especially in his assessment of Wagner's standing as a philosopher, whilst maintaining his unswerving loyalty to Wagner's supremacy as an artist.

2. Legacy and influence

These individuals proved a fractious group, but despite their differences they showed a common devotion to Wagner's art and an unshakable belief in his artistic greatness. They were generally more interested in Wagner the social thinker and cultural prophet than Wagner the composer, and it was through their varying activities that Wagner's unsystematic and wayward philosophy gained something approaching canonical status amongst conservative thinkers. It is tempting to see them as a group of cranks and pseudo-intellectuals, as little more than a myopic gathering of right-wing extremists and ANTI-SEMITES gathered around a center of *völkisch*, conservative thought. But this is misleading: Stein, Schemann, and Thode were highly regarded in academic and cultural circles; Chamberlain was a widely read author and, following the success of his signature work *The Foundations of the Nineteenth Century*, and his studies of such cultural giants as Kant and GOETHE, a highly regarded literary figure in his own right, and an invaluable publicist for the Bayreuth cause.

The significance of the Bayreuth Circle in the history of the dissemination of Wagner's ideas is that it created the mechanism by which the unsystematic ideology of Bayreuth meshed with the complex machine of conservative, *völkisch* thought in the final decades of the long nineteenth century. This corrupt idealism of Bayreuth was based not on critical engagement with Wagner's dramatic works but on selective appropriation of his legacy: ideological capital was made out of the NATIONALIST and racist elements in later Wagnerian thought whilst the radical elements that had informed his writings on REVOLUTION and the initial conception of the *RING* were conveniently downplayed or ignored. The shared assumption of the circle was that Wagner's art was a source of political and cultural regeneration. As Winfried Schüler states in his invaluable book, which has yet to be translated into English, the idea of cultural regeneration formed the ideological *LEITMOTIV* that bound the group together under an increasingly conservative, anti-modernist, and nationalist banner. These ideas were by no means limited to the closed world of Bayreuth; such thinking was part of the *lingua franca* of the time and resonated strongly with the *Zeitgeist* of the Wilhelmine Reich. Thus Bayreuth became a stronghold of what Fritz Stern aptly called the "politics of cultural despair." It was this hardened ideological position that, after being tempered by the humiliations of World War I and its aftermath, became politically exploitable, and such a powerful weapon in the hands of the growing forces of extreme nationalism. Thus could HITLER write to Siegfried Wagner following the Nazi successes in Bayreuth in the elections of 1924, "Great pride filled me when I saw the *völkisch* victory in the city wherein first the Master and then Chamberlain had forged the spiritual sword we now wield [*das geistige Schwert geschmiedet wurde, mit dem wir heute fechten*]" (Hitler to Siegfried Wagner, 5 May 1924).   ROGER ALLEN

Winfried Schüler, *Der Bayreuther Kreis von seiner Entstehung bis zum Ausgang der Wilhelmisichen Ära. Wagnerkult und Kulturreform im Geiste völkischer Weltanschauung* (Munster: Aschendorff, 1971).
Frederic Spotts, *Bayreuth* (see bibliography).
Fritz Stern, *The Politics of Cultural Despair: A Study in the Rise of the Germanic Ideology* (Berkeley: University of California Press, 1961; repr. 1974).

Bayreuth Festival, announcements for. As final preparations for the first launch of the BAYREUTH FESTIVAL got under way, J. Zimmermann, editor of the local paper, the *Bayreuther Tageblatt*, began a series of what ended up as twenty-three press releases to report on the events. Every fourteen days between May and August 1876, these articles under the heading "Bayreuther autographische Korrespondenz" were distributed by the Festival Board to approximately 180 press outlets throughout Germany. The releases covered a wide variety of topics: chronicling the arrival of the performers, preparations by the town for the anticipated massive influx of visitors, the progress of the final rehearsals, listings of the dignitaries in attendance and the various honors they bestowed on the performers. The press releases were capped by a description of the performances themselves and an account of the audience response. Approximately halfway through the series, as the full stage rehearsals began, the musician and critic Heinrich PORGES, an integral member of Wagner's rehearsal team, also began contributing to the reports, offering authoritatively written "behind-the-scenes" glimpses of the coming attractions.

NICHOLAS VAZSONYI

Susanna Großmann-Vendrey, *Bayreuth in der deutschen Presse* (see bibliography): esp. 1:44–6.
Nicholas Vazsonyi, "Press Releases from the Bayreuth Festival, 1876: An Early Attempt at Spin Control," *Wagner and His World*, ed. Thomas Grey (see bibliography): 391–408.

Bayreuth Festival, history of the. The annual festival devoted exclusively to the works of Richard Wagner that takes place in the purpose-built FESTIVAL THEATER between 25 July and 31 August each summer in the Franconian city of BAYREUTH, Germany. The festival was launched on 13 August 1876 with a performance of *Das RHEINGOLD* and, though interrupted by two world wars, continues to run today, still managed by the Wagner family. The Bayreuth festival was preceded by several decades of thought and planning, starting with an initial idea in the late 1840s, accompanied by proposals for festivals in a number of different locations, including the RHINE, ZURICH, WEIMAR, and MUNICH, the city which even saw the aborted construction of a theater, specially designed for the purpose by Gottfried SEMPER. The result of all this became the model for summer music festivals all over the world, but it retains its own unique features, foremost its dedication to the mature work of a single composer, a place of pilgrimage with a set of traditions and rituals, most of which were put in place from the start, and conceived by Wagner himself. All this accounts in part for the waiting list which, according to rumor, currently runs about ten years.

The history of the Bayreuth festival can be broken up into a series of discrete segments, each one a reflection of the person or team in charge.

Though it is still run by a Wagner descendant, the battle to retain it as a family business has been in jeopardy from its earliest days.

1. The first festivals, 1876 and 1882

When it became clear that Wagner would not be able to hold his planned summer festival in Munich for the ideal performance of his epic RING OF THE NIBELUNG cycle, he started to look for a new location. It needed to be in the state of Bavaria in order to retain the protection and support Wagner had been receiving from its King, LUDWIG II. In 1870, Wagner settled on the small city of BAYREUTH, initially because of the ornate Opera House that was already there. Upon inspection, the house turned out to be unsuitable, and so a brand new Festival Theater was built starting in 1872, very much along the lines originally conceived by Semper for Munich. After many false starts, and launches promised as early as summer 1873, the first festival was held in August 1876 with three complete runs of the *Ring* cycle starting 13 August and to a mostly full house. Dignitaries and celebrities from the all over the world were in attendance, including Kaiser Wilhelm, Dom Pedro II of Brazil, King Ludwig (who attended in secret), other members of the nobility, as well as BRUCKNER, Grieg, Tchaikovsky, and LISZT.

Although the first festival was in many respects the musical event of the century, it was a financial loss and Wagner was not happy with the production, promising that he would want to do it all differently next time around. There was to be no next time for him and the *Ring*, and another festival was not mounted until 1882 for the premiere of PARSIFAL, the only opera Wagner wrote specifically with the acoustics and ambience of the theater in mind. Indeed, Wagner had stipulated that *Parsifal* was only to be performed in that hall. Anything else would amount to a form of sacrilege. That second season, the festival opened on 26 July, and this earlier start has generally been maintained ever since. There were a total of sixteen performances of *Parsifal* that season, and, for the last one, Wagner took the baton for the concluding scene. That was to be his last Bayreuth festival.

2. The Cosima era, 1883–1906

When Richard Wagner died on 13 February 1883, he left no instructions as to what should happen to the Bayreuth Festival. It was unclear whether the festival would continue at all and, if so, under whose leadership. The idea that a woman would run it seemed preposterous. Nevertheless, the Wagner family legal counselor, Adolf von GROß secured the Wagner inheritance for COSIMA and SIEGFRIED, also meaning that Cosima became de facto owner of the Bayreuth festival theater. Thus leadership of the festival passed to her and has remained in the hands of the Wagner family to this day. But Cosima was very shrewd and, though totally in control, stayed very much in the background. Through sheer force of will, she managed to mount a festival that same year, 1883 and the following year 1884, with a total of twelve and ten performances respectively of *Parsifal*. With these productions began also the tradition under Cosima of total fidelity to Wagner's wishes, meaning that nothing from the 1882 production was to be changed.

There was no festival in 1885, which began the tradition of often having one and sometimes two "pause" years between festivals, a tradition that lasted until the festival of 1936, after which there was an annual festival interrupted only by the German collapse of 1945. This was another shrewd tactic of Cosima's, which served to ensure that, when held, the festival would continue to attract a substantial audience. With the 1886 festival, in addition to the obligatory performances of *Parsifal*, Cosima began the practice of adding Wagner works to the Bayreuth repertoire, starting with *Tristan und Isolde*, which she produced with careful attention to detail. It was during this season that her father Franz Liszt paid his last visit to Bayreuth and would die under miserable circumstances unattended by his daughter in a house very close to WAHNFRIED. In 1888, Cosima added *Die* MEISTERSINGER, then TANN-HÄUSER (1891), and LOHENGRIN (1894). The 1896 festival saw the first performance of the *Ring* cycle since the 1876 premiere. *Der* FLIEGENDE HOLLÄNDER was added in 1901, and with that the so-called Bayreuth canon that endures to this day had been establish entirely under Cosima's direction. Though she has been criticized for an overly rigid attachment to the perceived wishes of her husband, Cosima did actually exercise some artistic license, even inviting Isadora DUNCAN for *Tannhäuser* in 1904, but she never took credit for any of the productions.

Although Cosima would live until 1930, a series of heart attacks prompted her to withdraw after the 1906 festival and turn its running over to her son, Siegfried.

3. The Siegfried era, 1908–1930

The years that Siegfried Wagner ran the festival were perhaps its most turbulent. In 1913, the *Parsifal* copyright was set to expire, and thus the exclusivity with which it was performed in Bayreuth (at least in Europe). Despite petitions and efforts by some leading artists and celebrities, the Reichstag (German parliament) refused to extend the copyright. At the same time, there was a dynastic dispute launched by Siegfried's sister ISOLDE, who had married Franz Beidler in 1900. They had a son (Franz Wilhelm BEIDLER) in 1901: at the time, Richard Wagner's only grandchild. A court case to prove Isolde's paternity failed amidst threats to expose Siegfried's homosexuality. The struggle reached such a point that in June 1914 Siegfried announced that the entire Wagner estate – including Wahnfried and the Festival Theater – would be turned over to a "Richard Wagner Foundation for the German People" with a board of directors headed by the mayor of Bayreuth. But, with the outbreak of World War I on 28 July 1914, the proposal was silently dropped and never reopened, since Siegfried did eventually get married in 1915 and had two sons. That year's festival was already under way, but as country after country entered the war, audience members gradually started evacuating Bayreuth and returning home. The festival ended abruptly after a performance of *Parsifal* on 1 August 1914, not to reopen until 1924.

Reopening in 1924 proved to be a huge challenge, because the entire Wagner estate had been wiped out by the double shock of the war and the uncontrolled inflation that followed. So Siegfried and his wife WINIFRED assiduously raised funds in order to reopen with productions of the *Ring*, *Parsifal*, and *Meistersinger*, which opened the festival on 22 July. At the conclusion of that first performance, the audience spontaneously rose and sang the German national anthem. This preview of the coming politicization of the Bayreuth festival and the Wagner name had already been prepared by the extreme right-wing publications of the so-called BAYREUTH CIRCLE, not to mention that Adolf HITLER had paid the first of what would be many visits to Wahnfried already in 1923. Siegfried responded to the singing by posting the following announcement: "Das Publikum wird herzlich gebeten, nach Schluss der *Meistersinger* nicht zu singen. Hier gilt's der Kunst!" (The public is urged not to sing at the conclusion of the *Mastersingers*. Art is what matters here!).

Siegfried, though criticized throughout his life for not being as great as his father, nevertheless introduced many innovations to the productions. But all this was brought to an abrupt end in 1930 when, a few months after his mother's passing, Siegfried died on 4 August, after having collapsed during a rehearsal of *GÖTTERDÄMMERUNG* in mid-July.

4. The Winifred era, 1931–1944

Once again the future leadership of the festival was in question, and once again it was a woman who took the lead. Although Winifred's solution would be different from Cosima's, it was no less inspired. She put together a triumvirate of Wilhelm FURTWÄNGLER as music director, Heinz TIETJEN as artistic director, and Emil PREETORIUS as scenic designer to jointly run the festival. Nevertheless, it was Winifred who was increasingly in charge, and quite publicly so. Productions now increasingly bore their own stamp, rather than slavishly following any perceived tradition stemming from the Master himself, though the Nazi takeover of 1933 also had its impact on some productions, such as *Die Meistersinger*, which reflected the government ideology and served to make a connection between the work of Richard Wagner as a prefiguration of Germany's National Socialist destiny. Adolf Hitler became a frequent visitor both to the festival and as a guest at Wahnfried.

After World War II broke out on 1 September 1939, Winifred assumed that the festival would have another hiatus, as with the previous world war. But Hitler insisted that the festival continue as a matter of national pride, and instituted the so-called wartime festivals (*Kriegsfestspiele*) starting in 1940, which he funded, providing free tickets for war wounded, a program run through the *Kraft durch Freude* (KdF) program headed by Bodo LAFFERENTZ, who was married to Winifred's daughter, VERENA. During the last two wartime festivals, 1943 and 1944, *Die Meistersinger* was the only work performed.

The Americans occupied Bayreuth in April 1945, and requisitioned the Festival Theater, which was first looted and later used for light entertainment.

In 1946, it was turned over to the City of Bayreuth and used to house German refugees. The future of the festival was again in doubt, especially because of the close ties between the Wagner family and Hitler.

5. Wieland and New Bayreuth, 1951–1966

After denazification proceedings, and various proposals for the revival of the festival, including a team that would include uncompromised people such as Franz Beidler and Thomas MANN, Winifred turned the festival over to her two sons, Wieland and Wolfgang, also thereby cutting her daughters out of the inheritance and sowing the seeds for future conflict. There followed what was, on the surface at least, a successful partnership between the two brothers, with Wieland managing artistic issues and Wolfgang in charge of the business.

The Festival reopened on 30 July 1951. Wieland and Wolfgang adapted their father's injunction with a note reading: "Im Interesse einer reibungslosen Durchführung der Festspiele bitten wir, von Gesprächen und Debatten politischer Art auf dem Festspielhügel freundlichst absehen zu wollen. 'Hier gilt's der Kunst'" (For the sake of a smooth progression of the festival, we kindly request that you refrain from all conversation and debates of a political nature on the festival hill. "Art is what matters here"). This gesture of depoliticizing Wagner and Bayreuth was then enacted on the stage by Wieland's daringly spare productions, which replaced the conventional scenery and costumes with abstract shapes and lighting. The result is what has generally been referred to as "New Bayreuth," greeted by some as a revelation of Wagner's timelessness, and roundly rejected by others as an abomination that flew in the face of Wagner's intentions as specified in the score. Rather than perpetuate Bayreuth as the guardian of convention and tradition – as Cosima, Siegfried, and Winifred had done to varying degrees – Wieland inaugurated a tradition of adventurous and experimental productions that continues to be a hallmark of Bayreuth, for better or worse.

Wieland died prematurely and suddenly of cancer just after the 1966 festival, and thus left Wolfgang in sole charge.

6. The Wolfgang era, 1967–2008

Wolfgang, who had neither the training nor the artistic talent of his brother, began his leadership by trying to emulate the Wieland style, but was roundly criticized for his lack of inspiration. With a knack for survival that would stand him in good stead later as well, he started the practice of inviting guest stage directors to Bayreuth. Called "Werkstatt Bayreuth" (Bayreuth Workshop), the idea was that productions would be considered a work-in-progress during their entire run, and subject to change and improvement over the years. In the end, and even more extremely than Wieland, Wolfgang's workshop model turned Bayreuth into a stage that is constantly renewing itself. Most controversial of all was his decision to invite the French team of Patrice CHÉREAU and Pierre Boulez to mount the centenary production of the *Ring* in 1976. Scandal soon turned to acclaim, and the seal was set on the Wolfgang era, which lasted longer than anyone else's and racked up an astounding 1,268 performances during his reign alone (not including the co-directorship with Wieland), compared to 274 under Cosima.

There was, however, mounting pressure concerning the legal succession of the Festival. In 1973, after several years of negotiations, the Wagner family and the various governmental authorities and foundations – on whose financing the Festival increasingly depended – reached an accord. The Wagner estate – theater, Wahnfried, and the Wagner archive – was turned over to the RICHARD WAGNER FOUNDATION of Bayreuth (Richard-Wagner-Stiftung Bayreuth). Wahnfried was transformed into the Richard Wagner MUSEUM. The archive was sold to federal, Bavarian, and local governments, which presented it to the Foundation "on permanent loan." The critical and controversial element – authority to appoint the Festival's director – was vested in the Foundation. Although the Foundation was obliged first to consider a member of the Wagner family for the position, the arrangement came close to ending the Festival as a family enterprise. Nevertheless, as part of the deal, Wolfgang insisted on being appointed director for life.

7. Katharina and beyond

As Wolfgang grew older, he became more insistent about staying on or at least selecting his successor. Initially, he wanted his second wife, GUDRUN to take over. In 2001, the Foundation appointed Eva WAGNER-PASQUIER, a daughter by Wolfgang's first marriage, to the position, but Wolfgang refused to step down, citing his contract for life. After Gudrun passed away suddenly in 2007, Wolfgang agreed to step down following the 2008 festival, but only because the Foundation agreed to appoint both Eva and his daughter KATHARINA as joint directors, over the competing team of NIKE WAGNER and Gerard Mortier. Since 2009, the two women have run the festival (Wolfgang died in 2010), though by all appearances Katharina is in control. There have been mounting criticisms of her management style and artistic decisions, but this is nothing new in the history of the festival. Their contract expires in 2015. One issue hotly debated in recent years is whether the Bayreuth canon should be expanded to include Wagner's pre-*Holländer* works, not to mention the works of other composers.   NICHOLAS VAZSONYI

See also BAYREUTH FESTIVAL, RITUALS AND TRADITIONS; FESTIVAL, IDEA OF;

Herbert Barth, *Der Festspielhügel: Richard Wagners Werk in Bayreuth* (Munich: dtv, 1976).
Jonathan Carr, *The Wagner Clan* (see bibliography).
Michael Karbaum, *Studien zur Geschichte der Bayreuther Festspiele* (see bibliography).
Geoffrey Skelton, *Wagner at Bayreuth: Experiment and Tradition* (London: Barrie & Rockliff, 1965).
Frederic Spotts, *Bayreuth: A History of the Wagner Festival* (see bibliography).

Bayreuth Festival, rituals and traditions of the. Traditions have permeated the Festival since 1876 with the first cycle of *Der RING DES NIBELUNGEN*. According to wishes Wagner outlined in a letter to Ludwig II of 1 October 1874, performances start at 4pm and there is a significant intermission between acts, allowing audience members plenty of time to refresh themselves at any one of a number of places to eat and drink on the Festival Hill complex. Nowadays, one can even eat a three-course meal at the Steigenberger restaurant; meals must be ordered in their entirety before the performance. These dining facilities were not yet in place at the 1876 opening, and visitors complained about the lack of food.

During the 1882 premiere of *PARSIFAL*, applause was deemed unseemly at the conclusion of the first act with the Hall of the Grail. At one performance, however, clapping and calls of "bravo!" rang out from the back of the auditorium, resulting in a massive "shushing" by the audience. Unbeknownst to the assembled public, the malefactor was none other than Wagner himself. Nonetheless, the tradition of silence prevails to this day (see *KUNSTRELIGION*).

Several traditions manifest themselves before the curtain rises. With all performances already sold out, people – especially students – gather by the box office early in the day at the west side of the Festspielhaus and hold signs with the inscription "Suche Karte" (seeking a ticket), hoping that someone either will sell or, with luck, simply give the ticket as a gift. In order to impede the black market transfer for tickets, the management has been known to check personal identification before allowing admittance to the auditorium.

Fifteen minutes before the initial curtain rises and at the end of each intermission, a brass fanfare plays a recognizable theme from the next act of the evening's opera. Played from the balcony at the front of the theater by members of the Festival orchestra, the fanfare sounds twice at the 10-minute mark and three times at the 5-minute mark. This tradition dates back to the first festival, again as outlined in his letter to Ludwig of 1 October 1874; Wagner composed the fanfares for the *Ring* (WWV, Appendix, 561–).

Despite Wagner's original intentions for a less formally dressed and more egalitarian public, after 1930 the tradition of formal and fashionable evening attire became *de rigeur*. Men favored tuxedos (along with a smattering of white ties and tails, replete with pinned decorations and awards). Women tend to dress in formal, long dresses, later including elegant pantsuits. (Jeans are frowned upon.) Every year in the last week of July at the formal, red-carpeted opening of the Festival, personalities from the worlds of politics (usually including the German Chancellor and the Head of the State of Bavaria), the arts, sports, and fashion parade to the theater. Each is greeted by the Festival director(s) at the steps at the front of the theater, with the viewing public stationed off to the side. During intermissions, voyeurism amidst the gathered public combines with eavesdropping on genteel and the occasional intense arguments (usually about the staging).

One significant tradition occurs at the end of each *Ring* cycle. After the conclusion of *Götterdämmerung* followed by several rounds of applause for the soloists and chorus, the curtain rises to reveal the entire orchestra assembled together with the conductor for their richly deserved and rousing approbation by the public. Of interest and amusement is the attire of the players. Because the orchestra is hidden from view of the public, no formal dress is required, and since the Festspielhaus is not air-conditioned (due to the noise of ventilator fans, fresh air is pumped silently into the auditorium) temperatures in the pit can rise to about 90 degrees with equally high humidity, and many players wear only shorts, sandals, and polo shirts.

For many, the most important tradition is the pilgrimage to Wagner's home, WAHNFRIED, now a MUSEUM. This includes a visit to Wagner's gravesite, located at the rear of the gardens behind Wahnfried. During the Festival, situated on the large granite slab resting atop the grave are mountains of wreaths from WAGNER SOCIETIES around the world, along with flowers, bouquets, and other offerings. Buried nearby is Russ, Wagner's favorite dog, who also receives a small tribute of flowers. After the season opens, the chorus from the Festival gathers one afternoon at the gravesite to sing in homage to the *Meister*.   EVAN BAKER

Bayreuther Blätter. A journal established by Wagner in 1878 and edited by Hans von WOLZOGEN until his death in 1938. Its sixty-one volumes, encompassing close to 20,000 pages and much convoluted thought and prose, are a compendium of the right-wing, nationalistic, *völkisch*, and ANTI-SEMITIC ideas typical of late Wagner and of the BAYREUTH CIRCLE after his death. Unquestionably and intentionally political, the *Bayreuther Blätter* nevertheless contains valuable material relating to Wagner and his works.

Wagner first discussed the establishment of a journal to promulgate his views with Theodor UHLIG in 1849, and obtained the support of LUDWIG II in 1865. Firm plans were made with Friedrich NIETZSCHE in the early 1870s only to be derailed by his break with Wagner in 1876, by which time Wolzogen had come to Wagner's attention as the author of the successful guide that explicated the *LEITMOTIVE* of the *Ring*. Wagner, pleased at having found a loyal disciple, invited him to move to Bayreuth in the fall of 1877 to become editor.

The first issue of the *Bayreuther Blätter* appeared in January 1878 under the title *Monatsschrift des Bayreuther Patronatvereins unter Mitwirkung Richard Wagner's redigirt von H. v. Wolzogen*. After Wagner's death and the dissolution of the *Patronatverein* (PATRONS' ASSOCIATION) in 1883, it was renamed *Bayreuther Blätter: Zeitschrift zur Verständigung über die Möglichkeiten einer deutschen Kultur* (Magazine to Communicate the Possibilities of a German Culture). From 1894, it bore the subtitle "Deutsche Zeitung im Geiste Richard Wagners" (German Newspaper in Richard Wagner's Spirit). During its first sixteen years, 8–12 issues were published annually; from 1901 it appeared quarterly. There were approximately 400 pages per issue until 1918, when it dropped to fewer than 150 in the early 1920s, after which time it settled at about 230 pages an issue for the remainder of its existence. At its peak in the late 1880s, it had a print run of about 1,500 copies, which dropped to 400–500 after 1900. Initially printed in roman type, the *Bayreuther Blätter* switched to *Fraktur* (old German script) in 1918 for nationalistic reasons. A survey published in 1898 reveals a readership drawn largely from the educated middle classes (*Bildungsbürgertum*): civil servants, doctors, teachers, musicians, philologists, writers, theologians, and the like.

Annette Hein's monograph on the *Bayreuther Blätter* includes an index of its contents, arranged by author and subject. Amongst the 421 authors are some well-known and respected figures such as Graf Albert Apponyi, Hermann Bahr, Max Dessoir, Romain Rolland, and Richard STRAUSS. Of the 141 regular contributors over its history, just eleven core Bayreuthians wrote almost two-fifths of the entire journal: Otto Braun, Houston Stewart CHAMBERLAIN, Carl Friedrich GLASENAPP, Wolfgang GOLTHER, Karl Grunsky, Richard von Schaukal, Ludwig SCHEMANN, Hermann Seeliger, Heinrich von Stein, Richard Wagner, and Hans von Wolzogen, with the latter contributing well over

400 signed articles in addition, likely, to the majority of the unsigned (115) and editorial contributions (353). Every issue also included a section devoted to the activities of the WAGNER SOCIETIES.

While most of Wagner's over 100 "contributions" took the form of posthumously published letters and other writings, he wrote twenty-two articles specifically for the journal. Apart from a few brief pieces, these fall into two principal categories: writings on AESTHETICS and MUSIC DRAMA (e.g., *Über das Dichten und Komponiren* [On Poetry and Composition, 1878] and *ÜBER DIE ANWENDUNG DER MUSIK AUF DAS DRAMA* [On the Application of Music to Drama, 1879]), and the so-called REGENERATION essays that reflect Wagner's increasingly anti-Semitic, conservative, and nationalistic views as well as his particular late beliefs (VEGETARIANISM, anti-VIVISECTION).

The *Bayreuther Blätter* was a vehicle to promulgate the idea of BAYREUTH. Its prose often employed religious and military metaphors (Bayreuth as a place of pilgrimage, for example, or its followers as "soldiers") and its subject matter covered all manner of nationalistic, anti-Semitic, *völkisch*, and racist topics, extending far beyond Wagner, music, art, or even culture and into the realm of POLITICS. The journal strongly supported Bismarck and the Second Reich, regarding its triumphs not only as military victories but also as victories for German culture and morals.

After the German defeat in 1918, the *Bayreuther Blätter*, like Bayreuth itself, became a haven for the anti-democratic, anti-Weimar, right-wing movement, supporting Adolf HITLER and the Nazis well before 1933. Many articles on more narrowly Wagnerian topics, such as MYTH or aesthetics, were refracted through this political lens or sought to underline connections between the works and racist, anti-Semitic thought (for example, by linking ALBERICH's lust for the gold in *Das RHEINGOLD* to a modern-day obsession with money that was then linked with Mammon and, of course, the JEWS). Hundreds of books on these topics were reviewed in its pages. In this way, the *Bayreuther Blätter* was an important vehicle in disseminating and legitimating such thought amongst its educated middle-class readership and, as such, played a role in the popular support for NATIONAL SOCIALISM.

The twin themes of anti-Semitism and German NATIONALISM, stemming from Wagner's own writings, recur frequently through its entire history, with the so-called "Jewish problem" being examined obsessively in all of its cultural, social, economic, religious, and racial guises. The "Jew" is generally presented in binary terms as the enemy of "the German." The problem of race served to link anti-Semitic and pro-German, Aryan, thought, with many writers being concerned with "degeneracy" and how the German race could be improved through selective breeding and racial selection. Great Germans, past and present, were celebrated and, indeed, from 1887 each issue began with an epigraph from one: the majority were taken from GOETHE, SCHILLER, SCHOPENHAUER, Wagner, LISZT, Carlyle, and Luther, but Clausewitz, Chamberlain, Hindenburg, Lagarde, and Hitler all make their appearance. In its last phase, the *Bayreuther Blätter* is noteworthy for its nazification of Wagner, with many articles connecting Wagner and his works to the new National Socialist Germany.

Nevertheless, the *Bayreuther Blätter* is still important for the many primary sources that were first published in its pages, including writings by Wagner not found in the *Gesammelte Schriften*, myriad CORRESPONDENCE to and from Wagner and his circle, and extracts from COSIMA WAGNER'S DIARIES. Heinrich PORGES' account of Wagner rehearsing the RING in 1876 appeared serially between 1880 and 1896, as did Friedrich von Hausegger's *Die Musik als Ausdruck* (1884) and Wolzogen's own *Musikalisch-dramatische Parellelen* (1894–1903). It also provides considerable information about WAGNERISM as a historical phenomenon, the activities of the Wagner societies, and Wagner's influence in general. In addition, the *Bayreuther Blätter* published some serious studies of Wagner's music and works; for example: Georg Capellen discussing the TRISTAN Prelude and Wagner's harmonic innovations (1902); Karl Wörner connecting Wagner with the wider tradition of German Romantic opera (1932 and 1933); Alfred LORENZ illustrating his analytical methodology (1927, 1933); and Otto STROBEL elucidating Wagner's prose sketch for *Der FLIEGENDE HOLLÄNDER* (1933) and musical sketches for "Winterstürme" (1930).

While Wagner occasionally disparaged Wolzogen and the *Bayreuther Blätter* in conversations that Cosima recorded faithfully in her diary, it is not accurate to claim that the views espoused by the journal throughout its history cannot, for the most part, be traced back to Wagner himself. From a vehicle read eagerly by young musicians and Wagnerians such as Gustav MAHLER in the late 1870s to a rather niche publication targeted at right-wing, conservative, and ultimately Nazi supporters and sympathizers, the trajectory of the *Bayreuther Blätter* reflects that of Wagner's reputation and influence as well as the Germany of the Second and Third Reichs.   STEPHEN MCCLATCHIE

Annette Hein, *"Es ist viel 'Hitler' in Wagner"* (see bibliography).
Winfried Schüler, *Der Bayreuther Kreis* (see bibliography).

Bayreuther Festspielführer (Bayreuth Festival Guide). The official guide to the BAYREUTH FESTIVAL, published by Georg Niehrenheim from 1897 until World War II, not to be confused with the so-called "Wild" editions, published by Friedrich Wild, appearing around the same time. The publication originated under the title *Bayreuther Festspiel-Anzeiger* (and later the *Praktischer Wegweiser für Bayreuther Festspielbesucher*) as a simple tourist guide with a brief introduction to the work(s) being performed; in 1906 the publisher started to include essays by BAYREUTH CIRCLE members such as Houston Stewart CHAMBERLAIN, Carl Friedrich GLASENAPP, Wolfgang GOLTHER, and Hans von WOLZOGEN. In 1924, the *Festspielführer* took its final form as a substantial, edited volume that provided a both musical-cultural-historical and practical guide to Wagner and Bayreuth.

Each *Festspielführer* fell into three main parts, followed by advertisements for Wagneriana, other musical events and festivals, travel, lodgings, restaurants and pubs. The longest part, a literary/scholarly section (average length: 320 pages), was followed by a practical section (with maps, train schedules, and suggestions for local tours), and a general section outlining the history of the town and surveying its main sights. The 1924 issue included a survey of the Festival from 1876 to 1914, with an index of all performances and artists.

Indices to the *Festspielführer* itself were provided for its 30th (1927) and 40th (1937) anniversaries. Other standard features were bibliographies and book reviews, obituaries, and historical photographs.

Particularly under the editorships of Karl Grunsky (1924–5) and Otto STROBEL (1933–9), the *Festspielführer* was notable for its strongly German national, right-wing orientation. Indeed, an anniversary article from 1937 celebrated its role in providing "intellectual and spiritual support" for the VOLK through its explicit dedication to Wagner's cultural and political significance. The cover of both of Grunsky's editions depicted a politically charged image of SIEGFRIED's sword and a (mis)quotation from SIEGFRIED: ("Nothung! Nothung! Nothung! Neu und Verjüngt! Zum Leben weckt ich dich wieder" [Nothung! Nothung! Nothung! New and rejuvenated! I have awakened you once again to life]). After the Nazi seizure of power in 1933, Strobel's editorial introduction concluded with an ecstatic paean to HITLER, and the *Festspielführer* printed the first of the photographs of Hitler that were to be found in all of the remaining issues. While there are only a few explicitly political essays (e.g., Georg Schott, "Richard Wagner und das neue Deutschland" [1934]; Otto Tröbes, "Mit Richard Wagner ins Dritte Deutsche Reich" [1938]), many articles made casual allusion to the reawakened German Reich and its *Führer*. (After 1936, the standard photograph of the orchestra and chorus taken outside the Festspielhaus included prominent swastika banners.)

Notwithstanding its tendentious politics, the *Festspielführer* published much of value. Important events, such as WOLZOGEN'S 80th birthday and the 50th anniversary of the BAYREUTHER BLÄTTER, Wagner's 120th birthday, COSIMA and SIEGFRIED WAGNER's deaths, and the 60th anniversary of the Festival were marked by articles and photographs. Siegfried Wagner's 1930 TANN-HÄUSER and the 1936 LOHENGRIN each received special sections. In addition to articles promulgating the ideology of Bayreuth and German culture in general, the *Festspielführer* not infrequently included analytical articles by serious scholars such as Alfred LORENZ and Wolfgang Golther. Its scholarly ambitions increased under Strobel's editorship: more facsimiles and studies of primary musical, textual, and historical documents were included, as well as more musical examples.   STEPHEN MCCLATCHIE

Otto Strobel, "Zum Geleit: Vierzig Jahre *Bayreuther Festspielführer*," in *Bayreuther Festspielführer 1937*, ed. Otto Strobel (Bayreuth: Georg Niehrenheim, 1937).

Beardsley, Aubrey Vincent (b. Brighton, 21 Aug. 1872; d. Menton, 16 March 1898), English artist, illustrator, and figurehead of the British decadent movement. Beardsley attended many Wagner performances in LONDON in the early 1890s, producing over twenty black-and-white drawings and one color poster on Wagnerian subjects during the decade. Subjects include characters and episodes from the dramas (particularly the RING, TRISTAN and TANNHÄUSER), the singers Max Alvary and Katharina Klafsky, and a TRISTAN audience. Early drawings were influenced by medievalism and Burne-Jones; later works veer towards PARODY, associating Wagner's dramas with EROTICISM, New Women, Francophilia, and effeminacy. Two larger incomplete projects appeared in *The Savoy* in 1896: *The Comedy of the Rhinegold* (six drawings in rococo and classical styles, intended to illustrate his uncompleted prose "version" of the drama) and *Under the Hill* (an erotic novella based on *Tannhäuser*; four heavily expurgated chapters and several drawings, with the Wagnerian source disguised, were published). Posthumous accounts often associated Beardsley, and decadents, with Tannhäuser.   EMMA SUTTON

See also WAGNER IN THE VISUAL ARTS

Victor Chan, "Aubrey Beardsley's *Frontispiece to 'The Comedy of the Rhinegold'*," *Arts Magazine* 57 (January 1983): 88–96.

Janet Jempson, "Aubrey Beardsley and the *Ring*," *Wagner* 17 (May 1996): 65–77.

Emma Sutton, *Aubrey Beardsley and British Wagnerism in the 1890s* (Oxford University Press, 2002).

Beckmesser. See SIXTUS BECKMESSER

Beethoven (1870). The year 1870, the centenary of Ludwig van BEETHOVEN's birth, was bound to elicit a tribute from his self-proclaimed rightful heir. But Wagner also sought to dignify the occasion through an original contribution to philosophy, declaring this intention at the outset. Indeed, this text was Wagner's most ambitious articulation of the changes in his aesthetic views since his ZURICH writings. Whereas earlier his argument had to do with the impact art could have on society, his interest now lay in articulating a theory of the special physiological and psychological processes involved in musical composition. Before, Wagner had deliberately downgraded music to only one of the arts necessary for MUSIC DRAMA, but now he raised music to the highest form of artistic expression, as described by Arthur SCHOPENHAUER. Wagner frequently diverts in this text to another topic that he consistently associated with Beethoven: the special character of German music, and of German national character in general, especially as opposed to the French (see GERMANNESS). This was a theme Wagner had been expounding ever since his PARIS years, but he could now present it with the new patriotic fervor occasioned by the FRANCO-PRUSSIAN WAR.

1. Schopenhauer and dreams
2. Seeing/hearing
3. Beethoven's inner world

1. Schopenhauer and dreams

Although Wagner had first encountered the writings of Schopenhauer in 1854 and immediately became an enthusiast, it was not until this essay, exactly ten years after the philosopher's death, that he attempted to summarize his reactions in writing. According to Klaus Kropfinger, Wagner believed that he, as a practicing poet and musician, was called to expand upon Schopenhauer's philosophy and correct various misconceptions. Presumably Wagner aimed to reconcile Schopenhauer's views on the primacy of music with his own pronouncements that music needed poetry to fully express itself.

Wagner quotes from *The World as Will and Representation* and emphasizes the special status of music that separates it from the other arts: music is a manifestation of the universal will, while the others are created by the individual will. Therefore music doesn't have to pass through the medium of an individual's conscious understanding. He also draws on Schopenhauer's long, rambling *Essay on Spirit Seeing and Everything Connected Therewith* from 1851 (in *Parerga and Paralipomena*). Since this essay does not address music or indeed any artistic matters, Wagner adds his own ideas about how the act of composing occurs through the "dream organ," described in Schopenhauer's spirit-seeing essay as the "ganglia" where all the different kinds of subconsciousness occur: second sight or clairvoyance, somnambulism, artificial magnetized somnambulism, and different kinds of DREAMS. Music is initiated by the composer's visual dream. Besides the dream organ, Wagner describes a second organ that works as an eye facing toward the dream, and as an ear facing outward; this organ translates the composer's visual dream into sound. Wagner also adds another stage to dreaming: there are actually two dreams, the deepest dream, and then that dream translated into something more understandable just before waking. Waking occurs with a scream: the sound originating in the eye/ear organ is the direct expression of the dream. The scream, although it can appear in attenuated form as a "cry of longing," is the source of all music.

By introducing extra levels into Schopenhauer's dream psychology, Wagner restates some important elements of his earlier writings on Beethoven and instrumental music. Two levels of dream, the "dream of deepest SLEEP" and the "lighter, allegoric" dream, have access to, respectively, harmony and rhythm (both conceived in the broadest sense). An exegesis of the C♯ Minor String Quartet (Op. 131) shows Beethoven, the dreamer, passing through various states of oscillation through the inner dream, most apparent in the Adagio sections, into waking (presumably through the outer dream) into the dancelike finale. This dichotomy reflects Wagner's traditional division of Beethoven's works into "absolute," DANCE-derived works and more dramatic compositions growing out of an inner poetic idea ("melody").

2. Seeing/hearing

Wagner makes a series of analogies to enforce his metaphysics of music: as the inner world is to the external world, dream is to consciousness, sound is to sight. Music gives us access to the innermost essence of ourselves; its language is feeling. Wagner had declared twenty years earlier in his Zurich writings that music was *only* feeling as opposed to thought, words and action, but now feeling falls on the superior side of the opposition. This change gave him the opportunity to attack (without naming him) HANSLICK, who had criticized theories of music as feeling and instead urged listeners to contemplate the beautiful forms played out in sound (*On the Musically Beautiful*, 1854). Wagner derided the concept of beautiful music as superficial and contrasted it with what he called a sublime experience of music, when our profound but obscure intimations are articulated aurally in the external world.

Wagner departs briefly from the perspective of the composer to consider the listener and makes the sweeping assertion that, when we listen to music, we "have fallen into a state essentially akin to that of hypnotic clairvoyance" (PW 5:75) where "our eyesight is paralyzed to such a degree by the effect of music upon us, that with eyes wide open we no longer intensively see" (74). Wagner's innovations at Bayreuth (the "invisible orchestra" and a completely dark house during the performance) worked to put this theory into practice.

3. Beethoven's inner world

Wagner finally comes back to his initial topic of how to understand Beethoven's music. Beethoven had the advantage of being protected from the outer world by his deafness and by the unusual thickness of his skull. This gave him greater access to the inner world, to the essence of things. He composed "like a man possessed; for to him in truth applies what Schopenhauer has said of the musician in general: he speaks the highest wisdom in a tongue his reason does not understand" (PW 5:83, repeated on 95). Then Wagner introduces a religious dimension: although Beethoven lived in Catholic Vienna, he was a German Protestant in spirit like the other great German artists BACH and Dürer. His late works reveal a period of blessed seclusion, a saint-like existence. The Ninth Symphony manifests the composer's fearful doubt and the return of his fundamental optimism in the last movement. Wagner asserts repeatedly that it is not the words that are important, but rather the introduction of the human voice. "With the anguished cry of one awaking from a nightmare, he speaks that actual Word whose ideal sense is none other than: 'Man, despite all, *is* good!'" (101). Wagner goes so far at this point as to reverse the requirement of his Zurich writings that the music serve the drama. But he forestalls the possibility that his own operas do not need words by arguing that since music is itself an Idea of the World, it includes drama. Drama as a product of music can have the same effect as music. For instance, SHAKESPEARE can be understood as "a Beethoven who goes on dreaming though awake" (108). Whereas Beethoven was clairvoyant, Shakespeare was a ghost-seer – he was able to see with his inner eye and regular eye at the same time. The immediacy and authenticity of Shakespeare's dramas are exactly like that of Beethoven's music. Although he does not spell it out, presumably Wagner considers his operas the equivalent of Beethoven's and Shakespeare's works combined. In a side comment Wagner points out that in the first printed edition of the Ninth, the phrase "Was die Mode streng geteilt" (What custom once strictly divided) was at one point replaced by "frech geteilt" (impudently divided). Although today the substitution is generally considered a copyist's error, Wagner interpreted it as highly significant, intended as a Protestant rebuke: "We might be looking on a *Luther* in his rage against the Pope!" (123).

The final section of the essay devolves into a rant against France, culminating with the lamentation that the downfall of the world started with the invention of writing, which led to printing and finally to newspapers that tell German wives how to dress in French fashions.

This text was considered Holy Scripture by late nineteenth-century Wagnerians, some of whom took it as a point of departure for their own metaphysics of music (Curt Mey, Friedrich von Hausegger, Felix WEINGARTNER). Before the backlash against Romanticism after World War I, composers Gustav MAHLER, Arnold SCHOENBERG, Richard STRAUSS, and others found the essay's mystical view of music and of the compositional process exactly to their taste. It certainly had an impact on the young Friedrich NIETZSCHE, who was going through an intense period of romantic intoxication brought on by music, Schopenhauer, and acquaintance with

Richard and COSIMA. The result was *The Birth of Tragedy*. Nietzsche praised the Beethoven essay in the dedication of his book to Wagner, although his different, more visually oriented and Apollonian interpretation of dream imagery is consistent with the problems he later perceived with Wagner's music.   SANNA PEDERSON

Carolyn Abbate, "Opera as Symphony, a Wagnerian Myth," *Analyzing Opera: Verdi and Wagner*, ed. Carolyn Abbate and Roger Parker (Berkeley: University of California Press, 1989): 92–124.

Thomas S. Grey, *Wagner's Musical Prose* (see bibliography).

Klaus Kropfinger, *Wagner and Beethoven* (see bibliography).

Edward A. Lippman, "Wagner's Conception of the Dream," *The Journal of Musicology* 8.1 (1990): 54–81.

Arthur Schopenhauer, *Parerga and Paralipomena: Short Philosophical Essays*, trans. E. F. J. Payne, (Oxford: Clarendon, 1974).

Beethoven, Ludwig van (b. Bonn, 16 or 17 Dec. 1770; d. Vienna, 26 March 1827), German composer and key figure in the transition from Viennese classicism to musical ROMANTICISM. Wagner invoked Beethoven's name continuously in his autobiographical and theoretical writings, making him an integral component of his own public persona. As a composer and pioneering conductor, Wagner became a conduit through which the prevailing late nineteenth- and twentieth-century understanding of Beethoven's cultural-historical significance was formed.

While other composers of his generation sought to broaden Beethoven's influence, Wagner demanded to be recognized as Beethoven's sole successor. Over the course of his career, he tried to show in varying ways how an opera composer could be the true heir to a composer of predominantly instrumental music. In doing so, he reworked the image of Beethoven and helped to consolidate the reputation of the Ninth Symphony as the most important of Beethoven's works.

1. Early exposure to Beethoven
2. Paris years
3. Dresden years
4. Zurich years
5. Wagner, Beethoven, and Schopenhauer
6. Wagner and the symphony after Beethoven

1. Early exposure to Beethoven

Beginning in 1835 in his "Red Pocketbook," Wagner documented the overwhelming impact Beethoven's music had on him. Klaus Kropfinger has shown how Wagner subsequently refashioned the account of his initial experiences of Beethoven many times. Kropfinger and other scholars question the veracity of such accounts as Wagner's anguished response to hearing about Beethoven's death, or his seeing *Fidelio* in 1829 with Wilhelmine SCHRÖDER-DEVRIENT as Leonore. A major part of his self-education as a composer involved completing a piano score of the Ninth Symphony in 1831 and writing in the next year a SYMPHONY IN C MAJOR, which could be called a study of Beethoven's style. In 1882, he conducted a private performance of this work and wrote that it was stylistically closest to Beethoven's Second Symphony, but also influenced by the Third, the Seventh, and the Adagio of the Fifth Symphony ("A Youthful Symphony," PW 6:320). Wagner worked on several other instrumental compositions in the early 1830s. He had his first opportunity to conduct Beethoven in RIGA, where as music director he conducted the Third through the Eighth Symphonies and the Leonore Overture No. 3 in 1838–9. It appears that he studied much more of Beethoven than just the symphonies; even in his early years he knew some of the string quartets (especially the late quartets Op. 127 and Op. 131), piano sonatas, and vocal music.

2. Paris years

During his years in PARIS (1839–42), Wagner heard the Ninth Symphony under the famous conductor François-Antoine Habeneck. Beethoven appears frequently in Wagner's Paris articles and short stories, accompanied by increasingly nationalistic sentiments. In Eine PILGERFAHRT ZU BEETHOVEN (A Pilgrimage to Beethoven), Wagner goes so far as to portray Beethoven conferring his blessing on the character named only by the initial "R." In Über die Ouvertüre (On the Overture) Wagner admires the Leonore Overture No. 3, where "one sole idea pervades the work: the freedom brought by a jubilant angel of light to suffering manhood" (PW 7:160). He argues that an opera overture should not try to portray coming events, but rather the main idea, "and bring it to a conclusion in anticipatory agreement with the solution of the problem in the scenic play," as in the Overture to Egmont. In subsequent writings as well, Wagner would emphasize the importance of Beethoven's use of an overarching poetic idea. This early essay also contains comments on the Overture to Coriolan, another work that Wagner returned to repeatedly as the one successful example of an overture depicting the events of the play.

3. Dresden years

As Royal Kapellmeister in DRESDEN, Wagner conducted the Ninth Symphony at the annual Palm Sunday concert of 5 April 1846, a bold programming choice as the Ninth was still considered one of Beethoven's problematic late works. To forestall these doubts, Wagner mounted an unprecedented PUBLICITY campaign to attract an audience for the concert and, for the performance itself, wrote PROGRAM NOTES specifically designed to help the uninitiated into an understanding of the work by interpreting the individual movements through excerpts from GOETHE's Faust. For his discussion of the fourth movement, Wagner coined the term "ABSOLUTE MUSIC," whose limits Beethoven transcends with the addition of SCHILLER's words. Perhaps because he regarded the Ninth with such reverence, he only conducted that work five times, each one a special "event": in Dresden (1846, 1847, and 1849); London (1855); and for the last time at the laying of the cornerstone at the Bayreuth FESTIVAL THEATER on 22 May 1872, without a doubt the most special event of all.

It was also as Kapellmeister in Dresden that Wagner met a violinist in his orchestra, Theodor UHLIG, whose enthusiasm for Beethoven initiated a friendship and an intense period of correspondence from 1849 through 1852. Uhlig wrote articles on Beethoven's symphonies for the NEUE ZEITSCHRIFT FÜR MUSIK that presented arguments he shared with

Wagner: that instrumental music was derived from DANCE, that symphonic movements should express one basic mood, and that the dramatic design of the work unfolds through short motives and motivic development. Uhlig showed some independence from Wagner's thought in also examining the structure of symphonic music after Beethoven; he pointed out the recurrence of motives across movements in Beethoven's Fifth and Schumann's Second Symphony as a significant unifying technique. Wagner's undertanding of his own use of motives and other "symphonic" techniques in his operas certainly owed much to his and Uhlig's analytic insights regarding Beethoven's procedures.

4. Zurich years

Wagner's ZURICH writings from 1849 to 1853 presented his revised version of MUSIC HISTORY in various ways. In every instance, all composers named come up short – with the sole exception of Beethoven. The famous image of the intrepid Beethoven as Columbus, sailing into uncharted waters with his Ninth Symphony and finally reaching the shore of verbal language in the last movement, appears in *Das KUNSTWERK DER ZUKUNFT* (The Artwork of the Future). This text also contains the description of the Seventh Symphony as "the apotheosis of the dance." While in Zurich, Wagner conducted and wrote program notes to the *Eroica* Symphony and *Coriolan* Overture. Besides the orchestral works, the Piano Sonatas Op. 106 ("Hammerklavier") and Op. 111 were championed by Wagner, especially as performed by LISZT, whom he commended as both performer and composer for bringing out the overall "idea" of the piece as a dramatic unity already apparent in the first few bars.

5. Wagner, Beethoven, and SCHOPENHAUER

Wagner's essay *BEETHOVEN* (1870) was written as part of the centenary celebrations of the composer. Wagner also used the occasion of the FRANCO-PRUSSIAN WAR then in progress to appeal to the German people to appreciate and defend their special national qualities, personified in Beethoven. In addition, this text uses Beethoven as an opportunity to develop Arthur SCHOPENHAUER'S AESTHETICS of music and theories about the unconscious. Wagner repudiated such previous writers as A. B. Marx, who had defined the essence of Beethoven's heroism by analogy with an outside subject. For Wagner, Beethoven's heroism lay in his own "defiant spirit." Wagner used Schopenhauer's theories to advance a paradoxical idea that Beethoven's deafness made him a better composer; it enhanced his ability to access the interior "DREAM world" that unlocks the connection of music with Schopenhauer's Will. While advancing his Schopenhauerian understanding of the supremacy of (instrumental) music, Wagner finds himself dismissing the importance of words, for instance in the Ninth Symphony. The fateful moment in the last movement when the human voice joins the instruments does not involve the words that the voice sings. Wagner then takes pains to distinguish between words, which are now clearly secondary to music, and drama, which can produce the same effect as music, using the example of SHAKESPEARE, whom he finds similar but not quite the same as Beethoven in his access to the unconscious.

6. Wagner and the symphony after Beethoven

Wagner's later writings often address other musicians' deviations from the true path set out by him and Beethoven. He attacks MENDELSSOHN, Hiller, BRAHMS, and lesser composers for inadequate performances or unwarranted imitations of Beethoven. In ÜBER DIE ANWENDUNG DER MUSIK AUF DAS DRAMA (On the Application of Music to Drama, 1879) Wagner reemphasizes Beethoven's status as the last composer of symphonies, and asserts that a symphonic unity formed of themes and motives is only possible in MUSIC DRAMA. However, an intriguing footnote to Wagner's Beethoven reception, and one that has fascinated modern scholars, are the sketches he made for possible symphonic works in the last years of his life.

Although there were many composers and critics in the nineteenth century engaged in the business of constructing Beethoven's image, Wagner's role was profound in part because of his own emerging stature as a musical giant, and partly because of the sheer quantity of his writings. In many ways, the strong, masculine, and above all German *Beethoven* we have inherited, and against whom we struggle (as opposed to the biographical composer), is a product of Richard Wagner. SANNA PEDERSON

Alessandra Comini, *The Changing Image of Beethoven: A Study in Mythmaking*, rev. edn. (Santa Fe, NM: Sunstone Press, 2008).

John Deathridge, "Unfinished Symphonies," *Wagner Beyond Good and Evil* (see bibliography): 189–205.

Hans-Joachim Hinrichsen, "'Seid umschlungen, Millionen': Die Beethoven-Rezeption," in *Beethoven Handbuch*, ed. Sven Hiemke (Kassel: Bärenreiter, 2009): 568–609.

K. M. Knittel, "Wagner, Deafness, and the Reception of Beethoven's Late Style," *Journal of the American Musicological Society* 51 (1998): 49–82.

Klaus Kropfinger, *Wagner and Beethoven* (see bibliography).

Nicholas Vazsonyi, *Richard Wagner: Self-Promotion and the Making of a Brand* (see bibliography).

Beidler, Franz Wilhelm (b. Bayreuth, 16 Oct. 1901; d. Zurich, 3 Aug. 1981). In addition to the four children from SIEGFRIED and WINIFRED, Wagner had one other grandchild, Franz Wilhelm Beidler, the only grandson of the "Master" for sixteen years until the birth of Wieland Wagner in 1917. Beidler referred to himself as the "lost grandson" in a letter to the Wagner biographer Ernest NEWMAN in October 1937 (Beidler, 1997, 364).

Beidler was the son of ISOLDE who, though legally the daughter of Hans von Bülow, was biologically Wagner's daughter. She married the Swiss conductor Franz Beidler in 1900. In 1906, there was a rift between Beidler Senior and Cosima, in which Isolde, who remained loyal to her husband, became involved. Though Isolde's relation to Wagner, and Franz Wilhelm's status as the "heir apparent," had been undisputed up to that point, there were subsequent attempts in WAHNFRIED to exclude her and her son from the line of succession. In 1913, Isolde tried desperately to fight her mother in the district court of Bayreuth, but she lost.

Beidler chose an academic career and received his Ph.D. with a dissertation on the history of German parliamentarism. He then began working with Leo Kestenberg, a Jewish music educator and cultural reformer, at the Prussian Ministry for Science, Art, and Public Education. The synthesis of art and socialism, which was Kerstenberg's personal philosophy, became Beidler's ideal. It was precisely in this spirit that Beidler understood the work of his grandfather, whom he forever thought of as a revolutionary of 1848/9. An open opponent of NATIONAL SOCIALISM, and married to the daughter of a Jewish Professor of Medicine (Sigmund Gottschalk), Beidler was dismissed from his position at the Prussian Ministry of Education and Cultural Affairs. His decision to go into exile was made easier by the fact that, through his father, he remained a Swiss citizen. He and his wife emigrated first to Paris and then in August 1934 – like his grandfather – to Zurich. He found a sense of home in the house of Thomas MANN, whom he knew from Munich.

Thomas Mann took an active interest in the publication of Beidler's work on Wagner's literary and ideological reception history and the *RING* tetralogy, which Beidler interpreted from a sociocritical and social utopian perspective. His magnum opus was supposed to be the biography *Cosima Wagner-Liszt: The Making of the Wagner Myth* (*Cosima Wagner-Liszt. Der Weg zum Wagner-Mythos*), which was conceived as a source-critical examination from a sociocultural and sociopsychological standpoint. According to a diary entry by Thomas Mann dated 1 September 1933, Beidler was inspired to write a novel about the influence of Wagner-Liszt-Cosima-Nietzsche. However, Beidler's position as the secretary of the Swiss Writer's Union did not leave him enough time for the extensive research needed for the biography, and he was also refused access to the Bayreuth archives. A source-critical study without sources was simply impossible. Although Beidler continued work on the biography after the war, the work remained fragmentary.

When the reopening of the Bayreuth Festival was considered in 1946, Beidler was put in charge of reorganizing it. That same year, he came up with the "Guidelines for the Reshaping of the Bayreuth Festival." The basic concept was to be the transition from the legacy of Richard and Cosima Wagner into an "autonomous foundation," with Thomas Mann as honorary president of the foundation council. The plan was abandoned, however, because it would have been tantamount to a legally unthinkable disinheritance of the recognized Wagner heirs. When the Festival was reopened in 1951, without Beidler's involvement, he spoke up one last time in the essay *Bedenken gegen Bayreuth* (Doubts about Bayreuth) as part of a publication of the German Academy of Language and Literature, which denounced Bayreuth's shared responsibility for National Socialism. His fragmentary Cosima biography, supplemented by other relevant texts, was published by his estate in 1997.　　DIETER BORCHMEYER

TRANS. HOLLY WERMTER

Franz Wilhelm Beidler, *Cosima Wagner-Liszt: Der Weg zum Wagner-Mythos. Ausgewählte Schriften des ersten Wagner-Enkels und sein unveröffentlichter Briefwechsel mit Thomas Mann*, ed. with Epilog by Dieter Borchmeyer (Bielefeld: Pendragon, 1997); rev. edn. as *Cosima Wagner. Ein Porträt. Richard Wagners erster Enkel: Ausgewählte Schriften und Briefwechsel mit Thomas Mann*, ed. and annotated Dieter Borchmeyer (Würzburg: Königshausen & Neumann, 2011).

Beidler, Isolde (née von Bülow, later Wagner) (b. Munich, 10 April 1865; d. Munich, 7 Feb. 1919). Isolde, or "Loldi" as she was known to the family, was presumably Wagner's first child and, reputedly, his favorite. She was born on the day of the first orchestral rehearsal of *TRISTAN UND ISOLDE*, while COSIMA WAGNER was still married to Hans von BÜLOW. The child was most probably conceived

during the time Cosima spent with Wagner at Villa Pellet by Lake Starnberg in the summer of 1864.

Isolde married the conductor Franz Beidler on 20 December 1900 in Bayreuth. They had a son, Franz Wilhelm BEIDLER, in 1901. Cosima had originally been pleased with the marriage, but had several disagreements with the couple over Beidler's duties and self-conduct at Bayreuth that culminated in a major confrontation in 1906 when Beidler asked to conduct a third *PARSIFAL*. Isolde sided with her husband, and a deep rift developed between mother and daughter. Attempts at reconciliation were made via letter but by this time Cosima was in ill health and all her correspondence went to SIEGFRIED WAGNER, or to EVA WAGNER and her husband Houston Stuart CHAMBERLAIN, who were not positively inclined toward Isolde. Eva blamed her mother's first heart trouble in 1906 on the argument with the Beidlers, and Chamberlain had an undying hatred for the Wagner sister who had rejected his romantic overtures and the obtuse Swiss conductor who had married her.

The end result was that Isolde, cut off financially and personally from WAHNFRIED, filed a paternity suit to be legally acknowledged as Wagner's daughter and to secure the rights of her son, the only Wagner grandson until the birth of WIELAND WAGNER in 1917. Although her status as Wagner's natural daughter was a long-accepted fact in the family, legally, Isolde had been baptized a von Bülow, and accepted a portion of her legal father's estate when he died in 1894. After a very public trial, Isolde's suit was denied. By this time she was physically and mentally broken, ailing from tuberculosis and serious depression. She died in 1919 without ever reconciling with the family.   LYDIA MAYNE

Jonathan Carr, *The Wagner Clan* (see bibliography).
Oliver Hilmes, *Cosima Wagner: The Lady of Bayreuth* (see bibliography).

Bel canto opera.
1. Context
2. Repertoire and style
3. Singers and training

1. Context

A term originally used for the light-toned, elegant, and often supremely virtuosic Italian vocal style ("bel canto" literally meaning "fine singing") of earlier ages, the currency of the term spread rapidly from the late nineteenth century onwards.

As working definitions of *bel canto* remain diverse, it is crucial to discuss this topic within Wagner's own attitudes toward Italian opera. For him, the term "bel canto" was used to describe the change in approaches to singing during the nineteenth century. When Wagner started his career in German theater, it was not only at the provincial companies that German opera played a marginal role compared to the Italian repertoire. Even bigger institutions like the Berlin and DRESDEN Hofoper only slowly departed from this emphasis, not to mention the European musical centers such as PARIS and LONDON, which sustained their opera houses with a thoroughly Italian repertoire. Giacomo MEYERBEER's success throughout Europe was grounded in his study of operatic form in Italy. By comparison, German composers such as Heinrich MARSCHNER or Louis SPOHR, who followed in the tradition of the recently deceased Carl Maria von WEBER, had little international standing. Similarly, the reign of the castrati – closely associated with *bel canto* opera of the seventeenth and eighteenth century – only gradually came to an end in the first third of the nineteenth century. As Wagner recalls in *MEIN LEBEN* (My Life, 1865–81), the castrato Sassaroli made a horrible impression on him as a child, when the singer visited his parents in Dresden. The castrato is described as part of a "ghostly machine" (*Spukmaschine*; ML 35) which Wagner identified as the ruin of the singing talent of one of his sisters (Klara Wolfram). Of course, this *ex posteriori* narrative serves to establish the composer's idiosyncratic views on Italian opera, but this is only one side of the coin.

2. Repertoire and style

Despite some twentieth-century notions that *bel canto* opera had come to an end with Gioachino ROSSINI, and that operas by Gaetano DONIZETTI and Vincenzo BELLINI should be attributed to ROMANTICISM, Wagner's understanding of *bel canto* opera with regards to these three has more in common with recent reception. When Wagner attended a performance of Bellini's *I Capuleti e i Montecchi* in Leipzig (1834), he was impressed by the use of pure song-like melodies, although later, in the *AUTOBIOGRAPHISCHE SKIZZE* (1842/3), he would call the music "insignificant" (SSD 1:9). Still, in 1834, he published an essay, *Pasticcio*, in the *NEUE ZEITSCHRIFT FÜR MUSIK* signed "Canto Spianato," which discussed and praised the essential skills for singing a Bellini opera. The pseudonym already suggests what Wagner admired most about the tradition of Italian "canto": the flawless use of legato and flowing melodious cantilenas. This, he claimed, was exactly what both German operas and singers lacked. He even praises ornaments such as trills and mordents for their intensification of the dramatic and emotional element in Bellini's operas. Wagner's early works evidently attempt to imitate this style, for instance the female parts and Friedrich's big aria in *Das LIEBESVERBOT*. But there is a considerable shift within Wagner's work: whereas at the end of Erik's cavatina in *Der FLIEGENDE HOLLÄNDER* the mordents are used for emotional intensification, they are increasingly used as rhetorical devices in later works (TANNHÄUSER insisting on his concept of love, or ISOLDE sarcastically depicting how TRISTAN might introduce her to King Marke). HAGEN's trill even turns out to be mockery when he asks the assembled Gibichungs to sacrifice sheep for FRICKA so she will grant a good marriage. However diverse these examples might be, they show that Wagner continued to use devices studied in *bel canto*, though he began to abhor the dramatic irrelevance of *canto fiorito*, with its coloraturas, runs, and scales, its excessive vocal virtuosity and ornamentation which increasingly conflicted with his aim of developing melodies as a perfect synthesis of word and tone.

In addition, the role of the orchestra in *bel canto* opera was exactly the opposite of what Wagner advocated. In *ZUKUNFTSMUSIK* (Music of the Future, 1860), Wagner remarks that, for the Italian operatic composer, "the orchestra is nothing but a monstrous guitar on which to accompany the air" (SSD 7:130). As a result, the orchestra lacks colors and delivers empty gestures, like the marches in operas such as *Norma* and *Belisario*, which must not be confused with Wagner's "Entry of the Guests" in TANNHÄUSER. It is still unclear whether Wagner understood that the large orchestras he called for might conflict with vocal beauty and coloring since, in several instances, he considered both the singers' volume and definition to be of greater importance well into casting the premieres of TRISTAN or the RING.

Wagner conducted Bellini's *Norma* while Kapellmeister in both MAGDEBURG and RIGA (where he enthusiastically advertised it). In addition to this and the aforementioned *Capuleti*, he also conducted *La straniera* and *I puritani*, as well as *Tancredi*, *Otello*, *Il barbiere di Siviglia*, and *Guillaume Tell* by Rossini, whom he met in Paris (1860). Their conversation revealed the aesthetic chasm that by then had developed between the mature Wagner and his earlier view of Italian *canto*. If his own search for pure melody after the Italian model had not ceased, his way of developing it from individualized musical declamation seemed irreconcilable with Rossini's position. In conversation with Wagner, Rossini is reported to have called it "the funeral oration of melody" (Weinstock 67).

3. Singers and training

Wagner's interest in *bel canto* opera diminished during his years in Paris (1839–42), in part because of experiences with the performance style of star singers such as tenor Giovanni Battista Rubini. In him, Wagner observed the virtuoso imitation of instrumental music as opposed to singing as the most natural means of human expression (i.e., singing should serve as the model for instrumental music). Much later, in *Über Schauspieler und Sänger* (Actors and Singers, 1872), he severely criticized the truncating of original scores in German opera houses in favor of standardized cadenzas and fermatas.

But, as is often the case with Wagner's pamphletizing, his attitude towards *bel canto* opera and singing is two-faced. There are hints that, for his own works, he wanted *bel canto* singers of the Parisian model. For instance, he sought a meeting with Pauline Viardot-García, sister of Maria Malibran and Manuel García whose *École de Garcia: Traité complet de l'art du chant par Manuel Garcia fils* (1840–7) remains a standard work on *bel canto*. Though Viardot-García's career was not limited to *bel canto*, it nevertheless constituted the basis of her technique as a singer. Wagner was disappointed that he was unable to engage her for more than private and semi-public salon performances. Clearly Wagner thought that the *bel canto* singing technique could be adapted to his own operas, and for German opera as a whole. In fact, the voice teacher Julius Hey, with whom he worked in both MUNICH and BAYREUTH, trained singers by the traditional Italian method of scales and solfege. Hey had been a pupil of Friedrich Schmitt, who in 1854 had written the *Große Gesangsschule für Deutschland*, itself an attempt to impart the principles of Italian *bel canto* technique to German singers. But this approach was an isolated episode, since Hey left Bayreuth after the first festival only to return in 1902, when he complained about the way singers were then prepared for their roles. The Bayreuth style had apparently shifted towards a *Sprechgesang* that neglected melody in favor of declamation, stressing syllables and dark vowels that Richard and later COSIMA thought essential for singing in German (see BAYREUTH BARK).

Towards the end of his life, Wagner recalled his impressions of Italian opera as a lost world, a typical perspective of *bel canto*. In a discussion with Hans RICHTER at TRIBSCHEN, he would not let himself be persuaded "that VERDI was no worse than Donizetti" (CWD 12 February 1871). And, a year later, Wagner apparently sang a cantilena from *I puritani* and remarked that "Bellini wrote melodies lovelier than one's dreams. The melody recalls Rubini to him, how wonderfully he sang it, and he observes: 'Our German singers have to go about it in an entirely different way, because they have not got this gift'" (CWD 3 August 1872). Finally, there is a report by Francesco Florimo referring to Wagner's visit to Naples in 1880, confirming his admiration for the music of Bellini that "comes from the heart, and is intimately bound up with the text" (quoted in Weinstock 507). Nostalgic quotations such as these once again reflect that Wagner tried to absorb a lot of what he admired (but also rejected) in *bel canto* opera, especially in comparison to German opera.

SEBASTIAN STAUSS

See also SINGERS, WAGNER'S RELATIONSHIP WITH/TO; WAGNER AS CONDUCTOR

Herbert Weinstock, trans. and ed., *Richard Wagner's Visit to Rossini (Paris 1860) and An Evening at Rossini's in Beau-Sejour (Passy) by Edmond Michotte* (Chicago University Press, 1968).

Bellini, Vincenzo (b. Catania, 3 Nov. 1801; d. Puteaux, 23 Sep. 1835), Italian opera composer. Wagner became acquainted with Bellini's music soon after coming to WÜRZBURG in 1833 – especially when his tenor brother ALBERT asked for the interpolation of an aria from *Il pirata* into *La straniera*. But Wagner could not obtain the full score, and his efforts to reorchestrate the piece were unsuccessful. In 1834, he attended a performance of *I Capuleti e i Montecchi* in Leipzig, with Wilhelmine SCHRÖDER-DEVRIENT singing the part of Romeo, an experience which remained with him for years. In a second attempt to interpolate a piece into a Bellini opera, Wagner composed an aria for the bass role of Oroveso in *Norma*. He – again unsuccessfully – offered it to Luigi Lablache in PARIS. Nevertheless, from the evidence, it seems as though Wagner liked Bellini and, specifically, *Norma*, most from the BEL CANTO OPERA repertoire. SEBASTIAN STAUSS

Berlioz, Hector (b. La Côte-Saint-André, near Grenoble, 11 Dec. 1803; d. Paris, 8 Mar. 1869), innovative composer who made pioneering contributions to the art of orchestration, among the first international virtuoso conductors, and leading music critic of his day.

The eminent Berliozian Jacques Barzun once succinctly observed that "Berlioz's maturity came early and Wagner's late" (2:177). More precisely, Berlioz composed his most AVANT-GARDE works in his thirties and forties, and later adopted a certain classical restraint; Wagner continued to evolve to the end. This, in addition to the obvious reasons of state and age, explains the gulf that exists between "the composer of *Roméo et Juliette*," as Wagner referred to Berlioz, and "the composer of *TRISTAN UND ISOLDE*," as Wagner referred to himself (in the dedication of the first edition of the full score of *Tristan* that Wagner gave to Berlioz in 1860).

Wagner's experiences with the French nation and people were conspicuously intense. He revered and came to embody the "holy German art" that

HANS SACHS celebrates at the close of *Die MEISTERSINGER*. There and elsewhere Wagner sets German mastery against "foreign majesty," using for "foreign" the word "wälscher" perhaps selected from the patriotic hymn "Die Wacht am Rhein" (1840), which exhorts protecting the Fatherland from the French. Such an ultimately defensive posture characterizes Wagner's tendentious relationship with Berlioz – the outstanding composer-critic of the generation of 1830, the enthusiast for GLUCK and BEETHOVEN with little time for musicians of the present and none for musicians of the future, and the face of music in France for international observers everywhere.

When the news of the July Revolution (1830) reached Leipzig, "history came alive" for the seventeen-year-old Wagner, already fascinated by Lafayette and the events of 1789 (ML/E 39). One year earlier, in the *Berliner Allgemeine musikalische Zeitung* (June/July 1829), he could have found a series of reviews of a German opera company's visit to the French capital crafted by the fledgling Paris correspondent who would soon compose the *Symphonie fantastique*. It was not that revolutionary French symphony, however, but French GRAND OPERA that captured Wagner's imagination both in 1829, when he saw AUBER and Scribe's *La Muette de Portici*, and in 1833, when, as chorus master in WÜRZBURG, he participated in the production of that seminal work. It was French grand opera that would bring Wagner to PARIS and that would nourish the notion of the GESAMTKUNSTWERK. Still, when Wagner arrived in Paris (17 September 1839), the name of Berlioz had to figure in his address book on the basis of essays published during 1835 in SCHUMANN's *NEUE ZEITSCHRIFT FÜR MUSIK* alone. Similarly, Berlioz might have noticed Wagner's name some six years earlier, when François-Joseph Fétis mentioned the LEIPZIG performance of Wagner's SYMPHONY IN C MAJOR in the *Revue musicale* (25 May 1833).

On an interior page of the autograph manuscript of Berlioz's *Roméo et Juliette*, completed on 8 September 1839, we find a note in the composer's hand: "Mr. Wagner / rue Monmartre." Wagner had thus made himself known to Berlioz almost immediately upon arrival, when the latter was preparing what was to become the greatest success of his career to date: three successive performances of his new "dramatic symphony" at the Conservatoire in November and December 1839. Singers are vital to *Roméo et Juliette*, but the love and death at the heart of the work are rendered exclusively by the orchestra. The aesthetic principle of the limitless expressive power of instrumental music, articulated in an Avant-Propos that is nothing if not a manifesto, rendered Berlioz forever unable to forgive Wagner's "crime" – of which he was guilty in theory but not in practice – of subordinating music to words.

It was during those crucial two and a half years in Paris that Wagner formed an enduring impression of Berlioz. He heard Berlioz's four symphonies (the *Fantastique*, *Harold en Italie*, *Roméo et Juliette*, and the *Funèbre et triomphale*) and observed their unsuspected audacity of orchestration and unbridled freedom of form. In his report from Paris, dated 5 May 1841, to the *Abend-Zeitung* (Dresden) (pub. 14 June), he praises Berlioz's originality and famously predicts that the *Symphonie funèbre et triomphale* "will continue to live and provide inspiration as long as a nation that calls itself France exists." In this same essay, in the *AUTOBIOGRAPHISCHE SKIZZE* (Autobiographical Sketch), in OPER

UND DRAMA (Opera and Drama), and elsewhere, Wagner tempers his enthusiasm for the composer, who cannot be a worthy disciple of BEETHOVEN because, in a word, he is French. In MEIN LEBEN (My Life, 1865–81), Wagner does admit, with considerable psychological insight, that beside Berlioz, in those early days, he felt like a "mere schoolboy."

In February 1843, Wagner welcomed Berlioz to DRESDEN, and they met again on half a dozen occasions, most notably in LONDON (1855), when both were sought-after visiting conductors and in Paris (1860–1), when both attempted to gain a slot in the rotation at the Paris Opéra. In countless letters to family, friends, and colleagues, Wagner records contradictory feelings towards Berlioz: admiration, irritation, pity. Berlioz, despite short-lived success and persistent financial insecurity, was nonetheless self-confident in the pursuit of his art. Wagner, in the end unimaginably triumphant, was more subject to self-doubt – his "self-serving evangelism" (Kolb 45) is a symptom – and less perpetually certain of his compositional path. It is for this reason that the word "Liebesangst" (love imbued with anxiety) seems aptly to qualify what Berlioz lastingly provoked in his younger German contemporary.

For Berlioz, with the chromaticism of TRISTAN and the revised TANNHÄUSER ringing in his ears, it was not difficult to quip: "Wagner is clearly mad!" (letter to Louis Berlioz, 5 March 1861). For Wagner, with the news of Berlioz's death fresh in his mind, no such compaction was possible. His final appraisal is tortured and incomplete: "If the true worth of an artist were not difficult to assess, correct judgment would be easy. Correct judgment becomes most difficult, however, if the artist's impact both upon his own day and upon posterity appears to be questionable, even when at the same time the artist's most outstanding qualities must be recognized without doubt" (*Fragment eines Aufsatzes über Hector Berlioz*, SSD 12: 310).   PETER BLOOM

Jacques Barzun, *Berlioz and the Romantic Century*, 2 vols. (New York: Columbia University Press, 1969): esp. chapter 24.

Peter Bloom, "Berlioz and Wagner," *The Cambridge Companion to Berlioz*, ed. Bloom (Cambridge University Press, 2000): 235–50.

David Cairns, *Berlioz: Servitude and Greatness* (London: Allen Lane, 1999).

S. Döhring, A. Jacobshagen, and G. Braam, eds., *Berlioz, Wagner und die Deutschen* (Cologne: Dohr, 2003).

Katherine Kolb, "Falling Leaves: Between Berlioz and Wagner," *19th-Century Music* 33 (2009): 25–61.

Betz, Franz (b. Berlin, 19 March 1835; d. Berlin, 11 Aug. 1900). Numbered among Wagner's favorite singers and admired for his diction, Betz premiered the roles of HANS SACHS in *Die MEISTERSINGER VON NÜRNBERG* (1868) and WOTAN in the first complete cycle of *Der RING DES NIBELUNGEN* (Bayreuth 1876). He also was known for his portrayals of the DUTCHMAN, King Marke (*TRISTAN*), and WOLFRAM (*TANNHÄUSER*). Although Betz was originally contracted in 1869 as Wotan for the premiere of *Das RHEINGOLD* at the Nationaltheater (Munich), LUDWIG II dismissed him for insubordination shortly before rehearsals were to begin; he was part of a group that attempted to usurp the authority of the theater administration so that Hans RICHTER would have ultimate authority as Wagner's personal representative.

EVAN BAKER

Böhm, Karl (b. Graz, 28 Aug. 1894; d. Salzburg, 14 Aug. 1981), conductor, close colleague of Richard STRAUSS and admired as an interpreter of MOZART. In 1964, Böhm was honored as Austria's first *Generalmusikdirektor*. He worked closely with WIELAND WAGNER in Bayreuth, conducting *TRISTAN* (1962) and his second production of the *RING* (1965) in performances which have since become classics of the Wagner discography. His style is notable for swift tempi and close attention to instrumental detail.   ROGER ALLEN

See also PERFORMANCE, CONDUCTORS; PERFORMANCE, RECORDING HISTORY

Boulez, Pierre (b. Montbrison, 26 March 1925), French conductor and composer. Boulez first conducted at BAYREUTH in 1966, collaborating with WIELAND WAGNER on a production of *PARSIFAL* that was in its swift tempi intentionally iconoclastic. In 1976, he and Patrice CHÉREAU were responsible for the centenary *RING DES NIBELUNGEN* at Bayreuth, which he conducted until 1980. Boulez returned there in 2004/5 to conduct *Parsifal* again in the Christoph Schlingensief production.   CHRIS WALTON

Karl-Ulrich Majer and Hella Preimesberger, eds., *Pierre Boulez in Bayreuth* (Bayreuth: Palladion/ Ellwanger, 2005).

Brahms, Johannes (b. Hamburg, 7 May 1833; d. Vienna, 3 April 1897). Brahms was introduced to the musical world by Robert SCHUMANN on the pages of the *NEUE ZEITSCHRIFT FÜR MUSIK* (39.18 [28 October 1853]: 185–6), in an essay entitled *Neue Bahnen* (New Paths). There, Schumann hailed the still-unpublished, twenty-year-old Brahms, whom he had met only weeks before, as a figure whose compositional mastery was not developing "step by step" but already "springing like Minerva fully armed from the head of Jove." Prophesying that Brahms would soon "lower his magic wand over the massed resources of chorus and orchestra," Schumann closed by proclaiming: "We welcome him as a staunch combatant." Schumann was engaged in a rhetorical battle against the so-called "NEW GERMAN SCHOOL" of Wagner, Franz LISZT, and Hector BERLIOZ. Brahms, Schumann defiantly declared, would heroically combat the self-proclaimed primacy of the "New Germans" in concert halls and in popular discourse. At stake in the fight, Schumann believed, was nothing less than the future of music itself.

A life-altering professional break for Brahms, Schumann's endorsement placed terrifying demands upon the shoulders of the young composer. And although Brahms would eventually emerge as a celebrated composer of symphonies, *Lieder*, and chamber works, his life and music would forever be tied in the popular imagination to those of Wagner. Brahms's first published compositions (1853–4) consisted of piano sonatas and songs, hardly sufficient ammunition to be used against the rhetoric of Wagner's followers. His sole foray into music criticism – to decry the New Germans' claims as "contrary to the most fundamental essence of music" – was a fiasco; leaked before it was ready for press, it was parodied before it appeared in print. In time, Brahms indeed turned to the genre of the choral symphony to which Schumann had alluded in *New Paths*, perhaps with Schumann's goal in mind: to reclaim the legacy of BEETHOVEN's Ninth from Wagner's self-serving appropriation of it in *Das KUNSTWERK DER ZUKUNFT* (The Artwork of the Future). However, each of Brahms's repeated attempts to compose such a work was aborted.

When Brahms's First Symphony was finally completed – without chorus – in 1876, critical responses to it fell into predictably partisan camps. Those who despised Wagner, like Eduard HANSLICK, were lavish in their praise, while Wagner's followers dismissed the symphony as inartistic and derivative. By 1876, however, Brahms had secured a prominent place in Austrian musical society, and the premiere of his symphony served to bolster his reputation as a powerful alternative to Wagner's creative voice. In his symphony's finale, he seemed deliberately to recast Beethoven's "Ode to Joy" for strings and winds alone, and thus to assert, contrary to Wagner's claims, the continued viability of the orchestral symphony as a genre. And in his Third Symphony, completed in the year of Wagner's death, Brahms conspicuously invoked Wagner's distinctive harmonic language, as if to demonstrate its perfect compatibility with classical symphonic forms. To the end, Brahms's attitude toward Wagner and his music remained deeply ambivalent. While he bristled at the ambitious, absolutist claims made on their behalf by the composer and his followers, he remained a respectful admirer of Wagner's art.

The most involved interaction between Brahms and Wagner occurred in June 1875, regarding Wagner's request for Brahms's return of the Paris autograph of the Venusburg music from *TANNHÄUSER*. The request for return had initially been made some ten years earlier, by COSIMA, and then by Peter CORNELIUS, both of whom Brahms rebuffed. When Wagner wrote directly in 1875, Brahms complied, but he requested in exchange a copy of *Die MEISTERSINGER*. Apparently, no copy of that opera was available, so Wagner sent instead the score of *Das RHEINGOLD*, for which Brahms was grateful, responding, "I give the best and most appropriate thanks daily to the work itself – it does not lie here without being utilized" (Brahms to Wagner, June 1875).   KEVIN C. KARNES

Walter Frisch and Kevin C. Karnes, eds., *Brahms and His World*, rev. edn. (Princeton University Press, 2009): esp. David Brodbeck, "Brahms, the Third Symphony, and the New German School" (95–116).

Brandt, (Johann Friedrich Christoph) Carl (b. Darmstadt, 15 June 1828; d. Darmstadt, 27 Dec. 1881). From 1849 to his death, Brandt was chief machinist at the Darmstadt Hoftheater, where his spectacular effects in GRAND OPERAS made him famous. Soon the foremost stage technician in German lands, he designed or modernized the machinery of twenty-four theaters, including MUNICH's Hoftheater (1869) and the BAYREUTH FESTIVAL THEATER. In 1869, he rescued the controversial *RHEINGOLD* premiere in Munich, where his brother Friedrich Carl ("Fritz senior," 1846–1927) was then engineer, and in 1870 he designed machinery for the *WALKÜRE* premiere, also in Munich. Wagner corresponded and met with Brandt regularly from 1871, entrusting him with the technical direction of the first Bayreuth *RING*. Wagner's high esteem of Brandt, whom he considered a genius and "his most important helper" (Wagner to LUDWIG II, 1 October 1874), wavered temporarily after the 1876 festival. Nevertheless Wagner put him in charge

of equipping *PARSIFAL*, including its famous *Wandeldekoration* (moving canvases). After Brandt's sudden death, his son, Friedrich Georg Heinrich ("Fritz junior," 1854–95), took over the technical direction at Bayreuth until 1884.
GUNDULA KREUZER

See also PRODUCTION HISTORY

Carl-Friedrich Baumann, *Bühnentechnik im Festspielhaus Bayreuth* (Munich: Prestel, 1980).
Hermann Kaiser, *Der Bühnenmeister Carl Brandt und Richard Wagner: Kunst der Szene in Darmstadt und Bayreuth* (Darmstadt: Roether, 1968).

Brangäne ([mezzo-]soprano; character in *TRISTAN UND ISOLDE*). ISOLDE's maid-servant, Brangäne assumes the classic role of confidante in the tradition of European theater and Italian opera. She represents the female equivalent to KURWENAL, TRISTAN's servant, and the two operate in parallel almost throughout the opera. Wagner adopted Brangäne's character from GOTTFRIED VON STRASSBURG'S Middle High German romance *Tristan*. Variously named "Brangain" in Béroul, "Brangien" in Thomas of Britain, and "Brangæne" in Gottfried, Brangäne plays a decisive part in all of the MEDIEVAL literary sources, but by no means the same one in Wagner's opera. In Gottfried, she is entrusted by her mistress Isolde the Wise, Queen of Ireland, with the love potion intended for Isolde the Fair, the Queen's daughter, and her husband-to-be King Marke. But she is kept ignorant of what the drink is all about. In a series of intrigues, she even poses as the Queen's daughter in Marke's bed on their wedding night in order to prevent Marke from finding out that his new wife, now passionately in love with Tristan, is no longer a virgin. Later fearing that Brangäne could be a witness if the deceit is exposed, Isolde the Fair tries to have her killed.

In Wagner's opera, the role of Brangäne is quite different, simplified in many details of plot in comparison with the medieval sources, yet at the same time expanded in terms of its emotional and narrative significance. In Act I, for instance, she relates much of the important epic narrative in dialogue with Isolde, just as Kurwenal does in Act III with Tristan. In more than one sense Brangäne serves as a kind of political diplomat, mediating between Tristan and Isolde in Act I and between the private and public realms (night and day) in Act II. Still, she motivates much of the plot in consequence of her actions, hastening the lovers' tragic outcome in her very attempts to avert it: in Act I she substitutes a love potion for the poison, contrary to her mistress's wishes and in the hope of saving her life, only to set the whole tragedy in motion.

In Act II, Brangäne is similarly powerless to keep Tristan and Isolde concealed from Mark, despite her best efforts. Her warning to the clandestine lovers in the second scene (*Einsam wachend*) has often been noted for its exquisitely wrought sonorous effects, such as the use of eleven solo string instruments and the deployment of the voice part itself. Wagner indicates in the score at this point that Brangäne should be invisible, sounding "from the watchtower" (*von der Zinne her, unsichtbar*); in performance, she is normally positioned at the back of the stage or off stage altogether. The total effect is to evoke an almost phantasmagoric glow suggestive of the very "twilight zone" that she occupies. And as an exercise in orchestral technique alone, this passage would exert a direct influence on modernist composers as diverse as

SCHOENBERG and Ravel. Brangäne's "call" is reiterated (*Habet Acht!*) in truncated form a semitone higher to make her admonition all the more urgent. Her scream that ends the scene – a last desperate signal to the lovers that Mark has surprised them – may also be analyzed as a displacement of Isolde's orgasm at precisely the moment excessive *jouissance* morphs into trauma (Žižek and Dolar 125).

Although designated soprano in the score, the role of Brangäne is more often sung by a dramatic mezzo-soprano. The voice part has a narrower range and a lower tessitura than that of Isolde, yet the two roles require similar versatility. Given its dramatic and musical richness, it is no surprise that the role has attracted some of the best operatic singers over the years, notably Margarete Klose, Kerstin Thorborg, Christa Ludwig, and more recently Waltraud Meier, before she took up the role of Isolde in 1993.

JEREMY COLEMAN

Slavoj Žižek and Mladen Dolar, *Opera's Second Death* (New York: Routledge, 2002).

Braune Buch, Das. Wagner's diary from 1865 to 1882, the so-called "Brown Book" was a gift from COSIMA to Wagner in which he would confide messages for Cosima to read later.

It includes the "Annals," notes he began in February 1868 for *MEIN LEBEN* (My Life, 1865–81; then in progress) that in effect rewrite the period 1846–67 contained in an earlier diary, the "Red Pocketbook." The rest contains a variety of important material, including musical sketches and drafts of prose and poetic works. EVA WAGNER (daughter of Richard and Cosima) subsequently destroyed some pages and pasted over others, presumably in an attempt to sanitize its contents. JEREMY COLEMAN

Joachim Bergfeld, ed., *Das Braune Buch: Tagebuchaufzeichnungen, 1865 bis 1882* (Zurich: Atlantis, 1975); trans. George Bird, *The Diary of Richard Wagner 1865–1882: The Brown Book* (London: Victor Gollancz, 1980).

Breitkopf & Härtel. The LEIPZIG-based music publishing firm established 1719 by Bernhard Christoph Breitkopf, purchased in 1796 by Gottfried Christoph Härtel, giving the company its present name. The firm (hereinafter: "Breitkopf") published many of Wagner's musical works and prose writings during his lifetime. His CORRESPONDENCE, usually addressed to the firm but sometimes specifically to Raymund Härtel or his older brother Hermann, dates from 1831 to 1874, representing a large chronological span which – with only a few exceptions – may be divided into five clear periods (Altmann 1911). The first accounts for just two letters from 1831 in which the eighteen-year-old Wagner offered to make piano arrangements of orchestral works for the firm. Although no further correspondence is recorded for ten years, two of Wagner's original works were published by Breitkopf in early 1832, namely his opus 1, the Sonata in B♭ major for piano (WWV 21) and his Polonaise in D major for four hands (WWV 23B). Breitkopf issued a second edition of these works in November 1862 and February 1866 respectively.

In the second period, from 1843 to 1844, Breitkopf declined Wagner's offer of Der FLIEGENDE HOLLÄNDER, but did accept *Das Liebesmahl der Apostel* (WWV 69), which was published in April 1845. Over the next three years, Breitkopf wrote to Wagner repeatedly requesting payment for a piano he had bought from the firm. Replying on 17 June 1848, Wagner offered several works for publication including *LOHENGRIN* in exchange for the cancellation of his debts. Breitkopf refused Wagner's proposal, on the grounds that the venture would be commercially unsustainable given the political climate. This exchange from 1848 constitutes the third period.

The fourth period, from 1851 to 1865, represents the years of most active correspondence between Wagner and Breitkopf. The year 1851 marked the start of negotiations concerning the publication of *Lohengrin*; while 1865, the year of the *TRISTAN UND ISOLDE* premiere, serves as a suitable end-point for the period in which the whole of *Tristan* was conceived and published in close collaboration with Breitkopf. Wagner finished each act and sent it off to the engravers before he had started on the next, and the numerous letters exchanged with Breitkopf between 1857 and 1860 show that Wagner was essentially working to publication (Deathridge). It was also during these years that Breitkopf published *Drei Operndichtungen nebst einer Mitteilung an meine Freunde* (consisting of the poems for *Der fliegende Holländer*, *TANNHÄUSER*, and *Lohengrin*, and a preface), as well as two versions of *Eine FAUST-OUVERTÜRE* (WWV 59) and Wagner's arrangement of GLUCK's *Iphigénie en Aulide* (WWV 77). Wagner even persuaded Breitkopf in March 1859 to engrave a new edition of *Tannhäuser*, but the task fell to Hermann Müller, the successor of C. F. Meser, who had already acquired the publishing rights to the work (Hopkinson). The letters of this period reflect Wagner's shrewd business sense as well as his acute interest in various aspects of publication, such as typography and script. In the fifth and final period, from 1869 to 1874, Wagner wrote to Breitkopf more often as a consumer of printed material (in particular, sheet music and copper-engraved portraiture) than as a composer negotiating publication of his own music. JEREMY COLEMAN

See also PUBLISHERS

Wilhelm Altmann, ed., *Briefwechsel mit seinen Verlegern, Band I: Richard Wagners Briefewechsel mit Breitkopf und Härtel* (Leipzig: Breitkopf & Härtel, 1911).

John Deathridge, "Public and Private Life: Reflections on the Genesis of *Tristan und Isolde* and the *Wesendonck Lieder*," in *Wagner Beyond Good and Evil* (see bibliography): 117–32.

Cecil Hopkinson, *Tannhäuser: An Examination of 36 Editions* (Tutzing: Hans Schneider, 1973).

Ludwig Strecker, *Richard Wagner als Verlagsgefährte: Eine Darstellung mit Briefen und Dokumenten* (Mainz: Schott, 1951).

Breker, Arno (b. Eberfeld, 19 July 1900; d. Düsseldorf, 13 Feb. 1991), German sculptor. After studies in Düsseldorf, he moved to Paris where he set up his first studio. In 1932, he was funded by the Prussian Ministry of Culture to spend a year in Rome. After the Nazis came to power, Breker's work was initially denounced as degenerate art. However, his neoclassical and monumental style was supported by many Nazi leaders, especially Adolf HITLER, and he maintained a friendship with Albert Speer. He joined the Nazi Party in 1937 and was made "official state sculptor" by Hitler, taking commissions from the Nazis from 1933 through 1942. He was provided a large property with studio and over forty assistants. After the war, he was classified as a "fellow traveler."

He produced a bust of Richard Wagner in 1955 that has been placed in front of the Bayreuth Festival Theater. Additional Wagner-related busts include ones of COSIMA WAGNER, WINIFRED WAGNER, and Franz LISZT.

NICHOLAS VAZSONYI

Brendel, Franz (b. Stolberg [Harz], 26 Nov. 1811; d. Leipzig, 25 Nov. 1868), journal editor, writer on music, critic. Franz's father, a mining engineer, moved the family to Freiburg, which Brendel considered his childhood home. There he studied music with composer and organist A. F. Anacker, a BEETHOVEN enthusiast and acquaintance of MENDELSSOHN. Between 1831 and 1835 he attended lectures in philosophy, art history, and aesthetics at the universities in LEIPZIG and in Berlin, where he came under the influence of HEGELIAN philosophy. Returning to Leipzig at the end of the decade, he came into contact with the SCHUMANN circle through author Julius Becker, and in the early 1840s he became firmly entrenched in the thought of the "Young Hegelians" of YOUNG GERMANY. Brendel would remain true to his philosophical and aesthetic training and convictions in later years, which would strongly influence his positions on Wagner.

He delivered a series of public music history lectures first in Freiburg and then in Dresden during the early 1840s, ultimately settling in Leipzig in late 1844 to take over the editorship of Robert Schumann's influential *NEUE ZEITSCHRIFT FÜR MUSIK*, a position he would hold until his death 24 years later. Brendel continued his activity as a lecturer on music history at the Leipzig Conservatory (beginning in 1846), where he remained employed for the rest of his life – these lectures, drawing from his earlier series, became the basis for his books *Grundzüge der Geschichte der Musik* (1848) and, most importantly, *Geschichte der Musik in Italien, Deutschland und Frankreich* (first edn. 1852).

By 1846, Brendel had drawn the attention of his journal readers to Wagner. He came to promote Wagner initially not as critic but as editor, enabling the Wagner propaganda of supporter Theodor UHLIG beginning in 1849, and publishing Das *JUDENTUM IN DER MUSIK* (Jewishness in Music) in 1850. The editor faced possible dismissal from the conservatory over the publication, which Wagner would publicly recognize in the supplement to the republication of the essay in 1869. Nevertheless, Brendel granted space in the *Neue Zeitschrift* to opposing opinions, which on the one hand reflected the dialogue (Hegelian dialectic) that he valued but on the other created personal tension with Wagner. Conflict over editorial policies, aesthetic positions (particularly regarding *GESAMTKUNSTWERK*) and even their respective character traits would make for a difficult working and personal relationship between the two men, which did not fully resolve itself during Brendel's life. Wagner faulted Brendel for caution, inconsistency, and failure to understand his ideas, while the editor felt that the composer did not comprehend how best to promote his cause. Aesthetically they disagreed primarily over the necessity for the continued existence of the *Sonderkunst* (separate arts; Brendel) or *Einzelkunst* (individual arts; Wagner).

These differences notwithstanding, Brendel and Wagner realized each other's value for their own cause, the former as editor of one of the most prominent music journals, the latter representing the leading edge of musical progress.

Thus Brendel's increasing recognition of Wagner's importance revealed itself in the pages of the *Neue Zeitschrift*, through his unqualified statement of support in the "Zum neuen Jahr" editorial for 1852, an extended article series of 1853, and many smaller aesthetic and critical essays. Moreover, other writers on music and critics from the progressive movement availed themselves of the journal to support Wagner, his music, and ideas during the early 1850s – most significant among them were members of Liszt's circle in Weimar, including Hans von Bülow, Joachim Raff, Richard Pohl, and – after 1854 – Liszt himself.

For his part, Wagner continued contributing to the journal despite his misgivings about Brendel and the publication, which he expressed in an open letter from February 1852, "Ein Brief an den Redacteur der Neuen Zeitschrift für Musik." Wagner's continued participation included open letters to Liszt about his *Goethe-Stiftung* project (1852) and the symphonic poems (1857), an essay about revising Gluck's overture to *Iphigenia in Aulis* (1854), and reprints of program notes (1853), all of which Brendel eagerly published. Wagner's growing absence from the journal during the balance of Brendel's editorship had less to do with their strained relationship than with the composer's progressive withdrawal from literary activity.

Meanwhile Brendel's *Geschichte der Musik* underwent successive revisions, in which the material on Wagner decidedly expanded, from ten pages in the first edition of 1852 (based on lectures from 1850) to the second of 1855, in which the composer receives a chapter of his own and over thirty pages of detailed discussion. In the important Leipzig *Tonkünstlerfest* address from 1859, entitled "Zur Anbahnung einer Verständigung," Brendel articulated the concept of the NEW GERMAN SCHOOL for the first time, although he had already argued for the aesthetic linkage of Wagner, Liszt, and BERLIOZ since the early 1850s. Wagner was crucial to this construct of German musical identity, based upon Beethoven's legacy – the composer himself kept his distance from the designation and from the organization that would arise around it in 1861, the Allgemeiner Deutscher Musikverein, organized by Brendel and associates and presided over by Liszt. Brendel nevertheless utilized the Allgemeiner Deutscher Musikverein to promote Wagner's music and cause, and he ensured that the major premieres of *TRISTAN UND ISOLDE* and *Die MEISTERSINGER VON NÜRNBERG* were extensively covered by the *Neue Zeitschrift*.   JAMES DEAVILLE

Franz Brendel, *Grundzüge der Geschichte der Musik* (1st edn. 1848) 6th edn. (Leipzig: Matthes, 1887).
 Die Musik der Gegenwart und die Gesammtkunst der Zukunft (Leipzig: Hinze, 1854).
James Deaville, "The Controversy Surrounding Liszt's Conception of Programme Music," in *Nineteenth-Century Music: Selected Proceedings of the Tenth International Conference*, ed. Jim Samson and Bennett Zon (Aldershot: Ashgate, 2002): 98–124.
Golan Gur, "Music and 'Weltanschauung': Franz Brendel and the Claims of Universal History," *Music & Letters* 93.3 (2012): 350–73.

Brockhaus family. The scion of the Brockhaus clan was Friedrich Arnold (1772–1823), a printer and publisher most closely associated with his eponymous company's *Conversations-Lexicon*, now known as the *Brockhaus Encyclopedia*. Based in LEIPZIG as of 1818, Brockhaus's company was one of the largest and most important in the German-speaking world. Friedrich Arnold had three sons, two of whom had direct links to Wagner. The eldest, Friedrich (b. 23 Sep. 1800; d. 8 Aug. 1865) married Wagner's sister, the actress Luise Konstanze (1805–72) in 1828. The youngest son, Hermann (b. 28 Jan. 1806; d. 5 Jan. 1877) married another Wagner sister, Ottilie (1811–83), in 1836.

Friedrich Arnold Brockhaus is said to have wished that "the eldest son should print the books, the second should publish them, and the third should write them." Friedrich worked with his next youngest brother Heinrich (1804–74) in the running of F. A. Brockhaus (Friedrich oversaw production and Heinrich editorial issues). After 1849, Friedrich removed himself from the running of the company. It was Heinrich's leadership that brought the company to its greatest heights of fame and influence. In the meantime, Hermann became an orientalist, known especially as a scholar of Sanskrit and Persian, and gaining a professorship at the University of Leipzig in 1848.

All three sons were active in liberal political causes. The firm published many of the works associated with the YOUNG GERMANY movement. Heinrich served in local and state government and as a delegate to the Frankfurt Parliament. Both brothers were engaged in the question of the Polish revolution and Friedrich's home was a meeting place for those sympathetic to the cause. Wagner was present at many of the "Polish" evenings and mentions them in his memoirs. In the Leipzig uprisings of 1830, the steam presses of F. A. Brockhaus were specifically targeted. Friedrich publicly promised to dismantle the machines thought to be putting skilled workers out of a job. Wagner clearly admired Friedrich's political abilities both during and after the uprisings, calling him a "Saxon Lafayette."

Wagner gained more than exposure to politics in the households of his brothers-in-law. He also acquired a lot of knowledge about the arts, in part but not entirely because F. A. Brockhaus published so many important contemporary writers. Buenaventura Genelli's *Dionysus with the Muses of Apollo*, seen in Friedrich's house, made a lifelong impression. Hermann's home was an important social gathering point for reading poetry and discussing ideas. Wagner was introduced to Friedrich NIETZSCHE there as well as Louis SPOHR.

Friedrich's and Hermann's homes remained a safe haven for the composer, and the brothers strove to support Wagner's career. Friedrich lobbied unsuccessfully to have Leipzig's theater produce *Die FEEN* in 1834. More concretely, the two brothers-in-law saw to it that Wagner remained in funds. Wagner had an early temporary proof-reading job at the company, but mostly the support was cash based: frequently in the form of an allowance (including the hefty sum of 200 Thaler lent at the time of the first production of *RIENZI*).

MARGARET ELEANOR MENNINGER

Brown Book, the. See *BRAUNE BUCH, DAS*

Bruckner, Anton (b. Ansfelden [near Linz], 4 Sep. 1824; d. Vienna, 11 Oct. 1896), Austrian composer. Bruckner first heard Wagner's music in the early 1860s, while organist at the Cathedral and *Stadtpfarrkirche* in Linz. A first production of *TANNHÄUSER* there, conducted by Bruckner's composition teacher Otto Kitzler, gave him the opportunity to rehearse the Pilgrims' Chorus with his local choral group, the *Liedertafel Frohsinn*. This experience appears to have sparked the ardent enthusiasm for Wagner that persisted throughout the rest of Bruckner's life; he attended every Wagner premiere from TRISTAN onwards, and met with the older composer on several related occasions – most notably at WAHNFRIED in September 1873, when Wagner accepted the dedication of Bruckner's Third (hence "Wagner") Symphony.

While there is little evidence that Bruckner took sustained interest in Wagner's philosophical and political thought, his absorption of Wagner's musical language appears to have been more extensive. The influence of Wagner's harmonic procedure (for example, extended chromatic sequence) and ORCHESTRATION (the use of WAGNER TUBAS in the last three symphonies) has often been noted; the conventional sonata exposition of Bruckner's First Symphony (1865–6, rev. 1890–1), likewise, is interrupted by a "breakthrough" theme that, in terms of scoring, resembles the culminating statements of the Pilgrims' Chorus in the *Tannhäuser* overture. Bruckner also borrows turns of melodic phrase from Wagner that, in certain cases (for example, the first version of the Third Symphony), may be intended as direct quotations and as homage; this latter category is certainly pertinent to the well-known case of the Adagio of the Seventh Symphony (1881–3), the composition of which Bruckner claimed was profoundly affected by the premonition and knowledge of Wagner's death.

After his meeting with Wagner in 1873, and now established in VIENNA, Bruckner became a member of the newly founded Wiener Akademischer Wagner-Verein (Viennese Academic WAGNER SOCIETY), where his friends – many of whom were also his students at the conservatory and university – actively promoted his music alongside Wagner's during the next decades. A particular highpoint came in December 1884 with the premiere of Bruckner's Seventh Symphony in Leipzig. Paraded – possibly contrary to audience reaction – as a stunning success, this performance followed closely on the publication of a *BAYREUTHER BLÄTTER* article by Josef Schalk that depicted Bruckner as the ideal German composer, free from the taint of the musical establishment and promoted (allegedly) by Wagner himself. This may have helped Bruckner's cause in his most immediate circles, but it undoubtedly also intensified the attacks aimed at him from the anti-Wagnerian ranks of Vienna's critical community.

Consequently, from Bruckner's lifetime onwards, a cautious distancing from Wagner has often been practiced by his apologists: Bruckner is presented as a symphonist who may have begun with Wagner's musical language and BEETHOVEN's classical form, but who ultimately founded a new ABSOLUTE MUSIC more philosophically profound than its sources. In the 1920s and 1930s, indeed, much Bruckner scholarship focused on anti-intellectual, "mystical" approaches that emphasized his ability to reveal an ineffable cosmos of feeling far beyond Wagner's word-bound genres. This claim lies behind Bruckner's contemporary appeal for Nazi ceremonial "experiences"; its residues are also found in many post-1945 assessments of Bruckner, and it may explain the pervasive popularity of the infamous (and very likely spurious) anecdote in which Bruckner, wholly absorbed in Wagner's music, inquires at the opera as to "why they are burning BRÜNNHILDE."

Approaches to Bruckner from the last two decades, aware of earlier cultural-political appropriations, have sought a more complex middle ground between the polarized labels of "Wagner-Symphonist" and the "most absolute of the absolute": Bruckner's symphonies as a sophisticated deployment of adapted aspects of Wagner's tonal language, in dialogue with the formal and rhetorical framework of the post-Beethovenian symphony and symphonic poem. This view is broadly in keeping with recent biographical revisions of Bruckner that transform him from a provincial simpleton into a canny, if clumsy, self-promoter; and even, in his symphonies, into an early modernist of the "maximalist" strain – seeking, rather like MAHLER, to assimilate Wagner's influence together with myriad others under the aegis of a single universal genre.   NICHOLAS ATTFIELD

Brückner, Max (b. Coburg, 14 March 1836; d. Coburg 2 May 1919) and **Gotthold Brückner** (Coburg 1844–92): scenic designers and painters. After establishing in the 1870s their studio in Coburg, the Brückner brothers received commissions to design and paint scenery for theaters throughout Germany, and served as chief designers for the Duke of Meiningen's important theater troupe. Wagner contracted the Brückners in 1874 to paint the settings for the first complete cycle of *Der RING DES NIBELUNGEN* to be designed by Josef HOFFMANN, sealing what became a long-term collaboration with the BAYREUTH FESTIVAL. Beginning with the *Ring* in 1896, Max alone provided all of the stage designs and his studio painted the settings for the Festival, an arrangement that lasted until 1911. With COSIMA's approval, Brückner published reproductions of his designs in small, individual portfolios labeled "Bayreuther Bühnenbilder." The designs, with the imprimatur of Bayreuth, served as models for other opera houses throughout the world.   EVAN BAKER

Max Brückner, *Richard Wagner's Werke im Bild* (Bayreuther Bühnenbilder) (Leipzig: Dr. G. Henning, 1902).
Fabian Kern, *Soeben gesehen. Bravo, Bravissimo: Die Coburger Theatermalerfamilie Brückner und ihre Beziehungen zu den Bayreuther Festspielen* (Berlin: Gesellschaft für Theatergeschichte, 2010).

Brünnhilde (soprano; character in *Der RING DES NIBELUNGEN*, with appearances in *Die WALKÜRE*, *SIEGFRIED* and *GÖTTERDÄMMERUNG*), daughter of WOTAN and ERDA, and one of the eight Valkyries. While the character of Brünnhilde appears in any number of NORDIC texts, these all predate the *Nibelungenlied*, and it was this original Brünnhilde that was likely Wagner's main source. In the *Nibelungenlied*, Brünnhilde is introduced as Gunther's object of desire, just as Hagen introduces her in Act I of *Götterdämmerung*. She is the queen of Iceland, nearly impossible to vanquish while still a virgin. Wagner took this rather straightforward character, a figure of amazonian femininity, an allegory of untamed nature, and turned her into one of the *Ring* cycle's most complex psychologies. More so even than her father Wotan, Brünnhilde undergoes an at times harrowing process of *Bildung* in the course of the cycle.

Where SIEGFRIED is buffeted about by the wiles of others, as well as by his own thoughtlessness and ignorance, Brünnhilde undergoes a bewildering gauntlet of reversals, all of them originating from her own psyche. She begins *Die Walküre* as an unambiguous, lively creature, but her filial piety to Wotan thrusts her into conflict when she recognizes that what he commands of her is not what he truly wants. After being punished, in Act III of *Die Walküre*, for heeding her love for Wotan rather than his explicit command, she is, when awakened by Siegfried in Act III of the following opera, a much more ambivalent and thoughtful figure, now a foil for Siegfried's own youthful exuberance. *Götterdämmerung* finally presents her outrage over a potion-addled Siegfried's betrayal, her wounded pride, and her fateful decision to join the scheme that Gunther and Hagen have hatched. No other figure in the *Ring* has so carefully calibrated a trajectory.

This is probably because Wagner allowed himself to be constrained by his sources only when it came to *Götterdämmerung* where, with some exceptions, Brünnhilde follows the trajectory of her namesake in the *Nibelungenlied*. The *Poetic EDDA* contains two different versions of how Sigurd won Brynhild, which Wagner used to have Brünnhilde won twice: first by being awakened through a kiss (in *Siegfried*), and then by being subdued (in *Götterdämmerung*). Where Wagner's superimpositions onto Siegfried made the character more compact, the opposite is true of Brünnhilde: In her case, Wagner cannily turned contradictory mythological accounts into a sequence, and thereby gave his heroine a complex and fractured biography.

The complexity of Brünnhilde's trajectory in the *Ring* is mirrored in her music as well. If the characters in the *Ring* are judged on the basis of the music they inspired in Wagner, there is much evidence to support the claim that Brünnhilde carries the day. The *Ring* began in 1848 as a story about the hero Siegfried and his relationship with Brünnhilde. In the final version, both Siegfried's role and Brünnhilde's stand at the pinnacle of the Wagnerian, heroic repertoire: vocally, musically, and dramatically demanding. Both have spectacular entrances: Brünnhilde's in Act II of *Die Walküre*, singing the climactic refrain of the Valkyries music, and Siegfried's rambunctious entrance in Act I of his eponymous opera, with high Cs for both. Both have powerful exits – together on high Cs at the end of *Siegfried*, of course, but also Siegfried with his touching tribute to Brünnhilde just before he dies, and the magnificent cadence at the end of her final monologue. But, following Carolyn Abbate (211), why is Siegfried so often considered the hero of the story, when that role so obviously belongs to Brünnhilde, dramatically as well as musically? Noble and commanding, or deeply touching, Brünnhilde's dynamic and emotional range spans the Valkyries music, the deeply personal scenes with her father, the *Todesverkündigung*, and the Revenge Trio, not to mention the fact that she has the last words in the overpowering Immolation Monologue.

Over the course of the 26 years it took for Wagner to compose the cycle, his sympathies – motivated in part by his reading of SCHOPENHAUER – shifted from Siegfried to Wotan, and critical opinion has long judged the portrayal of Wotan as the more psychologically and musically compelling. But even Wotan's music lacks the authority, as well as the brilliant and sharply etched contours, of Brünnhilde's. It is only Brünnhilde who in the end has experienced fully the very core of the tragedy that is the *Ring*, and it is only she who sees and understands it from within, it is indeed she whose music most convincingly embodies its essence.   ADRIAN DAUB AND PATRICK MCCRELESS

Carolyn Abbate, *Unsung Voices: Opera and Musical Narrative in the Nineteenth Century* (Princeton University Press, 1991).

Buddhism. See RELIGION

Bühnenfestspiel (stage festival play). Wagner developed the idea of a "stage festival" in essays written between 1849 and 1853. Conventional theater, he argued, was a commercial institution in which profit and social display were the primary concerns of practitioners and audiences. Inspired by the Athenian Festival of Dionysus, he conceived of a modern festival, with free admission, with no class divisions in the audience. The theater would be devoted to arousing in audiences an awareness of their common origin and identity as a "VOLK" while the MYTHS realizing that identity would be the drama on stage. To ensure that audiences were not distracted by urban life, the festival should take place in a semi-rural environment to which audiences travel solely to attend performances. These were the founding principles of the BAYREUTH FESTIVAL and they partly dictated both the site and design of the FESTIVAL THEATER. Unfortunately, admission to the festival has never been free.

SIMON WILLIAMS

See also AESTHETICS; ANCIENT GREECE; FESTIVAL, IDEA OF; *GESAMTKUNSTWERK*; PHILOSOPHY

Bühnenweihfestspiel (stage consecration festival play). Wagner's term for his final drama, PARSIFAL, whose staged performances he sought to restrict to the FESTIVAL THEATER at BAYREUTH. With some exceptions, such as the so-called "*Parsifal Raub*" (*Parsifal* theft) in New York in 1903, this restriction held force until thirty years after the composer's death. On 1 January 1914, the exclusive claim of Bayreuth officially expired, and in that year a flood of *Parsifal* performances took place in many of the world's leading opera houses. The Wagner family had benefited handsomely from their exclusive hold on *Parsifal*, and tried both legislative and executive action to have its monopoly extended or reinstated. As late as the 1930s, the Wagner clan still hoped that Adolf HITLER would intervene on their behalf.

Wagner's use of the term should be regarded in the context of the financial failure of the first Bayreuth Festival in 1876 with *Der RING DES NIBELUNGEN*, to which he gave the parallel designation "BÜHNENFESTSPIEL" (stage festival play). The huge resulting deficit had placed the future of the festival in jeopardy. The renewal of the enterprise with *Parsifal* in 1882 placed the festival on a sound footing for the first time, enabling it to prosper after Wagner's death.

Parsifal was the only work Wagner created with the unique qualities of the Bayreuth Festival Theater in mind, and its artistic realization in 1882 surpassed that of the 1876 performances. These circumstances as well as the work's theatrical qualities should be borne in mind in evaluating the expression "stage consecration festival play." Wagner described the Bayreuth theater to his indispensable supporter LUDWIG II in a letter of 28 September 1880 as the only appropriate setting for performances of the "sublime mysteries of Christian belief" contained in *Parsifal*, hinting at the "most consecrated mysteries" accessible to the initiated, but these comments are best understood in light of his desire to satisfy and flatter his royal patron, whom he referred to as "Parzival." By itself, the use of the term "Bühnenweihfestspiel" lends scant support to interpretations of *Parsifal* as a work of religious revelation, an approach that was exploited in self-serving fashion by the BAYREUTH CIRCLE during the first half of the twentieth century in the context of German nationalist politics.   WILLIAM KINDERMAN

See also *KUNSTRELIGION*; NATIONALISM

Bülow, Eva von. See CHAMBERLAIN, EVA WAGNER

Bülow, Hans Freiherr von (b. Dresden, 8 Jan. 1830; d. Cairo, 12 Feb. 1894), German pianist, conductor, and composer. One of Franz LISZT's most celebrated students, he played a leading role in promoting NEW GERMAN works across Europe, Russia, Britain, and America, giving the world premieres of WAGNER's *TRISTAN* and *MEISTERSINGER*, as well as Liszt's B minor Sonata. He was also first husband to COSIMA WAGNER, *née* Liszt.

1. Early career
2. *Ménage à trois*
3. Later career

1. Early career

Von Bülow began piano studies aged nine with Friedrich Wieck in DRESDEN. After meeting Liszt in 1842, he enrolled in MENDELSSOHN's LEIPZIG conservatory, but matriculated as a law student at Leipzig University (1848). Prior to this, he was present at the premiere of *RIENZI* (20 October 1842), saw Wagner conducting, and finally met the composer in 1846. These formative experiences led von Bülow to Weimar where he sought advice from Liszt, heard him play both of his *TANNHÄUSER* PIANO TRANSCRIPTIONS and – in 1850 – attended the premiere of *LOHENGRIN*. Wagner and Liszt both wrote to von Bülow's father supporting Hans's decision to pursue a career in music and drop legal studies.

Wagner promptly appointed von Bülow co-assistant (with Karl RITTER) of the ZURICH opera and, after a brief stint as Kapellmeister in St. Gall, von Bülow relocated to Weimar in 1851 for full-time piano studies with Liszt. During this time, von Bülow's excoriating reviews embroiled him in public spats, initially against the Berlin Royal Opera (1849) and Henriette Sontag (1852). These articles reflected his typically caustic literary style – both admired and despised – and set a pattern for von Bülow's lifelong relationship with the press.

Following his first recital tour in 1853, his widely reviewed Berlin debut in 1854 secured him a position as principle piano teacher at the Berlin Musikschule (now: Stern Conservatory), where he taught until 1864. Von Bülow's modern programs established him as a figurehead of the musical AVANT GARDE.

2. *Ménage à trois*

Von Bülow married Liszt's daughter Cosima on 18 August 1857, after a two-year relationship. The evidence suggests that von Bülow's moods and work ethic contributed to an unhappy marriage from the start ("in the very first year of my marriage I [Cosima] was in such despair at our misunderstandings that I wanted to die" [du Moulin Eckhart, 1:428]). Nevertheless, they had two daughters, Daniela and Blandine, born in 1860 and 1863 respectively.

Wagner reports first declaring his love for Cosima on 28 November 1863, and in 1864 – now enjoying King LUDWIG II's largesse – he invited the von Bülows to live with him in Munich. In July, von Bülow was duly appointed "court pianist" to Ludwig, later as Royal Kapellmeister; Cosima relocated first, with von Bülow following a week later. Court evidence from Wagner's housekeeper, Anna Mrazék, suggests that von Bülow knew almost immediately of Cosima's sexual relationship with Wagner, but covered it up (Walker, *Bülow*, 210). It was in these first weeks in Munich, furthermore, that Wagner and Cosima conceived ISOLDE, though even in his will, von Bülow treated Isolde as his own child. Liszt made several attempts to save von Bülow's marriage, admonishing Wagner, but Cosima's third and fourth pregnancies undermined them. When Wagner's daughter EVA was born (17 Feb. 1867), separation became inevitable. Cosima left von Bülow for good on 15 November 1868, and their Protestant divorce was finalized in Berlin on 18 July 1870.

Most histories typically label von Bülow an infamous cuckold, someone fawning over Wagner's genius even as the composer conducted an affair with – and eventually married – Cosima, in the face of public ridicule. It was a reputation von Bülow acknowledged, and one that caused him psychological anguish.

But von Bülow sharply distinguished personal from professional matters. While he never attended performances at Bayreuth, his concerts and donations raised 40,000 marks between 1877 and 1881 to help offset the deficit following the first BAYREUTH FESTIVAL; Wagner refused the gift, telling Cosima to invest it for their children.

The Cosima episode lasted barely a decade, but has become the prism through which history views von Bülow. Recent biographers (e.g., Walker) have, however, sought to emphasize von Bülow's subsequent career and professional legacy.

3. Later career

In Munich (court pianist 1864–7; Kapellmeister 1867–9), von Bülow conducted the successful world premieres of *TRISTAN* on 10 June 1865 (after producing the meticulous piano score in 1860), and *Die MEISTERSINGER* on 21 June 1868. He never saw Wagner again after the latter premiere. With these works von Bülow pioneered a graduated rehearsal technique – training répétiteurs, orchestral sectionals, work with individual singers, full orchestra, *Sitzprobe*, stage rehearsals, dress rehearsal – that remains standard in German opera houses today. He was also heavily involved with the establishment of the Royal Music School in Munich; Wagner appointed him director in 1865, and the first graduation concert took place on 31 July 1869, shortly before von Bülow left Munich, unable to cope with the scandal over Cosima.

After further concerts and two romantic liaisons, he resumed a full-time career as virtuoso in 1872, touring central Europe and the British Isles (1873–5) with notable programs of late BEETHOVEN, Wagner, Liszt, and BERLIOZ. As a critic, he penned a lengthy obituary of Carl TAUSIG (1871), and in 1875 famously dubbed VERDI's *Requiem* "an opera in ecclesiastical garb" (he would apologize to Verdi twenty-one years later).

In 1875, von Bülow embarked on a nine-month tour of America, during which he premiered Tchaikovsky's first piano concert in Boston, which was dedicated to him. He enjoyed a warm reception, but a minor stroke forced him to return to Europe, whereupon he accepted appointments as director of the Glasgow Choral Union (1877–8) and Hamburg Court Theater (1877–94), where he worked closely with MAHLER. During von Bülow's two final concert tours to America (1889–90), Thomas Edison recorded several cylinders of him playing and conducting. These are now lost.

Perhaps von Bülow's most notable appointment was as court conductor at Meiningen (1880–5). Under his meticulous regime, the orchestra became renowned for its precision and discipline, and premiered works by BRAHMS and Richard STRAUSS (his protégé) as well as regular performances of Beethoven and the New German repertoire.

In 1882, von Bülow married Marie Schanzer (1857–1941), an actress at the Meiningen theatre, who became his biographer and would edit his letters. Von Bülow's final appointment was at the Berlin Philharmonic (1887–92), where he established its international reputation, and set up a pension fund for its players. Weakened by exhaustion and suffering from an inflamed shoulder, he retired from Berlin in 1892 (not before controversially rededicating the *Eroica* Symphony to Bismarck). While convalescing in Cairo, he died of a massive stroke.   DAVID TRIPPETT

Richard Graf du Moulin Eckhart, *Cosima Wagner* (see bibliography).
Alan Walker, *Hans von Bülow* (New York: Oxford University Press, 2010).

Bülow, Isolde von. See BEIDLER, ISOLDE

Bulwer-Lytton, Edward George (Lord Lytton) (b. London, 25 May 1803; d. Torquay, 18 Jan. 1873), prolific Victorian novelist who famously persuaded Dickens to alter the ending of *Great Expectations*. Fashionable in nineteenth-century Germany, Bulwer's novel RIENZI formed the basis of Wagner's opera. Wagner attempted but failed to meet the writer in London in 1839. Bulwer's novels remained great favorites of Wagner's, particularly *Eugene Aram* (1832).

                                                    DAVID HUCKVALE

Burrell, Mary (b. London, 1850; d. London, 26 June 1898), Wagner collector and biographer. She was the only daughter of the prominent physician Sir John Banks, who held the Regius Professorship at the University of Dublin. In 1873, she married Willoughby Burrell, Captain of the Rifle Brigade (later called the 5th Baron Gwydyr). Her enthusiasm for Richard Wagner's work and her belief that the image of Wagner – strongly influenced by COSIMA – was partly based on fabrication motivated her go to Germany, where she began research for her own account of Wagner's life. In 1890, she became acquainted with Natalie Bilz, née PLANER, the illegitimate daughter of MINNA WAGNER, his first wife. Burrell purchased several of Wagner's documents from her, which Minna had taken with her to Germany after their separation. Natalie gained possession of them after her mother's death. However, Mary Burrell was only able to complete the first volume of her Wagner biography, which covered his life until 1834. It was published posthumously by her husband. Mary Burrell's collection of source materials remained in the family and was inaccessible until it was catalogued in 1929. In 1931, Mary Louise Curtis Bok (who later married the composer, conductor, and violionist Efrem Zimbalist) acquired the collection, and donated it to the Curtis Institute of Music in Philadelphia, which she also founded. A majority of the documents were published in 1950. In 1978, the collection, which now comprised 865 objects, was auctioned off by Christie's and the larger portion of the documents were purchased by the National Archive of the Richard Wagner Foundation in Bayreuth. In November 2011, the Bayreuth inventory increased, thanks to a donation of forty-two more documents by Mr. and Mrs. Jeffrey K. Brinck (New York).   WERNER BREIG

TRANS. HOLLY WERMTER

Auction catalog: 27 October 1978. Christie's: *The Richard Wagner Collection formed by . . . Mary Burrell; the property of the Curtis Institute of Music, Philadelphia*, London 1978.

Mary Burrell, *Richard Wagner: His Life & Works from 1813 to 1834, compiled from original Letters, Manuscripts & other Documents by The Honourable Mrs. Burrell née Banks and Illustrated with Portraits & Facsimiles* (London 1898; reprint Thalwil: TIMO, 2001).

Catalogue of the Burrell Collection of Wagner: Documents, Letters, and Other Biographical Material (London: Nonpareil Press, 1929).

Letters of Richard Wagner: The Burrell Collection, ed. with notes by John N. Burk (New York: Macmillan, 1950); German edition: *Richard Wagner Briefe: Die Sammlung Burrell*, trans. Karl and Irene Geiringer (Frankfurt am Main: Fischer, 1953).

C

Canzona. From the Italian and Provençal troubadour tradition, "canzona" was originally a term denoting a medieval poetic form divided into stanzas that would have been sung. The *Aufgesang* ("upsong") with its two *Stollen* ("posts") and the *Abgesang* ("downsong") are used with specific reference to German *Minnesang*, and function as the three components of the canzona strophe in European courtly love lyric (Ger. *Minnesang*). The canzona strophe opens with the *Aufgesang* and its two identical verse groups, the *Stollen*; the *Abgesang* provides a concluding verse group with a variant rhyme scheme and melody. For example, "Unter der Linden" by WALTHER VON DER VOGELWEIDE:

Under der linden	*a*	Under the linden tree
an der heide	*b*	in the meadow
dâ unser zweier bette was,	*c*	there was the bed of the two of us.
dâ mugt ir vinden	*a*	There you can find
schônebeide	*b*	beautifully
gebrochen bluomen unde gras.	*c*	broken both flowers and grass.
vor dem walde in einem tal,	*d*	In front of the forest in a valley,
tandaradei,	*x*	tandaradei,
schône sanc diu nahtegal.	*d*	beautifully sang the nightingale.

The first six lines above are the *Aufgesang* with the two identical *Stollen* (abc + abc) and the final three lines the variant *Abgesang* (dxd). Many other rhyme schemes are possible in the canzona strophe as long as the three components are clearly delineated.   RAY M. WAKEFIELD

Walther von der Vogelweide, "Under the Linden Tree," in *Vom frühen Mittelalter bis zum Sturm und Drang: An Anthology of German Literature*, ed. Kim Vivian, Frank J. Tobin, and Richard H. Lawson (Prospect Heights, IL: Waveland, 1998): 223.

Caricature. See PARODIES, SATIRE, CARICATURES; WAGNER AND POPULAR CULTURE

Carolsfeld, Ludwig Schnorr von (b. Munich, 2 July 1836; d. Dresden, 21 July 1865) and **Malwina Schnorr von (née Garrigue)** (b. Copenhagen, 7 Dec. 1825; d. Karlsruhe, 8 Feb. 1904). Son of the painter Julius Schnorr von Carolsfeld, Ludwig developed early as a singer; his artistry combined a powerful, dark, but pleasing tenor voice, excellent diction, and intelligent acting that helped listeners disregard his corpulent figure. Wagner was deeply impressed when he first heard Schnorr as LOHENGRIN in 1862, soon thereafter worked through TRISTAN with him, and cast him and his wife Malwina in the title roles for the premiere of *TRISTAN UND ISOLDE* (1865). Four performances took place, but less than a month later Schnorr died, becoming a Wagnerian martyr and unapproachable ideal in the process. The next year Malwina disturbed Wagner by reporting to him that she was able to communicate with her dead husband, and that she desired to help Wagner achieve his artistic aims, on which (in her view) COSIMA was a malign influence.

DAVID BRECKBILL

Einhard Luther, *Biographie eines Stimmfaches* (see bibliography): 1:150–65.
Ernest Newman, *Life of Richard Wagner* (see bibliography): 4:3–37.
Richard Wagner, "Meine Erinnerungen an Ludwig Schnorr von Carolsfeld" (1868, see Appendix 5: Prose works).

Chamberlain, Eva Wagner (b. Tribschen, 17 Feb. 1867; d. Bayreuth, 26 May 1942). Although called "von Bülow" at birth, Eva was the second daughter of RICHARD and COSIMA WAGNER. After Wagner's death, she served as her mother's secretary and companion. In 1908, she married Houston Stewart CHAMBERLAIN, staunch member of the BAYREUTH CIRCLE, and with him became an avid supporter of the nascent National Socialist party. In an effort to protect Wagner's image, Eva Chamberlain destroyed portions of his correspondence (including letters to and from Cosima) and inserted a codicil in her will which ensured that COSIMA WAGNER'S DIARIES would remain embargoed for thirty years after her own death. With her sister, Daniela Thode-von Bülow, she exemplified the old Bayreuth orthodoxy that resisted WINIFRED WAGNER's new production of *PARSIFAL* at the 1934 Festival.

STEPHEN MCCLATCHIE

Oliver Hilmes, *Cosimas Kinder: Triumph und Tragödie der Wagner-Dynastie* (Munich: Siedler, 2009).
Cosima Wagner: The Lady of Bayreuth, trans. Stewart Spencer (New Haven, CT: Yale University Press, 2010).

Chamberlain, Houston Stewart (b. Southsea, 9 Sep. 1855; d. Bayreuth, 9 Jan. 1927).

1. Biography
2. Chamberlain's Wagner writings
3. Chamberlain's legacy

1. Biography

Houston Stewart Chamberlain's father was an English admiral and his mother was of aristocratic Scottish descent. As a boy he proved to be temperamentally unsuited to the boarding school education normal for the sons of the Victorian upper middle class; instead he spent his formative years travelling widely and acquiring a broad experience of European languages and culture. An important early influence was that of Otto Kuntze, a young German theology student who introduced Chamberlain to Germanic ideas and culture. Chamberlain's formal musical education was limited to introductory lessons in piano and music theory; yet in his autobiography *Lebenswege meines Denkens* he relates that it was through the magic of Beethoven's art that he was first introduced to the innermost shrine of music (161). He first became aware of Wagner during a boat trip on Lake Lucerne (summer 1870) and subsequently read the texts of the RING operas.

The young Chamberlain was unable to attend the first BAYREUTH FESTIVAL (1876) due to lack of funds. His first encounter with a performance of the Ring was in MUNICH (1878), after which he submitted an essay to Hans von WOLZOGEN for possible publication in the BAYREUTHER BLÄTTER. He subsequently attended the premiere of PARSIFAL (1882) and was swept away by the artistic utopianism of Bayreuth and the cultic atmosphere generated by Wagner's final work. His first essays on Wagnerian matters were published in the REVUE WAGNÉRIENNE which he edited jointly with Édouard Dujardin during a sojourn in Paris. His contributions to this short-lived but highly influential journal brought him to the attention of Bayreuth. He first met COSIMA in DRESDEN on 12 June 1888, and thus began an association with WAHNFRIED which, though far from unproblematic, lasted until his death. In 1908, he married EVA WAGNER and moved permanently to Bayreuth; from that point on he became an indispensable member of the so-called BAYREUTH CIRCLE, gathered around the ageing Cosima, and a prime mover in the development of Bayreuth's nationalistic ideology. On 30 September 1923, he met with Adolf HITLER and subsequently became the first figure of national standing to endorse publicly the nascent Nazi movement.

2. Chamberlain's Wagner writings

Chamberlain was a natural scientist by discipline, evident in his fondness for organic metaphors. His published output covers a vast range and includes major studies of Kant (1905) and GOETHE (1912) in addition to his increasingly strident political tracts. His Wagner writings mostly belong to the period prior to the publication of his best-known work, *The Foundations of the Nineteenth Century* (1899). His earliest extant though unpublished essay, written in winter 1878–9 in Florence, after his first experience of the *Ring* in performance, is critical of the newly founded *Bayreuther Blätter* for attaching extraneous philosophical and social ideas to Wagner's art: "it is completely wrong and reprehensible to derive specific philosophical teachings from a work of art. We do not have to consider the personal views of the artist when contemplating his creations, for they breathe a higher spirit; and there can hardly be an unhappier idea, or one more detrimental to the Society's cause, than to 'demonstrate philosophical attitudes on the basis of his works'," (essay pub. in Allen, "All Is Here Music," 174). Chamberlain's subsequent contributions to the *Revue wagnérienne* were not only important in establishing his Wagnerian credentials, they also acted as preliminaries for his first full-length study of Wagner, *Das Drama Richard Wagners* (1892). Its central thesis is that Wagner was essentially a dramatic poet; words and music play an equal part in what Chamberlain designates as the "Word-Tone drama." "Yes, the REDEMPTION of music! The redemption of the 'inner man'! – that was Wagner's great achievement; the redemption of music in and through the drama" (*Wagnerian Drama*, 45).

Chamberlain's full-length biography, *Richard Wagner* (1896), was covertly commissioned by Cosima to provide an accessible study of the composer suitable for the bourgeois marketplace. The elaborate ICONOGRAPHY of the published work supports a hagiography which conveniently glosses over Wagner's revolutionary past in order to emphasize his Reichsdeutsch credentials and make him acceptable to the bourgeoisie; in contrast, the criticisms of the operas themselves make no attempt to support an ideological position and are informed by a thoroughgoing knowledge of the texts and scores. It is in the chapter on Wagner's writings and teachings where the process through which the late Wagnerian thought of the REGENERATION essays can be seen to be supporting a hardening Germanic ideology. The content and style of *Richard Wagner* was clearly compliant with the requirements of Wahnfried. However, Chamberlain aroused Cosima's ire by giving a lecture "Richard Wagners Philosophie" on 16 December 1898 to a learned philosophical society in Vienna (later pub. *Münchener Allgemeine Zeitung*, 25–28 February 1899) in which he cast Wagner as a philosophical dilettante. In spite of his loyalty to the Wagnerian cause, Chamberlain was no uncritical Wagnerian and, at least before his move to Bayreuth in 1908, strove to maintain some degree of intellectual distance between himself and Wahnfried orthodoxy.

The publication of *The Foundations of the Nineteenth Century* (1899) marked the turning point in Chamberlain's career as an ideologue and established him as a figure of national importance. The *Foundations* made scant reference to Wagner, and Cosima declared the intellectual debt had been insufficiently acknowledged. The art historian and Bayreuth ideologue Henry THODE took up the cudgels and accused Chamberlain of having plagiarized his main thesis from Wagner's late essays; Chamberlain responded by publishing an extensive preface to the third edition of the *Foundations* (1901) in which he refutes Thode's argument by demonstrating his intellectual distance from Wagner. This public encounter between two of Cosima's closest associates ensured that Wagner and Bayreuth became synonymous in the public mind with this toxic mix of world history and racially inspired anthropology which was to have such far-reaching influence as a precursor of Nazi ideology.

3. Chamberlain's legacy

Chamberlain is a complex and uncomfortable yet unavoidable figure in the history of the dissemination of Wagner's ideas. His writings of the 1880s and 1890s are among the earliest attempts to engage with the phenomenon of Wagner's art, and still merit close critical attention; his subsequent career as a publicist and cultural historian nourished the development of a cultural chauvinism and racially inspired ideology that irrevocably linked Wagner and Bayreuth with forces of political extremism.   ROGER ALLEN

Roger Allen, "*Die Weihe des Hauses*: Houston Stewart Chamberlain and the Early Reception of *Parsifal*," *A Companion to Wagner's "Parsifal"*, ed. Kinderman and Syer (see bibliography): 245–76.

"'All Is Here Music': Houston Stewart Chamberlain and *Der Ring des Nibelungen*," *wagnerspectrum* 2.1 (2006): 155–77.

Houston Stewart Chamberlain, *Das Drama Richard Wagners* (Leipzig: Breitkopf & Härtel, 1892); Eng. trans. *The Wagnerian Drama* (London: John Lane The Bodley Head, 1923).

Die Grundlagen des Neunzehnten Jahrhunderts (Munich: Bruckmann, 1899); Eng. trans. *The Foundations of the Nineteenth Century*, trans. John Lees (London: John Lane The Bodley Head, 1911).

Lebenswege meines Denkens (Munich: Bruckmann, 1919); abridged as *Mein Weg nach Bayreuth*, intr. Paul Bülow (Munich: Bruckmann, 1937).

Richard Wagner (Munich: Bruckmann, 1896); Eng. trans. G. Ainslie Hight (London: Dent, 1900).

Geoffrey Field, *Evangelist of Race: The Germanic Vision of Houston Stewart Chamberlain* (New York: Columbia University Press, 1981).

Champfleury, Jules (b. Laon, 10[?] Sep. 1821; d. Sèvres, 6 Dec. 1889), *nom de plume* of Jules François Felix Fleury-Husson; French author and art critic; early supporter of Wagner in FRANCE. From 1845 to 1868, Champfleury was a contributor to the influential arts-and-literature journal *L'Artiste* (1831–1904). He was a proponent of realism (*réalisme*) in the literary and visual arts, and of the painter Gustave Courbet in particular. After hearing excerpts of *LOHENGRIN, TANNHÄUSER, Der FLIEGENDE HOLLÄNDER*, and *TRISTAN UND ISOLDE* in PARIS, January 1860, and contemporaneous with BAUDELAIRE's efforts, Champfleury wrote *Richard Wagner* (1860), a brief but vigorous defense of the composer against French detractors who had heard little of Wagner's music. Of the music, Champfleury wrote: "Beauty, grandeur, and calm seem to be the pedestals on which he has placed his legends. Each of his operas is an aspiration to this *MUSIC OF THE FUTURE* that these fools and frivolous people have spoken of without knowing it." WILLIAM GIBBONS

Chéreau, Patrice (b. Lézigné, 2 Nov. 1944). Working with his long-time designer Richard Peduzzi, Chéreau directed the centenary production of the *RING* at BAYREUTH in 1976. Wide-ranging historical allusions incited furor amongst conservatives. The portrayal of WOTAN as a nineteenth-century capitalist resonated with ideas in circulation since George Bernard SHAW's reading in the *Perfect Wagnerite*. Chéreau's intense, realistic acting style proved highly influential, inspiring many theater-oriented opera directors. Most active as a theater/film director, Chéreau returned to Wagner with *TRISTAN UND ISOLDE* in 2007 (La Scala) and a semi-staged re-interpretation of the *WESENDONCK LIEDER* (Louvre, 2010). KATHERINE SYER

Chorus. Wagner rarely had nice things to say about the chorus. In one famous formulation, from *OPER UND DRAMA* (Opera and Drama, 1851), he dismissed it as a metonym for operatic spectacle itself, a loud lump of bodies whose presence on stage was unmoored from any dramatic necessity: "The massive chorus of our modern opera is nothing else but … the mute splendor of scenery converted to moving noise" (PW 2:63). His polemic was directed primarily toward French opera, and its alleged reliance on the chorus to provide sonic and scenic spectacle; by contrast, Wagner vowed to banish the chorus from his works, whittle down the number of onstage bodies to a few principals, and assign the traditional choral roles of reflection and commentary to the orchestra.

To some extent, Wagner made good on his promise: there is no chorus in most of the *RING* cycle, and its deployment in *TRISTAN UND ISOLDE* – an empty, diatonic embodiment of the world the lovers emphatically reject – is clearly one of derision. But like most of Wagner's reformist proclamations, the public pledge belies a much more complicated reality. For all his bluster about banishing the chorus, the majority of his operas still rely on one – *Die*

MEISTERSINGER VON NÜRNBERG spectacularly so. The chorus is a vital participant throughout much of *LOHENGRIN* and *TANNHÄUSER* (as Wagner himself boasted), and it lies at the heart of *Der FLIEGENDE HOLLÄNDER* as well; indeed, the thrilling choral confrontation beginning Act III of that opera was some of the first music Wagner wrote for the work, and essentially encapsulates the piece as a whole. *PARSIFAL* is more complicated, in that it presents both a feisty men's chorus (the knights) as well as a mysterious and sclerotic treble chorus (the voices "from above"); neither role, however – the former active, the latter reflective – is without precedent in the operatic repertory. *HAGEN*'s vassals in *GÖTTERDÄMMERUNG* might be Wagner's most traditional – and traditionally uninteresting – chorus, but it should also be noted that many directors have effectively imbued the silent chorus of Gibichungs left on stage at the end of that work (and thus the *Ring* cycle as a whole) with significant political and dramaturgical weight.

Yet if Wagner rarely succeeded in banishing the chorus, he did demote it. With few exceptions, his choruses tend to inhabit a limited diatonic space, in marked contrast to the "advanced" chromaticism, and attendant libidinal and metaphysical striving, of the operas' principals. Similarly, Wagner's choruses typically repeat, rather than generate, thematic material; most of the famous choral moments in his operas (the march in *Tannhäuser*, the bridal procession in *Lohengrin*, the "Wach auf" chorus in *Die Meistersinger*) simply restate music already essayed by the principals or the orchestra. Ironically, this tendency to deny the chorus a sense of musical or dramatic sovereignty ultimately reproduces, rather than replaces, mass spectacle. Certainly the end of *Die Meistersinger* – the procession of guilds followed by a massive chorus of Nuremberg patriots loudly intoning C major arpeggios – bears more than a passing resemblance to the French practices of *GRAND OPERA* Wagner so strenuously sought to discredit. RYAN MINOR

Werner Breig, "Zur Geschichte des Chores im musikdramatischen Werk Wagners," *Bayreuther Festspiele 1989. Programmheft VI. "Götterdämmerung"* (Bayreuth: Bayreuther Festspiele, 1989): 1–22.

Ryan Minor, "Wagner's Last Chorus: Consecrating Space and Spectatorship in *Parsifal*," *Cambridge Opera Journal* 17.1 (2005): 1–36.

Christianity. See RELIGION

Collectibles. See MEMORABILIA

Communication to my Friends, A. See *MITTEILUNG AN MEINE FREUNDE, EINE*

Cooke, Deryck (b. Leicester, 14 Sep. 1919; d. Surrey, 27 Oct. 1976): English composer and writer on music. Best known for his "performing version" of Mahler's Tenth Symphony, Cooke was regarded by many during his life as an authority on Wagner, one with special insight and sensitivity to the music. In 1967, he recorded "An Introduction to *Der Ring des Nibelungen*," released by Decca in the following year alongside Georg SOLTI's studio recording, and had planned a multi-volume study of Wagner's *Ring* in two main parts, the first an analysis of the poetic text and literary sources, the second an analysis of the score. It remained unfinished at his death, and only the first half of the first main part was published, under the title *I Saw The World End*. The allusion here to the so-called SCHOPENHAUERIAN ending of the *Ring*, drafted in 1856 but deliberately rejected by Wagner in the final text, is arguably misleading for a study that claims to articulate the "composer's intentions." However, what Cooke's study may lack in interpretative and critical sophistication, it makes up for with a broad command of Wagner's mythological sources.   JEREMY COLEMAN

Deryck Cooke, *I Saw The World End: A Study of Wagner's "Ring"* (London: Oxford University Press, 1979).
An Introduction to Der Ring des Nibelungen, Re-release Audio CD (Decca, 2005).

Cornelius, Peter (b. Mainz, 24 Dec. 1824; d. Mainz, 26 Oct. 1874): composer, writer on music, poet, translator. Both Cornelius's parents were actors, and his father prepared him for a dual career in music and drama. His music teachers in Mainz were Joseph Panny (violin) and Heinrich Esser (composition). Although Cornelius left school in 1838, he possessed and developed literary abilities that would eventually manifest themselves in the writing of poetry and prose, and in translation (he learned Latin, Italian, Spanish, and above all French). Beginning in the mid-1840s Cornelius was composing music for poetry he had written, *Lieder* that were inspired by often unrequited love interests. Cornelius relocated to Berlin after the death of his father – under the aegis of his uncle, noted painter Peter von Cornelius, he pursued music studies under the tutelage of Siegfried Dehn (1844–9). He undertook critical writing about music for Berlin journals and papers during his last two years there (1851–2), with a review of LISZT's Chopin book that brought him to the composer's attention. Cornelius visited Weimar in 1852 and settled there in November 1853, after having met Wagner one month earlier in Basel.

Liszt put him to work as translator of articles and literary texts, while Cornelius worked on composition under his oversight and wrote primarily for the *NEUE ZEITSCHRIFT FÜR MUSIK* on behalf of the NEW GERMAN cause. It was in Weimar that he acquired a reputation as a linguist, propagandist, and poet-composer (*Dichter-Komponist*), resulting in translations for BERLIOZ, journalistic writing in support of Liszt, Berlioz, and Wagner, a series of his own song cycles, and the opera *Der Barbier von Bagdad*. A scandal at the work's premiere in December 1858 helped Cornelius decide to leave Weimar, moving in April 1859 to Vienna, where he would remain until the end of 1864.

There Cornelius worked on his second opera *Der Cid* and, after 1861, entered into an important friendship with Wagner, whose influence would dominate the rest of his life. He undertook various tasks for Wagner in VIENNA, especially with regard to the rehearsals for *TRISTAN UND ISOLDE*, but he also served as Wagner's friend and confidant. Thus Wagner famously had Cornelius attempt (unsuccessfully) to retrieve a manuscript copy of *TANNHÄUSER* from BRAHMS. Just as with Liszt, Cornelius eventually found Wagner's friendship and influence oppressive – in his desire for independence, he positioned himself as an outsider among the partisans of the New German School. His financial need nevertheless motivated him to accept the composer's invitation from late 1864 to join him in MUNICH, where Cornelius would spend the last decade of his life.

Under those feelings, the composition of *Der Cid* became an act of defiance towards Wagner (the opera's premiere in Weimar in May 1865 hindered

Cornelius from attending the premiere of *Tristan und Isolde*). A position in harmony and rhetoric at the Royal School of Music in Munich afforded him the financial stability to marry. However, the demands of teaching and of family life significantly curtailed any major compositional activity. During the Munich years he did find time and inspiration to publish several larger Wagner articles, about *LOHENGRIN*, *Tannhäuser*, *Die MEISTERSINGER*, and Wagner's position in the development of German art, and to begin work on the Wagnerian opera *Gunlöd*. Cornelius died of diabetes two months short of his fiftieth birthday. JAMES DEAVILLE

James Deaville and Günter Wagner, eds., *Sämtliche Schriften von Peter Cornelius* (Mainz: Schott, 2004).

Correspondence
1. Letters as personal testimonials
2. Wagner as writer and receiver of letters
3. Types of letters
4. Addressees and topics: case studies

1. Letters as personal testimonials

In the introduction to the planned complete edition of Richard Wagner's letters, Julius Kapp characterized these documents as "a great autobiography that shows the entire, checkered scale of suffering and happiness," more "original and sincere" than the "actual" autobiography *MEIN LEBEN* (My Life, 1865–81) (Kapp and Kastner 6). As such, the letters can be compared to other first-person texts in which Wagner explains his thoughts, actions, and intentions. Added to these, COSIMA WAGNER'S DIARIES are an essential – albeit indirect – personal testimonial of Wagner's life because she was concerned with recording his comments as thoroughly and precisely as possible.

However, the letters assume a special status within this group of documents because of their sheer quantity. They constitute a finely woven network that stretches from Wagner's youth (the first letters we have were written when he was seventeen) until his death. Still, letters do not necessarily deliver the "boundless sincerity" that Kapp claims. Indeed, sincerity is often sacrificed for the sake of certain interests, particularly with regard to MONEY matters. For example, when Wagner asks to borrow money, he is often unrealistic about his ability to pay it back. Nevertheless, what connects these letters (and diaries) to reality – in contrast to the autobiographies – is their portrayal of life in the moment. Events are not carefully selected and there is no evident attempt to color them. Nor are they affected by the discrepancies in memory inevitable when describing events in the distant past. The combination of letters and extensive commentary currently being attempted in the latest edition of *Sämtliche Briefe* will come close to realizing Kapp's notion of a biography based on documents.

2. Wagner as writer and receiver of letters

At their root, letters are pieces of a written dialogue between two people who usually participate equally in the process. With regard to Richard Wagner's correspondence, we have today nearly all the letters he wrote, but not all the letters he received. Wagner's correspondence partners seemed to know early on that these letters were valuable and saved them carefully. Many of the letters Wagner received were lost in part because he was not able to keep the growing number of letters during his many moves (see Appendix 3: Wagner's addresses). However, even when this was no longer a problem, he did not put much stock into saving letters. After his death, his heir and widow COSIMA destroyed many letters to Wagner, for example from those from whom he was later estranged (e.g., Peter CORNELIUS, Friedrich NIETZSCHE, Hans von BÜLOW). She also destroyed her own letters to him. However, not all losses can be attributed to these personal differences, because several correspondence partners who never had a falling out with him and Bayreuth are also affected, such as August RÖCKEL, Theodor UHLIG, and many others. It seems that, as far as Cosima was concerned, the words of the "master" had their own value, independent of the dialogue in which they were written. Perhaps she even thought that letters from others could cast a shadow on Wagner's words. There are only four correspondence partners who are nearly as equally represented as Wagner himself: LUDWIG II King of Bavaria, Franz LISZT, and the publishing houses BREITKOPF & HÄRTEL and SCHOTT. The letters from the publishing houses still exist today only because the publishers themselves kept copies of business letters. Only the letters from Ludwig II and Liszt were carefully saved, a lacuna Wagner biographers must accept.

3. Types of letters

Wagner's letters are for the most part standard; in other words, the message is directed at an individual or a small group of people and delivered via mail. At mid-century, a new form of sending messages spread throughout Europe – the electric telegraph. Wagner began using this method during his ZURICH years and later used it as an important tool for organizing his musical performances.

Another variation of written communication was the so-called billets, actually communications written on small slips of paper and delivered by messenger, who often returned quickly with an answer. This kind of exchange was possible when sender and receiver lived in the same city. From his time in Zurich, many such messages from Mathilde and Otto WESENDONCK still exist today.

Wagner wrote his letters himself (for instance in contrast to GOETHE, who almost always dictated his). When Cosima assisted him with his correspondence, she wrote in her own name and not in Wagner's. This was sometimes the case with Schott, Ludwig II, and Nietzsche. With regard to the latter two, an actual parallel correspondence emerged.

Wagner's letters are for the most part written in German, the only language with which he felt completely comfortable. However, his command of French was also so good that, during his time in PARIS (1859–61), he wrote a number of letters in that language, a skill that proved useful later for his correspondence with Judith GAUTIER (1865–78).

Wagner wrote very quickly in a fluid and legible handwriting, which became even easier for us to read after 1848 when he shifted from German to Latin script. Letters to high-ranking people sometimes had a rough copy; for the most part, however, the first (i.e., fair) copies of letters were sent, which underscored their spontaneity and personal tone.

(The typewriter was invented during Wagner's lifetime, but played no role in his correspondence.)

Occasionally Wagner kept diaries for short periods, which he later sent as letters. The diary entries written in VENICE (1858–9) subsequently sent to Mathilde Wesendonck also fall into this category of hybrid texts, as well as the diary entries sent to Ludwig II in September 1865.

One kind of text that, despite its name, has nothing to do with personal communication is the so-called "open letter." These were treatises, manifestos, polemics, and so forth that were varied in length and intended for the public. However, they have the form of a letter addressed to a specific person. Wagner was particularly fond of this literary form because it gave him the opportunity to present general ideas in a relaxed, conversational tone. His addressees were people who were on his side regarding the issue in question, for example the treatise addressed to Princess Marie von Wittgenstein (Marie Fürstin zu HOHENLOHE), *ÜBER FRANZ LISZTS SYMPHONISCHE DICHTUNGEN* (On Franz Liszt's Symphonic Poems, 1857). Other examples include the open letter to Friedrich Nietzsche in which Wagner defended *The Birth of Tragedy* against the harsh criticism from Ulrich von Wilamowitz-Möllendorf (1872), and, in the late Bayreuth period, the *Offenes Schreiben an Herrn Ernst von Weber* (Open Letter to Mr Ernst von Weber, 1879), in which Wagner rejected the practice of VIVISECTION.

Other text types similar to a "letter" are public statements, meaning printed circulars addressed to artists, letters in the form of a poem, dedications, acknowledgments, contracts, and so on. These documents – hundreds of which survive today – are significant as biographical sources although they are not letters in the narrow sense of the word (see the Appendix of the WAGNER-BRIEFE-VERZEICHNIS [WBV] for these).

4. Addressees and topics: case studies

Wagner wrote nearly 10,000 letters in his almost seventy-year lifespan. In WBV there is evidence of 9,030 letters and 694 letter-like documents. A supplement published online in 2009 contains 192 additional letters. The number of correspondence partners is even more difficult to determine than the number of letters. The WBV counts about 1,200 named addressees; 400 letters are directed to unknown recipients. Since the letters to unknown addressees included many directed to the same one, it can be assumed that there are approximately 1,500 correspondence partners. Wagner only exchanged one or two letters with most of them. However, even these isolated letters sometimes contain important information or creative ideas, for example the letters to Eduard HANSLICK (1 January 1847) or Adolf STAHR (31 May 1851). Some correspondence was maintained over a long period; Wagner wrote more than one hundred letters to 15 people (approximately 1 percent of all his correspondence partners). In order of frequency, these are:

> MINNA WAGNER, Ludwig II, Franz LISZT, Friedrich FEUSTEL, COSIMA WAGNER, Hans von BÜLOW, Schott, Ernst Wilhelm FRITZSCH, Lorenz von DÜFFLIPP, Mathilde MAIER, Mathilde WESENDONCK, BREITKOPF & HÄRTEL, Hans RICHTER, Adolf von GROß, Josef STANDHARTNER.

Most importantly, these "major correspondences," which make up about 30 percent of all his letters, show how important letter-writing was to Wagner and powerfully reveal how different the phases of his life were. Four selected exchanges (with three of the most important correspondents) serve as an example.

The largest quantity of Wagner's letters went to his first wife Minna; we know of 414 (most of her responses have been lost). The correspondence is so voluminous because, during their time apart, the letters helped them stay in touch. It continued even after their separation until shortly before her death (1866). Wagner had a similarly close-knit correspondence from 1849 to 1852 with Theodor Uhlig, a Dresden friend who died early.

Wagner's second most important exchange was with Ludwig II. Today we have 334 letters by Wagner and a corresponding number of replies. Wagner's initial enthusiasm about the friendship with the young king, who he thought would help him escape his disastrous financial situation as well as enable him to realize his artistic objectives, faded because the relationship was riddled with misunderstandings. However, Wagner was so financially dependent on Ludwig II that "without the king, he and his works would no longer exist" (CWD 25 June 1869). For this reason, he felt coerced to continue the correspondence, in which he dealt with topics ranging from artistic to political issues, in the rather pious tone the king wanted. Cosima's diaries often reveal his uneasiness and even humiliation at this state of affairs.

Wagner's third most extensive correspondence was with Franz Liszt. These letters are among the most important documents concerning Wagner's private life, philosophy, and artistic work. They exchanged thoughts about everything, and the letters also document crises and estrangement. Liszt was one of the few correspondence partners Wagner treated as an equal (Liszt was allowed to call Wagner "friend"). As Wagner himself realized, this correspondence was special because it turned out to be a more effective way for the two to exchange ideas than actual conversation. In the diary addressed to Mathilde Wesendonck, he wrote that he did not think it was good to be in Liszt's presence for too long because he "was afraid that our differences [would] become too obvious. From a distance, we gain a lot from each other" (1855).

Among Wagner's letters, there was one that was met with great enthusiasm by the public, which read them like a work of literature, meaning those letters and diary entries addressed to his "muse" in Zurich, Mathilde Wesendonck, supplemented by several letters written in return. Their correspondence continued until 1865, the year of the *Tristan* premiere and came to an end with the beginning of his relationship with Cosima. The reception of this correspondence was based on Wagner's openness to Mathilde about his feelings and artistic plans, unlike any other correspondence. Mathilde Wesendonck stimulated him to compose the music for the *Ring* and was the inspiration behind *Tristan und Isolde*. She also learned of the re-working of TANNHÄUSER for Paris from Wagner's letters, and was the first to hear about his plans for PARSIFAL. It is the only correspondence that does not show that Wagner continually had money problems. (Mathilde's husband Otto supported him financially.) The exchange with Mathilde Wesendonck gave him the opportunity to present an ideal image of himself as the inspired artist and to see this reflected in the words of his understanding correspondence partner.   WERNER BREIG

TRANS. HOLLY WERMTER

See also CORRESPONDENCE, EDITIONS OF; *WAGNER-BRIEFE-VERZEICHNIS*

Julius Kapp and Emerich Kastner, eds., *Richard Wagners Gesammelte Briefe*, vol. 1 (Leipzig: Hesse & Becker, 1914).

Correspondence, editions of

1. Inventory
2. Original editions of letters
3. The first attempt at a complete edition (Kapp/Kastner)
4. Editions of individual correspondence
5. *Sämtliche Briefe*

1. Inventory

A majority of the letters that Richard Wagner wrote between 1830 and 1883 – about 10,000 – still exist today, preserved in libraries and archives, or by private collectors. This happy state of affairs is a reflection of Wagner's fame during his lifetime.

By contrast, fewer than 2,000 letters written *to* Wagner still exist today. Since Wagner certainly did not receive fewer letters than he wrote, we have to assume that many have been lost. Reasons for this include Wagner's nomadic existence as well as his uninterest in saving them. However, some were also deliberately destroyed by COSIMA (e.g., the letters from Friedrich NIETZSCHE). Only four sets of correspondence which include both sides of the exchange have been preserved and published almost in their entirety: those with LUDWIG II King of Bavaria, Franz LISZT, and with the publishers BREITKOPF & HÄRTEL and SCHOTT.

The inventory of Wagner's known letters has been catalogued in the *WAGNER-BRIEFE-VERZEICHNIS* (WBV), published in 1998, which appeared in conjunction with the *Sämtliche Briefe* edition, and account for 9,030 letters. A list of letters identified after the publication of this catalog can now be found online, accessible through the homepage of the Richard-Wagner-Briefausgabe at the University of Würzburg.

2. Original editions of letters

Just a few years after Richard Wagner's death (1883), Cosima started to publish his letters, beginning with those from her father, Franz Liszt (1887). A year later, she published the letters to his Dresden friends (Theodor UHLIG, Ferdinand HEINE, Wilhelm Fischer), which she also edited herself. As a result of her efforts, a large portion of Wagner's correspondence was made public quite quickly. The most important letters were published by Breitkopf & Härtel in a seventeen-volume series entitled *Richard Wagners Briefe in Originalausgaben* (1911). The series was divided into two parts and included the following (Wagner is abbreviated as "RW"; the editor's name [unless it is a WAHNFRIED edition] and publication year appear in parenthesis):

Part I: Vols. 1–2: RW to MINNA Wagner (1908); Vol. 3: Letters to the family from RW (Glasenapp, 1907); Vol. 4: RW to Theodor Uhlig, Wilhelm

Fischer and Ferdinand Heine (1888); Vol. 5: RW to Mathilde WESEN-DONCK (Golther, 1904); Vol. 6: RW to Otto Wesendonck (Golther, 1905); Vol. 7: Correspondence between RW and Breitkopf & Härtel (Altmann, 1911); Vol. 8: Correspondence between RW and B. Schott's Sons (Altmann, 1911).

Part II: Vol. 9: Correspondence between Wagner and Liszt (1887); Vol. 10: RW to Theodor APEL (Apel, 1910); Vol. 11: RW to August RÖCKEL (La Mara [= Marie Lipsius], 1894); Vol. 12: RW to Ferdinand PRAEGER (Chamberlain, 1894); Vol. 13: RW to Eliza WILLE (E. Wille, 1887); Vol. 14: RW to his artists (= 2nd volume of the Bayreuth letters, Kloss, 1908); Vol. 15: Bayreuth letters from RW (Glasenapp, 1907); Vol. 16: RW to Emil HECKEL (Heckel, 1899); Vol. 17: RW to friends and contemporaries (Kloss, 1909).

Although all of these letters were published in the same collection, there are stark editorial differences. Cosima Wagner – who edited Volumes 4 and 9, and the letters to Minna – made considerable changes. For example, she removed some of Wagner's political and anti-religion polemic from his letters to Uhlig; in the letters to Minna, she concealed identities by replacing names with initials. By contrast, the letters edited by Wilhelm Altmann (director of the music department of the National Library in Berlin) and Wolfgang GOLTHER were unchanged.

3. The first attempt at a complete edition (Kapp/Kastner)

Shortly after completion of the *Originalausgaben*, Julius Kapp and Emerich Kastner planned a complete edition. Kapp criticized the Breitkopf version for its haphazard organization, and complained that several volumes were incomplete and that parts of letters, particularly those to Uhlig, were missing. He wanted them presented in chronological order, and unexpurgated.

Two volumes of Kapp's project were published in 1914: volumes 1 (letters to 1843) and 2 (letters 1843–50). The project was abandoned because of World War I and was not taken up again. However, it remains important, even as a fragment, and set new standards for later editions.

4. Editions of individual correspondence

In the years that followed, the *Originalausgaben* were supplemented by a series of editions dedicated to other recipients, including Hans von BÜLOW, Julie RITTER, Hans RICHTER, Mathilde MAIER, Anton PUSINELLI, and Judith GAUTIER. In general, the editors no longer altered the texts, and had no critical ambitions. At the same time, while making a wealth of material available to Wagner research, these editions provide no information about the whereabouts of the letters, and set no new standards for editing.

The most important edition, after Kapp's attempt, was the publication of Wagner's correspondence with Ludwig II (5 vols. 1936–9), edited by Otto STROBEL, who can be considered the founder of philological Wagner research. As in Kapp's edition, the principles of completeness and fidelity to the original were key. The letters are also complemented by extensive commentary, which constitutes a substantial contribution to Wagner's biography.

5. *Sämtliche Briefe*

In 1962, an edition of the complete letters was planned by WINIFRED WAGNER, then head of the Wagner clan, and the State-owned Deutscher Verlag für Musik in Leipzig (GDR). At the time, the editors estimated that there were approximately 5,000 letters in existence, and that the edition would comprise fifteen volumes. The first volume was published in 1967, edited by Gertrud STROBEL (the archivist of the Bayreuth Richard Wagner Archive) and the Leipzig musicologist Werner Wolf. Strobel was responsible for compiling and selecting the letters as well as the source catalog, and Wolf was in charge of the introduction, commentary, and the index. The introductions were rather extensive (e.g., 48 pages for vol. 1), but had less to do with the actual letters, instead providing biographical information from the time in Wagner's life when the letters were written. These introductions, if combined, would constitute a new Wagner biography. By comparison, the comments about the letters are brief.

Since 1986, Hans-Joachim Bauer and Johannes Forner have replaced Strobel and Wolf. The RICHARD-WAGNER-STIFTUNG assumed control of the Richard Wagner family archives in partnership with the publisher.

The collapse of the East German state in 1989 affected the economic conditions for the project. The Deutscher Verlag für Musik was taken over by Breitkopf & Härtel, which was willing to continue the project. The board of directors of the Richard Wagner Foundation selected Werner Breig to assume editorial responsibility.

As the basis for the continuation of the project, an index of letters was first created (WBV). Published in 1998, it became the basis for the new edition, to comprise a planned 34 volumes (volumes appearing as they are completed). Unlike previous editions, which were arranged according to biographical caesuras, each of the newer volumes contains the letters from a particular year, beginning 1860 (vol. 1), and continuing to 1882–3 (vol. xxxiv).

For vols. x onwards, new editing guidelines were established, the main features of which are explained in the opening paragraphs of each volume. Commentary plays a significant role, and constitutes approximately half of every volume. The work was begun in Bochum, but moved to Erlangen in 1998, and then to Würzburg in 2008. Among the editors are Dr. Martin Dürrer, Dr. Andreas Mielke, Dr. Isabel Kraft (until 2006), and Dr. Margret Jestremski (since 2007). At first, Werner Breig was the editor-in-chief, but after the move to Würzburg this task was assumed by the editorial team. Since 2006, the project has been sponsored by the German Research Foundation (DFG). For more information, please consult the *Wagner-Briefe-Verzeichnis* (28–47).

WERNER BREIG

TRANS. HOLLY WERMTER

See also CORRESPONDENCE; *WAGNER-BRIEFE-VERZEICHNIS*

Werner Breig, "Probleme einer Gesamtausgabe der Briefe Richard Wagners," *Der Brief in Klassik und Romantik: Aktuelle Probleme der Briefedition*, ed. Lothar Blum and Andreas Meier (Würzburg: Königshausen & Neumann, 1993): 121–53.

Martin Dürrer, Margret Jestremski, and Andreas Mielke, "'Wenn ich nur nicht so entsetzlich viel Briefe zu schreiben hätte!' The Erlangen Edition *"Sämtlicher Briefe"* Richard Wagners," in: *Erlanger Editionen: Grundlagenforschung durch Quelleneditionen: Berichte und Studien*, ed. Helmut Neuhaus (Erlangen: Palm & Enke, 2009): 409–26.

Catalogs and indexes

Wilhelm Altmann, *Richard Wagners Briefe nach Zeitfolge und Inhalt: Ein Beitrag zur Lebensgeschichte des Meisters* (Leipzig, 1903).

Werner Breig, Martin Dürrer, and Andreas Mielke, *Chronologisches Verzeichnis der Briefe von Richard Wagner: Wagner-Briefe-Verzeichnis (WBV)* (Wiesbaden: Breitkopf & Härtel, 1998).

Emerich Kastner, *Wagneriana: Beiträge zur Richard-Wagner-Bibliographie*, vol. 1: *Briefe Richard Wagner's an seine Zeitgenossen (1830–1883)* (Wien, 1885).

Briefe von Richard Wagner an seine Zeitgenossen: 1830–1883 (Berlin, 1897).

Complete editions

Richard Wagners gesammelte Briefe, ed. Julius Kapp and Emerich Kastner, 2 vols. (out of print) (Leipzig, 1914) abbreviated as Kapp/Kastner.

Richard Wagner, *Sämtliche Briefe* (abbreviated as SB): Vols. 1–5, ed. Gertrud Strobel and Werner Wolf (Leipzig, 1967, 1969, 1975, 1979, 1993); Vols. 6–8, ed. Hans-Joachim Bauer and Johannes Forner (Leipzig, 1986, 1988, 1991); vol. 9, ed. Klaus Burmeister and Johannes Forner (Leipzig, 2000); Vols. 10–19, ed. Andreas Mielke (Vols. 10, 14, 15, 17, 18), Martin Dürrer (Vols. 11–12, 16, 17), Martin Dürrer and Isabel Kraft (vol. 13), and Margret Jestremski (vol. 19) (Wiesbaden, 1999–2011).

Cosima Wagner's diaries. Cosima wrote her diaries for her son, SIEGFRIED. The entries which begin on 1 January 1869 and end with Richard Wagner's death on 13 February 1883 comprise approximately 5,000 pages. They thus commence during the time Cosima and Richard had begun to live together in TRIBSCHEN, and include the move to Bayreuth and the first festivals, ending abruptly with his death in Venice. Beyond the significant events in the life of the Wagner family, the diaries also shed light on daily life, and convey a sense of the time. They also record everything the couple heard, played, and read.

Cosima had no intention of making the diaries public, given that they also contain a panorama of experiences and comments that are sometimes private, sometimes banal, as well as revealing remarks Wagner made about other composers and his own compositional work. Shared readings, the joys and frustrations of parenthood, music performed by guests or Wagner himself, his essays, observations about politics and current events, about the reception of his works: all these are presented in a colorful mix, seasoned with Wagner's own sharp wit. Wagner's entire worldview is on display, and Cosima did her best to faithfully record Wagner's legendary loquaciousness: her entries get longer and more detailed with each passing year.

Wagner also made sweeping, often cruel or even stupid comments, especially about other composers such as MENDELSSOHN, which Cosima again notes with full agreement. As such, Wagner is presented as the autonomous genius, an image she herself had helped to establish. Cosima recognized Wagner's stature and accepted his authoritarian ways – or, rather, she adjusted herself to them. As far as she was concerned, her most important task was to enable Wagner to compose: "The theater of his thinking is a temple and the present theater a fairground stall, he speaks the language of the priest, and shopkeepers are supposed to understand him! I have to dedicate my whole life to him, for I have recognized his position" (CWD 4 October 1869).

Wagner was an artist for whom the devotion of a woman was a prerequisite for his creative process. Cosima complied, and so her sense of mission meant that she overlooked a lot: Wagner's moodiness, his many HEALTH problems, his frequent irritation over trivialities, his increasing inability to let her leave his side, even for short periods. When she once did not give him a present for his birthday, because the household was strapped for money, he reproached her (CWD 27 May 1874). He showered her with signs of love and affection, but could just as quickly get offended and become venomous. True, he did not hold a grudge for long, and always begged for forgiveness the following day. All this is noted, and so Wagner actually appears in a rather human light, since his moods were surely also affected by the demands of his creative work as well as the imponderables of daily life, such as recurring MONEY issues, problems with performances, and so forth.

When talking to Cosima about his earlier relationships with women, Wagner was understandably less than honest. The fact that he had conceived his most important works during his marriage with MINNA was suppressed. His disdainful portrayal of her (also in MEIN LEBEN [My Life, 1865–81]) set the stage for the future scholarly appraisal of her as a narrow-minded and uncomprehending bourgeois woman, unsuited for him as a partner. He also did not sufficiently acknowledge Mathilde WESENDONCK's role in the conception and composition of TRISTAN, and he downplayed the significance of their relationship for his creative work whose influence reached all the way to MEISTERSINGER.

When Cosima and Richard's second daughter, EVA, married Houston Stewart CHAMBERLAIN in 1908, Cosima allegedly gave her the diaries. However Eva's own notation in the manuscript catalog of the Wahnfried Archive states that she received them on 22 October 1911. She defaced the text by making 50 deletions, of which 41 have been restored. One example: Cosima wrote: "We talk of Hans's character, and R. admits to me that from the beginning there was always something alien about it for him, *amounting almost to a repulsion*" (CWD 13 March 1882; the portion in italics was crossed out). In June 1935, Eva turned the diaries over to the City of Bayreuth "as a donation to the Richard-Wagner-Gedenkstätte," specifying certain conditions, for instance that they were only to be published thirty years after her death (which occurred on 26 May 1942). The diaries were edited and annotated by Martin Gregor-Dellin and Dietrich Mack; the first volume (1869–77) appeared in 1976, the second (1878–83) the following year, published by Piper (Munich). The handwritten original is in the Richard-Wagner-Gedenkstätte in Bayreuth. The English translation is by Geoffrey Skelton and includes an excellent index, missing from the German edition.   EVA RIEGER

TRANS. NICHOLAS VAZSONYI

Cronaca wagneriana. A short-lived periodical (OCLC 503757328), published four times in 1893, six times in 1894, and twice in 1895 on behalf of the WAGNER SOCIETY Sezione Bolognese dell'Associazione Universale Richard Wagner. According to Axel Körner (238), the *Cronaca*'s "contextualization of Wagner" corresponded to that of other contemporaneous European publications in political-social terms as a "conspirator of 1848" and friend of Mikhail BAKUNIN.   MICHAEL SAFFLE

Axel Körner, *Politics of Culture in Liberal Italy: From Unification to Fascism* (New York: Routledge, 2009).

Culshaw, John (b. Southport, 28 May 1924; d. London, 27 April 1980), English record producer. An influential and idealistic champion of Wagner on record in the first decade of the stereo era, Culshaw masterminded the Decca *Ring* (recorded in Vienna, 1958–65, with SOLTI conducting), the most ambitious operatic recording of its time both in scope and in its aim to "produce" opera for the home listener. DAVID BRECKBILL

John Culshaw, *Ring Resounding* (London: Secker & Warburg / New York: Viking, 1967).
The Golden Ring (1965 BBC film, dir. Humphrey Burton, documenting the recording of the Decca *Götterdämmerung*).

D'Agoult, Countess Marie Cathérine Sophie (b. Frankfurt am Main, 31 Dec. 1805; d. Paris, 5 March 1876), liberalist aristocrat, writer (pen name: Daniel Stern), and journalist, mistress to Franz LISZT and mother to COSIMA WAGNER, *née* Liszt. During her affair with Liszt (1833–44), d'Agoult lived openly as his mistress (1835–9), later documenting this bitterly in *Nélida* (1846). They conceived three children, though Daniel and Blandine died aged 20 and 26 respectively. Marie came into contact with WAGNER only through her relationship to Cosima.   DAVID TRIPPETT

Dahlhaus, Carl (b. Hanover, 10 June 1928; d. Berlin, 13 March 1989), musicologist. No single scholar in the second half of the twentieth century produced more on Wagner than Dahlhaus. Besides being Editor-in-Chief of the Richard Wagner collected edition (*SÄMTLICHE WERKE*), which began appearing in 1970, Dahlhaus co-authored with John Deathridge the Wagner entry in the 1980 (6th edn.) of *The New Grove Dictionary of Music and Musicians*, which was issued in book form in 1984. He also produced a monograph, edited books about Wagner, and published at least twenty additional free-standing articles on Wagner.

Dahlhaus was particularly important for taking German music scholarship in a new direction that focused on Wagner's innovative compositional processes, although he never adopted the densely analytical approach characteristic of American music theorists. In doing so, Dahlhaus explicitly tried to steer away from biographical, cultural, and political issues and instead focus on technical and aesthetic concerns.   SANNA PEDERSON

Carl Dahlhaus, ed., *Das Drama Richard Wagners als musikalisches Kunstwerk* (Regensburg: Bosse, 1970).
Richard Wagner: Werk und Wirkung (Regensburg: Bosse, 1971).
Richard Wagner's Music Dramas (see bibliography).

Daland (bass; character in *Der FLIEGENDE HOLLÄNDER*), the merchant-captain father of the heroine SENTA. Daland promises his daughter Senta as a bride to the titular DUTCHMAN in exchange for the incalculable wealth stored aboard his ship. The character is modeled on the merchant "Scotsman" in the play briefly described in Heinrich HEINE's satirical "fable of the Flying Dutchman." Wagner develops Daland into an emblem of the good-natured, materialistic bourgeois philistine. In the opening and closing scenes of the opera, Daland's part consists of short bits of naturalistic musical dialogue or declamation. Otherwise, as in his duet with the Dutchman in Act I or his short, semi-buffo aria in Act II, Daland's music is bluff and tuneful, though still tending toward a kind of conversational melodic style Wagner may have assimilated from the comic operas of composers such as Daniel AUBER and Albert Lortzing.   THOMAS S. GREY

Dance

1. Wagner's concept of dance
2. Dance in Wagner's operas
3. Choreographers

1. Wagner's concept of dance

Richard Wagner's concept of dance was developed most clearly in his early theoretical writings: *Die KUNST UND DIE REVOLUTION* (Art and Revolution, 1849), *Das KUNSTWERK DER ZUKUNFT* (The Artwork of the Future, 1849/50), and *OPER UND DRAMA* (Opera and Drama, 1851). For Wagner, dance, together with tone and poetry, was one of three primeval sisters that would combine to become the ideal, total, universal dramatic work of art – the *GESAMTKUNSTWERK*.

Wagner distinguished between *Bewegung* (movement), *Tanz* (dance), *Ballet(t)* (ballet), and *Gebärde* (gesture). Ballet, now separate from its sister arts, alienated from its original, ANCIENT GREEK model, and isolated from a natural folk environment, was thus an empty activity. Ballet represented everything Wagner despised: French artificiality, fashion, commercialism, loss of national identity. Wagner described ballet as unoriginal, without inner meaning, and performed for material success, the same terms he used to describe assimilated JEWS in *Das JUDENTUM IN DER MUSIK* (1850). Both ballet dancers and Jews appear as the embodiment of alienation and displacement. Since the height of Romantic ballet's success in France coincided with Wagner's ambivalent relationship to MEYERBEER and GRAND OPERA, he was compelled to reject ballet as its integral part and develop an idea of dance that circumvented his contemporary experience.

Das Kunstwerk der Zukunft contains an entire section devoted to dance, described as "the most realistic of all arts" that "includes within itself the condition for the enunciating of all remaining art" (SSD 3:71; PW 1:100). Through the expression of "corporeal-man" all other arts – tone, poetry, sculpture, architecture – become sensible and meaningful. Movement and dance provide the mimetic glue through which sung and spoken word can be represented on stage. Form, the human body, is necessary to articulate and express essence; corporeal form thus determined the possibility of the realization of Wagner's drama. Dance as summation of the physical, sensuous translation of ideas – embodiment of thought and the mind – was a vital part of the total work of art. The passages on dance end with the judgment: "O glorious dance! O shameful dance!" (SSD 3:81; PW 1:110). This statement summarizes Wagner's attitude to dance, both in its ideal form, and as a nasty commercial practice. Clearly, Wagner never underestimated the importance of dance, but he also did not invent new dance forms, either as a new stage art or as a reawakened art of the VOLK.

Instead, in *OPER UND DRAMA* Wagner explored the power of gesture, which plays a much greater role in the realization of his operas. Gesture takes on the function of dance by fusing movement with performance on and off stage, including that of the orchestra. Gesture – "das Unaussprechliche" (that which cannot be articulated) – eventually speaks as movement of rhythm and tone, put into bodily action or dance. Ideally, gesture develops from its origins of pure sensual dance movement into spiritual mimesis, as spirit translated into physical movement, an interpretation that proved a more modern and radical concept than a mere reimagination of dance.

2. Dance in Wagner's operas

Wagner's use of dance in his operas did not live up to his own ideals of a *Gesamtkunstwerk*. His operas have few dedicated "dance" scenes and do not find a new place for movement. The most famous remains the Venusberg scene in TANNHÄUSER (see Wagner to Mathilde WESENDONCK, 10 April 1860). Otherwise, dance plays hardly any role in the embodiment of his music-word drama.

But if instead of "dance," we consider Wagner's ideas of "gesture," then his operas demonstrate a new relationship to movement. He demanded a new "Gebärdenspiel" (*Oper und Drama*) of his singers and of the orchestra, and he envisioned a new experience for the audience. Together, this represented the new corporeal unity of performing and experiencing his works, an ongoing project within the constant evolution of his revolutionary work of art. Thus the completed performance as incarnation of gesture becomes the essence of the *Gesamtkunstwerk*.

3. Choreographers

In the process of staging his operas, Wagner employed choreographers to varying degrees of satisfaction. But only in the twentieth century were his compositions, which he never meant as musical illustration for dance outside of opera, appropriated to accompany dance and ballet. To the many choreographers who used (often a very random selection of) Wagner's music, belong Isadora DUNCAN, Rudolf von Laban (1879–1958), and Maurice Béjart (1927–2007), who consistently returned to Wagner's oeuvre and took up the challenge of the *Gesamtkunstwerk*. He created a "spectacle total" with dance at its center. In pieces such as *Bahkti* (1968), *Ring um den Ring* (1990), or *Also sprach Zarathustra* (2006), he incorporated Wagner's philosophy as well as his libretti and music.   MARION KANT

See: FRICKE, RICHARD

Theresa Cameron, "The Bayreuth Productions of the Tannhäuser Bacchanale, 1904–1967," in *Ausdruckstanz: Eine mitteleuropäische Bewegung der ersten Hälfte des 20. Jahrhunderts*, ed. Gunhild Oberzaucher-Schüller (Wilhelmshaven: Heinrichshofen, 1992).

Carl Dahlhaus and Egon Voss, eds., *Wagnerliteratur: Wagnerforschung* (Chapter 5; see bibliography).

Sybille Dahms, "Der Einfluss von Wagners Werk und Kunsttheorie auf Tanz und Ballett," in *Richard Wagner 1883–1983: Die Rezeption im 19. und 20. Jahrhundert*, ed. Ursula Müller (Stuttgart: Stuttgarter Arbeiten zur Germanistik, 1984).

Dannreuther, Edward George (b. Strasbourg, 4 Nov. 1844; d. Hastings, 12 Feb. 1905), German pianist, pedagogue, and writer on music, resident in England from 1863. Dannreuther championed Wagner's cause, translating his *Über das Dirigiren* (On Conducting, 1869) and ZUKUNFTSMUSIK (Music of the Future, 1860) into English and, in 1872, founded the London WAGNER SOCIETY. Wagner stayed with him during his visit to LONDON in 1877. In 1895, he became professor of piano at the Royal College of Music.

DAVID TRIPPETT

Edward Dannreuther, *Richard Wagner: His Tendencies and Theories* (London: Augener, 1873). *Richard Wagner and the Reform of Opera* (London: Augener 1904).

Debussy, Claude (b. Saint-Germain-en-Laye, 22 Aug. 1862; d. Paris, 25 March 1918), French composer. During his years at the Conservatoire (from 1872), Debussy familiarized himself with Wagner's works and became a fervent admirer. In 1888, he went to BAYREUTH, and heard *Die MEISTERSINGER VON NÜRN-BERG* and *PARSIFAL*. The following year, he returned to see *TRISTAN UND ISOLDE* and *Der RING DES NIBELUNGEN*. Marked by this experience, he began to criticize in particular the system of LEITMOTIVE in the *Ring*. From 1888/9 – both peak and turning point of his Wagner frenzy – he began to detach himself from the German composer's suffocating influence. He conceived an entirely antithetical technique of composition, privileging a dramaturgy where music is a "discreet person" rather than dominant. Between 1893 and 1902, he worked on *Pelléas et Mélisande* (1902), the first French opera to transcend WAGNERISM. Even if he continued to criticize Wagner's AESTHETICS, he remained, till the end of his life, an ardent admirer of *Tristan* and, especially, *Parsifal*.   HERMANN GRAMPP

Claude Debussy, *Debussy on Music: The Critical Writings of the French Composer Claude Debussy*, intro. F. Lesure, trans. and ed. R. L. Smith (Ithaca, NY: Cornell University Press, 1988). Robin Holloway, *Debussy and Wagner* (London: Eulenburg Books, 1979).

Decadence. Wagner's importance for decadent art has been richly documented. The Venusberg music from *TANNHÄUSER*, the eroticism-death symbolism of *TRISTAN UND ISOLDE*, the image of the debased and degraded SIEGFRIED in *GÖTTERDÄMMERUNG*, the sickness-REDEMPTION oppositions in *PARSIFAL*, were all vital examples for *fin-de-siècle* decadent topics and AESTHETICS. BAUDELAIRE's description of Wagner's "Venus" music in terms of "will, desire, concentration, nervous intensity" in his essay *Richard Wagner and "Tann-häuser" in Paris* (1861) is seminal, not only in shifting Wagner reception towards decadent thematics, but also in influencing definitions of decadence which emerged from the 1880s. The exquisite sensuous surface, ecstatic intensifications, and morbid desire heard in *Tristan und Isolde* were highly prized by important artists of decadence – Aubrey BEARDSLEY, Thomas MANN, Gabriele d'Annunzio, Joséphin Péladan, and others. Wagner's art attracted decadents through its "DEGENERATIVE" figures (for example, KLINGSOR and HAGEN), its miniaturism in which large-scale form seems to collapse into expressive extremes concentrated in beautiful moments, and the fatalistic or catastrophic preoccupation with "ending."

The decadent character of *Parsifal* is often identified with the preoccupation with algolagnia (conjunctions of pleasure and pain, commonly related to Wagner's description of the suffering AMFORTAS in a letter to

Mathilde WESENDONK of 30 May 1859 as "my third-act Tristan inconceivably intensified"). *Parsifal* is also frequently raised as the quintessential "late work," with its associations of artifice, mannerism and decaying forms. And Klingsor's magic garden, the artificial paradise of the Flower Maidens in Act II, is a site rich with decadent suggestiveness. For NIETZSCHE, however, the redemptive yearning represented a fundamental aspect of its decadent "sickness." In *The Case of Wagner* (1888), Nietzsche declared *Parsifal* to be "*the stroke of genius* in seduction," as the supreme example of Wagner's "persuasion of sensuousness which in turn makes the spirit weary and worn-out" (183–4). In *Parsifal*, Nietzsche continued, Wagner exhibits masterly cunning in his alliance of beauty and sickness, and confirms his status as the "greatest *miniaturist* in music who crowds into the smallest space an infinity of sense and sweetness" (171).

Wagner and decadence preoccupied Nietzsche in the years before his final mental collapse. Historical narratives incorporating notions of decadence have often fallen into disrepute, but with Wagner, the French *décadence*, Christianity, and Greek and Roman antiquity as central stimuli, Nietzsche saw decadence as the major modern cultural malaise, but one which is not simply to be equated with, or defined by, decline. He shifted decadence from abject marginality to ambivalent prominence in MODERNITY. Decadence thus rises above the merely topical or fashionable. Famously, Nietzsche declared the crucial role of decadence in modernity and its central significance in his own development: "I am, no less than Wagner, a child of this time; that is, a decadent" (155). For Nietzsche in the 1880s, Wagner's art of neurosis, atomization, artifice, sensuousness, and "histrionics" ("an expression of physiological degeneration") (169) "sums up modernity" (156). Nietzsche's notion of "convalescence" from Wagnerian sickness and the necessity of a full experience of decadence are powerfully resonant in many ambivalently post-Wagnerian works of the late nineteenth and early twentieth centuries.

STEPHEN C. DOWNES

Friedrich Nietzsche, *The Birth of Tragedy and The Case of Wagner*, trans. Walter Kaufmann (New York: Vintage, 1967).

Degeneration and regeneration. Degeneration, though not reducible to a single definition, can be understood as a process that operates either from the surface inwards or from the depths to outer appearance, as a transitory force which moves towards grotesque, sacrilegious, or perverse deformations, the adoption of intermediate or hybrid states (e.g., human figures metamorphosing into artificial, misanthropic, or misogynist forms), the prematurely aged or decayed, or the racially debased. The degenerate figure is typically one which embodies the abject, feared, yet fascinating "Other." Degeneration can also have wider implications, denoting general cultural, moral, racial, national, or social decline.

In the second half of the nineteenth century Bénédict Augustin Morel's *Traité des dégénérescences physiques, intellectuelles et morales de l'espèce humaine* (1857) became widely influential. It spawned some notorious tracts (e.g., Cesare Lombroso's *Genius and Insanity* [1863] and Richard von Krafft-Ebing's *Psychopathia Sexualis* [1886]). From this discourse emerged Max Nordau's widely translated *Entartung* (*Degeneration*, 1892), which described the weakness of the "degenerate" who withdraws from the struggles of life into an artificially enclosed environment of self-indulgent despair. For Nordau, Wagner is the most degenerate of all. By contrast, in NIETZSCHE's 1876 essay *Richard Wagner in Bayreuth*, Wagner's art is celebrated as a model for cultural regeneration: styptic (it stops bleeding) and contracting (strengthening through tightening), Wagner's art is an antidote to the "degeneration," "degradation," and "corruption" which Nietzsche saw as symptomatic of modern art.

At a fundamental level the enormous narrative of the *Ring* cycle is driven by the repercussions of interfering with the double forces of nature (degenerative and regenerative) which should continually operate in balanced opposition. When this equilibrium is broken or destabilized, the dangers of decay or degeneration must be held back through the imposition of unnatural powers. More specifically, the character of HAGEN epitomizes Wagner's fascination with the notion of a pure race threatened by degenerate corruption. Meticulously portrayed as the physiological opposite of SIEGFRIED, the grotesque, enfeebled, scheming Hagen embodies the horror of racial, degenerate deviance (see Weiner). Wagner's portrayal of Hagen relates to Nietzsche's discussion, in *Twilight of the Idols*, of beauty and ugliness in aesthetic judgment. Nietzsche states that the ugly "recalls decay, danger, impotence ... The ugly is understood as a sign and symptom of degeneration ... Every token of exhaustion, of heaviness, of age, of weariness, every kind of unfreedom, whether convulsive or paralytic, above all the smell, color and shape of dissolution, of decomposition, though it be attenuated to the point of being no more than a symbol – all this calls forth the same reaction, the value judgment 'ugly'." This ugliness arouses in the observer "the profoundest hate there is" because it springs from a recognition, the foresight that this is the "decline of his type" (90).

In a famous letter to August Röckel, Wagner writes: "to be real, to live – what this means is to be created, to grow, to bloom, to wither and to die; without the necessity of death, there is no possibility of life" (25/26 January 1854). Here Wagner summarizes his belief in the necessary coexistence of degeneration and regeneration, in the opposing organic processes of development and decay which drive the natural cycle of life and death. In RHEINGOLD, the tragic end of the gods is foreshadowed in the section of scene 2 in which the threatened loss of their source of eternal vigor, the golden apples, reaches its climax with the giants demanding possession of Freia, the keeper of these fruits, as the promised payment for the construction of Wotan's castle. Freia's apples possess symbolic associations with natural energy, naivety, and libidinal love. The loss of this fruit of vitality would be a fatal blow to the gods. The predicament marks the beginning of Wotan's tragedy (at least as presented in *Rheingold*). Brünnhilde's ultimate understanding of Wotan's fate at the end of GÖTTERDÄMMERUNG is knowledge that momentarily and spectacularly allows the counteracting forces of regeneration to be released as she rides her horse to the ultimate sacrifice at her immolation.

There are many images of regeneration in Wagner's works. The sprouting of the previously lifeless staff as symbol of REDEMPTION in the final scene of TANNHÄUSER is an obvious example, but we might also include the ecstatic state achieved in Isolde's "Transfiguration" (see *LIEBESTOD*). Perhaps the most famous, however, is the pastoral "Good Friday Music" in Act III of *PARSIFAL*. The passage is a late stage in a long-range process in the music drama which can be traced in both local motivic detail and large-scale tonal relationships. William Kinderman has analyzed the operation of musical symbols of regeneration within the redemptive narrative. In the opening phrase of the Prelude to Act I the A♭–G semitone descent "sounds, momentarily, like the flat sixth of C minor" and is thereby a motive presenting, in "germinal form," the tonal pairing of A♭ and C which parallels the relationship between the Grail's purity and degenerating anguished torment. A transformation of this motive into a rising appoggiatura subsequently supports the enunciation of the word "Wunde" (wound) and later informs the crucial moment in Act II of Kundry's kissing of Parsifal, when the source of the wound and the pollution of the sanctuary in her previous seduction of Amfortas is revealed. Kinderman describes how, in Act III, this sinful semitonal wound is "purged" from the communion theme, how it is "cleansed" as the semitone is replaced by a rising, regenerative whole tone: regeneration for the degenerate. In the essays that make up *Religion und Kunst* (Religion and Art), contemporaneous with the composition of *Parsifal* and often referred to as the "Essays on Regeneration" (*Regenerationsschriften*), Wagner expounded his conviction that, in the face of the historical decline and inadequacies of religion, "Art," and (because he retains a Schopenhauerian worldview) especially music, can and must reveal divine truths and thus fulfill a fallen and degenerate mankind's desire for regeneration and redemption from suffering.

STEPHEN C. DOWNES

See also GOBINEAU, ARTHUR, COMTE DE; *KUNSTRELIGION*; RELIGION

William Kinderman, "Wagner's *Parsifal*: Musical Form and the Drama of Redemption," *Journal of Musicology* 4 (1985): 431–46.

Friedrich Nietzsche, *Twilight of the Idols and The Anti-Christ*, trans. R. J. Hollingdale (Harmondsworth: Penguin, 1990).

Marc A. Weiner, *Richard Wagner and the Anti-Semitic Imagination* (see bibliography).

Devrient, Philipp Eduard (b. Berlin, 11 Aug. 1801; d. Karlsruhe, 4 Oct. 1877), actor, director, theater historian, and reformer. Devrient worked at the DRESDEN Court Theater during part of Wagner's tenure as Kapellmeister there, and he introduced reforms with regard to costume design and rehearsals that anticipated Wagner's own later theatrical practices and theories. Appointed director of the Karlsruhe Court Theatre in 1852, Devrient undertook several reforms with the intention of creating unified and integrated productions. Wagner's relationship with Devrient was never easy. He considered Devrient's staging of the chorus in Act II of *TANNHÄUSER* to be a betrayal of the work, and tensions between the two men led them to abandon plans to stage the first production of *TRISTAN UND ISOLDE* in Karlsruhe. Devrient, whose artistic tastes were more conservative than Wagner's, is remembered today for his great history of German theater – *Geschichte der deutschen Schauspielkunst* (1848–74). Wagner published a hostile review of Devrient's memoir of Mendelssohn in 1869. Devrient's diaries mention

Wagner frequently, and include details of his participation in the DRESDEN UPRISING (1849). SIMON WILLIAMS

Eduard Devrient, *Aus seinen Tagebüchern*, ed. Rolf Kabel (Weimar: Böhlau, 1964).

Diet / eating habits / food. Wagner's dietary habits were dictated partly by pecuniary considerations, fluctuations in HEALTH, and various fads unexceptional for the era. On the whole his intake was frugal. He drank wine regularly, occasionally beer (his favorite brand being *Weihenstephan*), spirits rarely, but seldom to excess; inebriate occasions were rare enough to merit a diary entry. He was a moderate smoker from at least 1851 – mostly of cigars or cheroots – and he took snuff habitually in later life.

Symptoms of poor digestion were evident from at least 1842: the previous 30 months of near-starvation in PARIS cannot have helped. To alleviate persistent bowel problems, he submitted himself to lengthy and rigorous hydrotherapy at spas in Bohemia (e.g., MARIENBAD) and later SWITZERLAND, where the typical diet was enormous quantities of cold water supplemented by dry biscuits and cold milk.

Released from such strictures he much enjoyed meat (especially veal and roast beef) and seafood (notably herrings, trout, lobster, and other shellfish), and he was self-confessedly over-fond of butter and cheeses (his favorite breakfast being coffee, lots of good bread, and lashings of butter). In LONDON, Ferdinand PRAEGER recalled a moderate eater but one who unwisely ate very quickly and consequently suffered terrible dyspepsia. Wendelin WEISSHEIMER also observed that when Wagner was agitated he bolted his food almost unchewed.

Certain foods induced positively Proustian bouts of creativity, as evidenced by his hymn of praise to the *Zwieback* (a kind of intensely toasted rusk bread; see letter to Mathilde WESENDONCK 9 May 1859). For others he had an aversion: witness the bizarre interview in Lauchstädt with the Bethmann company's stage director, who "was continually reaching through an open window to the branch of a cherry tree, picking and chewing cherries one after the other, and spitting out the cherry-stones with an explosive noise. This last activity had a decisive effect on me [i.e., to leave Lauchstädt], for curiously enough I have an inborn distaste for fruit" [*da ich sonderbarer Weise eine angeborene Abneigung gegen Obst habe*] (ML/E 87).

Another curious taste was noted in 1876 at WAHNFRIED by Ludwig Strecker, owner of SCHOTT's publishing house: "At table I was struck by the fact that from time to time he would impale morsels of food on his fork and dip them in a salt cellar placed there for that purpose" (Spencer 237). Lilli LEHMANN wrote of COSIMA's attempt to "educate" the 62-year-old composer for failing to use his knife at table in the proper English fashion – such remarks often causing dinners to come to an abrupt end.

Judith GAUTIER claimed to have inaugurated the habit of evening dinner being served at the Wagners'. Unlike the French, Germans took their hearty main meal at lunchtime. On first visiting TRIBSCHEN for an evening, she and her friends were surprised on being offered only tea and biscuits. Subsequently supper became the habit at 8.00pm: cold meats, salad, cakes, and fruit, lubricated with champagne sent by Chandon, who presented

Wagner "with more than he could use" (Gautier 47). Wagner's felicitous friendship with Paul Chandon (dating from February 1858) won him not only an ardent admirer of his music, but an almost constant supply of the best champagne – joyously quaffed whenever possible. In his last weeks at the Palazzo Vendramin-Calergi, cases of fine champagne in half-bottles were obtained "on doctor's orders" from his favorite Hotel Europa.

Felix MOTTL dined at Wahnfried on 9 June 1876: "Asparagus soup. Fish. Roast beef. Charlotte russe. Dessert. Malaga. Rosé. Hock. Champagne" (Spencer 242). When not travelling or entertaining, the family lived more modestly: Susanne Weinert's diary confides the Wahnfried supper menu for 2 September 1875 – "veal steak and macaroni."

His famous late espousal of VEGETARIANISM was less a dietary decision than a philosophical one, fulfilling his lifelong rapport with animals and embracing the reverence for life enshrined in BUDDHISM and SCHOPENHAUER. Having previously criticized NIETZSCHE's abstention from meat, Wagner's conversion was motivated in January 1880 by reading *Thalysia* by Jean Antoine Gleizès (1773–1843). COSIMA WAGNER'S DIARY gives his immediate reaction: "World history begins at the point where man became a beast of prey and killed the first animal" (8 January 1880). The DEGENERATION of the human race is thus attributable to meat-eating. However it is not evident that Wagner followed any strict vegetarian regime despite his doctrinaire writings on the subject.   DEREK WATSON

Patrick Forbes, *Champagne: The Wine, the Land, and the People* (London: Victor Gollancz, 1967).
Judith Gautier, *Wagner At Home*, trans. Effie Dunreith Massie (New York: John Lane, 1911).
Stewart Spencer, *Wagner Remembered* (see bibliography).

Dietsch, Pierre-Louis (b. Dijon, 17 March 1808; d. Paris, 20 Feb. 1865), French composer and conductor. The librettists for Dietsch's opera *Le Vaisseau fantôme* (1842), P. Foucher and H. Révoil, purchased Wagner's sketch for his *Der FLIEGENDE HOLLÄNDER* in July 1841, though this was just one of many sources for their work. Dietsch conducted the fateful Paris premiere of *TANNHÄUSER* in 1861; Wagner later complained of his "incompetence" ("Unfähigkeit," ML 646).   CHRIS WALTON

Dingelstedt, Franz von (b. Halsdorf/Hesse, 30 June 1814; d. Vienna, 15 May 1881), German poet, novelist, journalist, and stage director. Dingelstedt first came to public attention as a writer associated with the YOUNG GERMANY movement. However, he made his name as an Intendant and stage director, first at the MUNICH Hof- und Nationaltheater (1851–7), then at the Weimar Hoftheater (1857–67), finally in VIENNA, where he simultaneously directed the Hofoper (1867–80) and the Burgtheater (1870–81). Dingelstedt was one of the theatrical pioneers of the Romantic-realistic style, in which Wagner conceived all his MUSIC DRAMAS. He developed his mode of total theater, in which all elements blend into a harmonious whole, mainly through the production of SHAKESPEARE and German and European classics, but his production of *TANNHÄUSER* in Munich was particularly successful and did much to further the cause of that work in Germany. Later he directed both *Tannhäuser* and *Die MEISTERSINGER* at the Vienna Hofoper. Unlike many of his contemporaries, Dingelstedt focused primarily upon establishing the mood and atmosphere of a production, less on historicist detail.   SIMON WILLIAMS

Doepler, Carl Emil (b. Warsaw, 1824; d. Berlin, 1905) costume designer for the first complete *Der RING DES NIBELUNGEN* at Bayreuth. Wagner made contact with Doepler in December 1874, and subsequently engaged him to create the costumes and props for the *Ring*. Cosima makes mention of them in her diaries, frequently positive, though she also notes some dissatisfaction: "the costumes remind one of Indian chiefs and so much ethnographical nonsense that carries the mark of small-time theaters!" (CWD 28 July 1876). He drew more than 500 designs and, in 1889, published a now very rare portfolio of forty colored lithographs of his *Ring* costume designs.   EVAN BAKER

Donington, Robert (b. Leeds, 4 May 1907; d. Firle [Sussex], 20 Jan. 1990), English musicologist and instrumentalist. Donington's study *Wagner's "Ring" and its Symbols: The Music and the Myth* interprets the *Ring* scene by scene in terms of Jungian psychology. In particular, Donington identifies mythic-psychological archetypes in the work's symbols, be they individual characters, tangible objects, or more abstract images: for example, Wotan is "an image of the self," Loge "a mercurial 'trickster,'" and the Tarnhelm "a symbol of unconscious fantasy." These symbols correspond in turn to a network of *LEITMOTIVE*, re-labeled by Donington and listed in an Appendix. If Donington's hermeneutics is insightful, his reading of Wagner's letters and biography, by contrast, is largely uncritical, as are his speculations on the role played by "intuition" and the "unconscious" in Wagner's working method. Significantly, however, Donington's view of MYTH as both transhistorical and universal resonates with the precepts of structuralism, especially as propagated by Claude Lévi-Strauss.   JEREMY COLEMAN

Robert Donington, *Wagner's "Ring" and its Symbols* (see bibliography).
Carl Jung, "Wotan," *Neue Schweizer Rundschau* (March, 1936): 657–69; republished in *Aufsätze zur Zeitgeschichte* (Zurich: Rascher, 1946) 1–23; trans. Elizabeth Welsh, Barbara Hannah, and Mary Briner, *Essays on Contemporary Events* (London: Kegan Paul, 1947) 1–16.

Donizetti, Gaetano (b. Bergamo, 29 Nov. 1797; d. Bergamo, 8 April 1848), Italian opera composer. Wagner mostly mentions Donizetti alongside BELLINI and ROSSINI. However, he did not conduct a Donizetti opera in his early Kapellmeister years (as he did with the other two). Among Wagner's modest commissions in PARIS, where Donizetti was highly successful at the time, was to proof-read the score of *La favorite* in the winter of 1840/1, as well as to make instrumental arrangements from it. Being of no evident influence on Wagner's composing style, *La favorite* is invoked in his essays as a paradigm for the decline of Italian BEL CANTO OPERA within the Paris scene. As a theater practitioner and in private, Wagner tended to be more moderate: back in DRESDEN, he once considered staging *Dom Sébastien*. In Switzerland, he recommended *L'elisir d'amore* and *Belisario* to conductor Heinrich Sczadrowsky in St. Gall.   SEBASTIAN STAUSS

Dorn, Heinrich Ludwig Egmont (b. Königsberg, 14 Nov. 1804; d. Berlin, 10 Jan. 1892), conductor, composer, and pianist. Dorn studied in Berlin, but worked in KÖNIGSBERG and RIGA. In Königsberg (1828–33), Dorn reorganized the theater orchestra along the lines of the Berlin Hofkapelle. In Riga, Dorn became the city music director in 1834 and the conductor of the German Theater in 1836. He retained his influential position until 1843. Dorn helped to form the first *Liedertafel* and, from 1834 onwards, served as director of the local *Singakademie*. In order to revive Riga's musical fortunes, Dorn established the Duna Music Festival in 1836, and made a significant contribution to the local operatic scene by giving the local premiere of MEYERBEER's *Robert le diable*. Dorn's own musical works include, for example, operas *Abu Kara* (1831), *Der Schöffe von Paris* (1838), *Das Banner von England* (1842), and *Die Nibelungen* (1854). Already in Riga, Dorn and Wagner became rivals, especially after Dorn had written a critique of Wagner's concert on 19 March 1838 for the NEUE ZEITSCHRIFT FÜR MUSIK. Later, Dorn's opera *Die Nibelungen* increased tensions, given Wagner's plan for a work based on the same theme.

HANNU SALMI

Draeseke, Felix (August Bernhard) (b. Coburg, 7 Oct. 1835; d. Dresden, 26 Feb. 1913), German composer, writer on music, and teacher. The LEIPZIG-trained Draeseke first came into contact with Wagner through a performance of LOHENGRIN in Weimar (1852). He subsequently became associated with the NEW GERMAN cause and wrote a Wagner-inspired opera, *König Sigurd*. His 1859 meeting with Wagner in Lucerne was momentous for his direction, but the radical style of Draeseke's "Germania March" caused a scandal at the 1861 *Tonkünstler-Versammlung* in Weimar, and Wagner himself called the work "truly miserable" (ML/E 656). Draeseke moved to Switzerland in 1862, visiting MUNICH for the 1865 premiere of TRISTAN. The composer returned to Germany in 1876, settling in DRESDEN, where he spent the rest of his life. He remained true to the harmonic principles of LISZT and Wagner in his later operatic, chamber, and symphonic works, but could not reconcile himself with the innovations of Richard STRAUSS. JAMES DEAVILLE

Dream. See SLEEP / DREAM

Dresden. Located on the Elbe River and first mentioned in chronicles in 1206, Dresden became the residence of the Margrave of Meissen in 1270. Upon the division of Saxony in 1485, it became the capital of the Albertine line, evolving first into one of the seven electorates (*Kurfürstentum*) and eventually into the Kingdom of Saxony. Dresden became famous for its baroque architecture and its extraordinary art collection, developed mostly during the reign of August II (r. 1694–1733). In the later eighteenth century, Dresden's court sported a strong reputation for theater and music, albeit dominated by Italian direction and musical tastes while bourgois-supported theatrical troupes presented German operas and *Singspiele* (including Mozart's *Die Entführung aus dem Serail* in 1785). It was Carl Maria von WEBER's tenure as director of the opera (1817–26), and his development of German romantic opera, that made Dresden's theater so important within the German-speaking states.

Wagner first moved to the city (pop. circa 57,000) in late 1814, when he lived for a time on the same street as SCHOPENHAUER. Ludwig GEYER got Wagner small parts in several plays ranging from a walk-on in Friedrich Kind's *The Vineyard on the Elbe* to speaking parts in *William Tell* (family legend tells of Wagner missing his one line) and Kotzebue's *Misanthropy and Remorse*. Wagner entered Dresden's Kreuzschule in 1822 and was rapidly kicked out, whereupon he moved back to LEIPZIG to complete his education.

In April 1842, Wagner returned to Dresden. The enormous success of RIENZI that year and the friendly if restrained reception of *Der* FLIEGENDE HOLLÄNDER resulted in Wagner's appointment as *Kapellmeister* in February 1843 at a salary of 1,500 thalers, a position held jointly with Carl Gottlieb REISSIGER, and under the leadership of August von LÜTTICHAU. The position placed Wagner at the center of Dresden musical life, which he embellished by taking on the directorship of the men's chorus *Liedertafel*, a position he received through the sponsorship of Maximilian Leopold Löwe (1795–1865). Wagner used this chorus to help stage his oratorio *Das Liebesmahl der Apostel* (Love-Feast of the Apostles) in the Frauenkirche on 6 July 1843. The piece showcased an orchestra of hundreds and a choir of 1,200.

Wagner staged three other important theatrical festival performances in Dresden. The first was a welcoming ceremony for the return of Friedrich August II from England at Pillnitz on 12 August 1844. Wagner and Reissiger together (and without consultation with von Lüttichau) organized the transport of 200 singers and 106 musicians to perform a specially composed anthem to the sovereign. In December of the same year, Wagner participated in the reinterment of Weber's remains, composing both a funeral march and a men's chorus. The third outsize production of Wagner's was his performance of BEETHOVEN's Ninth Symphony during the annual Palm Sunday concert on 5 April 1846. Despite predictions of failure, the concert was a huge success.

Wagner was frequently in conflict with musicians and management at the court. At the same time, his interests in political reform, awoken in Leipzig in the 1830s, matured. In 1848, he began publishing newspaper articles and making speeches calling for the reform of Dresden's theater and Saxony's government. Wagner participated in the DRESDEN UPRISING of May 1849, for which he paid with exile, fleeing Dresden and leaving behind enormous debts. Granted amnesty in 1862, Wagner returned to Dresden in 1873 for a production of *Rienzi* in his honor.   MARGARET ELEANOR MENNINGER

Dresden library. This library consists of 169 works collected by Wagner between 1842 and 1849. The library's acquisition and custom rebinding cost Wagner more than he could afford, but was a great source of pride and inspiration. Absent of marginalia (apart from scattered pencil marks), the works consist primarily of dramas, histories, classical literature, and German mythology, but also include Dante and Gibbon. Wagner himself pointed to two works that were of essential importance to him in the 1840s: Jakob Grimm's *Deutsche Mythologie* and Johann Gustav Droysen's *Des Aischylos Werke*.

After Wagner fled from Dresden, the library was transferred to the ownership of Heinrich BROCKHAUS as security for an unpaid loan of 500 thalers (originally lent in 1846). While Brockhaus did return several of Wagner's own scores and one particularly valuable work (the nine-volume *Romans des douze pairs de France*) to Wagner, the rest of the library remained in the hands of the Brockhaus family, which published an inventory in 1966 (see Westernhagen).   MARGARET ELEANOR MENNINGER

See also READING

Curt von Westernhagen, *Richard Wagners Dresdener Bibliothek 1842–1849: Neue Dokumente zur Geschichte seines Schaffens*, Mit 6 Abbildungen und Kundstdrucktafeln (Wiesbaden: Brockhaus, 1966).

Dresden uprising (May 1849). This was one of the final wave of revolts during the 1848–9 REVOLUTIONS, parallel to uprisings in Baden and the Bavarian Palatinate, all quelled by Prussian armed intervention. Across Europe, the "springtime of peoples" had witnessed liberal, constitutional victories. Rhetorical liberty, however, proved just that: initial coalitions – revolutionary socialists such as Wagner and *laissez-faire* Rhenish industrialists; pan-Slavists such as BAKUNIN and *völkisch* German nationalists; monarchists and republicans, and so on – proved irreconcilable. Moreover, the old order proved stronger than either it or its opponents had believed – and for many bourgeois seemed less threatening. Representatives to the Frankfurt *Vorparlament* moved toward national unity, promulgating a German constitution (28 March) and offering the imperial crown to Prussia's Frederick William IV. His refusal (3 April) to "pick up a crown from the gutter" threw them into disarray. Emboldened, Frederick Augustus II of Saxony rejected the constitution and dissolved the Saxon parliament (30 April), elected in January with a democratic majority. Unlike Prussia, Saxony had long been a constitutional monarchy, and a reform ministry had governed from March 1848 to February 1849. But the king's appointment of a reactionary movement, headed by Friedrich von Beust, and rejection of the constitution, ultimately provoked democratic opponents into a hurried response. On 3 May, the town council organized the Communal Guard into a defense committee. Loyalist troops opened fire. Early on 4 May, king and government escaped to Königstein; townsmen formed a provisional government.

Even at the time, the extent of Wagner's involvement was obscured. Eduard DEVRIENT reports MINNA visiting him in desperation for advice concerning her husband, implicated yet not directly involved (diary entry for 17 May 1849). Devrient is clear that she has been deceived. Wagner would downplay his role further in *MEIN LEBEN* (My Life, 1865–81), yet nevertheless admits considerable involvement. He had the printer of RÖCKEL's *Volksblätter* print appeals to the Saxon army: "Are you with us against foreign troops?" (ML/E 394). Wagner probably ordered hand-grenades; he certainly served on the barricades and acted as look-out, observing street-fighting from the Kreuzkirche tower, whilst engaging in animated politico-philosophical discussion. Prussians entered the Neustadt on 6 April. "Immediately the troops, supported by several cannon, opened an attack on ... the people's forces on the new marketplace" (ML/E 397). On 7 April, miners from the Erzgebirge singing the *Marseillaise* arrived to reinforce the opposition. However, Prussian and loyalist troops outnumbered the rebels and were gaining ground, even though barricades meant that every street was hard fought. As the provisional government began an unsurprisingly abortive attempt to retreat to the Erzgebirge, to encourage revolt across Germany, Dresden's streets, including the opera house, were ablaze. In his Introduction to Marx's *The Class Struggles in France*, Engels would bracket Dresden's barricade heroism with that of Paris and Vienna, yet also pointed to the inevitable, once politics gave way to the "purely military standpoint."

Repression was brutal. Many leaders, participants, and sympathizers were killed or punished: Bakunin, Röckel, and even Wilhelmine SCHRÖDER-DEVRIENT were arraigned. By chance, and with LISZT's help, Wagner escaped into Swiss exile, intending in the RING, as he explained, to "make clear to the men of the Revolution the *meaning* of that Revolution, in its noblest sense" (Wagner to Uhlig, 12 November 1851).   MARK BERRY

Eduard Devrient, *Aus seinen Tagebüchern*, ed. Rolf Kabel (Weimar: Böhlau, 1964).
Frederick Engels, "Revolution and Counter-Revolution in Germany," in Karl Marx and Frederick Engels, *Selected Works*, 3 vols. (Moscow: Progress, 1970): 1:300–89.
Jonathan Sperber, *The European Revolutions, 1848–1851* (Cambridge University Press, 1994).

Drexel, Ellen (b. Wiesbaden, 20 Aug. 1919; d. Eppstein im Taunus, 17 Apr. 2002), first wife of WOLFGANG WAGNER (married 1943), mother of EVA (b. 1945) and GOTTFRIED (b. 1947). Drexel starred as a child at the State Theater, Wiesbaden, and was later a solo dancer at the Berlin State Opera. She regretted giving up her ballet career after marriage, and suffered under the closeness of the Wagner family to HITLER. She was divorced in 1976 when Wolfgang married GUDRUN Mack.   EVA RIEGER

See also Appendix 1: Wagner family tree

Gottfried Wagner, *Wer nicht mit dem Wolf heult* (see bibliography).

Düfflipp, Lorenz von (b. 1820; d. 9 May 1886), Royal Court Secretary of Bavaria 1866–77. When Wagner had to leave MUNICH and LUDWIG II, Düfflipp became their middleman. Although he showed understanding for Wagner, Düfflipp was charged with conveying the king's intentions, such as the first staging of the RING in Munich and the limited financial support for the BAYREUTH FESTIVAL.   SEBASTIAN STAUSS

Duncan, Isadora (b. San Francisco, 26 May 1877; d. Nice, 14 Sep. 1927), dancer who did not create modern DANCE but became its incarnation. Hardly another dancer inspired so many works of art, charmed intellectuals across Europe, and evoked so many utopian projects. Under the influence of Friedrich NIETZSCHE's *The Birth of Tragedy* (1872), Duncan declared herself the heir of Greek tragedy, and cultivated a "free dance" that rejected ballet as a representation of the bourgeois constraints of Western civilization's social rules and morality. Her fluid movement AESTHETICS contained the notion that human beings had to reconnect to nature's beauty and harmonious rhythmic impulses to find existential "truth."

Duncan referred several times to: "the three great precursors of the Dance of our century – BEETHOVEN, Nietzsche and Wagner" (243), and wrote her most influential essay *Der Tanz der Zukunft* (Dance of the Future, 1903) the year before she was drawn into the Wagner circle at Bayreuth. Beyond the title, it has several ideas in common with Wagner's *Das KUNSTWERK DER ZUKUNFT* (1849/50). Both disdain ballet, share the vision of artistic REVOLUTION, emphasize that rhythm drives movement, and idealize ancient

Greek tragedy as the source of cultural REGENERATION. Her pamphlet sings a hymn to cosmic movement and the naked female body.

Duncan performed as *First Grace* in the production of the TANNHÄUSER Bacchanal at the 1904 Bayreuth festival. SIEGFRIED WAGNER had seen her dance in Munich in 1903, and suggested an invitation to his mother, COSIMA. Duncan interpreted the Bacchanal as an imagined event, a fantasy of the brain or "cerebrale." She resurrected Wagner's initial ideas of the Bacchanal as feverish expressions of TANNHÄUSER's disturbed mind, a view he had set out in a letter to Mathilde WESENDONCK (10 April 1860). Duncan danced her *Grace* in a see-through Grecian tunic with bare legs and feet.

Her autobiography describes the Bayreuth stay, where she switched allegiance from ANCIENT GREECE to Wagnerian operas: "The ... Temple on the hill of Bayreuth, with its waves and reverberations of magic, had entirely obliterated Athena's Temple," and "My soul was like a battlefield where Apollo, Dionysus, Christ, Nietzsche and Richard Wagner disputed the ground. At Bayreuth I was buffeted between Venusberg and the Grail" (107/111).

She used Wagner's songs and arrangements from piano scores in her recitals throughout the 1910s and 1920s: in post-revolutionary Soviet Russia she paired Wagnerian music (*Walkürenritt, Isoldes Liebestod, Bacchanal*) with the *Marseillaise* or the *Internationale*.   MARION KANT

See also EXCERPTS (FROM WORKS); PIANO ARRANGEMENTS AND REDUCTIONS

Isadora Duncan, *My Life* (London: Victor Gollancz, 1928).

Dutchman, The (bass-baritone; title role of *Der* FLIEGENDE HOLLÄNDER), the earliest of the canonic bass-baritone parts in Wagner's works, first performed by Johann Michael Wächter. The Dutchman's only solo number is the great monologue ("Die Frist ist um") delivered by the Dutchman when he sets foot on shore after the last of his long series of seven-year sea voyages. The number, mostly in C minor, is composed of accompanied recitative, arioso, and aria-like sections that can still be identified to some extent with the multi-section "scene and aria" designs of contemporary French or Italian opera, here loosened and expanded. (In the production notes on the opera Wagner drafted in 1852, he included detailed directions for the blocking of this monologue.) The Dutchman adapts his brooding, agitated, Byronic musical persona to the more conventional lyricism of DALAND in the subsequent duet with him. The long duet scene with SENTA in Act II, the musical centerpiece of the opera, also bears traces of the progression from *scena* through cantabile to cabaletta styles, grounded in E major, but infused with a strong overall trajectory from stillness to exalted dynamic momentum. In Act III, the role is limited to a concentrated dramatic confrontation with Senta after her "fidelity" has been claimed by her first suitor, Erik.

The figure of the Dutchman, a sea-captain forced to sail the seas forever with his phantom crew as punishment for some act of blasphemy or hubris, did not achieve literary form until some twenty years before Wagner's operatic treatment. The captain's identity as a "Dutchman" is posited in the tale "Vanderdecken's Message Home" printed in Blackwood's *Edinburgh Magazine* of May 1821. (Wagner's Dutchman is never given a proper name.) Edward Fitzball's nautical melodrama *The Flying Dutchman; or, the Phantom Ship* (1827) preserves his identity as the Dutch captain Vanderdecken. Slightly earlier references to a "Flying Dutchman" and his ghost ship can be found in poems by Thomas Moore and by Sir Walter Scott ("Rokeby," 1813), while a still earlier and better-known variant of the story is that told in Samuel Taylor Coleridge's ballad "The Rime of the Ancient Mariner" (1798).

Most bass-baritones known for roles such as WOTAN and HANS SACHS in the later music dramas have also been well-known interpreters of the Dutchman: Anton van Rooy (the first Bayreuth Dutchman), Friedrich Schorr, Hans HOTTER, George London, Norman Bailey, and more recently James Morris, Robert Hale, and Falk Struckmann. The versatile baritone Dietrich Fischer-Dieskau recorded the role though he did not perform it in the theater. Conversely, leading contemporary Wagnerian bass-baritone Bryn Terfel has performed the role on stage to great acclaim since 2006, though not yet recorded it.   THOMAS S. GREY

$$\boxed{E}$$

Edda. The title *Edda* is used to designate two different works from the thirteenth century in Old Norse literature: the *Prose Edda*, a handbook of poetics written in the vernacular sometime during the 1220s by the Icelandic chieftain Snorri Sturluson, and the *Poetic Edda*, a collection of vernacular mythological and heroic poetry thought to have been written down about 1270 by an unknown scribe. Together these two works constitute the main literary sources for our knowledge of pre-Christian Norse mythology and heroic legend.

As a poetic handbook dedicated to preserving the creation and understanding of the centuries-old traditional Norse poetic genre known in modern use as skaldic poetry, the *Prose Edda* is a unique medieval Icelandic work. It is divided into a prologue and three sections, each with a title and a different function in the project of preserving and explaining the poetic diction and meters. In the first section of the work, called "Gylfaginning" (The Tricking of Gylfi), Snorri presents a systematic and comprehensive account of Norse mythology from the creation of the world to its ultimate destruction, and here is related the story of the building of the gods' fortification against the giants by a giant master builder, which Wagner adapted so successfully in *Das* RHEINGOLD.

Wagner is known to have possessed two translations of the *Prose Edda*: *Die Edda, nebst einer Einleitung über nordische Poesie und Mythologie* by Christian Friedrich Rühs (Berlin, 1812), and *Mythologische Dichtungen und Lieder der Skandinavier* by Friedrich Majer (Leipzig, 1818) (Cooke 116).

The *Poetic Edda* contains twenty-nine poems and several prose inserts. Eleven of the poems treat mythological subjects, beginning with a prophetic poem forecasting the Nordic Doomsday *ragnarök* and concluding with a dialogue between Thor and a dwarf. These poems, most of them told in a mixture of narrative and dialogue, focus on tales of the gods Odin, Thor, Frey, and Loki, and include a range of native Norse poetic genres, including prophecy, gnomic verse, wisdom contests, flytings (verbal insult contests), curses, and mnemonic lists. The eighteen heroic poems follow chronologically the tragic story of the Volsungs, Gjukungs, and Budlungs. Seven of these poems relate the central episode of Sigurd's slaying of the great dragon Fafnir, which wins him lasting fame and a fabulous treasure, and his subsequent involvement with and betrayal of Brynhild, which bring about his downfall and death. We have no way of determining the age of any of the poems in the *Poetic Edda*, but all the poems clearly circulated in oral tradition and can therefore be said to possess the veneer of age. Wagner certainly consulted the poems in developing his characters for *Der* RING DES NIBELUNGEN.

Various German translations of the *Poetic Edda*, published between 1814 and 1851, were available to Wagner. In his library were translations by Jacob and Wilhelm Grimm, *Lieder der alten Edda* (Berlin, 1815) as well as the edition by Friedrich Majer (Cooke III).   KAAREN GRIMSTAD

See also NORDIC MYTHOLOGY; VÖLSUNGA SAGA

Deryck Cooke, *I Saw the World End* (see bibliography).

Einleitung. See OVERTURE / PRELUDE

Eisenstein, Sergei Mikhailovich (b. Riga, 23 Jan. 1898; d. Moscow, 11 Feb. 1948), Russian film director and film theorist, especially renowned for his pioneering uses of film montage. Eisenstein's experience staging *Die WALKÜRE* for the Bolshoi Theater in 1940 strongly influenced his approach to using sound and color in film, as reflected in his next (and final) film, *Ivan the Terrible* (*Part I*, 1944; *Part II*, 1946, released 1958). While working on *Walküre*, Eisenstein wrote his seminal theoretical article on "vertical montage," and articles discussing Wagner's relevance to cinema. With *Ivan the Terrible*, Eisenstein sought to find a motivic film language that would unify the work in the manner of Wagner's musical motives. Accordingly, *Ivan* presents the viewer with a dense web of audiovisual LEITMOTIVE – recurrent visual symbols, sound effects, and (in *Part II*'s color sequence) motivic uses of color.   HILAN WARSHAW

Rosamund Bartlett, "The Embodiment of Myth: Eizenshtein's Production of *Die Walküre*," *Slavonic and East European Review* 70.1 (1992): 53–76.

Patrick Carnegy, *Wagner and the Art of Theatre* (see bibliography): 226–33.

Sergei Eisenstein, "From Lectures on Music and Colour in *Ivan the Terrible*," trans. William Powell, *The Eisenstein Reader*, ed. R. Taylor (London: British Film Institute, 1998): 167–86.

Elisabeth (soprano; character in *TANNHÄUSER*), first performed by the nineteen-year-old Johanna Jachmann-Wagner, the adopted daughter of Wagner's older brother ALBERT. The saintly Elisabeth, niece of the Landgraf Hermann of Thuringia, is the antipode to Venus, the pagan goddess of love to whom TANNHÄUSER has given himself at the time the opera begins. Elisabeth's role is centered above all in Act II, with the solo aria "Dich, teure Halle," a duet scene with Tannhäuser, and a key part in the monumental ensemble finale that develops after Tannhäuser derails the Song Contest with his immoderate praise of Venus. After she has been seeking in vain for the penitential hero among the returning pilgrims in the first scene of Act III, Elisabeth's part concludes with the slow, woodwind-accompanied prayer "Allmächt'ge Jungfrau, hör' mein Flehen!"

Just as he adapted the historical and legendary versions of the Tannhäuser figure, Wagner combined the historical figure of St. Elisabeth of Hungary (1207–31) with other legendary and fictional figures, such as the Landgräfin Sophia in Ludwig Bechstein's account of the "Song Contest at the Wartburg" (in *Die Sagen von Eisenach und der Wartburg*, 1835) and the character of Mathilde in E. T. A. HOFFMANN's *Kampf der Sänger* (1818), object of the rival affections of Tannhäuser and "Wolfframb von Eschinbach." The historical Elisabeth of Hungary became the daughter-in-law of Landgraf Hermann of Thuringia when she was betrothed in childhood to Hermann's son, Ludwig, who succeeded him as Landgraf in 1217. Elisabeth was widowed already at age twenty when Ludwig died while away in the Crusades. She devoted the remainder of her brief life to poverty and charitable works, becoming canonized as early as 1235. Numerous stories about Elisabeth's piety and miracles are recounted in Bechstein's *Sagen von Eisenach und der Wartburg*. Both Bechstein and Wagner's other "scholarly" source, C. T. L. Lucas's *Über den Krieg von Wartburg* (1838), identified the Contest of Song with an astrological prediction by the magician KLINGSOR of Elisabeth's birth.

Prominent interpreters of the role in the earlier twentieth century include Johanna Gadski, Lotte Lehmann, Elisabeth Rethberg, and Maria Müller, followed by Dutch soprano Gré Brouwenstijn at Bayreuth in the 1950s. Birgit NILSSON and Gwyneth Jones, Wagnerian sopranos noted for their vocal and dramatic range, have sung both Elisabeth and Venus (though the latter is closer to a mezzo role), thus inviting for a reading of these roles as polarized manifestations of a female ideal that Tannhäuser strives, but fails, to reconcile.

THOMAS S. GREY

Ludwig Bechstein, *Die Sagen von Eisenach und der Wartburg, dem Hörseelberg und Reinhardsbrunn* (Hildburghausen: Kesselring'schen Hofbuchhandlung, 1835).

Ellis, William Ashton (b. London, 20 Aug. 1852; d. London, 2 Jan. 1919), translator into English of Wagner's prose works and letters, biographer of and propagandist for Wagner. Ellis was never personally acquainted with Wagner. His was among a number of wreaths sent from London to Bayreuth for Wagner's funeral, and there is some poignancy in his account of being in VENICE to witness the musical tribute conducted by Anton SEIDL on the Grand Canal a month after Wagner's death. In their own time, Ellis's translations became notorious for their over-faithfulness to Wagner's sense with their use of archaisms and idiosyncratic compound words. However, as John Deathridge has commented, Ellis's translations "are closer in time to the original and capture a part of the historical 'aura' of the texts that a modern translation never could" (Deathridge xliii). For this reason, no modern English translation of the complete prose works has been contemplated, and Ellis's remains acknowledged as standard. It is usually abbreviated bibliographically as "PW," though in a rare flash of irony Ellis himself affected concern about confusion with *Pearson's Weekly*.

William Ashton Ellis was a son of Robert Ellis (1823–77), a Welsh-born obstetric surgeon with learning broad enough to qualify him to become the "scientific editor" of the Catalogue of the Great Exhibition of 1851. Educated as a Queen's Scholar at Westminster School, Ellis at first fulfilled his father's evident intention that he should follow a medical career, and he was a prizewinning student at St. George's Medical School. Appointed Resident Medical Officer at the Western Dispensary on Rochester Row in Westminster, this put him in direct contact with the material world and its discontents, and by 1885 he was prominent in the campaign to extend representation to the Members (in addition to the Fellows) on the Council of the Royal College of Surgeons. But as a theosophist he had meanwhile succumbed to the transcendental attractions of both Wagner and Madame Blavatsky. In 1887, he gave up his medical officer's post, first to save Blavatsky from near fatal illness in Ostend, and then to accept the position of editor of the London WAGNER

SOCIETY's quarterly journal, *The MEISTER*, between 1888 and 1895. This decision cost him a secure income, as George Bernard SHAW pointed out to both the public and the government. Thanks to Shaw's efforts, Ellis was eventually awarded a modest civil list pension in 1908.

In 1891, the London Wagner Society commissioned Ellis to translate Wagner's complete prose works, first periodically, then as bound volumes, eight in all. Having completed this task in 1899, Ellis moved to the village of Horsted Keynes in Sussex to pursue his second major project, the translation of Carl Friedrich GLASENAPP's *Life of Wagner*. After the second volume (1902), Ellis found that his own researches compelled him to continue on his own, and Glasenapp's name was dropped from the title page. By 1909 (and his sixth volume) Ellis had reached only 1859 in Wagner's life when adverse circumstances, not entirely explained, caused him to break off the work. He relocated, first to Brighton, and then in 1915 back to London, where, remarkably, his offer to take up his old job as Resident Medical Officer at the Western Dispensary was accepted because of war labor shortages. He published three linked articles on Wagner in the *Musical Times* in 1915 (in which he sought to rescue "our Wagner" from German "barbarism"), but in literary terms his life's work was done. Ellis died aged 67 in his rooms at the Dispensary on 2 January 1919. Possibly a victim of the flu pandemic that swept the world after World War I, he was buried in the churchyard of St. Nicholas, Tooting Graveney, five days later. DAVID CORMACK

David Cormack, "Faithful, all too Faithful," and "William Ashton Ellis: Completing the Picture," *Wagner* 14.3 and 15.2 (1993–4): 104–37 and 62–8. Also available at: http://users. belgacom.net/wagnerlibrary/articles/wlar0250.htm.

"'Or is he a mere translator?': Bernard Shaw's agitation for William Ashton Ellis's civil list pension," *Wagner* 23.2 (2002): 81–112.

The Family Letters of Richard Wagner, trans. W. A. Ellis, enlarged edition with Introduction and Notes by John Deathridge (London: Palgrave Macmillan, 1991).

Elmendorff, Karl (b. Düsseldorf, 25 Oct. 1891; d. Hofheim am Taunus, 21 Oct. 1962), conductor. Elmendorff worked at opera houses throughout Germany including Mainz (1923–5), the Bavarian State Opera (1925), and the State Opera of Saxony (1941–5). He appeared regularly at Bayreuth from 1927 to 1942. His recorded legacy includes near complete versions of *TRISTAN* (1928), and *TANNHÄUSER* (1930), *GÖTTERDÄMMERUNG* (1942), and a notable *Die WALKÜRE* Act I from Dresden (1944). His style is notable for lean textures and transparency of orchestral sound. ROGER ALLEN

See also PERFORMANCE, CONDUCTORS

Elsa (soprano; character in *LOHENGRIN*). Elsa, the young heiress of Brabant, is the operatic stereotype of persecuted innocence. Her role is characterized by a high range, lyricism (her solos "Einsam in trüben Tagen" and "Euch Lüften" were and are performed as concert arias), tender woodwind accompaniment, and shy speechlessness when she first appears on stage. This is supported by Wagner's appraisal of the role when he imagined the performance of the soprano Louise Köster, whom he characterized as virginal, feminine, and very graceful (letter to Minna, 26 September 1847). Elsa is, however, not merely a passive figure, since the central conflict of the opera – between LOHENGRIN's and ORTRUD's spheres of influence – is actually located within her. This is apparent in the ensemble at the close of Act II, "In düsterm Brüten," when she ponders her love for Lohengrin against Ortrud's insinuations. Although the work is entitled *Lohengrin*, Wagner declared Elsa a "most important role, actually the main role, ... the most delightful and affecting in the world" in one of his earliest written statements about the opera (letter to ALBERT WAGNER, 4 August 1845). Though this was probably intended to recommend the role to his niece Johanna Jachmann-Wagner (who, in the end, sang the role of Ortrud in the first Berlin production), he acknowledged Elsa's centrality to his music drama project by singling out her DREAM narration in his late treatise ÜBER DIE ANWENDUNG DER MUSIK AUF DAS DRAMA (On the Application of Music to Drama, 1879) in order to justify the bold harmonic strategies when juxtaposing Elsa's signature key of A♭ major with Lohengrin's A major.

Modern interpretations of her character have likewise centered on the dream narration: Carolyn Abbate argues that Elsa makes Lohengrin enter her world through the power of her voice enhanced by instruments (29–31). Mary A. Cicora takes this idea further by suggesting that Elsa's dream narration turns him into a fictional character in her own world (88). In its power to "conjure" her champion, Elsa's dream parallels SENTA's ballad that makes the DUTCHMAN appear, while her anguished vision of the returning swan in Act III is comparable to SIEGLINDE's hallucinations of HUNDING's dogs; in all three works the imaginative power of the female character directly influences the story. Wagner highlighted this visionary trait when he characterized Elsa in *Eine Mitteilung an meine Freunde* (A Communication to My Friends, 1851) as "the unconscious, involuntary" side of human nature, from which the conscious, intellectual nature of Lohengrin seeks redemption. This recourse to GENDER echoes theories on the respective roles of music and language explained in *OPER UND DRAMA* (Opera and Drama, 1851), where they are associated with the feminine and masculine aspects of creativity. Wagner even declares Elsa "the spirit of the people," who transformed him into the "perfect revolutionary," highlighting *Lohengrin*'s preparatory role for his later music dramas. At the same time he acknowledges that the overwhelming greatness of her love forces Elsa to transgress Lohengrin's insistence on unconditional acceptance. Wagner's version of the story highlights this urgency by having Elsa ask the forbidden question during the wedding night, while in some medieval sources the couple remain together for several years. Thus no happy ending is possible for Lohengrin and Elsa, in contrast to Weber's *Euryanthe*, which in many other aspects provided an important model for Wagner, especially in the musical characterization of the heroine. BARBARA EICHNER

Carolyn Abbate, *In Search of Opera* (Princeton University Press, 2001).

Mary A. Cicora, *Modern Myths and Wagnerian Deconstructions: Hermeneutic Approaches to Wagner's Music-Dramas* (Westport, CT: Greenwood, 2000).

Nila Parly, *Vocal Victories: Wagner's Female Characters from Senta to Kundry* (Copenhagen: Museum Tusculanum Press, 2011).

Eva Rieger, *Richard Wagner's Women* (see bibliography).

Ende in Paris, Ein (A Death in Paris). Novella, written as a sequel to *Eine PILGERFAHRT ZU BEETHOVEN*, at the suggestion of Maurice SCHLESINGER, publisher of the *REVUE ET GAZETTE MUSICALE* (PARIS), because of the latter novella's success. It appeared originally in that journal under the title *Un musicien étranger à Paris* (later in German in the *Abend-Zeitung* of Dresden together with *A Pilgrimage*) and recounts the final days of "R...," a "poor German composer" who dies poverty-stricken and unrecognized in a Montmartre garret. His deathbed speech, delivered to the narrator (also an expatriate composer), is a harangue against the commercialization and commodification of music – which has become an industry – and a glorification of "art music" composed for its own sake. The classic articulation "R..." gives of KUNSTRELIGION begins with the famous line: "I believe in God, Mozart and Beethoven" (*Ich glaube an Gott, Mozart und Beethoven*, SSD 1:135).

NICHOLAS VAZSONYI

Endless melody (*unendliche Melodie*). The term originates in Wagner's essay ZUKUNFTSMUSIK (Music of the Future; originally *Lettre sur la musique* as preface to *Quatre poèmes d'opéra*, 1861), in which Wagner aimed to summarize his notorious theories of a "musical dramatic artwork of the future" for the Parisian audience of his revised TANNHÄUSER. After glossing some of the main themes of *Das KUNSTWERK DER ZUKUNFT* (The Artwork of the Future, 1849/50) and OPER UND DRAMA (Opera and Drama), Wagner appends some new reflections on musical form and "melody" based above all on his experience with the recently completed TRISTAN UND ISOLDE. He is at pains to distinguish between the symmetrical periodicity (based on predictable antecedent-consequent schemata) of conventional, "DANCE-based" instrumental and operatic melody, on the one hand, and the ideal of a continuously evolving motivic discourse he traces back to BEETHOVEN's symphonies (paradigmatically, the opening movement of the *Eroica*), on the other. Now, Wagner claims, he has discovered how a dramatic poem, such as his *Tristan*, might encourage and even "pre-determine" a continuous melodic-motivic unfolding that would yield much greater, freer (but nonetheless coherent) expanses of musical form than anything imaginable within the symphonic tradition, let alone the conventions of the operatic aria or duet. The poet of such a drama will invite the musician to unleash his melodic invention "so that it pours through the whole work like an uninterrupted stream" (Jacobs 40; SSD 7:129). Wagner admits he is thinking specifically in terms of the orchestra's role, expressing the ineffable or "great Unsaid" that lies implicit beneath the poetic verses of the drama. "The unmistakable form of this resounding silence," in Wagner's deliberately paradoxical formulation, "is *endless melody*" (Jacobs 40; SSD 7:130). The idea is reinforced with a METAPHORICAL image: this new "endless melody" is like the impression made by the murmurings of a great forest at sunset. The cumulative texture of sounds, sights, and feelings there is experienced as a process whose "wholeness" is intuited, though not easily interpreted in diagrammatic or schematic terms.

From the time Wagner coined the term in 1861, "endless melody" caught on as a catch-word to denote many aspects of his musical style: the characteristic evasion of full harmonic cadences, the role of motivically accompanied arioso textures in place of traditional melodic periodicity, and continuity of scene and act structures in place of closed musical numbers. At first, critics were likely to deploy the phrase negatively, to parody what they viewed as the amorphousness resulting from Wagner's abandonment of periodic syntax and closed musical numbers. "The 'infinite [i.e., endless] melody' is the dominant, musically undermining power in *Die MEISTERSINGER*, as in *Tristan und Isolde*," wrote Eduard HANSLICK in his review of the former work; "anxiously omitting every conclusive cadence, this boneless tonal mollusk [*knochkenlose Ton-Molluske*] floats on toward the immeasurable, renewing itself from its own substance" (Hanslick 127–8). Although in *Zukunftsmusik* Wagner spoke of such melody "spanning the whole compass of a music drama" (*das ganze dramatische Tonstück*), both Wagner's account and the traditional reception of the term can be illustrated by such individual examples as the Act I Preludes to *LOHENGRIN* and *Tristan und Isolde*, Isolde's "Transfiguration," or the extended love-duet from Act II of *Tristan*. THOMAS S. GREY

See also MUSIC THEORY

Eduard Hanslick, *Vienna's Golden Years of Music, 1850–1900*, trans. H. Pleasants (New York: Simon & Schuster, 1950).

Robert Jacobs, *Three Wagner Essays* (see bibliography).

David Trippett, *Wagner's Melodies* (Cambridge University Press, 2013).

England. See LONDON

Erda (mezzo-soprano; character in *Der RING DES NIBELUNGEN*, with appearances in *Das RHEINGOLD* and *SIEGFRIED*). Primordial earth-goddess, and mother of the Norns and BRÜNNHILDE, Erda is an invention of Wagner's, a skillful amalgam of several divinities, assembled from NORDIC sagas, Jakob Grimm's *Deutsche Mythologie* (1835), and the *EDDA* (though Icelandic sources refer to the goddess as "Jörd"). Wagner may have relied on Greek mythology as well: in particular, the earth-goddess Gaia, as well as the Eumenides in the *Oresteia* bear striking resemblances to Wagner's characterizations of Erda. Like the former, Erda is more senior than the gods of Valhalla and understands the world in ways they do not. Like the latter, Wagner also made his Erda omniscient and all-seeing, the *Vala*, an oracle the more action-oriented Wotan petitions and yet fails to heed at crucial points.

Erda's irruption into the *Ring*'s plot is a late addition – only in the 1851 prose-drafts to *Der junge Siegfried* did Wagner incorporate her as an actual character rather than simply a reference. Once Wagner had decided to add the *Vorabend* of *Das Rheingold* later that year, Erda became pivotal to the cycle's plot, appearing out of the earth and warning WOTAN about the destructive power of the Ring. The scene in which Wotan awakens Erda from her slumbers in *Siegfried* is drawn from the eddic *Baldrs draumar* (Baldr's Dreams), where Odin travels to Helheim, the realm of the dead, to resurrect the *Völva*, a "wise-woman" who can help him interpret his son Baldr's "baleful dreams." Just as in Erda's appearance in *Siegfried*, these visions eventually point towards Ragnarök (the end of the gods). Beyond providing a foil for Wotan's incomplete perspective on the events of the cycle and his hubris, Erda thus also provides a convenient bracketing mechanism for the cycle: she knows what came before Wotan, and she knows what will come after ("Wie alles war – weiß ich; wie alles wird; wie alles sein wird").

In the first of Erda's two appearances in the *Ring*, when she arises from the depths to warn Wotan to relinquish the Ring (*Rheingold*, Scene 4), she is in control both dramatically and musically. The distinctive key of C♯ minor seems to arise with her into consciousness – a key that has not yet been heard in *Das Rheingold*, but that, significantly, is the parallel minor of the D♭ major of Valhalla. The motive that ascends in dotted rhythms through the C♯ minor triad (mm. 3478–9; see Appendix 4: *Leitmotive in Der Ring des Nibelungen*; CWE 10) is conventionally associated with Erda herself, while the descending motive that falls through the Neapolitan harmony, introduced near the end of her appearance (mm. 3502–3), is associated with, and usually designated as, the Twilight of the Gods (or *Götterdämmerung*, CWE 11). Both motives are crucial in the later parts of the *Ring*, once Wotan has decided to renounce his power. Central in this regard is Erda's other appearance, in Act III, Scene 1, of *Siegfried*. Here the ascending and descending versions of her dotted arpeggio motive serve as the basic materials of the Prelude to Act III, and undergird much of the opening dialogue between her and the Wanderer. Here, in contrast to the scene late in *Das Rheingold*, Wotan acts, and Erda reacts. He sets the key and the motives, and he makes the heroic decision, while she hardly seems to be all-wise and all-knowing; unable to awaken, she seems melodically and tonally confused and unfocused.

Responses to Erda have often been critical: Nietzsche disliked the casualness with which Wotan reawakens the mother of all things in *Siegfried*, only to send her back to sleep (§9). Ernest Newman poked fun at her appearances as nice pseudo-philosophy, but "inappropriate … to a drama" (231n). Adorno meanwhile casts Erda's supplementary character, the fact that Wotan's dismissal of her in *Siegfried* in no way constitutes his emancipation from her, in terms of Wagner's retrograde celebration of cyclical myth (111).

ADRIAN DAUB AND PATRICK MCCRELESS

Theodor W. Adorno, *In Search of Wagner* (see bibliography).
Ernest Newman, *A Study of Wagner* (London, 1899).
Friedrich Nietzsche, "*The Case of Wagner*" (see bibliography).
Susanne Vill, "Erda: Mythische Quellen und musikalische Gestaltung," in *Alles ist nach seiner Art*, ed. Udo Bermbach (Stuttgart: Metzler, 2001): 198–224.

Eva Pogner (soprano; character in *Die MEISTERSINGER VON NÜRNBERG*). In some ways the least important female lead in any Wagner opera, Eva's function within the plot is largely decorative. She is granted neither the heroism of BRÜNNHILDE or SENTA nor the metaphysical introspection of ISOLDE, and her amorous world lacks the human complexity of ELISABETH'S or ELSA'S. Eva's father, Veit Pogner, presents her as young, virginal chattel to the man who will win the song contest, and it is as such that the rest of the characters, and indeed the work more generally, treat her. Wagner's source material offered little inspiration for the role; accordingly, some of the opera's early drafts simply refer to her as "the beloved."

Yet if Eva is beloved, she also loves back – and does so in more complicated ways than the simple mechanics of the plot require. Most obviously, Eva's relationship with HANS SACHS is blatantly libidinal, and although she ultimately chooses the younger WALTHER VON STOLZING, it is Eva's renunciation of her feelings for Sachs (as much as it is Sachs's for her) that provides emotional texture to an otherwise hackneyed love story. The intensity of this love triangle – and the ambivalence of its dissolution – are often ignored on the stage, although Götz Friedrich's production for the Deutsche Oper Berlin

(1995) and Andreas Homoki's for the Komische Oper Berlin (2010) have both highlighted Eva's split loyalties in effective ways.

Once Eva chooses Walther, however, she reassumes her supporting, and supportive, role: she functions not only as Walther's love object and artistic muse, but also as the model spectator for his singing. It is Eva who first repeats (in the Quintet) the melody of his Prize Song, conferring onto it a recognition that extends beyond that of Sachs and, ultimately, the mastersingers. In both inspiring Walther's song as well as crowning it with spectatorial approval – thereby anticipating its enthusiastic reception by the VOLK in the opera's final scene – Eva jumpstarts a feedback loop of artistic inspiration that is virtually identical to the one Wagner's writings promoted between the artist and the *Volk*.

Given the musical and dramatic manifestations of these three functions – Walther's young lover, repressed paramour of the older Hans Sachs, and idealized bourgeois spectator – it is hardly surprising that Eva is a difficult role to cast convincingly. The Quintet in particular requires a combination of sheer vocal stamina, razor-sharp precision of pitch, and floating upper register that is rarely found in any singer, let alone the younger ones who might provide some measure of youthful verisimilitude. As a result, many of the more successful vocal interpreters of the role (at the moment, Emily Magee and Karita Mattila; historically, Elisabeth Schwarzkopf) are less persuasive as Walther's teenage love interest than they are in the scenes with Sachs. Still, some directors and singers have successfully emphasized Eva's youth; most notably the 23-year-old Anja Silja, in WIELAND WAGNER's 1963 production for Bayreuth, portrayed a scrappy and headstrong young woman whose iconoclastic vitality served as metaphor for the New Bayreuth project itself.   RYAN MINOR

See also WOMEN

Excerpts (from works). Even in the early stages of his career, Wagner planned and prepared excerpts from his works: first, when complete performances were not yet possible, and, second, to popularize them. He already had such plans for his first opera, *Die FEEN* (composed 1833, premiered 1888). As for *Das LIEBESVERBOT*, after the first performance (Magdeburg, 1836), there was a production of three numbers from the work in 1840. From *RIENZI*, Wagner arranged the famous "Introduction and Prayer" and several other parts of the work for his ZURICH concert series in 1853; however, they were published much later (1870–4). Still today, the Overture and the Prayer are performed in concerts. As for *Der FLIEGENDE HOLLÄNDER*, Wagner arranged the *Lied* of the Norwegian sailors for four-part male chorus in 1851.

In 1853, desperately needing MONEY, Wagner suggested the publication of excerpts to BREITKOPF. Although the OVERTURES of this composer's early operas (up to *LOHENGRIN*) were planned as independent concert pieces and performed separately early on, Breitkopf was reticent; he understood the problems of Wagner's scores whose through-composed structure impeded the lucrative "morceaux détachés" (detached pieces) common in works of his contemporaries. Therefore, for the Zurich concerts of 1853, Wagner arranged, as an early "model," *Senta's Ballade*, adding an orchestral introduction and ending. This simple procedure of adding a musical frame to a vocal or instrumental set piece, extracted from a through-composed score, is characteristic for all the excerpts he prepared himself, and becomes an issue of authenticity for concert performances today. Wagner was consistent. He wrote to LISZT (as Breitkopf's intermediary): "Only I, as the composer, may undertake to detach several popular vocal excerpts by arranging and resizing them with [new] introductions and endings" (16 November 1853). The result was the *Lyrische Stücke für eine Gesangsstimme aus Lohengrin ausgezogen und eingerichtet vom Componisten*, published in 1854 and containing nine pieces for voice and piano, which served as the model for all further arrangements of this kind. Out of this, as orchestral analogies, Wagner arranged the *Brautzug* (Bridal Procession, with special orchestral ending) and *Brautlied und Hochzeitsmusik* (Bridal Song and Wedding Music, with interlude and concert ending). Wagner's autograph full scores of such (mostly short) introductions and endings indicate the exact intersection with the published score; therefore he did not need to write full scores of these excerpts. Most of these autograph additions are mentioned in the WAGNER WERK-VERZEICHNIS (WWV, published 1986), though it provides limited information on the location of these mostly unpublished autographs. Fortunately, since 1986, others have found their way to the Bayreuth archives, thus throwing new light on the complicated question of authentic excerpts from Wagner's works.

After the Zurich concerts of 1853, there were further opportunities for Wagner's self-promotional concerts, for instance in PARIS (1860), as preparation for the spectacular performance of *TANNHÄUSER* (1861), and 1862–3 in VIENNA, where Wagner tried in vain to have *TRISTAN UND ISOLDE* premiered. Other concerts followed in 1875 in preparation for the Ring in 1876, and in 1877 to raise funds to settle the debts from the first festival. For these occasions, between 1859 and 1875, Wagner prepared further orchestral excerpts. Except for *Tristan*, he generally avoided publishing them, in order to retain control. As for excerpts and arrangements made by others, none may be regarded as "authentic" even if some of them may be considered "legitimate" arrangements by those closely associated with the composer, such as LISZT, TAUSIG, or RUBINSTEIN.   ULRICH DRÜNER

The following is a list of later excerpts prepared by Wagner not mentioned in the entry above.

Rheingold (1853–4): *Der Raub des Rheingolds* (The Theft of the Rhinegold), and *Einzug der Götter in Walhall* (The Gods' Entry into Valhalla; Vienna, 1862).

Walküre (1854–6): *Siegmunds Lenzeslied* (Siegmund's Spring Song), *Walkürenritt* (The Ride of the Valkyries), *Wotans Abschied und Feuerzauber* (Wotan's Farewell and Magic Fire; Vienna, 1862; Ride of the Valkyries, published 1877).

Siegfried (1855–7 and 1864–71): *Schmiedelieder* (Forging Songs; Vienna, 1862).

Tristan (1856–9): Prelude with concert ending (published 1860), and *Liebestod* (Love Death, alternatively attached to the Prelude; Paris 1859–60, published 1882/8).

Meistersinger (1862–7): *Versammlung der Meistersingerzunft* (Gathering of the Mastersingers' Guild [orchestral only]) and *Pogners Ansprache* (Pogner's Address; Vienna, 1862); *Schusterlied* (Cobbler's Song; Vienna, 1863); *Fanget an!* (Begin!; Munich, 1865).

Götterdämmerung (1869–76): *Hagens Wacht* (Hagen's Watch), *Siegfrieds Tod* (Siegfried's Death), *Trauermarsch* (Funeral March), and *Schlußszene* (Final Scene; Vienna, 1875).

Parsifal (1877–82): Choruses (only privately performed 1880); Prelude with concert ending (published 1882).

See also ORCHESTRAL CONCERTS

F

Fantin-Latour, (Ignace-)Henri(-Théodore) (b. Grenoble, 14 Jan. 1836; d. Buré [Lower Normandy], 25 Aug. 1904), French painter and printmaker, occasional exhibitor with the Impressionists. Musical subjects (allegorical, scenes from BERLIOZ, and tributes to SCHUMANN) appear throughout his life, and Wagnerian subjects from 1862. Fantin-Latour visited BAYREUTH only once (in 1876) but produced over a hundred Wagnerian images, often repeating scenes in different media (principally lithographs, oils, drawings, and pastels). His subjects – temptation scenes, *femmes fatales* (particularly from the RING, TANNHÄUSER, and LOHENGRIN), the pastoral, and vision – were imaginative, and unrelated to stage productions. Wagnerian images (several shown at the Salon) proliferated in the 1870s and 1880s, and became fashionable by the 1890s. He provided a frontispiece for the commemorative 1884 BAYREUTHER BLÄTTER, and illustrations for La REVUE WAGNÉRIENNE (1885) and Adolphe Jullien's study (1886). *Autour du piano* (1885), depicting friends from "le petit Bayreuth" including Emmanuel Chabrier, Vincent d'Indy, Edmund Maître, and Antoine Lascoux, was celebrated at the Salon.   EMMA SUTTON

> See also WAGNER IN THE VISUAL ARTS

V. M. C. Bajou, "Les Sujets musicaux chez Fantin-Latour" (dissertation, Paris, École Louvre, 1988).

Victoria Fantin-Latour, ed., *Catalogue de l'œuvre complet (1849–1904) de Fantin-Latour* (Paris: Henri Floury, 1911; repr. New York: Da Capo, 1969).

Janet Jempson, "Henri Fantin-Latour and Wagner," *Wagner* 18 (January 1997): 20–31.

Faust-Ouvertüre, Eine (A Faust Overture; WWV 59). A concert overture on the subject of GOETHE's *Faust* or, more particularly, a character study of the brooding, solitary Faust as depicted in the opening scenes of Goethe's play. The work was originally composed in PARIS in January 1840, influenced in part by works of BEETHOVEN and BERLIOZ as performed by the Conservatoire orchestra under François Habeneck. Under Liszt's encouragement, Wagner slightly revised his score for publication in the early 1850s, at the same time Liszt was composing his series of "symphonic poems." (Wagner's reference to his own work as a *Tongedicht* in a letter to Liszt of 9 November 1852 may have had some influence on the nomenclature of Liszt's works.) Originally Wagner had thought to compose a multi-movement program symphony along the lines of Liszt's later *Faust* Symphony (1854). By the time he published the revised score in 1855, Wagner had long since abandoned those plans, and he would certainly not want to have been seen as competing directly with his friend and advocate, Liszt. Aside from the semi-private SIEGFRIED IDYLL (WWV 103) and occasional works such as the *Imperial March* (*KAISERMARSCH*) and the *American Centennial March* (WWV 104 and 110), the *Faust* overture is Wagner's only mature orchestral composition. The music manifests at various levels the young Wagner's enthusiasm for such Beethoven works as the Ninth Symphony and the *Coriolan* overture.　　　　THOMAS S. GREY

Feen, Die (The Fairies; WWV 32), grand Romantic opera in three acts, premiered at the Königliches Hof- und Nationaltheater, MUNICH, 29 June 1888. Wagner completed *Die Feen* in 1834 but could not convince the director Franz Hauser to mount the work in LEIPZIG. He vigorously defended his opera and noted that the staging requirements were not greater than for MEYERBEER's *Robert le Diable*. At twenty, and unproven in the theater, he was already highly ambitious. Another performance possibility for *Die Feen* encouraged Wagner to recast the opera, originally through-composed, as a *Singspiel* with spoken text, but that effort failed. Wagner never again tried to have the work staged. The premiere of *Die Feen* took place posthumously in 1888 with substantial cuts made to the score. Resultant plot gaps were patched up with Wagner's additional *Singspiel* text. Musically a success, the production was especially impressive on account of Karl Lautenschläger's magical lighting designs and scenic transformations. Revivals reached a total of seventy performances by 1899.

Wagner's libretto is based on Carlo Gozzi's theatrical fable *La donna serpente* (The Lady as Snake, 1762). The Venetian playwright's meta-theatrical style combining *commedia dell'arte* with serious elements and elaborate stage effects attracted many early Romantics, including Richard's uncle ADOLF WAGNER and E. T. A. HOFFMANN. Like Gozzi's play, Wagner's opera centers on a mortal prince who, while hunting, encounters an enchanting doe that later becomes his shape-shifting supernatural wife. After being forbidden to do so, Prince Arindal discovers the name of his wife Ada and is expelled from her realm. A series of bizarre illusions cause him to distrust Ada wrongfully and curse her. This triggers her magical transformation into a serpent in Gozzi's play. Wagner opted for a metamorphosis into stone and a Gluck-oriented Orphic conclusion, with Ada restored to human form through Arindal's passionate song. His choice to have Gozzi's invisible magician provide the hero with a magical lyre and sword nods in the direction of Theodor Körner's volume of patriotic lyrics *Leyer und Schwert* (1814). Wagner remained attracted to aspects of Gozzi's tale for the rest of his career, most conspicuously in *LOHENGRIN*.

The musical heritage of *Die Feen* spans the range of Wagner's idols in his youth: MOZART, BEETHOVEN, MARSCHNER, Meyerbeer, MENDELSSOHN, and above all WEBER. Wagner's proclivity towards embedded reflective narratives follows Gozzi's cues in Act I, with realizations that feature musical motive and tonalities that later resurface in different guises and contexts. Far-reaching is Wagner's shaping of Arindal in Act III in a complex of scenes launched by a CHORUS praying for his REDEMPTION. Deranged, Arindal recalls in distorted form the fateful hunt (F minor) before he envisions a transcendental reunion with his wife (E major) which, in turn, connects to her response heard from afar (in E, modally inflected) once he has fallen asleep. Upon waking he rescues Ada, following verbal guidance from an offstage magician. Wagner's tonal framework for these scenes involving a third-related tonal pair (E–C) anticipates his later large-scale tonal language. Dramaturgical echoes reverberate in SIEGFRIED, GÖTTERDÄMMERUNG, and TRISTAN UND ISOLDE.

Soon after completing a prose draft of PARSIFAL in 1865, Wagner gave the score of *Die Feen* to LUDWIG II. Traces of Gozzi can be found in the elaborate transformation scenes in the framing acts of *Parsifal* and in the characterization of the shape-shifting KUNDRY, while stage directions for the collapse of KLINGSOR's magic garden replicate the end of Act I of *La donna serpente* – a scenic effect Wagner had initially avoided in *Die Feen*.

KATHERINE R. SYER

Thomas S. Grey, "Meister Richard's Apprenticeship: The Early Operas (1833–1840)," in *The Cambridge Companion to Wagner* (see bibliography): 20–6.

Michael von Soden and Andreas Loesch, eds., *Richard Wagner: "Die Feen"* (Frankfurt am Main: Insel, 1983).

Katherine R. Syer, "'It left me no peace': From Carlo Gozzi's *La donna serpente* to Wagner's *Parsifal*," *The Musical Quarterly* 94.3 (2011): 325–80.

Festival, idea of. Wagner's idea of a theatrical festival was born out of intense frustration with the theatrical practice of his day. Most opera houses at the time were largely sites of social spectacle, places where one could see and be seen while sampling the art. In a typical baroque opera house, the auditorium lights remained at least partly lit throughout the performance, a ring of hierarchically arranged boxes reinforced social display, and an ornate interior provided gilded distractions from the stage performance. Infuriated by such practices in PARIS and DRESDEN, Wagner came to believe that a new form of theater demanded not just new libretti and new music, but also new artistic organizations, new architecture, and new audiences.

In *Die KUNST UND DIE REVOLUTION* (Art and Revolution, 1849), written in ZURICH in the wake of the DRESDEN UPRISING, Wagner argued that modern society had become fragmented by hierarchy and corrupted by commerce, its decadence only reinforced by a superficial and commodified art. A partial solution to this crisis lay in reawakening the tragedies of ANCIENT GREECE, where festivals of ancient myth had once unified the VOLK. This reawakening would be no mere return, but a new synthesis of the Attic spirit with the age of BEETHOVEN.

Wagner concretized this idea in a series of letters written in the 1850s. To Ernst Benedikt KIETZ on 14 September 1850, he described a plan to build a temporary theater in Zurich, invite the public to attend three free performances spaced over a week, and then demolish the whole business once it was over. By the next year, Wagner's dream had only grown. In a letter to Theodor UHLIG of 12 November 1851, he imagined creating a four-day dramatic festival that would take place only "after the Revolution" (*nach der Revolution*) and that would "make clear to the people of the Revolution the *meaning* of that Revolution, in its noblest sense." Writing more practically to LISZT on 30 January 1852, Wagner urged that his NIBELUNG drama be performed in "some beautiful wilderness" (*irgendeiner schönen Einöde*) far from the smog of industrial civilization.

Once King LUDWIG II became his patron, however, Wagner was under pressure to build his FESTIVAL THEATER as a permanent structure in the Bavarian capital of MUNICH. While this 1865 project was eventually cancelled, it quite literally set the stage for BAYREUTH. Working together with the architect Gottfried SEMPER, Wagner planned a new kind of theater building, one that combined amphitheater seating with a double-proscenium stage and hid the orchestra from the audience's view. The design realized, in architectural form, the union of ancient Greece and modern Germany that Wagner had first called for during his Zurich years.

MATTHEW WILSON SMITH

Simon Williams, *Richard Wagner and Festival Theatre* (Westport, CT: Greenwood, 1994).

Festival Theater, Bayreuth (Festspielhaus; built 1872–5). Wagner is unique in constructing a theater for the performance of his own works. No existing stage, he considered, could meet the scenic demands of the *RING*, while the configuration of conventional theater auditoria reflected invidious class difference, and they were suited more for the socialization of the audience than for viewing operatic performance. The Bayreuth Festival Theater was based, in part, on Gottfried SEMPER's plans for the FESTIVAL THEATER in MUNICH, but was designed by architect Otto Brückwald (1841–1917) with input from Wagner. The site on the so-called "Green Hill" (*grüner Hügel*) was suggested by Bayreuth's mayor, Theodor MUNCKER, who also helped Wagner acquire the plot free of charge, donated by the municipality of Bayreuth. Ground was broken on 29 April 1872, but the official ceremony for the laying of the cornerstone (*Grundsteinlegung*) was on Wagner's birthday, 22 May 1872, during which Wagner enclosed the following motto:

Here do I enshrine a secret	Hier schließ' ich ein Geheimniß ein,
And may it rest for many hundred years:	da ruh' es viele hundert Jahr':
As long as this stone holds it confined,	so lange es verwahrt der Stein,
It will reveal itself to the world.	macht es der Welt sich offenbar

(SSD 9:326)

That evening, there was a gala concert performance of BEETHOVEN's Ninth Symphony at the MARGRAVIAL OPERA HOUSE, with Wagner conducting. Rehearsals for the world premiere of the complete Ring cycle were begun on 1 July 1875.

The cost of the theater was 428,384.09 marks (approximately 3.29 million euros in 2013) financed by King LUDWIG II and with funds from various private sources, including WAGNER SOCIETIES. The original building covered 3,319 square meters (approximately 35,700 square feet). According to Wagner's wishes, it was to be a "provisional structure" that eschewed all architectural ornamentation and ostentatious furnishing, so as not to take attention away from the artwork. The provisional nature of the building has over time diminished with several phases of additional construction and reinforcement, starting in 1882, when a front portico (*Königsbau*), with separate access to the royal box, was added in time for the world premiere of *PARSIFAL*.

In 1888, electric lighting replaced the original gas fixtures. A complex of additional buildings for rehearsal rooms, set storage, and dining facilities were constructed. The original seating capacity of 1,345 plus an additional 300 seats in the galleries was increased to a current total of 1,925 seats.

Acoustically and visually the auditorium is unique. As the orchestral music emerges from the sunken pit (the MYSTISCHER ABGRUND), its precise source cannot be determined by the audience, and as it bounces off the wooden facings, it sounds slightly muted in contrast to conventional houses. This favors the singers, who need not project a massive volume of sound. The steeply raked, wedge-shaped amphitheater and the double proscenium arch repeated on the side walls allow the audience to feel themselves part of the illusory stage world. The entire auditorium therefore enhances the experience of the GESAMTKUNSTWERK. The theater is now the site of the annual BAYREUTH FESTIVAL. SIMON WILLIAMS

Festival Theater, Munich. This project for a monumental theater (1864–6), planned by LUDWIG II, designed by Gottfried SEMPER, and intended to house the performance of Wagner's music dramas, was never realized. The theater would have been built on a site above the Isar, overlooking the center of Munich, but the vast expense of the project and Wagner's lack of enthusiasm for it meant the theater was never built. Nevertheless, the plan incorporated several features that would later be included in the Bayreuth FESTIVAL THEATER, including the sunken orchestra pit and the arrangement of the audience in tiers, reminiscent of the Greek amphitheater. SIMON WILLIAMS

Feuerbach, Ludwig Andreas (b. Landshut, 28 July 1804; d. Rechenberg [near Nuremberg], 13 Sep. 1872), philosopher, attended Berlin lectures by HEGEL and Friedrich Schleiermacher. Feuerbach lectured at Erlangen but failed to obtain a university position, an ambition rendered impossible following revelation of his authorship of the atheistic *Thoughts on Death and Immortality* (published anonymously, 1830); he relied upon income from his wife's factory. A key member of the "Young Hegelian" school, Feuerbach inspired many 1848 radicals, whilst remaining personally aloof from REVOLUTION. Following the factory's bankruptcy, Feuerbach's later years were spent in relative poverty. Having read Marx's *Capital*, he joined the Social Democratic Party in 1870.

Feuerbach's interests remained founded upon the theology of his youth. Unmasking the "secret" – a typical Young Hegelian conceit – of religion as inversion, he proceeded to anthropological criticism of philosophy, understood as abstraction from theology, itself abstracted religion. Man had transferred all his greatest qualities to an imagined, transcendental being, God. Humanity was impoverished; LOVE, the essence of religion, was perverted, even denied. Love must therefore be brought back down to earth, as Wagner attempted in the RING, most clearly in SIEGMUND's rejection of Valhalla, of immortality as promised by BRÜNNHILDE, and, subsequently, her Siegmund/love-inspired rebellion against WOTAN. She loses divinity but gains humanity.

Feuerbach had become, for Wagner, "the proponent of the ruthlessly radical liberation of the individual from the bondage of conceptions associated with the belief in traditional authority" (ML/E 430). The title of *Das*

KUNSTWERK DER ZUKUNFT (The Artwork of the Future, 1849/50) echoed its dedicatee's *Principles of the Philosophy of the Future*. Like many of his generation, Wagner not only followed Feuerbach's critique of RELIGION, but extended it to political and economic life. ALBERICH transforms value-free Rhinegold into possessed – in more than one sense – capital, a classic case of Feuerbachian inversion. What should be loved, enjoyed, and possessed though not owned by all, enslaves the Nibelungs as if it were divine. Likewise, Wotan enjoys not only religious but political power through the fortress of Valhalla. Principles that were, at least for a time, potentially good, have come to rule over mere mortals. Those principles, sapped of life just like the World-Ash tree, have hardened into law. Wotan and Alberich battle for possession of a ring whose imagined power rules the world. As Wagner explained to August RÖCKEL, "the essence of change is the essence of reality, whereas only the imaginary is changelessly unending" (letter of 25/26 January 1854). Liberation "from the bondage of [such] conceptions" was the task of the DRESDEN UPRISING and its dramatic counterparts: Volsung revolution and Brünnhilde's elevation to the "purely human." Such sentiments remained part of Wagner's conception until completion of the *Ring* and indeed of PARSIFAL too, neither supplanted by nor vanquishing newer, metaphysical concerns.

To take one example, that sympathy for fellow human beings (SCHOPENHAUER's *Mitleid*) which Brünnhilde exhibits in her benedictory Immolation Scene is prefigured in Feuerbach's "species being." Consciousness of fellow suffering or indeed joy is what distinguishes man from beast, and what must once again be ascribed to man rather than God. Brünnhilde's example is intended for the "watchers" – as well as us – who might therefore heed Wagner's Feuerbachian words of 1849: "We see that man is utterly incapable in himself of attaining his destiny, that in himself he has not the strength to germinate the living seed distinguishing him from the beast. Yet, that strength, missing in man, we find, in overflowing abundance, in the totality of men ... Whereas the spirit of the isolated man remains eternally buried in deepest night, it is awakened in the combination of men" (SSD 12:242). Wagner's dialectic between Feuerbach and Schopenhauer harks back to their common Romantic roots in Schleiermacher's theology of love, creating something dramatically new.   MARK BERRY

See also POLITICS

Mark Berry, *Treacherous Bonds and Laughing Fire* (see bibliography).
Ludwig Feuerbach, *Principles of the Philosophy of the Future*, trans. Manfred Vogel (Indianapolis, IN and Cambridge: Hackett, 1986).
The Essence of Christianity, trans. George Eliot (Amherst, NY: Prometheus, 1989).

Feustel, Friedrich (b. Egern am Tegernsee, 21 Jan. 1824; d. Bayreuth, 12 Oct. 1891), prominent banker, National Liberal politician, and chairman of BAYREUTH's town council. Friedrich Feustel was also a distant relation of Richard Wagner's brother-in-law, Hermann BROCKHAUS. Wagner used this connection to promote his festival plans for Bayreuth. Feustel became one of Wagner's most important local advocates; he also backed the Festival financially, and was a founding member of the Festival's three-person management committee (*Verwaltungsrat*). His daughter married Adolf von GROß.

ANTHONY J. STEINHOFF

Film music. Max Steiner, doyen of Hollywood film music, always claimed that it was Wagner who was the true father of film music. Indeed, Wagner's approach to composition has many things in common with the techniques of film music. The idea of the "underscore" is a direct descendant of Wagner's ENDLESS MELODY. The requirement of film music to serve the narrative and events on screen, at the expense of traditional musical form, is another. Nevertheless, Steiner's desire to "catch" every action on screen with music (a technique eventually labeled "Mickey Mousing" due to its highly developed use in animation), has perhaps more in common with ballet music, though Wagner did also write ballet music (the Bacchanal in *TANNHÄUSER* eventually finding its way into the Bugs Bunny cartoon called *What's Opera Doc?* [1957]).

SIXTUS BECKMESSER's pantomime in *Die MEISTERSINGER VON NÜRNBERG* is an excellent example of the way in which Wagner influenced later film scoring. Because of its comic action, conveyed by the actor entirely by means of mime rather than by singing, and the music's accurate synchronization to the actor's physical actions, its onomatopoeic imitations and the kaleidoscopic array of *LEITMOTIVE* employed make it similar to the way in which Carl Stalling later scored Warner Brothers cartoons.

LEITMOTIV is often regarded as one of the principal connections between Wagner's compositional method and that of film music, though few, if any, film composers have ever used *Leitmotive* in quite the complex and exhaustively metamorphic manner that we encounter in Wagnerian MUSIC DRAMA. Film scores more typically subject a main theme to metamorphosis. When a *Leitmotiv* system is employed, it is generally much simpler than Wagner's approach. Bernard Herrmann based his score for *Citizen Kane* (dir. Orson Welles, 1941) on two principal themes, which are metamorphosed in the highly un-Wagnerian manner of what amounts to a dance suite. Herrmann chose to do this in order to impose a strict musical logic over Welles's many montage sequences, in a bid to create greater structural cohesion; but the story of *Citizen Kane* is a highly Wagnerian one, contrasting the need for LOVE with the lust for power. Consequently, Herrmann's two themes connoting these oppositions are stated at the outset. "Power," unsurprisingly, contains a Wagnerian tritone (as in HAGEN's motive) to symbolize corruption.

Herrmann, like Steiner, also quoted Wagner's own music at appropriate places. In Alfred Hitchcock's *Vertigo* (1958), a story of obsessive love, Herrmann refers to the ethereal double thirds in the string writing of the Act III Prelude to *TRISTAN UND ISOLDE*. Steiner had previously quoted the "Liebesnacht" music in a love scene in *Now Voyager* (dir. Irving Rapper, 1942). Such quotations suggest that both composers were sympathetic to Wagner's musico-dramatic approach, even if their own stylistic idioms were rather different. Of course, Wagner's emotional mission, to overwhelm the audience with oceanic waves of sound, was immediately taken up by Hollywood and developed into a post-Romantic idiom that lasted well into the 1950s.

Electronics, jazz, pop, and serialism influenced the 1960s soundtrack, particularly in England (though Hammer horror films kept the flag of Wagnerian sonority flying in typically lurid colors throughout that decade). The musical style of Hollywood's Golden Age was then suddenly revived by John Williams for *Star Wars* (dir. George Lucas, 1977), and this style has largely prevailed in popular cinema ever since.

Star Wars was indebted to the style of Steiner's main colleague and rival at Warner Brothers' Studios, Erich Wolfgang Korngold. Indeed, the main theme of *Star Wars* bears a strong resemblance to Korngold's main theme for *Kings Row* (dir. Sam Wood, 1942). Korngold also looked to Wagner as a model for his operatic approach to film scoring, which was consistent with the operas he himself wrote in Vienna before emigrating to Hollywood. The only major difference in Hollywood was that the performers spoke rather than sang their dialogue. Korngold's film scores are by far the most complex from this period of Hollywood cinema, and they indeed employ *Leitmotiv*, Wagnerian sonority, and a correspondence between action and musical structure, which, via the more Viennese elements in Richard STRAUSS's style, can indeed be traced back to Wagner's example.

Considering the influence of Wagner's method on film music, it is perhaps surprising that Wagner's actual music has had a limited appeal for the cinema itself. Obviously it appears in Wagner bio-pics. Korngold somewhat schmaltzily arranged sections of the Wagner canon for *Magic Fire* (dir. William Dieterle, 1954), condensing the *Ring* cycle into a mere four minutes. By contrast, Tony Palmer's television bio-pic (*Wagner*, 1983) played Wagner's music straight. "The Ride of the Valkyries" made its first significant movie appearance in Carl Briel's compiled score for D. W. Griffith's silent classic *Birth of a Nation* (1915), where it accompanied shots of the Ku Klux Klan. Its use in German newsreels (*Wochenschau*) from World War II to accompany footage of Luftwaffe air raids might have inspired a similar juxtaposition in the famous American helicopter raid in Francis Ford Coppola's *Apocalypse Now* (1979). John Boorman also used Wagner to add mythic and emotional resonance to his re-telling of the King Arthur legend in *Excalibur* (1981), while Werner Herzog, who directed a rather cinematic production of LOHENGRIN at Bayreuth in 1990, brought Wagner to the soundtrack of his remake of F. W. Murnau's *Nosferatu* in 1979 to emphasize Murnau's specifically German ROMANTIC take on Bram Stoker's *Dracula*.

On a purely dramatic level, Wagner's penchant for the crushing visual effect (which he shared with the GRAND OPERAS of his *bête noire*, MEYERBEER) also has much in common with Hollywood disaster movies such as *The Towering Inferno* (dir. Irwin Allen, 1974). The democratic amphitheatrical seating plan of BAYREUTH has been adopted by cinemas the world over. Wagner was also one of the first directors to plunge his theater into complete darkness, and this, along with the FESTIVAL THEATER's sunken orchestra pit, has much in common with the experience of hearing the soundtrack music of a film emerge from loudspeakers in a pitch-black cinema.

DAVID HUCKVALE

Jeongwon Joe and Sander Gilman, eds., *Wagner and Cinema* (see bibliography).

Films about Wagner

1. Narrative films
2. Documentaries

1. Narrative films

Cinematic portrayals of Wagner date back to the mimic Leopoldo Fregoli; in such short films as *Maestri di musica* (1898) and *L'Homme Protée* (1899, dir. George Méliès), Fregoli impersonated Wagner, among other celebrated figures. The first feature-length dramatic depiction came in 1913 with Carl Froelich's *The Life and Works of Richard Wagner*. Approximately 80 minutes long – a nearly unprecedented duration at the time – this ambitious production was filmed on location in BAYREUTH and elsewhere. The realism did not extend to the soundtrack, however; given the prohibitive licensing fees demanded by the Wagner family, Froelich eschewed Wagner's music and commissioned an original score from the young composer Giuseppe Becce – who also portrayed Wagner in the film.

Magic Fire (1955), Republic Pictures' film on Wagner's life, was one of the last of the glossy, sentimentalized composer biographies that once proliferated on American and British screens. Directed by German émigré William Dieterle with music direction by the venerable Erich Korngold (who also briefly appeared as Hans RICHTER), the film featured Alan Badel (Wagner), Yvonne de Carlo (MINNA Planer [WAGNER]), and Rita Gam (COSIMA Liszt [WAGNER]). Despite lavish settings and some well-written dialogue, the film was a box-office failure; it is most often seen today in a severely abridged version that sometimes strains coherence.

The 1970s brought a wealth of Wagner narratives on film. West German TV produced *Die Barrikade* (1970), about Wagner's participation in the DRESDEN UPRISING, and *Auf den Spuren von Richard Wagners "Tristan und Isolde"* (1973), dramatizing the story of Wagner and Mathilde WESENDONCK alongside excerpts from TRISTAN. In Luchino Visconti's visually sumptuous *Ludwig* (1972), Trevor Howard plays Wagner as a crafty, acquisitive showman, bemoaning his financial straits to LUDWIG II while sitting in lush dwellings afforded by the king's patronage. By contrast, Hans-Jürgen SYBERBERG's *Ludwig: Requiem for a Virgin King* (1972) is not primarily interested in narrative, but in historical argument presented in a ruminative, consciously theatrical style. The film contemplates Ludwig's mythic ROMANTICISM (a worldview that Syberberg clearly empathizes with), as well as what Syberberg sees as the eventual perversion and discrediting of that tradition by HITLER. Syberberg expanded on the same subject matter and cinematic techniques in his seven-hour *Hitler: A Film from Germany* (1977). Suffused with Wagnerian music and references, *Hitler* was quickly recognized as Syberberg's most significant achievement, although many viewers were uncomfortable with the grandeur Syberberg sometimes invests in his subject.

Paul Nicholas played Wagner in Ken Russell's *Lisztomania* (1975), a wildly irreverent rock musical about LISZT (Roger Daltrey). Underlying the film's relentlessly excessive style is a cogent insight about the Romantic cult of the artist as a progenitor of both rock-star culture and totalitarian hero worship. The point is most clearly expressed in the treatment of Wagner; in one scene,

Wagner croons lyrics about the future Aryan redeemer while dressed in a Superman costume and thrashing a machine-gun-shaped guitar. At least one image in *Lisztomania* later recurred, to considerably different effect, in Syberberg's *Hitler*: Hitler rising from Wagner's grave.

Tony Palmer's nine-hour *Wagner* (1983) starred Richard Burton in one of his final performances, leading an eminent cast that also featured Vanessa Redgrave, Laurence Olivier, John Gielgud, and many others. Past his years of peak energy, Burton nevertheless brilliantly captured the implacable self-confidence and burning intensity that so many contemporaries noted in Wagner. The film's lavish recreations of scenes from the composer's life (luminously filmed by veteran cinematographer Vittorio Storaro) are bound to give Wagner enthusiasts pleasure. Charles Wood's screenplay does not shy away from depicting Wagner's flaws, although it often takes Wagner's accounts at their word; for instance, the PARIS *TANNHÄUSER* SCANDAL OF 1861 is depicted as the work of saboteurs brought to the performance by MEYERBEER. Subsequent dramatizations have included the German-French production *Wahnfried* (1986), in which Otto Sander played Wagner opposite Tatja Seibt as Cosima and Christoph Waltz as Friedrich NIETZSCHE. In *Celles qui aimaient Wagner* (2011), a contemporary woman escapes her mundane reality by imagining encounters with Wagner (Jean-François Balmer) and members of his circle.

2. Documentaries

Near the opening of the television documentary *Great Composers: Wagner* (1997), Daniel Barenboim notes that Wagner's renown has, if anything, been bolstered by the fact that many people have serious reservations about him. Judging from the numerous documentaries about controversial aspects of Wagner, Barenboim's refreshingly candid observation has some basis in fact.

Hans-Jürgen Syberberg's *Winifred Wagner und die Geschichte des Hauses Wahnfried von 1914–1975* (1975; The Confessions of Winifred Wagner), based on filmed interviews with WINIFRED, garnered widespread attention due to Winifred's unapologetically fond recollections of Hitler. Her onscreen efforts to shape the perception of her family's history (often leading to a battle of wills with Syberberg, her questioner) make for powerful and disquieting viewing. More recently, Tony Palmer's *PARSIFAL: The Search for the Grail* (1998) presented a broad overview of the Grail legend and the most contentious aspect of *Parsifal*'s reception history, Hitler's enthusiasm for the work. Palmer's *The Wagner Family* (2010) concentrated not only on the Nazi years, but on the quarrels among the family's younger generations. Also in 2010, *Stephen Fry: Wagner and Me* chronicled Fry's infectious passion for Wagner's work, as well as his personal reckoning with Wagner's anti-Semitism and posthumous appropriation by Hitler. More conventional introductions to Wagner's work and life include *Great Composers: Wagner* (mentioned above), *Famous Composers: Wagner* (1996), and the German production *Richard Wagner und die Frauen* (2005), which included re-enacted scenes involving prominent women in Wagner's life.

Numerous documentaries have focused on the staging of Wagner productions. Among them are *The Making of "Der RING DES NIBELUNGEN"* (1983), about Patrice CHÉREAU's centenary production; *A to Z of Wagner* (1995), which

follows David Alden's TANNHÄUSER in Munich; and Werner Herzog's *Die Verwandlung der Welt in Musik* (The Transformation of the World into Music, 1996), about Herzog's LOHENGRIN in Bayreuth. *Sing Faster: The Stagehands' Ring Cycle* (1999) provides a unique perspective on Wagnerian performance: the San Francisco Opera's *Ring* as seen through the eyes of its union stagehands. *The Golden Ring* (1965) documents the recording sessions for the superlative GÖTTERDÄMMERUNG that John CULSHAW produced for Decca, with Birgit NILSSON and Dietrich Fischer-Dieskau under the direction of Sir Georg SOLTI. Susan Froemke's *Wagner's Dream* (2012) chronicles the rehearsals for Robert Lepage's Ring cycle at the Metropolitan Opera.   HILAN WARSHAW
See also Appendix 9: Documentaries and films

Jeongwon Joe and Sander L. Gilman, eds., *Wagner and Cinema* (see bibliography).

John C. Tibbetts, *Composers in the Movies: Studies in Musical Biography* (New Haven, CT: Yale University Press, 2005).

Hilan Warshaw, "'The Dream Organ': Wagner as a Proto-Filmmaker," in *Wagner Outside the "Ring": Essays on the Operas, Their Performance and Their Connections with Other Arts*, ed. John L. DiGaetani (Jefferson, NC: McFarland, 2009): 184–98.

Flagstad, Kirsten (b. Hamar, 12 July 1895; d. Oslo, 7 Dec. 1962), Norwegian soprano. Her spectacular debut as SIEGLINDE at the Metropolitan Opera on 2 February 1935 turned her overnight into the most celebrated Wagner soprano (especially ISOLDE and BRÜNNHILDE) of her era, particularly at the Metropolitan Opera (1935–52) and Covent Garden (1936–51). Her rich, ample, and freely produced voice remains (via recordings) an iconic Wagner sound.

DAVID BRECKBILL

Edwin McArthur, *Flagstad: A Personal Memoir* (New York: Knopf, 1965).

Fliegende Holländer, Der (The Flying Dutchman, WWV 63). Romantic opera in three acts, libretto and music by Richard Wagner. Libretto completed May 1841; music composed primarily July–November 1841. First performance: Dresden, Royal Saxon Court Theater, 2 January 1843, cond. Richard Wagner. For cast information, see Appendix 10: Stage productions. Overture and corresponding conclusion of Act III revised 1860 (overture by 19 January, Act III conclusion by 16 March). One-act version first performed Bayreuth Festival 1901.
1. Sources, genesis of libretto, and composition
2. Synopsis
3. The music
4. Premiere, performance history highlights, and interpretation.

1. Sources, genesis of libretto, and composition

The biggest adventure of Wagner's early life was the month-long sea voyage he undertook with his wife MINNA and their Newfoundland dog, Robber, from the Baltic coast of East Prussia to LONDON and finally Boulogne-sur-mer in the late summer of 1839. Narrowly avoiding shipwreck during a spell of rough weather in the North Sea, their vessel sought shelter in a Norwegian fjord near a village called Sandviken. Whether or not the calls of the sailors aboard the *Thetis* provided an accurate model for the choral singing of the sailors in Acts I and III of *Der fliegende Holländer* (as Wagner claimed in MEIN LEBEN [My Life, 1865–81]) and whether or not he heard the "legend of the

Flying Dutchman" recounted by the crew (as he told his first audiences in 1843), the voyage must have been the principal impetus to choosing the story as the subject for his next opera. (Quite possibly, though, the connection did not occur to him until after arriving in PARIS, where he had occasion to read or be reminded of Heinrich HEINE's version of the "Dutchman" story.) The folkloric motifs of a ghost ship haunting the seas with its spectral crew and a sea-captain cursed for some act of blasphemy or hubris may date back, as Wagner surmised, to the great age of European maritime exploration between the fifteenth and seventeenth centuries. The endless journeying of the Dutchman figure as a form of divine punishment could also be traced back, as Wagner also noted, to Homer's Odysseus or the medieval Christian legend of Ahasuerus, the "Wandering Jew" (SSD 4:460–2; PW 1:307–8; see also Grey 181–2).

Essentially, though, the story of the *Flying Dutchman* was a "modern" myth, and its literary manifestations date only from the early nineteenth century. Of these, it is clear that Wagner relied primarily on the prose vignette forming chapter 7 of Heinrich Heine's *Aus den Memoiren des Herren von Schnabelewopski* (published in *Der Salon*, vol. 1, 1834) which describes the performance of a popular play on the Dutchman story in a theater Heine locates in Amsterdam. Shorn of its sardonic narrative frame, Heine's fictional drama provides all the key ingredients of Wagner's libretto: the Dutchman and his crew released once every seven years from their cursed wanderings, a Scottish merchant and his unnamed daughter strangely obsessed with the heirloom portrait of a sea captain "dressed in the style of the Spanish Netherlands," her vow to remain true to the real Dutchman, when he appears at their door, and her concluding act of self-sacrifice to ensure that she may never betray her vow. Among numerous English and German versions of the story in circulation before Wagner's opera, he could well have known Wilhelm Hauff's *Die Geschichte von dem Gespensterschiff* or Walter Scott's poem "Rokeby." It is conceivable that the prototype for Heine's "Schnabelewopski" play was the semi-farcical melodrama *The Flying Dutchman; or, the Phantom Ship* published before 1829 and playing in London while Heine was visiting there in April 1827. *The Phantom Ship*, a novel on the *Flying Dutchman* theme by Captain Frederick Marryat, was serialized in the British *New Monthly Magazine* between 1837 and 1839; although it was published in German translation only in 1844 (as *Der fliegende Holländer*), several early critics of Wagner's opera assumed this novel to be his source.

Wagner sketched a scenario for a one-act opera, *Le Hollandais volant*, in the spring of 1840; at the time he was still completing the score of RIENZI. Realizing that the chances of a production of *Rienzi* in Paris were slim, he hoped to interest the director of the OPÉRA, Léon Pillet, in a shorter work that could be paired with a ballet or another shorter opera in one to three acts. The rights to his French-language scenario were purchased by the Opéra for 500 francs, but the commission for the opera itself was given to librettist Paul Foucher and conductor-composer Pierre-Louis Dietsch, whose *Vaisseau fantôme* (not closely modeled on Wagner's draft proposal, in the end) premiered on 9 November 1842, shortly before Wagner produced *Der fliegende Holländer* in DRESDEN.

Wagner worked out his own German libretto in May 1841 and spent the following summer composing the score, the bulk of which he drafted within a period of about two months in the seclusion of a rented house in Meudon, outside Paris. By 21 October 1841 he had completed the orchestration of the opera, with the overture (composed last) following in November. Upon MEYERBEER's recommendation, Wagner sent the score to the manager of the Berlin Court Theater, Count Wilhelm von Redern. Ultimately the signal success of *Rienzi* at the Dresden Theater paved the way for a premiere of Wagner's newest work there, where he had settled in April 1842. Until a few weeks before the 2 January 1843 premiere, Wagner had left the setting of his opera on the coast of Scotland, following the example of Heine's *Schabele-wopski*, with the local characters named "Donald" and "Georg" instead of "DALAND" and "Erik" (the "Anna" of the prose draft had since been changed to "Senta"). Wagner ends his *AUTOBIOGRAPHISCHE SKIZZE* (Autobiographical Sketch, 1842/3) with a description of his dramatic sea voyage and some claims about its influence on the conception of his newest opera; it may have occurred to him in planning the piece to underline the biographical connections of his new opera by relocating it in accordance with his own experiences.

2. Synopsis

Act I

A storm rages off the coast of Norway. The ship of the Norwegian merchant-captain Daland has taken refuge in a narrow fjord, a short distance from his home port. As the storm dies down, the helmsman remains alone on board to keep watch. He dozes off, to be awakened by lingering surges from the storm and a "terrible crash" with which the phantom ship the *Flying Dutchman* has just cast anchor nearby, though unseen by the helmsman. The ghostly crew of the Dutchman's ship lowers their sails.

The DUTCHMAN strides slowly ashore from his deck. In an extended monologue, accompanied by musical figures relating to him and his storm-tossed voyages, he meditates on the fate that forces him to sail about the world forever until the final Judgment Day. Daland notices the dark stranger on shore and is amazed to hear of the vast wealth stored in the hold of the Dutchman's ship; the Dutchman, in turn, eagerly seizes on the information that Daland has an obedient, faithful daughter at home. "Let her be my wife!" he proposes. With thoughts of the Dutchman's treasure running through his head, Daland immediately strikes a deal. The helmsman announces the arrival of the propitious south wind and Daland's ship prepares to set sail again.

Act II

In a large room in Daland's house his daughter, Senta, her nurse, Mary, and a group of local girls are sitting at their spinning wheels. The girls sing of their absent sweethearts and the precious trinkets they hope to receive when the ship returns home. Senta participates neither in their song nor in the industrious activity it accompanies, instead asking Mary for the ballad of the "Flying Dutchman." When Mary refuses to comply, Senta begins it herself. As she recites the legend of the doomed sea captain (whose portrait adorns the wall of the room) the other girls listen with increasing raptness, involuntarily taking up her refrain. Senta herself breaks out of the song as she suddenly proclaims that she will be the one to rescue the doomed Dutchman from his endless cycle of wandering. At that same moment her local suitor, the huntsman Erik, appears with news of the sighting of Daland's ship. Mary tells the girls to prepare for its homecoming.

Erik upbraids Senta for her strange fixation with the old portrait and the legend around it. He tells her of a troubling dream: he imagined a foreign ship arriving on their coast carrying Daland and a dark stranger. The stranger, as Senta guesses, matches the figure in the portrait. At the end of his dream he saw Senta fall to her knees, embrace the stranger, and speed away with him across the sea. "He looks for me!" she cries out. "I must find him, I must perish with him!"

No sooner has Erik rushed off in despair than the Dutchman himself, identical to the dark figure of the portrait, appears at the threshold. Senta barely acknowledges her father's return, except to ask about the stranger. Daland introduces him and explains his purpose, then leaves the couple to become acquainted. For a while they remain transfixed in silent mutual contemplation. Gradually they begin to express their feelings, and their understanding of the fate that brings them together. The encounter between the Dutchman and Senta grows ever more animated, until Daland returns. Will he be able to announce their betrothal? Senta holds up her hand in token of a pledge, and all three rejoice in the vows exchanged.

Act III

In the harbor, the ships of Daland and the Dutchman lie at anchor. The Norwegian crew is making merry aboard their ship while the Dutchman's is immersed in an uncanny, brooding silence. The village girls arrive and mock the sailors, who are dancing among themselves. Gradually, stirrings are heard within the hold of the Dutchman's ship, until the ghostly crew breaks out in loud calls ("Johohoe!"). They sing a macabre song of their own. The singing of the two crews clashes in a tempestuous counterpoint until the Norwegian crew at last flees in terror. The Dutchman's crew falls suddenly silent once more.

Senta and Erik rush out of Daland's house, where Erik has returned to plead with her. He claims that she has sworn to be "eternally faithful" to him, recalling how they used to roam the highlands together watching the ships sail away. Senta's father would leave her in Erik's care, and she, in turn, promised to be true to him. The Dutchman overhears Erik's recollections, steps forth and announces his resolve to depart and to free Senta of her (he believes) conflicting vows. He explains to Senta the conditions of his salvation and warns her to save herself: any woman who accepts him but fails to remain true will have to share his cursed fate. Alerted by Erik's cries, the sailors and villagers assemble on the shore. The Dutchman reveals his identity to all. As he leaps back aboard his ship, Senta runs to the edge of a nearby cliff and leaps off, thus remaining "true unto death." The Dutchman's ship is seen to sink beneath the waves while his transfigured image, embracing that of Senta, rises upward, bathed in celestial light.

3. The music

The originality and forward-looking quality of the *Holländer* score owe something to a confluence of practical and aesthetic impulses. The Parisian conductor François Habeneck advised Wagner that he might have better luck with a small-scale work in one act. At the same time, the frustrations he was experiencing in the Parisian musical world initiated a reaction against the status quo he had initially been willing to embrace. If *Rienzi* had been Wagner's attempt at a Hollywood blockbuster, so to speak, *Der fliegende Holländer* was something like a turn towards experimental independent film. The generic basis for this "independent" turn was that of German romantic opera, in such works as BEETHOVEN's *Fidelio*, WEBER's *Freischütz*, MARSCHNER's *Hans Heiling*, or Wagner's own first opera, *Die FEEN*. In particular, he claimed to have conceived the whole work as a kind of "dramatic ballad," a musical-theatrical amplification of the ballad on the Dutchman legend sung by Senta at the center of the opera. "The wide wild ocean with its far-flung legends is an element which cannot be reduced compliantly and willingly to a modern opera," Wagner wrote (somewhat tendentiously) to his Dresden colleague Ferdinand Heine (undated: August 1843), some months after the work's premiere: "From the outset I had to abandon the modern arrangement of dividing the work into arias, duets, finales, etc., and instead relate the legend in a single breath, just as a good poem should be."

This is wishful thinking, but that Wagner should already be presenting his work in these terms at the time is not without interest. The score is conceived in three discrete acts, although devised in a way that allows the end of Acts I and II to be dovetailed with the openings of Acts II and III respectively (an option only realized when Cosima added the opera to the Bayreuth repertoire at the beginning of the twentieth century). The acts themselves are subdivided into numbers or scenes, but the ideal of a larger continuity is suggested by such composite designations as "Scene, Duet, and Chorus" (end of Act I), "Song, Scene, Ballad, and Chorus" (beginning of Act II), "Aria, Duet, and Trio" (end of Act II), or "Duet, Cavatina, and Finale" (end of Act III). The progression from freely declamatory "scenes" through solo, ensemble, and choral configurations, it should be noted, was something Wagner had observed in contemporary French GRAND OPERAS. Now, however, he makes a consistent point of eliding even these larger aggregates within each act and suppressing the "applause points" that would normally be provided in other operas of the day.

If *Der fliegende Holländer* is still more a Romantic-era number opera than a leitmotivic "MUSIC DRAMA" in the later Wagnerian sense, it does make more consistent use of a small collection of melodic-motivic materials than any of Wagner's previous works. The closest thing to a recurring associative LEITMOTIV would be the hollow resounding call-figure denoting the Dutchman himself (Example 1).

1. The Dutchman's motive

2. Senta's Ballad, verse theme

3. Senta's Ballad, refrain theme

4. Echo effect with "3–2–1" motive, Sailors' Chorus, Act I

5. "3–2–1" and "5–6–5" motive in Sailors' Chorus, Act III

The "elemental" quality of the figure, composed of perfect fourths and fifths, and its initial positioning on the dominant and tonic scale degrees of D minor in the overture evoke the first movement of BEETHOVEN's Ninth Symphony, a work the young Wagner heard through the lens of a musical "mysticism" inspired by his enthusiasm for E. T. A. HOFFMANN. Senta's ballad of the Dutchman answers the Dutchman's "call" with an inversion, of sorts, in related compound meter (Example 2)

The refrain of her ballad, expressing the promise of the Dutchman's ultimate REDEMPTION, includes two simple motivic contours – a descending 3–2–1 (tonic) figure and a 5–6–5 (dominant) oscillation (marked "a" and "b" respectively in Example 3) that are echoed in the singing and dancing of Daland's crew in Acts I and III. In the first case (opening of Act I) this involves a literal echo effect, suggesting the cries of the sailors rebounding off the rocky walls of the fjords (Example 4).

From this initially "natural" environment the figures are later domesticated in the rough and ready dance theme of the sailors in Act III (Example 5). Indoors, the Norwegian maidens echo the 5–6–5 oscillating figure in their "Spinning Chorus" that opens Act II (Example 6).

6. Spinning Chorus, theme (with "5–6–5" motive)

The construction of these basic motives from the simplest triadic, diatonic materials anticipates Wagner's strategy in the *Ring* dramas of providing a core of "natural" motives drawn from the triad and major scale as the basis for more complex motivic evolutions, and as a foil for chromatic, disruptive materials introduced by antagonistic forces within the drama.

The simple, even banal basis of this melodic "intertextuality" linking the world of the sailors with that of their doting lasses on shore underlines the distance that separates them from the Dutchman and his existential wanderings. The melodic idiom characterizing the solo numbers of Daland and Erik is similarly plain and direct, Erik's tending toward the sentimentally florid while Daland's is more bluff and hearty. The loose, harmonically unstable, declamatory style of the "dream" Erik describes to Senta, on the other hand, is explained by its subject: a vision of her escaping into another world together with the Dutchman. (Sequential iterations of the Dutchman's "call" motive form the only unifying melodic content of the dream.) The conflict between external and internal values, the ordinary and the visionary, or the human and the supernatural, is given thrilling musical-dramatic expression in the great choral tableau that forms the first half of Act III. Here the *gemütlich* singing and dancing of the Norwegian community serves as an explicit provocation of the mysteriously silent crew of the Dutchman's ship. However we evaluate its position on the continuum of opera to music drama, the *Holländer* score confirms that Wagner's musical-dramatic genius lay less in his powers of lyrical invention than in the dramatic deployment of his melodic-motivic ideas – their "orchestration" in both literal and figurative terms, as we might put it.

4. Premiere, performance history highlights, and interpretation

The premiere of *Der fliegende Holländer* (Dresden, 2 January 1843) occurred in the shadow of Wagner's first major success, *Rienzi*. The smaller, less spectacular, darker-hued, cautiously "experimental" *Holländer* scored little more than a *succès d'estime*. In Dresden, and in the production mounted under the composer's direction in Berlin a year later, the opera enjoyed (in each case) a mere four performances. The demanding scenic requirements of the outer acts – with two "practicable" ships, swelling seas, and whistling storms – were scarcely met at the premiere, though Wagner expressed his satisfaction at the way these effects were realized in Berlin and in a presumably modest production in ZURICH he oversaw in the spring of 1852. The role of Senta was created in Dresden by Wagner's youthful idol, Wilhemine SCHRÖDER-DEVRIENT. Vocal and dramatic aspects of the role were likely inspired by her famous interpretation of Leonore in Beethoven's *Fidelio*, a heroine fanatically committed to the rescue of her imprisoned husband. Wagner found the appearance and dramatic conception of his first Dutchman, Johann Michael Wächter, underwhelming, by comparison.

Despite its relatively modest dimensions, the work was slow to be taken up in Germany. A Vienna production in 1860 and a large-budget revival in Munich, sponsored by Wagner's new patron LUDWIG II (1864), were two significant events. For the latter, Wagner was able to include the revised ending of the overture he created for concert performances in Paris in 1860, consisting of more involved sequential development of the "redemption" theme in the coda and an elaborated transformation of the idea (with harps) over an extended plagal cadence, aptly reminiscent of ISOLDE's "Transfiguration." The representation of Senta and the Dutchman rising "transfigured" above the waves at the conclusion of the opera (where the same revised ending was deployed) remained a sticking point for many early productions, however. George Bernard SHAW's mocking description of awkwardly designed effigies of the main characters hoisted into the flies in an 1891 London production resonates with numerous other complaints about the way this sentimental phantasmagoria was realized in the nineteenth century.

In 1901, *Der fliegende Holländer* became the earliest, and to date the last, of Wagner's works to enter the repertoire of the Bayreuth festival. Cosima insisted on the one-act structure although Wagner himself had never tried this. Since then it has remained a common but by no means universal option. The opera was the vehicle for one of the signal early experiments in modernist opera staging when designer Edward Dülberg and director Jürgen Fehling created for the Berlin KROLL OPER a dark-hued, constructivist interpretation influenced by the contemporary Bauhaus idiom, played in modern dress. The production met with considerable resistance, though it anticipated the dominant aesthetic of early postwar productions under Wagner's grandson WIELAND.

The "point of view" experiment of Jean-Pierre Ponnelle's 1975 San Francisco Opera production, in which the sleepy helmsman of Act 1 "dreams" the appearance of the Dutchman's ship and subsequent events, was taken up in an influential and widely viewed 1978 Bayreuth production (one of the first disseminated on film and video) directed by Harry Kupfer, where the drama is a projection of Senta's obsession with the Dutchman's portrait and his legend. (The casting of African-American baritone Simon Estes as the Dutchman underlined the transgressive nature of Senta's obsessions.) This production also initiated a still-prevailing preference for Wagner's original 1842 ending of the opera (and overture), which can serve – even if against the composer's presumed intentions – to highlight anti-sentimental, even brutally graphic versions of Senta's suicide that have become popular among modern directors.

Wagner justifiably regarded *Der fliegende Holländer* as the decisive turning point in his career as an opera composer and as a dramatic "poet." While his sources were all modern ones, he recognized in the material the distinctively malleable, psychologically suggestive symbolic values of MYTH that would continue to define all his subsequent works. Like the other protagonists of the "Romantic" operas from the Dresden period, TANNHÄUSER and LOHENGRIN, the Dutchman is easily construed as a figure of Romantic alienation from the world of everyday bourgeois reality. Like them, but still more emphatically, he longs for integration into the sphere of "normal" domestic and social relations, while fearing the impossibility of this integration. Senta, like her counterparts ELISABETH and ELSA, is driven by a self-sacrificing instinct to "redeem" the alienated, suffering hero through her own demise. Like Elsa, in particular, she seems to "will" this hero into her presence from some other, numinous realm. Senta's ballad thus functions like Elsa's "dream" narration. The reflexive relation of the ballad to the opera as a whole, emphasized by Wagner in his *Eine Mitteilung an meine Freunde* (A Communication to My Friends), makes it a structural axis of the drama, musically and dramaturgically.

As a bass-baritone role, the Dutchman has affinities with non-Romantic roles such as WOTAN, HANS SACHS, or even AMFORTAS – all of them featuring extended musical-dramatic monologues reminiscent to some degree of the Dutchman's opening scene. Wagner's interest in the Dutchman as a manifestation of the legendary trope of the "Wandering Jew" – cursed to live on through endless generations as witness to the unceasing historical cycle of human *WAHN* – prefigures his interest in the philosophy of Schopenhauer and its influence on *TRISTAN* and *PARSIFAL*. While the music of *Der fliegende Holländer* only offers occasional glimpses of the mature Wagner, the affinity of its dramatic conception with the later music dramas has helped to ensure its place in the canon. THOMAS S. GREY

Attila Csampai and Dietmar Holland, eds., *Richard Wagner, "Der fliegende Holländer"* (see bibliography).
Thomas Grey, ed. *Richard Wagner: "Der fliegende Holländer"* (see bibliography).
The Opera Quarterly 21:3 (Summer 2005). Special issue on *Der fliegende Holländer.*
Simon Williams, *Wagner and the Romantic Hero* (Cambridge University Press, 2004).

Flying Dutchman, The. See FLIEGENDE HOLLÄNDER, DER

Fortuny y Madrazo, Mariano (b. Granada, 11 May 1871; d. Venice, 2 May 1949), Spanish designer, painter, etcher, and photographer. Fortuny visited Paris in the 1890s, where he heard Wagner's work and befriended Proust. After he attended BAYREUTH in the early 1890s with the Spanish Wagnerian painter Rogelio de Egusquiza, Wagnerian subjects and AESTHETICS dominated his work. His numerous oils, etchings, and engravings on Wagnerian subjects include *Parsifal: Fanciulle fiore* (which won the gold medal at the Munich international exhibition, 1896). His interest in pictorial and theatrical lighting and in multimedia projects was greatly indebted to Bayreuth. Highly influential as a stage designer and lighting engineer, he aspired to unite light, music, and scenic effects, developing the "Fortuny dome," "cupola" or "celestial vault," and techniques of indirect lighting using a model of the *Festspielhaus*. Designs for theater include: *TRISTAN* at La Scala (1901); a cupola for the KROLL OPER, Berlin, inaugurated with *Tristan* (1907); and *MEISTERSINGER* at Rome's Teatro dell'Opera (1931). EMMA SUTTON

See also WAGNER IN THE VISUAL ARTS

Maurizio Barberis, Claudio Franzini, Silvio Fuso, and Marco Tosa, eds., *Mariano Fortuny* (Venice: Marsilio, 1999) [Exhibition catalog].
Patrick Carnegy, *Wagner and the Art of the Theatre* (see bibliography).
Vittorio Pica, "Gli scenari del *Tristano e Isotta*," *Emporium* 73 (January 1901).

France. In Wagner's lifetime, PARIS was considered the cultural center of the civilized world, the "Capital of the nineteenth century" (as Walter Benjamin called it in the title of his famous essay collection). Wagner wanted to be successful in Paris in order to be successful in the whole world. During his two longer stays there (1839–42 and 1859–62), he experienced failure. Nevertheless, even if his personal ambitions were thwarted, Wagner considered France the country of culture where international artistic standards were set. Toward the end of his life, he witnessed a growing Wagnerian movement in France.

This particular strand of Wagner reception was – ironically – born during the greatest failure of Wagner's art in France, the TANNHÄUSER SCANDAL of March 1861. Provoked and ashamed by the Paris audience who made this opera performance a complete fiasco, France's leading AVANT-GARDE poet, Charles BAUDELAIRE, defended Wagner in a famous article, which became the founding document of the French *wagnérisme*. The beginnings are symptomatic for the history of the whole movement: a defense of Wagner by illustrious representatives of France's avant-garde literary scene.

Throughout the 1860s, Wagner's music was played in concerts of conductor Jules Étienne PASDELOUP (Concerts Pasdeloup), whilst a growing number of articles and publications furthered a debate for and against Wagner. When Pasdeloup staged RIENZI in 1869 at the Théâtre-Lyrique, its success and a growing understanding of the new AESTHETICS seemed to pave the way for a dissemination of Wagner's music in France. However, the FRANCO-PRUSSIAN WAR OF 1870–1 proved a major break. The role of politics in Wagner's reception history is not only a German phenomenon, but also integral to French WAGNERISM, though at the other end of the ideological spectrum. Since the German left wing had no space for culture in their political program, it gave the nationalist and folkish (*völkisch*) movement the opportunity to take complete possession of Wagner. This seems absurd considering the fact that Wagner's art theory was entirely based upon politically progressive ideas. By contrast, in France, it was the Republican nationalists who were fiercely opposed to Wagner in his role as the cultural representative of the German enemy, whilst an intellectual, literary avant-garde regarded Wagner as the prophet of a new era of art, which was considered universal and not necessarily limited to its German origins.

One of the reasons for the fierce anti-Wagnerism in France was the latter's unfortunate "comedy" entitled *Eine Kapitulation*, a satire in the tradition of Aristophanes, in which Wagner openly mocked the besieged Parisians (including Victor Hugo and Gambetta). Even if he had intended to caricature the German theater system, and deplored until his death that his comedy was chronically misunderstood, the French, even his friends, felt insulted. In addition, Wagner's role as cultural representative of the new German *Reich* explains the official ban of his operas on French national stages between 1871 and 1891 – a ban which can be compared to the ongoing prohibition of Wagner's music in ISRAEL. There was only one performance of LOHENGRIN in Nice (21 November 1881), and two performances of the same opera at the Eden-Théâtre in Paris in 1887 (3 and 5 May), after which the conductor Charles Lamoureux withdrew the work due to political protest. In September 1891, Lamoureux repeated his project to stage *Lohengrin*, this time at the OPÉRA. Politically organized mass demonstrations in front of the Paris Opéra vanished quickly, and *Lohengrin* enjoyed wide success, serving as a starting point for the staging of all Wagner operas in France until 1914. Indeed, Wagner's operas were performed more than those of any other composer before World War I.

The basis for this unparalleled triumph was laid, paradoxically, during the years of the Wagner ban (1871–91), when Wagner's music could only be heard at the Concerts Pasdeloup, Concerts Colonne, Concerts Lamoureux, and in private circles, and not on the stage. Significant musical writers such as Édouard SCHURÉ and Adolphe Jullien published important books about Wagner, the literary group of symbolists around Édouard Dujardin founded the famous periodical *REVUE WAGNÉRIENNE* (1885–8), and French composers such as Ernest Chausson, Édouard Lalo, Emmanuel Chabrier, and Vincent d'Indy created operas that were clearly influenced by Wagner's aesthetics. Wagner had an impact on the pictorial arts, too, provoking Wagner-inspired paintings by artists such as Henri FANTIN-LATOUR or Odilon Redon. At the same time, Wagner's increasing popularity became the basis for the success in the late 1890s. The sheer quantitative scale of French Wagner admiration can be observed indirectly from the visitor's book (*Fremdenliste*) which lists all those attending the Bayreuth Festival from 1876 on. The large French contingent reaches its apex in 1896 with 840 visitors.

World War I constituted yet another radical break in the official French reception of Wagner, and meant a total ban on Wagner's music on stage and in concert halls between 1914 and 1919. Nevertheless, Wagner's music had become irrevocably part of France's cultural heritage. Despite the caesura between 1914 and 1919, and despite opposition of the musical avant-garde such as the Groupe des Six, Wagner's works soon returned to French theaters, and France's interest in Wagner continued. Even World War II and the German occupation did not interrupt the French Wagner tradition, which continues to this day.

In the twentieth century, France produced important Wagnerian singers such as Germaine Lubin, Ernest Blanc, and Régine Crespin, and sent two Frenchmen to Bayreuth (Patrice CHÉREAU and Pierre BOULEZ) to stage the "Centennial RING" of 1976. French literature – even if no longer at the height of *fin-de-siècle* Wagnerian frenzy – has continued to be infused with Wagnerian elements, from Marcel Proust to Julien Gracq. Wagner remained an important topic for postwar French thought: the anthropologist Claude Lévi-Strauss (1908–2009) viewed Wagner as the father of the structural analysis of MYTH, and the anti-postmodern philosopher Alain Badiou (b. 1937) has maintained a strong interest in the German composer throughout his career. Wagner is still widely popular with French audiences, and the Bayreuth Festival continues to enjoy a large French contingent.　　　　　　　　　　　　　HERMANN GRAMPP

Annegret Fauser and Manuela Schwartz, eds., *Vom Wagner zum Wagnérisme: Musik, Literatur, Kunst, Politik* (Leipziger Universitätsverlag, 1999).

Martine Kahane and Nicole Wild, eds., *Wagner et la France*, exhibition, Paris, Théâtre national de l'Opéra, 26 October 1983–26 January 1984 (Bibliothèque Nationale, Théâtre national de l'Opéra de Paris: Éditions Herscher, 1983).

Wagner et la France, Numéro spécial de la *Revue musicale*, 1 October 1923.

Franco-Prussian War of 1870–1. The war was a result of tensions over Prussia's drive to unify the German states. Otto von Bismarck maneuvered Napoleon III into war, and then rallied the Germans against French "aggression." France was defeated, and a unified German state was established with Prussian King Wilhelm I as emperor. The war occasioned Wagner's satirical libretto about the French defeat, *Eine Kapitulation* (WWV 102).   CELIA APPLEGATE

See also GERMAN UNIFICATION

Frantz, (Gustav Adolph) Constantin (b. Börnecke, 12 Sep. 1817; d. Blasewitz, 2 May 1891), historian and political theorist. Prussian civil servant, from 1862 a full-time writer. Although he was initially Hegelian, SCHELLING's influence turned him rightward. Like many contemporaries, Frantz addressed the "German question": how to reconcile cultural nationhood with German *Klein-staaterei* (petty-statism). This he described, with typical national modesty, as the most obscure, most involved, and most comprehensive problem in all of modern history. Note the German conflation between national and universal, also present in Wagner's and others' writings.

Critical of liberal, instrumentalist conceptions of state and monarchy, which he viewed in natural, organic terms, Frantz opposed both the National Liberals (associated with Jewish hegemony), and Bismarck's *kleindeutsch* policy, meaning unification as a Prusso-German nation-state, excluding Austria. Instead, Frantz advocated particularism within a pacifistic confederation to include Switzerland, Belgium, the Netherlands, and Scandinavia. Austria and Prussia would act from within rather than as would-be great powers. This federal model for Europe as a whole would defend against French and Russian expansionism, and protect traditional Western Christendom. Latterly claimed as a forerunner of the European ideal, Frantz was romantically nostalgic for the Holy Roman Empire: not a state, but a set of legal institutions, through which sovereign entities, ranging from electorates to imperial knights, might thrive, as much culturally as politically. It was Germany's particular privilege and calling, Frantz believed, to form a living connection between state and international law in the development of continental Europe. GERMAN UNIFICATION (1871), he believed, ignored German historical development, transplanting foreign constitutional forms in the name of a national principle.

Frantz may have influenced a surprisingly rare expression of blatant nationalism in Wagner's dramatic oeuvre: HANS SACHS's peroration in *Die MEISTERSINGER VON NÜRNBERG*. Even if the Empire fell to a French (*welsch*) threat, Sachs exclaims, "holy German art" would endure. Wagner had encountered Frantz's work during the 1860s, dedicating the second edition of *OPER UND DRAMA* (Opera and Drama) to him and proposing to LUDWIG II in 1866 that he assume leadership of the German Confederation. Cosima records: "R. says, 'Who suffered more than I did under the drawbacks of life in Germany? Indeed, I even got to the stage of wishing to see the whole nation dissolved, but always in the hope of building something new, something more in line with the German spirit. It was a great joy to me to get a glimpse through Constantin Frantz of the German Empire; and who cannot feel at least some hope, now that the Germans have shown such strength?'"

(CWD 14 February 1871). When Wagner's initial enthusiasm for Bismarck's *Reich* faltered, this almost metaphysical *Reich* remained an alternative.

In 1878, Wagner republished WAS IST DEUTSCH? (What is German?) requesting Frantz's response. Frantz's *Open Letter to Richard Wagner* (June 1878), also published in the BAYREUTHER BLÄTTER, argued that the new *Reich* was as un-German as could be. Importantly, he distinguishes between (German) "metapolitics" and conventional politics (analogously with metaphysics and physics). Metapolitics must have a higher aim than mere political ends, a privileging characteristic in the idealism of the later BAYREUTH CIRCLE.   MARK BERRY

See also GERMANNESS / GERMAN IDENTITY

Fricka. (mezzo-soprano; character in *Der RING DES NIBELUNGEN*, with appearances in *Das RHEINGOLD* and *Die WALKÜRE*; wife of WOTAN). Fricka does not appear as a character in her own right in the 1848 *Nibelungen*-draft, and makes her first appearance in the drafts for *Siegfrieds Tod*. The figure of Fricka has her origins in the NORDIC sagas, though Wagner dresses up the Germanic goddess of marriage and motherhood in the garb of the nineteenth century. Snorri Sturluson's *Prose EDDA* features the goddess Frigg as Odin's partner and equal, and as Baldr's mother; meanwhile, the *Oedisdrecka* in the VÖLSUNGA SAGA suggests that she had children with gods other than Odin. Wagner's Fricka, by contrast, is a scold, a prude, and a shrew, furious at her husband's transgressions. She is also childless – while her husband procreates almost uncontrollably out of wedlock, the marriage that she seeks to protect above all – her own – remains without offspring.

Wagner's transformation of the sparse *Edda*-material about Fricka suggests in the first place a turn towards Greek mythology: The raging jealousy with which Fricka chases down the products of her husband's infidelities in *Die Walküre* is not that of the Nordic Frigg, but rather of Hera. Second, however, Fricka is the most contemporary of the *Ring*'s divine characters: jealous, greedy, and cantankerous, she is so clearly the domineering matron of nineteenth-century literature and culture that she even turns the other gods bourgeois. The oft-noted similarities between Wotan and the bourgeois patriarch exist because of Fricka. Not for nothing do the scenes in which she intervenes into the cycle's action (the second scenes of *Rheingold* and *Walküre*) deal with the two chief elements of nineteenth-century domestic disturbance: in *Rheingold*, the gods' obsession with status is on the brink of bankrupting them; in *Walküre*, her husband's infidelity threatens to destroy the family's credibility.

In her two scenes in *Das Rheingold*, Fricka's music rarely rises above the level of recitative, inasmuch as it primarily portrays her as either hectoring Wotan or fretting about Freia. In her only other scene – Act II, Scene 1 of *Walküre* – she is a formidable opponent to Wotan, musically and dramatically. Beginning again with recitative, her music rises with increasing declamatory power as the scene proceeds, leading ultimately into what is in effect an aria, or monologue, of rage, beginning with "O, was klag ich / um Ehe und Eid." Her monologue is a tonally closed piece in G♯ minor (the only use of this key as an extended tonal center in the *Ring*), and is a clear Lorenzian Barform (a = m. 283; a′ = m. 300; B = m. 315). No *Leitmotive* are associated with her, but a referential key is, at least in *Walküre*. As the goddess who upholds the laws of marriage and custom, she is given the conventional key of C – but C in its dark form of C minor; this is the principal key of her scene, the one in which she enters and exits. C minor is also the key of Hunding's scene in Act I – and appropriately so, since she is the goddess whose laws he has strictly upheld, and to whom he has appealed for vengeance on SIEGMUND and SIEGLINDE.

The interpretation of Fricka's conception and role has changed in tune with the sensitivity to matters of GENDER and sexuality in Wagner's oeuvre. For those contemporaries of Wagner who understood the *Ring* as a straightforward and fairly faithful recasting of Germanic myths, the misogyny of Wagner's characterization of the goddess was largely ignored in favor of her domesticity and loyalty to her husband. Those who understood Wagner's depiction of Wotan's marriage to implicitly criticize the institution often cast her as an embodiment of all that was wrong with that which she is sworn to protect.

With the advent of feminism, more attention was paid to Fricka's role vis-à-vis Wotan's design, and what moral valuation Wagner's poem suggests: is Fricka Wotan's moral compass and corrective (Schickling 222), or does Wagner displace all the strictures of conventional morality on women? With either reading, the argument Fricka offers in *Walküre* Act II serves to refute Wotan's dreams of autonomy, confronting him with the commitments he has made in the name of the new order he has created (Borchmeyer 227). As Shaw put it in *The Perfect Wagnerite*: "Fricka is absolutely right when she declares that the end of the gods began" with Wotan's wayward procreation (Shaw 41). For most twentieth-century observers, Wagner essentially invites us to shift our approval from one side to the other (Ewans 128).

Apart from parallels to Wagner's own marriage to his first wife Minna, whom he even compares with Fricka (see letter to Minna 30 September 1854), many observers have also noted that the program Fricka querulously disrupts – Wotan's domination and wanton procreation – is heavily gendered, making her Wotan's sexual bad conscience. For Slavoj Žižek, Fricka and BRÜNNHILDE are externalized and opposed "libidinal components" of Wotan's psyche, his erotic superego and his impulse to uncontrollable free love (250). More narrowly, the *Ring*'s two recognizably "bourgeois" marriages (HUNDING-Sieglinde and Wotan-Fricka), barren, disharmonious, and unhappy, allow Wagner to suggest that "family relations inevitably reflect the bourgeois-capitalist system in which they are situated" (Deathridge 59).

ADRIAN DAUB AND PATRICK MCCRELESS

Dieter Borchmeyer, *Drama and the World of Richard Wagner* (see bibliography).
John Deathridge, *Wagner Beyond Good and Evil* (see bibliography).
Michael Ewans, *Wagner and Aeschylus: The Ring and the Oresteia* (Cambridge University Press, 1983).
Eva Rieger, *Richard Wagner's Women*, trans. Chris Walton (Woodbridge: Boydell, 2011).
Dieter Schickling, *Abschied von Walhall* (Munich: Deutsche Verlags-Anstalt, 1983).
George Bernard Shaw, *The Perfect Wagnerite* (see bibliography).
Slavoj Žižek, *Contingency, Hegemony, Universality* (London: Verso, 2000).

Fricke, Richard (b. Leipzig, 10 March 1818; d. Dessau, 29 April 1903), German choreographer and movement specialist. Wagner first encountered Fricke in

Dessau in 1872, when he attended a strikingly unified production of GLUCK's *Orfeo* at the Court Theatre, directed by Fricke. As a result, he invited Fricke to Bayreuth to supervise the movement of the actors in the first production of the *RING*. Fricke proved invaluable to the production, making many contributions that are now considered to be in the domain of the stage director. Fricke instructed Wagner's children in dance and became a close family friend. On Wagner's recommendation, he directed *LOHENGRIN* in Turin in 1877. He returned to Bayreuth in 1882 to choreograph the Flower Maidens in *PARSIFAL*. Fricke's memoir of his time in Bayreuth, *Bayreuth vor Dreissig Jahren* (Dresden 1906), is one of the key sources for Wagner's own work as a stage director.

SIMON WILLIAMS

Richard Fricke, *Wagner in Rehearsal 1875–1876: The Diaries of Richard Fricke*, trans. George Fricke, ed. James Deaville and Evan Baker (Hillsdale, NY: Pendragon, 1998).

Friendship. Wagner's friends have left us reports near-incompatible in character, telling of loyalty and disloyalty of equal intensity. Praised on the one hand as a paragon of unstinting empathy (thus Verena "Vreneli" Weidmann), he was accused on the other of dropping those whose usefulness had expired (thus Peter CORNELIUS). Friends were undoubtedly exploited for personal benefit as Wagner showed little hesitation in his endeavors to appropriate their finances and their wives. Reminiscences of friends in *MEIN LEBEN* (My Life, 1865–81) are laced with condescension, while COSIMA'S DIARIES record Wagner's assertions that he had "no friends who really showed sympathy for my life" and that it was always they who had "abandoned him when he expected too much of them" (CWD 7 August 1879, 16 September 1878). It can thus be tempting to read fair-weather-friendliness into most of Wagner's actions. But many sources suggest a more differentiated view would be fairer by far.

Wagner was gregarious by nature, a fact reflected in his early CORRESPONDENCE with friends such as Theodor APEL in which he meanders serenely from work to the weather, from cures to the epicurean, finances to philosophy and from the musical to the menstrual. Later correspondence and reminiscences suggest that such openness among friends was a trait he long retained.

Whenever debt or scandal forced him to move, Wagner found new friends with apparent ease. He bestowed the familiar form of address "Du" readily, though not indiscriminately. While his preferences might later have lain with those whose birth afforded them the higher social status to which he himself aspired, his lifelong friendly relations with "lower" classes, from orchestral musicians to serving staff, reflect a desire and a need to engage with his fellow men and women that went beyond considerations of either caste or personal gain. SERVANTS such as Vreneli Weidmann, and Anna and Franz Mrazek followed him across borders and through near-bankruptcies in testament to relationships that were ostensibly unequal, though seemingly founded more on affection than on mere subservience. Nor did his friendships center solely on matters musical or intellectual, for from early on he favored the company of others when he traveled, went HIKING, or took the waters. In later years, he counted family doctors such as Josef STANDHARTNER among his close friends, their intimate knowledge of his physical frailties no doubt serving as a natural conduit for emotional intimacy. Yet more than any other musician of the age, Wagner also enjoyed the friendship (albeit seldom untroubled) of great minds in diverse fields, from Franz LISZT to Gottfried SEMPER and Friedrich NIETZSCHE. It is largely in letters to friends such as Theodor UHLIG that we learn of Wagner's artistic development. And despite his late tendency to misogyny and his earlier rapacious SEXUALITY, it was also often in his correspondence with platonic women friends (such as Julie RITTER, Eliza WILLE, and Mathilde WESENDONCK) that he was at ease enough to impart information vital to an understanding of his life and art.

Wagner's loyalty to friends is seen in his efforts to provide them with employment, organizing the ZURICH appointments of von BÜLOW and Semper in 1850 and 1855 respectively, then the call to MUNICH of von Bülow, RÖCKEL, and Cornelius a decade later (though personal loyalty here coincided with their usefulness to his purpose). During his Zurich exile, Wagner began associating mostly with men several years younger than he, from von Bülow to Wilhelm BAUMGARTNER, Jakob SULZER, Karl RITTER, Carl TAUSIG, and others, perhaps as a form of *Ersatz* for the sons that MINNA had never borne him. His subsequent friendships with artists and intellectuals of the caliber of Nietzsche, Engelbert HUMPERDINCK, Hans RICHTER, and others prove the extraordinary devotion that he could inspire in the most gifted members of the younger generation.

Platitudes from Wagner's early correspondence such as his insistence to Gottfried Engelbert ANDERS (on 10 July 1841) that "my happiness and that of my friends is one and the same thing" do not disappear from later letters to friends, though what are here clichés of minimum significance later become signifiers of manipulation as Wagner becomes increasingly adept at gauging his language to the addressee in order to achieve maximum gain (most notably with LUDWIG II). The designation "friend" itself acquires added meaning. Ludwig is addressed specifically thus, though with adjectives ranging variously from "illustrious" to "only" and in a style latently homoerotic. In that same correspondence, Cosima becomes "die Freundin" (feminine of "friend"), the definite article both concealing and revealing her status as far more than connoted by the noun alone. Wagner's Zurich exile also saw him use the word in partisan fashion, as in his *MITTEILUNG AN MEINE FREUNDE* (Communication to My Friends), where he begins to divide the world into those who are capable of understanding his art (the "friends" to whom he deigns to communicate) and those who are not.

Wagner's generosity to friends found expression in sundry gifts, from clothes to lighters, cufflinks, and the like, though such largesse was often greatest when he could least afford it (as at Christmas 1863) and in some cases he resorted to begging wealthy friends (such as the Wesendoncks) to provide him with gifts for others. Certain friendships seem to have ceased when Wagner became too demanding of money (as with Julie Ritter) or meddled too much in private matters (as with Karl Ritter and, to an extent, with Nietzsche), though such lost friendships could trouble him for long afterwards: thus he was hurt when Karl Ritter rebuffed his efforts to meet him in VENICE after a hiatus of twenty years. But in other cases, mutual respect and affection were retained on both sides over several decades, especially among those who regarded Wagner's financial entreaties as occasional distractions to be tolerated, not an insurmountable obstacle to companionship (as with Karl Franz Anton PUSINELLI, Jakob Sulzer, and the KIETZ brothers).

CHRIS WALTON

Stewart Spencer, *Wagner Remembered* (London: Faber & Faber, 2000).

Fritzsch, Ernst Wilhelm (b. Lützen [Saxony-Anhalt], 24 Aug. 1840; d. Leipzig, 14 Aug. 1902), German publisher. Fritzsch was the son of a miller and alderman, but, having been taught piano and violin from an early age, decided to study at the conservatory in LEIPZIG. After graduating in 1862 and working as an orchestral musician in Bern (Switzerland), he returned to Leipzig in 1866. That same year, he took over a music store and lending library next to the Gewandhaus. In 1870, Fritzsch established himself as the publisher and editor of the *Musikalisches Wochenblatt*. In it, Wagnerian works and performances were given more space than in most other journals of the time, which soon attracted the composer's attention. Wagner's publication projects and plans in the 1860s had in many cases been unsatisfactory or, regarding his plans for an edition of his collected writings also dating from the mid-1860s, unsuccessful. So, when Fritzsch proved skillful in publishing Wagner's *Beethoven* essay (1870), Wagner also approached him about the collected writings. They came to an agreement in spring 1871, with Wagner returning to his original concept of a chronological (rather than systematic) order of volumes. For his part, Fritzsch made the acquaintance of Friedrich NIETZSCHE, via Wagner, and also became his publisher. Wagner and Fritzsch were on friendly terms, and the composer became a godparent to Fritzsch's son (b. 1872).

During the editorial process, Fritzsch did not have it easy, as Wagner kept nagging the clearly inexperienced publisher not only about the quality of paper, type prints, and luxurious binding, but especially about the delayed proofs and the postponement of release dates. Nevertheless, Fritzsch largely kept within the timeframe, so that the last of nine volumes of Wagner's writings was published in August 1873 with only a month's delay, due in part to Wagner's own changing ideas about the volumes and their contents.

Fritzsch's enterprise declined soon after the last of the nine volumes of Wagner's collected works appeared, in part because of the economic crisis (following a boom) of 1873. He sold the rights to Nietzsche's writings to Ernst Schmeitzner, who (after also publishing the *BAYREUTHER BLÄTTER*) had to sell them back in 1886. But Fritzsch held on to the Wagner rights throughout – even when faced with bankruptcy in 1878/9. Only five years later and half a year after Wagner's death (and with the approval from Bayreuth), Fritzsch published a supplementary tenth volume of Wagner's collected works. Even before his death, Wagner was still occasionally contributing to the *Musikalisches Wochenblatt*, and Fritzsch in turn published some of the composer's minor works, such as *An Webers Grab* or *In das Album der Fürstin M[etternich]*.

SEBASTIAN STAUSS

Christa and Peter Jost, *Richard Wagner und Sein Verleger Ernst Wilhelm Fritzsch* (Tutzing: Schneider, 1997).

Furtwängler, Wilhelm (b. Berlin, 25 Jan. 1886; d. Baden Baden, 30 Nov. 1954), one of the most influential conductors of his generation. Becoming a leading figure in 1922 upon his election to succeed Artur Nikisch as Chief Conductor of the Berlin Philharmonic Orchestra, he led acclaimed performances of the RING at Covent Garden during the Coronation season (1937) and was an important figure in the politicization of Wagner performances in Third Reich Bayreuth, conducting grandiose productions of LOHENGRIN (1936) and Die MEISTER-SINGER (1943/4). After the war, his most significant Wagner performances were given in Italy (*Ring* cycles at La Scala, Milan [1950] and for Rome Radio [1953]). He also made two important studio recordings for EMI: TRISTAN UND ISOLDE (1952) and DIE WALKÜRE (1954).

Furtwängler's place in the pantheon of Wagner interpreters is assured; his contribution to Wagner polemics is less well known. He was a product of the cultured intellectual elite of Wilhelmine Germany and was thoroughly imbued with the philosophical traditions of German idealism as represented in music above all by BEETHOVEN. He thus retained a healthy degree of skepticism toward Wagner whom, as a young musician, he regarded with suspicion (Furtwängler 1980, 30). His first experiences of the *Ring* as recounted in his *Notebooks* were disappointing: "Theatre, nothing but theatre" (91). His later essay, *The Case of Wagner freely after Nietzsche* (1941) modifies his earlier views and is an important contribution to the aesthetic debate begun by NIETZSCHE in 1888 with the publication of *The Case of Wagner*. "Nietzsche allowed himself to become bogged down in arguments relating to details of content. We must take the argument beyond this and discuss it in terms of the real Wagner, Wagner the poet, the dramatist, the composer – in short, of Wagner the artist" (Furtwängler 1991, 96).   ROGER ALLEN

See also PERFORMANCE, CONDUCTING

Wilhelm Furtwängler, *Furtwängler on Music: Essays and Addresses*, trans. and ed. Ronald Taylor (Aldershot: Scolar Press, 1991).

Notebooks (1924–54), trans. Shaun Whiteside, ed. Michael Tanner (London: Quartet Books, 1989).

Wilhelm Furtwängler: Briefe (Wiesbaden: F. A. Brockhaus, 1980).

G

Gaillard, Karl (b. Potsdam, 13 Jan. 1813; d. Berlin, 10 Jan. 1851), journal editor, writer, poet, music critic, music store owner. He was one of the editors of the *Berliner musikalische Zeitung* from its founding in 1844 until its absorption into the *Neue Berliner Musikzeitung* in 1847. Upon witnessing a performance of *Der FLIEGENDE HOLLÄNDER* in Berlin in 1844, Gaillard enthusiastically promoted Wagner in the journal and maintained a friendly CORRESPONDENCE with the composer, as Wagner's sole Berlin supporter during the 1840s.   JAMES DEAVILLE

Gautier, Louise Charlotte Ernestine, better known as Judith Gautier (b. Paris, 24 Aug. 1845; d. Dinard, 26 Dec. 1917). The daughter of author Théophile Gautier and his mistress, the contralto Ernesta Grisi, Judith Gautier was an orientalist who translated Chinese poetry and became famous for her oriental novels. She was not only a leading writer of the Romantic period but also a woman of outstanding beauty. She and her husband, author Catulle MENDÈS, were enthusiastic proponents of Wagner's music in FRANCE. They visited COSIMA and Richard in TRIBSCHEN in 1869 and 1870. However, Gautier's book of memoirs (*Wagner at Home*, 1911) is unreliable, especially after 1876, when, now divorced, she attended the opening of the BAYREUTH FESTIVAL and an intense relationship developed with Wagner. She is credited as being his "muse" for *PARSIFAL*, and translated the text into French. When Cosima discovered their correspondence, Wagner stopped writing to her and Judith's letters to Wagner were destroyed.   EVA RIEGER

Gender. "Gender is a primary field within which or by means of which power is articulated" (Scott 45). Wagner's work participates in the cultural construction of gender. This is particularly so in his concept of LOVE, which cannot be compared to the conventional emotion at the center of many other operas of his contemporaries. For Wagner, "love" was the fundamental human relationship which dominated all else. Living in the nineteenth century, he was convinced that patriarchy was the natural state of society. As he regarded women to be self-sacrificing, this meant that love relationships between the sexes were imbued with a structural inequality. By dividing women into idols of purity (Irene, ELSA, ELISABETH) and those who use their sexual power over men (Venus, KUNDRY) or show independence (ORTRUD), he reflects the ideology of his times. His *RING DES NIBELUNGEN* presents insoluble conflicts between an unblighted, unspoiled nature and the struggle to achieve power. Women were regarded as a part of nature in the nineteenth century, and Wagner equipped them with the special ability of love. Thus, ideally, they live only for their lover rather than striving for power. This fundamentally restricts them to a subordinate position, from which they can only escape by virtue of moral superiority, as BRÜNNHILDE demonstrates. At an early stage, before he had read SCHOPENHAUER, Wagner idolized SIEGFRIED as a heroic character. (Brünnhilde claims in her final praise of him that he is the most honest of men, a great maker of treaties, the best of all heroes.)

The love affair between Brünnhilde and Siegfried provides a glimpse of the utopian potential of a relationship which is built on true love. However, the structural difference between Siegfried and Brünnhilde is remarkable. Siegfried is protected by Wagner from suffering, whereas Brünnhilde is punished for having read her father's thoughts, is betrayed by Siegfried and, responsible for his death, commits suicide. Gender-encoding can also be found in the music: whereas Siegfried has seven motives allotted to him, nearly all of which lead upwards in large intervals or triads, demonstrating his innate nobility and versatile personality as well as his physical strength, Brünnhilde only has the general motive of the Valkyries, which she shares with her sisters. After Siegfried finds her and cuts away her armor with his phallic sword, that motive is abandoned (only to be heard afterwards in combination with her horse as an echo of her past) and she is from then on associated with a love motive. Her metamorphosis into a compassionate woman with no other ambition than to love her partner shows that Wagner "is caught in the very ideology of domination he attempts to criticize" (Corse), as her dependence on her father's law is now exchanged for dependence on her love for Siegfried.

The *Ring* cycle ends with the destruction of the old world of contracts, yet Brünnhilde's singing and the music show a different picture. She sees in Siegfried the great hero, a man who could destroy an order that violates nature. Wagner is more concerned with women's ability to love than with all else, as his choice of text and motives for the ending of the *Ring* proves. By asserting the REDEMPTIVE power of love, Wagner deviates from the conventional method of demonstrating love affairs on the opera stage.

Even in *TRISTAN UND ISOLDE*, this structural imbalance is evident, although the union of the two protagonists is usually regarded as one in which their individual identities fade, apparently melting into each other. However, by betraying his king, Tristan loses all traditionally male-identified qualities such as fame, honor, friendship, gallantry, loyalty, and virtue, essential in the public world. Isolde's nocturnal world is described in traditionally female-identified terms such as desire, bliss, insatiable yearning, craving, wishing, sighing, hoping, and lamenting. The public world of "day" is musically diatonic, often with chordal accompaniment, symbolizing healthy convention, and the rule of (commonsense) paternal law. As in *TANNHÄUSER*, the cult of the night, sexuality, and death are allocated to the female, musically depicted with suspensions, diminished sevenths, haunting chromatics, and harmonic diversity. The male protagonist cannot survive if he dives too deeply into this world which he also desires. Whereas TANNHÄUSER manages to escape, Tristan cannot, because the love potion makes his love for Isolde eternal. Tristan is far more endangered than Isolde, as he not only disobeys his king, but enters into a feminine world of sexuality, thereby losing his honor.

It follows that he welcomes Melot's sword and subsequently curses himself in despair before he dies.

Gender analysis shows that Wagner used traditionally feminine traits for men when describing shabby or weak characters. MIME brings up Siegfried, feeds him, cooks for him, and makes his bed. He lacks the power to forge a sword and later mixes poison – all feminine characteristics which, when associated with a man, make him unlikeable, to say the least. Likewise, when women are attributed with male traits, as the Valkyries (musically shown by upwards soaring triads and large orchestral accompaniment), they can only be likeable if they do not endanger man's essential predominance (as Ortrud does). The Valkyries can be positive, because they are both dependent on WOTAN and asexual. EVA RIEGER

Sandra Corse, *Wagner and the New Consciousness. Language and Love in the "Ring"* (Madison, NJ: Fairleigh Dickinson University Press, 1990).

Eva Rieger, *Leuchtende Liebe, lachender Tod: Richard Wagners Bild der Frau im Spiegel seiner Musik* (Düsseldorf: Artemis & Winkler, 2009).

Joan Wallach Scott, "Gender: A Useful Category of Historical Analysis," in *Gender and the Politics of History* (New York: Columbia University Press, 1988).

German history. As with many of Wagner's ideas, it is all too easy to present, selectively or unwittingly, an assemblage of quotations "proving" a certain line, whereas one might just as readily demonstrate the contrary. Was Wagner "nationalist" or "universalist"? Does he properly belong to "the Right" or to "the Left"? The answer has often been formulated beforehand in essentialist terms, dependent on whether one wishes to convict a monster or absolve a genius. The twentieth-century "German catastrophe" (Friedrich Meinecke) looms ominously over such decisions, not just in sensationalist popular treatments, but in the work of Theodor ADORNO – just as in more general controversies concerning nineteenth-century German history, above all the claim of a *Sonderweg*, or "special [German historical] path," at its most extreme, viewing the Second Reich merely as a prelude to the Third. Unsur-prisingly, Wagner's attitudes towards a German nation, which, for most of his life, lacked concrete political unity except in the past, proved mixed, complex, and subject to development. However, one thread running through his ideas remained historical: the state of the German nation was in many respects to be attributed to its particular history, which remained very much an ongoing tale, awaiting resolution.

1. Napoleon, France, and the Wars of Liberation
2. Saxony and Germany
3. Wagner, Bismarck, and German unification
4. Wagner's writings on German history
5. Wagner and German history after 1883

1. Napoleon, France, and the Wars of Liberation

Thomas Nipperdey opened his history of nineteenth-century Germany with the words "In the beginning was Napoleon." They might also hold the secret to *Wagner*'s history of nineteenth-century Germany. The year 1813 saw the Battle of Leipzig and also Wagner's birth in LEIPZIG. Napoleon's defeat, following his retreat from Russia, hastened the collapse of the First Empire, resulting in a withdrawal of French forces from German soil. Those German states allied to France now joined the opposing coalition. The legend of the Wars of Liberation, in which free Germans rather than their princes vanquished the French foe, began to be told and re-told, memorialized in popular rather than official monuments across a "nation," a concept given new life by the French Revolution. One can trace Franco-German enmity as far back as one wishes, but the Thirty Years War (1618–48) and subsequent French political and cultural hegemony cast lengthy shadows. Eighteenth-century princes might imitate Versailles, but national aspirations pointed away from civilized court and salon to a truer, more honest culture, grounded, for instance, in the forests of the Brothers Grimm – or that from which untainted SIEGFRIED emerges.

"Germany" often had truer existence as an opposing cultural force to France than as a political entity, not least during the 1840 Rhine crisis. Wagner's miserable, homesick sojourn in Paris (1839–42) sharpened that tendency in his case. If meretricious entertainment (MEYERBEER) were French, then true art might be German. A performance of *the* German Romantic opera, WEBER's *Der Freischütz*, made a huge impression at this time: "It seems to be the poem of those Bohemian Woods themselves" (SSD 1:212).

2. Saxony and Germany

Crucial to understanding Wagner, though often overlooked, are his birth and childhood in the Saxon cities of Leipzig and DRESDEN. Transformed by Napoleon from an electorate into a useful allied kingdom in 1806, Saxony had the misfortune to emerge from the Battle of Leipzig on the losing side. Most Saxon troops defected to the allied forces; King Frederick Augustus I was imprisoned; the state itself seemed imperiled, Saxony proving the great loser from the German states at the 1814–15 Congress of Vienna. Though Prussia failed to absorb her entirely, the remnant of the Wettin kingdom held but three-quarters of the territory of the new Prussian province of Saxony.

As Germans, looking askance at recent French cultural and political domination, increasingly wished for some form of national unification, questions arose: in what form and under whose aegis? A German Confederation formed part of the postwar settlement. Would this safeguard individual states' rights, or furnish a battleground upon which Austria and Prussia would fight for supremacy? Would there be popular unification founded upon a national movement, as desired by many of the 1848–9 revolutionaries, Wagner included, or a traditional power-political aggrandizement by one or both of the two great German powers? And where would this leave other German states, members of the so-called "third Germany," such as Saxony and Bavaria? Nineteenth-century history did not lead inevitably to BISMARCK's German Empire which, by excluding Austria, divided rather than unified the German nation. Until the Battle of Königgrätz (1866), there was everything to play for, and the French enemy, now under Napoleon III, remained to be defeated.

When Wagner, then, came to advise LUDWIG II, earlier experience informed his judgment. Wagner remained at best ambivalent concerning the other German princes, yet suspicion of Prussia, a "barracks state" for many other Germans, always formed a crucial part of his outlook. Bismarck secretly made indirect contact with Wagner, attempting unsuccessfully to have him secure Bavaria's neutrality between Prussia and Austria (Salmi 197–9). The contrast, however exaggerated, between Prussian militarism and the cultural achievement of other states (Bavarian, Saxon, etc.) was a mainstay of discourse within those states. "Nationalism" involved many competing strands.

Moreover, though one does not necessarily associate Wagner later in life with Saxony, we find him in Leipzig, publicly and otherwise, more often than we might suspect. NIETZSCHE wrote to his friend Erwin Rohde of attempts to effect a first encounter: Wagner was staying with relatives in Leipzig, unbeknown to the press. When they met, Nietzsche was enchanted by Wagner's reading from *MEIN LEBEN* (My Life, 1865–81) a scene from his Leipzig student days and observed, not for the last time, Wagner's fondness for the local dialect (letter of 9 November 1868).

3. Wagner, Bismarck, and GERMAN UNIFICATION

Wagner and Bismarck were both Germans; neither would have denied that, nor wished to do so. However, particular and particularist identities – both Protestant, but in many respects opposed – counted too. Wagner, on account of his role in the DRESDEN UPRISING, was barred for eleven years even from entering the German Confederation. It would take longer still before he would be permitted to return to Saxony. The grudging nature of the Saxon king's initial concession was mirrored in Wagner's claim – irrespective of whether one believes him – that he felt no emotion upon his return to German soil (12 August 1860). During exile, Wagner had been a German outcast, indeed outlaw, just like *Die WALKÜRE*'s revolutionary SIEGMUND: "I was always outlawed."

When German unification, such as it was, came from above, through Prussian aggrandizement, it is therefore unsurprising that Wagner's initial approbation – again, one should not neglect the power of anti-French sentiment in the FRANCO-PRUSSIAN WAR OF 1870–1, witnessed in *Eine Kapitulation* – soon turned sour. Admiration for the Chancellor's achievement – "an honest Prussian who succeeded in carrying out a diplomatic coup: 'At that time he still knew nothing about the German swindle, he was a complete Prussian'" – is more than balanced a fortnight later by: "That is why I curse Bismarck – for dealing with all these very important problems like a Pomeranian Junker." "Curse" was obliterated by an unknown hand and replaced by "deplore," testimony to family sensitivities concerning Wagnerian German identity (CWD 31 October 1882 and 14 November 1882). Karl Marx could not have been further from the truth, political as well as aesthetic, when answering, at the time of the opening Bayreuth Festival, the persistent question, "What do you think of Wagner?" with the dismissal: highly characteristic of the "New German-Prussian empire-musicians" (letter to Jenny Marx, August/September 1876).

4. Wagner's writings on German history

Wagner's writings expressed such ambivalence and ambiguities. *Die deutsche Oper* (On German Opera, 1834), his first published piece, expresses the wish that German opera were more open to French and Italian influences. However, during his "revolutionary" period, it becomes clear that the universal artwork of the future will transcend mere national style not so much through synthesis as by development of largely Teutonic art. An intriguing and often confusing companion to the aesthetically inclined essays is Die WIBELUNGEN. A conflation of history and myth presents correspondences between, for instance, Emperor Frederick Barbarossa and Siegfried, not only as historical-mythological figures but as revolutionary inspirations. It is hoped that these German heroes, asleep in the Kyffhäuser Mountains, might return, though an original (1848) exhortation for such an awakening was omitted in a subsequent published version, indicative perhaps of Wagner's disillusionment concerning national revolution. Whoever Barbarossa and Siegfried may have been, they were not Prussians.

Subsequent interest in German history tended, in the spirit of Die MEISTERSINGER VON NÜRNBERG, to extol German art at the expense of German politics. A collection of essays written for Ludwig II was published in 1867, its title, Deutsche Kunst und deutsche Politik, reflecting this shift, likewise the contemporary essay, WAS IST DEUTSCH? (unpublished until 1878) asking, "what is German?" Influence and regard of Constantin FRANTZ are marked. Just as HANS SACHS proclaims that holy German art will endure no matter what political calamity might befall the Holy Roman Empire, so Wagner now chooses the forlornly French-periwigged BACH as epitome of the German spirit, his music triumphing despite both his wretched, unrecognized existence as choirmaster and organist, and Germany's catastrophic political fortunes. (Lutheran-Bachian chorales loom large in the Meistersinger score, likewise neo-Bachian counterpoint.) Even when the Germans subsequently attempted democracy and revolution, they merely aped the French; German achievement lay with GOETHE and SCHILLER. Enemies within were as much to blame as those without; what remained of the German spirit was imperiled by an alliterative trinity of Js: jurists, Junkers, and JEWS, elsewhere joined by Jesuits and journalists (SSD 10:61).

5. Wagner and German history after 1883

Subsequent generations have often striven to dissolve these ambiguities, or simply failed to notice them. NATIONAL SOCIALISM provides perhaps the most flagrant example, but it is far from alone. When Thomas MANN challenged hardening nationalist orthodoxy by presenting a more interesting, complex Wagner in a 1933 address, Leiden und Größe Richard Wagners (Sufferings and Greatness of Richard Wagner), he was rebuked in an indignant "Protest by the Richard Wagner City Munich," which spoke on behalf of a "national restoration of Germany ... [having] taken on definite form." Though signatories, including Richard STRAUSS, Hans KNAPPERTSBUSCH, and Hans Pfitzner, were not all National Socialists, this was one example of an effort to dissolve the ambiguities sketched above, or a failure to notice them. Such elision of Wagner with Nazi goals has continued to haunt Wagner scholarship and reception into the twenty-first century. The anti-Reich Wagner of Was ist deutsch? let alone more universalist writings, would surely have objected.

However, performance may herald a degree of hope. Some stage directors, such as Stefan Herheim and Peter Konwitschny – notably both musicians themselves, able to confront Wagner's dramas musically – have grappled more seriously with the multifaceted view of German history evinced by Wagner and his role within it. Exemplary in this respect was Herheim's PARSIFAL at Bayreuth, simultaneously re-telling Wagner's story of Parsifal and the work's reception story. Electrifying was the unfurling of swastikas, long absent from the Festival, as Weimar-*artiste* KLINGSOR cast his spear, but still more of a challenge to New Bayreuth orthodoxy was the reproduction on stage in the third act of WIELAND and WOLFGANG WAGNER's 1951 claim that politics had no place in such a festival. German history always was more interesting than that, as Herheim's contradiction bravely demonstrated. MARK BERRY

Thomas Mann, "Sufferings and Greatness of Richard Wagner," in *Essays of Three Decades*, trans. H. T. Lowe-Porter (New York: Knopf, 1976): 307–71.

Friedrich Meinecke, *The German Catastrophe: Reflections and Recollections*, trans. Sidney B. Fay (Cambridge, MA: Harvard University Press, 1950).

Friedrich Nietzsche, *Selected Letters* (see bibliography).

Thomas Nipperdey, *Deutsche Geschichte*, 3 vols., vol. 1, *1800–1866: Bürgerwelt und starker Staat* (Munich: Beck, 1998).

"Protest der Richard-Wagner-Stadt München," *Münchner Neueste Nachrichten*, 16/17 April 1933, repr. and trans. in Sven Friedrich, "Ambivalenz der Leidenschaft: Thomas Mann und Richard Wagner. Zum 125. Geburtstag Thomas Manns," in *Programmhefte der Bayreuther Festspiele* (2000).

Hannu Salmi, *Die schriftstellerische und politische Tätigkeit Richard Wagners* (see bibliography).

Hans-Ulrich Wehler, *The German Empire, 1871–1918*, trans. Kim Traynor (Oxford: Berg, 1997).

German unification. Unification into a single German state took place formally on 18 January 1871 in the Hall of Mirrors at Versailles in France. Unification at this time and place represented the victory of German armies over the French in the FRANCO-PRUSSIAN WAR and the victory of the Prussian-led version of German unity. Its most notable feature was the exclusion of the Habsburg (Austrian) Empire from influence over German affairs. This ended a decades-long process of debating various kinds and means of German unification. Germans before 1871 had a strong sense of cultural commonality but disagreed about its political implications. The Prussian solution was less democratic and less Catholic than many nationalist activists had envisioned. Liberal nationalists consoled themselves with the constitution and its parliament (the *Reichstag*), and those unhappy about Prussian dominance, Richard Wagner among them, could point to the new Empire's federal structure, a hoped-for guarantee of Germany's diversity. CELIA APPLEGATE

See also NATIONALISM

Germanness / German identity. Throughout Wagner's lifetime and beyond, the question of what constituted "Germanness" was hotly debated, prompting Friedrich NIETZSCHE to remark in 1874 that "It is characteristic of the Germans that the question 'what is German?' never dies out among them" (*Beyond Good and Evil* §224). From the late eighteenth century onwards, artists and intellectuals sought to define the commonalities of the German-speaking people – politically divided into dozens of small states – through a shared language, culture, and history. This search for a German identity gained urgency through the dissolution of the Holy Roman Empire of the German Nation in 1806, and became a widespread, popular movement during the anti-Napoleonic "Wars of Liberation," culminating in the Battle of Leipzig in 1813, the year of Wagner's birth.

The discrepancy between a strong sense of national identity on the one hand and the lack of a politically unified nation-state on the other remained a central issue throughout the nineteenth century and had an impact on Wagner's life at various points. The revolutions of 1848/9, which he vigorously supported (see Dresden uprising), were intended to forge a liberal German state, but failed due to the resistance or indifference of most German rulers. Later, like the majority of his contemporaries, Wagner greeted the German victories in the Franco-Prussian war of 1870–1 and the subsequent foundation of the German Empire with enthusiasm, but was quickly disenchanted with the resulting state which, in his opinion, did not sufficiently address the lack of centralized support for the arts and especially his music festival project. During the last years of his life and after his death, Wagner's music dramas and writings in turn strongly influenced the debate on "Germanness," and although nowadays his works are not a core constituent of German identity, few public debates dispense with them entirely. Because of the many facets of the issue, it will be useful to separate Wagner's own attitude towards (his) German identity from the role he played in contemporary and posthumous discourse.

1. Wagner and German identity
2. German identity and Wagner

1. Wagner and German identity

While Wagner is nowadays mainly remembered for radical political statements, in his ideas about Germanness he concurred with the majority of middle-class Protestant Germans. He differed, however, in the central role he accorded to music and especially the theater in the formation of the German character and society, as witnessed in his proposals for a national theater in Dresden (1849) or for the education of singers for German stages. Like many German intellectuals, he fervently believed in historical continuity rooted in a shared language: "our German language, the only heritage retained intact from our forefathers" (SSD 10:273; PW 6:272), which in turn gave rise to the sagas and myths emanating from "the people" (Volk) and embodying the essence of the German spirit (Herder). In turn those who – in Wagner's opinion – could not partake in this historical-linguistic community were to be excluded from the true art based on folk traditions. Though Wagner's radical anti-Jewish views were not (yet) widely shared at mid-century, he, like many contemporaries, found it easier to define Germanness negatively – that is, in binary opposition to groups construed as hostile, such as the French, Jews, or Jesuits. The positive attributes he ascribed to Germans, summarized for example as "seriousness, depth and unspoiled nature" (PW 3:280; "Ernst, Tiefe und Ursprünglichkeit," SSD 6:279), similarly resonated with contemporary sensibilities, as did the conviction that the Germans were the true heirs of Greek culture and civilization (e.g., *WAS IST DEUTSCH?*, 1865–78).

Throughout his life, from the early *Über deutsches Musikwesen* (1840) to the REGENERATION essays of his last years, Wagner remained convinced that the German spirit had a special ability to integrate and synthesize all cultural influences. Therefore German art and especially music, inspired by the model of BEETHOVEN, had the universal mission to lead all other nations peacefully towards a higher mode of existence: "for the bringer of happiness for the world [the artist] ranks higher than the world conqueror!" (PW 5:126; *denn dem Weltbeglücker gehört der Rang noch vor dem Welteroberer!* SSD 9:126). Wagner's nationalism is therefore not identical with simple patriotism – in fact he normally disdained its popular manifestations (*ÜBER STAAT UND RELIGION* [On State and Religion], 1864) – but an ingrained conviction of the superiority of the German spirit and culture that masks itself as universalism. Wagner's claim that being German meant doing a thing for its own sake was likewise rooted in his conception of good and valuable music: because the Germans excelled in serious study and rejected shallow virtuosity (in *Über deutsches Musikwesen* Wagner opposes self-content German *Hausmusik* with the glamour of international concert platforms), they were the inventors and true owners of instrumental music.

Despite this manifest belief in the superiority of the German character, Wagner frequently points out its shortcomings, again agreeing with popular discourse. Due to their seriousness and thoughtfulness, Germans tend to be phlegmatic, ponderous, and disinclined to take concrete action (e.g., *Beethoven*, *Was ist deutsch?*). The provincialism of German musical life hinders artists to make a nation-wide impact, and the lack of natural singing voices puts the Germans at a disadvantage on the operatic stage (though this makes them turn to the more valuable pursuit of music drama and instrumental music). Wagner frequently praises – and envies – the Italian and French operatic traditions as well as the superior organization of the great opera houses of London and Paris. He is not opposed to foreign models *per se*, but consistently berates his fellow countrymen for their blind emulation and imitation of foreign "fashion" (*Mode*), again a trait that permeates his writings. In contrast to these continuities, the last decade of his life saw a shift towards a conception of German identity that stresses its innate characteristics, thus preparing a more general acceptance of ethnic or racial conceptions of Germanness.

2. German identity and Wagner

Wagner's followers and detractors alike noted his pivotal role in the development of a German operatic tradition early on, but it was not before the last decades of his life that his works were more widely welcomed as the (temporary) solution to the embattled issue of German music. In some circles, the Bayreuth project was considered a national enterprise, and the German WAGNER SOCIETIES propagated support for the festival and frequent "pilgrimages" as a national duty. In many countries, such as the UNITED STATES OF AMERICA, performances of Wagner's works were first organized by native German artists and thus associated with German culture as such. While it is pointless to claim that Wagner's music dramas are inherently "German" (though in the nineteenth century this was widely taken for granted), his operatic figures contributed to pervasive clichés about the "old Teutons" and shaped how many Germans envisaged their ancestors, demonstrated in the "Teutonic" costumes displayed in historical pageants. Although Wagner himself admitted to misgivings about the national role ascribed to Bayreuth (*Das Bühnenfestspielhaus zu Bayreuth*, 1873), after his death the BAYREUTH CIRCLE around COSIMA WAGNER and her supporters emphasized Bayreuth's centrality to the national discourse, for example arguing for Wagner's importance for German culture in the lawsuit concerning the protection of PARSIFAL. Through the BAYREUTHER BLÄTTER and especially the writings of WOLZOGEN, GLASENAPP, and CHAMBERLAIN, Wagner's oeuvre was claimed for right-wing, pessimist, and often ANTI-SEMITIC takes on Germanness. In such circles, one's attitude to Wagner's work was considered a touchstone of Germanness (or lack thereof), as Thomas MANN had to experience after his critical speech of 1933, *Leiden und Größe Richard Wagners*. Conversely, Wagner's works were considered an obvious target – or culprit – when German politics impacted on the performance of German music outside Germany. Notable examples are the boycotts of his works at the beginning of World War I, and in ISRAEL in the aftermath of the Third Reich, when Wagner's music had served propaganda purposes, such as the gala performances of *Meistersinger* on 21 March 1933, the so-called Day of Potsdam, and during the NUREMBERG Rallies. With a changed political climate and declining significance of "high culture" in the public discourse, Wagner's music has largely lost its defining power for contemporary Germanness, although the Wagner family is still of wide media interest and the opening night of the Bayreuth festival is a fixture in the summer calendar of politicians and public figures. At the same time, his works and writings continue to fuel animated scholarly and popular debates about the interrelationship between culture and (national) identity, but now mainly from historical rather than personal or confessional perspectives.   BARBARA EICHNER

Celia Applegate and Pamela Potter, eds., *Music and German National Identity* (University of Chicago Press, 2002).

Hermann Danuser and Herfried Münkler (eds.), *Deutsche Meister – böse Geister? Nationale Selbstfindung in der Musik* (Schliengen: Argos, 2001).

Barbara Eichner, *History in Mighty Sounds: Musical Constructions of German National Identity, 1848–1914* (Woodbridge: Boydell & Brewer, 2012).

Nicholas Vazsonyi, "Marketing German Identity: Richard Wagner's Enterprise," *German Studies Review* 28.2 (May 2005): 327–46.

Gervinus, Georg Gottfried (b. Darmstadt, 20 May 1805; d. Heidelberg, 18 March 1871), liberal historian and journalist. One of the "Göttingen Seven," removed from their teaching posts at the University of Göttingen for political reasons in 1837. Though he was a deputy at the 1848 National Assembly, his moderate liberalism later gave way to radical republicanism, and he abandoned his advocacy of Prussia by espousing federalism. His work, animated by the conviction that historians must serve the future, became eclipsed by the historicist dogma of objectivity. A source for the RING, Gervinus' five-volume history of German literature situated works within their social context. It ended by highlighting signs of artificiality and exhaustion in contemporary culture and by urging Germans to renounce aesthetic inwardness in favor of political action. As Wagner recalls in MEIN LEBEN (My Life, 1865–81), *Die* MEISTERSINGER VON NÜRNBERG was inspired in part by Gervinus' treatment of the MASTERSINGERS and his portrayal of HANS SACHS as a wise ironist embodying German virtues.   MÁRTON DORNBACH

G. G. Gervinus, *Geschichte der poetischen National-Literatur der Deutschen*, 5 vols. (Leipzig: Wilhelm Engelmann, 1846).

John Warrack, *Richard Wagner: "Die Meistersinger von Nürnberg"* (see bibliography).

Gesamtkunstwerk

1. Common parlance
2. Origins and sources
3. Wagner's articulation of the concept

1. Common parlance

The term "Gesamtkunstwerk," or "total work of art," is often used to signify the exalted unification of a variety of art forms into some form of cultural spectacle: a seamless melding that overwhelms spectators' emotions, impedes the possibility of critical thought, and molds a group of individuals into a powerless mass. The concept is often conflated with "WAGNERISM," as if Wagner, who famously promulgated the exalted unification of the arts in two treatises of 1849, *Die* KUNST UND DIE REVOLUTION (Art and Revolution) and *Das* KUNSTWERK DER ZUKUNFT (The Artwork of the Future), held a consistent theoretical view for more than three decades until his death in 1883. Yet Wagner was neither the first to theorize the *Gesamtkunstwerk* nor the first to name it; indeed, he himself used the term in his writings only a few times and in later years strongly disavowed it. The concept is nevertheless associated primarily with his name, owing not only to the nature of his arguments but also to the force of his personality, the vehemence of his claims, their artistic elaboration in his own MUSIC DRAMAS, the construction of a FESTIVAL THEATER in BAYREUTH in which these works could be experienced, and the receptive environment in which his ideas were expressed.

2. Origins and sources

The term *Gesamtkunstwerk* has been traced to 1827, when the Berlin philosopher Karl Friedrich Eusebius Trahndorff described "a striving toward a total work of art [*zu einem Gesamt-Kunstwerke*] on the part of all the arts," citing especially four art forms ("wordsound, music, facial expression, and the art of dance") that together demonstrated and encouraged a broader expression of artistic interrelation oriented fundamentally toward performance (*Aesthetik oder Lehre von der Weltanschauung und Kunst* [Berlin: Maurer, 1827], quoted in Neumann 192–3). More famous philosophical sources for Wagner's understanding of the concept abounded, some consciously chosen and others absorbed more passively in the era of German Romanticism. In a lecture of 1803, Friedrich Wilhelm Joseph SCHELLING had described his vision of a combination of poetry, music, and dance recreating the achievements of ancient drama to produce the hypothetical opera of the future. In the musical sphere, one model for considering the interrelation of the arts was provided by Carl Maria von

WEBER, who in 1817 defined opera as a combination of the arts, their formal distinctions dissolved to create a "new world" (review of E. T. A. Hoffmann, *Undine*).

While eighteenth-century theorists had cautioned against the interrelation of the arts (most famously Gotthold Ephraim Lessing, in his "Laocoon" of 1766), the theme appeared more positively in subsequent decades in the work of a range of German thinkers. Prominent among them were Clemens Brentano, Georg Wilhelm Friedrich HEGEL, E. T. A. HOFFMANN, Friedrich Hölderlin, Novalis, Friedrich SCHILLER, Friedrich von Schlegel, and Ludwig Tieck and Wilhelm Heinrich Wackenroder, most of whose works Wagner read in the years preceding the 1848 Revolution. While Hegel had valued tragic drama above all other art forms, Schlegel had placed the novel at the artistic pinnacle; these precursors inspired Wagner and, more generally, demonstrate the importance of the idea of artistic interrelation to early nineteenth-century German AESTHETICS.

Philosophical and literary sources merged with political ideals to produce an orientation in Wagner's own presentation of the *Gesamtkunstwerk* that was simultaneously aesthetic and political. Arthur SCHOPENHAUER's *Die Welt als Wille und Vorstellung* (The World as Will and Representation), sometimes considered a central source for the composer, in fact first came to Wagner's attention in 1854, more than three decades after its initial publication; this encounter both confirmed the composer's ideas and prompted a shift away from overt and optimistic political radicalism and the sublation of such sympathies within his music dramas.

3. Wagner's articulation of the concept

Wagner's primary articulation of the *Gesamtkunstwerk* appears in *The Artwork of the Future*, written in late 1849 while the composer was exiled in Zurich following his participation in the failed DRESDEN UPRISING that spring. Foregrounding its utopian nature, he situated the concept at the crossroads of a fictionalized past in ANCIENT GREECE and an imagined German nation of the future. He described three sister arts in this model – poetry, music, and DANCE (*Poesie*, *Ton*, and *Tanz*) – which derived from the human faculties of speaking, listening, and looking; forming the central components of Greek drama, these stood for a wider range of creative activity. Other art forms could also be included, the number of participants in this communal effort being less relevant than the fact of their collaboration.

In this utopian proposal of artistic unification, individual art forms would recapture and even surpass the glory they had achieved in ancient Greece. With the rhetoric of democratic reform, Wagner described how, by joining the effort to produce the *Gesamtkunstwerk*, each art form would develop itself more fully, becoming enriched and ennobled by the process: "Not one richly developed faculty of the individual arts will remain unused in the *Gesamtkunstwerk* of the future; precisely in it will each one attain its full value for the first time" (SSD 3:157; PW 1:190). Each art form would become stronger and more independent by struggling to define itself against the others and, ultimately, by working in conjunction with them. Alone, for example, music vainly attempted to reproduce the attributes more properly and effortlessly achieved by other arts; it attained the freedom to be its true self only in association with them. The interrelation of the arts thus provided the necessary conditions for ensuring the autonomy of each; each art form would come into its own by abdicating self-control.

The completion of this unified work of art ultimately required its presentation to an audience; just as the *Gesamtkunstwerk* would unite a variety of art forms, so, too, would individual spectators be brought together to encounter this achievement, becoming a unified audience through their shared aesthetic experience. The *Gesamtkunstwerk* would foster a more direct artistic communication between the creative artist, the work of art, and the audience – all of which would combine to achieve the grand unifying experience at which Wagner believed artistic creation ultimately aimed. Interweaving aesthetic, national, and political aspirations, conflating production and reception, and fundamentally utopian, Wagner's discussion of the communal activity of artistic production and reception that helped create both the total work of art and its audience would prove central to modern aesthetics and artistic practice – often as a counter-model or fuzzy conceptual foil – for well over a century and a half. JULIET KOSS

See also PHILOSOPHY; MUSIC DRAMA

Juliet Koss, *Modernism after Wagner* (Minneapolis: University of Minnesota Press, 2010).
Alfred R. Neumann, "The Earliest Use of the Term 'Gesamtkunstwerk,'" *Philological Quarterly* 35 (1956): 191–3.
Matthew Wilson Smith, *The Total Work of Art* (see bibliography).

Gesellschaft der Freunde von Bayreuth, Die (The Society of the Friends of Bayreuth). This organization was founded on 22 September 1949, shortly after plans were confirmed for revival of the festival, for the primary purpose of providing it with financial support. With its help, the first postwar festival was held in 1951. Since then it has raised over 60 million euros for the preservation of the FESTIVAL THEATER, technical improvements, and production costs. The association, which has its office at the theater, makes no artistic decisions. At the time of the fiftieth postwar festival (2010) its membership stood at over 5,300, including major German corporations. Also, in 2010, it began to publish an annual *Almanach der Freunde von Bayreuth* to replace the formerly extensive tri-lingual Festival program booklets, a tradition abandoned by KATHARINA WAGNER. A glossy overview of current productions, the *Almanach* includes interviews with performers, and essays by scholars and lay experts on aspects of Wagner. DEREK WATSON

See also BAYREUTH FESTIVAL, HISTORY OF

Gesture. See DANCE

Geyer, Johanna. See WAGNER, JOHANNA

Geyer, Ludwig Heinrich Christian (b. Eisleben, 21 Jan. 1779; d. Dresden, 30 Sep. 1821), actor, painter, playwright; officially Richard Wagner's stepfather. Geyer moved to LEIPZIG in 1801, where he became friends with Carl Friedrich Wagner. After Friedrich's death, Geyer married his widow, JOHANNA WAGNER, on 28 August 1814, and moved the family to DRESDEN, where he worked as an actor in the court theater. Richard took Geyer's last name until the age of fourteen. There has been some speculation that Geyer may have been the composer's father.   ALEXIS LUKO

Glasenapp, Carl Friedrich (b. Riga, 3 Oct. 1847; d. Riga, 14 April 1915), German writer on music. Educated in linguistics, philology, and history of art in Dorpat, Glasenapp taught in Pernau from 1873 to 1875 before returning to his home city of RIGA to teach language and literature. He first heard Wagner's music when he was sixteen years old, and began preparing a biography of the composer while still a student. His first Wagner biography was published in two volumes to coincide more or less with the first Bayreuth festival in 1876. Subsequently he was accepted as Wagner's unofficial "house biographer" and given unprecedented access to family documents, including COSIMA WAGNER'S DIARIES. He eventually expanded the biography to six volumes, incorporating an impressive range of documentary material. His researches were clouded by uncritical and hagiographical interpretations, however, which conformed readily to a sanitized view of the composer promoted by the BAYREUTH CIRCLE at the time. The industrious Wagner scholar William Ashton ELLIS began a free translation and expansion of Glasenapp's six-volume biography, elaborating it to such an extent that the project gradually changed into an independent study of Ellis's own (1900–8). Glasenapp himself revised the biography perennially for republication up until his death. He also prepared two monumental reference volumes, the *Wagner-Lexicon* (1883 with Heinrich von Stein) and the *Wagner Enzyklopädie* (1891), both of which consist almost entirely of excerpts from Wagner's prose writings. The semblance of authority and objectivity that Wagner's words lend to these publications conceals the critical fact that the passages are highly selective, the titles of the entries alone betraying xenophobic views far cruder than Wagner might have allowed. For instance, ten separate titles in the *Wagner-Lexicon* contain the word "Volk." The *Enzyklopädie* is less explicit in content, but nonetheless an imposing pair of volumes, placing it firmly in the nationalist camp that would dominate German culture in the first half of the twentieth century.

                                                                    JEREMY COLEMAN

William Ashton Ellis, *Life of Richard Wagner: Being an Authorised English version by William Ashton Ellis of C. F. Glasenapp's "Das Leben Richard Wagner's,"* 6 vols. (London: Kegan Paul, Trench, Trübner & Co., 1900–8).
Carl Friedrich Glasenapp, *Das Leben Richard Wagners in sechs Büchern* (see bibliography).
Richard Wagner's Leben und Wirken (see bibliography).
Wagner-Enzyklopädie: Hauptserscheinungen des Kunst- und Kulturgeschichte im Lichte der Anschauung Richard Wagners, 2 vols. (Leipzig: E. W. Fritzsch, 1891).
Carl Friedrich Glasenapp and Heinrich von Stein, *Wagner-lexicon: Hauptbegriffe der Kunst- und Weltanschauung Richard Wagner's* (Stuttgart: J. G. Cotta, 1883).

Gluck, Christoph Willibald Ritter von (b. Erasbach, 2 July 1714; d. Vienna, 16 Nov. 1787), composer and reformer of eighteenth-century Italian and French opera. After settling in Vienna, he started a fruitful collaboration with the Italian poet Ranieri Calzabigi to reform the conventions of opera seria. They produced three operas together: *Orfeo ed Euridice* (1762), *Alceste* (1767), and *Paride ed Elena* (1770). The principle of this reform was "to restrict music to its true office of serving poetry by means of expression and by following the situations of the story, without interrupting the action or stifling it with a useless superfluity of ornaments" ("Dedication for Alceste" [1769]). In *OPER UND DRAMA* (Opera and Drama, 1851), Wagner claimed that Gluck's reforms were merely a revolt against the "willfulness of the singer" (PW 2:26). Wagner's own reform ideas, however, owe much to Gluck's work.

In 1773, Gluck went to Paris to conduct his *Iphigénie en Aulide* at the Académie Royale de Musique. During his five-year period of activity there, the city became embroiled in a pamphlet war, *la Querelle des Gluckistes et des Piccinnistes*, which involved Gluck's changes to French opera and his competition with Niccolò Piccinni, and which contributed to his image as a revolutionary composer in the nineteenth century. Gluck composed four new works for the Académie – *Iphigénie en Aulide* (1774), *Armide* (1777), *Iphigénie en Tauride* (1779), and *Écho et Narcisse* (1779) – and he revised and adapted *Orfeo* (*Orphée et Euridice*, 1774) and *Alceste* (1775). In 1779, Gluck returned definitively to Vienna, where he participated in the city's musical life on a limited basis. After suffering a series of strokes, he died in 1787.

Most of Gluck's Parisian operas remained in the repertoire of leading German and Austrian opera houses throughout the nineteenth century. Wagner recalled hearing *Iphigénie en Tauride* in Vienna in 1832, remarking that it "bored me as a whole" (ML/E 62). Prior to this performance, Wagner's only other experience with Gluck was through E. T. A. HOFFMANN's writings about the composer, including the novella *Ritter Gluck*.

Shortly after Wagner became Hofkapellmeister in DRESDEN, he conducted *Armide*, on 5 March 1843. In 1847, Wagner revised *Iphigénie en Aulide* for the Dresden stage (WWV 77), providing a new German translation, orchestration, instrumental interludes, and a new coda to the overture for concert performances (SSD 5:111–22; PW 3:153–66; orig. NZfM 40.1 [I July 1854]). In the original ending of the opera, the characters Iphigenia and Achilles prepare for their marriage; Wagner changed the ending, so that the goddess Artemis (Diane, in Gluck's version) orders Iphigenia to serve in her temple at Tauris, thereby creating a link with *Iphigénie en Tauride*.

Throughout his writings, Wagner linked Gluck and Wolfgang Amadeus MOZART as composers trying to transform eighteenth-century opera, but who were "absolutely unable to ignite the fire" for real change (PW 1:153–4). According to Wagner, Gluck's operatic revolution was finally coming to fruition in his own music dramas, a claim music historians in the later nineteenth century such as Franz LISZT and Ludwig NOHL tried to confirm.

ERIC SCHNEEMAN

William Gibbons, "Music of the Future, Music of the Past: *Tannhäuser* and *Alceste* at the Paris Opéra," *19th-Century Music* 33.3 (2010): 232–46.

Ludwig Nohl, *Gluck und Wagner* (Munich: Finsterlin, 1870).

Wolf Gerhard Schmidt, "'Einsamer Leitstern' oder 'machtloser Revolutionär'? Strategische Divergenzen in Richard Wagners Gluck-Rezeption," *Die Musikforschung* 54.3 (2001): 255–74.

Gobineau, (Joseph) Arthur, Comte de (b. Ville d'Avray, 14 July 1816; d. Turin, 13 Oct. 1882), novelist, diplomat, essayist, ethnologist. Protégé of Alexis de Tocqueville, who as Foreign Minister appointed Gobineau his Cabinet Head. Gobineau's diplomatic career took in Germany, Persia, Brazil, and Sweden. In *Essai sur l'inégalité des races humaines* (The Inequality of Human

Races, 1853–5), Gobineau made racial distinction – white (intelligent, courageous), black (sensual, brutal), and yellow (materialistic, feeble) – history's guiding principle. The white race, whether Germanic, ancient Greek, or Indo-European ("Aryan"), enabled civilization. Apparent exceptions, such as China, were ascribed to white influence. Civilization partly depended upon miscegenation, interracial breeding, yet in that dilution lay its downfall. Gobineau was not anti-Semitic; he admired the effort of "white" Jews through Mosaic Law to maintain their "purity." Tocqueville protested that Gobineau's argument was probably wrong and certainly pernicious.

The Wagners briefly met Gobineau in Rome in 1876. There is neither evidence nor likelihood that Wagner read Gobineau or learned of his ideas until after their 1880 meeting in VENICE; Wagner makes no mention of Gobineau's theories before 1880, nor does COSIMA in her diaries. Thus, despite the claims of writers such as Robert Gutman (chapter 13), the possibility of influence upon PARSIFAL, whose poem was essentially completed in 1877, its "orchestral sketch" in 1879, tends towards zero. Gobineau visited WAHNFRIED in 1881 (when Wagner presented his collected writings to "the Count") and in 1882.

"Scientific" fatalism might appeal to Wagner as SCHOPENHAUER's disciple, though not as revolutionary. Gobineau presented not a political program, but an alleged scientific truth, echoing the Enlightenment project of discerning fundamental historical laws, akin to those of Newton – or, as later racists would prefer, Darwin. Gobineau believed in human DEGENERATION; Wagner varied. Whereas Gobineau's driving force was miscegenation, Wagner, in a late echo of Feuerbach, pointed to dietary change. Though Wagner seems to have come to attribute some importance to miscegenation, he introduced a gendered element and retained the prospect of REGENERATION or REDEMPTION through art and RELIGION. Thus, in an 1881 BROWN BOOK entry, possibly intended in part to correct Gobineau's non-racial essay, La Renaissance, he wrote: "In the mingling of races, the blood of the nobler males is ruined by the baser feminine element: the masculine element suffers, character founders, whilst the women gain as much as to take the men's place. (Renaissance). The feminine thus remains owing deliverance: here art – as there in religion; the immaculate Virgin gives birth to the Savior" (BB/E, 23 October 1881). Gobineau denied universality and founded morality upon ontology: Aryan deeds were good because they were performed by Aryans. Wagner, however, desired universal redemption, JEWS included; morality should transform ontology.

Yet, as with Schopenhauer, Wagner found "confirmation" of previously held views, and "corrected" instances in which both writers erred. Cosima describes Wagner, during Gobineau's 1881 visit, as "downright explosive in favor of Christian theories in contrast to racial ones" (CWD 3 June 1881). Correspondence demonstrates mutual respect but with both men standing their intellectual ground. Despite some writers' claims, Gobineau's influence on Wagner was minimal, differences revealing more than correspondences. However, the pan-Germanist Ludwig SCHEMANN and other members of the BAYREUTH CIRCLE founded a Gobineau Association in 1894, transforming Gobineau's pessimism into a racial and political opposition between Aryan and Jew. Cosima dissociated herself and the Festival.

MARK BERRY

See also VEGETARIANISM

Eugène Eric, ed., *Richard et Cosima Wagner/Arthur Gobineau: Correspondance 1880–1882* (Saint-Genouph: Nizet, 2000).

Robert W. Gutman, *Richard Wagner: The Man, His Mind, and His Music* (New York: Harcourt, Brace, & World, 1968).

Ludwig Schemann, *Gobineau. Eine Biographie*, 2 vols. (Strasbourg: Trübner, 1913–16).

Goethe, Johann Wolfgang von (b. Frankfurt am Main, 28 Aug. 1749; d. Weimar, 22 March 1832), German poet, dramatist, and statesman. According to Wagner, the paradigms of German culture were Goethe and BEETHOVEN. In his PROGRAM NOTES for the 1846 Palm Sunday performance of the Ninth Symphony in DRESDEN, he interpreted the music with verses from *Faust*, thereby interweaving elements of these two supreme works of German culture. For Wagner, Goethe's Weimar – or the "Weimar miracle" as he describes it in his essay DEUTSCHE KUNST UND DEUTSCHE POLITIK (German Art and German Politics, 1867/8) – represented the pinnacle of German culture. Wagner almost had the opportunity to repeat this miracle with Franz LISZT. Even though this illusion was shattered in the end, Weimar remained a cultural, political, and aesthetic ideal, and in many respects the model for the organization of the BAYREUTH FESTIVAL. Weimar was proof for the idea that a universal art could be realized and created in a provincial setting that was protected and supported by a royal patron who ensured material and intellectual independence.

Wagner's interest in Goethe is a recurrent and lifelong theme in his writings, letters, and conversations. Even his career as a dramatist began with hints of Goethe. For example, the tragedy *Leubald*, written when Wagner was thirteen, is strongly influenced by *Götz von Berlichingen*. His first attempt at an opera in 1830, which he called a "Shepherd Opera" (WWV 6), was also inspired by a work from Goethe, namely his pastoral play *Die Laune des Verliebten*. When he was arranging Gluck's *Iphigénie en Aulide* for the Royal Saxon Court Theater in 1846/7 (WWV 77), he replaced its *lieto fine* with lyrics set to music – the rapture of *Iphigénie in Taurus* is modeled on Euripides – and in doing so he created a bridge between the opera and Goethe's drama. Wagner's canonical, dramatic works contain innumerable traces of Goethe: whether it be the affinities between *Faust* and TANNHÄUSER, the strong echoes of the final scene of *Faust II* in the love duet of TRISTAN and ISOLDE, the inspiration of Goethe's poem *Hans Sachsens poetische Sendung* for MEISTERSINGER, or lastly the full range of mystical voices from the dome in PARSIFAL praising love and faith that are reminiscent of the last scene of *Faust II*. The constant re-readings of *Faust* are one of the most consistent aspects of Wagner's life, in his later years with particular interest in the "classical Walpurgis night" of Part Two. It is also important to note his own attempts to create music for Goethe's opus summum: *Seven Compositions from Goethe's* Faust (WWV 15; 1831), composed in Goethe's lifetime, and *A FAUST OVERTURE* (WWV 59; 1840/55). In turn, this inspired Franz Liszt's *A Faust Symphony* (1854/7). Both works have an indefinite article in the title to express the fact that the music can only be "an" approximation of Goethe's incommensurable work and never "the" musical version of it. In conversations with COSIMA, Wagner repeatedly linked his concept of MUSIC DRAMA with *Faust*. Again and again, he referred to Goethe's comment about the "barbaric advantages" in his remarks on *Rameaus Neffe* (Rameau's Nephew), which the modern artist cannot abandon. When Cosima once again mentioned this comment in a conversation on 8 February 1872, Wagner remarked: "Yes, *Faust*, the Ninth, Bach's Passion music are barbarian works of that kind, that is to say, works of art which cannot be compared with a Greek Apollo or a Greek tragedy." He also ascribed them to his concept of the "artwork of the future." Wagner was convinced that the parallels between the Ninth Symphony, *Faust*, and music drama show that the absence of perfection in the sense of a Greek aesthetic ideal – the "barbarian" deviation from the normative, classical model – revealed a new, higher, aesthetic model. For Wagner, it was precisely the deviation from the norm with regard to *Faust* and the RING that necessitated a break with theatrical convention. From the start, the tetralogy was intended for performance during a festival, because its demands differed so radically from what standard theater could offer. So, it is no surprise that Wagner believed a unique and unconventional theater – like his Bayreuth FESTIVAL THEATER – was needed for Goethe's *Faust*. This idea of a "Faust-Theater" – developed in Wagner's essay *ÜBER SCHAUSPIELER UND SÄNGER* (Actors and Singers, 1872) and in conversations with Cosima – would break with the tradition of the proscenium stage in favor of a modernized Shakespearean stage, surrounded on all sides by the audience.

The encounter with the final scene of *Faust* was one of Wagner's most profound and aesthetic experiences. Nevertheless, in a letter to Mathilde WESENDONCK, he criticized Goethe for allowing Faust to "completely forget" his love for Gretchen in Part Two:

> so that the real world, the world of classical art, the practical world of industry can now be *acted out* before his highly objective gaze in the greatest possible comfort. As a result I can regard this Faust really only as a missed opportunity; and the opportunity that has been missed is nothing less than the unique chance of salvation and REDEMPTION. This is something that the grey-haired sinner feels for himself in the end, when he seeks, somewhat obviously, to make good his early omission in the final tableau – so extraneous, after death, when it no longer embarrasses him but where it can only be an agreeable experience to let the angel draw him to its breast and no doubt waken him to a new life. (7 APRIL 1858)

Wagner repeated this critique in conversations with Cosima. The main point is the fact that the apotheosis of LOVE in the final scene of *Faust* was presented as a contrived postscript to Faust's earthly existence and does not follow from itself. In the *Ring*, however, the redemption through female love develops immanently out of SIEGFRIED'S tragedy. In Wagner's eyes it is not a transcendental, postmortem postscript, as in *Faust*. Nevertheless, it is love that links the endings of both mythical dramas. This is Thomas MANN's conclusion in his essay *The Eternal Feminine* (1903): "The ending of *Faust* and what the violins sing in the final moments of *GÖTTERDÄMMERUNG* is the same thing, and it is the truth. The eternal feminine draws us onward [*Das Ewig Weibliche zieht uns hinan*]."

DIETER BORCHMEYER
TRANS. HOLLY WERMTER

Dieter Borchmeyer, *Drama and the World of Richard Wagner* (see bibliography).

Golther, Wolfgang (b. Stuttgart, 25 May 1863; d. Rostock, 4 Dec. 1945) was a Germanist particularly known for his writings on NORDIC and Germanic MYTHOLOGY and the German literature of the MIDDLE AGES. Golther held the chair in German philology in Rostock from 1895 until 1935 and was associated with the BAYREUTH CIRCLE from the mid-1880s. On his 75th birthday, he was awarded the GOETHE Medal by Adolf HITLER and made an honorary citizen of BAYREUTH.

Golther was a core contributor to the BAYREUTHER BLÄTTER (35 essays and reviews between 1885 and 1936) and also wrote for the BAYREUTHER FESTSPIELFÜHRER (annually except for 1930) and other music journals. Many of these essays dealt with the roots of Wagner's dramas in German or Norse myth or literature. Other topics explored by Golther include: Faust, SCHILLER, LISZT, and SIEGFRIED WAGNER. In 1913, Golther published a new edition of Wagner's *Gesammelte Schriften*, for which he wrote an introduction, notes, and an index. His biography *Richard Wagner: Leben und Lebenswerk* appeared in 1926.

STEPHEN MCCLATCHIE

See also PROSE WORKS, EDITIONS OF

Annette Hein, *"Es ist viel 'Hitler' in Wagner"* (see bibliography).
Winfried Schüler, *Der Bayreuther Kreis* (see bibliography).

Goodall, Sir Reginald ("Reggie") (b. Lincoln [UK], 13 July 1901; d. Bridge, Kent [UK], 5 May 1990) conductor and coach, and an early collaborator of Benjamin Britten. In June 1945, Goodall conducted the premiere of *Peter Grimes*. He subsequently specialized in Wagner, and established himself in London as a distinguished operatic coach and, later, as a conductor with acclaimed performances of *Die MEISTERSINGER* (1968) sung in English, followed by a complete English *RING* (1973). His highly expressive style was notable for expansive tempi, lyrical phrasing, and beauty of sound.

ROGER ALLEN

See also PERFORMANCE, CONDUCTORS

John Lucas, *Reggie: The Life of Reginald Goodall* (London: Julia MacRae, 1993); paperback repr., *The Genius of Valhalla: The Life of Reginald Goodall* (Woodbridge: Boydell, 2009).

Götterdämmerung (Twilight of the Gods, WWV 86d). "Third Day" (*Dritter Tag*), in three acts with a two-scene prologue, and fourth part of Wagner's *Der RING DES NIBELUNGEN*. Premiered as part of the first performance of the complete *Ring* cycle, 17 August 1876, at the Bayreuth *Festspielhaus*.
1. Genesis, sources, and development
2. Composition
3. Plot summary
4. Musical structure
(Note: For issues applicable to the entire cycle – including publication, first staging, and significant performances – please consult the entry for *Der Ring des Nibelungen*.)

1. Genesis, sources, and development

While it didn't assume its final shape until 1874, *Götterdämmerung* contains the material that motivated Wagner's initial drafts of the *Ring* operas, namely Siegfried's death and the dawning of a new world. This was what first drew Wagner to the Siegfried myth, and it was to be the plot of *Siegfrieds Tod*, the opera that eventually grew into the *Ring* cycle. Wagner first discovered Siegfried as a possible topic for an opera in 1848, though he seems to have mulled over the Siegfried materials ever since 1843, when he encountered them in Jacob Grimm's *Deutsche Mythologie*. In October 1848, Wagner wrote *Die Nibelungensage (Mythus)*, although it was not intended as the prose sketch for the cycle, but rather as background for a single opera of more limited scope. At the suggestion of Eduard DEVRIENT, he expanded that more limited opera, *Siegfrieds Tod*, with a prologue that would spell out some of the background contained in *Die Nibelungensage (Mythus)* and his other prose outlines. This revised libretto was completed in November 1848 (*Zweitschrift des Textbuches*), but Wagner revised his drafts yet a third time in December (the *Drittschrift*), adding Hagen's vision of Alberich, which once again connected the more self-contained *Siegfrieds Tod* to the wider context adumbrated in the prose outlines.

At this point, Wagner abruptly shelved the project in favor of other musical, political, and essayistic endeavors. When the project reemerged (Wagner was by now exiled in SWITZERLAND), it had far outgrown the confines of *Siegfrieds Tod* and included the notion of a dedicated site for the project, ideas that all emerge in Wagner's letters of October and November 1851 to UHLIG (see also FESTIVAL, IDEA OF). Simultaneously, Wagner wrote a *Viertschrift* of the text. As its context widened, *Siegfrieds Tod* underwent a transformation in line with Wagner's course of READING: in 1852, Wagner revised the ending under the influence of Ludwig FEUERBACH's philosophy, giving it an anarchic bent, in which the corrupt rule of the gods is replaced by the rule of humanity. In 1856, he provided another ending written under the influence of his reading of SCHOPENHAUER – here, BRÜNNHILDE interprets the end of the gods as a renunciation of the Will. The ending we hear today is closest to the 1852 ending, though Wagner decided to drop all of the overtly philosophical lines when he set the words to music. The opera did not receive its final title until 1856.

2. Composition

Wagner began the musical composition of *Götterdämmerung* in the fall of 1870, a few months after completing *SIEGFRIED*, and he composed it straight through, completing it on 14 November 1874.

3. Plot summary

Götterdämmerung breaks down into three acts and a two-scene prologue. The opera opens at the Valkyrie rock, where *Siegfried* ended. The three Norns (daughters of ERDA) are weaving the fate of the world: past, present, and future. As they predict that WOTAN will set fire to his palace Valhalla, their rope suddenly ruptures. They disappear and, as the sun rises, SIEGFRIED and

Brünnhilde appear in domestic bliss. Siegfried sets out down the RHINE in search of adventure, but leaves Brünnhilde the Ring as a token of his undying love.

Act I opens on the Gibichung court, where King GUNTHER and his sister GUTRUNE are counseled by HAGEN – the siblings are in search of mates, and Hagen proposes they marry Brünnhilde and Siegfried respectively. Hagen gives Gutrune a potion of forgetting, which he suggests she use on Siegfried – once Siegfried has forgotten his love for Brünnhilde, Gutrune can manipulate him into securing Brünnhilde for Gunther. Soon, Siegfried appears, and the plan is set into motion. Drugged, Siegfried indeed offers to win Brünnhilde for Gunther in exchange for Gutrune's hand. He even swears blood brotherhood with Gunther in a ritual Hagen oversees but does not partake in.

The Valkyrie Waltraute encounters a waiting Brünnhilde on her rock, and attempts to persuade her to help Wotan. Resigned after the shattering of his spear and under the influence of ALBERICH's curse, the god has barricaded himself in Valhalla, which he has filled with the branches of the world-tree, called Yggdrasill (NORDIC MYTHOLOGY). Waltraute asks Brünnhilde for the Ring, but Brünnhilde demurs, regarding it as her marriage ring. After Waltraute has left, Siegfried appears, though, using the *Tarnhelm*, he has given himself the appearance of Gunther. Brünnhilde resists the man she believes to be a stranger, but he overpowers her and takes the Ring.

Act II finds Hagen half-asleep by the Rhine, when his father Alberich appears and exacts from his son the promise to kill Siegfried and secure the Ring for him. Hagen summons Gunther's vassals to greet the returning Siegfried, Gunther, and Brünnhilde. As the Gibichung court prepares for a wedding, Brünnhilde catches sight of Siegfried, who is no longer wearing the *Tarnhelm*. She notices the ring on his finger and accuses him of having slept with her. Siegfried, still under the influence of the memory potion, not only denies this, but swears to that fact on a spear, another oath engineered by Hagen. By the rules of the oath, his life will be forfeit if he has lied. As Siegfried walks off to prepare his own nuptials with Gutrune, Hagen convinces Gunther that only killing Siegfried would expunge Gunther's shame. They are joined in their plot by a furious Brünnhilde, who suggests that Siegfried can be killed by a stab in the back. Brünnhilde and Gunther, joined by Hagen, swear an oath to avenge themselves on Siegfried.

Act III opens once more on the banks of the Rhine. Siegfried has been separated from his hunting party and comes across the Rhinemaidens, who try to convince him to return their gold. He refuses. Reunited with Hagen, Gunther, and the hunting party, Siegfried regales them with the story of his life. At the crucial moment, Hagen uses another potion to restore Siegfried's memory. When Siegfried recalls the discovery of Brünnhilde, Hagen stabs him with a spear. He explains that Siegfried has just confessed to perjuring himself, making his life forfeit. Siegfried dies remembering Brünnhilde and is borne away by Gunther's host. Back at Gunther's court, Gunther blames Hagen for Siegfried's death, and when he resists Hagen's claim to the Ring, Hagen kills him. Before Hagen can take the Ring from the dead Siegfried's hand, Brünnhilde appears. She has the courtiers amass a funeral pyre, and tells the Rhinemaidens that Siegfried's fire will purge the Ring of its curse and that it will be theirs. She sets fire to the pyre and to the Gibichung Hall, then rides her horse Grane into the flames. Wotan, who has received word of events through his ravens, simultaneously sets fire to Valhalla. Hagen drowns trying to secure the Ring for himself. The Rhinemaidens disappear into the river with the Ring and Wotan's fortress burns in the background as the curtain falls.

4. Musical structure

(Note: music examples [CWE #] can be found in Appendix 4: *Leitmotive* in *Der Ring des Nibelungen*.)

The *Ring* concludes with the massive *Götterdämmerung*, which, in its much earlier version as *Siegfrieds Tod*, was to be a stand-alone opera until Wagner decided to precede it with *Der junge Siegfried* in May of 1851. An oddity frequently noted about the work is that, even though Wagner, as he developed the text of the *Ring* between 1848 and 1852, and beyond, made some important changes in the text of *Siegfrieds Tod / Götterdämmerung* (for example, he had trouble deciding how to end it – see above), much of the original text is intact, so that long stretches of the libretto of *Götterdämmerung* remain just as they were in 1848. The opera thus retains a number of vestiges of an older conception of opera, such as a lively, C major chorus of vassals in the middle of Act II, and a rather conventional revenge trio at the end of the same act. And so, paradoxically, in *Götterdämmerung* we have the earliest of the *Ring*'s texts – the libretto was composed *before* Wagner set down his new theories of musical drama in the essays of 1849 and OPER UND DRAMA (Opera and Drama, 1851) – set to the last of its music.

When Wagner began the composition of the opera in 1870, he brought to the old libretto the weight of all the music that he had already composed before it in the cycle – ten to eleven hours, including a staggering array of *Leitmotive*, thematic and harmonic transformations of all sorts, and a tightly knit web of tonal relations. When we experience *Götterdämmerung* in the context of a complete *Ring* cycle in the theater, or even when we hear it knowing all the music that precedes it, we may well experience a sense of unremitting heaviness. To be sure, this heaviness comes in part from the heft of the opera itself: it is a long, ponderous, brutally tragic, motivically and harmonically saturated work, in Wagner's latest, most chromatic style. But, if we know the *Ring*, much of the heaviness is also produced by our own memories – a result not only of our having heard so much of the material many times before, but from the fact that we have accumulated within us the weight of all the emotional and psychological associations that earlier iterations of the material have planted in us.

To these musical ideas already heard are added a number of *Leitmotive* introduced only in *Götterdämmerung*, among which are Hagen (CWE 15), Gutrune (CWE 16), and Siegfried's Death (CWE 17). Three aspects of the usage of these motives – and indeed, motivic usage in the opera in general – are of critical importance. First, even more than in the previous three operas of the *Ring*, it is difficult to specify a particular reference for some motives, and especially misleading to do so. Second, more than ever before, new motives are built out of transformations of old ones, and the musical texture is extraordinarily rich, even saturated, with motives and with dramatically based transformations of motives, all with their associated emotional resonances. And third, even the tiniest fragment – two or three notes – if used with sufficient rhetorical emphasis and with sufficient consistency, can become a motive that projects the most devastating musical effect.

A single example must suffice: the motive designated as "Hagen and the Gibichungs." The motive is the first music we hear in Act I, and there is no question as to whom it initially refers. But it – or at least a part of it – quickly assumes a far broader role, one that eludes a single description. The crucial element in the motive is the descending two-note figure, from a strong beat to a weak beat, usually in triple meter. This figure is ubiquitous in Act I, to the extent that the descending interval can be almost any interval, so long as the rhythmic gesture is present. Early on we hear the names "Ha-gen" and "Grim-hild" sung to it. It recurs many times just after Hagen introduces his plot of betrayal that will follow Siegfried's drinking the potion of forgetfulness. When Gutrune brings the potion to Siegfried in Scene 2, her motive, which sounds here for the first time, uses the same descending figure with the same rhythmic accentuation, but now gentle, and robbed of its gruffness. But there is even more at play. Gutrune's motive is in parallel thirds, and it ranges through (though not in order) a series of descending thirds a third apart; it is thus strongly reminiscent of the Ring motive. At the same time, its first few notes outline the inversion of Siegfried's Horn. Immediately after Siegfried has drunk the potion and he looks at her with desire, we hear her motive again, and it conjures up everything noted thus far: Hagen, the Gibichungs, the potion, the deception, the betrayal of Siegfried, the gentle Gutrune, and in general the now-turned-upside-down world that will prevail in the opera until Hagen gives Siegfried the potion that will restore his memory late in Act III, a few hours hence. Yet there is still more. After Siegfried has violently wrested the Ring from the stunned Brünnhilde at the end of Act I, he draws his sword to place between them as the two-note figure recurs, in octaves, in B minor, *forte*, with heavy accent (Act I mm. 2696ff.), hammering home the violent violation of Brünnhilde – though not without the gentle Gutrune motive, an essential element of the deception, occurring a few measures later in mm. 2709ff., and some final, brutal, B minor octaves to clinch the final cadence of the act.

On a far broader level, *Götterdämmerung* plays a critical role in the large-scale formal and tonal plan of the *Ring*. Its structure of {prologue + three acts} mirrors that of the "Preliminary Evening" of the cycle, *Das RHEINGOLD* {scene at bottom of Rhein with Rheinmaidens and Alberich + 3 scenes with the gods, Valhalla – Nibelheim – Valhalla}. Above all, this 1 + 3 structure is that of the entire cycle, with its "Preliminary Evening" and "Three Days." What is more, *Rheingold* begins in E♭ major, the key of the Rhine and the natural world, and ends in D♭ major, the key of Valhalla and the gods. *Götterdämmerung* also begins in E♭, though in the appropriately darker minor mode, and it also ends in D♭ major. Accordingly the entire cycle also begins in E♭ and ends in D♭. Tonally associative relations are in play in other aspects of the opera as well. The first four chords in the Norns' Scene, and thus in the entire work, are E♭ minor, C♭ major, E♭ minor, D♭ minor: an exact semitone below the chords that articulated the awakening of

Brünnhilde in Act III, Scene 3, of *Siegfried*, and an immediate sign that the C major of the new reign of love at the end of that opera will not last. Like the many *Leitmotive* in the work and the many hundreds of their transformations, the associative keys and chords build up associations every time we hear them, contributing in the process to an experience like no other.

ADRIAN DAUB AND PATRICK MCCRELESS

Gottfried von Strassburg (flourished 1210). Gottfried is not mentioned in contemporary documents, so our knowledge of him is limited to the evidence contained in his masterpiece, the courtly romance *Tristan*. It reveals him to be a highly educated writer with a secure knowledge of French and Latin, of medieval rhetorical gestures, of theology, and of courtly practices. His *Tristan* is acknowledged to be the most brilliant medieval telling of the tragic love story of Tristan and Isolde. In his prologue, he lifts the two lovers above the conventions of courtly love and courtly society, and places them in a supernatural realm of Tristan-Love, an eternal exemplum for the love of noble hearts. Gottfried's version of the story is told as a sublime allegory on love, and, though his work is only seven-eighths complete, the tragic ending with Isolde's *LIEBESTOD* is most certainly also the conclusion of his narrative.

RAY M. WAKEFIELD

Gottfried von Strassburg, *Tristan*, trans. A. T. Hatto, rev. edn. (London: Penguin, 1967).

Grand opera. Among Anglophone writers during the nineteenth and much of the twentieth centuries, the term "grand opera" was often used to describe any sufficiently monumental operatic work, in contradistinction to lighter forms such as operetta. With regard to Wagner, however, it is more appropriate to use the term in its narrower sense, as a specific operatic genre centered at the PARIS OPÉRA and especially popular during the 1830s and 1840s. Although prefigured by works such as Spontini's *Fernand Cortez* and Rossini's *Guillaume Tell*, the genre is most clearly typified by works such as Auber's *La Muette de Portici*, HALÉVY's *La Juive*, and MEYERBEER's *Les Huguenots*. BERLIOZ's *Les Troyens*, VERDI's *Don Carlos*, and Wagner's *RIENZI* may be considered distinct and perhaps idiosyncratic adaptations of the form.

1. The genre
2. Influence on Wagner
3. Wagner on grand opera
4. Critical reception

1. The genre

Grand opera in this sense was typified by a number of salient characteristics. Plot material was usually drawn from events of the late medieval or early modern period, and often hinged upon large-scale political or religious conflict. *Les Huguenots*, to take one example, unfolds against the Huguenot/Catholic rivalry in late sixteenth-century France, and culminates with the St. Bartholomew's Day massacre. With their complex plots and expansive five-act structure, they were typically the longest works in the repertoire of mid-nineteenth-century opera houses, employing large choral and orchestral forces, and often calling for extravagant scenic effects (such as the volcanic eruption in Auber's *La Muette de Portici*). The genre also attracted the most famous and highly paid singers of its day. The most influential librettist for the genre, Eugène Scribe, often centered his plots around moments of *frisson*: sudden shifts designed to elicit extraordinary audience response. A famous example comes in Act v of Halévy's *La Juive*, in which the eponymous heroine is revealed to be the long-lost daughter of the Cardinal Brogni (and is hence Christian rather than Jewish) just at the moment in which she is cast into the fire. The intense dramaturgy and spectacular stage effects helped to make grand operas enormously popular, not only in Paris, but also in other European centers such as Berlin and DRESDEN.

2. Influence on Wagner

The influence of grand opera on Wagner's works was profound. Although the similarity between his *Rienzi* and the operas of Meyerbeer has occasionally been overstated, Wagner's "breakthrough work" is very much in the tradition of the genre. Like *Les Huguenots*, *La Juive*, and *Le Prophète*, *Rienzi* is cast in five acts; like these operas, its plot material derives from late medieval/early modern European history. As in *Les Huguenots* and *La Muette de Portici*, the tragedy of *Rienzi* is as much political as personal. Just as the seventeenth-century Neapolitan revolt against the Spanish viceroy forms an integral part of *La Muette de Portici*, so Wagner's opera narrates an ultimately unsuccessful attempt to overthrow the oligarchical rule of the aristocracy in late fourteenth-century Rome. Like the grand operas of Meyerbeer and Halévy, Wagner's *Rienzi* calls for massed choral and orchestral forces, and includes spectacular stage effects such as the burning of the Capitol (in Act v). In *Eine MITTEILUNG AN MEINE FREUNDE* (A Communication to My Friends), Wagner acknowledged (although in ambivalent terms) that grand opera had served as a musical and dramatic exemplar for *Rienzi*, and the work can certainly be understood – for instance by Hans von BÜLOW – as an intensification of the Meyerbeerian model.

Though completed in Paris, *Rienzi*'s enormously successful world premiere in Dresden helped to pave the way for Wagner's later appointment as Kapellmeister in the city. But despite (or perhaps because of) the significance of grand opera in the development of his career, Wagner never returned to the five-act structure that was so typical of the genre. That is not to say, however, that the styles and conventions of grand opera had no significance for his later works. Scenes such as the "Gathering of the Nobles" from Act II of *TANNHÄUSER* and the elaborate processions with which the finales to *LOHENGRIN* and *Die MEISTERSINGER* begin can certainly be understood within the context of grand opera. Unlike *Rienzi*, the plot material for these later Wagnerian works is not directly political; nevertheless, all three unfold against a specific historical backdrop, and *Meistersinger* is set in the early modern period. Like Rienzi (or John of Leyden, for that matter) some of the characters in these works (e.g., WOLFRAM in *Tannhäuser*, King Henry in *Lohengrin*, HANS SACHS in *Die Meistersinger*) were historical personages. More significant than these (arguably) superficial similarities are the ways in which Wagner evokes the dramaturgy of grand opera in these later works. Most notable in this regard is perhaps the Finale from Act II of *Lohengrin*, in which first ORTRUD and then Telramund interrupt the bridal procession with false claims and accusations. The sense of sudden shock and surprise (more evident perhaps in the music than in the libretto) evokes those moments of *frisson* that were so important to the genre of grand opera. The penultimate scene in Act II of *GÖTTERDÄMMERUNG* – in which a violated BRÜNNHILDE appears at the court of the Gibichungs – also belongs to this tradition. The dramatic swearing of oaths with which this scene climaxes finds parallels in numerous other operas (e.g., the "Sanctification of the Swords" scene from *Les Huguenots*), and in many ways reproduces the dramaturgy of the Parisian grand operas from the 1830s and 1840s. WALTHER's initial refusal to accept membership in the guild of the Mastersingers might also be regarded as one of these moments, when the plot trajectory of the drama undergoes – or rather seems to undergo – an abrupt reversal. In sum, then, while none of Wagner's works apart from *Rienzi* can be placed wholly within the narrow limits of the genre, we may certainly identify points of convergence between Wagner's later oeuvre and the grand operas of Meyerbeer, Halévy, and Auber.

3. Wagner on grand opera

Any consideration of these points of convergence is conditioned by the role that the term "grand opera" has played in the reception of Wagner's works, a role that is often highly polemicized. As is often the case, the reception history of a particular term or topic with regard to these works begins with the composer himself. Wagner's opinion of Parisian grand opera was not wholly negative. In his *Erinnerungen an Auber* (1871), for instance, he acknowledges the musical and dramatic power of *La Muette de Portici*, and although his review of *La Reine de Chypre* (1841) is largely critical, he nevertheless praises many aspects of Halévy's music. Even though Meyerbeer often appears in his writings as a *bête noire*, Wagner clearly admired certain aspects of Meyerbeer's music (in particular, the Raoul/Valentine duet from Act IV of *Les Huguenots*). More typical, however, is Wagner's evaluation of grand opera in the various accounts that he gives of his own stylistic development. In *Eine Mitteilung an meine Freunde*, for instance, Wagner emphasizes the abrupt shift that took place between *Rienzi* and *Der FLIEGENDE HOLLÄNDER*. *Rienzi*, and the genre of grand opera that it represented, was consigned to the prehistory of the MUSIC DRAMA. By virtue of the fact that its foremost practitioner (Meyerbeer) was Jewish, moreover, Wagner's evaluation of grand opera also became bound up with the ANTI-SEMITIC polemic that is such a notorious part of his theoretical work. The continued popularity of *Rienzi* during Wagner's lifetime was thus a source of embarrassment to the composer, and the work has subsequently occupied an awkward place in the Wagnerian canon. In Wagner's prose writing, "grand opera" is typically a term of opprobrium: a shorthand way of referencing all that was superficial, materialistic, inauthentic, and gaudy about nineteenth-century opera: all of those qualities, in other words, against which he wanted to define his own works.

4. Critical reception

Late nineteenth- and early twentieth-century writers frequently reproduced Wagner's own evaluation of grand opera and its influence on and presence within the Wagnerian canon (SHAW's discussion of the RING operas in *The Perfect Wagnerite* is an anomaly). This attitude is especially clear in the work of writers (such as GLASENAPP and CHAMBERLAIN) who were closely allied with the BAYREUTH enterprise, but it also informs (for example) the highly influential work of Ernest NEWMAN. Beginning in the second half of the twentieth century, scholars began to take a more nuanced and less categorical approach to the relationship between Wagner's works and the Parisian grand operas of the 1830s and 1840s. The works of Gutman, Deathridge, and Grey are particularly important to this more recent reevaluation, which has recognized the central role of grand opera in the creation and reception of Wagner's works.   STEPHEN MEYER

John Deathridge, *Wagner's "Rienzi"* (see bibliography).
Thomas S. Grey, "Richard Wagner and the Legacy of French Grand Opera," *The Cambridge Companion to Grand Opera*, ed. David Charlton (Cambridge University Press, 2003): 321–43.
John Warrack, "The Influence of Grand Opéra on Wagner," *Music in Paris in the Eighteen-Thirties*, ed. Peter Bloom (Stuyvesant, NY: Pendragon, 1987): 575–88.

Gravina, Count Biagio (b. Palermo, 5 Dec. 1850; d. Palermo, 14 Sep. 1897), Sicilian noble who courted Blandine von Bülow, Wagner's stepdaughter, in early 1882. Despite concerns about his weak finances, they were married in Bayreuth that August. They visited the Wagners in VENICE in October. Pregnancy prevented their attending Wagner's funeral. Living in Palermo, they had three children. Despairing over money problems, Gravina committed suicide. Descendants include active German musicians.   JOHN W. BARKER

John W. Barker, *Wagner and Venice* (see bibliography)

Greece, ancient. See ANCIENT GREECE

Groß, Adolf von (b. Bamberg, 25 March 1845; d. Bayreuth, 5 June 1931), banker. Groß worked for Friedrich FEUSTEL, whose daughter he married in 1872. Beyond handling Wagner's finances, he became an intimate member of the household. After Wagner's death, Groß worked closely with COSIMA as the children's guardian and as chief financial officer of the BAYREUTH FESTIVAL. He secured continuation of festival funding after the death of Ludwig II (1886), despite Bavarian government opposition. After World War I, tensions with then festival director SIEGFRIED WAGNER forced Groß to step down.

NICHOLAS VAZSONYI

Gunther and Gutrune (bass-baritone and soprano; characters in *Der RING DES NIBELUNGEN*, appearing only in *GÖTTERDÄMMERUNG*). Wagner took the sibling characters Gunther, King of the Gibichungs, and Gutrune from the *Nibelungenlied* (where their names are Gunther and Kriemhild; the name Gudrun is taken from the EDDIC *Lay of Atli*), and, unlike HAGEN, Wagner transposed their characters and motivations more or less directly into the context of the *Ring* cycle. In the *Nibelungenlied*, Gunther resides at Worms with his sister Kriemhild – she will eventually become SIEGFRIED's wife; he lusts after BRÜNNHILD, the Queen of Iceland. The *Ring* presents them as a good deal less active, however: in the *Nibelungenlied* the siblings dupe Siegfried into participating in the intrigue to secure Brünnhilde for Gunther, and Hagen suggests Siegfried's use of the *Tarnhelm* simply as good strategy – the calamitous wooing of Brünnhilde is essentially the siblings' fault. Where the *Nibelungenlied* makes Gunther an active (if at times irresolute) ruler, Wagner presents the Gibichung king as hopelessly out of his depth – none of the evil schemes to which he is party really originates with him. Rather his cupidity and vainglory make him an easy mark for much more capable schemers.

The reasons for this shift in agency have to do with the wider context in which Wagner placed his initial ideas for *Siegfrieds Tod*. Specifically, the pair constitutes the cycle's counterweight to SIEGMUND and SIEGLINDE. They are the cycle's only two "full" humans, and they behave accordingly: their plots, their evil, and their comeuppance all seem banal when measured against the scale of the cycle as a whole. Where *Die WALKÜRE* presented the two Volsung twins' reunion as one dictated by nature and an expression of an attraction that superseded conventional morality, Gunther and Gutrune's togetherness seems altogether pathetic. They appear in most of their scenes together as a couple, because they have the same problem: they need mates, and they are willing to do anything to get them. Their erotic desperation makes them welcome tools of their scheming half-brother Hagen, who is in turn a tool of ALBERICH's revenge. Whereas the Volsungs and their love were an expression of autonomy vis-à-vis outside determination and manipulation, the Gibichungs are entirely at the mercy of forces they do not understand.

There are hints of impotence in the way both siblings, but particularly Gutrune, automatically turn to manipulation to achieve their erotic aims: "How could I bind Siegfried?" Gutrune asks, immediately pointing out that "the world's most lovely women" have surely already approached this champion, and that she would stand no chance against them.

Second, however, Wagner is also intent on contrasting the schoolgirl crush Gutrune has on Siegfried with the much deeper love he presented at the end of *Siegfried*. *Götterdämmerung* gives Gutrune very little to do: even her "courtship" with Siegfried proceeds by glances alone, thanks to the fact that she gives him the love potion after exchanging one word with him. Even her longer scenes with him emphasize that this is no rapturous love-dialogue in the vein of Siegfried's and Brünnhilde's at the conclusion of *Siegfried*: Their longest duet consists merely of her prompts and his narration (of Brünnhilde's capture) – scenes of this nature Wagner usually gives to the lowliest of his characters. Compare this to the ecstatic, and incredibly wordy, dialogue that seals the union of Brünnhilde and Siegfried, or the idyll that opens *Götterdämmerung*.

Gunther makes as weak a musical impression as he does a dramatic one. He lacks the sharply etched melodic and vocal character that is so recognizable in most of the lead roles in the *Ring* (e.g., Wotan, Alberich, Siegfried, Brünnhilde, LOGE, and MIME). Although he sings the first lines in Act I of *Götterdämmerung*, he never really leads, dramatically and musically; he only follows. One might consider the dotted figure that dominates the first few pages of Act I to be his *Leitmotiv*, but an equally plausible interpretation is that the motive represents the Gibichung Hall and the Gibichungs in general.

Similarly, we hear in the orchestra, just before his first entrance, the strong, descending downbeat figure, quarter note (crotchet) – half note (minim), quarter note (crotchet) – half note (minim) (or strong–weak, strong–weak), and this motive is sometimes associated with him (see Appendix 4: *Leitmotive in Der Ring des Nibelungen*; CWE 15). But, as the act progresses, it becomes more clearly attached to Hagen: although Gunther uses it in his very first phrase, on a descending fifth, he uses it to utter the name *Hagen*. Then, as the fierce and rhythmically aggressive motive jabs itself into the texture again and again, Hagen, the villain to which the motive is really attached, reveals his treacherous plan; Gunther, and later Siegfried, simply accede to it.

Oddly, the strong–weak figure also connects Gunther to his sister Gutrune, whose motive also begins with a descending perfect fifth on a downbeat. Her motive, however, is a more extended lyrical melody, and it projects an entirely different expressive character – it is always gentler, more fluid, and more delicately orchestrated (CWE 16). Gutrune's motive portrays her as an innocent and hopeful, but also passive, gullible, and ambitious young woman. The consistency with which she is represented by her motive, in its associative key of G major, has been noted countless times. There are reasons to see her as a deeper character, though – more so than her brother Gunther. Surely it is significant that, in the first scene of the opera, she sings, but her motive is not yet sounded. It occurs only when she has already met Siegfried, well into Act I, Scene 2, and when, at the coaxing of Hagen, she begins to imagine winning him for herself – by magic, if not by her own powers. A simple motive it is not, because it bears curious and intriguing relationships with more important motives: it is a loose inversion of the first notes of Siegfried's Horn Call, and it shares the crucial, strong–weak descending fifth with a rougher motive of Gunther and Hagen. It also proceeds entirely in parallel thirds, thereby connecting it closely to the Ring motive.

ADRIAN DAUB AND PATRICK MCCRELESS

Gurnemanz (bass; character in *PARSIFAL*). The key narrator role in the outer acts of *Parsifal*, Gurnemanz is the most extensive single vocal part in the work. Although Wagner used the spelling "Gurnemans" in his prose draft of 1865, he eventually decided to adopt the form of the name used in his principal source, WOLFRAM VON ESCHENBACH's *Parzival*. Wagner's Gurnemanz is a composite of two figures from Wolfram's epic poem: Gurnemanz, the knight who teaches Parzival about chivalry, and Trevrizent, the hermit who gives him theology instruction on Good Friday. Trevrizent is the primary model for Gurnemanz in Act III.

Another important but far less familiar model for Gurnemanz is found in Wagner's youthful first opera *Die FEEN* (The Fairies) from 1834. Katherine Syer has observed that "Gurnemanz's Act I narration . . . reveals unmistakable roots in the pair of reflective narratives for Gunther and Gernot in Act I of *Die Feen*" (363). Gernot is the companion of Prince Arindal, and witnessed the prince having been drawn into the fairy realm after chasing an enchanting doe into a river; the miraculous animal then transformed into a beautiful yet accursed woman: Princess Ada. When the action of this opera begins, Arindal has been banished from the fairy realm but longs to return to Ada, while

Gernot (aided by Gunther) seeks to free him from his powerful attachment to her. To this end, Gernot relates the tale of the witch Dilnavaz, whose ravishing beauty was revealed to be illusory magic when a piece of her hand was severed. The parallel dramatic construction in *Parsifal* is Gurnemanz's role as companion to AMFORTAS when the unfortunate Grail-King was seduced by the beautiful yet accursed KUNDRY. Gurnemanz's Act I narration gains much weight from his eyewitness account of Amfortas's calamitous experience at Klingsor's castle, the musical setting of which foreshadows PARSIFAL's encounter with Kundry in Act II. At the same time, the dignified gravity of Wagner's Gurnemanz also suggests a parallel to Sarastro in MOZART's *Zauberflöte*.

As the curtain opens in Act I, Gurnemanz appears in a Morning Prayer scene with two squires. This passage is punctuated by musical motives played on stage emanating from the Grail Temple, and otherwise draws on related motives taken from the Prelude and played from the orchestra pit. Throughout the first act up to the entrance into the temple, Gurnemanz plays a central role. It is to Gurnemanz that Kundry presents the balsam for Amfortas. Although Gurnemanz defends Kundry against taunts from the squires, he too harbors doubts about her, asking pointedly: "Where were you wandering, when our lord lost the spear?" The music heard at this juncture is the chromatic coiling figure that Wagner once described as a "tragic, serpentine motive of love's desire which acts destructively, like poison" (CWD 4 June 1878). Soon thereafter, this "serpentine" is developed in the first part of the great narrative, as Gurnemanz describes how Amfortas "is held in thrall [by] a gorgeous, fearsome woman ... in her embraces he lies drunken, he lets the spear fall." At the dropping of the spear (*entsunken*) the rising semitones from Kundry's motive of seduction lead to the dissonant inflection or chromatic contamination (*Schmerzensfigur* or "pain" motive) lodged at the center of the Communion theme, that musical subject related to the Grail that is first heard at the outset of the Prelude. This points to the prehistory of the drama – Kundry's earlier seduction of Amfortas – as the source of these dramatic tensions, while preparing for Parsifal's very different response to Kundry's embrace in the following act.

Although Gurnemanz scolds Parsifal for his misdeed in slaying the swan, he senses potential in the stranger, and decides to lead him to the Grail Temple. "You see my son, here time becomes space," Gurnemanz comments as the two of them approach the castle to the stirring accents of the orchestral transformation music. Nevertheless, Parsifal's outwardly passive response to the Grail ceremony and to Amfortas's anguished predicament cause Gurnemanz to lose patience. To a clipped, parodied version of the Prophecy theme, he declares: "You are then nothing but a fool! Leave, away with you!"

In Act III, Gurnemanz encounters a more experienced, matured Parsifal, but still recognizes him as the one "who once killed the swan." Like Wolfram's Trevrizent, Gurnemanz instructs Parsifal about the spiritual meaning of Good Friday. His first urgent request is for Parsifal to remove his armor, unfitting as it is to carry weapons on this holiest of days. Gurnemanz's response to Parsifal's return of the Holy Spear triggers his narrative about the grim state of the Grail community and the death of Amfortas's father,

Titurel. Later, when Parsifal comments on the beauty of the surrounding meadows, Gurnemanz explains: "That is Good Friday's magic." In response to Parsifal's pessimistic thoughts about Good Friday as the "day of greatest grief," Gurnemanz describes the REDEMPTION of all living things; the scene unfolds as an almost pantheistic vision celebrating a renewed innocence of the natural world. Turning Parsifal's thoughts away from despair, Gurnemanz prepares him for his return to the temple for the long-awaited fulfillment of the Grail's prophecy. Wagner especially disliked the prominence of a healing question posed by Parzival to Anfortas in Wolfram's version of the myth. In Wagner's *Parsifal*, the quest of the hero largely concerns the recovery of the spear, while the Grail represents the still center of the drama. Unlike Amfortas, who recklessly carried the spear into combat against the evil magician Klingsor, Parsifal avoids using it aggressively. He instead employs the spear in the closing ceremony to heal Amfortas's wound, while reuniting spear and Grail in a symbolic integration of male and female principles. This sense of enhanced integration is richly embodied in the closing music of *Parsifal*, in which the motives associated with the Grail are joined into a larger synthesis. Wagner's musical-dramatic strategies often involve a varied recapitulation of earlier events leading to a new outcome. On his decisive return to the Grail Temple, Parsifal shows himself ready at last to relieve Amfortas and assume leadership, owing to the indispensable guidance of Gurnemanz.

WILLIAM KINDERMAN

Katherine Syer, "'*It left me no peace*': From Carlo Gozzi's *La donna serpente* to Wagner's *Parsifal*," *The Musical Quarterly* 94.3 (2011): 325–80.

Gutrune. See GUNTHER AND GUTRUNE

Gutzkow, Karl (b. Berlin, 17 March 1811; d. Sachsenhausen, 16 Dec. 1878), writer. Alongside Heinrich LAUBE and Heinrich HEINE, Gutzkow was a prime protagonist of the so-called YOUNG GERMANY. A student of HEGEL's and Schleiermacher's, he emerged early as a literary star and a political firebrand, and was jailed for several months. In 1847, Gutzkow relocated to DRESDEN to advise the court theater, where his path crossed Wagner's. Initially, the two young men, from the same generation and politically in tune, seem to have felt immense mutual respect, which quickly gave way to an enmity that endured for decades – in 1878, Wagner could still fly into a rage at an approving mention of Gutzkow (CWD 11 April 1878). Competing aesthetic conceptions seem to have been at stake, with Wagner and Gutzkow both seeking to mark their territory. From Wagner's perspective, the dispute concerned matters of aesthetic form: the interaction between opera and drama – Wagner recounts how Gutzkow borrowed the orchestra for "a melodramatic part" in his play *Uriel Acosta*, the results Wagner thought "equally derogatory for the music and the drama" (ML 336–7; ML/E 323).

ADRIAN DAUB

H

Hagen (bass; character in *Der Ring des Nibelungen*, with appearances in *Götterdämmerung*; son of Alberich and half-brother of Gunther). The version of Hagen Wagner presents in the *Ring* is drawn from both the *Lay of Atli* in the *Poetic Edda* and from the *Nibelungenlied*, where he is not just a different character, but has a much more minor role. In the *Atlakvida*, Högni is the brother of Gunnar and a valiant fighter. In later texts from the *Edda*, Högni is seen actually counseling against killing Sigurd, and only the *Nibelungenlied* portrays him as a conflicted accessory in the murder of Siegfried. Wagner instead makes him Siegfried's true antagonist and the ultimate author of his demise. This is also why Wagner's Hagen is only Gunther's half-brother: he is Siegfried's perfect analogue in that both men have one foot in the realm of humans and one in the realm of the supernatural. Siegfried is son to Wotan and a human woman, Hagen the son of Alberich, conceived as the "anti-Siegfried" ("to spite the gods," as Alberich explains to his son in *Götterdämmerung*).

If both Siegfried and Hagen remain plugged in to a wider dramatic frame than the petty Gibichungs, Hagen's understanding of that wider frame is altogether different from Siegfried's, in particular when it comes to the ramifications of Siegfried's destruction of Wotan's spear. If the shattering of the spear of contracts represents the vanishing of an old order, then the beginning of *Götterdämmerung* finds Siegfried in connubial bliss with Brünnhilde, either unaware that it is up to him to create a new order in its place, or unwilling to do so. Hagen, aware of the spear's destruction thanks to his father, immediately grasps the new options this development opens up. Hagen's successes (and even the possibility that his schemes come into being in the first place) are dependent on Siegfried's failings. In elevating Hagen vis-à-vis *Edda* and *Nibelungenlied*, Wagner also creates two antagonists shaped by the same fluid situation, and who each respond in opposite ways to that situation.

The music in *Götterdämmerung* lends the character further gravity still: Wagner's Hagen is one of the great incarnations of evil in opera. His is by far the most developed and dramatic bass role in the *Ring* – the other two, Fafner and Hunding, in the first three operas of the cycle, being far smaller roles. The descending, two-note, strong–weak figure (see Appendix 4: *Leitmotive* in *Der Ring des Nibelungen*; CWE 15) at the beginning of Act I of *Götterdämmerung*, though associated to a degree with Gunther, is primarily Hagen's, reappearing in Scenes 1 and 2 at all the critical moments of decision in his plotting of the double marriage: Gunther's "gepriesen sei Grimhild";

the first sound of Siegfried's horn (here Hagen's descending, strong–weak perfect fifths emerge ominously out of the closing fifth of Siegfried's Horn Call); Gunther's welcoming of Siegfried; GUTRUNE's motive as she welcomes Siegfried (her motive has not one but *two* consecutive descending fifths, suggesting both her innocence and the calamity that her entering into Hagen's plan will bring about); and as Siegfried and Gunther prepare to depart by boat. The brutal two-note trochaic motive even comes into play at the end of the act, when Siegfried pulls his sword after ripping the ring off of Brünnhilde's hand, and in the closing measures; all this is Hagen's work.

Three terrifying moments in *Götterdämmerung* exemplify the overwhelming musical power of evil that Hagen is able to summon. The first is his welcome of Siegfried at the beginning of Act I, Scene 2: the horrific tension between his words ("Heil! Siegfried, theurer Held!") and the motive of the Curse (CWE 9), which accompanies in the trombones, and of which he sings the last three notes, is a central moment in the drama. The second is his summoning of the vassals at the beginning of Act II, Scene 3 – the combined effect of the cowhorn that he blows, the pedal F♯, and his shouted monotone on C, most characteristic when it is preceded by the upper neighbor D♭, is shattering (CWE 17). The harmonic strangeness of the passage gives a hint as to the power of his music: the D♭, because of its rhythmic placement, and because of the incessant repetition of C, sounds like a dissonant neighboring tone resolving to a consonance. Yet what could be more representative of Hagen's twisted mind than the fact that the "resolution" (C over F♯) is a tritone, while the "dissonance" (D♭ over F♯) is a faux-perfect fifth (really a diminished sixth)? Third, this figure – D♭–C over F♯ – becomes the *Leitmotiv* for Siegfried's murder – hence its designation in Appendix 4 as "Siegfried's Death." It recurs many times through the rest of the opera, always with the sinister suggestion of Siegfried's impending death, and it is stated three times successively, along with the Curse, as Hagen spears Siegfried in the back. It never returns.

Much of the interpretation of Hagen has centered on the question of the villain's agency. This is because, unlike Siegfried's response to the absence of established authority, Hagen's opportunism appears so quintessentially "modern." What is more, while Wagner's progressive thickening of the *Ring* plot may have added to the stature of most characters, it also had the (probably unintentional) effect of weakening Hagen's. When he appears, he is not Siegfried's self-styled antipode as in the drafts for *Siegfrieds Tod*, but rather a tool of his father's revenge, four operas in the making. Early interpretations often either glossed over this shift (since it emphasized that Wagner had created a new mythology rather than faithfully bringing back an original Germanic mythology), or they tended to regard the reduced Hagen of *Götterdämmerung* as Wagner's last word on the subject (Shaw). Subsequent generations of critics were instead fascinated by the ambivalence in Hagen's character, his cunning, controlling power that seems to spring from complete submission.   ADRIAN DAUB AND PATRICK MCCRELESS

See: SLEEP /DREAM

George Bernard Shaw, *The Perfect Wagnerite* (see bibliography).

Halévy, Fromental (b. Paris, 27 May 1799; d. Nice, 17 March 1862), French composer of Jewish birth who, along with MEYERBEER, was a leading creator of GRAND OPERA. Halévy's *La Juive* (The Jewess) was one of the most popular operas of the nineteenth century. During his first PARIS sojourn, Wagner completed various arrangements of Halévy's *La Reine de Chypre* (1841), and wrote extensive reviews of the work. Although Wagner is dismissive of the opera's libretto, he gives qualified approval to Halévy's music: praising the decorous grace and simplicity of the vocal lines even while criticizing certain aspects of the ORCHESTRATION. Wagner retained a generally positive view of Halévy, especially of *La Juive*: in *MEIN LEBEN* (My Life, 1865–81) he recounts a cordial meeting with the French composer during his visit to Paris in 1860. In Wagner's later writings, it is Meyerbeer rather than Halévy who is the target of ANTI-SEMITIC aesthetic attacks.   STEPHEN MEYER

See also JEWS

Hans Sachs (bass; character in *Die MEISTERSINGER VON NÜRNBERG*). A nearly ubiquitous presence in an opera about art and love, Sachs somewhat paradoxically is never shown pursuing either one: he does not sing in the song contest – in fact he never formally sings one of his mastersongs – and he renounces any claim on EVA POGNER's affections. But Sachs stage-manages the proceedings all the same, ensuring that the right man wins the song contest and the wrong man humiliates himself. Most of the opera conforms to Sachs's views, and when it does not – for example, the riot ending Act II, or Walther's refusal of the mastersingers' wreath – he is granted two long monologues to set matters straight. Although *Die Meistersinger* is not necessarily about Hans Sachs *per se*, it is about his values and the complicated, even troubling, ways in which those values react to the proceedings around him. It is in this sense that Sachs serves as the opera's *spiritus rector*.

Not surprisingly, then, Sachs is also the character with whom Wagner seemed most to identify. He referred to himself as "Hans Sachs" on multiple occasions, most notably in the latter stretches of his affair with Mathilde WESENDONCK – a relationship whose erotic charge, like that of Sachs and Eva, was ultimately renounced. On a less personal level, however, Wagner's depiction of Sachs as a man of the people, an artist of and for the VOLK, obviously resonated with his own claims about the ideal relationship between artist and his public; if WALTHER VON STOLZING is a Wagnerian, Sachs is Wagner himself.

This view of Sachs as a kind of "people's artist" would not have been possible, of course, if the historical Hans SACHS (1494–1576) did not already come pre-packaged with a long reception history portraying the cobbler-poet in precisely these terms. Primed in part by Lortzing's 1840 opera *Hans Sachs* (based on the eponymous play of 1827 by Johann Ludwig Deinhardstein), and in part by GERVINUS's monumental history of German literature from roughly the same time – both of which stress Sachs as a sympathetic man of the *Volk*, in contrast to aristocratic foppery – Wagner's audiences would have had little trouble placing his character within a familiar constellation linking together Sachs, NUREMBERG, Dürer, and indeed an entire nexus of German Protestant identity. Nor is Sachs's air of melancholy an exclusively Wagnerian accretion; it is already in Gervinus to some degree, just as popular histories portrayed the mature Sachs mourning his status as a widower. (Perhaps because it was well known, this biographical detail does not receive much playtime in the opera, but it can be dealt with effectively on stage; David McVicar's 2011 Glyndebourne production achieved a poignant *coup de théâtre* in having Sachs look at a portrait of his deceased wife during the Act III Prelude.)

What is largely missing from Wagner's Hans Sachs is his confessional politics. Although in Act III the *Volk* greets Sachs's arrival on the meadow by singing part of "Die WITTEMBERGISCHE NACHTIGALL," the historical Hans Sachs's effusive paean to Martin Luther and polemic against the Catholic Church, the excerpt Wagner chose to set is not overtly confrontational. As much as the opera celebrates a storybook image of Protestant cultural patrimony, the explicitly anti-Catholic rhetoric of the real Hans Sachs is mainly absent, as is the intense confessional strife of sixteenth-century Nuremberg more generally. And though he claims, vaguely, that his values are beset by unnamed outside forces (the "falscher welscher Majestät" decried in his final monologue), Wagner's Hans Sachs inhabits a relatively placid world – one in which, if anything, *he* is the dominant authority. As Klaus van den Berg has pointed out, Lortzing's Hans Sachs had to be rescued by the emperor from the clutches of his aristocratic rival; Wagner's Hans Sachs, by contrast, needs no *deus ex machina* – he is already god of his own Nuremberg.

Sachs's closing monologue, praising "Holy German art" as the best defense against foreign domination, has been a sore spot in the opera's postwar reception and production history (see Die MEISTERSINGER VON NÜRNBERG). But Sachs's xenophobic hectoring is not the only problem with his character; his active role in SIXTUS BECKMESSER's humiliation is another. Although an earlier draft of the opera had Sachs actively lying to Beckmesser about the authorship of Walther's poem, Sachs is still duplicitous in the final version. More critical stagings have emphasized this issue, starting with WIELAND WAGNER's 1956 production for Bayreuth, which highlighted Sachs's behavior with menacing lighting. Most recently, Bayreuth's 2007 staging by KATHARINA WAGNER and dramaturge Robert Sollich crystallized the reading of Sachs as a fundamentally malevolent character, not only in his dealings with Beckmesser but more ominously in his demagogic sway over Walther and an adoring *Volk*.

Both Sachs's potential demagoguery and his backroom manipulations are related to the vocal demands of the role. Because Sachs sings more than any other character, yet is often not the immediate focus of attention, he is typically given a *parlando* style of declamation (in opposition to more melodic material assigned Walther, Eva, and Beckmesser) that often wears the singer out long before the opera's end. And precisely because Sachs's closing monologue comes after nearly five hours' worth of declamatory singing, his tirade often results in barking. Indeed, the default casting of the role with a WOTAN (James Morris or Donald McIntyre) has tended to reinforce the sense that Sachs's final address is the curse of an angry old man. And yet hearing younger singers in the role (Wolfgang Brendel or Tómas Tómasson), and especially those trained in *Lieder* or Mozart (Dietrich Fischer-Dieskau or Gerald Finley), leaves the impression of a Sachs whose sermons are rather the birth cries of an energetic German nationalism that was just finding its voice.   RYAN MINOR

Klaus van den Berg, "*Die Meistersinger* as Comedy: The Performative and Social Signification of Genre," in *Wagner's "Meistersinger": Performance, History, Representation*, ed. Nicholas Vazsonyi (see bibliography): 145–64.

Hanslick, Eduard (b. Prague, 11 Sep. 1825; d. Baden [Vienna], 6 Aug. 1904), the most significant music critic of the nineteenth century. Hanslick was famous for his conservative AESTHETICS, outlined in his book *Vom musikalisch-Schönen* (On the Beautiful in Music), and for opposing Wagner and the NEW GERMAN SCHOOL in what became the most important Viennese newspaper of the late nineteenth century, the *Neue Freie Presse*. He was born in Bohemia to German-speaking parents; his mother was Jewish and converted at the time of her marriage to Catholicism. His musical education was supervised primarily by V. Tomášek and he became an excellent pianist. While a law student in Prague and VIENNA, he began writing music reviews. When he was twenty-one, he produced a long (twelve installment), laudatory review of the first production of *TANNHÄUSER* in DRESDEN for the *Wiener Allgemeine Musik-Zeitung*. Here he proclaimed Wagner the next great opera composer. He continued to write criticism after becoming a civil servant. His 1854 book *Vom musikalisch-Schönen* received a great deal of publicity and made him a name in the musical world. Even though it appeared to counter Wagner's and LISZT's arguments that music alone was incomplete and needed the assistance of other art forms, it was not originally written with those composers' ideas in mind. In 1855, Hanslick started writing for *Die Presse* in Vienna, then joined the newly formed *Neue freie Presse* in 1864 and stayed there until his official retirement in 1896, continuing to contribute occasionally until 1900. When a position lecturing at the University on the aesthetics and history of music turned into a professorship in 1861, he was able to give up his day job and devote his time fully to lecturing and criticism.

1. Hanslick's arguments against Wagner's music
2. The Jewish question
3. Hanslick's influence on the reception of Wagner

1. Hanslick's arguments against Wagner's music

When *LOHENGRIN* was finally premiered in Vienna in 1858, Hanslick issued the first of his negative views of Wagner's new musical techniques. In his reviews of subsequent works, he would remain steadfast in his objection to what he saw as a lack of melody and form. Hanslick was familiar with Wagner's writings as well as his music, and they seem to have convinced him all the more to dispute his arguments for the reform of opera. For instance, Hanslick described Wagner's concept of "ENDLESS MELODY" as "formlessness elevated to a principle, a systematized non-music, a melodic nerve fever written out on the five lines of the staff" ("Seine Lehre von der 'unendlichen Melodie,' d.h. die zum Princip erhobene Formlosigkeit, die systematisierte Nicht-musik, das auf 5 Notenlinien verschriebene melodische Nervenfieber" [Hanslick, *Vom musikalisch-Schönen*, x]). He further objected to the use of *LEITMOTIVE* instead of thematic development. On the other hand, he acknowledged that Wagner knew how to stage scenes effectively and gave him credit for visual effect.

2. The Jewish question

Any personal cordiality between Wagner and Hanslick ended at their meeting in 1862 in Vienna at the home of Josef STANDHARTNER, where a reading of a draft of the libretto to *Die MEISTERSINGER VON NÜRNBERG* included the pedantic, untalented (and possibly intended to be Jewish) character "Veit Hanslich," changed later to SIXTUS BECKMESSER. Wagner did not take Hanslick's subsequent negative review of *Die Meistersinger* well and "outed" Hanslick as a Jew in his 1869 edition of *Das Judentum in der Musik*. (This sequence of events, the particulars of which are still disputed, is documented in Grey, "Masters and their Critics.") Although in his memoirs Hanslick denied he was Jewish, Leon Botstein has argued that the *Neue Freie Presse* and the sophisticated, light feuilleton style that Hanslick cultivated were both understood to be Jewish. Indeed, Hanslick's colleagues at the newspaper included Theodor Herzl – the founder of the Zionist movement – and other prominent Jewish writers. According to Wagner and his supporters, everything that undermined the Wagnerian cause could be traced to what they saw as the all-powerful Jewish press and the feuilleton section in particular.

3. Hanslick's influence on the reception of Wagner

Hanslick's reviews of Wagner were translated and reprinted in many other music journals, especially London's *Musical World* and Boston's *Dwight's Journal of Music*. His entertaining and informative reports on the 1876 premiere of the RING at BAYREUTH were a prime source of information on that event. Hanslick also reviewed the Vienna production two years later. But after listing all the performances he attended and all the effort he put into trying to appreciate the *Ring*, Hanslick admitted in the end it was complete torture. The only other opera of Wagner's besides *Tannhäuser* that Hanslick grew to appreciate was *Die Meistersinger*.

In the 1880s, Hanslick wrote about the expansion of the Wagnerian worldview as exemplified in the BAYREUTHER BLÄTTER. He predicted, "The future cultural historian of Germany will be able to give authentic testimony, on the basis of the first five volumes of this journal, how strongly the *delirium tremens* of the Wagnerian intoxication raged among us, and what sort of abnormalities of thought and feeling it occasioned in the 'cultured' people of the time" (Hanslick, "Wagner-Kultus," 339).

Hanslick's critiques were vehemently countered by the Wagnerians. An article on the occasion of Hanslick's 70th birthday in 1895 commented: "Hanslick has always had a strongly aggressive nature and has never made a secret of his convictions, so it is no wonder that with the years not only the honors but also the enemies have increased. None of our music writers has been so frequently, so strongly and so insistently attacked as Hanslick ... within the Wagner literature the number of feuilletons, lead articles, essays, etc. that are directed specifically against Hanslick count in the hundreds" (*Signale für die musikalische Welt* [1895]: 690).

Of all Wagner's critics, Hanslick stands out as the most significant. Since the beginning, their names have been linked together as mortal enemies and stand-ins for the conservative and progressive poles of the second half of the nineteenth century.　　　　　　　　　　　　　　　SANNA PEDERSON

Leon Botstein, "German Jews and Wagner," *Richard Wagner and His World*, ed. Thomas S. Grey (see bibliography): 151–97.

Thomas S. Grey, "Hanslick, Eduard," *Grove Music Online.* www.oxfordmusiconline.com (accessed 16 March 2011).

"Masters and Their Critics: Wagner, Hanslick, Beckmesser, and *Die Meistersinger*," in *Wagner's "Meistersinger"*, ed. Nicholas Vazsonyi (see bibliography): 165–89.

Eduard Hanslick, *Vom musikalisch-Schönen*, 3rd edn. (Leipzig: Rudolph Weigel, 1865).

"Wagner-Kultus," *Aus dem Opernleben der Gegenwart* (Berlin: Allgemeiner Verein für Deutsche Litteratur, 1884).

Health. A topic that recurs throughout Wagner's letters: health good and ill, his endeavors to turn the latter into the former, and the effects that both had on his creativity. With the exception of a possible bout of typhoid fever in PARIS in late 1860 (mentioned briefly in ML 641–2), Wagner remained free from major illnesses throughout his life. This is perhaps a little surprising, given his large number of SEXUAL partners (a consequence of his considerable sex drive, well documented in his letters, and his lifelong belief that masturbation was detrimental to one's health and to be avoided at all costs). While Wagner for decades complained repeatedly of poor health, he nevertheless possessed a constitution robust enough for him to embark on highly taxing, extended mountain HIKING into his early 40s, and his lifelong fondness for going on walks ensured that he always got frequent exercise. He drank alcohol regularly and smoked cigars and cigarettes, but it seems he took none of these to excess, nor can it be proven that they had any significant impact on his health. Wagner did, however, suffer from certain specific complaints for the greater part of his adult life: intestinal problems and all that went with them, from flatulence to diarrhea, constipation and hemorrhoids (it has been suggested that he suffered from irritable bowel syndrome [see Thiery and Seidel]); erysipelas (which S. J. London has suggested was in fact atopic dermatitis, a type of eczema); a hernia on the right-hand side for which he wore a truss from the 1840s onwards; and in his final years heart problems, probably angina pectoris, culminating in his final, fatal heart attack on 13 February 1883. Not surprisingly, given the rudimentary understanding of medical conditions in his day, Wagner's own descriptions of his ailments are also vague. He often refers to his various bowel problems generically as a "stomach catarrh." At other times he also writes of assorted "nervous complaints" (e.g., letters during the summer of 1852) that cannot be more precisely identified. While his CORRESPONDENCE and COSIMA WAGNER'S DIARIES reveal bouts of depression and elation, plus intermittent insomnia, these events seem not to have been of greater intensity than is the norm among much of the population (though his general condition did deteriorate in his final years). Wagner himself all but admitted in *MEIN LEBEN* (My Life, 1865–81; ML 504–5) and his CORRESPONDENCE with Josef STANDHARTNER that various of his illnesses might have been psychosomatic.

Wagner followed the bourgeois trend of his day by taking the waters in order to alleviate his assorted sufferings. He first did so in the summer of 1834 in Teplitz, along with Theodor APEL, though he claimed that it was Apel who needed treatment, whereas he had gone for pleasure (it is also possible that he really went to try and find a cure for his erysipelas, which is first mentioned in his correspondence in February 1834). Wagner sought spa relief for his bowel problems in the mid-1840s, though the creative results in each case outweighed the medicinal benefits: In Teplitz in the summer of 1842 he wrote the prose sketch of *TANNHÄUSER*; his cure there in mid-1843 saw him embark on his studies of German mythology; and his cure in MARIENBAD in 1845 resulted in the prose sketches of both *LOHENGRIN* and *Die MEISTERSINGER*. His doctor in DRESDEN was Karl Franz Anton PUSINELLI, who became a lifelong friend.

The general therapeutic possibilities of water began to interest Wagner while still in Dresden, from drinking it to excess in 1843 to pouring ice-cold buckets over his body in 1844. In PARIS in early 1850 he made the acquaintance of Karl Lindemann, a proponent of hydrotherapy. Thus it should not surprise us that Wagner decided in the summer of 1851 to embark upon a full-scale water cure in Albisbrunn, several miles outside ZURICH, at an institute founded in 1839 by one Christoph Zacharias Wilhelm Brunner (1805–85), who had already treated members of Europe's high society. Wagner's puritanical cure lasted ten weeks and comprised daily baths, daily colonic irrigation, and a diet of water, milk, dry bread, and fruit. There was much walking, but no intellectual pursuits more taxing than card-playing were allowed. Wagner claimed in a letter to Ferdinand HEINE of 20 December 1851 that the cure had given him a "foretaste of complete physical health" and for a while he was a vociferous convert, recommending hydrotherapy to all his friends. In early 1853, Wagner was plagued by stomach problems and hoarseness. His new Zurich doctor, Hans Conrad Rahn-Escher (1802–81), cured him by prescribing nothing more than rest, quiet, keeping warm, and drinking tea. This seems to confirm a psychosomatic element to Wagner's bouts of ill health, as Wagner himself all but admitted in *Mein Leben*. His erysipelas and bowel problems by no means disappeared for good, though a treatment under the less rigid hydrotherapeutic regime of a Dr. Vaillant in Geneva in 1856 seems to have provided longer-lasting relief.

Wagner's doctor in VIENNA in the early 1860s was Josef Standhartner, physician to the imperial family and a man who shared with Rahn-Escher the good sense not to treat an illness where treatment was not absolutely necessary. They too became close and Wagner fell in love with Standhartner's niece, Seraphine Mauro. Wagner continued to consult Standhartner by letter long after he had left Vienna, telling him of his recurrent bowel problems and his enemas, asking advice on the best diet to follow, suggesting that an over-indulgence of "Swiss cheese" might be his problem, and suchlike. Wagner also became friends with the royal physician in MUNICH, Oscar Schanzenbach, and while their relations were dominated by court intrigues in which Schanzenbach seems to have sided with Wagner, the latter also consulted him about his bowels and was prescribed certain "powders" that eased the symptoms (as he claimed in a letter to Hans von BÜLOW of 18 March 1868).

On his first visit to BAYREUTH in April 1871, Wagner took ill with fits of shivering and was treated by Carl Hermann Landgraf (1820–1910), a former student of the universities of Vienna, Prague, and Paris. Wagner was impressed, and so appointed Landgraf as the family doctor after their move to Bayreuth. Wagner's complaints over the next ten years still centered on his bowels, though there was apparently an attack of gout in 1874, a swollen nose in 1879 that turned out to be a return of his erysipelas (for which Landgraf prescribed a steam inhalation of hibiscus tea plus cold compresses), and the usual gamut of headaches, colds, and sniffles. COSIMA's diaries mention various mineral water "cures" that Wagner undertook at home in these last years. In the summer of 1877, Wagner went once more to a spa, this time at Bad Ems, though it gave his bowels little relief.

Cosima first mentions Wagner's tightening of the chest (*Herzbeklemmungen*) on 9 August 1872, though we should beware of interpreting this as an early sign of his later heart problems, as it might just as well have been some form of panic attack (Wagner himself had occasionally mentioned such "Beklemmungen" in his chest long before, e.g., in a letter to Minna of 21 April 1862). However, references to chest pains increase in Cosima's diaries from about 1878 onwards, suggesting that this was indeed the onset of the heart condition that would in the end prove fatal. During his visit to Naples in 1880, Wagner consulted Otto von Schrön (1837–1917), a noted professor at the local university whose work against cholera had brought him the freedom of his adopted city. Another prominent physician was brought onto the scene by Landgraf, who was increasingly concerned about Wagner's bowel problems. He organized a consultation with Wilhelm Olivier Leube (1842–1922), a professor in Erlangen who had specialized and published in the field of stomach and intestinal disorders. Cosima noted after his examination on 26 October 1881 that the results were excellent: "R.'s organs quite healthy; only a strict diet and much fresh air are necessary" – though that diet apparently involved lots of meat and ample quantities of sparkling wine. Wagner further informed LUDWIG II that the doctors advised a milder climate, so he spent the winter with his family in Sicily, where he finished PARSIFAL. Landgraf, however, remained convinced that there was a cardiac problem, and he warned by letter against warm baths and also prescribed daily doses of quinine.

Wagner's chest cramps became increasingly frequent in his last year, and his bowel problems did not leave him. During his last winter in VENICE he was attended by Friedrich Keppler, a German doctor with a practice in the city. A month after Wagner's death on 13 February 1883, Keppler wrote that Wagner had suffered from a dilation of the heart, especially of the right ventricle, an enlarged stomach and a hernia on the right-hand side (the same for which Pusinelli had prescribed a truss many years before) and claimed that the thoracic cavity had become constricted on account of a "massive accumulation of gas in the stomach and intestines." He had treated Wagner by arranging for a suitable truss and by massaging the abdomen regularly, but stated that he had refrained as much as possible from prescribing medicines since Wagner "had the bad habit of taking many strong medicines in higgledy-piggledy fashion, often in large quantities, that had been prescribed to him by various doctors whom he had consulted previously." His death, claimed Keppler, had been caused by a rupture of the right ventricle.

There are certain obvious parallels between Wagner's state of health and his works, the most obvious being the infirm AMFORTAS with his healing baths in *Parsifal*, though we must also recall that the first draft of the RHEINGOLD libretto, in which the waters of the RHINE feature large, was written at the spa of Albisbrunn (whose waters, as it happens, eventually flow into the Rhine several miles downriver), while the close of GÖTTERDÄMMERUNG sees the Rhine break its banks to wash the whole world clean again in a kind of meta-hydrotherapy. And as noted above, it seems that Wagner's spa visits in the 1840s acted as a creative stimulus. It has further been suggested that the Bayreuth Festival itself was modeled on the nineteenth-century sanatorium, each being situated in a place of relative isolation where visitors could enjoy a purifying regimen, here aesthetic, there physical; and as Vogt has observed, the *Festspielhaus* was conceived without a foyer, thus forcing its audiences into the fresh air between the acts.

Perhaps more significantly, Wagner's ill health afforded him the friendship of doctors who proved among his most steadfast, lifelong allies. There is no doubt that close links existed (not least in his own subconscious) between Wagner's muse and his health – in particular, the health of his bowels. Wagner on occasion used the word "Verstopfung" (constipation) to denote both the physical condition and a writer's block. One should again beware of drawing simplistic parallels, though it is noteworthy that in the summer of 1853, when Wagner was wrestling with how to compose the *Ring*, he suffered from prolonged constipation; the sudden flood of inspiration for the *Rheingold* that autumn coincided with a major bout of diarrhea; and in a letter to Karl Lindemann in the following April, he announced in the same breath the completion of *Rheingold* and a "congestion of blood in the anus," implying that the creative and alimentary flows were somehow linked, and that each had ceased again. "The most important thing," Wagner once told Theodor Kirchner in the 1850s, "is that a man has good bowel movements. Everything else isn't so important."   CHRIS WALTON

Friedrich Keppler, foreword to Henry Perl, *Richard Wagner in Venedig: Mosaikbilder aus seinen letzen Lebenstagen* (Augsburg: Gebrüder Reichel, 1883): vi–viii.

S. J. London, "Anton Pusinelli, M.D. (1815–1878): Janissary to a Genius," *New York State Journal of Medicine* 69.12 (1969): 1451–61.

Joachim Thiery and Dietrich Seidel, "'I Feel Only Discontent': Wagner and His Doctors," *Wagner* 16.1 (1995): 3–22.

Matthias Theodor Vogt, "Die Geburt des Festspielgedankens aus dem Geist der Bäderkur," in *Welttheater, Mysterienspiel, rituelles Theater "Vom Himmel durch die Welt zur Hölle,"* ed. Peter Csobádi, Gernot Gruber, et al. (Anif/Salzburg: Ursula Müller-Speiser, 1992): 343–64.

Chris Walton, *Richard Wagner's Zurich* (see bibliography).

Heckel, Emil (b. Mannheim, 22 May 1831; d. Mannheim, 28 March 1908), music publisher and owner of a shop for music instruments in Mannheim. Son of Karl Ferdinand Heckel, who started the business in 1821. Emil worked in the firm from 1857, for a while together with his brother Karl, taking over sole management after his father's death in 1870. Emil was an admirer and eventually a friend of Wagner's, and pioneered the idea of WAGNER

SOCIETIES, founding the first one in Mannheim on 1 June 1871. He was instrumental in the founding of the first BAYREUTH FESTIVAL (1876). His firm issued the first edition of *Die FEEN* (1888). An annotated edition of Emil's CORRESPONDENCE with Wagner merged with his reminiscences of the composer was published by his son, Karl.   NICHOLAS VAZSONYI

Karl Heckel, ed., *Briefe Richard Wagners an Emil Heckel: Zur Entstehungsgeschichte der Bühnenfestspiele in Bayreuth* (Berlin, 1899; Eng. trans. William Ashton Ellis, *Letters of Richard Wagner to Emil Heckel*, 1899).

Hegel, Georg Wilhelm Friedrich (b. Stuttgart, 27 Aug. 1770; d. Berlin, 14 Nov. 1831), philosopher. He studied alongside Friedrich Hölderlin and Friedrich SCHELLING at Tübingen, and taught at Jena, NUREMBERG, and Heidelberg. In 1818, he succeeded Fichte as Professor of Philosophy at the University of Berlin, his lectures attracting students from across Europe. SCHOPENHAUER scheduled clashing Berlin lectures, an empty hall awaiting. A conflict embodied in Wagner's oeuvre had already been dramatized.

As Aristotle stands to Plato, Hegel does to Kant. Hegel's philosophy restored dynamism to neo-Aristotelian ontology (philosophy of being), long encumbered by scholastic encrustation. At the heart of Hegel's system lies the dialectical method, owing something to Fichte and instantiated in *Phenomenology of Spirit*. As Hegel worked on it in Jena in 1806, Napoleon entered the city, the Consul-Emperor a model for Hegel's "world-historical" individual, unconscious vehicle of Spirit itself. Whereas mathematics depend upon the principle of non-contradiction, Hegel's ontology proclaims that contradiction exists, thereby going beyond Kant. Hegel's dialectic places conflict between subject and object at the heart of being, expressed in history – revelation in time of God/Spirit – through alienation of mind. The vulgar Hegelian thesis-antithesis-synthesis has nothing to do with Hegel's philosophy, which posits objects growing through necessary *self*-negation into their full potentiality. Contradiction lies within; it is not applied from without. That radical dialectical method, rather than his accommodationist "positive philosophy" – though one should distinguish Hegel's ideal, rational state from its empirical counterpart – proved Hegel's greatest legacy to radical successors: first "Young" or "Left" Hegelians such as David Friedrich Strauss, Ludwig FEUERBACH, Bruno Bauer, and Max Stirner; thereafter, figures such as Wagner, Mikhail BAKUNIN, Karl Marx, and beyond. Others, for instance, Søren Kierkegaard and Friedrich NIETZSCHE, revolted, yet always consciously.

Wagner's acquaintance with Hegel(-ianism) may be categorized as follows: (i) what we know he read; (ii) what he may have read; (iii) what he learned second-hand from Bakunin, Georg HERWEGH, *et al.*, and the general intellectual milieu; (iv) internal evidence from dramas and writings such as *OPER UND DRAMA* (Opera and Drama, 1851), themselves a significant contribution to Hegelian aesthetics. From the mid-1850s, following Schopenhauer, Wagner tended to disparage Hegel, minimizing his influence. Yet Wagner's works, including *PARSIFAL* and the late "REGENERATION essays," speak differently: Hegel, Schopenhauer, and other intellectual currents coexist, modify, transform, even do battle, no one "side" claiming victory.

Hegel's *Philosophy of History* was the sole work of modern philosophy in Wagner's DRESDEN LIBRARY – though we know that he read others, including Hegel's *Phenomenology*. The latter's identification of transformations in consciousness with historical eras is replicated in Wagner's prose writings, especially those written in ZURICH exile, for instance in Wagner's typology of Greek state and tragedy, Christian negation and subjectivity (cloister replacing amphitheater), and modern imperative to reconciliation (the ARTWORK OF THE FUTURE). Hegelian contradiction forms the material of WOTAN's *WALKÜRE* monologue – better, dialectical self-dialogue. Negation of Wotan's original political intent, a monarchical state under rule of law, is revealed as implicit in that state's founding, yet revelation may only, in Hegelian spirit, come *historically*, contradictions having become apparent. "The owl of Minerva only takes flight at the onset of dusk," that *Dämmerung* prophetic of *Götterdämmerung* itself ("die Eule der Minerva beginnt erst mit der einbrechenden Dämmerung ihren Flug," Hegel, 7:28). Hegel's master-slave dialectic is proclaimed with thoroughgoing anarchism: "Lord through contracts, now am I enslaved to those contracts" (*Walküre* Act II, scene 2).

Hegel was unwilling to negate the principle incarnate in the *Rechtstaat* (legal state); Leftist successors, Wagner and Bakunin amongst them, prepared to forge and to wield swords of anarchism. Wagner's world-historical individual, SIEGFRIED, re-forger of Nothung and rebel without a consciousness, serves both as celebration and as critique not only of the REVOLUTIONS of 1848–9, but of the Hegelianism in which Wagner conceived his chronicle. BRÜNNHILDE's Immolation Scene interpretative wisdom, voiced as ravens take flight, dawns only at twilight: hers, the *Ring*'s, societal. We cannot predict what that final scene's "watchers" will (re-)build, yet one day it will be understood in light of what they saw on the Rhine, Minerva's owl once again spreading its wings.

The conflict between individual and totality inherent in Hegel's system – or, as Marx argued, inherent in its engendering bourgeois capitalism – is, consciously or otherwise, dramatized in verbal and musical terms in Wagner's dramas. Dynamic material resists and yet is molded by demands of the whole: a prelude to subsequent analytical controversies, which might fruitfully be probed for sociopolitical and philosophical meaning – and *vice versa*.   MARK BERRY

See also WAGNER AS ESSAYIST

Mark Berry, "Is it here that Time becomes Space? Hegel, Schopenhauer, History, and Grace in *Parsifal*," *The Wagner Journal* 3.3 (2009): 29–59.

Georg Friedrich Wilhelm Hegel, *Grundlinen der Philosophie des Rechts*, in *Werke*, 20 vols., ed. Eva Moldenhauer and Karl Markus Michel (Frankfurt: Suhrkamp, 1969–72).

Heim, Emilie (b. 1830; d. 1911), soprano, wife of the choral conductor Ignaz Heim. Sang several times under Wagner, including SENTA's Ballad in ZURICH (1853). Sang SIEGLINDE to Wagner's HUNDING and SIEGMUND at the private first performance of the *WALKÜRE* Act I on 26 April 1856 in Zurich, accompanied by Theodor Kirchner, and again to LISZT's accompaniment on 22 October 1856. Wagner wrote that she "possessed

a truly lovely voice and a warm tone ... but was thoroughly unmusical"
(ML 545; ML/E 532).   CHRIS WALTON

Chris Walton, *Richard Wagner's Zurich* (see bibliography).

Heine, Ferdinand (17??–18??), was employed at the DRESDEN Court Theater as both
a comedian and a costume designer, and served in the latter capacity for
RIENZI. He corresponded with Wagner between 1841 and 1868. Described
by Wagner as "staunch ally," Heine and his wife frequently hosted the
impoverished Wagners at dinners consisting mainly of potatoes and herring
(Gregor-Dellin 112, 115). Heine was one of Wagner's consistent correspondents from Dresden.   MARGARET ELEANOR MENNINGER

Martin Gregor-Dellin, *Richard Wagner: His Life, His Work, His Century* (see bibliography).

Heine, Heinrich (b. Düsseldorf, 13 Dec. 1797; d. Paris, 17 Feb. 1856), German-Jewish
poet, essayist, journalist, and literary critic. Of all the contemporary poets and
writers, none left their mark on Wagner's work as much as Heinrich
Heine, though Wagner later denied this because of his ANTI-SEMITIC
resentments. For NIETZSCHE, Heine and Wagner – like HEGEL and
SCHOPENHAUER in philosophy – were evidence of the great de-
provincialization of German culture, which continued Goethe's European
influence.

Heinrich LAUBE introduced Wagner to Heine in PARIS in 1839/40. Around
this time, Wagner set a French translation of Heine's poem *The Two Grenadiers*
to music and dedicated to him a copy of the composition published in the
summer of 1840. This was also to thank Heine for allowing him "to use as the
subject of an opera" a three-act play based on the saga of the FLYING
DUTCHMAN, which appeared in the book *From the Memoirs of Herr von Schnabelewopski*, a fact he describes in his *Autobiographische Skizze* (Autobiographical
Sketch, 1842/3). As he concedes in *MEIN LEBEN* (My Life, 1865–81; ML/E
198), his Paris articles for the *Abend-Zeitung* (Dresden) were inspired by the style
Heine used in his own articles (sometimes on the identical subject matter) that
had appeared in the *Allgemeine Zeitung* (Augsburg). Wagner also adopted this style
for his feuilleton pieces and novellas for the *Revue et gazette musicale* that were
written during his Paris years (1839–42). By the same token, Wagner's feuilletons
allegedly reminded Heine of E. T. A. HOFFMANN's prose. According to Wagner,
Heine said: "Hoffmann himself could not have written such a thing" (ML/E 191).

Wagner's intimate acquaintance with Heine is evident over and again in
conversations and letters, and also in his humorous verses for his birthday on
22 May 1840 or 1841 that parodied a stanza of Heine's *Lyrical Intermezzo* (Im
wunderschönen Monat Mai), "In the wonderful month of May, / When all the
buds were bursting open, / My love burst forth from my heart," which Wagner
adapted with remarkable self-deprecation:

Im wunderschönen Monat Mai	In the wonderful month of May
kroch Richard Wagner aus dem Ei;	crawled Richard Wagner out of the egg;
ihm wünschen, die zumeist ihn lieben	those who love him the most think
er wäre besser drin geblieben	it had been better had he stayed in.

Political and moral opposition to the reactionary state of affairs in Germany united Heine and Wagner during this time. In an article from Paris for the *Abend-Zeitung* (Dresden) dated 6 July 1841, Wagner emphatically takes Heine's side against those who tried to exclude him from German culture: "We see a talent come out of our midst, like few Germany has seen ... Those of our young nation who hold a pen in their hand ... try ... to imitate Heine, because never has a phenomenon, so suddenly evoked and so fully unexpected, controlled its course as compellingly as Heine. And yet we stand back and patiently watch 'how our police drive this magnificent talent from our fatherland' [and that] 'his deep roots, which could nourish us all, are ripped out of the earth.' Yes, we are forcing him to stop being German, whereas he can never become Parisian."

Heine and Wagner's loose friendship admittedly did not continue after the latter left Paris for what Heine in *Lutetia* describes as "the German potato-country." The fact that Heine had little regard for Wagner's later dramatic music principles is clear in the satiric poem "Jung-Katerverein für Poesie-Musik" (Young Tomcats' Society for Poetry-Music, 1854), which alluded to Wagner, though it directly referred to Franz LISZT. Nevertheless, traces of Heine in Wagner's musical-dramatic oeuvre are apparent from *Das LIEBESVERBOT* to *PARSIFAL*. Wagner is indebted to Heine not only for the material for *Der FLIEGENDE HOLLÄNDER*, but also for *TANNHÄUSER*. The prose draft of *Die MEISTERSINGER* (1845) bespeaks Heine's influence; Wagner draws on ideas in Heine's essay "Ende der Kunstperiode" (The End of the Period of Art), and the concept of KUNDRY in *Parsifal* was at the very least inspired by the "she-devil" Herodias in Heine's *Atta Troll* (Caput XIX). Despite this, Wagner increasingly denied Heine's influence, and made disparaging remarks, even going so far as to exclude his name from *Mein Leben* as a source for his stage works, like *Der fliegende Holländer*. He also plays an ambivalent, but important role at the end of Wagner's essay *Das JUDENTUM IN DER MUSIK* (Jewishness in Music, 1850) where, according to Wagner, the Jews, "had brought forth no true poet." Wagner saw Heine in the "office" of a "highly-gifted poet-Jew" to lay bare the unpoetic aridity of MODERNITY, until "he duped himself into a poet, and was rewarded by his versified lies being set to music by our own composers" (PW 5:100). Wagner fails to mention that he himself is one of these composers who had set Heine to music.

Wagner endorsed Heine as long as he could use him for the satirical negation of modern society. However, Wagner rebuffed him when he seemed to become a positive poet. With regard to this polemic relationship, Wagner's attitude is not only negative, but contradictory. His remark to Cosima, which she recounts in a diary entry from 13 December 1869, is telling. Wagner read aloud from a volume of Heine's posthumous writings and concluded: "As always things of incomparable genius, but also very repulsive pieces. 'He is the bad conscience of our time,' R. says, 'the most unedifying and demoralizing matters one can possibly imagine, and yet one feels closer to him than to the whole clique he is so naively exposing'." One could say that Heine is not only the bad conscience of his own time, but of Wagner as well.

DIETER BORCHMEYER
TRANS. HOLLY WERMTER

Dieter Borchmeyer, *Richard Wagner: Ahasvers Wandlungen* (see bibliography): 117–42, 144–96, and esp. 371–91.

Joseph A. Kruse: "Richard Wagners Heine: Zwischen Anregung, Parodie und Verdrängung," in *Heine-Zeit* (Stuttgart: Metzler, 1997): 363–80.

Heldentenor. Although Wagner did not coin this term, it has come to designate the type of voice that possesses the combination of power, stamina, and weight necessary to cope successfully with certain of his heroic tenor roles, particularly TANNHÄUSER, TRISTAN, SIEGMUND, and the two SIEGFRIEDS. With a few notable exceptions in the Siegfrieds, the top note of these roles is a', but Wagner demands considerable power in the top third of the range, and also requires that declamatory passages in the middle and lower registers possess heft and solidity. Thus it is scarcely surprising that some singers in this category either began their careers as baritones before moving to Heldentenor roles (notably Rudolf Berger, Lauritz MELCHIOR, Set Svanholm, and Ramón Vinay) or else possessed a dark timbre (Ludwig Schnorr von CAROLSFELD, Alfred von Bary, Ludwig Suthaus, Hans Hopf, Spas Wenkoff), although true tenors with powerful voices have also been renowned Heldentenors (Albert NIEMANN, Heinrich VOGL, Ernst Kraus, Max LORENZ). DAVID BRECKBILL

Einhard Luther, *Biographie eines Stimmfaches* (see bibliography).

Hendrich, Hermann (b. Heringen, 31 Oct. 1854; d. Schreiberhau, 18 July 1931), German painter. Conceived the *Nibelungenhalle* (Hall of the Nibelungs) located midway up the so-called *Drachenfels* (Dragon's Rock) on the river RHINE just south of Bonn where, according to legend, SIEGFRIED killed the dragon Fafner. The *Nibelungenhalle* was opened in 1913 to mark the centenary of Wagner's birth, and contains twelve paintings by Hendrich on themes from *Der RING DES NIBELUNGEN.* NICHOLAS VAZSONYI

See also WAGNER IN THE VISUAL ARTS

Herder, Johann Gottfried (b. Mohrungen, East Prussia, 25 Aug. 1744; d. Weimar, 18 Dec. 1803), theologian, linguist, literary critic, pioneering ethnologist and cultural anthropologist. Wagner found in Herder's exploration and praise of native cultures and notion of *Volksgeist* (folk spirit), a scholarly basis for his own celebration of Germanness, and his contempt for Germans who "aped" foreign, above all French, fashion. *Siegfrieds Tod* and *Die MEISTERSINGER* in particular are unthinkable without Herder's writings on culture and language. In Herder, Wagner also found his notion of STABREIM, allegedly the essential ingredient of the German tongue.

Nonetheless Herder's theories avoid extreme (Wagnerian) NATIONALISM and metaphysics. Though there are times when Herder can sound xenophobic, he in fact celebrates each culture in its own terms. This leads, for instance, to an admiration for Judaism, tenaciously preserved over the centuries; an admiration which Wagner perversely shares while remaining fiercely ANTI-SEMITIC. Therefore, to see Herder either through Wagner's fanciful eyes or in the light of fascist nationalism distorts his attempt at a practical anthropology and produces a reactionary characterization rejected by his growing number of admirers. BARRY EMSLIE

Herwegh, Georg Friedrich Rudolph Theodor (b. Stuttgart, 31 May 1817; d. Baden Baden, 7 April 1875) and **Emma (née Siegmund)** (b. Berlin, 10 May 1817; d. Paris, 24 March 1904). Georg was a political poet particularly associated with the *Vormärz*-movement in Germany. An outspoken radical democrat, he clashed repeatedly with the retrenched authorities that dominated Germany after the Carlsbad Decrees, and was forced to flee to Switzerland on three separate occasions. He encountered Wagner during the third exile in ZURICH. By the time he met Wagner there, Herwegh's star as a poet was on the wane – he produced little in the way of poetry after his seminal "Gedichte eines Lebendigen" (1841–3), but remained an intellectual fixture among European socialists until his death. In 1843, Georg married Emma Siegmund, who matched his revolutionary fervor and followed him into exile. When Wagner met Georg, the couple was temporarily separated, but before long they brought together a motley group of artists and intellectuals in their Zurich home. While his association with the Herweghs was brief, Wagner retained much affection for the two for the rest of his life – in 1873, two years before Herwegh's death, a short poem amiably describes him as "der demokrat'sche Bänkelsänger" (the minstrel of democracy; SSD 12:374). From the beginning, Wagner's association with Georg was to have an impact on the composer's philosophical development: his first mention of the poet occurs in a letter to UHLIG about the philosopher Ludwig FEUERBACH (January 1850) – Herwegh and Wagner even seem to have schemed to bring the philosopher to Zurich (Walton 53). It was the worldly Herweghs who introduced Wagner to the writings of SCHOPENHAUER. Personally acquainted with Marx, BAKUNIN, George Sand, Lamartine, and many other politically active poets and thinkers, Herwegh became the exiled Wagner's lifeline to a wider world.   ADRIAN DAUB

Chris Walton, *Richard Wagner's Zurich* (see bibliography).

Hiking and walking. When Wagner fled from DRESDEN to SWITZERLAND in 1849, the country was already profiting from tourism. He undertook many tours, either on his own, or together with friends such as Georg HERWEGH, Theodor UHLIG, and Karl RITTER. Central Switzerland was within easy reach by horse carriage, boat, or by foot from ZURICH, where Wagner lived. Being in early manhood, he enjoyed climbing up the Säntis, Faulhorn, Rigi, Grosses Sidelhorn, and Pilatus mountains, some of them more than once. In 1852, he passed through the Alps on his way to ITALY. He did not want to use the main paths, tried to find other unspoiled routes, and sometimes took serious risks. Brunnen on Lake Lucerne was his favorite destination, and Fehr remarks that he planned to erect a provisional theater and perform the *RING* cycle there because of the superb view of the lake and the mountains in the background. In 1853, he took his friends Franz LISZT and Georg Herwegh to Lake Lucerne, and they visited the places mentioned by SCHILLER in his drama *William Tell*. Nature was a source of inspiration for him, and the grandeur of the mountains between Chur and St. Moritz inspired him to create the Valhalla motive with its majestic impetus (it also describes WOTAN), played by thirteen brass instruments (trumpets, trombones, and tubas). He was impressed by the Swiss landscape and his frequent use of the expression "Erhabenheit" (majesty, sublimity), a term used in the eighteenth century to describe the mountains, shows how he judged the scenery aesthetically. Josef HOFF-MANN's stage designs for the first BAYREUTH *Ring* (1876) with their many mountains, cliffs, woods, valleys, and so on, contain much alpine scenery and were obviously influenced by Wagner. In his stage directions, many associations are also made to the Swiss nature scenes he loved so much, and his music often refers to nature: the tempest in *Der FLIEGENDER HOLLÄNDER*, the green summer scenery when TANNHÄUSER escapes from the underworld, the spring night surrounding the lovers in the first act of *Die WALKÜRE*. The nature motives serve to symbolize the inner state of the protagonists. Wagner had planned a long oboe solo for Tannhäuser's escape from the underworld which was probably influenced by shepherds playing the shawm. When his opera *Tannhäuser* was performed in Paris on 3 March 1861, the solo was scorned and Wagner shortened it, however choosing the long version once more for the performance in Vienna in 1875. Wagner lets a shepherd boy play the cor anglais in Act III of *TRISTAN UND ISOLDE*; he would however have preferred the alphorn and the melody is similar to those which Swiss shepherds used to play. These examples show how important nature effects were for him, and how they influenced his music.

When he was forced to leave Munich in 1865, Wagner searched for a house next to Lake Geneva, but could not find the right one. In 1866, he discovered a villa in TRIBSCHEN in Lucerne, where he spent five years before the family moved to Bayreuth. He undertook outings with his family but no longer went on climbing tours. EVA RIEGER

Max Fehr, *Richard Wagners Schweizer Zeit*, 2 vols. (Aarau/Leipzig: Sauerländer, 1934–53).
Eva Rieger and Hiltrud Schroeder, *Richard Wagners Wanderungen in der Schweiz* (Cologne: Böhlau, 2009).

Hiller, Ferdinand (von) (b. Frankfurt, 24 Oct. 1811; d. Cologne, 11 May 1885), German composer, pianist, conductor, and teacher. From an early age, Hiller displayed a pronounced aptitude towards music, and eventually succeeded MENDELSSOHN as director of the LEIPZIG Gewandhaus Orchestra (1843). In 1844, Hiller became closely acquainted with Wagner, who was then Kapellmeister in DRESDEN. In October 1845, Hiller assisted with the premiere of *TANNHÄUSER*. Although Wagner wrote condescendingly of him in his autobiography *MEIN LEBEN* (My Life, 1865–81), other sources, particularly Hiller's own diaries, portray their relationship as being quite cordial; Wagner visited him frequently. Nonetheless, Wagner's opinion of Hiller would eventually sour: in a footnote of his translation of *Eine Mitteilung an meine Freunde* (A Communication to My Friends, 1851), W. A. Ellis notes that the "former friend" who advised Wagner to avoid politics was Hiller. DANIEL SHERIDAN

Ferdinand Hiller, *Mendelssohn: Letters and Recollections* (1874), trans. M. E. von Gehn (New York: Vienna House, 1972).

Hitler, Adolf (b. Braunau [Austria], 20 April 1889; d. Berlin, 30 April 1945). Leader of the National Socialist German Workers' Party (Nazi Party) from 1921 on, Hitler was appointed chancellor of Germany in 1933 and adopted the title of *Führer* (leader) of the newly designated Third Reich (1933–45). His expansionist and racist anti-Semitic policies led to World War II and the annihilation of

European Jewish populations (Holocaust). Hitler committed suicide in a bunker in Berlin as the city fell to Allied troops.

1. Early connections to Wagner (1901–1933)
2. The Führer and Bayreuth (1933–1945)
3. The Wagner-Hitler connection: fact and fiction

1. Early connections to Wagner (1901–1933)

In his autobiographical and ideological tract *Mein Kampf*, Hitler identified a 1901 performance of *LOHENGRIN* in Linz as his first exposure to Wagner and the point at which he became thoroughly enchanted by the composer's works. Years later, when Albert Speer asked why he insisted on opening the Nazi party rallies with the overture from *RIENZI*, Hitler recalled that the performance he had heard in his youth inspired him to "unify" Germany through the annexation of Austria (he also received the autograph full score for his fiftieth birthday and reportedly took it with him to the bunker, where it was most likely destroyed). Otherwise, most other accounts of Hitler's early exposure to Wagner come from the memoir of his friend August Kubizek, but have been largely discredited for their historical inaccuracies and exaggerated accounts of Hitler deriving inspiration for his later political goals from the messages conveyed in Wagner's stage works and prose. If Hitler's exposure to Wagner's ANTI-SEMITISM is questionable, however, there is no doubt that he was very taken with the anti-Semitic writings of Wagner's son-in-law, Houston Stewart CHAMBERLAIN, author of the most influential racially based anti-Semitic treatise of the time, *The Foundations of the Nineteenth Century*. When Hitler visited Bayreuth in 1923, he deeply impressed the ailing Chamberlain and managed to forge friendships with SIEGFRIED and WINIFRED, the latter of whom not only idolized Hitler, but also provided him access to Munich's social elite. Following the 1923 putsch that led to Hitler's imprisonment, Winifred publicly defended him while sending food and paper during his incarceration (contrary to the widespread myth, this was probably not the same paper used to write *Mein Kampf*).

2. The Führer and Bayreuth (1933–1945)

Although Hitler had to distance himself from Bayreuth in the late 1920s to keep the establishment free from politics, within two weeks of becoming chancellor on 30 January 1933, he publicly renewed his ties with the family by celebrating the fiftieth anniversary of Wagner's death in LEIPZIG with Winifred, WOLFGANG, and other political and cultural leaders at his side. Hitler was not only a frequent and honored guest at Bayreuth, as well as a paternal figure to the Wagner children from that point on (their father Siegfried having died in 1930), he also purchased tens of thousands of marks' worth of tickets, provided over 50,000 marks for each new production, and in 1940 provided ten times that amount to keep the festival running. When Winifred wanted to suspend the festival after the war broke out, Hitler averted its closure by designating it an official wartime festival, opening it up to soldiers and workers and thereby facilitating government subsidies.

It is undeniable that Bayreuth became a showpiece for the Third Reich as well as one of Hitler's pet projects, but mythology further embellished the relationship both during and after the Third Reich. Alleged ties between Wagner and Hitler drew not only on NATIONALISM, anti-Semitism, and an ideal of racial purity, but also on Hitler's attraction to Wagnerian heroes (including the supposition that the "Führer" designation was inspired by the conclusion to *Lohengrin*), his modeling the title of *Mein Kampf* on that of Wagner's autobiography MEIN LEBEN (My Life, 1865–81), and even their common VEGETARIANISM and love of DOGS. Rumors of the impending marriage between Hitler and Winifred proliferated, and Winifred's undying devotion to Hitler long after the end of the war was the unsettling centerpiece of Hans-Jürgen SYBERBERG's 1975 film (*Winifred Wagner und die Geschichte des Hauses Wahnfried von 1914–1975*). The next generation of Wagners (specifically Winifred's sons) initially shunned or downplayed that relationship, but their children felt the need to denounce the family's ties with Hitler, inspired by their aunt FRIEDELIND's rejection of the family's complicity.

3. The Wagner-Hitler connection: fact and fiction

The musings of a few influential Germans in exile first planted the seeds that would flower after the war into theories about Wagner's influence over Hitler, the Germans, and the extermination policies of the Nazi government. In 1937–8, exiled philosopher Theodor W. ADORNO wrote an extensive musical and sociological analysis of Wagner's oeuvre and its impact on Germany, proposing that Wagner's *Ring* served the important function of providing the Germans with a much needed mythology, and claiming to read anti-Semitism not only in Wagner's prose but also in several of his musical works. In 1938, Thomas MANN's essay "Brother Hitler" placed the dictator within an artistic lineage that could be traced back to Wagner. The connection was further strengthened when, in November 1938, the Palestine Symphony Orchestra decided to refrain from performing the overture to *Meistersinger* after learning of the *Kristallnacht* pogrom, a decision that later sparked a hotly disputed ban in ISRAEL on playing Wagner's music that has lasted to the present day.

The Wagner-Hitler connection attracted attention once again in 1976, the centennial year of the Bayreuth festival, when Hartmut Zelinsky came out with a daring attempt to trace "Bayreuth idealism" as an unbroken tradition from Wagner down to Hitler and a rich source of inspiration for Hitler's worldview. That same year witnessed the shocking revelations of Winifred Wagner, whose testimony to her undying loyalty to Hitler was cunningly caught on film by director Hans Jürgen Syberberg. More recently, Joachim Köhler's provocatively titled book *Wagner's Hitler* fully explored the possibility of Hitler's fulfillment of Wagner's prophecies, citing Wagner as the chief source for Hitler's anti-Semitism and program of genocide. Yet clear evidence of direct connections between the two is difficult to pin down beyond Hitler's documented enthusiasm for Wagner's music. Dina Porat has painstakingly exposed the futility of seeking concrete connections between Wagner and Hitler, insisting that any of Hitler's inspirations drawn from Wagner were highly personal, limited to his admiration for Wagner's music, and without explicit reference to any of Wagner's published anti-Semitic statements such as Das JUDENTUM IN DER MUSIK (Jewishness in Music, 1850).   PAMELA M. POTTER

See also BAYREUTH FESTIVAL, HISTORY OF THE

Saul Friedländer and Jörn Rüsen, eds., *Richard Wagner im Dritten Reich* (Munich: C. H. Beck, 2000).

Brigitte Hamann, *Winifred Wagner: A Life at the Heart of Hitler's Bayreuth* (see bibliography), chapters 3 and 5: 122–32.

Joachim Köhler, *Wagner's Hitler: The Prophet and His Disciple*, trans. Ronald Taylor (Oxford: Polity, 1999).

Dina Porat, "'Zum Raum wird hier die Zeit': Richard Wagners Bedeutung für Adolf Hitler und die nationalsozialistische Führung," in *Richard Wagner und die Juden*, ed. D. Borchmeyer, et al. (see bibliography): 207–20.

Frederic Spotts, *Hitler and the Power of Aesthetics* (London: Hutchinson, 2002).

Hartmut Zelinsky, *Richard Wagner – ein deutsches Thema* (see bibliography).

Hoffmann, E. T. A. (Ernst Theodor Amadeus) (b. Königsberg, 24 Jan. 1776; d. Berlin, 25 June 1822), author, music critic and composer, and one of the most important exponents of German ROMANTICISM. While he served for much of his life as a member of the Prussian civil service, he began dedicating himself primarily to writing and composing in the early 1800s. His efforts as a composer and dramaturge went largely unrecognized in his time, but his music criticism in LEIPZIG's *Allgemeine Musikalische Zeitung*, especially of the still living Ludwig van BEETHOVEN, was influential. Indeed, Hoffmann inaugurated a descriptive and romanticized style of music criticism, as well as a deeply psychological approach to the discussion of composers, that became a model, also for much of Wagner's prose writings on music and musicians during the Paris period (1839–42), such as the *PILGERFAHRT ZU BEETHOVEN* (Pilgrimage to Beethoven, 1840).

Hoffmann served as musical director in Leipzig, taking up the post in the month and year of Wagner's birth. Hoffmann, a friend of Wagner's uncle, ADOLF, never met young Richard, but his poetic works exercised a tremendous influence over young Wagner's imagination. In his *AUTOBIOGRAPHISCHE SKIZZE* (Autobiographical Sketch, 1842/3) Wagner writes that at the age of sixteen "my reading of Hoffmann inspired my most excited mysticism" (SSD 1:6). Hoffmann's stories seem to have retained their fascination for Wagner even as an adult – he refers to them both in his essays and in his private conversations. Though Wagner tended to underplay this debt, at least the early drafts and completed operas owe much to Hoffmann: in 1842, he embarked on an opera version of *Die Bergwerke zu Falun* (The Mines of Falun, WWV 67) based on Hoffmann's story of the same name. The *MITTEILUNG AN MEINE FREUNDE* (Communication to My Friends, 1851) credits Hoffmann's "The Singers' Contest" (published as part of the *Serapionsbrüder* in 1819–21) as one of the sources for *TANNHÄUSER*. Ultimately, it was Hoffmann's role as a music theorist that had the most enduring impact on Wagner. Not only did his blend of music, criticism, and fiction point ahead to Wagner's own hybrid oeuvre, but the term "musical drama" itself appears in a short story by Hoffmann (Borchmeyer 100).   ADRIAN DAUB

Dieter Borchmeyer, *Das Theater Richard Wagners* (see bibliography).

Hoffmann, Josef (b. Vienna, 22 July 1831; d. Vienna, 31 Jan. 1904), landscape and scenic painter. Hoffmann attracted attention for his designs of *Die Zauberflöte* and *Der Freischütz* in Vienna. After considering the work of many artists, Wagner asked Hoffmann to submit designs for the first production of the RING. He was greatly impressed by the heroic atmosphere of Hoffmann's conception when he saw the sketches in November 1873; with one or two exceptions, they fully complemented his conception of the *Ring*. Hoffmann was to have painted the sets himself, but he fell out with the BRÜCKNER brothers over their translation of his sketches into scenery and left the production team. He was highly critical of the sets, based on his sketches, when he saw the *Ring* in 1876; Wagner did not like them either. No photographs of the sets have survived, but from Hoffmann's sketches it is clear that they were conceived in the Romantic-realistic style of the time.

SIMON WILLIAMS

Oswald Georg Bauer, *Josef Hoffmann: Der Bühnenbildner der ersten Bayreuther Festspiele* (Munich: Deutscher Kunstverlag, 2008).

Hohenlohe, Marie Fürstin zu (b. Woronince [Ukraine], 18 Feb. 1837; d. Stainach [Austria], 21 Jan. 1920), patron of the arts, and the only daughter of Carolyne zu SAYN-WITTGENSTEIN and Prince Nicholas Sayn-Wittgenstein-Berleburg-Ludwigsburg. Following her mother's relationship with Franz LISZT, she grew up within the rich artistic circle at Weimar from 1849. Gatherings at the Altenburg brought her into frequent contact with WAGNER, BERLIOZ, Hebbel, and Kaulbach, among others. Wagner describes her often in MEIN LEBEN (My Life, 1865–81), relating how, after having heard the SIEGFRIED poem, she demanded to hear the remainder of the RING cycle. It was to Marie, furthermore, that Wagner addressed his open letter ÜBER FRANZ LISZTS SYMPHONISCHE DICHTUNGEN (On Franz Liszt's Symphonic Poems, 1857). From 1855, her vast inheritance meant she was financially secure, despite her parents' separation. Four years later, she married Prince Konstantin zu Hohenlohe-Waldenburg-Schillingsfürst; the pair settled in VIENNA, where they had six children. Marie's artistic philanthropy sought to spread the "Weimar spirit," part of which entailed her German translation of Liszt's (and Carolyne's) biography of Chopin.

DAVID TRIPPETT

Holländer, Der. See DUTCHMAN, THE

Hotter, Hans (b. Offenbach am Main, 19 Jan. 1909; d. Munich, 6 Dec. 2003), German bass-baritone. Although he sang many Wagner roles frequently (especially the DUTCHMAN, HANS SACHS, and GURNEMANZ), Hotter was most important as the dominant WOTAN of his day at the world's leading opera houses. He recorded much of *Die WALKÜRE*, Act II as early as 1938, served as Bayreuth's almost exclusive Wotan in 1952–8 (with more appearances through 1966), and in the 1960s recorded two-thirds of the role in Decca's RING.

DAVID BRECKBILL

Hans Hotter, *"Der Mai war mir gewogen..." – Erinnerungen* (Munich: Kindler, 1996), trans. *Memoirs* (Hanover, NH/London: University Press of New England, 2006).

Huldigungsmarsch (Homage March, WWV 97) in E♭ major is a five-minute concert piece originally for military band. Composed in August 1864 in Starnberg (near MUNICH), the work was dedicated to LUDWIG II of Bavaria on the occasion of his nineteenth birthday, and as such represents the first public gesture of gratitude on Wagner's part to his new royal patron. The first performance took place in Munich on 5 October 1864, although it had originally been planned for the birthday itself, on 25 August. In 1865, Wagner tried to persuade SCHOTT to publish the piece arguing that it would find "a very popular uptake [through] garden concerts and military performances" (letter to Schott, 11 February 1865, my translation). Wagner began work on a version for orchestra in February 1865, but broke off at around bars 70/1. Continued by Joachim RAFF and completed in 1871, the orchestral version was published in July 1871 and received its first performance on 12 November, in VIENNA.   JEREMY COLEMAN

Humperdinck, Engelbert (b. Siegburg, 1 Sep. 1854; d. Neustrelitz, 27 Sep. 1921), composer. As a talented student composer at the conservatories of Cologne and Munich, Humperdinck became enamored with Wagner's music at the time of the first BAYREUTH FESTIVAL in 1876, joining a student Wagner society in Munich, the "Orden vom Gral" (Order of the Grail). Receipt of the Mendelssohn Prize in 1879 enabled an extensive trip to ITALY, and it was there, in March 1880, that Humperdinck paid an uninvited visit to Wagner at the Villa d'Angri (Naples). Though lasting only half an hour, that visit, Humperdinck later recalled, was "one of the most exciting and uplifting moments of my life" (quoted by Wolfram Humperdinck 89). Wagner responded warmly if bemusedly to his rapt admirer, reportedly calling out to his wife, "Look here, Cosima: Here we have a knight in Naples, Herr Engelbert Humperdinck, a Knight of the Holy Grail in Munich" (Humperdinck to Oskar Merz [undated letter, spring 1880], quoted in Irmen 36). After speaking about Wagner's work and Humperdinck's plans, Wagner invited Humperdinck to return to Angri at the end of his travels later that spring. Humperdinck did so and took part in Wagner's birthday celebrations in May, after which he received an invitation to join the Wagners in Bayreuth to help with preparations for the upcoming premiere of *PARSIFAL*. Again, Humperdinck accepted Wagner's invitation, and when he arrived in Bayreuth (January 1881), he felt as though his wildest dreams had come true. As he reported in a letter to his parents, he worked as if enveloped "in a rosy mood and under a heaven filled with violins" (9 January 1881, quoted in Irmen 40).

Humperdinck spent the next twenty months in almost daily contact with the Wagner family. He lunched with Wagner and his Bayreuth friends, assisted in rehearsals for the upcoming premiere, and studied SCHOPENHAUER at Wagner's behest. But his primary charge was to prepare a copy of Wagner's manuscript score. Humperdinck's recollections of his work as Wagner's principal copyist during this period provide some of our most important records of the composer's working methods during the final years of his life (*Parsifal-Skizzen*). After the *Parsifal* premiere (29 August 1882), Humperdinck's work at Bayreuth came to a natural conclusion, and he departed for Italy soon thereafter.

The next few years were difficult for Humperdinck, spent in travel, creative searching, and several unsuccessful attempts to secure a steady and rewarding appointment as a composition teacher or a conductor. As a composer who was strongly drawn to opera, he also felt the need to distance himself from Wagner's domineering presence. A solution came slowly, with a song-cycle of 1890 based on texts by the Brothers Grimm, adapted into poetry by his sister Adelheid, which Humperdinck elaborated first into a *Singspiel* and then, in 1893, into his fairy-tale opera *Hänsel und Gretel*. Premiered in Weimar (23 December 1893) under Richard STRAUSS's baton, Humperdinck's opera was an instant success, quickly staged in opera houses throughout central Europe. Humperdinck followed with the fairy-tale melodrama *Königskinder* (1897), which was likewise an international success. With his third fairy-tale composition, *Dornröschen* (1902), the fashion for such works had run its course, and Humperdinck never regained the popular standing he enjoyed at the turn of the century. KEVIN C. KARNES

Engelbert Humperdinck, *Parsifal-Skizzen*, ed. Eva Humperdinck (Koblenz: Görres, 2000).
Wolfram Humperdinck, *Engelbert Humperdinck: Das Leben meines Vaters* (Frankfurt am Main: Waldemar Kramer, 1965).
Hans-Josef Irmen, *Die Odyssee des Engelbert Humperdinck: Eine biographische Dokumentation* (Siegburg: F. Schmitt, 1975).

Hunding (bass; character in *Der RING DES NIBELUNGEN*, with appearances in *Die WALKÜRE*). SIEGLINDE's husband, who protests his case to FRICKA, and with her aid slays SIEGMUND in a duel, has been given comparatively short shrift in interpretations of the *Ring*. Hunding is one of Wagner's pseudo-antagonists, who are catalysts for the plot, but are only accidental external triggers (like the giants, Daland, etc.) instead of fully realized personalities. It matters little that Hunding is married to Sieglinde; in other words, it only matters that she be married. What is more, Wagner's libretto portrays him as altogether reactive and lacking initiative: he bands together with his clan to hunt the *Wölflinge*, he follows and blindly enforces the law in hospitality and marriage, he calls on Fricka in his fury over the Völsung's betrayal, and even fights his climactic duel with Siegmund in Fricka's stead ("Fricka fälle dich hier").

Wagner derived the character of Hunding from the *VÖLSUNGA SAGA*, where he is a king in his own right and an enemy of King Sigmund. In the saga, both King Hunding and King Sigmund are ultimately slain by each other's sons – and, just as in *Die Walküre*, Odin intervenes in these killings. In condensing these parallel fates (the two kings and their two sons) into three people (Hunding, Siegmund, Sieglinde), Wagner's libretto instead construes an asymmetry between Hunding and Siegmund: Hunding and Siegmund do not meet as equals, but rather as exact opposites – the former a successful chieftain of sorts, the latter a homeless wretch on the run, the former with an exemplary household, the latter without any remaining family he is aware of.

This asymmetry is intentional on Wagner's part: Hunding is the perfect antipode to the tribe of humans Wotan conceives of in his "grosser Gedanke" at the end of *Rheingold* – where they reject established authority (Fricka's, Hunding's, and ultimately even Wotan's), Hunding hews closely to all established authority. Unlike the other clear villain of the *Ring*, Hagen, Hunding does not represent an "affront [*Hohn*]" to the Gods, but rather works his evil in servitude to them.

The musical portrayal of Hunding is at one with his limited dramatic function in the *Ring:* he fills the role required of Sieglinde's husband – that is, to be the grim enforcer of the laws of marriage and social custom, the obedient servant of Fricka. Act 1, Scene 2 of *Die Walküre* takes place on his turf, in his presence; it is his only scene in the cycle, with the exception of his brief appearance in Act 11, Scene 5, where he kills Siegmund. His is the music of authority and convention, albeit authority and convention harshly enforced. The motive that announces his first appearance and is associated with him throughout the scene (see Appendix 4: *Leitmotive* in *Der Ring des Nibelungen*; CWE 13) is emblematic of this authority: minor mode, $\frac{4}{4}$ meter, military rhythms, simple and conventional harmony, low brass orchestration, and absolutely predictable four-measure phrase lengths. He grounds the scene firmly in C minor at the beginning and end – a whole step down from the D minor/ major of Scene 1. In Acts 1 and 11 of *Die Walküre*, which focus on the relationship of Siegmund and Sieglinde, and which begin and end in D minor, C minor nevertheless plays a significant symbolic and musical role, as the key of Hunding and Fricka. It returns to ground Fricka's scene with Wotan early in Act 11. Indeed, as Fricka approaches, to insist on the sacredness of Hunding's marriage contract, Wotan quotes the musical line of Hunding's "Heilig ist mein Herd" (Act 1, Scene 2, mm. 408–11) in C minor. At the end of the act, when Wotan orders Hunding to kneel before Fricka, his "Heilig ist mein Herd" melody is heard once more, now pulled up to the D-minor key that dominates the two acts.

Full interpretations of the character of Hunding are fairly rare. One of the most influential comes in the shape of fiction, Thomas MANN's *Wälsungen- blut* (1906, published 1921). Here, Hunding's stand-in, the ministerial clerk von Beckerath, is not only ignorant of the nature of Siegmund and Sieglinde's relationship, he also seems too "trivial" (the twins' favorite taunt) to perceive it. Mann thus reads Hunding as a typical nineteenth-century philistine, beholden to convention because he is too unimaginative to think beyond it.   ADRIAN DAUB AND PATRICK MCCRELESS

I

Iconography. Wagnerian iconography is a vast field for research, with much material previously inaccessible but now available for viewing through ubiquitous offerings on the Internet. Iconographies appear in the form of ephemera for sale: lithographs, engravings, figurines, and photographs of portraits, caricatures, and images of not only Wagner, but also his operas (see also MEMORABILIA). The historical value of Wagnerian iconography cannot be underestimated. Frequently, nineteenth- and early twentieth-century images provide the only accurate documentation of past productions.

Allegorical representations or photographs of stage productions, and documents such as AUTOGRAPH MANUSCRIPTS, libretti, and CORRESPONDENCE accompanied images derived for POPULAR CULTURE that include figurines of LOHENGRIN and the swan, portraits on beer mugs, and plain kitsch. In 1908, the MUNICH bookshop Ackermann boasted of its specialty for "Wagneriana" as well as an art gallery for "the works of Richard Wagner in single sheets [*Einzelblättern*], portfolios [*Mappen*] and other formats [*Werken*]." Much of the ephemera are rare and highly sought as collector's pieces.

In contrast, drawings and paintings of portraits and scenes remained hidden in private collections or were thought lost, only to surface in public institutions, such as Friedrich Pecht's portrait of Wagner found in the early 1970s at the Metropolitan Museum of Art, New York (now on loan to the Metropolitan Opera). Josef HOFFMANN's original oil paintings for the designs for the 1876 RING were thought to be long lost, but were recently found in a private collection. The Bavarian government assisted by financial institutions purchased the paintings and they are now at the Richard Wagner MUSEUM in WAHNFRIED.

Since 1976, each new *Ring* at Bayreuth was documented by a single publication that included extensive iconography detailing the preparation and production of the operas. During the 1990s other theaters followed the Bayreuth example, publishing iconography of their own productions of the *Ring*.

1. Published collections of iconography
2. Portraits during Wagner's lifetime
3. Facsimiles
4. Production iconography
5. Allegorical scenes and popular culture
6. Collections of Wagnerian iconography

1. Published collections of iconography

Among the earliest extensively illustrated biographies was that penned in French by the musicologist and opera historian Adolphe Jullien (1886) as *Richard Wagner, his life and works; book decorated with fourteen lithographs by M. Fantin-Latour, fifteen portraits of Richard Wagner, four etchings and 120 engravings, scenes from operas, cartoons, views of theaters, autographs, etc.*, followed by an English edition in 1892. Houston Stewart CHAMBERLAIN (1896) published perhaps the first biography of Wagner with wide-ranging documentation from the archives of Haus Wahnfried that included iconography of portraits, scenes, facsimiles of music, and correspondence. Mary BURRELL (1898) produced in a very rare "elephant folio" format a prodigious and magnificent biography covering the composer's early years with numerous illustrations of documents never seen before, from both public archives and the author's own collection (now in the Nationalarchiv, Bayreuth). Erich Engel (1913) published an important two-volume biography of the composer richly illustrated, with equally rare images from a variety of sources. The first publication dedicated solely to Wagnerian iconography is by Julius Kapp (1933) followed by an even larger contribution by Robert Bory (1938), which included portraits, caricatures, and documents, many for the first time. The value of these early publications cannot be underestimated; the originals of numerous images were lost or destroyed during World War II. Among the greatest losses are selected facsimile pages of the autograph full scores of *Die FEEN, Das LIEBESVERBOT, RIENZI, Das RHEINGOLD,* and *Die WALKÜRE* presented to HITLER in 1939. The trio of Herbert Barth, Dietrich Mack, and Egon Voss (1975) presented a lavishly illustrated biography of the composer complete with reproductions of documents, facsimiles, portraits, and caricatures, many in color. An extraordinarily valuable and enormous volume with reproductions of the designs, stage models, and documents for the first productions of Wagner's operas in Munich was provided by Detta and Michel Petzet (1970). Dietrich Mack provided an equally valuable iconography and documentary study of the productions at Bayreuth 1876–1976 (1976).

2. Portraits during Wagner's lifetime

Ernst Benedikt KIETZ's pencil drawing of Wagner (Bory 74, Geck 3) during his Paris sojourn in 1842 formed the basis for the earliest published portrait of the composer that appeared in the newspaper *Zeitung für die Elegante Welt* (1843). The same portrait appeared six months later in the *Illustrirte Zeitung* as part of a report of the first performances of *Rienzi*. A version was posted by the authorities in May 1849 as the infamous *Steckbrief* (criminal "wanted notice"; Bory 94) when Wagner's revolutionary activities forced him to flee DRESDEN. In 1851, the Zurich publisher Füssli printed over 100 lithograph copies of the portrait for sale to the public. Clementine Stockar-Escher, a Swiss artist, painted a portrait in 1853, which appeared in an April issue of *Illustrirte Zeitung* and several months later was issued by BREITKOPF & HÄRTEL as a lithograph for public sale (Bory 97).

The first series of photographic portraits were made during Wagner's sojourn in Paris, 1860, by Pierre Petit and Trinquart (Bory 122). During

Wagner's abortive attempts to stage TRISTAN UND ISOLDE at the Vienna Court Opera, Viktor Angerer prepared a series of photographs of the composer in different poses (Bory 136, Geck 11a–e). All photographs appeared for public commerce in different sizes, primarily as "carte de visite" (c. 3.5″ × 2.4″) and "cabinet" (c. 6″ × 4.25″) formats.

After Wagner's rescue by LUDWIG II in 1864, his visage became far better known. Joseph Albert, a court photographer, prepared two series of photographs in 1864 and 1865 respectively (Bory 137). One of the photographs included Wagner, with his dog Pohl at his feet, surrounded by fourteen friends shortly before the postponement of the Tristan premiere (Bory 143). Franz Hanfstaengel began a long relationship with Wagner issuing photographs of the composer standing in an overcoat; one was later published as a print and as a photo-engraving (Geck 18a–d).

Among the best-known portraits are those of Wagner wearing his black velvet beret. The first appeared in 1867 during a return visit to Paris from the studio of Pierson (Bory 166); the second series during Wagner's Swiss exile at his villa TRIBSCHEN in Lucerne, issued by Bonnet. The most famous is Wagner seated in front of the villa, another while holding Eva, his newborn daughter (Geck 19a–d). Hafstaengel published in 1871 what became probably Wagner's most recognizable photographs with and without his beret (Geck 22a–f); Franz von Lenbach used the photographs as models for his red chalk drawing and paintings (Bory 185, 183) of the composer, now in Wahnfried. Wagner's first portrait together with COSIMA was made during his 1872 visit to Vienna, where Cosima sat looking up at Wagner for a portrait in Fritz Luckhardt's atelier (Geck 25c). One year later, the family friend Adolph von GROß photographed Cosima and Wagner with their son, SIEGFRIED, along with another married couple, this time with Wagner wearing his beret (Geck 28a–b, Bory 181). Later portraits show an aged composer from a series published by Elliot & Fry in 1877 during his London visit (Bory 213). In 1881, Gross photographed Wagner with his family standing on the steps that led from the garden into Wahnfried (Geck 35a–c). During Wagner's last visit to Munich in 1882, he sat once more for Joseph Albert (Geck 40a–b).

Paintings of Wagner during his lifetime were less publicly known, for they remained largely in private hands; most are now in public institutions. These include the oil painting of Friedrich Pecht, commissioned by Wagner as a gift for Ludwig II. The painting, long out of sight but which surfaced during the early 1970s in the collections of the Metropolitan Museum, is now on loan at the Metropolitan Opera Gallery (Geck 16, III). Auguste RENOIR sketched and painted portraits of Wagner during his 1882 sojourn in Palermo (Geck 38, VII). Previously unknown drawings and painted portraits, once inaccessible in private collections, continue to surface on the antiquarian market, most recently a portrait pencil sketch by Henry Holiday during Wagner's London visit in 1877 (Föttinger 167).

Portraits are also in the form of busts by Caspar von Zumbusch (Munich, 1864) and GUSTAV ADOLPH KIETZ (Bayreuth, 1873) both in Wahnfried (Geck 14, 27). Wagner's final rendition is the death mask made by August Benvenuti the day following the composer's death in VENICE on 13 February 1883 (Geck 42, Bory 237).

3. Facsimiles

Reproductions of Wagner's autographs – music and correspondence – are important sources for iconography studies, particularly if one is unable to study the originals housed in Bayreuth, public institutions, or private collections that remain inaccessible. In the 1920s, the Munich publishing firm of Drei Masken Verlag performed the singular duty of publishing full facsimiles of Wagner's autograph scores for *Tristan und Isolde*, *Die MEISTERSINGER VON NÜRNBERG*, and *PARSIFAL*. In 1893, SCHOTT issued a facsimile of the composer's autograph libretto to *Die Meistersinger von Nürnberg* and reissued it exactly ninety years later. The autograph libretto of *Siegfrieds Tod* is available for study at the digital library of the Beinecke Library at Yale University. Otto STROBEL, former archivist of the Haus Wahnfried, published an important study of the development of the *Ring* libretto, which included over thirty high-quality facsimiles of Wagner's prose drafts material and libretti beginning with *Siegfrieds Tod* and rounding the circle to *Das Rheingold*.

4. Production iconography

Nineteenth-century German newspapers, particularly the *Illustrirte Zeitung* (LEIPZIG), portrayed scenes from Wagner's operas. These are often the only documentation of the early productions of *Rienzi*, *Fliegende Holländer*, and *Tannhäuser* at Dresden, and the Weimar premiere of *Lohengrin*. As Wagner's operas became better known, other journals began publishing illustrations of scenes and costumes, particularly Theodore Pixis's illustrations of the Munich productions of *Rheingold* and *Walküre* that appeared in the *Illustrirte Zeitung* in October 1869 and January 1871. Before and during the 1876 *Ring* cycles, newspapers published not only illustrations of performances, but also images of rehearsals, scenes in and about the Festspielhaus, and daily life in Bayreuth.

Josef Hoffmann published in 1878 portfolios of fourteen photolithographs of the stage designs. Almost twenty years later, Max BRÜCKNER prepared his own color reproductions, equally in their own portfolios, of his *Dekorationsentwürfe* for the Bayreuth *Ring* staged by Cosima Wagner. Beginning in 1902, Gotthold Henning issued the series of portfolios entitled *Bayreuther Bühnenbilder*, which included facsimiles of Brückner's designs for all of the productions up to 1905.

For the 1908 Wagner festival at Munich's Prinzregententheater, the Kunstverlag Jos. Paul Böhm produced four "Richard Wagner Album[s]" of iconography for the *Ring*, *Die Meistersinger*, *Tristan und Isolde*, and *Tannhäuser*. Most followed the designs from their first performances in the Hoftheater. The iconography for the performances of *Tristan und Isolde* revealed a setting completely different from that of the first performances. Willi Wirk, the stage director, noted his goal that the settings should create an "atmosphere, not phony naturalism or illusion" (*geheuchelte Naturwahrheit oder Illusion*), thusly following a new scenic style, instead of the original 1865 settings.

Production photographs form an important part of Wagnerian iconography. The Bavarian court photographer Hans Brand, based in Bayreuth, produced a portfolio of photographs of the settings for *Parsifal* (1889) and *Tannhäuser* (1892). Postcards of many productions up to the 1940s were issued by the photography firm Ramme & Ulrich, also of Bayreuth.

Before the advent of photography, many singers posed in Wagnerian costume published as lithographs; among the best known are those of Josef TICHATSCHEK as Rienzi and Tannhäuser, and Ludwig Schnorr von CAROLSFELD as Lohengrin. Portraits of singers in their Wagnerian roles appeared at first as photographs, and then proliferated as postcards. During the 1876 *Ring* cycle, Hans Brand photographed the soloists and chorus members in costume and issued for sale twenty-four photographs in a decorated portfolio, with an additional eleven photographs sold separately (one of which was Amalie MATERNA posed as Brünnhilde with her horse, Grane).

5. Allegorical scenes and popular culture

Wagnerian iconography abounds in popular culture, frequently reinforcing operatic stereotypes, particularly large female singers, and the winged helmets and metal breastplates of BRÜNNHILDE and the Valkyries. Much iconography imagined scenes depicting events during the operas, including Lohengrin's arrival by swan, WOTAN's farewell to Brünnhilde, or the Holländer's ghost ship flying into port.

Artists at the beginning of the twentieth century including Hugo Braune, Ferdinand Leeke, and Franz STASSEN produced illustrations in now very rare large broadside formats (up to *c.* 32″ × 24″) of scenes, framed often by decorative motives and occasionally by extracts of music. Many of the images were later scaled to the popular postcard size. Book illustrators provided iconic designs, the best known being Arthur RACKHAM with his interpretation of the *Ring*, and Willy Pogány for *Tannhäuser, Lohengrin*, and *Parsifal*. In the early 1900s, Schott published vocal scores that included a portrait of Wagner and photographs of the Bayreuth productions. The *Ring* scores appeared bound in red covers embossed with a dragon-shaped "Ring" of the Nibelung.

Ceramic and bronze figurines depicting characters from the operas were popular. Wagner's patron Ludwig II assembled a collection of figurines dedicated to his favorite opera, focusing on Lohengrin and his swan. Large cups appeared on the market, with scenes from Wagner's operas. Objects of the quality of kitsch also abounded in the form of carved pipes with Wagner's portrait along with advertisements, such as Alberich seizing the "gold," being a cup filled with beer. In the first decades of the twentieth century, Liebig advertised its *Fleischextrakt* (concentrated meat stock, similar to today's bouillon cubes) on small cards – similar to today's sports cards – illustrating a series of six scenes from each of Wagner's operas and his private life. Contemporary advertisements utilize the Wagnerian stereotype of the Valkyrie in print and broadcast media. One communications company touted its digital qualities with a headshot of a "Valkyrie" (complete with the horned helmet and braided locks) ostensibly "singing" a high note, shattering a nearby wine glass.

6. Collections of Wagnerian iconography

Herbert Barth, Dietrich Mack, and Egon Voss, eds., *Wagner: A Documentary Study* (New York: Oxford University Press, 1975).

Robert Bory, *Richard Wagner: Sein Leben und sein Werk in Bildern* (Leipzig: Huber, 1938).

Mary Banks Burrell, *Richard Wagner, his life & works from 1813 to 1834 compiled from original letters, manuscripts & other documents by Mrs. Burrell née Banks and illustrated with portraits & facsimiles* ([London: A. Wyon,] 1898).

Houston Stewart Chamberlain, *Richard Wagner: Mit zahlreichen Porträts, Faksimiles, Illustrationen und Beilagen* (Munich: Verlagsanstalt für Kunst und Wissenschaft, 1896).

Erich W. Engel, *Richard Wagners Leben und Werke im Bilde*, 2 vols. (Vienna: Engle, 1913).

Gudrun Föttinger, "Neues aus dem Nationalarchiv der Richard-Wagner-Stiftung Bayreuth. 'Ich bin zu wechselnd in meinem Ausdrucke.' Neuere Anmerkungen zur Wagner Ikonografie," *wagnerspectrum* 7.1 (2011): 143–70.

Adolphe Jullien, *Richard Wagner, sa vie et ses œuvres: Ouvrage orné de quatorze lithographies originales par M. Fantin-Latour, de quinze portraits de Richard Wagner, de quatre eaux fortes et de 120 gravures, scènes d'opéras, caricatures, vues de théâtres, autographes, etc.* (Paris: J. Rouam, 1886). Eng. Trans. *Richard Wagner, his life and works; tr. from the French by Florence Percival Hall. With an introduction by B. J. Lang. Illustrated* (Boston: J.B. Millet company, 1892).

Julius Kapp, *Richard Wagner, sein Leben, sein Werk, sein Welt in 260 Bildern* (Berlin: Max Hesse, 1933).

Dietrich Mack, *100 Jahre Bayreuther Festspiele: Der Bayreuther Inszenierungsstil 1876–1976* (Munich: Prestel, 1976).

Michael and Detta Petzet, *Die Richard Wagner-Bühne König Ludwigs II.* (Munich: Prestel, 1970).

Portraits

Martin Geck, *Die Bildnisse Richard Wagners* (Munich: Prestel, 1970).

Newspaper iconography

Illustrirte Zeitung (Leipzig, 1843–1944); the years 1843–71 can be searched at: http://de.wikisource.org/wiki/Zeitschriften (accessed 21 September 2012).

Early published stage and costume designs of Wagner's operas

Joseph Albert, *Costüm-Portraits sämtlicher das Bayreuther Bühnenfestspiel "der Ring des Nibelungen" darstellenden Künstler & Künstlerinnen, unter Leitung des Prof. C.E. Doepler aus Berlin, aufgenommen in Theater zu Bayreuth ... 24 Cabinet-Photographien in elegantester Enveloppe mit Namensverzeichnis* (Munich: Joseph Albert, 1876).

Max Brückner, *Der Ring des Nibelungen: zur Aufführung in Bayreuth im Jahre 1896 von Richard Wagner; Dekorationsentwürfe von Max Brückner* (Bayreuth: Heuschmann, 1896).

[Max Brückner], *R. Wagner's "Parsifal." Scenische Bilder nach den für die Bayreuther Aufführung gefertigten Decorations- und Costümskizzen. Neun Lichtdrucke von Naumann & Schröder* (Leipzig: Buch- und Kunstverlag von Albert Unflad, [after 1883]).

Carl Emil Doepler, *Der Ring des Nibelungen: Figurinen* ([Berlin]: Berliner Kunstdruck- und Verlags-Anstalt, [1889]).

Hermann Hendrich, *Der Ring des Nibelungen in Bildern von Hermann Hendrich* (Leipzig: J.J. Weber, [c. 1909]).

Gotthold Henning (ed.), *Max Brückner, Bayreuther Bühnenbilder: Farbige Reproduktion der in Coburg für das Bayreuther Festspielhaus gemalten Originale* (Leipzig: 1902–5).

Josef Hoffmann, *Der Ring des Nibelungen* (Vienna: V. Angerer, [1878]).

Hans Thoma, *Costume designs for Richard Wagner's Ring des Nibelungen, with an introd. by Henry Thode* (Leipzig: Breitkopf & Härtel, 1897).

Early published production photographs

Hans Brand, *Richard Wagnertheater: Dekorationen aus Parsifal* (Bayreuth: Hans Brand, 1889).

Tannhäuser: Bühnen-Dekorationen und scenische Bilder aus Richard Wagners Bühnenfestspielhaus (Bayreuth: Hans Brand, 1892).

Allegorical representations of Wagnerian scenes and figures (selections)

Hugo L. Braune, *Richard Wagners Bühnenwerke in Bildern dargestellt* (Leipzig: Emil Hermann senior für C. F. W. Siegels Musikalienhandlung R. Linnemann, 1906).

Ferdinand Leeke, *Richard Wagner-Werk: Ein Bildercyklus* (Munich: Franz Hanfstaengl, 1894–5). *Richard Wagners Heldengestalten* (Leipzig: Kunstverlag L. Pernitzsch, 1900).

Willy Pogány (illustrator) and Thomas William Hazen Rolleston, *Parsifal or the Legend of the Holy Grail: Retold from Ancient Sources with Acknowledgement to the "Parsifal of Richard Wagner"* (London: Harrap, 1912).

(illustrator) and Thomas William Hazen Rolleston, *The Tale of Lohengrin, Knight of the Swan after the Drama of Richard Wagner* (London: Harrap, 1913).

(illustrator) and Thomas William Hazen Rolleston, *Tannhäuser: A Dramatic Poem by Richard Wagner. Freely Translated in Poetic Narrative Form by T. W. Rolleston. Presented by Willy Pogány* (London: Harrap, 1911).

Arthur Rackham (illustrator), *The Ring of the Nibelung: A Trilogy with a Prelude, by Richard Wagner. Translated into English by Margaret Armour*, 2 vols. (London: W. Heinemann, 1910–11).

Ferdinand Staeger, *Die Meistersinger von Nürnberg* (Munich: Othmar Kern, 1921).

Franz Stassen, *Parsifal: 15 Bilder zu Richard Wagners Bühnenweihfestspiel* (Berlin: Fischer & Franke, 1901).

Der Ring des Nibelungen: 1. Das Rheingold, 24 Original-Lithographien zu Richard Wagners Dichtung (Berlin: Adolf Forker, 1914).

Tristan und Isolde: 12 Bilder zu Richard Wagners Tondichtung (Berlin: Fischer & Franke, 1900).

EVAN BAKER

Improvisation. The spontaneous creation of what is outwardly perceivable as art. It connotes a synchrony of inspiration and production, thereby collapsing the hierarchical distinction between composer-creator and performer-executant. Lacking a written record by definition, improvisation is conceived for the moment, and hence conveys an event-status; typically viewed as an emblem of mental inspiration, it is nevertheless mediated – for musicians – by the tactile dimensions of an instrument, and – for actors – by the interactive engagement with an audience.

Wagner's interest in concepts of improvisation relates to (i) stage acting and writing; (ii) musical composition; (iii) drama arising from spontaneous interaction with the VOLK.

His chance encounter with *Kasperltheater* (improvised street puppet theatre, similar to Punch & Judy) on 14 May 1871 exerted a discernible influence on his late conception of drama. From this stems Wagner's developing theory of the birth of art out of the spirit of improvisation – "the natural process in the beginnings of all art" (SSD 9:142; PW 5:143) – which had no precedent in his ZURICH writings. He came to regard improvisation as the key to understanding the irrationality of dramatic art as well as its historical origin as folk-art; specifically, this concerns mimetic improvisation, the improvising mime, who embodies the collectively poeticizing *Volksgeist*, from whom all legitimate artistic expression – after HERDER – stems, and to whom all artists are to feel themselves related in this sense.

Accordingly, Wagner recommends that aspiring actors: "Practice improvising scenes and whole pieces. Indisputably, in improvising lies the root and kernel of all mimetic gifts, of all true acting talent. The dramatic actor to whom it has never occurred what force would flow from his work if only he could see the whole thing improvised before him, has never felt within him the true calling to dramatic poetry" (SSD 9:142; PW 5:143).

What led Wagner to regard *Kasperltheater* as a "last ray of hope for the German folk's productive spirit" (SSD 9:182; PW 5:182), was the interaction between audience and stage, and, above all, the single figure – "a wonder-working genius of this most genuine of all the stage-shows I ever have witnessed" (SSD 9:182; PW 5:182) – unifying the roles of an improvising poet, theater director, and actor. This unity of artistic agency finds a precedent in the ironic trialogue of Goethe's stage prologue to *Faust*, in which Wagner claimed to see "all the art of the future" (CWD 24 July 1872) and about which he comments to COSIMA: "One sees to what extent GOETHE always had the puppet show in mind" (CWD 7 November 1872).

For Wagner, improvisation evinces unconscious inspiration. Hence an improvising mime also becomes the arbiter of unconscious, unmediated creativity, analogous to the unconscious imagination of ROMANTICISM (see SCHOPENHAUER), in which a poetic idea loses potency the instant it attains conscious, reflective thought. Wagner understood his own compositional methods as essentially non-conscious in this sense, complaining regularly of feeling alienated by notation. He defined SHAKESPEAREAN drama accordingly as "a fixed mimetic improvisation of the highest poetic worth" (SSD 5:143; PW 5:144), and duly extends the paradox to BEETHOVEN's late quartets: "what is the thing written down as compared with the inspiration? ... in [Beethoven's] last quartets he was able to remember and record improvisations, which could only be done through art of the highest, highest order. With me it is always the drama which flouts convention and opens up new possibilities" (CWD 4 December 1870). It may seem contradictory that Wagner asked at times for strict adherence to his rhythmic notation, and at other times for singers to abandon the metrical beat and "give the freest play to one's natural sensibility" (SSD 5:129; PW 3:175). Yet, as he argues in 1871, it is precisely the dialectic between the unconscious, improvising *Volksgeist* and consciously notated artistic production that gives rise to the artwork of the future.

DAVID TRIPPETT

Dieter Borchmeyer, "Inspiration durch Kasperltheater: Richard Wagners Idee des improvisatorischen Dramas," *Euphorion* 74 (1980): 113–33.
Theory and Theatre (New York: Oxford University Press, 2002): 250–86.

Incest. See LOVE

Isolde (soprano; title role in *TRISTAN UND ISOLDE*). Isolde is an ancient name going back to Essyllt in the MEDIEVAL Welsh triads, which are texts that sought to preserve oral traditions by grouping objects in threes. In Triad 80, for example, we read of "Essyllt Fair-Hair (Trystan's mistress)" as one of the "Three Faithless Wives of the Island of Britain." The three Isoldes in GOTTFRIED VON STRASSBURG's medieval romance *Tristan* (c. 1210) – Wagner's main source – clearly relate to the device, except that they have in common not so much faithlessness as the love potion and its aftermath: Isolde the Elder invents it; her daughter Isolde the Fair drinks it by accident, falling fatally in love with Tristan; and Isolde of the White Hands is its victim, filled with anger about her husband Tristan. Having drunk the potion, he still cannot consummate his marriage to her because of his ongoing obsession with Isolde the Fair.

Thomas of Britain's *Tristran* (*c.* 1170) – Gottfried's model and also known to Wagner – has but two Isoldes, probably because only a sixth of the text survives. Nevertheless, it had just as great an impact. The vivid episode at the end of the narrative when Isolde of the White Hands cruelly lies to Tristran that the boat she sees is carrying a black flag, when in fact it has a white flag indicating the arrival of Isolde the Fair, the woman he really loves, results in the deaths of both her rival and her husband. Wagner hinted in a letter to Liszt (16 December 1854) that he was going to include it. He decided in the end, however, that there was to be only one Isolde, albeit with many contradictory attributes that both Thomas and Gottfried had already astutely crafted into their own characters with that name: serial faithlessness alongside miraculous powers of healing, for example, and sublime beauty combined with utterly ruthless political cunning.

The blindly murderous anger of Isolde of the White Hands is certainly part of the Isolde in Act I of Wagner's opera. And so is the way Isolde the Fair herself resorts to criminal methods in Gottfried's *Tristan*. Here the author attributes her deviance to the effects of the love potion. But Wagner dispenses with the excuse: his Isolde does not have to drink anything before insisting to BRANGÄNE's horror in Act I, Scene 4 that TRISTAN must be killed by poison, and moreover in the guise of a drink of reconciliation. A potential murderess, and moreover a wily one bent on her own destruction, she takes the "poison" herself (Brangäne has meanwhile replaced it with the love potion) and all of a sudden – at a tricky moment dramatically – becomes an epitome of sexual abandon. In turn, this provocative trait in the character of Isolde the Fair is placed on a collision course with the reappearance of Wagner's heroine in Act III, Scenes 2–3 when, on witnessing Tristan's dead body disfigured by a wound that only she could have healed, her former reckless passion is discarded just as suddenly for the protective, now tragic, instincts of her mother, Isolde the Elder.

Birgit NILSSON, one of the finest sopranos ever to perform Isolde, once quipped that the secret is "comfortable shoes" (Obituary, *New York Times*, 12 January 2006). Wittily as ever, she was making a serious point. There are eleven scenes in *Tristan und Isolde*, in six of which Tristan sings. (He is in a seventh, but conspicuously dead.) In contrast, Isolde sings in all of the scenes but one (Act III, Scene 1) where, admittedly, Tristan's role is vocally taxing in the extreme. Still, the harder task is hers: she is on stage more than he is and has to be not only in command of a variety of vocal styles and registers, but also able to act out all the contrasting parts of her character from murderous rage to utmost rapture convincingly over a long stretch of time.

The Shakespearean tensions in the character of Isolde that derive from Wagner's manipulation of the multiple Isoldes in his sources can easily lead to irritating inconsistencies in performance. But any singer who can still lend a sense of logical dramatic purpose to her final Love-Death (see *LIEBESTOD*) after one of the longest acting and singing journeys in opera will always convince audiences of the cogency of Wagner's most daring theatrical adventure. The first Isolde, Malvina Schnorr von CAROLSFELD, noted in a letter to her mother-in-law (12 May 1865) the rapt attention of the audience throughout a full rehearsal of the "epoch-making" work, to which her powerful voice and dramatic aura must have contributed. Later Rosa Sucher, renowned for her singing and acting abilities, first created the role in London (1882) and Bayreuth (1886) with a similar response, and another notable soprano, Olive Fremstad, also famous for her dramatic presence, sang it just as memorably at the Metropolitan Opera in New York (1908) in performances conducted by Gustav MAHLER.

Other illustrious Isoldes from the early twentieth century are Lilli LEHMANN and Anna von Mildenburg, who were in turn models of fine singing and acting for a younger generation that included Frida LEIDER (for some, the best Isolde ever), Marjorie Lawrence and Helen Traubel. The most outstanding Isolde of the twentieth century is considered to be Kirsten FLAGSTAD, whose interpretation is immortalized in a studio recording of *Tristan und Isolde* conducted by Wilhelm FURTWÄNGLER (1952). But her voice in this performance is no longer at its best – more Isolde the Elder perhaps than Isolde the Fair.

Wary of the reputation of Isolde as a heavy soprano role, more recent generations of sopranos have been reluctant to take it on. A pivotal moment came when Margaret Price, renowned for her supple and wonderfully sensual performances of Mozart, agreed to take on the role in Carlos Kleiber's famous recording (1982). Susan Bullock and Nina Stemme originally thought their voices unsuitable for Isolde, but took inspiration from Price's example and have since given utterly convincing performances in many full-scale productions in the opera house. The irony – one that sums up the many dramatic strands Wagner wove into Isolde and the utopian demands of the part – is that Price herself refused to perform the role in the theatre. "I'm not a long-distance runner," *The Guardian* reported her as saying (24 September 2009). "I'll sing it to my dogs."   JOHN DEATHRIDGE

Israel. Attempts to perform Richard Wagner's music in Israel have met with opposition since 1938 when the OVERTURE to *Die MEISTERSINGER VON NÜRNBERG* was removed from the program of the season opening of The Palestine Symphony Orchestra, later to become The Israel Philharmonic Orchestra (IPO). News of *Kristallnacht*, which took place in Nazi Germany three days prior to the concert, caused Bronisław Huberman (the orchestra's founder) and the orchestra's management to ask conductor Eugen Szenkar not to perform the piece. Identifying Wagner with the then current events was the result of his ANTI-SEMITISM, the fact that HITLER admired him, and the nazification of BAYREUTH and the FESTIVAL in the late 1920s.

Since that time, the Wagner controversy has appeared on the Israeli agenda at least once every decade. Regardless of their political affiliation, ministers of education present a united front: they do not encourage performing Wagner publicly, but leave the decision to the musical bodies. Attempts by the leading orchestras have aroused fierce debate. In these conflicts, Wagner's worldview and musical works are intertwined with the ideas of NATIONAL SOCIALISM and the Holocaust, combined with current events that relate to Israeli society and the state's foreign policy. The issue is primarily discussed in the Knesset or its Education, Culture, and Sports Committee, and in the media (mainly the print media). The conflicts cross party lines, and opinions vary even among Holocaust survivors – some in favor and others against performing Wagner.

In the 1950s and 1960s, the desire to perform Wagner's music was bound up with an attempt to perform the works of Richard STRAUSS, who headed the Nazi *Reichsmusikkammer*. The arguments against performing Wagner focused on the cultural boycott which the Nazis imposed on the JEWS and their work, and the traumatic memories of Holocaust survivors who claimed that Wagner's music was performed in the forced labor, concentration, and death camps.

The most scathing controversy of those years followed an article "On the Importance of Wagner" by Uri Toeplitz, which appeared in the IPO's program in June 1966, and which explained that "We feel the time has come for a change, not only because of the paramount demands of artistic freedom, but also because opposition to Wagner has become a mere gesture." This announcement came fifteen years after Israeli society had been in turmoil over German-related issues: the 1952 reparations agreement between Israel and West Germany, the Yad Vashem Law (1953), the Holocaust and Heroism Remembrance Day Law (1959), and the Nazis and Nazi Collaborators Punishment Law (1950), which made it possible to convict war criminals, among them Adolf Eichmann.

The 1966 controversy showed that, even twenty years after World War II, Israeli society still rejected the person whom many perceived as the symbol of Nazism. Ministers, Knesset members, publicists, and Holocaust survivors participated in the debate. On behalf of the Minister of Education, who had been asked a parliamentary question on the matter, his deputy responded that "The Government of Israel does not intend to engage in cultural censorship," although "had [the IPO] asked its advice, the Ministry would have recommended excluding the works of Wagner and Strauss from orchestra repertoires" (Interpellation 846, 28 June 1966). He differentiated between establishing diplomatic ties with Germany (1965) and the emotions related to the problematic history.

Subsequent attempts to lift the boycott on Wagner and Strauss were buried even before they matured. In 1981, Zubin Mehta, the IPO musical director, announced that the orchestra would perform the *Liebestod* from TRISTAN UND ISOLDE as an encore. Although Mehta suggested that the musicians and those members of the audience who did not wish to listen to the piece leave the hall, tempers flared. Once again the matter was discussed in the press, reaching new heights, perhaps influenced in part by the conflict between Prime Minister Menachem Begin and West German Chancellor Helmut Schmidt, who declared Germany's commitment to resolve the suffering of the Palestinians, as he believed that his country was indirectly responsible for their situation. The passionate mood was also focused on the conductor, whose foreignness caused some to accuse him of being insensitive to Jewish suffering.

This was the first time that the press presented the public with Wagner's biography and the effect of his work on National Socialism. Thenceforth more works by Wagner were heard on radio and television, arousing only a moderate reaction.

The insulting attitude toward Mehta, as a foreigner, encouraged Daniel Barenboim to take on lifting the boycott. At the end of 1991, he held a special concert devoted to Wagner's music, thus preventing opposition by the captive audience of subscription holders. The public responded with anger. During the Gulf War (1991), Iraq threatened to launch missiles with German-made gas warheads at Israel. One of the IPO's musicians, a Holocaust survivor, played *Kaddish* at the entrance to the hall. Politicians and publicists attacked the orchestra for not showing consideration for the feelings of Holocaust survivors.

At the end of 2000, the Rishon Lezion Symphony Orchestra performed the *SIEGFRIED IDYLL*. Before the concert, the issue was heard for the first time by the Tel Aviv district court. Its ruling was compatible with the approach of the ministers of education: the decision should be left to the musical bodies.

Barenboim tried to lift the boycott again in 2001 when he was invited to the Israel Festival with the Berlin Staatskapelle. Tickets to the concert that included the first act of *Die WALKÜRE* were quickly sold. The planned concert prompted a debate in the Knesset and its Education and Culture Committee. The tense meeting of the committee concluded with an agreement with the heads of the festival and Barenboim not to perform the piece. At the end of the substitute concert that concluded the entire festival, Barenboim asked the audience to discuss the matter and listen to an excerpt from *Tristan und Isolde*. Some members of the audience, mainly people in their 30s and 40s, left the hall and the piece was performed in relative peace and quiet.

The management of the Bayreuth Festival twice approached Israel in an attempt to encourage reconciliation. In 1998, the University of Bayreuth, the Bayreuth Festival, and Tel Aviv University organized a conference, the subject of which was Wagner and the Jews. The participants were intellectuals from Germany, Israel, and other countries. At the end of 2010, it became known that the management of the Festival wished to host the Israeli Chamber Orchestra at its opening. In both instances the argument was renewed, albeit on a smaller scope.   NA'AMA SHEFFI

See also BAYREUTH FESTIVAL, HISTORY OF THE

Dieter Borchmeyer et al., eds., *Richard Wagner und die Juden* (Stuttgart: Metzler, 2000).
Na'ama Sheffi, *The Ring of Myths* (see bibliography).

Italy, Wagner's view of and reception in

1. Wagner's view of Italy
2. Italian Wagner reception to 1871 and Bologna's *Lohengrin*
3. Wagner's works in Italy to 1914
4. Twentieth-century trends and beyond

1. Wagner's view of Italy

Like many German-speaking intellectuals of his time, Wagner esteemed Italy for its classical heritage and Renaissance art while disdaining contemporary Italian culture. His contempt was aimed particularly at Italian opera. To Wagner's chagrin, opera – an Italian invention – was being cultivated more fruitfully in Italy and FRANCE than in Germany. Yet Wagner dated the beginning of the alleged current decline of Italian music precisely to the rise of opera, an argument he sets out in OPER UND DRAMA (Opera and Drama, 1851): Italian opera had decayed into mere entertainment and spoiled the Italians' natural musical vein; ROSSINI epitomized the climax of this development and, hence, the death of opera. This bleak outlook helped Wagner clear a space for his "true" (and German) MUSIC DRAMA. Yet despite using Italian opera as a negative aesthetic foil, Wagner – like so many German artists before him – carried forth the idea of "beautiful Italy" whose warm climate, southern landscapes, and historical sites increasingly offered respite from his work, the rough Franconian weather, and German seriousness.

2. Italian Wagner reception to 1871 and Bologna's Lohengrin

Wagner's personal fondness for Italy was fostered by his appreciation of the surprisingly vivid discourse about, and recognition of, his art in Italy, which he contrasted positively with his tenuous reception in France. Beginning in the mid-1850s, this discourse initially addressed mostly his writings. These were appropriated for contrasting positions within an ongoing debate about the necessity and direction of an OPERATIC REFORM, which in turn became linked to larger issues such as post-unification Italian identity, economic concerns, internationalism, and experiences of MODERNITY. The association of Wagner with cosmopolitanism and progress, as opposed to Italian provincialism, was particularly pronounced among the *scapigliati* (the "unkempt" or Bohemian ones), a Milanese group of young musicians and writers including Arrigo Boito, who translated several Wagner libretti. More decidedly Wagnerian was the critic Filippo Filippi; in 1870 he undertook, and reported on, one of the first Italian pilgrimages to Wagner performances in Germany.

Polemics about the "musica dell'avvenire" (music of the future) skyrocketed with the triumphant premiere of LOHENGRIN at Bologna's Teatro Comunale on 1 November 1871, the first performance of a Wagner opera in Italy. Several factors helped make Bologna the capital of Italian WAGNERISM, including the partisanship of its (then) liberal mayor Camillo Casarini, the promotion by the music publisher Giovannina Lucca, who in 1868 had acquired the Italian rights to Wagner's works, and the meticulous musical direction by Angelo Mariani, who had brought the Comunale to international acclaim. All three (and the entire production team) had attended Wagner's own production in MUNICH. Moreover, some considered Wagner a means to outdo Milan as a cultural center. So much attention (and revenue) did Lohengrin garner that the production was exported to Florence and, in 1872, Wagner was named honorary citizen of Bologna. However, the press remained divided. Hostile critics devalued Wagner from the nationalist perspective of an opposition between the "true," melodic, and instinctual Italian opera and symphonic, intellectual German music – an antagonism resembling, with inverse preferences, contemporaneous Germanic responses to Italian opera.

3. Wagner's works in Italy to 1914

Anti-Wagnerian patriotic demonstrations increased during the Italian premiere of TANNHÄUSER in Bologna the following year and, in 1873, nearly drowned out the first *Lohengrin* at Italy's foremost theater, La Scala in Milan. Here, hostilities were boosted by VERDI's publisher Ricordi, owner of the leading Italian music periodical. Not until Ricordi acquired its rival Lucca in 1888 did La Scala rehabilitate *Lohengrin*, followed by the first Italian *MEISTERSINGER* in 1889. Bologna meanwhile resumed its Wagnerian advocacy with *RIENZI* (1876, following Venice two years earlier) as well as the Italian premieres of *Der FLIEGENDE HOLLÄNDER* (1877), *TRISTAN* (1888), and *PARSIFAL* (1914). The *RING* cycle was successfully introduced to five Italian cities by Angelo NEUMANN's touring Wagner Theater in 1883. By the mid-1890s, virtually every theatre had staged *Lohengrin*, while *Holländer*, *Tannhäuser*, and *Die WALKÜRE* gradually entered the repertory. In Bologna, a WAGNER SOCIETY (founded in 1887) furthered the Wagnerian cause with annual Wagner concerts and the *CRONACA WAGNERIANA* (1893–5). Turin came a close second in the number of Wagner performances, which were here supported, among others, by the composer-conductor Carlo Pedrotti, the impresario Giovanni Depanis, and the critic Giuseppe Depanis.

From 1876, when several Italian notables attended the first BAYREUTH FESTIVAL, both detractors and the minority of supporters of Wagner produced book-length studies, some translated into German. Apart from nationalist prejudices (continually buttressed in many daily or popular music papers), key points of contention were the extent of innovation in his works (as opposed to his theories), the nature or lack of melodies, orchestral "realism," an absence of theatricality, and the perceived overall monotony of his later operas; even some Wagnerians such as Francesco D'Arcais and Enrico Panzacchi favored the pre-*Tristan* oeuvre. Amidst popularizing writings, Luigi Torchi's voluminous biography of 1890 heralded a more positivist, "scientific" discussion of Wagner and his German context. During the 1890s, a number of young Italians became – sometimes temporarily – glowing Wagner adepts, such as the poet Enrico Thovez. Although Wagner's persona received less attention than in German discourse, leftist and proto-nationalist writers looked favorably upon his revolutionary past, most notably Gabriele D'Annunzio. Epitomizing the thriving literary Wagnerism that peaked in Italy around 1900, his novels were stylistically influenced by, and saturated with references to, Wagner's works.

4. Twentieth-century trends and beyond

From around 1910, Wagner began to represent outmoded political and aesthetic ideas. Linked to a revival of sixteenth- to eighteenth-century Italian music and, later, a revaluation of nineteenth-century Italian opera, the antagonism between pro- and anti-Wagnerians turned into a more general argument about modernism and *italianità*. As elsewhere, reactions against ROMANTICISM and the perceived cultural DECADENCE associated with Wagner fed a growing disillusionment with him among musicians, intellectuals, and the AVANT-GARDE; instead, a Mediterranean, melodious, non-mystical music drama was envisioned. By the 1920s, despite some musicological efforts and isolated literary proponents such as Arturo Onofri, Wagnerism in Italy was largely marginalized.

Nevertheless, the decades following World War I brought an ever-growing number of Wagner performances. At La Scala, at least two of his works were usually programmed each season; Arturo TOSCANINI advocated uncut performances; and anti-illusionist directorial approaches were tried, including the only staged realization of Adolphe APPIA's visionary *Tristan* (1923) and, in 1964, WIELAND WAGNER's rendition. Wagner was an integral part of Florence's *Maggio musicale* (launched in 1933) and initially both eponym and main focus of the Ravello Festival, founded in 1953 to mark the seventieth anniversary of Wagner's death. Beginning in the late 1930s, theaters shifted towards performances in German. After the 1950s, Wagner productions decreased and tended to be less committed to new conceptual readings than elsewhere in Europe. More recently these trends have been fading, in line with a global theatrical reemphasis on Wagner.   GUNDULA KREUZER

John W. Barker, "A Forgotten Early Champion of Wagner: Venetian Bandmaster Jacopo Calascione," *Journal of Band Research*, 43 (2007–8): 1–37.

Adriana Guarnieri Corazzol, *Tristano, mio Tristano: Gli scrittori italiani e il caso Wagner* (Bologna: Il Mulino, 1988).

Ute Jung, *Die Rezeption der Kunst Richard Wagners in Italien* (Regensburg: Gustav Bosse, 1974).

Axel Körner, *Politics of Culture in Liberal Italy: From Unification to Fascism* (New York and London: Routledge, 2009).

Marion S. Miller, "Wagnerism, Wagnerians, and Italian Identity," in *Wagnerism in European Culture and Politics*, ed. Large and Weber (see bibliography): 167–97.

Museo teatrale alla Scala, ed., *Il caso Wagner al Teatro alla Scala, 1873–1991* (Milan: Selís, 1994).

Wagner und Italien, *wagnerspectrum* 6.1 (2010).

Italy, Wagner's travels to. When able to travel for pleasure, not professional reasons, Wagner invariably chose Italian destinations.

Wagner's first journey solely for his own recreation was a HIKING tour through the Swiss Alps in 1852 (10 July–5 August), ending at the Borromean Islands in Lago Maggiore. The following year he made a more substantial inroad (14 July–10 September 1853). Tormented by ill HEALTH and by difficulties in beginning composition of the RING, he toured alone through Turin to Genoa, which delighted him as his first "genuine Italian city." Moving to LA SPEZIA, he had an almost visionary experience that inspired the opening pages of *Das RHEINGOLD*.

Wagner's first extended Italian residence was in Venice (August 1858–March 1859). Still a political exile, he sought escape from his romantic entanglements with Mathilde WESENDONCK. In a rented flat in the Giustiniani Palaces on the Grand Canal, he set to work composing Act II of *TRISTAN UND ISOLDE*, tightly restricting his social life. He quickly succumbed to the Lagoon City's magic. A gondolier song, he later admitted, influenced the Shepherd's pipe tune that opens Act III. Indifferent to visual art at that time in his life, he enjoyed Venice's theater offerings but ignored its limited musical world, though he ventured contacts with the military bands of the Austrian army, then occupying the city. He did, however, become disillusioned with Venice's winter weather.

In November 1861, Wagner returned briefly to Venice, on invitation from the Wesendoncks, who first drew him to Venetian painting. He later claimed that the great *Assumption* by Titian inspired him to begin composing *Die MEISTERSINGER*, a statement still puzzling analysts. With his first wife

MINNA dead (1866), and scandalously involved with COSIMA, Wagner took the latter on a sentimental visit to her birthplace at Lake Como in 1868, adding stops in the Borromean Islands and Genoa.

Wagner renewed travels to Italy only in 1876. Exhausted following the *Ring* premiere at the first BAYREUTH FESTIVAL, he took Cosima and their children for an extended tour around the peninsula (14 September–29 December), most of which was totally new for both. Passing through Verona, they spent a week in Venice (20–27 September) at its Europa Hotel. Entranced by the city, Cosima reinforced Wagner's enthusiasm for it. She spurred his interest in its art and monuments, and, captivated by Titian's *Assumption*, initiated their preoccupation with it in subsequent visits.

Briefly in Bologna, Wagner was welcomed in this first Italian city to give his music warm reception. On initial encounter (29 September–5 October), Naples gave pleasure, but the fullest rest was found during a month's residence in Sorrento (6 October–7 November). NIETZSCHE was also staying nearby, and his tumultuous conversation with Wagner began their parting of paths. By way of Naples, the Wagners moved to Rome (9 November–3 December), where they toured the sites – reacting with Lutheran disgust to St. Peter's – and pursued personal contacts. Cosima socialized uncomfortably with Princess SAYN-WITTGENSTEIN, the *inamorata* of her father, Franz LISZT. Suppressing his usual scorn for Italian musical life, Richard met with composers Giovanni Sgambati and Paolo Tosti, plus composer-conductor Luigi Mancinelli. There, too, he encountered the Comte de GOBINEAU. Another new city for the Wagners was Florence (3–17 December), with a brief rush back to Bologna (4–5 December) allowing Richard to attend a performance there of *RIENZI*. In Florence, he crossed paths with a past romantic interest, Jessie LAUSSOT. By train, via Bologna again, the family returned to Munich and Bayreuth.

Subsequently, Richard and Cosima discussed a wide range of various travel destinations around the Mediterranean world, but their thoughts invariably returned to Italy. By 1880, in bad health, despairing of another Bayreuth winter, with the orchestration for *PARSIFAL* still not begun, Wagner took his family for their longest Italian sojourn (3 January–31 October). They traveled by train to Naples, outside of which they rented the Villa d'Angri, residing there for the bulk of the trip (4 January–8 August). Initially nursing his health, Wagner indulged his curiosity about the Neapolitan law courts.

Again overcoming his disdain for Italian musical life, Wagner visited the Naples Music Conservatory during Holy Week (25–26 March), admiring performances of music by Leonardo Leo and Clément Jannequin. He also thawed the hostility of anti-Wagnerian critic Francesco Florimo by praising the latter's idol, BELLINI. Sgambati was welcomed as a visitor, and Engelbert HUMPERDINCK, now a Bayreuth assistant, came to consult on *Parsifal*. Wagner even discussed possible scenic designs with the painter Arnold Böcklin. Most important, however, was the beginning of Wagner's friendship with the Russian-born painter Paul von JOUKOWSKY, who soon became a regular family companion. On an excursion with Joukowsky, by way of Amalfi, Wagner found at Ravello his model for KLINGSOR's magic garden.

Problems of health and weather soured the Naples experience, and the Wagners departed, via Rome, to Tuscany where they eventually settled at the Villa Torre Fiorentino outside Siena (22 August–1 October). Wagner was overwhelmed by Siena's grand Duomo, which he assigned Joukowsky to use as the scenic model for his Grail Temple. Renewing his own work on the *Parsifal* scoring, he also completed his dictation to Cosima of his autobiography, *MEIN LEBEN* (My Life, 1865–81). Finally, the Wagners devoted nearly a month to Venice (4–30 October), staying first at the Hotel Danieli and then the Palazzo Contarini delle Figure on the Grand Canal. With Joukowsky, the Wagners again relished the sights and art.

Despite various travel ideas, the Wagners undertook their next vacation again in Italy (November 1881–May 1882), and in a long-considered city, Palermo in Sicily, residing first in its Hôtel des Palmes, then in the suburban Villa Porazzi (Villa Gangi). During this stay (5 November–19 March) Wagner completed the scoring for *Parsifal*, and was sketched by the artist RENOIR. There began the courting of Cosima's daughter, Blandine von Bülow, by the impoverished Sicilian nobleman, Count Biagio GRAVINA. Meanwhile, to thank his Sicilian hosts, Wagner organized and conducted a private performance of his *SIEGFRIED IDYLL*, and two of his marches, using local musicians.

From Palermo, the Wagners moved to Catania and Acireale (20 March–10 April 1882), where they witnessed a rail passage by the dying Garibaldi, and enjoyed an excursion to Taormina. By steamship to Naples and by train north, they made a substantial stay in Venice (15–29 April), again at the Hotel Europa. While there, at a concert in the Piazza San Marco by the Municipal Band, Wagner first encountered its bandmaster, Jacopo Calascione. By now the Wagners had succumbed completely to Venice, and, despite fantasies about far-flung and exotic places, they made plans for a return visit to Venice the following winter.

That would represent their recuperation following the *Parsifal* premiere in the summer of 1882. After a temporary stop at the Hotel Europa (16–18 August), they settled into a large suite of rooms in the mezzanine of the Palazzo Vendramin-Calergi. Their life was tight-knit and semi-isolated. Joukowsky became an added member of the family, though not residing with them. Some visitors did so, however, such as the conductor Hermann LEVI and, above all, Franz Liszt. His stay at the Vendramin (19 November–13 January) was often disruptive, especially to Wagner's restrictive social life.

Regularly more comfortable in the company of painters than musicians, Wagner still held the Italian musical scene in general contempt, and likewise its personalities – with a few exceptions, such as bandmaster Calascione. He accepted contacts with the local Liceo, the Conservatorio di Musica Benedetto Marcello. Coming to respect its faculty and student musicians, he engaged them for a performance of his youthful Symphony in C major, as a birthday/Christmas gift to Cosima. Humperdinck arrived from Bayreuth to assist. A series of rehearsals, at first kept secret from Cosima, culminated in the performance on Christmas Eve for a small audience of family and friends, in the Fenice Theater's Sala Apollonea – Wagner's last performance as a conductor.

Liszt left before the Venetian Carnival in January, in whose revelry Wagner and his family joined more than once, especially for the dramatic closing night. Richard is described as being unusually vigorous at the time, despite the general fragility of his health – then being monitored by Dr. Friedrich Keppler, a physician and gynecologist resident in Venice who had become the family doctor. Rainy weather disrupted Wagner's plans of a tour of some regional cities with his son, SIEGFRIED. Then on the afternoon of Tuesday, 13 February, one of his recurrent heart spasms proved fatal. His death immediately became international news, but the family forbade any commemorations or ceremony as the embalmed corpse was taken off by special train to Bayreuth.

Venice, Wagner's favorite non-German city, seems to have opened his mind and sensitivities as did no other. He read deeply into its history. He relished Venetian theater, especially the plays of Goldoni and Gozzi. With Cosima he enjoyed paintings at the Accademia and elsewhere. He was particularly inspired by Venice's architecture and monuments, and pontificated on them to his family. Above all, he appreciated the inherent theatricality of the Venetian ambience.

Conversely, Venice incorporated Wagner into its mystique. For decades, an annual commemoration of his death was offered, especially by bandmaster Calascione. There are more monuments and markers to Wagner around the city than to any other foreigner, and his personal rooms are now restored in the Palazzo Vendramin.   JOHN W. BARKER

John W. Barker, *Wagner and Venice* (University of Rochester Press, 2008).
Paul Gerhardt Dippel, *Richard Wagner und Italien: Vom Zaubergarten zur Lagune* (Emsdetten: Lechte, 1966).
Carlo de Incontrera, "I viaggi di Wagner in Italia," in *Wagner in Italia*, ed. Giancarlo Rostirola (Turin: RAI, 1982): 9–54, plus 68 plates.

Jews. Wagner's attitudes towards the Jews as a collective have been well explored in the extensive literature on his ANTI-SEMITISM. His relationship with individuals who self-identified or were identified as Jews is less clear. Indeed, who was considered "Jewish" and what that term actually meant in Wagner's time was not a clear-cut matter. The nineteenth century was for European, especially for German, Jews the best of times and the worst of times. Civil emancipation, increased economic and social mobility, and access to secular education were slowly acquired by European Jews: all balanced by the rise of political anti-Semitism (which desired to reverse civil emancipation), and the reappearance in altered form of older forms of anti-Semitism in the shape of the "blood libel." Political realities in the Russian Empire led to massive pogroms and the flight of millions of Eastern and mainly unacculturated Jews west to travel and settle in the cities of western Europe and beyond. Yet this also led to the rise of a range of Jewish responses to these political realities from assimilation and conversion, to the rise of political and cultural Zionism, to the establishment of secular Jewish political parties (at least in the Austro-Hungarian Empire). This snapshot is both reductive as well as accurate.

Between Wagner's birth in 1813 and his death in 1883 the very question "who is a Jew?" became ever more difficult to answer, yet it was asked ever more frequently. Many Jews, even those in Wagner's musical circle, such as the Viennese musicologist Guido Adler, remained Jewish in their religious and ethnic identity. Some Jews in his circle, such as the conductor Hermann LEVI, though the son of a rabbi, had left the Jewish community as adults and were "without confession," yet with an ambiguous relationship to their Jewish background. Some, such as Michael Bernays, the greatest Goethe scholar of his time, also the son of a rabbi, had simply converted as a young man. Some, such as Heinrich HEINE, one of Wagner's *bêtes noires*, whom he met in the 1840s and about whom he initially wrote with enthusiasm, also converted to Christianity (read: Protestantism) and yet remained very much Jews in their own eyes as well as the eyes of contemporaries such as Wagner. Later, Wagner excoriated the convert Heine as "the conscience of Judaism, just as Judaism is the evil conscience of our modern Civilization" (PW 3:100). Some, who had been raised outside the Jewish community, such as Felix MENDELSSOHN BARTHOLDY and his sister Fanny, were labeled as Jews no matter their own self-identification. Indeed, some Jews were more Jewish than others, both in the estimation of the world in which they lived (Eastern Jews were seen through Western eyes as especially "Jewish") as well as often in their own.

Wagner's relationship to living "Jews" is much more complex than his denigration of Jews as a collective. We can take three examples. One is the case of Fromental HALÉVY, where Wagner's admiration trumped his own attitude towards both the Jews and French GRAND OPERA. Son of a cantor, Halévy's Jewish background was reflected in what may well have been the most popular opera of the day, *La Juive* (1835) as well as his first major work, the *Marche funèbre et de profundis en Hébreu* (1820).

Wagner met Halévy in 1840 and 1841, during his Paris years, and mentions him in *MEIN LEBEN* (My Life, 1865–81), noting that he had undertaken a piano score of his opera *La Reine de Chypre* (1841), about which he had written an essay in 1842. Wagner clearly admired Halévy and, in his essay on French opera, he praises the German reception of *La Juive* as having "awakened that kind of innermost profound sympathy, which, if truthfully aroused, indicates close kinship. In delighted surprise and true edification the German can recognize in this creation ... the clearest and loveliest traces of BEETHOVEN's spirit which represents the quintessence of the German school" (SSD 12:142). Cosima records Wagner praising *La Juive* as the opera that "restored to [him his] taste for clean [*saubere*] music, after it had been totally corrupted in Paris" (CWD 16 June 1874). One needs to add that the figure of Eléazar in *La Juive*, whose aria "Rachel, quand du Seigneur" remains a standard ornament of the tenor repertoire, is a complex and difficult representation of the Jew. More in the mold of Shakespeare's Shylock than that of Walter Scott's Isaac, Eléazar presents the negative image of the Jew on the stage.

Halévy functions as the "good Jewish operatic composer" in contrast to Giacomo MEYERBEER, whom Wagner also knew in Paris in the 1840s and who is the focus of Wagner's initially anonymous essay *Das JUDENTUM IN DER MUSIK* (Jewishness in Music, 1850).

Wagner's relationship to Felix Mendelssohn Bartholdy was equally complex. By 1850, he served alongside Meyerbeer as the focus of "Jewishness in Music": "Mendelssohn [in contrast to Beethoven] reduces these achievements to vague, fantastic shadow-forms, midst whose indefinite shimmer our freakish fancy is indeed aroused, but our inner, purely-human yearning for distinct artistic sight is hardly touched with even the merest hope of a fulfillment" (PW 3:96) And yet Wagner acknowledges (unlike with Meyerbeer) his sympathy toward Mendelssohn: "This, as we have said, is the tragic trait in Mendelssohn's life-history; and if in the domain of Art we are to give our sympathy to the sheer personality, we can scarcely deny a large measure thereof to Mendelssohn, even though the force of that sympathy be weakened by the reflection that the Tragic, in Mendelssohn's situation, hung rather over him than came to actual, sore and cleansing consciousness" (PW 3:96). Wagner had met Mendelssohn when the latter attended a performance of *Der FLIEGENDE HOLLÄNDER* in Berlin, and afterwards went backstage to congratulate Wagner. Wagner wrote to Mendelssohn after that evening that "I am really happy that you like me. If I have come a little closer to you, that is the nicest thing about my whole Berlin expedition" (quoted in Werner 179). Yet well after Mendelssohn's death, Wagner continued to see him as a hated rival (as in 1850), and therefore dismissed any originality in his work. Cosima records that: "One evening Richard sees the 'Songs without Words' by Mendelssohn on the piano. He shows me the 'Venetian Barcarole' where Mendelssohn, omitting the main part uses the refrain of [Rossini's] *Otello* and passes it off as a folk tune" (CWD 16 October 1882). A truly "Jewish" trait, according to Wagner: the inability to be original in the writing of Western music.

Wagner's personal anti-Semitism colored his relationship with actual, living Jews. Yet he was quite willing to have both a social and a professional relationship with those self-same Jews. At the time, the long term anti-Semitic mayor of Vienna, Karl Lueger (1844–1910), defined his similar relationships with Jews by remarking: "I decide who is a Jew" – Wagner did much the same. Typical of this is his difficult and aggressive relationship to Hermann Levi, the royal music director, and the conductor LUDWIG II demanded be given a central role at Bayreuth. Levi's relationship to Wagner was in his own estimation pathological, as he wrote to his friend, the Nobel Laureate Paul Heyse, himself half-Jewish: "I am addicted to that man [Wagner] body and soul" (Gay 216). (Indeed, the support of Wagner's music on the part of Jews of all shades has been remarked upon, then as now. But one must add that while Jews were present among the musical avant-garde, most Jews as well as non-Jews in the German-speaking lands had little or no interest in Wagner's music at the time.) Levi, often a guest at WAHNFRIED, was regularly humiliated by the Wagner family at the dinner table because of his Jewish background. Cosima noted in her diary following a visit to Bayreuth: "When we were alone, we discussed the strange attraction of Wagner to certain Jews; he said: 'We shall yet have a synagogue in Wahnfried'" (CWD 13 January 1879). One can add here that Levi was buried in the public park in Garmisch-Partenkirchen (Bavaria). The Nazis destroyed his monument and vandalized his grave – a comment on the problematic ambiguity of social and political anti-Semitism in nineteenth-century Germany and its real-political results in the twentieth.

SANDER L. GILMAN

Laurence Dreyfus, "Hermann Levi's Shame and Parsifal's Guilt: A Critique of Essentialism in Biography and Criticism," *Cambridge Opera Journal* 6.2 (July 1994): 125–45.

Peter Gay, "Hermann Levi: A Study in Service and Self-Hatred," in *Freud, Jews, and Other Germans: Masters and Victim in Modernist Culture* (New York: Oxford University Press, 1978): 189–231.

Diana R. Hallman, *Opera, Liberalism, and Antisemitism in Nineteenth-Century France: The Politics of Halévy's "La Juive"* (Cambridge University Press, 2002).

Eric Werner, "Jews around Richard and Cosima Wagner," *The Musical Quarterly* 71.2 (1985): 172–99.

Joukowsky, Paul von (1845–1912), Russian-German painter who was a close family friend for the last three years of Wagner's life, often travelling with them to ITALY. Joukowsky designed four of the five sets for the first production of *PARSIFAL* at the FESTIVAL THEATER (1882). He proved to be an ideal collaborator as he was fully prepared to modify his designs at Wagner's behest. Although the sets are not entirely free of a historicist obsession with detail, they display a level of abstraction and a concern with atmosphere that anticipate symbolist stage design. Joukowsky sketched a portrait of Wagner on the evening before his death in the Palazzo Vendramin in VENICE.

SIMON WILLIAMS

Judentum in der Musik, Das (Jewishness in Music, also: Judaism in Music). This essay was first published in the NEUE ZEITSCHRIFT FÜR MUSIK (3 and 6 September 1850) under the pseudonym "K. Freigedank" (*free thinking*), and reissued in 1869 with the author's name, appearing in several translations and new editions thereafter (French 1850; Italian 1897; English 1898). The essay has been cited as the primary source for demonstrating Wagner's ANTI-SEMITISM in his works, POLITICS, and cultural legacy. It started out as an attack on the unnamed composer Giacomo MEYERBEER and grew into a diatribe against the alleged destructiveness of all Jewish influence in contemporary European culture. Wagner at first chose to exclude it from an edition of his collected writings, but then later added it in.

1. The essay
2. Wagner's anti-Semitism
3. The influence of *Das Judentum*

1. The essay

The ideas in this essay were largely in line with other contemporary reactions against Jewish emancipation that exaggerated the supposed threats to German culture posed by JEWS' successes in the arts and letters. Wagner argued that the Jew had been held back from contributing to true German art because of his language and cultural background, but in recent times had managed to influence European culture, owing to the latter's inherent weakening. Despite the poisonous tone of much of the essay, in the end Wagner does not suggest that the Jew be excluded from a thriving German cultural life, and even proposes the Jew overcome his cultural inferiority, albeit not through religious conversion alone but through total self-denial and assimilation. He uses the term *Untergang* ("going under") to describe this, a term which unfortunately has taken on more violent implications in post-Holocaust analyses of the text.

What does distinguish this essay from others of its time, however, is the ambitious and detailed exploration of supposed Jewish traits, some of which could be tied to physical characteristics. Presuming that one harbors a "natural revulsion" toward the Jews, Wagner refers to their "unpleasantly foreign" physical appearance and launches into a lengthy examination of Jewish speech, claiming that Jews can never acquire fluency in modern European languages. He details the "repulsiveness" of Jewish speech tones and purports the Jews' inability to engage in meaningful dialogue or express deep emotions. Jews have, in Wagner's view, nevertheless managed to dominate the musical world, and he attributes their success to the relative ease by which musical style can be imitated, leaving it vulnerable to Jewish appropriation. He argues that such Jewish "imitations" are doomed to failure, however, since Jews can only draw upon sterile and outmoded synagogue chant for inspiration. He claims to detect such emotional emptiness and superficiality in the works of MENDELSSOHN and the unnamed Meyerbeer.

Wagner's views never quite cross over into identifying the Jews as a distinct race, and he endorses a process of REDEMPTION by which Jews such as the political satirist Ludwig Börne (1786–1837) had supposedly freed themselves from their burdensome legacy. Nevertheless, the explicit descriptions of Jewish traits that can be linked to physical characteristics, the ambiguity of the term *Untergang* as the solution to the Jewish "problem," the evocation of biological metaphors (he refers to Jewish-dominated German music as a "worm-infested corpse"), and the violent recommendation for "the forceful ejection of this destructive foreign element" that he puts forth but immediately rejects as impracticable in the preface to the 1869 reissue, could serve as validation for later arguments promoting racial anti-Semitism and, ultimately, the extermination of European Jewry.

2. Wagner's anti-Semitism

Despite the support and assistance Wagner had received from Jews, he published *Das Judentum* in 1850, around the same time that like-minded conservatives had linked democratic movements with the Jewish community because of a few prominent Jews in their ranks. Most puzzling is the fact that he chose to publish the essay first under a pseudonym, and then reissued it in 1869 under his own name (apparently against COSIMA's advice), all the while maintaining close and fruitful relationships with Jews. A statement by NIETZSCHE first suggested that Wagner's anti-Semitism was a form of self-hatred stemming from a suspicion that his biological father was a Jew (*The Case of Wagner*), but more systematic studies, especially that of Jacob Katz, have offered compelling arguments that Wagner's anti-Semitism grew out of an uncontrollable artistic paranoia rather than self-hatred, racism, or even a consistent political anti-Jewish agenda. Yet the coincidence of his public reissue of the essay in 1869 with the rise of organized anti-Semitism in Germany made him appear as a pioneer of the movement and gave him occasion to exploit this position toward his own self-advancement.

Prior to penning *Das Judentum*, Wagner was not known to be an outspoken anti-Semite but instead admired and befriended a number of Jews, though some of his earlier writings already contain anti-Semitic references. *Das Judentum* arose in response to an ongoing debate in the *Neue Zeitschrift für Musik* and other journals over the tremendous success of Meyerbeer's *Le Prophète* and the ensuing anti-Semitic attack on its composer, instigated by Wagner's friend Theodor UHLIG in the late spring of 1850. However, Wagner also gave vent to his own strained professional relationship with Meyerbeer, his failures in PARIS despite Meyerbeer's assistance, and his desire to liberate himself from this perceived subservience. Wagner's discomfort had reached a climax when critics found striking similarities between his own musical works and those of Meyerbeer while simultaneously castigating Meyerbeer's music for its alleged "Hebraic" traits (Uhlig's term). Unwilling to attack Meyerbeer openly, Wagner never named him directly in the essay but instead expanded his criticism to include the inherent failings of all Jewish creations and, in the process, compromised the work of artists he had previously admired, including Felix Mendelssohn and Heinrich HEINE.

Thereafter Wagner seems to have let his paranoia get the better of him, assuming that his identity as author must have been known, and interpreting any negative reception of his music thereafter as "Jewish conspiracies" in retribution for its publication. When he decided to republish the essay nineteen years later, this was done as a gesture of openly confronting his imagined Jewish adversaries. Ironically his identity as author of the 1850 essay was not as widely known as he had assumed, and its re-publication sent shock waves among his many Jewish admirers. Yet Wagner's unveiling as the author of this rabid attack also had the opposite effect of attracting the attention of anti-Semitic writers such as Paul Lagarde, Constantin FRANTZ, and his own future son-in-law Houston Stewart CHAMBERLAIN, as well as that of the Jewish musician Joseph RUBINSTEIN, who successfully appealed to Wagner to aid him in finding "redemption" from his supposed Jewish failings. The establishment of the BAYREUTH FESTIVAL later created a forum for anti-Semitic dialogue with the publication of the first *BAYREUTHER BLÄTTER* in 1878.

Wagner was emboldened to weave his anti-Semitic ideas into the arguments of later essays, such as *WAS IST DEUTSCH?* (What is German?, 1865/78) and *ERKENNE DICH SELBST* (Know Thyself, 1881). Yet even at the peak of his fame as a prophet of the anti-Semitic movement, Wagner continued to cultivate close relationships with Jews, especially the conductor Hermann LEVI. Realizing the importance of appeasing his Jewish admirers, in 1880 Wagner cautiously refused to sign a petition to revoke Jewish rights. With such gestures, Wagner managed to maintain a public image more or less of neutrality toward the Jews, even though in his private life he was known at times to express shocking anti-Semitic sentiments, as documented in the diaries of his wife Cosima.

3. The influence of *Das Judentum*

By virtue of this essay, Wagner's impact on later anti-Semitic views was considerable, resonating in publications not only in Germany but also in other countries thanks to numerous translations of the essay. The links between HITLER and Wagner have become a source of heated controversy in which Wagner has been, on the one hand, designated as a prophetic architect of the Third Reich and, on the other hand, exonerated as a mere mouthpiece of the commonplace anti-Jewish sentiments of his times. In the Third Reich, "Das Judentum" was cited as one of the first German attempts to come to terms with the problems of the Jewish race in Europe, and musicologists were implored to continue Wagner's mission of getting to the bottom of the "Jewish question" although only a small number actually heeded the call. Instead they focused on analysis and critical editions of Wagner's works, biographical and genealogical studies, and documentary projects, many of which were to be carried out under the auspices of the incipient Richard Wagner Research Center at Bayreuth (Richard-Wagner-Forschungsstätte), a one-man operation founded by Otto STROBEL in 1938 under Hitler's edict. Still, the exaltation of Wagner in Nazi Germany provoked the exiled philosopher and music critic Theodor ADORNO in 1937 to write an extensive musical and sociological analysis of Wagner's impact on Germany. In this essay, Adorno was the first to detect anti-Semitism not only in Wagner's prose but also in several of his musical works. Almost simultaneously, there was a last-minute decision by the Palestine Symphony Orchestra in November 1938 to refrain from performing the overture to Wagner's *MEISTERSINGER VON NÜRNBERG* after learning of the *Kristallnacht* pogrom, a decision that grew into a hotly disputed ban on Wagner's music in ISRAEL. This ongoing controversy, combined with Adorno's suggestions that the roots of racial theory are laid out in Wagner's operas and that certain characters can be interpreted as anti-Semitic caricatures, have inspired a wealth of analyses that seek to expand or to discredit Adorno's assumptions and raise serious questions about the ethical implications of performing Wagner's music.   PAMELA M. POTTER

Theodor W. Adorno, *In Search of Wagner* (see bibliography).
Jens Malte Fischer, *Richard Wagners "Das Judentum in der Musik"* (see bibliography).
Jacob Katz, *The Darker Side of Genius* (see bibliography).
Na'ama Sheffi, *The Ring of Myths* (see bibliography).

Kaisermarsch ("Imperial March," WWV 104) in B♭ major, a single-movement concert piece for large orchestra with optional chorus. Composed between February and mid-March 1871, the work was first performed on 14 April in Berlin, to celebrate the proclamation of King Wilhelm I as "German Emperor." Originally it was scored for military band and conceived as a march for the return of the victorious German troops from the FRANCO-PRUSSIAN WAR, but Wagner subsequently revised it as an orchestral concert work. Between 14 and 16 March Wagner drafted a poetic text (*Volkslied*) to be sung from memory at the closing iteration of the main theme by a unison chorus consisting of the whole Prussian army ("Heil! Heil dem Kaiser!"). The work's emphatic nationalist purpose is made all the more explicit by the repeated quotation of Luther's *Ein feste Burg ist unser Gott*. It was performed at the ceremony for the foundation (*Grundsteinlegung*) of the Bayreuth Festspielhaus on 22 May 1872, in an arrangement for four-part chorus.   JEREMY COLEMAN

Karajan, Herbert von (b. Salzburg, 5 April 1908; d. Anif, 16 July 1989), one of the most influential conductors in Europe following World War II. He first came to prominence as a Wagnerian with a performance of *TRISTAN* at the Berlin State Opera on 21 October 1938 which prompted a laudatory review by the critic Edwin von der Null under the banner headline, "Das Wunder Karajan." At the first postwar Bayreuth Festivals in 1951/2, Karajan conducted the *RING*, *Die MEISTERSINGER*, and *Tristan* in performances acclaimed for their dramatic intensity. He later both stage-directed and conducted important Wagner performances at the Salzburg Easter Festival with the Berlin Philharmonic Orchestra, and in association with the stage designer Gunther Schneider-Siemssen. Karajan has left an impressive legacy of Wagner recordings. His style is notable for refined musicianship, clarity of instrumental texture, and beauty of sound. "You knew with Karajan that he would pick up the color and emotion of the phrase. He could reflect that in the orchestra" (Osborne 548).   ROGER ALLEN

See also PERFORMANCE, CONDUCTORS; PERFORMANCE, RECORDING HISTORY

Richard Osborne, *Herbert von Karajan: A Life in Music* (London: Chatto & Windus, 1998).

Keilberth, Joseph (b. Karlsruhe, 19 April 1908; d. Munich, 20 July 1968), conductor, acclaimed for performances of Wagner and Richard STRAUSS. He began his career in Karlsruhe where, in 1935, he was appointed Germany's youngest general music director. He later became Chief Conductor of the Berlin Staatskapelle and of the Bamberg Symphony orchestra, an ensemble made up of German musicians displaced from Czechoslovakia after the end of World War II. Keilberth established his Wagnerian credentials with his first RING cycle in 1936. In 1952, he was invited to Bayreuth, where he appeared regularly until 1956. His Wagner style, evident in the acclaimed Ring cycle recorded in 1955 but not issued until more than fifty years later, was in marked contrast to his Bayreuth contemporary Hans KNAPPERTSBUSCH: his predilection for swift tempi and lean textures was more in the manner of his early mentor Felix MOTTL. Keilberth died of a heart attack on the podium of the Bavarian State Opera whilst conducting a performance of TRISTAN.

ROGER ALLEN

Kietz, Ernst Benedikt (b. Leipzig, 9 March 1815; d. Dresden, 31 May 1892), German painter and lithographer. A pupil of Paul Delaroche, he lived in Paris from 1838 to 1870. One of Wagner's closest friends during his first PARIS stay (1839–42). Kietz made a few portraits of Wagner and a drawing of New Year's Eve 1841, when Wagner is depicted standing on a chair amidst his fellow Paris friends. Kietz was an unsuccessful painter whose fame is due exclusively to his friendship with Wagner. Wagner dedicated a piano album in E major to him, presumably in December 1840. Back in Dresden, Wagner also got to know Kietz's younger brother GUSTAV ADOLPH, a sculptor, who also became a close acquaintance of the Wagners. Wagner corresponded with Ernst Benedikt Kietz for about twenty years and visited him each time he travelled to Paris in the 1850s. After 1861, the former close contact withered and died completely.

HERMANN GRAMPP

Kietz, Gustav Adolph (b. Leipzig, 26 March 1824; d. Dresden, 24 June 1908), sculptor, who studied with Ernst Rietschel. Gustav was the younger brother of the artist ERNST BENEDIKT KIETZ, with whom Wagner developed a close friendship during his PARIS stay (1839–42). Gustav Adolph was a frequent guest at the Wagner household in DRESDEN, and participated in the DRESDEN UPRISING (1849). Later he sculpted busts of Wagner and COSIMA. Kietz's chatty and vivid recollections (published 1905) include documents from his brother Ernst Benedikt's estate.

MARGARET ELEANOR MENNINGER

Gustav Adolf Kietz, *Richard Wagner in den Jahren 1842–1849 und 1873–1875: Erinnerungen von Gustav Adolf Kietz, aufgezeichnet von Marie Kietz* (Dresden: Carl Reissner, 1905).

Klindworth, Karl (b. Hanover, 25 September 1830; d. Stolpe [Oranienburg], 27 July 1916), pianist of great accomplishment and successful conductor of concerts. Klindworth is remembered today for his series of Wagnerian vocal scores. He was a star pupil of LISZT; Wagner was much impressed by him, both musically and personally: "if the man had a tenor voice, I'd not shrink from abducting him; he's got everything else, especially the physical appearance, that it takes to be SIEGFRIED" (letter to Otto WESENDONCK, 21 March 1855). A man of immense energy, when the second act of his vocal score of GÖTTERDÄMMERUNG was lost in the post from Moscow, where Klindworth taught, he duly arrived at WAHNFRIED to start another one from scratch. Politically, Klindworth was right-wing and nationalistic, writing in 1907 "I believe that only a terrible world war can ... bring our people back to prudence and moderation, faith and moral aspiration" (quoted in Hamann 5). His adopted English daughter, the orphaned WINIFRED Williams, eventually married Wagner's son, SIEGFRIED, and later befriended HITLER.   DAVID HUCKVALE

See also PIANO ARRANGEMENTS AND REDUCTIONS

Brigitte Hamann, *Winifred Wagner: A Life at the Heart of Hitler's Bayreuth* (see bibliography).

Klingsor (bass; character in PARSIFAL), demonic magician, who holds KUNDRY in bondage and seeks to destroy the Grail community. Klingsor is a distinctive creation with roots in the medieval sources. Klingsor's Magic Garden is a sensual reincarnation of WOLFRAM VON ESCHENBACH's "Schastel Marveile" in his epic poem *Parzival*, and the Flower Maidens are counterparts to the four hundred maidens held captive by Clinschor in Wolfram's saga. In the medieval poem, Clinschor's castration by a cuckolded husband helped enable him to develop magic powers. In Wagner's version, Klingsor's castration is self-inflicted; the magician is a fallen angel, a former member of the Grail community who has devoted himself to black magic. As Wagner's drama begins, Klingsor has already seized the Holy Spear and used it to deal the Grail-King AMFORTAS a wound that will not heal. Having gained the spear, Klingsor covets the Grail as well, and plans to ruin PARSIFAL by exploiting his control over the temptress Kundry, who had earlier helped him to damage Amfortas.

Another, little-known source was C. T. L. Lucas's 1838 treatise *Ueber den Krieg von Wartburg*, which the composer obtained around 1840 while living in PARIS. Lucas's speculations about the names in the medieval sagas clearly attracted Wagner's attention. According to Lucas, the name "Clinschor," as it appears in Wolfram, signifies "Clin-jour" or "daybreak." Lucas identifies the magician as an enemy of LOVE, which is here associated with night, while thereby linking the name of the character with Lucifer. This interpretation resonates with Wagner's handling of the demonic Klingsor in *Parsifal* as well as with the allegorical treatment of night that he would develop in TRISTAN UND ISOLDE. On the other hand, a "Klingsor" character also appears prominently in the saga material about the Wartburg song contests that Wagner assimilated into the second act of TANNHÄUSER. Wagner's interest was surely aroused as well by Lucas's observations about the musical implications of the German variant of the name as "Klings-Ohr" or "Klingsohr" (ear sound).

In *Parsifal*, Klingsor represents the anti-Grail, and he dominates the middle act of the drama, which is set in his *Zauberschloss* (magic castle). His associated tonality is B minor, which begins and closes this act. Klingsor's primary theme is a twisting, highly chromatic subject. The coiling, chromatic motive of Kundry's seduction (the so-called *Zaubermotiv* or Magic motive) is closely linked to Klingsor's music, pointing to his control over her. The first notes of this serpentine motive are heard as B–D–E♯–F♯ when Klingsor first appears, declaiming the words "Die Zeit ist da" (The time has come; Example 7).

7. Klingsor motive "Die Zeit ist da"

These same words are spoken by Kundry when she disappears in the previous act, which confirms a direct link between these events. Just before Klingsor calls up Kundry in Act II, we hear her motive of seduction combined with chromatic scales in B minor. In the work as a whole, Klingsor's chromatic music is pitted against the diatonic themes associated with the Grail.

Of all Wagner's characters, Klingsor perhaps most strongly resembles an opera director. His Magic Castle serves as the setting to lure Parsifal, whose rout of Klingsor's knights and dalliance with the Flower Maidens lead up to his crucial encounter with Kundry, who is acting as Klingsor's agent. Parsifal's resistance to Kundry's seduction and his compassionate identification with Amfortas foil Klingsor's plan; the Holy Spear when hurled by Klingsor does not harm Parsifal, but remains suspended over his head. Nevertheless, the second act closes in Klingsor's key of B minor, since Parsifal's return path to the Grail has been blocked by Kundry's curse and he faces years of torturous "pathless wandering" before reaching his elusive goal. WILLIAM KINDERMAN

Knappertsbusch, Hans (b. Elberfeld [now Wuppertal], 12 March 1888; d. Munich, 25 Oct. 1965), conductor. Highly regarded as an interpreter of Wagner, BRUCKNER, and Richard STRAUSS. He studied philosophy at the University of Bonn, conducting at the Cologne Conservatory, and as a young man assisted SIEGFRIED WAGNER and Hans RICHTER at the BAYREUTH FESTIVAL. In 1923, he became Director of the Bavarian State Opera, a post he held until replaced by Clemens Krauss in 1936. Knappertsbusch was a signatory to and generally believed to be the instigator of the polemical *Protest from Richard Wagner's Own City of Munich* in response to Thomas MANN's essay *The Sufferings and Greatness of Richard Wagner*. In 1951, Knappertsbusch was invited to Bayreuth and, with the exception of 1953, appeared there every year until 1964. His style was in general notable for spacious tempi and grandeur of approach. He was effectively the General Music Director of the New Bayreuth and was particularly associated with WIELAND WAGNER's epoch-making production of *PARSIFAL*. ROGER ALLEN

See also PERFORMANCE, CONDUCTORS

Köhler, (Christian) Louis (Heinrich) (b. Brunswick, 5 Sep. 1820; d. Königsberg, 16 Feb. 1886), writer on music, composer, pianist, and teacher. He was closely associated with the NEW GERMAN SCHOOL, especially LISZT. His 1853 book *Die Melodie der Sprache* (The Melody of Speech) attempted to create a practical example for Wagner's conception of the "POETIC-MUSICAL PERIOD" from *OPER UND DRAMA* (Opera and Drama, 1851). However, his creation of a "natural melody" from music and word was overly reminiscent of more traditional conceptions of musical phrasing, and the book received Wagner's disapprobation. JAMES DEAVILLE

Thomas S. Grey, *Wagner's Musical Prose* (see bibliography).

Königsberg, the capital of East Prussia, present-day Kaliningrad. Königsberg was the home of Immanuel Kant and a lively cultural center in the eighteenth and nineteenth centuries. For Wagner, the town was particularly important as the birthplace of E. T. A. HOFFMANN, one of his central paragons. After appointment as music director of Heinrich Bethmann's touring company, Wagner moved to Königsberg in June 1836, following his fiancée MINNA Planer, whom he married there. In a letter to Robert SCHUMANN, Wagner described himself as being "exiled to Siberia" (3 December 1836), though he was soon to move even further east to RIGA. In Königsberg, Wagner composed his overture *Rule Britannia*. Interesting sketches have survived in the blank pages of its first draft. These refer to three musical numbers: an Introduction, a Chorus of Priests, and a Chorus of Youths, as well as Baltic influences, including the names of Baltic deities Picullos, Percunos, and Potrimpos. HANNU SALMI

Kroll Oper, Berlin. The Kroll entertainment complex (located in what is today called the Platz der Republik, next to the Reichstag) was converted in 1894 into a royal opera theater that would offer more popular fare than the royal opera on Unter den Linden. Following the Depression, it became impossible to operate two opera houses, and the less lucrative Kroll Oper had to close its doors in 1931. The building then became the seat of the Nazi government in December 1933 after the burning of the Reichstag. It was badly damaged in 1945, and was demolished in 1951.

Despite the conventional wisdom that the Kroll's closure was a harbinger of HITLER's rise, the measure was introduced by the right on purely budgetary grounds and was supported by the Center party and the Social Democrats. Furthermore, although Otto Klemperer's tenure as director is commonly singled out for its progressive repertoire, more conventional offerings were also the norm. Nevertheless, the notorious Nazi exhibit on

"Degenerate Music" of 1938 cited his controversial FLIEGENDE HOLLÄNDER production in 1929 as an instance of Jews "defiling" Wagner, even though the controversy at the time centered on Ewald Dülberg's stage designs.

PAMELA M. POTTER

See also NATIONAL SOCIALISM; PERFORMANCE, CONDUCTING; PRODUCTION HISTORY

Hans J. Reichardt, ed., *Bei Kroll 1844 bis 1957* (Berlin: Transit, 1988).

Kundry (mezzo-soprano; character in PARSIFAL), the enigmatic female figure, is perhaps the most complex of all Wagner's characters. In the genesis of the work, which lasted several decades, Kundry long remained a crucial missing ingredient in the dramatic scenario. She serves to connect AMFORTAS and PARSIFAL, motivating the downfall of the one and triumph of the other. Kundry is a fascinating amalgam who absorbs content from several characters in Wagner's main source, WOLFRAM VON ESCHENBACH's *Parzival*. These include "Cundrie la sorcière," a Grail messenger of mysterious and sinister aspect; Orgeluse, a seductress held in the power of the sorcerer Chinschor (see KLINGSOR); and Parzival's cousin Sigune, a melancholy maiden and penitent. These three characters serve as models for Wagner's Kundry in each of the three acts. As a bringer of news (*Kunde*), Kundry also partakes in Eschenbach's character Trevrizent, an old knight who also served as one model for GURNEMANZ. Yet there are dimensions of Kundry that have no basis in Eschenbach's *Parzival*, and her dramatic relationship to Parsifal rewards close attention. In the Good Friday scene in which she is baptized by Parsifal, Kundry undergoes a final transformation, unmistakably becoming a silent re-embodiment of Mary Magdalene – the Mary Magdalene both of the Bible and of Wagner's incomplete drama *Jesus von Nazareth*.

Kundry also reflects aspects of the character of the young woman Savitri in Wagner's unfinished BUDDHIST drama *Die Sieger* (The Victors, WWV 89) from 1856. The plot of *Die Sieger* centers on the relation of sensuous and godly LOVE, of Eros and Agape. In a previous incarnation, the beautiful Savitri had spurned, with mocking laughter, a Brahmin's son. She passionately loves the chaste young man Ananda, but is influenced by the Buddha to renounce him, while being admitted into the Buddha's community. Similarly, the cause of Kundry's curse and domination by Klingsor was her sin of *Schadenfreude*, her spiteful laughter at the redeemer on the cross.

Yet another unfamiliar model for aspects of Kundry is the character Ada in Wagner's first opera, *Die FEEN* (The Fairies) from 1834, which is based in turn on Carlo Gozzi's eighteenth-century play, *La donna serpente* (The Snake Woman). As Katherine Syer has observed, Gozzi's works exerted an enduring influence on Wagner, and the figure Cherestaní in *La donna serpente* displays affinities to Kundry that cannot be coincidental. Like Kundry, Cherestaní suffers from a curse and undergoes metamorphosis, moving between antithetical realms. The motive of serpentine transformation from Gozzi's drama seems reflected in Kundry's snakeskin belt and her animalistic qualities: in Act I she is accused of being "like a wild animal." Wagner himself once described the twisting chromatic musical motive heard when she kisses Parsifal in Act II as a "poisonous serpentine motive of love's desire" (CWD

4 June 1878). Kundry's motive – often described as the *Zaubermotiv* (Magic motive), and closely associated with Klingsor's music – circles around the dissonant interval of the tritone; its circular motion evokes the image of the biblical serpent ready to strike.

Beyond the well-known letter Wagner wrote to Mathilde Wesendonck on 29/30 May 1859, his letter of August 1860 in which he describes Kundry at some length (while not yet giving her this name, and using Eschenbach's spelling of the names of the other characters) conveys the following:

> Did I tell you already that the legendary wild messenger of the Grail should be one and the same being as the seductive woman of the second act? Since this has occurred to me, almost everything about this material has become clear . . .
>
> When Parzival arrives, the stupid lad, she can't take her eyes off him . . . What takes place in her? Does she fear some age-old curse; does she yearn to be freed from it? . . . – Huddled in a corner she witnesses the torturous scene with Anfortas: she looks with wonderful penetration (sphinx-like) at Parzival . . .

> (RICHARD WAGNER AN MATHILDE WESENDONK, 243–4, MY TRANSLATION)

What stands out is Wagner's inquiry into the existential state of Kundry, whereby he refers to her "sphinx-like" regard of the "pure fool," Parsifal. A sphinx is a mysterious compound being – part human, part animal. Inasmuch as Kundry consists of a complex amalgam of conflicting character types, she does indeed seem strangely "sphinx-like." In the long history of the sphinx, that "symbol of the symbolic itself" in Hegel's formulation, it is rare for a commentator to probe the soul of the sphinx-like protagonist, as does Wagner. This unusual perspective helped him to fill out the dramatic psychology of *Parsifal* in unprecedented fashion, moving far beyond Wolfram von Eschenbach. The timeless, primeval aspect of Kundry, who had already been discovered by the Grail founder Titurel, and whose incarnations included Herodias and Gundryggia, belongs to this rich symbolic context. Because of her curse, Kundry must serve in bondage to the demonic Klingsor, but she instinctively yearns for an end to her servitude. A normal human being should be unable to resist her seduction, to see beyond the sensuous entanglement of Klingsor's magic realm. Parsifal's compassion for and inward identification with Amfortas become his means of resistance, whereby the sphinx-like riddle of Kundry's seduction is answered by SCHOPENHAUERIAN renunciation, ultimately setting her free from Klingsor.

Kundry's attempted seduction of Parsifal in Act II is the most formidable of the challenges on his path toward the role of redeemer: its success would doom him. As she delivers her poisoned kiss, the aforementioned "poisonous serpentine motive of love's desire" sounds in the orchestra. The alert listener can perceive how this theme represents a dissonant, chromatic transformation of the Communion theme heard from the outset of *Parsifal* and at the revelation of the Grail later in Act I. Instead of a stable, consonant rise through the triad to the sixth degree, the shape of this serpentine motive unfolds as two minor thirds followed by semitones, which in the example rise through D♯ to E and then fall back through D♯ to D, the pitch poised a tritone higher than G♯, the initial note of the preceding and following measures (see measures

3–5 of Example 13 in PARSIFAL). The dissonant turn to the minor within the Communion theme – a striking element of chromatic contamination associated dramatically with Amfortas's wound – is derived from Kundry's poisoned kiss, reminding us in turn of her earlier seduction of Amfortas, which occurred before the beginning of the action. The last two measures of the example show the emergence of the so-called "Schmerzensfigur" (pain motive) associated with Amfortas's wound from Kundry's chromatic music, as the ascending semitone F to F♯ is inverted to G♭ to F at "Sehr belebend." Hence the drama's crucial turning point comes in this replay of the earlier seduction scene, with Parsifal taking the place of Amfortas.

Kundry curses Parsifal's return path at the end of Act II, but Klingsor's control over her is limited, and she eventually reappears in the Grail realm, enabling Parsifal's return. This sets the scene for her baptism, her presence at the closing Grail scene, and death in the final moments. Kundry's role in Act III is mainly pantomime, with her text limited to the single repeated word "Dienen, dienen" (to serve, to serve). The end of *Parsifal* is especially controversial, and some directors have kept Kundry alive at the conclusion, departing from Wagner's stage directions. Some commentators regard Kundry as a Jewish figure, and the motif of the wandering Jew is relevant, but the models for this character are diverse and far-reaching, as we have seen. An ideological quandary pertains to her death, since even after being converted Kundry cannot endure a confrontation with the renewed spiritual force of the Grail. As Joseph Chytry puts it, "there are good reasons for finding distasteful a redemption of woman which, to be blunt, first renders her dumb and then liquidates her" (309). Alternatively, Kundry's death can be seen to stand for her disappearance from the level of the visible action to another, metaphysical level, whereby she is released at last from her cycle of reincarnations and removed once and for all from Klingsor's grip, diminishing his sway.   WILLIAM KINDERMAN

See also ANTI-SEMITISM; REDEMPTION; RELIGION

Joseph Chytry, *The Aesthetic State: A Quest in Modern German Thought* (Berkeley: University of California Press, 1989).

William Kinderman, *Wagner's "Parsifal"* (New York: Oxford University Press, 2013).

Katherine Syer, "'It left me no peace': From Carlo Gozzi's *La donna serpente* to Wagner's *Parsifal*," *The Musical Quarterly* 94.3 (2011): 325–80.

Richard Wagner an Mathilde Wesendonk: Tagebuchblätter und Briefe 1853–1871 (see bibliography).

Kunst des Übergangs. See ART OF TRANSITION

Kunst und die Revolution, Die (Art and Revolution), the first of the three major ZURICH writings, the others being *Das KUNSTWERK DER ZUKUNFT* (1849/50) and *OPER UND DRAMA* (1851). According to *MEIN LEBEN* (My Life, 1865–81), it was written in a few days at the end of July 1849, just two months after the DRESDEN UPRISING and Wagner's escape from the law, published by WIGAND in Leipzig. When the three Zurich pieces are considered together, *Die Kunst und die Revolution* functions as a general preface to the other two, which are much longer and go into increasing detail about how and why opera must be reformed. Although the themes are basically the same in all three texts, *Die Kunst und die Revolution* contains the most rhetoric of political exhortation, being written so soon after Wagner's participation in the REVOLUTION.

It reads like an inspirational speech at a socialist political gathering. It does not address music or any of the other arts specifically; instead, it critiques the role of art in contemporary society by contrasting it with that of the ancient Greeks. Wagner was following a long German tradition of using ANCIENT GREECE as the measuring stick. His version would inspire NIETZSCHE's *Die Geburt der Tragödie* (Birth of Tragedy) twenty years later. He begins by comparing art's central role in the public sphere of the Greeks to the decadence of the nineteenth century, where art only serves as entertainment. With the Greeks, the arts were unified, all playing a role in its highest form – the drama, specifically the tragedy: here Wagner uses the term GESAMTKUNSTWERK for the first time. Ever since, civilization has become fragmented and so have the arts. Wagner then turns more political and argues that, despite being unrivaled by subsequent eras, there was a fatal flaw to ancient Greek civilization: it was dependent on slave labor. Not everyone was free, and in order to have true art, there must be true freedom. Next Wagner jumps to Christianity and describes it also as enslavement, in that it does nothing to help people on earth except to give them hope for a better afterlife. Today we are all slaves, to religion and to a commercial, industrial economy predicated on profit. The ARTWORK OF THE FUTURE must stand in opposition to the public state of things and be revolutionary. Then art and society will transcend categories of nation and will include everyone. Each person will grow freely and naturally into an artist. The public will not have to pay for their theater tickets because the state should pay for production costs; there should be no monetary considerations. In the last sentences it turns out, surprisingly – given that Christianity has been discussed mostly in a negative way – that art will be the brotherly union of Apollo and Jesus.

This publication could have hardly come at a worse time: practically no one wanted to hear about revolution and utopian visions of the future just after a revolution had failed and the future looked a lot like the past. However, Wagner was paid well for it, and he decided for the time being to try making more money by writing about the artwork of the future.   SANNA PEDERSON
See also OPERATIC REFORM

James Garratt, *Music, Culture and Social Reform in the Age of Wagner* (Cambridge University Press, 2010).

Stefanie Hein, *Richard Wagners Kunstprogramm im nationalkulturellen Kontext: Ein Beitrag zur Kulturgeschichte des 19. Jahrhunderts* (Würzburg: Königshausen & Neumann, 2006).

Kunst und Klima (Art and Climate). An early review of *Das KUNSTWERK DER ZUKUNFT* published in the *Augsburger Allgemeine Zeitung* on 15 January 1850 remarked that Wagner's speculations about the future of art "in relation to the progress of the human race towards true freedom" had failed to take into account "the influence of climate on the artistic capacities of mankind," and had erroneously attributed to the "modern northern-European nations a prospective faculty of artistic apprehension and creativity entirely incompatible with their natural environment" (SSD 3:207; PW 1:251). Wagner's brief essay entitled *Art and Climate* was written in late February 1850 in response to these criticisms, in an attempt to "expose as utterly baseless this lazy, cowardly, and tasteless objection of 'climate'" (Wagner to Theodor UHLIG, 8 February 1850).

The essay was published in the Stuttgart journal *Deutsche Monatsschrift für Politik, Wissenschaft, Kunst und Leben* 1.4 (April 1850), where the following year some pre-publication excerpts from the long essay OPER UND DRAMA (Opera and Drama, 1851) were to appear.

Wagner maintains that so long as early human populations remained "coddled" in the tropical climates of equatorial regions they remained in a state of figurative childhood, morally and intellectually. Human history and culture, properly speaking, did not begin until mankind was weaned from this child-like dependency on nature and established a relative level of independence from his immediate environment. Hence historical and cultural man first emerged in "the naked, sea-washed rocky coasts of ancient Greece [*Hellas*], upon the stony soil and beneath the sparse shade of the olive groves of Attica" (SSD 3:209; PW 1:253). Where his critic had suggested that northern European nations could never recapture the happy equilibrium of man and nature enjoyed by the ancient Greeks in their "sunny Ionian climes," Wagner represents the climatic conditions of ANCIENT GREECE as merely the first stage of man's hard-won independence from the conditions of his natural environment. The remainder of the essay mostly recapitulates ideas from *Das Kunstwerk der Zukunft* contrasting the idealized relation of man to art in ancient Greece with the corrupting influence of commerce and industry in modern art. Since the time of the Greeks a "post-natural" mankind, so to speak, has developed in relation to history and civilization. Wagner calls for a future "culture" to be established in an improved relation to "our climatic nature," replacing the corrupt "civilization" that emerged from the religious and political institutions of the European MIDDLE AGES, which the artificial "renaissance" of classical culture in the early modern era was incapable of truly reforming. (This semantic distinction between "civilization" and "culture" is not systematically developed, but emerges somewhat accidentally in the course of the essay.)   THOMAS S. GREY

See also AESTHETICS; MODERNITY

Kunstreligion (Art religion / Religion of art). Around 1750 secularization and the emancipation of the arts from social and religious convention combined into a trend that Friedrich NIETZSCHE later summarized in *Human, All-Too Human*, the book that sealed his break with Wagner: "the feelings expelled from the sphere of religion by the Enlightenment throw themselves into art" (Aphorism No. 150). It was indeed a small step from Hamann's and HERDER's view of the Bible as a poetic text to Klopstock's redefinition of the poet as a prophet communicating a religious truth.

Kant's and SCHELLING's AESTHETICS lent further momentum to speculation about the power of artistic genius to intimate the absolute. While Protestant theologian Friedrich Schleiermacher's *Speeches On Religion* introduced the term "Kunstreligion" in 1799 to evoke an ideal future in which art would show an experiential path to a religiosity freed from dogma, contemporaries drawn to Catholicism such as Wackenroder, Tieck, Novalis, and Friedrich Schlegel more boldly celebrated art, and especially music, as a revelation of the divine. Similarly to these Romantic writers, the young HEGEL hoped that a religion enlivened by art would overcome the abstraction and fragmentation of MODERNITY. By 1800, however, Hegel understood that the progressive differentiation of cultural spheres in the modern age made the divorce between religion and art irreversible. It was thus in ANCIENT GREECE that Hegel's 1807 *Phenomenology of Spirit* located art religion, superseded first by the transcendent God of Christianity and then by conceptual thought.

Steeped in ROMANTICISM and Hegelianism but inoculated by FEUERBACH against dogmatic religion, Wagner remained obsessed with the ideal of individual and cultural REDEMPTION. His thinking about renewal through art revolved around two signal achievements: Greek tragedy as a total art (*GESAMTKUNSTWERK*) rooted in a people's religious life and the Christian idea of an absolute that no art but music can convey. To remedy the cultural decline brought about by the death of tragedy and by the Christian hostility to the senses, Wagner's ZURICH writings called for a universal art religion that would re-establish the shattered unity of the arts and reintegrate them into the communal life of the people.

Following SCHOPENHAUER's metaphysics of music, Wagner's essay *BEETHOVEN* (1870) argues that music relates to the other arts as religious faith does to institutionalized churches. Beethoven is portrayed as a Catholic awakened through Bach's music to his Protestant spirituality, and indeed as a saint who realized the redemptive significance of suffering and transcended the limitations of ABSOLUTE MUSIC. In the late essay *RELIGION AND ART* (1880), Wagner lamented the rigidification of Christian symbolism to a dogmatic system and proclaimed: "when religion becomes artificial it falls to art to salvage the kernel of religion" (PW 6:213). The undertaking to release Christian allegories from theological dogma and reimagine them as spiritually charged symbols resulted in Wagner's *BÜHNENWEIHFESTSPIEL* (stage consecration festival play) *PARSIFAL*.

From the outset the quasi-religious posture of Wagner's works has divided audiences, eliciting cultic devotion from some and suspicious resistance from others, with many Wagnerians attesting to a mix of these extreme reactions.

MÁRTON DORNBACH

See also *PILGERFAHRT ZU BEETHOVEN, EINE*; RELIGION

Albert Meier, Alessandro Costazza, and Gérard Laudin, eds., *Kunstreligion: Ein ästhetisches Konzept der Moderne in seiner historischen Entfaltung, Band 1: Der Ursprung des Konzepts um 1800* (Berlin: De Gruyter, 2011).

Kunstwerk der Zukunft, Das (The Artwork of the Future). Finished in late 1849, published in Leipzig by WIGAND in 1850, this text makes up 135 pages and is therefore much longer than *Die KUNST UND DIE REVOLUTION* (Art and Revolution) of earlier that year, but much shorter than *OPER UND DRAMA* (Opera and Drama, 1851).

Divided into five chapters, it moves from a general critique of Western civilization, which is lamented as no longer whole and complete, to a more specific discussion of the corresponding lost unity of the arts. The artwork of the future is also described in passing as a *GESAMTKUNSTWERK*, and a "Drama" (not "Musikdrama"). The lengthy dedication to the philosopher Ludwig FEUERBACH is reflected in the text's emphasis on LOVE as the force that restores unity.

The first chapter bemoans Man's separation from nature. Once upon a time, people (the *VOLK*) naturally formed groups such as tribes and clans, and created art out of a true need for it. Since then, RELIGION and government have imposed artificial definitions on groups and their need for art has been artificial ever since. The artwork of the future will come into being naturally to fulfill the *Volk*'s need for it.

The second, most important, chapter discusses in succession the three "purely human" arts: DANCE, music, and poetry. Originally these three "sisters" could not be separated because they were connected by love for each other; they were arts that merged to form a single Art. Dance and music were linked through rhythm. Poetry joined in via music, which is most vitally expressed through the voice and words. But dance has since become separated from its sisters and has become depraved. In moving from dance to a discussion of music, Wagner switches from the visual image of three sisters to the ocean, which separates and connects lands, just as music stands between dance and poetry – the tone itself being the fluid, primal element. This METAPHOR leads to another image, of Columbus discovering a new continent, thus finding the ocean's other shore; this is compared to BEETHOVEN's achievement, reuniting the arts in his last symphony, significant because it makes ABSOLUTE MUSIC – that is, instrumental music – obsolete. The history of poetry shows that it was initially always accompanied by music and dance, as in Tragedy, the first communal artistic creation of the *Volk*. As poetry became a written rather than spoken art, it dwindled into thought, cut off from the natural senses of the body. This second chapter ends with a new image of how the arts are unified: it is like a man giving himself entirely to woman, creating a child made up of both mother and father. Only when the arts love each other and give themselves up entirely to each other can there again be a unified, complete art.

The third chapter tells the history of the rise and fall of architecture, sculpture, and painting, which have also become corrupt. The fourth chapter sketches the artwork of the future. The architect must design a building only with the aim of making the drama as effective as possible. The landscape painter will try to recreate nature as a backdrop to Man on stage. The orchestra will add an emotional dimension to the common goal of all these arts, which is the drama.

Chapter 5 asks: Who will be the artist of the future? Answer: It will be an association of artists, and ultimately, the *Volk* of which they are a part. Wagner ends with what he calls "the outline of a glorious saga," *Wieland the Smith*. Wieland is forced to forge objects for his king, who has crippled him to keep him from escaping. Wieland, who once had a swan as a wife, comes upon the idea of forging wings. Because of his utmost need, he was able to create wings that allowed him to fly away, kill his oppressor, and reunite with his swan wife. In his final sentence Wagner explains that Wieland is the *Volk*, who need to do the same. SANNA PEDERSON

See also AESTHETICS; ANCIENT GREECE; MUSIC DRAMA; PHILOSOPHY; SCHILLER, FRIEDRICH

Rainer Franke, *Richard Wagners Zürcher Kunstschriften* (see bibliography).
Jürgen Kühnel, "The Prose Writings," in *The Wagner Handbook*, ed. Ulrich Müller and Peter Wapnewski, trans. John Deathridge (see bibliography): 565–651.

Kurwenal (baritone; character in *TRISTAN UND ISOLDE*), TRISTAN's servant. Kurwenal represents the male counterpart to BRANGÄNE. Wagner based the character on GOTTFRIED VON STRASSBURG's *Tristan*, where the name Kurwenal had been translated from the Old French "Gorvenal" in Thomas of Britain's earlier version of the story. Arguably a role of unsatisfactory proportions, Kurwenal has limited dramatic function in Acts I and II. Like Brangäne, he acts as a kind of diplomat in Act I, relaying stiff proposals and replies between Tristan and ISOLDE, and in Act II, during the central *imbroglio*, he scarcely utters three words ("Rette dich, Tristan!"). It is in Act III that Kurwenal comes to the fore both expressively and in terms of narrative, as he tends to the fatally wounded Tristan. Whereas in Act I, Brangäne prompts Isolde to recall previous events in the narrative for the sake of dramatic exposition (as in the *RING*), in Act III it is Kurwenal who is forced to remind Tristan of the recent occurrences he has forgotten. Faithful to the end, Kurwenal avenges Tristan's death in Act II, Scene 3 by killing Melot, but dies himself in the attempt. Despite its deceptive challenges, the role has been sung as often by bass-baritones with strong upper registers (Friedrich Schorr and Hans HOTTER, to name but two) as it has by true baritones such as Bernd Weikl and Dietrich Fischer-Dieskau, for which voice register the role was conceived.   JEREMY COLEMAN

L

La Spezia, coastal town in Liguria (ITALY), which Wagner visited in 1853. La Spezia has an outsize role to play in the composer's own mythmaking. *MEIN LEBEN* (My Life, 1865–81), written decades later, recounts a synesthetic vision the composer supposedly experienced on 5 September 1853, which contained in it the germs of the *RHEINGOLD* Prelude. Returning from a hike in the "dreary and desolate" Italian countryside, Wagner fell into a "somnolent state" on the couch, and "suddenly felt as though I were sinking in swiftly flowing water," which was transformed into the undulating E♭ major triads of the Prelude. "It must," Wagner concludes, "long have lain latent within me, though it had not been able to find definite form" (ML 512; ML/E 499).

Scholarship has tended to cast doubt on Wagner's version of the story, which accords neither with his letters around the time (which record nothing of the vision until more than a year after the fact), nor with the musical development of the musical sketches for the *Rheingold* Prelude. Opinions diverge on the reasons for Wagner's embellishment, but it is generally agreed that the idea of "latent" oceanic feeling welling up into consciousness is owed to SCHOPENHAUER's notion of music as the expression of the proto-individual "will," and reflects Wagner's discovery of Schopenhauer in the months after the supposed incident at La Spezia.   ADRIAN DAUB

Lafferentz, Bodo (b. Kiel, 27 July 1897; d. Überlingen, 17 Jan. 1975), married Richard Wagner's granddaughter VERENA (1943). He was taken prisoner during World War I and held in England 1918–20; he joined the Nazi party in 1933 and, later, the SS, and was put in charge of the KdF (*Kraft durch Freude*, "Strength through Joy") program, which organized recreational facilities and programs for German workers. Lafferentz was appointed to the supervisory board of the Volkswagen project in 1938. He organized KdF visits to Bayreuth for the *Kriegsfestspiele* (war Festivals) and, in 1942 as SS-Obersturmbannführer, appointed his future brother-in-law WIELAND WAGNER to the "Institute for Physical Research," a division for highly trained prisoners of the Flossenbürg concentration-camp complex, devising guidance systems for the V-2 rocket. After the war, he often sided with Verena and FRIEDELIND, sisters of the BAYREUTH FESTIVAL managers Wieland and WOLFGANG, in quarrels over the Festival organization, but never intervened in aesthetic issues.

EVA RIEGER

Albrecht Bald and Jörg Skriebeleit, *Das Außenlager Bayreuth des KZ Flossenbürg: Wieland Wagner und Bodo Lafferentz im "Institut für physikalische Forschung"* (Bayreuth: Rabenstein, 2003).

Lafferentz, Verena (b. Bayreuth, 2 Dec. 1920), daughter of Richard Wagner's son SIEGFRIED and WINIFRED WAGNER. She studied medicine until World War II thwarted these plans, and then worked as a nurse. She married Bodo LAFFERENTZ (1943) and they had five children: Amélie (1944), Manfred (1945), Winifred (1947), Wieland (1949), and Verena (1952).   EVA RIEGER

See also Appendix 1: Wagner family tree

Langford, Laura Carter Holloway (née Carter) (b. Nashville, Tennessee, 22 Aug. 1843; d. Canaan, NY, July 1930), founder and leader of the Seidl Society. Langford was Brooklyn's leading impresario, and prime mover towards a "Brooklyn Bayreuth." The Society was begun in 1889 to support Anton SEIDL's floundering summer season at Coney Island's Brighton Beach resort. In 1894, it became producer of these concerts, offered fourteen times weekly for two months: a visionary enterprise with a famous conductor, world-class orchestra, ZUKUNFTSMUSIK (music of the future) repertoire dominated by Wagner and LISZT, and 25-cent tickets. Beginning in 1890, the Society presented up to sixteen Seidl concerts annually at the Brooklyn Academy of Music; Wagner excerpts predominated. The Society twice presented truncated concert performances of PARSIFAL (1890, 1891). Langford's plan for staged opera performances expired with Seidl's death.   JOSEPH HOROWITZ

See also UNITED STATES OF AMERICA

Joseph Horowitz, *Moral Fire: Portraits from America's Fin-de-Siecle* (Berkeley: University of California Press, 2012).

L'art pour l'art (art for art's sake), nineteenth-century doctrine that privileged art (of any kind) created purely for the purpose of being beautiful. The phrase seems to have originated with the French philosopher Victor Cousin as early as 1818 (though possibly as early as 1804), but the idea gained credence in later years, particularly after the 1848 revolution, with artists including the poets Théophile Gautier and Charles BAUDELAIRE – both ardent Wagnerians. Proponents of *l'art pour l'art* believed that, as Gautier wrote in the preface to his poem *Albertus* (1832): "As a general rule, when something becomes useful, it ceases being beautiful." *L'art pour l'art* was a reaction against what many artists perceived to be an increasing bourgeois domination of French culture in the nineteenth century. They detested the idea that art could become simply a commodity for mass consumption or that it might be put to use as a moralistic or didactic tool for the public. In retaliation, these artists retreated from society, devoting themselves entirely to the contemplation and creation of beauty. Aspects of the doctrine of *l'art pour l'art* persisted into the twentieth century in France, shaping, among others, the Parnassian and symbolist movements. Outside France, proponents included Edgar Allen Poe, and the English aesthetic movement typified by Oscar Wilde and James McNeill Whistler. Critics of *l'art pour l'art* found the movement fundamentally elitist and decadent. Friedrich NIETZSCHE, among the most vocal critics, agreed that art should not be subject to public morality, but rejected the exaltation of purposelessness; the philosopher wrote in 1888 that "Art is the great stimulant to life: how could one conceive of it as purposeless, aimless, *l'art pour l'art?*" Walter Benjamin and Theodor ADORNO were influential twentieth-century critics of *l'art pour l'art*, rejecting the possibility of separating art entirely from POLITICS or culture.

Although Wagner never used the term and was not part of the movement, he adopted many concepts from *l'art pour l'art*, evident especially in the prose works written during the Paris stay 1839–42, when he began to rail against the commodification of art. This in part may explain why he had such a passionate following amongst French authors of the mid- to late nineteenth century. In a somewhat ironic twist, he even appropriated the concept of creating art "for its own sake" and recast this as a specifically German trait. WILLIAM GIBBONS

See also GERMANNESS; *ENDE IN PARIS, EIN*; *KUNSTRELIGION*; *PILGERFAHRT ZU BEETHOVEN, EINE*; *WAS IST DEUTSCH?*; WAGNERISM

Laube, Heinrich (b. Sprottau [Silesia], 18 Sep. 1806; d. Vienna, 1 Aug. 1884), writer, journalist, and theater administrator associated with the YOUNG GERMANY movement. From 1832 onwards he was an editor of the *Zeitung für die elegante Welt*, which he used not only for political expression, but also to promote the young Richard Wagner. Wagner's *MEIN LEBEN* casts Laube as one of the group of writers and administrators who, through their incomprehension of the opera form, compelled him to write his own libretti. Shortly after his laudatory review of Wagner's work, Laube approached the composer with plans for an opera based on the life of Tadeusz Kosciuszko, the Polish freedom fighter, which he had initially drafted for MEYERBEER. Wagner later cast his opposition to Laube's plans in aesthetic terms, claiming he felt it was inappropriate for a musical telling, but Laube seems to have detected political expediency in the young composer's inclinations: instead of the story of a Polish revolutionary, Wagner embarked on *Die FEEN*, his first completed opera, a magical tale inspired by an Italian play, much better adapted to the repressive climate in Germany at the time. Still, *Mein Leben* recasts Laube's suspicion of opportunism as a suspicion of the emergent notion of the GESAMTKUNSTWERK – Laube, Wagner insists, "never really forgave me for writing my own poems" (ML/E 71). Wagner's association with Laube endured, and Laube's *Zeitung* published several of the young composer's writings, including the *AUTOBIOGRAPHISCHE SKIZZE* (Autobiographical Sketch, 1842/3). Their friendship seems to have cooled following Wagner's unsuccessful attempt to bring Laube to DRESDEN – the post went to Wagner's detested GUTZKOW. ADRIAN DAUB

Laussot, Jessie (née Taylor) (b. London, 27 Dec. 1826; d. Florence, 8 May 1905). Laussot studied piano together with Hans von BÜLOW in DRESDEN, and married Eugène Laussot, a wealthy wine merchant (1844). In 1850, the couple invited Wagner to their home in Bordeaux, offering him an annuity. Wagner and Jessie fell in love. Nothing came of the affair, as Jessie's husband found out and prevented their eloping to Greece and Asia Minor. Wagner later commented that she was too immature to undertake such a step. She moved to Florence, where she founded the choir "Società Cherubini," which she conducted. She introduced German chamber music in Florence, especially that of Franz LISZT, for which he was grateful. She also helped von Bülow when he turned his back on Germany (1869) and visited her in a state of great exhaustion. After Eugène Laussot died in 1878, she married the cultural historian Karl Hillebrand, who died in 1884. EVA RIEGER

David Cormack, "An Abduction from the Seraglio: Rescuing Jessie Laussot," *The Wagner Journal* 6.1 (2012): 50–63.

Lehmann, Lilli (b. Würzburg, 24 Nov. 1848; d. Berlin, 17 May 1929). One of the greatest sopranos of her time, Lehmann possessed a stylistic diversity that permitted her to excel as Violetta, Norma, ISOLDE, BRÜNNHILDE, and in many other roles. She sang in Berlin (1870–85), but also in LONDON, the Metropolitan Opera, VIENNA, and Salzburg. At BAYREUTH, she sang minor roles in the 1876 *RING* premiere and Brünnhilde in the 1896 revival.

DAVID BRECKBILL

Lilli Lehmann, *Mein Weg* (Leipzig: Hirzel, 1913), trans. *My Path Through Life* (New York: Putnam, 1914; repr. New York: Arno, 1977).

Lehmann, Lotte (b. Perleberg, 27 Feb. 1888; d. Santa Barbara, 26 Aug. 1976), German soprano. Her repertory encompassed art song and many non-Wagner operatic roles (her Marschallin in *Der Rosenkavalier* was especially acclaimed), but appearances as ELISABETH, ELSA, EVA, and especially SIEGLINDE made her one of the leading Wagner singers of the 1920s–1940s. DAVID BRECKBILL

Alan Jefferson, *Lotte Lehmann, 1888–1976* (London: MacRae, 1988).

Lehrs, Samuel (Born: Levi, Samuel) (b. Königsberg, 1806; d. Paris, 13 April 1843), German philologist. Lehrs was among Wagner's closest friends during the latter's years in PARIS (1839–42). He inspired Wagner to read ANCIENT GREEK literature, and indirectly inspired him to fuse the two characters of TANNHÄUSER and Heinrich von Ofterdingen, by pointing him to C. T. L. Lucas's work *Über den Krieg von Wartburg* (1838). Wagner eternalized him as the "German philologist" in his novella Ein ENDE IN PARIS (A Death in Paris). Lehrs died impoverished. HERMANN GRAMPP

Leider, Frida (b. Berlin, 18 April 1888; d. Berlin, 4 June 1975), German soprano. Early in her career she sang at Hamburg (1919–23) but then moved to Berlin, her home base during an era that also found her achieving triumphs – especially as BRÜNNHILDE, ISOLDE, and KUNDRY – at Covent Garden (1924–38), BAYREUTH (1928, 1933–8), the Metropolitan Opera (1933–4), Chicago, and elsewhere. DAVID BRECKBILL

Frida Leider, *Das war mein Teil* (Berlin: Herbig, 1959), trans. *Playing My Part* (London: Calder and Boyars / New York: Meredith, 1966).

Leipzig. Richard Wagner's birthplace, was Saxony's largest city in the nineteenth century. The thrice-annual fairs, begun in the twelfth century, propelled the city into an important commercial power, and the foremost center for publishing in German-speaking lands by the eighteenth century, a position it held well into the twentieth. Leipzig's university was founded in 1409 and numbers amongst its prominent alumni GOETHE, Lessing, Fichte, and NIETZSCHE. With respect to music, the city's fame rests on several important personages and institutions. Johann Sebastian BACH was Cantor at the Church of St. Thomas (*Thomaskirche*) from 1723 to 1750. Felix MENDELSSOHN BARTHOLDY conducted the Gewandhaus Orchestra from 1835 to 1843. Robert SCHUMANN studied at the university, met and married Clara Wieck, and founded the *NEUE ZEITSCHRIFT FÜR MUSIK* while a resident.

Saxon politics frequently interfered with Leipzig's economic as well as its cultural development. The Seven Years War (1756–63) resulted in a Prussian occupation of the city, and this was repeated with magnified results following Napoleon's loss at the "Battle of the Nations" in October 1813, when Saxony fought on the side of the Emperor. Leipzig was placed under Russian and then Prussian administration, and the kingdom lost a substantial portion of its territory. Longstanding resentment against DRESDEN in Leipzig found further expression in the unrest of the 1830s and 1840s.

Wagner's relationship to Leipzig is connected to all these factors. He and his family had strong ties to Leipzig's cultural scene, particularly the theater, administration of which was finally wrested away from Dresden in 1817. It was located only a few houses away from Wagner's birthplace on the Brühl. When Wagner returned to Leipzig for schooling, he studied at both the main church schools, St. Nicholas and St. Thomas. His university studies in Leipzig were paired with his composition instruction with Christian Theodor WEINLIG, one of Bach's successors as *Thomaskantor*. Wagner's ties by marriage to the BROCKHAUS publishing dynasty gave him a supportive family network as well as entrée into a wider world of politics including those of YOUNG GERMANY.

Some of Wagner's early compositions were written, published, and performed in Leipzig. His OVERTURE in D minor (WWV 20) was premiered on 25 December 1831 in the concert hall at the Gewandhaus, albeit by the music society Euterpe. The same group premiered his Overture in C major (WWV 27) in the following April, 1832, but the piece was repeated to wider acclaim in January 1833 by the Gewandhaus Orchestra. This early start did not translate into immediate success; the efforts by Friedrich Brockhaus to sponsor a performance of *Die* FEEN (The Fairies) in 1834 failed.

Generally speaking, Wagner's recollections of his natal city are not particularly positive; he was quite critical of Leipzig's musical life. Conversely, Leipzigers' interest in Wagner was tepid. Admittedly, through the efforts of Angelo NEUMANN, it was the first city to mount a complete production of the *RING* cycle outside Bayreuth (1878), but in 1885 local government also demolished Wagner's birth house.   MARGARET ELEANOR MENNINGER

Leitmotiv (pl. *Leitmotive*), literally, "leading motive." A term used to identify the most important thematic materials in Wagner's later works which are associated with events, objects, feelings, and characters and which recur in varied forms, bringing an evolutionary continuity to the drama. That association might be straightforwardly pictorial, as with the flowing material suggesting the waters of the RHINE in the *RING*, or less obviously literal – for example, the motives representing such concepts as "death" and "day" in *TRISTAN UND ISOLDE*.

1. Before Wagner
2. Wagner's motivic methods
3. The term in history
4. Later perspectives
5. Redressing the balance

1. Before Wagner

In opera, from the time of Monteverdi onwards, the design of constituent scenes and acts involved distinct generic forms – most basically, recitative, aria, ensemble – any one of which would have a duration determined by the number of constituent phrases, which was often substantial. The seeds of future developments, to which the concept of *Leitmotiv* would become appropriate, can be found in accompanied recitative. Recitatives in seventeenth- and eighteenth-century opera are often classed either as *secco* (dry) or *accompagnato* (accompanied). *Secco* recitative was not literally unaccompanied, but harmonic backing was kept to a minimum, with sharply articulated chords in continuo instruments, and the vocal lines were syllabic and unmelodic. *Accompagnato* involved fuller instrumental support, which could share the thematic material to some extent, and the vocal writing could also embrace elements of that more lyrical, flowing vocal style called *arioso* – something midway between the speech-like rhythms of *secco* recitative and the fully fledged melodic phrases of an aria.

2. Wagner's motivic methods

Wagner did not immediately jettison the operatic form-schemes he found in BEETHOVEN, WEBER, and others. But, in gradually moving further away from traditional aria style, with its often ornate vocal writing and extensive *da capo* repetitions, he reduced musico-dramatic design to its most essential building block, the short thematic phrase or melodic motive. Clearly, that musico-dramatic structure was not simply a concatenation of such motives, stuck end-to-end with no thought for the larger formal units that might arise. But critical commentary on Wagner's work, from the earliest times, has tended to find itself polarized between relatively specialized accounts of POETIC-MUSICAL PERIODS and more anecdotal discussions in which *Leitmotive* are the main focus. In either case, however, the usefulness of the result will depend on the ability of the reader to summon up the sound of the materials in question.

There can also be some ambiguity about how brief or extended a Wagnerian *Leitmotiv* might be. To take one of the most memorable, the *Ring* cycle's "Valhalla" motive: strictly speaking, this should probably be identified primarily with the initial two-bar phrase heard at the beginning of Scene 2 of *Das RHEINGOLD*, rather than with the developmental treatment of that motive which constitutes the scene's first 20-bar poetic-musical period, before the dialogue between Wotan and Fricka begins (see CWE 4 in Appendix 4). But little harm is done if motive and period are "confused" in this way. The whole process of critical analysis of musical materials involves such ambiguities, inevitable consequences of the fundamental differences between words and musical sounds.

3. The term in history

Music historians delight in pointing out that Wagner himself did not invent the term *Leitmotiv* – and also that, when he became aware of it, he responded dismissively, as he did to most things which he couldn't claim to have created himself. Motive, as in "thematisches Motiv" or "Hauptmotiv" (main motive), can be found before 1870, in Wagner and innumerable other writers, while commentators as close to Wagner as LISZT and UHLIG had discussed his music's thematic materials. But it was the music historian August Wilhelm AMBROS who, in his *Culturhistorische Bilder aus dem Musikleben der Gegenwart*

(Leipzig, 1860), hit on a new term for the description of how Wagner, in the stage works that were known by then, and also Liszt in his symphonic poems, sought "to establish a higher unity across the whole by means of consistent *Leitmotive*" (*durchgehende Leitmotive*). It was the promise that these vast amounts of continuous dramatic music, which so obviously lacked the kind of hefty cadential articulations found in number operas, were nevertheless unified, and therefore coherent, that served to motivate those early commentaries in which the term gained the currency it has never subsequently lost.

Crucially, the term appears in Hans von WOLZOGEN's *Thematischer Leitfaden durch die Musik zu Richard Wagner's Festspiel "Der Ring des Nibelungen"* (Thematic Guide to the Music of Richard Wagner's *Der Ring des Nibelungen*), published at the time of the cycle's first complete performance at Bayreuth in 1876. Von Wolzogen was an important member of Wagner's BAYREUTH CIRCLE, but this didn't save him from the rebuke which is implicit in an essay Wagner penned three years later, ÜBER DIE ANWENDUNG DER MUSIK AUF DAS DRAMA (On the Application of Music to Drama): "one of my younger friends ... has devoted some attention to the characteristics of *Leitmotive*, as he calls them, but has treated them from the point of view of their dramatic import and effect rather than as elements of the musical structure."

Wagner might have longed to mesmerize the entire community by way of his art, as he believed to have been the case with ANCIENT GREEK theater, and to do so without the need for conscious, analytical thought on the part of listeners: yet, like most if not all composers, he also craved appreciation for the originality, subtlety, and richness of his approach to "musical structure." Sticking simple pictorial labels onto themes as aids to orientation and comprehension – the critical equivalent of a stage production which required banners with the appropriate label ("sword," "spear") to be brandished whenever the text even hints at a particular object – risked devaluing as well as oversimplifying something more ambiguous and allusive. Yet the idea of a truly symphonic form of drama which owed more to BEETHOVEN's orchestral and choral masterworks (i.e., the Ninth Symphony!) than to any earlier operas was itself an over-simplification; the true richness of Wagner's invention required the kind of interaction between representational transparency (text and production) and complex musical processes which he managed to sustain in his work from *Das Rheingold* through to PARSIFAL.

4. Later perspectives

Since 1876, and von Wolzogen's first demonstration of what a leitmotivic analysis of Wagner might be like, an elaborate historiography of Wagner interpretation has evolved in which discussions of terminology in general, and of *Leitmotiv* in particular, have been prominent. While it is only relatively recently, in writings by Thomas S. Grey and Christian Thorau, that the historical context of the concept's emergence and exploitation has been fully excavated, attempts to explain, clarify, and even on occasion fruitfully complicate Wagner's practice by way of leitmotivic analysis and categorization have been a common practice, often extending into commentaries on other opera composers too.

The basic theme of such commentaries is nothing less than the ways in which words and music, verbal concepts and musical sounds, might connect with each other: weighty aesthetic, philosophical, and psychological issues are involved. The problem, like many others in musicology, was pithily pinned down by Carl DAHLHAUS: "the practice of giving Wagnerian *Leitmotive* names which fix an identity to them once and for all is as questionable as it is unavoidable: questionable, because the translation of musical expression into precise verbal terms is never satisfactory; unavoidable, because the idea of wordless, instinctive understanding of musical motives without the need for mediation through language, is an illusion. The name that half-misses the object altogether is nevertheless the only way to get at it . . . Thus the uncertainty over nomenclature . . . is not a matter that would be solved by more exact exegesis, but is the reflection and consequence of one of the characteristics of leitmotivic technique itself" (Dahlhaus 61).

Dahlhaus makes much of the contrast between what he terms "allegorical" motives, such as those associated with the important verbal-dramatic topics of death and day in *Tristan*, but which can offer no direct connection by way of shape or style with the concepts concerned, and other representational motives where, for example, it is easy to provide analogies in sound for such physical and emotional states as restlessness or despair. Yet such representations and analogies can never be absolutely fixed when the musical drama requires the developmental treatment of basic images and ideas, so that they shade into quite different images and ideas, and can even be perceived as something primarily musical, floating free from the explicit, extra-musical associations (a river, a ring) that might have inspired them in the first place. Hence the bold claim by Carolyn Abbate that "Wagner's motives have no referential meaning; they may, and of course do, absorb meaning at exceptional and solemn moments, by being used with elaborate calculation as signs, but unless purposely maintained in this artificial state, they shed their specific poetic meaning and revert to their natural state as musical thoughts" (Abbate 45).

This view is worth keeping in mind when responding to the various classifications of thematic types which have been presented, for example by Robert DONINGTON and F. E. Kirby. Donington claimed that "there is no motive in the *Ring* which cannot be traced either directly or indirectly to the simple arpeggio figure (it is scarcely yet a motive) with which *Rhinegold* opens" (Donington 275). Nevertheless, in Donington's listing of ninety distinct motivic shapes (some subdivided), the elementary contrast between his No. 1 ("The depths of the Rhine as undifferentiated nature") and No. 3 ("Erda the Earth-Mother as ancestral wisdom") is surely even more potent than the similarity of their common "broken-chord" or ascending arpeggio (see CWE 1 and 10 respectively in Appendix 4). Similarly, Kirby accepts that the transformation and development of basic themes in *The Ring* reflect "the complexity and ambiguity in many of the characters and the situations in which they find themselves" (Kirby 90). The value of leitmotivic analysis is therefore in helping to highlight the constant and constructive flux to which Wagner's materials are subject.

5. Redressing the balance

Critical discussion of the nature and scope of Wagner's compositional methods, with *Leitmotiv* as central, has often suffered from giving too little emphasis to the composer's own basic intentions as revealed in his writings. Christian Thorau has redressed the balance, stressing that "Wagner's ideal was a mode of aesthetic perception in which conceptual, rational comprehension is resolved in favor of an understanding at an emotional level": it is therefore "emotional understanding" that should make "the rational sensuously perceptible, intelligible." For this reason, as – according to Thorau – Wagner attempted to explain in *OPER UND DRAMA* (Opera and Drama): "the musical *motives* are supposed to transfer the dramatic *motives* of the plot into the nonverbal artistic expression of the music. The semantic referential dimension of the motives, its function of reminiscence and anticipation, should not rise into awareness as a conceptual definiteness but should remain part of the total effect, where that which is shown is understood in a holistic, integrated manner" (Thorau 138).

Yet such theoretical ideals would be brought abruptly down to earth by a dramatic practice in which "conceptual definiteness" could no more be excluded from the listeners' perception than it could be assumed to occur throughout as listeners attend to a Wagner performance. Thorau is clear that "a listener who is in command of a conscious verbalized knowledge that seems to transfer the profoundest secrets of the poetic intent to the referential level of linguistic meanings ... becomes an initiate who is no longer the immediate but the *mediated* partner in the realization," and "Wagner's original intention is turned on its head: a means to motivate emotional understanding becomes a means to rationalize this very process" (Thorau 139). However, if that is so, it simply demonstrates the impracticality of Wagner's "original intention."

Thorau observes that Wagner "never considered that it might be the traditionally educated middle class itself that – by establishing a listening code through musical knowledge – was going to define an adequately prepared Wagnerian audience" (Thorau 145). Nevertheless, by the time he had completed and performed both *The Ring* and *Parsifal*, it is possible that Wagner could see that his chosen path for moving away from traditional operatic devices was amply justified, despite his inability to realize the extravagant aesthetic ideals of 1850. The late essay *Über die Anwendung der Musik auf das Drama* indicated just such a recognition, even if it also retained a degree of nostalgia for a view of these works which concerned itself much more with "musical structure" than with mere "*Leitmotive*."   ARNOLD WHITTALL

See also Theodor W. ADORNO; MUSIC THEORY; WAGNER AS COMPOSER

Carolyn Abbate, "Wagner, 'On Modulation,' and *Tristan*," *Cambridge Opera Journal* 1 (1989): 33–58.

Carl Dahlhaus, *Richard Wagner's Music Dramas* (see bibliography).

Robert Donington, *Wagner's Ring and its Symbols* (see bibliography).

Thomas S. Grey, "...*wie ein roter Faden*" (see bibliography).

F. E. Kirby, *Wagner's Themes: A Study in Musical Expression* (Warren, MI: Harmonie Park, 2004).

Christian Thorau, "Guides for Wagnerites: Leitmotifs and Wagnerian Listening," in *Richard Wagner and his World*, ed. Thomas S. Grey (see bibliography): 133–50.

Leitmotiv guides. Motivic guidebooks that lead through a musico-dramatic work of art appeared in the context of Wagner's stage works and were a literary genre new to opera history. The first of its kind was published in 1876 a few weeks before the Bayreuth premiere of the *RING*. The author of the hundred-page booklet, entitled *Thematischer Leitfaden durch die Musik zu Richard Wagners Festspiel "Der Ring des Nibelungen"* (Thematic *Leitfaden* [leading threads] through the music of Richard Wagner's festival drama *The Ring of the Nibelung*) was Hans von WOLZOGEN, an amateur musician and trained philologist who became Wagner's devotee and confidant from the Bayreuth years on. Together with an introduction to the plot, the *Leitfaden* offered a detailed musical analysis of the entire work. By naming, systematizing, and interpreting all of the principal musical motives of Wagner's score, Wolzogen wove a "leading thread" through the fourteen-hour cycle of MUSIC DRAMAS. Wolzogen subsequently published a *Leitfaden* for *TRISTAN* (1880) and *PARSIFAL* (1882).

His texts formalized a method of analyzing Wagner's works already explored by Theodor UHLIG and Franz LISZT in the 1850s, and further developed in the early 1870s by Gottlieb Federlein, but now made accessible and broadly available to the general public. This would remain the dominant musical-critical approach to his oeuvre up to World War I. They served as a model for many similar and imitative publications addressed to a growing Wagner audience at the end of the nineteenth century. Within two decades after the *Ring* premiere, all Wagner operas going back to *TANNHÄUSER* came to be discussed and analyzed using the so-called *LEITMOTIVE*. Translations or adaptations appeared in English, French, and Italian; Wolzogen's *Parsifal* guide even reached its twenty-third edition in 1918. By subjecting all his mature works to the same explanatory method, the *Leitfaden* literature contributed to the popular conception that Wagner used one uniform compositional method. Yet, the relation between naming and labeling melodic phrases as a way of accessing the music and Wagner's possible intentions is problematic. Regarding the listening experience, Wagner had a more unconscious or at least pre-conceptual perception in mind when he called the motives "Gefühls-wegweiser" (signposts for the emotions). Moreover, there is no evidence in his compositional sketches that Wagner named his musical ideas. The composer might have sensed that, by naming a motive, he would be verbalizing and thus explicitly rationalizing a possible "poetic intent" which in turn would eliminate the idea of a more fluid and emotional motivation provided by the music. Thus it seems reasonable to suggest that Wagner tolerated but never welcomed or praised the dense scholastic and hermeneutic conceptualization Wolzogen had offered in his booklets. He was also worried about such aids being misunderstood by critics. In fact, the *Leitmotiv* guides were also used as a way to criticize Wagner. While Eduard HANSLICK and later Igor Stravinsky argued that the "need" for such verbal aids was proof of Wagner's flawed aesthetic conception, Claude DEBUSSY simply assumed Wagner had written the guides himself.

Neither Wagner nor Wolzogen could prevent the technique from being increasingly identified with Wagner's musical style, and virtually merged with the work. In libretti of the major Wagner works, appearances of motives were correlated with the text of the drama and *Leitmotiv* tables were printed at the front of piano-vocal scores. The integration of the interpretative method into the text of the work served as a surrogate notation for educated amateurs, but was also a crucial technical step for the *Leitmotiv* to become the trademark of

Wagner's music. Such libretti and piano scores, as well as guidebooks using Wolzogen's labels, are still in use today or have been transformed by means of digital presentation ("motive training" on CD and through internet websites). Undoubtedly, the motive perspective remains a popular path to the work because it offers graspable units and a comprehensible structure given the vast and overwhelming dimensions of Wagner's music. But it seems that the typical manner of Wagnerian listening – identifying, interpreting, and discussing *Leitmotive* – has lost its former importance. One reason is certainly that scholarly work on Wagner's music has shifted away from motive analysis to questions of form, sound, performance, and staging. Another reason could be the competition between the visual and the audio. Since the advent of *Regietheater*, theatrical presentations of Wagner's works often create a dense and suggestive network of symbols and allusions that appeal to the eye and that compete with the leitmotivic references emanating from the orchestra pit.

CHRISTIAN THORAU

Thomas S. Grey, *Wagner's Musical Prose: Texts and Contexts* (see bibliography).

Christian Thorau, "Guides for Wagnerites: Leitmotifs and Wagnerian Listening," in *Richard Wagner and his World*, ed. Thomas S. Grey (see bibliography): 133–50.

Semantisierte Sinnlichkeit: Rezeption und Zeichenstruktur der Leitmotivtechnik Richard Wagners (Stuttgart: Steiner, 2003).

Levi, Hermann (b. Giessen, 7 Nov. 1839; d. Munich, 13 May 1900), German conductor. The son of a rabbi, Levi attended the LEIPZIG Conservatory in his late teens, then took up conducting posts in Saarbrücken, MANNHEIM, and Rotterdam before becoming Kapellmeister at Karlsruhe (1864–72) and finally MUNICH (1872–96). While in Karlsruhe, he became a close friend of Clara Schumann and Johannes BRAHMS, but Levi's increasing association with Wagner in the course of the 1870s finally caused a permanent breach in his relationship with the more conservative circle. Wagner had been aware of Levi since at least 1870, when he wrote the conductor to thank him for not participating in the Munich premiere of *Die WALKÜRE* (letter of [28] April 1870). Thereafter Wagner continued to cultivate the relationship, and Levi, who both professionally and aesthetically was becoming increasingly committed to opera and Wagner's dreams for society, responded with ever greater enthusiasm. Not until LUDWIG II's funding of the premiere of *PARSIFAL* stipulated the participation of the conductor, orchestra, and stage personnel of the Munich Court Theater, however, did Levi and Wagner work directly with one another.

Their relationship nearly foundered in 1881, when the composer showed Levi an anonymous note expressing outrage at the idea that the "Christian" *Parsifal* should be conducted by a Jew, a sentiment that echoed the composer's own view and that caused him to encourage Levi to be baptized. Levi offered to withdraw, but Wagner eventually stopped short of making this request a demand, and Levi led the first performance of *Parsifal* at BAYREUTH in 1882, remaining the work's primary conductor through 1894. His position at Bayreuth was not ideally serene, however: although COSIMA Wagner's rigid conception of authenticity demanded that she retain Levi as her *Parsifal* conductor – and although she clearly valued his company and his musicianship – it also prompted her to make his Jewishness an ongoing point of contention, and the ill feeling her attitude engendered again prompted him to offer to step down on at least one occasion.

Levi was nearly the only conductor of his day to conduct all of Wagner's important works (*Parsifal* at Bayreuth, everything else in Munich), but his musical interests and commitments ranged widely, from GLUCK and MOZART to living French composers. Having separated from Brahms, Levi became an advocate for the symphonies of BRUCKNER, who held Levi's opinion in such high regard that when the conductor roundly criticized the Eighth, the composer was plunged into self-doubt and spent years revising that and other works – time posterity wishes he might rather have spent on creation. As an interpreter, Levi seems to have been extremely cultured and musical. Although he was not a flamboyant figure on the podium, his early training and aspirations as a composer allowed him to recognize the special characteristics of each work he led, resulting in performances of great perceptiveness and empathy. The fact that Wagnerians of the time regarded his conducting as "spiritual" may thus have to more to do with the effect he achieved in *Parsifal*, with which he was so closely associated, than with his musical approach in general.   DAVID BRECKBILL

See also ANTI-SEMITISM; JEWS

Laurence Dreyfus, "Hermann Levi's Shame and *Parsifal*'s Guilt: A Critique of Essentialism in Biography and Criticism," *Cambridge Opera Journal* 6.2 (1994): 125–45.

Frithjof Haas, *Zwischen Brahms und Wagner: Der Dirigent Hermann Levi* (Zurich: Atlantis, 1995).

Stephan Mösch, "'Leidens- und Freudenszeit': Zum Verhältnis zwischen Hermann Levi und Bayreuth," *WagnerSpectrum* 5.1 (2009): 65–104.

Weihe, Werkstatt, Wirklichkeit: Wagners "Parsifal" in Bayreuth (see bibliography): 255–315.

Egon Voss, *Die Dirigenten der Bayreuther Festspiele* (see bibliography).

Levine, James (b. Cincinnati, 23 June 1943), American conductor and pianist. Levine studied at the Juilliard School and was George Szell's assistant at Cleveland, then artistic director of the Metropolitan Opera in New York, 1986–2004. He gave his BAYREUTH debut with PARSIFAL in 1982 in a Götz Friedrich production notable for its slow tempi. He was further responsible for Alfred Kirchner's production of the RING DES NIBELUNGEN at Bayreuth (1994–8) and conducted the Metropolitan *Ring* in the productions by Otto Schenk (1986) and Robert Lepage (2011).   CHRIS WALTON

Robert C. Marsh, *Dialogues and Discoveries: James Levine: His Life and His Music* (New York: Scribner, 1998).

Liebestod (love-death). Normally refers to the concert version of ISOLDE's final monologue at the end of Act III of TRISTAN UND ISOLDE. The habit of referring to one of Wagner's most famous pieces of music in this way probably began with the PIANO ARRANGEMENT of it by Franz LISZT issued in 1867 with the title *Isolden's Liebestod*. But Wagner himself never used the word "Liebestod" to describe the music either in its concert form or in the complete work. He first thought of performing it as a separate item, preceded by the *Tristan* PRELUDE, in the early 1860s (see EXCERPTS). He conducted the beginning and ending of *Tristan* in concert a total of nineteen times in many European cities between March 1863 (ST. PETERSBURG) and May 1877 (LONDON). In surviving programs, however, he consistently describes the Prelude as the "Liebestod" and not the ending, which, instead, he describes as "Verklärung" (transfiguration).

The word "Liebestod" occurs only once in the whole of *Tristan und Isolde*, in the middle of the love duet in Act II. Attaching it to the *Tristan* Prelude, Wagner clearly wanted the listener to associate the music with the protagonists' state of mind (and body) at the center of the work. Placing the Prelude side by side with the music of Isolde's final monologue from Act III, however, he also wanted to convey the sense of moving beyond the idea of "Liebestod" to something else. The word "Verklärung" he used to describe the second half of the concert version has a religious aura about it that suggests Isolde is finally released from "die Liebe als Qual" (LOVE as torment) – a phrase standing out in Wagner's sketches for Act III like words from a modern psychoanalyst's notebook – to achieve something akin to divine status. Put another way: the concert version is a powerful musical expression not just of a single anguished condition the protagonists themselves describe as a "Liebestod" in Act II of the complete work, but of a transition *in nuce* to an altogether different emotional state that gives the ending a sense of sacred enactment.

Isolde's orgasmic death has caused so much voyeuristic excitement that the reasons for its distinctive place in *Tristan* have become blurred. (According to a famous 1985 essay by media theorist Friedrich Kittler, TRISTAN's far-from-dead body, to which Isolde sings, even has an erection made abundantly visible by the surging thrust of the music as she herself dies.) Thus the encyclopedist is tempted to cast lexicographical niceties to the winds and – for the sake of clarity and a modicum of sanity – to refer to the *Tristan* ending as posterity always has. Worries about what to call it in any case can blind us to the fact that, strangely for such a well-known piece of music, it is still little understood. Wagner's description of it in his sketches for the third act as "ascending melodies of love, rising up as if out of Tristan's soul like a sea of blossoms, into which Isolde throws herself and – dies" can certainly help us to understand its ambiguities and dramatic sense. The image is in all likelihood a reference to the moment in GOTTFRIED VON STRASSBURG's *Tristan* – Wagner's main MEDIEVAL source – when Isolde's "secret song" steals "with its rapturous music hidden and unseen through the windows of the eyes into many noble hearts." The reversal is significant. The melody initiated by Tristan in the love duet of Act II with his words "So starben wir" (Thus might we die; Example 8) is taken up by Isolde with her words "Mild und leise" (Softly and quietly; Example 9) at the start of the *Liebestod*.

ACT II

8. Theme from *Tristan und Isolde* Act II, "So starben wir..."

ACT III

9. Theme from *Tristan und Isolde* Act III, "Mild und leise..."

Instead of Isolde's melody quietly invading other noble hearts, it is now Tristan's "secret song" that steals "unseen" through Isolde's eyes (and ears) into her heart, leading her to commit suicide in a "sea of blossoms." Wagner had no trouble in converting the aquatic and vegetal image into a welter of gorgeous sound in the *Liebestod* that has held the world in thrall ever since.

Like the rest of the remarkable score of *Tristan*, the power of the *Liebestod* has always resided in its ability to conjure up visual and acoustic allusions: Narcissus dying after falling in love with his own reflection in the waters of a spring, for example, or the *mater dolorosa* weeping over the body of the dead Christ. The Virgin's "glowing head" in Titian's *Assunta dei Frari* reminded Wagner, according to COSIMA WAGNER'S DIARIES, of the sexual urge "now freed of all desire" (25 April 1882), a striking comparison suggesting an analogy between the Assumption of the Virgin Mary and Isolde's sumptuous acceptance of death as she transcends earthly sexual longing. PARSIFAL, the hero who renounces sexual desire, was due to visit Tristan on his sickbed in the early sketches of *Tristan und Isolde* until Wagner decided to devote a separate work to him. The two heroes are indeed closely related, not only because of their motherless condition, but also because of their eventual escape from sexual passion into an enraptured world of divine grace. The *Liebestod*'s magnificent irony is that Isolde's religious ecstasy and rapturous escape from the torment of love is composed on the wings of Tristan's "secret song" – music that has already entered her ear during their greatest sexual arousal in Act II.

Luis Buñuel played a gramophone record of Wagner's *Liebestod* at the 1929 premiere of the silent version of his and Salvador Dali's notorious film *Un chien andalou*. (It was also part of the soundtrack added later.) Without any intended surrealist fantasy, the Hollywood star Joan Crawford, her character married unhappily to an older man and thwarted in passion by her lover, commits suicide in full evening attire at the end of the film *Humoresque* (1946) by deliberately walking into a stormy ocean accompanied by a version of the *Liebestod* arranged and conducted by Franz Waxman. The *Liebestod* has been used in many films since with varying degrees of success and even lent its name to a psychoanalytical theory ("*Liebestod* fantasy") coined by J. C. Flugel in 1953. It has also been recorded by many outstanding sopranos – by far the best are in the complete *Tristan* recordings with Kirsten FLAGSTAD (1952) and Margaret Price (1982) – and is still regularly performed in the concert hall. In modern times it usually includes the soprano voice, in contrast to a nineteenth-century tradition that Wagner did his best to uphold, according to which it should be played outside the opera house as a purely instrumental work. JOHN DEATHRIDGE

Robert Bailey, ed., *Prelude and Transfiguration from "Tristan und Isolde"* (see bibliography).
John Deathridge, *Wagner Beyond Good and Evil* (see bibliography).
Roger Scruton, *Death-Devoted Heart: Sex and the Sacred in Wagner's "Tristan und Isolde"* (see bibliography).

Liebesverbot, Das, oder Die Novize von Palermo (The Ban on Love, or The Novice of Palermo; WWV 38), Wagner's second opera, written in 1834–5 during his tenure with the Bethmann company. It was given just one performance in his lifetime by that company in MAGDEBURG on 29 March 1836. This *grosse komische Oper* is based on SHAKESPEARE's *Measure for Measure*.

Wagner shifted the action from Vienna to Palermo, a land of sunshine and hedonistic pleasure; the King of Sicily is absent and a German governor, Friedrich (bass), rules in his place. The puritanical Friedrich has banned all pleasure, including drink, carnival, and sexual congress outside marriage; those who indulge will be punished by death. A young nobleman, Claudio (tenor), has been arrested for getting Julia pregnant and both of them are to be executed. Claudio has dispatched his friend Luzio (tenor) to ask his sister Isabella (soprano) to intercede for him with Friedrich. Luzio meets Isabella and, enchanted by her beauty, makes an offer of marriage, which she refuses. On hearing of Claudio's sentence, Isabella, in a private meeting, begs Friedrich to pardon Claudio, which Friedrich agrees to do if Isabella sleeps with him. She refuses, and tells Claudio to prepare for death. But on returning to the convent, she plans to save him by employing the services of her fellow novice Mariana (soprano), who was secretly married to and then abandoned by Friedrich. Isabella tells Friedrich she will sleep with him and in the darkness has Mariana take her place. The action comes to a climax in the *corso* of Palermo where, despite Friedrich's ban, carnival is taking place. In a series of maskings and unmaskings Friedrich is revealed to be the hypocrite he is, Isabella accepts Luzio as her lover, and the crowd rejoices at the news that the King of Sicily, the guardian of their pleasures, has just returned to his realm.

Das Liebesverbot was written under the influence of the writers of YOUNG GERMANY, such as Heinrich LAUBE and Friedrich Heinse, who were fervent advocates of free LOVE. Wagner's opera has none of the darkness and ambiguity of Shakespeare's work, his vision of unbridled sexuality being largely unproblematic. The score shows him to have been remarkably adept in mastering the Italian and French operatic idioms, AUBER and BELLINI being the major influences. Theatrically there are allusions to MOZART, the final scene being based on Act IV of *Figaro*, while a comic subplot, in which Friedrich's henchman Brighella is seduced by Dorella, is pure *commedia dell'arte*, its music recalling ROSSINI. The later Wagner is anticipated in the use of several LEITMOTIVE, most notably a heavy descending theme for the "ban on love," which is heard in various forms throughout the action. More strikingly, Shakespeare's quasi-tragic dramatic atmosphere is caught in a lengthy aria for Friedrich in which he determines to sacrifice his life rather than forego the delights of Isabella's body. In the intensity of its utterance, Friedrich's predicament, in which physical love overwhelms all other considerations, looks forward to the conflicted situations of such figures as TANNHÄUSER, SIEGMUND, and TRISTAN.   SIMON WILLIAMS

Liszt, Franz (b. Raiding [Doborján], 22 Oct. 1811; d. Bayreuth, 31 July 1886) was a Hungarian pianist, composer, and teacher. Influential as the most famous pianist of the century, he became a central figure in European musical life, and was arguably the most important living artist for Richard Wagner's professional development. Literary narrative, anecdote, myth, and hagiography abound in the Liszt literature of the nineteenth and twentieth centuries. Historically, Liszt's multivalent identity saw him assume status as a French literary Romantic, Great German composer, Hungarian patriot, ascetic Catholic priest, and libidinous womanizer. Yet amid such contradictory poses, he consistently pursued an AVANT-GARDIST agenda, whether manifest in terms of a piano-technical imagination, revival of plainchant, program music, atonality, or the promotion of progressive opera. He remains a charismatically flexible figure in scholarly discourse.

1. Early life
2. Weimar and Rome
3. Relations with Wagner
4. From "devoted admirer" to "Bayreuth's poodle"
5. Posterity
6. Liszt's piano transcriptions of Wagner (ordered by date of composition)

1. Early life

Following piano lessons from his father, Adam, Liszt studied with Carl Czerny in Vienna. A student of BEETHOVEN, Czerny accompanied Liszt and Adam when Anton Schindler arranged for them to meet the revered composer in April 1823. While Beethoven did not attend the concert of Liszt's to which he had been invited, the two had met earlier in the composer's rooms, though the legend that Beethoven kissed Liszt on the head after hearing him play ("kiss of consecration" / *Weihekuss*), though still debated, remains unlikely, lacking any affirmative evidence.

Following several successful concerts in Vienna, Liszt (mimicking Mozart's travels) journeyed with his father via MUNICH, Augsburg, Strasbourg, and Stuttgart arriving in PARIS in December 1823. After making the acquaintance of piano maker Sébastien Érard, Liszt applied to the Paris Conservatoire but was refused: foreigners were not permitted. Instead he received private tuition from Anton Reicha (theory) and Ferdinando Paer (composition). Further tours were punctuated by the premiere in Paris of Liszt's opera *Don Sanche* (1825).

Following the July revolution of 1830 – after Liszt's thwarted infatuation with Countess Caroline de Saint-Cricq, a breakdown, and a period of introspection in which he contemplated entering a Catholic seminary – he began reading widely, gave fewer concerts, and was increasingly drawn to the ideas of the Saint-Simonians, and later to the revolutionary teachings of Abbé Felicité de Lamennais. The heady milieu Liszt encountered in Paris included many of French Romanticism's principal architects, including Sainte-Beuve, Victor Hugo, Eugène Delacroix, Honoré de Balzac, and George Sand. In 1830, Liszt met BERLIOZ, encountered Chopin the following year, and in 1832 first heard Paganini, which inspired his own compositions.

That same year, Liszt first met Marie D'AGOULT. Already estranged from her husband, she became Liszt's lover shortly thereafter, and during their relationship (1835–9) would bear him three children, Blandine-Rachel (1835–62), COSIMA (1837–1930), and Daniel (1839–59). An initial elopement to Switzerland was punctuated in 1837 by Liszt's return to Princess Belgiojoso's salon in Paris for a much-discussed, inconclusive virtuoso "duel" with Sigismond Thalberg. During this period Liszt rose to European fame as both a supreme virtuoso pianist, whose charisma aroused admiration to the point of hysteria (HEINE's *Lisztomania*) on his unprecedented concert tours, and a philanthropist who raised large sums of money for the public good: victims of flooding (Pest 1839), and a Beethoven monument (Bonn 1845).

2. Weimar and Rome

At the apex of his pianistic fame in 1847, Liszt ceased giving paid recitals and settled into an entirely different position in Weimar as "Kapellmeister im ausserordentlichen Dienst," an appointment made in 1842, but only taken up full-time in 1848. That year, he also met the Ukrainian Princess Carolyn zu SAYN-WITTGENSTEIN, who would relocate to Weimar in 1848, becoming Liszt's long-term partner. At the Weimar court, Liszt's professional identity shifted from performer-virtuoso to serious composer, reflecting the dominant European aesthetics that increasingly promoted the formation of a canon of great, immanent works. The classicism of GOETHE and SCHILLER was within living memory in the town, and with the support of the Grand Duke Carl Alexander (1818–1901), Liszt aspired to create in post-classical Weimar "a new Athens," reviving the spirit of the town's artistic heritage through a renovating agenda for musical progress. This effectively established Weimar as the seat of NEW GERMAN aesthetics, and liberal students such as Peter CORNELIUS, Joachim RAFF, and Hans von BÜLOW were attracted accordingly, working as copyists, secretaries, and essayists, as well as musicians at the Altenburg, Liszt's grand residence.

A Hegelian through and through, Liszt pursued a self-consciously progressive musical agenda as Kapellmeister, completing the major corpus of his orchestral repertoire: twelve symphonic poems, *Eine Symphonie zu Dantes Divina Comedia* (1857), and *Eine Faust Symphonie* (1856). As (an emerging) conductor at the Hoftheater, he gave prominent performances of new works by contemporary composers such as Wagner and Berlioz, as well as revivals of older repertoire. Throughout the 1850s, Franz BRENDEL remained a close advocate and loyal defender of Liszt's ambitions in the pages of the *NEUE ZEITSCHRIFT*. Following tensions over Liszt's partnership with Princess Carolyn, and hostile relations with Franz von DINGELSTEDT over control of the Hoftheater, however, Liszt resigned his Weimar post in 1858, finally leaving for Rome in 1861.

His reason for relocating was ostensibly to secure his Catholic marriage to Carolyn, though they abandoned nuptial plans after the promise of another decade of litigation. Now Liszt cultivated his interests in plainchant, the music of Palestrina, and the Caecilian movement, gave weekly masterclasses, and continued composing. Following the death of two of his children, Daniel and Blandine-Rachel, he entered the Dominican monastery of Madonna del Rosario in 1863. In 1865, he received the tonsure and took the four minor holy orders, becoming thereafter "Abbé Liszt."

What Liszt later dubbed "ma vie trifurquée" began in 1869 and involved continuous shuttling between his three homes of Weimar (summer), Rome (autumn), and Budapest (winter and spring): in Budapest he was appointed the first president of the newly formed National Hungarian Royal Academy of Music; in Weimar he gave masterclasses at the Hofgärtnerei, attracting droves of students each summer; in Rome he composed at the idyllic Villa d'Este, giving rise to a number of experimental, non-tonal piano works, whose stylistic reach is often connected to SCHOENBERG and DEBUSSY. But the travelling was tiring, and Liszt's poor health was compounded by what was likely a broken hip in 1881, and increasing blindness (cataracts) by 1886. Following a final tour to England in 1886, and despite a fever, he travelled to BAYREUTH in July of that year to support the struggling Festival, now run by his estranged daughter (and in need of continued celebrity endorsement). After witnessing performances of *Parsifal* and the Bayreuth premiere of *Tristan*, he died of what seems to have been a heart attack. He was buried in Bayreuth, though competing interests argued for his final resting place to be Weimar, Raiding, Rome, and Budapest.

3. Relations with Wagner

Liszt first met Wagner in 1841, when the latter briefly introduced himself in an "awkward" exchange in Paris following Heinrich Laube's cynical recommendation "to lose no time in looking [Liszt] up, as he was 'generous'" (ML/E 239). After Liszt had heard *RIENZI* in DRESDEN (1844), a second meeting followed in Berlin, mediated by Wilhemine SCHROEDER-DEVRIENT. Thereafter, Wagner contacted Liszt in 1845 about funds for the planned Weber memorial in Dresden, and again in 1846, when he sent the scores of *Rienzi* and *TANNHÄUSER* in dogged pursuit of Liszt's esteem: "I proceed quite openly to rouse you up in my favor" (Wagner to Liszt, 22 March 1846). By 1848, he began requesting personal financial help from Liszt, initially selling the copyright to his extant operas and accepting commissions, but thereafter simply requesting a series of bailouts, often in uncomfortably obsequious, manipulative prose. The year 1849 marked a sea-change: Liszt conducted the first performances of *Tannhäuser* since the Dresden premiere (as a late substitution for Schubert's *Alfonso und Estrella* that Liszt – on point of resignation – forced on the Grand Duchess for her birthday), and gave Wagner a supreme endorsement by publishing two PIANO TRANSCRIPTIONS from the opera, declaring to its salivating composer: "Once and for all, number me in future among your most zealous and devoted admirers; near or far, count on me and make use of me" (Liszt to Wagner, 26 February 1849).

This Wagner did. Often. Liszt had the fame, influence, resources, and financing to rescue Wagner from critical and political ignominy as a composer-criminal, ingloriously expelled from Germany in 1849. Perhaps most significantly, he was a key figure in securing Wagner's eventual amnesty and in promoting the first fledgling Bayreuth festivals. While Liszt allowed himself to be exploited in ways political, fiscal, and personal, he also benefitted by tapping the progressive repertoire he felt most reflected his ambitions for post-classical Weimar. After *Tannhäuser*, Liszt mounted the ambitious premiere of *LOHENGRIN* (1850), planned to perform *Siegfrieds Tod* (had Wagner managed to complete it), and encouraged Wagner in 1856 to let him premiere *Tristan und Isolde*, even voicing the notion that the completed *RING* cycle be premiered at the Hoftheater in 1859 (Liszt to Agnes Street-Klindworth, 30 January 1857). Above all, Liszt admired Wagner's music immensely, speaking of: "your valiant and superb genius ... [reflected in] the blazing and magnificent pages of your *Tannhäuser*" (Liszt to Wagner, 26 February 1849). Nevertheless, the relationship was decidedly asymmetrical, and Wagner knew it, writing dismissively to Theodor UHLIG: "remarkable that a friend, who is quite distant from me in many important aspects of life and thinking nevertheless with unshakable loyalty and attentiveness takes such an unusual interest in my entire existence ... and seems to have dedicated his entire being to one thing only: to help me and to publicize my works" (27 July 1850).

4. From "devoted admirer" to "Bayreuth's poodle"

As a writer, Liszt penned lengthy, panegyrical essays on *Tannhäuser* and *Lohengrin* (published together as a brochure in French [1851] and German [1852]), initiating a new didactic strain of opera criticism and (in *Lohengrin*) *Leitmotiv* analysis. To be sure, Liszt also published a series of essays about the history of modern opera based on other composers' works he performed at Weimar, but arguably not with the same eye to international propaganda.

By contrast, Wagner's comments on Liszt were mixed; he famously admitted that after becoming acquainted with Liszt's music, he became "quite a different fellow in terms of harmony," though disdained Richard POHL for "blurt[ing] out this secret for the whole world to hear, right at the head of a short notice on the Tristan Prelude" (Wagner to Bülow, 7 October 1859). Yet Wagner also disparaged Liszt's "apotheosis obsession" in symphonic music, and would dismiss his late piano works as "completely meaningless" and "budding insanity" (CWD 2 August 1869 and 28–29 November 1882). Wagner's reticence in publicly evaluating Liszt's music is further glimpsed in his open letter on the Symphonic Poems (1857), where, after suggesting that mental representations of Orpheus or Prometheus could replace the dance or march as the arbiter of "form" on which music's ability to communicate depends, he nevertheless unveils his skepticism: "[one] may point to the difficulty of extracting an intelligible form for musical composition out of such exalted representations" (77). In other words, Wagner's operatic aesthetics were substantively at odds with Liszt's symphonic path.

Yet in composition, the cross-fertilization of musical ideas between the two men worked both ways. Liszt made no fewer than fifteen piano transcriptions of Wagner's music (see 6. Liszt's piano transcriptions of Wagner) employing varying degrees of arrangement and re-composition to disseminate images of Wagner's music among the European bourgeoisie; he regularly sent new works to Wagner during the 1850s for feedback, incorporating, for instance, Wagner's advice not to portray paradise through a planned choral finale in his "Dante" symphony (Liszt's ensuing dedication read: "as Virgil guided Dante, so have you guided me through the mysterious regions of those worlds of sound that are steeped in life"). While acts of direct borrowing appear more traceable on Wagner's side, the *Reminiscenzenjägerei* of the 1850s and 1860s is not always what it seems, as Liszt noted: "Wagner and I adopted the same theme for *Faust* before we even knew each other – I give you my word on this" (quoted in Göllerich 172). Over and above debates about the openings of *Tristan* in Liszt's "Die Lorelei" and *Parsifal* in his "Die Glocken des Strassburg Munsters," recent scholarly attitudes have tended to see these borrowings less as thievery, and more as "a type of criticism – a compelling musical commentary" (Hamilton 44), for Liszt reincorporates the borrowed material in *Parsifal* back into his piano work *Am Grabe Richard Wagners*, for example, together with the Montsalvat bells, in a final tributary "statement."

A misreading of tone over Liszt's comments about *Tristan* caused an unprecedented rift in 1859, and five years later a yet more serious rupture occurred over the Cosima affair. Liszt intervened twice in the matter, and, following an abrasive confrontation with Wagner, the latter wrote in his diary with sickly irony: "I shall finally come to hate my friend completely! . . . Your father is repugnant to me" (BB/E, 1 September 1865).

Despite the ensuing years of silence between the two composers, they resumed correspondence in 1872, though this was long since voided of a tone of innocent friendship. During the 1870s and 1880s, aesthetic differences further splintered their putative artistic unity to the point where the mere fact that Cosima and Liszt conversed in French irritated Wagner. Liszt came to resent his subordinate role at the Bayreuth festivals, calling himself "not a composer, but a publicity agent" and – after Wagner's death – "Bayreuth's poodle" (reported by Carl Lachmund, 342).

5. Posterity

Ever since Nietzsche lumped Liszt together with Wagner as his historical sidekick – "In a formula: 'Wagner and Liszt'" ("Case of Wagner" 635) – the friendship and shared aesthetic outlook between the two has been exaggerated in biographical writing. The thorny reality of their mutual interdependence betrays this fiction, and more recent portraits, from scholarship and pop culture alike, emphasize Liszt's unwittingly sacrificial role in reception history: "as John the Baptist to Wagner's Messiah" in Kenneth Hamilton's words (44), or as the helpless victim of Wagner-as-vampire, in Ken Russell's film *Lisztomania*. Like many aspects of Wagner's behavior, it is difficult for historians to separate Wagner's calculated public persona from his sincere beliefs, and this is the enduring double-vision with which we assess his public encomiums to Liszt, first in 1851: "[O]ne Friend . . . lifted me from out my deepest discontent . . . [thus did he] make me anew, and now entirely, an Artist. This wondrous Friend of mine is Franz Liszt" (SSD 4: 337–8; PW 1:385). And twenty-five years later, at a banquet celebrating the conclusion of the first complete cycle of the Ring at Bayreuth: "He is the one who first had faith in me when I was as yet unknown, and without whom you would perhaps not have heard a note of mine, my dear friend Franz Liszt" (Glasenapp 5:298).

Ultimately, then, the Liszt-Wagner relationship retained its asymmetry: Liszt was unambiguous in his praise of Wagner's music; Wagner was unambiguous in his praise of Liszt's role as "my second self" (SSD 4:340; PW 1:388). Wagner's gratitude in 1854 is revealing in this respect: "*You*, for the first and only time, have disclosed to me the joy of being wholly understood. My being has passed into yours" (Wagner to Liszt, 7[?] October 1854).

6. Liszt's piano transcriptions of Wagner (ordered by date of composition)

1849:   Ouvertüre zu *Tannhäuser* / Overture to *Tannhäuser* (S 422)
1849:   "O du mein holder Abendstern," Rezitativ und Romanze aus der Oper *Tannhäuser* / Recitative and Romance "Evening Star" from *Tannhäuser* (S 444)

1852:   Zwei Stücke aus *Tannhäuser* und *Lohengrin* | Two pieces from *Tannhäuser* and *Lohengrin* (S 445)

     i. Einzug der Gäste auf der Wartburg | Entry of the Guests

     ii. Elsas Brautzug zum Münster | Elsa's bridal procession

1854:   Aus *Lohengrin* | From *Lohengrin*

     i. Festspiel und Brautlied | Festival and Bridal Song

     ii. Elsa's Traum | Elsa's dream

     iii. Lohengrins Verweis | Lohengrin's admonition

1859:   Phantasiestück über Motive aus *Rienzi* "Santo Spirito cavaliere" von Richard Wagner | Fantasy on Themes from *Rienzi* (S 439)

1860:   Spinnerlied aus dem *Fliegenden Holländer* | Spinning Chorus from *Der fliegende Holländer* (S 440)

1861:   Pilgerchor aus *Tannhäuser* | Pilgrims' Chorus from *Tannhäuser* (S 443)

1867:   Isoldes Liebestod aus *Tristan und Isolde* | Isolde's Liebestod from *Tristan und Isolde* (S 447)

1871:   "Am stillen Herd" aus den *Meistersingern* | "Am stillen Herd" from *Die Meistersinger* (S 448)

1872:   Ballade aus dem *fliegenden Holländer* | Ballad from *Der fliegende Holländer* (S 441)

1875:   "Walhall" aus dem *Ring des Nibelungen* | "Valhalla" from *Der Ring des Nibelungen* (S 449)

1882:   Feierlicher Marsch zum heiligen Gral aus *Parsifal* (Marche solennelle du Saint Gral de Parsifal) | Solemn March to the Holy Grail from *Parsifal* (S 450)

DAVID TRIPPETT

Nicolas Dufetel, "Liszt et la 'propagande wagnérienne': Le Projet de deux livres en français sur l'histoire de l'opéra et sur Wagner (1849–1859)," *Acta musicologica* 82 (2010): 263–304.

Carl Friedrich Glasenapp, *Das Leben Richard Wagners in sechs Büchern* (see bibliography).

August Göllerich, *Franz Liszt* (Berlin: Marquard & Co., 1908).

Kenneth Hamilton, "Wagner and Liszt: Elective Affinities," in *Richard Wagner and His World*, ed. Thomas S. Grey (Princeton University Press, 2009): 27–64.

Jonathan Kregor, "Liszt's Wagner," *The Wagner Journal* 5 (2011): 17–43.

Carl Lachmund, *Living with Liszt: From the Diary of Carl Lachmund* (Stuyvesant, NY: Pendragon, 1995).

Franz Liszt, *Sämtliche Schriften*, ed. Detlev Altenburg, 5 vols. (Wiesbaden: Breitkopf & Härtel, 1989–)

Franz Liszt and Agnes Street-Klindworth: A Correspondence, 1854–1886, ed. and trans. Pauline Pocknell (Hillsdale, NY: Pendragon, 2000).

Richard Wagner, "Wagner's Open Letter to Marie Wittgenstein on Liszt's Symphonic Poems," trans. Thomas S. Grey, *The Wagner Journal* 5 (2011): 65–81.

Alan Walker, *Franz Liszt*, 3 vols. (London and Boston: Faber, 1983–97).

Loën, Baron August von (b. Dessau, 27 Jan. 1828; d. Jena, 28 Apr. 1887). After a distinguished career in the Prussian army, Loën opted to pursue his literary and dramatic interests, most notably as director of Weimar's Court Theater (1867–87). In that capacity, he was Wagner's guest at the Munich premiere of RHEINGOLD (1869), and in 1877 floated the idea of staging *Rheingold* in Weimar. Wagner also tapped Loën in 1871 to oversee the PATRONS' ASSOCIATION (*Patronatverein*).   ANTHONY J. STEINHOFF

Loge (tenor; character in *Der RING DES NIBELUNGEN*, with appearances in *Das RHEINGOLD*. Half-god of fire). In Loge, Wagner created an outsider god who represents in many respects the bad conscience of the gods of Valhalla. Loge is unique among the *Ring*'s cast of characters in that he appears in corporeal form only in *Das Rheingold*, and absconds into his own element, fire, at the end of that opera. In the cycle's main "days" Loge is present only musically, for instance when Wotan invokes him at the end of *Die WALKÜRE*, in the famous *Feuerzauber*. In conceiving the character Wagner superimposed a number of divinities, only one of which was his NORDIC namesake Loki. Wagner relied on Jakob Grimm's *Germanische Mythologie* (1835) in elaborating the *Ring*'s cosmology, and imbued Loge's character with the traits of gods Grimm's tome identified as similar. Wagner's Loge is a trickster, a messenger god like Hermes, a promethean figure, or a Lucifer in the mold of GOETHE's Mephistopheles.

As befits a god associated with fire, Loge appears in the *Ring* as an amoral, elemental, and deeply anarchic force – "who knows what I'll do?" Loge asks in parting at the end of *Rheingold*. He is bound by Wotan's system of laws and contracts, but willing to interpret them in ways antithetical to their spirit. His contempt for the gods of Valhalla is evident, although his is the most persistent voice of caution as WOTAN sets off the calamitous chain of events that will eventually lead to the gods' demise. At the same time, Loge's caution does not spring from any affection he holds for the other gods. When Loge gleefully comments on the gods' triumphant entry into their new palace by saying that "here they rush to their end," he seems Mephistophelian in the pleasure he takes in destructions – nevertheless Wagner, in a letter to August Röckel, made it clear that he thought Loge was essentially correct (25/26 January 1854).

Loge is associated with some of the most distinctive and instantly recognizable music in the *Ring*: the rapid, parallel, chromatic, major $\frac{6}{3}$ chords in semiquavers that introduce him (*Rheingold*, Scene 2, mm. 1184 ff.; see Appendix 4: *Leitmotive* in *Der Ring des Nibelungen*, CWE 6a), and the gossamer, dotted neighboring-chord figures that immediately follow (mm. 1192 ff. and 1203 ff.; see CWE 6b). These motives are the Fire or Loge motive, and the Magic Fire motive, respectively. They articulate, even without Loge's actual presence, some of the central scenes of the cycle: Wotan's putting BRÜNNHILDE to sleep at the end of *Walküre*, Siegfried's passing through the fire to reach Brünnhilde at the top of the mountain in Act III of *Siegfried*, his "Rhine Journey" back through the fire between the prologue and Act I of *GÖTTERDÄMMERUNG*, and, at the very end, the burning of Valhalla.

Given that Loge disappears into Wagner's construction, becomes part of the *Ring*'s furniture, where Wagner stands vis-à-vis the character and his motivation becomes a central question in Loge's reception. Shaw was the first to suggest that Wagner's opinion of Loge may have shifted over time. The god started out a "shifty, unreal, delusive" pessimist that typified "the reasoning faculty," but after his encounter with SCHOPENHAUER Wagner became "bent on proving that he had always been a Pessimist at heart, and that Loki was the most sensible and worthy advisor to Wotan" (119).   ADRIAN DAUB AND PATRICK MCCRELESS

George Bernard Shaw, *The Perfect Wagnerite* (see bibliography).

Lohengrin (WWV 75), Romantic opera in three acts. Text written in 1845, composition 1846–8, first performed at the Weimar Court Theater on 28 August 1850. Cond. Franz LISZT. For cast information, see Appendix 10: Stage productions.

1. Sources
2. Development of the text
3. Composition
4. Plot summary
5. Musical structure
6. Publication, first staging, and significant performances
7. Critical reception and problems of interpretation

1. Sources

Like the majority of Wagner's dramatic works, *Lohengrin* is based on medieval poetry, in this case notably an eponymous epic poem from the 1280s, as well as *Parzival* and *Titurel* by WOLFRAM VON ESCHENBACH. However, he thoroughly reworked these sources. According to MEIN LEBEN (My Life, 1865–81), Wagner first came across the story in 1841/2 in the Annual Proceedings of the Königsberg Germanic Society (1838), containing also the account of the *Wartburgkrieg* which inspired TANNHÄUSER. While working on the prose draft in the summer of 1845, and the libretto later that year (see below), he probably drew on the contemporary editions of Wolfram's poems by Karl Simrock (1842) and San-Marte (1833), as well as Joseph von Görres's edition of the anonymous *Lohengrin* (1813). Wagner, however, repeatedly stressed that he had to "purify" the – as he thought – convoluted and contaminated courtly poetry and return to a putative folk (*VOLK*) tradition, which he sought in the retellings in the *Niederländische Sagen* (ed. Johann Wilhelm Wolf, 1843), the *Deutsche Sagen* by Jakob and Wilhelm Grimm (1816/18), and the fairy tales of Ludwig Bechstein. Undoubtedly the story of the swan knight shows parallels to fairy tales of the "Tierbräutigam" type, where the enchanted partner stays until asked to reveal their secret, and the "Melusine" type about the impossible love story of a human and supernatural partner. Wagner's own comparison of *Lohengrin* with the Greek myth of Zeus and Semele (*Eine MITTEILUNG AN MEINE FREUNDE* [A Communication to My Friends], 1851) was probably made from hindsight; the parallel is first mentioned in a letter of 1846, but it is not clear whether it informed the genesis of the opera. Other literary and operatic conventions also entered the text, such as the quarrel of the queens outside the church, which is modeled on a scene in the *Nibelungenlied* (and absent from the *Ring*), or the motive of the interrupted wedding, which was a staple of GRAND OPERA.

2. Development of the text

Wagner wrote the text of *Lohengrin* quickly, which explains why there are few changes from prose draft to verse libretto. According to *Mein Leben*, the idea for the opera came to him fully formed while he was recovering at the Bohemian spa MARIENBAD. This account is supported by a letter to his brother Albert (4 August 1845), stating that he finished a detailed plan for *Lohengrin* the day before. The versified version was completed on 27 November 1845; Wagner read the text on 17 December to Ferdinand HILLER, Robert SCHUMANN, and several painters. A slightly changed version was sent to MEYERBEER in 1846, and the autograph fair copy, which incorporates the changes made during composition (e.g., shortening ORTRUD's speech at the end of Act III), was written in late 1848. The finale of the first act was included in a concert program of 22 September 1848; a full text was sold at the Weimar premiere in 1850 and published in the *Gesammelte Schriften und Dichtungen*, volume 2.

3. Composition

The composition of *Lohengrin* proceeded as speedily as the text. For the first time, Wagner composed the individual acts from beginning to end, finishing the first complete draft on 30 July 1846. The second complete draft, which outlines the ORCHESTRATION, began with Act III (September 1846–March 1847); Acts I and II were completed in June and August 1847 respectively. Wagner started writing the full score on 1 January 1848 and finished it on 28 April 1848. He later changed only details and never considered recasting the opera to the extent that *Tannhäuser* was reworked. The second stanza of Lohengrin's "Grail Narration" was cut at the Weimar premiere, which necessitated a new transition. Wagner also arranged EXCERPTS for concert performances in ZURICH (1853), LONDON (1855), PARIS (1860), St. Petersburg, Moscow, and Budapest (1863), as well as for the *Lyrische Stücke aus Lohengrin* printed in 1854.

4. Plot summary

Act I. A meadow on the banks of the river Schelde: When King Heinrich – the historical Heinrich I "the Fowler" (d. 936) – arrives in Brabant to gather support for a campaign against the Hungarians, he learns that Brabant is without a duke. The heir Gottfried has disappeared, and Friedrich Graf von Telramund, who claims the title through his wife Ortrud (a descendant of the previous ruling family), accuses the heiress ELSA of killing her brother. Asked to defend herself against these charges, Elsa recounts a vision of a knight in shining armor whom she expects to be her champion, offering herself and her country as a reward. In response to her fervent prayer, Lohengrin arrives in a boat drawn by a swan, while the chorus hails the miraculous apparition. He promises to fight for her in the trial by combat on the condition that she never ask for his name and origin. Elsa readily agrees; Lohengrin defeats Telramund and is welcomed as Elsa's husband and Brabant's ruler by everybody except Ortrud, who wonders why her magical powers are ineffective against the stranger.

Act II. The courtyard of the citadel of Antwerp. Telramund blames Ortrud for his disgrace by lying about Elsa's involvement in her brother's death. Ortrud, however, plans a dual strategy for Lohengrin's destruction: she will work on Elsa to break her promise to Lohengrin, while Telramund should injure the swan knight in order to destroy his magical powers. Together they vow revenge. Elsa appears on the balcony and dwells on her happiness and love. Ortrud appeals to her compassion, whereupon Elsa descends to the courtyard. Alone, Ortrud triumphs and swears to bring the pagan gods back to power. However, when she tries to kindle Elsa's doubts about her future husband, Elsa declares that her love and trust are above such doubts.

At daybreak the herald gathers the Brabantians, declaring that Telramund is outlawed, that Lohengrin will rule as "protector of Brabant," and that he will lead them into battle the next morning. This news is greeted with universal acclaim; only four noblemen pledge to support Telramund, who is hidden among the crowd. Elsa appears with her wedding retinue and slowly proceeds to the church, but Ortrud interrupts the procession by challenging Elsa about Lohengrin's descent and right to rule. Elsa rebuffs her and appeals to Lohengrin for protection. Together they continue towards the church, but now Telramund accuses Lohengrin of falsifying the trial by combat with magic and repeats Ortrud's question, which Lohengrin refuses to answer: only Elsa has the right to ask. Elsa is deeply troubled but finally, after agonizing contemplation, renews her pledge of trust, and the wedding train proceeds to the church.

Act III, Scene 1. Elsa and Lohengrin are escorted to the bridal chamber by the King and attendants. Alone they first delight in their mutual affection, but then Elsa's nagging doubts compel her to beg Lohengrin to reveal his name to her at least in private. He responds that his secret is not shameful and that he has given up much in exchange for her love. This alarms Elsa even more; she doubts her ability to make him stay and envisages the swan's return to take her husband away. Driven to desperation she asks for his name. At that moment Telramund and his supporters attack Lohengrin, but he kills Telramund. He commands Elsa's attendants to take her away and promises to reveal his identity at the King's judgment seat.

Scene 2. A meadow on the banks of the river Schelde. Nobles and soldiers gather in the morning and hail the King and Lohengrin. Lohengrin, however, declares that he will not lead the campaign. He explains that he killed Telramund in self-defense and that Elsa asked the fatal question, forcing him to reveal his identity: he is a knight of the Grail, the son of Parzival, and was sent to Brabant to fight for Elsa's innocence on the condition that he remained anonymous. Because of Elsa's breach of promise he has to return to Montsalvat, leaving behind a horn, sword, and ring for her brother. The swan returns; Ortrud triumphs and reveals that the swan is the lost heir, transformed by her sorcery. Lohengrin kneels down and prays silently, whereupon Gottfried is restored to human form. While Elsa embraces her brother and everybody marvels at this miracle, Lohengrin leaves; Elsa collapses amid general exclamations of woe.

5. Musical structure

Since *Lohengrin* was composed after *Der* FLIEGENDE HOLLÄNDER and *Tannhäuser* and before the ZURICH aesthetic writings, most discussions of its music center on the question of whether it is a "progressive" MUSIC DRAMA or a "backward-looking" opera, although such binary oppositions do not do justice to the stylistic balance that makes *Lohengrin* – labeled "romantic opera" – such an engaging artwork. Although it is, like Auber's and Meyerbeer's GRAND OPERAS, conceived in scenes and tableaux rather than individual numbers, it is easy to identify self-contained lyrical utterances that function like arias within the drama (e.g., Elsa's dream "Einsam in trüben Tagen," "Euch Lüften, die mein Klagen," Telramund's "Durch dich mußt' ich verlieren," and

10. "Forbidden Question" motive

Lohengrin's "Atmest du nicht mit mir"). These solo scenes were frequently singled out for stand-alone performance and individual publication. The CHORUS plays an important if conventional role in the massed scenes of each act, where the men-at-arms, Elsa's attendants, and "the people" mainly react to the actions of the protagonists, although they are also capable of making up their own mind, for example in their condemnation of Elsa's lack of trust in the final act. The six- and eight-part choral writing is highly inventive, makes unique use of different tone colors (e.g., in the doubling of high tenors and altos in "Wie faßt uns selig süßes Grauen"), and reaches a level of contrapuntal complexity that Wagner does not attempt again before *Meistersinger*.

Another staple in the debate of opera versus music drama is the use of motives and the extent to which they constitute a through-composed fabric. Here *Lohengrin* stands in the tradition of earlier Romantic operas, such as WEBER's *Euryanthe* (1823) or MARSCHNER's *Der Vampyr* (1828). Motives, such as the memorable "Forbidden Question" (Example 10), are mainly used to trigger reminiscences rather than as structural units, although their use, such as in the last bars of Act II, is highly effective. Uniquely amongst Wagner's dramatic works, *Lohengrin* is conceived in a recurring pattern of corresponding four-bar phrases in common time, which is partly dependent on the consistent use of rhymed tetrameters. A notable exception is the dialogue between Ortrud and Telramund in Act II, where a combination of rhymeless, flexible blank verse and motivic interweaving allows the composer to experiment with freer declamation. This scene is also outstanding in its use of the orchestra to evoke a somber, uncanny atmosphere. *Lohengrin*, in its entirety, has rightly been considered the first of Wagner's works where the ORCHESTRATION is central, rather than adjunct, to the conception of its sound world. The main characters are associated with recognizable instrumental combinations and keys: Lohengrin and the Grail – divided strings and A major; King Heinrich – brass and C major; Elsa – woodwind instruments and Ab major; Ortrud – bassoon, bass clarinet, cellos, and F♯ minor. In addition, off- and onstage ensembles and the careful gradation of the orchestral dynamics are frequently used to indicate relative distance and open spaces, expanding the enclosed stage in ways that Wagner further explores in the *Ring* dramas and especially PARSIFAL.

6. Publication, first staging, and significant performances

The vocal score (arranged by Theodor UHLIG) was advertised by BREITKOPF & HÄRTEL in February 1852. Unusually for the time, the publishers agreed to lithograph a full score, a copy of which Wagner received in early August 1852. This score is, like the autograph, dedicated to Franz Liszt, thanking him for making the first full performance possible. A partial performance of Act I had taken place in Dresden on 22 September 1848, and as late as January 1849 the court theater advertised the premiere, but the outbreak of the DRESDEN UPRISING and Wagner's flight from Germany prevented its realization. Wagner's absence from the preparations in Weimar has, however, been fortuitous for research, since he discussed his ideas at length in letters to Liszt and to Ferdinand HEINE, whose designs were published in 1853. *Lohengrin* was staged on 28 August 1850 during the celebrations of Goethe's birthday, with extra rehearsals, new stage design (Angelo II Quaglio), an augmented orchestra, and a celebratory prologue.

Wagner conducted excerpts in ZURICH in 1853, but he did not hear *Lohengrin* in its entirety until 15 May 1861 in VIENNA. He also oversaw the performances in MUNICH 1867 (cond. Hans von BÜLOW) and Vienna 1875 (cond. Hans RICHTER). At the first BAYREUTH performance in 1894, COSIMA Wagner altered the staging for the first time from the customary thirteenth-century style to the historically accurate tenth century.

After the Weimar premiere, *Lohengrin* was quickly taken up by German and international theatres (Vienna, 1856; Berlin, 1859; St. Petersburg, 1868) and paved the way for Wagner's other works. It was the first of his works to be performed in ITALY (Bologna, 1871; Milan 1873) and reached New York as early as 1871, and London in 1875 in Italian (1880 in English). In Paris, where Wagner's works were not staged in the aftermath of the FRANCO-PRUSSIAN WAR, the first performance in 1887 caused a predictable scandal and took place under police protection. For almost a century *Lohengrin* remained the Wagner opera most popular with audiences; only in the second half of the twentieth century was it overtaken by the later music dramas, notably the *Ring*.

7. Critical reception and problems of interpretation

Opinions about the first performance were predictably divided between Wagner's followers and detractors, but the vigorous debate helped to catapult him to the center of critical and popular attention. By the 1870s, *Lohengrin* was firmly established as a staple of the operatic repertoire; Cosima commented: "*Lohengrin* maintains its position as Richard's most profitable opus" (CWD 14 January 1871). Its success was not restricted to the German-speaking countries but was a worldwide phenomenon. This international reception contrasts ironically with the efforts of *völkisch* groups, such as the BAYREUTH CIRCLE, to promote *Lohengrin* as a particularly "German" work. This tendency was pilloried in Heinrich Mann's novel *Der Untertan* (1914/18), where the "loyal subject" Diederich Hessling revels in the military glamour of a *Lohengrin* performance. The German-nationalist reading was encouraged not only by the male choruses of Acts I and III, but also by the very idea of a messianic hero who comes to the aid of the threatened fatherland. Political figures such as LUDWIG II and Adolf HITLER thus identified with the swan knight to varying degrees, conveniently overlooking that Lohengrin never leads the Brabantians to victory.

The fact that Lohengrin achieves his political goals – restoring the succession of the Brabant dukes – but fails in his relationship with Elsa is a result of, in Carl Dahlhaus's apt summary, the mixing of "a fairy-tale subject [with] a tragic outcome and the outward trappings of a historical drama" (35). The ending of the opera was criticized early on; Wagner himself admitted to misgivings when Hermann Franck challenged Elsa's punishment and death, but defended them as dramatic necessities in a detailed letter (30 May 1846). In contrast to *Tannhäuser*, Wagner afterwards never considered changing the ending, though he was puzzled by continued criticism of his hero as cold and inhuman. This impression is partly rooted in a dramatic-musical problem of the finale: its musical climax is undoubtedly the "Grail Narration," which shows Lohengrin in the full glory of Montsalvat, rather than his expressions of loss and regret. Elsa gets no opportunity to voice her own perspective, unlike ISOLDE or BRÜNNHILDE, whose final monologues swing the balance of their dramas towards elation and redemption. Thus Gottfried's miraculous transformation is just a brief (musical) point of rest in a tableau of agitation and consternation, and its credible depiction remains a problem for contemporary stagings adverse to religious symbolism. In his writings, Wagner dissociates himself from a Christian-medieval reading of *Lohengrin*, prominent for example in Liszt's essay of 1850. In doing so he ignores that he himself had carried the sharp contrast between the "Christian" world of the Grail and Ortrud's "pagan" sphere into the medieval story, a contrast which permeates the musical fabric at its most impressive moments (Prelude, Act II, Scene 1, Grail Narration). By 1879 he could look back to his last "romantic opera" with greater equanimity. According to Cosima, he had "come to the conclusion that in it he has provided a complete portrait of the MIDDLE AGES. Among other things he mentions the sentries sounding their trumpets, and also the preceding fight. I add that *Lohengrin* is the only monument that shows the *beauty* of the Middle Ages" (CWD 6 June 1879).   BARBARA EICHNER

Attila Csampai and Dietmar Holland, eds., *Richard Wagner, "Lohengrin": Texte, Materialien, Kommentare* (Reinbek bei Hamburg: Rowohlt, 1989).

Carl Dahlhaus, *Richard Wagner's Music Dramas* (see bibliography).

John Deathridge, "Wagner the Progressive: Another Look at *Lohengrin*," in *Wagner Beyond Good and Evil* (see bibliography): 31–44.

Volker Mertens, "Wagner's Middle Ages," in *The Wagner Handbook*, ed. Ulrich Müller and Peter Wapnewski, trans. John Deathridge (see bibliography): 236–68.

Lohengrin (tenor; title role in LOHENGRIN). The hero of the eponymous opera – which revolves, ironically, around his desire for anonymity – is the son of Grail King Parzival who journeys from Montsalvat in order to defend ELSA of Brabant against the false charges laid against her, on condition that she never ask for his name and descent.

Elsa, however, cannot conquer her doubts entirely, and asks the forbidden question, thus forcing Lohengrin to reveal his identity and return to the Grail community; before his departure he restores the enchanted swan – Elsa's brother Gottfried – to his human form.

His miraculous arrival in a boat drawn by a swan signals that Wagner was inspired by a wide range of literature including fairy tale and folk traditions as well as the medieval epic poems *Parzival*, *Titurel*, and *Lohengrin*. The obvious musical model for the swan knight was Adolar, the male protagonist of Carl Maria von WEBER's *Euryanthe*. Adolar, however, has no transcendent background and clearly overreacts when he accuses Euryanthe of betraying a family secret; this requires his catharsis but also makes a happy ending for the lovers possible. Lohengrin, by contrast, cannot change his superhuman nature into a purely human existence, thus making the tragic outcome unavoidable, as Wagner explained in a letter to his friend Hermann Franck (30 May 1846). Unlike the DUTCHMAN and TANNHÄUSER, the male leads in Wagner's earlier "romantic operas," Lohengrin is an outsider but not an outcast. He does not have to be integrated or initiated into a self-contained community (like WALTHER VON STOLZING or PARSIFAL); rather he is gratefully welcomed by everybody (except ORTRUD and Telramund) and immediately accepted as Elsa's husband, "protector of Brabant," and military leader. His relationship with the worldly authority of the King is characterized by mutual respect. While the King bows gladly to the superior forces he recognizes behind Lohengrin, the swan knight in turn integrates himself easily into the feudal hierarchy of the Holy Roman Empire. If he cannot stay, it is not because of a dark secret – as Elsa is led to suspect – but because he is literally too "bright" for the mundane world. This is apparent not only from Wagner's detailed stage directions, such as the resplendent silver armor in Act I and the association with a swan, but even more from the music. Beside his personal musical motives – for example, the exuberant fanfares first heard in Elsa's dream vision and then accompanying his arrival – Lohengrin is also intimately associated with the sound world of the Grail, the ethereal sounds of divided strings. They surround his first appearance and his central musical scene in Act III, the "Grail Narration" revealing his identity, with a radiant musical halo, lending him a messianic aura. This aura and his otherworldliness, together with unique attributes such as a swan boat, made Lohengrin a perfect target for satire and caricature in the nineteenth century; best known today is the PARODY *Lohengrin* (1859) by the Viennese playwright Johann Nestroy.

Wagner was at pains to point out that the Christian symbolism, which includes the Grail, the trial by combat, and the descending dove, is only skin deep. While in a letter to the literary critic Adolf STAHR (31 May 1851) he acknowledges that he had embraced a Christian position with artistic naivety, he stresses in *Eine MITTEILUNG AN MEINE FREUNDE* (A Communication to My Friends, 1851) that the category "Christian-Romantic" describes only incidental appearances, not Lohengrin's true inner being. In contrast, Wagner compares Lohengrin's situation with the plight of the true artist who wants to be understood and accepted unconditionally, but is rejected by the hostility of contemporary society. This reading of Lohengrin as a socio-political allegory is supported by the King's behavior towards the swan knight; worldly power cedes precedence to the transcendent realm of art (e.g., in Lohengrin's refusal to reveal his identity to the King). However, it is equally obvious that Wagner's interpretation of Lohengrin as the misunderstood and unappreciated artist reflects the composer's biographical situation in 1851 as an exile in ZURICH, rather than that of the esteemed *Kapellmeister* he was at the time of composition. In his letters and *Eine Mitteilung*, Wagner saw Lohengrin in need of REDEMPTION from his superhuman loneliness through the unconditional love of a woman, and he was hurt when others criticized his hero as cold and unfeeling. This interpretation of Lohengrin as the true artist has been perpetuated in Wagner literature ever since but, as with many of the composer's writings, it should be taken as only one amongst many possible readings.

As an operatic role, Lohengrin is traditionally classified as "jugendlicher HELDENTENOR" (youthful heroic tenor), encapsulating the demands made on the singer who needs both a heroic attitude for the interaction with the King, Telramund, and male choir, and lyrical qualities for the tender dialogues with Elsa. Amongst the tenor roles in Wagner's oeuvre, Lohengrin and Walter von Stolzing most closely approach the ideal of a German BEL CANTO, in contrast to the greater vigor and stamina required for the "true" heroic tenors TRISTAN and SIEGFRIED. While Lohengrin was premiered with Karl Beck from the Weimar ensemble in the title role, Wagner probably had conceived Lohengrin with the DRESDEN tenor Joseph TICHATSCHEK in mind, who had already successfully sung the title roles in RIENZI and Tannhäuser. Wagner's preference for his old friend Tichatschek caused a conflict during the new production of the opera in Munich in 1867, when LUDWIG II was disappointed with the singer's unassuming appearance and demanded an artist who would match vocal with physical beauty. In the end, the role was given to the young Heinrich VOGL, who became one of the most important Wagner tenors in the second half of the nineteenth century, and debuted as Lohengrin at the Metropolitan Opera in 1890. Other important singers include Jean de Reszke, whose Lohengrin dominated Covent Garden in the 1890s; Ernest van Dyck, who was scheduled to sing at the first Bayreuth performance but had to be replaced at the last minute with Emil Gerhäuser; Lauritz MELCHIOR, who embodied the heroic Wagner tenor for his generation and selected Lohengrin's farewell for his last stage performance in 1950; Leo Slezak, of the famous swan anecdote; Wolfgang Windgassen; Jess Thomas; James King; Gösta Winbergh; René Kollo; Peter Hofmann, whose appearance conformed to the ideal of the Wagnerian hero; Siegfried Jerusalem and Peter Seiffert.   BARBARA EICHNER

Simon Williams, *Wagner and the Romantic Hero* (Cambridge University Press, 2004).

"Loldi." See BEIDLER, Isolde

London. After being blown about by a gale en route from RIGA via Pillau to PARIS in August 1839, Wagner and MINNA found themselves with an unexpected week to spare in London while the ship and crew of the *Thetis* recovered at Gravesend. According to *MEIN LEBEN* (My Life, 1865–81), the surreptitious sea voyage "was arranged mainly out of consideration for our dog," the Newfoundland Robber, but it had also the advantage of evading Wagner's creditors. In London Wagner tried unsuccessfully to look up the Philharmonic Society's chairman Sir George Smart to inquire after the fate of his *Rule Britannia* overture. (Doubtless he would also have probed him on his recollections of BEETHOVEN and the Ninth Symphony, and of WEBER, who had died in Smart's house in 1826.) Wagner next tried to seek out Lord (BULWER-) LYTTON "to come to some agreement" about his proposed treatment of *RIENZI*. Lytton was out of town, but playing on his poor English and the good nature of the officials Wagner blustered his way into the Strangers' Gallery of the then provisional House of Lords (reconstruction of the Houses of Parliament following the fire of 1834 had not yet begun). There he saw and heard, albeit uncomprehendingly, orators including the prime minister Lord Melbourne and the near legendary Duke of Wellington in a debate on enforcing the slave trade ban on Portugal. "After this," he would write, "I thought I knew all there was to know about the capital of the British Empire" (ML 178; ML/E 168). This week-long first visit was too short to alter Wagner's opinion of the English as venal and superficial, as reflected the following year in *Eine PILGERFAHRT ZU BEETHOVEN*, in which an affluent "Englishman" tries to buy access to Beethoven. (The penniless German composer "R" eventually wins the coveted access through his artistic affinity with the great man.)

Wagner's second visit to London, in 1855, was made on his own, but now as guest conductor of the Philharmonic Society. This time the objectionable Englishman Wagner found in his way was *The Times*'s music critic James Davison. This was to be Wagner's lengthiest visit, lasting from March to June. He became acquainted with Ferdinand PRAEGER, Karl KLINDWORTH, and Malwida von MEYSENBUG, and was glad to encounter Gottfried SEMPER again. He was also able to complete the scoring of the first act of *Die WALKÜRE*. But he was miserably unhappy. He hated the climate (spring, he complained, never arrived). Wagner refused to offer Davison the customary bribes (dinners and cigars, at least), and though the Queen and Prince Albert, and indeed the general public, proved friendly, Wagner left London after eight under-rehearsed concerts in the Hanover Square Rooms with his prejudices about the English establishment and press reinforced – as were theirs about him.

His third London visit, with COSIMA in May 1877, was made as a supplicant, albeit a famous one. Reluctantly he had been persuaded that a significant defrayal of the losses at Bayreuth the previous year could be obtained through a series of concerts at the Royal Albert Hall conducted by, or at least in the presence of, the composer. (Hans RICHTER's conducting generally salvaged the concerts.) The eight concerts made only a small profit, but of lasting benefit to Wagner was the cementing of relations with a new generation of Englishmen keen to promote his cause. Even Davison had been largely won over, but Wagner's English champions were now Edward DANNREUTHER, Julius Cyriax, and Davison's successor at *The Times* Franz Hueffer. Though originally expatriate Germans they became naturalized British subjects; and from this time Wagner knew that his cause had been internationalized.

Had the author of *The Perfect Wagnerite* and *Back to Methuselah* lived to be one hundred and twenty, he would have rejoiced to discover Cosima's record in her *Diaries* of the "tremendous impression" made on Wagner of London as "Alberich's dream come true – Nibelheim, world domination, activity, work, everywhere the oppressive feeling of steam and fog" (CWD 25 May 1877). For herself, Cosima confided that "If I had to choose a large city, it would be London" (CWD 1 May 1877). The Wagners were flattered to be introduced to George Eliot and George Henry Lewes, Robert Browning, Edward and Georgiana Burne-Jones, John Everett Millais, William Morris, and, again, Queen Victoria. Henceforth Wagner's feelings towards the English-speaking world were positive, to the extent of encouraging performances of his works in English (to an Australian correspondent) and entertaining the notion of relocating personally to the UNITED STATES OF AMERICA (to his American dentist).

Dannreuther had founded an independent London WAGNER SOCIETY in 1872, with the antiquarian Lord Lindsay as its president. Soon after the composer's death, a Universal Richard Wagner Society (Allgemeiner Richard Wagner-Verein) was formed under the ensconced authority in Bayreuth. In 1884 the London Wagner Society was re-established as a "branch" of the parent *Verein*, with the barrister Benjamin Lewis Mosely as its secretary. Its committee comprised English establishment figures from its president the Earl of Dysart, through accomplished musicians and critics including Walter Bache, Joseph Barnby, H. F. Frost, A. J. Hipkins, Frank Schuster, and J. S. Shedlock, to individuals eminent in other fields such as the art dealer Charles Dowdeswell, the actress Alma Murray, and the Anglican cleric H. R. Haweis. George Bernard SHAW became a wary member, and his published music criticism during the time contains both acerbic and sympathetic comments on the society's activities.

In 1887 the "London correspondent" of the *Revue wagnérienne*, Louis N. Parker, complained that England lacked a journal to rival its celebrated Paris counterpart. Soon afterwards William Ashton ELLIS gave up a promising medical career to accept appointment not only as the editor of the society's quarterly *THE MEISTER*, but also as translator of the *Prose Works of Richard Wagner*, sponsored by the society. As an early theosophist, Ellis transferred a zealotry first displayed toward the still living Helene Petrovna Blavatsky to the recently deceased Wagner. Displacing Mosely as secretary of the London Wagner Society, Ellis became a self-anointed English ambassador for Bayreuth, having reason to believe that Cosima Wagner had endorsed him as the English translator of the collections of Wagner's letters, which she gradually sanctioned for publication. (Ellis was not, however, the "authorized" translator of *Mein Leben* in 1911, as has been suggested.) After Ellis collaborated with Houston Stewart CHAMBERLAIN in the demolition of Ferdinand PRAEGER's overstated personal acquaintance with Wagner, he forced the resignation in 1895 of Praeger's former patron Lord Dysart. This brought about the collapse of the London Wagner Society. (Its last surviving member was probably the novelist Eden Phillpotts, who died in 1960.)

Dannreuther returned for a time to try to keep the Wagner Society going, until his death in 1904. In 1910 a completely new "Wagner Association" was formed in London by the then celebrated playwright Louis N. Parker. It looked forward to the Wagner centenary in 1913, and somehow it seems to have reconciled some of the antagonists of the older society (though not Ernest NEWMAN and Bernard Shaw). But it could not survive the onset of World War I. While Wagner's music had notable individual British adherents between the wars (many of them literary rather than musical figures) it was only after the establishment in 1951 of WIELAND and WOLFGANG Wagner's "New Bayreuth" that Ernest Newman would consent to become the first President of the (current) London Wagner Society, founded in 1953 by the distinguished war hero Major Harry Edmonds (1891–1989).   DAVID CORMACK

David Cormack, "Of Earls and Egypt: Founders of the First Wagner Societies," *Musical Times* 150.1907 (Summer 2009): 27–42.

D. H. Laurence, ed., *Shaw's Music*, 3 vols., 2nd edn. (London: Bodley Head, 1989).

Anne D. Sessa, *Richard Wagner and the English* (Cranbury, NJ: Associated University Presses, 1979).

Stewart Spencer, "Wagner in London (1)," *Wagner* 3.4 (October 1982): 98–123.

"Wagner's Addresses in London," *Wagner* 26.1 (January 2005): 33–51.

Lorenz, Alfred (b. Vienna, 11 July 1868; d. Munich, 20 Nov. 1939), Wagnerian theorist. Lorenz began his career as a conductor and composer at the court of Saxe-Coburg Gotha before turning to academia in the wake of World War I, and writing a doctoral dissertation on the musical form of *Der RING DES NIBELUNGEN* (1922). A revised version of the dissertation was published as the first volume of *Das Geheimnis der Form bei Richard Wagner* (1924); in three additional volumes, Lorenz applied his analytical methodology to *TRISTAN UND ISOLDE* (1926), *Die MEISTERSINGER VON NÜRNBERG* (1931), and *PARSIFAL* (1933). Lorenz also published shorter analyses on aspects of Wagner's three Romantic operas as well as works by BACH, BEETHOVEN, BRUCKNER, and, in his two-volume *Habilitationsschrift*, the early operas of Alessandro Scarlatti (1927).

Instead of being formless, as Wagner's previous critics had charged, Lorenz argued that Wagner's works comprised a series of "POETIC-MUSICAL PERIODS" (a concept originating in Wagner's *OPER UND DRAMA* [Opera and Drama, 1851]), each of which was organized into one of several formal types, principally "Bar" (AAB) and "Bogen" (i.e., arch; ABA), through the repetition of *LEITMOTIVE* and other musical material. Smaller formal types could be combined to form "potentiated" forms (such as a *Bar* form in which each section is itself a smaller *Bar* form) or "composite" forms (in which the sections of a *Bogen* form could be made up of a *Bar*, a *Bogen*, and another *Bar*); these larger forms were often extended to encompass an entire act or indeed an entire work (e.g., *Die Meistersinger* as a gigantic *Bar* form). Many of these higher forms do cohere along dramatic lines and are perceived as a whole in the theater. In order to make his formal types work, Lorenz developed the concepts of "substitution" and "free" and "opposite" symmetry in which, for example, the outer sections of a *Bogen* form could be deemed the "same" even though the motives were not (e.g., Licht-ALBERICH [WOTAN] and Schwarz-Alberich, as opposites, could balance each other).

As a result of these, and other, feats of analytical sleight of hand, critics after World War II have been dismissive of what they saw as Lorenz's "Procrustean" approach. Yet in most cases they have missed or minimized the idealistic roots of his methodology in the Wagnerian-SCHOPENHAUERIAN expressive aesthetic and ideology of genius. Here the ultimate goal is to make the analysis superfluous by training the sympathetic listener to intuit the formal perfection of the work in an instantaneous flash of insight. To evaluate Lorenz's approach without understanding its philosophical and aesthetic basis is to fundamentally misrepresent it.

In other writings, Lorenz applied the historiographical approach developed by his father, Ottokar, in which history is seen as series of waves of actions and reactions articulated by different generations. He was an early and vocal supporter of the Nazis, joining the Party in 1931 and publishing a series of articles on racial and genealogical research as well as on Wagner's Aryan ancestry. He also edited a two-volume selection of Wagner's writings and letters (1938) in which proto-Nazi thoughts were highlighted in a different typeface. In its totalizing desire to subsume each smaller element of a musical work into a larger entity, it can be argued that Lorenz's methodology has certain similarities to NATIONAL SOCIALIST ideology.

STEPHEN MCCLATCHIE

See also MUSIC THEORY

Stephen McClatchie, *Analyzing Wagner's Operas: Alfred Lorenz and German Nationalist Ideology* (University of Rochester Press, 1998).

Lorenz, Max (born Max Sülzenfuß; Düsseldorf, 10 May 1901; d. Salzburg, 12 January 1975), the foremost Wagner tenor in Germany in the 1930s–40s. Irreplaceable at Bayreuth (1933–44; later appearances in 1952), particularly as SIEGFRIED, TRISTAN, and WALTHER VON STOLZING, he also appeared in Vienna, New York (Metropolitan Opera, 1931–4 and 1947–50), Covent Garden, and at La Scala. During the Nazi era, Lorenz was spared prosecution, despite his homosexuality, and managed to save his Jewish wife, Lotte Appel, from deportation.

DAVID BRECKBILL

Wagner's Mastersinger – Hitler's Siegfried: The Life and Times of Max Lorenz, a film by Eric Schulz and Claus Wischmann (EuroArts Music, 2008).

Lost works. See WORKS, LOST

Love. Love is ubiquitous in Wagner's work, whether as a driving force in the dramas or as an elevated theoretical concept in the writings. No matter its form and context, the fundamental significance of love is not to be denied, even though Wagner cannot – nor does he want to – contain it within consistent and unambiguous parameters. In *Das KUNSTWERK DER ZUKUNFT* (The Artwork of the Future, 1849/50), Wagner wrote: "Now as Man is not free except through Love, neither is anything that proceeds ... from him ... [T]he highest freedom is the satisfaction of the highest need: but the highest human need is *Love*" (PW 1:97). We can see then that love is at the taproot of all that is good, and we might easily, and correctly, infer that it escapes an exclusively romantic context. That is, love explains and underpins more than just the relationship between two lovers, although it certainly does that as well.

In order to appreciate this, we can turn to Wagner's most problematic character: SIEGFRIED. In a letter to August RÖCKEL (25/26 January 1854) we are told that "Siegfried never ceases to love." Now *we* might not think this his most striking characteristic and, even if we did, might not make that kind of extravagant claim. And yet Siegfried's love is highly revealing, for it covers all the varied territory relevant for Wagnerian love. It is instinctual; it is subjectively focused on a revelatory sexual union; it leads to otherworldly REDEMPTION; it is a quality racially possessed by the (original) German VOLK; it evokes an idealized communist brotherhood; it is incestuous; and it functions as a radical challenge to conventional social mores.

The union with Brünnhilde is self-evidently crucial. It leads to spiritual redemption which is, as Wagner repeatedly insists, the product of sex – that is, of "real sensuous love." For "only through love ... do man and woman become human" (Wagner to Röckel, 25/26 January 1854). He even goes so far as to claim they become one; that they lose their individual egos, which is something we observe with his most mutually obsessed loving couple. TRISTAN and ISOLDE adopt each other's identity at the climax of their duet. This type of love is focused on an ascent into an otherworldly realm. It has its first upfront expression with SENTA and the DUTCHMAN, "transfigured" in a projection following their deaths. Wagner also describes ISOLDE's last solo (mislabeled *LIEBESTOD*) as a "transfiguration," and even at one time planned a Dutchman-like projection for BRÜNNHILDE and SIEGFRIED. Nevertheless, when Brünnhilde says of Siegfried that "none was more pure in love" (*GÖTTERDÄMMERUNG* Act III), she is not downgrading sex. The transcendence she is about to engineer in the Immolation is only conceivable because of their sexual union.

But this is hardly the end of it. In the "Siegfried-man," Wagner thinks he has found the archetypical German hero, unsullied and deeply embedded in the natural world. It is therefore his axiomatic state to be loving, and in *Die WIBELUNGEN* he is linked to that most absolute, loving figure: Christ. Furthermore, Siegfried is a personification of the *Volk*, which is consequently also portrayed as innately loving; a version, albeit highly romanticized, of the communist community. Elsewhere, Wagner explains how the ideal Man is reconciled with his "species" identity, and becomes "an integral factor in the totality of Nature," yielding himself "to wide Love itself." As a result the "egotist becomes a communist" (PW 1:94). Also relevant here is *Jesus von Nazareth* (1849), where Wagner puts the argument for something approaching free (sexual) love, and attacks private property. However, if love is the defining characteristic of the original German *Volk*, then that people most dreaded by Wagner would be stamped by its antithesis. And indeed they are. He insists that the JEWS, like Judas in *Jesus von Nazareth*, are "loveless." This is why it makes so much sense to regard ALBERICH in the *RING* as a figure representative of Jews, even though Wagner does not specifically describe him as such.

The communal notion of love spills over into the ideal of Brotherhood. For instance, in *Eine MITTEILUNG AN MEINE FREUNDE* (A Communication to my Friends, 1871), Wagner tells us at length how important love and fellowship are to him. So, although he appears to reject "Greek" love as un-German (CWD 26 April 1870; PW 1:170), we find deep platonic relationships in the dramas. Psychologically interesting, for instance, is the death cry of Melot, voicing a love for Tristan that has turned malicious. Yet more interesting in purely ideological terms is the relationship between AMFORTAS and PARSIFAL. Although neither has anything directly to do with the other until the climactic scene, their shared association with Christ in a drama drenched in explicit Christian iconography and implicit sexuality makes their bonding more overtly loving and lofty than that, say, between Parsifal and KUNDRY or – for that matter – that between Amfortas and Kundry, which predates the drama but still powerfully drives it.

However, perhaps the most striking function of love in Wagner is REVOLUTIONARY; but not revolutionary merely with regard to his wishy-washy 1840s communism. Rather it is revolutionary with respect to sexual freedom. Breaking sexual taboos is an unmistakable ingredient in the Wagner project – it might indeed be its most essential – and this includes the many vital incestuous relationships in the music dramas. Incest enriches the love of the twins SIEGMUND and SIEGLINDE; Siegfried and Brünnhilde's blood relationship determines their special status; Tristan and Isolde become virtual siblings in Act II; Parsifal succumbs to Kundry's revelatory kiss when he is seduced into thinking of her as his mother; FRICKA explicitly accuses Wotan of incestuously desiring Brünnhilde; and even EVA and HANS SACHS play with the notion of an ersatz incestuous relationship. Whether this is a confirmation of the supposed universal role of Freud's Oedipus Complex is pure speculation, but there can be no denying Wagner's interest in the Oedipus story. He has a good deal to say about Sophocles' play in OPER UND DRAMA. Whatever the case, incest is part of Wagner's wide-ranging and deep engagement with love, a commodity which in his hands covers a multitude of virtues ... and sins.   BARRY EMSLIE

Barry Emslie, *Richard Wagner and the Centrality of Love* (Woodbridge: Boydell & Brewer, 2010).

Ludwig II, King of Bavaria (b. Nymphenburg Palace, Munich, 25 Aug. 1845; d. Lake Starnberg, near Munich, 13 June 1886; reign 10 Mar. 1864 to 13 June 1886). Ludwig succeeded his father, Maximilian II, but was closer in artistic ambition to Maximilian's deposed father, Ludwig I. Aestheticism was a hallmark of Ludwig's reign, which witnessed construction of neo-Romantic, "fairy-tale" castles such as Linderhof, Herrenchiemsee, and Neuschwanstein; the latter's wall frescoes depict Wagnerian scenes. Though Ludwig was hardly devoted to the more mundane of his duties and was no consummate politician, Bavaria under his rule nevertheless successfully held out for a high price even when there was no alternative to GERMAN UNIFICATION. Ludwig won a private, secret income from Bismarck's Guelph fund in return for putting his name to Bismarck's "Kaiser letter," bidding Prussia's William I to "reestablish a German Empire and German imperial dignity." His extensive correspondence, with both Wagner and COSIMA, is an invaluable source for the Wagner scholar.

At thirteen, Ludwig was enthralled by reports of LOHENGRIN in MUNICH. He heard it there in 1861 and, inspired by the swan knight (see "Neu*schwan*stein"), engaged in study of Wagner's writings. Increasingly tormented by his homosexuality, he would sooner withdraw from society, always preferring to experience private performances of Wagner's works. In response to Wagner's 1863 call for a German prince to fund model operatic performances of the RING, Ludwig dispatched his Cabinet Secretary, Franz von PFISTERMEISTER, only a month after his accession (1864), to bring Wagner to Munich. The King's "Friend" received a generous stipend, so that he might compose and perform his works. Soon exiled, if temporarily, to TRIBSCHEN, following machinations by Pfistermeister and Ludwig von der PFORDTEN, Wagner's counsel persisted. Such was his influence that BISMARCK attempted to have him ensure Bavarian neutrality between Prussia and Austria in 1866. In this context, and partly influenced by Constantin FRANTZ, if not Bismarck, Wagner penned WAS IS DEUTSCH? (What is German?, 1865/78) for Ludwig's instruction. Wagner counseled Ludwig against abdication, apparently strengthening his resolve – not least since, as king, he would be better placed to assist Wagner.

Ludwig paid the most pressing of Wagner's debts, afforded him free residence, and supported the world premieres of TRISTAN UND ISOLDE (1865), Die MEISTERSINGER (1868), Das RHEINGOLD (1869), and Die WALKÜRE (1870), the latter two against Wagner's will. Plans for a Munich FESTIVAL THEATER by Gottfried SEMPER were thwarted, yet land for the BAYREUTH FESTIVAL THEATER was provided at no cost and the first BAYREUTH FESTIVAL was saved by Ludwig's loan of 100,000 thalers. Ludwig also sponsored land-purchase and construction costs for WAHNFRIED.

Ludwig grew heavily indebted, though Wagnerian expenses totaled under a seventh of the Civil List. (He funded artistic projects personally.) In 1886, exasperated by Ludwig's refusal to economize and fearful of dismissal, ministers presented a medical report signed by four psychiatrists, none of whom had ever met Ludwig, declaring him unfit to rule – for life. Maximilian's brother, Leopold, was declared Regent; Ludwig was transported to Schloss Berg. The cause of his tragic drowning in adjacent Lake Starnberg remains unclear: suicide, accidental death through escape, or murder?   MARK BERRY

Detta Petzet and Michael Petzet, *Die Richard Wagner-Bühne König Ludwigs II.* (Munich: Prestel, 1970).

Otto Strobel, ed., *König Ludwig II. und Richard Wagner. Briefwechsel. Mit vielen anderen Urkunden,* 5 vols. (Karlsruhe: Braun, 1936–9).

Lüttichau, (Wolf Adolph) August Freiherr von (b. Ulbersdorf bei Schandau, 15 June 1785; d. Dresden, 16 Feb. 1863), Director of the Dresden Court Theater from 1824 to 1862. He was instrumental in Wagner's appointment to Kapellmeister in February 1843, and oversaw the premieres of RIENZI and Der FLIEGENDE HOLLÄNDER, but figures primarily as a foil to Wagner's own expectations. Lüttichau opposed Wagner's Palm Sunday performance of Beethoven's Ninth Symphony in 1846, which was wildly popular.

MARGARET ELEANOR MENNINGER

Magdeburg. City on the Elbe river, capital of Sachsen-Anhalt (in Wagner's day, the province of Prussian Saxony). Wagner's second professional post was as the music director of the theatrical company of Heinrich Bethmann, which he had first joined during their 1834 summer season in the resort of Bad Lauchstädt. (Wagner conducted his first opera there, *Don Giovanni*.) Bethmann's troupe made its winter headquarters in Magdeburg, whither Wagner followed them. The fortified town included a large Prussian military presence and had a population of about 39,000 in Wagner's time, according to an 1840 *Konversations-Lexikon* ("with 2,932 houses and 12 churches," mostly Protestant, including the large medieval *Dom*). MINNA Planer, an actress and singer with the troupe, was assiduously courted by the young Wagner during the later months of his engagement there, from the fall of 1835 until he departed in May 1836; they were married in East Prussia on 22 November 1836.

The wide repertoire conducted by Wagner in Magdeburg included ROSSINI's *Barber of Seville* and *Tancredi*; AUBER's *La Muette de Portici*; Cherubini's *Les Deux Journées*; BELLINI's *Norma* and *La straniera*; Hérold's *Zampa*; WEBER's *Oberon*; SPOHR's *Jessonda*; and MARSCHNER's *Templer und Jüdin*. In addition, he convinced the celebrated Wilhelmine SCHRÖDER-DEVRIENT to make guest appearances as Leonore (*Fidelio*), Desdemona (Rossini's *Otello*), and Agathe (*Freischütz*). Wagner conducted occasional orchestral concerts under the auspices of the town's Masonic lodges, "Harpokrates" and "Ferdinand zur Glückseligkeit." Schröder-Devrient appeared at one benefit concert.

Wagner composed a large OVERTURE for a *Columbus* drama written by his wealthy young friend Theodor APEL, which the theater produced at Apel's expense. His principal creative work during the Magdeburg period was his second completed opera, *Das LIEBESVERBOT*, composed over the period of a year between January 1835 and New Year's 1836. The disastrous attempt at a premiere, drawing on volunteer services of the small troupe in March 1836, is memorably described in *MEIN LEBEN* (My Life, 1865–81). As Ernest Newman aptly put it: "Wagner's career in Magdeburg, as in practically every other town with which he was associated for any length of time, ended in disaster" (1:206). He left for Berlin on 18 May 1836, soon afterwards following Minna Planer north to KÖNIGSBERG.   THOMAS S. GREY

Ernest Newman, *The Life of Richard Wagner* (see bibliography).

Mahler, Gustav (b. Kalischt/Kaliště [Bohemia], 7 July 1860; d. Vienna, 18 May 1911), Austro-German composer and conductor. Wagner's MUSIC DRAMAS and his AESTHETICS were a predominant influence on Gustav Mahler throughout his life. With Richard STRAUSS and Hugo WOLF, Mahler belonged to the first generation of composers who came to maturity under his influence. As a student in VIENNA in the 1870s, he studied Wagner's works, heard *TANNHÄUSER* under the composer's baton in 1875, and was a member of the Vienna Academic WAGNER SOCIETY and the Wagnerian Pernersdorfer circle.

Although Mahler did not complete an opera, in *Das klagende Lied* and the symphonies he showed himself to be an adherent of the Wagnerian-SCHOPENHAUERIAN expressive aesthetic position which held that, as the highest of the arts, music allowed the properly attuned listener a glimpse of the Ideal, ultimate truth and that its principal essence was expression. As a result, in Mahler's symphonies, just as in Wagner's music dramas, the musical means is dictated, and justified, by the expressive intent; the content determines the form. Mahler employs a Wagnerian orchestra in most of his works, although his orchestral technique moved beyond Wagner in his later works. Like the Wagnerian *LEITMOTIV*, Mahler's themes occasionally appear in more than one work.

Mahler's renown as a conductor of Wagner was acknowledged even by the ANTI-SEMITIC press and the anti-Semitic Vienna Academic-Wagner-Society. He typically chose Wagnerian works for his debuts: *LOHENGRIN* in LEIPZIG (1886); *Der RING DES NIBELUNGEN* (in Hungarian) as Director of the Royal Budapest Opera (1889); *TANNHÄUSER* in Hamburg (1891); *Lohengrin* for Vienna (1897); and *TRISTAN UND ISOLDE* for New York (1907). Mahler preferred his Wagner unadulterated: in Vienna, he immediately began opening the usual cuts in all the works; his first *RHEINGOLD* omitted the traditional Viennese intermission between scenes 2 and 3; and the *GÖTTERDÄMMERUNG* Norns' scene was performed in Vienna for the first time in his September 1898 *Ring* cycle. Like Wagner, he took operatic staging seriously and rejuvenated the existing productions in Vienna before embarking on ambitious new productions with Alfred ROLLER.

Mahler attended the BAYREUTH FESTIVAL in 1883 (*PARSIFAL*), 1889 (*Parsifal, Tristan, MEISTERSINGER*), 1891 (*Tannhäuser, Parsifal* twice), and 1896 (*Ring*), and had a cordial relationship with the Wagner family until his death. He supported COSIMA's efforts to restrict *Parsifal* for Bayreuth and, particularly in his Hamburg years, coached singers for the Festival (e.g., Anna von Mildenburg for her debut as KUNDRY in 1897). Later, as Director of the Vienna Hofoper, he generally approved requests for its personnel to appear in Bayreuth. Mahler also conducted SIEGFRIED WAGNER's opera *Der Bärenhäuter* in Vienna (1899) despite his misgivings about the score. Despite his fame as a Wagner conductor, as a JEW Mahler was never invited to conduct at the Bayreuth Festival.   STEPHEN MCCLATCHIE

See also ORCHESTRATION; WAGNER AS CONDUCTOR; WAGNER SOCIETIES

Stephen McClatchie, "Mahler's Wagner," in *Mahler im Kontext / Contextualizing Mahler*, ed. E. W. Partsch and M. Solvik (Vienna: Böhlau, 2011): 407–36.
Eduard Reeser, "Briefe an Cosima Wagner," *Gustav Mahler: Unbekannte Briefe*, ed. Herta Blaukopf (Vienna: Zsonlay, 1983): 211–40; Eng. trans. *Mahler's Unknown Letters*, ed. Herta Blaukopf, trans. R. Stokes (Boston: Northeastern University Press, 1987): 199–225.

Maier, Mathilde (b. Mainz, 1834; d. Mainz, 29 June 1910), friend of Wagner. They met in 1862 and Wagner asked her to live with him as housekeeper and partner. She declined, since Wagner was still officially married. Maier's conservative opinions vexed him. Wagner's love for her was not passionate; he saw in her a housewife and companion. When COSIMA arrived in MUNICH to visit Wagner (1864), he immediately dropped Mathilde. However, they remained good friends for life.   EVA RIEGER

Hans Scholz, ed., *Richard Wagner an Mathilde Maier (1862–1878)* (Leipzig: Weicher, 1930).

Makart, Hans (b. Salzburg, 28 May 1840; d. Vienna, 3 Oct. 1884), painter. By the 1870s Makart had become one of the most sought-after artists in central Europe, and his Viennese atelier became a destination for cultural elites not unlike Wagner's BAYREUTH (Richard and COSIMA visited in 1875). Makart's large-scale history paintings, his modern variants of multi-panel old master genres such as triptychs or narrative frescoes (sometimes using experimental pigments or even photographic elements), and his extravagant historicizing designs for an 1879 Viennese pageant celebrating the Habsburg imperial family contributed to a reputation as Wagner's counterpart in the field of visual arts, a sort of visual *Gesamtkünstler*. In particular, Makart's extravagant and sensual use of color was frequently compared with Wagner's treatment of orchestral timbres. Wagner himself (perhaps with Cosima's encouragement) had thought at one point to approach Makart to design sets and costumes for the first *RING* cycle. Elements of the first Bayreuth *PARSIFAL*, above all Paul von JOUKOWSKY's designs for KLINGSOR's magic garden, distinctly evoke the lush, colorful, and busy "Makart style." Makart did paint a series of scenes from the *Ring* cycle as part of an interior design project (now preserved in the Latvian National Museum of Art, RIGA). The "Makart style" remained a byword into the time of Thomas MANN for that aspect of Wagner's art appealing to the luxurious appetites of the late-capitalist bourgeoisie.
THOMAS S. GREY
See also WAGNER IN THE VISUAL ARTS

Malten, Therese (b. Insterburg, 21 June 1855; d. Neuzschieren, 2 Jan. 1930), German soprano. Based in DRESDEN, she nevertheless gained fame at BAYREUTH (KUNDRY at every festival, 1882–94, plus appearances as ISOLDE and EVA), in LONDON, and in ST. PETERSBURG, where she sang in the *RING* production mounted by Angelo NEUMANN (1889).   DAVID BRECKBILL

Michael Letchford, *Therese Malten: Wagner's Devoted Kundry* (Letchford: Goar Lodge, 2010).

Mann, Thomas (b. Lübeck, 6 June 1875; d. Zurich, 12 Aug. 1955), Germany's preeminent twentieth-century writer, a consummate practitioner of literary WAGNERISM, and a key figure in Wagner's politically contested afterlife. An anthology of his writings on Wagner can be found in *Pro and Contra Wagner* (Mann), a more complete collection in *Im Schatten Wagners* (Vaget, *Schatten*). In 1920, Mann declared: "Wagner is still the artist I understand best, and in whose shadow I continue to live" (Mann 67); and in 1952 he admitted to Theodor ADORNO: "I have imitated Wagner a great deal" (Vaget, *Schatten*, 222).

Mann received a rudimentary musical education playing the violin, his love of music having been awakened by his mother, Julia, who played the piano and sang to him. She also took the boy to the opera, where *LOHENGRIN* became the seminal experience of his lifelong passion for Wagner. When Mann moved to MUNICH in 1894, he found himself in the capital of the German Wagner cult, and for a number of years he immersed himself in it. He attended the BAYREUTH FESTIVAL in 1909 in order to see *PARSIFAL*. This was to be his only visit to the Wagner shrine.

After his decision in 1922 to lend his support to the embattled Weimar Republic, Mann's view of Wagner and his attitude towards the Bayreuth phenomenon became more critical. During his exile in Switzerland (1933–8, 1952–5) and the United States (1938–52), Wagner remained at the center of his critical reflections on Germany, while his allegiance to Wagner's art remained unbroken.

Initially Mann's understanding was shaped by his sophisticated reading of NIETZSCHE's "immortal critique of Wagner," which he took to be "a pan-egyric in reverse" (Mann 100). Nietzsche showed him in what sense "Wagner sums up modernity" – which caused Mann to agree that, even as a writer, "one must first become a Wagnerian." The author of *The Case of Wagner* also made Mann see that Wagner's heroes and heroines, their archaic garb notwith-standing, were actually contemporaries of Madame Bovary and lent themselves to parody when transplanted into contemporary settings.

Mann's literary Wagnerism manifests itself in essentially three ways. First, on the level of narrative technique, starting with *Little Herr Friedemann* (1898), Mann employs the *LEITMOTIV* in order to illuminate subconscious mental and psychic processes – a crucial goal of literary MODERNISM. Leitmotivic narration is prominent in *Buddenbrooks*, *Death in Venice*, *The Magic Mountain*, and *Joseph and His Brothers*. The technique becomes more subtle as Mann moves from a primarily descriptive to a more symbolic and "symphonic" use of the *Leitmotiv*.

Second, on the level of structure, Mann parodies Wagner. Two novellas do so overtly: *Tristan* (1903), which is set in a sanatorium, and *The Blood of the Walsungs* (1906), which revisits Act I of *Die WALKÜRE* relocated into the milieu of an arriviste Jewish family in Berlin. Three novels do so less obviously; *The Magic Mountain* bears some resemblance to *TANNHÄUSER*, while *Buddenbrooks* and *Joseph* are to some degree modeled on *The RING*.

Third, Mann, as a participant and later as a critic of the Wagner cult, became a leading voice in the analysis of Wagner as a man and artist. Commemorating the fiftieth anniversary of Wagner's death, Mann's *The Sorrows and Grandeur of Richard Wagner* (1933) is an elegantly written summary of his larger assessment, which has Wagner as the quintessential representa-tive of the nineteenth century, a figure fully comparable to literary giants such as Tolstoy, Ibsen, and Zola. While rejecting some of the implications of the doctrine of the *GESAMTKUNSTWERK* – the notion, for instance, that SIEGFRIED is superior to Goethe's *Torquato Tasso* – this essay remains a sophisticated and generous expression of Mann's unstinting admiration. At the same time, it firmly rejects the attempt to claim Wagner as the patron saint of a "troglodytic Teutonism" (Vaget, *Schatten*, 75), including NATIONAL SOCIALISM. Another major text, "Richard Wagner's 'Der Ring des Nibel-ungen'" (1937), was occasioned by a new production of that work in ZURICH.

Although serious reservations about Wagner may be found in the writings of 1908–11, notably in "Coming to Terms with Richard Wagner," the Wagner passages in *Reflections of a Nonpolitical Man* (1915–18), written in defense of the German cause in World War I, betray a certain closeness to the nationalist cult of Wagner in the spirit of Bayreuth. Among Mann's later writings, his letter to the editor of *Common Sense* (1940), in response to Peter Viereck, stands out; here he speaks for the first time of "the intricate and painful interrelationships which undeniably exist between the Wagnerian sphere and the National Socialist evil" (Mann 196).

A key event in Mann's biography and German cultural history was the public protest against his lecture at the University of Munich (culled from *The Sorrows and Grandeur*, delivered on 10 February 1933) by an opportunistic alliance, led by Hans KNAPPERTSBUSCH, of prominent cultural figures and a handful of local Nazi officials. In the infamous "Protest of Richard Wagner's Own City of Munich," Mann was accused of having besmirched "our great German musical genius" (Mann 150). To some extent this was an act of revenge for what the Munich Wagnerians saw as his "betrayal" of their camp by throwing his support in with the Weimar Republic and the Social Democrats, and for his attacks on Munich's reactionary cultural establishment. The "Protest" denounced Mann as un-German, as someone for whom, in the new Germany under HITLER, there was simply no room. Mann concluded that this was tantamount to a "national excommunication"; he thus wisely decided not to return to Germany from a lecture tour abroad. Indeed, he would remain in exile for the rest of his life. Asked to return to Germany immediately after the war, he refused, citing among other reasons the "Wagner-Protest" of 1933.

Thomas Mann's importance for a critical engagement with the legacy of Wagner is impossible to overstate. When Germany embraced a nationalist interpretation of Wagner, Mann emphasized the cosmopolitan character of his work. When the ideology of the BAYREUTH CIRCLE threatened to monopolize Wagner, Mann invoked Nietzsche and BAUDELAIRE. And when Wagner's work was in any way exploited politically, Mann insisted on its essentially aesthetic qualities. When, after the war, Germans were seeking ways to reconnect with Wagner, Mann's writing proved indispensable.

HANS RUDOLF VAGET

Walter Frisch, *German Modernism: Music and the Arts* (Berkeley: University of California Press, 2005), "Thomas Mann, Wagner, and Irony," 186–203.

Thomas Mann, *Thomas Mann: Pro and Contra Wagner*, trans. Allan Bunden, intro. Erich Heller (University of Chicago Press, 1985).

Holger Pils and Christina Ulrich, eds., *Liebe ohne Glauben: Thomas Mann und Richard Wagner* (Göttingen: Wallstein, 2011).

Hans R. Vaget, ed., *Im Schatten Wagners: Thomas Mann über Richard Wagner. Texte und Zeugnisse 1895–1955*, selected, and with commentary and an essay, by Hans R. Vaget, 3rd edn. (Frankfurt am Main: Fischer, 2010).

"National and Universal: Thomas Mann and the Paradox of 'German' Music," in *Music and German National Identity*, ed. Celia Applegate and Pamela Potter (University of Chicago Press, 2002): 155–77.

Mannheim. City on the confluence of the Rhine and Neckar rivers, in the north-western corner of modern Baden-Württemberg. Mannheim enjoyed a distinguished musical history under the aegis of Prince-Elector Karl Theodor

(1724–99), and a distinguished theatrical history following the Elector's initiative to establish a "national theater" there, sponsoring important premieres of plays by SCHILLER and others from the 1780s on. The Mannheim theater produced TANNHÄUSER in 1855, LOHENGRIN in 1859, and a somewhat abridged MEISTERSINGER in 1869. Emil HECKEL, a piano manufacturer and music dealer in Mannheim, founded the first WAGNER SOCIETY (*Wagnerverein*), conceived to support the BAYREUTH FESTIVAL project. On 20 December 1871, Wagner conducted a concert in Mannheim of his own works (Preludes to *Lohengrin*, TRISTAN UND ISOLDE, *Die Meistersinger*, Isolde's "Transfiguration," and the recent KAISERMARSCH) together with works by Mozart (overture to *The Magic Flute*) and BEETHOVEN (the Seventh Symphony) in conjunction with Heckel's efforts on his behalf. Friedrich NIETZSCHE was present at this first of Wagner's Bayreuth benefit concerts, as well as at a private performance in Mannheim of the SIEGFRIED IDYLL.   THOMAS S. GREY

Marbach, Rosalie. See WAGNER, ROSALIE

Margravial Opera House. See MARKGRÄFLICHES OPERNHAUS, BAYREUTH

Marienbad (today Mariánské Lázně), spa in Bohemia (Czech Republic), the site of curative mineral springs reputed to bring relief to various disorders of the liver and digestive organs. Marienbad became fashionable when GOETHE frequented the place in the early 1820s. On the recommendation of his DRESDEN physician, Anton PUSINELLI, Wagner, accompanied by MINNA and their PETS (their dog and their parrot), spent the better part of the summer of 1845 (3 July–9 August), lodging in a modest boarding house, known as the "Kleeblatt" (cloverleaf).

Finding tedious the prescribed routines of this "health factory" (so dubbed by Mark Twain, who visited the spa after attending the BAYREUTH FESTIVAL in 1892), Wagner instead read a great deal and produced prose drafts for two new operas. The cure provided only temporary relief of the intestinal disorders that had troubled him since his years in PARIS (see HEALTH). On the other hand, the five weeks spent in this invigorating atmosphere led to an explosion of creativity that forever links Marienbad to the genesis of at least two of his operatic works.

First, Wagner took up his earlier idea of a comic opera that would be a satyr play to follow (in the manner of ANCIENT GREEK drama) the tragedy of TANNHÄUSER. Inspired by the lively accounts in Georg Gottfried GERVINUS's *Geschichte der poetischen National-Literatur der Deutschen* (1835–42) of the works of the Renaissance poet Hans SACHS and of the NUREMBERG guild of the "MASTERSINGERS," Wagner set down a detailed prose draft for *Die MEISTERSINGER VON NÜRNBERG* (translated in Ennis). He shelved the "Marienbad draft," dated 16 July, until 1861. Wagner recounts the conception of the draft in *Eine MITTEILUNG AN MEINE FREUNDE* (A Communication to My Friends) and in *MEIN LEBEN* (My Life, 1865–81). Then Wagner turned to a prose draft, dated 3 August, for *LOHENGRIN*, culled from the anonymous thirteenth-century courtly epic edited by Joseph Görres, *Lohengrin, ein altdeutsches Gedicht* (1813).

In addition to these two projects, Wagner read the works of WOLFRAM VON ESCHENBACH, *Parcival* (1836) and *Der jüngere Titurel* (1841), in the modernized versions by San-Marte. We may also conclude, then, that the origins of Wagner's last work for the stage, PARSIFAL, likewise lie in his readings of the summer of 1845.

While in Marienbad, Wagner made the acquaintance of a 20-year-old law student and music enthusiast from Prague, Eduard HANSLICK, who was to become his most formidable opponent. As we know from Hanslick's memoir *Aus meinem Leben* (1894), he introduced himself as an admirer. Their relations were cordial: "At that time he [Wagner] wasn't yet god."

HANS RUDOLF VAGET

See also HEALTH

Jane Ennis, "The Prose Drafts of *Die Meistersinger von Nürnberg*" (1), *Wagner* 8 (1987): 13–22.

Markgräfliches Opernhaus, Bayreuth. Constructed between 1745 and 1748 by court architect Joseph Saint-Pierre, with a late baroque interior by the Italian father-son team of Giuseppe and Carlo Gallo da Bibiena, the Margravial Opera House is a magnificent testament to the cultural politics of Margrave Friedrich von Brandenburg-Prussia and his spouse, Wilhelmina of Prussia, Frederick the Great's oldest sister. The theater's splendid auditorium and deep stage (27 meters) – and the fact that it had no resident opera company – led Wagner to consider holding his RING festival there. He abandoned this notion after discovering that the pit space was insufficient for the size of orchestra he required, but remained in favor of holding his festival in Bayreuth, in a new, purpose-built FESTIVAL THEATER. Yet, when the laying of the new theater's foundation stone was celebrated on 22 May 1872, most of the attendant festivities – speeches, gala dinner, and concert featuring BEETHOVEN's Ninth Symphony – took place in the venerable Opera House.

ANTHONY J. STEINHOFF

Marschner, Heinrich August (b. Zittau, 16 Aug. 1795; d. Hanover, 14 Dec. 1861), significant composer of German Romantic opera. Marschner's activity fell between the death of WEBER (1826) and Wagner's ascendancy in the 1840s. His most important operas were *Der Vampyr* (1828), *Der Templer und die Jüdin* (1829), and *Hans Heiling* (1833). It was as a chorus master in WÜRZBURG (1833–4) that Wagner first became acquainted with Marschner's music. The stage works of Marschner – especially *Der Vampyr* and *Hans Heiling* – influenced Wagner's early operas through *Der* FLIEGENDE HOLLÄNDER, particularly in their use of supernatural plots, increased role of the orchestra, and less rigid divisions between operatic "numbers." For a performance of *Der Vampyr* in Würzburg in 1833, Wagner composed extra music as the finale for an aria that his brother Albert sang.

JAMES DEAVILLE

Ulrich Weisstein, "Heinrich Marschner's 'romantische Oper' *Hans Heiling*: A Bridge between Weber and Wagner," *Music and German Literature*, ed. James M. McGlathery (Columbia, SC: Camden House, 1992): 154–79.

Mastersingers. As their name implies, mastersingers were practitioners of *Meistersang* (mastersong), a highly formalized union of verse and song that flourished in German-speaking Central Europe from the fifteenth through the seventeenth century. At its zenith in the mid-1500s, over twenty guild-like mastersong "schools" existed in prominent cities such as Mainz, NUREMBERG,

Augsburg, Strasbourg, MUNICH, and Frankfurt; some guilds survived well into the eighteenth century, with the final school in Memmingen lasting until 1875. Nonetheless, mastersingers traced the roots of their art back to the MIDDLE AGES: the tripartite *Bar* form of their stanzas, consisting of two metrically identical *Stollen* followed by an *Abgesang* (see also CANZONA), is that of the courtly love lyric (*Minnesang*), and all mastersingers honored twelve medieval *Meister* as the founders of their art. These included thirteenth-century minnesingers such as WALTHER VON DER VOGELWEIDE and WOLFRAM VON ESCHENBACH alongside later gnomic poets, above all the four "crowned masters" Regenbogen, Marner, Heinrich von Mügeln, and Frauenlob. When WALTHER VON STOLZING notes in *Die MEISTERSINGER VON NÜRNBERG* that he learned what he knows of singing by studying an old book of songs by Walther von der Vogelweide, he thus lays claim to a direct lineage from one of the twelve old masters.

Despite such courtly forebears, *Meistersang* was a quintessentially bourgeois institution, based upon the belief that artistic expression could be codified according to established rules. Most mastersingers were tradesmen, although the membership of more prestigious schools might also include jurists, teachers, and members of the lower nobility. Each school held regular singing competitions, traditionally on Sundays after church, divided into the "main singing" (*Hauptsingen*) for religious songs and the "convivial singing" (*Zechsingen*) for secular themes. The title *Meister* was reserved for a singer who composed a new *Ton*, an original melody with metrically unique verse and rhyme. A *Meister* could also judge competitions as a "marker" (*Merker*), who enforced the metrical rules codified for each school in a *Tabulatur*. At competitions, the singer entered a pulpit-like *Singstuhl*, while the markers sat behind curtains in the so-called *Gemerk*, from which they deducted points for every violation of the *Tabulatur* rules. If a singer collected more than seven violation points, he had "sung incorrectly" (*versungen*).

The Nuremberg mastersong *Singschule* existed from around 1450 to 1774. At its peak in the sixteenth century, it claimed over 250 members and was the most influential of all mastersong guilds, not least due to the prodigious output of its most famous member, the shoemaker Hans SACHS. Most regional schools created a list of twelve local masters whom they honored alongside the original masters, and the Nuremberg *Meister* listed by Sachs in 1515 include his teacher in the art of mastersong, the weaver Lienhard Nunnenbeck (d. *c.* 1527), and his apparent role model, the barber-surgeon Hans Folz (d. 1513). Indeed, all of the mastersingers portrayed in *Die Meistersinger* are among the twelve Nuremberg masters, including SIXTUS BECKMESSER, author of one surviving song, but about whom nothing more is known.

GLENN EHRSTINE

Materna, Amalie (b. St. Georgen, 10 July 1844; d. Vienna, 18 Jan. 1918), Austrian soprano. Engaged in VIENNA (1869–94), she portrayed BRÜNNHILDE at the first productions of the *RING* in BAYREUTH (1876) and Berlin (1881), and in the Metropolitan Opera's premiere of *Die WALKÜRE* (1885). She was also the first KUNDRY (Bayreuth 1882 and each subsequent festival through 1891), and appeared in Wagner's LONDON concerts (1877).   DAVID BRECKBILL

Medieval. See MIDDLE AGES

Mein Leben (My Life), Wagner's most substantial autobiographical statement. It was begun at the request of King LUDWIG II of Bavaria on 17 July 1865 and the last of its four parts completed on 25 July 1880. It was first printed in a private edition in four volumes (1870, 1872, 1874, and 1880), as Wagner intended it solely for the eyes of his most intimate friends and colleagues. The first public edition appeared in 1911. One of the most influential publications in Wagner's literary output, it left an indelible mark on the first film about him directed by Carl Froelich (released in the US, 1913), as well as countless biographies and studies.

Wagner dictated *Mein Leben* to his "friend and wife," as he put it in the foreword, "who wished me to tell her the story of my life." That it was not COSIMA but Ludwig II who asked him to write it prompted Martin Gregor-Dellin, the editor of the modern edition, to note that the statement is "one of the inexactitudes, the bland artifices, that we encounter in dealing with this book" (ML/E 741). Indeed, it is the relatively innocuous start of a gradual avalanche of misinformation and theatrical distortion that becomes increasingly clear when letters, sketches, diaries, and other documents relevant to the events in the narrative are critically examined. To name just three instances: the one-way journey from history to myth that supposedly marked the genesis of the RING is far less straightforward when other projects he worked on at the time are considered. As for his activities during the 1849 DRESDEN UPRISING or the relations he enjoyed with his left-wing *confrères* during his subsequent exile in SWITZERLAND, there is nothing in *Mein Leben* to suggest that they were anything but artistically logical and positive. In fact they were reckless and baffling (Lippert, Evans).

Mein Leben ends with the call to Munich by King Ludwig II in 1864. According to COSIMA WAGNER'S DIARIES, Wagner told her three days before he died (9 February 1883) that he still intended "to finish the biography." He probably meant his earlier promise to the king about ending *Mein Leben* at the moment his wife began her famous diaries on 1 January 1869, thus providing a seamless "official" account of his life from beginning to end. It was not to be. His notes for the eventful intervening four years remain in diary form in the so-called Annals (see *Das BRAUNE BUCH*). Nor can Cosima's diaries count as a proper autobiographical narrative, despite what many would like to think. In terms of genuine autobiography, Wagner's life remains a fragment.

The integrity of *Mein Leben* itself has sometimes been in doubt. Wagner's early biographer Mary BURRELL obtained a clandestine copy in 1892 from the printer of the private edition, promptly declaring that Wagner was "not responsible" for the book (Deathridge 16). Cosima herself had some qualms that the unvarnished frankness of parts of the text could fall into the wrong hands, and soon after Wagner's death requested all recipients of the private edition (about fifteen of them) to return their copies to Bayreuth, where most of them were destroyed. Even the king obliged. The first public printing in 1911 was followed by a swirl of invective accusing its deceased author, or his Bayreuth family, of chicanery, censorship (the cuts were actually minor), embarrassing self-revelation, and sometimes all three. The story was so fantastic that nearly thirty years after its author's death many still found it hard to accept.

A modern edition of *Mein Leben* that does justice to its remarkable place in nineteenth-century letters, and provides a detailed scholarly counterbalance to its many idiosyncrasies, does not exist. The apparatus in the modern edition by Gregor-Dellin (ML) is inadequate and the generally excellent English translation (ML/E) does not even have an index. For an excellent index, the anonymous English edition published in two volumes in 1911 by the London firm of Constable & Co. should be consulted.   JOHN DEATHRIDGE

John Deathridge, *Wagner Beyond Good and Evil* (see bibliography).
Tamara S. Evans, "Am Mythenstein: Richard Wagner and Swiss Society," *Re-Reading Wagner*, ed. R. Grimm and J. Hermand (Madison: University of Wisconsin Press, 1993): 3–22.
Woldemar Lippert, *Wagner in Exile: 1849–62*, trans. Paul England (London: Harrap, 1930).

Meister, The. Periodical (OCLC 220766300) devoted to Wagner, published in eight volumes (London: George Redway, 1888–95) as the "quarterly journal of the London Branch of the Wagner Society." *The Meister* was edited throughout its run by William Ashton ELLIS. Among its contents were Ellis's translation into English of Wagner's *Die* KUNST UND DIE REVOLUTION (Art and Revolution, 1849) as well as SCHOPENHAUER's *World as Will and Idea* (1818, rev. 1844), "reminiscences" of Wagner by Gounod and LISZT, poems in Wagner's honor, and so on. A decade before publishing *The Perfect Wagnerite* (1898), George Bernard SHAW joined the Wagner Society and began reading *The Meister*; in 1889 he attended at least one lecture given by Ellis in London.

MICHAEL SAFFLE

Meistersinger von Nürnberg, Die (The Mastersingers of Nuremberg, WWV 96), opera in three acts, to Wagner's own libretto; first performed on 21 June 1868 at the Königliches Hof- und National-Theater, Munich. Cond. Hans von BÜLOW; see Appendix 10: Stage productions for original cast. Wagner oversaw the production.

1. Synopsis
2. Genesis and sources
3. Music and dramaturgy
4. Reception and performance history

1. Synopsis

The opera takes place in NUREMBERG, in the middle of the sixteenth century. Following a festive, if stentorian, Prelude that previews many of the coming themes (so many, in fact, that it resembles the potpourri overtures common to operettas), Act 1 begins in St. Catherine's Church, with a chorale sung by the congregation. Between verses of this largely diatonic chorus, a pointedly chromatic theme in the orchestra depicts the amorous yearnings of WALTHER VON STOLZING (a knight, newly arrived in town) and EVA POGNER (daughter of Veit Pogner, a prominent goldsmith and mastersinger), who are exchanging vaguely illicit glances during the church service. This contrast between the musical language of the community and that of the young lovers forms one of the central animating tensions of the opera to come.

If the opening Prelude, chorale, and orchestral interludes lay out much of the work's musical landscape – both literally the thematic material itself as well as the dialectics between tradition and innovation, form and expression, and diatonicism and chromaticism – the subsequent plot of Act I now elaborates these themes in words. Walther inquires about Eva's marital status and we learn that Eva will be offered as bride to the mastersinger who wins the song contest on the following day. Walther, headstrong and impetuous, decides he will compete for Eva's hand, but his resolve is soon complicated by the explanations of the mastersingers' elaborate rules essayed in exacting detail by David – the love interest of Magdalene (Eva's nurse), and himself a mastersinger in training as well as apprentice to the cobbler-poet HANS SACHS.

After a lovingly pompous entrance and roll-call of the mastersingers, Walther is introduced by Veit Pogner to his colleagues. SIXTUS BECKMESSER – town clerk and resident pedant, but also competitor for Eva's hand – is immediately suspicious of Walther. As the latter is subjected to various queries by the mastersingers about his training, credo, and provenance, it becomes clear that he is not only an outsider, but also ignorant and disdainful of the mastersingers' rules. Walther is asked to sing a "Trial Song," which is graded harshly by Beckmesser (donning his official cap as Marker, a kind of musical scorekeeper). Spurred on by Beckmesser, most of the mastersingers reject the newcomer's candidacy out of hand. The act ends in chaos and consternation for all but Sachs, who has located in Walther the breath of fresh air he feels the cloistered guild has long needed.

Act II functions largely as an interregnum, positioned between the old order of Act I – represented by the hidebound traditions of Beckmesser – and the new order, represented by Walther, that the opera's formal requirements as comedy will ensure take hold in Act III. Eva learns that Walther's interactions with the mastersingers did not go well; Sachs, in his "Flieder" (Elder) monologue, reflects on the meaning of Walther's failure. Reunited, Eva and Walther decide to elope, but have to retreat when the Nightwatchman makes his rounds and Sachs shines his lamp on their pathway. Beckmesser appears, lute in hand, to woo Eva in advance of the next day's singing competition; he is unaware that it is Magdalene in disguise he sees in Eva's window. Sachs, who needs to finish cobbling a pair of shoes, interrupts Beckmesser's serenade and proposes to serve as Marker while Beckmesser sings to Eva/Magdalene. The combined ruckus of Beckmesser's performance and Sachs's cobbling first attracts the attention of David – who sees Beckmesser serenading his Magdalene. After David assaults Beckmesser, a large group of townspeople find themselves drawn into a strange midnight brawl set to a chaotic fugue.

Act III begins with a moving Prelude introducing both the despondent "WAHN" (madness, delusion) theme in the low strings as well as a hopeful chorale melody in the brass serving as its antidote; both themes will return in the course of the act. The most self-consciously soulful music of the opera, the Prelude is typically played to an open curtain revealing a brooding Sachs lost in thought (though not written in the score, this is a performance practice that began with Wagner himself). After a lighthearted scene with David, who realizes belatedly that the day's festival and singing contest coincide with

Sachs's name day (Johannistag / St. John's Day), Sachs returns to his ruminations; in the subsequent "Wahn" monologue, he decides to channel the madness of the previous night into more expedient ends. As if on cue, a recently awoken Walther enters the room and relates his dream; he is then coached by Sachs on how to express his dreams in a song form the masters will understand.

After Walther and Sachs leave, Beckmesser enters, discovering the slip of paper on which Sachs wrote down the text of Walther's new song. Believing the text to be proof that Sachs himself plans to sing for Eva's hand in the song contest, Beckmesser steals it. He is caught by Sachs, who lets him keep the sheet of paper and does nothing to correct Beckmesser's mistaken attribution of the song. After Beckmesser leaves, certain of his coming victory, Eva enters. Her interactions with Sachs are awkward, and it is both an emotional and a musical relief when Walther joins them and sings the remaining third verse of his prize-song to be. Eva's relief culminates in an impassioned outburst of gratitude to Sachs, who responds by quoting the "desire motive" from Wagner's *TRISTAN UND ISOLDE*, whose tragic outcome Sachs wishes to avoid. After David and Magdalene enter, the scene ends with a contemplative quintet. The only such ensemble in Wagner's oeuvre, this quintet is an unabashed set piece. But in quoting the melody of Walther's Prize Song, it also installs Eva and the other characters as model spectators of Walther's performance – the outcome of which is increasingly a foregone conclusion.

The final scene opens on the meadows outside of Nuremberg, as the VOLK gather for the song contest. After the guilds enter, the combined chorus greets Sachs by singing the monumental "Wach auf" (Awaken) chorale, set to words from the historical Hans SACHS's famous 1523 poem about Martin Luther. The competition then begins, with Beckmesser the first to sing, but he has difficulty remembering the words he has stolen from Sachs's atelier; the result is a spectacularly surreal garbling of Walther's text. Humiliated, Beckmesser lashes out at Sachs, who – having stage-managed the entire proceedings – is happy to introduce Walther. Not surprisingly, Walther sings the correct version of the song to the hearty approval of the *Volk*, Eva, and the mastersingers. Technically Walther must now join the mastersingers if he is to receive Eva's hand, but he rejects this prospect. Sachs, wounded by Walther's dismissal of the mastersingers, sings a defense of "holy German art" that is enthusiastically parroted back by all on stage in the firmest of C major affirmations.

2. Genesis and sources

Initially conceived in 1845 as a light-hearted satyr-play to follow *TANN-HÄUSER*, *Die Meistersinger* was not finished until 1867 – well after Wagner had composed *TRISTAN UND ISOLDE* and much of the *RING* cycle. By this point, the opera had changed shape; if nothing else, it is longer and more serious than the 1845 outlines suggest. And yet even these early sketches contain most of the elements that would ultimately form the backbone of the opera: a young man and woman in love, pedantic mastersingers, a Marker who also has designs on the young woman, burghers drawn into a nighttime brawl, Hans Sachs's ruminations on the worrying decline of German art, a triumphant prize song by the young man, and general acclaim for Sachs at the work's end. How precisely these pieces fit together in each stage of the opera's genesis is best dealt with elsewhere (see Warrack), but what is notable is that they were all more or less present from the beginning – a state of affairs that is partially attributable to Wagner's literary forebears.

Wagner pointed to two chief inspirations for the opera: GERVINUS's *Geschichte der poetischen National-Literatur der Deutschen* – which paints an admiring portrait of the historical Hans Sachs and the MASTERSINGERS – and an incident Wagner claims to have witnessed in Nuremberg, when an overly confident singer was publicly humiliated to the degree that a riot formed in the street. Like many of Wagner's latter-day narrations of artistic inspiration, this one is only partially true; most notably, it leaves out Johann Ludwig Deinhardstein's play *Hans Sachs* (1827) which Wagner did see, and which was later adapted for the operatic stage by Lortzing. One additional source Wagner admitted to reading was WAGENSEIL's *Von der Meister-Singer holdseligen Kunst* (1697), which helped him flesh out the rituals and rules of the mastersingers.

Although Wagner undoubtedly drew on other writings, not to mention his own imagination, most of the libretto's details – particularly some of the more convoluted ones that might otherwise be attributed to the author himself – stem from these sources alone. Wagenseil, for instance, provided the elaborate rules for the mastersingers: not only the form of mastersong itself, but also the special chair in which one sang, the "Fanget an" (begin) as a signal to start singing, and the role of the Marker. The baptism of a new song – surely one of the more precious moments in Act III – was already in Gervinus, as was Veit Pogner's complaint that the mastersingers were no longer held in sufficient respect outside Nuremberg. The insistence on a fundamental distinction between Hans Sachs and an out-of-touch social superior is in both Gervinus and Deinhardstein/Lortzing, just as the latter's dramatization of a Beckmesser-like character claiming authorship of a poem he did not write, then botching its recitation to the point of surreal absurdity, clearly provided Wagner with one of the opera's most ingenious (if cruel) moments.

Walther does not appear in any of the sources mentioned above, but, as Lydia Goehr has recently argued, one the most significant predecessors for the character – the young prophet with a sword – comes from MEYERBEER's wildly successful *Le Prophète*: an opera, and a Jewish composer, that Wagner had publicly denounced. In fact, *Meistersinger* draws heavily on the traditions of grand opera, that genre he scorned above all others: the procession of guilds and general spectacle of the final scene most obviously, but also on the level of structure in each act's progression towards dramatic and striking tableaux.

3. Music and dramaturgy

Die Meistersinger is Wagner's only comedy. But that designation does not reflect any comedic content as such (Loge's comments in *Das* RHEINGOLD after WOTAN steals the ring are probably more humorous than any moment in *Meistersinger*). Rather, it indicates the work's form – the happy ending, "correct" pairing of lovers, and public humiliation of the pretender. *Meistersinger* is also the only mature Wagner opera in which nobody dies. Yet in many ways the opera encapsulates the entire Wagnerian oeuvre: moments of sheer tedium as well as those of utter sublimity, Wagner's most thorough-going exploration of the "ART OF TRANSITION," and, perhaps above all, a demonstration of his idealized relationship between art, artists, and the *Volk*.

What is unique about *Meistersinger* is its head-on confrontation with the music and traditions of the past – a confrontation that results in ambivalence and derision as well as homage. If the opening Prelude's genial revue of the opera's thematic material is in keeping with the work's generic designation as a comedy, so, too, does it announce the opera's altogether serious aim to interrogate the status and viability of traditional artistic forms. When, towards the end of the Prelude, Wagner famously combines three C major themes ("Mastersinger," the "march" or "King David" motive, and a snippet from Walther's Prize Song) – thus announcing the opera's contrapuntal ambitions as well as its unique brand of diatonicism – it is difficult to say where homage ends and critique begins. After all, each theme consists mainly of an arpeggiated C major triad – in other words, the same three notes – such that weaving them together is not especially difficult; the implication is that contrapuntal showmanship is child's play. While the Prelude fulfills its historical function of announcing the music to come, so, too, does it announce the work's critique of historical forms and procedures themselves. (Not surprisingly, it is this moment from the overture that resurfaces at the end of the opera to accompany Sachs's insistence that Walther honor his "German masters," since by this point it is clear that older traditions are no longer the only viable means of composition.)

The critique is more or less on the surface for most the opera, including virtually all the scenes with the mastersingers or Beckmesser, but it lingers on even at the end of the work, after Walther accepts Sachs's spirited defense of the mastersingers and agrees to join their ranks. For Walther's success in mastering the *Bar* form was remarkably fast and effortless, and was undertaken primarily for amorous reasons. If the opera does not entirely dismiss an art form that could be learned so quickly, and out of sheer expedience, nor does it entirely endorse it, either. A similar ambivalence about the expressive capabilities of older music surfaces in the work's hazy diatonicism, which, as Carl Dahlhaus pointed out, is more a reimagining – second nature, not first – than it is an uncomplicated return to an earlier musical language (205). There is almost always a citational quality to the diatonic moments, which tend to be juxtaposed against a much more expressive and agile chromaticism (the opening chorale and orchestral interludes depicting Walther's longing glances are typical in this regard). Indeed, it can hardly be an accident that what are arguably the two most intensely felt moments of the work – the Act III Prelude and the Quintet – have virtually nothing to do with earlier music. If Walther and Sachs need to pay obeisance to the past, *Die Meistersinger* suggests, the work's listeners in the opera house can be spared such a burden.

4. Reception and performance history

Die Meistersinger's annexation by – and, for some, anticipation of – Nazi propaganda has understandably overshadowed its entire reception since World War II. And although the claim that *Meistersinger* was Hitler's favorite

opera is a canard, the point is clear enough: more than any other Wagner work
this one is tarnished, perhaps indelibly so, by the historical resonance of its
nationalist sentiments, particularly in conjunction with the characterization
of Beckmesser, which some have argued is anti-Semitic (see SIXTUS
BECKMESSER). But it should also be noted that *Meistersinger*'s status as the
political hot potato within Wagner's oeuvre is a recent accretion. Certainly the
opera's initial success throughout Europe showed no signs of a stigma, and
even in those times and places when one would imagine that anti-German
sentiment might preclude the work's performance, *Meistersinger* remained
strangely immune to censure: it was performed in the USA during both world
wars, and received new productions at La Scala just ten days after World
War II, and again in 1947. Similarly, performances of the opera seem not to
have been quite the ubiquitous agent of nationalist sentiment within Germany
that one might assume. Between the Bayreuth festival's founding in 1876 and
the "Kriegsfestspiele" – the performances intended to boost Nazi morale
during the war – both the *Ring* cycle and *Parsifal* were each performed there
about four times as often as *Meistersinger*. Similar statistics emerge at other
German houses.

All the same, the work's attractions for German nationalists were clear.
Although neither the treatment of Beckmesser nor an acknowledgment of
Wagner's anti-Semitism played an explicit role in the far right's adoption of
Meistersinger, Sachs's closing rant formed an obvious and well-traveled point
of entry. At the reopening of the Bayreuth festival in 1924, after the extended
hiatus occasioned by World War I, the audience felt moved to sing "Deutschland über alles" in enthusiastic response to the closing scene – a practice that
Siegfried Wagner soon forbade. The monumental "Wach auf" chorus, with its
promise of a new day, appealed to Nazi sentiments; Goebbels cited the
moment approvingly in a 1933 radio broadcast of the opera from Bayreuth,
and that same year – the first of Nazi rule – during a performance at the Berlin
Staatsoper the chorus turned away from Hans Sachs, and towards Hitler in
the audience, to sing the chorale. Perhaps most infamously, the opera was
performed repeatedly at the Nuremberg rallies (which Hitler insisted take
place on the same meadows as the opera's final scene), and the Act III
Prelude also made a notable appearance in Leni Riefenstahl's *Triumph of the
Will*. The list goes on.

Yet despite a Nazi embrace that did not, perhaps, represent an entirely
willful misreading of the opera's politics, *Die Meistersinger* had little trouble
reentering the repertory throughout Europe and America following the war.
What changed was the way the work was staged. WIELAND WAGNER's
1956 production for Bayreuth stripped away the charged setting – it was
famously dubbed the "Meistersinger ohne Nürnberg" (Mastersingers without
Nuremberg) – but just as important was the staging's pervasive atmosphere of
viciousness and foreboding, particularly in Act II. Subsequently, and presumably due to increasing public scrutiny of Wagner's anti-Semitism, the locus of
directorial attention shifted to the final scene. In WOLFGANG WAGNER's 1984
Bayreuth staging, Wolfgang himself joins Beckmesser's and Sachs's hands in
appeasement, the *Volk* seem genuinely shocked by Sachs's rant, and, when
Sachs finally leaves the stage, the chorus waves vigorously, as if to welcome an

overdue exorcism. Less conciliatory, if also more controversial, is Peter Konwitschny's 2002 Hamburg production, which comes to a halt during the infamous speech as the mastersingers query Sachs as to the meaning and implications of his nationalist fear-mongering. Those implications – at least in their most familiar and dystopian reading – are highlighted in the 2007 Bayreuth staging by KATHARINA WAGNER and dramaturge Robert Sollich, who portray Sachs as a ruthless demagogue presiding over the symbolic execution of his enemies while the chorus sings the "Wach auf" chorale. Predictably, both the Konwitschny and Wagner/Sollich productions were *succès de scandale*, but it is perhaps an index of changing times that their critical reception seems to have been generated as much by the sense that staging Sachs as a proto-Nazi is old hat as it was shock over a startling, new revelation. And indeed, two stagings from 2011 by David McVicar (Glyndebourne) and Andreas Homoki (Komische Oper Berlin) suggest that some directors' interests have moved more towards character studies than the opera's political baggage. Whether this trend can be sustained responsibly, without suppressing the work's politics, remains to be seen.   RYAN MINOR

Carl Dahlhaus, *Nineteenth-Century Music*, trans. J. Bradford Robinson (Berkeley: University of California Press, 1991).

Lydia Goehr, "'– wie ihn uns Meister Dürer gemalt': Contest, Myth, and Prophecy in Wagner's *Die Meistersinger*," *Journal of the American Musicological Association* 64.1 (2011): 51–118.

Arthur Groos, "Constructing Nuremberg: Typological and Proleptic Communities in *Die Meistersinger*," *19th-Century Music* 16.1 (1992): 18–34.

Nicholas Vazsonyi, ed., *Wagner's "Meistersinger": Performance, History, Representation* (University of Rochester Press, 2003).

John Warrack, *Richard Wagner: "Die Meistersinger von Nürnberg"* (New York: Cambridge University Press, 1994).

Melchior, Lauritz (b. Copenhagen, 20 March 1890; d. Santa Monica, 18 March 1973), Danish tenor. Originally a baritone, he became the quintessential HELDENTENOR at BAYREUTH (1924–31, as PARSIFAL, SIEGMUND, SIEGFRIED, TRISTAN), the Metropolitan Opera (1926–50), and Covent Garden (1926–39) by means of his commanding, baritonal sound with ringing high notes. In the course of his career, he made 223 appearances as TRISTAN.

DAVID BRECKBILL

Shirlee Emmons, *Tristanissimo: The Authorized Biography of Heroic Tenor Lauritz Melchior* (New York: Schirmer, 1990).

Melos (τέλειον μέλος), the Greek term for singing, song, and rhythmically intoned poetry. *Melos* forms the root of Wagner's theory of musical communication. In German musical discourse, however, the concept of melody had become a daunting philosophical monstrance (Wackenroder, Schlegel, SCHELLING, SCHOPENHAUER), and Wagner emerged from a tradition that viewed "beautiful" melody as anathema to German composition, which was itself increasingly defined (via climate and national temperament) in opposition to Italianate lyricism. Consequently no complaint was more widely or more bitterly touted during the mid-century than Wagner's alleged incapability of writing such melody; his melodies were dismissed merely as a dense weave of ceaselessly modulating, characteristic motivic fragments. But Wagner – perhaps defensively – consistently asserted the primacy of melody as "music's only form … it is not even thinkable apart from melody" (SSD 7:125; PW 3:333). Since 1834, he located this primarily in Bellinian BEL CANTO, chastising his compatriots' skepticism: "Let's drop the joke for once, spare ourselves the sermon, and hold fast to what it was that so enchanted us … especially with BELLINI, it was the clear melody, the simple noble and beautiful song; surely it would not be a sin if, before going to bed, we prayed that heaven would one day give German composers such melodies and such a mode of handling song" (SSD 12:20; PW 8:68). From this early Italian orientation, Wagner took the notion of melody's tactile sensuality (*Sinnlichkeit*), by which a plastic musical utterance could access listeners' "feelings" directly, without recourse to reflexive interpretation.

But it was in *OPER UND DRAMA* (Opera and Drama, 1851) that Wagner fully individuated his concept of *melos*, redefining it as a linguistic concept specific to the German tongue – that is, *Versemelodie*: a melodic-poetic amalgam that ignores poetic meter, end-rhyme, periodic structure, and architectonic form, in favor of instinctive speech rhythms, phrasal units determined by breath, and melodic pitches determined by intoned speech roots, which are themselves organized according to alliterative correspondences (*STABREIM*). Wagner conceives this as an historic reintegration (after Pindar) of poetry and music, and along the way issues a veritable taxonomic mania of aberrant melodic types: absolute melody (typified by ROSSINI), Patriarchal melody (BEETHOVEN's setting of SCHILLER's *An die Freude*), quadratic melody (periodic structure), instrumental melody (derived from the heritage of dance forms), orchestral melody (continuous instrumental fabric / accompaniment), and in 1860, "ENDLESS MELODY" (*unendliche Melodie*), to name but a few. Wagner complements these WITH an equally extensive set of poetic METAPHORS for melody, from "wave-born reflection [of the poet]" to "boat [on the sea of harmony]" and "love-greeting of the woman to the man."

Pragmatically speaking, Wagner's notion of *melos* was also a cipher for understanding the motivic structure of Beethoven's works. In order to demonstrate "endless melody" to Felix DRAESEKE in 1859, Wagner reportedly sang through the opening of the first movement of the "Eroica," switching between parts from theme to theme, as though a single melodic line formed a vital structural thread (he would comment similarly on Op. 131, and the first movement of the Ninth Symphony) (Draeseke 179–80). Melody in this sense becomes an arbiter of form, which explains Wagner's comments that *TRISTAN*'s form was a function of its melody – in other words, the conjunction of (vocal) *Versemelodie* with (instrumental) orchestral melody. DAVID TRIPPETT

Felix Draeseke, "Was tut der heutigen musikalischen Produktion not?," *Signale für die musikalische Welt*, 11/12 (1907): 177–81.
Thomas Grey, *Wagner's Musical Prose* (see bibliography).
David Trippett, *Wagner's Melodies: Aesthetics and Materialism in German Musical Identity* (Cambridge University Press, 2012).

Memorabilia. The market for memorabilia has always been an important aspect in the reception of celebrated composers. Therefore, many similarities may be found in MUSEUM holdings and exhibition stores devoted to composers, frequently displaying kitsch tendencies: dishes and pastry with fanciful composer-related names (*tournedos Rossini*) or their portraits (*Mozart candy*); busts; cups, plates, pipes, medals, engravings, and postcards with portraits, playing cards, and other games, to which nowadays we have added plastic statues, mouse pads, T-shirts, pullovers, and so on, with their portraits or facsimile handwriting. Last, but not least, all kinds of books, albums, calendars, and other printed (and now digitized) methods have greatly contributed to the popularization of composers.

These trends can largely be traced back to the Romantic period. Previously, musicians were regarded as highly skilled craftsmen, whose products were the property of their employers. These views changed with BEETHOVEN who, however, did not fully profit from the emerging discourse of genius, authentic creativity, and artistic property. Early examples of those who did benefit were Jenny Lind (who was commercialized through a wide range of handicrafts), LISZT, Paganini, and ROSSINI, who were all icons of popular imagination and feverish social interest. For Wagner, things are somewhat different. After the founding of the Bayreuth Festival in 1876, he became an object of self-identification for large segments of the German-speaking upper classes. Therefore, in addition to the early forms of marketing described above, new forms of "souvenirs" became popular. Starting with photographs and albums of the Bayreuth productions and their artists, editors soon understood that graphic ICONOGRAPHY and painting increasingly proved the most effective media for allegoric and coded representation. From single postcards to expensive albums, hundreds of works and series of works were offered on the Wagner market. Indeed, many of the dramaturgical plots of Wagner's operas not only told stories about Teutonism and anti-Teutonism; in artistic presentations, these contents sometimes moved imperceptibly to pure fairy tale, immature myth, quasi-historical narrative, and even to racial social utopia. The most striking examples of the latter tendency are Arthur RACKHAM's illustrations of the *RING*, sixty-six unsurpassed masterworks published in 1910–11. The second most important name is Franz STASSEN, a close friend of SIEGFRIED WAGNER. In 1908, Stassen started illustrating most of Richard Wagner's works. Beside the aesthetic perfection, the ideological association of his dazzlingly beautiful Teutonic figures contrasted the "otherness" of the ugly and suggested an artistic language Richard Wagner might have hoped for but could not achieve with the naturalistic stagecraft of the 1870s. Symbolistic and impressionistic styles enabled other artists such as Hugo Braune, Henri FANTIN-LATOUR, Hermann HENDRICH, Ferdinand Leeke, and many others, to create highly interesting illustrations and large-scale albums.

These collections are valuable today. Even more prized is the market for manuscripts, which, with the "invention" of the Romantic artist, became a valuable commodity. Before 1800, entries in "friendship books" were primarily made for the artist's host and contain (clichéd or original) sayings about life in general. With Beethoven, WEBER, BERLIOZ, and MENDELSSOHN, new forms of artistic presents and souvenirs became popular; the Romantic "autograph book" became a reliquary for guests containing specimens of human genius. The emerging category of album leaf (*Albumblatt*) does not quote just *any work*, but the latest *great work* of the composer, thus representing in one or two lines the essence of genial invention. Signed and/or inscribed engravings (later photographs), books, and scores achieved immense popularity and are fascinating for collectors as well as antiquarian dealers. The role of CORRESPONDENCE also changed radically, especially in Wagner's case. In addition to being a tool of communication, it became an object of value. The hasty composer frequently signed a letter dictated to and written by a secretary; in contrast, Wagner always seems to have been thinking of posterity. He *never* dictated letters; he always wrote himself in a very fine and decorative handwriting, thus creating objects of veneration for centuries to come.

ULRICH DRÜNER

Mendelssohn Bartholdy, Felix (b. Hamburg, 3 Feb. 1809; d. Leipzig, 4 Nov. 1847), composer, organist, pianist, and conductor. His life was marked by enormous productivity as a composer of symphonies, overtures, concerti, piano and chamber music, and oratorios, as well as ceaseless labor as a conductor and reformer of European musical life. In LEIPZIG (1843), he established the first conservatory in German-speaking Europe, and became the recognized leader in the nineteenth-century revival and study of music of the past, a testimony to the impact of his 1829 revival of BACH's *St. Matthew Passion* as well as to his many performances of Bach's music. The grandson of the famous Jewish philosopher Moses Mendelssohn, Felix was baptized a Christian in his childhood; many of his compositions expressed his Protestant faith. He travelled frequently in Europe and was particularly revered in Great Britain, a country he visited ten times. He was "the greatest child prodigy the history of Western music has ever known" (Rosen 569) but also became a forceful musical presence in his adulthood. As a composer, he excelled in "understatement, chiaroscuro, nuance, and subtle, coloristic orchestration," which often evoked images of places with the sensibilities of a painter (Todd xxvii).

A near contemporary of Richard Wagner (born four years later), Mendelssohn and his legacy loomed large in Wagner's conception of his own place in the musical world. His initial encounters with Mendelssohn reflected genuine admiration for Mendelssohn's music as well as a whiff of ingratiating himself with this acknowledged star. Wagner once considered Mendelssohn's *Hebrides* overture (Op. 26) a masterpiece, "one of the most beautiful works of music that we have" (PW 6:144). In the 1830s, several of Wagner's early works (*Die FEEN* and incidental music) showed Mendelssohnian influences to the point of imitation. In 1836, he sent Mendelssohn the score of his 1831 SYMPHONY IN C MAJOR; receiving no acknowledgment, he concluded that Mendelssohn feared him as a rival. Their later encounters were strained and infrequent, despite geographic proximity after Wagner's 1842 return to DRESDEN. Mendelssohn himself was discreet in expressing his opinion of Wagner's compositions, though he hinted to colleagues that it was not wholly favorable. He conducted the OVERTURE to TANNHÄUSER in an 1846 concert with the Leipzig Gewandhaus orchestra. The work was not well received, and Wagner blamed Mendelssohn's "morose demeanor" for its failure (Todd 511).

Wagner's most significant engagement with Mendelssohn came after the latter's untimely death at the age of 38. Wagner's 1850 essay *Das JUDENTUM IN DER MUSIK* (Judaism in Music) made the Jewish heritage of this pious

Protestant central to his alleged failure as a creative artist. In Wagner's critique, Mendelssohn had everything Wagner had lacked – wealth, education, connections, early success – but because born a JEW he could never achieve real German profundity. Mendelssohn's "aesthetic of creative restoration" (Botstein 16) expressed pedantry and imitation, his compositional subtleties became insincerities and the beauty of his compositions mere prettiness. "Judaism in Music" initiated the destruction of Mendelssohn's reputation, a process that culminated in the Third Reich and has only since the 1980s fully reversed itself.   CELIA APPLEGATE

Leon Botstein, "The Aesthetics of Assimilation and Affirmation: Reconstructing the Career of Felix Mendelssohn," in R. Larry Todd, ed., *Mendelssohn and his World* (Princeton University Press, 1991).

Charles Rosen, *The Romantic Generation* (Cambridge, MA: Harvard University Press, 1995).

R. Larry Todd, *Mendelssohn: A Life in Music* (New York: Oxford University Press, 2003).

Mendès, Catulle (b. Bordeaux, 22 May 1841; d. Paris, 8 Feb. 1909), French Parnassian poet, novelist, and critic. Mendès was married to two of the most prominent Wagnerians of his day: Judith GAUTIER (making him the son-in-law of poet Théophile Gautier) and later to the composer Augusta Holmès. Acutely concerned with musical dramas, Mendès contributed libretti to many of the leading opera composers of his time, including Chabrier (*Gwendoline* and *Briséïs*), Messager (*Isoline*), Hahn (*La Carmélite*), Erlanger (*Le Fils de l'étoile*), and Massenet (*Ariane* and *Bacchus*). He was an early advocate for Wagner in France, defending the composer tirelessly both before and after the TANNHÄUSER SCANDAL OF 1861, including in the short-lived *Revue fantaisiste* (1861), in the REVUE WAGNÉRIENNE (1885–7) and later in his *Richard Wagner* (Paris, 1886). In a letter to his friend Stéphane Mallarmé, Mendès demonstrated his adulation for Wagner: "I am pleased to initiate you into the new art, which is neither poetry nor music, yet which is at the same time both music and poetry, created by Richard Wagner. This man – if that term applies to someone of his hyper-divine nature – is truly at once precursor and redeemer" (letter of 27 May 1870).   WILLIAM GIBBONS

See also Charles BAUDELAIRE; Jules CHAMPFLEURY

Metaphor. As a writer, Wagner was always given to the cultivation of extended metaphors, in his theoretical writings no less than in his dramatic texts.

Especially when engaged in aesthetic speculation, he seems to have seized on metaphor as a means of "realizing" abstract ideas for the visual or sensory imagination (as he himself might have put it). Two key examples would be the metaphor of music as "ocean" dominating the section on music (*Tonkunst*) in relation to poetry and DANCE in *Das KUNSTWERK DER ZUKUNFT* (The Artwork of the Future) and the metaphor of music as "woman" introduced at the end of Part 1 of *OPER UND DRAMA* (Opera and Drama).

Metaphorical constructions of music in *Das Kunstwerk der Zukunft* illustrate the labile, shifting character of Wagner's figurative language. Initially, music is presented as one of the three "purely human" arts, together with poetry and dance. These are pictured as sisters entwined in a loving embrace in the ideal days of ANCIENT GREECE, suggesting traditional images of the "three graces" (SSD 3:67–8). Later, in describing the medium of music itself, Wagner turns to the image of music as an "ocean" separating the shores of poetry and dance. Conceiving music as a fluid medium also suggests to him a notion of music as the life-blood of artistic man, nourishing all of his creative organs: tone is the "heart" of the artistic body, music (*Tonkunst*) its circulating medium. Turning back to the figure of the musical ocean, Wagner develops its spatial dimensions: harmony represents the unfathomable depths of the ocean; the illuminated surface is melody, with its linear, wave-like contours; the winds ("breath") blowing from the shores of poetry and dance condition the rhythm of those melodic waves. Melody and rhythm are also identified with the shores themselves, however, as the respective points of contact between music and poetry (melody) and dance (rhythm). Finally, on the basis of the ocean metaphor Wagner introduces an analogy between Columbus and BEETHOVEN, "that hero who traversed the wide open seas of ABSOLUTE MUSIC to their furthest limit" (SSD 3:85–6). In *Oper und Drama* Wagner recalls the Beethoven-as-Columbus analogy within his critique of the "errors" of modern musical culture (SSD 3:278). Beethoven discovered a new world of expressive possibilities while merely seeking, like Columbus, a new route to a remote part of the known world ("absolute" instrumental music, the East Indies). But the truth behind his discovery could not remain hidden for long: he had found the way toward the new world of the "musical drama of the future."

In *Oper und Drama* as a whole, Wagner exchanges the elemental metaphor of the musical "ocean" for a nexus of organic and specifically GENDERED and sexual metaphors centering on that of "music as woman." The complete musical organism is to be found in "melody." Beethoven's music had tried to show the listener the conception or birth of melody as a self-contained process, realized entirely within the musical medium itself (SSD 3:315). This again was a misconception: music is in fact only the passive, nurturing receptacle for the "poetic intent," the male seed that is needed to fertilize it (SSD 4:101–3). By the time this latter term is introduced at the end of Part 2, it is not quite clear whether the product of this metaphorical intercourse represents "melody" (as first implied), "dramatic melody" more specifically, or the "musical drama" as a whole. Consistent with the earlier ocean metaphor is the implication that music on its own lacks a means for either formal or semantic determination. As a fluid, passive body of inchoate expressive substance it requires some outside force to give it shape and meaning.

Oper und Drama is rife with yet other organic and physiological metaphors. Vowels are likened to the blood circulating within the "flesh and bones" provided by consonants (within the theory of poetic STABREIM); the poet speaks to the "eye" of hearing, the musician to its "ear"; appropriately conceived dramatic situations represent the diverse members that constitute the whole, living "body" of the drama – and so on. The folk-song that provided the melodic model for modern art music is a "wildflower" from which composers distilled only the scent (the melody) but ignored the living plant itself and its delicate organs of reproduction (the poetry). Later, in the essay ZUKUNFTSMUSIK (Music of the Future, 1861) Wagner would try to evoke the new genus of ENDLESS MELODY he had since cultivated in TRISTAN UND ISOLDE with the metaphor of a whole forest, and the subtle polyphony of sensory impressions experienced in contemplating the "resounding" silence of the woods on a quiet summer evening (SSD 4:131–2).

WALTHER VON STOLZING works this same image into his "trial song" in Act I of *Die MEISTERSINGER* ("es schwillt und schallt, / es tönt der Wald / von holder Stimmen Gemenge"), reinforced by HANS SACHS's response when he tries to recall that elusive "melody" in his "*Flieder* monologue" in Act II ("kann's nicht behalten, – doch auch nicht vergessen; / und fass' ich es ganz, – kann ich's nicht messen"). When Sachs teaches Walther the principles of *Meistergesang* in Act III, he calls on the metaphors of marriage and reproduction from *Oper und Drama*. When Walther's Prize Song is afterwards "baptized," the reproductive figure from Wagner's treatise is joined to a figure (baptism) that frames the whole opera. The self-reflexive poetics of *Die Meistersinger* make it a natural locus for the migration of metaphors from the domain of Wagner's theoretical writings into the creative sphere. *Tristan und Isolde*, by comparison, is characterized by a more "autonomous" figurative world, operating mostly in dichotomous pairings such as night-day, love-death, I-thou, self-world. Here, and even more in *Parsifal*, however, the role of metaphor is subsumed into that of symbol.   THOMAS S. GREY

Michael Dyson, "Sea, Mirror, Woman, Love: Some Recurrent Imagery in *Opera and Drama*," *The Wagner Journal* 5.3 (November 2011): 16–33.
Frank Glass, *The Fertilizing Seed: Wagner's Concept of the Poetic Intent* (Ann Arbor, MI: UMI Research Press, 1983).
Thomas S. Grey, *Wagner's Musical Prose* (see bibliography): esp. chapter 3.
Jean-Jacques Nattiez, *Wagner Androgyne* (see bibliography).
Holly Watkins, *Metaphors of Depth in German Musical Thought from E. T. A. Hoffmann to Arnold Schoenberg* (Cambridge University Press, 2011).

Metternich, Princess Pauline [von Metternich-Winneburg zu Beilstein, Princess Pauline Clémentine] (b. Vienna, 25 Feb. 1836; d. Vienna, 28 Sep. 1921), Austrian noble and patron of arts. Wife of the Austrian ambassador in Paris, Prince Richard von Metternich, who was son of the powerful Austrian State Chancellor Klemens von Metternich. She was a decisive figure during the TANNHÄUSER SCANDAL OF 1861. It was at her intervention that Napoleon III ordered Wagner's work to be staged at the Paris OPÉRA. She was supportive during the tiresome and drawn-out process, and remained faithful to Wagner even after she became the object of public scorn in the aftermath of the scandal.   HERMANN GRAMPP

Meyer, Friederike, German actress whom Wagner met in Frankfurt in early 1862. Meyer so impressed Wagner with her talents that they quickly became romantically involved. In November of that year, Meyer accompanied Wagner to VIENNA, and thus began what Wagner later described as his "very painful entanglement" with her (ML/E 685). The previous year, Wagner had engaged Meyer's estranged sister, the soprano Luise MEYER-DUSTMANN, to sing the lead role in his planned Vienna premiere of TRISTAN UND ISOLDE. When Luise learned of Wagner's relations with Friederike, the singer's enthusiasm for Wagner and his project cooled considerably, and it has been suggested that this turn of events may have played a role in scuttling Wagner's plans for *Tristan* in the Austrian capital. Persuaded by Wagner, Meyer soon departed for VENICE. Meyer later made several attempts to reunite with the composer, but Wagner did not reciprocate her overtures, and the two fell out of touch.

KEVIN C. KARNES

Meyerbeer, Giacomo, orig. Jacob Liebmann Beer (b. Tasdorf [near Berlin], 5 Sep. 1791; d. Paris, 2 May 1864), one of the most famous and successful composers of his day. Meyerbeer influenced Wagner's career in numerous highly significant ways. Born near Berlin into a wealthy Jewish family, Meyerbeer spent much of his early career in Italy. Here he absorbed many elements of Italian operatic style, and scored an important success with his opera *Il crociato in Egitto* (1824). It was with his monumental French works, however, that Meyerbeer had the most significant influence on the history of opera. With his *Robert le diable* (1831) and especially with the immensely popular *Les Huguenots* (1836), Meyerbeer articulated the new forms and musical dramaturgy of GRAND OPERA: patterns that he further developed with his grand operas *Le Prophète* (1849) and *L'Africaine* (1865). In 1842, Meyerbeer returned to Berlin to take the post of General Music Director of Prussia. Although he gave up this position in 1848, Meyerbeer remained the director of Royal Court Music, and wrote many works for the Prussian court. With his mastery of different national idioms and his unsurpassed international reputation, Meyerbeer's impact on his contemporaries and successors was both wide and deep.

Wagner first experienced Meyerbeer's music during the 1830s as a part of the repertoire of various provincial theaters at which he was employed, and the older composer's works clearly had a formative influence on the development of Wagner's style. Indeed – as Wagner himself makes clear in his AUTOBIOGRAPHISCHE SKIZZE (Autobiographical Sketch, 1842/3) and in *Eine MITTEILUNG AN MEINE FREUNDE* (A Communication to My Friends, 1851) – he crafted his RIENZI on the model of the five-act grand opera that Meyerbeer had perfected with *Les Huguenots*. Meyerbeer was an acknowledged master of orchestral and choral effects, and the influence of his innovative approach to texture may be heard in many of Wagner's works (although, curiously not so much in *Rienzi* itself). The chorus of infernal demons in *Robert le diable*, for example, finds an echo in the dead sailors of *Der FLIEGENDE HOLLÄNDER*, and Wagner's ORCHESTRATION of brass and wind instruments is in many ways prefigured by Meyerbeer's practices. Although Meyerbeer's influence on Wagner's style is clearest in his early operas – up to and including LOHENGRIN – it can be heard in later works as well (especially *Die MEISTERSINGER*, with its large choruses, complex plot and mise-en-scène). Indeed, one could argue that Meyerbeer's music (rather than that of BEETHOVEN or WEBER) and sense for theater had the most lasting impact on Wagner's style.

In the early part of his career, Wagner regarded Meyerbeer as a mentor and fellow artist. The tone of his letters to Meyerbeer during this period is adulatory and occasionally fawning. In an 1837 letter from RIGA, for instance, Wagner praised Meyerbeer's stylistic course and asked him directly to help him establish himself in PARIS. Wagner first met Meyerbeer in 1839 in the seaside resort town of Boulogne, while en route to the French metropolis.

Meyerbeer treated his younger colleague with his characteristic courteous respect: listening to parts of *Rienzi* and introducing Wagner to other musicians in the city. Meyerbeer continued his support of the younger composer during Wagner's Paris years: writing letters of recommendation to the director of the Paris Opéra and to François Habeneck (its principal conductor), and introducing Wagner to influential men in the musical world of Paris such as the publisher Maurice SCHLESINGER. Meyerbeer occasionally gave Wagner MONEY, and in general helped Wagner in his attempts to break into the world of the Paris OPÉRA (an attempt that was eventually unsuccessful). When Wagner decided to leave Paris, Meyerbeer continued to support his younger colleague with a letter to LÜTTICHAU, director of the DRESDEN court theater, recommending a production of *Rienzi* there.

Insofar as we may judge by early essays such as *Über Meyerbeers Huguenotten*, Wagner's attitude towards Meyerbeer's music during this period was extremely positive. By 1850, however, this attitude had radically changed. It was in this year that Wagner published perhaps his most notorious essay, *Das JUDENTUM IN DER MUSIK* (Jewishness in Music). Wagner's ANTI-SEMITISM is rooted in stereotypical descriptions of the Jewish body and the Jewish voice. It is also expressed through familiar dichotomies between commercialism and authenticity, and between false mimicry and authentic creativity. Meyerbeer's name does not appear in this essay; Wagner speaks instead of a "certain Jewish composer." In his *OPER UND DRAMA* (Opera and Drama, 1851), however, Wagner drops this mask of anonymity. Chapter 6 of Book One contains an extensive critique of Meyerbeer's style, which climaxes with the famous description of Meyerbeer's musical dramaturgy as consisting of nothing but "effects without causes" (PW 2:95; *Wirkung ohne Ursache* SSD 3:301). Wagner takes the very quality that many of Meyerbeer's contemporaries singled out for special praise – namely his ability to synthesize elements of different national operatic styles into a seamless work of art – and turns it on its head, stigmatizing Meyerbeer's cosmopolitanism as a mark of inauthenticity. Here, as in later prose works, it is not too much to say that Meyerbeer takes on something close to mythic status: the archetypal JEW creating works of beguiling superficiality; works that were the embodiment of everything false, derivative, and commercial.

Elements of Wagner's critique, it should be noted, are found in other mid-nineteenth-century writings: most notably in Robert SCHUMANN's comparison between *Les Huguenots* and MENDELSSOHN's *St. Paul*. Nevertheless, the ingratitude and antipathy that Wagner showed toward Meyerbeer was extraordinary, even in the more hostile German critical environment. Indeed, Wagner's vilification of the older composer in his mid and late career is so violent that many biographers have tried to understand his relationship to Meyerbeer in quasi-Freudian terms: as a response to an "anxiety of influence" or as a desire to attack a surrogate father. However it is to be explained, Wagner's critique of Meyerbeer cast a long shadow. It was not dispelled until the 1960s and 1970s, when scholars such as Heinz and Gudrun Becker pioneered a reevaluation of Meyerbeer's contributions. Their work laid the foundation for a more nuanced investigation of the vital and complex relationship between Wagner and his cosmopolitan precursor. STEPHEN MEYER

Heinz and Gudrun Becker, *Giacomo Meyerbeer: A Life in Letters*, trans. Mark Violette (Portland, OR: Amadeus, 1989).

Mark Everist, *Giacomo Meyerbeer and Music Drama in Nineteenth-Century Paris* (Burlington, VT: Ashgate, 2005).

Giacomo Meyerbeer: Briefwechsel und Tagebücher, 8 vols., ed. Heinz Becker, Sabine Henze-Döhring, et al. (Berlin: De Gruyter, 1959–2006).

Helmuth Weinland, "Wagner und Meyerbeer," *Musik-Konzepte 59: Richard Wagner zwischen Beethoven und Schönberg* (Munich: edition text + kritik, 1988): 31–72.

Meyer-Dustmann, Luise (b. Aachen, 22 Aug. 1831; d. Berlin, 2 March 1899), German singer. Struck by Meyer-Dustmann's singing, Wagner provisionally cast the soprano, in 1857, in the role of SIEGLINDE in *Die WALKÜRE*, and in a letter to Franz LISZT (28 June 1857) he envisioned her singing the role of ISOLDE. In May 1861, Wagner traveled to VIENNA in search of singers for the premiere of *TRISTAN UND ISOLDE*, and upon meeting and hearing Meyer-Dustmann as ELSA in a rehearsal for *LOHENGRIN*, he wrote excitedly to his wife MINNA of his intention to employ her in his new opera: "no question of it!" (13 May 1861). However, when Wagner moved to Vienna in November 1862 to arrange for the premiere of the work, he brought with him his new lover, the actress Friederike MEYER, Meyer-Dustmann's estranged sister. Displeased with Wagner's relations with Friederike, Luise's enthusiasm for Wagner's project cooled considerably, possibly contributing to the collapse of his plans for a Viennese premiere.   KEVIN C. KARNES

Meysenbug, Malwida Freiin von (b. Kassel, 28 Oct. 1816; d. Rome, 26 April 1903), German writer and political radical. Malwida first met Wagner in LONDON during his conducting visit in 1855. Exiled there from Hamburg since 1852 as a dangerous democrat, she had been living with the Russian revolutionary writer Alexander Herzen. (She became the adoptive mother of his daughter, Olga.) Her acquaintance with Wagner was renewed in Paris in 1860, and by 1868 she had become an intimate of both him and COSIMA. She was witness, with Hans RICHTER, to their wedding in Lucerne in 1870. She met NIETZSCHE in Bayreuth (1872), and developed what has been described as a motherly affection for him. She observed the subsequent disintegration of his relationship with Wagner without diminution of her feelings towards either. In later years, Malwida became close to the writer Romain Rolland. She died in Rome in 1903, and has a tomb in the protestant "Cimitero degli Inglesi."

DAVID CORMACK

Malwida von Meysenbug, *Memoiren einer Idealistin* (orig. 1869–76), ed. R. Wiggershaus (Königstein/Ts: Helmer, 1998); trans. Monte Gardiner, "Malwida von Meysenbug's Memoirs of an Idealist," (Ph.D. thesis, Brigham Young University, 1999).

Middle Ages, historical period beginning with the socioeconomic breakdown of the Roman Empire and ending with the weakening and gradual disappearance of medieval institutions. It is always difficult to agree on precise dates, but the Middle Ages roughly cover a thousand-year time span between AD 500 and 1500. In the wake of Rome's dissolution, the early Middle Ages puts its mark on continuing Roman institutions, in particular the Christian Church and the concept of Empire. Charlemagne is crowned by the pope as "Emperor of the Romans" in 800, setting a precedent which leads to centuries of contentious relations between the medieval Papacy and the medieval Empire. By the tenth century, the emperor is viewed as the "Holy Roman Emperor." In the high Middle Ages, the characteristic medieval institutions are well established: a dominant and united Catholic Church, a powerful Empire as its secular counterpart, competing feudal monarchies in France and England, and a rural, socioeconomic system grounded in feudalism and controlled by the landed aristocracy.

In the late Middle Ages, medieval culture wanes. During the fourteenth century, in particular, catastrophic developments in Europe lead to dramatic changes in European society. Successive waves of the Black Death sweep through Europe at this time, and it is estimated that nearly half the population succumbs, leading to labor shortages and a disruption of the rural economy. During this same period, the French and the English engage in the "Hundred Years War," a conflict which has a devastating effect on the flower of medieval French and English chivalry. By the end of the fifteenth century, the characteristic institutions of the high Middle Ages are on the way out: the Church is rocked by scandal and schismatic reformers, the Empire has lost meaningful central authority, economic growth has moved to urban areas undermining the power of the landed aristocracy, and the unifying power of Latin is giving way to vernacular languages.

Interest in the Middle Ages revives early in the nineteenth century with the rediscovery of medieval manuscripts and a Romantic interest in the narratives of warriors, dragons, Arthurian knights, and courtly damsels. Serious scholarly work is paralleled by popularizing historical novels, paintings, dramas, and operas. Richard Wagner's oeuvre has an especially important role in interpreting medieval narrative and passing it on to succeeding generations. His eclectic combination of the NORDIC and German versions of the dragon-slayer master narrative in Der RING DES NIBELUNGEN becomes a new version which influences artists, writers, and filmmakers throughout the twentieth century. In Fritz Lang's two-part silent film Die Nibelungen (1924 and 1926), we have an example of a narrative which has more in common with Wagner than with either of the main medieval source texts. Wagner's Tristan has a similar impact on later writers and artists. In effect, his operas become a kind of conduit through which medieval narratives pass on their way to later adapters and interpreters.   RAY M. WAKEFIELD

See also GOTTFRIED VON STRASSBURG; PARZIVAL; WALTHER VON DER VOGELWEIDE; WOLFRAM VON ESCHENBACH

Benjamin Arnold, *Medieval Germany: 500–1300* (Toronto University Press, 1997).

Mime (tenor; character in Der RING DES NIBELUNGEN, with appearances in *Das RHEINGOLD* and *SIEGFRIED*. Brother of ALBERICH, adoptive father of SIEGFRIED, Nibelung smith). While there is a character named Mime in the VÖLSUNGA SAGA, the *Ring*'s Mime constitutes a marked demotion in importance and dignity. In the *Poetic EDDA*, Mimir appears as a guardian of wisdom and prophecy – his name means "the rememberer" or "the sage." Odin sacrifices his eye at Mimir's well to gain the gift of foresight. It also tells of Mimir's death in the struggle between the Aesir and Vanir. Odin finds Mimir decapitated and retrieves the head, which continues to counsel him.

Given Mimir's clairvoyance, it is rather ironic that Wagner transforms him into a bumbling and incompetent schemer, buffeted about by forces he barely understands.

Mime appears twice in the *Ring*, each time the object of another's power and violence: in *Das Rheingold* it is his own brother who abuses him; in *Siegfried* it is the ward who cannot believe himself Mime's son. Mime is the consummate victim, and one who seems to deserve his victimhood. Adorno located in Mime's pathetic exclamations of *Weh! Weh!* in *Das Rheingold* the schizophrenic nature of Wagner's attitude towards the downtrodden: honest concern over the injustice perpetrated upon them, and disgust at them and their fate.

It does not help that Wagner gives Mime few attributes that are not outright pathetic. It may go too far to claim, as some have suggested, that Mime is an ANTI-SEMITIC caricature (see Danuser, Weiner), which puts him in the same category as Alberich and *Die MEISTERSINGER*'s SIXTUS BECKMESSER. His inferiority and his evil are staged in the terms of nineteenth-century racism; his squeaky voice is redolent with Wagner's infamous description of "Jewish" vocality in *Das JUDENTUM IN DER MUSIK* (Jewishness in Music, 1850). And the "cunning" smith's inability to do his job right and reforge Nothung smacks of Wagner's critique of "Jewish" composers' lack of originality and creativity. Mime is an unskillful schemer, who confronts WOTAN with questions about the gods without realizing who Wotan is. Unlike his brother, he wants power without having to pay for it. ADORNO touches on Mime (alongside Alberich and Beckmesser) when he discusses the strange dialectic of humor in Wagner's works. Adorno suggests that there is something sadistic and brutalizing whenever Wagner tries to create straightforwardly funny characters – and indeed Mime's comedy in *Siegfried* works only when confronted with the more and more outlandish abuse the smith's young ward heaps upon him.

Nevertheless, Mime is closely associated with many of the central musical ideas of the *Ring*: the Nibelheim/Forging motive of Scene 3 of *Rheingold* and the Prelude to Act I of *Siegfried* (see Appendix 4: *Leitmotive* in *Der Ring des Nibelungen*; CWE 7), the Tarnhelm (CWE 8), and the Ring (CWE 2). Musically, as well as dramatically, he is a crafty villain of low comedy – a whining tenor rather than a HELDENTENOR. His music is, with few exceptions, deliberately ugly (dissonant, grating, rhythmically ungainly), virtually always in the minor mode, and often unstable tonally. Ugly or not, he and his music dominate Act I of *Siegfried*, as he plots to have Siegfried re-forge Siegmund's sword, so he can engineer the death of Fafner and gain the gold and the Ring for himself.

ADRIAN DAUB AND PATRICK MCCRELESS

Hermann Danuser, "Universalität oder Partikularität: Zur Frage antisemitischer Charakterzeichnung in Wagners Werk," in *Richard Wagner und die Juden*, ed. Dieter Borchmeyer (Weimar: Metzler, 2000): 79–100.
Marc Weiner, *Richard Wagner and the Anti-Semitic Imagination* (see bibliography).

Minnesota. Although Wagner never visited the UNITED STATES OF AMERICA, he entertained ideas of traveling there as early as the 1850s. Aware that Americans appreciated his music and, typically, attracted by the idea that he might find MONEY there to support his projects, he thought about emigration after the late 1870s, when he worried that his own dreams and plans might go unrealized in an ungrateful Germany. According to his American dentist, Dr. Newell Sill Jenkins, in 1878 Wagner "fancied he might be able to find the support he longed for by going with his works to settle permanently in America," an idea that Jenkins found "wildly impractical" (245). COSIMA Wagner reported that Wagner wished to move to Minnesota, where he would build a "drama school and a house" by using half of the million-dollar subscription that he expected from American admirers (CWD 1 February 1880). Apparently Wagner also considered dedicating *PARSIFAL* to the American people. Nothing came of these plans. Still, given Wagner's penchant for luxuries such as silk and velvet, as well as his declining HEALTH after the 1870s, one wonders how he would have dealt with the asperities of the Minnesota frontier and the rigors of that state's climate. The theater in Red Wing, Minnesota (built 1906), contains a bust of Wagner, so certainly he had admirers in the American Midwest, including the current Richard Wagner Society of the Upper Midwest.

DAVID E. BARCLAY

Newell Sill Jenkins, "Recollections of Villa Wahnfried from Wagner's American Dentist," in *Richard Wagner and His World*, ed. Thomas S. Grey (see bibliography): 237–47.

Mitteilung an meine Freunde, Eine (A Communication to My Friends). In 1871, in the preface to volumes 3 and 4 of his *Gesammelte Schriften*, Wagner called this essay the "conclusion" of the period of furious literary activity that began after his flight from Germany in 1849 and included such major works as *OPER UND DRAMA* (Opera and Drama, 1851) and *Das KUNSTWERK DER ZUKUNFT* (The Artwork of the Future, 1849/50). Originally published as the preface to the libretti of *Der FLIEGENDE HOLLÄNDER*, *TANNHÄUSER*, and *LOHENGRIN*, it was written in the summer of 1851 and appeared in December of that year after a delay due to the publisher BREITKOPF & HÄRTEL's objections to certain political passages.

Wagner begins with the announcement that he intends to tell the story of his life as an artist in an attempt to clear up misunderstandings of how his theories relate to his works. He later, more accurately, characterizes the essay as an account of the evolution of his thought. Anticipating trouble, he opens by dividing his readers into critics who cannot understand what he tries to express and those who can understand because they love him. Consequently, he writes this essay only for his loving friends. Love becomes a theme that surfaces in different ways throughout the substantial essay (36,000 words; 123 pages in the English translation). Related to this theme is Wagner's repeated insistence that he stays true to his inner needs for true love and understanding, even though they are completely at odds with his financial success and the demands of the public. Ideas that had originally been sketched as independent pieces – on genius and on the monumental – are also inserted in this preliminary section.

The main section recounts his first attempts at opera, his first success with *RIENZI*, and the projects begun while at DRESDEN (1842–9). Wagner notes that he immediately recognized the inner price he would have to pay to be outwardly successful and almost turned down the Dresden position. He relates the plans and ideas that resulted in *Der fliegende Holländer*, *Tannhäuser*, a sketch for *Die MEISTERSINGER*, and *Lohengrin*. He goes into almost as much detail about unrealized projects (*Die Sarazenin, Siegfrieds Tod, Friedrich I, Jesus von Nazareth*; see STAGE WORKS, INCOMPLETE). He provides some keys to interpreting his operas in order to correct misunderstandings, emphasizing in particular the importance of MYTH. His romantic operas all have mythic counterparts and they all have to do with REDEMPTION through LOVE. The DUTCHMAN, a wandering Odysseus-like figure, can be redeemed only by "the Woman of the Future." TANNHÄUSER, another Odysseus, this time enticed by Calypso, longs for the highest form of love. LOHENGRIN's story is that of Zeus and Semele; like Zeus, he wanted to love and be loved as a mortal person rather than as a god. It is absurd to think that either *Tannhäuser* or *Lohengrin* is about CHRISTIANITY.

Wagner's account of the REVOLUTIONS of 1848/9 deemphasizes his political participation and focuses instead on his crisis of disillusion with the theater. Although he was frustrated by what opera had become, he realized that a spoken play could never capture the "purely human" aspect; this could only be supplied by music, the language of emotions. Music and words have a reciprocal dependence on each other: music can only be focused with words, and words must be shaped with the intent to express emotions. He recognized that the form of opera had to be changed: he needed to dispense with the traditional organization by numbers and instead differentiate each scene by a distinct change of mood. Wagner declares he will write "no more operas"; instead, his works will be called dramas. Melody will be affected by his allowing it to take shape from the "feeling utterance of the words." While writing *Siegfrieds Tod* he came upon the idea of STABREIM, alliterative verse, as a means to give shape to the melody.

The final section begins with a mention of the DRESDEN UPRISING of 1849, explaining briefly that his participation was the consequence of his decision long before to turn his back on the world. He then gives very pithy summaries of his recent publications *Die KUNST UND DIE REVOLUTION* (Art and Revolution: art and society develop in parallel ways), *Das Kunstwerk der Zukunft* (separation of the arts made real art impossible), and *Oper und Drama* (the current relationship between the poet and musician must be reversed). Now that Wagner's account has caught up with his latest thoughts, it occurs to him to express lavishly his gratitude to LISZT, the ideal friend who helped him continue his career. The very end announces his most recent idea of turning *Siegfrieds Tod* into three dramas with a lengthy Prelude to be performed at a FESTIVAL over four days – in other words, the basic concept of the *RING*.

In sum, Wagner's account at this turning point in his career contains important aesthetic ideas that are woven into his depiction of himself as a misunderstood victim. By drawing in the reader through this style of personal narrative, he aims to create the impression that he is giving special access to a community of like-minded supporters. Compared to the other Zurich writings, *Eine Mitteilung* is surprisingly easy to read; as Ernest NEWMAN put it, it "elucidates so gratefully for us so many dark passages of Opera and Drama."   SANNA PEDERSON

John Deathridge, "Wagner Lives: Issues in Autobiography," *Wagner Beyond Good and Evil* (see bibliography): 3–17.

Rüdiger Krohn, "The Revolutionary of 1848–49," in *The Wagner Handbook*, ed. Ulrich Müller and Peter Wapnewski, trans. John Deathridge (see bibliography): 156–65.

James Treadwell, *Interpreting Wagner* (see bibliography).

"The *Ring* and the Conditions of Interpretation: Wagner's Writing, 1848 to 1852," *Cambridge Opera Journal* 7.3 (1995): 207–31.

Modern music.

1. Boulez on Wagner
2. Wagner and the modern
3. Progress and prose
4. Wagner as model
5. The spirit of Wagner

1. Boulez on Wagner

In an essay accompanying his 1970 BAYREUTH FESTIVAL recording of *PARSIFAL*, the eminent composer and conductor Pierre BOULEZ described Wagner's music as "in a perpetual state of becoming," and declared that it places the emphasis for the first time "on *uncertainty*, indeterminacy, a definite rejection of *finality* and an unwillingness to stabilize musical events before they have exhausted their potential powers of evolution and renewal" (Boulez 254).

Boulez's view of *Parsifal* reflected his own compositional priorities at that time, as found in such major compositions as *Pli selon pli* (1957–62, with later revisions), *Éclat/Multiples* (1970), and *Rituel in memoriam Maderna* (1974–5). Such an emblematic way of understanding Wagner's progressiveness was also evident in an essay of 1963 by the influential philosopher and critic Theodor W. ADORNO, who wrote of "the feeling of leaving solid ground, of drifting into uncertainty" as "precisely what is exciting and also compelling about the experience of Wagnerian music" (Adorno 591).

2. Wagner and the modern

The use of such images to connect Wagner with the world of mid-twentieth-century composition – a world in which traditional "BACH to BRAHMS" ideas about fixed forms and technical processes, which culminated in resolution rather than dissolution, remained subject to radical reappraisal – showed how important it was for more progressive thinkers about modern music to connect Wagner to developments that had taken place since his own time, and to imply that such developments were sanctioned – even made necessary – by Wagner's own progressiveness, his refusal simply to endorse the artistic status quo.

In Wagner's time, the principal institutions of musical life concerned with both performance and academic study were beginning to attach more and more value to the music of the past. "Modern music" was therefore ceasing to be the kind of contemporary composition which owed little or nothing to earlier styles: instead it was beginning to develop those features of dialogue with and opposition to old or earlier music that have become even more sharply defined throughout the era of musical MODERNISM since the late nineteenth century. Nevertheless, when Wagner conceived of

Das KUNSTWERK DER ZUKUNFT (The Artwork of the Future, 1849/50), and later – if only in a spirit of disapproval – of *ZUKUNFTSMUSIK* (Music of the Future, 1860), he did not envisage something so radically different from what was then acceptably contemporary as to abandon such staple features as recognizable thematic materials, regular rhythmic patterns, forms involving prominent use of exact or closely related repetition, and clearly audible distinctions between consonance and dissonance.

3. Progress and prose

Wagner's attitude to progress was rooted more in aesthetic ideals and (in his earlier years) sociopolitical principles than in technical radicalism. He was more concerned to reject what he saw as ideological superficiality and mechanical virtuosity than to promote new levels of technical complexity which would leave his works at risk of lacking that fundamental appeal to the mass of the people which he believed to be the essence of ANCIENT GREEK theater. At the same time, however, his compositional innovations, born of disdain for the glib, stagey effects and stylistic mannerisms of ROSSINI and MEYERBEER, eroded the relatively clear-cut formal elements of earlier opera (aria, recitative, ensemble) in favor of a more intensely expressive process involving many different degrees of connection and juxtaposition, in order to absorb and inspire audiences, not just entertain them. The resulting "uncertainty [and] indeterminacy" (Boulez 254) were balanced to a far greater extent than would be the case in the high modernist music of the twentieth century by the sublimely consonant closural resolutions of the later music dramas.

Nevertheless, from *Das RHEINGOLD* onwards, Wagner adumbrated a kind of "musical prose," as SCHOENBERG termed it in his essay "Brahms the Progressive," which contains a good deal about other composers, including Wagner (416). This musical prose, comprising POETIC-MUSICAL PERIODS of constantly varied phrase-lengths, became associated with an approach to harmony foreshadowing the "emancipation of the dissonance" from its traditional need to resolve onto consonance, and also with the abandonment, after 1909, of many of the harmonic conventions associated with the tonal key system. Those "rhetorical dialectics" – the term devised by Wagner in his late essay *ÜBER DIE ANWENDUNG DER MUSIK AUF DAS DRAMA* (On the Application of Music to Drama, 1879) to describe how dramatic juxtapositions of different materials in the MUSIC DRAMAS were complemented by the smoothest of transitional processes – were therefore available as evidence of an emergent, "post-tonal" modernism which has, arguably, remained the mainstream mode of progressive musical expression ever since.

4. Wagner as model

More immediately, this late nineteenth-century understanding of the nature of Wagner's progressiveness opened up a direct route to the kind of expressionistic post-tonal techniques pioneered by early generations of "post-Wagnerian" composers, including (for a short time) Richard STRAUSS, as well as Berg, Schreker, and Schoenberg himself. And although it was clear that Wagner was not alone in pioneering a progressive approach to harmony – LISZT was is some ways even more radical – it was Wagner's unique compositional achievements, especially in the opera house, and his embodiment of the ideal of the successful creative personality in society who was not primarily a virtuoso performer, which ensured his pre-eminence as a role model for composers who came after. Such pre-eminence was reinforced by the iconic status accorded to the so-called TRISTAN CHORD – often quoted as a specific acknowledgment of its potency, whether in the intensely serious context of Alban Berg's *Lyric Suite* for string quartet (1926) or as a comic allusion to incipient inebriation in Benjamin Britten's opera *Albert Herring* (1947). Many composers from Debussy onwards have used brief Wagner quotations as a means of establishing their own apparent independence from what is quoted, while at the same time acknowledging its continued power: Shostakovich's Symphony No. 15 (1971) is a good example.

During the first three decades after Wagner's death, there was an increasing disparity between composers such as Strauss and MAHLER, who advocated a kind of modern music that acknowledged some aspects of the balance between old and new found in Wagner himself, and those such as Debussy who sought to profit from Wagnerian innovations in form and harmony while rejecting what they felt to be the more blatant and overemphatic expressive characteristics of Wagner's dramatic style. There is a case for saying that Wagner's impact on modern music, whether modernist or otherwise, was so fundamental that he was as responsible for provoking such profoundly anti-Wagnerian initiatives as Erik Satie's Dadaism (a source in turn of John Cage's experimentalism), Stravinsky's neoclassicism, and Bartók's nationalism, as for inspiring the large-scale operatic enterprises (often involving mythic, non-realistic subject-matter) of later German composers such as Hans Werner Henze, Karlheinz Stockhausen, and Wolfgang Rihm. In the same way, even the most prominent opera composers between 1920 and 1970 – Janáček and Britten – who could be said to owe more to Mussorgsky, VERDI, or Puccini than to Wagner, were not unaffected, positively as well as negatively, by what they knew of Wagner's work and thought.

5. The spirit of Wagner

Given that serious music since the nineteenth century evolved into a uniquely pluralistic phenomenon (and even though the twenty-first century is showing signs of a retreat from this) it would be absurd to ascribe that pluralism to a single root cause – the Wagner (or anti-Wagner) style. But it would be equally unwise to deny the defining impact of the model which Wagner provided of an individual driven by an overwhelming creative ambition, and extraordinarily successful (as much from luck as from judgment) in enabling that ambition to be realized as a continued and valued presence on a scene whose institutions and aesthetic ideals have perhaps changed less since his time than they might have done had that presence been less palpable.

A recent demonstration of Wagner's abiding significance for modern music is to be found in his appearance as a (speaking, not singing) character in the opera *Wagner Dream* (2006) by the British composer Jonathan Harvey (b. 1939). *Wagner Dream* is wholly of its time in its progressive, state-of-the-art combination of live and electronic sound, and in the way it allows for the juxtaposition and interaction of two separate yet interdependent dramatic elements – the VENICE of Wagner's last day and the enactment of a version of the Buddhist drama which Wagner only sketched in outline, *Die Sieger*. Had Wagner himself composed any music for *Die Sieger* it would obviously have been utterly different from Harvey's. Yet Harvey's celebration of the Wagnerian spirit, as it confronts a seismic crisis involving spiritual and bodily forces, demonstrates not simply its continued artistic relevance but its ability to retain a core of identity within an infinite adaptability. Two centuries after his birth, modern music – and not just modernist music – remains in thrall to much of what was valued and explored by Wagner as a unique creative force.

ARNOLD WHITTALL

Theodor W. Adorno, "Wagner's relevance for today," in *Essays on Music* (see bibliography): 584–602.
Pierre Boulez, *Orientations*, ed. Jean-Jacques Nattiez (London: Faber & Faber, 1986).
Arnold Schoenberg, "Brahms the Progressive," in *Style and Idea* (see bibliography): 398–441.
Arnold Whittall, "Wagner and 21st-Century Opera," *The Musical Times* (Summer 2008): 5–16.

Modernism. Beginning in the late nineteenth century and particularly associated with the period after World War I, "modernism" denotes a range of movements that advocated a radical break with past conventions and the invention of methods more suited to modernity. This hodgepodge of schools, circles, scholars, and artists – many of whom fiercely disagreed with one another and some of whom resisted identification with "isms" of any kind – is better seen as a complex network than a single stream.

The story of Wagner's impact on modernism begins in nineteenth-century France. Charles BAUDELAIRE's *Richard Wagner et "Tannhäuser" à Paris*, in which the poet approvingly noted the composer's "[a]bsolute, despotic taste for a dramatic ideal . . . in which every detail must ceaselessly contribute to the total effect" (121), planted the seeds of the French cult of Wagner as early as 1861. While the FRANCO-PRUSSIAN WAR temporarily interrupted enthusiasm for things German, French WAGNERISM would burst into full flower with the establishment of the Symbolist journal *La REVUE WAGNÉRIENNE* in 1885. The journal published Stéphane Mallarmé's *Richard Wagner, rêveries d'un poète français* (August 1885), a devotional essay-prose-poem that embraced a vision of theater as a sacred rite for the masses. Odilon Redon's lithograph "Brünnhilde" (1885) and Paul Verlaine's poem "Parsifal" (8 January 1886) would appear in the journal's pages as well, alongside Wagner-inspired works by a virtual catalog of the *fin-de-siècle* AVANT-GARDE, including René Ghil, Stuart Merrill, Charles Morice, J. K. Huysmans, Algernon Swinburne, and Téodor de Wyzewa. Though most strongly identified with the Symbolist movement, French Wagnerism was by no means limited to it, and indeed the Wagner Society of Marseilles counted Émile Zola and Paul Cézanne among its members from the mid-1860s.

The fact that Baudelaire and Zola were both Wagner enthusiasts indicates just how broad and various the composer's influence was. To proclaim oneself a "Wagnerite" implied a certain rejection of bourgeois convention, but beyond that the term might imply anything from revolutionary to reactionary POLITICS, from scientific to mystical attitudes, from the stance of the decadent to that of the *engagé*. Thus an aesthete such as Aubrey BEARDSLEY could compose a series of illustrations of the *RING* cycle while, elsewhere in London, George Bernard SHAW was interpreting the *Ring* as a socialist allegory of capitalism. At times a mutual appreciation for the composer helped bridge significant differences. Writing to Paul Gauguin around 22 January 1889, Vincent van Gogh described his desire to mirror in painting Wagner's achievement in music. Gauguin returned the enthusiasm, describing Wagner as a herald of sacred art and, by October 1889, Gauguin had begun a practice of copying out passages by and about the composer.

One of the most characteristic forms of modernism, the interior monologue, is deeply indebted to the Symbolist reception of Wagner's use of *LEITMOTIV*. The founder of *La revue wagnérienne*, Édouard Dujardin, was explicitly seeking a literary analogue of Wagner's *Leitmotiv* structure when he wrote his pioneering stream-of-consciousness novel *Les Lauriers sont coupés* (We'll to the Woods No More, 1887). James Joyce credited Dujardin's novel for having inspired the narrative form of *Ulysses*, a novel that (like *Finnegans Wake*) includes several references to Wagner. Two other pioneers of internal narrative, Thomas MANN and Virginia WOOLF, attended Wagner performances regularly, were frequent visitors to Bayreuth, and wrote novels rife with Wagnerian allusion. In playwriting, stream-of-consciousness structure emerged with August Strindberg's *Et drömspel* (A Dream Play, 1901) and *Spöksonaten* (Ghost Sonata, 1907), the former of which references *Die MEISTERSINGER* and the latter of which incorporates *Die WALKÜRE*. But perhaps the most clearly indebted literary work of high modernism is T. S. Eliot's *The Waste Land*. The poem, with its motivic structure and episodes of interior monologue, includes two passages from *TRISTAN UND ISOLDE* and two from *GÖTTERDÄMMERUNG*, a section that echoes Act III, Scene 1 of *Götterdämmerung*, and a quotation from Verlaine's "Parsifal" poem. Beneath these surface allusions, of course, lies a rich vein that connects Eliot's use of MYTH to that of Wagner.

The aesthetic form perhaps most strongly associated with Wagner is the *GESAMTKUNSTWERK*, and here too the influence on modernism is profound. A self-proclaimed "Wagner fanatic" until the atmosphere of post-1914 PARIS made such allegiances unfashionable, Sergei Diaghilev sought to marry the most modern forms of music, DANCE, painting, and costuming in his Ballets Russes productions. Similarly, Diaghilev's countryman Wassily Kandinsky decided to devote his life to art after hearing a production of *LOHENGRIN*. Wagner particularly inspired in Kandinsky a passion for the combination of music and the visual arts, a union he explored explicitly in his play *Der gelbe Klang* (Yellow Sound, 1912) and essay *Über das Geistige in der Kunst* (On the Spiritual in Art, 1911), and implicitly in his painting.

Many of Kandinsky's colleagues at the Bauhaus were equally inspired by the *Gesamtkunstwerk* idea, although there was little agreement on just what the term meant. In his 1919 opening address to Bauhaus students, Walter Gropius described the goal of the school as the creation of a "große[s] Gesamtkunstwerk" that would organically unify art-form with art-form, art with technology, art with the people, and the people with one another. For László Moholy-Nagy, on the other hand, the "Theater of Totality" was a fully automated machine, capable of producing "SIMULTANEOUS, SYNOPTICAL, and SYNACOUSTICAL reproductions of thought (with motion pictures, phonographs, loud-speakers)" (62). It is with Moholy-Nagy's vision in particular that we glimpse the role that the *Gesamtkunstwerk* idea will come to play for pioneers of multimedia in the second half of the twentieth century.

The influence of Wagner on modernism, like modernism itself, underwent a profound change after 1933. Given HITLER's promulgation of a Nazified Wagner cult and his attempt to mold the German state into a mass *Gesamtkunstwerk*, many modernists came to see aesthetic totality – and even the entire legacy of Wagner – as inextricable from totalitarianism. Wagner's influence on modernism after 1945, while still pervasive, would become more subterranean.   MATTHEW WILSON SMITH

See also NATIONAL SOCIALISM; NEW MEDIA; WAGNER IN LITERATURE; WAGNER IN THE VISUAL ARTS

Charles Baudelaire, *The Painter of Modern Life*, trans. Jonathan Mayne (London: Phaidon, 1964).
Juliet Koss, *Modernism after Wagner* (Minneapolis: University of Minnesota Press, 2010).
David C. Large and William Weber, eds., *Wagnerism in European Culture and Politics* (see bibliography).
László Moholy-Nagy, "Theatre, Circus, Variety," in *The Theater of the Bauhaus*, ed. W. Gropius and A. S. Wensinger, trans. A. S. Wensinger (Baltimore: Johns Hopkins University Press, 1961).
Matthew Wilson Smith, *The Total Work of Art* (see bibliography).

Modernity. In an essay published in 1878, Wagner noted that the word "modern" in German is both an adjective describing the "new" and a verb meaning "to decay." With the punning title "Modern," the essay set out to describe modernity as a movement that had supposedly begun by striving optimistically for "an entirely new world that has nothing at all to do with the worlds preceding it" (SSD 10:55) only to succumb to debilitating confusion, and above all to JEWS.

This late ANTI-SEMITIC jeremiad, however, shows the ageing Wagner in denial about his earlier involvement with modernity. He writes, for example, that he merely observed "the flowering of the plant" in the literary circles of the YOUNG GERMANY movement in the 1830s, whose members were intent on creating a "new" art opposed to the "orthodoxy" of the old order (SSD 10:56). Nearer the truth is that the young Wagner was heavily influenced by the idea, whose adherents at the time fervently believed that feudal Germany was living in a fatal time warp compared with more progressive societies in England and France.

As Wagner became more attracted to the so-called Left Hegelians in the 1840s, the belief grew. The work of Bruno Bauer and Ludwig FEUERBACH in particular, who were critical of HEGEL's positive attitude to RELIGION and his assumption that the dialectic of history had already come to an end, offered Wagner plenty of ammunition in his ZURICH writings (1849–51) to promote his anti-Christian views and his "new" KUNSTWERK DER ZUKUNFT (Artwork of the Future) that was to triumph in the name of the German spirit (*Geist*) over symphony and opera. BEETHOVEN's "error" – the Young Hegelian mind was never less than eager to point out supposed mistakes made by others about the true course of history – was that he had tried to overcome a bourgeois and naïve Christian belief system in the Ninth Symphony with an instrumental genre that had long since fulfilled its historical task. Opera too, had never escaped the confines of ABSOLUTE MUSIC. ROSSINI sacrificed drama for the sake of melody and MEYERBEER was still demoting his librettist to the role of poetic private secretary. Thus opera could be neither truly dramatic nor socially critical, let alone serve as an adequate vehicle for the utopian drama of the future. The banishment of symphony and opera to the past was therefore deemed to be logical, desirable, and above all irrevocable.

Wagner's role in the "philosophical project of modernity" (Jürgen Habermas) has still to be properly assessed. Wagner was himself only too well aware that his severe Left Hegelian espousal of its values in his Zurich writings was in danger of creating its own orthodoxy. Needless to say, given his sensitivity about positive external relations, he never made these doubts explicit in public. As if to compensate for the lack, the young NIETZSCHE clearly refers to them in the second of his *Untimely Meditations* ("The Use and Abuse of History for Life") where – using the third act of TRISTAN UND ISOLDE as an example – he suggests that Wagner's work is entwined in a paradox. History is dependent on modernity because it needs it for its regeneration. Modernity cannot convincingly assert itself, however, without at the same time being swallowed up by history, thus finding itself unwillingly reintegrated into history's regressive course. The younger Nietzsche presents *Tristan* as a brilliant – and tragic – expression of the dilemma.

An older and more skeptical Nietzsche exhorted his readers on the last page of his polemical *Case of Wagner* (1888) to make a "resolute incision" into Wagner in order to isolate modernity's "antagonistic values." Only in this way can we arrive at a *"diagnosis of the modern soul"* (192; original emphasis). All the tables are turned. In a final *coup de grâce* – probably Nietzsche's most telling point – Wagner is light years away from being a victim of modernity, as his later writings monotonously insist. On the contrary, he is to the last, including the notion of a "good conscience" based on contradictory values arising from an inability to tell the difference between "yes" and "no," its *"most instructive case"* (192; original emphasis). JOHN DEATHRIDGE

John Deathridge, "Moderne," *Wagner und Nietzsche: Kultur – Werk – Wirkung*, ed. Stefan Lorenz Sorgner, H. James Birx, and Nikolaus Knoepffler (Reinbeck bei Hamburg: Rowohlt, 2008): 106–20.

Friedrich Nieztsche, *The Birth of Tragedy and The Case of Wagner*, trans. W. Kaufmann (New York: Vintage, 1967).

Money. Echoing the Bible, Wagner viewed the love of money as the root of all evil, specifically the cause of society's greatest evil – lovelessness. Like Dickens, he required no sacred or philosophical text to arrive at such a view: only bitter experience of hard times.

The composer was born in an age which still generally regarded musicians as little more than servants. The era of patronage altered radically during his lifetime, but that did not open up avenues of easy income for independent musicians. Similarly, when slavery was abolished, how then to feed, clothe, and house the liberated? A freelance career in music was fraught with perils (witness the cases of Schubert and BERLIOZ); orchestral and theater wages were miserable; even a successful composer-conductor such as Lortzing died in penury partly as a result of inadequate pay, partly through being forced to sell his works to theaters for pitifully small sums. Neither in publishing nor in performance were there systems of commissioning, copyright, royalties, or performing rights comparable to more recent times. Standard practice was that with a single payment the management of each theater bought its right to perform a work in perpetuity; sales to each were negotiated separately, and the sums paid varied considerably. Publishers' fees also diverged widely and, without assured success of financial return, they were cautious about paying advances. Only a few composers and virtuosi successfully broke the mold and were able to dictate terms to publishers and theater directors, and they did so pugnaciously: BEETHOVEN, WEBER, SPOHR, MEYERBEER, and LISZT, for example, as well as "star" singers guaranteed to fill the house.

Wagner was acutely conscious of inequalities and injustices ruling the salary system for musicians. His own sources of income were fourfold: (1) from conducting, (2) from publication of his works, (3) from their performance, and (4) from his published writings. He fully realized the potential of money, and understood well the disparate systems governing payment for such talents as his own, which varied considerably not only in the many German states (German copyright law was not regulated until 1870) but in other countries where laws pertaining to performance rights differed widely.

He could be as enterprising as any capitalist; Hans von BÜLOW thought he possessed financial genius fit for a career as a banker. But optimism fatally blinded him to any real business sense. The recurring trap into which he fell was that his idealism always overstepped reality. Without that idealism, total self-conviction, and ambitious determination there would have been no Richard Wagner, no Bayreuth. These qualities however outstripped social realities and mundane practicalities. His utter belief in himself, the unshakable certainty that he was creating works of the highest importance and beauty to be enjoyed by the world for ever more, led him always to expect pecuniary support. Fortunately there were those who shared his belief in himself: a succession of well-meaning, disinterested creditors and generous benefactors over several decades, the most important from his Swiss exile onward being Franz Liszt, Julie RITTER, Otto WESENDONCK, and LUDWIG II of Bavaria, none of whom expected material return for their investment in him.

Wagner's income before 1850 mostly derived from conducting (see WAGNER AS CONDUCTOR). Income from the podium after 1849 was much more sporadic, undertaken mainly to sustain him during the composition of his works, and subsequently as fundraising for Bayreuth. Pay in his first posts was negligible and patchy; in each town he accrued debts. The thirty months in Paris proved financially disastrous, his only earnings being work for Maurice SCHLESINGER and the occasional sale of a song or text. He narrowly escaped debtors' jail. On taking up his DRESDEN court appointment, he was pursued by creditors, who never ceased to worry him. His Dresden salary was good: 1,500 thalers per annum. (His senior colleague REISSIGER received 2,000 thalers, as did Otto Nicolai in Berlin in 1847.) A financially prudent married man could have lived comfortably on this. The rent on his Ostra Allee apartment (see Appendix 3: Wagner's addresses) was 220 thalers per annum, which the court theater director thought extravagant in cost and furnishings. A piano was bought from BREITKOPF & HÄRTEL for 440 thalers with a down-payment of 240 thalers. (Breitkopf had to wait until 1851 for the rest of their money, when they acquired the rights to publish LOHENGRIN in liquidation of the debt.) To help him pay what he considered his principal debts of honor, mainly to friends and family, SCHRÖDER-DEVRIENT of her own accord lent him 1,000 thalers. Other income was a generous 300 thalers from the Dresden Hoftheater for their performing rights for RIENZI plus their fee for FLIEGENDER HOLLÄNDER. Beyond Dresden in the 1840s, interest in his works was slow and sporadic; consequently he earned little from sales of them to theaters.

The disastrous decision to publish *Rienzi*, *Holländer*, and *Tannhäuser* at his own expense (i.e., on credit) led to ever-increasing debts not only to the music-seller Meser but to a widening circle of creditors. Schröder-Devrient suddenly demanded repayment of her loan. He proposed to Breitkopf that they buy the rights to these published scores by agreeing to pay off Meser. In declining, they missed a golden opportunity they would rue later. In August 1846, the Dresden Theater Pension Fund lent him an unprecedented 5,000 thalers at 5 percent interest; repayments to be 500 thalers annually, with the composer also taking out a life insurance policy at 3 percent on the capital amount. To adhere to such a scheme would have required rigorous economy. Two years later things were so much worse that Wagner appealed for a salary increase of 500 thalers per annum. It is difficult to estimate the potential consequences of the financial catastrophe that loomed when Wagner was forced to flee in the wake of the DRESDEN UPRISING of May 1849. One of his firmest friends to lend him aid at this time and afterwards was Dr. Anton PUSINELLI.

For Wagner, the legendary Nibelung Hoard was present in the modern world like some monstrous curse through the worship of gold and money which enslaved the ordinary man, corrupted the aristocracy, severed friend from friend, and so undermined society. He deeply detested accumulated wealth. He was well aware too that his indifference to the value of money and his inability to save it had led him to unspeakable personal suffering (letter to Pusinelli, 13 January 1870).

In ZURICH, his fairly regular orchestral conducting (1850–5) saw him well paid: by 1854 earning 100 Swiss francs [SF] per concert – a sum amounting to over a month's rent for an apartment. From 1851 to 1859 he benefited from an annual pension provided by Julie Ritter of 800 thalers (= SF 3,000; half of his old Dresden salary). Living expenses in Zurich he calculated at SF 17 per week (including rent). The rent on his ground floor flat in the Zeltweg from September 1851 was moderate; but in April 1853 he and MINNA removed to a larger second-floor apartment, involving more expense and the purchase of rich furnishings on credit. They were able to entertain guests more easily and, although by all reports their hospitality was not ostentatious, Wagner acknow-ledged that Liszt on his first Zurich visit "was startled into admiration of what he termed my *petite elegance*" (ML/E 495).

All this comfort was procured with great expectation of income from the "hailstorm" of interest in *Tannhäuser* among German theaters. In 1852–3 he did indeed earn a respectable amount from these performances (Ernest NEWMAN computed it as SF 7,500) but it was insufficient to meet needs at home, costs of recent foreign travel, and debts to local tradesmen. Ernest Newman, whose four-volume *Life* remains one of the most balanced guides through the composer's complex finances, comments: "Before the modern world censures Wagner for his borrowings, it ought ... to remember that had German composers in those days received anything like justice at the hands of theaters, a continuing royalty being paid to them as is the case today, Wagner would have been able to live comfortably for a considerable time on *Tannhäuser* alone" (Newman 2:411). The pattern of lavish purchases and luxurious accommodation, furnished on borrowed money in misplaced expectation of impending prosperity, was to repeat itself almost exactly in Paris and Penzing (VIENNA) during the next decade.

Meanwhile, by summer 1854 he was borrowing desperately from Jacob SULZER, Liszt, and others. To the rescue came Otto Wesendonck that fall, clearing Wagner's declared debts of SF 7,000, and guaranteeing him a quarterly income of SF 500. Sulzer was appointed to handle Wagner's financial affairs. In April 1856, Otto increased the quarterly income by SF 250, thus matching Julie Ritter's annual allowance of SF 3,000. Wesendonck always ensured his dealings with Wagner were entered into as "business arrangements" for the sake of propriety, but knew he was effectively the composer's patron, being wise enough to realize he had need of a certain degree of comfort that brought tranquillity for creative work. The "Asyl" property was a case in point: it was rented to the Wagners for SF 1,000 per annum, an amount only partly defrayed.

Wesendonck also joined the quite complex chain of investment in the *RING* scores. When Breitkopf backed off from involvement with them (although they had published *Tristan und Isolde*, paying Wagner 6,000 francs for his score) Otto offered Wagner another loan. The composer declined this one and suggested instead a business arrangement (August 1859): that he sell Otto the copyright for the *Ring* dramas at the same rate of 6,000 francs per score. Otto immediately paid 12,000 francs for the first two operas, and another 6,000 for the as yet unfinished *SIEGFRIED* in 1860. SCHOTT bought the publishing rights to *Das RHEINGOLD* in January of that year for 10,000 francs. By rights 6,000 of this was due to Otto, but Schott's entire fee had been swallowed up by the losses on Wagner's ORCHESTRAL CONCERTS in Paris. Wagner's shrewd solution was to offer Otto a receipt for the sum due to him some day for the final opera of the *Ring* cycle, as a means of paying back the 6,000 francs for *Rheingold*. Otto acquiesced. And so on it went. With the Bavarian government in 1864, an entirely new contract for future performance rights of the cycle was negotiated in exchange for generous further payments to Wagner.

Meanwhile Franz Schott advanced 10,000 francs for *Die MEISTERSINGER* in December 1861, Wagner promising them the complete score (not a note of which had been written) a year hence. There followed a six-year history of the work's creation, punctuated by pleas from Wagner to the publisher for further advances. This of October 1862 from Biebrich:

> You are mistaken, my dear Herr *Schott!* You are greatly mistaken as to the way in which a man like me may be treated. Many things may be extorted by hunger, but not works of a higher nature. Or do you think that when my cares prevent me from sleeping at night, I shall be serenely cheerful the next

day, and full of good ideas for my work? The "Mastersingers" would have been very close to completion by now if you had taken due care of me since the date when I first settled here for that very purpose.

Schott's stiff rejoinder was to point out that not he, but only some enormously rich banker or a prince with millions to spend could provide for Wagner's needs and comforts.

Despite the lucrative success of his RUSSIAN tour Wagner was drawn again into a vortex of debt by spring 1864. His summons to MUNICH and Ludwig II's patronage entirely altered his financial future. But in stating such a well-known fact it must be remembered that anxiety over monetary matters never really left him. As long as Ludwig reigned, Wagner and his family were certain of a home and necessary comfort. Yet, the TRIBSCHEN idyll aside, pecuniary cares large and small were omnipresent. The Munich period was fraught with fiscal scandal and the reawakening of the specters of creditors from over three decades. In the Bayreuth years, the nagging toll of funding the building of the theater, the initial festivals, and the recouping of the losses of 1876 echoes through the pages of his CORRESPONDENCE and his wife's diary.

On almost no other artist in history has the weight of unthinking moral opprobrium rested so heavily as on Richard Wagner. His borrowing and his profligacy have been untiringly criticized and caricatured. An unbiased observer of his affairs should see that his financial calamities were overwhelmingly the result of his altruism and his innate need to achieve recognition. As early as his MAGDEBURG job, large-hearted devotion to the cause of art is evident in his tour in search of singers for the company through southern Germany and Austria, undertaken (foolishly) at his own expense. The Meser misadventure again illustrates more than anything the venturesome altruist.

He was frequently prodigal to others in need. He never could be accused of being mean. To quote Robert von Hornstein: "Throughout his life he suffered from fits of generosity and sympathy, when he would give away a thaler instead of a groschen; this did not pay the bills" (Spencer 96).

Gregarious by nature, he strove ever to be a kind host, especially to the talented young people who almost always surrounded him. In turn, he was notably demonstrative, frequently effusive, in expressing gratitude to those who had helped him as to those who meant much to him. To Minna, after their separation, and for Natalie (PLANER) too, he made sound provision. In his letters of support, through his practical help, by way of gifts, and quite selfless, genuine acts of affection, he can rarely be called an ingrate.

DEREK WATSON

Robert von Hornstein, *Memoiren* (Munich: Süddeutsche Monatshefte, 1908).

Hanjo Kesting, ed., *Das Pump-Genie: Richard Wagner und das Geld* (Frankfurt am Main: Eichborn, 1993).

Ernest Newman, *The Life of Richard Wagner* (see bibliography).

Stewart Spencer, *Wagner Remembered* (see bibliography).

Chris Walton, *Richard Wagner's Zurich* (see bibliography).

Morality. Historians often adopt a tone of prurient hypocrisy with figures of whom they disapprove. The Russian Empress Catherine the Great long endured persistent references to her "scandalous" love life: that is, she was a successful female ruler with the temerity to take lovers. It has become the practice for moral custodians, FRICKAS *de nos jours*, to berate Wagner for his easy way with other men's money and women. Understanding both as property is instructive, betokening a narrow conception of "morality," typical of the public opinion and commercial press by which Wagner not unreasonably considered himself hounded. Wagner believed consistently that private property distorted every relationship between man and man, likewise man and woman. Shortly before his death, he lauded Wilhelm Heinse for having depicted in his novel *Ardinghello* (1787) a society in which institution of property had never been permitted (CWD 30 September 1882).

French socialism, directly and through intermediaries such as Heinrich LAUBE, August RÖCKEL, and Mikhail BAKUNIN, was a pervading influence. As early as *Das LIEBESVERBOT*, Wagner tells us, "all I cared about was to uncover the sinfulness of hypocrisy and the artificiality of the judicial attitude toward morality" (ML/E 83). Friedrich, prudishly shocked by popular licentiousness, employs state power to enforce an unnatural moral code, whilst transgressing it himself. Röckel, during their DRESDEN discussions, provided theoretical ballast: "On the basis of the socialist theories of Proudhon and others ... he constructed a whole new moral order of things to which ... he little by little converted me ... I began to rebuild upon it my hopes for the realization of my artistic ideals." Wagner questioned Röckel about his desire "to do away completely with the institution of marriage as we knew it," and was "particularly struck" by the claim that, only after eradication of coercion by money, rank, and family prejudice, would sexual morality be possible (ML/E 373–4). He returned in his final essay *Über das Weibliche* to the subject. Marriage – to COSIMA, at least? – raised man and his moral faculties far above the animal world, yet he was dragged far beneath it by "conventional marriage" (*Konventionsheiraten*), an "abuse" (*Mißbrauch*) founded upon property (SSD 12:343–4).

Self-justification? Perhaps, for instance when Wagner tells us that Minna "became increasingly perplexed at my seemingly incomprehensible conception of art and its relative importance," and at his "higher delicacy in regard to moral questions," being "unable to understand and approve my freedom of thought in such matters" (ML/E 130–1). Only up to a point, though, for the contrast between Minna's need for financial stability and the moral purpose Wagner sought in art is real enough. That they were ultimately unsuited need not send one scurrying for blame. There is, moreover, no mistaking Wagner's moral outrage at his perception of modern art as "industry, its moral purpose the acquisition of money, its aesthetic purpose the entertainment of the bored" (SSD 3:18).

Under the influence of YOUNG GERMAN and Young Hegelian ideas, most likely including Max Stirner's anarchistic manifesto, *The Ego and its Own* (1844), Wagner created in the *RING* an artwork that dramatizes alternative moral possibilities. Fricka, Wagner writes, represents custom (*Sitte*) (Wagner to Uhlig, 12 November 1851). Her marriage to WOTAN is fruitless; his children are sired outside wedlock. One of them, SIEGLINDE, experiences both brutal treatment as chattel by her husband HUNDING, and passionate convention-flouting fulfillment with her twin brother, SIEGMUND. Fricka is outraged: "My heart trembles, my mind reels: bridal embrace between brother and sister!

When was it ever heard of that siblings were lovers?" (*Walküre*, Act II, Scene I). As the gods' – religion's – hold on society falters, moral prohibitions dependent upon their power are insisted upon ever more stridently. The gods would go to ruin, Fricka insists, were her moral law not to be obeyed; they already have. Wagner echoes Stirner and prefigures NIETZSCHE, providing a crucial link in the inversion of HEGEL's elevation of customary over individual morality: "Note how a 'moral man' behaves, who today often thinks he is through with God ... a customary-moral shudder will come over him at the conception of one's being allowed to touch his sister also as a woman ... Because he *believes* in those moral commandments" (Stirner 45); and "They have rid themselves of the Christian God, and thus believe that they must cling all the more firmly to Christian morality ... one must, in response to the smallest emancipation from theology, reassert one's position in awe-inspiring fashion as a moral fanatic" (Nietzsche 80).

What, then, of the pre-eminent "affair," with Mathilde WESENDONCK? One can deplore Wagner's ingratitude towards her husband, Otto, who had offered considerable financial support, only to find himself cuckolded – at least metaphysically. Wagner opposed marriage as legal setting in stone or ring. Moreover, Wagner's insistence that the world owed him a living – why should someone be favored because he dealt in silks instead of composing the *Ring*? – is borne out even in capitalist terms by the industry he created for and bequeathed that world. It has done incalculably better from him than *vice versa*.

One might also consider it significant that, when Wagner condensed the action of TRISTAN UND ISOLDE into a few words for Mathilde Wesendonck, he did not even mention King Marke's forgiveness. Were the sacrifices of men such as Wesendonck and Hans von BÜLOW as naught to such a monstrous ego? Yet Wagner sees the "custom of the time" leading to the sin of marriage for POLITICS' sake. The action of *Tristan* is not, moreover, really of this phenomenal world at all, but metaphysical. By now (1859), Wagner had partially converted to a morality founded upon SCHOPENHAUER's teaching. Though immediately taken by Schopenhauer's AESTHETICS, "the moral principles" of *The World as Will and Representation* had been more difficult initially to accept, "for here the annihilation of the Will and complete self-abnegation are represented as the only true means of redemption from the constricting bonds of individuality in its dealings with the world" (ML/E 509). Either way – in practice, both – Wagner rejected the dictates of bourgeois morality.

MARK BERRY

See also LOVE

Mark Berry, "The Positive Influence of Wagner upon Nietzsche," *The Wagner Journal*, 2.2 (2008): 11–28.

Friedrich Nietzsche, *Twilight of the Idols / The Anti-Christ*, trans. R. J. Hollingdale, with an introduction by Michael Tanner (Harmondsworth: Penguin, 1990).

Max Stirner, *The Ego and its Own*, trans. Steven Byington, ed. David Leopold (Cambridge University Press, 1995).

Mottl, Felix (b. Unter-St. Veit [near Vienna], 24 Aug. 1856; d. Munich, 2 July 1911), Austrian conductor. As a student at the Vienna Conservatory, Mottl was an ardent admirer of Wagner's works. After impressing the composer with his piano rendition of several passages from the as yet unperformed *RING*, he became one of the members of the so-called NIBELUNG CHANCELLERY that helped to prepare its first performances. Mottl was charged in particular with helping to coach Emil SCARIA in the role of HAGEN (although Scaria ultimately was unable to participate in the festival for financial reasons) and Amalie MATERNA in that of BRÜNNHILDE. In the wake of this BAYREUTH experience, which he recognized as the cornerstone on which his career and vocation were built, Mottl moved on to several appointments as a conductor before settling in Karlsruhe (1881–1903), which he elevated to one of the leading and most innovative operatic centers in Germany, producing to great acclaim operas by BERLIOZ, CORNELIUS, Chabrier, Schubert, and many other modern or neglected composers. Even so, Karlsruhe became known as "little Bayreuth" because of Mottl's tireless championing of Wagner's works.

COSIMA WAGNER first called on Mottl to conduct at Bayreuth in 1886, when she prepared the first production there of TRISTAN UND ISOLDE. He became the conductor with whom Cosima worked most closely, and his career at Bayreuth lasted until 1906 (her final season as festival director). He appeared at eleven of the thirteen festivals during those two decades, being entrusted with the Bayreuth premieres of TANNHÄUSER (1891), LOHENGRIN (1894), and Der FLIEGENDE HOLLÄNDER (1901), and conducting MEISTERSINGER in 1892, the Ring in 1896, and PARSIFAL in 1888 and 1897. To this day, he remains the only conductor to have led all ten of the canonical Wagner operas at Bayreuth. Of the leading conductors there, it was he who earned the most opprobrium for the so-called "Bayreuth tempi," regarded in many circles as slow and dragging. Other observers, however, recognized in his performances a remarkable ability to coordinate musical effects with the drama playing out on the stage, and certain of his singers found his interpretations unmatched because of the Dionysian intensity that emerged from the lyrical breadth and sonorous depth he cultivated.

Mottl conducted several times in LONDON (notably the Ring at Covent Garden in 1898 and 1900), and at the Metropolitan Opera in New York in the 1903–4 season, but his last major appointment was at the MUNICH Hofoper (1903–11), which like Karlsruhe profited immensely from his advocacy of novelties, his passionate attachment to the works of Wagner, and his enviable powers of musical preparation and identification. He suffered a heart attack during his 100th performance of TRISTAN and died eleven days later.

Mottl was a prolific composer and orchestrator; his most notable contribution to the Wagner canon is his version (which has become standard) of the four WESENDONCK LIEDER, which Wagner himself did not orchestrate. In the latter years of his life, Mottl prepared editions of eight of Wagner's operas, which remain valuable for the inclusion of instructions Mottl gleaned from Wagner during rehearsals for performances he supervised, as well as for reflecting Mottl's own practical experience with the works.

DAVID BRECKBILL

Frithjof Haas, Der Magier am Dirigentenpult: Felix Mottl (Karlsruhe: Info, 2006).
Thomas Seedorf, "Ein treuer Diener seines Herrn: Richard Wagner und Felix Mottl," wagnerspectrum 5.1 (2009): 47–63.
Egon Voss, Die Dirigenten der Bayreuther Festspiele (see bibliography).

Mozart, Wolfgang Amadeus (b. Salzburg, 27 Jan. 1756; d. Vienna, 5 Dec. 1791), child prodigy and Viennese classicist composer who wrote for all instrumental combinations and musical genres, including landmark operas. Wagner's engagement with Mozart reaches back to the earliest stages of his career when, for his debut as a conductor on 2 August 1834 at Bad Lauchstädt near Weimar, he performed on short notice *Don Giovanni*, an opera that continued to preoccupy him to the end of his life. Mozart's *Requiem* had by this time already made a deep impression on the young musician. Another Mozart opera that exerted an impact was *Die Zauberflöte* (The Magic Flute), which influenced features of Wagner's first opera, *Die FEEN* (The Fairies, 1834). Both *Die Zauberflöte* and *Die Feen* draw on the legacy of the eighteenth-century Venetian dramatist Carlo Gozzi. Gozzi's dramatic fables blend richly symbolic fairy-tale plots with the farcical improvisatory practice of the *commedia dell'arte*. In *Die Feen*, based on Gozzi's *La donna serpente*, Wagner incorporated into Act II a duet for Gernot and Drolla that recalls Papageno and Papagena in *Zauberflöte*. The trials endured by Arindal leading to his reunion with Ada as the couple assumes leadership of the Fairy Realm at the conclusion also parallel events in *Zauberflöte*. Wagner's early passion for Gozzi and Mozart alike was stimulated by his keen admiration of E. T. A. HOFFMANN's writings. Hoffmann had recommended the use of Gozzi's theater pieces as opera plots, and his enthusiasm for Mozart was so great that in 1813 – the year of Wagner's birth – he changed his third name to Amadeus in homage to the composer.

By the end of his period at RIGA in 1839, Wagner had conducted Mozart's *Die Entführung aus dem Serail* (The Abduction from the Seraglio) and *Le nozze di Figaro* (The Marriage of Figaro) as well as further performances of *Don Giovanni* and *Die Zauberflöte*. In his own operas from his years at DRESDEN during the 1840s, an affinity to Mozartian models sometimes surfaces, as for instance in ORTRUD's scornfully triumphant final passage in LOHENGRIN, which suggests the influence of Elektra's vengeful concluding aria in *Idomeneo*. While in ZURICH (1850), Wagner produced his own performing version for a new production of *Don Giovanni*.

For the composer of TRISTAN UND ISOLDE, Mozart was "the great *Chromatiker*." An aspect of *Don Giovanni* that captivated Wagner was the uncanny, pervasively chromatic, D minor music associated with the death of the Commendatore, the masked avengers, and the great scene near the conclusion when Don Giovanni confronts the Stone Guest. Its expressive power, enhanced by syncopations and subtleties in orchestration, foreshadows certain features of Wagner's mature musical style. The all-embracing, large-scale continuity of Mozart's musical-dramatic conception also stirred Wagner, who referred in various writings to the overture – with its two sharply contrasted moods, the imposing *Andante* foreshadowing the scene of Giovanni's downfall, followed by the *Molto Allegro* in D major – as well as to the swift pacing of the ensuing scene leading to the slaying of the Commendatore in D minor.

Wagner marveled at the power of Mozart's melodic invention, which he understood as derived from the style of classical Italian singing. Wagner found this melodic quality generally lacking in the music of his own contemporaries. In his treatise *Über das Dirigiren* (On Conducting, 1869), Wagner writes that Mozart's musical originality "shows to greatest advantage in the vocal character of the melodies," and he insists that interpreters must seek to convey the "extraordinarily expressive vocal character of [Mozart's] instrumental themes." In the same treatise, Wagner stressed the importance in performance of making adjustments in tempo, as for example at the end of the overture to *Don Giovanni* (see WAGNER AS CONDUCTOR).

Wagner's passionate response to *Don Giovanni* was conditioned by Hoffmann's haunting "Don Juan" narrative from his *Fantasiestücke in Callot's Manier* (1810). Hoffmann's vivid retelling of Mozart's and da Ponte's opera decisively revises the conclusion, changing the destiny of Donna Anna, who becomes the consecrated bride of the doomed, demonic Don Giovanni. As related by Hoffmann, the power of the narrative transcends the sphere of art; the singer of Donna Anna, obsessed with her role, dies during the night following the performance. The dramatic parallel to a Wagnerian heroine such as SENTA is unmistakable. COSIMA Wagner describes in her diary their evening reading of Hoffmann's "Don Juan" on 26 September 1870, stating that "Donna Anna and her death reminded me of *Tristan* and Schnorr," alluding thereby to the death after a performance in MUNICH in 1865 of Ludwig Schnorr von CAROLSFELD, who premiered the role of Tristan. Hoffmann's depiction of the death of the soprano singing Donna Anna was reportedly based on a real incident that occurred at Posen around 1800.

COSIMA WAGNER'S DIARY entries from the last decade of Wagner's life often preserve his comments about Mozart. As she recorded in her diary entry of 7 August 1874, Wagner felt that "in the whole figure of Sarastro – Mozart for the first time sounded the note of a masculine dignity and cordiality which one might describe as German, which had been unknown before his time." In composing his final drama, PARSIFAL, Wagner evidently drew on the precedent of Mozart's Sarastro in lending gravity to the important bass role of his narrator figure GURNEMANZ. The thoughtful, dignified bearing of Gurnemanz supports this association, and his stepwise ascending vocal line in B major in Act I ("selbst zu ihm erkoren"), as he takes PARSIFAL with him to the Grail Service, bears comparison to passages in Sarastro's E major aria "In diesen heil'gen Hallen" (Act II, *Zauberflöte*). Another individual number from that same Mozart opera that impressed Wagner was Pamina's heartbreaking G minor aria "Ach, ich fühl's," as Cosima noted after a performance they attended on 11 November 1880.

A bias on Wagner's part against Mozart's purely instrumental forms surfaces in her entry from 5 January 1881: "R[ichard] considers the form of the Mozart concertos extraordinarily clumsy, with some nice ideas scattered throughout." To the end of his life, Wagner's undiminished admiration for his artistic predecessor remained grounded in those two operas that had so aroused his enthusiasm as a young man. On 23 February 1878, she writes that "After lunch R[ichard] comes back to Mozart, and particularly *Die Zauberflöte*; he says that certain things in it marked a turning point in the history of art; Sarastro introduced dignity of spirit in place of conventional dignity. – Certain things in Mozart will and can never be excelled, he says." Later that year, on 12 November, while reflecting on Donna Anna's music in *Don Giovanni*, Wagner proudly declared himself "the last of the Mozartians."   WILLIAM KINDERMAN

See also WAGNER AS CONDUCTOR

Muchanoff-Kalergis, Marie von (née von Nesselrode) (b. Warsaw, 7 Aug. 1822; d. Warsaw, 22 May 1874), Polish pianist and patron of the arts. Wagner's *Das JUDENTUM IN DER MUSIK* (Jewishness in Music) of 1850 was reissued in 1869 by J. J. Weber (LEIPZIG), with a new introduction and a new dedication to Marie Muchanoff, the former Countess Kalergis, an intimate friend who had offered generous support to Wagner during his sojourn in PARIS in and around 1860. In Paris, Countess Kalergis – the niece of Count Nesselrode (foreign minister for the Russian tsars Alexander I and Nicholas I) – belonged to the circle of Princess METTERNICH and the emperor Napoleon III. She had studied piano with Chopin, who said she played "very well," and was praised both by BERLIOZ and by LISZT. It was for her that Wagner, during the summer of 1860, organized a private reading of the second act of *TRISTAN UND ISOLDE* with Karl KLINDWORTH at the piano, Pauline Viardot as Isolde, Wagner as Tristan, and Berlioz as auditor.

By dedicating the new version of his pamphlet to the Countess, and arranging it to satisfy her curiosity, Wagner surely assumed that Muchanoff-Kalergis was sympathetic to his "cause." Her biographer nonetheless claims that she was surprised, on Easter Sunday 1869, to receive the extravagant dedication of *Das Judentum in der Musik*. PETER BLOOM

Marie von Mouchanoff-Kalergis, *Briefe an ihre Tochter. Ein Lebens- und Charakterbild,* ed. La Mara [Marie Lipsius], 2nd edn. (Leipzig: Breitkopf & Härtel, 1911).
Constantin Photiadès, *La "Symphonie en blanc majeur": Marie Kalergis née Comtesse Nesselrode* (Paris: Plon, 1924).

Muck, Karl (b. Darmstadt, 22 Oct. 1859; d. Stuttgart, 3 March 1940), conductor, studied classical philology in Heidelberg and music in Leipzig. His first major position was at the Landestheater in Prague, where he acquired a reputation as a conductor of Wagner before joining the Berlin Royal Opera as Kapellmeister (1892) and *Generalmusikdirektor* (1908). He conducted operas throughout Europe and had considerable success in America with the Boston Symphony Orchestra (1906–8; 1912–18), although his final season was marred by political controversy which resulted in his temporary internment. In 1922, he became conductor of the Hamburg Philharmonic, which he directed until his retirement in 1933. His last important appearance was in 1933 at a concert in LEIPZIG marking the 50th anniversary of Wagner's death. Muck assisted both COSIMA and SIEGFRIED WAGNER at BAYREUTH, conducting *PARSIFAL* at every Festival from 1901 until 1930. He was one of the first conductors to advocate fidelity to the score over the older, more subjective tradition of conducting. His extensive legacy of Wagner recordings is amongst the most important from the early electrical era. ROGER ALLEN

See also PERFORMANCE, CONDUCTORS; PERFORMANCE, RECORDING HISTORY

Harold C. Schonberg, *The Great Conductors* (London: Victor Gollancz, 1968): 216–22.

Müller, Christian Gottlieb (b. Nieder-Oderwitz near Zittau, 6 Feb. 1800; d. Altenburg, 29 June 1863), violinist, composer, conductor, and teacher. Müller was a member of the LEIPZIG Gewandhaus Orchestra, and conducted Leipzig's amateur Euterpe Society. Wagner studied harmony with Müller between 1828 and 1831; these lessons were initially carried out in secret. JAMES DEAVILLE

Muncker, Theodor (b. Bayreuth, 29 May 1823; d. Bayreuth, 14 Feb. 1900), long-serving mayor of Bayreuth. After legal studies at Erlangen and Munich, Muncker joined Bayreuth's municipal administration, becoming the town's mayor on 29 March 1863, a position he held until his death. As mayor, Muncker promoted schooling, public health, and a modernization of the communal infrastructure. Encouraged by his friend and colleague, Friedrich FEUSTEL, he also became a key supporter of Wagner's BAYREUTH FESTIVAL idea. The mayor repeatedly used his influence and connections to win the necessary administrative approvals for Wagner's undertaking. He personally recommended the site on the Green Hill for the FESTIVAL THEATER, facilitated Wagner's acquisition of the plot on which WAHNFRIED was built, and was a founding member of the Festival's three-person management committee (with Feustel and Dr. Käfferlein). Muncker was also the first and long-serving president of the Allgemeine Richard-Wagner-Verein as well as chairman of the association's Bayreuth chapter.   ANTHONY J. STEINHOFF

Munich, originally settled in the twelfth century and, since 1506, the capital city of Bavaria. It is located on the River Isar north of the Bavarian Alps, today the third largest city in Germany. After 1864, given the financial support of LUDWIG II, King of Bavaria, Munich became a focal point of Richard Wagner's life.
1.   1864–1865
2.   After 1865

1. 1864–1865

On March 24/25 1864, Wagner stopped in Munich during his escape from creditors in VIENNA. A few weeks later, on 3 May, the Bavarian cabinet secretary Franz Seraph von PFISTERMEISTER caught up with him in Stuttgart to present an official invitation from the newly crowned Ludwig II. The next day Wagner and his new patron met in Munich. Less than five months later, the composer seized the opportunity to move into a luxurious new home at 21 Brienner Straße, not far from the royal residence.

Since the 1820s, opera had become increasingly popular in the Bavarian metropolis through construction of the National Theater and the work of Franz Lachner (1803–90), first as a Court Kapellmeister and then as music director (*Generalmusikdirektor*). Both ensured an up-to-date and aptly urban music theater and a sophisticated orchestral culture. In 1855 and 1858 respectively, *TANNHÄUSER* and *LOHENGRIN* were staged in the National Theater – one of their later performances on 2 February 1861 is said to have been the epiphanous experience of the then crown prince Ludwig.

In 1864 Wagner added to the Munich Wagner repertoire by conducting the first performance of Der *FLIEGENDE HOLLÄNDER*. He also brought in two of his closest musical companions, Hans von BÜLOW and Peter CORNELIUS. In February of 1865, however, there appeared the first critical newspaper comments about Wagner's hold over the king to the detriment of the people and the state treasury. To the horror of the royal Bavarian cabinet, Gottfried SEMPER was commissioned by the king to draw up plans and build a model for a FESTIVAL THEATER on the Isar's high bank (not far from where the

Munich Philharmonic Hall at the Gasteig opened in 1985). By the end of 1864, another opponent of Wagner's besides Pfistermeister, Bavaria's Prime Minister Ludwig Freiherr von der PFORDTEN, had joined the cabinet's ranks (Wagner called this couple "Pfi" and "Pfo").

Wagner's relationship with Ludwig went through several periods of estrangement, the first maybe as early as February of 1865, when the king did not attend performances of *Der fliegende Holländer* and *Tannhäuser*. As a consequence, the king did not attend a special performance of *Tannhäuser* starring Ludwig Schnorr von CAROLSFELD. But, soon after that, the preparations for the world premiere of *TRISTAN UND ISOLDE* began. The birth of Wagner's and COSIMA's first child, ISOLDE (10 April 1865), coincided with the rehearsal period. During the following summer, as Wagner started to dictate *MEIN LEBEN* (My Life, 1865–81) to Cosima and wrote the prose draft of *PARSIFAL*, the political situation came to a head in terms of both Ludwig's inner circle and the pressure Bavaria faced in its precarious position between the feuding states of Prussia and Austria-Hungary. The fact that Wagner expressed his political opinions not only privately but in writing – *ÜBER STAAT UND RELIGION* (On State and Religion, 1864) and *WAS IST DEUTSCH?* (What is German?, 1865/78) – that he tried to exert influence over the composition of the king's cabinet, and that he supposedly received a large amount of money to pay off his debts in addition to receiving a royal pension, finally made the government issue an ultimatum to the king: to choose between the love of the people or to continue his friendship with the composer, which, given the monarch's shy behavior, seemed even more intimate than it was. Ludwig gave in, and on 10 December 1865 Wagner left Munich in secret.

2. After 1865

When on 22 May 1866 Ludwig paid Wagner a secret birthday visit at his home in TRIBSCHEN, Wagner managed – yet again – to conceal the true nature of his relationship to Cosima (though rumors abounded) and to convince his patron not to abdicate, as a telegram to Wagner from 15 May 1866 proves. But there were tensions again between Ludwig and Wagner regarding the Munich *Lohengrin* production (summer 1867), namely about the casting of Wagner's companion Joseph TICHATSCHEK, 60 years old at the time, in the title role. At the hugely successful world premiere of *Die MEISTERSINGER VON NÜRNBERG* on 21 July 1868, Wagner sat in the royal box, but this was the last glow of a fading fire. When the relationship between Wagner and Cosima became public, the correspondence between Wagner and the king was suspended. The world premieres of *Das RHEINGOLD* and *Die WALKÜRE* strained the relationship between the two even further, because Ludwig II insisted on them despite Wagner's protests.

During the 1870s, the Munich Wagner repertoire grew, first with *RIENZI* (1871), and in November 1878 with the first complete performance of the *RING* cycle outside of Bayreuth. On 12 November that year, when Wagner conducted the Prelude to *Parsifal* in a private performance, he and Ludwig II met for the last time. Hermann LEVI's appointment as Court Kapellmeister in 1872 was another milestone in the Wagnerization of Munich.

After Wagner's death, the gap between Bayreuth and Munich grew larger, exemplified by another private performance of *Parsifal* for Ludwig II, this time in violation of Wagner's copyright, though he did not live to see the posthumous world premiere of *Die FEEN* on 29 June 1888. The opening of the Prinzregententheater (1901), which can be compared to the Bayreuth Festival Theater in design, was greeted with great suspicion by Cosima. The inauguration of the Munich Opera Festivals in 1904 once again unsettled the hitherto sole reign of the "Green Hill," even more so as Felix MOTTL left his indelible mark on the Munich Festival in its early years. Since then this tradition has continued. A special highlight of this tradition was the performance in 1983 of all Wagner's operas under the baton of Wolfgang Sawallisch.

SEBASTIAN STAUSS
TRANSLATED BY ULRICKE LELICKENS

Museums and archives. During the last years of his life, Richard Wagner spent a great deal of energy recovering manuscripts, CORRESPONDENCE, and other documents from earlier decades of his career. Although the AUTOGRAPH SOURCES of nearly half the works from his youth are still missing, the record of his works as a whole is much better than in the case of composers such as BACH, Haydn, MOZART, and many others. The documents left at the deaths of Richard and COSIMA Wagner formed the basis of the Richard-Wagner-Familienarchiv, which included autographs of all the composer's main works with the exception of those donated by Wagner in the 1860s to LUDWIG II. This archive became public property in 1973, when the Wagner family formed the RICHARD WAGNER FOUNDATION. As a supplementary National institution, the Richard-Wagner-Forschungsstätte was founded in 1939 for Wagner research (see Otto STROBEL); it became part of the Richard-Wagner-Gedenkstätte der Stadt Bayreuth in 1953. This was established in 1924 first as a private Wagner memorial in Bayreuth on the basis of several collections including those of C. F. GLASENAPP (Wagner's biographer) and Hans von WOLZOGEN (editor of the *BAYREUTHER BLÄTTER*). It was acquired in 1927 by the City of Bayreuth; in 1976, it became part of the Richard-Wagner-Museum at WAHNFRIED, Richard and Cosima Wagner's home in Bayreuth.

Currently, there are two organizations: the Richard-Wagner-Gedenkstätte, which owns part of Wagner's original manuscripts, and the Nationalarchiv der Richard-Wagner-Stiftung in Bayreuth (formerly the R.-W.-Familienarchiv), run out of the Siegfried-Wagner-Haus (next to WAHNFRIED), which owns several thousands of Wagner's manuscripts and letters. Parts of these holdings are exhibited in the R.-W.-Museum as well. The complicated structure of properties and locations is the consequence of the severe rift within the Wagner family since the 1930s.

Additional manuscripts and documents are spread across the world in approximately fifty public and a few private museums, libraries, and archives, of whose contents only a few examples will be mentioned here. The best-known museum outside Bayreuth is the Richard-Wagner-Museum at TRIBSCHEN, the scenic home on the shores of Lake Lucerne where Wagner lived from 1866 to 1872. In addition to numerous objects and documents relating to Wagner's life in SWITZERLAND, including his Érard piano, this collection includes several important autographs such as letters, a libretto of *Der FLIEGENDE HOLLÄNDER*, and the full autograph score of the *SIEGFRIED IDYLL* (first performed there on 25 December 1870).

The Reuter-Wagner-Museum, in Eisenach (Saxony), is the largest Wagner memorial outside Bayreuth. This is the former collection of the Wagner bibliographer Nikolaus OESTERLEIN, who opened his private museum in 1887 in Vienna with around 20,000 items. It was acquired by the City of Eisenach in 1895 and publicly displayed in 1897 in the Villa Fritz Reuter (Reuter was a north-German poet, 1810–74). In addition to a large stock of printed editions, programs, playbills (partly unique copies), engravings, busts, and early photographs, there are also autograph letters and musical manuscripts.

A small Wagner museum is located in Graupa (near DRESDEN) in the house where the composer completed the first draft of all three acts of *LOHENGRIN*. This museum documents Wagner's Dresden years (1842–9). An additional museum is currently being planned in VENICE, at the Palazzo Vendramin Calergi, where Wagner died in 1883.

As for historic Wagner collections, three further names must be mentioned: Ludwig II of Bavaria and Adolf Hitler, but first, the early Irish Wagner biographer, Mary BURRELL (1850–98). Unhappy with the "official," rather hagiographic biography by Glasenapp, heavily influenced (and partly falsified) by Cosima Wagner, Mrs. Burrell wanted a more critical view. For that purpose, she acquired all the documents she could throughout Europe: hundreds of autograph letters by Wagner and nearly all of his family and relatives, most of them coming from Wagner's stepdaughter Natalie PLANER, whose financial difficulties ended thanks to Burrell's generosity. After the latter's death, the collection became the property of The Curtis Institute of Music (Philadelphia, USA), but was sold by auction at Christie's in 1978. The most important items were acquired by the Bayreuth Archives: autograph excerpts from *Das LIEBESVERBOT*, drafts for *Die Hochzeit* and *Der fliegende Holländer*, the libretti of *Leubald* and *RIENZI*, the ouverture WWV 20, and so on (see auction catalog under BURRELL).

More dramatically, several of Wagner's most important manuscripts became part of private collections, of which invaluable parts are lost today. Between 1864 and 1868, on various occasions, Wagner gave Ludwig II the full autograph scores of *Die Feen*, *Das Liebesverbot*, *Rienzi*, *Das RHEINGOLD*, *Die WALKÜRE*, and the first draft of *Der fliegende Holländer*. After the king's death, these manuscripts became part of the Archive of the Royal Bavarian Family, the *Wittelsbacher Ausgleichsfond*. However, in 1939, the Bavarian *Industrie- und Handelskammer* (Chamber of Industry and Commerce) had the unfortunate idea of offering these six treasures to Adolf Hitler on the occasion of his fiftieth birthday. Hitler owned them until his death on 30 April 1945, and they are now lost.

Wagner's publisher SCHOTT in Mainz also had an archive of materials left after Wagner's death. But their whereabouts are not known at this time. On the other hand, several important documents such as correction pages for *Tristan* found a new home in the Collection Bodmeriana in Coligny, Switzerland. One of the last important private collections, owned by Paul

Richard, is now at the Universitätsbibliothek Bern (Switzerland). Its special focus is on iconography, artefacts on Wagnerian themes, playbills, letters, and editions.

As for public libraries, rather important autograph manuscripts such as *Entracte* (WWV 24), *Liebesmahl* (prose draft WWV 69), *Gruß an seine Getreuen* (WWV 71), and *Trauermusik* (WWV 73) are at the Staatsbibliothek Preussischer Kulturbesitz, Berlin. Further German institutional owners of autograph material are the Landesbibliothek and the Staatsarchiv, Dresden, and the Bayrische Staatsbibliothek, MUNICH.

Further European autograph holdings may be found at The British Library, London (lieder, Overtures *Rule Britannia* WWV 42 and *Polonia* WWV 39, libretto and drafts of *Das Liebesverbot*); the Bibliothèque Nationale, Paris (Overtures *Columbus* WWV 37 and *Polonia* WWV 39, most of the *Paris arrangements* WWV 62); the Zentralbibliothek, Zurich; and the Österreichische Nationalbibliothek and Gesellschaft der Musikfreunde, Vienna. In the USA, the New York Public Library owns drafts for *Rienzi*; other collections can be found at Yale University (New Haven, CT), the Heinemann Collection at the Pierpont Morgan Library, New York (Lieder WWV 50, 53, 55, 57), and The Library of Congress, Washington, DC (excerpts from PARSIFAL and *Die Walküre*, symphony WWV 29).

For first and early performances of Wagner's works, copyists' manuscripts may be extremely important. Such materials, often not part of the Bayreuth collections, are found in Dresden, Landesbibliothek (*Rienzi, Holländer,* TANNHÄUSER first version); Paris, Bibliothèque de l'Opéra (*Tannhäuser,* 2nd version); Zurich, Zentralbibliothek; Munich, Staatsbibliothek; Mainz, Schott Archive (Der RING DES NIBELUNGEN, *Parsifal*); Milan, Ricordi Archive; Berlin, Staatsbibliothek; London, The British Library (*Holländer*); Chicago, Newberry Library; Yale University; Harvard University; Library of Congress (*Liebesverbot*). ULRICH DRÜNER

See also Appendix 12: Archives and museums

Music critics and criticism. Wagner brought about major changes in music criticism. Beginning with his ZURICH writings, he broadened dramatically the parameters of musical discussion with the unprecedented claim that the future of civilization depended on the future of music. His writings sparked a strong response, generating years of polarized and polemical music criticism. By the end of Wagner's lifetime, mainstream music criticism was still centered on him, while the specialized Wagner literature had become a whole industry unto itself. Nor from that point on has writing on Wagner ever abated.

During the second half of the nineteenth century, music criticism developed along with other journalism by expanding and diversifying. Helmut Kirchmeyer's ambitious project to reprint all the significant German music criticism from the end of the eighteenth century to towards the end of the nineteenth century unsurprisingly faltered at the point where Wagner's presence in the music journals took off. The volumes documenting the contemporary criticism of Wagner only cover about the first ten years, from 1842 to 1852, leaving the last thirty years of Wagner's lifetime unpublished in his series.

Music criticism not only expanded but also changed in ways that specifically served Wagner's needs. With Wagner, for the first time, a music journal became openly partisan, when the *NEUE ZEITSCHRIFT FÜR MUSIK* (NZfM) declared that it officially supported Wagner in 1852. Early anti-Wagner critics reacted energetically; François-Joseph Fétis published a long article that year in *La REVUE ET GAZETTE MUSICALE* that formed the basis of French objections to Wagner for decades to come. Ludwig Bischoff in the *Rheinische* (later *Niederrheinische*) *Musik-Zeitung,* and several writers for the LEIPZIG weekly *Die Grenzboten* carried on feuds with the *Neue Zeitschrift.* Later, in 1878, Wagner approved the founding of a journal, the *BAYREUTHER BLÄTTER,* created expressly to serve his causes.

Premieres and publications offered opportunities for media blitzes, beginning with the efforts of Franz LISZT, who not only premiered *LOHENGRIN* (Weimar, 1850) and organized the festival at BALLENSTEDT (1852), but also wrote long publicity pieces on *TANNHÄUSER* and *Lohengrin* that propelled Wagner's works onto center stage of German musical life. The delayed premieres of *Tannhäuser* and *Lohengrin* in other cities were further occasions, over the years, for renewed discussion of those works: *Tannhäuser* was not premiered in Berlin until 1856, and VIENNA in 1857; *Lohengrin* was not premiered in Vienna until 1876.

Another way Wagner was kept in the limelight was to have his Zurich writings repeatedly discussed, paraphrased, and translated. A second edition of *OPER UND DRAMA* (Opera and Drama, 1851) was issued in 1869. Even though Wagner's views had evolved significantly from this book's arguments, he did not revise or renounce them, which led to confusion and the need for even more articles that accounted for discrepancies among his writings. When Wagner published his collected works (*Gesammelte Schriften und Dichtungen*) for the first time in 1871, another round of discussion ensued.

Wagner himself published pieces in music journals, often in the form of "open letters," despite frequently denouncing and ridiculing music criticism. As a young man, he had published some essays in German and French music journals. While living in Paris from 1839 to 1842, his journalism, which included three novellas, was one meager source of scarce income.

Wagner's most infamous article, *Das JUDENTUM IN DER MUSIK* (Jewishness in Music), appeared in the *NZfM* in 1850 and unleashed a storm of controversy in the musical press. Although the work was published under a pseudonym, the author's identity was known by some critics (see Fischer 31). The reissue of the piece in 1869 under his own name was in the form of a pamphlet.

The Viennese music critic Max Graf observed in his history of music criticism that "the battle against Wagner moved from town to town, from country to country, from continent to continent. The same arguments for and against him were to be read in papers all over the world" (Graf 252). Therefore, "Wagner, the greatest enemy of musical criticism in his time, increased the importance of criticism in the dailies. His curse was transformed into a blessing. Hundreds of music critics lived on Wagner" (Graf 24).

As Graf indicates, in the big cities of Vienna and Berlin, most of the music criticism appeared in the feuilleton section of the daily newspapers. The number of newspapers at that time is astounding. According to Graf, Berlin had 45 daily newspapers in 1900. Music journals were also now more numerous and more specialized, catering to specific types of musicians. Of the general music journals, most were based in either Berlin or Leipzig: the *Musikalisches Wochenblatt* (1870–1908, Leipzig, ed. Ernst Fritzsch) was populated by Wagnerian writers such as Hans von WOLZOGEN, Richard POHL, Heinrich PORGES, Friedrich von Hausegger, and Arthur SEIDL. The *Allgemeine Musikalische Zeitung* (1863–82, Leipzig, ed. Friedrich Chrysander) represented a more conservative, scholarly approach, and occasionally criticized the Wagnerians.

The BAYREUTHER BLÄTTER (1878–1938) was not only able to focus on Wagner's music, but also issued articles expanding on his writings or thought. In the following decade other countries followed with their own periodicals: *Deutsche Worte* in Vienna, REVUE WAGNÉRIENNE in Paris (1885–7), THE MEISTER in London (1888–95), and CRONACA WAGNERIANA in Italy (1893–5).

Despite the fact that Wagner was so controversial, music criticism in the nineteenth century was overwhelmingly dominated by pro-Wagnerian writers. By far the most famous music critic to oppose Wagner and the Wagnerians was Eduard HANSLICK, writing for the Viennese in the *Neue freie Presse*. There is not a single other comparable figure who stood out against the Wagnerian tide.   SANNA PEDERSON

See also RECEPTION, IN THE GERMAN-LANGUAGE PRESS

Jens Malte Fischer, *Richard Wagners "Das Judentum in der Musik"* (see bibliography).
Max Graf, *Composer and Critic* (New York: Norton, 1946).
Helmut Kirchmeyer, *Situationsgeschichte der Musikkritik* (see bibliography).

Music drama. If LEITMOTIV represents one extreme of Wagnerian terminology, music drama marks the other: the totality within which those small thematic elements play a defining role.

A commonsense distinction between Wagner's "romantic operas" (the works up to and including LOHENGRIN [1850]) and "music dramas" (*Das RHEINGOLD* and after) seems to make good sense. Yet ironies and paradoxes abound when the history and meaning of the term "music drama" are traced. It might be supposed that the concept arose simply to signal that music drama was not opera – or not exactly the same as opera, if by opera is understood the form as developed and exploited by composers during the seventeenth, eighteenth, and early nineteenth centuries, in the time of Monteverdi to ROSSINI and beyond, and which had originally been designated *dramma per musica*.

Opera was not so much something defined by its dramatic subject-matter – tragedy (*opera seria*, GRAND OPERA) and comedy (*opera buffa*) were equally possible – as by its formal design. Opera meant "number opera," with clear if not always literal separation between arias, recitatives, and ensembles, and it was a genre which had no problem with showcasing vocal display (coloratura, BEL CANTO). Music drama might not always completely avoid such operatic elements, any more than it would completely abandon all connection with the song-like forms of the German *Singspiel* or French *opéra comique*. However, music drama did avoid the spoken dialogue that those forms of opera allowed, for the simple reason that *sung* dialogues, and the flexible musical structures they required, tended to be more prominent features of music drama than of opera. Moreover, even when music drama included extended solo passages, it became preferable to think of these as soliloquies or monologues rather than as arias, since they often lacked the formal or stylistic characteristics of the operatic aria: a comparison between, for example, HANS SACHS's *Flieder-monolog* from *Die MEISTERSINGER VON NÜRNBERG* and the "Largo al factotum" from Rossini's *Il barbiere di Siviglia* will indicate the issues involved when such terminological distinctions are applied.

One could therefore argue that music drama is closer to spoken drama than it is to opera. In opera, the verbal text can be subject to the kind of ornamented drawing out of syllables and repetitions of words which suggest that the composer is not primarily concerned for the text as such to be heard and followed: rather, the opera libretto, and the situations the libretto text describes, are used as sources for expressive excursions whose character and quality are (almost) entirely musical. *Prima la musica, dopo le parole* is the tag conventionally applied to opera: "first the music, then the words." Music drama might therefore logically be expected to aim for the opposite emphasis, with the music merely making sure that the general import of the verbal text, the dramatic poem, can be understood. But logic has little place in the world of music theater, and the world of Richard Wagner is no different.

Just as Wagner failed to invent the term *Leitmotiv*, so too "music drama" originated elsewhere, in seventeenth-century Italy as *dramma per musica*, in eighteenth-century England as "musical drama" (Handel), and in early nineteenth-century Germany as "musikalisches Drama" (E. T. A. HOFFMANN). The ZURICH writings spend much time underlining the gulf between opera as one thing and spoken drama as something else. And because drama, as established by the ANCIENT GREEKS, could use musical elements without requiring a different label, Wagner in 1851 had no doubt that "I shall write no more operas: but as I do not care to invent an arbitrary name for these [new] works, I will simply call them dramas" (SSD 4:345). Two decades later, in 1872, with TRISTAN and *Meistersinger* composed, and with work on The RING nearing completion, he took time to pen a short essay (*ÜBER DIE BENENNUNG "MUSIKDRAMA"* [On the Term "Music Drama"]) making the eminently sensible suggestion that the single German word was merely a convenient conflation of "musikalisches Drama": so, in English, "music drama" is just a short form of "musical drama." The possibility of this term being shortened in turn to "musical" has of course been realized, although in a context closer to Broadway than to Bayreuth.

None of this should detract from the virtuosity of Wagner's sustained attempt to ensure that dramatic music in a theatrical setting was granted the pre-eminence previously accorded by the public to spoken verse and stage plays. Music's lack of the explicit conceptual significations accorded to words was a strength rather than a weakness, especially if the best modern drama could be understood, in Wagner's famously enigmatic phrase, as "acts of music made visible": not, it should be noted, "acts of poetry made (musically) audible." The passionate and abiding conviction that in the drama was the deed led to a further verbal swerve when Wagner categorized *Tristan und Isolde* as a *Handlung*, the kind of "action" or "deed" that could only be adequately realized – shown visibly as well as audibly – in the musical form given to it by Wagner.

In the 1872 essay, Wagner made a dramatic show of being lost for words when it came to the best way of determining what his works should be called, and concluding that "I must send my poor works into the world without any name for their genre: and that is how I intend to leave it, while I work with our contemporary theaters, which ... know nothing but operas, and which, if you provide a real *music drama*, will make an *opera* out of it" (PW 304). That was how he felt a few years before the BAYREUTH FESTIVAL, and the prospect of a self-constructed performing tradition for his works became realities. By 1879, he was more concerned with showing how his "new form of dramatic music" engaged with symphonic as well as dramatic qualities, and with reiterating the deficiencies of opera. In the end, his own non-operas were offered as models for how drama should be practiced in the future, and the degree of influence they have exercised demonstrates just how seriously those offerings – even if they remain generically nameless – have been taken by composers since Wagner's own time.   ARNOLD WHITTALL

Music of the Future. See *Zukunftsmusik*

Music history. Wagner's interest in music history was not that of a scholar, but rather that of a composer with two motives: to track down the origins of music so that he could tap into that vital source, avoiding the ways music went into a decline and fall; and to position himself as the only composer who could revitalize music – the only composer who could give music a future.
1. Origins of music
2. Reasons for the downfall of music
3. Beethoven and music after Beethoven
4. Wagner as music historian

1. Origins of music

Over the course of his theoretical writings, Wagner varied his account of the origins of music. Beginning with *Die KUNST UND DIE REVOLUTION* (Art and Revolution, 1849), he took ANCIENT GREECE as the point of departure. This was in keeping with the privileged place afforded to classical antiquity in eighteenth- and nineteenth-century Germany, especially in the Weimar classicism of GOETHE, SCHILLER, and HERDER. Wagner was influenced in particular by Friedrich Schiller's *On the Aesthetic Education of Man* (1795), in which the Hellenic ideal consisted of unity on two levels: art integrated into sociopolitical life, and the arts themselves indivisible within the genre of tragedy. With the decline of ancient Greek tragedy and the increasing fragmentation of society, the arts went through a corresponding process, becoming more specialized and independent from each other. This set the stage for Wagner to proclaim a new and final stage in history that would recover that ancient unity and make art relevant to society again. In *Das KUNSTWERK DER ZUKUNFT* (The Artwork of the Future, 1849/50), Wagner again followed Weimar classicism in elaborating on the original unity of the arts, describing how music, poetry, and DANCE originally were inseparable. However, in this text and in the following *OPER UND DRAMA* (Opera and Drama, 1851) he substituted "the people" (*VOLK*) for the Greeks as the point of origin of music. Wagner speculated that, before civilization, humans formed groups naturally and created music spontaneously. Ever since, however, the artificial impositions of society and musical institutions had corrupted any kind of naturally motivated music-making.

Wagner pursued this theory of the natural origins of music with conjectures (indebted to Rousseau) about expressive vocal utterances that are pre-verbal and pre-musical. The spontaneously emitted groans and cries generated by strong feelings form the primal basis for both music and language, in that these utterances contain the pitches and vowels that make up the simplest melodies and words. Wagner echoed Herder's pioneering cultural theory here in proposing that the act of communication through sound, variously embodied in both music and language, is the foundation of all human societies. MUSIC DRAMA, which combines music and language, therefore has the all-important mission of binding isolated individuals to their cultural and historical communities.

In the late essay BEETHOVEN (1870), Wagner recast the origin of music: instead of its occurring in a distant past, he now located it deeply buried within the human being's psyche. He described the compositional process in terms of accessing the unconscious through dreams. There is still a primal utterance, now taking the form of a scream: upon waking from the DREAM, the sound of the scream gives the composer his starting point for making music in the conscious world.

2. Reasons for the downfall of music

In his revolutionary-era writings, Wagner drew on contemporary YOUNG GERMAN writers in grounding the history of art in its social context. In *Die Kunst und die Revolution*, the downfall of art is attributed to its being severed from sociopolitical life and becoming art for entertainment and profit. In *Das JUDENTUM IN DER MUSIK* (Jewishness in Music, 1850), opera's transformation into a capitalistic enterprise is blamed on the JEWS. Various other writings make the French responsible for turning opera into an entertainment industry (as part of their general destruction of civilization that Wagner attributes to them). CHRISTIANITY also plays a role in music's downfall in the first ZURICH writings, and is equated with the musical development of counterpoint, which for Wagner represents ABSOLUTE MUSIC – that is, music completely cut off from any relation to other arts and social significance. This initially hostile portrayal of Christianity and counterpoint made it difficult for Wagner to find a favorable place in history for a composer he otherwise revered: J. S. BACH. However, at other times when he used German national ideology as the basis for his historical narrative, Wagner could enshrine Bach, chorales, and even counterpoint within the positive historical context of the German Reformation.

The most detailed account of the decline of opera appears in Part One of *Oper und Drama*. Here Wagner's history of opera begins with the eighteenth century and two lines of development: serious and frivolous. GLUCK, Cherubini, Méhul, and Spontini represent the first, with their struggles to make the singer an instrument of the composer's intention. However, none of them went far enough to displace the emphasis on music itself. The frivolous development includes MOZART, ROSSINI, AUBER, and MEYERBEER. Mozart wrote beautiful music, but did not understand that the traditional forms prevented him from making a connection to the drama. Rossini represents the ultimate in frivolity, where there is no drama and the music does not even have an expressive function. Opera has degenerated into "absolute melody" or simply memorable tunes.

Wagner's idiosyncratic account of opera omits the seventeenth century entirely. It appears that at this time he was not yet aware of the roots of opera in Italian Humanism and the revival of ancient Greek ideals. (Later writings acknowledge early Italian opera, but dismiss its emphasis on words at the expense of the music as deluded and monotonous.) In his account of the eighteenth century, one would think that he would have wanted to claim Gluck, Weber, and Mozart as important predecessors: Gluck because of his insistence on the precedence of words over music, Weber for his goal of creating a national German opera, and Mozart for his acknowledged master-works. However, Wagner judged them to have remained first and foremost composers, which meant their aspirations for opera did not go far enough beyond purely musical concerns.

3. Beethoven and music after Beethoven

The most important composer by far in all of Wagner's accounts is BEETHOVEN. He casts Beethoven's historical significance in various ways that always point towards a single successor: himself. In *Das Kunstwerk der Zukunft* Wagner used Beethoven's Ninth Symphony to mark the end of the whole misbegotten history of absolute music, or music separated from its sister arts. By bringing words and voices back in to join with the instrumental music, Beethoven sent the clear message that a new era was to begin where the arts were once again united. Therefore, all composers after Beethoven who continued to pursue instrumental music, such as SCHUMANN, MENDELSSOHN, and BRAHMS, were dismissed as trying to progress beyond a dead end. Furthermore, for Wagner, Beethoven was GERMANNESS personified, and therefore the French, Italian, and English nations were by definition unable to produce any great composers. Wagner's support of the compositions of his presumed allies and fellow Beethoven worshippers BERLIOZ, LISZT, and BRUCKNER was ambiguous. It can be safely inferred that Wagner considered only his own works to represent a true development in the history of music after Beethoven.

4. Wagner as music historian

The absurdity of calling Wagner a music historian calls attention to the way he conveyed his strong views successfully while scorning the newly scientific and scholarly rigor of the emerging discipline of musicology. It is difficult to categorize the genre of his writing; he seems to have envisioned a whole new class of readers who could partake of densely intellectual discourse without circulating within professional academic institutions. In taking this stance, Wagner dismissed the more philological approach embodied in such monumental works of nineteenth-century music history as Otto Jahn's bio-graphy of Mozart and Alexander Wheelock Thayer's *Life of Beethoven*. But already as early as his Beethoven novellas (e.g., *Eine PILGERFAHRT ZU BEETHOVEN*; A Pilgrimage to Beethoven, 1840) and projected Beethoven biography around

1840, Wagner had rejected the scholarly approach as missing the essence of any aesthetic object. Wagner's one-time disciple NIETZSCHE more famously articulated this attitude about the deadly consequences of musicology and historical inquiry beginning in the 1870s in his critiques of modernity and rationality. Only after Wagner's death did a younger, more Wagner-friendly generation of musicologists such as Guido Adler attempt to integrate his works and ideas into the standard scholarly historical narrative.

It has been argued that another source for Wagner's historical narrative of music is told through his own operas. Jean-Jacques Nattiez has matched up moments in the RING cycle with Wagner's theories in *Oper und Drama*, beginning with *Das RHEINGOLD*'s famous opening E♭ as the primordial sound from which music emerges.

In sum, Wagner's various accounts of the history of music can be traced to several sources: Weimar classicism for the ideal of ancient Greece, Rousseau and Herder for the theory of music in a "natural setting," and earlier music critics on the importance of Beethoven. However, his composite version, taken up by his followers, has had an impact on music historiography beyond any of these individual sources. Wagner's efforts to rewrite music history in order to construct a lineage that validated his own music was surely the most direct source for subsequent composers, who increasingly supplemented their music with written justification. The most successful was SCHOENBERG, who dubbed himself the heir of both Wagner and Brahms and the only composer who could ensure the supremacy of German music. Richard Taruskin has located a historiographical trend in Schoenberg's writings where "ontogeny" becomes "phylogeny" – that is, an individual composer presents his trajectory as having such significance that it simultaneously embodies the development of music itself. This trend is almost inconceivable without Wagner's example.   SANNA PEDERSON

Alan Roy Anbari, "Richard Wagner's Concepts of History" (PhD dissertation, University of Texas at Austin, 2007).
Thomas S. Grey, *Wagner's Musical Prose* (see bibliography).
Klaus Kropfinger, "Nachwort," in Wagner, *Oper und Drama*, ed. Kropfinger (Stuttgart: Reclam, 1994): 430–532.
Wagner and Beethoven (see bibliography).
Jean-Jacques Nattiez, *Wagner Androgyne: A Study in Interpretation*, trans. Stewart Spencer (Princeton University Press, 1993).
Anthony Newcomb, "*Ritornello Ritornato*: A Variety of Wagnerian Refrain Form," in *Analyzing Opera: Verdi and Wagner*, ed. Carolyn Abbate and Roger Parker (Berkeley: University of California Press, 1989): 202–21.
Richard Taruskin, *The Oxford History of Western Music*, vol. 4 (New York: Oxford University Press, 2005).

Music theory. Wagner's music, life, and writings have invited inquiry from a wide range of disciplines. *Der RING DES NIBELUNGEN*, for example, has served as a touchstone for sociopolitical commentaries by George Bernard SHAW and Theodor ADORNO, Jungian psychological readings by Robert Donington and Jean Shinoda Bolen, mythological source studies by Jessie Weston and Deryck COOKE, and artistic interpretations by graphic artist Arthur RACKHAM and stage director Patrice CHÉREAU, to name but a very few. Among disciplinary approaches to Wagner, however, music theory (a subfield of musicology) stands apart as the only one to engage with the music itself on a technical level.

1. Theoretical approaches to Wagner's music
2. Theme
3. Tonality
4. Form

1. Theoretical approaches to Wagner's music

"Music theory" is, perhaps, a bit of a misnomer. While it is true that scholars working in the field certainly posit theories of musical structure, behavior, meaning, coherence, and composition both prescriptive and descriptive, a large component of the work many theorists do comprises analysis – the disassembling of musical materials to understand how they function. This analytical work often informs, or is informed by, music theories, but it remains nevertheless a distinct activity, one predicated on empirical investigation, labeling, categorizing, and model creation for specific pieces of music, or portions thereof.

Regarding Wagner's music, the composer himself is the first music theorist we must consider. While Wagner rarely spoke in technical terms about the materials of music and their functions, there are a few concepts he developed in works he wrote around 1850 that shed light on his art and that remain relevant to present-day discussions of his music. In this regard, Wagner exhibits one important function of the music theorist: to theorize prescriptively about new compositional practices. That Wagner was also the composer who essayed these practices suggests that there is an especially close connection between theory and musical product. While this is true for some of Wagner's works (the first two MUSIC DRAMAS of *The Ring*, for instance), like all artists, Wagner developed across his career, and thus we find that many of his theories remain imperfectly or incompletely realized even in his own compositions.

There are five of Wagner's musico-theoretic concepts that remain the most relevant to modern-day theory and analysis. They are: (1) ENDLESS MELODY, the idea that the musical narrative should comprise significant or meaningful melodic content, by extension avoiding stock formulas of melodic-harmonic articulation (cadences), and other hackneyed or meaningless melodic materials; (2) musical prose, the notion that musical phrases should not exhibit metrical regularity (e.g., pervasive four-bar grouping), but rather remain fluid and flexible, the way that written prose avoids the regular metricality native to much poetry; (3) motifs of presentiment and reminiscence (often referred to as *LEITMOTIVE*, though this was not Wagner's terminology), musical thoughts articulated by the orchestra that either foreshadow or, more often, recall emotion-rich moments of vocal expression; (4) *STABREIM*, the use of alliteration and assonance to group together ideas associated with the same semantic content; and (5) the POETIC-MUSICAL PERIOD, a formal unit predicated on tonal and dramatic unity. More recent music analysis has adopted and adapted each of these Wagnerian ideas; many of these will be discussed below.

Scholars working since Wagner's death have attempted to explain his music, *ex post facto*, using a descriptive approach. That is, they have spoken not about potential compositional techniques one might use in creating new works, the way Wagner did, but rather about how Wagner's already extant music operates. In so doing, these scholars often broach the realm of criticism as well, citing analytic data to explain why they find Wagner's music to be successful or not. While there are many facets of Wagner's music worthy of investigation, the bulk of the theorizing, analysis, and criticism predicated on a technical understanding of the materials of Wagner's music centers loosely on three interrelated topics: theme, tonality, and form.

2. Theme

More than any other development in dramatic music, it is the *Leitmotiv* that Wagner is remembered for. Though precursors of the *Leitmotiv* are evident both in the works of composers before Wagner and in Wagner's early works, it was with the completion of the *Ring* that the concept was introduced to audiences at large. This was accomplished by the efforts of Hans von WOLZOGEN, who published a guide to the themes of the *Ring*, in so doing popularizing the term *Leitmotiv*. It is he, too, who can be credited with (or blamed for) the popular understanding of this term.

The most banal definition of *Leitmotiv* – one all too appropriate for many examples of the technique – is "a signature tune," a theme that appears to signal the presence or mention of a certain character, object, action, place, or emotion. In its more subtle manifestations, though, the *Leitmotiv* is a tool of the musical dramatist's art, a method by which musical developments may parallel dramatic developments, emotional residue may be collected and recalled, and twists of musical meaning such as irony and revelation may be achieved. Despite the popular misconception of leitmotivic technique as little more than a musical catalog – a misconception spawned not only by Wolzogen's guide and its many progeny, but also by contemporaneous artists and critics eager to misrepresent Wagner's work – musicologists working in recent decades have tried to clarify the flexibility, nuance, and importance of the *Leitmotiv*. Scholars such as Deryck Cooke, Warren Darcy, and Matthew Bribitzer-Stull have explained not only the *Leitmotiv*'s developmental nature and dramatic subtlety, but also its relationship to musical form. Others, such as Thomas Grey, have indicated the centrality of the *Leitmotiv* in the reception history of Wagner's music dramas. In short, audiences have viewed the *Leitmotiv* both as the problem and as the solution when trying to understand Wagner's music dramas.

3. Tonality

When musicians speak of "tonality," they can mean a number of things. Most often, though, "tonality" refers to the concept of tonic key – how one triad (such as E♭ major) serves as the central, most stable sonority that abstractly controls the music of a given section, and how harmony and counterpoint contribute to supporting that triad as tonic. In Wagner's music (especially the later works such as TRISTAN UND ISOLDE, GÖTTERDÄMMERUNG, and PARSIFAL) both harmonic function and tonal center are fluid and ambiguous. Counterpoint, too, often functions not according to the time-worn contrapuntal principles propagated throughout

Europe since the late fourteenth century, but rather as an ad hoc art guided by the demands of drama and thematic association.

Two Austro-German music theorists working early in the twentieth century were among the first to describe Wagnerian tonality, albeit in different terms from one another. Arnold SCHOENBERG characterized Wagner's tonality as "wandering" – that is, not grounded in one tonic key but rather feinting first at one tonic and then at another. Ernst Kurth, on the other hand, approached Wagner's tonality in terms of harmony, specifically the manner in which the energies of Wagner's harmonies affected the mind of the listener in a psychological sense. Ambiguous harmonies (such as Wagner's "TRISTAN" CHORD) were, for Kurth, symbolic of Romantic-era attitudes.

While Schoenberg's and Kurth's approaches to the analysis of Wagnerian tonality have remained largely undeveloped by modern scholars, the work of two other Austro-German theorists – Hugo Riemann and Heinrich Schenker – has enjoyed a wide application and development in recent years. Though neither man spent much time analyzing Wagner's music, many would argue that neo-Riemannian and Schenkerian methods have proved valuable to understanding Wagner's art. The elements of greatest interest to modern scholars culled from Riemann's wide-ranging theoretic prose are two: (1) the categorization of harmonies into one of three functions (tonic, dominant, or subdominant) related abstractly to one tonic chord; and (2) the coherence of harmonic progressions via common-tone connections between harmonies. Anglo-American music-theorists such as David Lewin, Brian Hyer, and Richard Cohn have applied adapted Riemannian analytic techniques to the music of Wagner in order to explain the coherence of chromatic and harmonically or tonally ambiguous passages.

Tonality for Schenker, on the other hand, was not based on harmonic function or common tones, but was rather predicated on the composing-out of a tonic triad through the union of contrapuntal and harmonic means. Schenker's early work celebrated Wagner's music, but in later writings he turned against Wagner, considering him to be a "dramatic" composer rather than one capable of competently handling the structures of ABSOLUTE MUSIC with the genius of composers such as J. S. BACH, BEETHOVEN, or Chopin. Arguments continue about what repertories Schenkerian analysis is best adapted to. Some scholars feel that Schenker's methods are most revelatory when applied to clearly functional, monotonal music (like much of W. A. MOZART's oeuvre) rather than the "wandering," "energetic," or ambiguous tonality of Wagner. On the other hand, theorists such as Warren Darcy and Patrick McCreless have argued that Schenkerian analysis is appropriate for certain passages in Wagner's music, and that the understanding of musical structure gleaned from Schenkerian analysis may be relevant to the dramatic context as well.

Finally, it would be remiss to conclude this discussion of music theory, tonality, and Wagner, without mentioning the American scholar Robert Bailey. Bailey, while building on notions of earlier theorists such as Alfred LORENZ, is widely credited with classifying three dramatic uses of tonality in Wagner's works. These classifications were disseminated by Bailey's students in a variety of publications, both extending Bailey's rudimentary explanations and applying his ideas to other repertories (e.g., those of Gustav MAHLER and Hugo

WOLF). In short, Bailey's forms of dramatic tonality comprise: (1) associative tonality, in which a tonic key, harmonic sonority, harmonic function, timbre, or even a single pitch is associated with an element of the drama; (2) expressive tonality, in which systematically rising or falling tonic pitch levels symbolize rising or falling dramatic intensity; and (3) directional tonality, in which a given section of music moves from one tonic key to another, paralleling a concomitant dramatic motion. A related, under-defined concept promulgated by Bailey is the notion of the double-tonic complex (sometimes called "double tonality," or "tonal pairing") in which two tonic centers consistently vie for supremacy across a span of music, creating a sense of tension and/or ambiguity often correlated with the drama.

4. Form

Both theme and tonality feature prominently in discussion of Wagnerian form. In fact, music theorists' discussions of form in common-practice music (i.e., the art music of western Europe from the late seventeenth to late nineteenth centuries), while often complex and nuanced, sometimes boil down to just these two facets of musical composition – that is, how and when thematic material is repeated (variation being a form of repetition) and what tonic keys are locally operative.

Perhaps the most notorious student of Wagnerian form was Alfred LORENZ. Lorenz's work can be characterized as morbidly formal; his studies of Wagner's mature music dramas divide the works exhaustively into formal chunks and then describe these chunks in terms of recurring formal patterns such as the *Bar* (AAB) and *Bogen* ("arch," or palindrome) form. Lorenz's ultra-formalism has been criticized by scholars such as Carl DAHLHAUS, who react to it as an artefact of NATIONAL SOCIALISM. (Lorenz was a member of the Nazi party and depicted Wagner as its forefather.) Others criticize Lorenz for the misapplication of Wagner's "poetic-musical period" to mammoth spans of music never intended by the composer to be formally united. Others, however, see in Lorenz's work an attention to thematic, dramatic, textural, and metric unity useful in parsing the continuities (i.e., "endless melody") of Wagner's later music dramas. Among those to adopt Lorenzian formal logic are Patrick McCreless, whose study of *SIEGFRIED* includes form charts for various nested units, and Warren Darcy, whose study of *Das RHEINGOLD* divides that work into twenty tonal-dramatic episodes largely isomorphic to Lorenz's poetic-musical periods.

Finally, recent work in Anglo-American music theory has propounded other formal paradigms in describing Wagner's music. Anthony Newcomb, for one, traces Wagner's use of refrain structures in which a given theme or thematic complex serves as a refrain, alternating with contrasting material. A related concept, developed by James Hepokoski in describing the music of Jean Sibelius, is the rotational form, in which contrasting chunks of music are repeated in the same succession (ABC, ABC, ABC, etc.). The rotational idea has proved useful to Warren Darcy and others, who have used it to explain the form of passages from the *Ring*. Finally, the development of Wagner's smaller, phrase-level forms has enjoyed the reapplication of Wagner's notion of "musical prose." William Rothstein, for example, traces the development of

Wagner's metric groupings, from the clunky, four-bar units of the early operas, to the fluidity of the mature works.   MATTHEW BRIBITZER-STULL

Robert Bailey, "The Structure of the *Ring* and its Evolution," *19th-Century Music* 1.1 (1977): 48–61.

Wagner: Prelude and Transfiguration from "Tristan and Isolde" (New York: Norton, 1985).

Warren Darcy, "The Ursatz in Wagner: Or, Was Wagner a Background Composer After All?" *Intégral* 4 (1990): 1–35.

Wagner's "Das Rheingold" (New York: Oxford University Press, 1993).

Patrick McCreless, *Wagner's "Siegfried": Its Drama, History, and its Music* (Ann Arbor: University of Michigan Press, 1982).

Mystischer Abgrund. In his "Bayreuth" essay of 1873, Wagner wrote that he and his architect, Gottfried SEMPER, had developed a plan for the empty space between the proscenium and the front row of seats, a space they dubbed "the 'mystic gulf,' because it is to separate reality from ideality" (*den 'mystischen Abgrund', weil er die Realität von der Idealität zu trennen habe*) (SSD 9:337). Theory was put into practice when the FESTIVAL THEATER was constructed with a deeply sunken orchestra pit that extended beneath the stage and out of spectators' view. This "mystischer Abgrund" realized Wagner's desire to give the illusion of music welling up uncreated, as if emerging from "Gaia's holy ur-womb" (*heiligen Urschooße Gaia's*, SSD 9:338). While not entirely unprecedented (precursors may be found in Claude-Nicholas Ledoux's theatre in Besançon [1778–84] as well as at the opera house in RIGA where Wagner conducted), the "mystic gulf" remains one of the most innovative and influential features of the Festival Theater, and is central to its strategy of occultation of the means of theatrical production.   MATTHEW WILSON SMITH

Matthew Wilson Smith, *The Total Work of Art* (see bibliography): 30–6.

Beat Wyss, "Ragnarok of Illusion: Richard Wagner's 'Mystical Abyss' at Bayreuth," trans. Denise Bratton, *October* 54 (1990): 57–78.

Myth / mythos. The term "myth" was not part of our general vocabulary until the beginning of the twentieth century, although it had, by the end of the nineteenth century, begun to find a place in dictionaries and lexicons (although usually with the Latinized ending "myth*us*"). In any case, it stood in the shadow of the term "mythology," which is the historical account of pagan gods and legends. It was left to Richard Wagner to first juxtapose the word "mythos" with "mythology." In OPER UND DRAMA (Opera and Drama, 1851) he consistently uses the term with the Greek ending, a form not even NIETZSCHE, a classical philologist, employed.

Wagner wanted nothing to do with the term "mythology" and its antiquated and didactic implications. According to Wagner, whose definition survives to this day, the concept of mythos was an unchanging explanation of reality: "The incomparable thing about the Mythos is, that it is true for all time, and its content, however close its compression, is inexhaustible throughout the ages. The only task of the Poet was to expound it" (PW 2:191). There are four points of significance to note here about mythos: (1) its timelessness; (2) its compressed structure; (3) its inexhaustibility, in the sense that its fundamental truth is never revealed in any particular interpretation; (4) the fact that an individual poet does not create mythos, but "merely" expounds it.

In *Die WIBELUNGEN* (1848), Wagner defined mythos as the epitome of the "people's insight" (PW 7:266), thus keeping in line with HERDER and the Romantics. Based on etymological speculations about the alleged identity of the Nibelungen as the old Frankish dynasty of the Wibelungen (= Ghibellines), he sought to follow the romantic tradition by regarding mythos as consistent with the "beliefs" of the *VOLK*. For this reason, Wagner posited that the Frankish dynasty and the Nibelungen of the saga shared an "if not genealogical, then certainly mythical identity" (PW 7:263), a connection which could be discovered by examining the dynastic names which issued from the German "folk-mouth" (PW 7:268).

Wagner said that the Franks' self-proclaimed Trojan ancestry should also be understood as a "mythical identity." Ancient Troy was the "ur-town," which according to folk belief was "built by the earliest human races and circled by Cyclopean walls to guard their holiest fetish," and it held the "well-spring of all patriarchism" (PW 7:281). The idea that history is, in a sense, the recapitulation of mythical prototypes, which was developed using the example of the "ur-town," left its mark throughout the *Wibelungen*, which is subtitled *World-History as Told in Saga*. Another prototype is the idea of the "ur-kinghood," based on the stem-father who had "sprung from the gods" (PW 7:259). The Wagnerian prototypes (ur-kinghood, ur-heroism, ur-town) correspond exactly to the "numinous prototypes" (Hübner) of modern myth research. One such prototype is prehistory, in which a numinous being carries out a particular action for the first time, which is thenceforth repeated in an identical fashion. In the first place, this applies to recurrent acts of nature, upon which Wagner developed his concept of mythos. Wagner's way of thinking is structurally mythical: history presents itself as a cyclical repetition of an archetypical pattern of events, in a process diametrically opposed to linear progress.

In *Oper und Drama*, Wagner's definition of mythos goes in another, more structural direction as the "concentrated image of the things themselves" (PW 2:153). "Thus in mythos all the shaping impulse of the folk makes toward realizing to its senses a broadest grouping of the most manifold phenomena, and in the most succinct of shapes" presented in "plastic" form (PW 2:154). This process of consolidation already seen in mythos culminates in the art form of drama, and Greek tragedy is the paradigm: "Tragedy is nothing other than the artistic completion of the Myth itself" (PW 2:156).

Wagner saw history as a derived form of mythos in that it repeats mythical prototypes. However, he described the present – which is marked by natural catastrophes, a nihilistic thirst for power, the corruption of human relationships through an obsession with money, and the abstraction and anonymity of social relationships – as an era estranged from mythos. He conjured up mythos in its pure form once more in *Der RING DES NIBELUNGEN*, in the unspoiled mythical age at the beginning of *RHEINGOLD*. This is evident in the musical cosmogony of the overture and the scene with the three Rhinemaidens. The mythical age – the true "Golden" Age – is corrupted and collapses following Alberich's curse on LOVE and the theft of the Rhine gold. This is reversed at the end of *GÖTTERDÄMMERUNG* and transformed into a new state of mythical integrity. The desacralized, prosaic state of the modern world, dominated and fragmented by science, politics, and history, can no longer be made whole. Consequently, the art form that corresponds to modernity is not tragedy, which is shaped by the condensed anatomy of mythos, but rather the open structure of the novel. However, the dominant form of the new age should be the MUSIC DRAMA, the "artwork of the future," which assimilates the historical experiences of the modern world reflected in the novel, but now as myth. If mythos is "the beginning and end of history," then this evolutionary process "is no retrogression, but a progress to the winning of the highest human faculty" (PW 2:224). This transpires programmatically in the *Ring*, where the world of Germanic gods functions as a symbolic representation of modernity as reflected in the complex structure of the novel. Just as mythos becomes a sublimated form of history, so too the music drama functions as a symbolic consolidation of the sublimated form of the novel.   DIETER BORCHMEYER

TRANSLATED BY HOLLY WERMTER

See also ANCIENT GREECE; WAGNER AS LIBRETTIST

Udo Bermbach and Dieter Borchmeyer, eds., *Richard Wagner. Der Ring des Nibelungen. Ansichten des Mythos* (Stuttgart: Metzler, 1995).
Kurt Hübner, *Die Wahrheit des Mythos* (Munich: Beck, 1985).

Naples. See ITALY, WAGNER'S TRAVELS TO

National Socialism, musical life during. The National Socialist German Workers' Party (Nazi Party) dominated Germany's government from 1933 to 1945. On the surface, the party aimed to superimpose an ideology of NATIONALISM and racism on all areas of culture, including music, and the 1938 convocation in Düsseldorf known as the *Reichsmusiktage* (Reich music days) with its notorious exhibit on *Entartete Musik* (degenerate music) stood out as the single most concerted effort to set such ideological criteria. Yet the far greater impact of National Socialism actually lay in the more tangible policy measures of reforming music professions, patronizing elite musical institutions, and purging German musical life of JEWS and political opponents. The Reichsmusikkammer (Reich Music Chamber), established in 1933 as a branch of the Propaganda Ministry and first presided over by composer Richard STRAUSS, became the obligatory union for practitioners in all facets of music production. Within a relatively short time, it set wages for professional musicians, regulated certification, and established an old-age pension plan. By requiring proof of Aryan lineage for membership, it also aimed systematically to exclude Jews from taking part in German musical life. Massive purges of "undesirables" from performance, composition, and music education affected gypsies, non-whites, political, social, and sexual "deviants," and most of all Jews. Their exclusion was carried out first by publicly humiliating prominent figures such as SCHOENBERG, Bruno Walter, and Otto Klemperer (accused of "defiling Wagner"), and then through bureaucratic means: by 1935, all non-Aryans were excluded from the Reichsmusikkammer, and in 1937 Jews were officially banned from attending public cultural events (this could be enforced only after 1941, when every Jew was required to wear a yellow badge).

Yet this comprehensive policy of exclusion sometimes came into conflict with the parallel mission to maintain high levels of artistic quality, especially in connection with Wagner productions. The Nazi government made concerted efforts to revitalize high-profile musical institutions that had found themselves in serious financial straits prior to 1933, including the BAYREUTH FESTIVAL. HITLER's admiration for Wagner and close ties with the family prompted him to rescue the festival from its financial difficulties, subsidizing new productions and averting its closure during the war, but also to retain the director Heinz TIETJEN and stage designer Emil PREETORIUS despite their former Marxist connections, as well as singers Max LORENZ and Frida LEIDER, and conductor Herbert Janssen, despite their marriage to Jews. Hermann Göring similarly exercised his authority as Prussian head of state in choosing artistic personnel for the Prussian State Opera in Berlin, and contracted Lorenz and Leider, while Caspar Neher continued to stage Wagner operas in Germany despite his close associations with communists such as Bertolt Brecht.

Beyond these administrative and institutional reforms, however, Nazi leaders had little if any impact on musical consumption. Hitler's Wagner obsession did little to reverse a steady decline in the popularity of Wagner productions since the 1920s. A few feeble attempts during the Third Reich to re-popularize Wagner's music had only limited success (the best known instances were the Wagner quotations in the score to Leni Riefenstahl's *Triumph of the Will*), although certain works enjoyed special status at state and party events, with *Die MEISTERSINGER* and the *RIENZI* overture earning special prominence. PAMELA M. POTTER

See also GERMANNESS

Michael H. Kater, *The Twisted Muse. Musicians and Their Music in the Third Reich* (Oxford University Press, 1997).

Pamela M. Potter, "Nazism," *Grove Music Online*, www.oxfordmusiconline (accessed 23 March 2013).

"Wagner and the Third Reich: Myths and Realities," in *Cambridge Companion to Wagner*, ed. Thomas S. Grey (see bibliography): 235–45.

National Socialism, Wagner propaganda during. National Socialist propaganda consistently claimed correspondences between Richard Wagner and the major themes of HITLER's movement. Contributors to party-controlled newspapers and journals – including leading scholars – were adamant that there were parallels between Wagner's works (both prose and stage) and the Nazi world-view. Since the nineteenth century, German political movements from left to right have consistently staked claims to "German masters" as high-cultural validation of their ideals. By the end of that century, Wagner was invoked by activists of every political persuasion, nationalistic and right-wing interpretations being particularly strong. Supporters, especially around the BAYREUTH CIRCLE, intensified these associations into the twentieth century. By the time Hitler became a Wagnerian, views of the composer as a *völkish* icon constituted a significant strain of Wagner RECEPTION.

Hitler was respected among Nazi Wagnerians as a true aficionado. Besides his highly symbolic attendance at performances including the BAYREUTH FESTIVAL, however, Hitler did not make public statements about the meanings that Wagner had for him or his movement. Doubtless, the Nazi leader was influenced by notions deemed Wagnerian by the *völkish* right. But debate continues as to whether "Hitler's Wagner" had any relationship to Wagner, thus holding the composer responsible for actions this construct inspired.

Clearly, though, in a cultural-historical version of "working toward the Führer," Nazi scholars, critics, and journalists strove to link Wagner directly to their ideology. In this effort, they paid special attention to Wagner's writings. As described in the main Nazi party newspaper, the *Völkischer Beobachter* (*VB*), his polemics were "weapons for today's final battle" (*VB* 16 June 1934) which "seem as though they were written expressly to address our struggle" (*VB* 23 May 1928). Overall, they held, "one always runs into National Socialist views" in his writings, so much that "it seems he divined our movement"

(*VB* 17 April 1939). From its earliest cultural coverage on, the Nazi press focused most of all on Wagner's notorious article *Das JUDENTUM IN DER MUSIK* (Jewishness in Music, 1850). Underscoring Wagner's ANTI-SEMITIC views, Nazi ideologues designated him "one of the few who early and clearly recognized the cultural dangers of Judaism and, without any consideration for his own person, steadfastly went into battle" (*VB* 12 February 1933).

But Wagner's music dramas were equally important to Nazi propagandists. While not every one of his works was appropriated in strong political terms, *LOHENGRIN* and *Die MEISTERSINGER VON NÜRNBERG* were – mainly as celebrations of GERMANNESS, and not as attacks on JEWS (however much SIXTUS BECKMESSER may appear to be stereotyped). The Nazi implication of Wagner's work as eliminationist anti-Semitic plot appears primarily in the reception of the *RING*. There, ALBERICH incarnated the "dark spirit of Jewish Mammonism" and SIEGFRIED the "embodiment of National Socialism, which alone possesses the courage to break the chains of slavery around the German people" (*VB* 17 August 1929). "Truly," the foremost Nazi propaganda outlet warned, "if you don't take this seriously, you're going to go down in the fall: now is the time to recognize and fight the enemy." This "is what Wagner tells us" (*VB* 23 August 1928). It was in the *Ring* cycle, therefore, that National Socialist Wagnerians perceived their *Meister*'s voice as harmonizing most perfectly with their *Führer*'s.   DAVID B. DENNIS

See also ANTI-SEMITISM; NATIONALISM; *VOLK*

David B. Dennis, "Crying 'Wolf'? A Review Essay on Recent Wagner Literature," *German Studies Review* 24.1 (2001): 145–58.
Inhumanities: Nazi Interpretations of Western Culture (Cambridge University Press, 2012).
"'The Most German of all German Operas': *Die Meistersinger* through the Lens of the Third Reich," in *Wagner's "Meistersinger": Performance, History, Representation*, ed. Nicholas Vazsonyi (see bibliography): 98–119.

Nationalism. The history of German nationalism has no clear starting point in the modern era, a circumstance reflecting long centuries of political fragmentation and collective powerlessness. Germany's central geographical position made it an essential area of cultural and economic transmission and, at the same time, contributed to a history marked by constant tension, discontinuity, and the absence of stable sources for collective identity. It made Germany an incoherent term or, in the estimation of many a frustrated observer, a mere geographical expression. German Europe's overarching state, the Holy Roman Empire of the German Nation, embodied the incoherence of German national identity. In 962, its founder King Otto I chose diffuse imperial grandeur over monarchical centralism, and from then until 1806, when its remaining members dissolved it, its hundreds of princes, dukes, cities, and bishops, none of them with the means to reform this pseudo-empire, chose instead to preserve their own authority, even at the cost of internal insecurity and vulnerability to outside powers.

Wagner was born less than a decade after the Empire dissolved and in the immediate wake of the Battle of the Nations (1813). The name of this event expressed the new political realities of Europe, suggesting the future course that German political development should take – towards a unified national state. German nationalism had already begun to cohere as a movement during the years of French domination (1792–1815). It was grounded in the patriotism of language and culture – a passionate interest in the commonalities of speech, history, art, and custom among the German-speaking people (*VOLK*). For nationalists, the German language most clearly expressed the nation's identity, and the culture of a people was "the flower of its being" (HERDER, quoted in Sheehan 166). Not surprisingly, the POLITICS associated with such views were inchoate, and a nationalist movement hardly existed before the French revolutionary invasion of the Rhineland in 1792. Its adherents did not represent a cross-section of the population but rather a small, self-consciously enlightened number of people drawn mainly from the middle strata of society.

Wagner's background matched this social and educational profile; moreover, he grew up in the city renowned among nationalists for the battle that had roused their hopes for a unified German state, hopes subsequently dashed by the restoration of decentralized princely states. As Wagner recognized, his own process of coming to self-consciousness and maturity, learning, striving, creating, and experiencing defeat then vindication seemed to mirror the development of the German nation itself. His nationalism, while having its origins in his unhappy years in PARIS (1839–42) and containing elements with a uniquely Wagnerian cast, nevertheless flowed in the mainstream of national feeling, as it changed and adjusted from the period of French revolutionary and Napoleonic incursions through to the wars of unification.

Like early nationalist propagandists Johann Gottlieb Fichte and Friedrich Ludwig Jahn, he believed that the German people and their nation had a special mission to secure the future of Europe on a higher moral plane. Like them, he saw the Germans as an original, unadulterated people, capable of much greater achievements as a people than their enemies (ranging from petty, self-interested princes, to the French, the Catholics, and the JEWS) had so far allowed them. Like them he thought Germany needed to awaken to its own greatness and assert itself in a world of nations, thereby bringing about the REGENERATION not just of Germans and German culture, but of the entire world. Unlike them, he regarded his own role in this regeneration – through the MUSIC DRAMAS he gave to Germany and the world – to be essential, and therein lay the seeds of both his own ultimate disappointment with the fruits of nationalism and his followers' missionary zeal.

Wagner's nationalism thus had a strongly utopian caste to it, shaped by his reading of GERMAN HISTORY and MYTH and sustained by the ambiguity of political developments toward a national state during his adult years. Influenced by German Universalist thinkers such as Constantin FRANTZ, Wagner was never an enthusiastic adherent of the "small-German" solution, which entailed a unified state formed under Prussian leadership. In his ZURICH writings (1849–51), products of his years of political exile, he still proclaimed that the social revolution was needed before the ARTWORK OF THE FUTURE could be created and consumed. Later, he expressed vaguer ideas about a forthcoming unity between state and culture at the heart of which was GERMANNESS, a quality he repeatedly attempted to define in his writings from the 1850s and 1860s, such as *WAS IST DEUTSCH?* (What is German?). Germans were, among other things, brave, solid, true, honest, free, and purely human, and had no desire to rule over foreign peoples. Discussions of legal regimes, forms of government, and electoral politics came to hold no place in his efforts to describe a German national future. What mattered was the establishment of conditions in which the unified art works (*GESAMTKUNSTWERK*) he imagined could come into being and be given to the public. Artistic regeneration could even lead the way to political regeneration or at least make it imaginable; the German nation would be realized first in the unified art work, thus paving the way for a more far-reaching unity of the German people.

In a sense, Bismarck beat Wagner to the finish line, with *Realpolitik* outpacing the *Gesamtkunstwerk* every step of the way. After centuries of catching up and delays, most Germans were eager to embrace the so-called second Reich of 1871 as the long-awaited embodiment of their national identity. Artistic rebirth could wait, or follow. But for Wagner, GERMAN UNIFICATION under Bismarck could only bring disappointment, though different in kind from the disappointment of republicans or "great-German" nationalists, who had hoped for a German state embracing Austria. Yet, as the Master turned ever further away from political involvement, his followers were determined to graft WAGNERISM onto the national tree. In the words of the Academic Wagner Society of Berlin, the opening of Bayreuth in 1876 signified a "massive artistic monument to the German spirit" that formed the counterpart to the political achievement of 1871. The "German festival" at Bayreuth represented a "second triumph" for the "world-historical calling of the Germanic peoples," and Richard Wagner, "the bard of German greatness," had had "unfailing reformatory impact in the art world" that could "only be compared to Bismarck's political achievements" (quoted in Vazsonyi 180). Wagner's importance to German nationalism and the German nation was thus declared self-evident.   CELIA APPLEGATE

See also GERMAN HISTORY; POLITICS

James J. Sheehan, *German History 1780–1866* (Oxford: Clarendon, 1989).
Nicholas Vazsonyi, *Richard Wagner: Self-Promotion and the Making of a Brand* (see bibliography).

Naumann, Emil (b. Berlin, 8 Sep. 1827; d. Dresden, 23 June 1888), music scholar, composer, and grandson of composer Johann Gottlieb Naumann (1741–1801). His cousin, Ernst Naumann (1832–1910), was also a music scholar and composer, and his sister, Ida Naumann Becker, was a singer and a composer of *Lieder*. Between 1842 and 1844, Naumann studied with MENDELSSOHN, who was a lasting influence on Naumann's work as a composer; these compositions included three operas, several sacred works, *Lieder* collections, and a few instrumental pieces. From 1850, he served as *Hofkirchen-Musikdirektor* (music director for the court church) in Berlin, and edited a psalm cycle for the church year in 1855. Naumann received a doctorate from Berlin University in 1867. Upon moving to DRESDEN in 1873, he began lecturing on music history at that city's conservatory and was eventually appointed professor.

As a scholar, Naumann wrote numerous essays and books on music history and aesthetics, often from a German nationalist standpoint. His most widely known scholarly work was his *Illustrierte Musikgeschichte* (Illustrated History of Music, 1880–5), which was translated into many languages and went through several editions. In this volume, Naumann argued that music had entered "the age of the epigones" and he saw little chance for further progress of the "classical" musical genres, such as the symphony. Moreover, "tonal art" as an organic whole was "complete and finished." This aesthetic conservatism also manifested itself in Naumann's reception of the first BAYREUTH FESTIVAL (1876). This is evident in his essay *Musikdrama oder Oper?* (Music Drama or Opera?, 1876), in which Naumann argued that Wagner's ideas about operatic reform showed no genuine innovation or originality, and in fact simply replicated the ideas of the Florentine Camerata, the late sixteenth-century group of Italian artists and intellectuals whose discussions on musical and dramatic trends originated the genre of opera. Nonetheless, Naumann conceded Wagner's musical talent, such as his aptitude for creating orchestral effects. For example, his description of the orchestral PRELUDE to *Das RHEINGOLD* compliments Wagner's orchestration and the effect of the covered orchestra pit. Naumann's 1877 essay *Zukunftsmusik und die Musik der Zukunft* ("Music of the Future" and the Music of the Future) reiterates the claim that there is nothing radically innovative in Wagner's AESTHETIC paradigm, and that the concept of "music of the future" could be traced back to the ideas espoused by the significant composers of previous generations.

DANIEL SHERIDAN

Emil Naumann, *Musikdrama oder Oper? Eine Beleuchtung der Bayreuther Bühnenfestspiele* (Berlin: Oppenheim, 1876).
"Zukunftsmusik und die Musik der Zukunft," Ein Vortrag gehalten am 6. Januar 1877 im wissenschaftlichen Verein zu Berlin, *Deutsche Zeit- und Streit-Fragen* 6.82 (1877).

Nazi. See NATIONAL SOCIALISM (with subheadings)

Neudeutsche Schule. See NEW GERMAN SCHOOL

Neue Wagner-Forschungen. Journal of the Richard-Wagner-Forschungsstätte (RWF; Bayreuth) established by HITLER's edict on 22 May 1938. Edited by RWF director Otto STROBEL, its sole issue (Karlsruhe: G. Braun, 1943) embodies the RWF's curious tension between scholarly objectivity and Nazi ideology. The contents combine scholarly articles and critical editions of primary documents with more tendentious material, such as an obituary of Wagner analyst and long-time Nazi party member Alfred LORENZ that stresses his connections with the National Socialists.

A second volume of *Neue Wagner-Forschungen* remained unpublished because of the war and survives in Strobel's *Nachlaß* in the Nationalarchiv of the RICHARD WAGNER FOUNDATION. It was to include over 100 unpublished letters from Wagner to Eduard DEVRIENT, Gustav Schmidt, and others, and entries from Hans RICHTER's diary. Plans for a third volume can be reconstructed from Strobel's correspondence. STEPHEN MCCLATCHIE

Neue Zeitschrift für Musik (*NZfM*, 1834–). The primary German-language music periodical of the mid- and late nineteenth centuries, and the longest-running music journal in Germany. Robert SCHUMANN established the journal in LEIPZIG in 1834, as an alternative to the musically conservative *Allgemeine Musikalische Zeitung* (*AMZ*), which was published in the same city by BREITKOPF & HÄRTEL. Due to Schumann's literary abilities, the *NZfM* flourished in its initial years, even though its subscription base did not challenge that of the *AMZ*. One of Schumann's associates, Karl Franz BRENDEL, bought the journal in late 1844 and – while retaining the original title – started transforming it from a repository for "wholly personal perspectives and opinions" (Brendel, *NZfM* 22.1–2 [1845]: 10) into a vehicle for musical reform in accordance with the editor's scholarly and philosophical (i.e., Hegelian) leanings.

As early as 1846, Brendel had brought Wagner to the attention of his readers, but it was not until June 1851 that the editor clearly wrote in Wagner's favor ("Wagner has made the most significant contribution of the present in the field of opera"), and January 1852 that he unequivocally dedicated his journal to the composer's cause. The first substantial PUBLICITY campaign for Wagner in the journal was by Theodor UHLIG, who published articles about Beethoven's symphonies (1850) and Wagner's aesthetic writings (1850–2) with the latter's full approbation. Wagner himself took up the pen with his controversial *Das JUDENTUM IN DER MUSIK* (Jewishness in Music, 1850), which appeared under the pen name "K. Freigedank" and caused Brendel considerable difficulties (as Wagner recognized in the *Aufklärungen über "Das Judentum in der Musik"* from 1869).

Despite ongoing misgivings over the *NZfM* and Brendel's editorship, Wagner continued to make submissions to and allow his writings to be reprinted in the journal in the form of open letters and short essays. The journal reprinted excerpts from *Ein THEATER IN ZÜRICH* (A Theater in Zurich, July 1851), and Brendel published in 1852 Wagner's letters about music criticism/journalism (addressed to Brendel) and about LISZT's Goethe Foundation project (*ÜBER DIE "GOETHE-STIFTUNG"* [Concerning the Goethe Foundation, 1851]), as well as serial excerpts from his pamphlet about the performance of *TANNHÄUSER* (continued into 1853), reprints of his Zurich PROGRAM NOTES regarding the OVERTURES to *Tannhäuser* and *Der FLIEGENDE HOLLÄNDER*, and the "instrumental introduction" to *LOHENGRIN*. In 1854, Wagner once again wrote specifically for the *NZfM* with a detailed communication to Brendel about revising the conclusion of GLUCK's overture to *Iphigenia in Aulis* (replete with musical examples). Later *NZfM* publications initiated by Wagner include: *Ein Brief von Richard Wagner über Franz Liszt* (April 1857, later titled: *ÜBER FRANZ LISZTS SYMPHONISCHE DICHTUNGEN* [On Franz Liszt's Symphonic Poems]), *Meine Erinnerungen an Ludwig Schnorr von Carolsfeld* (June 1868), and *Über das Dirigieren* (November 1869–January 1870). The journal also reprinted the foreword to the *Gesammelte Schriften und Dichtungen* (1871) and the *BEETHOVEN* essay (1870, republished in 1874).

Wagner's ongoing presence in the *NZfM* would seem to contradict his own misgivings over Brendel and the journal, as stated in letters to Uhlig and Liszt: he chided Brendel's inconsistency in supporting his cause, and the editor's lack of understanding for the aesthetic issues at stake (for example, Brendel insisted on the need to retain the *Sonderkunst* [separate arts]). Brendel's policy of opening his columns to free debate resulted in the journal's erstwhile publication of opposing viewpoints (e.g., those of Eduard Krüger), which led to Wagner's corrective letter about criticism from 1852. Despite Wagner's serious doubts, the *NZfM* was influential and thus, as he wrote to Uhlig

(20 September 1850), "for lack of something better, you use it." Wagner's name did appear as a contributor in the journal's semi-annual masthead beginning in January of 1852.

Besides Wagner's participation as author during the early 1850s, the *NZfM* gave every indication of being the publication organ for the early Wagnerians. Uhlig's intense and methodical promotion, and Brendel's eventual full support for Wagner laid the cornerstones between 1850 and 1852 for the pro-Wagner contributions from the Liszt circle in Weimar, beginning with Hans von BÜLOW in 1852. He was joined by Joachim RAFF in 1853, and Peter CORNELIUS and – above all – Franz Liszt in 1854, all of them producing favorable literature about Wagner. NEW GERMANS from outside of Weimar similarly added to these efforts, including the self-proclaimed "oldest Wagnerian" Richard POHL in DRESDEN, and Louis KÖHLER in KÖNIGSBERG. More often than not, the *NZfM* contributions of these critics involved skirmishes with anti-Wagnerian polemics in the newspapers and journals of the day, most notoriously the *Grenzboten* of Leipzig – Bülow and Raff were particularly adept combatants, but Brendel and Pohl also challenged Wagner's opponents.

During the crucial years of the 1850s and 1860s, the journal also carried (favorable) reviews of Wagner performances, aesthetic assessments of his writings and thought, and even close analyses of specific works: Uhlig's multi-part review of the *LOHENGRIN* premiere (1850), Brendel's discussion of Weimar performances of *Lohengrin* and *Tannhäuser* (1852), and – later – Brendel's 1859 article series about *Lohengrin*, and his address about the New German School. In terms of broader evaluations, Brendel published his *Die bisherige Sonderkunst und das Kunstwerk der Zukunft* (The Separate Arts and the Artwork of the Future) as an article series in 1853, and Pohl followed up with his reflections on "die Musik der Gegenwart und die Gesammtkunst der Zukunft" (Music of the Present and the Total Art of the Future) in 1854 and 1855. Liszt's brief introduction to *Das RHEINGOLD* appeared in the *NZfM* of 1 January 1855, while his more detailed discussion of *Der fliegende Holländer* took up five issues in 1854.

By the late 1850s, the attention of the journal – in the absence of new compositions or writings by Wagner – turned towards Liszt and the New German School. The activity of the Allgemeiner Deutscher Musikverein (founded 1861) took up considerable space in the *NZfM*, and even though the premieres of *TRISTAN* (1865) and *Die MEISTERSINGER VON NÜRNBERG* (1868) received extended reviews (the latter by Cornelius), the journal never recovered the intensity of its initial Wagner promotion.   JAMES DEAVILLE

See also MUSIC CRITICS AND CRITICISM; RECEPTION

James Deaville, "The Controversy Surrounding Liszt's Conception of Programme Music," in *Nineteenth-Century Music: Selected Proceedings of the Tenth International Conference*, ed. Jim Samson and Bennett Zon (Aldershot: Ashgate, 2002): 98–124.

James Garratt, *Music, Culture and Social Reform in the Age of Wagner* (Cambridge University Press, 2010).

Nicholas Vazsonyi, *Richard Wagner: Self-Promotion and the Making of a Brand* (see bibliography).

Neumann, Angelo (b. Vienna, 18 Aug. 1838; d. Prague, 20 Dec. 1910), singer, impresario, opera director. Neumann gave his baritone debut in Krakow in 1859. Following short engagements in Pressburg (Bratislava), Ödenburg

(Sopron), and Danzig (Gdansk), he was an ensemble member of the Vienna Hofoper between 1862 and 1876, where in 1875 he witnessed Wagner direct *LOHENGRIN* and *TANNHÄUSER*. In 1876, Neumann was called to LEIPZIG as opera director. Having opened his tenure with a new *Lohengrin*, Neumann attended the first BAYREUTH FESTIVAL and immediately worked towards "transplanting" its *RING DES NIBELUNGEN* to Leipzig (Neumann 22). Despite cumbersome negotiations, Wagner's refusal to release the Bayreuth décor, and prevailing opinion that the *Ring* was impossible in ordinary theaters, Neumann in 1878 succeeded in staging the first complete *Ring* cycle outside Bayreuth and MUNICH. The success of this production, which closely imitated the Bayreuth model, earned him Wagner's trust, as did his willingness (by contrast to his chief rival, Bernhard Pollini of Hamburg) to accommodate as much as possible the composer's wishes regarding cast and staging.

Notwithstanding occasional conflicts, Neumann now became Wagner's most important entrepreneurial advocate. In May 1881, he brought his *Ring* to Berlin's Victoria-Theater, with Wagner attending two of four sold-out cycles; a year later he took it to LONDON. After concluding his Leipzig directorship in June 1882, with performances of all Wagner's operas from *RIENZI* to *GÖTTERDÄMMERUNG*, Neumann formed a touring "Richard Wagner Theater" with conductor Anton SEIDL, an orchestra of sixty to seventy, two casts (including such leading Wagner singers as Amalie MATERNA, Emil SCARIA, and Heinrich and Therese VOGL, as well as Katharina Klafsky and Hedwig Reicher-Kindermann, both of whom Neumann had discovered), chorus, technical staff, and the original Bayreuth décor that Wagner was now willing to sell. Between September 1882 and June 1883, the company performed twenty-nine *Ring* cycles in twenty-five cities across Germany, Holland, Belgium, Switzerland, Italy, and Austro-Hungary, as well as individual operas or promotional concerts (for a [mostly correct] list of performances, see Rubow & Stump). Regardless of inevitable artistic compromises, this unprecedented tour demonstrated widely that the *Ring* was economically and technically viable, and how it was to be staged (Wagner to Neumann 16 October 1881). Promoting "Muster-Aufführungen" (model performances), it became Bayreuth's "ambulant" counterpart. Wagner clearly appreciated the managerial skills of his "friend and benefactor" (*Freund und Gönner*) and considered entrusting him with an American tour (he was less convinced about Neumann's idea of a permanent Wagner Theater in Berlin). A decisive motivation was Wagner's recognition that – ironically in view of his ANTI-SEMITISM – he owed his then most important revenues to the Jewish-born Neumann (Wagner to Neumann, 13 June 1882, 13 January and 11 February 1883; see also CWD).

Following the tour, Neumann revitalized the Wagner repertory in Bremen as director of its Stadttheater. From 1885 to his death, he managed the Deutsches Landestheater (since 1888 Neues Deutsches Theater) in Prague, which – like Leipzig – he brought to European fame with his talent for discovering singers and conductors, his cyclic performances of masters including GLUCK, MOZART, MEYERBEER, VERDI, and (repeatedly) Wagner, as well as the annual May Festival he instituted in the 1890s. That same year Neumann revived the "Wagner Theater" for *Ring* productions in ST. PETERSBURG and Moscow. His *Erinnerungen an Richard Wagner* (1907) is an important, if somewhat grandiloquent, source on the tour and Wagner's artistic and financial interests. GUNDULA KREUZER

Josef Juhász, *Das Richard Wagner-Theater in Italien. Erinnerungen an die Aufführungen des "Ring des Nibelungen"* (Berlin: Deutsche Bühnen- und Concert-Agentur, 1884).

Der Ring des Nibelungen: Erinnerung an die 100 Aufführungen des Richard Wagner-Theaters (Darmstadt: Herbert, 1883).

Gundula Kreuzer, "Authentizität, Visualisierung, Bewahrung: Das reisende 'Wagner-Theater' und die Konservierbarkeit von Inszenierungen," in *Angst vor der Zerstörung: Der Meister Künste zwischen Archiv und Erneuerung*, ed. Robert Sollich, Clemens Risi, Sebastian Reus, and Stephan Jöris (Berlin: Theater der Zeit, 2008): 139–60.

Angelo Neumann, *Erinnerungen an Richard Wagner* (see bibliography).

Markus Rubow and Susanne Stump, "Das wandelnde Bayreuth: Das Richard-Wagner-Theater Angelo Neumanns," in *Der Ring des Nibelungen in Münster: Der Zyklus von 1999–2001*, ed. Klaus Hortschansky and Berthold Warnecke (Münster: agenda, 2001): 191–205.

New German School (*Neudeutsche Schule*), designation for the progressive movement in music around Wagner and LISZT, especially during the 1850s and 1860s. Coined by *NEUE ZEITSCHRIFT FÜR MUSIK* editor Franz BRENDEL in 1859 as an alternative to the derisive nickname *ZUKUNFTSMUSIK*, the phrase came to apply to those composers and writers on music who espoused the general principle of music as possessing expressive and descriptive qualities. For Brendel, BACH and Handel represented what he identified as the Old Germans (Protestant church music) – Wagner, Liszt, and BERLIOZ served as the coryphaei for the new movement. Trying to link the three into a united German artistic movement was problematic, however, because Wagner was the only one of the triad born German, and both Berlioz and Wagner distanced themselves from the term and its tangible manifestation in the society called the Allgemeiner Deutscher Musikverein (ADMV, established 1861). Well before Brendel's neologism, already at the start of the 1850s, a circle of like-minded progressive musicians had begun to form, with a hub of activity around Liszt in Weimar, an ideological center in Wagner and his aesthetic writings, and a publication vehicle in Brendel's LEIPZIG-based *Neue Zeitschrift*. Those in Weimar designated themselves as *Neu-Weimar*, while contributors to Brendel's journal used the term *Fortschrittspartei* (progressive party) and their opponents called them *Zukunftsmusiker* (musicians of the future). They pursued the goal of musical reform through a closer union of music and word, which occasioned significant opposition from such figures as Eduard HANSLICK and Johannes BRAHMS, among others, who refused to recognize the validity of the designation "New German School."

Wagner may not have adopted Brendel's term, nor developed close ties with members of the New German School other than Liszt, Peter CORNELIUS, and Hans von BÜLOW, but he did benefit from its dedication to him, including premieres of *LOHENGRIN* under Liszt (1850) and of *TRISTAN UND ISOLDE* (1865) and *Die MEISTERSINGER VON NÜRNBERG* (1868) under Bülow, and publication of a number of his open letters and short essays (including *Das JUDENTUM IN DER MUSIK*; Jewishness in Music) through Brendel in the *Neue Zeitschrift* of the 1850s. Furthermore, New Germans Liszt (in the 1850s) and Cornelius (in the 1860s) published extended essays about Wagner that earned his praise. The ADMV tangibly demonstrated its dedication to Wagner by performing excerpts from his works at its annual *Tonkünstlerversammlungen* – for example, at the preliminary festival in Leipzig in 1859, attendees heard the PRELUDE to *Tristan*, while the 1865 festival in Dessau featured the Prelude to *Die Meistersinger* (both performances before the premieres of those works). With the establishment of the Bayreuth FESTIVAL THEATER, the creation of the *BAYREUTHER BLÄTTER*, and the development of his BAYREUTH CIRCLE of supporters, Wagner ultimately did not need to rely upon the institutions of the New German School to promulgate his cause.

To the extent that the designation New German came to be associated with orchestral program music, especially the symphonic poem, the movement and its *spiritus rector* Liszt exerted considerable influence upon composers of other national compositional schools in Europe and the United States. At the end of the century, Richard STRAUSS was mentored by Liszt's pupil Alexander Ritter, and thus has been associated with the New German movement by virtue of his tone poems, as have other members of the so-called Munich School. However, the appropriateness of the designation "New German" for the late nineteenth century is a matter of debate, given the term's historical roots and its increasingly vague meaning over the course of the century.   JAMES DEAVILLE

Detlef Altenburg, ed., *Liszt und die Neudeutsche Schule*, Weimarer Liszt-Studien, vol. 3 (Laaber Verlag, 2006).

James Deaville, ed., "Franz Brendel's Reconciliation Address," in *Richard Wagner and His World*, ed. Thomas S. Grey (see bibliography): 311–32.

New media. See WAGNER AND NEW MEDIA

Newman, Ernest (b. Everton [Lancashire], 30 Nov. 1868; d. Tadworth [Surrey], 7 July 1959), born William Roberts. He first used the pseudonym Ernest Newman when he began writing for the *National Reformer* in 1889, thereby signaling his desire to be known as a "new man in earnest." He adopted the name permanently in 1899 and went on to become the pre-eminent English music critic in the first half of the twentieth century, and the author of some twenty books, including several on Wagner.

Newman attended Liverpool College and University, planning for a career in the civil service in India. Prevented from entering the colonial service for health reasons, Newman went into banking. In fourteen years as a clerk at the Bank of Liverpool, he taught himself music and learned several foreign languages.

His first book, *Pseudo-Philosophy at the End of the Nineteenth-Century* (1897), written under the pseudonym Hugh Mortimer Cecil, was a spirited attack on some theologically tinged opponents of Darwin. This kind of debunking would remain characteristic of Newman's criticism in general.

Before his appointment in 1920 as music critic for *The Sunday Times*, where he remained until 1958, Newman taught briefly at the Midland Institute School of Music in Birmingham and wrote music criticism for the *Manchester Guardian*, the *Birmingham Daily Post*, and *The Guardian*, championing Richard STRAUSS, Elgar, Hugo WOLF, and Sibelius. His first foray into Wagnerian territory was *A Study of Wagner* (1899), a monograph he later disowned. A more comprehensive and probing book, *Wagner as Man and Artist*, followed in 1914. *Fact and Fiction about Wagner* (1931) addresses issues only touched upon in the previous book and cleared the way for Newman's *opus magnum*, *The Life of Richard Wagner* (4 vols., 1933–47). A magisterial introduction to the operatic works, *Wagner Nights*, followed in 1949.

Although much new information has since become available, and the critical focus on Wagner has been sharpened considerably, and although his treatment of SCHOPENHAUER and NIETZSCHE is inadequate, Newman's monumental work is widely considered to be the standard biography on account of his sound methodology, his commonsensical assessment of the composer's character flaws, and his disavowal of any pretensions to finality. In the Foreword to volume one, he insists that a biography must be based on "the whole evidence available at the time of writing" – an unmistakable rejection of the manipulation of information practiced by Wagner's descendants, and invalidating much German scholarship on Wagner.

Although Newman's *Life* has not been translated into German, it was much admired by Theodor ADORNO, Thomas MANN, and Franz BEIDLER, the composer's disinherited grandson. When Beidler, the only Wagner descendant aside from FRIEDELIND who remained untainted by Nazism, was charged to draw up plans for a completely de-nazified BAYREUTH FESTIVAL, he placed Newman, a Bayreuth regular for half a century, at the top of an international advisory board. For legal reasons, that plan came to naught.

HANS RUDOLF VAGET

Vera Newman, *Ernest Newman: A Memoir by His Wife* (New York: Knopf, 1964).
Hans R. Vaget, "The Importance of Ernest Newman," *The Wagner Journal* 1.3 (2007): 19–34.

Nibelung Chancellery, from the German "Nibelungen Kanzelei." Group of originally four musicians – Hermann ZUMPE, Anton SEIDL, Joseph RUBINSTEIN, and Demetrius Lalas – who helped Wagner with musical preparations for the first full performance of the *RING* in BAYREUTH (1876). In a letter to LUDWIG II, Wagner remarks: "Parcels intended for them are already arriving addressed to: 'Nibelung Chancellery in Bayreuth.' I am also training the four of them to be capable of conducting my work in the future by insisting that they help me in everything now. I then invite these apprentices of mine to make music for us of an evening" (1 October 1874). NICHOLAS VAZSONYI

Niemann, Albert Wilhelm Karl (b. Erxleben, 15 Jan. 1831; d. Berlin, 13 Jan. 1917), German singer. Arguably the most significant Wagner tenor during the composer's lifetime, Niemann sang the title role in the ill-starred PARIS production of *TANNHÄUSER* (1861). His lengthiest engagement was at Berlin (1866–88), where he was the first WALTHER VON STOLZING (1870) and TRISTAN (1876). He was SIEGMUND in the first productions of the *RING* at BAYREUTH (1876) and LONDON (1882), and appeared in the Metropolitan Opera premieres of *TRISTAN UND ISOLDE* (1886) and *GÖTTERDÄMMERUNG* (1888). DAVID BRECKBILL

Einhard Luther, *Biographie eines Stimmfaches* (see bibliography): 1:166–89.

Nietzsche, Friedrich Wilhelm (b. Röcken, 15 Oct. 1844; d. Weimar, 25 Aug. 1900), German philosopher.

1. Nietzsche and Wagner
2. After Wagner
3. Critique of Wagner

1. Nietzsche and Wagner

At heart a musical conservative, sixteen-year-old Nietzsche was introduced to Wagner's music in 1861 by his more adventurous friend, Gustav Krug (whose father was a friend of Mendelssohn). Four years before its first performance, they purchased Hans von BÜLOW's PIANO REDUCTION of *TRISTAN UND ISOLDE* and played through the entire opera, singing all the parts. Doubtful at first, Nietzsche only became fully converted to Wagner's "brilliant deeds and plans for [aesthetic and social] reform" (Young 40) in 1864, and not fully converted to his music until October 1868, when he was swept off his feet by the Prelude to *Tristan* and the overture to *Die MEISTERSINGER VON NÜRNBERG*. The following month (November 1868), in LEIPZIG, he met Wagner in person. The latter was delighted to find a brilliant young graduate student so versed in his music, while Nietzsche found in Wagner "the most vivid illustration of what SCHOPENHAUER calls a 'genius'" (Young 78). Nietzsche had recently undergone a Schopenhauerian conversion; Wagner had been a disciple since 1854.

Appointed as professor of classics in Basel (1869), Nietzsche quickly accepted the invitation to visit the Wagners in TRIBSCHEN, about three hours away by train. Soon adopted as a member of the family, he had his own bedroom and an invitation to visit whenever he wished. Wagner, the same age as Nietzsche's long-dead but greatly missed father, became his emotional and intellectual mentor; COSIMA Wagner, the object of an "impossible love" in the romantic tradition of GOETHE's Werther. In the three years prior to their departure for BAYREUTH, Nietzsche visited the Wagners in Tribschen twenty-three times. In the evenings, he and Cosima would play four-handed piano pieces and there would be intense, three-sided discussions of SCHOPENHAUER, Wagner's recently published *BEETHOVEN* essay (1870), and of Nietzsche's preparatory work for his first book, *The Birth of Tragedy* (1872). In its Preface, he describes this book as the continuation of a "conversation" with Wagner, one he could have with no one else. Heartbroken by the Wagners' move to Bayreuth, Nietzsche gave thanks that, in *The Birth*, he had at least "memorialized the world of Tribschen." Nietzsche disliked Bayreuth, and his personal intimacy with the Wagners never recovered from their, as he felt, desertion of the "isle of the blessed" (*Ecce homo* 3; Human, All-too-Human §2).

Although Nietzsche continued to work for the Bayreuth cause until 1876 (*Richard Wagner at Bayreuth* was an essay intended as his contribution to the first Bayreuth Festival), the first hints of Wagner-criticism occur in the privacy of his notebooks as early as the beginning of 1874. So, for example, while still finding much to admire in Wagner, he also writes that "the tyrannical [in him] allows validity to no other individuality save his own and that of his intimates. The danger for Wagner is great, when he does not allow BRAHMS to be valid. Or the JEWS" (Young 186).

This rejection of the "tyrannical" in Wagner, as well as being a judgment upon Wagner's thought and art, was the expression of a personal need. Nietzsche needed to escape the shadow of Wagner's towering personality and intellect in order to, in the phrase of Pindar's he liked to quote, "become what he was."

In August 1874, Nietzsche turned up at WAHNFRIED, the Wagners' house in Bayreuth, with a copy of Brahms's "Song of Triumph" in his suitcase. Placing the red-covered score on the piano, he must have known that, to the irascible Wagner, it would be, in Wagner's own later, rueful words, "a red rag to a bull." Wagner duly exploded while Nietzsche withdrew into cold politeness. Though this rupture of their friendship was never healed, Nietzsche attended the first Bayreuth Festival in 1876, only to depart halfway through. (Contrary to the portrait of a decisive act of Wagner-rejection he presented in *Ecce homo*, however, he actually returned eight days later.)

One of the sources of Nietzsche's alienation from Wagner was that, some months before the Festival, he had decided to reject Schopenhauer's (and Wagner's) metaphysical idealism, together with the "life-denial" that it facilitated. In its place, he adopted the positivist spirit and naturalistic metaphysics that was the dominant current of the times. In 1878, he published *Human, All-too-Human*, which Wagner loathed since it rejected everything – Schopenhauer, pessimism, metaphysical idealism, and the deification of art – that he believed in. The final meeting between the two former friends, a restrained affair, occurred in Sorrento on 5 November 1876.

In February 1883, on hearing of Wagner's death, Nietzsche wrote to a friend that "Wagner was by far the fullest man I have known, and in this sense I have suffered terribly from his absence these six years. But something resembling a deadly insult came between us" (Young 239–40). The "insult" was this. In October 1877 Nietzsche had visited a Dr. Eiser and an ophthalmologist in Frankfurt on account of his multiple health, above all eye, problems. Astonishingly, Eiser, a keen Wagnerian, exchanged letters with Wagner concerning Nietzsche's condition. Wagner informed Eiser of his own view that Nietzsche's progress towards blindness was the result of "masturbation" (Wagner to Eiser, 23 October 1877). Nietzsche got to hear of this letter and, connecting it with Wagner's earlier insinuation that he had homoerotic leanings (Young 183), wrote to a friend that Wagner had informed his doctor that he was guilty of "unnatural debauchery, with indications of pederasty." Wagner's former disciple was, in other words, (a) incipiently gay, (b) going blind because he masturbated too much, and, such is the further implication, (c) straying from the straight and narrow of Wagnerian thinking on account of (a) and (b).

2. After Wagner

Human, All-too-Human marked Nietzsche's public defection from the Wagnerian camp. A careful reading of his notebooks and letters, however, reveals that, in an important sense, he *never* ceased to be a Wagnerian. Thus in the privacy of his notebooks for 1878 – contemporaneous with his public defection from the "Bayreuth horizon" in *Human, All-too-Human* – he still writes that what "we want [is] to be better Wagnerians than Wagner" (Young 360). After Wagner's death, he continued to maintain strong links with leading Wagnerians such as Heinrich von Stein and Rheinhart von Seydlitz, and as late as October 1886 – after, that is, *Beyond Good and Evil*'s dismissal of Wagner as a "ponderous," "neurotic," "anti-Semitic" decadent – he is still capable of describing himself as "to a great extent Wagner's heir," and of observing to a friend that: "It is wonderful how all these followers of Wagner remain true to me. You know,

I think, that today I still believe in the ideal in which Wagner believed as firmly as ever – why should it be important that I stumbled over the many human-all-too-human obstacles that R[ichard] W[agner] placed in the path of his ideal?" (Young 360). What these and other remarks show is that, though Nietzsche's criticisms of Wagner became ever more savage as he approaches the collapse of his sanity at the end of 1888, they remain, always, "in-house" criticisms. In Nietzsche's view, there is some "ideal" to which both he and Wagner had once subscribed, to which he has remained loyal but Wagner has betrayed.

Shortly after Wagner's death, Nietzsche wrote to a friend that "In the end it was the *aged* Wagner against whom I had to protect myself" (Young 359; emphasis added). What he rejected was, then, the *later*, Schopenhauerian Wagner. In their first intimacy, two things had rendered Nietzsche and Wagner comrades-in-arms: first, Schopenhauerianism and, second, the REGENERATION of community through rebirth of Greek tragedy in the form of the "ARTWORK OF THE FUTURE" (*Birth of Tragedy* 23) (see PHILOSOPHY). Though he had tried to reconcile these positions in *The Birth of Tragedy* (Young, chapter 7), Nietzsche came to see that they are, in fact, absolutely incompatible, since the former, with its idealism and pessimism, is "life-denying" while the latter is "life-affirming." And so he rejected Wagner's, and his own former, Schopenhauerianism while retaining to the end the "rebirth of tragedy" project. This thesis can be substantiated by observing that the unifying subtext to all of Nietzsche's major criticisms of Wagner is that of *apostasy*, betrayal of the Bayreuth project in its original conception.

3. Critique of Wagner

Three principal lines of criticism can be distinguished in Nietzsche's Wagner-critique. First is the "actor" critique. Wagner's artworks, claims Nietzsche, purport to be full of deep content, but all he is actually interested in is having a powerful *effect* on the audience (*Case of Wagner* §§7, 8). This accounts for the "colossal" character of his works – the aim is to overwhelm the audience, to "intimidate" it (Young 186). And it accounts, too, for the "hypnotic," "narcotic" character of the "sorcerer's" music: in case the audience is not bullied into acknowledging Wagner's genius, the intention is that they be *seduced or drugged* into doing so through the magic potion that is the music. The effect of such art is, however, damaging: it provides the *décadent*, the "neurotic" and "exhausted," with a momentary escape from reality but, like all drugs, ends up making them sicker than they were before (*Case of Wagner* §§5, 7; *Genealogy* 3:20).

Nietzsche's second charge is one of musical incompetence. In spite of a genius for small-scale "affect-painting" (Young 186), Wagner suffered, Nietzsche claims, from an "inability to create organic forms," an inability which makes him "our greatest *miniaturist*" in music (*Case of Wagner* §7; *Gay Science* 87). His so-called "development" is "so miserable, so awkward, so amateurish" that the best he can do is to take "things that have not grown *out of* each other" and "jumble them *in* with each other" (*Case of Wagner* §7). The result can only be described as a "musical polyp" (*Case of Wagner* §1) – surely an intentional echo of HANSLICK's description of Wagner's music as a "boneless tonal mollusk" (127–8). Inability to provide form marks Wagner's relation not only to melody but also to rhythm. No one could DANCE or march to Wagner, not even to his "Imperial March" (*Gay Science* 368). On account of this lack of "measure" and "limit" – of audible bar-lines – all we can do with Wagner is to "swim" in the wandering "infinity" of his sea of "continuous melody" (Young 186–7).

Nietzsche's final major line of criticism (dubiously consistent with the "actor" critique) accuses Wagner of "asceticism." It concerns Wagner in his "old age" (*Genealogy* 3:1), above all, the composer of PARSIFAL. Though marveling at its musical effects, Nietzsche hated its libretto more than any other of Wagner's works. In its "insane hatred of knowledge, mind and sensuality" it is, he claims, almost a parody of "the ascetic ideal" – Nietzsche's term for "life-denial," the desire to exit this world, the "will to death." What is important about the "asceticism" critique in the *Genealogy of Morals*, however, is that Nietzsche explicitly calls *Parsifal* "an apostasy":

> an actual self-denial, self-cancelation on the part of an artist who had hitherto wanted the opposite with all the force of his will, namely for his art to be the *highest intellectualization and sensualization*. And not just in his art: his life too. Recall how enthusiastically Wagner followed in the footsteps of the philosopher FEUERBACH in his day: Feuerbach's dictum of "healthy sensuality" – that sounded like the pronouncement of salvation to the Wagner of the 1830s and 1840s, as to so many Germans (– they called themselves the "*Young* Germans").

(ANTI-CHRIST 276)

The earlier Wagner had been an enthusiastic life-affirmer. But *Parsifal* makes clear that love of life has turned to "hatred" (*Genealogy* 3:3). Nietzsche knows, of course, that Wagner's turn "against life" happened long before *Parsifal*, indeed had already happened in 1856, with the replacement of the "Feuerbach ending" to the RING with the "Schopenhauer ending" (*Case of Wagner* §4). The point must be that *Parsifal* reveals Wagner's Schopenhauerianism *more clearly* than any other work. In *Tristan*, Wagner still has the un-Schopenhauerian idea of sexuality as a path to REDEMPTION, whereas in *Parsifal* he finally joins Schopenhauer in the absolute rejection of sexuality.

The subtext that runs through all these criticisms is the accusation of betrayal, apostasy. In the "asceticism" critique, it is explicit. But it is implicit in the "actor" critique as well, for Nietzsche is here attempting to hoist Wagner with his own petard. It was, that is, *Wagner* who in OPER UND DRAMA (Opera and Drama, 1851) had initiated the critique of Franco-Italian opera as a "narcotic" (PW 2:46) and, in *Die* KUNST UND DIE REVOLUTION (Art and Revolution, 1849), as a momentary "distraction," an escape from life for the bored and exhausted (PW 1:44). The subtext of the "actor" critique is thus the claim that, in spite of Wagner's "brilliant deeds and plans for reform" Nietzsche had admired in 1864, the later Wagner had ended up producing nothing more than a new version of what, according to his ideal, he wished to abolish. Again the charge is one of apostasy.

The "musical incompetence" critique might seem to be unrelated to the apostasy theme, but it is, in fact, Nietzsche's attempted explanation of why, fundamentally, Wagner fell short of his ideal. The key to seeing this is to understand Nietzsche's complex concept of DECADENCE. Nietzsche associates it first of all with the "will to death" (*Case of Wagner* §4). Wagner is decadent because his post-Schopenhauerian works, like those of his admirer BAUDELAIRE, are in love with death, "life-denying." (*The Case of Wagner* carefully avoids mentioning *Meistersinger*, which will not fit Nietzsche's thesis, though he does mention it in other works.) But he is also decadent because his music – a mirror of his soul and of the modern soul in general – is "formless," an "anarchy of atoms," a "chaos" (*Case of Wagner* §7, Second Postscript). These notions are connected. The reason that the decadent "wills death" is that, like Jesus and the Buddha (*Anti-Christ* 30, 42), they lack the strength to face and overcome opposition. The reason they lack the strength to cope with life is precisely the "chaos" in their souls. Chaos in the soul is a "morbid" condition (*Twilight* 9:35). For, as Plato showed in the *Republic*, unless one has become "one man," unless one has disciplined the drives of the soul into a single organic hierarchy, one cannot cope with life, and for that reason one will, together with the two arch-"Romantics" Schopenhauer and Wagner, yearn for "quiet, stillness, calm seas, redemption from [one]self through art" (*Gay Science* 370), in other words, for death. The decadence of Wagner's music reveals the decadence of his soul. This is the major, "human-all-to-human" reason he was unable to live up to his early, life-affirming "ideal" of the rebirth of community through the rebirth of Greek tragedy.   JULIAN YOUNG

Eduard Hanslick, *Vienna's Golden Years of Music, 1850–1900*, trans. H. Pleasants (New York: Simon & Schuster, 1950).

Friedrich Nietzsche, *The Birth of Tragedy and other Writings*, ed. R. Geuss and R. Speirs, trans. R. Speirs (Cambridge University Press, 1999).

The Case of Wagner, in *The Anti-Christ, Ecce Homo, Twilight of the Idols and Other Writings*, ed. A. Ridley, trans J. Norman (Cambridge University Press, 2005).

The Gay Science, ed. B. Williams, trans. J. Naukhoff (Cambridge University Press, 2001).

On the Genealogy of Morals, ed. K. Ansell-Pearson, trans. C. Diethe (Cambridge University Press, 1994).

Julian Young, *Friedrich Nietzsche: A Philosophical Biography* (New York: Cambridge University Press, 2010).

Nilsson, Birgit (b. Västra Karup, 17 May 1918; d. Västra Karup, 25 Dec. 2005), Swedish soprano. Nilsson was the most internationally acclaimed singer of BRÜNNHILDE and ISOLDE from the late 1950s through the 1970s, with appearances in those roles at all the important opera houses of the world. Her uniquely powerful, bright, gleaming sound also made her a renowned exponent of the title role in Puccini's *Turandot*.   DAVID BRECKBILL

Birgit Nilsson, *La Nilsson: My Life in Opera*, trans. Doris Jung Popper (Hanover, NH: University Press of New England, 2007).

Nohl, (Karl Friedrich) Ludwig (b. Iserlohn, 5 Dec. 1831; d. Heidelberg, 15 Dec. 1885), German writer on music. Trained in both law and music, he first joined the civil service and then, after receiving the Promotion in 1859 and the Habilitation in Heidelberg in 1860, unsuccessfully applied for a position in musicology in MUNICH, only to be called back for an honorary professorship (1864–8) by LUDWIG II. After a period in Badenweiler (till 1872), Nohl returned to Heidelberg, becoming professor there in 1880 while also teaching in Karlsruhe. Nohl was best known for his biographies of and letter editions for composers such as Haydn, MOZART, BEETHOVEN, and LISZT. The staunchly nationalist Nohl was also noted for his intense devotion to Wagner; in dedicating his Beethoven biography to Wagner, Nohl lauded him as "the master of masters," though COSIMA WAGNER'S DIARIES reveal that Wagner had criticized the Beethoven book. The study *Gluck und Wagner* (1870) seeks to trace the development of MUSIC DRAMA before Wagner, while the strongly nationalistic *Richard Wagner's Bedeutung für die nationale Kunst* (Richard Wagner's Significance for the National Art, 1883) positioned the composer as solidifying a coherent German identity (see GERMANNESS). He also wrote a short biography of Wagner (1869) and a number of other studies about or referring to Wagner.   JAMES DEAVILLE

Nordic mythology. The term used to designate a body of myths about the gods presumed to have been worshipped in some form or another in the Nordic countries (Sweden, Norway, Denmark, and Iceland) in the pre-Christian period. We are unusually fortunate in our information about Nordic mythology because we have the record of four literary sources from Denmark and Iceland written down in the thirteenth century, well after conversion to Christianity in these societies, but before all the oral stories and poetry that related pre-Christian mythological traditions had been forgotten.

1. Sources
2. Mythology

1. Sources

From Denmark, we have the Latin work *Gesta danorum* of the cleric Saxo Grammaticus, who wrote sixteen books on the history of Denmark in the early thirteenth century under the patronage of the king and the archbishop of Denmark. Of these, the first eight cover a legendary history up to the time of conversion in the mid-tenth century. Saxo praises the story-telling abilities of the Icelanders and claims that he has used them as sources for his early history of Denmark. Among the tales he relates from the legendary period are three that recur in different versions from the later Icelandic sources: the death of the god Balder and the encounters of Thor with the giants Geirrod and Utgarda-Loki. Saxo portrays the gods as magicians and illusionists as one would expect from a cleric working for an archbishop.

The remaining three written sources are Icelandic: the *Prose EDDA*, written by Snorri Sturluson some time in the 1220s; the *Poetic Edda*, an anonymous collection of traditional mythological and heroic poems from the late thirteenth century; and *Ynglinga Saga*, the first saga in the historical survey of the kings of Norway called *Heimskringla* (The Circle of the World), attributed with some certainty to Snorri Sturluson. The scope of *Heimskringla* covers the time of the early mythological kings of Scandinavia to the historical time of the late twelfth century. *Ynglinga Saga* gives an account of the mythical and legendary ancestors of the Ynglings, the kings of Sweden. The original ancestor of the royal line, which later devolved into the royal line of Norway as well, is Yngvi-Frey, whom Snorri presents as one of a group of chieftains from Asia who migrated north to Sweden under the leadership of Odin. When they reached the north, they were worshipped as gods because of their superiority.

Snorri employs a similar euhemeristic explanation for the origin of the gods in his Prologue to the *Prose Edda*.

Finally, we have the testimony of the traditional oral Nordic poetic genre known in modern use as skaldic poetry. Thanks to Snorri's *Edda* and other written sources, we have the names and an extensive corpus of the poetry of many of the professional court poets who composed skaldic poetry in honor of kings and earls going back into the ninth century.

In addition to German translations of the *Poetic Edda* and Snorri's *Edda*, Wagner had access to information about Nordic mythology for his R I N G cycle through the work *Deutsche Mythologie*, Jacob Grimm's reconstruction of ancient Germanic mythology.

2. Mythology

Based on the systematizing efforts of Snorri and the redactor of the *Poetic Edda*, we may describe the mythology as a narrative that comprises a description of the creation of the world, the introduction of the three major social groups (the Aesir, Vanir, and the giants), the ongoing struggles between the gods (Aesir and Vanir) against the giants, and the destruction of the world, termed *ragnarök* (the doom of the gods), in the final gigantic battle between the gods and the giants. Both Snorri's *Edda* and the *Poetic Edda* depict a new world rising from the flames and flood of the old, populated by the few gods and humans who have somehow survived the holocaust.

The major gods are Odin, Thor, Balder, Tyr, Njord, Frey, and Loki; the major goddesses are Frigg (wife of Odin) and Freyja (sister to Frey). In addition to these, Snorri lists a large number of other divinities whose names figure in poetic periphrasis, but about whom there is little other information. The gods inhabit the center of the world and live in a city named Asgard. Opposed to the gods and inhabiting the periphery of the world are the giants and cosmic monsters. There are several giants named in the stories, but the monsters are especially important, for they are the children of Loki and a giantess. They are the fearsome wolf Fenrir, which will break loose from his bonds before the final battle and swallow Odin; the giant snake Midgardserpent, which lies coiled around the earth deep in the ocean and will rise up and be the death of Thor; and Hel, Loki's daughter, who presides over the land of the dead.

Scholars have identified two basic spatial models of the cosmos described in the sources for Nordic mythology: a vertical model based on the notion of the world-tree, called Yggdrasil, with three levels of cosmos, where the dwellings of the gods and Valhall ("hall of the slain"), the upper kingdom of dead warriors ruled over by Odin, are located at the top of the tree, humans inhabit the middle level, and at the roots lies the lower kingdom of the dead ruled over by Hel; and a horizontal model based on the concept of a place called Midgard (the middle space), inhabited by gods and men, and a place called Utgard (the outer space), inhabited by giants and chthonic monsters. The horizontal model has generated most of the individual myths, where the focus is on what scholars have called the "negative reciprocity" that obtains between the insider social group (the gods) and the outsider social group (the giants and monsters). This negative reciprocity inhibits the peaceful circulation of cultural goods and of women as marriage partners in the system, forcing each side to resort to trickery, theft, and force to obtain what they want from the other group. In this state of continuous social tension the gods prevail over the giants through their superior cunning and brute force until the final apocalyptic battle between the two opposing groups, which brings death and destruction to both sides.   KAAREN GRIMSTAD

See also VÖLSUNGA SAGA

Nuitter, Charles-Louis-Étienne [Born: Truinet, Charles-Louis-Étienne] (b. Paris, 24 April 1828; d. Paris, 23 Feb. 1899), French translator and agent. Trained as a lawyer, he started working for the Paris OPÉRA as librarian around 1860, before he was officially appointed to this post in 1866. In 1882, he created the Bibliothèque de l'Opéra. He also wrote dramas and libretti, and translated operas. He reworked *TANNHÄUSER* for the 1861 production and later translated *Der FLIEGENDE HOLLÄNDER, RIENZI*, and *LOHENGRIN*. He became the personal agent of Richard, and later COSIMA, Wagner in Paris.

                    HERMANN GRAMPP

Correspondance: Richard et Cosima Wagner, Charles Nuitter, ed. and annotated P. Jost, R. Feist, and P. Reynal (Sprimont: Mardaga, 2002).

Nuremberg

1. The "most German" city
2. Wagner and Nuremberg
3. After Wagner

1. The "most German" city

By the end of the eighteenth century, with the publication of Wilhelm Heinrich Wackenroder and Ludwig Tieck's *Herzensergießungen eines kunstliebenden Kloster-bruders* (Confessions from the Heart of an Art-Loving Friar, 1796), the foundational text of German ROMANTICISM, the city of Nuremberg had become a symbol of what was perceived by the Romantics as authentic German spirit. Wackenroder and Tieck's book celebrated late medieval and early modern Nuremberg as "the vibrantly teeming school of native art" and proclaimed that "a truly fruitful, overflowing spirit of art lived and thrived within your walls: – when Master HANS SACHS ... and so many other highly praised men of honor were still living!" (Wackenroder 112).

The supposedly authentic and organic GERMANNESS represented by Nuremberg was based on the city's status as one of the best-preserved great medieval cities in Germany, and paired with a critique of the Enlightenment and of the rigorous, orderly grid patterns of other cities, such as nearby Erlangen. The first half of the nineteenth century saw a vigorous and successful effort to erect a statue to Albrecht Dürer in Nuremberg (foundation stone laid in 1828, on the tercentennial of Dürer's death), as well as to preserve Dürer's house (originally restored in 1826). Throughout much of the nineteenth century, Germans in Nuremberg and elsewhere celebrated the artistic heritage of Nuremberg by engaging in historical pageants and parades where they dressed up in costumes thought to be authentic to the fifteenth and sixteenth centuries. Baron Hans von Aufsess worked for decades to create the Germanic National Museum in Nuremberg (ultimately founded in 1853) in an effort to "cultivate a love for the history of" the "fatherland ... [and]

everything beautiful and grand that its art and history have to offer" (Brockmann 63). Especially after the end of the Holy Roman Empire of the German Nation (1806), Nuremberg and its history were seen by many German patriots as a reminder of purportedly better times when the nation had been unified under the leadership of strong and art-loving emperors. This was the message of Johann Ludwig Deinhardstein's play *Hans Sachs* (1828), as well as of Albert Lortzing's opera of the same name (1840) in both of which the shoemaker-poet Hans SACHS is presented as an honest, hard-working German supported by an understanding emperor Maximilian.

The popular celebration of Nuremberg as a *locus amoenus* for German culture reached its high point in 1861, when the city hosted a massive festival of amateur singers from throughout Germany under the motto: "In word and song the German banner goes forth / Uniting in love both south and north." The guiding idea behind the celebration was that German musical culture could help to bring about national unity; as one slogan proclaimed, "Music overcomes distance wherever we are, / Stronger than an army's might; / Music brings us together from near and far / To defend and protect and fight" (Brockmann 73).

2. Wagner and Nuremberg

Less than a month after that singers' festival, Richard Wagner, who had returned to Germany in 1860 after over a decade in political exile following his participation in the DRESDEN UPRISING (1849), passed through Nuremberg where, as he reported in his autobiography, he saw "a number of the city's curiosities," and where he was probably moved to begin work on the opera about Nuremberg that he had envisioned as early as 1845 (ML 674). That opera, *Die MEISTERSINGER VON NÜRNBERG*, was to be the crowning Romantic apotheosis of the city and the major artistic statement on German identity at the moment of the nation's belated unification. As Wagner wrote in a diary entry intended for his patron LUDWIG II, "we must show them clearly and unequivocally, in golden letters of fire, what is truly German, what the genuine German spirit is: the spirit of all that is genuine, true and unadulterated" (27 September 1865). Six years after the premiere of *Die Meistersinger* in MUNICH (1868), the opera was first performed in Nuremberg; and in the same year, 1874, the city unveiled a statue to the shoemaker-poet Hans Sachs. As one poem written in honor of the event proclaimed, "Richard Wagner's opera already honored the man, / Leaving a monumental musical trace; / But today the eye of the German can scan / Father Sachs's honorable and noble face" (Brockmann 115).

3. After Wagner

The celebration of Nuremberg as the capital of an authentically German spirit continued well into the twentieth century, with another singers' festival in 1912, the so-called "Deutscher Tag" (German Day) of 1923, and the four-hundredth anniversary celebrations of Dürer's death in 1928. Adolf HITLER's National Socialist German Workers Party (NSDAP) held two party congresses there during the Weimar Republic (1927 and 1929), as well as all of the party congresses after the NSDAP came to power in 1933; these party congresses were memorably captured in Leni Riefenstahl's documentary *Triumph of the Will* (1935), which features a partly Wagnerian soundtrack. As Hitler proclaimed in 1933: "In order to awaken the movement's devotion to these honorable traditions of our struggle, we will therefore for all eternity celebrate the Reich party rallies in this place" (Brockmann 140). According to the Wagner-lover Hitler, the choice of Nuremberg signaled "a connection to the mighty past" and a declaration "that our movement is nothing but the continuation not just of German greatness but of German art and German culture" (Brockmann 140). Unsurprisingly, one of the major components of the opening of each Nazi rally in Nuremberg was a solemn performance of *Die Meistersinger* in the presence of Hitler himself.

When Americans chose Nuremberg as the site of the International Military Tribunal (IMT) against leading Nazi war criminals in 1945–6, they began a process of rebranding the city that continues to this day. Today the city that was once considered "the most German of all German cities" proclaims itself the "City of Peace and Human Rights." Nuremberg now has a "Street of Human Rights" designed by the Israeli artist Dani Karavan and located in front of the Germanic National Museum; it hosts an annual festival of human rights; awards an international prize for human rights every other year; and offers fellowships to persecuted writers from abroad.   STEPHEN BROCKMANN

See also NATIONAL SOCIALISM, MUSICAL LIFE DURING

Stephen Brockmann, *Nuremberg: The Imaginary Capital* (Rochester, NY: Camden House, 2006).
Wilhelm Heinrich Wackenroder, *Confessions and Fantasies*, trans. Mary Hurst Schubert
    (University Park: Pennsylvania State University Press, 1971).

Oesterlein, Nikolaus Johannes (b. Vienna, 4 May 1841; d. Vienna, 7 Oct. 1898), administrator, collector of Wagneriana, and writer about music. Nephew of Nikolaus Oesterlein (1804–39), journalist, author, and founder of Austria's first armaments factory. After completing his basic education, the younger Oesterlein became director of the Nußdorfer Brewery in Vienna's 19th District even as he continued studying music. He wrote favorably about the works of LISZT and BRUCKNER; after 1868, however, and especially after a visit to BAYREUTH in 1876, he concentrated on Wagner's career and compositions. By 1883, the year his idol died, Oesterlein had amassed thousands of Wagnerian artifacts in his Vienna apartment; in 1895, with support from investors, he opened a Wagner Museum in Eisenach, close to the Wartburg. Today he is best known for his Wagner publications, especially his massive bibliography in four volumes, which catalogues over 10,000 Wagner-related publications by the year of Wagner's death.   MICHAEL SAFFLE

See also MUSEUMS AND ARCHIVES

Nikolaus Oesterlein, *Entwurf zu einem Richard Wagner-Museum* (see bibliography).
Nikolaus Oesterlein, *Katalog einer Richard-Wagner-Bibliothek*, 4 vols. (see bibliography).

On the Application of Music to Drama. See *ÜBER DIE ANWENDUNG DER MUSIK AUF DAS DRAMA*

On Franz Liszt's Symphonic Poems. See *ÜBER FRANZ LISZTS SYMPHONISCHE DICHTUNGEN*

On State and Religion. See *ÜBER STAAT UND RELIGION*

On the Term "Music Drama." See *ÜBER DIE BENENNUNG "MUSIKDRAMA"*

Oper und Drama (Opera and Drama), the third and longest of the so-called "ZURICH writings," following Die *KUNST UND DIE REVOLUTION* (Art and Revolution, 1849) and Das *KUNSTWERK DER ZUKUNFT* (The Artwork of the Future, 1849/50). It was begun in September or October 1850 with the provisional title *Das Wesen der Oper* (The Nature of Opera). The critique of traditional opera suggested by that title came to form the first of three large parts, as "Die Oper und das Wesen der Musik" (Opera and the Nature of Music). The general title *Oper und Drama* was in place by December 1850, a complete draft finished in early January 1851. A fair copy of Part 1 was sent to Wagner's friend Theodor UHLIG on 20 January 1851. Part 2, "Das Schauspiel und das Wesen der dramatischen Dichtkunst" (The Play and the Nature of Dramatic Poetry), followed at the beginning of February, and Part 3, "Dichtkunst und Tonkunst im Drama der Zukunft" (Poetry and Music in the Drama of the Future), was sent to Uhlig around 15 February 1851. Large portions of Part 2 were published under the title "Über moderne dramatische Dichtkunst" (On Modern Dramatic Poetry) in the second issue of Adolf Kolatschek's *Deutsche Monatsschrift für Politik, Wissenschaft, Kunst und Leben*, and the whole book was issued by J. J. Weber of Leipzig in November 1851.

Wagner's "Zurich writings" were a reflection of his highly active, not to say overwrought, state of mind during the early months of his political exile in Switzerland following the DRESDEN UPRISING of May 1849. This exile coincided with the origins of his plan for an operatic epic based on the *Nibelungenlied* and the MYTHS of the hero SIEGFRIED. Echoing the opinions of such contemporaries as Pierre-Joseph Proudhon, Mikhail BAKUNIN, and Karl Marx, Wagner was convinced that all aspects of European politics, society, and culture were poised to undergo radical changes. In Wagner's view, these changes would be intimately linked with the revolutionary nature of his own ideas for a post-operatic "musical drama." The first two Zurich essays had presented a general critique of modern European society and culture (contrasted with the achievements of ANCIENT GREECE) and a broad outline of past, present, and necessary future attempts to unite the separate "sister" arts of poetry, DANCE, and music into a single "combined art-work" responding to the true cultural needs of society. *Oper und Drama* sought to move the argument more specifically onto the terrain of opera, as currently practiced and as Wagner believed it must now be reformed.

To some extent the essays of 1849–51 were a kind of therapy for Wagner, an attempt to purge his own mind of "critical reflection" before he moved on to create his great "Siegfried" drama in a style unconstrained by existing operatic conventions. This therapy was at the same time an attempt to work out some of the creative parameters of the new genre of musical drama he had in mind. These parameters included the role of alliterative verse or *STABREIM*; a newly fluid approach to the harmonic-formal syntax of vocal melody, responding to metrical and rhetorical structures of dramatic verse; and a network of expressive-associative musical themes or motives, which later became known as *LEITMOTIVE*. These ideas are all taken up in Part 3 of the essay – "a piece of work," he wrote to Uhlig, "that gets to the heart of things" (20 January 1851).

"The error of opera as an artistic genre lies in the fact that a means of expression (music) has been made an end, while the end of expression (drama) has been made the means" (PW 2:17). This manifesto-like pronouncement from the introduction to Part 1 of the essay challenges modern composers who suppose that they might eventually "create a true drama on the basis of absolute music" by continuing along the path of traditional operatic practice. Part 1 is taken up largely with a relentless, if not always perfectly cogent, critique of "operatic melody" as practiced over the previous hundred years or so. GLUCK is praised for resisting the demands of vain virtuoso singers and concentrating as best he could on the demands of expression. MOZART's innate, naïve musical genius succeeded even better in matching musical beauty to apt settings of the poetry he was given. WEBER is credited with a special feeling for the natural idioms of "folk" (*VOLK*) music and the ability to elevate these to a fully artistic plane. The opera aria, as opposed to the artificial experiment of recitative, derives ultimately from "folk" melody. The result is the "absolute melody" of Rossinian BEL CANTO. While Wagner acknowledges the more dramatically, poetically inclined traditions of French opera, he is unwilling to admit any connection with the GRAND OPERAS of MEYERBEER, let alone any resemblance of those operas to his idea of a new musical drama. Meyerbeer's desperate attempts to infuse traditional operatic forms with pseudo-historical, regional, or other topical "character" has only led to a complete DEGENERATION of these forms. Wagner famously denounces the basis of Meyerbeer's works – citing the example of the electrically lit sunrise in *Le Prophète* – as "effects without causes" (PW 2:95; *Wirkung ohne Ursache*, SSD 3:301). BEETHOVEN meanwhile had sought to develop a newly "speaking" quality of melodic expression in instrumental music, an example pursued even more radically by BERLIOZ. Those efforts reflected a genuine impulse in the historical development of music generally, though they failed to acknowledge the imperative of articulate language, as song, in any truly integrated form of musical expression. In section 7 (of Part 1) Wagner develops his METAPHOR of music as "woman," requiring the "fertilizing seed" of the word, provided by poetry, as its male partner. Only in this way can music bear the fruit of genuinely expressive, organically conceived melody as Wagner understands it. The GENDERED metaphor inspires a semi-satirical typology of national operatic styles according to which Italian opera is a promiscuous "strumpet," French opera a "coquette," and German opera a "prude" who condemns the other two while secretly envying them, incapable of entering into any properly loving relationship with poetry.

Part 2, "The Play and the Nature of Dramatic Poetry," consists mainly of a critique of modern (post-classical) spoken drama, forming a counterpart to the critique of opera in Part 1. This is conducted in similarly schematic, generalized terms. The final goal of Wagner's arguments in Part 2 is a demonstration of why MYTH is the necessary source material for a drama that would convey a purely human content directly to the faculty of emotion or feeling, and why music (*Tonsprache*) must necessarily supplement spoken language (*Wortsprache*) in achieving this end. The first two sections of Part 2 look at how medieval and early modern European "romance" influenced modern drama in its desire to represent a broad array of imaginative and historical incident. Section 3 analyzes the stories of Oedipus and Antigone (as dramatized by Sophocles, though Wagner is little concerned with text or authorship here). The conflict of the state and the individual will is represented as a foundational myth of classical drama. At the same time it is clear that Wagner is thinking about his own WOTAN as representative of the state's authority (and the preservation of custom or *Gewohnheit*, as he puts it here) in conflict with motives of individual, purely human feeling embodied in BRÜNNHILDE, as a variation on Antigone. The dynamic conflict of reason (the state) with feeling (the individual) paves the way to Wagner's poetics of the musical drama "of the future" (more specifically, the anticipated RING cycle). He begins with a description of alliterative verse (*Stabreim*) as a poetic means of mediating between conventional verbal signs and instinctive "feeling," or between language as meaning and language as sound. Alliterative verse and an effective condensation of poetic "motives" both require music to complete the "realization for the senses" they strive for. Returning to his gendered metaphors from Part 1, Wagner identifies the "poetic intent" (*dichterische Absicht*) as a form of male seed required to fertilize the female musical organism. This poetic intent is related to the "condensed" (*verdichtete*) nexus of poetic-mythical motifs on which the drama should be based. Music is the expressive solution in which this "condensed" content can be most fully and effectively reconstituted.

Part 3, "Poetry and Music in the Drama of the Future," is of particular interest for the insight it gives us into Wagner's ideas about the composition of the *Ring* cycle while the project was still in gestation. Precisely because he had not advanced beyond a few abortive musical sketches and ideas for a handful of eventual *LEITMOTIVE*, however, the theoretical blueprint set forth in Part 3 cannot be applied in any literal way to the finished works. What seems to have been hovering in Wagner's mind at this time was something between the style of *LOHENGRIN* and the fully leitmotivic music dramas of the *Ring*, where a tonally migratory, rhetorically flexible "musical prose" replaces most vestiges of the stable, periodic "operatic melody" critiqued in Part 1. Wagner is still much preoccupied with the musical possibilities of the alliterative verse he has chosen for the *Ring* libretti (sections 1 and 2) which, in their final form, employ a free alternation of two-stress and three-stress lines, the latter giving weight to the end of a speech or rhetorical "period." In this he sees the secret to a new kind of "natural" musical speech or *Worttonsprache*, freed from the "shackles" of iambic tetrameter and end-rhyme. Drawing on Enlightenment speculations about the origins of language (Rousseau, Condillac, and HERDER, though without directly citing any of them), Wagner suggests how music will restore an element of the original, directly expressive sonorous value of vowel sounds, the primal organism of meaning to which the alliterating consonants provide a kind of semantic exoskeleton. In moving from issues of vocal setting (*Versmelodie*) to harmony and tonality, in sections 3 and 4, Wagner proposes an anthropological METAPHOR of musical modulation: the tonic key represents a "patriarchal" domain from which the melody will gradually break free in order to establish exogamous ties outside the immediate family, and so extend the realm of expressive possibilities. The new music drama will be composed of a network of POETIC-MUSICAL PERIODS exemplifying this principle, as it relates to the setting of poetic *Stabreim*. A preliminary theory of *LEITMOTIV* evolves from the discussion of the "speech capacity of the orchestra" in sections 5 and 6. The orchestra in the new musical drama is charged with realizing "for the ear" what the actors' gestures communicate to the eye, in addition to underscoring the sense of the poetic text itself. Key gestures, dramatic utterances, or other expressive nodes of the drama – collectively designated as "plastic elements of feeling" (*plastische Gefühlsmomente*) – will find an appropriate musical correlate in orchestral motives whose dramatically conditioned exposition and recurrence will result in a vast, quasi-symphonic web or network encompassing the whole drama. Wagner envisions a temporal scheme whereby these motives or "melodic elements" (what we now call *Leitmotive*) may be anticipated in the orchestra before they are explicitly defined by some present dramatic context, after which they may be infinitely recalled and varied as the drama demands.

In the closing section of Part 3, Wagner tries to clarify how these ideas relate to his earlier operatic practice, his own present plans, and the potential of a new kind of musical drama more generally. He admits to the utopian tendency of the theories he has outlined, and he turns to thoughts about institutional reforms, the training of singers, and the conditions of performance necessary to the realization of his vision. As Wagner's correspondence of the period demonstrates, he was already forming ideas for the FESTIVAL THEATER project that would be realized in BAYREUTH a quarter of a century later.

THOMAS S. GREY

Carl Dahlhaus, *Wagners Konzeption des musikalischen Dramas* (Regensburg: Bosse, 1971).

Frank Glass, *The Fertilizing Seed: Richard Wagner's Concept of the Poetic Intent* (Ann Arbor, MI: UMI Research Press, 1983).

Thomas S. Grey, *Wagner's Musical Prose* (see bibliography).

Jack Stein, *Richard Wagner and the Synthesis of the Arts* (see bibliography).

James Treadwell, "The *Ring* and the Conditions of Interpretation: Wagner's Writing, 1848–52," *Cambridge Opera Journal* 7 (1995): 207–31.

Opéra, Paris. In Wagner's time, the term "PARIS Opéra" generally referred to the foremost lyric stage of the French capital, located at the Salle le Peletier. The official name of the theater changed many times during this period, usually in conjunction with shifts in the political regime. Until Napoleon III proclaimed the "liberty of the theaters" in 1864, theatrical licenses generally delimited specific repertoires for individual stages, and the Opéra was typically dedicated to large-scale operas with recitatives (rather than dialogue). Despite occasional financial difficulties, the Opéra was in its day the most technically advanced and prestigious operatic venue in Europe.

Throughout his career, the Paris Opéra served Wagner as both a model and a *Gegenbild* against which he could define his ideals and aspirations. But it was particularly important at two points in his artistic development. The first of these came during the period 1839–42, in which Wagner was attempting to forge a career for himself in Paris as a composer, arranger, and journalist. Although Wagner sold a prose scenario for an opera on Der FLIEGENDE HOLLÄNDER (intended as a one-act curtain-raiser) to the Opéra establishment, and was nearly able to place Das LIEBESVERBOT at the Théâtre de la Renaissance, his hopes of triumphing as an opera composer in Paris (described in Eine MITTEILUNG AN MEINE FREUNDE; A Communication to My Friends, 1851) were ultimately frustrated.

Wagner returned to Paris in 1859, and spent much of the following year supervising preparations for a production of TANNHÄUSER. For this production, Wagner had the support of the Emperor, and all of the resources of the Opéra were put at his disposal. Wagner rewrote large sections of his original score, making important alterations to the role of Venus and to the first-act Venusberg scene. But Wagner was unwilling to adapt his work fully to the conventions of the institution. The performances of TANNHÄUSER – which took place in March of 1861 – were disrupted by members of the Jockey Club, and Wagner's second attempt to establish himself at the Opéra ended in fiasco.

In his *Bericht über die Aufführung des "Tannhäuser" in Paris*, Wagner describes these performances and the preparations that led up to them, focusing on the malevolence of the aristocratic claque, while praising certain singers and other elements of the production. In this sense, the *Bericht* may serve as a microcosm of Wagner's ambivalent attitude towards the Paris Opéra as a whole. Wagner admired and envied the exceptional technical possibilities of the theater, as well as the high quality of the musicians whom it employed. But Wagner is deeply critical of the Opéra's sociopolitical position, and the AESTHETICS with which he felt this position was bound up. This negative evaluation of the Opéra appears as early as the *AUTOBIOGRAPHISCHE SKIZZE* (Autobiographical Sketch, 1842/3), and may be found (among other places) in his satirical play *Eine Kapitulation* (1871). In these and other essays, Wagner's attitude towards the theater is very much bound up with his more general critique of contemporary French and Italian operatic styles.   STEPHEN MEYER

See also *TANNHÄUSER*, PARIS SCANDAL OF 1861

Operatic reform. Mostly linked to Wagner's ZURICH writings, especially *OPER UND DRAMA* (Opera and Drama, 1851) Wagner's more practical reforms (such as dimming the auditorium lights, and the invisible orchestra) only became evident much later. Nevertheless, Wagner's desire to fundamentally change the genre, and the development of his compositional and dramaturgic style, was a continuous process, his argumentative attempts coming in (often polemic) flashes. In the theoretical writings of the early 1850s, and already as a young opera composer, Wagner realized that the balance between music and text had to be restored and, in Germany, created anew.

As far as Wagner was concerned, "Opera" as such had come to an end with ROSSINI. Christoph Willibald GLUCK had already attempted to reform opera in the mid-eighteenth century and, in many respects, Wagner's approach a century later was similar: the avoidance of repetition (textual and musical), a continuity of musical sections and an attempt to counteract the arbitrary displays of celebrated singers, a practice Wagner particularly disparaged because they were, in his view, symptoms of the shallowness favored by nineteenth-century audiences dominated by the "'philistine,' the most willful, the cruelest, the dirtiest bread-giver of the artist" (SSD 4:226). Typical for the philistine public, according to Wagner's view and experience, was the bourgeois French culture he found in PARIS. To counteract Paris's enormous influence on German theater, Wagner stressed the necessity of returning to national themes and forms. He emphasized, for instance in *Über die Bestimmung der Oper* from 1871, SHAKESPEARE and BEETHOVEN as aesthetic models: the former because of the originality and incalculability of his pieces, which Wagner considered a unique form of "a fixed mimic improvisation" (SSD 9:143); the latter as the paradigm for musical immediacy to be reproduced in opera. As an Englishman, Shakespeare was closer to reflecting the German spirit than the French.

While Wagner advocated abolishing the mixture of styles evident in the repertory of German opera houses, he did concede that, to a large extent, German translations of French GRAND OPERA and Italian BEL CANTO opera were inadequate. Thus, the effects and virtuosity of the singing parts depended not only on the skills of the singers they had originally been written for, but also on prosodic congruency. So, Wagner was being consistent when he called for operatic reform by the "word-tone-artist" who would unify music and poetry in a so-called GESAMTKUNSTWERK. Achieving this goal also required social REVOLUTION, as well as improving the conditions of theater production and the basic organization of the theater.

Wagner called frequently for the reorganization of theater companies; in Zurich, Wagner opted for an advisory board for the local theater, and, in DRESDEN and MUNICH, he proclaimed the need for singers with a dramatic education. In general, there was a notable shift in concepts of a German "Nationaltheater" around 1850, strongly influenced by the YOUNG GERMANY movement, who were indebted to Friedrich SCHILLER's definition of theater as the optimal site for the creation and education of a national audience. The more aggressive nationalism of the later nineteenth century added to these ideas by turning to ANTI-SEMITISM and REGENERATION.

SEBASTIAN STAUSS

Orchestral concerts. The music of Richard Wagner acquired a larger and more diverse public in concert halls than in opera houses during the late nineteenth century. EXCERPTS from his operas were played over and over again at a wide array of orchestral series, band concerts, informal "promenade" concerts, and even recitals and "benefit" concerts. The best-known pieces – the TANNHÄUSER OVERTURE and the "Ride of the Valkyries," for example – acquired a commercially more potent public than the staging of TRISTAN UND ISOLDE or GÖTTERDÄMMERUNG. Since concert-goers often had little knowledge of the dramatic structure of the operas, they appreciated the music in symphonic terms, rather as they did pictorial genres such as the suite, rhapsody, or tone poem. Still, orchestras which served particularly educated publics offered notable vocal selections – the LIEBESTOD or HANS SACHS's Monologue – or even devoted a concert to a complete act. The idea of GESAMTKUNSTWERK had little to do with all this, for the Wagnerian concert repertory took on a life of its own. For that matter, even though Wagner condemned performance of excerpts from his works, he followed that common practice himself. For example, prior to the failed premiere of TANNHÄUSER in PARIS in 1861, he put on three concerts of his own music.

Some elite orchestras kept their distance from Wagner. The Vienna Philharmonic went a long time before going beyond the *Faust Overture* (1840); the Society of Concerts in Paris performed little more than the *Tannhäuser* overture and CHORUSES from PARSIFAL, pieces which fit its choral-orchestral ensemble. But the Philharmonic Society of London and the Gewandhaus Concerts in LEIPZIG paid more attention to opera selections generally and Wagner in particular. Wagner was heard the most in burgeoning concerts of low-priced orchestral series, where performing standards were often quite high. The Popular Concerts of Classical Music in Paris played a piece by Wagner as early as 1863, and the Concerts-Colonne offered a program with excerpts from ten of his major works in 1901. Indeed, one can argue that Wagner's music was treated in canonic terms by his death in 1883, prior to the epochal Parisian premiere of LOHENGRIN in 1891.

Wagner's OVERTURES became standard repertory at band concerts throughout Europe, holding company thereby with works in that genre by

371

WEBER, AUBER, Hérold, and Adam. In Bremen in 1879, for example, the Kapelle of the Hanseatic Infantry-Regiment No. 75 offered the overture to RIENZI and pieces from *Lohengrin* along with a *fantaisie* on *Les Huguenots* and Johann Strauss Jr.'s *Fledermaus-Quadrille*. TRANSCRIPTIONS of Wagner's works also appeared in benefit concert programs, forming part of a repertory dominated by pieces from GRAND OPERA and medleys of tunes from those works. Many listeners in fact came to know Wagner's music chiefly through LISZT'S transcriptions, some of which are best seen as *fantasies*. Indeed, the German violinist August WILHELMJ composed a *Romanza* for violin and orchestra upon the *Albumblatt* for piano Wagner wrote for Princess Pauline METTERNICH in 1861. The year before that the Bonn Beethoven-Verein presented the piece transcribed for piano along with pieces by BEETHOVEN, MENDELSSOHN, and Ferdinand HILLER, suggesting Wagner's incipient canonic reputation.   WILLIAM WEBER

See also EXCERPTS (FROM WORKS); PROGRAM NOTES; RECEPTION; VIENNA

Orchestration. Wagner is justifiably recognized as one of the most influential figures in the history of orchestration. His ability to create unique sonic landscapes was already evident in his early operas, and his skills began to flourish with the extraordinary innovations of the RING, TRISTAN UND ISOLDE, Die MEISTERSINGER VON NÜRNBERG, and PARSIFAL. Wagner's orchestral palette drew together some of the best instrumental innovations of the industrial revolution. Most importantly, Wagner expanded the range and flexibility of the wind and brass sections such that they achieved a true balance both with the strings and with each other. In the words of Richard STRAUSS, Wagner "perfected the modern orchestra" after Berlioz had "created it" (Berlioz ii).

Wagner had a keen instinct for sensual, richly textured harmonies and there are, without question, distinctly "Wagnerian" orchestral sounds – one thinks, for instance, of themes such as "The Ride of the Valkyries," where the deep, primal melodies in the brass are accompanied by wild, swirling strings. Nevertheless, it is hard to generalize about Wagner's work. Each of the operas distinctively offers its own lush and vibrant sound world, which can range from the intimate subtleties of a solo violin to the full force of more than a hundred musicians. Indeed, the metaphor of a "sound world" is especially important. The orchestration of Wagner's works is intimately linked to his central innovation in the design of the Bayreuth FESTIVAL THEATER: the submersion of the orchestra beneath the stage such that the audience can be enveloped in darkness and experience the music as a vital part of the fictional space. Even before this idea materialized, Wagner produced tone colors that seem almost tangible, a physical presence within which the opera's characters think, move, and feel. But these sound worlds did not arise *sui generis*. Wagner's orchestration drew from a variety of contemporary trends and ultimately influenced generations of composers after his death.

1. Size and structure of Wagner's orchestras
2. Orchestration and MUSIC DRAMA
3. Wagner's influence

1. Size and structure of Wagner's orchestras

In terms of orchestral dimensions, Wagner's operas from RIENZI to LOHEN-GRIN are not terribly dissimilar to the many operas and symphonies that Wagner conducted throughout his early career – works by composers such as BEETHOVEN, WEBER, MARSCHNER, MEYERBEER, HALÉVY, DONIZETTI, and BELLINI. There are many examples of striking orchestral writing in the early operas – consider, for instance, the emerging *tutti* of the OVERTURE to *TANNHÄUSER*, with its magisterial trombone melody, or the striking use of woodwinds in *Lohengrin*, which Strauss called "the apex of true perfection" (Berlioz ii) – but the orchestral make-up itself, in terms of size and structure, was fairly unremarkable.

Everything changed, however, with the *Ring*. Wagner demanded a string section of sixty-four players: sixteen first violins, sixteen second violins, twelve violas, twelve cellos, and eight double basses. Few orchestras had ever used a string choir of this size, and the effect when its full power is unleashed is arresting (see, for instance, the opening storm of *Die WALKÜRE*). Wagner also enlarged the woodwinds, quadrupling every part other than the bassoons. This allowed for a powerful, homogeneous woodwind texture that can effectively counterbalance the other sections of the orchestra. But the most distinctive orchestral expansions in the *Ring* involve the brass section.

In his early operas, Wagner had already begun exploring the potential of the new valve horns, which allowed for greater melodic flexibility (as opposed to the natural horns of the eighteenth and early nineteenth centuries, which had a more restricted range of notes). In the *Ring*, Wagner continued to expand the melodic and harmonic potential of these instruments, but he also greatly increased their size. Most remarkably, Wagner called for eight horns, each of which participates in the generative unfolding of E♭ major at the outset of the Prelude to *Das RHEINGOLD*. Four of these horns are occasionally substituted for the so-called "WAGNER TUBAS." These instruments – described by Wagner as tenor and bass tubas – were variants of instruments that Wagner had seen in Paris in 1853 (presumably the saxhorns of the famous brass designer Adolphe Sax). They provide extra depth and color as can be heard quite prominently in the famous "Valhalla theme" at the outset of *Das Rheingold*, Scene 2. The Wagner tubas, however, are not the only brass innovation in the tetralogy. Wagner also used four trumpets, one of which was a bass trumpet specifically designed for the *Ring*. And the brass section is further filled out with four trombones and a contrabass tuba. All of this is then enriched by a large and varied percussion section, including eighteen anvils (used creatively to depict the slave labor of the Nibelungs) and six harps, which are put to stunning effect at the end of *Das Rheingold* for the appearance of the "Rainbow Bridge."

Wagner used slightly more subdued orchestras for *Tristan und Isolde* and *Die Meistersinger*, works originally conceived – if not realized – as practical, access-ible operas that could be produced and performed more easily than the operas of the *Ring*. In *Tristan*, Wagner blends the various sections of the opera more thoroughly than he ever had before, as typified by the extraordinary swirling tone colors of "Isolde's Transfiguration" (*LIEBESTOD*). *Die Meistersinger* shows similar sensibility but with moments of colorful and surprising contrast, such as we find in the procession of the guilds in the opera's final scene. With *Parsifal*, which was designed for the new Bayreuth Theater, Wagner again used a massive orchestra similar to the *Ring*. This allowed him to infuse his novel, chromatic harmonies with remarkable grandeur. In addition to the main orchestra, the opera's grail ceremony calls for four bells, which are notoriously difficult to deal with; real church bells are impractical because of their size and weight and few of the familiar substitutes – including the use of pianos, gongs, and synthesizers – have proven fully satisfactory (see Burton 1992, 346).

2. Orchestration and music drama

The instrumental make-up of Wagner's operas tells us something of his scope and ambition, but the actual sounds of the opera cannot be separated from other aspects, including harmony, counterpoint, singing, and staging. Indeed, it is impossible to understand Wagner's orchestration without appreciating his compositional innovations in general. When ALBERICH reveals the "Tarnhelm" in *Das Rheingold* – the magic helmet that makes him invisible – the sounds are unforgettably eerie not simply because of the unique muted horns, but also because of the stunning harmonic juxtaposition of G♯ minor and E minor triads (harmonies that rarely occur together in classical or early Romantic practice). And, more importantly, the moment is dramatically effective because these sounds don't arise as isolated accompaniment to a particular aria or duet. Rather, they are thoroughly fused with the flowing and continuous sound world of the entire opera.

In that sense, the best way to appreciate Wagner's orchestration is to study how it evolves over the course of a single scene rather than looking at a collection of isolated moments. The final scene of *Die Walküre*, Act III, Scene 3, offers a powerful example. It begins with a sorrowful woodwind choir, led by a prominent bass clarinet. WOTAN is enraged that BRÜNNHILDE had disobeyed his commands by protecting SIEGMUND and SIEGLINDE from HUNDING. He has decided to punish Brünnhilde by taking away her powers as a Valkyrie and banishing her to the world of humans, where she will spend the rest of her days in shame and servitude.

The opening music features an intricate counterpoint of sorrowful LEITMOTIVE that pass between the lower ranges of the woodwind section – a strong evocation of the despair that hangs over both characters. When Brünnhilde begins to sing, she takes over the melody of the bass clarinet and sings without any accompaniment. Thus begins an extraordinary orchestral arc that shifts, over the course of thirty minutes, from a trembling, unaccompanied solo voice to one of the most dazzling explosions of orchestral energy in the entire *Ring*.

Throughout this scene, one gets the sense that Brünnhilde and Wotan actually begin to *control* the music around them. Indeed, immediately after her initial solo entry, Brünnhilde begins to shape the winds and strings such that they form a delicate accompaniment to her pleas for mercy. Wotan frequently interjects, often with assertive brass and strings, trying to shield himself from any sympathetic emotion. But Brünnhilde gradually becomes more and more effective in her command of the orchestra. She eventually transforms the orchestra's key from a despondent E minor to a bright E major and surrounds herself with luminescent brass and wind accompaniment while reminding Wotan, ecstatically, about his capacity for love and compassion (she addresses him at this point as "He who breathed love into my heart" [*Der diese Liebe mir in's Herz gehaucht*]). Wotan refuses to yield and, as he reasserts her punishment, the orchestra darkens with jagged, minor-mode motives in the brass and strings. But Brünnhilde maintains her control over the orchestra and eventually arrives at a massive *fortissimo* climax. She demands that Wotan encircle her by fire so that only a hero can take her for his bride, and her voice, originally weak and unaccompanied, now sings with full command of the entire orchestra, every section combining in a dizzying array of thematic fragments, all sounding forth at full volume. Wotan ultimately overflows with compassion in response to this music and sustains the shimmering orchestral effects to close out the opera.

The overall scene, then, creates a massive orchestral swell, but it does so in a way that is carefully calibrated to the unfolding psychological drama of the two central characters. And we sense that the orchestra is not merely "background" music. Nor does it simply play the role of a "Greek chorus," commenting on the action from an objective distance (a common metaphor in Wagner reception). Rather, it becomes a vital part of the opera's fictional space, something that the characters can manipulate and command for the sake of power and persuasion (see BaileyShea).

3. Wagner's influence

Those most obviously indebted to Wagner's orchestral technique were his immediate successors, composers such as BRUCKNER, MAHLER, Strauss, and DEBUSSY. These composers amplified the Wagnerian orchestral palette with new instrumental timbres and denser polyphonic writing (it is far easier, for instance, to create a PIANO REDUCTION of a Wagner opera than it is a Mahler Symphony or a Strauss tone poem). But influence can work in both positive and negative directions, and thus Wagner's shadow also extends over those who actively rejected the gradual swelling of orchestral proportions. Arnold SCHOENBERG is an especially interesting case. His *Gurrelieder*, with its gargantuan orchestra, is, in some sense, a culmination of Wagnerian ambition. But he also turned toward smaller, more intimate combinations in an apparent rejection of the Wagnerian ethos, as with his First Chamber Symphony, Op. 9, with its fifteen solo instruments. And yet even then we hear echoes of Wagner's SIEGFRIED IDYLL, a piece whose small ensemble enfolds the *Ring*'s magic into the light, contrapuntal web of its eleven instruments (see Hopkins 699).

With composers such as Stravinsky, we get a much stronger rejection of the Romantic orchestral tradition (note, for instance, the absence of violins and violas in his *Symphony of Psalms*). But even after the many twists and turns of modern and postmodern trends, we still continually find traces of Wagner's influence, whether it be in the size and scope of projects such as Stockhausen's *Licht* (a sequence of seven operas) or the more direct appropriations of Wagner in the Hollywood FILM MUSIC of composers such as John Williams and Hans Zimmer.

All of this reinforces Wagner's basic legacy. Put simply, he infused the familiar nineteenth-century orchestra with a new energy, such that – as in the Prelude to *Das Rheingold* – the sound world of the orchestra appears to have been created for the very first time.   MATT BAILEYSHEA

See also MODERN MUSIC

Matthew BaileyShea, "The Struggle for Orchestral Control: Power, Dialogue, and the Role of the Orchestra in Wagner's *Ring*," *19th-Century Music* 31.1 (2007): 3–27.

Hector Berlioz, *Treatise on Instrumentation*, revised and enlarged Richard Strauss, trans. Theodore Front (New York: Kalmus, 1948).

Jonathan Burton, "Orchestration," in *The Wagner Compendium*, ed. Barry Millington (see bibliography): 334–47.

G. W. Hopkins, "Orchestration," in *The New Grove Dictionary of Music and Musicians*, ed. Stanley Sadie (London: Macmillan, 1980): 13:691–700.

Ortrud (mezzo-soprano, character in LOHENGRIN). Although the figure of the envious, scheming woman who contributes to ELSA's downfall – in some accounts the Duchess of Cleve, in others the wife of Count Telramund, in the French tradition Matabrune – existed already in the medieval *Lohengrin* sources, Wagner developed her significantly. He gave her a pagan background, which allowed for the darkly threatening atmosphere surrounding her, and made her the pivotal figure who actively drives the plot. She enchants Gottfried, incites Telramund to accuse Elsa of Gottfried's murder and attack LOHENGRIN, and makes Elsa ask the forbidden question. Unlike Eglantine, her obvious predecessor in Carl Maria von WEBER's *Euryanthe*, she is not motivated by spurned love but by a desire to regain the power due to her family. Wagner famously summarized this aspect of her personality in a letter to Franz LISZT (30 January 1852): "Ortrud is a woman who – *does not know love* ... Her nature is politics. A *male* politician disgusts us, a *female* politician appalls us: it was this appallingness which I had to portray." Apparently Wagner himself thought, with hindsight, this aberration from his feminine ideal uncanny, since he characterizes her as his personal adversary, as "a reactionary, a woman concerned only for what is outdated and for that reason is hostile to all that is new," displaying an attitude towards women's increasing public role that is, in Hans Mayer's perceptive analysis, reactionary in itself (Mayer 251–2). Wagner then goes on to speculate about Ortrud's "stunted" and "undeveloped" longing "deprived of an object," which has led modern commentators to assume that she is sexually repressed. This is, however, not borne out by the opera; for Ortrud power is not a substitute for love, unlike for WOTAN and ALBERICH. She is unique amongst Wagner's female figures in that she pursues entirely her own goals, not those of a beloved man, and, if she fails, this is due to the unforeseen interference of the greater supernatural powers of the Grail.

Although her voice type – the mature, dangerous mezzo-soprano – was already well established by the 1840s, the depiction of her "murderous fanaticism" and "terrible madness" inspired Wagner to some of his most adventurous music (letter to Liszt, 30 January 1852). Her musical motives are derived from diminished chords, which destabilize the harmonic framework but take on a structural quality in the first scene of Act II. Ortrud's scene with Telramund is driven by the horizontal, melodic impulses of her serpentine motives, not the harmonic progressions that are typical of Elsa, Lohengrin, or the King (Parly 94). Like these other protagonists in *Lohengrin*, she has a characteristic key, F♯ minor, the parallel minor to Lohengrin's A major, indicating that the two main adversaries are in fact closely related: Both have access to supernatural powers and belong to a pre- or meta-historical world that contrasts sharply with the courtly world of tenth-century Brabant.

BARBARA EICHNER

Hans Mayer, "Die politische Frau: Ortrud und Lohengrin [1975]," in *Richard Wagner, "Lohengrin": Texte, Materialien, Kommentare*, ed. Attila Csampai and Dietmar Holland, (Reinbek bei Hamburg: Rowohlt, 1989): 249–53.

Nila Parly, *Vocal Victories. Wagner's Female Characters from Senta to Kundry* (Copenhagen: Museum Tusculanum, 2011).

Eva Rieger, *Richard Wagner's Women* (see bibliography).

Overture / prelude. Overture (*Ouvertüre*), prelude (*Vorspiel*), and introduction (*Einleitung*) are the terms Wagner used to denote the different forms of orchestral music that precede an opera or MUSIC DRAMA, or that begin one of its acts. Differences in nature and function between these pieces can be substantial: Wagner's orchestral openings vary widely in duration and in their relationship to the music that follows them. Moreover, different types of opening music are associated with different stages in his career.

1. Until 1845: from the early concert overtures to TANNHÄUSER
2. After 1845: from LOHENGRIN to PARSIFAL
3. Concert endings by Wagner

1. Until 1845: from the early concert overtures to *Tannhäuser*

It is not an exaggeration to claim that Wagner was a composer of overtures before he became a composer of operas. By the time Wagner entered the scene around 1830, the overture had become a musical genre of considerable prominence. In the concert overtures of Felix MENDELSSOHN BARTHOLDY and Hector BERLIOZ, the genre had definitively left behind its modest roots as an operatic or theatrical "noise-killer," so much so that in 1835 Robert SCHUMANN could hail it as a way out of the post-Beethovenian crisis of the symphony.

It is no coincidence, therefore, that in the early stages of his career, Wagner felt attracted to the genre of the overture. Between 1830 and 1845, he began no fewer than seventeen overtures for concert, theater, or opera (twelve of which have survived), and it is in these works that one can see Wagner mature from a young composer learning his craft to a master of the genre: the difference in quality between his earliest surviving attempt, the Concert Overture in D minor of 1831 (WWV 20), and the first version of *Eine FAUST-OUVERTÜRE* (1839–40) is stunning; the overtures to *Der FLIEGENDE HOLLÄNDER* (1841) and *Tannhäuser* (1845) rank among the major instrumental works of the mid-nineteenth century.

The five operatic overtures that Wagner wrote during these years do not differ essentially from those of other nineteenth-century German composers: cast in sonata form and often stretching that form's conventions for expressive purposes, they are independent orchestral pieces that precede the opera as a whole (the open-ended version of the *Tannhäuser* overture, which omits the

377

framing return of its slow introduction in order to merge with the Bacchanal that opens Act I, was first performed only in 1875). While in PARIS in 1841, Wagner articulated his ideas about the function and layout of an opera overture in an essay titled *Über die Ouvertüre* (On the Overture): the overture should present "the drama's characteristic idea" (*die charakteristische Idee des Dramas*) and preferably include themes and motives that come back in the opera (SSD 1:204). Without exception, Wagner's opera overtures establish thematic connections to the rest of the opera. The presentation of the drama's "characteristic idea," however, ranges from a full-blown symphonic narrative (e.g., *Der fliegende Holländer*) to a selective preview of important scenes or ideas (e.g., *Tannhäuser*). In spite of their close connection to the operas they introduce, these overtures are also significant as symphonic works in their own right. Especially those to *Der fliegende Holländer* and *Tannhäuser* had a decisive influence on the development of orchestral music in the second half of the nineteenth century and formed a major inspiration for Liszt's symphonic poems of the 1850s.

Wagner's overtures differ fundamentally from the orchestral introductions to later acts in the early operas, which are usually much shorter and directly linked to the act they introduce. Many of these later-act openings are similar to the brief orchestral introductions that, following the overture, begin the opening scene of the first act. There are exceptions. In *Der fliegende Holländer*, the second and third acts are preceded by short entr'actes that begin by recalling the music from the end of the previous act, then gradually lead into the new act's opening scene, thus echoing Wagner's original conception of the work as a brief one-act opera. In *Tannhäuser*, the "Einleitung" to Act III is a self-contained musical tableau that depicts Tannhäuser's pilgrimage to Rome and foreshadows the "Rom-Erzählung" later in the opera.

2. After 1845: from *Lohengrin* to *Parsifal*

From *Lohengrin* onwards, Wagner abandoned the traditional overture, re-placing it with a variety of shorter and longer formats that may be identified in the score as "Vorspiel," or "Einleitung," or not identified at all. The "Vorspiel" to *Lohengrin* was most likely begun as the slow introduction to a full-fledged overture and then turned into a self-sufficient piece. Like the earlier overtures, it stands entirely separate from the first act, which begins with its own brief orchestral introduction. This is an exception in Wagner's later operas: typically, an orchestral opening is directly connected to the act it precedes. In consequence, the categorical difference that existed between an overture and an introduction in the earlier operas disappears, a tendency that is reflected in Wagner's use of the same terms "Vorspiel" and "Einleitung" for any orchestral opening, regardless of which act it precedes.

In TRISTAN UND ISOLDE, Die MEISTERSINGER VON NÜRNBERG, and *Parsifal*, it is still possible to distinguish between the more extended, substantial, and self-contained orchestral opening that precedes the first act, and the more condensed introductions or preludes to later acts. Formally, however, only the *Meistersinger* "Vorspiel" adopts the sonata-form layout of the traditional overture. The "Einleitung" to the first act of *Tristan* is a unique musical form that gradually builds up to an enormous climax by freely cycling through a number of recurring themes; the "Vorspiel" to *Parsifal* has a ternary design in which the concluding section is not a recapitulation, but a development of the opening section. Together with the (unnamed) Prelude to Act III in *Lohengrin* (which, exceptionally, is thematically unrelated to any other music in the opera) and the "Vorspiel" to Act III in *Die Meistersinger*, these orchestral openings can be called "separable": although connected to subsequent music, they could easily be (and have often been) turned into stand-alone pieces. It is no coincidence that, for several of them, Wagner himself provided alternative concert endings (see listing below).

No such extended introductory pieces occur in *Der RING DES NIBEL-UNGEN*. Without exception, orchestral introductions in the *Ring* are short and lack sufficient formal independence and musical substance to stand on their own. Even the temporally more extended introductions, such as the "Vorspiele" to *Das RHEINGOLD* and to Act II of *SIEGFRIED*, appear inseparable from the act they introduce. In spite of their uniform brevity, however, these orchestral introductions are essential to the *Ring*'s musical construction, constituting highly charged nodes in the network of *LEITMOTIVE* that spans the entire tetralogy.

3. Concert endings by Wagner

Gluck, Overture to *Iphigénie en Aulide*: new concert ending composed, performed, and published 1854 (WWV 87).

Lohengrin, Prelude to Act III: concert ending composed and performed in 1853 – WORK LOST.

Tristan und Isolde, Prelude to Act I: concert ending composed 1859, first performed and published 1860.

Die Meistersinger von Nürnberg, Prelude to Act I: concert ending (i.e., original version of the prelude) composed and first performed 1862, published 1866.

Parsifal, Prelude to Act I: concert ending (i.e., original version of the prelude) composed and first performed 1878, published 1882.

STEVEN G. VANDE MOORTELE

Thomas S. Grey, "Wagner, the Overture, and the Aesthetics of Musical Form," *19th-Century Music* 12 (1988): 3–22.

Reinhard Strohm, "Gedanken zu Wagners Opernouvertüren," in *Wagnerliteratur-Wagnerforschung*, ed. Carl Dahlhaus and Egon Voss (Mainz: Schott, 1985): 69–84.

Paris. Amongst the cities that played a major part in Richard Wagner's life, Paris was the crucial one, prompting Nietzsche to remark that "Paris was the actual *soil* for Wagner" (*dass Paris der eigentliche* Boden *für Wagner ist*; *Nietzsche contra Wagner*, "Wohin Wagner gehört" [Where Wagner is at home]). And in 1867, Wagner wrote to LUDWIG II, King of Bavaria:

> As the world now is, Paris is the culminating point: all other cities are simply stations along the way. It is the heart of modern civilization, drawing in the blood before sending it out again to the limbs ... When I decided to become a famous opera composer, my good angel sent me straight to that heart: there I was at the source, and there I was able to grasp at once things which at the wayside stations would perhaps have taken me half a lifetime to learn.
>
> (18 JULY 1867)

The relationship between Wagner and Paris was, for various reasons, a strained one. No other city provoked in Wagner the same artistic ambition, and no other city inflicted on him the same degree of disappointment. The importance of Paris for Wagner was twofold: first, as a place of residence. Wagner's ambition to "conquer" Paris as the cultural capital of his time brought him there twice for extended periods (1839–42; 1859–62). In addition, he made nine brief visits lasting no longer than three weeks.

Second, its importance is rooted in the evolution of the French Wagnerian movement, which originated and developed in Paris as France's intellectual center of gravity. In its literary scene, a specific form of *wagnérisme* came into being which was unique in the history of Wagner reception.

1. First stay, 1839–1842
2. Second stay, 1859–1862
3. Last visit and after

1. First stay 1839–1842

At the end of the 1830s, Paris was the ultimate goal of Wagner's artistic endeavors. His calculation was that German court theaters were bound to accept his operas once they had been successfully staged at the Grand Opéra. He arrived in Paris on 17 September 1839, after an odyssey travelling from RIGA – to flee his creditors – via RUSSIA, East Prussia, the Baltic Sea, Norway, and LONDON. Armed with letters of introduction from Giacomo MEYERBEER, whom he had met on his arrival in Boulogne-sur-Mer, Wagner was determined to succeed. During the following two and a half years, Wagner took residence in Paris and made several futile attempts to have his works staged. His encounter with the director of the Paris Opéra came to nothing, the rehearsal of the *Columbus* Overture with François-Antoine Habeneck's Société des Concerts du Conservatoire was as much a failure as the inclusion of this piece into a concert series of the REVUE ET GAZETTE MUSICALE DE PARIS on 4 February 1841. Finally, the Théâtre de la Renaissance agreed to stage *Das LIEBESVERBOT*, but this enterprise failed, too, due to the theater's bankruptcy in April 1840.

In order to survive financially, Wagner had to accept odd jobs such as scoring musical arrangements for Maurice SCHLESINGER's music publishing house. Among these, his piano reductions of Donizetti's *La Favorite* and HALÉVY's *La Reine de Chypre* stand out. Between 12 July 1840 and 1 May 1842, Wagner contributed ten articles to the *Revue et gazette musicale*. Among those, many excel in dramatic structure and style, in particular *Eine PILGERFAHRT ZU BEETHOVEN* (A Pilgrimage to Beethoven, 1840). In the novella *Ein ENDE IN PARIS* (A Death in Paris, 1841) Wagner semi-autobiographically presents a sociocultural criticism of the Parisian musical scene, and does so for the first and perhaps last time in a journalistic style that is both elegant and readable. Apart from these publications, Wagner reported on Parisian music life for German journals and magazines (*Abend-Zeitung* [Dresden], *Europa*, and Schumann's *NEUE ZEITSCHRIFT FÜR MUSIK*).

Wagner had four different addresses in Paris (Appendix 3: Wagner's addresses). In September 1839, he moved to 3 rue de la Tonnellerie, falsely called "Molière's birth house." On 15 April 1840, he took a bigger apartment at 25 rue du Helder, in the hope of artistic success at the Théâtre de la Renaissance, which failed the same month. On 29 April 1841, he moved to the suburb of Meudon (27 Avenue du Château), and finally, back to Paris on 30 October 1841 (14 rue Jacob, in the Quartier Latin), where he stayed till his final departure, 7 April 1842.

Wagner lived a meager life with his wife MINNA, and struggled to survive. However, he likely never went to the debtors' prison in rue de Clichy, as suggested by Minna in a letter to impress a potential creditor, since no trace of such incarceration can be found, either in the Police Archives or in the National Archives of Paris. Wagner enjoyed the company of friends who shared his modest life, and who formed an artists' circle not unlike that in Henri Murger's story collection *Scènes de la vie de bohème*, dating from the same period. The circle comprised the scholar Samuel LEHRS, the librarian and musical historian Gottfried ANDERS, the painters Ernst Benedikt KIETZ and Friedrich PECHT, and Wagner the composer. He was acquainted with Heinrich HEINE and met (in Schlesinger's music shop) Hector BERLIOZ and Franz LISZT, though the friendship with Liszt did not commence until later.

The most important outcome of Wagner's first Paris stay was – apart from prose writings – his compositions. He continued work on *RIENZI*, completing it on 19 November 1840. More importantly, he wrote and composed large parts of *Der FLIEGENDE HOLLÄNDER* in the summer of 1841 in Meudon and finished the score in November 1841. He financed the Meudon apartment and the rental of a piano by selling *Holländer* to the Paris Opéra for 500 francs. Thus, the first of the ten "Bayreuth operas" was conceived, written, and composed in the French capital, which makes Paris the birthplace of an AESTHETICS that ultimately resulted in Wagner's reconceptualization of opera.

In addition, Wagner composed *Lieder* based on French poems by Hugo, Ronsard, and Reboul, as well as Heine's *Les Deux Grenadiers* (published by Schlesinger in 1840). Finally, he finished his FAUST-OVERTÜRE on 12 January 1840.

2. Second stay, 1859–1862

In the period between his two longer Paris stays, Wagner only made brief stops there in 1849, 1850, 1853, 1855, and 1858. While Wagner passed through Paris in 1849 on his flight from Saxony following the failed DRESDEN UPRISING, he visited from his exile in ZURICH during the 1850s hoping in vain for Paris performances of his works, paying social visits, or simply as intermediate stops, for instance, on the way to London (1855). During the 1850s, since he still was not allowed on German soil, he decided to make a second attempt to "conquer" Paris with a production under his personal guidance. His initial plan was to find a theater to stage his recently finished *TRISTAN UND ISOLDE*.

When Wagner arrived in Paris on 15 September 1859, he moved to 4 rue Matignon, and was to stay, with a long interruption in the summer and autumn of 1861, in the French capital until 1 February 1862. Between 7 October 1859 and 15 October 1860, he lived at 16 rue Newton, near the Arc de Triomphe. Thereafter, he moved to 3 rue d'Aumale, a building which still exists today, and in which he resided during the *TANNHÄUSER SCANDAL OF 1861*. Between 3 December 1861 and 1 February 1862, Wagner resided at the Hôtel (du Quai) Voltaire across the river from the Louvre.

Initially, he wanted to stage *TANNHÄUSER* and *LOHENGRIN* to pave the way for *Tristan und Isolde* at the Salle Ventadour. He even contemplated staging *Das RHEINGOLD* in May 1861 (letter to B. Schott's Söhne, 7 January 1860). Wagner wanted to prepare Paris as the ground on which his operas would receive model performances – sung in German – since there was, in his eyes, no hope to do so in Germany: Paris was to fulfill the role taken on by MUNICH after 1865.

In Paris, Wagner was known – if at all – through his prose writings of the early 1840s. Only a small circle of experts knew some of his music and his theoretical essays. In order to become known by the Paris audience, he rented the Salle Ventadour at the Théâtre-Italien for three ORCHESTRAL CONCERTS on 25 January, 1 February, and 8 February 1860. He presented EXCERPTS from *Der fliegende Holländer, Tannhäuser, Lohengin*, and the PRELUDE of *Tristan und Isolde*, which startled most listeners, even Berlioz. This created a lot of publicity and provoked both fierce opponents and ardent admirers. The enormous deficit caused by the concerts seemed to jeopardize Wagner's plans for full opera performances but, unexpectedly, on 11 March 1860, the Emperor Napoleon III gave the order to stage *Tannhäuser* at the Paris Opéra, at the intervention of Princess Pauline METTERNICH, wife of the Austrian ambassador in Paris.

Wagner prepared this event by further expanding his hitherto considerable acquaintances in Paris. During 1860, he fostered his social network with Wednesday soirées in his home in rue Newton, where many personalities of Paris's musical, intellectual, and political life were frequent guests, such as the composers Camille Saint-Saëns and Charles Gounod; the musician Ernest Reyer; the critic and later director of the Opéra Émile Perrin; the writers Léon

Leroy, Catulle MENDÈS, and Malwida von MEYSENBUG; or the lawyers (and later politicians) Jules Ferry and Émile Ollivier.

The rehearsals for *Tannhäuser* started in September 1860, but the premiere was postponed repeatedly for various reasons, leaving the opera staff, Wagner's friends – many of whom had travelled long distances – and the composer himself tired and strained. After 164 rehearsals, the premiere finally took place on 13 March 1861. However, Wagner had failed to organize support from the claqueurs and press, since he thought the music would speak for itself. At the same time, the political opposition to Napoleon III (the ultra-conservative old aristocracy of the Jockey Club) was prepared to make this enterprise a failure. After three evenings of almost constant noise, shouting, and whistling, Wagner withdrew the opera in order to save the singers and musician this disgrace.

This scandal constituted Wagner's biggest lifetime theatrical failure, but triggered, paradoxically, the beginning of the French Wagnerian movement, starting with a famous article by Charles BAUDELAIRE. Wagner spent most of the summer and autumn in Germany (which he was allowed to enter again) before returning to Paris in December 1861 and January 1862, completing the first version of the text of *Die Meistersinger von Nürnberg*, and leaving for good on 1 February 1862.

3. Last visit and after

Wagner visited Paris for the last time from 28 October to 4 November 1867. He came to visit the Universal Exhibition and stayed at the Grand Hôtel near the construction site of the Opéra Garnier. He would never return to the French capital, but stayed in close contact with the growing number of Parisian Wagnerians such as Judith GAUTIER, Catulle Mendès, Édouard SCHURÉ, or Auguste Villiers de l'Isle-Adam. Wagner was able to witness the French Wagnerian movement grow steadily until his death in 1883, but did not live to see its peak around 1900, which made Paris the capital of international WAGNERISM. HERMANN GRAMPP

Robert L. Jacobs and Geoffrey Skelton, eds. and trans., *Wagner Writes from Paris: Stories, Essays and Articles by the Young Composer* (London: Allen & Unwin, 1973).

Danièle Pistone, "Dossier: Wagner et Paris," *Revue internationale de musique française* 1 (1980): 7–84.

Parodies, satire, caricatures. It is not only Richard Wagner's operas that offer a rich trove of sources ripe for caricature, parody, and satire, but also the physiognomy of the man himself. His short stature, prominent nose, and beret, not to mention the events in his tumultuous professional and personal life, proved irresistible for caricatures easily understood, particularly for those in the know. Nevertheless, parodies and satires of Wagner's prose writings, opera texts, and music are for non-German speakers problematic at best. This difficulty throws into sharp relief the enormous struggle to translate texts of diverse dialects and *Kosenamen* (terms of endearment) into idiomatic English. Translations simply cannot reflect the full meaning of puns, word play, double-entendres, tongue twisters, and topical commentaries. Interpretations also fail fully to convey the *auditory* humor of distinctly different dialects, including Viennese, Bavarian, "Plattdeutsch" of northern Germany, and Berlin's Prussian.

Wagner did not spare himself or his operas, often shifting into his thick native Saxon dialect for jokes. During his composition of TRISTAN UND ISOLDE, Wagner wrote in a letter to Mathilde WESENDONCK (9 July 1859) poking fun at the deaths of the title pair: "Sie starben frei, sie starben gern / im Schweizerhof zu Luzern" (They die freely, they die gladly / in the Schweizerhof in Lucerne), the Schweizerhof being a high-class and expensive hotel where the composer resided. COSIMA recorded in her DIARIES many of Wagner's humorous asides. During the composition of PARSIFAL, he quipped "Now then, I shall have my *Monsieurs* [Knights of the Grail] shuffle to the 'Radetzky-marsch' [by Johann Strauss Sr.]" (25 January 1878). In another remark, Wagner quipped: "Oh, that is my salvation, that I have been given the ability to quickly change all seriousness into silliness" (6 August 1878). During the 1876 rehearsals for *Die WALKÜRE*, when asked where FRICKA should enter the scene, Wagner replied, "from the left; the devil always enters from the left," a reflection of an old theater practice of the villain always entering from that side of the stage (Fricke 104).

Wagner's prose writings, particularly the works of the "future," *Das KUNSTWERK DER ZUKUNFT* (The Artwork of the Future, 1849/50) and *ZUKUNFTSMUSIK* (Music of the Future, 1860), formed targets for parody. The French particularly mocked the "music of the future" being without melody or rhythm. In reaction to numerous writings about the composer, a concert of Wagner's music (6 December 1868), and the premiere of *RIENZI* in PARIS at the Théâtre Lyrique (6 April 1869), a full-page caricature by André Gill appeared on the cover of *L'Éclipse* (18 April 1869) showing Wagner ferociously hammering a quarter note into a giant ear spurting blood (Kahane and Wild 28). The memories of Wagner's TANNHÄUSER SCANDAL at the Opéra (1861) were still fresh.

Among the earliest surviving stage parodies of Wagner's operas is Hermann Müller's *Tannhäuser and the Brawl on the Wartburg* (Breslau, 1854). The plot occurs "at the same time in different centuries; Act I in Venus' basement restaurant with Pschörr beer" in Munich, "the second act some-where else, the third in *Schiesswerdehalle* on the Wartburg, and the fourth [act] after the third." Landgrave Pietsch ("a gentle tyrant, uncle [of Elisabeth], and otherwise a bourgeois") sings a peroration to the hall to the tune of Sarastro's "In diesen heil'gen Hallen" from MOZART's *Die Zauberflöte*. University profes-sors judge the song contest and issue passing or failing grades. Three years later, Johann Nestroy reworked the Wollheim text into what became one of the best-known parodies: *Tannhäuser: A Farce of the Future with Music of the Past and Groups of the Present in Three Acts*. The Landgrave is Purzel (colloquialism for "cute little fellow") portrayed by Nestroy himself in the first performances, speaking and singing with a thick Viennese accent. The entry of the guests in Act II included not only Tannhäuser and his fellow minnesingers, but also "nobles of both sexes, vassals, knights, giants, trainbearers, heralds, nymphs, hunters ... and pallbearers" together with characters from well-known operas including *Robert le diable* (MEYERBEER), *Guillaume Tell* (ROSSINI), *Norma* (BELLINI), and Mozart's *Le nozze di Figaro*. At the end of the final scene, Venus brings Elisabeth and Tannhäuser back to life, but warns, "with their first [marital] spat, they will die once more!"

Der RING DES NIBELUNGEN did not escape the pen of parodists. One year after the Bayreuth premiere, P. Gisbert [recte Gisbert Prinower] published Der Ring der nie gelungen (The Ring that Never Worked). In the first part, Mein, dein, sein Gold (Mine, Yours, His Gold; recte Das Rheingold), the Rhein maidens are transformed into Oochgelinde, Willhunde, and Flußwilde, "female Rhine guards acting as young Rhine virgins but will gladly show off a bit of humor." The parody begins with a spoof of the original "Weia Waga Woge, du Welle walle zur Wiege" as Oochgelinde sings the tongue twisting "Wir Wiener Wäscherinnen waschen weiße Wäsche..." and adds commentary on Wagner's literary devices "O, für fünfzehn Thaler monatlich auch noch immer in Alliterationen sprechen!" (We Viennese laundry maids wash white laundry ... Oh, for fifteen thalers monthly always to continue speaking in alliterations!). Gisbert's thoroughly humorous Ring text is also filled with pithy social and political commentary, similar to George Bernard SHAW's The Perfect Wagnerite (1898).

During World War II, Wagner was mercilessly lampooned as an agent of the Nazis. Spike Jones and his band, City Slickers, parodied the overture to MEISTERSINGER along with the "Ride of the Valkyries," entitled The Flight of the Valkyries for an American propaganda film, Der Führer's Face, with Disney's Donald Duck. In 1943, the actress Pola Negri starred as Genya Smetana[!], a willful opera singer in Hi Diddle Diddle. In one scene, the figure of Wagner wearing his beret and sitting under a tree is seen as part of a wallpaper pattern. At a social gathering in the final scene of the film, Negri and friends proceed to massacre the Pilgrims' chorus from Tannhäuser. The figure of Wagner in the wallpaper comes to life, jumps up and down, and complains bitterly, followed by howling dogs and whinnying horses.

In the 1960s, the German cabaret team of Helmut Qualtinger and Carl Merz with music by Jeff Palme lampooned the American musical theater genre, combining elements from Wagner and George Gershwin entitled, Siggy und Bess: Der Swing der Nibelungen. Eine teutonische Jazzoper für Orchester und fünf Pistolen. Included are filmic references to Frankenstein and Cecil B. de Mille; Siggy is an auto mechanic in a New Orleans garage. Allusions to the Ring surface with the "Rhinesisters," a funeral company named "Feuerzauber" (cremation by "Magic Fire"), and "Siegfried's Mississippi Journey." Instances of the Ring text are mangled: for example, from Die Walküre, "Einen Ford verhieß mir der Vater" (My father promised me a Ford; recte Siegmund's "Ein Schwert [sword] verheiß mir der Vater"). The piece ends with Siggy and Bess disappearing into the Mississippi amidst a water ballet complete with Esther Williams and her massive chorus of water-skiers.

The first of the two of the greatest parodies of Wagner in English occurred in 1957 with the cartoon What's Opera, Doc? The Wagnerian stereotypes in the guise of Bugs Bunny and Elmer Fudd attired in Teutonic costumes complete with the horned helmets, blond braided hair, and spears wreak musical and visual havoc upon Tannhäuser, Tristan und Isolde, and Die Walküre. Fudd sings "Kill da wabbit" to the tune of the "Ride of the Valkyries." Then, during the 1970s through the 1990s, Anna Russell performed a sketch that, in the space of forty minutes, proceeded to explain the plot and the music of the entire nineteen hours of the *Ring*. Her droll descriptions of many characters included "WOTAN and Mrs. Fricka Wotan" and "that little dwarf, ALBERICH ... You do remember Alberich, don't you?" The greatest of her *bon mots* of the entire lecture zeroed in towards one crucial and believable observation of the entire cycle – "I'm not making this up, you know!" – that delighted Wagnerians throughout the world.   EVAN BAKER

See also WAGNER AND POPULAR CULTURE

Dieter Borchmeyer and Stephan Kohler, eds., *Wagner Parodien* (Frankfurt: Insel, 1983).
Manfred Eger, "Richard Wagner in Parodie und Karikatur," in *Richard-Wagner-Handbuch*, ed. Ulrich Müller and Peter Wapnewski (see bibliography): 760–76.
Richard Fricke, *Bayreuth vor dreißig Jahren: Erinnerungen an Wahnfried und aus dem Festspielhause* (Dresden: Bertling, 1906).
Eduard Fuchs and Ernst Kreowski, *Richard Wagner in der Karikatur* (Berlin: Behr, 1907).
Martine Kahane and Nicole Wild, *Wagner et la France* (Paris: Bibliothèque Nationale, 1983).
Andrea Schneider, *Die parodierten Musikdramen Richard Wagners: Geschichte und Dokumentation Wagnerscher Opernparodien im deutschsprachigen Raum von der Mitte des 19. Jahrhunderts bis zum Ende des Ersten Weltkrieges* (Anif/Salzburg: Müller-Speiser, 1996).
Hey Diddle, Diddle is available at www.archive.org for download.

Parsifal (WWV 111), *BÜHNENWEIHFESTSPIEL* (stage consecration festival play) in three acts, first performed at the FESTIVAL THEATER, BAYREUTH, 26 July 1882. Cond. Hermann Levi. For cast information, see Appendix 10: Stage productions.
1. Background, sources, and development of the text
2. Composition and first performances
3. Plot structure
4. Musical structure
5. Production history
6. Critical reception and problems of interpretation

1. Background, sources, and development of the text

Parsifal was Wagner's final work, and the culmination of his efforts to bring medieval MYTH and MODERN MUSIC together in a dynamic relationship. The composer himself once described the opera as his "last card," in recognition both of his failing health and of the fact that *Die Sieger* (The Victors, WWV 89), the BUDDHIST drama that was to have followed *Parsifal*, would never be composed. Nevertheless, Wagner's preoccupation with themes related to *Parsifal* stretched over much of his career. His very first opera, *Die FEEN* (The Fairies, 1834), closely based on Carlo Gozzi's *La donna serpente* (The Snake Woman), foreshadows certain elements of *Parsifal*, especially the parallel between the main female figure KUNDRY (*Parsifal*) and Ada (*Die Feen*).

Around 1840, while Wagner was in PARIS, he came into possession of stimulating sources on medieval saga material, contained especially in an 1838 publication from KÖNIGSBERG by Christian Theodor Ludwig Lucas entitled *Über den Krieg von Wartburg* (About the Wartburg War). Lucas's book is an underestimated work in relation to Wagner's TANNHÄUSER and LOHEN-GRIN, as well as aspects of *Parsifal*, for instance in the character KLINGSOR.

Wagner's first engagement with the mythic saga material thus predated his close reading at MARIENBAD in 1845 of his main source, WOLFRAM VON

ESCHENBACH's thirteenth-century epic poem *PARZIVAL*. During the 1850s, Wagner contemplated and then rejected the idea of introducing the character of Parsifal into the third act of *TRISTAN*, and he even sketched music for "Parzival's Refrain." The episode in question concerned Parzival as wandering pilgrim seeking the Grail. At the urging of his patron, LUDWIG II, Wagner wrote out a detailed prose draft in 1865. Twelve years later, in early 1877, he wrote out a second, still more detailed prose draft; the completion of the poem followed in April 1877. During this period, he changed the names of several of the characters: "Parzival" became "Parsifal," while "Gurnemans" was altered to "GURNEMANZ," "Anfortas" to "AMFORTAS," and "Chinschor" to "Klingsor."

2. Composition and first performances

The composition of the music was begun tentatively in 1876 and sustained over the period from August 1877 to April 1879, with the writing of the full score and revision or insertion of certain passages occupying Wagner until January of 1882. Research on Wagner's manuscripts has shown that the last extended musical passage he conceived was actually the second half of the transformation music in Act I, which was added to his drafts in March 1881 (see Kinderman and Syer 158–65). *Parsifal* was painstakingly rehearsed and given a series of exemplary performances to reopen the Bayreuth Festival in July and August 1882, six months before Wagner's death. Wagner called it a *Bühnenweihfestspiel* and meant to confine staged performances of the work to Bayreuth.

3. Plot structure

Wagner characteristically departed from his sources to create a highly concentrated drama, heavily laden with symbolic import. He viewed the wounded Grail King in *Parsifal*, Amfortas, as analogous to the wounded TRISTAN of Act III of *Tristan und Isolde* but with an enormous dramatic intensification. Amfortas's wound will not heal because it is the outward symbol of his inward state of moral impurity, and whenever he serves his duty of revealing the Holy Grail the wound opens afresh. This dilemma of Amfortas threatens to cause the downfall of the Order of Knights and bring the Grail into the hands of the diabolical Klingsor, who has already seized the Holy Spear and covets the Grail as well. Amfortas's inability to perform his office after the communion scene in the second half of Act I eventually causes the death of his father, Titurel, founder of the Grail Temple, whose funeral procession forms the transformation music at the change of scene in Act III. Only the intervention of Parsifal as redeemer prevents this dissipation of the Order of the Grail in the final moments of the drama, as Parsifal returns the Spear, heals Amfortas's wound and assumes the role of leader of the Order.

The drama of *Parsifal* thus turns on the conflict between two opposing and incompatible realms, the spheres of the Grail and the anti-Grail. The crucial encounter that decides the outcome of this struggle is Kundry's attempt to seduce Parsifal in Klingsor's magic garden in Act II. Only in this great duet scene are the deeper layers of symbolic meaning unveiled. Kundry, the sole principal female figure in *Parsifal* and perhaps the most fascinating and complex of all Wagner's characters, was developed mainly as an amalgam of characters in Wolfram von Eschenbach's poem: in Act I she is a wild heathen, distrusted by the knights but nonetheless bound to serve Amfortas for some mysterious and yet undisclosed reason; in Act II, she is an apparently irresistible temptress and unwilling agent of the evil Klingsor in his magic castle; and in Act III, she is a penitent who comes to resemble Mary Magdalene in the Good Friday scene and who attains release through death in the opera's closing moments. As Kundry reveals toward the close of Act II, she is under a curse and has experienced untold reincarnations through history, as Herodias and others. The cause of her curse and domination by Klingsor was her sin of *Schadenfreude*, her spiteful laughter at the redeemer on the cross. Paradoxically, she can only be set free of her curse if her seductive charms are resisted, but no such protagonist with an insight transcending the sway of the senses ever emerges until Parsifal. The seduction attempt, centered on the delivery of Kundry's poisoned kiss to Parsifal, acts like a replay of her earlier seduction of Amfortas, which led to his loss of the Spear and his wounding by Klingsor. Unlike Amfortas, Parsifal resists the temptation of her seduction because his capacity for compassion, as predicted in the prophecy of Act I ("Knowing through compassion, the Pure Fool"), enables him to identify with the agony of Amfortas, and gradually to grasp the significance of his calling to the Grail. Since the seduction has failed, and the protective shield of Parsifal's purity remains intact, the Spear when thrown by Klingsor cannot harm him. As Parsifal makes the sign of the cross with the Spear, Klingsor's illusory magic realm is destroyed.

Parsifal's return journey to the Grail is tortuous, since his path – cursed by Kundry – is blocked. His eventual return to the Grail, on Good Friday, coincides with Kundry's reincarnation as a penitent, and his first duty as redeemer is to baptize her. Act III concludes, as did Act I, with the Communion service and revelation of the Grail, now no longer under threat from Klingsor.

4. Musical structure

The music of *Parsifal* assumes great dramatic weight and importance, especially in view of the ritualistic nature of the Grail scenes, the sparsity of text in portions of Act III, which approach pantomime, and the inward, psychological nature of the Parsifal-Kundry encounter in Act II. The largest single vocal part, on the other hand, is given to the narrator, Gurnemanz. At a formative stage in composition, Wagner described the "core of the drama" as the first Grail scene, and it is indeed the music for this section that is anticipated in the Prelude to Act I and eventually reinterpreted and resolved in the concluding Grail scene of Act III. Noteworthy in this respect is Wagner's control of tonal relations on different levels of the musical structure. The opening Communion or Last Supper theme (Example 11) thus begins and ends in A♭ major, but turns prominently to C minor in its third measure, in a motivic gesture later associated with Amfortas's wound and hence with the threat to the Grail. Wagner also employs this A♭/C axis or tonal pairing to generate the ensuing tonal sequence of the entire theme beginning in C minor, with its internal dissonances intensified; and on the most gigantic level, he

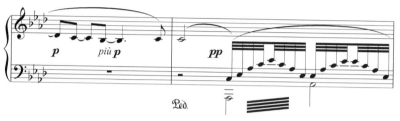

11. Communion or Last Supper theme

plans the entire first act to modulate to the major mode of C at the entrance into the Grail Temple, where this tonality is affirmed by the fixed pitches of the temple bells. A grim reinterpretation of the fixed pitches of the bells occurs during the funeral procession for Titurel in Act III, in the key of E minor. The second act, on the other hand, begins and ends in B minor, a key associated with Klingsor. Wagner portrays the dramatic irony at Parsifal's destruction of Klingsor's castle at the end of Act II through the tonal clash of C major against B minor – Grail against anti-Grail – since bleak trials and "pathless wandering" still await Parsifal. When the castle crumbles and the "Grail" motive rises up in C major at Parsifal's word "Pracht" (pomp), a dissonant F♯ emerges in the bass, turning the tonal equilibrium toward Klingsor's dark key of B minor (Example 12).

For his Communion theme Wagner drew upon the opening motive of the "Excelsior!" Prelude in *The Bells of Strasburg Cathedral*, a choral work composed by his father-in-law, Franz LISZT. Liszt's cantata was inspired in turn by *The Golden Legend*, a poem by the American poet Henry Wadsworth Longfellow, who had met Liszt at Rome in 1868. Wagner first heard Liszt's work at their joint concert at Budapest in March 1875; he later acknowledged his borrowing or even his "theft" of this motive from Liszt, and COSIMA WAGNER'S DIARY entry of 28 December 1878 refers to his looking at Liszt's cantata to see whether he had committed "plagiarism," a circumstance likely connected as well to the treatment of the bells in each work. It was surely the poetic intention in Longfellow's work that fascinated both composers, particularly the association of the Excelsior motto with endless striving toward what is "higher" and "higher yet": the promise of immortality and progress ever upward (see Marget). This is reflected musically in Wagner's theme through its rising contour through the triad to the sixth degree, a pattern that further ascends to a decisive resolving cadence in Act III, once Parsifal returns with the Spear to the Grail realm, the threat posed by Klingsor by then removed.

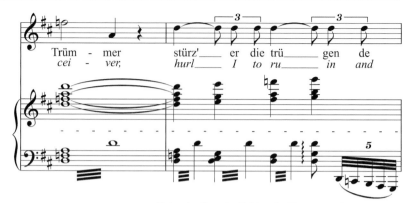

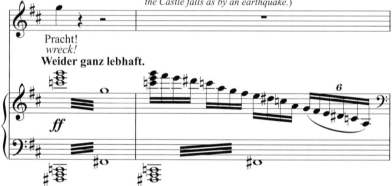

12. Act II, Klingsor's castle crumbles

The music associated with Kundry and Klingsor, with Amfortas's agony, and with Parsifal's tortuous journey back to the Grail in the Act III Prelude, displays a dissonant chromaticism sometimes even more advanced than in *Tristan* but which nevertheless retains contact with the music of the Grail. The so-called Magic motive (*Zaubermotiv*) (Example 13), heard when Kundry delivers her kiss to Parsifal, outlines the dissonant interval of the tritone, instead of rising through the perfect fifth to the major sixth, as does the Communion theme; its intervallic configuration is devised as a chromatic distortion of the latter. (Here too, the model of Liszt's music exerted influence on Wagner; one is reminded how the themes associated with Faust in the opening movement of Liszt's "Faust" Symphony are parodied through chromaticism in the closing "Mephistopheles" movement as an embodiment of Goethe's idea of "der Geist, der stets verneint" [the spirit that always negates].) At Parsifal's response to Kundry's kiss, furthermore, this chromatic material is juxtaposed with the familiar dissonant inflection within the Communion theme itself (often described as the "Schmerzensfigur" or "pain" motive), which enables the listener to hear that inflection with new insight as a "chromatic contamination" – stemming from Kundry's earlier seduction

13. Magic motive (*Zaubermotiv*)

of Amfortas – of the otherwise diatonically pure music of the Grail (this is also shown in Example 13). This "chromatic contamination" is purged from the music of the Grail in Act III, motivated dramatically by Parsifal's aforementioned return of the Spear, and the head of the Communion theme receives a new ascending resolution.

The enormous time-scale of Wagner's drama requires an appropriately massive musical resolution of tensions, which is supplied in part in the "Good Friday" music and capped by the closing music to Act III, with its choral text "Erlösung dem Erlöser!" (Redemption to the Redeemer!). Here the various themes and motives heard successively in the Act I Prelude are combined in a larger formal synthesis symbolizing the wholeness of the REDEMPTION. In both Grail Temple scenes but especially in Act I, Wagner enhances the sonority through hidden choruses heard from halfway up and atop the dome.

5. Production history

The restriction of staged performances to Bayreuth was broken by the 1903 production of *Parsifal* in New York, where the Berne copyright agreement was not in force. A decade later, at the end of 1913, the copyright officially expired, and a flood of *Parsifal* productions ensued in many of the world's leading opera houses. One landmark production was the 1914 Freiburg *Parsifal* designed by Ludwig Sievert, a follower of the modernistic Swiss theater theorist Adolphe APPIA, whose ideas had been rejected by COSIMA in order to maintain the original 1882 production. Appia's emphasis on nuanced lighting, abstract geometric sets, and mythic rather than historical aspects of the dramas was carried forth by WIELAND WAGNER, whose 1951 production marked the resumption of the Bayreuth Festival after World War II.

Since the 1970s, directors have tended to take more interventionist approaches to staging *Parsifal*, often departing from the composer's stage directions. During the 1975 run of his Bayreuth production, for instance, WOLFGANG WAGNER decided to keep Kundry alive at the conclusion. She also remained alive in Götz Friedrich's 1976 Stuttgart production, whereas in Uwe Wand's *Parsifal* from Leipzig in 1982 Kundry's destiny was joined with Amfortas following the onstage death of Parsifal. In Harry Kupfer's imaginative 1992 Berlin production, Amfortas dies instead of Kundry. An especially provocative reinterpretation of the drama's close occurs in Nikolaus Lehnhoff's production, which has reached the stage in London, San Francisco, Chicago, and other cities since 1999. In this version, the Grail Knights break into two groups: a conservative faction stays with Gurnemanz, to whom Parsifal has entrusted the Holy Spear as an admired symbol of orthodoxy; other individual knights break away to follow Kundry and Parsifal, who depart toward a lighted but ominous undisclosed destination, following a railway track.

6. Critical reception and problems of interpretation

The controversy that has always surrounded *Parsifal* is connected in part to its close relationship to Christianity, an issue already raised by a severely disappointed NIETZSCHE. However, "Christ" is never mentioned by name, and there is no need to interpret *Parsifal* within a Christian framework. (To be sure, the analogy between "Adam and Eve: Christ" and "Amfortas and Kundry: Parsifal" lies close at hand, and was drawn by the composer himself in a letter to King Ludwig II of 7 September 1865, whereby Wagner stressed the need for great caution with the comparison.) *Parsifal* is a major monument to the aesthetic of the sublime and to Wagner's conviction as expressed in his essay *Religion und Kunst* (Religion and Art, 1880) that art could "salvage the kernel of religion" through its "ideal representation" of mythic religious images (see KUNSTRELIGION). The role of compassion is central to this framework, and is conveyed in part through varied musical recapitulation. Following Kundry's kiss, Parsifal's compassionate identification with the wounded Grail King is represented through the recall of passages drawn from Amfortas's lament in Act I. More weighty still is Parsifal's quotation of the savior's distressed cry that originally led him to the realm of the Grail: "Redeem, rescue me from hands defiled by guilt!" Parsifal's selfless identification with the Other and realization of the nature of his mission leads him on a path opposed to that of the guilt-ridden Grail King. Whereas Amfortas had aggressively carried the Spear into combat against Klingsor, Parsifal wisely holds the Spear in protective concealment until he at last regains access to the Grail. At the conclusion, the reunification of Spear and Grail stands for a symbolic integration of male and female principles, and some commentators have offered more sweeping affirmative interpretations. For Jean-Jacques Nattiez, the character of Parsifal himself becomes here "the symbolic embodiment of an angelic androgyny, proclaiming a new civilization and culture" (170).

The theme of REDEMPTION, which obsessed Wagner throughout his career, is developed and radicalized in *Parsifal* to concern not just individuals but a collective society. The resulting political and ideological overtones have seemed sinister to some commentators, especially in view of subsequent German history, and not without reason. In 1923, Wagner's son-in-law Houston Stewart CHAMBERLAIN hailed Adolf HITLER as Germany's savior. A decade later, Alfred LORENZ sought to identify Wagner's "prophetic thoughts" with the "march to victory of a racially highly bred people" following Hitler's rise to power (153). Nevertheless, Parsifal's qualities of pity, pacifism, and renunciation are incompatible with fascism, and performances of the work at Bayreuth were discontinued during World War II. The NATIONAL SOCIALIST ideologist Alfred Rosenberg found that "*Parsifal* represents a church-influenced enfeeblement in favor of the value of renunciation" (139).

Another critical issue is the imbalance between *Agapē* and *Eros*; the brotherhood of knights leaves no place for SEXUALITY, and the "redemption" of Kundry renders her dumb before eliminating her. As Joseph Chytry has pointed out, Wagner's planned Buddhist drama *Die Sieger* would have confirmed the compatibility of *Agapē* and *Eros*, but it remained unrealized (308–11; see STAGE WORKS, INCOMPLETE). A number of modern opera directors have departed from Wagner's stage directions for the conclusion, keeping Kundry alive as mentioned above. Wagner himself weighed the possibility of having the dead Titurel stir in his coffin when Parsifal takes over as leader and reveals the Grail in the closing moments. Some commentators have regarded Kundry as a Jewish figure, but she is not so identified by Wagner, despite the relevance of the motif of the wandering Jew. Kundry is based on multiple characters in Wolfram von Eschenbach's *Parzival*, and, as noted above, she also parallels in certain respects Ada in Wagner's first completed opera *Die Feen*, a figure based in turn on Cherestanì in Wagner's model, the play *La donna serpente* by the eighteenth-century Venetian playwright Carlo Gozzi (see Syer).

It is above all the music of *Parsifal* that represents a summation of Wagner's achievement in its exquisite textures and orchestration, richness of allusion, and the gigantic simplicity of its large-scale formal relations, and as an unconsummated symbol for those aspects of the drama that transcend action and concepts to embrace the ineffable and the numinous.

WILLIAM KINDERMAN

Joseph Chytry, *The Aesthetic State: A Quest in Modern German Thought* (Berkeley: University of California Press, 1989): esp. 308–11.
William Kinderman, *Wagner's "Parsifal"* (New York: Oxford University Press, 2013).
William Kinderman and Katherine Syer, eds., *A Companion to Wagner's "Parsifal"* (see bibliography).
Alfred Lorenz, *Der musikalische Aufbau von Richard Wagners "Parsifal"* (Berlin: Max Hesse, 1933).
Arthur W. Marget, "Liszt and *Parsifal*," *Music Review* 14 (1953): 107–24.
Jean-Jacques Nattiez, *Wagner Androgyne: A Study in Interpretation* (see bibliography).
Alfred Rosenberg, *Selected Writings*, ed. with intro. by Robert Pois (London: Jonathan Cape, 1970).
Katherine Syer, "'*It left me no peace*': From Carlo Gozzi's *La donna serpente* to Wagner's *Parsifal*," *The Musical Quarterly* 94 (2011): 325–80.

Parsifal (tenor; title character in PARSIFAL). Wagner's treatment of the title character of his final drama reflects his fascination with names and naming, a preoccupation he shared with the author of his main mythic source, WOLFRAM VON ESCHENBACH. Wolfram employs a total of over six hundred names in his *PARZIVAL* and *Titurel*. Wagner deliberated intensely over the name of his hero. Up to the second prose draft (early 1877), he retained the name "Parzival"; the change to "Parsifal" was made while he was at work on the poem. His alteration was based on the notion that "Fal parsi" meant "foolish pure one" in an Arabic dialect. In the introduction to his 1813 edition *Lohengrin, ein altdeutsches Gedicht*, Joseph Görres had written that "We don't know whether it's an accidental circumstance that the name of the hero Parcifal can be derived in a completely unforced way from Arabic: Parsi or Parseh Fal, in other words, the pure or poor dumb one, or 'thumbe' in the language of the poem, in which character he is excellently maintained throughout the narrative" (vi). Although not correct, this etymological idea found its way into a memorable passage in Act II of *Parsifal*. Even when the inaccuracy of this etymological speculation was pointed out to Wagner by Judith GAUTIER, the composer insisted on retaining the idea, since he had incorporated this derivation into a key moment of the drama. At the beginning of the seduction scene in Act II, KUNDRY dwells upon her earlier electrifying call of "Par-si-fal," the first time his name is heard in the work. Through the conceit of the inverted form of the name "Fal parsi" with its invented derivation, Wagner coordinates the emphasis on "Par-si-fal" with a characteristic three-note triadic musical motive, the same motivic element that in the Prophecy theme had been set to the words "reine[r] Tor," or "pure fool." Example 14 shows the motive as it appears in the uppermost voice when sung by four squires, immediately preceding Parsifal's initial appearance in Act I, and Example 15 reproduces the threefold treatment of the motive after Kundry's entrance in Act II. Her elaborate ritual of naming Parsifal thus confirms his role in the unfolding prophecy of the Grail.

"rei - ne   Thor"

14. "reine(r) Tor" (pure fool)

KUNDRY: "Par   -   si - fal!"

PARSIFAL: "Par   -   si - fal?"

KUNDRY: "Par - si - fal!"

15. "Par-si-fal"

Parsifal first appears in the drama in an inverted role to that of the swan-knight LOHENGRIN (Parzival's son in the mythic sources): he commits a "murder" of the swan, which – since he finds himself in the Grail realm, where such animals are considered sacred – is shocking. When GURNEMANZ points out his misdeed, Parsifal displays his capacity for compassion, discarding his bow and arrow. Sensing Parsifal's spiritual potential, Gurnemanz leads him to the ceremony in the Grail Temple, where Parsifal witnesses the terrible agonies of the wounded Grail King AMFORTAS. When Parsifal observes these events yet remains outwardly passive, Gurnemanz loses patience, declares him to be "nothing but a fool," and sends him angrily on his way.

The drama as a whole can be understood as a special type of *Bildungsroman*, with the education of the hero prolonged over the course of the action. Parsifal's path parallels that of Amfortas, but leads to a different outcome. He is tested above all by his encounter in Act II with Kundry, who is cursed to serve the evil magician KLINGSOR. Parsifal's routing of Klingsor's knights and his encounter with the flirtatious Flower Maidens lead – just as the sorcerer has planned – to Kundry's crucial double role of mother substitute and lover, delivering a "final mother's blessing" in the form of a "first kiss of love." As a major threshold event in Parsifal's character development, Kundry's poisoned kiss occupies a central dramatic position. Her seduction attempt is the most formidable of all Parsifal's psychological challenges on his path toward the role of redeemer: its success would doom him. Yet Kundry's kiss also unlocks Parsifal's awareness of his prophesied role. A normal human being should be unable to resist her, to see beyond the sensuous entanglement of Klingsor's magic realm. Parsifal's compassion for Amfortas enables him to resist Kundry, whereby the sphinx riddle of Kundry's seduction is answered by Schopenhauerian renunciation, ultimately setting her free from Klingsor. A key moment is his recall of the original summons from the Grail: "Redeem me! Rescue me from hands defiled by guilt!," words Parsifal declaims to the poignant chromatic inflection lodged in the opening Communion theme. His response to Kundry represents an altered replay of her earlier successful seduction of Amfortas, when Klingsor had seized the Holy Spear and dealt him the dolorous blow that will not heal. Parsifal's quest in Wagner's drama involves retrieval of this spear. Since the seduction has failed, the weapon cannot harm him and remains suspended over his head when hurled by Klingsor at the end of Act II.

Parsifal's return path with the spear is long blocked by Kundry's spiteful curse; his "pathless wandering" in search of the Grail is conveyed musically through the Prelude to Act III, a highly chromatic passage linked to his later narrative. In this music, the gradual emergence of the rhythmically energized Prophecy motive signals the approach of Parsifal, whose heroism in this phase is a triumph of endurance, of not succumbing to shadows of uncertainty and illusion. Gurnemanz's discovery of Kundry on Good Friday signals the breaking of Klingsor's sway over her, thereby granting Parsifal access at last to his goal. When he shows the Holy Spear to Gurnemanz, the Communion or "Last Supper" theme from the outset of the entire work for the first time sheds its dissonant harmonic turn to the dark minor mode; this new resolved form of the theme is set to the choral text "Redemption to the Redeemer" in the last moments of the entire work. The integrative closing passages are initiated by an emphatic D major transformation of the motive first heard at Parsifal's entrance in Act I. Unlike Amfortas, who had recklessly carried the Holy Spear into combat against Klingsor, Parsifal has avoided using it aggressively. In this final scene, he employs the spear instead as a healing instrument to cure Amfortas's wound while he assumes the role of Grail King. Apart from illustrating the prophesied correct path through his capacity for compassion and avoidance of aggression, Parsifal's deed consists in a restoration of the threatened Grail involving a symbolic integration of male and female principles, as is reflected through the reunification of spear and Grail.

WILLIAM KINDERMAN

Joseph von Görres, ed., *Lohengrin, ein altdeutsches Gedicht, nach der Abschrift des Vaticanischen Manuscripts von Ferdinand Gloekle* (Heidelberg: Mohr & Zimmer, 1813).
William Kinderman, *Wagner's "Parsifal"* (New York: Oxford University Press, 2013).

Parzival. The acknowledged masterpiece of the medieval German poet WOLFRAM VON ESCHENBACH. Internal evidence in the text suggests that the romance was probably begun around 1200 and not completed until midway through the second decade of the thirteenth century. *Parzival* is often listed alongside Dante's *Divine Comedy* as among the most important works of the high MIDDLE AGES. Wolfram takes as his source Chrétien de Troyes's *Perceval* and then proceeds, in a manner atypical for medieval authorship, to create new material and to take freedoms with his source text. In Wolfram's hands, the narrative becomes the first *Bildungsroman* (novel of inner development) in German literature. The protagonist, Parzival, has a twofold lineage: his father is of the secular, Arthurian world, whereas his mother is of the spiritual, Grail world. Parzival's task over the course of the romance is to unite these two worlds, to become whole by reconciling two antagonistic forces which literally threaten to tear him apart.

Since the prologue informs us that Parzival will be slow on his journey toward wisdom, he is made to wander in search of advice and instruction. Those who offer advice are firmly grounded in the Grail or the Arthurian realm. Therefore, whenever he attempts to follow the advice from the one realm, it has disastrous results when he arrives in the other. His mother (Grail), for example, sends young Parzival out into the world and advises him to win a woman's ring and greeting, and to kiss as well as embrace her. When he meets Lady Jeschute (Arthurian), he forces himself upon her, kisses her, and steals her ring, thereby bringing shame on himself and on Lady Jeschute. Moreover, following thorough training in the ways of the chivalric world from Gurnemanz (Arthurian), Parzival arrives at the Grail castle and, following Gurnemanz's advice, fails to ask the critical question which would finally release his uncle Anfortas from the torment of an eternally festering wound. Finally, Parzival engages his half-brother Feirefiz in single combat and, when Feirefiz's identity is revealed, realizes that he has been fighting his own blood lineage his whole life and that wisdom can only come from within. At this point, he is called back to the Grail and is able to ask the question which releases his uncle Anfortas from his suffering and makes Parzival the king of the Grail.

At the end, the narrator takes us back to the prologue and the introduction of his protagonist as a man graced by both white and black, the color of heaven and the color of hell. The narrator concludes that it is possible to live a life which gains the favor of the world, and experiences the faults of being human, and still does not rob God of the soul. Parzival has finally embraced the double heritage introduced in the prologue by staying true to his secular lineage while recognizing the priority of the spiritual realm.

RAY M. WAKEFIELD

Arthur Groos, *Romancing the Grail* (Ithaca, NY: Cornell University Press, 1995).
Wolfram von Eschenbach, *Parzival*, trans. Helen M. Mustard and Charles E. Passage (New York: Vintage, 1961).

Pasdeloup, Jules Étienne (b. Paris, 15 Sep. 1819; d. Fontainebleau, 13 Aug. 1887), French conductor, concert organizer, and composer. In 1852, he founded the Société des jeunes artistes, later renamed the Société des jeunes artistes du Conservatoire (1856). On 27 October 1861, he conducted the first of his Sunday Concerts populaires de musique classique at the Cirque Napoléon in Paris, which had 5,000 seats. These concerts, later known as Concerts Pasdeloup, represent a revolution in the French orchestral concert tradition, since they rendered classical music accessible and affordable to large numbers of listeners. They became the most important concert series in France during the Second Empire and shaped audiences' musical knowledge and taste until 1870 by introducing composers such as BERLIOZ, Wagner, and contemporary French composers. After the FRANCO-PRUSSIAN WAR OF 1870–1, Pasdeloup was increasingly under pressure from two main competitors. The technical superiority of the Concert national (from 1873) by Édouard Colonne, and the Société des nouveaux concerts (from 1881) by Charles Lamoureux made his enterprise go bankrupt in 1884.

Pasdeloup pioneered the performance of Wagner's music in France. Having played the first Wagner piece with the Société des jeunes artistes du Conservatoire in 1861, he increasingly included Wagner in his concert programs throughout the 1860s, which acquainted the Paris audience with Wagner's music after the TANNHÄUSER SCANDAL in 1861. In 1869, Pasdeloup staged a widely acclaimed production of RIENZI at the Théâtre-Lyrique, which received thirty-eight performances in 1869 and 1870. His plans to play all of Wagner's works (the next two projects with fixed dates were LOHENGRIN and Die MEISTERSINGER VON NÜRNBERG) failed due to the theater's bankruptcy. After the war of 1870–1, when Wagner's standing in France reached a new low, Pasdeloup once again started to conduct Wagner's music in 1873. He conducted the first performance of the SIEGFRIED funeral march (GÖTTERDÄMMERUNG) in France (29 October 1876). Since it was only five years after the war, Pasdeloup was accused of being an anti-patriotic pro-Wagnerian traitor, some even suggesting that he was a German agent named "pas de loup" (a translation of the German: "Wolfgang"), a foolishness which Saint-Saëns repeated as late as October 1916. Together with the Concerts Colonne and the Concerts Lamoureux, which both excelled in Wagner, these were the "golden years" of the French orchestral tradition, with three major Wagner orchestras on offer each Sunday for the Parisian general public.

Pasdeloup was in personal contact with Wagner, attended the *Meistersinger* premiere in MUNICH in 1868, visited Wagner in TRIBSCHEN on 15 March 1869 to prepare his *Rienzi* production, and gave him the manuscript of his "Polonia" overture, deemed lost. In 1879, Wagner sent him a signed portrait.

HERMANN GRAMPP

"Richard Wagner et les parisiens," supplement of *L'Éclipse* 19 (1876).

Patronatverein. See PATRONS' ASSOCIATION

Patron certificate (*Patronatschein*). Idea proposed in 1871 as a means to raise the estimated 300,000 thalers (about 9 million euros in 2012) needed to build the Bayreuth FESTIVAL THEATER. One thousand patron certificates each costing 300 thalers would be issued by a PATRONS' ASSOCIATION. The owner of each *Patronatschein* would be guaranteed a seat for all three of the *Ring* cycles planned for the first festival. Should three individuals share the cost of a single certificate, each of them would be able to attend one complete cycle. Wagner was delighted with the plan that would allow him to "collect contributions for the realization of a national idea" (*Beiträge sammeln zur Verwirklichung einer nationalen Idee*, SSD 16:119), charting a middle course between older and newer forms of funding: a conglomerate of small-scale patrons instead of a single benefactor or the mercantilism of selling tickets at a box office. Concerned that people would be unable to afford even the 100 talers for a one-third share in a certificate, Emil HECKEL devised the idea of WAGNER SOCIETIES, which would make group purchases of certificates using funds collected from much more modest annual dues.

NICHOLAS VAZSONYI

Patrons' Association. In 1871, shortly before his untimely death, the German-Jewish pianist and Wagner devotee Carl TAUSIG, together with COSIMA's friend and wealthy socialite Marie von SCHLEINITZ, came up with an idea to create a *Patronatverein* (Patrons' Association) whose members would purchase a total of 1,000 PATRON CERTIFICATES for 300 thalers each, to raise the estimated 300,000 thalers needed to build the Bayreuth Festival theater. The owner of each *Patronatschein* would be guaranteed a seat for all three of the *Ring* cycles planned for the first festival. Should three individuals share the cost of a single certificate, each of them could attend one complete cycle.

Two circulars, dated 12 and 18 May 1871, quickly followed. In the first, Wagner optimistically announced the forthcoming festival for the summer of 1873, proclaimed Bayreuth as the location, and declared the formation of a "Society of Friends" (*Verein von Freunden*) called the "Patrons of the Stage Festival in Bayreuth" (*Patronen des Bühnenfestspieles in Bayreuth*) (SSD 16:131). The second flyer explains the financial details for the "Patron certificate" scheme (*Aufforderung zur Erwerbung von Patronatsscheinen*, SSD 16:132).

Public reaction was mixed, and many thought the Patrons' Association was offering stock shares for profit. Wagner was not entirely blameless in provoking comparisons with business ventures. Only about 340 certificates were sold, many of them to the WAGNER SOCIETIES formed to enable those who could not afford the 100 thalers for a one-third share the chance to participate in the Bayreuth venture.

The fiscal failure of the first festival in 1876 prompted a lengthy appeal on 1 January 1877 in which Wagner suggested a two-pronged approach to maintaining the Bayreuth idea in the long term. Part of the necessary funds would be raised through a newly formed "Patrons' Association." Wagner, widely ridiculed in the press for seeking state support, conceived of a public-private sponsorship that was yet again ahead of its time.

At the meeting of delegates on 2 April 1877 in Leipzig, the "General Patrons Association for the Maintenance and Preservation of the Stage Festivals in Bayreuth" (*Allgemeiner Patronat-Verein zur Pflege und Erhaltung der Bühnenfestspiele zu Bayreuth*) was formed, and assumed some significant goals, outlined in its charter: to maintain and preserve permanently the Bayreuth Festival according to Wagner's intentions, to secure the funding for the annual recurrence of the Bayreuth Festival, and to spread better understanding of Wagner's artwork in general, and specifically the *Nibelung* tetralogy.

The statutes of the new centralized society combined the original focus on funding with the educational and propagandist mission of the Wagner societies. Wagner gave a speech on this occasion, saying: "I always thought that the Wagner Society would be charged with promoting my direction. I consider this to be its most important function" (SSD 12:324–32).

One month after Wagner's death in February 1883, the Wagner Society in Munich released a circular "To the representatives of the Former Bayreuth Patron's Association" with the idea of restructuring the former *Patronatverein* and consolidating the Richard Wagner Societies into one General Richard Wagner Society (Allgemeiner Richard-Wagner-Verein).

In 1921, after the bankruptcy following World War I, SIEGFRIED WAGNER founded the Deutsche Festspiel-Stiftung, which sold more than 3,000 patron certificates, in an effort to revive the Festival.

In September 1949, again with a view to reviving the festival, the GESELLSCHAFT DER FREUNDE VON BAYREUTH, which functions as a latter-day Patrons' Society, was founded. It contributed a considerable amount for the reopening of the festival in 1951. Today, it continues to play a major role in the existence of the Festival.   NICHOLAS VAZSONYI

Hans von Wolzogen, *Grundlage und Aufgabe des Allgemeinen Patronatvereins zur Pflege und Erhaltung der Bühnenfestspiele zu Bayreuth* (Chemnitz: Schmeitzner, 1877).

Pecht, (August) Friedrich (b. Constance, 2 Oct. 1814; d. Munich, 24 April 1903), painter and art critic. He was part of Wagner's inner circle in both PARIS and DRESDEN. Pecht eventually relocated to MUNICH where he continued to paint, including a portrait of Wagner. He also published widely on the subject of art in newspapers and national journals such as *Die Gartenlaube*.
          MARGARET ELEANOR MENNINGER

Performance, conductors
1. Wagner and his assistants
2. After Wagner
3. Wilhelm Furtwängler, Hans Knappertsbusch, and Karl Böhm.
4. Two case studies: Otto Klemperer and Reginald Goodall
5. Solti, Karajan, and the advent of the studio recording

6. The future

7. Conclusion

1. Wagner and his assistants

The history of conducting Wagner's ten canonical operas spans over a century and a half of evolving PERFORMANCE PRACTICE and tradition. The premieres of *Der FLIEGENDE HOLLÄNDER* and *TANNHÄUSER* were conducted by Wagner himself in his capacity of Court Kapellmeister to the Royal Theater in DRESDEN. *TRISTAN* and *Die MEISTERSINGER VON NÜRNBERG* were first given in MUNICH and conducted not by the composer but by Hans von BÜLOW, who had prepared the singers and orchestra under Wagner's personal supervision. The premiere of *Die Meistersinger* in particular won the composer's unqualified approval: "the evening of the first performance of the *Mastersingers* was the high point of my career as man and artist. Just as it will be found, in time, that this work of mine is the most perfect of all that I have written so far, so must I declare that this performance of it ... was the best that has been given of my works" (letter to LUDWIG II, 14 October 1868). In the following year (1869) Wagner published his widely admired treatise *Über das Dirigiren* (On Conducting) in the course of which he carefully describes the way in which the Prelude to *Die Meistersinger* should be played. He stresses the importance of *MELOS* as "the sole guide to the right tempo" (SSD 8:274; Wagner/Dannreuther 19). Wagner's concept of *melos* incorporates all musical and dramatic aspects of a work rather than just melody in its narrower sense and is crucial to understanding his theory of conducting. In a later response to Wagner's essay, the conductor Felix WEINGARTNER wrote that "Wagner says very truly that just as the right comprehension of the melos of a piece of music suggests the right tempo for it, so the right way of conducting an opera presupposes the true comprehension of the dramatic situation on the part of the conductor" (Weingartner 44). It was for this reason that Wagner was dissatisfied with Hans RICHTER's conducting of the first *RING* cycles in Bayreuth in 1876. Reporting to LUDWIG II in February 1879, he described his "horror at realizing that my conductor – in spite of the fact that I consider him the best I know – was not able to maintain the correct tempo, however often he got it right, – because he was incapable of *knowing why* the music had to be interpreted in one way and not the other" (letter to Ludwig II, 9 February 1879). Wagner was more satisfied with Hermann LEVI's conducting of *PARSIFAL* (1882), describing the Flower Maidens' scene as "utterly unsurpassable, and probably the most masterly piece of direction in terms of music and staging that has ever come my way ... Thanks to the zeal of our admirable conductor, Levi, whose enthusiasm I cannot praise highly enough, this was a total success" (letter to Ludwig II, 8 September 1882). Bülow, Richter, and Levi are seminal figures in the history of conducting. Through their direct association with Wagner and in response to the interpretative demands of his later operas, the act of performance became separated from the act of creation and led through the work of such as Artur Nikisch directly to the establishment of the conductor as autonomous artist with a degree of artistic authority independent of the composer.

2. After Wagner

In the years following Wagner's death, COSIMA sought to reify Wagner performance practice by gathering around her in Bayreuth a group of conductors she regarded as faithful to the Bayreuth ideal. In addition to Richter and Levi, Felix MOTTL became the third member of the triumvirate who worked closely with her during her directorship of the Festival. Outside the immediate orbit of Bayreuth, MAHLER was making a strong impact in VIENNA in conjunction with the scenic designer Alfred ROLLER, whilst Anton SEIDL was carrying the Wagner torch in the UNITED STATES OF AMERICA. It is not possible to know how early Wagner performance sounded under the direction of these conductors; all we can do is construct assumptions on surviving documentary evidence.

With the advent of Richard STRAUSS and Karl MUCK, we encounter the first important executants that have bequeathed significant recorded evidence of earlier Wagnerian performance practice. Strauss was a highly influential conductor who learned his craft as assistant to Bülow in Meiningen. His recorded legacy of Wagner is not large, but his performance of the Prelude to *TRISTAN UND ISOLDE* (1928) is a significant primary source. Strauss takes an underlying tempo of two dotted quarter-note beats in a bar rather than the more usual six eighth notes, and there are noticeable instances of the type of tempo modification which exceed the normal *tempo rubato* and are known to have been practiced in the symphonic repertoire by Bülow (see Weingartner 17). Any claim that Strauss's reading may represent Bülow's (and by extension Wagner's) performance of the *Tristan* Prelude must be treated with healthy skepticism; there are simply too many assumptions and imponderables in the way. Nevertheless, this recording by Strauss is of the first importance to the student of early Wagnerian performance practice.

The same is true of the early electrical recordings made in Bayreuth and Berlin by Karl ELMENDORFF and Karl Muck. Elmendorff conducted regularly at Bayreuth from 1927, where he made his debut with *Tristan und Isolde*, until 1942. His recorded legacy is substantial: there exist almost complete readings of *Tristan* (1927) and *Tannhäuser* (1930), and a complete *GÖTTERDÄMMERUNG* (1942), which are notable for dramatic urgency and attention to musical detail. Karl Muck is a major figure in the history of Wagner conducting who was fortunately active into the era of electrical recording. Born in 1859, his formative musical experiences coincided with the high point of the Wagner/Bülow tradition, yet he was with Weingartner and later TOSCANINI one of the early protagonists of the objective style in which the letter of the score is the ultimate authority. Muck's recorded legacy is of unique importance amongst these early primary sources. It consists of a collection of OVERTURES and preludes, "Siegfried's Rhine Journey" and the "Funeral March" from *Götterdämmerung*, the *SIEGFRIED IDYLL*, extracts from Act I of *Parsifal* captured in the Bayreuth Festspielhaus in 1927, and an almost complete Act III recorded a year later in Berlin. These performances present a paradox. On the one hand, Muck's readings of the overtures and preludes have an urgency and vibrancy which energizes the music through taut rhythmic control and a brisk tempo. The overture to *Der fliegende Holländer* conjures up a ferocious tempest whilst the

Meistersinger Prelude in particular is lean textured and characterized by a subtlety of tempo inflection rather than tempo modification which is closely compliant with Wagner's instructions for the performance of this piece in *Über das Dirigiren* (On Conducting, 1869). In striking contrast is his reading of the *Parsifal* Prelude, which is notable for its slow tempo. It may be that Muck's long association with this work at Bayreuth under Cosima and then SIEGFRIED WAGNER encouraged a monumental, almost reverential approach compliant with its iconic status. The Act I Transformation Music has extraordinary cumulative power; the almost complete Act III (recorded a year later in Berlin) is notable for Muck's control of expressive line and close attention to details of balance and texture. The American critic Herbert Peyser described Muck's *Parsifal* as "the only and ultimate *Parsifal*; the *Parsifal* in which every phrase is charged with infinities; the *Parsifal* which was neither of this age nor of that age but of all time" (quoted in Schonberg 221).

3. Wilhelm Furtwängler, Hans Knappertsbusch, and Karl Böhm

To the generation after Strauss and Muck belong some of the most significant names in the history of Wagner conducting: FURTWÄNGLER, KNAPPERTSBUSCH, and BÖHM occupy a central position in the troubled middle years of the twentieth century which, as is well known, saw both Wagner's work and the act of its performance politicized by an extremist ideology. Furtwängler's surviving recorded performances transcend the limitations of the medium in intensity of expression. Amongst the most significant are extracts from *LOHENGRIN* (Bayreuth, 1936) and the *RING* (London, 1937), which include a complete *WALKÜRE* Act III timed at under an hour. Furtwängler is often considered to be the last exponent of the nineteenth-century Romantic style: his two extant *Ring* cycles (La Scala Milan, 1950 and Rome, 1953) captured in live performance or from radio broadcasts provide compelling evidence of his flexible approach to tempo although, as with Muck, it is a question of tempo inflection rather than modification in the manner of Richard Strauss's reading of the *Tristan* Prelude. Furtwängler's lasting legacy is undoubtedly his complete studio recording of *Tristan und Isolde* (1952) with Kirsten FLAGSTAD and the Philharmonia Orchestra of LONDON, a justly famous reading which stands today as something of a watershed in the history of Wagnerian performance in spite of strong competition from later rivals.

Hans Knappertsbusch's reputation rests largely on his work in WIELAND WAGNER's "New Bayreuth" from its inception in 1951 until his last appearances there in 1964. Knappertsbusch had been an assistant to Hans Richter and thus could claim a direct connection to a royal tradition of Wagner conducting; yet it is difficult to see any justification in earlier performance practice for his broad tempi in the *Ring*. To think of Knappertsbusch entirely as a proponent of slow tempi, however, is misleading: his recording of *Tristan* captured at a live performance in Munich in 1950 has an urgency not usually associated with his more measured approach. Knappertsbusch is principally remembered today as a distinguished exponent of *Parsifal*, a work he made his own during his time at Bayreuth and to which he brought deep expressive insight born of long experience in the theater.

Karl Böhm was steeped in the performing traditions of Karl Muck; his *Ring* performances captured live at Bayreuth in 1966–7 and his *Tristan* performance with Birgit NILSSON and Wolfgang WINDGASSEN have the same fleetness of tempi and close attention to matters of texture and timbre evident in Muck's recordings of the overtures and preludes. Böhm was a leading Mozartian: his sprightly rhythms and transparency of texture provided Wieland Wagner with a sought-after change from the saturated orchestral sound of Knappertsbusch.

4. Two case studies: Otto Klemperer and Reginald Goodall

Two important figures of this generation somewhat outside the mainstream of Wagner conducting are Otto Klemperer (1885–1973) and Reginald GOODALL. Klemperer's conducting of the Berlin KROLL OPER's production of *Der flie-gende Holländer* (1929) represented in its use of the 1843 Dresden performing version an early attempt to rediscover some of the raw dramatic power of Wagner's early work through the application of historically informed perform-ance practice. Klemperer's conducting was roundly attacked in the press: "Tempi were ridiculously overdriven, finer dynamic shadings eliminated and all expression reduced to a minimum" (quoted in Millington and Spencer 13). An important recording of *Der fliegende Holländer* (1968) gives a vivid idea of the intensity of Klemperer's visceral approach to the score and some clue as to how it might have sounded to the shocked audiences of Weimar Berlin. Klemperer also made a significant recording of the SIEGFRIED IDYLL using the original chamber instrumentation specified by Wagner. Later in his career, Klemperer's indifferent health prevented him from conducting full-length Wagner productions in the theater.

Between 1968 and 1986, Reginald Goodall presided over performances of Wagner's last seven operas in London and Cardiff which were widely acclaimed for their expressive power and dramatic impact. Goodall's *Ring* (sung in English) owed much to Knappertsbusch in its broad tempi and grandeur of approach; yet through patient coaching and detailed rehearsal with singers and orchestra, "Reggie" achieved a degree of ensemble not always apparent in Knappertsbusch's extant recordings. His *Meistersinger* was spacious and lyrical, in striking contrast to his reading of *Tristan*, which is more akin to the incandescence of Furtwängler. It is only in his reading of *Parsifal* that his predilection for slow tempi can result in a loss of momentum detrimental to overall musical cohesion.

5. Solti, Karajan, and the advent of the studio recording

Thus far, all the recorded evidence considered, with the exception of Furtwängler's *Tristan*, is associated with the act of live performance in the theater. The work of conductors was captured through either live perform-ances (usually through the medium of the radio broadcast) or recordings made as adjuncts to the act of live performance, as with Muck's *Parsifal*. Furtwängler's *Tristan* stands alone for it represented two artists (Furtwängler and Flagstad) coming together at the end of long association with the work to set down for posterity an artistic legacy through the medium of studio recording. There was no sense in which this was conceived as a performance for the gramophone as an autonomous medium. In marked contrast, the studio recording of the complete *Ring* by the Decca Company in full stereophonic sound conducted by George SOLTI represents a sea change in the history of conducting Wagner. These performances were made *for* the gramophone rather than captured *by* the gramophone and effectively brought Wagner out of the theater and into the public domain. The effect on Wagner conducting was far reaching. This essay is not the place to consider the wider implications of this except to say that Georg Solti's dynamic conducting for the microphone rather than the theater was a major factor in the success of these recordings in the global marketplace. It is no exaggeration to say that the Decca *Ring* marked a paradigm shift in the way Wagner is heard. Herbert von Karajan's cycle dating from the 1960s was made in conjunction with performances at the Salzburg Festival and is thus representative of the older tradition. Pierre Boulez's musical direction of *Parsifal* and subsequently the centenary *Ring* in Bayreuth was in marked contrast to the weighty approach of Knappertsbusch and initially met with a mixed reception. Other conductors active in Bayreuth and the major opera houses of the world who have made significant contributions to Wagner interpretation and whose performances have been recorded for posterity include Bernard Haitink, James LEVINE, Daniel BARENBOIM, and Antonio Pappano.

6. The future

What are the issues arising from this brief survey of the history of Wagner conducting? David Breckbill deftly identifies the fundamental problem: "For no composer of the nineteenth century is the concept of 'authentic' performance practice more problematical than it is in the case of Wagner" (350). The "sound" of the Wagner orchestra heard in the opera house today and on post-1950 recordings of the stereo and digital era is entirely different to anything Wagner himself would have recognized or imagined. Wagner's strings would have been strung with gut, the sound of the wind and brass certainly less in volume, and the all-important timpani less powerful and more incisive. In a telling memoir of the making of Karl Muck's *Parsifal* recordings in Bayreuth in 1927 with the orchestra on the stage, the sound engineer W. S. Barrell describes how the engineers captured the sound.

> It is interesting to compare the recording technique of those early days with that of today [1959]. We used only one microphone and had no tone controls of any kind. Alterations in balance, etc., could be made only by changing the orchestral seating or the positioning of a single microphone. Today, a battery of microphones with individual treble and bass controls are on tap: one often feels that much of the art of recording has been replaced by the "knob" and screwdriver.
>
> (BARRELL 390)

Herein lies the immense importance of the early electrical recordings of, *inter alia*, Strauss, Elmendorff, and Muck. Even taking into account (or perhaps thanks to) the limitations of 1920s technology, the lean textured sound of the orchestra is far closer to the world of Wagner's imagination than the products of the stereo age when the aesthetic of performance is so often driven by commercial considerations. Thus one of the challenges facing Wagner conductors of the future is to make use of the evidence of past practice of a period far closer to Wagner's world than our own and cast new light on Wagner's scores rather than adding to the already saturated catalogue of recordings. Roger Norrington and Simon Rattle have begun to address this issue by making a cautious beginning in exploring the possibilities of period-instrument Wagner; Christian Thieleman's live recording of the *Ring* from Bayreuth in 2008 incorporates elements of historically informed performance practice.

7. Conclusion

This necessarily selective survey of representative figures in Wagner conducting challenges a number of received opinions accumulated over nearly a century and a half since the composer's death. First, there is no royal road stretching back to the composer himself, in spite of Cosima Wagner's attempt to create such a tradition. Second, the myth of the long Wagnerian line supposedly espoused by conductors such as Knappertsbusch has no foundation in Wagnerian theory but is in essence an uneasy mismatch between *melos* and the Schenkerian idea of *Urline* (Allen 5). What is significant is that almost without exception leading Wagner conductors have also been leading symphonic conductors. That is not to say that Wagner's operas are essentially symphonies with voices: as Wagner himself demonstrates in the essay *ÜBER DIE ANWENDUNG DER MUSIK AUF DAS DRAMA* (On the Application of Music to Drama, 1879), they are operas in which the dynamic of musical form and content is entirely defined by the need for dramatic expression. Thus approaches as diverse as Knappertsbusch and Furtwängler, Boulez and Barenboim, Rattle and Thieleman, to name but a few, can be said to be equally authentic in that through seeking to realize the Wagnerian *melos* in the broadest sense of the term they achieve a degree of expression in accordance with the composer's dramatic intentions.   ROGER ALLEN

See also PERFORMANCE, RECORDING HISTORY

Roger Allen, "Of Bridge-Builders, Arch-Critics and Miniaturists: The Art of Wagner Conducting," *The Wagner Journal* 2.2 (2008): 3–10.

W. S. Barrell, "I Was There," *Gramophone* (January 1959): 390.

David Breckbill, "Performance Practice" and "Wagner in Performance," in *The Wagner Compendium*, ed. Barry Millington (see bibliography): 350–74.

Barry Millington and Stewart Spencer, *Wagner in Performance* (New Haven, CT: Yale University Press, 1992).

Harold C. Schonberg, *The Great Conductors* (London: Victor Gollancz, 1968).

Richard Wagner, *On Conducting*, trans. Edward Dannreuther (London: William Reeves, 1887).

Felix Weingartner, *Weingartner on Music and Conducting*, trans. Ernest Newman (New York: Dover, 1969): 3–56.

David Wooldridge, *Conductor's World* (London: Barrie and Rockliff, The Cresset Press, 1970).

Performance, recording history. *Der RING DES NIBELUNGEN* received its first complete performances at BAYREUTH in 1876. The next year, Charles Cros (in France) imagined and Thomas Edison (in the UNITED STATES OF AMERICA) invented a process that could record, preserve, and reproduce sound. It was originally envisioned as a "talking machine," but within little more than a decade the phonograph's potential for documenting the work of leading musicians began to be recognized, and Johannes BRAHMS, Anton Arensky, Sergei Tanayev, Anna Essipova, and the teenaged Josef Hofmann are among the musical luminaries who had performed for this new technological marvel by the mid-1890s. When the recording industry was subsequently launched around the beginning of the twentieth century, WAGNERISM was a potent cultural phenomenon, and from that day to this Wagner's massive, complex, and enduringly popular works have posed special challenges to the ingenuity and creativity of those who wish to represent their aural dimensions in a satisfying recorded form. In turn recordings have immeasurably enriched – and, for better and for worse, even helped to shape – listeners' perceptions of Wagner's works.

1. The acoustical era, c. 1900–c. 1925
2. The electrical era, c. 1925–c. 1950
3. The LP and CD era, c. 1950 onward
4. The emergence of non-commercial recordings
5. Concluding thoughts

1. The acoustical era, c. 1900–c. 1925

Although the advent of recording opened a new world of experience and documentary potential, two technological limitations distorted perception of Wagner's works in the early era. First, in order to be recorded clearly and vividly, performers needed to be positioned very near a single point (the recording horn) – a reality that favored solo performers, especially vocalists, rather than Wagner's elaborate, seductively scored textures, but one that also caused the process of recording to seem clinical and inhibiting to singers accustomed to live performance settings. Secondly, the outer limit of uninterrupted duration was four or (no more than) five minutes for a 12-inch (30 cm) disk, which was (a few exceptions notwithstanding) the largest size generally used during this period – other standard sizes, with correspondingly shorter time limits, included 7-inch (18 cm), 10-inch (25 cm), 27 cm (Odeon, Fonotipia), and 28 cm (Pathé). This time limit remained intractable despite much experimentation with disk diameter and cylinder size, playback speeds ("78 rpm" was, if ever, a later standard), size of grooves, and density of groove threading throughout this period. Lilli LEHMANN's 1907 Odeon recording of the *LIEBESTOD* (*TRISTAN UND ISOLDE*) fell victim to these limitations: although often included on historical reissues since its first public appearance in 1993, it remained unreleased in its day at least in part because, to accommodate a playing time of nearly 5½ minutes, the grooves spiraled so far into the center of the 12-inch disk as to leave no room for a label.

The earliest vocal recordings featured piano accompaniment, but by about 1905 it became increasingly customary to employ a more vivid "orchestral" background. String instruments did not record well at a distance, however, and so string parts in recording orchestras were often doubled by or rescored for wind instruments – a procedure that misrepresented the sonic character of Wagner's scoring and thus prevented recordings of orchestral excerpts from attaining much credibility despite occasional contributions by famous conductors (Leo Blech, Fritz Busch, Albert Coates, Karl MUCK, Leopold Stokowski, SIEGFRIED WAGNER, Bruno Walter, and Henry Wood are among those who made acoustical Wagner recordings). Since each cylinder or side was regarded as an independent unit, a decisive beginning and ending was expected – so much for ENDLESS MELODY! Further, to later ears, numerous recordings of this era seem intent on pushing the tempo ahead in order to fit as much music onto the recording as possible, thereby falsifying or limiting the expressive inclinations of the performers. Cuts were also frequently employed as a means of fitting an overly long passage on a single side. One can generally expect acoustical recordings of ELISABETH's "Dich, teure Halle" (*TANNHÄUSER*) or SIEGMUND's "Winterstürme" (*Die WALKÜRE*) to contain all the vocal lines in those arias, but WOLFRAM's Song to the Evening Star (*Tannhäuser*) might begin at any of three different points ("Wie Todesahnung" or "Da scheinest du," or "O du, mein holder Abendstern"), and LOHENGRIN's Narration ("In fernem Land") might be presented complete or with any of at least thirteen different abridgements of the vocal part. Many other excerpts as well often incorporated cuts of expedience.

Given the prevailing side-as-unit mindset, there were not many attempts at creating continuity over the course of several sides. Even the Gramophone Company's extensive *PARSIFAL* series (released to coincide with the expiration of the ban on staging the work outside Bayreuth on 1 January 1914 – smaller *Parsifal* series by Odeon, Anker, and Pathé also appeared at that time) and the 1922–3 *Ring* series by HMV (sung in English) consist mostly of passages that are continuous for only a side or two (and often featuring cuts within sides), although the former includes most of the Act I Grail Scene. Two early exceptions are the 1909 Odeon recordings of *Tannhäuser*, Act II (twenty sides) and the Bridal Chamber Scene from *Lohengrin* (nine sides), while the thirty-side HMV *Die MEISTERSINGER VON NÜRNBERG* from 1923–4 (sung in English, and one of the best-sounding acoustical Wagner recordings) includes enough of the score to achieve a greater sense of continuity. A little-known 1913–14 Anker recording of *Die Walküre*, Act I cuts portions of some orchestral passages.

Although the fundamental limitations of sonority and duration cause acoustical recordings to seem primitive to modern listeners, in their day they offered the opportunity to digest important passages of Wagner's music in an unprecedented way, and all the major record companies – Berliner/G&T/ Gramophone/HMV, Victor, Columbia, Pathé, Edison, Odeon, Fonotipia, Parlophon(e), Polyphon, Anker, Favorite – and numerous minor ones made and released significant Wagner recordings, including some with singers Wagner himself had admired or supervised (including Lilli Lehmann, Marianne Brandt, Hermann WINKELMANN, and Julius Lieban). For historians and connoisseurs of operatic singing, these thousands of recordings (which include dozens and even hundreds of versions of important arias) constitute a rich resource for understanding the ways in which singers steeped in local and national styles of singing coped with the vocal and expressive challenges of Wagner's music; the variety of styles (and languages – one can hear Wagner sung in at least ten tongues besides German on acoustical recordings) is especially instructive given the fundamental stylistic homogeneity that predominates in the early twenty-first century.

2. The electrical era, *c.* 1925–*c.* 1950

The advent of the electronic process of recording decisively altered the quality of the recordings offered to the public. No longer were orchestras too unwieldy to record effectively or efficiently, and since much classical music consists of works that cannot be contained on a side or two, the concept of the recording "unit" in classical music began to expand from a single side or disk to a multi-disk album – obviously an important development in the ability of recordings to deal with Wagner's gargantuan works.

The first decade of the electrical era was nevertheless transitional in many respects. It took engineers some time to wean themselves from practices common in the acoustical era, such as doubling a pizzicato in the low strings, or a timpani stroke, with a staccato tuba note. Rushed tempi and cuts to tauten the musical material often persisted. And many of the "performances" released in set form were actually collections of recordings made by different performers at different times, so that orchestra, conductor, or the singer of a certain role could switch from one side to the next. This seemingly haphazard approach to recording was an understandable carry-over from the acoustical concept of recording a side at a time. Eventually, however, recordings of complete acts with consistent orchestras and casts began to appear: the (not quite complete) Karl Muck *Parsifal*, Act III (1928) was a pioneer, followed by Bruno Walter's *Walküre*, Act I (1935, featuring Lotte LEHMANN and Lauritz MELCHIOR), Böhm's *Meistersinger*, Act III (1938), and Rodzinski's *Walküre*, Act III (1945). The cachet of Bayreuth also attracted record companies at this time: Columbia recorded studio-made excerpts from the *Ring* and *Parsifal* at the festival in 1927, and expanded to somewhat abridged recordings of *Tristan* (1928) and *Tannhäuser* (1930), while Telefunken followed with excerpts from *Walküre*, *Siegfried*, and *Lohengrin* (1936). (A few recordings featuring Bayreuth singers performing their festival roles had been made there in 1904 by G&T; because they used piano accompaniment, they were not retained long in the catalog and became instant rarities.)

Despite certain obvious limitations, some recordings in this era continue to be regarded as classics in the annals of Wagnerian recordings. Although there had been outstanding Wagner singers before this time, the best of those active in the 1920s and 1930s were situated chronologically and stylistically at a productive confluence of alternative approaches (see PERFORMANCE, SINGERS), and the work of Ivar Andresen, Rudolf Bockelmann, FLAGSTAD, Alexander Kipnis, Herbert Janssen, LEIDER, Lotte Lehmann, Max LORENZ, Melchior, Maria Müller, Elisabeth Rethberg, Schorr, Franz Völker, and others continues to attract admiration and loyalty. Likewise, the famous conductors of the day (see PERFORMANCE, CONDUCTORS), including WEINGARTNER, Richard STRAUSS, MUCK, FURTWÄNGLER, TOSCANINI, and Stokowski (whose "symphonic syntheses" of Wagner scores represented the last word in recorded opulence), made recordings that begin to show the expressive refinements and sonic effects possible when making recordings under controlled conditions.

3. The LP and CD era, *c.* 1950 onward

Already by the 1940s numerous recordings were being taped rather than cut onto disks, which offered the hope of expanded duration and increased continuity if a new format for disseminating recordings could be found. American Columbia introduced commercial long-playing records in 1948 to mixed reaction – typically, some traditionalists disliked this change, and in Great Britain HMV/Columbia catered to this conservative demographic longer than most other companies. Columbia's release of the 1951 Bayreuth *Meistersinger*, however, definitively proved the older format to be a dinosaur where large-scale Wagner recordings were concerned: in its (British) 78 rpm format this recording appeared on thirty-four fragile double-sided disks, while on American LPs it occupied only five vinyl disks – a vastly more convenient and durable format that soon carried the day.

During the early LP era several kinds of full-length Wagner recordings appeared: studio recordings made originally for radio broadcast but distributed on commercial labels; studio recordings made by a record company with the intention of commercial release; and recordings made by a commercial recording company in association with live stage performance(s), often at Bayreuth. The performance and sonic standards of the radio broadcasts were generally low, and few of these recordings made significant impact even in their day apart from giving Wagner's works full-length representation. The first exemplary studio recording of a complete Wagner opera was the Furtwängler *Tristan* of 1952 (EMI); the conductor reportedly recognized that the contribution of producer Walter Legge (a notorious perfectionist) was as decisive as his own in the success of this recording, which featured a very strong cast headed by the already legendary Kirsten Flagstad, outstanding sound and technical standards, and (controversially) interpolations from another singer of high notes that Flagstad could no longer manage. This was Legge's only attempt at a complete Wagner opera, however; his conviction that vocal standards of the 1950s could not justify a recording of the *Ring* left the field to Decca and its younger producer John CULSHAW. Except for its early studio recording of *Meistersinger* from Vienna, Decca's forays into complete Wagner recording had been made at Bayreuth (*Parsifal* in 1951, *Lohengrin* in 1953, and in 1955 both a FLIEGENDE HOLLÄNDER that was promptly released and a *Ring* that did not appear for half a century), but Culshaw envisioned producing Wagner for the home listener in a way that would realize Wagner's dramatic aims more successfully than the theatrical apparatus of Wagner's day permitted, and the idealistic illusion for which Culshaw strove was not well served by extraneous noise from audience and stage, live performance inaccuracies, and other manifestations of (corpo)reality. His studio recordings of the *Ring* operas (1958–65) and *Tristan und Isolde* (1960), all with SOLTI conducting the Vienna Philharmonic, were captured in vivid stereophonic sound when that technology was new and exciting, and he liberally provided (sometimes spectacular) sound effects either requested or implied by the score.

The remarkable commercial success of Decca's stereo Wagner recordings made other companies eager to cash in on the benefits of having strong Wagner catalogs of their own, and studio recordings proliferated for the next several decades. (The lure of Bayreuth also continued to exert its spell on the record industry: Deutsche Grammophon and Philips in particular recorded frequently at Bayreuth during the 1960s–80s.) Thereafter, however, the expense of making studio recordings became increasingly prohibitive, and thus new recordings of complete Wagner operas released in audio format tended to be taken either from live performances (whether staged or in concert form) or from video productions (again, sometimes taken from live staged performances, but at other times recorded as videos under studio conditions – most commercial Bayreuth videos are of this sort). Ongoing technological advances such as quadraphonic sound, digital stereo, and super audio compact disks (SACD) went hand in hand with both improved playback formats (CD permitted more internal access points and longer uninterrupted spans of time than had LPs) and increasing standards of cosmetic perfection (several decades after the fact, the orchestral intonation of the Solti *Ring* sounded ragged by comparison with that achieved in more recent recordings) to assure that new currents in interpretation and new generations of performers were enshrined in recordings whose outer trappings suggested progress.

4. The emergence of non-commercial recordings

The relatively limited number of complete Wagner recordings available during the first two decades of the LP era permitted all interested listeners to have fixed points of reference for evaluating new recordings. For example, there was no legitimate recorded *Siegfried* until Decca's was released in 1963, and consequently the second to appear (Karajan's for DG, released six years later) was inevitably heard against widespread prior knowledge of that earlier recording. Most Wagner operas were represented by at best a handful of commercially available versions into the 1970s, making it possible for anyone to know, savor, and ponder the relative virtues of the recordings then on the market. Individual sets at the time seemed to have a canonic status, but in the course of the 1970s three new realities emerged to undermine that perception. First, it turned out that no new recordings were likely to pursue in any depth the kind of "production" concept that Culshaw had both practiced and mistakenly seen as the wave of the future; second, the generation of Wagner singers that followed the one in which Birgit NILSSON and Wolfgang WINDGASSEN were pre-eminent seemed to lack performers who could challenge those illustrious predecessors on the level playing field recordings created; and third, it became apparent that there existed a vast body of non-commercial recordings of live performances that would permit listeners to hear performers who either pre-dated or were unjustly underrepresented by the recording industry's relatively limited ability to market complete recordings.

Already in the 1930s the Mapleson cylinders (recorded in 1900–3 during performances at the Metropolitan Opera) started to receive public dissemination, thereby making known the existence and value of unofficial recordings (at least to those patient enough to listen through heavy surface noise for dimly captured singing). In the 1960s a number of "pirate" labels began to release Wagner and other operatic recordings taken from live performances and/or broadcasts (dating from the 1930s on) at leading venues including Covent Garden, La Scala, the Metropolitan Opera, Salzburg, the Vienna State Opera, and others. Such recordings featured singers and conductors whose abilities and performances compared favorably with those who could be heard on current recordings, and in settings that allowed the spontaneity and intensity of live performances to offset imperfections of execution and sound quality that would have been unacceptable in a studio recording.

The documentary and sentimental value of such recordings was also a powerful lure. The definition of "pirate" recordings was murky, because differing copyright laws in different countries meant that some labels could legally release recordings made as recently as just over two decades earlier; consequently, Bayreuth broadcasts from the 1950s (for example) became well known in the 1970s–80s. As all of these unofficial recordings began to circulate, the hegemony of commercially made recordings began to crumble. EMI acquired rights to tapes of Wilhelm Furtwängler's Rome concert performance of the *Ring* from 1953 and issued it as their own in 1972; individual institutions (Bayreuth, Covent Garden, the Met) eventually released noncommercial recordings from their archives on their own labels or in agreements with existing record companies; and all the while companies who had never made any recordings of their own flooded the market with dozens of non-commercial recordings of each Wagner opera. The consumer and the historian undoubtedly reap enormous benefits from having so many recordings readily available along with plentiful reissues of commercial recordings, but this infinite variety means that there is no longer an incontestable canon of important Wagner recordings, and discourse about favorites becomes problematical when those involved in the discussion cannot be expected to have a common point of reference.

5. Concluding thoughts

In 1922, after nearly four decades of experiencing Wagner in the theater, George Bernard SHAW provocatively asserted that his "favorite way of enjoying *The Ring* is to sit at the back of a box, comfortable on two chairs, feet up, and listen without looking ... The truth is, a man whose imagination cannot serve him better than the most costly devices of the imitative scenepainter, should not go to the theatre" (ix). Toward the end of his life, knowing full well that Wagner's works were fundamentally dramatic rather than musical, conductor Wilhelm Furtwängler nevertheless maintained that unstaged concert performances of Wagner's operas were the best way in which to reveal that drama. And although the rise of *Regietheater* has expanded the meaning(s), significance, and relevance of Wagner's works, many Wagnerians (for many reasons) persist in finding that visual representations or realizations (of whatever kind) of Wagner's dramas often limit or contradict (rather than clarify or enhance) the dramatic implications of the aurally perceivable dimensions of his works. This attitude both undergirds and rises from the passions aroused by over a century of Wagner recordings, and despite the impressive popularity of Wagner on video in recent decades, audio recordings seem destined both to flourish and to continue to provide a helpful, even central way of studying and experiencing Wagner's vast, perpetually stimulating works.   DAVID BRECKBILL

See also Appendix 7: Selected sound recordings

Nicholas Cook, Eric Clarke, Daniel Leech-Wilkinson, and John Rink, eds., *The Cambridge Companion to Recorded Music* (Cambridge University Press, 2009).

John Culshaw, *Ring Resounding* (London: Secker & Warburg/New York: Viking, 1967).

Timothy Day, *A Century of Recorded Music: Listening to Musical History* (New Haven, CT: Yale University Press, 2000).

Roland Gelatt, *The Fabulous Phonograph, 1877–1977*, 2nd rev. edn. (New York: Collier, 1977).

George Bernard Shaw, *The Perfect Wagnerite* (see bibliography).

Performance, singers. From the time his important operas were first produced up to the present day, performing any of Wagner's major roles has been regarded as among the most demanding tasks a singer can undertake. The enterprise requires unusual vocal power, stamina, range, and expressivity along with exemplary diction, psychological acuity, and histrionic inventiveness. Throughout the history of Wagner performance, even the most renowned singers have generally fallen short in one or more of these parameters. Given this reality, it would be pointless to insist either that the glory days of Wagner singing occurred during a certain era in the distant past, or that what singers can achieve today is better than anything our forebears encountered. Instead, the history of Wagner singing might more profitably be understood as a story of changing standards, practices, and values that reflect different understandings of the artistic, dramatic, and cultural essence of Wagner's works and, consequently, that successively explore different facets of the challenges Wagner's roles present. This remains so partly because other dimensions of Wagner in performance – including staging and production, conducting and orchestral PERFORMANCE PRACTICE (see also PRODUCTION HISTORY and PERFORMANCE, CONDUCTING), to say nothing of audience expectations – likewise continue to change, thereby requiring different skills or emphases from singers.

1. Realities and challenges
2. Development and early history
3. Recordings and Wagner singing
4. Wagner singers as actors

1. Realities and challenges

In the centuries leading up to Wagner's career, composers of operas often wrote roles geared to the talents of specific singers. Unless one generalizes the influence of Wilhelmine SCHRÖDER-DEVRIENT, however – and as late as during preparations for the first *PARSIFAL* production in 1882, Wagner was imagining how she (who died in 1860) would have uttered specific lines in his new work – Wagner's roles lack such definite models. Consequently, they might be said to be written for idealized singers rather than actual ones, and the process of turning them into flesh and blood has prompted many sorts of provisional and/or ideologically motivated solutions. On one level, the notes of each role represent only a part of a larger theatrical portrayal, and, from Wagner's description of his reaction to Schröder-Devrient on to the performers with whom he worked, he demonstrated a willingness to overlook vocal shortcomings if singers/actors demonstrated understanding of the characters they portrayed. But seen strictly on its own terms, Wagner's vocal writing struck initial observers as paradoxical: most of his roles demand high notes but often dwell extensively in the middle or lower part of the voice, and the declamatory nature of much of the writing requires that the text be comprehensibly projected over a heavily scored orchestra. Consequently many of the leading roles have been sung by singers who possess the vocal weight for the majority of the role but who have also (mostly) managed to sing the requested high notes. Singers who possess a darker tonal coloring have often been favored, but it is also frequently the case that the roles attract singers "from below" – Pogners sometimes switch to HANS SACHS, basses attempt WOTAN, singers who initially trained as baritones become HELDENTENORS, (not-quite) converted mezzo-sopranos have essayed ISOLDE or BRÜNNHILDE, and so on. Since most of Wagner's leading roles employ a full two-octave range or more, it is not surprising that singers of different sorts have attempted them, especially since some are notoriously unclassifiable where vocal type or range is concerned (for example KUNDRY in *Parsifal*, which Herbert von KARAJAN went so far as to cast with two different singers in his 1961 Vienna production). In any case, given the musically seamless nature of Wagner's works, transposition of specific passages (although not unknown) has not been as frequent a choice in Wagner as in number operas, so that re-pitching or deemphasizing notes at the extremes of the range has been the preferred solution for performing passages that call for notes a singer cannot easily command.

The primary method of making life easier for Wagner singers in live performance, however, has been abbreviating the works so as not to overtax vocal stamina. It would be difficult to determine whether the comfort of audiences or singers has been the primary motivation in instituting most abbreviations; surely the two have gone hand in hand, but singers have often been at least "enthusiastically acquiescent" (to use David Hamilton's memorable phrase) in adopting cuts. Now that live performances are generally complete (in order to compete with recordings, where completeness is expected), it is difficult for contemporary audiences to realize the extent to which Wagner's works were abbreviated in earlier times (although generally not at BAYREUTH). Reliable reports suggest that Anton SEIDL's celebrated Metropolitan Opera performances of the 1880s–90s did not exceed four hours (including intermissions), and many Met broadcast recordings of the 1930s–70s contain frequent and/or major excisions. Even now, a ten-minute omission in the early stages of the Act II love duet in *Tristan und Isolde* frequently persists in live performances.

Cutting the operas down to size was an early and ongoing strategy for managing Wagner vocally, but other features of his writing proved less easily solved. Wagner's chromatic harmonies were initially quite perplexing to singers – Lilli LEHMANN (the first Bayreuth Woglinde) believed that the Rhinemaidens' music was filled with errors at the passage beginning "So weise und stark" (*Götterdämmerung*, III/I) until hearing the context, and claimed that both Wagner and LISZT were astonished that she and her fellow Rhinemaidens were able to master such harmonic complexity. A veteran critic hailed Marie Wittich in 1904 as the best Kundry Bayreuth had ever had, in part because she (unlike her nine illustrious predecessors) had finally mastered harmonically challenging leaps at "beim Küssen bang" and "sei hold der Hüldin" (*Parsifal*, II/2). And lest it be thought that difficulties of this kind have disappeared, one must note (among many possible examples) the high percentage of times King Marke's last line ("Der Wahn häufte die Not!," *Tristan*, III/3) goes awry, or that the unaccompanied augmented triad at the end of SIEGFRIED's "Warum aber starb sie da?" (*Siegfried*, II/2) does not arrive on the proposed unison with the clarinet. Perhaps, however, such difficulties with fine points of intonation and harmonic awareness can best be understood as endemic to the kinds of voices Wagner's major roles were from the beginning assumed to require: voices possessing power, size, and projection are not always the most precisely tuned instruments.

2. Development and early history

Wagner's persistent dream of a school (SCHULE FÜR STYL UND TRADITION) that would provide comprehensive instruction for performers of his works never came to pass during his lifetime, and the vocal pedagogues with whom he worked most closely were never linked so publicly with him as to cause their pronouncements on Wagner singing to carry special weight (although much of what Julius Hey taught, with Wagner's input and blessing, emerged in his influential treatise on vocal pedagogy, *Deutscher Gesangs-Unterricht*). As a result, in the era when Wagner's mature works were making their way into widespread circulation, there was no generally approved understanding of the best way to sing his music, and various regional and national styles were left to treat it as they may. Against the background of these many diverse approaches, however, was an overriding bifurcation. It seemed to some that the largely declamatory nature of the vocal writing combined with the heavy ORCHESTRATION constituted a threat to good singing as it had long been understood, which meant that some singers became specialists in Wagner roles while others remained committed to stylistic viability in a wider repertory, and therefore either restricted the amount of Wagner they sang or else employed something close to their customary style in singing Wagner. (Through subsequent generations many singers who were known for stellar Wagner portrayals, such as Anna Mildenburg, Frida LEIDER, Birgit NILSSON, Jon Vickers, and James Morris, resisted being pigeonholed as Wagner specialists, and maintained wide-ranging repertories.)

The primary controversy surrounding Wagner singing during the years just after Wagner's death concerned the nature of diction. To the extent that Wagner expressed himself on this point, clear diction was to serve as a means of combating the vagueness of pronunciation (and dramatic expression) that he observed in traditional operatic performances of his day. But whereas he envisioned a kind of singing in which the notes were all to be declaimed and/ or sung expressively, without being preconceived by the singer as belonging to either recitative or aria, his widow COSIMA determined that emphatic clarity of diction was to be the chief contribution of singing to Wagnerian drama, and made the Bayreuth Festival the setting in which this approach was most extensively practiced. She and her assistant Julius Kniese (1848–1905), the chorus master and chief répétiteur for the solo singers at Bayreuth from 1888 until his death, insisted on explosive consonants and (with certain singers) a hard, dry timbre in singing Wagner.

Established singers often found these methods unproductive or harmful, and consequently many of the singers most associated with Bayreuth – who then became widely known thanks to the Bayreuth imprimatur – had as their chief virtues youth and stylistic malleability rather than exceptional endowment of voice or technical prowess. Not surprisingly, audiences in the great international opera houses of London and New York, which sponsored Wagner performances in German but boasted the best singing the world had to offer, were not pleased by the brittle singing style that stemmed from the Bayreuth orbit. Thus those centers employed versatile singers such as Lilli Lehmann or recruited singers known for their work in other repertories (the signal coup in this regard was persuading Jean de Reszke, the greatest celebrity among tenors in the 1890s, to learn TRISTAN and Siegfried in German) in addition to importing the best German singers they could find (not many of whom found lasting international success). The stylistic range on display in Wagner performances in London and New York was thus sometimes extreme, but allowing these different approaches to coexist and giving the singers who represented them an opportunity to interact paved the way for an ultimately satisfying synthesis several decades into the twentieth century. In the meantime, there were some singers, notably Anton van Rooy and Ernestine Schumann-Heink, who were valued both at Cosima's Bayreuth and in London/ New York; these and several other singers left recordings showing how fine voices and powerful artistic personalities could transform Bayreuth diction into a style that became vividly expressive, sometimes in a remarkably detailed way, while remaining technically sound and sophisticated.

The period between the two world wars is sometimes regarded as a Golden Age for Wagner singing; during these decades a vital, productive synthesis of the Bayreuth and BEL CANTO approaches emerged, in conjunction with the arrival of numerous remarkably endowed and skilled vocalists. Tempi were generally faster and more fluid during this period than they have since become, and although this pace required singers to navigate quick notes alertly, it also permitted them to make Wagner's vocal writing sound like eloquent, elevated speech. The leading exponents had the technical command necessary to portray contrasting emotions with remarkable point and specificity, and possessed vocal resources that enabled them to rise to extroverted moments with seemingly boundless energy. This threefold dispensation of voice, vocal technique, and a vibrant and extensive (if stylized) range of expression characterizes the work of dozens of singers in this period to one extent or another. Some of the most notable included Frida Leider, bright of tone and incandescent of temperament as Isolde and Brünnhilde; Lotte LEHMANN, whose heartfelt abandon was unforgettable as ELISABETH, ELSA, EVA, and SIEGLINDE; Friedrich Schorr, the very embodiment of authority and dignity but also notable for subtlety and humaneness of expression as Wotan and Hans Sachs; and Alexander Kipnis, a bass whose juicy, imposing timbre encompassed remarkable gradations of tone and was at the service of an interpretative imagination of the first order. Lauritz MELCHIOR divides opinion: despite his powerful, magnificently baritonal voice with ringing high notes, which some regard as the quintessential Heldentenor sound, his notoriously slapdash and unreliable rhythmic sense does not recommend itself to modern listeners, and his *Sprechgesang* in wordy passages preserves the unlovely portions of the Bayreuth style. But his best – enormous stamina and the ability to portray with great intensity and vocal mastery a wide range of powerful emotions – makes him a signal phenomenon in the history of Wagner singing. His most celebrated partner, Kirsten FLAGSTAD, had a magnificently rich voice and remarkable musical security, but her way with words was less vivid than these other paragons, and her temperament more aristocratic, placid, or phlegmatic, depending on one's point of view. In the wake of these several decades of stylistic synthesis, it was she who became an important model for subsequent generations of Wagner singers.

3. Recordings and Wagner singing

Our ability to analyze the singing of this and subsequent eras is immeasurably enhanced thanks to audio recordings. Nevertheless, the existence and influence of this medium have altered audience expectations profoundly, thereby transforming live Wagner performance in significant ways. Live performance grants a singer numerous means of communication with an audience, but on recordings it is only the aural dimension that matters. As a way of compensating for this deprivation, balance is generally engineered in the singers' favor on recordings, which permits the singing to be perceived with greater immediacy and detail. Unfortunately, not all voices reveal their characteristic timbre when heard in recorded form, and some distinctive voices are not "phonogenic." Given the ability of recordings to adjust balance, a large voice – once a *sine qua non* of Wagner singing – becomes less crucial, and the kind of detail that lither voices can achieve becomes increasingly important (there are a few famous complete recordings of leading Wagner roles performed by singers who could not have undertaken stage performances of the role in question). Studio-made "performances" disguise the fact that vocal stamina remains one of the chief challenges of Wagner singing. Finally, unless one knows how to listen to them, recordings reward performers who emphasize calculation and accurate detail over spirit and spontaneity. Some singers chafe at such exacting demands, sensing that there is a significant disjunction between what makes a good live performance and a good recording. Not every singer is skilled in meeting these double demands, but as recordings have become more fundamental a part of musical life, live performances have gradually taken on more of the features that make for effective recordings.

The generations following the so-called Golden Age contained few voices that possessed equivalent caliber (among the leading figures, Hans HOTTER's imposing sound was not ideally steady or focused and Wolfgang WINDGASSEN's tenor was far lighter than Melchior's, although Birgit Nilsson's gleaming soprano produced top notes with a brilliance and ease that Leider and Flagstad could not match), but with recordings revealing the wondrous details of Wagner's orchestral scoring it became important for singers of this era to sing the music more smoothly than had some of their forebears, especially when performing under conductors who favored expansive tempi, such as Hans KNAPPERTSBUSCH, Reginald GOODALL, and James Levine. Herbert von Karajan's desire for beautiful singing in his Wagner performances was often stymied by the shallow pool of available talent, and he countered by casting singers who could produce a pleasing sound but whose vocal equipment was far too modest for their assignments according to the standards of just a few decades earlier. The 1970s–80s constituted a generation in which, as perceived via recordings, and with a few notable exceptions, Wagner singing seemed to be in sharp decline. By the beginning of the twenty-first century, however, the decades-long goal of sounding both polished and expressive enough in live performance to result in a satisfactory recording yielded a general standard in which singers' stamina, accuracy, and communicative skills met such requirements – and the dark days of the 1970s and 1980s showed signs of receding for good.

4. Wagner singers as actors

Part of the explanation for the increasingly convincing Wagner singing around the turn of the twenty-first century can be attributed to the rise and triumph of *Regietheater*. Whatever the intellectual or theatrical virtues of any individual production, singers' central involvement with the process of thinking through and realizing stimulating new dramatic conceptions of Wagner's works redirected their focus to something larger than the pressure of competing on strictly vocal terms with the giants of the past, and, paradoxically, but as Wagner himself might have predicted and appreciated, the general standard of singing as such became a less central issue.

Although much operatic acting has been notoriously routine and unaccomplished – an obituary of Hermann WINKELMANN recalled that he never quite lost the habit of beating time in order to stay with the orchestra in Act III of *Tristan und Isolde* – there have always been Wagner singers who, whether gifted vocalists or not, made gripping figures on stage according to the dictates and expectations of the time. Up until about the mid-twentieth century, however – that is, during the period in which Wagner's own dramaturgical suggestions held nominal sway – much of the responsibility for effective drama was assumed to rest with the individual singers rather than the stage director, whose task was largely predetermined. Singers, too, were expected to coordinate certain actions with mimetic instructions or implications in Wagner's scores. But there is much for which specific instructions are not given, which left room for published manuals of advice about how to treat specific passages as singer, actor, or both – and which also gave scope for the genius of gifted performers. Accordingly, W. J. Henderson could report that Albert Niemann "poured into the last act of *Tristan* . . . the vials of all agonies. He was heart-rending" (493). Oscar Thompson remembered that, in the Act I curse from *Tristan und Isolde*:

> Mme. [Olive] Fremstad, with her back to the audience, raised first one clenched fist at the end of an extended arm, with the words "Fluch dir, Verruchter"; then the other at "Fluch deinem Haupt"; and both hands at "Rache! Tod! Tod uns Beiden!" Staggering down stage, she dropped to one knee and buried her face in an elbow, while clutching her head. It appeared spontaneous, tragic, regal. In its execution there was no semblance of pose.
>
> (233–4)

Beyond evoking the histrionic style of a bygone era, these passages demonstrate the assumption that any novelty or departure from well-established traditions was the singer's initiative. Often this extended even to costumes – when, at his Met debut as Siegmund in 1914, Rudolf Berger appeared with what was called a "Psyche knot," it was he who needed to explain that "the old Teutonic warriors wore their hair that way, as he had found by reference to paintings and historical writings" (*New York Times* obituary, 28 February 1915).

Although changing standards and increasingly sophisticated stage technology made productions more unified over the course of the twentieth century, it was the eventual prominence of opera productions on film and telecasts that transformed acting in Wagner. Oversized gestures and stylized poses needed to be abandoned when the camera made close-ups (with the greater subtlety they permit) into a basic perspective for opera audiences. Whereas in earlier times vocal attributes were chiefly responsible for determining the roles for which a singer was cast, now physical appearance, acting ability, and suitability for the character came to be crucial – sometimes more so, in fact, than vocal qualifications, since sound engineers could be relied upon to keep singers audible.

In short, since Wagner first produced his works a whole host of developments and changed conditions has transformed the nature of the demands placed upon Wagner singers – and as long as Wagner's musical dramas continue to justify ongoing performance and imaginative engagement, other changes too are likely to occur. The manifold variety of perspectives from which the work of Wagner singers is preserved and can be perceived provides a rich fund of possibilities on which to build.   DAVID BRECKBILL

Hans Bélart, *Gesangsdramatische Wagnerkunst (nach Richard Wagners Tradition)* (Dresden: Carl Reissner, 1915).

W. J. Henderson, *The Art of Singing* (New York: Dial, 1938).

Julius Hey, *Deutscher Gesangs-Unterricht* (Mainz: Schott, 1884–7).

Einhard Luther, *Biographie eines Stimmfaches* (see bibliography).

Conrad L. Osborne, "Karajan Closes the Ring," *High Fidelity* (September 1970): 77–9; repr. *Records in Review, 1971 Edition* (Great Barrington, MA: Wyeth, 1971): 406–10.

Michael Scott, *The Record of Singing*, 2 vols. (London: Duckworth, 1977–9; repr. Boston: Northeastern University Press, 1993).

J. B. Steane, *The Grand Tradition: Seventy Years of Singing on Record, 1900 to 1970*, 2nd edn. (Portland, OR: Amadeus, 1993).

Oscar Thompson, *The American Singer* (New York: Dial, 1937).

Performance practice. The performance practice of Wagner's music has not been studied to the same extent as his scores, his libretti, his PROSE WORKS, and the staging of his dramas. Whereas different stage productions and their aesthetic and ideological implications have triggered heated discussions over the years, the question of musical performance has created less scholarly debate. For several reasons, this is something of a paradox. The style of musical performance has gone through considerable changes since Wagner's pieces were first played. Wagner's own practice exerted a lasting impact on the general culture of performing practice in Western art music. Furthermore, one might say that Wagner anticipated the "performative turn" in musicology by stating that the work does not consist in the written score, but rather in its performance.

The performance history of Wagner's music may be approached through a variety of sources: the scores, his own writings on musical performance, contemporaneous reports on how this music may have sounded, the knowledge of general performing styles and traditions as documented in written sources since the early nineteenth century, and the ever increasing stock of musical recordings.

1. Orchestral sound
2. Wagner on performance practice
3. After Wagner

1. Orchestral sound

As can be seen from the scores, Wagner initiated changes in the orchestra's instrumental resources (see ORCHESTRATION). From the 1840s, he expanded the size of his woodwind and brass sections, and increased the string sections accordingly. By the time he had moved to DRESDEN (about 1843), he had created a more blended arrangement of strings and winds by changing the seating of the instruments. From 1847, as conductor, Wagner placed himself in the pit in front of the orchestra and the singers (see WAGNER AS CONDUCTOR). He also modified existing musical instruments and invented new ones such as the WAGNER TUBA. Finally, by the time of the opening of the FESTIVAL THEATER in Bayreuth in 1876, the covered orchestral pit had been realized, further contributing to the blending of instrumental groups and timbres and to the general dampening of the orchestra in favor of the singers.

2. Wagner on performance practice

It was mainly in his essays on conducting that Wagner expressed his views on musical performance. These are devoted to the interpretation of individual works spanning GLUCK's and BEETHOVEN's music to his own. Important insights can also be drawn from his musical scores, where technical prescriptions of playing became increasingly detailed throughout his oeuvre. Notably, Wagner was one of the first to emphasize that, although the written text must be respected, the conductor is a creative force alongside the composer. One main idea is that the tempo should spring from an adherence to the intuitively felt *MELOS* or melodic substance of the work. This would imply that the music should be articulated according to phrases, not bar lines, and that tempo fluctuations are of prime importance in creating a compelling and meaningful musical expression. Wagner exerted a powerful impact on the culture of performance practice concerning tempo, string bowing, dynamics, and the role of principals in the orchestra. As surprising as it might seem today, he was reticent about the use of vibrato and *portamento*, saving these for moments of extraordinary musical expression.

Though published sources show an abundance of responses to Wagner's music by his contemporaries and successors, including BAUDELAIRE, NIETZSCHE, Mallarmé, Bernard SHAW, Proust, and Thomas MANN, who offered often ardent descriptions of their aesthetic experience of his music, specific comments on musical interpretation were left for critics in daily newspapers. A systematic study of these sources with regard to performance practice still remains to be done.

3. After Wagner

From the early nineteenth century and well into the era of musical recording, a multitude of local and national orchestral schools and performance traditions existed side by side. This situation differs considerably from today's homogenized uniformity across cultural and national borders. Apparently, the tempo fluctuations that are often associated with so-called Romantic performance practice were not a general trait in the early Romantic period. In orchestral conducting, the expressive use of speeding up and slowing down came in as something new with Wagner and LISZT in the 1840s. This aspect of Wagner's own practice was a strong influence on subsequent generations of conductors such as Nikisch, MAHLER, and Richard STRAUSS, each of whom cultivated, in their own ways, an increased malleability of tempo and phrasing. Simultaneously, Mahler was strongly opposed to the blended timbre (*Mischklang*) of Wagner's orchestra and instead struggled for analytic clarity and differentiation.

TOSCANINI, who belonged to the same generation as Mahler and Strauss, introduced a quite different practice, emphasizing metronome-based tempi and a singing melody line, probably influenced by his early years as Kapellmeister in Italian opera houses. Mahler's students Bruno Walter and Otto Klemperer, in their earlier phases, continued the Romantic performance practice, but went over to a more objective style during the general anti-Romantic turn after World War I, influenced by the *Neue Sachlichkeit* advocated by Stravinsky and Hindemith. This new objectivity, however, must not be confused with Toscanini's style. FURTWÄNGLER in turn clung to the Romantic idea of the visionary "creating" conductor at a time when musical objectivism had become hegemonic.

From the 1920s to the 1950s, Toscanini and Furtwängler were widely regarded as archetypal opposites in the world of musical interpretation. As such they were both invited to Bayreuth and were analyzed in contemporary reports and reviews.

Since the 1890s, recordings have become an indispensable source for studying Wagnerian performance history. Early recordings, usually with brief vocal excerpts accompanied by piano, often expose an astonishing art of flexible intonation and timing, with an occasional heroic tone. The electric microphone's advent from the mid-1920s resulted in the first more reliable takes with larger orchestral forces. Toscanini and Furtwängler, alongside several of their contemporaries such as KNAPPERTSBUSCH and Erich Kleiber, were reasonably well documented in the interwar period, normally presenting just preludes and other excerpts from the works. Tempi were generally swift, as in the case of Strauss and early Walter. Live recordings of whole scenes and acts were sometimes made, such as Beecham's *GÖTTERDÄMMERUNG* with the London Symphony Orchestra at Covent Garden in 1936. However, complete music dramas were rarely successfully recorded until the LP was launched after World War II.

Furtwängler epitomized the notion of sensitive articulation, long-distance hearing, and in-depth understanding of formal structures, as can be noted for example in his late recordings of *TRISTAN* (1952) and *Die WALKÜRE* (1954). SOLTI's landmark studio recording of the *RING* (1958–65) revealed remarkable musical control, sometimes verging on the bombastic. Other milestones included the *Tristans* of Böhm (1966), Karajan (1972), and Carlos Kleiber (1980–2), the latter two more acclaimed for their orchestral conducting than for their singers. BOULEZ, who conducted the Bayreuth *Ring* from 1976 to 1980, established an increased rhythmic exactness and analytical transparency, also countering the leading role of the strings in Karajan and Bernstein. While Giuseppe Sinopoli achieved a shimmering clarity and attention to detail, and Daniel BARENBOIM a more feverish expressivity and fluctuation of tempo,

Christian THIELEMANN has more recently exhibited a tendency for moderation and balance. In the last decades of the twentieth century, tempi generally slowed, as can be noted in James Levine's performances at the Metropolitan Opera and in Bayreuth.

The historically informed performance practice that emerged fully in the 1950s has so far had little impact on Wagner performance. The "performative turn" in musicology from the 1980s has revived certain imperatives that were already promoted in Wagner's writings. This turn implies that the assumed hierarchy between work and performance, or between the alleged "original" and its "representation," is reversed. Wagner similarly regarded performance as constitutive of the very idea of what the musical work means, or is. This view runs contrary to the idea of *Werktreue* (fidelity to the work), where the performer's role is to give little more than a faithful rendering of the composer's original idea. Wagner's attitude towards *Werktreue* has been the subject of debate because of his often quoted invocation: "Kinder! Macht Neues! Neues! und abermals Neues!" (Children, do something *new*! something *new*! and again something *new*!; often misquoted as "Kinder! schafft Neues!"; Letter to Liszt, 8 September 1852).

Information from the many different sources on the performance practice of Wagner's music can hardly be synthesized into a single coherent picture. Neither can it provide us with any assurance as to how his music really was played, nor produce complete prescriptions as to how it ought to be played. In line with Wagner's own aesthetic thinking, the musical work remains an open and virtual object in need of continual reinterpretation.

ERLING E. GULDBRANDSEN

See also PERFORMANCE, CONDUCTORS; PERFORMANCE, RECORDING HISTORY

Pets. The boy Richard displayed boundless love for animals – notably dogs. The mature composer was never truly content without "something to bark around him" (Ellis 1:81). Dogs played a major role in his life, such as Rüpel, "a very intelligent brown poodle," in MAGDEBURG (ML/E 100), and the splendid Newfoundland "Robber" in RIGA, who joined the Wagners' dramatic escape and subsequent perilous sea voyage from there. MEIN LEBEN (My Life, 1865–81) tells of the early Riga months: "Inasmuch as our marriage always remained childless and we were compelled to enliven our hearth by enlisting the help of a dog, we this time hit upon the eccentric idea of taking in a baby wolf, which had been brought to our door as a tiny cub. As we found that this expedient did not augment our domestic felicity, we gave it up after a few weeks" (ML/E 147). Robber's disappearance in PARIS is memorably described in *Mein Leben* and he assumes heroic status in the short story *Ein ENDE IN PARIS* (A Death in Paris).

The DRESDEN household included Peps (a kind of spaniel) and a parrot Papo who, trained by MINNA, excelled at performing extracts from *RIENZI* and scolding Richard's misdemeanors. Both joined the Wagners in ZURICH and were succeeded by Fips, another little spaniel dog, and a parrot Jacquot (also known as "Knackerchen"), whose repertoire included the start of BEETHOVEN's Eighth Symphony. In Penzing (VIENNA), Wagner's landlord gave him an old hunting dog called Pohl. The deaths of these companions, notably of Papo (February 1851), Peps (July 1855), Fips (Paris, June 1861), and Pohl (January 1866), assume tragic proportions in both his CORRESPONDENCE and his autobiographies, attesting to true grief and affection. Such strong affinity with, indeed reverence for, animals is a trait Wagner shared with SCHOPENHAUER. It led both men to oppose VIVISECTION, and was a factor in Wagner's latter-day espousal of VEGETARIANISM.

In his VENICE diary for Mathilde WESENDONCK, 1 October 1858, Wagner's account of witnessing the cruel killing of poultry in the street continues with significant reflections about man's duty to the animal kingdom, the importance of never being dead to pity, but consciously retaining fellow-feeling for all suffering creatures, and the nature of compassion itself, all of which "will become clear to you from the final act of *Parzival*."

Guests received by COSIMA or Wagner were always introduced first to the dogs. TRIBSCHEN hosted quite a menagerie: Russ (or Rouzemouk) – another Newfoundland; Cos (or Koss: its name chosen by Cosima to prevent people from familiarly abbreviating her own) – a terrier; also Fritz the horse; Wodan and Frigga, who were proud peacocks; plus two golden pheasants, several sheep, hens, and a cat. The grave of the Russian Russ (who died in 1875), near that of the Wagners at WAHNFRIED, bears the inscription "Hier ruht und wacht Wagners Russ" (Here rests and guards Wagner's Russ). He was succeeded by two Newfoundlands: Branke (Brangäne) and Marke at BAYREUTH, where lived also a Spitz dog called Putzi and some ornithological exotica gifted by LUDWIG II.   DEREK WATSON

William Ashton Ellis, *Life of Richard Wagner* (see bibliography).

Stewart Spencer, ed., *Wagner Remembered* (London: Faber & Faber, 2000).

Richard Wagner an Mathilde Wesendonck (see bibliography).

Hans von Wolzogen, *Richard Wagner und die Tierwelt*, 3rd edn. (Berlin: Schuster & Loeffler, 1910).

Pfistermeister, Franz Seraph von (b. Amberg, 14 Dec. 1820; d. Munich, 2 March 1912), Bavarian Cabinet Secretary. In May 1864, as Wagner fled VIENNA to escape his debts, Pfistermeister practically hunted him down in a Stuttgart hotel with the invitation for an audience with LUDWIG II. Two years later, Wagner had Pfistermeister removed from his MUNICH post for having intrigued against the composer.   SEBASTIAN STAUSS

Pfordten, Ludwig Karl Heinrich, Freiherr von der (b. Ried im Innkreis, 11 Sep. 1811; d. Munich, 18 Aug. 1880), politician and jurist. Held professorships in WÜRZBURG and LEIPZIG. Appointed Minister of Education by Frederick Augustus II of Saxony in 1848. Wagner failed to interest him in his "Plan for the Organization of a German National Theatre for the Kingdom of Saxony." Bavarian Minister-President and Foreign Minister during 1849–59 and 1864–6. During the 1850s, Pfordten failed to unite the smaller German kingdoms under Bavarian leadership against Prussia and Austria. He advised Maximilian II against a MUNICH staging of *TANNHÄUSER*, a slight LUDWIG II held against him. Suspicious of Wagner's influence upon the king, and horrified at his plans for a music school and FESTIVAL THEATER, Pfordten and colleagues manufactured a public scandal in 1865, compelling Ludwig to choose, in

Pfordten's terms, between the love and respect of his faithful subjects and the friendship of Richard Wagner. Pfordten's second ministry proved disastrous, Bavaria emerging on the losing side in the Austro-Prussian War (1866).

MARK BERRY

Philosophy. Wagner's philosophical thinking was dramatically transformed by his discovery of SCHOPENHAUER in 1854 (see also REDEMPTION). Earlier, while deriving general inspiration from FEUERBACH, Proudhon, and more remotely HEGEL, he had been, in his own right, an original philosophical thinker. After the discovery of Schopenhauer, which he likened to a religious conversion, he abandoned original thinking and became Schopenhauer's disciple and interpreter, a discipleship which had a profound impact on his artworks.

Wagner took an active part in the attempted revolution of 1848–9 as a self-declared "communist" (footnote on PW 1:167). He had, however, no interest in Marx's kind of state-mediated communism for, together with his revolutionary companion, Mikhail BAKUNIN, he was an anarchist. Anarchism, he believed, was the obvious route to communism. With the abolition of the instruments of force belonging to the state, private property as an institution would simply disappear.

Wagner's belief in the need for revolution was based on a thoughtful critique of modern society, a critique, in particular, of the state and of capitalism. The critique of the state is focused on Prussia, then the most extreme manifestation of the totalizing character of the modern state. The state, Wagner observes, is oppressively bureaucratic. By compelling us all to submit to a host of identical procedures it enforces a "red-tape uniformity" (PW 1:203). Permanently aggressive and militarized, it seeks, through control of education, to determine the culture and values of its citizens: "So shall you think and act!" (PW 2:196) and not otherwise, it says. The effect is social homogenization. The modern state disciplines individuals into nothing more than functions of itself.

Industrial capitalism has, in its own domain, the same kind of effect. In pursuit of "the holy five percent" (PW 1:42) workers are reduced to mere "steam power for the machine" (PW 1:54). Though we deplore the slavery of the ancient world, capitalism has created its own kind of slavery. One might think that while the workers are undoubtedly miserable, at least the "slave owners," the bourgeoisie, lead flourishing lives. But this is not so. Since capitalism requires a materialist conception of happiness, the bourgeoisie conceive of happiness as "luxury," as consumption. But once genuine desires are satisfied, the acquisition of unnecessary things produces diminishing degrees of pleasure and becomes, in fact, boring. The bourgeoisie are "bored to death by pleasure" (PW 3:306).

Another product of capitalism is social atomization, loss of community. By making a "religion of egoism" (PW 1:155), by creating *and evaluating positively* a society of individuals in which each pursues private advantage to the exclusion of all other considerations, it destroys community.

A further strand in Wagner's cultural criticism alleges the death of LOVE in MODERNITY. Partly this is a product of capitalism – the object of love needs to be a person but capitalism transforms people into mere "steam power," mere, as we say, "human resources." But partly, too, it is due to the fact that the language of modernity has become emotionally inarticulate. The first language, Wager claims, was essentially song: in the simple world of our prehistoric ancestors objects could be identified simply by pointing, so that the main function of language (like the babble of babies) was to express feeling. As, however, the world became more technical and complex language perforce turned outward. It became a device for the coordinated manipulation of the outer world, its capacity to express feeling increasingly atrophied. Modernity therefore cannot love because it cannot *express* love – or any other emotion (PW 2:224–36).

The final strand in Wagner's critique brings us to the heart of his concern – the condition of art, above all of opera, in modernity. Two strands in his critique can be distinguished, one concerning commodification the other loss of "wonder."

Since capitalism shapes modernity in general, it shapes in particular art. "Mirroring," as always, the condition of the society that produces it (PW 1:24), art has become a commodity, a consumer product. Opera, in particular, has been reduced to the "opera industry" (Wagner to Gustav Klemm, 20 June 1845). Whereas the art of the past has sought to educate, or at least elevate, its audience, modern opera has become simply a part of the entertainment "industry": "When the prince leaves a heavy dinner, the banker an exhausting financial operation, the working man a weary day of toil and go to the theater, what they ask for is rest, distraction, and amusement, and are in no mood for renewed effort and fresh expenditure of force" (PW 1:44).

The most significant consequence of this for opera is that all the audience really care about is the music. Though the creators of opera in sixteenth-century Italy had, commendably, thought to bring about the rebirth of Greek tragedy – a rebirth that, if genuine, would give primacy to words – in Franco-Italian opera all that matters is the aria – a lovely tune for easy listening. The plot is relegated to the recitative – that it makes no attempt at psychological interest or even plausibility does not matter since the audience talk through it anyway. After the big aria it demands six encores, which of course further destroys whatever dramatic continuity might survive the stop-start character of the aria-recitative division. The evening is thus reduced to a "chaos of disconnected sensations" (SSD 3:20; PW 1:44).

Turning to the issue of "wonder," Wagner observes that, in the past, art had possessed a charismatic power of religious or quasi-religious intensity which had raised it "high above" daily life and preserved it in the memory (PW 2:321). Reverence for the artwork meant that the audience brought to it a very high quality of attention. But now that opera has been reduced to a cheap "narcotic" (PW 2:46) all that has been lost. Interestingly, Wagner adds another reason for art's loss of "wonder" – the mechanical reproduction of artworks. In an age in which "even the humblest citizen has the opportunity of placing the noblest types of art before his eyes upon his mantelpiece, whilst the beggar himself may peep at them in the art-shop windows" (PW 5:120), and in which repertory theater and piano reductions are making music increasingly available on demand, the performance or viewing of an artwork is losing the sense of being a "special occasion" on which its wonder had depended in the past.

What was to be done about this dismal state of art and life? What, after the "fire-cure" (Wagner to UHLIG, 22 October 1850) of revolution has swept all this away, is to replace it? Though he of course rejects Greek slavery, Wagner's motto, as for almost all German thinkers since GOETHE, is "back to the Greeks." Wagner's aim was to secure the "noble" form of life for all people (PW 1:56), an ideal approached more nearly by the Greeks than by any other human civilization.

Particularly after the Greek temple had declined into empty ritual, the heart of Greek life was the tragic festival. It is here that Wagner finds "the perfect artwork" (PW 1:53), "the exemplary model of that ideal relation dreamt of by me between theater and public" (PW 3:306). Why, we must now ask, does Wagner make Greek tragedy the paradigm of great art, the template to which any truly great – "world-historically" significant (PW 1:75) – artwork such as the "artwork of the future" he himself aspires to create must conform? Six features define the greatness that was the Greek artwork and which is to return in the form of his own KUNSTWERK DER ZUKUNFT (Artwork of the Future).

First, far removed from the triviality of the modern "opera industry," the tragic festival was a religious occasion, performed in the presence of the gods, in particular Apollo, the musician, and Dionysus, the poet. It was the most important event in the Greek year; everything stopped for it – shipping, government, law, and even warfare – so that the entire citizenry of the *polis* could gather in the amphitheater. The importance of the occasion meant that the audience brought to the work an unparalleled level of seriousness and attention (PW 1:32–4).

The awesomeness of the occasion – this is the second defining feature of the great artwork – was dependent on the fact that tragedy occurred only occasionally, "only on special, sacred feast days" (PW 3:306–7). Greek tragedy did not suffer the over-exposure of modernity's repertory theatre but was performed exclusively as a FESTIVAL. Here, of course, lies the genesis of the BAYREUTH FESTIVAL: Wagner believes, as we have seen, that only the "wonder" that attaches to a special occasion gives art the power to influence people's lives.

The third feature that makes Greek tragedy the paradigm of the great artwork is that it is, to use Wagner's celebrated term, a GESAMTKUNSTWERK (PW 1:162, 166, 194), a "total" or, better, "collective artwork" in one of the two senses implicit in the term: it collected together, synthesized, all the individual arts into one collaborative work – painting in the form of set-design, sculpture in the form of "living sculpture" (see PW 1:170 and 186–8) of acting, and DANCE in the form of the ritualized movements of the actors and chorus. Above all, it collected together words and music. Though the music is lost, which makes us think of them as plays, Greek tragedies were actually MUSIC DRAMAS, almost operas. Within the collective artwork, Wagner emphasizes, the most important element is the words since is it they that convey the "message" of the work (see PW 2:17). But the music is an essential element, too, since it lends the words a life-affecting emotional intensity no non-musical art-form can achieve.

Over whom was the power of the artwork exercised? Over the entire community. The fourth defining feature of great art is thus that it is a "collective artwork" in a second sense – it "collects," gathers together, the entire community.

What was the point of this gathering-in of community? Like Hegel, Wagner views Greek tragedy as a clarifying exposition of communal ethos – of the Greeks' "life-view in common" (PW 2:156), their "own noblest essence," the "abstract and epitome" of what it was to be a Greek (PW 1:32–4, 52). Tragedy of course deals in mythic figures rather than abstract principles. It was, nonetheless, a "concrete meditation" (PW 2:60) upon, a working through of, ethical dilemmas. This is the fifth defining feature of the great artwork.

Because what is expounded is communal, "the people's" conception of the good life, it follows that in a certain sense (the sixth and final defining feature of the great artwork) the artwork is authored by the people as a whole. An authentic work must be "inspired by the spirit of the Volk" (PW 1:136). If it is not the people's ethos that is expounded then the work is merely manipulative propaganda that is inconsistent with there being the gathering of a *"free community"* (PW 1:35).

Early Wagner's project was, then, the rebirth of an artwork possessing all these features. The central aim is therefore the overcoming of atomization, the rebirth of a shared and living ethos that defines authentic community. Why, we may ask, is this so important? Wagner's explicit answer is that only within community can there be genuine flourishing of individuals. Only "necessary" action can, he claims, give meaning to our lives, and necessary action is that which "recognizes individual want in collective want or finds it based thereon." All else is "artificial," "caprice" (PW 1:75–6). Only if we regard our lives as centered upon a contribution to the flourishing of our community can we live meaningful, flourishing, lives.

A second answer is implicit in Wagner's anarchism. One of Proudhon's dictums to which Wagner subscribed is "Property is theft." But another is "Anarchy is order" (see PW 2:204). The question he confronts is, therefore: what, in the absence of the state, can be the principle of order? Wagner's implicit answer is: Art. A community bound by the *Gesamtkunstwerk* has no need of the instruments of the state.

Thus, in brief, Wagner's first philosophy is what we might call "the philosophy of the *Gesamtkunstwerk.*" While critical of the present, it is nonetheless hopeful for, "optimistic" about, the future of mankind (Wagner to RÖCKEL, 23 August 1856). With the conversion to Schopenhauerianism, however, optimism gives way to pessimism, Wagner becomes convinced of the futility of all attempts at REDEMPTION. The "festival" project went ahead, but its original, inner meaning had been eviscerated. The rebirth of the authentically Greek was now off the table.   JULIAN YOUNG

See also AESTHETICS; FESTIVAL, IDEA OF; *KUNSTRELIGION*

Piano arrangements and reductions. In an age before sound recording, Wagnerians were indebted to piano reductions of the MUSIC DRAMAS, if they wished to hear Wagner's works more frequently than theatrical performances and concerts permitted. NIETZSCHE was one of these. "From the moment there was a piano score of *Tristan*," he wrote in *Ecce Homo*, " – my compliments, Herr von Bülow! – I was a Wagnerian." Hans von BÜLOW in fact made relatively few transcriptions of Wagner's music, but Bülow's teacher, Franz LISZT, was far more prolific, and his popular piano versions of famous moments from the music dramas set the tone for his competitors in this once thriving industry.

The Wagnerian piano reduction exists in three basic forms: (1) the vocal score, which is primarily designed for practical rehearsal, with the orchestral material condensed for the répétiteur into a part for piano, and the vocal lines accurately reproduced above; (2) the self-contained concert or salon piece based on musical themes from Wagner's oeuvre, of which Liszt's PIANO TRANSCRIPTIONS and paraphrases are the best-known examples; and (3) the piano score, which differs in style and intention from the other two, existing in a strange "middle earth" between the vocal score and piano piece. Now rarely heard and seldom reprinted, piano scores have no vocal lines, these being assimilated into the piano reduction so that a single pianist can recreate an impression of an entire music drama alone.

Even the most accomplished transcriber has virtually insurmountable difficulties when confronting some of Wagner's most luminous orchestral effects. Vocal recitative is also problematic in piano transcription. One of the most prolific Wagnerian transcribers was Karl KLINDWORTH, who transcribed, among others, a complete RING, PARSIFAL, and TANNHÄUSER. Another of Liszt's star pupils, Klindworth was well versed in the "orchestral" piano style pioneered by his teacher. His arrangements are not as virtuosic as Liszt's but nonetheless require an excellent technique.

Richard Kleinmichel (1846–1901) was also a man of extraordinary energy. A composer in his own right, he also completed vocal scores for the Ring and TRISTAN, as well as a piano score of LOHENGRIN; but the most prolific of all these men must surely be Otto Singer (1863–1931), who furnished the PUBLISHERS BREITKOPF & HÄRTEL with many Wagnerian vocal scores for their lavishly produced editions of 1914, with elaborate Jugenstil Franz STASSEN frontispieces.

As the Wagner cult grew, the market was soon flooded with Wagnerian "salon" pieces by the likes of Gustav Lange, Albert Heinz, Johannes Doebber, Friedrich Ferdinand Brissler, Hans Sitt, and, alas, many uncredited musicians, who labored for this once voracious market. Vocal scores are still needed, of course, but most opera companies rely on the celebrated nineteenth-century versions. The market for salon pieces and the piano score in particular has now been almost entirely replaced by CDs, DVDs, and the internet; but we should not ignore these piano versions as they reveal a great deal about what it meant to be a WAGNERIAN before the invention of recording technology.

DAVID HUCKVALE

Piano transcriptions. Along with PIANO ARRANGEMENTS AND REDUCTIONS, these were the principal means by which an educated public became acquainted with Wagner's music during the nineteenth century. Pianos were a staple of bourgeois domesticity, and transcriptions served both as a souvenir of a performance event and as a medium for provincial audiences to access music otherwise unavailable to them. In 1830–1, Wagner himself made a two-hand transcription of BEETHOVEN's Ninth Symphony, but it was primarily Franz LISZT who developed the genre of Wagner transcription. Beginning in 1849, with two excerpts from TANNHÄUSER, Liszt produced fifteen transcriptions in all, ranging from virtuosic warhorses (*Tannhäuser* overture) to modest arrangements (*Elsa's Dream*), opera fantasies (*RIENZI Fantasy*) to note-for-note transcriptions (*LIEBESTOD*). Indeed, so powerful was Liszt's endorsement and dissemination of Wagner's music that the *Liebestod* is so named by his designation (not Wagner's, which was *Verklärung*). But transcriptions could also mock: Emmanuel Chabrier's four-hand *Souvenirs de Munich*, and Gabriel Fauré's / André Messanger's quadrille *Souvenirs de Bayreuth* are wickedly funny send-ups of *TRISTAN* and the *RING*, respectively. Other notable contemporaries who published transcriptions include Hans von BÜLOW, Carl TAUSIG, Moritz Moszkowski, and Louis Brassin; more recent contributions come from Glenn Gould and Zoltan Kocsis.   DAVID TRIPPETT

Jonathan Kregor, *Liszt as Transcriber* (Cambridge University Press, 2010).

Helmut Loos, "Liszts Klavierübertragungen von Werken Richard Wagners: Versuch einer Deutung," in *Franz Liszt und Richard Wagner: Musikalische und geistesgeschichtliche Grundlagen der neudeutschen Schule* (Munich and Salzburg: Katzbichler, 1986): 103–18.

Pilgerfahrt zu Beethoven, Eine (A Pilgrimage to Beethoven), novella, first published by Maurice SCHLESINGER in French as "Une visite à Beethoven, épisode de la vie d'un musicien allemande," in the *REVUE ET GAZETTE MUSICALE* during November–December 1840. It was subsequently published in its German original between July and August 1841 in the *Abend-Zeitung* (DRESDEN) together with *Ein ENDE IN PARIS* (A Death in Paris) under the collected title: "Zwei Epochen aus dem Leben eines deutschen Musikers."

The novella follows the story of "R. . ." a "poor German composer," who realizes BEETHOVEN is still alive and decides to journey on foot to visit him. Beethoven becomes an iconic figure, and music the ultimate expression of KUNSTRELIGION. After enduring many hardships, "R. . ." manages to gain an audience with the composer, and a conversation between "R. . ." and the fictionalized Beethoven ensues. Several topics are covered which will be of crucial importance for the remainder of Wagner's development as a composer.

The conversation begins with *Fidelio*, and quickly turns to Beethoven's views on contemporary opera, which he rejects as being a ridiculous patchwork. If he were to write another opera, it would be quite different in form and content. "R. . ." even refers to the new form Beethoven is suggesting as a "musical drama" (*musikalisches Drama*, SSD 1:109). Next, Beethoven shows "R. . ." the score to his last symphony which, in the timeframe of the novella, has not yet been premiered. A discussion of Beethoven's Ninth Symphony ensues, in which Beethoven explains the necessity for introducing text in the last movement, as the only possible solution remaining for the symphony. "R. . ." leaves feeling blessed by Beethoven and realizing that he has been granted nothing less than a revelation.

There have been many interpretations of this rich work, which contains the seeds and justification for much of Wagner's future theoretical and compositional work. Speculation concerning the model for "R. . ." has included Johann Friedrich Reichardt and Ludwig Rellstab. However it makes more sense to think of "R. . ." as a projection of Richard Wagner, and not just because "R. . ." is born in a medium-sized German city, beginning with the letter "L" (i.e., LEIPZIG). Written at the height of Wagner's desperate and ultimately unsuccessful attempt to launch himself in the existing opera market of PARIS, the novella represents the moment at which Wagner transforms himself from the aspiring composer of GRAND OPERA (i.e., *RIENZI*) and begins instead to carve out his own niche as a distinctly German composer who has understood the true significance of the Ninth Symphony's last movement and, taking up Beethoven's implicit directive (made explicit in the novella), will henceforth attempt to forge a new kind of opera that aspires to the highest expression of symphonic music, now made even more expressive with the addition of dramatic text (i.e., MUSIC DRAMA).   NICHOLAS VAZSONYI

K. M. Knittel, "Pilgrimages to Beethoven: Reminiscences by his Contemporaries," *Music & Letters* 84.1 (2003): 19–54.

Karl Kropfinger, *Wagner and Beethoven* (see bibliography).

Nicholas Vazsonyi, "Beethoven Instrumentalized: Richard Wagner's Self-Marketing & Media Image," *Music & Letters* 89.2 (2008): 195–211.

Planer, Christine Wilhelmine "Minna." See WAGNER, MINNA

Planer, Natalie (b. 22 Feb. 1826; d. 1892), illegitimate daughter of one Herr von Einsiedel and Wagner's first wife MINNA WAGNER, who presented Natalie as her sister to the general public. She lived for many years with her mother and Wagner and, late in life, married a man named Bilz. When Minna died (1866), Natalie inherited various Wagner-related documents, which she kept, despite COSIMA Wagner's request for their return. Twenty-four years later, Mary BURRELL visited her in a house for underprivileged women in Leisnig, and purchased 128 letters from Richard to Minna. Cosima, on the other hand, destroyed most of Richard's letters to Minna. The tales Natalie Planer told Mary Burrell about Wagner's life are not considered reliable.   EVA RIEGER

Plüddemann, Martin (b. Kolberg, Pomerania [now Kołobrzeg, Poland], 29 Sep. 1854; d. Berlin, 8 Oct. 1897). Born into a musical family, Plüddemann studied voice and composition at Leipzig and later emerged as an accomplished ballad writer and teacher. A favorite of Wagner's who visited the composer both at WAHNFRIED and in NAPLES, Plüddemann advocated Wagner's cause in such publications as *Die Bühnenweihfestspiele in Bayreuth, ihre Gegner und ihre Zukunft* (1876) and *Aus der Zeit – für die Zeit* (1880).   ANTHONY J. STEINHOFF

Poetic-musical period, a term coined in Part 3 of *OPER UND DRAMA* (Opera and Drama, 1851) to denote a hypothetical structural unit that would form the fundamental building-block of the "musical dramatic artwork of the future" outlined there (with implicit reference to plans for *Siegfrieds Tod* and the eventual *RING* cycle). Specifically, Wagner is trying to describe (or better, imagine) how rhetorically unified sections of poetic text will interact with harmonic progressions and tonal design to create a fluid but still coherent structure in place of traditional operatic "numbers" (recitative and aria, duet, chorus, finale, etc.). As described in *Oper und Drama* (SSD 4:152–4), a "poetic-musical period" consists of a speech or series of verses (presumably the utterance of a single character), the musical setting of which begins and ends in a particular ("tonic") key, while it may traverse any number of intermediate tonal areas in between, reflecting the shifting affective contours of the overall text.

Initially, Wagner is concerned with the way in which modulation might serve to complement the role of alliteration or STABREIM in structuring patterns of similarity and difference on both semantic and affective levels. In the model line "Die Liebe gibt Lust zum Leben" (Love gives pleasure to life), the alliterative consonant "L" underwrites a single, overall affect. The composer should set these words all within a single appropriate key (say, C major). The same alliteration could serve to unify a simple affective contrast in the variant line "Die Liebe bringt Lust und Leid" (Love brings pleasure and sorrow). Here the composer would shift toward an appropriately contrasting, but harmonically proximate key (say, A minor) on the intermediate term, *Lust*. If the poetic utterance were further extended to return to the opening affective stance (*Hauptempfindung*), the pattern of alliteration would likely need to change, as in the expanded model: "Die Liebe bringt Lust und Leid, doch in ihr Weh auch webt sie Wonnen" (Love brings pleasure and sorrow, but with its pain it also weaves delight). The musician, however, could return to the original key (say, C major) in setting the second line, enfolding the changing pattern of alliteration within a larger tonal unity. The same could apply over a still longer series of verses, accompanied by a free-roaming series of harmonic or tonal shifts: all the local poetic and musical contrasts would be understood within the unifying light of a principle key (*Haupttonart*).

When he came to composing the *Ring* dramas, Wagner was not particularly concerned with coordinating *Stabreim* and musical modulation in just these terms. It is often possible, however, to identify passages of variable length unified by a controlling tonic and representing a rhetorically coherent unit – that is, something akin to the "poetic-musical period." (Apart from the issue of *Stabreim*, it is also easy to relate the terms of the *Oper und Drama* passage to the compositional idiom of LOHENGRIN.) Alfred LORENZ appealed to the idea of tonally rounded "periods" as the basis for the grandiose, hierarchical assemblages of "bars," "arches," and refrain forms into which he parceled Wagner's entire later oeuvre. The question of tonal closure, and at what levels it might legitimately be recognized in the later scores, is one that has continued to preoccupy Wagnerian analysis ever since. At the least, Wagner's hypothetical account of a network of "poetic-musical periods" in *Oper und Drama* confirms that he was concerned with creating a new, dramatically justified, but also musically coherent, tonal practice as he contemplated a new "post-operatic" genre of musical drama.   THOMAS S. GREY

See also MUSIC THEORY; WAGNER AS COMPOSER

Thomas S. Grey, *Wagner's Musical Prose* (see bibliography): esp. chapter 4 and Appendix 1, 375–7 (translation from *Oper und Drama*, Part 3, section 3).

Pohl, Richard (b. Leipzig, 12 Sep. 1826; d. Baden-Baden, 17 Dec. 1896), writer on music, critic, translator. After early activity in LEIPZIG (collaboration with SCHUMANN), Pohl moved to DRESDEN, where he took up the cause of the befriended Wagner, LISZT, and BERLIOZ in contributions to Brendel's *NEUE ZEITSCHRIFT FÜR MUSIK*, publishing under the pseudonym "Hoplit." In 1854, he moved to Weimar, where he translated for Liszt and co-edited with Brendel the *Anregungen für Kunst, Leben und Wissenschaft* (1856–61). He was a driving force behind the establishment of the Allgemeiner Deutscher

Musikverein in 1861, a performance society that promoted Wagner's music. Pohl settled in Baden-Baden in 1863, where he continued to agitate for Wagner, most significantly with a bid for the FESTIVAL THEATER. He published memoirs of BAYREUTH (1877) and a collection of his Wagner essays (1883) and wrote a novel about Wagner (*Richard Wiegand*, 1904). As Wagner publicist, he never produced a major study, yet his consistent, reliable partisanship as author of articles and reviews, journal editor and event organizer earned Pohl the praise of Wagner, who allegedly called him the "älteste Wagnerianer" (oldest Wagnerian, Seidl 116).   JAMES DEAVILLE

Arthur Seidl, "Richard Pohl," *Bayreuther Blätter* 20 (1897): 116–21.

Politics. Aristotle's contention that man is by nature a political animal (ζῷον πολιτικόν) might have been formulated with Wagner in mind (Aristotle I.1253a2). Whatever he claimed on occasion, for instance when seeking amnesty for his revolutionary deeds, or writing MEIN LEBEN (My Life, 1865–81) for LUDWIG II, Wagner's life and oeuvre were intimately and often explicitly concerned with political questions. "Questions" is the moot word, for, whilst Wagner rarely hesitated to proffer answers, he ultimately found them wanting. Political involvement arose from artistic need and *vice versa*, art and politics being inextricably related in Wagner's conception. Inspired by Attic tragedy, Wagnerian musical drama was necessarily political: communal celebration and perhaps incitement. Wagner also treated with political ideas in essays, CORRESPONDENCE, and the dramas themselves.

1. Karl Marx, German idealism, and French socialism
2. The *Ring*
3. The *Ring*: political order
4. The *Ring*: heroic challenges
5. After Wagner

1. Karl Marx, German idealism, and French socialism

Wagner was a contemporary of Marx (b. 1818) in more than a chronological sense. They shared influences, not least the philosophy of Friedrich SCHILLER, G. F. W. HEGEL, and Young Hegelians such as Ludwig FEUERBACH; they shared friends and acquaintances, such as Mikhail BAKUNIN and Georg HERWEGH; they denounced many of the same social ills, not least nineteenth-century bourgeois capitalism. Both, moreover, were master dramatists; even *Capital* is as much psychopathological history as work of economic analysis. The differences between Marx and Wagner are, however, equally telling. That Marx would have dismissed Wagner's work largely as "ideology" does not mean that we should do so, yet there lies therein much of that "true socialism" Marx and Engels excoriated in favor of their "scientific" variety. Wagner's politics concern themselves with some issues of lesser importance to Marx, for instance despoliation of the natural world ("green politics," one might say) and a pre-Nietzschean conception of the will to power (*Liebesgelüste*; see Wagner to UHLIG, 11/12 November 1851).

For Wagner, standing firmly in the tradition of German idealism, the Athenian *polis* had embodied harmony between individual and society, private and public. Tragic enactment represented the supreme manifestation of harmony – in every sense. The problem of modern political life, for both Wagner and idealism, was how to reconcile the apparently idyllic communal integration of Hellenic life with post-classical, Christian subjectivity (individual souls: the Lutheran priesthood of all believers). Art, as life in general, fragmented following the political decline of Athens. A higher unity – Wagner aimed not at a *restoration* of tragedy but at its *renewal* – entailed wholesale transformation of the public realm: individuality would flourish, but not the empty, mercenary individualism as abetted by modern civilization. Socialization of art and aestheticization of society would be one and the same. As for Schiller and the German Romantics, art was the paradigm of free, productive activity – or would be when liberated from forcible division of labor. For the divorce of "opera" from "drama" was as much a dehumanized and dehumanizing consequence as factory wage-slavery: REVOLUTION would overcome both.

French socialism – "utopian" according to the typology inherited from Marx and Engels – played an important role here too, not least via August RÖCKEL, though Wagner also read much for himself, returning to Pierre-Joseph Proudhon after the DRESDEN UPRISING. In *Mein Leben*, Wagner recalls having questioned Röckel in DRESDEN about his "new moral order of things," founded upon "the annihilation of the power of capital by direct productive labor." Where, asked Wagner, would the "free spirits, let alone artists," be found, "if everyone were to be swallowed up into the one working class"? Röckel replied "that if everybody participated in the work at hand according to his powers and capacities, work would cease to be a burden, and would become an occupation which would eventually assume an entirely artistic character, just as it had already been proven that a field worked laboriously by a single peasant with the plough was infinitely less productive than when cultivated by several persons according to a horticultural system." This utopian socialism stood closer to Marx than one might think, for division of labor is to be transformed into something voluntarist rather than merely abandoned in Romantic reaction. Wagner thus "took pleasure in developing conceptions of a possible form of human society which would correspond wholly, and indeed solely, to my highest artistic ideals" (ML/E 373–4). The "ZURICH reform writings" – Die KUNST UND DIE REVOLUTION (Art and Revolution, 1849), *Das KUNSTWERK DER ZUKUNFT* (The Artwork of the Future, 1849/50), and *OPER UND DRAMA* (Opera and Drama, 1851) – do just that.

2. The *Ring*

One might say that Wagner's politics are expressed most clearly, or rather most probingly, in *Der RING DES NIBELUNGEN*. This is true and misleading: there is no single doctrine to be expressed, but a continual, questioning process of development. Dramatic form, radicalizing rather than resolving – there are harmonic implications here too – arguably proved better suited than essay-writing to such development, at least for Wagner, though we should never reduce the dramas to tracts.

There nevertheless remains much political truth in Wagner's encouragement to LISZT, "Mark well my new poem – it contains the beginning of the world and its destruction!" (Wagner to Liszt, 11 February 1853). At the heart of the *Ring*'s action lie the foundation of modern state and society, and their dissolution, the latter seeming increasingly uncertain following the apparent failure of revolution in 1848–9, yet never abandoned. Even in the 1880s, Wagner would record, recalling his earlier, highly political *Jesus von Nazareth*: "Jesus could foresee nothing but the end; we no less. Materially and empirically composed, we await the destructive forces which, even, for the Roman world, did not fail to appear" (BB/E 201). Annihilation remains political as well as metaphysical, the Christian dialectic between cyclical (Greek) and linear (Jewish), at least as understood by Wagner, SCHOPENHAUER, and many other German idealists, reimagined, just as in PARSIFAL.

3. The *Ring*: political order

In WOTAN's winning the *Ring*'s "world," the necessity of its end (*GÖTTERDÄMMERUNG*) is already clear. The Norns recall him fashioning his spear, political instrument of domination, from the World-ash tree: Nature raped in founding the artificial state. In 1849, Wagner noted, under the heading, "On the Principle of Communism," that, historically, such arbitrary (*willkürlich*) deeds of possession, on the part of a people or an individual, were invariably justified by religious, mythical, or otherwise spruced-up contracts (SSD 12:254). When we hear of Wotan's subsequent actions, we understand them as inevitable consequences of that original political sin against Nature (and humanity). His spear shattered in combat by Siegfried's sword of (would-be) revolution, Wotan has commanded his tamed heroes to fell the withered boughs of the World-ash. "The ash fell; the spring ran dry eternal!" (*Götterdämmerung*, Prelude). Domination achieved, disaster has ensued, not least for Wotan himself, now surrounded by the ash-tree logs, awaiting their final all-consuming blaze: further wanton natural despoliation. The state, as Bakunin insisted, "is not a direct product of Nature; it does not, like society, precede the awakening of thought in man." Instead, it "dominates society and tends to absorb it altogether" (Bakunin 137–8).

Wotan, however, is no mere gangster. We sense the religious aura and majesty of Valhalla: the ideological defenses of the gods' stronghold should not be underestimated, especially as it emerges in Wotan's musical dream. Wotan's vision is not, moreover, of "might is right." He restrains Donner from resolving the problem of the giants as in the *Prose EDDA*: "Stop, you savage! Nothing through force! My spear protects contracts: spare your hammer's power" (*RHEINGOLD*, Scene 2). Such is a remnant of the originally creative urge that led him to inscribe contracts upon his spear; the problem with laws is that as soon as they are rendered unalterable, human creativity is stifled. They are transformed into their opposite; they entrap, as Wotan laments in his *WALKÜRE* monologue. Conflict between love and the Law is a constant refrain in Wagner's plans for *Jesus von Nazareth*. Indeed, Wagner portrays Jesus, who proclaims that his death will also bring about that of the Law, as an heir to Proudhon and Bakunin (SSD 11:290). Law has, in a classical case of Feuerbachian inversion, acquired divine power over the men whose original creation it was, as Valhalla (or Heaven) has in religious terms. The temporary and imaginary have become feared and obeyed as eternal and super-real. And yet, as we read in the 1848 prose sketch (*Der Nibelungen-Mythus: Als Entwurf zu einen Drama*), though the purpose of the gods' "higher world order is moral consciousness . . . they are tainted by the very injustice they hunt down." From the oppressed "depths of Nibelheim consciousness of their guilt echoes threateningly" (SSD 2:157). Wagner originally intended that the oppressed Nibelungs be liberated by revolution; experience taught him the struggle would be harder.

In Nibelheim lies a more modern – at least to Wagner – instantiation of domination, and a threat to the gods' relatively enlightened variety. For, as Marx observed, though Wagner might readily have done, "the relationship of industry and, in particular, the world of wealth to the political world is a principal problem of modern times" (Marx, "Zur Kritik der Hegelschen Rechtsphilosophie"). Both extended Feuerbach's critique of religious alienation, this time into the realm of capital. ALBERICH's parallel rape of Nature – there are two creation myths in the *Ring* cosmos – is theft of the Rhine gold. Value-free in its natural state, Alberich transforms it into capital in the Nibelung hoard, and would-be totalitarian power in the ring, with which he enslaves his kinsmen and would vanquish *ancien régime* Valhalla. He may not accomplish that himself, yet his bourgeois challenge, born of his lowly place endured in its feudal order, hastens its destruction.

4. The *Ring*: heroic challenges

Subsequent challenges issue from SIEGMUND and SIEGFRIED, both standing in Wagner's line of charismatic revolutionary heroes from RIENZI (indeed from the hero of the FAUST-OVERTÜRE) to PARSIFAL. Enthusiasm for the figure of Siegfried was widespread amongst *Vormärz* radicals, including the young Engels, for whom nineteenth-century "heroic deeds" (*Heldentaten*) might be endeavored by "sons of Siegfried" (see his essay *Siegfrieds Heimat*). Brünnhilde, we might note, sends Siegfried out into the world: "to new deeds, dear hero" (*Götterdämmerung*, Prelude).

If our opening quotation might have been made for Wagner, so, in the VÖLSUNGA context, might Aristotle's subsequent words: "And he who by nature and not by mere accident is without a state, is either a bad man or above humanity; he is like the 'Tribeless, lawless, heartless one,' whom Homer [*Iliad*, Book IX] denounces – the natural outcast is forthwith a lover of war; he may be compared to an isolated piece at draughts" (Aristotle I.1253a2–6). Siegmund and Siegfried both appear out of nowhere, or rather out of the Teutonic forest, suggesting a world in which Franco-Roman rules (laws) do not apply – that is, a stateless place of anarchy. Wagner does not consider them "bad men"; foes such as HUNDING and FRICKA do. In Wagner's attempt, confounded by state power, to have them transcend or at least transform existing society, they echo Aristotle's "above humanity" – and prefigure NIETZSCHE's *Übermensch*. Both heroes stand opposed to "tribe" and "law," and are, in the face of society and its institutions, "lovers of war." Such was Wotan's intention, having turned against his own laws and attempted to free himself from the merciless dialectic of power-politics. "Heartless" the Volsung heroes are too, whereas Hunding – his second line, "Holy is my hearth" – prides himself upon his outwardly respectable, internally repressive (bourgeois-equivalent) household (*Die Walküre*, Act I).

Siegmund's rescue of SIEGLINDE from Hunding's domination therefore represents dramatic progress; it is blessed with heroic progeny. By contrast, BRÜNNHILDE's wish that Siegfried settle down attempts (again) to render permanent what should be temporary. Marriage, symbolized with cruelest irony by possession of Alberich's ring of power, would pervert and destroy their love through intervention of law and property. Her need to constrain Siegfried thus helps initiate, in alliance with Gibichung state corruption, the tragedy of *Götterdämmerung*, the undoing of all concerned. Nothing could be further from the truth than George Bernard SHAW's claim that, in *Götterdämmerung*, Wagner relinquished his political vision; his politics, however, stood far from Shaw's Fabian variety.

Instead, there persisted a vision of free LOVE inspired by Young German and Young Hegelian "sensualism," and by French socialists such as Charles Fourier and the Saint-Simonians – despite Wagner's Schopenhauerian recognition of love itself as a form of power. Fourier lamented: "Our legislators want to subordinate the social system to ... the Family," which he contrasted with "groups" of honor, friendship, and love, and "which God has almost entirely excluded from influence in Social Harmony, because it is a group of forced or material bonds, not a free, passionate gathering, dissoluble at will ... Since all constraint engenders falsehood ... both civilized and patriarchal society, where this group is the dominant one, are the most duplicitous" (80). It is no coincidence that conventional marriages in Wagner are duplicitous – and barren. Siegfried, if unconsciously, destroys the bonds of law and state as much through his betrayal of Brünnhilde as through his defiance of Wotan.

5. After Wagner

Wagner was not the first to treat with political ideas in his musical dramas, yet those coming after tended to take their leave from him. That might lie in rejection – for example, Igor Stravinsky and even Richard STRAUSS, in his marriage of Wagnerian musico-dramatic construction to decidedly Nietzschean aestheticism – or in continuation. Alban Berg's *Wozzeck* and *Lulu* dealt explicitly with sociopolitical concerns, likewise Arnold SCHOENBERG's *Moses und Aron*, an exemplar regarding difficulties and opportunities provided by the Wagnerian-modernist tradition. Schoenberg contrasts Moses, at a loss for words, and therefore lacking power, with Aron, whose dangerous political power lies in BEL CANTO ease of communication and its catastrophic consequences. If Bertolt Brecht and Kurt Weill reckoned themselves resolutely anti-Wagnerian, they could hardly have done so without him; there remained, in any case, more than a little residue. Postwar "engaged" composers such as Hans Werner Henze and Luigi Nono were compelled to confront Wagner's legacy: in Henze's case almost equally through inescapable homage and angry confrontation.

Wagner's dramas have also stood at the forefront of political *Regietheater*. There are specific historical reasons for this, not least a postwar Adornian desire to "salvage" them from their fraught relationship to GERMAN HISTORY, but content and political purpose have proved equally important. If WIELAND WAGNER's "New Bayreuth" understandably downplayed the taint of politics – itself a political act – then directors such as Joachim Herz, Ruth Berghaus, Patrice CHÉREAU, and Stefan Herheim have continued, in Wagnerian tradition, to question the dramas, to venture out to "new deeds." Man remains a ζῷον πολιτικόν.

MARK BERRY

See also GENDER; MODERN MUSIC; PHILOSOPHY

Aristotle, *The Politics*, trans. Jonathan Barnes, ed. Stephen Everson (Cambridge University Press, 1988).

Mikhail Bakunin, "State and Society," *Selected Writings*, trans. Steven Cox (London: Jonathan Cape, 1973).

Udo Bermbach, *Der Wahn des Gesamtkunstwerks* (see bibliography).

Mark Berry, "Is it here that Time Becomes Space? Hegel, Schopenhauer, History, and Grace in *Parsifal*," *The Wagner Journal* 3.3 (2009): 29–59.

Treacherous Bonds and Laughing Fire (see bibliography).

Charles Fourier, *The Theory of the Four Movements*, ed. G. Steadman Jones and I. Patterson (Cambridge University Press, 1996).

Karl Marx and Friedrich Engels, *The German Ideology, including Theses on Feuerbach and Introduction to the Critique of Political Economy* (Amherst, NY: Prometheus, 1998).

Popular culture. See WAGNER AND POPULAR CULTURE

Porges, Heinrich (b. Prague, 25 Nov. 1837; d. Munich, 17 Nov. 1900), Czech-Austrian writer on music, editor, and choirmaster. In 1863, he assumed the role of co-editor with Franz BRENDEL of the NEUE ZEITSCHRIFT FÜR MUSIK, a journal whose editorial slant at the time was as a partisan advocate for the progressive leanings of the so-called NEW GERMAN SCHOOL. In 1867, Porges took over, along with editor Julius Fröbel, the arts pages of the MUNICH-based *Süddeutsche Presse* and, in 1880, became the music critic for the *Neueste Nachrichten*, also based in Munich. The "Porges Choral Society" was formed in 1886 in order to promote his favored contemporary composers, including BERLIOZ, LISZT, CORNELIUS, and BRUCKNER, in addition to works by Palestrina and BACH. Porges first came to Wagner's attention in VIENNA in 1863, by arranging and publicizing a financially successful ORCHESTRAL CONCERT. He also assisted in selling Wagner's effects after he was forced to flee from his Viennese creditors. Although Porges turned down Wagner's invitation to join him in Munich as a private secretary the following year, he would soon become a prominent disciple of Wagner. He wrote a piece on LOHENGRIN for the *Süddeutsche Presse* in 1867 when the work was performed in Munich, and later a short monograph on TRISTAN UND ISOLDE (published in 1906). Wagner expressed admiration for Porges's *Tristan* essay in a letter (15 May 1867), later included as the preface to the published monograph. While serving as Wagner's assistant during the rehearsals for the 1876 premiere of the RING cycle at BAYREUTH, Porges helped with promotion of the festival by writing bi-weekly updates about preparations, which were distributed under the title "Bayreuther autographische Korrespondenz." At Wagner's request, he also chronicled the rehearsal activities in detail in *Die Bühnenproben zu den Bayreuther Festspielen des Jahres 1876* (Wagner to Porges, 6 November 1872). These were initially published in installments in the BAYREUTHER BLÄTTER and then in book form, one for each opera in the cycle, the 1896 publication of the section on GÖTTERDÄMMERUNG coinciding with the second production of the *Ring* at Bayreuth. Porges's writings, in addition to recording Wagner's interactions with the singers and the orchestra, also effectively functioned as a repository of Wagner's ideas on how the cycle should ideally be staged and performed, which Wagner hoped would establish a paradigm for future interpreters of the cycle to follow. Porges also assisted with the rehearsals for the premiere of *PARSIFAL* at the 1882 Bayreuth Festival and studiously documented those proceedings; most of the notes recorded by Porges pertain to matters of musical performance rather than staging. Following Porges's death in 1900, Wagner's son SIEGFRIED delivered the funeral oration, which was subsequently reprinted in the *Bayreuther Blätter*.

DANIEL SHERIDAN

See also BAYREUTH FESTIVAL, ANNOUNCEMENTS FOR

Heinrich Porges, *Tristan und Isolde, nebst einem Briefe Richard Wagners*, intro. Hans von Wolzogen (Leipzig: Breitkopf & Härtel, 1906).
Wagner Rehearsing the "Ring" (see bibliography).

Praeger, Ferdinand (Christian Wilhelm), (b. Leipzig, 22 Jan. 1815; d. London, 2 Sep. 1891), German-born composer (briefly a pupil of Hummel), pianist, teacher, and writer. Settled in LONDON in 1834, where he taught music and was correspondent for a number of music journals including the *NEUE ZEITSCHRIFT FÜR MUSIK*. He became a British subject in 1854. Praeger claimed the credit (unjustifiably) for the Philharmonic Society's invitation to Wagner to conduct eight concerts in London from March to June 1855. On the recommendation of the London-based father of his DRESDEN comrade August RÖCKEL, Wagner trusted Praeger enough to be his house guest on arrival. In his autobiography, Wagner wrote that he found him "an unusually considerate fellow, yet a bit over-excited for the level of his education" (ML 527; ML/E 514). When Praeger visited him in ZURICH two years later, Wagner was put out to find he had become "extremely nervous and imagined himself persecuted by fate" (ML 565; ML/E 552). In a letter to George Hogarth, the secretary of the Philharmonic Society, dated 3 March 1855 (the day before Wagner's arrival), Praeger had confessed to "not being a Wagnerite, having never heard his operas yet" (British Library, unpublished). Overawed at the time, Praeger would subsequently exaggerate the degree of his acquaintance with Wagner, especially in his posthumously published *Wagner as I Knew Him* (1892). But however unreliable as to dates and facts, Praeger clearly got to know Wagner, and his book contains some convincing aperçus on Wagner's character. Praeger sought unsuccessfully to be recognized as a composer in his own right: there are pathetic appeals to the conductor William George Cusins and the directors of the Philharmonic Society to have his orchestral works considered in 1879 and 1881 (British Library, unpublished). Praeger died in 1891 shortly before Houston Stewart CHAMBERLAIN and William Ashton ELLIS publicized his relationship to Wagner.

DAVID CORMACK

Houston Stewart Chamberlain, *Richard Wagner an Ferdinand Praeger*, 2nd edn. (Leipzig, 1908).
W. A. Ellis, *The Life of Richard Wagner*, vol. 5 (London, 1906).
Ferdinand Praeger, *Wagner as I Knew Him* (London, 1892).

Preetorius, Emil (b. Mainz, 21 June 1883; d. Munich, 27 Jan. 1973), stage designer. Before being appointed head of design at BAYREUTH in 1932, Preetorius was widely known as an illustrator of books and a scenic designer in major

German opera houses. For the remainder of the 1930s, with Heinz TIETJEN as stage director, Preetorius provided Bayreuth with designs that mediated between the romantic realism of the nineteenth century and the severely modernist vision of Adolphe APPIA. The starkly delineated Valkyrie Rock, for example, was offset by a realistic pine tree. In his attempt to compromise between the realistic tradition of design in Wagnerian production and a realization of the symbolic, ahistorical aspects of MYTH, Preetorius arguably became the most influential designer in the decades prior to the spread of WIELAND WAGNER'S minimalism. He continued to work for several years after World War II, his last major project being the abstract sets for Herbert von KARAJAN's production of the *RING* in VIENNA (1958).   SIMON WILLIAMS

Preface to the Publication of the Poem of the Festival Stage Play "The Ring of the Nibelung."
See *Vorwort zur Herausgabe der Dichtung des Bühnenfestspiels "Der Ring des Nibelungen"*

Prelude. See OVERTURE / PRELUDE

Pringle, Carrie (Caroline Mary Isabelle) (b. Linz, 19 Mar. 1859; d. Brighton, 12 Nov. 1930), soprano. One of the six solo *Blumenmädchen* in the first performances of *PARSIFAL* at BAYREUTH in 1882, Carrie Pringle is notoriously the "English Flowermaiden" who so infatuated Wagner that an alleged dispute with COSIMA over her return to Bayreuth in 1883 precipitated his fatal heart attack. Reliable evidence in support of this theory has not been found, but as recently as 2007, Jonathan Harvey reworked it in his opera *Wagner Dream*. Carrie's "Englishness" can be traced to a great-grandfather in the Scots Brigade in Holland and a grandfather, captain in the (British) King's German Legion who saw service against Napoleon in the Peninsular Wars. She was born in Linz, the daughter of Basil John Charles Pringle (1825–86), a gentleman of inherited private means with some reputation as a "violin virtuoso." Carrie's mother was Isabelle *née* Latinovics de Borsod (1830–1906), of minor nobility from Hódság, Hungary (now Odžaji, in Serbia). After further domiciles in Gotha, Munich, and Milan, the family came to London (for the first time) following Carrie's failure to be re-cast in *Parsifal* in 1883. In England, Carrie made occasional appearances as a singer, but by 1896 was reduced to advertising (as a "Bayreuth artiste") for engagements in "Holiday Concerts on Piers &c." Her last reported engagement was in 1913. Where she was during World War I is unknown, but she eventually turns up in the Brighton voters' list in 1929, living near two of her younger sisters. She was clearly ill by this time. She died soon after of ovarian cancer, and was cremated privately at Brighton's Woodvale Cemetery.   DAVID CORMACK

David Cormack, "English Flowermaidens (and other transplants) at Bayreuth," *Musical Times* 150.1909 (2009): 95–102.
 "'Wir welken und sterben dahinnen': Carrie Pringle and the Solo Flowermaidens of 1882," *Musical Times* 146.1890 (2005): 16–31.
Stewart Spencer, "'Er starb, – ein Mensch wie alle': Wagner and Carrie Pringle," in *Festspielbuch 2004*, ed. P. Emmerich (Bayreuth, 2004): 72–85.

Production history
1. *Werktreue* versus *Regietheater*
2. Early productions
3. The first productions of *Der RING DES NIBELUNGEN* and *PARSIFAL*

4. From Wagner's death to National Socialism
5. After World War II
6. Recent experiments

1. *Werktreue* versus *Regietheater*

"Kinder! Macht neues! Neues! Abermals neues!" (Children! Do something *new!* something *new!* and again something *new!*) So noted Richard Wagner in a letter to Franz LISZT (8 September 1852) expressing his exasperation over a report of a composer reworking an earlier opera, rather than being inspired to create an entirely new work. This exclamation by Wagner himself lies at the heart of a longstanding and ongoing debate about the most appropriate way to stage Wagner's works.

Since the nineteenth century, new productions of Wagner's operas with stagings that departed from the original or from Wagner's indications in the published score have frequently stirred enormous controversy and outrage. Only later were many acknowledged as "classic" and accorded cult status. Since World War II scenic styles have evolved from a near pictorial realism to increasing abstraction or to transpositions in time and place: space age "science fiction," pop art, emphasis upon political, social, sexual commentaries or concepts otherwise rendered incomprehensible to all but a select few. Many of these same productions, however, have provided crucial impetus toward the evolution of theater architecture, production technology, and, above all, stage lighting (see also STAGE DESIGN).

The debate revolving around the concepts of *Werktreue* (true to the original) and *Regietheater* (director's theater, sometimes called "Eurotrash") applied to opera stagings and productions is one that has existed since the beginning of the twentieth century. Essentially, the question is whether directors should follow exactly (*Werktreue*) the detailed scenic descriptions and stage directions noted by Wagner in his printed scores, or whether the director remains truer to Wagner's call for innovation by following a new path (*Regietheater*).

Stage directors are only a part of an entire production, albeit providing much of the artistic vision. While a staging in its artistic entirety includes the dramaturgy, stage direction, scenic settings, costumes, and lighting design, one additional but crucial aspect governs the success of a production, and that is the theater itself. The size of the stages, their technical capabilities and, above all, the budget determine how much of a production can be realized. What may be an effective staging in one theater, however, may not be so in others due to artistic, cultural, technical, and budgetary restraints.

Productions of Wagner's operas require a commitment of huge physical resources and manpower. Table 1 displays the number of separate scenes required for each opera.

The number of settings may not seem demanding. Those numbers, however, are deceiving. Not only do stage productions demand enormous technical efforts combined with "Wagnerian" singers, each opera requires a large orchestra and chorus. The financial costs of the performers often offset possible savings from the production budget.

Table 1

Opera	Acts	Static scenes	Live changes or special effects within an act
RIENZI	5	6	0 (Act v, The collapse of the Capitol is a special effect)
Der FLIEGENDE HOLLÄNDER	3	3	0 (the arrival of the Dutchman's boat and its sinking is a special effect)
TANNHÄUSER	3	4	1 (Act I, the *Venusberg* to valley of the Wartburg)
LOHENGRIN	3	4	1 (Act III, the bridal pair's bedroom to the Scheldt riverbanks)
TRISTAN UND ISOLDE	3	3	0
Die MEISTERSINGER VON NÜRNBERG	3	4	1 (Act III, Sachs's *Schusterstube* to Pegnitz)
Das RHEINGOLD	3	3	0 (revealing the rainbow bridge and Valhalla after Donner's "forging" the rainbow bridge is a special effect)
Die WALKÜRE	3	3	0
SIEGFRIED	3	4	1 (Act III, Mountain pass to Brünnhilde's *Fels*)
GÖTTERDÄMMERUNG	3 (including Vorspiel)	3	1 (*Vorspiel* plays in front of Brünnhilde's *Fels*; Act III, Siegfried's funeral march from the banks of the Rhine to the *Gibichunghalle*)
PARSIFAL	3	5	3 (Act I, *Aue* to *Gralstempel*; Act II, *Zaubergarten* to *Wüste*; Act III, Gurnemanz's hut to *Gralstempel*)

Despite the logistical burdens and financial requirements, the statistics reflecting the "performability" of Wagner's operas remained consistent over the decades. The numbers for the entire 1898–9 season reveal 7,939 presentations of 205 operas in more than 350 public and private German-speaking theaters in Germany, Switzerland, and the Austrian Empire. Wagner's eleven operas – not including *Parsifal* – received almost 1,300 performances (Table 2). *Tannhäuser* was the most popular, closely followed by *Lohengrin*.

Table 2

Title	Performances (1,293)
Tannhäuser	277
Lohengrin	273
Der fliegende Holländer	177
Die Walküre	120
Die Meistersinger von Nürnberg	110
Das Rheingold	84
Siegfried	73
Götterdämmerung	71
Rienzi	60
Tristan und Isolde	44
Die Feen	4

(*Parsifal* was not included in the statistics, as the opera remained under copyright protection and was not performed outside of Bayreuth until 1914.) Data: Held

During the 2003–8 seasons in seventy public theaters solely in Germany, the available statistics reveal that *Der fliegende Holländer* and *Tannhäuser* racked up 496 and 392 performances respectively in a listing of the thirty most popular operas. As a point of comparison during the same time span, *Die Zauberflöte* totaled 2,729 performances (data: Jacobshagen). Within a century following the premiere of *Lohengrin* at the Teatro Comunale Bologna in 1871, there were over 1,200 performances of Wagner works in Italy (data: Jung).

Three historical factors have played crucial roles in the evolution of Wagnerian opera production: the invention of electric light, the application of Adolphe APPIA's theories of stage and lighting design, and the consequences of WIELAND WAGNER's stagings starting in the 1950s. With the moral legitimacy as a direct descendant of the composer, and as co-director with his brother WOLFGANG of the Wagner Festival in BAYREUTH, Wieland paved the way for other stage directors to experiment with new, different, and sometimes radical, if not outrageous, productions.

A detailed production history for an encyclopedia is not possible; for further investigation, the best resources are listed in the bibliographical references. The website "Werkstatt Wagner" offers a multitude of images of past and current productions (www.richard-wagner-werkstatt.com/inszenierungen). Many stagings post 1982 are available on DVD with an enormous amount of snippets at the YouTube website (see also Appendix 10: Stage productions).

2. Early productions

(For more information on the world premiere of Wagner's operas, see the entry under the work's title.) The performances of Wagner's early operas began inauspiciously. His first stage composition, *Die FEEN* (completed 1834) never received a production during the composer's lifetime. *Das LIEBESVERBOT*, Wagner's second opera, premiered (albeit only with fragments) at the MAGDEBURG Stadttheater on 29 March 1836, with a second performance on 6 April; the result was a flop. The opera was not revived until well after Wagner's death.

Success came to Wagner for the first time at the DRESDEN Hoftheater on 20 October 1842 with the premiere of *RIENZI*. A grandiose work in five acts filled with trappings of French GRAND OPERA, the production demanded the utmost of the Hoftheater's stage resources as well as the patience of the audience with performances lasting almost five hours. Several presentations found the opera split into two evenings as *Rienzis Größe* and *Rienzis Fall*. Despite the difficult musical and scenic requirements (and Wagner's later disavowals of the opera, calling it *Schreihals*, a "throat shrieker"), by 1903 *Rienzi* had received over 200 performances in Dresden.

Der FLIEGENDE HOLLÄNDER anchored in Dresden on 2 January 1843, but remained in port for only three performances, not returning until 2 March 1862. On 5 June 1843, Louis SPOHR, the noted composer and conductor at the Kassel Hoftheater, produced *Holländer*, the first staging of Wagner's operas outside of Dresden. Berlin followed on 7 January 1844, with the composer conducting the first two performances. Like Dresden, the opera did not succeed, and disappeared from the repertory until December 1868.

Despite the arrival of several important pieces of scenery to the Dresden Hoftheater from Paris after the premiere of *TANNHÄUSER* on 19 October 1845, the opera was a success and recorded more than 500 performances by 1913. Due to his participation in the political upheavals in May 1849, Wagner fled to exile in Switzerland and the authorities cancelled all further performances of his operas along with the planned premiere of *LOHENGRIN*

In the summer of 1850, Franz Liszt began preparations for the premiere of *Lohengrin* at the Weimar Hoftheater. While Wagner was unable to supervise personally the rehearsals and the scenic preparations, in a letter to Liszt dated 2 July 1850, he enclosed stage sketches for each scene. Despite the limited stage space of the Weimar Hoftheater and an orchestra of forty-five players, *Lohengrin* was a success. The opera was slow to travel outside of Weimar due, in part, to Wagner's past political activities. Three years elapsed before another theater staged the opera, this time at the Hoftheater in Wiesbaden (2 July 1853); within three years, more than fifteen theaters produced *Lohengrin*. In 1853 BREITKOPF & HÄRTEL published Wagner's detailed staging instructions as part of a scenario that became the basis for future stagings by other theaters.

The VIENNA Court Opera staged its first performance of *Lohengrin* on 19 August 1858 to the designs of Theodor Jachimovicz, Carlo Brioschi, and Moritz Lehmann with more than 680 performances in different productions through 1936. On 23 January 1859, the Berlin Court Theater produced the opera to the designs of Carl Gropius. ALBERT WAGNER (brother of the composer) staged the production, and his daughter Johanna Jachmann Wagner sang ORTRUD. *Lohengrin* received over 745 performances in Berlin until 1935.

Between 1853 and 1855, over forty theaters throughout Europe produced *Tannhäuser*. Despite these numbers, reports of substandard performances reached Wagner. Consequently, in August 1852 Wagner published an important essay, *Über die Aufführung des "Tannhäusers": Eine Mitteilung an die Dirigenten und Darsteller dieser Oper*, filled with precise staging and musical instructions as well as observations on the characters and chorus (see also WAGNER AS STAGE DIRECTOR).

During his Swiss exile, Wagner staged and conducted *Holländer* at Zurich's Aktientheater on 25 April 1852. Even with the best efforts of the theater, the performances left Wagner dissatisfied and prompted him to write *Bemerkungen zur Aufführung der Oper: "Der fliegende Holländer."* The tract (along with that of *Tannhäuser*), with its numerous and exacting observations on the dramaturgy, acting, and staging, is still worth reading today.

The most significant productions of the decade were the stagings of *Tannhäuser* and *Lohengrin* at the Nationaltheater in MUNICH with the settings designed by Angelo II Quaglio and Heinrich Döll. *Tannhäuser* premiered there on 12 August 1855 with forty-four subsequent performances. On 28 February 1858, *Lohengrin* premiered with the production by the same design team. Unbeknownst to Wagner, his operas in Munich provided the catalyst for his future: on 2 January 1861, the future King LUDWIG II attended a performance of *Lohengrin*, his first opera ever and his life-long favorite.

The decade of the 1860s proved both fraught and rewarding for Wagner. In 1860, the Paris Opéra beckoned with the offer of a premiere for *Tannhäuser* with all the trappings of French grand opera for elaborate scenery and costumes. After more than 160 difficult rehearsals with diffident performers, an incompetent conductor, and a violent audience response to Wagner's inclusion of ballet music in the first act instead of its usual place in the third act, the entire enterprise was doomed (see also TANNHÄUSER, PARIS SCANDAL OF 1861). After its tumultuous premiere on 13 March 1861 and two subsequent performances, Wagner withdrew the opera. *Tannhäuser* did not to return to the Opéra until 1895; by the end of the century, the opera had received 100 performances.

Upon Ludwig II's accession to the throne of the kingdom of Bavaria in 1864, Wagnerian operatic production reached a turning point. Ludwig's rescue of Wagner that same year set the path for standard scenic representations for virtually all theaters until the end of the nineteenth century. The key productions – with the composer's direct and indirect participation – included the first Munich production of *Der fliegende Holländer* (4 December 1864), the world premiere of TRISTAN UND ISOLDE (10 June 1865) followed by revivals with new scenery for *Lohengrin* (16 June 1867) and *Tannhäuser* (1 August 1867). Wagner personally staged the first performance of *Die MEISTERSINGER VON NÜRNBERG* (26 June 1868). The veteran scenic artists Angelo II Quaglio and Heinrich Döll provided each opera with new stage designs. Against Wagner's wishes, Ludwig commanded the first productions of *Das RHEINGOLD* (22 September 1869) and *Die WALKÜRE* (26 June 1870).

3. The first productions of *Der RING DES NIBELUNGEN* and *PARSIFAL*

On 13 August 1876, the first complete cycle of *Der Ring des Nibelungen* at the Festspielhaus opened the Wagner Festival in Bayreuth. The Viennese landscape artist Josef HOFFMANN created the designs for the settings, but after a falling out with Wagner he departed from the Festival. Max and Gotthold BRÜCKNER completed the details of transferring the designs into reality and painted the scenery, sealing a collaboration with the Wagner Festival that lasted up to 1915.

At first, Wagner did not release the performance rights for the *Ring* to other theaters until he realized that another cycle would not soon occur in Bayreuth. Angelo NEUMANN obtained Wagner's permission to stage the *Ring* in Leipzig, commencing with *Das Rheingold* (28 April 1878) and ending with *Götterdämmerung* on 22 September that same year. The first complete cycle in seven days, however, occurred at the Hoftheater in Munich (17–23 November 1878) with new settings by Angelo II Quaglio, Heinrich Döll, and Christian Jank.

Neumann's greatest contribution to Wagnerian production history was two-fold: first, his staging of the *Ring* for the first time in Berlin in 1881 with four cycles at the Viktoria Theater (the Hoftheater did not stage the complete cycle until 1888); Wagner himself observed the rehearsals prior to the premiere on 5 May. The second, and even more significant contribution, was a tour of the *Ring* from September 1882 to June 1883. After securing the rights from Wagner, Neumann purchased the original 1876 production as well. The *Richard-Wagner-Theater*, a troupe of over 135 singers, stagehands, and musicians with five railroad freight cars filled with scenery, costumes, and musical instruments traveled to over twenty-five cities throughout Europe, which included the first Italian performances of the *Ring* in Venice. The impact of the tour cannot be underestimated. The public, theater *Intendants*, stage directors, and scene designers were given a unique opportunity to attend a *Ring* cycle for the first time. Anton SEIDL, a veteran of the Neumann traveling ensemble, conducted the first North American *Ring* cycle at the Metropolitan Opera (3–11 March 1889).

Wagner's final opera, *Parsifal* (26 July 1882), was composed and scenically envisioned expressly for the Festspielhaus. Although Paul von JOUKOWSKY produced several designs, Gotthold and Max Brückner created the scenic effect of the *Verwandlungsszene* (transformation scene) from the forest into the Hall of the Grail in Act 1. This effect, visible to the audience and coordinated with the music, was achieved through the means of rolling extended canvas drops from one side of the stage to the other.

4. From Wagner's death to National Socialism

Naturalistic staging styles continued, receiving their imprimatur at the Bayreuth Festival with COSIMA WAGNER's Bayreuth productions of *Tristan und Isolde* (25 July 1886), *Die Meistersinger von Nürnberg* (23 July 1888), *Tannhäuser* (22 July 1891), and *Lohengrin* (20 July 1894). Her greatest work followed two years later with the new production of *Der Ring des Nibelungen* (premiere cycle, 19–22 July 1896). Gotthold and Max Brückner created the settings and incorporated some elements of the Munich productions into their own designs, which were published and served as models for other theaters. Before the 1886 summer season, electric lighting was installed in the Festspielhaus. Despite the thousands of lamps, technology for stage illumination remained primitive, the artistic possibilities unimagined.

During the decade of 1890, Adolphe Appia published an essay and a book that would profoundly change the visual aspects of Wagnerian staging: *La Mise en scène du drame wagnérien* (Paris, 1895) and his major work, *Die Musik und die Inszenierung* (Munich, 1899). His ideas of using light as an artistic device at first found support from Gustav MAHLER and his designer Alfred ROLLER at the Vienna Hofoper; its full effect, however, was not truly felt until the 1951 reopening of the Bayreuth Festival.

On the occasion of the twentieth anniversary of the death of Wagner, Gustav Mahler staged and conducted *Tristan und Isolde* to the iconoclastic designs of Alfred Roller, which premiered on 21 February 1903 at the Vienna Court Opera. Roller's production was the first to use stage lighting as an integral part of the overall artistic concept. Skillful application of light greatly assisted in the creation of the dramatic atmosphere suggested by the music, particularly the nighttime scene of Act II with the evening stars and its gradual transition to the grey dawn.

The year 1914 marked a milestone in Wagner opera production: the expiration of the copyright protection for *Parsifal* at midnight, 31 December 1913, when Barcelona's Gran Teatre del Liceu staged *Parsifal* in Italian; the following evening, nine theaters simultaneously performed the opera. The Berlin Hoftheater followed on 5 January. At the end of June 1914, more than twenty opera houses had staged their first productions of *Parsifal*. Earlier, the Metropolitan Opera contravened the copyright with its own production on 24 December 1903 with a faithful reproduction of the Bayreuth staging, including the mechanical *Verwandlungseffekt*.

At Arturo TOSCANINI's invitation, Appia revised the original designs published in his *Die Musik und die Inszenierung*, for a staging of *Tristan und Isolde* on 20 December 1923 at the Teatro alla Scala, Milan. Despite the lack of comprehension by the production staff and the public, Appia saw his cherished designs realized for the first time and professed satisfaction.

On 21 November 1924, the Basel Stadttheater produced *Das Rheingold* set to Appia's designs and staged by Oskar Wäterlin, followed by *Die Walküre* on 1 February 1925. At first, the production seemed successful, but at later performances of *Die Walküre* the traditionalists organized demonstrations and press campaigns against Appia's designs. Such was the vehemence that the Stadttheater cancelled the planned stagings of *Siegfried* and *Götterdämmerung* and removed *Rheingold* and *Die Walküre* from the repertory.

One of the most significant productions of *Der fliegende Holländer* occurred during the Weimar Republic on 17 April 1928 at the KROLL OPER. Struck out were all references to the "rocky" seashore and folkloric elements including elaborate sails, ropes, and rigging of old, resulting in minimal stage settings. The women wore pullover sweaters, and their spinning wheels were banished from the scene. Such a staging created an outpouring of controversy and rage with calls from the public for government intervention.

The ascent of the National Socialists in Germany ended AVANT-GARDE stagings. Naturalistic productions remained *de rigueur*, particularly for *Die Meistersinger von Nürnberg*. In 1935, the Berlin Städtische Oper and the Staatsoper each staged the opera, with emphasis upon "das Volk" in the final scene with faithful reproductions of medieval Nuremberg. The army supplemented the regular crowd of choristers and supernumeraries, packing the stage with hundreds of people for the final scene with the Meistersingers at the Pegnitz meadow.

5. After World War II

In 1951, two significant events played a fundamental role in the history of Wagnerian opera production: the postwar reopening of the Richard Wagner Festival on 30 July with Wieland Wagner's stagings of *Parsifal* and the *Ring* (31 July–4 August). Equally influential was the first effective application of Appia's theories, particularly the artistic use of light. Wieland's productions stripped the stage of all but essential scenery, placing emphasis upon lighting and singers gifted with thespian talents. Additionally, the principles of "Werkstatt Bayreuth" came into being, allowing stage directors over a period of four to five summers to modify and improve productions. Applying the ideals of "Werkstatt Bayreuth" in July 1952, Wieland removed the remaining naturalistic elements from the *Ring* production (24–29 July), leaving only a bare, oval stage; lighting and projections became dominant.

The issues of *Werktreue* versus *Regietheater* came to the fore with Wieland's 1956 staging of *Die Meistersinger von Nürnberg* (24 July). Not a single representation of old NUREMBERG was present throughout the opera, particularly the street scene of Act II; only a raked kidney-shaped stage painted with cobblestones. A huge linden bough floated above the stage, and two benches on both sides of the raked stage represented the dwellings of SACHS and Pogner. The Festival meadow was an arena with the seated chorus on risers dressed in all white, segregated by sex. Reactions from the public were extraordinarily vociferous. Wieland took advantage of the *Werkstatt Bayreuth* concept to refine the production the following year and included minimal, but recognizable references to old Nuremberg.

Such upheavals occurred again on 23 July 1959 with Wieland Wagner's iconoclastic production of *Der fliegende Holländer* with the first act set completely on Daland's ship, with the quarterdeck facing the audience. The skeletal prow and hull of the Dutchman's vessel flew up from behind the quarterdeck. No folkloric elements were visible, and it was clear that life among the villagers was impoverished and exceedingly difficult.

The decade of the 1970s provided unusual productions that changed and challenged Wagnerian staging not only visually, but textually. On 29 January 1970, Sadler's Wells Theatre (precursor to the English National Opera, London) began producing its own *Ring*. This included commissioning Andrew Porter's superb singing English translation of Wagner's libretto. Thus, the *Ring* became far more accessible to the English-speaking public, particularly in the United States. Even small cities such as Flagstaff, Arizona staged the *Ring* (20–26 June 1996) with Porter's translation. In 1974, the Seattle Opera began a tradition of staging the *Ring* with Porter's translation that continues to this day.

Among the significant non-*Ring* stagings was Götz Friedrich's *Tannhäuser* for the 1972 Bayreuth Festival (21 July). The dramaturgy focused on the "insider-outsider" dichotomy but with elements of staging that brought forth uncomfortable dialectics of then East and West German societies. For the 1974 Salzburg Easter Festival, Herbert von Karajan and his longtime collaborator

Günther Schneider-Siemssen created a detailed and naturalistic Nuremberg – particularly the Act II street scene – utilizing the vast stage of the Grosses Festspielhaus. At the San Francisco Opera in 1974, Jean-Pierre Ponnelle staged *Der fliegende Holländer* as a dream of the Steuermann that played entirely on the quarterdeck of the ship. Harry Kupfer, in 1975 also at the Bayreuth Festival, produced the opera that was a reflection of Senta's mind, grasping the Dutchman's portrait throughout the opera, with houses spinning and lights flashing during the Ghost Chorus. In 1976, Ulrich Melchinger at the Staats-oper Kassel staged *Holländer* as a satanic black mass. On 22 December 1977, the Metropolitan Opera presented *Tannhäuser* staged by Otto Schenk. Günther Schneider-Siemssen's designs provided a contrast to abstract productions by using ultra-realistic settings complete with lavish medieval costumes.

Beginning in 1973, Joachim Herz presented a *Ring* at the Leipzig Stadttheater that emphasized the human drama influenced by the dialectics of societal differences such as those revealed by George Bernard SHAW's *The Perfect Wagnerite*. The intensity of the human drama was displayed during SIEGFRIED's funeral march, as WOTAN wanders alone in his vast halls of Valhalla mourning the death of Siegfried and his dreams of the future. Many of Herz's ideas remained mostly unknown to the West due to the isolation of Leipzig in former East Germany, but presaged those of Patrice CHÉREAU's centennial staging of the *Ring* in Bayreuth (1976). He focused on the human drama amidst the social and economic issues of the industrial revolution during Wagner's lifetime. At first, the production created an uproar, with fistfights and bomb threats, but by the end of its cycle in 1981, the staging was accorded cult status and acknowledged as one of the finest ever.

Among the most significant productions of the 1980s was the Metropolitan Opera's staging of the *Ring* by Otto Schenk to the designs of Günther Schneider-Siemssen, which was begun in 1986 and completed in three years. Schenk focused on naturalistic settings, a contrast to virtually all other current productions. It became a favorite with the public; Wagner enthusiasts from all over the world travelled to the Met in search of *Werktreue*, a staging that seemed to follow Wagner's dictates.

Arguments pro and contra *Werktreue* continued in the 1990s with the Zurich Opera presenting Robert Wilson's exacting choreography of *Lohengrin* where a single bird's wing represented the swan. At the end of the decade, Peter Konwitschny and the Bayerische Staatsoper presented *Tristan und Isolde* with the first act placed on the deck of a cruise ship. The second act was a cartoon-like deep red forest with old-fashioned ceiling lights and exposed bulbs representing the nighttime stars. In the final scene, coffins for the lovers were placed on biers at the center of the stage; Tristan was resurrected in the final moments of the opera. King Marke and Brangäne stood as silent mourners while Tristan and Isolde walked off into the distant darkness of the stage during the last moments of the *Liebestod*. The prestigious German periodical *Opernwelt* named this production as "best of the year."

6. Recent experiments

A summer festival in the small Austrian provincial town of Wels deserves notice for its productions providing a respite for many from *Regietheater*.

Founded in 1995, the Richard Wagner Festival offers *Werktreu* stagings with flying ships complete with sails and rigging, clearly delineated forests of trees, and temples.

A stark contrast appeared at the Stuttgart Staatstheater, which successfully undertook the courageous experiment of presenting the *Ring* (1999–2000) with one stage director for each opera: Joachim Schlömer (*Rheingold*), Christoph Nel (*Walküre*), Jossi Wieler (*Siegfried*), and Peter Konwitschny (*Götterdämmerung*).

On 22 September 2002 in Würzburg, KATHARINA WAGNER, the newest generation of Wagner's descendants, debuted as a stage director of *Der fliegende Holländer*; among notable moments was the second act set in an office with whirring computers from the 1970s.

Peter Konwitschny continued his iconoclastic path on 3 November 2002 at the Hamburgische Staatsoper with a production of *Die Meistersinger*. All male soloists, except WALTHER VON STOLZING, were garbed in silk jackets and velvet berets favored by Wagner, resulting in startling resemblances to the composer. An enormous controversy arose over the staging, with its interruption during Sachs's final peroration of the "foreign" influence upon what is "German and genuine." The music stopped and a lively debate ensued between the Masters, which continued until the conductor demanded the music should resume.

During the 2007–9 seasons at the Palau de les Arts Reina Sofia in Valencia, Spain the performance group "La Fura dels Baus" with the co-director Carlos Padrissa staged an extraordinary *Ring*. A stunning mixture of multimedia projections, acrobats, cranes for Wotan and the Valkyries, along with LOGE scooting about the stage on a Segway are only a few of the many ideas forming the staging.

The decade beginning with 2010 has been less auspicious for Wagnerian production. Warsaw's Teatr Wielki produced *Der fliegende Holländer* on 16 March 2010 that included a shallow water tank covering the entire stage floor. Women in Act II frolicked like fish, with Senta attired in a white wedding gown, carrying a rifle, and splashing through the settings. At the Teatro alla Scala one day later, La Fura dels Baus staged *Tannhäuser* and placed the opera vaguely somewhere in India with a giant hand dominating the Hindi settings and multiple scenic projections; ELISABETH was dressed in a chic sari. On 27 July at the Bayreuth Festival, Hans Neuenfels staged *Lohengrin* with the chorus costumed as laboratory rats.   EVAN BAKER

Evan Baker, *From the Score to the Stage: An Illustrated History of Continental Opera Production and Staging* (University of Chicago Press, 2013).

"Richard Wagner and his search for the ideal theatrical space," in *Opera in Context: Essays on Historical Staging from the Late Renaissance to the Time of Puccini*, ed. Mark A. Radice (Portland, OR: Amadeus, 1998): 241–78.

"'Wir welken und sterben dahinnen': Carrie Pringle and the Solo Flowermaidens of 1882," *Musical Times* 146.1890 (2005): 16–31.

Oswald Georg Bauer, *Richard Wagner: The Stage Designs and Productions from the Premières to the Present* (New York: Rizzoli, 1983).

Patrick Carnegy, *Wagner and the Art of the Theatre* (see bibliography).

Berthold Held, "Was leistet das gegenwärtige deutsche Theater?," in *Bühne und Welt* II (1899–1900): 1:144–56; here 150.

Arnold Jacobshagen, "Musiktheater," in *Deutsches Musikinformationszentrum* (2009): 1–13 (www.miz.org/static_de/themenportale/einfuehrungstexte_pdf/03_KonzerteMusiktheater/jacobshagen.pdf, accessed 31 August 2012).

Ute Jung, *Die Rezeption der Kunst Richard Wagners in Italien* (Regensburg: Bosse, 1973).
Ditta and Michael Petzet, *Die Richard Wagner-Bühne König Ludwigs II.* (Munich: Prestel, 1970).

Program notes. In programming, promoting, and conducting ORCHESTRAL CONCERTS of his own music and selected classics at various times in his career, Wagner became one of the first exponents of the modern "program note." For him, however, the genre had an exclusively hermeneutic function; his notes contain none of the factual data on genesis, premiere, or other biographical matters we expect today. The earliest and most elaborate of his notes was a gloss on BEETHOVEN's Ninth Symphony for a performance in one of the annual "Palm Sunday" concerts in DRESDEN (5 April 1846). Here, in an effort to provide a "text" for the first three movements to supplement the role of SCHILLER's "ode" in the finale, Wagner excerpts passages from GOETHE's *Faust.* These, and Schiller's *An die Freude,* are interspersed with descriptive accounts linking the texts with the music of each movement. (Wagner's explanation of the introductory passage to the choral finale includes the first significant use of the term ABSOLUTE MUSIC.) Beethoven was in fact the only composer, other than himself, to be accorded this treatment. Wagner contributed no such notes, for example, to the concerts he conducted with the London Philharmonic Society in 1855, whose programs were too varied and too many for such input on his part, and not under his direct control. For concerts given during his earlier years in ZURICH, he provided substantial programmatic exegeses of Beethoven's *Eroica* Symphony (1851) and *Coriolan* Overture (1852), as well as his own overtures to *TANNHÄUSER* (1852), *Der FLIEGENDE HOLLÄNDER* (1853), the Act I Prelude to *LOHENGRIN* (1853), and the introduction to Act III of *Tannhäuser* ("Tannhäuser's Rome Journey"). The Zurich concerts of May 1853 also included choral-orchestral excerpts such as the "Entry of the Guests at the Wartburg" from *Tannhäuser,* and Elsa's procession to the Münster with double men's chorus (Act II) and the Act III Prelude and Bridal Chorus from *Lohengrin.* For these, as for some "preview" excerpts from the *RING* dramas presented in Vienna (1875) and privately for LUDWIG II in 1869, Wagner's objective was mainly to describe the dramatic context of the pieces, and to provide texts or incipits for the vocal portions. The most significant later note is that written for the performance of the *TRISTAN* Prelude in Wagner's Parisian concerts of 1860 (replaced by a shorter note for the actual program). He also provided short evocations of the orchestral preludes to *Die MEISTERSINGER* and *PARSIFAL* for private performances under the auspices of Prince Konstantin of Hohenzollern-Hechingen and King LUDWIG II, respectively, on 2 December 1863 and 12 November 1880.　　　　　　　　　　　THOMAS S. GREY

Thomas S. Grey, trans., "The Complete Program Notes of Richard Wagner," *Richard Wagner and his World,* ed. Thomas S. Grey (see bibliography): 479–522.
Nicholas Vazsonyi, *Richard Wagner: Self-Promotion and the Making of a Brand* (see bibliography): esp. chapter 2.

Projects. Wagner's "projects" are defined here as either (1) works for which plans are mentioned by Wagner, but for which no sketches or drafts survive; or (2) sketches that cannot be identified as part of a particular "work." In later years, Wagner had ideas for stage works based on the lives of various historical figures, including Alexander the Great, Bernhard von Weimar, Frederick the Great, Hans SACHS ("second marriage"), and Andreas Hofer. However, entries from COSIMA WAGNER'S DIARIES suggest that Wagner was far from certain about whether these works should be set to music (CWD 18 March 1870; 30 October 1870). In late 1839 Wagner had the idea of writing a "great Faust symphony," but *Eine FAUST-OVERTÜRE* in D minor (WWV 59) – originally conceived as the first movement – was all that became of the project. Single sketches for "symphonies" (WWV 78) dating 1846–7 may have been intended as incidental music, while Wagner's later plans for symphonies (WWV 107) represent a more serious and ongoing preoccupation (Deathridge, "Unfinished Symphonies").

A further late orchestral project consisted of a series of "overtures" (WWV 107) on various literary subjects, including *Lohengrin's Voyage*, *Tristan the Hero*, *Epilogue to Romeo and Juliet*, *Brünnhilde*, and *Wieland der Schmied* – planned between January 1874 and February 1875 in contract with SCHOTT publishers. The overture *Romeo und Julie*, in particular, developed out of a project on the same subject (WWV 98) that Wagner had started in April–May 1868. Even after he had abandoned the overtures, Wagner continued to work on the WWV 98 project, which he later planned as a funeral dirge for the fallen German soldiers in the FRANCO-PRUSSIAN WAR. The nonexistent "Starnberg Quartet" mentioned in Cosima's diaries is not a myth of Wagner's making, but rather the product of scholars' subsequent misunderstandings. Intended by Wagner as a dedication piece to Cosima, the project was misidentified by Ernest NEWMAN as a putative early version of the *SIEGFRIED IDYLL*, and Gerald Abraham even undertook a "reconstruction" of the quartet, published by Oxford University Press in 1947.   JEREMY COLEMAN

Gerald Abraham, "Wagner's String Quartet: An Essay in Musical Speculation," *The Musical Times* 86 (1945): 233–4.

John Deathridge, "Cataloguing Wagner," *The Musical Times* 124.1680 (1983): 92–6.

"Unfinished Symphonies," *Wagner Beyond Good and Evil* (see bibliography): 189–205.

Richard Wagner, *Quartet Movement*, reconstructed by Gerald Abraham (London: Oxford University Press, 1947).

Prose works, editions of. Wagner contemplated a collected edition of his essays as early as 1844. The idea of bringing together everything he had written during his PARIS years (1839–42) into a single volume seemed like a good idea at the time. But it was soon outpaced by the sheer copiousness of his literary output, which demanded a multi-volume edition. This idea experienced several stops and starts until a young publisher, Ernst Wilhelm FRITZSCH, offered Wagner the chance of editing his libretti and writings in several volumes. This was called a "collected" (*Gesammelte*) rather than a "complete" (*Sämtliche*) edition for two cogent reasons: first, the difficulty of obtaining manuscripts of unpublished writings or of those only published in French; second, the desirability of presenting a specific NATIONALIST image of the author (and editor) that did not always correspond with what he had published in the past. The second was especially true of his early enthusiasms for Italian and French opera, and in particular for Giacomo MEYERBEER, who in the meantime had become a *bête noire* and central target of his ANTI-SEMITIC views.

The *Gesammelte Schriften und Dichtungen* edited by Wagner himself appeared between 1871 and 1873 in nine volumes with new introductions to the first six. A tenth was added posthumously in 1883 – edited probably by Wagner's chief propaganda guru, Hans von WOLZOGEN, "according to the wishes of the Master" – when interest in Wagner's prose works began to increase. The first nine volumes (print run 2,000) had sold surprisingly slowly. But now after Wagner's death it was time to start publishing a new collection "gathered from unpublished papers" (edited by Wolzogen, 1885) and to reprint the ten-volume Fritzsch edition a further three times (2nd edn. 1887–8; 3rd edn. 1897–8; 4th edn. 1907) before adding two further volumes to its fifth edition (1912) with notes by Richard Sternfeld and a new title: *Sämtliche Schriften und Dichtungen*. A sixth edition called the "Volks-Ausgabe" (People's Edition) appeared shortly after (1912–14) under the same title with the addition of another four volumes that included the text of Wagner's autobiography MEIN LEBEN (My Life, 1865–81) and a richly stocked index.

The "Volks-Ausgabe" formed the basis of all succeeding multi-volume editions. These range from Julius Kapp's fourteen-volume collection *Richard Wagners Gesammelte Schriften* (1914) to the ten-volume "centennial edition" (1983) edited by Dieter Borchmeyer – a controversial publication that pointedly omitted the anti-Semitic writings. Ironically, Borchmeyer's edition was a return to the view behind the collection edited by Wagner in the 1870s that the author should be presented in the way the author (or editor) thinks the current age should see him with contrary evidence discreetly suppressed. Anti-Semitism is notably present in the one, but just as notably absent in the other.

Objective critical editions of the prose writings are painfully rare. Notable exceptions include the edition of, and detailed commentary on, OPER UND DRAMA by Klaus Kropfinger (1984) and Jens Malte Fischer's edition of *Das JUDENTUM IN DER MUSIK* (2000) with a wealth of documentation about the essay's reception before and after Wagner's death.   JOHN DEATHRIDGE

See also WAGNER AS ESSAYIST

Publicity and self-promotion. Although several composers of the early and mid-nineteenth century engaged in and were adept at making themselves and their works known, Richard Wagner was arguably the first to make self-promotion a cornerstone of his artistic enterprise. In this, he was consistent from about the 1840s until his death in 1883. He availed himself of several means, none of which was wholly original but which, when combined, created an impact on the public sphere that has endured in ways that may never have been equaled by any celebrity in history.

Wagner's contemporaries and immediate predecessors who were most talented at managing their own publicity included virtuoso-composers such as Niccolò Paganini and Franz LISZT, as well as Giacomo MEYERBEER and Hector BERLIOZ. It is no small irony that Wagner was highly critical of all these men while often engaging in tactics they had mastered. Indeed, one of the challenges in the nineteenth century was to negotiate the fine line between seeking publicity while still being taken seriously as an artist.

Even a cursory look at Wagner's correspondence reveals that he never stopped talking about himself and his projects, and contemporary eyewitness accounts corroborate this impression of the composer. But Wagner also formalized the activity by several means. First, he published a series of autobiographies, starting in 1842/3 with the AUTOBIOGRAPHISCHE SKIZZE (Autobiographical Sketch), then ten years later, *Eine* MITTEILUNG AN MEINE FREUNDE (A Communication to My Friends, 1851), then ZUKUNFTSMUSIK (Music of the Future, 1860) and finally MEIN LEBEN (My Life, 1865–81). All of these works serve to present a finely crafted image of Wagner, his life story, and the compositional history of his stage works. So powerful and evocative is the narrative that its most significant moments have become a permanent feature of Wagner lore and continue to be repeated to this day. These include the rough sea voyage to England in 1839 that would become the inspiration of *Der* FLIEGENDE HOLLÄNDER's stormy overture, as well as the semi-feverish half-sleep Wagner experienced in LA SPEZIA (1853) during which the opening sounds of *Das* RHEINGOLD apparently came to him. Though such stories contain embellishment if not outright invention, they live on despite scholarly intervention and correction. Wagner's autobiographies also present an image of the composer in turns as rebel, outcast, victim, fugitive, misunderstood and underappreciated genius, and true German.

Beyond the autobiographies, Wagner wrote a series of theoretical essays, the most important of which were drafted during a lull in his compositional output directly following his escape after the DRESDEN UPRISING of 1849 and his arrival in ZURICH. These essays, which include *Das* KUNSTWERK DER ZUKUNFT (The Artwork of the Future, 1849/50) and the book-length OPER UND DRAMA (Opera and Drama, 1851), set out the aesthetic path he intends to follow for his mature works. Though they conform in many ways to the existing genre of aesthetic manifesto, their size, scope, and detailed argumentation serve to present Wagner and his work as a form of unique brand that breaks with everything hitherto known in the operatic world. As a result of these, a new vocabulary specifically applicable to Wagner's operas came into being, including terms like LEITMOTIV, MUSIC DRAMA, GESAMTKUNSTWERK (total work of art), *Festspiel* (festival play), ENDLESS MELODY, and so on.

Later on in his life, Wagner supplemented his aesthetics with a series of essays that ventured into areas of history, politics, and ideology. These include the so-called REGENERATION essays that make up *Religion und Kunst* (Religion and Art), which served as a sort of founding document for the members of the BAYREUTH CIRCLE who went on to advocate an increasingly right-wing, nationalistic, and ANTI-SEMITIC ideology with Wagner as its spiritual guide. Herein lie the seeds for the appropriation of Wagner as an icon of the Nazi movement and his tarnished image and reputation since World War II.

Beyond his writings, Wagner engaged in actual publicity campaigns. A famous example would be his effort to ensure the success of his performance of BEETHOVEN's Ninth Symphony at the 5 April 1846 Palm Sunday concert in DRESDEN. Since many thought the piece was unperformable, there was considerable anxiety and dismay which Wagner countered by placing a series of four anonymous announcements (on 24 and 31 March, and 2 and 4 April) in the personals section of the local newspaper (*Dresdener Anzeiger*), each seemingly written by a different person, and each designed to encourage attendance at the concert or inform the public about the piece. The concert was sold out, and such a success that Beethoven's Ninth became a staple at future Palm Sunday concerts. The term "Wagnerianer" also dates from this period, used for the first time, though pejoratively, in an article that appeared in the *Signale für die musikalische Welt*.

Thirty years later, there was a similar effort to announce and publicize the first Bayreuth festival, including several essays and announcements by Wagner himself, advertisements placed by local WAGNER SOCIETIES, as well as bi-weekly press releases, written by *Bayreuther Tageblatt* editor J. Zimmermann and Wagner's assistant Heinrich PORGES, distributed between May and August 1876 all over Germany under the heading "Bayreuther autographische Korrespondenz."

Wagner had already received significant assistance in publicizing his projects earlier in his career. This included a series of articles by Wagner's Dresden friend, Theodor UHLIG, that appeared over a three-year period between 1849 and 1852 in the *NEUE ZEITSCHRIFT FÜR MUSIK*, whose editor, Franz BRENDEL, had decided to make Wagner the centerpiece of the journal's aesthetic agenda. After his move to Weimer, Franz Liszt also became a tireless supporter of Wagner, not only premiering *LOHENGRIN*, but writing significant essays about it and other works which were published all over Europe in several languages.

The last element in Wagner's effort to publicize his works were ORCHESTRAL CONCERTS he gave in major European cities (e.g., LONDON, PARIS, VIENNA, ST. PETERSBURG) that programmed EXCERPTS and discrete sections from his operas. Such concerts had the double-edged effect of at once creating tremendous interest in the full operas while also serving to undermine Wagner's own argument that he had composed continuous works that were precisely not the sort of patchwork of set pieces and recitative/dialog characteristic of all other opera.   NICHOLAS VAZSONYI

See also, BAYREUTH FESTIVAL, ANNOUNCEMENTS FOR

Nicholas Vazsonyi, *Richard Wagner: Self-Promotion and the Making of a Brand* (see bibliography).

Publishers. Wagner's early contacts with publishers suffered from both the young composer's hubris and his inexperience in publishing. From the 1830s onwards, French, and to some extent German, music publishing practices were governed by the rules of the early capitalist era. Therefore, operas by celebrated and successful composers were paid up to ten- or twentyfold the median annual income of a musician, whilst young unknown composers were, at best, not paid for a new score, or, worse, had to pay at least part of the publication costs.

Before *RIENZI*, Wagner's third but first successful opera, several of his songs and piano works had been published, of which only few references have survived in the early CORRESPONDENCE. On 16 May 1843, he unsuccessfully offered *RIENZI* to B. Schott's Söhne in Mainz, one of Germany's leading publishing houses. Two months later, Wagner contacted the firm of BREITKOPF & HÄRTEL; the directors offered only a profit-sharing option instead of a fee. Wagner's refusal was one of the major errors of his early life. Without knowing the exact costs of music engraving and printing, he decided to organize the publication of Rienzi, Der FLIEGENDE HOLLÄNDER, and TANNHÄUSER himself, and to delegate marketing to the DRESDEN firm of Meser, a small local vendor with neither the commercial scope nor the necessary contacts. In 1848, Wagner offered the three operas to Breitkopf & Härtel, but at that time, they were still considered too difficult to perform in small opera houses and thus not profitable. Finally, after a seven-year struggle with mounting debts, Wagner's ultimate inability to repay the loans for the publishing costs was sealed by his flight following the DRESDEN UPRISING. Thus the copyrights became the property of his debtors – a major loss of income in later successful years. In 1859, the debtors sold the rights to Hermann Müller, Meser's successor, who sold them to Adolph Fürstner in Berlin in 1872.

Having understood that his works were not about to become part of the German operatic repertory, Wagner changed his strategy with Lohengrin and all those that followed, pitching them not primarily as commercial objects, but as works of "high art," and later as embodiments of the "deutsche Geist" (German spirit), composed as "gifts to the [German] nation" (letters to Breitkopf 8 April 1851 and 10 July 1856; letter to Schott 25 December 1859). Thus, in 1851, Breitkopf was offered Lohengrin as a remedy against artistic degeneration (8 April 1851). After having heard LISZT's performance in Weimar and fully aware of its outstanding quality, Breitkopf accepted it for the ridiculous fee of 200 thaler (a musician's salary for three months), given that the publication of a complex 400-page score, that had only been performed in one theater (Weimar), and written by a composer with a police arrest warrant, was an uneconomical long-term investment.

In 1856, Breitkopf began negotiations with Wagner for the publication of the Der RING DES NIBELUNGEN, only two-thirds complete at the time and still very far from being performed. However, the publishers immediately recognized the "compelling force" of this project. Initially, they accepted a fee of 10,000 thaler for the four planned operas, but wanted to pay in an extended series of installments. However, Breitkopf lost courage and interrupted negotiations. Two years later, in 1858, Wagner offered TRISTAN for a fee of 3,000 thaler; Breitkopf accepted for 500 thaler plus 50 percent of all profits; the score was published in 1860. In 1859, Breitkopf again tried to obtain the Ring on a profit-sharing basis, but in December 1859 negotiations were broken by Wagner who accused the publisher, in a letter to a friend, of showing "repulsive pettiness and tenacity" (Strecker 71). He was looking for a sponsor to cover his living expenses, an unrealistic plan for any commercial publisher.

However, a partial miracle did occur in late November 1859, when Heinrich Esser, Kapellmeister of the Vienna Hofoper, informed Wagner that Franz Schott, the owner of B. Schott's Söhne in Mainz, wished to contact him. Esser was Franz Schott's musical advisor. Most importantly, Schott's wife, Betty, was a professional pianist and a committed "WAGNERIAN." She exerted enormous influence on her husband to support Wagner. Franz Schott was aware that publishing Wagner, Germany's most discussed composer, might be a highly profitable long-term investment, but understood quickly that Wagner's excessive monetary needs might also imperil his firm. Still, he had learned from Esser that, for Wagner, the sensuality of a luxurious lifestyle was a *sine qua non* for artistic work (Strecker 173), so Schott tried his best to satisfy Wagner's needs.

As early as his very first letter to Schott (11 December 1859), Wagner appeals to the publisher's "faith" in the destiny of his mature works and demands 10,000 francs for each of the four parts of the *Ring* (which equals the previous total fee of 10,000 thaler for the entire cycle), begging for the first of an endless series of down payments. Schott accepted all of Wagner's conditions and signed the contract, even though the rights of the *Ring* were already sold to Otto WESENDONCK. (Looking ahead, this sale to Schott did not hinder a third, still more expensive sale of the *Ring* to Ludwig II. Wagner would eventually sort out of all these complications.)

A letter of 30 October 1861 contains Wagner's first mention of the MEIS-TERSINGER to Franz Schott. On 1 December, Wagner first met the Schott family, signed the contract (for another 10,000 francs), and, on 5 February, returned to Mainz to read the libretto at a dazzling private party. Close contact started which, however, soon suffered from interminable financial demands. Wagner eventually lived for nearly a year near Mainz (Bieberich). In the face of Wagner's almost extortive letters, Schott lost his temper and stopped payments in late October 1862. Composition of *Meistersinger* was interrupted for nearly a year, and contact with Schott adopted a rather businesslike tone for several years thereafter, with improvement following 1868, after the opera was first performed. However, new difficulties arose with the composer and his new agents Voltz and Batz. Only Wagner's letters to Betty Schott convey real friendship; she played the role of "muse" for *Meistersinger*.

Franz Schott died on 8 May 1874, and Betty just eleven months later on 5 April 1875. They had no direct heirs and considered their nephews unsuitable for the firm's direction. Therefore their wills granted one fifth of the firm and the directorship to the 22-year-old Dr. Ludwig Strecker (1853–1943), a highly gifted jurist with well-developed musical tastes, who had admired Wagner's works since his youth. He joined the firm on 2 January 1875 and, after a three-month "crash course," took over the firm following Betty's death and would soon prove that he was the best choice as Franz Schott's successor. After only one year at Schott's, Strecker felt ready to assume the firm's most important asset, Wagner's works. Hence, the difficult interim period of Wagner's contact with the firm's clerk, Mazière, ended with Strecker's first visit to the "Master" in BAYREUTH on 17–18 January 1876. Wagner expected an elderly morose attorney and was stunned to meet a handsome man of 22 with dazzling intellect, polished manners, and a deep understanding of artistic concerns. Strecker attended the first Bayreuth Festival (1876) and was a frequent guest of the Wagner family. Hidden under the balcony of the Munich Royal Opera House, he also attended the first private performance of the PARSIFAL Prelude for Ludwig II along with Wagner's family and a few intimate friends.

Strecker's first challenge was the negotiations for the publication of *Parsifal*. He was immediately aware of the work's cultural significance and yet of the enormous fiscal loss occasioned by the stipulation that performances be limited to Bayreuth. On 30 August 1881, Strecker received Wagner's letter demanding a fee of 100,000 marks for *Parsifal* (formerly 33,000 thaler, equivalent to the annual salary of fifteen Hofkapellmeisters). This was the highest fee for any musical work in nineteenth-century Germany and, probably, in Europe; Gounod's fee of 100,000 francs (= 75,000 marks) for the oratorio *The Redemption*, to which Wagner refers in his letter, was the previous maximum which, of course, now had to be surpassed. Strecker immediately travelled to Bayreuth, where he learned that Wagner was in Dresden. There, he was badly received by the Master, who overwhelmed him with increasingly violent accusations, which mystified Strecker. But neither he nor COSIMA could stop the composer. When the storm was over, Strecker said that he had just come to sign the contract for 100,000 marks. According to COSIMA WAGNER'S DIARIES, Wagner, totally puzzled, asked why he did not say this earlier (Strecker 311).

Strecker was anxious to publish the vocal score as soon as possible since it had to appear prior to the *Parsifal* premiere on 26 July 1882. As soon as the vocal score reached Schott, engravers were pulled out from other projects, and the plates were prepared so hastily that the first issue had to be accompanied by a correction list of over a hundred errors. (A first edition may be determined by the number of errors in the text.) This was Wagner's last publication; after his death, all publishing decisions were made by Cosima and her musical consultants. ULRICH DRÜNER

Ludwig Strecker, *Richard Wagner als Verlagsgefährte: Ein Abschnitt der Geschichte des Musikverlages B. Schott's Söhne* (Mainz: Schott, 1951).

Pusinelli, (Karl Franz) Anton (b. Dresden, 10 Jan. 1815; d. Dresden, 31 March 1878), a graduate of the *Kreuzschule*, a pediatrician and court doctor, and Wagner's lifelong financial supporter and confidant. Their CORRESPONDENCE began in 1843, the year after they met during the choral festival where Wagner's *Das Liebesmahl der Apostel* (Love-Feast of the Apostles) premiered (Pusinelli was a member of the *Liedertafel*, which Wagner later conducted), and continued until Pusinelli's death.

Pusinelli's comprehensive sponsorship and stalwart devotion included support of Wagner's 1862 application for amnesty from the King of Saxony. He also mediated the break-up of Wagner's first marriage to MINNA, communicating with both parties about her health and his consideration of a divorce. Pusinelli underwrote Wagner via loans, gifts, purchase of copyrights (which he then renounced), and efforts to manage the publishing of Wagner's early operas. At Pusinelli's death, Wagner still owed him more than 5,000 thaler. MARGARET ELEANOR MENNINGER

See also MONEY

—————————————— R ——————————————

Rackham, Arthur (b. London, 19 Sep. 1867; d. Limpsfield [Surrey], 6 Sep. 1939), English illustrator of literary classics, fairy tales, and children's books. Rackham travelled widely in Germany and Austria, attending the RING at BAYREUTH in 1879 and again in 1899, when he also saw PARSIFAL and MEISTERSINGER. His two-volume *Ring* (Margaret Armour's translation) for Heinemann appeared in 1910 (*The Rhinegold* and *The Valkyrie*) and 1911 (*Siegfried* and *The Twilight of the Gods*). The volumes comprised sixty-four full-page color and twenty-three black and white illustrations in total, combining naturalistic settings and fantastic subjects using a restricted palette; Rackham acknowledged their "grimness." Accompanying exhibitions were held at the Leicester Galleries, London; Rackham received gold medals at the Barcelona International Exhibition (1911) and from the Société Nationale des Beaux Arts (1912). The drawings' debts to German art caused controversy; more recently, ANTI-SEMITIC elements have been identified. SIEGFRIED WAGNER (who met Rackham in London in 1927) and C. S. Lewis were admirers, and the images influenced filmmakers Fritz Lang and Lotte Reiniger.   EMMA SUTTON
See also WAGNER IN THE VISUAL ARTS

James Hamilton, *Arthur Rackham: A Life with Illustration* (London: Pavilion, 1990).
Derek Hudson, *Arthur Rackham: His Life and Work* (London: William Heinemann, 1960; repr. 1974).
Marc A. Weiner, *Richard Wagner and the Anti-Semitic Imagination* (see bibliography).

Raff, (Joseph) Joachim (b. Lachen [near Zurich], 27 May 1822; d. Frankfurt, 24/25 June 1882), composer, critic, and teacher. Raff's father trained him in music, but he did not decide to become a musician until the age of 20, after which he developed into an accomplished pianist and organist, and began composing for the piano. In 1843, he submitted early piano works to MENDELSSOHN for comment; they received praise from the composer, who recommended them to BREITKOPF & HÄRTEL for publication (Opp. 2–6). The summer of 1845 brought Raff's first encounter with LISZT, who helped the young composer find work in a Cologne music and piano store. During his two years in Cologne, Raff met Mendelssohn (1846) and remained in contact with Liszt, whom he ultimately followed to Weimar in 1850. There he served as amanuensis to the Kapellmeister, assisting with instrumentation and in the copying and preparation of manuscripts, above all for the symphonic poems.

It was through Liszt that Wagner first became aware of Raff, around 1850. Raff's first major published comments about Wagner, however, earned the composer's scorn: an open letter to the editor of the *NEUE ZEITSCHRIFT FÜR*

MUSIK, Franz BRENDEL (11 February 1853), criticized aspects of Wagner's theories. Later that year, Raff's series of articles in defense of Wagner against critic Otto Jahn misfired, in that he likewise misunderstood or resisted core principles of Wagner's writings. The differences came to a head with the publication of Raff's book *Die Wagnerfrage* (1854), which revealed on the one hand continued misunderstandings and mis-applications of Wagner's theoretical work, on the other a strong dose of self-importance and independence. The book resulted in alienation from the NEW GERMAN circle, which led to Raff's departure from Weimar, where he had already felt oppressed by Liszt's commanding figure (despite Liszt's promotion of Weimar performances of the opera *König Alfred*, Psalm 121, and the choral fairy tale *Dornröschen*).

In 1855, he moved to Wiesbaden, where his fiancée Doris Genast occupied a position as actress at the court theatre and where Raff himself taught piano, singing, and harmony for over 20 years. He came into closer personal contact with Wagner during the latter's residence in Biebrich in 1862, but Raff's disdain for *TRISTAN* and Wagner's reciprocal aversion towards Raff as a person kept the relationship distant. There is no evidence of further dealings between them after Wagner departed from the middle Rhine, although Raff valued *Die MEISTERSINGER* and Wagner gives Raff credit in *MEIN LEBEN* (My Life, 1865–81) for having inspired the publication of the *WESENDONCK LIEDER*.

In Wiesbaden, Raff produced the majority of his numbered compositions, and achieved his first broad public recognition. By the 1870s, he was arguably the most performed living composer in Germany, having published a large amount of music in a variety of genres and styles. However, it was just that eclecticism and quantity of production that became the primary sources of criticism of Raff's compositional activity. While eschewing the more radical approaches of Wagner (MUSIC DRAMA and *LEITMOTIV*) and Liszt (symphonic poem and thematic transformation), he nevertheless cultivated the field of program music through descriptive symphonies, for example.

Raff became director of the new Hoch Conservatory in Frankfurt in 1878, which caused a slowing of compositional production. He died of a heart attack in the night of 24–25 June 1882. After his passing, Raff's music fairly quickly disappeared from the repertoire. His personal distancing from Wagner, Liszt, and the New German School undoubtedly contributed to this loss of influence, although his legacy lived on in pupils such as Edward MacDowell and Alexander Ritter. JAMES DEAVILLE

Ravello. See ITALY, WAGNER'S TRAVELS TO; KLINGSOR; *PARSIFAL*

Reading. Of all the great composers in the history of music, Wagner was one of the most avid readers. For a productive musician, it is unusual that he was able to engage himself with such a broad spectrum of world literature. As a young boy who dreamed of becoming a poet, he read a wide range of literature. This left a strong impression on the 14-year-old Wagner's first literary work, the tragedy *Leubald* (WWV 1), in which he intertwined elements of GOETHE'S *Götz von Berlichingen* with excerpts from several SHAKESPEARE plays. The extensive library of his uncle ADOLF Wagner in LEIPZIG served both as Wagner's first literary treasure trove and as the model for his own libraries in DRESDEN and BAYREUTH. His uncle introduced him to ANCIENT GREEK tragedy and, through his *Parnasso italiano*, to the literature of the Italian Renaissance. He also acquainted him with contemporary Romantic literary circles, to which he had personal contact. Indeed, he laid the foundation for Wagner's literary development.

Classical Greek antiquity was the sustained focus of his literary interests from the start (he had a more distanced attitude toward Roman antiquity, and the Christian late antiquity played almost no role). He became interested in ancient Indian literature after encountering SCHOPENHAUER'S philosophy, and he was also fascinated by Old Norse (NORDIC) and German literature of the MIDDLE AGES, as well as Dante and (very eclectically) the literature of the Italian Renaissance. He also read Shakespeare, the literature of the Spanish Golden Age, German literature from the Classical and ROMANTIC periods – von Heinse to HEINE – and a few important works of the nineteenth century, including Walter Scott and Balzac. Wagner lifelong considered Balzac to be the epitome of the modern novelist and an "incomparable figure" (SSD 8:91–2).

Wagner also read philosophical texts, particularly by Germans – beginning in 1854 primarily with the work of SCHOPENHAUER. He also read the works of his friends, which is how he and COSIMA came to study the early works of NIETZSCHE, and treatises particularly in relationship to the sources of his own works. However, his readings on "aesthetic" topics, aside from the sources for his opera texts, were in no way primarily for research purposes, but were rather part of his general intellectual development. He paid only sporadic attention to the literature of his time. Nevertheless, he avidly read Tolstoy's *War and Peace* in French just a few weeks before his death (CWD 3–9 December 1882). Wagner's DRESDEN LIBRARY prior to his exile and the one in WAHNFRIED are reflections of his literary cosmos, but nevertheless do not represent a complete the picture of his literary interests.

Wagner read mostly in German. The only other language he felt really at home with was French, which he mastered during his exile. Otherwise, he had only limited knowledge of other languages, such as ancient Greek, Latin, English, and Italian. For texts in these and other languages, he usually resorted to translations – even of Greek, which he had learned as a schoolboy.

For ancient Greek literature, he often referred to translations particularly by Johann Heinrich Voß (Homer) and Johann Gustav Droysen (Aeschylus). He also read modern German translations of Medieval German and Old Norse literature (particularly by Karl Simrock), although he always compared the translation with the original. Wagner had great respect for seventeenth-century Spanish literature, but he was completely dependent on translations; the Romantics, for whom Spanish literature had paradigmatic significance, published first-rate translations. During the *Tristan* period, he was particularly taken with Calderón, but later Lope de Vega and especially Cervantes were the focus of his reading.

Wagner could not have imagined a life without reading or books, and he often compared his relationship to them with human relationships. On 31 July 1860 he wrote to Cäcilie AVENARIUS: "Believe me, the company of people costs more than it's worth: for the most part it just wears me out. A book by a noble spirit is the most precious friend one can have." Wagner attempted to engage in a lively dialogue with every author, which explains why he carefully read books from cover to cover, even those he was not looking at for research purposes. On 24 February 1869, he wrote to LUDWIG II that, after his daily work composing, he needed to turn his attention to "our great minds" – Homer, Shakespeare, Calderón, Goethe, and SCHILLER – in order to preserve them through his "nightly prayers": "I am in good company and know which friends I can depend on." It is clear here that it was important for him to surround himself with only the most important writers. For that reason, he had little interest in contemporary literature, which had not yet proven itself against the test of time.

Wagner's enthusiasm for reading stands in strange contrast to the theoretical hostility towards reading found in his ZURICH writings. For example, in OPER UND DRAMA (Opera and Drama, 1851) he polemicizes against mere "literature" – that is, books that amount to nothing more than pure readability and are stripped of sensuality. He calls mere narration something that appeals "to the imagination and not the senses" – which Thomas MANN found particularly outrageous – and the "exiguous phantom" of the true "sensuous" artwork, meaning the dramatic (SSD 4:2; PW 2:119). After his conversion to Schopenhauer – who valued art the more it was distinct from the physical world and thus reflected will – and even more when, as an older composer, he was no longer forced to continuously defend his own work, he could once again pay tribute to imagination and encourage reading. However, Wagner preferred reading aloud to an audience rather than reading alone (as for instance when he recited Aeschylus's *Oresteia* in the Villa Angri near Naples in 1880). Thus, even reading should be a "performance."

During his final years, Wagner became increasingly focused in his reading activities and developed a canon of the most significant writers and works of world literature (as evidenced in conversations with Cosima on 4 June 1871 and 9 June 1878). Among them were Homer, Aeschylus, and Sophocles; Plato's *Symposium*; Dante; "everything by Shakespeare"; *Don Quijote*; Goethe's *Faust* (especially the "Classical Walpurgisnacht") was the only German work (CWD 4 June 1871). In a conversation on 10 November 1878 Wagner radically reduced his literary canon once again. He laughed and said that he could destroy his "entire library": one only needs "Shakespeare and *Don Quijote*." Cosima, however, wanted to add *Faust*, though only with Wagner's approval. Cervantes's novel was one of the few books that Wagner read often and with such enthusiasm in his last years – "and with much laughter and untold joy" (CWD 15 November 1879). In his opinion it, along with Shakespeare, represented the epitome of the novel, though he also much enjoyed Cervantes's *Novelas Ejemplares* and *Entremeses*.

The last image of Wagner is of him reading. It is a drawing that Paul von JOUKOWSKY completed during Wagner's reading of Fouqués's *Undine*, the day before he died. Underneath, Cosima wrote: "R[ichard] reading."

DIETER BORCHMEYER

TRANS. HOLLY WERMTER

Dieter Borchmeyer, *Richard Wagner. Ahasvers Wandlungen* (see bibliography)
  Das Theater Richard Wagners. Idee – Dichtung – Wirkung (see bibliography).
Yvonne Nilges, *Richard Wagners Shakespeare* (Würzburg: Königshausen & Neumann, 2007).

Curt von Westernhagen, *Richard Wagners Dresdener Bibliothek 1842–1849: Neue Dokumente zur Geschichte seines Schaffens*, Mit 6 Abbildungen und Kunstdrucktafeln (Wiesbaden: Brockhaus, 1966).

Reception. The musical and extra-musical storms that have surrounded Richard Wagner in life and death, coupled with the sheer range of his artistic, cultural, and intellectual activities, make the discussion of his reception a complex venture. It does not suffice to talk in turn of Wagner the composer, Wagner the writer, Wagner the theater visionary, and so on, because these were never discrete parts of Wagner's life and work, not for Wagner, nor for his contemporaries, and still less for his latter-day admirers and detractors. But neither do the parts of Wagner add up, or always add up, to a consistent whole, and this too has vexed many who have encountered the man, his works, and his legacy.

1. Wagner's reception during his lifetime
2. Wagner and his legacy
3. Twentieth-century trends

1. Wagner's reception during his lifetime

Public recognition of Wagner's talents came first not for his operatic offerings (the early operas *Die FEEN* and *Das LIEBESVERBOT* were failures), but rather for orchestral compositions such as the warmly received SYMPHONY IN C MAJOR (1832) and the musical criticism from his first stint in Paris. Only in 1842, with the enthusiastic response to *RIENZI*'s premiere in DRESDEN, did Wagner's star as an opera composer begin to rise, a reputation that increased, especially in German-speaking Europe, with the successes of *Der FLIEGENDE HOLLÄNDER* (1843), *TANNHÄUSER* (1845), and *LOHENGRIN* (1850). Elsewhere in Europe, a broader appreciation for Wagner's music materialized only during the 1860s, and it was largely based on these early works. The pieces' historico-mythic themes helped generate public interest, as did the accessibility of their form and musical style. But their attractiveness also resulted from their relatively modest demands on theaters and orchestras, thereby facilitating performance even at some of Europe's smaller houses.

Early on, print culture exerted a powerful influence over Wagner reception, pro and contra. Robert SCHUMANN, Franz BRENDEL, and Franz LISZT established one trend: using an influential journal (*NEUE ZEITSCHRIFT FÜR MUSIK*) to praise and promote the composer's musical progressivism. Wagner himself pursued another: the publication of numerous texts, starting with the theoretical manifestos he wrote in Zurich between 1849 and 1851 (e.g., *Das KUNSTWERK DER ZUKUNFT* [The Artwork of the Future] or *OPER UND DRAMA* [Opera and Drama]), in which he explained and defended his musico-dramatic vision and asserted its broader sociocultural importance. Although the turgid prose style that characterized these post-1848 texts may have impaired a full understanding of Wagner's views, what contemporaries did grasp sufficed to provoke partisan debates over the composer and his operas, particularly the works from *Die WALKÜRE* to *PARSIFAL*. While critics such as Vienna's Eduard HANSLICK acknowledged Wagner's extraordinary gifts, they faulted his post-*Lohengrin* creations for their non-musical dimensions and hybridity (accusations that could be supported by the ZURICH writings) and their lack of originality. These voices too, and those of composers such as Hector BERLIOZ and Giuseppe VERDI, also found outlet in the contemporary press. Conversely, Wagner's embrace of Germanic MYTH won him admirers such as King LUDWIG II and, for a time, Friedrich NIETZSCHE. His ideas on music and theater attracted such diverse personalities as Charles BAUDELAIRE, August von LOËN, and Gustav MAHLER. Wagner's NATIONALIST and ANTI-SEMITIC sentiments, evident in such essays as *Das JUDENTUM IN DER MUSIK* (Jewishness in Music, 1850) and *WAS IST DEUTSCH?* (What is German?, 1865/78), were more problematic. Public perception of him as a German composer, in particular, kept even the earlier Wagnerian operas off Paris's stages from the late 1860s until the 1880s.

For all the importance of the published word, direct encounters with the music were no less significant in shaping public reception of Wagner. For those who could, the experience of attending a live production was especially impressive. But, as Hanslick noted in his review of the *Ring* at Bayreuth in 1876, more people were won over to the operas by the stagecraft than by the music, which frequently overwhelmed "lay" listeners. Inasmuch as relatively few could afford to hear opera at the theater, growing familiarity with Wagner's dramas ultimately resulted not from stage, but rather from performances at ORCHESTRAL CONCERTS. Wagner himself started the practice of offering bite-size morsels of his works and, by his death, EXCERPTS from the operas had become standard and highly popular fare on concert programs across Europe. Changes in musical publishing, moreover, allowed for mass consumption of Wagner's music, in the form of TRANSCRIPTIONS and ARRANGEMENTS designed for private performance of every sort (solo piano, piano four hands, wind ensemble, etc.).

2. Wagner and his legacy

By the 1870s, and continuing into the early twentieth century, it becomes almost impossible to separate Wagner reception from considerations of his legacy. In large measure, this resulted from Wagner's own efforts, from the publication of his collected writings in 1871 (*Gesammelte Schriften und Dichtungen*) to the press campaigns for Bayreuth, to promote a particular, highly emotional response to himself and his works. But the program of developing a recognizable Wagner "brand," premised on the composer's status as a unique German musical-cultural hero, was pursued even more passionately by his disciples, the so-called BAYREUTH CIRCLE, after his death. Under widow COSIMA's management, the BAYREUTH FESTIVAL produced definitive versions of the operas. Hans von WOLZOGEN published *LEITMOTIV* GUIDES to the music dramas (*Meistersinger* excepted), thereby shaping both reception and analyses of these works for years to come. Moreover, in the *BAYREUTHER BLÄTTER*, edited by Wolzogen, and the growing network of WAGNER SOCIETIES and associations, the Bayreuth Circle had instruments not just for maintaining and spreading the Wagner cult, but also (at least into the 1940s) for disseminating a Wagner image that stressed both chauvinistic, conservative nationalism and intense anti-Semitism.

But there also emerged, shortly after Wagner's death, a more cosmopolitan, pan-European WAGNERISM that remained vibrant into the 1920s. Overall, non-musical considerations figured prominently. The French *wagnériens*, a generally literary and philosophical lot including Baudelaire, Stéphane Mallarmé, and Joris-Karl Huysmans, were especially interested in Wagner's AESTHETICS and symbolic language. With its articles on Wagner's works and translations of his writings, the REVUE WAGNÉRIENNE (1885–8), edited by Édouard Dujardin, helped make it acceptable for non-Germans to know and admire Wagner. In RUSSIA, Sergei Diaghilev's Ballets Russes took inspiration from the idea of GESAMTKUNSTWERK (total work of art) to pursue a unification of Russian culture. Wagnerian themes, images, and symbols also proved tantalizing subjects for literary invention, tempting not just French symbolists such as Paul Verlaine and Huysmans, but also such noted MODERNIST authors as T. S. Eliot, James Joyce, Thomas MANN, Oscar Wilde, and Virginia WOOLF.

Still, Wagner's influence as composer and theater man endured long after his death. His experiments with harmony, tonality, form, and rhythm led directly to the late romanticism of Antonín Dvořák, Gustav Mahler, Jean Sibelius, and Richard STRAUSS; they also played a key role in Arnold SCHOENBERG's development and eventual move to atonality. Wagner's mark in the world of opera was so immense that numerous admirers, including Hugo WOLF and Alexander Scriabin, avoided it altogether, toiling rather in genres Wagner had neglected: symphony, symphonic poem, chamber music, and art song. And while he wrote no plays, Wagner's approach to theater and stagecraft had attained such eminence in German-speaking Europe that in the 1920s Bertolt Brecht made Wagner the central target of his dramaturgical-theatrical reforms.

3. Twentieth-century trends

Although the attention given to Wagner in considerations of music, opera, and German culture abated considerably after the centenary of his birth in 1913, scholarly and popular fascination with the man and his works remains lively. One of the most significant developments was Adolf HITLER's appropriation of Wagner and his music to promote NATIONAL SOCIALIST understandings of German national identity (GERMANNESS) and race. Not only did this tend to promote Die MEISTERSINGER VON NÜRNBERG as the greatest of the composer's works (rather than PARSIFAL), but it has also made it almost impossible since 1945 to separate Wagner from discussions about Nazism and the Holocaust. Thus, for decades, Wagner's music has been effectively banned in ISRAEL. In the 1960s, scholars began to contend that Wagner's anti-Semitism also infused his operas, especially the RING, Meistersinger, and Parsifal.

But the twentieth century also witnessed a veritable, if still uneven, revolution in how Wagner has been performed, heard, and comprehended. Adolphe APPIA, Alfred ROLLER, and Otto Klemperer directly challenged Bayreuth traditions, especially in terms of STAGING and PERFORMANCE PRACTICE, Appia largely at the level of theory, Roller and Klemperer in their productions for, respectively, Vienna and Berlin (KROLL OPER). With his path-breaking productions for the postwar Bayreuth festival, Wagner's own grandson, WIELAND, further encouraged directors to take an open mind to performing Wagnerian opera. Under this admonition, the Ring has appeared at

Bayreuth as both mystery play (W. Wagner) and anti-capitalist allegory (Patrice CHÉREAU, at the 1976 centenary). And with his controversial *Parsifal* (1983), Hans-Jürgen SYBERBERG demonstrated film's potential to interpret Wagner's creations along entirely new lines and for new audiences. Lastly, among intellectuals and musicologists, there has been a clear postwar trend away from the totalizing assessments epitomized by Alfred LORENZ's monumental *Das Geheimnis der Form bei Wagner* and towards small-scale and thematic analyses, evident in studies by such figures as Theodor ADORNO, Carl DAHLHAUS, and Jean-Jacques Nattiez, as well as in efforts to subject Wagner to Schenkerian analysis and apply structuralist approaches to his employment of myth.   ANTHONY J. STEINHOFF

See also MODERN MUSIC; MUSIC CRITICS AND CRITICISM; PIANO TRANSCRIPTIONS; PUBLICITY; WAGNER AS ESSAYIST

Patrick Carnegy, *Wagner and the Art of the Theatre* (see bibliography);
Carl Dahlhaus, "Wagner's Musical Influence," in *The Wagner Handbook*, ed. Ulrich Müller and Peter Wapnewski, trans. John Deathridge (see bibliography): 547–62.
Saul Friedländer and Jörn Rüsen, eds., *Richard Wagner im Dritten Reich* (Munich: Beck, 2000).
Susanna Großmann-Vendrey, *Bayreuth in der deutschen Presse* (see bibliography).
David C. Large and William Weber, eds., *Wagnerism in European Culture and Politics* (see bibliography).
Hannu Salmi, *Wagner and Wagnerism in Nineteenth-Century Sweden, Finland, and the Baltic Provinces* (see bibliography).
Matthew Wilson Smith, *The Total Work of Art* (see bibliography).
Nicholas Vazsonyi, *Richard Wagner: Self-Promotion and the Making of a Brand* (see bibliography).

Reception, in the German-language press. After 1850, Wagner would become the focus of cultural debates that continued after his death, but the artistic aspects soon took a back seat. In unparalleled fashion, all of his operas from RIENZI on became repertoire pieces, their success surpassing that even of MEYERBEER. The pros and cons of the debates that surrounded Wagner can only be briefly touched on in an encyclopedia article, particularly since time has clouded contemporary historical contingencies. In addition, Wagner today (2011) is held accountable for his transgressions far more than many of his now forgotten contemporaries. Contemporary journalistic opposition has been almost insignificant both for the assessment and for the circulation of Wagner's operas. But it has also shifted attention from the artwork onto the composer as a person.

The *Rienzi* debate is typical for the period of a battle between supporters and opponents of Meyerbeerian opera, which was then already in decline. The then all but unknown Wagner was instantly recognized as a composer with exceptional talent, who was writing in the so-called "noble style" of Spontini. In two almost paradigmatic articles, the pros and cons of *Rienzi* were debated in the pages of the *NEUE ZEITSCHRIFT FÜR MUSIK* (LEIPZIG) and the *Rheinische Zeitung* (Cologne).

The Christian reinterpretation of the *FLIEGENDE HOLLÄNDER* material, directed against Heinrich HEINE, had the Dutchman given his promised redemption from an angel for overcoming his egoism. This, however, remained unnoticed around the time of the premiere only to be misappropriated later by the increasingly atheistic interpretation of Wagner within the BAYREUTH CIRCLE.

The Catholic tenor of the TANNHÄUSER saga stirred up the Protestant elite, who were internally already theologically at odds and who perceived re-catholicizing tendencies in the opera. Nevertheless, the significance of *Tannhäuser* as a game-changing opera soon became apparent: Wagner had created full-blooded characters, continued Weber's tradition of integrating numbers into extended scenes, and treated instrumentation as a compositional element of textual interpretation to the point that it could even invert the meaning of what was being sung. Wagner's opponents came almost exclusively from Biedermeier circles, the last proponents of the old BEL CANTO Italian opera (which had run its course by 1840) and of the still contemporary French opera.

LOHENGRIN, which came in the wake of *Tannhäuser* (*Lohengrin* was never performed before *Tannhäuser* on a German stage), confirmed the tendency of *Tannhäuser* by remaining tied to a set of issues that had little to do with what the majority of German intellectuals wanted from the new German national opera. As a result, Wagner lost the YOUNG GERMAN friends he made during the *Vormärz* (pre-March) era, including Heinrich LAUBE, and STAHR could cope with *Lohengrin* only by changing its meaning to fit its mythological opposite. In several extended articles, Wagner is accused not only of not recognizing German national interests, but also of hindering others in their implementation, because of the indisputable success of his operas (for instance Heinrich DORN's initially successful opera *Die Nibelungen* [1854], or the works of the anti-Wagnerian Vincenz Lachner). The opera triggered a polarized worldview that became ever more strident in the course of the century in which musicology emerged as a discipline.

In Germany, musicology has traditionally been critical of the respective *Zeitgeist*. The Wagnerian operatic reform, presented in his theoretical writings, ends the notion of music as an abstract art comprising indefinable emotions, an idea popular with Kant and Michaelis. Instead, Wagner (along with Romantics such as E. T. A. HOFFMANN) claims music as not only aesthetically literature's equal, but actually its superior. Additionally, Wagner's libretti can be considered poetry, demanding both a new interpretive method and also a new type of listener. Because of the musical setting, the new listener must be capable of and willing to engage in analytical thought (*Reflexionsmusik*).

In this vein, Franz BRENDEL, editor of the NEUE ZEITSCHRIFT FÜR MUSIK, was committed to promoting Wagner and his direction, beginning in 1850, and also raised the status of art criticism to the level of cultural philosophy. Hence, a Wagnerian bloc emerged that increasingly took on the character of a faction and even understood itself this way.

Despite political (Berlin, DRESDEN, VIENNA), artistic (MUNICH), and ideological (Cologne, LEIPZIG) opposition, Wagner had established himself on the German stage by 1856, and his works were performed increasingly with each passing year. All the noise of his detractors – often unoriginal and conservative post-MENDELSSOHN composers, as well as diehard opera music directors, envious of Wagner's success – served to fuel the decline of Meyerbeerian opera and increase Wagner's standing.

Not much changed until the Paris TANNHÄUSER SCANDAL OF 1861, when the debates took on a sharper tone, also in response to the RING and TRISTAN. Hegelian dialecticians approved of Wagner's unexpected abandonment of Christian ideas shaped by the Middle Ages, and proclamation of an atheistic worldview – where God is no longer sent to redeem human-kind, but rather that a man, begotten through incest, is chosen to redeem the gods – in which humans and the gods interfere with nature, and where love and power are seen as irreconcilable opposites.

Wagner had represented a failed, compulsively self-destructive world in the *Ring*. Tristan and Isolde suggested utter hopelessness. They may find their ultimate fulfillment in a lethal flush of love, but the Christian idea of REDEMPTION, as represented in *Der fliegende Holländer*, here becomes despairing pessimism, simultaneously excused as the workings of irrational magic, not unlike the *Ring*. Wagner garnered the passionate disapproval of those who perceived the music (tonal language) as impracticable. The text encountered non-comprehension and ridicule, the use of STABREIM as more strange than poetic. When Wagner had Otto Brückwald design and build him his own theater between 1872 and 1875, and when he gave his operas the aura of a surrogate religion (see KUNSTRELIGION [art religion]), he was declared an inveterate megalomaniac. Not that this negatively affected his artistic success. But the outrage over his supposed arrogance now knew no bounds, heightened by Wagner's offensive declaration that the European opera houses offered nothing more than amusement and, therefore, could not be taken seriously in a cultural sense. As a result, Wagner had to deal with being presented as mentally ill in a sixty-seven-page "psychiatric study" by Dr. Puschmann (1873). CARICATURES were increasingly in circulation after 1856, mostly based on his appearance and portraying the demeanor of especially zealous and, therefore, unpleasant WAGNERIANS. The characteristic *Stabreim*, subject to chronic imitation and parody, remained a source of amusement, while *Kunstreligion* remained a special problem.

After 1873, the battle of Bayreuth was decided. The same man, to whom no reigning ruler and no academic institution dared bestow even the smallest honor (other than financial support), was now receiving emperors, kings, and grand dukes. Furthermore, the public regarded him as the most important dramatist, not only the creator of a new type of singer, but the composer who had elevated German opera to world-class status. His influence went far beyond the realm of music and the boundaries of Germany, and had an impact on many other aspects of culture (see WAGNER IN LITERATURE; WAGNER IN THE VISUAL ARTS). Contemporary composers, including BRAHMS and VERDI, studied Wagner's scores, but the reverse cannot be said. Wilhelm I, the German emperor victorious in the FRANCO-PRUSSIAN WAR, recognized him as a national symbol. Journalists and fellow composers who had malevolently or offensively spoken about Wagner now saw themselves ridiculed (TAPPERT). After all German music journals had sided with Wagner, his opponents retreated to the last remaining anti-Wagner bastion, the *Neue Berliner Musikzeitung* published by Bote and Bock. Here, Wagner's old adversaries had the floor for the last time, led by his arch-rivals Heinrich Dorn, Richard Wuerst, and Berlin academia.

The last controversy during Wagner's lifetime was sparked by the libretto and setting of PARSIFAL. In the *Meistersinger*, Wagner had left behind the hopelessly delusional world of the *Ring* and, in *Parsifal*, returns to Christian ideas. Redemption no longer takes place in combination with a construed erotic act, but is rather the result of compassion and merciful innocence. Amorous love is now understood as *caritas*, benevolent love, reviving the religious debates of the 1840s and 1850s, particularly those surrounding *Tannhäuser*. In the 1880s, Wagner would have overlooked what his more militant followers were saying, but not the renewed suspicion of re-catholicizing tendencies. NIETZSCHE's reaction was characteristic. He went from Wagner admirer to Wagner adversary, wanting nothing to do with him anymore, though without denying his artistic significance. His strident and provocative reevaluation of Wagner set a sharply distinct tone on Wagner reception that emphasized a different set of those qualities and achievements that, even today, shape how Wagner is regarded by those who admire him. However, in so doing, Nietzsche provided material for a line of Wagner criticism that also continues to have a major impact on the way Wagner is perceived and discussed today.　　　　HELMUT KIRCHMEYER

TRANS. HOLLY WERMTER

Susanna Großmann-Vendrey, *Bayreuth in der deutschen Presse* (see bibliography).
Helmut Kirchmeyer, *Situationsgeschichte der Musikkritik und des musikalischen Pressewesens in Deutschland, IV. Teil. Das zeitgenössische Wagner-Bild* (Regensburg: Bosse, 1968–85).
Wilhelm Tappert, *Ein Wagner-Lexikon: Wörterbuch der Unhöflichkeit* [etc.] (see bibliography).

Redemption. In Wagner's worldview, redemption seems almost to function as a technical term. Certainly it is hard to overstate its importance in both the dramas and the essays. An electronic search in the complete works, for instance, gives over 500 hits for "redemption" and "redeemer" (*Erlösung* and *Erlöser*). However if one were to compare it with other technical terms, such as the LEITMOTIV and STABREIM, a simple difference would soon become clear. Whereas Wagner modifies and even dispenses at will with the last two, redemption is indispensable and is consistently, in his eyes at least, employed across an astonishingly wide intellectual and dramatic terrain. Nonetheless, its full significance was not initially clear to him. The key stage work is his fourth: Der FLIEGENDE HOLLÄNDER. And the key theoretician, although only discovered ten years later, is SCHOPENHAUER.

Der *fliegende Holländer* is the first of Wagner's redemption-based dramas and the word *Erlösung* and its derivatives crop up repeatedly, though only out of the mouths of the DUTCHMAN and SENTA. What we have here is the model on which, emotionally and philosophically, the MUSIC DRAMA as genre is dependent. The determining ingredients are the otherworldly nature of redemption, and the theatrical and conceptual means by which it is brought about.

True Wagnerian redemption means leaving the everyday world by virtue of ecstatic death. It is an ascent – sometimes quite literally, in that we see the Dutchman and Senta projected in a transfigured state after their deaths. Something similar was planned at one time for SIEGFRIED and BRÜNNHILDE, while ISOLDE's so-called LIEBESTOD is saturated by the idea of ascending to join the already transfigured TRISTAN. And this leads us to the means by which redemption is engineered. This is heterosexual LOVE and it is explicitly sex-based. In the principal examples (Siegfried/Brünnhilde, Tristan/Isolde) the physical consummation of the relationship is a necessary part of the agenda, and therefore Wagner is being wholly consistent when, in his writings, he insists on the unparalleled revelatory significance of the heterosexual act. As a result the metaphysical goal of redemption, by which the meager world is left behind, is expressive of arguably the most intimate of material (or bodily) experiences.

This anomaly becomes all the clearer when we consider Schopenhauer. It seems Wagner first read *The World as Will and Representation* in 1854, whereupon it became almost holy writ for him. He claimed for instance that his three early music dramas (he means *Der fliegende Holländer*, TANNHÄUSER, and LOHENGRIN) were Schopenhauerian *avant la lettre*; that he has only now "really understood" them. And all this has happened because he has been "faithful to [his] intuitions." Above all, he recognizes the similarity between his own notion of redemption and Schopenhauerian renunciation of the world, and goes so far as to claim that the "single poetic feature" of the first three redemption-based dramas is "the high tragedy of renunciation" (Wagner to RÖCKEL, 23 August 1856). But exactly this is the problem.

Schopenhauerian renunciation is a denial of the earthly world, which is a place of near unremitting misery. Fortunately it can be transcended; that is, there is an escape from the quotidian (phenomenal) world to a higher (or noumenal) realm. Now all of this sounds very Wagnerian. However, the anomaly lies in the manner in which this is accomplished. Schopenhauerian escape and ascension are products of lonely contemplation. Renunciation is attained by the individual alone. In other words, sex is certainly not the royal road to Schopenhauerian renunciation, as it is to Wagnerian redemption. And on this discrepancy the intellectual webbing between the composer and the philosopher (they never met) unravels and no amount of rationalizing on Wagner's part can put the weave back together. This is something he was much bothered by when working on *Tristan und Isolde*, and in 1858 he even attempts a letter (aborted) to the philosopher in which he fancies he can put him to rights.

This struggle with Schopenhauer draws our attention to another characteristic of Wagnerian redemption, at least as he imagined it in the mid-1850s. He now says that our arbitrary and suffering encounter with the world is transcended by the sexual act to the degree that we approach reality in a deeper way in the here and now. He claims we come close to the Kantian thing-in-itself, in that the empirical world ceases to be for us merely a representation of the alienating (Schopenhauerian) Will. Instead we come to know the Will in its purest, innate form. However, this implies an experience that is both open to everyone and, more to the point, realizable in earthly life – assuming social mores allow the free exercise of sexual love. So, redemption for Wagner is not just embodied in the sexual act between a man and a woman but, more broadly, is connected to his earlier community-based celebration of the German tribe both in his first work on Siegfried (*Der Nibelungen-Mythus* [The Nibelungen Myth], 1848) and in *Das KUNSTWERK DER ZUKUNFT* (The Artwork of the Future, 1849/50), where redemption is intimately and repeatedly expressed in VOLK-based terms. It is even equated with communism. It also recalls *Jesus von Nazareth* (1849), where the Redeemer argues against property and for the free expression of love. Redemption, in short, does not lose its racial, or communal, character once the 1840s are behind Wagner. He was, for instance, never in any doubt that JEWS are denied redemption. If salvation is an option for them, it is not an ascension but an *Untergang* – a downfall.

This communal character appears in its most extraordinary form in Wagner's last stage work. *PARSIFAL* is an incessant peroration on redemption, but its intellectual and dramatic realization is anything but straightforward. By blending redemption deeply within Christian iconography and yet by subtlety subverting Christian thought with the revelatory power of sex, Wagner effects his most astonishing, and unique, redemption-based reso-lution. Now Savior and Redeemer (terms that cover both AMFORTAS and PARSIFAL) survive in the community. The world is not transcended (although the female agent of this miracle is casually tossed aside), rather it is redeemed in the here and now and shown to bloom afresh. Clearly it is to be enjoyed, which must also mean sexually. We should not forget that Parsifal is to father LOHENGRIN just as Titurel has already fathered Amfortas. It is perhaps a pity that Wagner is only able to realize this quintessential manifestation of redemp-tion as experienced by an ideal German *Volk* in foreign (although European) surroundings, but by this time he had grown disillusioned with his own people. Nevertheless they remain, in one way or another, privileged in the redemption stakes. BARRY EMSLIE

See also AESTHETICS; ANTI-SEMITISM

Barry Emslie, "*Parsifal*: The Profanity of the Sacred," "*Parsifal*": *Richard Wagner*, Overture Opera Guides, ed. Gary Kahn (Richmond: Overture, 2011): 17–30.

Regeneration. See DEGENERATION AND REGENERATION

Reissiger, Carl Gottlieb (b. Belzig, 31 Jan. 1798; d. Dresden, 7 Nov. 1859), LEIPZIG-trained composer and conductor. Reissiger succeeded Carl Maria von WEBER as Court Kapellmeister in DRESDEN in 1828 and held the position for life, though he was compelled to share this post with Wagner between February 1843 and Wagner's flight following the DRESDEN UPRISING of May 1849. His tenure was marked by a great improvement in the technical capabilities of the orchestra. Reissiger conducted the premiere of *RIENZI*, and was a desig-nated foil for Wagner's unfulfilled ambitions in Dresden.

MARGARET ELEANOR MENNINGER

Reissinger, Gertrud (b. Kempten, 31 Dec. 1916; d. Aix-en-Provence, 16 Apr. 1998), studied ballet at the Günther School in MUNICH (Dir. Carl Orff). A childhood friend of WIELAND WAGNER, she married him (1941) and assisted him in his studies of opera production. She also choreographed Wieland's stage produc-tions (*TANNHÄUSER* [1954], *Die MEISTERSINGER VON NÜRNBERG* [1963]). They had four children: Iris (1942), Wolf Siegfried (1943), NIKE (1945), and Daphne (1946). EVA RIEGER

Renate Schostack: *Hinter Wahnfrieds Mauern: Gertrud Wagner, ein Leben* (Hamburg: Hoffmann und Campe, 1998).

Religion. Wagner's relationship to religion underwent dramatic changes. His think-ing moved from a Romantic understanding of Christianity, coupled with a strong critique of the Church, to a philosophy of religion based on

FEUERBACH's pantheistic ideas, and finally, influenced by SCHOPENHAUER, he returned to a form of Christianity synthesized with aspects of Buddhism.

1. Romantic Christianity
2. Revolution and critique of religion
3. A turn towards Buddhism
4. *Parsifal*: a synthesis of Buddhism and Christianity
5. *Religion und Kunst*

1. Romantic Christianity

If one believes the account in his autobiography MEIN LEBEN (My Life, 1865–81), Wagner experienced a (short) phase of mystical religiosity as a child. He writes that he "looked at the altarpiece of the Church of the Holy Cross with painful yearning and in [his] ecstatic excitement wanted to take the place of the Savior on the Cross" (ML 27; ML/E 20). During his Confirmation, he felt such a strong "shiver of sensation as [he] received the bread and wine" that he nearly gave up participating in Holy Communion for the rest of his life. He said this was to avoid the possibility of a weaker reaction to the Eucharist at a later time, but it was most likely because the initial excitement was soon replaced by a "noticeable change in sentiment" with respect to his "reverence for Church practices" (ML 27; ML/E 21).

The deep empathy for the Passion of Christ, which was to play a significant role in Wagner's later works (PARSIFAL as well as in his writings *Religion und Kunst* [Religion and Art] and *Heldentum und Christentum* [Heroism and Christianity]), undoubtedly stands in contrast to the pragmatic, Protestant, and enlightened religiosity of the family and vicarage where he lived as a child. Instead, it is reminiscent of the mysticism of Pietism portrayed in Romantic poetry (especially Novalis). The religious fascination of the young Wagner was largely aesthetic, which is evident in his Confirmation experience. The organ music and voices from above, the celebratory procession of the confirmands to the altar, and the liturgy are representative of the interaction between music, movement, and religious symbolism, and are characteristic of sacred theater. This experience finds expression in his monumental choral work *Das Liebesmahl der Apostel* (WWV 69, The Love Feast of the Apostles), in which the outpouring to the Holy Spirit is staged with a forceful entrance from the orchestra after a long interval of *a cappella* singing.

However, the young Wagner's literary and Romantic understanding of Christianity was unlike the idealization of Catholic liturgy and church-based institutions advocated by more "conservative"-minded Romantics. Instead, Wagner was closer to Heinrich HEINE's critical attitude, hence his ambivalent depiction of religion and the Church in the so-called "Romantic" operas. In TANNHÄUSER, ELISABETH's lived religion is irreconcilably divorced from the Church. TANNHÄUSER is not redeemed by papal absolution (which the pope denies him), but instead through Elisabeth's mystical martyrdom. This should be understood as a rebellion against the papal verdict and justifies a new religion of LOVE estranged from the Church. LOHENGRIN, on the other hand, takes place during a time of instability for the Christian faith. In tenth-century Brabant, the battle between paganism and Christianity rages on. In the figure of ORTRUD, the Germanic religion continues to bleed into the Christian world. LOHENGRIN does not arrive as a representative of the Church, but rather as an emissary of the Grail, who – in contrast to the official Church – symbolizes a transcendent power of which the world is again ultimately deprived. *Lohengrin* is a drama focused on mutually exclusive psychic forces, "faith" and "doubt," though "doubt" has the last word. In this respect, the work can be interpreted as a parable of the end of transcendence in MODERNITY.

2. Revolution and critique of religion

After *Lohengrin*, Wagner moved ever further away from his Romantic origins. In the course of the revolutionary events of 1848/9, and his encounter with Feuerbach's *Gedanken über Tod und Unsterblichkeit* (Thoughts on Death and Immortality), he developed a philosophical concept of the radical transience of everything that exists, which was diametrically opposed to Christian doctrine. Death was now no longer – as in Der FLIEGENDE HOLLÄNDER and *Tannhäuser* – an eagerly anticipated refuge for broken and suffering people to which one could flee from earthly fetters and where all conflicts are resolved. The paradox of death is that it means the irreversible end of the individual, but at the same time it is part of *Natura naturans*, the perpetual cycle of creation and destruction. Death is essential for all renewal, also in the social sphere.

In his revolutionary treatises, Wagner often equates death with holding on to the past, especially with regard to the propagation of social injustices. As long as antiquated forms of government focus on the benefit of the few to the detriment of the many, and continue to repress the fundamental human desire for freedom, then those who suffer under this repression are more or less buried alive. These unjust mechanisms of power – including the Church – must yield to a free, democratic, and self-organizing society, in which the individual can evolve without interference (see Bermbach and Dieckmann). In 1848, Wagner went so far as to call Christianity a necessary mistake of human history (SSD 12:258).

Nevertheless, at the time of the revolution, Wagner tried to understand the message of the New Testament independently from church dogma. In 1848, he carried out intensive studies of the New Testament and wrote a detailed draft of a five-act opera titled *Jesus von Nazareth* (WWV 80). In it, he presents a completely new interpretation of the Biblical text: Jesus is the son of God in a metaphorical sense; he preaches a religion of earthly love, communion of goods, and communism; he calls for freedom from the law and, with that, freedom from the state; and finally he demands the triumph over egoism, which Wagner held responsible for the inequality of men, obsession with property, hate, and repression. The draft of the drama is more than just a "retrieval of [Christianity's] honor." It is Wagner's attempt to penetrate the core of Christian doctrine, which he only reluctantly wants to abandon for himself and for the society he hopes to establish, set against the model of ANCIENT GREECE, often emphasized in his revolutionary writings, but which is only partly suitable as an ethical and religious foundation for a new society. After all, the freedom of the Greek polis was based on repression; slavery is the dark side of Greek democracy.

At the core of Wagner's revolutionary ideas is a radical critique of capitalism, which connects to his ANTI-SEMITISM, since Wagner wrongly believed that money was primarily in the hands of Jewish speculators. He called for the emancipation from capital, which he understood as the "God" of the modern world, and the declaration of war against "the demonic . . . with its abominable entourage of public and private profiteering, paper scams, interest, and the speculation of bankers." He sought a return to the roots of Christianity which would be "the *complete emancipation of the human* race; it will be the fulfillment of the pure teachings of Christ that hide enviously behind ostentatious dogma" (SSD 12:221).

However, Wagner was not exactly sure how the "pure teachings of Christ" could be realized as the foundation of a new political order, since he thought Jesus's teachings had nothing to do with the Church's interpretation of them. The fact that both denominations of the Christian church were in league with the state, and that they formulated their dogmas to fit the needs of secular rulers, had led to the bloody excesses of the Crusades and the Thirty Years War, and continued to characterize the alliance between the Church and capitalism: "to speed the rich, God has become our industry, which holds only the wretched Christian laborer to life until the heavenly courses of the stars of commerce bring round the gracious dispensation that sends him to a better world" (SSD 3:25; PW 1:49).

Wagner did not tire of strongly and cynically attacking the "lamentable effects of Christian dogma" on politics or invoking a democratic antithesis to Christ (SSD 3:25; PW 1:49). However, he did not always make a careful distinction between Christianity and the Church. For Wagner, Christianity *was* the Church, in contrast to Jesus, whom he believed the Church unjustly called its own. Wagner believed that Jesus heralded a secular religion of human kindness. He was "holy" only in the sense that Wagner defines holiness in his new confession of faith: "the free man alone is *holy* and nothing is higher than *Him*" (SSD 12:247).

This is in line with Feuerbach's critique of religion in *Das Wesen des Christentums* (The Essence of Christianity, 1841) making the rounds in intellectual circles at the time. According to Feuerbach, God is merely a projection – a form of wishful thinking – in which all things that people imagine are necessary for their happiness and completeness come together. Without realizing it, people glorify their own nature in God, while at the same time clinging to an artificial dependence on this abstract phantom. In this respect, religion is "the naïve nature of humankind" that should be overcome. According to Feuerbach, the deification of human beings should replace the worship of God: "*Homo homini Deus est* – this is the great practical principle – this is the axis on which revolves the history of the world." This idea was central to Wagner's understanding of a political utopia and set the tone for his participation in the revolution of 1848/9. If LOVE is no longer just a fantasy, but rather something real, it can ultimately lead to a new society in which the freedom of every person is guaranteed by mutual love and respect.

Nevertheless, Wagner abandons not only the idea of a personal creator God, but also ideas about the continued existence of the soul after death. Following Feuerbach, Wagner's *Jesus von Nazareth* begins not only with the vision of a social-revolutionary utopia, but also with an unusual metaphysical perspective. Death is "the last merging of the individual life into the aggregate life." It is the final and most definite revocation of egoism. In voluntary death, individuals engage in "self-sacrifice ... for the benefit and gain of all; the creature that carries out this sacrifice consciously then becomes a co-creator in that he uses his free will for the necessity of this sacrifice. Moreover, in that he uses his free will for the greatest moral significance, he becomes God himself" (SSD 11:299). When a person gives his life back to nature in willing agreement with death, a new albeit supra-individual form of immortality begins. He enters the eternal flow of life, and the cycle of *Natura naturans* continues.

As a result of his interest in NORDIC MYTHOLOGY beginning in the late 1840s, Christianity took a back seat for a while. In *Der RING DES NIBELUNGEN*, he combines his social critique with a pantheistic philosophy. The forces of nature are ensouled; gods, human beings, and the elements are an expression of the continuous cycle of birth and death. Both the tenacious hold the gods have on their own immortality and the struggle for power and lust are a manifestation of the egoism described above. The devastating consequences are made clear over the course of four evenings. In contrast to the gods, SIEGMUND, SIEGFRIED, and BRÜNNHILDE explicitly reject immortality for the sake of love and, in this way, prove that they are "free" even when being pushed by outside forces. A fatal set of actions is put into motion by an intelligible subject's awareness of his own mortality, the egoism of holding fast to power and possessions, and the fear of his own end. Ultimately, voluntary surrender to death as a guarantee of eternal renewal, and the hope for a new world of natural love – in the Feuerbachian sense – governs the drama. In this way, the *Ring* is a critique of society, a philosophy of nature, and a utopia all in one.

3. A turn towards Buddhism

After the failure of the DRESDEN UPRISING and his exile in ZURICH, Wagner took a renewed interest in religion around 1854. This was brought on by the works of Arthur Schopenhauer. As a result, Wagner discovered Indian philosophy, in particular Buddhism. In a famous letter to LISZT, Richard Wagner writes about his discovery of Schopenhauer's philosophy. Amidst the storms in his life he had "found a sedative which has finally helped me to sleep at night: it is the sincere and heartfelt yearning for death: total unconsciousness, complete annihilation, the end of all dreams – the only ultimate redemption!" (16[?] December 1854). With these words, Wagner paraphrased the final passages of the fourth book of Schopenhauer's magnum opus that end with the word "nothing," related to the Buddhist idea of *nirvāna*. According to Schopenhauer, life is essentially suffering. The source of this suffering is the hungry and self-destructive "will to live," which wages a bloody war against itself in countless ways. The only way to escape it is to deny this will and live an austere and ascetic life. Schopenhauer believed that "[b]efore us there is indeed only nothingness" (2:507). However, this "empty nothingness" is at the same time the only thing that can offer us solace. The mystical ecstasies of the saints in all religions are ultimately an expression of this "nothingness," which is parallel to the intentionally "meaningless words" that Indians use, such as the "reabsorption in *Brahman*, or the *nirvāna* of the Buddhists."

In theological writings of the eighteenth and the early nineteenth centuries, *nirvāna* was translated and defined as nothingness, non-existence, and extinguishment. This presented quite a challenge to, if not an unreasonable demand on, Western thinking, in which being is greater than nothingness. For this reason, Buddhism shared many commonalities with European nihilism. Friedrich NIETZSCHE later discussed this at length. Schopenhauer understood that "nothingness" in the form of "emptiness" (*shūnyata*) was at the same time an endless abundance (which the Zen Buddhists emphasize), and Wagner picked up this same idea, but he also associated these ideas with his earlier mysticism of death.

Schopenhauer saw the philosophy of ancient India – in the *vedānta*, though particularly in Buddhism – as a precursor to his own. He extracted the fundamental ideas of Buddhism from the resources available at the time (Indology was still in its infancy). This included the belief that life means suffering, and that one can overcome this suffering by changing one's outlook, as well as the ethics of compassion, particularly with regard to animals. Schopenhauer criticized Christianity and Judaism for their debasement of this idea because he believed that one cannot fundamentally distinguish between humans and animals. Overcoming the ego and the expansion of the consciousness to include all living (and suffering) things also has parallels in Buddhism. Recognizing the identity of all living things and the denigration of the world as a mere delusion (*WAHN*), as a "veil of maya," refers to the Vedantic philosophy of the Adavaita.

Like Schopenhauer, Wagner was drawn to Indian philosophy. In a letter to Mathilde WESENDONCK, he wrote: "You know how I have involuntarily become a Buddhist" (December 1858). Wagner belonged to a long line of artists and intellectuals brought to Indian philosophy by Schopenhauer. Shortly after reading *Die Welt als Wille und Vorstellung* (The World as Will and Representation), Wagner read the relevant Indian and Indological texts of the day, including the verses of the *Mahābhārata* and the *Rāmāyana*, Kālidāsa's drama *Shakuntalā*, Holtzmann's *Indische Sagen* (Indian Sagas), and much more. He studied Eugène Burnouf's comprehensive essay *Introduction à l'histoire du Buddhisme indien* (Introduction to the History of Indian Buddhism; Paris, 1844), the first standard work on Buddhism, as well as the two-volume study *Die Religion des Buddha und ihre Entstehung* (The Religion of Buddha and its Origins, 1857) by Carl Friedrich Koeppen (Left Hegelian and friend of Karl Marx). In countless letters, Wagner does not tire of explaining and presenting his own ideas about the tenets of Buddhism that he studied both in Schopenhauer's writings and in the research literature, for instance that the Buddhist cosmogony ("Ein Hauch trübt die Himmelsklarheit" / A breath clouds the clarity of the Heavens) is the source of the "desire" motive in *Tristan* (letter to Mathilde Wesendonck, 3 March 1860). He refers to Immanuel Kant's ideal of space and time as an expression of reincarnation. And, in contrast to Schopenhauer, he believed in the continuous identity of the soul, which helped him bring Christianity and Buddhism together in some ways (see, for example, letter to Mathilde Wesendonck, 10 August 1860).

In June 1878, Wagner immersed himself in the *Bhagavad Gītā* (the major Hindu religious text), prompting a remark about the superiority of ancient Indian philosophy over Greek philosophy which was, by comparison, limited by the notions of causality and materialism (CWD 21 June 1878). He maintained his fascination with Buddhism until his death, and spoke often and with great enthusiasm with COSIMA about it.

In the mid-1850s, after reading Schopenhauer, Wagner outlined three drama projects that in varying ways included Buddhist ideas: *Tristan und Isolde* (where Buddhist elements are more hidden), *Die Sieger* (The Victors; WWV 89), and *Parzival* (Wagner later changed the spelling to *Parsifal*). Buddhist ideas seem most obvious in *Die Sieger*. Here Shakyamuni, the historical Buddha, becomes a stage character. Because he has overcome his natural nescience (*avidyā*), Buddha can trace the fate of men back to their earliest incarnation. Buddha even recognizes that the maiden Prakriti (a Sanskrit word for nature, the primary matter from which the universe was created; later Wagner renames the girl after the Indian saga *Savitri*) is destined to suffer unrequited love for his pupil Ananda, because in an earlier life she had caused similar suffering in a young man by her haughty rejection of him. At the urge of his pupil, Buddha gives her the chance to follow her beloved as an ascetic and to be led to enlightenment as a follower of Buddha. The central ideas of Wagner's story are the overcoming of erotic desire for the sake of a higher love, which culminates in a liberated awakening, and the acceptance of a woman among Buddha's followers, whose basis (following the *Divyāvadāna*) Wagner found in Burnouf and Koeppen. But the sketch was never completed.

4. *Parsifal*: a synthesis of Buddhism and Christianity

The concept of Buddhist compassion is most pronounced in *Parsifal*. As early as 1855, Wagner wrote to Mathilde Wesendonck: "[I]f you wish to find out *my* religion, read Usinar. How shamed stands our whole Culture by these purest revelations of noblest humanity in the ancient East!" (30 April 1855). Wagner came across the story of King Ushinara – who cut out a piece of his own flesh to save a dove and a starving hawk – in Adolf Holtzmann's collection of *Indian Sagas*. Though this is not an original Buddhist story, it is analogous to tales about Buddha during his early incarnations as a rabbit; he would willingly sacrifice himself in order to feed a hungry Brahman. (Wagner read the story in 1882 while near Oldenberg and mentioned it to Cosima.) In a letter to Mathilde Wesendonck from Venice dated 1 October 1858 he writes that "compassion . . . is the strongest feature in my moral being, and presumably it is also the wellspring of my art." In a poultry shop, he had seen a chicken being slaughtered and heard its desperate cry, which caused him to feel a deep sympathy with the helpless animal. In the letter he wrote that human beings alone can lift themselves above suffering by means of philosophical insight and resignation, but the irrational, feeling animal is hopelessly at the mercy of it. In this way, mankind can become the "redeemer of the world" if it protects animals, recognizes the "error of existence," and accepts "animals' failed existence" within itself. In parentheses Wagner added: "This meaning will become clear to you someday on Good Friday morning from the third act of *Parzival*."

If we follow the development of *Parsifal* from Wagner's initial thoughts through the prose sketch from 1865 to the completed work of 1877–82, we see that the Buddhist elements, strong at first, eventually yield to Christian ideas. Buddhist ideals can be seen not just in KUNDRY's painful experience of being thrown from one incarnation (*saṃsāra*) to the next, or in the home of the Grail modeled on an Indian home for ascetics, a place of harmonious coexistence between human beings and animals, or that the daily ritual of revealing the Grail is similar to meditation (*dhyāna*), but above all in PARSIFAL's life. Wagner bases his character on the Indian *bodhisattvas*, enlightened beings who help others free themselves from "spiritual poisons" (ignorance, desire, hate, egoism) and guide them to self-realization. Crucial Buddhist concepts are interwoven in the formula "Durch Mitleid wissend der reine Tor" ("by compassion made wise, the pure fool"): *prajñā* (higher knowledge, intuition, enlightenment) and *karunā* (sympathy, compassion, gentleness). Additionally, there are clear parallels between Parsifal's development and the biography of Buddha.

On the other hand, at the center of the drama is the figure of the suffering Christ. Of the many definitions of the Grail that Wagner found in medieval epic poetry, he chose Robert de Boron's version, where the Grail is the cup from which Jesus drank at the Last Supper and that he passed to disciples as a sign of the new covenant. After Christ's side had been pierced by legionnaire Longinus's "Holy Lance," Joseph of Arimathea used the Grail to collect the blood. The ritual re-enactment of the "last love-feast" with the unveiling of the Grail and the illumination of the Blood are the only rituals of the Knights of the Grail. Good Friday as the day of compassion for the crucified Christ is also a moment when the suffering nature is "resolved of its sins." Wagner modifies an idea from one of Paul's epistles, where he writes that all creation has been groaning together in the pains of childbirth until now (Romans 8:19–22).

A complex of motives of the so-called *Heilandsklage* (Savior's Lament; sometimes falsely labeled the *Sündenqual* [Torment of sin] motive) that first occurs in the second part of the Prelude and, according to Wagner, symbolizes "the cold sweat at the Mount of Olives, the divine suffering at Golgatha" (SSD 12:347), is musically present at central points of the drama: during the lamentation of AMFORTAS, which explicitly refers to Christ; at the moment the Grail is unveiled; during Parsifal's moment of enlightenment; in Kundry's memory of her encounter with Christ; the Good Friday scene; and the healing of Amfortas, just to name a few examples.

Wagner's last MUSIC DRAMA ends with the suggestive phrase "Highest wonder of salvation: Redemption to the redeemer!," provoking much speculation. Undoubtedly, Wagner is referring to gnostic ideas. Within the context of Wagner's understanding of Christianity, as evident both in the music of *Parsifal* as well as in letters and writings, one can come to the following conclusion: the music of the *Heilandsklage* does not present Christ as triumphant, but rather as a suffering and self-sacrificing man, whose Passion will be forever repeated. According to Schopenhauer, although separated by time and space, he is nevertheless connected with suffering human beings through the mystery of compassion. However, because of their imperfections and indifference, he will perpetually be tormented and crucified. Therefore, their redemption is his redemption. In *Heroism and Christianity*, Wagner writes that Christ's voluntary suffering is brought full circle through imitation (see also SSD 10:215 and 10:202). However, Amfortas and the Knights of the Grail do not follow the example of loving compassion. They remain in utter isolation, they succumb to carnal temptation and therefore to narcissism, and they react to KLINGSOR's challenge with violence. As a result, Christ's act of salvation is called into question. The *Heilandsklage* is directed at the betrayal of the "violated sanctuary," which Parsifal hears in Amfortas's laments. By shouldering the conflicts of the guilt-ridden Kundry and Amfortas with his universal compassion and capacity to heal them, Parsifal reinforces Christ's act of salvation. In a letter to Mathilde Wesendonck, Wagner writes that Parsifal, like Christ, becomes the "redeemer of the world" (1 October 1848); not only that, but he also becomes the *redeemer of the Redeemer*.

The music that ends the drama expresses the same thing: "Highest wonder of salvation" variegates the proclamation of Amfortas ("by compassion made wise, the pure fool") and refers back to Parsifal. The "redemption of the Redeemer," however, is a variation of the *Abendmahlthema* and refers back to Christ. The head motive no longer turns into the *Schmerzensfigur* (pain motive), but instead the melodic movement rises diatonically. As a result, the *Abendmahlthema* (communion theme), which along with the *Schmerzensfigur* was previously a symbol of Christ's Passion and surrender, is simultaneously liberated and completed. With respect to this combination of motifs, it is important to note that Parsifal and Christ are melded into an imaginary union. Through his conscious compassion, Parsifal becomes the *redeemer of the Redeemer*. He is Christ's successor who completes His act of salvation by means of imitation. This is first evident when Parsifal brings the "undesecrated" spear back after a long odyssey. Here the *Abendmahlthema* sounds for the first time in its new form – freed from the vestiges of suffering and lament – followed by an ornamental variant of the *Heilandsklage*.

5. *Religion und Kunst*

Wagner's commitment to Christianity, as expressed in his later works, is still critical of the Church and is based on intense studies of Christian mysticism, in particular Master Eckhart and Jacob Böhme. Wagner also studied early Christianity and later Jewish traditions, including the Kabbala. Above all, however, he continued to be interested in a synthesis of Christian ideas with Buddhism. He believed that Buddha and Christ were analogous phenomena, even though he ultimately preferred Christ: "The suffering of Christ moves us more than the compassion of Buddha ... Christ wishes to suffer, suffers, and redeems us. Buddha looks on, commiserates, and teaches us how to achieve redemption" (CWD 28 October 1873). Throughout his life, Wagner held on to Schopenhauer's metaphysics of the will and remained an atheist in the sense that he rejected the idea of a creator God and was a follower of Darwin's theory of evolution.

Over time, Wagner tried to counter Schopenhauer's pessimism by looking for opportunities to overcome it. In his so-called "REGENERATION essays" (*Religion und Kunst* [Religion and Art] and the subsequent addenda), which accompany the composition of *Parsifal*, Wagner also draws political conclusions. He argues against VIVISECTION, and for VEGETARIANISM, ecology, and pacifism, which he bases on the ethics of compassion inspired by Schopenhauer and Buddhism.

Religion und Kunst (1880) highlights the relationship between a now non-credible, dogmatic ossification of religious institutions and the artistic (in particular musical) rebirth of the essence of religion (i.e., KUNSTRELIGION):

> One might say that where religion becomes artificial, it is reserved for art to save the essence of religion by recognizing the figurative value of the mythic symbols which the former would have us believe in their literal sense, and revealing their deep and hidden truth through an ideal presentation.
>
> (SSD 10:211; PW 6:213)

This "essence" can best be seen in the case of Christianity and Buddhism as the "recognition of the frailty of this world, and the consequent charge to free ourselves from it" (SSD 10:212; PW 6:213). Jesus expressed this in parables as well as in his example of voluntary suffering, since he could not expect the "poor in spirit" to grasp philosophical ideas – in contrast to Buddha, whose doctrine was meant for the "enlightened." Likewise, art symbolizes this in the depiction of the Christ Child as well as of the crucified Jesus. With Palestrina's style in mind, Wagner claims that church music resolves the contradictions of Church dogma in the melismas of sounds that transcend time and space, and delivers the divine message of Christianity ideally.

In the second half, Wagner asks why human behavior is so cruel both historically and in the present. The answer lies in the DEGENERATION of the once peaceful and fertile climate by means of natural disasters that drove human beings into inhospitable regions. It was only at this time that humans, who had happily nourished themselves with fruits, plants, and the milk of their herds, began slaughtering their domesticated animals and eating their flesh. This "ravenous and bloodthirsty race" that we encounter throughout history arose from these conditions. Further historical development reveals the thirst for power and violence that led to bloody conquests, and this continues even today (SSD 10:230). For Wagner, these so-called diseases of civilization are the result of an "unnatural" diet of "the limbs of murdered household animals dressed up beyond all recognition" (SSD 10:233; PW 6:234).

Even the Church joined in with this historical trajectory. However – as Wagner remarks with irony – the Church cannot invoke the gentle Savior, but instead must choose the bellicose heroes of the Old Testament as its patron saints of destruction. Wagner did not tire of pointing out that the link between Christianity and Judaism was a mistake with grave consequences, especially since he, like Schopenhauer, believed that Jesus of Nazareth was not Jewish and that Christianity may have originated from India, a theory often discussed during Wagner's lifetime.

Wagner does not admire history's winners, but rather the defeated. The "regeneration" of humankind, the restoration of its body and soul, the construction of a peaceful and non-violent society, and the blossoming of art, culture, and philosophy, therefore, must begin with a return to vegetarianism, the protection of all animals, a consistent form of pacifism, and to the roots of Christianity. With this discourse, which combined early ecological ideas with anti-Semitism, Wagner belonged to a cultural reform movement that expressed increasing disappointment with the Bismarck era's materialism and "social Darwinist" politics.

In *Heroism and Christianity*, Wagner addresses GOBINEAU's virulent theories on the degeneration of the superior "white races" as a result of mixing with other ethnicities. Though this seemed feasible to him from a scientific perspective, Wagner objected to its consequences. The highest form of development for a human being has nothing to do with "race," but rather reflects his ability to suffer willingly, Jesus being the best example. This entails a redefinition of the "hero" – now a person who greets suffering with resolve and without fear because he is aware of the frailty of the world. For Wagner, "blood" or "race" plays no role. On the contrary: "The blood of the Savior, flowing from his head, from his wounds on the Cross, – who would ask the outrageous question, whether it belongs to the white or some other race?" (SSD 10:280; PW 6:280). The "divine compassion" pours itself out "through the entire human species" and "cannot flow for the interests of one or a preferred race" (SSD 10:283; PW 6:283). With that, Gobineau's race theory is destroyed in Wagner's eyes. The message of the suffering Christ, which is valid for all, is a call to reject violence and resentment and gives a vision of a peaceful coexistence between humans and all other living things. Ultimately, this is the message of *Parsifal*.   ULRIKE KIENZLE

TRANS. HOLLY WERMTER

Udo Bermbach, *Der Wahn des Gesamtkunstwerks* (see bibliography).

Friedrich Dieckmann, "Ein Komponist im Aufstand: Richard Wagner und die deutsche Revolution," in *Zukunftsbilder*, ed. Hermann Danuser and Herfried Münkler (see bibliography): 19–46.

Ulrike Kienzle, "*...daß wissend würde die Welt!*" *Religion und Philosophie in Richard Wagners Musikdramen* (Würzburg: Königshausen & Neumann, 2005).

"*Parsifal* and Religion," in *A Companion to Wagner's "Parsifal"*, ed. William Kinderman and Katherine Syer (see bibliography): 81–130.

Arthur Schopenhauer, *Die Welt als Wille und Vorstellung*, Zürcher Ausgabe, 2 vols. (Zurich: Diogenes, 1977).

"Wagner und der Buddhismus," *wagnerspectrum* 3.2 (2007).

Religion und Kunst. See RELIGION,

Renoir, (Pierre-)August (b. Limoges, 25 Feb. 1841; d. Cagnes-sur-Mer, 3 Dec. 1919), French painter, printmaker, and sculptor, a founder and figurehead of Impressionism. He attended the ORCHESTRAL CONCERT performances of Wagner's work in PARIS in the 1860s (at one, fighting a French nationalist who criticized Wagner), producing an early portrait of Wagner from a photograph; Edmond Maître and Chabrier were friends. Music-making (especially girls at the piano) and theater boxes were recurrent subjects of his work. In 1879, he produced an oil, *TANNHÄUSER*, for the psychiatrist Dr. Emile Blanche's Paris dining room, and four panels (of which two, executed swiftly, were refused) on *Tannhäuser* scenes for the family's house in Dieppe. Wagner sat for Renoir (at Lascoux's introduction) in Palermo on 15 January 1882 for approximately 30 minutes: an oil (which Wagner disliked, and which Renoir copied in 1893), sketches, and a lithograph (*c.* 1900) resulted. Renoir attended BAYREUTH in 1896, leaving after *Das RHEINGOLD*, disgusted by the "boring" music and "tyranny" of the darkened theater.   EMMA SUTTON

See also WAGNER IN THE VISUAL ARTS

Willi Schuh, *Renoir und Wagner* (Erlenbach and Zurich: Rentsch, 1959).
 "Renoir und Wagner (neue Folge)," in *Umgang mit Musik: Über Komponisten, Libretti und Bilder* (Zurich: Atlantis, 1970).

Revolution was a constant specter for nineteenth-century Europeans, both a recurring, self-transforming event and a *Grundbegriff:* a "fundamental concept" (Reinhart Koselleck), an inescapable piece of sociopolitical vocabulary crystallized in a single term. Others relevant to Wagner include "state," "MORALITY," and "POLITICS." They require narration and interpretation, not analytical definition.

The French Revolution (1789) cast a shadow over the nineteenth century and posed a series of questions. Could feudal or aristocratic forms of government and society be maintained, reinvigorated even, with newfound popular conservative support? Were attempts to start anew doomed to bloody failure? Who should rule and how should government be structured? What of national sovereignty? The restorative model of revolution as a "wheel's turning" was replaced by modern revolution as violent rupture, transforming society, its omnipresence both new and persistent throughout Wagner's lifetime.

Indications were contradictory. The old order, apparently restored at the Congress of Vienna (1814–15), often had its much-vaunted "principle of legitimacy" breached: for example, the Holy Roman Empire not revived, two-fifths of Wagner's native Saxon territory ceded to Prussia. However, newer ideals of Liberalism and constitutionalism also encountered inveterate hostility, epitomized by Austrian Chancellor Metternich and his European "System." France's 1830 July Revolution commenced another wave, replacing ultra-legitimist Charles X with "citizen-king" Louis-Philippe. Constitutions were granted in Saxony, Baden, and elsewhere.

The seventeen-year-old Wagner, hitherto repelled by tales of French Revolutionary excess, drew inspiration from news of PARIS and DRESDEN: the "world of history came alive for me . . . naturally, I became a fervent partisan of the revolution" (ML/E 39). Increased and increasing public interest in social and political affairs characterized the period, "revolution" and reaction very much alive (YOUNG GERMANY). Few were surprised – Metternich wearily confessed to propping up rotten buildings – when revolution engulfed Europe in 1848–9, Wagner's experience culminating in the DRESDEN UPRISING.

Wagner's writings now breathed "Revolution," afforded a capital letter even when he abandoned the practice for other nouns. *Die Revolution* (1849), written for August RÖCKEL's *Volksblätter*, hymns the "sublime goddess *Revolution*," the "ever-rejuvenating mother of mankind," who prophesies a new world of LOVE (FEUERBACH's influence), in which "*all* as brothers" would be "*free* in their desires, *free* in their deeds, *free* in their pleasures" (SSD 12:245, 251). *Die KUNST UND DIE REVOLUTION* (Art and Revolution, 1849) and other Zurich writings look to a post-revolutionary *KUNSTWERK DER ZUKUNFT* (Artwork of the Future, 1849/50): essentially *Der RING DES NIBELUNGEN*.

However, the promise of revolution suggested by the *Ring* never materializes. Though SIEGFRIED the anarchist love-revolutionary shatters WOTAN's spear of state, he falls victim to HAGEN's spear. Yet, long after many '48ers lost faith, Wagner maintained his. Even after turning to SCHOPENHAUER, he continued to glorify revolution, above all in Siegfried's Funeral March, which dramatizes the conflict between revolution and resignation: challenging, not denying, revolutionary hopes. Wagner's chronicle never returns to the older meaning of revolution. The Ring is circular; the *Ring* is not, for, whether desirable or no, there can be no question of returning to the state of Nature depicted in the opening scene of *Das Rheingold* itself, which, as ALBERICH's fate illustrates, is far from straightforwardly idyllic. Too much has happened: the "watchers" of *GÖTTERDÄMMERUNG* – and the audience – must not forget, but learn from their witness. Indeed, the need to transform a moribund society is pursued in Wagner's final stage work, *PARSIFAL*.   MARK BERRY

Mark Berry, *Treacherous Bonds and Laughing Fire* (see bibliography).
Dieter Borchmeyer, *Die Götter tanzen Cancan: Richard Wagners Liebesrevolten* (Heidelberg: Manutius, 1992).

Revue et gazette musicale de Paris (1834–80), considered the most important French music periodical of its time; enjoyed a Europe-wide readership. Founded by Maurice SCHLESINGER as *Gazette musicale* on 5 January 1834, it merged with François-Joseph Fétis's *Revue musicale* (1827–34) and was renamed *Revue et gazette musicale de Paris* on 1 November 1835, running until 1880.

It was famous for its illustrious contributors, amongst whom where such distinguished musicians and musical writers as BERLIOZ, Fétis, LISZT, Rellstab, Sand, SCHUMANN, and Wagner. Richard Wagner contributed ten pieces to this periodical during his first PARIS stay (1839–42) – including the novellas *Eine PILGERFAHRT ZU BEETHOVEN* (A Pilgrimage to Beethoven, 1840) and *Ein ENDE IN PARIS* (A Death in Paris, 1841) – when he earned most of his money from minor jobs for Schlesinger's publishing house and music periodical. On 4 February 1841, Wagner's *Columbus* Overture was performed at the concert series sponsored by the *Revue et gazette musicale de Paris*.

HERMANN GRAMPP

Katharine Ellis, *Music Criticism in Nineteenth Century France: "La revue et gazette musicale de Paris," 1834–1880* (Cambridge University Press, 1995).

Revue wagnérienne, La. French literary journal published monthly from 1885 to early 1888; founded by the ultra-Wagnerian author Édouard Dujardin and the critic Théodor de Wyzewa. Created during the rise of *fin-de-siècle* Parisian WAGNERISM that followed the composer's death in 1883, the *Revue wagnérienne* was dedicated to disseminating Wagner's writings in France and exploring their impact on the arts, particularly literature. Since the 1860s, Wagnerism had largely been the province of Germanophiles and AVANT GARDE artists, who found the composer's music and writings compelling either despite or because of his rejection by mainstream French musical culture. Spurred on by figures such as Charles BAUDELAIRE, artists seeking to escape bourgeois AESTHETICS and embrace the idea of *L'ART POUR L'ART* were drawn to Wagner as a figurehead.

Consequently, despite its brief publication run, the *Revue wagnérienne* became one of the most significant journals for the Symbolist movement in France. Its contributors, in addition to Dujardin and Wyzewa, included most of the prominent Symbolists of the time: poets such as Paul Verlaine and Stéphane Mallarmé; author/critics like Joris-Karl Huysmans, Catulle MENDÈS, and Édouard SCHURÉ; and visual artists including Henri FANTIN-LATOUR and Odilon Redon.

The overall focus of the *Revue* on Wagner's theories is not surprising, given the lack of opportunity to actually see one of the music dramas on stage in France (although, from the 1870s on, EXCERPTS could be heard in various concert series). After the *TANNHÄUSER* SCANDAL (1861), it was not until the 1890s that Wagner's works were seen again at the Paris Opéra. Thus the authors, most of whom were not trained musicians, turned to poetic descriptions of the music dramas, relying on a kind of synesthetic analogy that fed into Symbolist thought. Huysmans, for example, sensuously blended sound with sight and smell in his description of the overture to *Tannhäuser* (March 1885), in a portion of which he experienced "an iridescent cloud of the morbid colors of rare flora," which "breathed out unknown fragrances, mingling the biblical scent of myrrh and the voluptuously complex perfumes of modern extracts."

Although it is often viewed as such today, the *Revue* did not exist entirely as a Symbolist mouthpiece; its contents, in fact, were extremely varied. In addition to the poetic or literary exaltations of Wagner's music and writings typically associated with the journal's Symbolist contributors, the *Revue* also contained Wyzewa's translations and commentaries on selections from Wagner's theoretical writings, as well as Dujardin's translations of excerpts from Wagner's libretti (sometimes with the aid of British Wagnerian Houston Stewart CHAMBERLAIN). Contributions of a more musicological nature were made by, for example, Adolphe Jullien, Charles Malherbe, and Victor Wilder, including commentary on Wagner's musical language and historical analyses of the subject matter of the music dramas. Each issue also contained the *Mois wagnérien* – a catalogue of European performances of Wagner's music (full productions and excerpts) taking place during the month – and, when applicable, reviews of the events at Bayreuth and notices of new books released on Wagnerian topics.   WILLIAM GIBBONS

Rheingold, Das (The Rhinegold, WWV 86a). One-act "Preliminary Evening" (*Vorabend*) to Der *RING DES NIBELUNGEN*, in four scenes, performed without intermission. First performed separately, at the insistence of King LUDWIG II and over Wagner's objections, in the Munich *Nationaltheater* on 22 September 1869 (cond. Franz Wüllner); first performance as part of the complete *Ring* cycle on 13 August 1876 to inaugurate the BAYREUTH FESTIVAL THEATER.
1. Genesis, sources, and development
2. Composition
3. Plot summary
4. Musical structure
(Note: For issues applicable to the entire cycle – including publication, first staging, and significant performances – please consult the entry for Der *RING DES NIBELUNGEN*)

1. Genesis, sources, and development

Wagner made the decision to add a *Vorabend* to what was at that point conceived as a trilogy (itself an expansion of, first, a single opera, then a pair of operas) sometime in the fall of 1851. In a letter Wagner wrote to Theodor UHLIG in 1851, he remarks that, as he started to sketch the music for his two

Siegfried operas, he began to feel that "the larger context, which alone lent the figures their immense, striking significance, was provided only through epic narration, by communication to thought," while it should indeed be "presented" "to the *senses*" (Wagner to Uhlig, 12 November 1851). While Wagner remained steadfast on the opera's dramatic content, its formal status and organization remained very much in flux: for years he still referred to the entire action as a *Vorspiel* (PRELUDE); at the same time a letter to Theodor Uhlig indicates that Wagner intended to make *Rheingold* a three-act opera of a length commensurate with the trilogy proper. By the time he completed his prose and verse drafts of the libretto in late 1852, however, *Rheingold* was by far the most compact of the *Ring* operas, consisting of four scenes to be performed without a break.

Das Rheingold's status as *Vorabend* is evident in the opera's cast of characters: of the driving actors of the story of the *Ring*, only WOTAN appears in the opera proper. ALBERICH, LOGE, and FRICKA may cast looming shadows over the action of the main "days," but those who will carry the drama in the coming works – SIEGMUND, SIEGFRIED, BRÜNNHILDE – are but distant consequences of the action of *Das Rheingold*. More importantly for a cycle that tells on some level the story of the passing of the regime of the gods in favor of the rule of humankind, there are no humans in *Das Rheingold*. Gods, dwarves, giants, and other mythical creatures vie for the Ring – significantly, when the Ring falls into human hands, it seems to unfold an entirely different power than in *Das Rheingold*.

2. Composition

Wagner composed the music of *Das Rheingold* in a concentrated effort of eleven weeks; he began the composition draft on 1 November 1853, and completed it 14 January 1854, and finished the full score on 28 May 1854.

3. Plot summary

As Wagner remarks in a letter to Uhlig, "the *Vorabend* is really a complete, rather action-packed drama" (14 October 1852). *Das Rheingold* opens upon the Rhinemaidens Woglinde, Flosshilde, and Wellgunde, who guard the titular gold at the bottom of the RHINE. Their carefree play is interrupted by the dwarf Alberich, whose advances they cruelly rebuff. As the sun rises, Alberich notices the shimmer of the Rhinegold, and the maidens let slip the secret key to the gold's possession: He who foreswears love will be able to use the hoard to rule the world. Alberich does so and absconds with the gold.

Meanwhile (scene 2), Wotan and Fricka are forced to grapple with a bad business decision: the giants Fafner and Fasolt have erected a new palace (Valhalla) for them and their fellow gods, but are now asking for payment. The parties had agreed to Fricka's sister Freia (the goddess of love) as their reward, but Wotan has sent out wily Loge to determine a suitable substitute. The giants point out that, as the guardian of treaties, Wotan can ill afford to break one he himself has made. When Loge interrupts the tense stand-off between Wotan, Fricka, Donner, and Froh on the one side and Fafner and Fasolt on the other, he does not bring the hoped-for resolution: he has scoured the earth for something that might replace love in the bargain, but his search has come up empty. He has found only one example where someone has recently given up love for another object – Alberich's renunciation in order to secure the Rhinegold.

Impressed, the giants amend their terms: they will accept this gold and the Ring Alberich has fashioned from it as a substitute for Freia, but are taking Freia as a token until Wotan can make good on his end of the bargain. Almost immediately, the gods start growing old – only Freia and her apples have given them their longevity and strength. Alarmed, Wotan and Loge head down to Nibelheim to win the gold and the ring. There (scene 3) Alberich has used the Rhinegold to fashion the Ring and a magic *Tarnhelm*, and uses both to lord over his fellow Nibelungs as their absolute master. Wotan and Loge confront Alberich and goad him into demonstrating the power of the *Tarnhelm* by transforming himself into different creatures. As his second transformation, and at Loge's instigation, Alberich turns himself into a toad, which makes him easy prey for Wotan and Loge. They capture and shackle him, and then return to Valhalla with him.

Back on the mountaintop across from Valhalla (scene 4), the gods force Alberich to bargain for his freedom. He is content to surrender the gold and the *Tarnhelm*, but refuses to relinquish the Ring. When Wotan grabs it from him anyway, Alberich curses it: "Whosoever owns it, may he be consumed by worry, and whosoever does not own it, may he be consumed by jealousy." The effects of this curse become immediately apparent: the giants agree to swap Freia for the loot but – like Alberich before him – Wotan holds back the Ring. Only when ERDA, the Earth goddess, older and wiser than Wotan himself, intervenes and foretells the doom that the Ring will bring to Wotan and his fellow gods, does he finally part company with it, only to have Fafner slay Fasolt over possession of the Ring almost immediately. The gods' triumphant entrance into their new palace is interrupted by the woeful song of the Rhinemaidens lamenting the loss of their gold; while Wotan shrugs them off, Loge seems similarly aware that this moment of triumph actually signals the inevitable decline of the gods of Valhalla.

If the Rhinemaidens and Loge are markedly pessimistic, Wotan thinks he has hit upon a solution: his "grosser Gedanke" (great thought), signaled by musical material that foreshadows the plot of *Die WALKÜRE* and the birth of SIEGFRIED, sets the stage for the *Ring*'s main three days, as Wotan attempts to solve through his offspring what he is no longer permitted to solve by himself.

4. Musical structure

(Note: music examples [CWE #] can be found in Appendix 4: *Leitmotive* in *Der Ring des Nibelungen*)

The music of *Das Rheingold* marks a new beginning in the history of opera. Gone is the division into separate numbers or closed lyrical pieces – arias, ensembles, and choruses – with recitative carrying along the dramatic action. Gone also is the foursquare phraseology of *TANNHÄUSER* and *LOHENGRIN* – the regular structuring of musical phrases in two-, four-, and eight-measure units. Rather, Wagner replaced end rhyme with *STABREIM*, and abandoned classical poetic meters (which tend to lend themselves to foursquare phraseology) in favor of a fluid accentuation and line-length. He thus strives for a new kind of declamation, ranging from something rather like conventional recitative at one end (as at the opening of Scene 2 in Valhalla), through a flexible, arioso vocal line with varying degrees of lyricism (as in much of Scene 4), to the occasional extended, fully symmetrical, musical statement (as in Fafner's description of Freia's golden apples, Scene 2, mm. 1111–24). Also noteworthy is the greatly expanded orchestra, which enables a vast panoply of timbral colors and dynamic shadings (e.g., the exceptionally rich, dark, brass sound of the Valhalla motive at the beginning of Scene 2).

But perhaps the most striking new aspect of *Rheingold* is its use of LEIT-MOTIVE. In OPER UND DRAMA (Opera and Drama, 1851) Wagner writes extensively about how, in his new "post-operatic" world, the creative intention is not so much to portray long and detailed sequences of action on stage, but to depict only as many actions as are necessary to convey a story, and then represent in words, melody, harmony, orchestral color, and gesture the emotional and psychological content of those few actions that are so chosen. At the center of this new AESTHETIC is the *Leitmotiv*, which is designed to capture the emotional essence of the object, place, idea, or person that it represents; which is plastic (*plastisch* is Wagner's word) in the sense that it can be transformed in various ways while still retaining its identity; and which is memorable, in the sense that its recurrences call up the various emotional resonances that its previous iterations have stored up in us. It is in *Das Rheingold* that we begin to build up the musico-psychological associations of these motives, the accumulation of which over the following sixteen or so hours constitutes the principal way in which the experience of the *Ring* is a radically new and essentially unequalled experience in opera.

In *Rheingold*, as in the *Ring* as a whole, some *Leitmotive* are purely local (for a particular scene), while others have ramifications for the entire opera, and/or for the entire cycle. *Leitmotive* in *Rheingold* also play a crucial role in the formal delineation of the work. As the "Preliminary Evening" (*Vorabend*) of the *Ring*, *Rheingold* is shorter than its companions, and it is divided into four interconnected scenes rather than separate acts. But, as in the other three works, it is frequently a leitmotivic association that determines the key of the individual scenes. Here the *Leitmotive* and their associative keys all refer to places: the E♭ major of the Rhine (see Appendix 4; CWE 1) for Scene 1, the D♭ major of Valhalla (CWE 4) for Scene 2, the B♭ minor of Nibelheim (CWE 7) for Scene 3, and a return to the D♭ major of Valhalla for Scene 4. Place, motive, and key all serve to link Scenes 2 through 4 as a quasi-ABA ternary structure (note that the tonal symmetry, D♭ to B♭ to D♭, articulates musically the symmetry of place), and exclude Scene 1 as separate, which it is both dramatically and musically: Alberich's theft of the Rhinegold in Scene 1 takes place at a distant time, previous to and locationally separate from that of the drama that unfolds in the rest of the opera.

An endlessly intriguing tension in *Rheingold*, and indeed in the entire *Ring*, plays out between psychological and musical continuity, on the one hand, and formal division on the other. In the theater, the drama unfolds before our eyes in unbroken continuity. Yet a study of the libretto and music shows clear divisions of the action and music, even in the complete absence of traditional operatic numbers and breaks between them. The American Wagner scholar Warren Darcy has, for example, divided *Rheingold* into exactly 20 "episodes" – formal divisions that are articulated by a single key (all the episodes but three are controlled by a single key), that are unified dramatically by playing out a specific dramatic action, and that display leitmotivic consistency (Darcy 59–60). Darcy cautions that his divisions are neither the "POETIC MUSICAL PERIODS" as described vaguely by Wagner in *Oper und Drama*, nor such periods as speculatively delineated by Alfred LORENZ in his well-known analysis of the *Ring* (1924). Nonetheless, the basic premise of both Darcy and Lorenz is the same: that the drama, however much it seems to be an undifferentiated wash of action and music that simply carries us along from start to finish, is also a relatively clearly delineated sequence of musico-dramatic actions.

ADRIAN DAUB AND PATRICK MCCRELESS

Warren Darcy, *Wagner's "Das Rheingold": Its Genesis and Structure* (Oxford University Press, 1993).

Rhine (Ger. *Rhein*), the longest river in Germany. Its source is in the Swiss Alps and it empties into the North Sea. The Rhine forms a portion of the long-disputed border between Germany and France and then continues its course through western Germany. From Roman times to the present day, the Rhine has been an important waterway and geo-political boundary.

English Romantics such as Ann Radcliffe, Mary Shelley, and Lord Byron made the ruined castles and rugged landscape of the Rhine a central image of European Romanticism. Other writers such as GOETHE, Hölderlin, HEINE, Brentano, Schlegel, Hugo, Dumas, Coleridge, BULWER-LYTTON, and Longfellow were also influenced by the idea of the Rhine. Artists such as Turner, Hans Thoma, and Max Slevogt depicted the river on canvas. The Rhenish landscape with its cliffs, vineyards, villages, and castles embodied romantic ideas of nature, the picturesque, and the sublime. The idealization of the MIDDLE AGES and unspoiled landscape was in part a reaction to the industrialization and urbanization of the nineteenth century. The ruined castles spoke to the military and political power of Germany's past and fed the growing movement of NATIONALISM in the nineteenth century.

While the Rhine was being idealized in its natural state by artists, it was also being redeveloped by engineers. The Congress of Vienna (1815) formed the Central Commission for Rhine Navigation, whose aim it was to facilitate the movement of people and freight on the river and to control its flow to prevent flooding and to provide water for agriculture and drinking. The goal of the chief engineer, Johann Gottfried Tulla, was to make the Rhine into a canal with a single, straight course and a predictable flow of water. To this end, the Tulla project eliminated oxbows and multiple-channel braids by dredging new or deeper channels and building dams and locks. This eliminated the romantic yet inconvenient meandering bends and sandbars, and the treacherous channels with fast water and submerged rocks. The canalization of the Rhine shortened it by approximately 105 kilometers and did away with many of the alluvial forests and floodplains, which allowed the Rhine to purge itself of toxins and waste.

In 1813, E. M. Arnt wrote, "The Rhine is Germany's river, not its boundary." While the French viewed the river as its eastern boundary, the linguistic border – which was an important indicator of nation for Europeans in the nineteenth century – lay far to the west of its banks. In 1840, French Prime Minister Adolphe Thiers declared that the borders of France should be extended to the "natural frontier on the Rhine." The ensuing Rhine crisis sparked intense anti-French sentiment as embodied in songs such as Nikolaus Becker's "Der freie Rhein" (The Free Rhine) and Max Schneckenburger's "Die Wacht am Rhein" (The Watch on the Rhine). The latter became a popular nationalist anthem during the FRANCO-PRUSSIAN WAR of 1870–1.

It is against this rich and complex cultural, historical, and political background that the full meaning of the "unspoiled" Rhine in *Der RING DES NIBELUNGEN* must be understood, on one level as a metaphor for the flow of life, time, and history, but on another as the fundamental source and resource that begins and ends Wagner's monumental drama.   LYDIA MAYNE

Richard-Wagner-Blätter. Periodical (OCLC 224497712) published quarterly in thirteen volumes from 1977 to 1989 (1990) on behalf of Bayreuth's AKTIONSKREIS FÜR DAS WERK RICHARD WAGNERS. For later issues Hans Schneider Verlag (Tutzing, 1983–8) served as publisher. Replaced in 1991 with the *Mitteilungen der Deutschen Richard-Wagner-Gesellschaft e.V.*

It is not to be confused with two other periodicals: the first, of the same name, published from 1949 to 1950 and possibly longer by the Schweizerischer Richard Wagner-Bund (formerly of Zollikon, Switzerland; later of Zurich); the second, known as the *Berliner Richard-Wagner-Blätter*, published from 1991 to 1992 and possibly longer by the Richard-Wagner-Verband, Berlin-Brandenburg.   MICHAEL SAFFLE

Raimund W. Sterl, Review [of vol. 12, nos. 1–2], *Musik in Bayern* 40 (1990): 102–3.

Richard Wagner Foundation (Richard-Wagner-Stiftung). In 1914, SIEGFRIED WAGNER proposed the BAYREUTH FESTIVAL become a national foundation. Political and economic events made this impossible in his lifetime. Siegfried's will stated that on WINIFRED WAGNER's death, his estate (including the FESTIVAL THEATER, WAHNFRIED, and the Wagner ARCHIVE) be divided equally between their children WIELAND, FRIEDELIND, WOLFGANG, VERENA, or their heirs. After World War II, the situation was affected by two factors: Winifred's delegation of managerial authority to her sons, and her sons' 1962 agreement that on the death of one of them the survivor would be sole director of the Festival. After Wieland's death (1966), his widow Gertrud (REISSINGER) and other family members disputed Wolfgang's sole rights. The ageing Winifred and her son realized the urgent necessity for a lasting legal framework to ensure the future stability of the Wagner inheritance, rather than have it disputed between Siegfried's descendants: by 1970 eleven grandchildren, as well as Friedelind and Verena (see Appendix 1: Wagner family tree).

After years of negotiations, the future of the Festival, Wahnfried, and the Archive was secured by the formation of the Stiftung in 1973. Richard's and Siegfried's legacy thus evolved into what they each had envisioned, a national institution. The governing members of the Foundation (with number of votes) are: Federal Republic of Germany (5), State of Bavaria (5), Wagner Family (4), City of Bayreuth (3), Die GESELLSCHAFT DER FREUNDE VON BAYREUTH (2), District of Oberfranken (2), Bavarian State Foundation (2), Oberfranken-stiftung (1).   DEREK WATSON

Richard-Wagner-Jahrbuch (LEIPZIG), a periodical (OCLC 5178199), edited by Ludwig Frankenstein, printed by the Deutsche Verlagsactiengesellschaft (Leipzig, 1906–13), and co-published by H. Paetel of Berlin (1907–8), and Hausbücher Verlag of the same city.

Five volumes, consisting of quarterly installments, appeared in print; none published between 1909 and 1911, however. Volumes included a supplement entitled "Bibliographie der auf Richard Wagner bezüglichen Buch-, Zeitungs- und Zeitschriften-Literatur." All five volumes were reprinted in a 1990 micro-fiche edition.   MICHAEL SAFFLE

Richard-Wagner-Jahrbuch, a single-issue periodical edited by Joseph Kürschner (Stutt-gart, 1886). Includes several interesting items, including original transcript of Wagner's 15 September 1877 Speech to the PATRONS' ASSOCIATION, titled "'Eine Rede Wagners,' mitgeteilt von Franz Muncker" (196–208), as well as the supplementary texts to Wagner's *Autobiographische Skizze* (Autobiographical Sketch, 1842/3) titled "Varianten und Ergänzungen zu Richard Wagners 'Autobiographischer Skizze,'" (286–92).

Not to be confused either with the RICHARD-WAGNER-JAHRBUCH (LEIPZIG and Berlin, 1906–13), or with the *Richard-Wagner-Jahrbuch* formerly *Nachrichten-blatt* (OCLC 224596380; ISBN 3-901149-07-4) published between 1988 and 2001 by the Österreichische Richard-Wagner-Gesellschaft, Graz.   MICHAEL SAFFLE

Richter, Hans (b. Raab, 4 April 1843; d. Bayreuth, 5 Dec. 1916), Austro-Hungarian conductor. As a student at the Vienna Conservatory in the 1860s, Richter was renowned for his broad musical abilities: although primarily a horn player, he was competent on all orchestral instruments save the harp. After a stint as a hornist at the Kärntnertortheater, in 1866 he was recommended to Wagner as a music copyist. Richter accordingly settled at TRIBSCHEN to work on *Die MEISTERSINGER VON NÜRNBERG,* and was of such incalculable assistance to Wagner in preparing the first production of that work (Munich, 1868) that the composer procured his appointment as a conductor at the Munich Hofoper. The next year Richter was scheduled to lead the first performance of *Das RHEINGOLD,* but backed out after the dress rehearsal as instructed by Wagner who, unhappy with the fact that the work was being produced singly rather than as part of the (as yet uncompleted) RING cycle, was moved to dissatisfaction with the staging and casting of the performance. LUDWIG II cut Richter loose for his involvement in this insubordination, but the young man made his way back to Tribschen to help Wagner with the copying of SIEGFRIED, then found a conducting position in Pest, and moved to VIENNA in 1875, where he reigned as the dominant conductor at the Hofoper, the Philharmonic concerts, and other institutions for nearly a quarter of a century, becoming a major figure in the biographies of BRAHMS, BRUCKNER, Dvořák, and many other composers of the day, as well as Wagner.

When planning the 1876 premiere of the *Ring* at Bayreuth, Wagner relied on Richter not only to serve as the conductor but also to assemble and rehearse the orchestra and to audition singers. After the performances, Wagner privately complained that Richter lacked intuitive understanding of his music, but he nevertheless also called him "the best [conductor] I know," and general knowledge that Richter was Wagner's chosen conductor enhanced his renown throughout Europe. Nowhere was this more apparent than in England. At the 1877 concerts arranged to defray the deficit from the *Ring* premiere, Wagner conducted some pieces, but the LONDON orchestra had difficulties deciphering his beat; by contrast, Richter led them with obvious mastery and his British reputation was made. He soon became a regular in London, supervising his own series of concerts, serving as the primary conductor of the season of (mostly Wagner) operas at the Drury Lane theatre in 1882 (including the British premiere of *TRISTAN UND ISOLDE*), and appearing frequently at Covent Garden. He eventually became most associated with the Hallé Orchestra (1899–1911) but also was crucial in helping to found the London Symphony Orchestra (1904). Apart from his enthusiastic championing of the music and career of Elgar, the longstanding preoccupation in his English activities was to produce the *Ring* in English as a means of founding an English National Opera. He achieved the first aim (at Covent Garden, 1908–9) but not the latter. At Bayreuth he was the most frequent conductor of the *Ring* and *Meistersinger* from 1888 until his retirement after the 1912 festival. His performances were not always meticulous in ensemble but were renowned for their authority and their grandeur of expression. DAVID BRECKBILL

Klaus Döge, "Lehrling, Geselle und Meister: Richard Wagner und Hans Richter," *wagnerspectrum* 5.1 (2009): 33–45.

Christopher Fifield, *True Artist and True Friend: A Biography of Hans Richter* (Oxford: Clarendon, 1993).

Egon Voss, *Die Dirigenten der Bayreuther Festspiele* (see bibliography).

Richard Wagner, *Briefe an Hans Richter*, ed. Ludwig Karpath (Berlin: Zsolnay, 1924).

Rienzi, der Letzte der Tribunen (Rienzi, the Last of the Tribunes; WWV 49). Grand Tragic Opera in five acts, premiered at the Königlich Sächsisches Hoftheater (Semperoper), DRESDEN, 20 October 1842. Cond. Carl Gottlieb REISSIGER. For cast information, see Appendix 10: Stage productions.

1. Genesis and sources
2. Development of the text
3. Composition
4. Plot summary
5. Critical reception and problems of interpretation
6. Publication and significant performances

1. Genesis and sources

Wagner based his libretto on Edward BULWER-LYTTON's novel, *Rienzi: The Last of the Roman Tribunes* (1835), which he first read in German translation in 1837. There had also been a drama *Rienzi: A Tragedy* (1828) by Mary Russell Mitford. Bulwer presents Rienzi as a tragic artist-leader, crushed by a perfidious public, but he was not solely responsible for the romantic canonization of this fourteenth-century political adventurer. Byron, in *Childe Harold's Pilgrimage*

(1812–18), had similarly regarded Rienzi in a positive light. On the other hand, in Gibbon's *Decline and Fall of the Roman Empire* (1776–89), Rienzi is described as "more eloquent than judicious, more enterprising than resolute," his faculties "not balanced by cool and commanding reason." Rienzi tainted "the desire of fame with puerile and ostentatious vanity" and "abused, in luxury and pride, the political maxim of speaking to the eyes as well as the understanding of the multitude" (268). Gibbon's criticism of Rienzi's love of regalia ("a parti-colored robe of velvet or satin, lined with fur" [269]) brings to mind not only Wagner's flamboyant personal wardrobe but also some of the more outrageous and equally effeminate costumes of Hermann Göring. For Gibbon, Rienzi was a megalomaniac, who allegedly had pointed the tip of his sword to the three parts of the known world, declaring: "And this too is mine!" (270). But Bulwer took issue with Gibbon's assessment, and blamed the popular uprising against Rienzi and his subsequent fall on an ungrateful people, an interpretation which Wagner echoes.

2. Development of the text

Wagner began work on the prose draft immediately after reading the novel in June 1837 and completed the score by the winter of 1840. Barry Millington writes that *Rienzi* "throws some interesting light on Wagner's social and political beliefs in the 1830s. Bulwer's novel, describing the irresistible force of a populace goaded beyond endurance by oppression and injustice, and swayed by the rhetoric of a charismatic leader (himself of plebeian origin), who overturns the old, corrupt order and puts in its stead a 'buono stato,' a Good Estate: all this made a direct appeal to Wagner's heart. However, neither Wagner's nor Bulwer's revolution was to establish an egalitarian society" (150–1). Indeed, Wagner seems to have seen himself as Rienzi, as revealed in a letter to TICHATSCHEK: "the figure of *Rienzi*, as I imagined him & attempted to depict him, should be a hero in the full sense of the word, – a visionary dreamer who has appeared like some beacon of light among a depraved & degenerate nation whom he sees it as his calling to enlighten & raise up. It is an historical fact that Rienzi was a young man of about 28 at the time he carried out this great undertaking" (6/7 September 1841). Actually, Rienzi was 34 at that time but, revealingly, Wagner was himself 28.

3. Composition

Wagner deliberately modeled *Rienzi* on the GRAND OPERA tradition exemplified by Giacomo MEYERBEER, though in Wagner's score march rhythms predominate, in both processional music and arias. The most inspired section is "Rienzi's Prayer" which is also heard at the beginning of the OVERTURE (Example 16).

This melody much impressed BERLIOZ when he heard *Rienzi* in DRESDEN in 1843, though he remained critical of Wagner's use of string tremolo, which suggested to him "a certain laziness of mind" which "calls for no invention on the part of the composer when there is no striking idea accompanying it above or below" (247).

4. Plot summary

Rienzi tells the story of the historical figure Cola di Rienzo (1313–54), who is outraged by the dissolute and corrupt aristocracy of Rome, one of whose

Rienzi.

Du stärk-test mich du gabst mir ho - be Kraft,
Thou gav - est me this charge from hea - ven sent,

16. Rienzi's prayer

families, the Colonna, was responsible for the death of his brother. When his sister Irene's virginity is also threatened by them, Rienzi takes matters into his own hands and inspires an uprising against the nobility. Adriano Colonna is persuaded to join Rienzi's cause and oppose his own father. In Act II, Rienzi appears as a Roman Tribune, and the Colonna plot their counter-attack. This is overheard by Adriano, who passes the information to Rienzi. After entertaining foreign ambassadors to a festival, Rienzi has the nobles taken prisoner and condemned to death, but Adriano successfully pleads for his father's life. The people now rise up in anger against this clemency and, when Colonna is finally executed, Adriano vows to avenge him, spreading rumors that Rienzi is no longer approved of by the church. The mob set fire to the Capitol and Rienzi dies in the flames.

5. Critical reception and problems of interpretation

Rienzi had an immense impact on Adolf HITLER. Reminiscing with his friend Kubizek on his first experience of the opera in Vienna in his youth, he declared, "In jener Stunde begann es" (In that hour it began) (64–6). Hitler was later presented with the manuscript of the opera, which has been lost, and presumably shared the same fate as its owner, going up in flames at the end of World War II.

There are further connections between Rienzi and later dictators. As a role model of the fascist super-politician, Rienzi redeems his country as if by a miracle. Rienzi also rises to power through his skill in oratory, that "miraculous and magic art, attested by the historians of the time, which Rienzi possessed over every one" (Bulwer-Lytton 385). Even Rienzi's demise anticipated the grisly ends of both Mussolini and Hitler: Rienzi's body was desecrated by the furious mob and then burnt to ashes. Rienzi shouts, "I will not die like a rat!" but does so nonetheless, and takes his sister with him, as Hitler took his wife, Eva Braun. The destruction of the Capitol around Rienzi is suitably Wagnerian – a *Götterdämmerung* played out with even greater effect in Berlin in 1945: "the fire burst out in volleys of smoke – the wood crackled – the lead melted – with a crash fell the severed gate – the dreadful entrance was opened to all the multitude – the proud Capitol of the Caesars was already tottering to its fall!" (Bulwer-Lytton 498). Rienzi, like an ominous foreshading of Hitler, blames the people for his downfall: "I have risked, dared, toiled enough for this dastard and degenerate race. I will yet baffle their malice – I renounce the thought of which they are so little worthy! – Let Rome perish! – I feel, at last, that I am nobler than my country! – she deserves not so high a sacrifice!" (Bulwer-Lytton 498).

6. Publication and significant performances

The full score (shortened version) of *Rienzi* was first published in Dresden in 1844. According to reports, original performances of the work ran a full six hours, including intermissions. Nonetheless an immense success, it catapulted Wagner to instant fame, a success that he compared to Rienzi's sudden "miraculous" rise. As he recalled: "I believe the whole crew of the theater, right down to the humblest employees, loved me as if I were some sort of miracle, and I am probably not far wrong in attributing much of this to the sympathy for and interest in a young man whose difficult circumstances were all well known to them, and who was now to step from utter obscurity into sudden glory" (ML/E 230).

Wagner was subsequently rather embarrassed by the work, deeply indebted as it was to the example of Meyerbeer, who had also arranged for the Dresden premiere. With its traditional division into recitatives, arias, duets, and trios, *Rienzi* flew in the face of Wagner's later aesthetic theories. Mistakenly regarded as unrepresentative of the Wagnerian canon, it has consequently never been performed at Bayreuth. The US premiere was at the Academy of Music, New York, on 4 March 1848. The first London performance was at Her Majesty's Theatre, 27 January 1879. The Overture was often performed on state occasions in communist bloc countries in the twentieth century, but performances in the West have been less frequent. One of the most successful was Nicholas Hynter's production in 1983 at English National Opera, which placed the action in a contemporary totalitarian setting.   DAVID HUCKVALE

Hector Berlioz, *The Memoirs of Hector Berlioz*, trans. David Cairns (London: Cardinal, 1990).
Edward Bulwer-Lytton, *Rienzi: The Last of the Roman Tribunes* (London: 1884/5).
John Deathridge, *Wagner's "Rienzi": A Reappraisal Based on a Study of the Sketches and Drafts* (Oxford University Press, 1977).
Edward Gibbon, *The Decline and Fall of the Roman Empire*, vol. 7 of 7 (London: Methuen, 1905).
David Huckvale, "Rienzi's Reich," *Wagner* 19.3 (September 1998): 103–16.
August Kubizek, *Young Hitler: The Story of our Friendship*, trans. E. V. Anderson (London: Mann, 1973).
Barry Millington, *Wagner* (see bibliography).

Riga, capital of Latvia. In Wagner's time, present-day Estonia and Latvia were divided into Estonia, Livonia, and Courland, which all belonged to the Russian Empire. Riga was one of the centers of the so-called Baltic provinces, and the capital of Livonia. When Wagner resided in KÖNIGSBERG (summer 1837), he was offered the post of music director in Riga. During his time in Livonia, he conducted operas and symphony concerts, gave guest performances in Mitau (today Jelgava), and completed his libretto for and began composition of *RIENZI*. In March 1839, Wagner's contract was not renewed and, because of creditors, he decided to escape, sailing from Pillau (East Prussia, now Baltysk in Russia) to LONDON. Wagner estimated that his own works would never be performed in Riga. He was wrong. The Riga German Theater became a regular performer of his work, starting with Der FLIEGENDE HOLLÄNDER in May 1843. Riga was also the home town of Wagner's biographer Carl Friedrich GLASENAPP and hosted a particularly active Wagner society.

HANNU SALMI

Ring des Nibelungen: Ein Bühnenfestspiel, Der (The Ring of the Nibelung: A Stage Festival Play, WWV 86). Cycle of four operas, technically a trilogy with a preface (*Vorabend*), comprising *Das RHEINGOLD, Die WALKÜRE, SIEGFRIED,* and *GÖTTERDÄMMERUNG*. Originally intended for performance on four consecutive days, the complete cycle was premiered at the BAYREUTH FESTIVAL THEATER between 13 and 17 August 1876, with a break on August 15 between *Die Walküre* and *Siegfried*. Cond. Hans Richter. For cast information, see Appendix 10: Stage productions.

1. Genesis, sources, and development
2. Composition
3. Plot summary (see also individual *Ring* entries)
4. Musical structure
5. Publication, first staging, and significant performances
6. Critical reception and problems of interpretation

1. Genesis, sources, and development

The *Ring* cycle occupied Wagner for the better part of his life: his first prose sketches for an opera about Old Norse mythology date from the late 1840s, but they soon expanded to a cycle of four operas, which Wagner completed in 1874.

Wagner's intentions to write a Nibelung-themed opera date back to the revolutionary year 1848. His short prose-sketch *Der Nibelungen-Mythos* (1848) already rehearses most of the plot of the eventual *Ring* cycle, and draws on five main Germanic sources. However, inspired by Romantic compilers and interpreters of MYTH, Wagner also took freely from sources foreign to his NORDIC setting, modeling his FRICKA not so much on her Eddic namesake Frigg, but on the Greek goddess Hera, and turning the fire-god LOGE (Loki) into a Lucifer-like figure.

The first of the sources that Wagner read, the *Nibelungenlied*, initially inspired him to compose a drama about SIEGFRIED and BRÜNNHILDE. It presents a sophisticated chivalric romance with kings and queens, and courtly love – hardly the world of the *Ring* in its final form. The other Germanic sources were the later *Thidriks Saga of Bern* (an anonymous prose narrative written in Old Norse, compiled in Norway around 1260–70), the *Poetic EDDA*, the *Prose Edda* of Snorri Snurluson, and the *VÖLSUNGA SAGA*, indispensable because they include not only the stories of the hero Sigurd (Siegfried), on which the later German sources are partly based, but also the mythology of the Scandinavian gods.

If most of the events Wagner included in his *Nibelungen-Mythos* sketch would find their way into the final version of the *Ring* cycle, they took a

493

circuitous route there. For Wagner did not intend all the events he had laid out in his sketch to end up as stage action – most of what he set down was meant as background, to be relayed narratively rather than presented dramatically. In general, his initial idea for the opera was limited to the plot of the first part of the *Nibelungenlied* – that is to say, Siegfried's tragic death. Strangely enough, although his plans soon spilled well beyond the rather traditional *Heldenoper* he had initially envisioned, he never seems to have considered including plot elements from the second part of the *Nibelungenlied*. Instead, Wagner looked backward in time, successively fleshing out dramatically what in earlier drafts had only been relayed in narrative form.

It is this dramatization of the backstory of Siegfried that slowly turned Wagner's single *Heldenoper* into a cycle that is more about WOTAN and Brünnhilde. In this shift, Wagner increasingly reworked or outright abandoned the plot of the *Nibelungenlied*, and began drawing on the Nordic sagas instead. After a futile attempt in the summer of 1850 to set the beginning of the tragic *Siegfrieds Tod* (comprising what became GÖTTERDÄM-MERUNG) to music, Wagner had the idea, in May of 1851, of preceding his *Heldenoper* with a comedic prequel, *Der junge Siegfried* ("Young Siegfried," corresponding to *Siegfried*). While Wagner began drawing on the Nordic sagas for this expansion (by bringing in MIME, based on the dwarf Mimir from the *Poetic Edda*), he seems to have been hesitant to dip too far into Eddic lore. This is why the opening of *Siegfried* draws neither on Edda nor on *Nibelungenlied*, but rather on a fairy tale, "The Boy Who Went out to Learn what Fear Was."

By the time Wagner had completed the text for *Der junge Siegfried*, he was already aware that too much backstory remained, and that his pair of operas would need to expand yet again. By the fall of 1851, the two Siegfried operas were joined by two more: *Die Walküre*, which provides the backstory for both Siegfried and Brünnhilde; and *Das Rheingold*, which portrays Wotan's and Alberich's cosmic struggle over the Rhinegold, and specifically the Ring. The libretti for all four operas were completed by the end of 1852, and Wagner circulated them to his friends by 1853.

2. Composition

Although the texts of the dramas were written in reverse order, the music was written beginning to end, though over a far longer period of time, with a pair of false starts, and not without detours and complications. In the summer of 1850, Wagner began to set the libretto of *Siegfrieds Tod* to music, but he soon abandoned it, in favor of other projects – including, in the fall and winter of 1850–1, the massive OPER UND DRAMA (Opera and Drama). The *Siegfrieds Tod* composition draft, which begins with the Norns's Scene, has been preserved, but none of this music survives in *Götterdämmerung*. After composing the text of *Der junge Siegfried* in the spring of 1851, he apparently embarked on the composition of the Prelude to Act 1: the composition draft of the Prelude begins on one side of a page and includes much of the present Prelude, but then stops, only to continue, in music obviously added at a later time, on the other side. This music is preserved in the *Ring*, and Robert Bailey has hypothesized that the opening of the Siegfried Prelude – that is, the measures on what appears to be the verso side of the composition draft – actually constitutes the earliest music in cycle to have been composed.

But the real composition of the music of the cycle did not begin until the fall of 1853, well after Wagner's completion of the texts of all four operas. Early on, his work went well. Wagner began composing the music of *Das Rheingold* on 1 November 1853 and completed the composition draft on 14 January, the full score on 28 May 1854. He immediately took up *Die Walküre*, beginning the composition draft on 28 June, and completing the draft on 27 December, and the full score by 23 March 1856. He then proceeded to *Siegfried* in September, completing the first act by March of 1857, and beginning the second on 22 May. By this time, though, all sorts of complications threatened the completion of the cycle. Now Wagner had two full operas and part of a third, but as yet he had no foreseeable chance of getting any of them performed or published; he was still in exile in Switzerland, with little hope of amnesty; and his perennial financial problems were worsening.

At the same time, he was gradually tiring of the musical material of the *Ring*, and his productivity was beginning to wane. His letters of late 1856 and 1857 make it clear that he was proceeding with *Siegfried* only with great difficulty, and that he was at times having to force himself to compose. Meanwhile, already in 1855, he had had his first idea about a musico-dramatic treatment of the Tristan story, and by mid-1856 this subject, and the music that he was beginning to imagine for it, threatened to take him over entirely. He began to think of the possibility of producing a shorter, smaller, "simple" work like *Tristan*, which he hoped could be brought to the stage quickly, and which could both relieve his financial situation and put his new work before the public again – no new work of his had been heard since Liszt's premiere of *LOHENGRIN* in Weimar in 1850. Wagner managed to work on Act II of *Siegfried* through the early summer of 1857, but then abruptly broke off composition on 27 June (at Act II, Scene 2, the "Forest Murmurs Scene"), only to take it up again on 13 July. Possibly because he feared losing the compositional thread if he were ever to return to the work, he worked quickly to finish the composition draft by 30 July, the orchestral draft by 9 August. However, he had orchestrated only the first act, not the second.

In the fall of 1857, he began work on *Tristan*, completing it in August of 1859. The completion of the new work failed to accomplish what Wagner intended; it was simply added to the growing stack of operas for which he could not secure a performance. In the difficult years from 1857 until he was summoned by Ludwig II of Bavaria in May of 1864, he performed individual EXTRACTS from the completed parts of the *Ring* (Siegfried's Forging Songs from Act I of *Siegfried*, for example); he found a PUBLISHER (B. Schott of Mainz), at least for the vocal score of *Das Rheingold*; and he was granted amnesty in 1862. In the flush of excitement around his sudden gain of a royal patron in 1864, he decided to complete the *Ring*. That being King Ludwig's first desire, Wagner promised to Schott the whole cycle by 1866, and to the king a performance by 1868. He did orchestrate Act II of *Siegfried* in 1864, but all the other plans came to naught, and he ultimately abandoned composition of the *Ring* again, focusing first on *Tristan* and then on *Die MEISTERSINGER VON NÜRNBERG*, which were premiered in Munich in 1865 and 1868, respectively.

In 1869, the successful performances of the two new operas behind him, and recently settled in TRIBSCHEN with COSIMA von Bülow, he was finally able to devote himself to the *Ring*, hoping to complete it and have the whole cycle premiered at a theater built by King Ludwig. But again complications arose. Ludwig was impatient, and insisted upon immediate performance of the two already completed works, *before* the completion of the whole. Wagner fought the initiative bitterly, and refused to have anything to do with it; but he was powerless to stop it, and so *Rheingold* and *Walküre* were premiered in Munich in 1869 and 1870 respectively. In the meantime, he began work on *Siegfried*, Act III, on 1 March, and completed the composition draft on 14 June. He began composing *Götterdämmerung* in October, completing the full score on 21 November 1874.

3. Plot summary

Following Wagner's development of his cycle, the *Ring*'s plot can best be understood in reverse. *Götterdämmerung* tells a fairly self-contained story, drawn in outlines from the *Nibelungenlied*: GUNTHER AND GUTRUNE, brother and sister rulers of Gibichung Hall on the Rhine, are told by their half-brother HAGEN that (a) a great hero named Siegfried will shortly arrive at their Hall, and (b) the most precious woman on earth, Brünnhilde, waits for a champion to claim her. The plot the siblings hatch, that Siegfried will claim Brünnhilde for the not-quite-heroic Gunther, and that Siegfried will get Gutrune as a reward, follows the plot of the *Nibelungenlied* quite exactly. By magic means Siegfried manages to claim Brünnhilde, but lets her believe that she was vanquished by Gunther. Upon her return to Gibichung Hall (Worms in the *Nibelungenlied*), Brünnhilde realizes that she has been tricked – together with her humiliated husband Gunther, she conspires to murder Siegfried by stabbing him in the back.

Wagner adds to this Brünnhilde's own death, and the return of the Rhinegold to its rightful owners, as well as the deaths of Hagen and Gunther, which in the *Nibelungenlied* occur only in the second part that deals with Kriemhild's (Gutrune's) revenge. These additions are necessary because Wagner alters the *Nibelungenlied* in one central respect: Brünnhilde feels betrayed not just because she has been tricked into marrying a man unworthy of her; she in fact knows Siegfried, and believes herself to be married to him. For where the *Nibelungenlied* makes Siegfried a co-conspirator in Kriemhild and Gunther's schemes, *Götterdämmerung* insists that he is a victim of the twins' guile, and they in turn of Hagen's. On first welcoming him to their Hall, the Gibichung siblings drug Siegfried with a potion that makes him fall madly in love with Gutrune, and wipes away any recollection of past loves – which (unbeknownst to Gunther and Gutrune, but not to Hagen) means Brünnhilde.

The story of their relationship is told in *Siegfried*. To be sure, Brünnhilde shows up only in the final scene of the opera, but in its three acts the opera presents a sort of *Bildungsroman* with Brünnhilde as its logical endpoint. Young Siegfried grows up in a forest with the villainous and pathetic dwarf Mime. The young man suspects that Mime is not his father, but his notions of family and gender are too confused for him to be sure (he has, importantly, never met a human woman before). Mime is grooming Siegfried for his own schemes: he wants the youth to slay the dragon Fafner who guards the Nibelung gold in a cave in the forest, and plans to murder him afterwards. He sends Siegfried, who professes that he does not know what fear is, on a mission to learn – from Fafner. Siegfried slays the dragon handily, but feels no fear. After coming into contact with the dragon's blood, Siegfried realizes he understands the song of a nearby bird. The bird helps him see through Mime's schemes, and Siegfried slays the dwarf.

The bird then tells him of a woman secluded away on a mountaintop, encircled by a ring of magical fire – Brünnhilde. During his journey to her, Siegfried comes upon an old man (in fact Wotan in his disguise as "wanderer"), and shatters his spear – by which Wotan guards all contracts and treaties. Arriving at Brünnhilde's rock, Siegfried fearlessly braves the fire, and reaches what he believes is a man in armor. When he takes off the armor and realizes that "this is no man," he feels fear for the first time. Brünnhilde awakens and rapturously welcomes her savior. Wotan, as we learn in *Götterdämmerung*, returns to his hall in Valhalla despondent and anticipating the twilight of the gods.

Die Walküre explains how Siegfried and Brünnhilde start off in *Siegfried* in such different positions, and why they nevertheless find each other with fated inevitability. At the same time it sets up Wotan's decisions and schemes that serve to unravel the old order in *Siegfried*, culminating in the shattering of his spear. Act I of *Die Walküre* introduces Siegfried's parents: Siegmund, a luckless fighter, arrives at the home of HUNDING, who turns out to be his sworn enemy. Hunding's wife Sieglinde is his twin sister, separated in early childhood, a fact the siblings only realize gradually, after Sieglinde has drugged her husband. The twins flee together and ultimately produce Siegfried.

Act II presents the divine fallout of Siegmund and Sieglinde's transgression: Wotan, the twins' father, wants to protect the two, and aid their escape from Hunding's grasp; his wife Fricka, as incensed about Wotan's infidelity as she is about the twins' incest, demands that Wotan intervene on Hunding's behalf. Brünnhilde, a Valkyrie, is caught in the middle, tasked first with helping Siegmund against Hunding, later with making sure Hunding wins out. Conflicted, Brünnhilde decides to heed what Wotan really wants, rather than what he has been compelled to order – she disobeys him and helps Siegmund. Wotan, however, makes sure Siegmund is slain, and punishes Brünnhilde severely for her transgression: the virginal demigod will become human and wait for a fearless man to rescue her, whilst she sleeps surrounded by a protective ring of fire.

Das Rheingold, the text of which Wagner drafted last and positioned as a preamble, a *Vorabend* rather than an evening in its own right, provides the cosmic context for Wotan's exertions. In the first scene, the dwarf Alberich steals the titular Rhinegold from the bottom of the river. He fashions from it a magic *Tarnhelm* and a magic Ring. Wotan, in debt to the two giants Fafner and Fasolt who have built his new palace, decides to take the hoard, including the Ring, from Alberich. Thanks to the fire-god Loge's cunning advice the plan succeeds, with one major hitch: Alberich curses the Ring. The curse immediately makes its effect felt: Wotan is loath to let go of it, but the intercession of the Earth Goddess Erda prevents him from reneging on his agreement. The moment Wotan hands the Ring over to the giants, Fafner slays Fasolt over it. As Wotan and his clan ascend to their new abode, the Rhinemaidens, guardians of the Rhinegold, lament its disappearance and demand its return.

4. Musical structure

(Note: music examples [CWE #] can be found in Appendix 4: *Leitmotive* in *Der Ring des Nibelungen*)

The *Ring* creates its own distinctive and immediately recognizable world of sound. The massive orchestra (far bigger than the orchestras for Wagner's other works), the web of LEITMOTIVE, Wagner's heroic vocal lines – all these testify to the success of the composer's intent, in the late 1840s, and in his treatise *Oper und Drama* (1851), to bring a new dramatic and musical world into existence. And just as the character of the ORCHESTRATION, *Leitmotive*, and vocal lines tells us that we are in the *Ring* at any particular moment in the cycle, so the unfolding of whole scenes and acts tells us that we are not in the world of conventional opera. There are no clearly marked recitatives and arias, and no separation of dramatic action and reflection on that action. We are carried along in a continuous wash of sound, always psychologically attuned to the drama, proceeding more in the rhythm of human emotion than in the stylized rhythm of traditional song and instrumental music. But this psychological sensitivity, dramatic realism, and seemingly unbroken continuity conceal an extraordinary musical artistry – an artistry that might be discussed in conventional terms such as melody, harmony, counterpoint, and rhythm, but can also be profitably discussed in terms of immediate sensation, memory and meaning, and formal structure.

As a composer Wagner had an uncanny ability to create musical moments rich in meaning and rhetorical power – immediate musical sensations that are instantly memorable. These *melodische Momente* (for us, *Leitmotive*), as he called them in Part III of *Oper und Drama*, were for him not musical *representations* of dramatic ideas or psychological states, but rather those ideas or states themselves, condensed into music, so that, at least as he would claim, the feeling actually *is* the music. A useful example is the motive of the Ring (see Appendix 4; CWE 2), as Woglinde first sings it in Scene 1 of *Das Rheingold*. Describing powers that could be used by anyone who could forge the Rhinegold into a ring, she first sings down through a minor seventh chord, E–C♯–A–F♯, then innocently ascends scale-wise, so that the relatively consonant chord resolves easily to the major tonic (E major) in the next measure (CWE 2a). In the following measure, though, beginning with the same descending musical figure, she colors it with C♮, adding an element of darkness and uncertainty and making the seventh chord half-diminished rather than minor (E–C♮–A–F♯), and then ascending up through the same chord rather than resolving it, and thus in a sense making a "ring" out of the whole, E–C♮– A–F♯– A–(B)–C♮–(A)– E (CWE 2b). The psychological point – that the gold is something seemingly harmless, but can be turned to sordid ends if someone forges it into a ring – is in the music itself. The *Ring* contains hundreds of comparable moments – moments in which emotional content is imparted in musical form.

Precisely because of the psychological and musical effectiveness of such moments, we remember them as *Leitmotive*; a distinctive motive having been heard once, we carry both its emotional and musical content in memory, such that a return of the motive can spark the memory, and the musical manipulation of the motive – altering its shape or rhythm, stating it in a different instrument or voice, changing its mode, and so forth – can color and develop the emotional content, so that now our memory will hold both the original motive and its altered restatement, and the emotional content of both. It is in part through carrying out this process on a massive scale that Wagner is able to achieve such a sense of continuity in the cycle, and such a sense of urgency and ongoing dramatic development. That the musico-dramatic process unfolds in this way over the sixteen or so hours of the *Ring* suggests that it is in important ways *about* memory; it is about how we retain psychological experiences, how we remember and re-experience them, and how these memories and experiences ramify and connect with other comparable experiences over time.

What may not be immediately apparent on the musical and dramatic surface of the cycle is how the process of memory and cross-reference contributes to large-scale musical form, and how there are elements of that form that simultaneously incorporate the ongoing psychological development, and answer to the dictates of purely musical form. Most of the central dramatic symbols or elements in the drama are associated with a particular musical key: the Rhine, in its primal state, is in E♭ major (CWE 1); Valhalla is in D♭ major (CWE 4), and Nibelheim in D♭'s relative minor, B♭ minor (CWE 7); the sword is in C major (CWE 12), the renunciation of love in C minor (CWE 3), and Alberich's Curse in B minor (CWE 9). Not only do the motives themselves recur across musical and dramatic time, but the keys do as well – the most central keys controlling vast stretches of musical time. Two examples must suffice. First, the half-diminished version of Woglinde's Ring melody noted above becomes a central symbol of evil in the cycle – most powerfully in that it is this very chord that Alberich intones in his Curse of the Ring in Scene 4 of *Rheingold*, but also that it recurs at the same pitch level, with increasingly desperate and tragic implications, throughout *Götterdämmerung*.

Second, associative musical keys combine with elements of musical-formal symmetry to articulate an overriding formal pattern to the entire cycle. *Das Rheingold*, which progresses from the initial scene in the bottom of the Rhine to the entrance of the gods into Valhalla, accordingly moves from the E♭ major of the Rhine to the D♭ major of Valhalla over the course of the opera. *Rheingold* is also structured such that the opening scene, with Alberich and the Rhinemaidens, is separate from the fundamental Valhalla – Nibelheim – Valhalla symmetry of the other three scenes. So *Rheingold* is structured as one scene plus three, moving from E♭ major to D♭ major. *Götterdämmerung*, though a work on a far vaster scale, also moves from E♭ (now in the minor mode) to D♭ major. It also, like *Rheingold*, has a one-plus-three format: a prologue followed by three acts. But the cycle as a whole is also structured by the one-plus-three principle: Wagner's "Stage Festival Play for Three Days and a Preliminary Evening." And, since both *Rheingold* and *Götterdämmerung* begin in E♭ and end in D♭, the entire cycle does the same. The keys that are grounded in dramatic symbols thus operate both on the level of the immediate presentation of those symbols, and on the level of the shape of the whole.

5. Publication, first staging, and significant performances

This aspect of the *Ring*'s history begins with Wagner's self-financed publication in February 1853 of fifty copies of the text, which he sent to select friends. Wagner soon came to regret publishing the libretto before it was set to music. The reaction among his friends was, for the most part, either antagonism or bemusement. In 1856, he offered publication rights for the scores of the *Ring* to BREITKOPF & HÄRTEL, but the negotiations led nowhere. After completing *Tristan* in 1859, and in desperate financial straits, he sold the publication rights of the *Ring* scores to Otto WESENDONCK, who immediately paid 6,000 francs each for *Rheingold* and *Walküre*, with 6,000 more to follow for *Siegfried* and *Götterdämmerung*, upon completion. Soon afterwards, early in 1860, Wesendonck also agreed to pay Wagner 6,000 francs for *Siegfried*, even though it was not yet finished. Fortunately, it was at the same time that the music publishing company B. SCHOTT'S SÖHNE in Mainz became interested in Wagner and his works, even the operas of the as-yet-incomplete *Ring*. The composer was thus able to sell publication rights for both the full score and the piano-vocal score of *Rheingold* to Schott for 10,000 francs; but he did so without compensating Wesendonck, who actually owned the rights. Schott acted quickly, and published the piano-vocal score of *Rheingold* (arr. Karl KLINDWORTH) in 1861.

Two years later, in 1863, with only *Rheingold* and *Walküre* complete, *Siegfried* two-thirds written, and *Götterdämmerung* not even begun, Wagner, boosted by the publication of the piano-vocal score of *Rheingold*, published the full poem of the *Ring*. His introduction to the volume, entitled "VORWORT ZUR HERAUSGABE DER DICHTUNG DES BÜHNENFESTSPIELS *DER RING DES NIBELUNGEN*," sets out his intentions for the cycle along with a plea for the means to bring it to the stage. Producing the work would require a new theatre built especially for the cycle, and a festival devoted to its performance.

Schott's Söhne, apparently pleased with the sales of *Rheingold*, issued Klindworth's piano-vocal score of *Walküre* in 1865, and that of *Siegfried* in 1871. At this point, still no full score of any of the works had been published. The performances of *Rheingold* and *Walküre* that Ludwig II demanded, and got, in 1869 and 1870, respectively, used scores copied from Wagner's fair copies by the conductor Hans RICHTER. As the year of the cycle's premiere (1876) approached, publication activity accelerated. The first edition of Wagner's complete works (*Gesammelte Schriften*, pub. 1871–3) included the complete *Ring* poem as volumes 5 and 6. Soon thereafter, Schott's produced the full score of *Rheingold* in 1873, *Walküre* in 1874, the piano-vocal score of *Götterdämmerung* in 1875, and the full scores of *Siegfried* and *Götterdämmerung* in 1876.

Wagner's original plan for his "Nibelung Drama," in the early 1850s, was to build a theater solely for the cycle, to present it in a festival dedicated to the event, and then to destroy the theatre. As he worked on composing the cycle in the years following, the idea of destroying the theatre gradually faded away, but the special theatre and exclusive festival remained central to his conception throughout. His rescue by Ludwig in 1864, along with his subsequent artistic successes with *Tristan* and *Meistersinger*, enabled him to fulfill this dream with the construction of the *Festspielhaus* FESTIVAL THEATER in Bayreuth for the premiere of the cycle in 1876.

For the premiere, Wagner's concept of stage production was dominated by the nineteenth-century "theatre of illusion" – the creation of an illusory dramatic space entirely separated from everyday experience. Hence his insistence on naturalistic theatrical effects; whatever he imagined must be literally brought to life on the stage: the Rhinemaidens must appear to be swimming in the Rhine, the rainbow bridge must be a real bridge, Fafner must appear in *Siegfried* as a real dragon, and so forth. To achieve such effects, he hired the Viennese landscape painter Josef HOFFMANN to produce landscape studies depicting what Wagner imagined as the scenic environment of the cycle; the BRÜCKNER brothers to realize the actual scenery from the paintings; Carl Emil DOEPLER, a professor of costume design in Berlin, to make the costumes; and Carl BRANDT, the leading German technical director of the time, to manage the difficult stage instructions. Given the demands upon them – Wagner was breaking new ground in German theater – the enterprise was extraordinarily successful.

Nevertheless, Wagner was not pleased, and immediately after the 1876 performances he began, as is clear from his letters of the time, to take account of what went wrong, and to make plans for improvements next time.

Two years after the premiere, Angelo NEUMANN persuaded the composer to grant him rights to produce the complete *Ring* in Leipzig in 1878, and Berlin in 1881. Wagner had originally planned that the cycle would only be performed in Bayreuth, but financial problems prohibited him from mounting another performance there in the foreseeable future. The Leipzig and Berlin performances were immensely successful, and demonstrated convincingly that the *Ring* would sell outside the narrow confines of Bayreuth – so convincingly, in fact, that in 1882–3 Neumann was able, with Wagner's blessing, to launch a travelling *Ring* production that brought the cycle to twenty-five European cities, from LONDON to ST. PETERSBURG, helping it to become known throughout the continent.

After Wagner's death in 1883, COSIMA took control of the Bayreuth Festival, with the self-proclaimed intent of producing Wagner's works exactly as he wanted them – something she considered herself uniquely positioned to do. She did not attempt to revive the *Ring* until 1896, twenty years after the premiere. As in most of her other productions, her conservative artistic tastes – her insistence on using essentially the same naturalistic sets and costumes as in 1876, and her obsession with clear diction and stylized gestures, and with slow tempi – brought her harsh criticism, as did her autocratic means of enforcing them. After the 1906 festival, she turned the reins over to SIEGFRIED WAGNER, who supervised twenty-one performances of the complete *Ring* cycle between 1908 and 1930. Though not exceptionally creative as a director, Siegfried did modernize the lighting, develop new scenic effects, and in general move away from the naturalism of the 1876 and 1896 productions.

Toward the end of his tenure, in the late 1920s, he began to use some of Adolphe APPIA'S ideas, whose work was introduced into the BAYREUTH CIRCLE by Houston Stewart CHAMBERLAIN. Appia despised naturalistic scenery and costumes and wanted to bring out the aesthetic values of the later Wagner, who realized the full power of his work in the music, as opposed to the values of the earlier Wagner of *Oper und Drama*, who imagined a total work of art guided by and subservient to the text.

The path towards increasingly abstract staging continued after World War II in WIELAND WAGNER's famous settings. More recently, as his approach fractured, several different strands of interpretation can be isolated. They generally differ along two axes. First, productions differ with respect to which character is considered the cycle's pivotal figure. Some earlier stagings emphasized Siegfried, but Wotan increasingly became the center of gravity. More recently, productions (such as the Copenhagen production of 2006) have given that role to Brünnhilde. This shift in emphasis also usually compels a parallel adjustment in the interpretation of the individual operas.

The second axis along which productions have differed started with the tumultuous Basel staging by Adolphe Appia, which launched the idea of increasingly spare *Rings*. While the Nazi years brought back the sumptuous GERMANNESS of the late nineteenth century, Wagner's heirs looked to productions like Appia's after the war. As swords, bearskins, and helmets faded into the background, productions generally treated the *Ring* as an allegory, but differed substantially in what kind of an allegory they understood the cycle to represent: political (as in CHÉREAU's centennial *Ring*), psychological (as in the Copenhagen *Ring*), or ecological (as in Francesca Zambello's San Francisco production).

Postwar stagings of the *Ring* cycle generally deemphasize the Germanic and mythological elements of Wagner's story, and those by Wagner's grandsons Wolfgang and Wieland preferred a generally psychologized approach. While "New Bayreuth" sought to periodize Wagner's cycle differently (pre-war stagings generally presented the *Ring* as a late Romantic work, while the Wagner brothers presented it as one of the earliest works of MODERNISM), other stagings emphasized the *Ring*'s connection to its own era. They followed critics such as George Bernard SHAW (and later Theodor W. ADORNO) in understanding the *Ring* as a reflection of Wagner's own frustrated political hopes, and a more general reflection on the nature of MODERNITY.

While traces of this reading go back to Wagner himself (Adorno points to Wotan's garb as "wanderer" in *Siegfried*, which rehearses the dress of the disappointed revolutionary), the first significant staging to make these ideas central was Patrice Chéreau's celebrated production of the centenary *Ring* at Bayreuth (1976). His characters inhabit an industrial wasteland rather than a Germanic forest. The Valencia production of the *Ring* updates this approach by situating the *Ring*'s world somewhere between the industrial age and the virtual world. Similarly, the Copenhagen production by the Royal Danish Opera House (2006) gives the cycle a decidedly feminist spin, and presents Wotan's rise and fall as that of a bourgeois patriarch. His Valhalla is a new company headquarters, Loge an unruly anarchist, and the failure of Wotan's plans the dissolution of a mercantile dynasty.

Stagings have also responded to Wagner's insistence that his unprecedented operas required an unprecedented kind of presentation. For a cycle that seems rather leery of technology, Wagner insisted on a technologically advanced mode of presentation, as he outlined in his preface to the first published version of the four operas' libretti. The hidden orchestra, the unusually elaborate sets, the so-called "Wagner-curtain," and his prodigious use of steam aimed at a kind of effect that Theodor Adorno called "phantasmagoric." As part of Wagner's legacy, Ring stagings have been forced to grapple with these technological demands. Some have done so by ignoring them – for instance in the well-regarded Stuttgart production in 1999/2000, which pointedly handed the staging to four different directors. They have also done so by controverting Wagner's demands, as in many early postwar Bayreuth productions – for instance Wieland Wagner's 1951 Ring, which borrows deliberately from Brechtian estrangement techniques; or they have instead embraced Wagner's technological demands, "updating" the Ring's "phantasmagoria" according to the latest technologies. The latter has emerged as a common theme recently, be it the Ring production in Valencia in 2007, or Robert Lepage's infamous "machine" in the 2010 Metropolitan Opera production of the cycle.

6. Critical reception and problems of interpretation

While the Ring's reception has been as varied as the gamut of its admirers and detractors, some general developments can be isolated. Given the Ring's multiple structure, the tragedy of Siegfried, the larger tragedy of Wotan, and the sacrifice and triumph of Brünnhilde, different times have lent themselves to different readings. Early on, listeners often saw in the Ring a Nibelungenlied opera and placed Wagner's cycle in the context of a whole range of Siegfried-themed art that proliferated after the rediscovery of the Nibelungenlied in 1755.

In keeping with the basic tenor of most of those works, they understood Wagner's cycle as an affirmation of Germanic spirit, as a German national opera (a view Wagner encouraged), and led them to latch onto Siegfried, ignoring or marginalizing those aspects of the dramatic whole that undercut both Siegfried's stature and his status as the cycle's center. Those who understood Wagner to be making a more complicated political, and a generally more pessimistic, statement necessarily emphasized Wotan's schemes and their eventual undoing. George Bernard Shaw seems genuinely uninterested in Siegfried himself. It is the story of Nibelungs, gods, Rheinmaidens, and Gibichungs that holds his interest.

Shaw also juxtaposes two major philosophical readings of the Ring. Once the cycle is understood not as the story of Siegfried's Bildung, but as the story of Wotan's tragic choices and their increasingly dire consequences, the question emerges whether we are meant to lament Wotan's undoing or not. This question is complicated by the fact that Wagner probably would have given a different answer to that question at different times. The younger Wagner, reader of Ludwig FEUERBACH and Heinrich HEINE, seems to have understood Wotan's undoing as a necessary step towards a more humane and humanistic world – the world of the gods reaches its "twilight" precisely because it cannot sustain the weight of its own internal contradictions. The later Wagner, influenced above all by the inveterate pessimism of Arthur SCHOPENHAUER, suggests that Siegfried's blithe destruction of the old order (by shattering Wotan's spear, engraved with all treaties), and his cavalier inability to replace that old order with a better new one (preferring domestic bliss with Brünnhilde), suggest that Wagner lost faith in the revolutionary narrative that animated his earliest drafts for both *Siegfrieds Tod* and *Götterdämmerung*. Readers such as Thomas MANN and Theodor W. Adorno understood the *Ring* as an allegory for the nineteenth century, for the process of modernization and the world of the bourgeoisie. Written between the revolutionary year of 1848 and the beginnings of the German Empire, during an era of industrialization and the ascendancy of the bourgeoisie, the *Ring* represented for them a kind of stocktaking, a diagnosis of the promise of bourgeois revolution and its eventual frustration. Other interpretations have emphasized the ecocritical aspects of Wagner's conception: for them, the *Ring* tells of a world brought into disarray when gold that delighted merely with its luster instead becomes a commodity to be exchanged, bartered, and eventually fought over.

Finally, Wagner's reception has shaped subsequent interpretations of his operas – most centrally, the Nazis' attraction to Wagner (and Wagner's heirs' own attraction to far-right politics). Alberich, *Walküre*, Wotan, and other *Ring* personages lent their names to the Nazis' crimes and their war. After the war, it became *de rigueur* to ask whether the *Ring* cycle had somehow elicited its instrumentalization in the Third Reich. Whether Wagner is fascist; whether his portrayal of Siegfried owes something to Nietzsche's "blonde beast" or the racial ideal of the Nazis; whether Mime or Alberich are modeled on Wagner's infamous characterizations of Jewish speech and song – all these questions began to be hotly debated even while war still raged in Europe.

ADRIAN DAUB AND PATRICK MCCRELESS

Robert Bailey, "The Structure of the *Ring* and Its Evolution," *19th-Century Music* 1.1 (1977): 48–61.

Deryck Cooke, *I Saw the World End: A Study of Wagner's "Ring"* (see bibliography).

Barry Millington, "*Der Ring des Nibelungen*: Conception and Interpretation" in Thomas S. Grey ed., *The Cambridge Companion to Wagner* (see bibliography): 74–84.

Ritter, Emilie (1825–63), daughter of Wagner's patroness JULIE RITTER, sister of Alexander and KARL. Corresponded with Wagner from 1850 to 1859. She attended the ZURICH Wagner festival of 1853. Wagner first recounted his "LA SPEZIA" vision for the opening of *Das RHEINGOLD* in a letter to her of 29 December 1854. His last letters, in 1859, begged for a large loan. Their correspondence then ceased. CHRIS WALTON

Ritter, Julie (b. Hamburg, 25 Nov. 1794; d. Pisa, 1869), mother of Alexander, EMILIE, and KARL. She lived in Narva until the death of her husband in 1840, and moved to DRESDEN with her children, where they became acquainted with Hans von BÜLOW and Wagner. In 1850, together with the LAUSSOTS, she gave Wagner an annual allowance of 3,000 francs (roughly equivalent to three years' rent for a ZURICH apartment). In 1851, an inheritance allowed her to take on sole responsibility for the allowance until circumstances caused her to discontinue it in 1859. CHRIS WALTON

See also MONEY

Ritter, Karl (also Carl) (b. Narva [Estonia], 8 Oct. 1830; d. Verona, 9 Oct. 1891), German composer and writer. Son of JULIE RITTER, brother of Alexander and EMILIE. Grew up in Dresden in the 1840s, where he studied composition with Robert SCHUMANN and became acquainted with Hans von BÜLOW and

Wagner. Moved to SWITZERLAND in mid-1850 to be close to Wagner, whom he joined on HIKING tours and on a water cure in Albisbrunn (see HEALTH). Attended the Weimar premiere of LOHENGRIN at Wagner's request. Ritter was instrumental in bringing Bülow to ZURICH. Wagner had him appointed to conduct at the Zurich theater, but stepped in when (according to Wagner) he proved incompetent. Ritter moved variously to St. Gallen, Lausanne, and Geneva, remaining all the while in Wagner's orbit. His dramatic sketch on TRISTAN AND ISOLDE (since lost) supposedly prompted Wagner's own interest in the topic. In 1857, Ritter published piano works and songs with BREITKOPF & HÄRTEL. In 1858, when COSIMA von Bülow was in a severe depression after her marriage, she and Ritter very nearly went through with a suicide pact in a boat on Lake Geneva. It was Ritter who suggested that Wagner move to VENICE for the winter of 1858/9. They travelled there together, but after Wagner left Venice they never met again. Wagner's attempt to visit him there in 1882 failed when Ritter apparently refused to see him. Wagner's later attitude to him was one of condescension, though their correspondence leaves no doubt as to the warmth of their FRIENDSHIP in the 1850s.   CHRIS WALTON

Peter Jost, "Karl Ritter, Komponist zwischen Schumann und Wagner," in *"Neue Bahnen": Robert Schumann und seine musikalischen Zeitgenossen*, ed. Bernhard R. Appel (Mainz: Schott, 2002): 182–204.

Chris Walton, *Richard Wagner's Zurich* (see bibliography).

Röckel, August (b. Graz, 1 Dec. 1814; d. Budapest, 18 July 1876), conductor, composer, pamphleteer; son of tenor Joseph Röckel. Assisted ROSSINI at the PARIS Théâtre Italien before assuming positions in Bamberg, Weimar, and finally DRESDEN (1843–9) as assistant to Wagner. Röckel withdrew his 1839 opera *Farinelli*, accepted for Dresden performance, as unworthy compared to Wagner's work. Dismissed for subversion, Röckel edited the socialist *Volksblätter*, to which Wagner contributed. Following the DRESDEN UPRISING, Röckel received a death sentence, commuted; his prison CORRESPONDENCE adds greatly to understanding of the RING. Wagner's letter of 25/26 January 1854 presents WOTAN (Wodan) rising to the tragic heights of willing his own destruction, a fundamental "pessimistic" shift in his conception. After release from prison in 1862, Röckel edited newspapers in Coburg, Frankfurt, Munich, and Vienna, and joined August Bebel's Verband Deutscher Arbeitervereine. FRIENDSHIP faltered during the later 1860s: Wagner held Röckel responsible for the dissemination of rumors concerning the relationship with COSIMA.

                                                                MARK BERRY

See also POLITICS; REVOLUTION

August Röckel, *Sachsens Erhebung und das Zuchthaus in Waldheim* (Frankfurt am Main: Adelmann, 1865).

Roller, Alfred (b. Brünn, 2 Oct. 1864; d. Vienna, 21 June 1935), Austrian painter and scenic designer. A leading practitioner of the Vienna Secession, Roller took up scenic design in collaboration with Gustav MAHLER, during the latter's directorship of the Vienna Court Opera (1897–1907). Their ground-breaking production of TRISTAN UND ISOLDE (1903) sustained the principles of the GESAMTKUNSTWERK but broke from the scenic models of BAYREUTH. The absence of historicist detail and high level of abstraction in the scenery, as well as the use of light as the main visual element, displayed the influence of APPIA's writings and represented one of the first successful realizations of scenic symbolism in European theater. Productions of *Das RHEINGOLD* (1905) and *Die WALKÜRE* (1907), though innovative, were less successful. In 1934, apparently at HITLER's request, Roller designed sets for *PARSIFAL* at Bayreuth, as the originals by Paul von JOUKOWSKY were no longer usable. But he effectively replicated the original sets and the production was a failure. Despite this, Roller remains one of the pioneering figures in modernist operatic production.   SIMON WILLIAMS

Romantic hero. The figure of the romantic hero is an early manifestation of the modern anti-hero, a character who inveighs against society rather than leads it toward utopian goals. As the central character or presence in much literature of the romantic age, in pre-revolutionary literature the romantic hero evinced several of the features of the Rousseauian "natural man" who, rejecting the civilized world, aspired to live at one with nature in small, self-sustaining rural communities. The later, post-revolutionary romantic hero was almost identical with the Byronic hero, the profoundly disaffected rebel who withdrew from society and, in his isolation, provided a radical critique of a corrupt and unjust world, but also destroyed himself due to his incapacity to reconcile his inner conflicts.

LISZT observed that *Der FLIEGENDE HOLLÄNDER* was a Byronic work, and the despair of the DUTCHMAN, who longs to find a home in society and yet is profoundly alienated from it, is perhaps Wagner's clearest embodiment of the later romantic hero. TANNHÄUSER also displays many features of this figure. He has indulged in sexual activities that are taboo to the strait-laced society of the Wartburg and his songs lack the restraint and poise this society favors. He dies an outcast, torn apart by his desire for fleshly pleasure and his need to repent, because in repentance he might find acceptance by the society that has ostracized him. Other manifestations of the late romantic hero in Wagner might include SIEGMUND, who fights against the cruelty of a world in which power and greed operate, but in his active defense of victims of oppression, he displays positive features that are not common in the figure. TRISTAN, whose LOVE for ISOLDE impels him to withdraw from the social and political arena, shows no need to be reconciled with society, but founders on his incapacity to come to terms with his growing sense that his desire for Isolde arises from the same physical and emotional bonds that tied him to his parents.

The earlier, pre-revolutionary manifestation of the romantic hero is not that common in Wagner, primarily because the idea of the "natural man" lacked potency in the mid-nineteenth century. Nevertheless, Wagner was familiar with and admired the writings of Rousseau, and at least one of his characters, SIEGFRIED, shares many of the features of "natural man." He grows up in the forest, with animals as his companions, and he senses that freedom resides primarily in living in nature. In Act II of *SIEGFRIED*, during the "Forest Murmurs" sequence, he becomes mesmerized by the sounds and playful appearances of nature, and longs for reunion with his mother. However,

Siegfried's later career, in the last part of *Siegfried* and throughout *GÖTTERDÄMMERUNG*, has little in common with either the early or late romantic hero.   SIMON WILLIAMS

Simon Williams, *Wagner and the Romantic Hero* (Cambridge University Press, 2004).

Romanticism (literary), held sway in German literature for more than 40 years. While the often theoretical texts of what is usually considered "early" Romanticism (1794–1801) were important though marginal, Romantic literature of various stripes became the mainstream in the early 1800s. "High" Romanticism (1801–15) and "late" Romanticism (1815–40), connected with names such as E. T. A. HOFFMANN, Ludwig Tieck, and Joseph von Eichendorff, signaled a kind of cultural dominance that was to persist well into the 1830s. By that time, more politically minded writers had broken with the poetics of "late" Romanticism and its emphasis on individual psychology, medieval settings, and the uncanny. Wagner's formative years straddle this divide as Romanticism gave way to newer, more overtly politicized impulses. He grew up with the texts of what is usually considered "high" and "late" Romanticism, but he articulated his own aesthetics (and his first musical projects) in the context of the first generation of poets, critics, and scholars – the so-called YOUNG GERMANY – to turn its back on Romanticism.

While Wagner's debt to the philosophy of Romanticism (SCHELLING, HEGEL, etc.), its tributaries and offshoots, has been clarified in recent years, Wagner's debt to the literature of German Romanticism has remained somewhat opaque. That is partly because German Romanticism itself was so varied, and partly because its legacy in Germany was so suffused and pervasive. To cite only a few instances: *Der FLIEGENDE HOLLÄNDER* is clearly a "Romantic" opera in the vein of WEBER, but it takes its plot from a parody of Romanticism, written by its great liquidator, Heinrich HEINE. The critique of the social division of labor implicit in the notion of GESAMTKUNSTWERK owes an incontrovertible debt to Romanticism; and yet Wagner's most explicit philosophical source was another anti-Romantic, Arthur SCHOPENHAUER. And while Wagner draws again and again on fairy-tale motifs, he seems highly ambivalent about their narrative structure and aesthetic value.

In *MEIN LEBEN* (My Life, 1865–81), Wagner highlights E. T. A. Hoffmann and Ludwig Tieck as early literary influences. While the opera projects they inspired (a version of *Die Minen von Falun*, among others) did not come to fruition, elements from the works of Hoffmann, Tieck, and the brothers Grimm can be found throughout Wagner's operas, especially once he discovered the MIDDLE AGES as a setting for his works. The poem to *TANNHÄUSER* incorporates ideas from Hoffmann (*Der Sängerkrieg*), Tieck (*Der getreue Eckhart und der Tannenhäuser*), and from Ludwig Bechstein's collections of fairy tales. While not every one of Wagner's mature operas owes such pronounced debts to Romanticism, individual plot points, character names, or settings can be traced either to the Romantic poets themselves, or to the literatures they had recuperated.

Beyond the individual motifs, the materials and epochs to which Wagner turned for his libretti more generally emerged from the quarry of Romanticism. It was the Romantics who systematically collected fairy tales and elevated them into a literary genre; it was they who led the rediscovery of the MIDDLE AGES and the early medieval epics; above all they turned the *Nibelungenlied* into a German national epic. August Wilhelm Schlegel and others had suggested detailed genealogies for MYTHS, pointing to commonalities and divergences among local folklores. While they studied these parallels theoretically, works such as the *Deutsche Mythologie* contain the blueprint for the kind of mythagogic syncretism Wagner would practice in elaborating above all the RING. When Wagner imbued his FRICKA with characteristics of Hera, or combined his LOGE with Hermes, Mephistopheles, and Prometheus, he was relying on the analyses of the Romantic theorists of myth. If they had suggested that parallel mythic constructions in different cultures pointed to common and forgotten ancestors to those myths, Wagner simply created these hypothetical ancestors out of whole cloth.

Even the plot mechanics of Wagner's operas owe a clear debt to German Romanticism: DREAMS, potions, and magic items had been plot devices of operatic story-telling well before Romanticism, but the way in which states of trance, forgetfulness, or dreaming put the subject in touch with a "deeper" reality was something Wagner took from Romantic novels and fairy tales. He took from them also a concern with language's and art's ability to adequately lay hold to "deeper" or more "absolute" truths. When LOHENGRIN forbids ELSA to ask for his name, when Wagner is concerned to reduce narration in the *Ring*, when obtuse PARSIFAL fails to understand the ritual he has witnessed, another worry looms in the background: if art is to plumb depths that go "beyond" the world of everyday experience (what Schopenhauer calls "representation"), then what in it needs to change to make this possible? This worry, which would eventually give rise to the idea of the *Gesamtkunstwerk*, is perhaps Wagner's most direct inheritance from German Romantic literature. Though he transformed their plots and myths, the sense that art had to change fundamentally if it were to penetrate to deeper structures of mind and world was one Wagner accepted wholesale.   ADRIAN DAUB

Rossini, Gioachino (b. Pesaro, 29 Feb. 1792; d. Paris, 13 Nov. 1868), Italian opera composer. When Wagner was still a child, his sister Klara (Wolfram) made her debut in *La Cenerentola* at the DRESDEN Hofoper in 1824. Later, he claimed that already then he had developed a strong preference for German over Italian opera. Yet his attitude towards Rossini remained as ambiguous as it was against BEL CANTO opera in general. In OPER UND DRAMA (Opera and Drama, 1851) he refers to Rossini as "the uncommonly handy modeler of artificial flowers" and that "[t]he only living thing he had come upon in Opera, was absolute Melody" (SSD 3:250–1). Rossini and his audience are characterized as reactionaries, opposed to OPERATIC REFORM and thus spelling the death of the genre. A personal meeting between Wagner and Rossini in PARIS (March 1860), arranged and documented by Edmond Michotte, proceeded with mutual respect, but did not lead to an aesthetic reconciliation.

SEBASTIAN STAUSS

Herbert Weinstock, trans. and ed., *Richard Wagner's Visit to Rossini (Paris 1860) and An Evening at Rossini's in Beau-Sejour (Passy) by Edmond Michotte* (Chicago University Press, 1968).

Rubinstein, Joseph (b. Starokonstantinov, 8 Feb. 1847; d. Lucerne, 15 Sep. 1884), pianist, composer, and arranger. In March 1872, Rubinstein, a Russian JEW, wrote to Wagner "demanding salvation" from his race (CWD 7 March 1872), by assisting with the RING at Bayreuth. He arrived on 21 April and joined the NIBELUNG CHANCELLERY, becoming what Wagner later called "Wahnfried's supreme court pianist!" (letter to LUDWIG II, 16 March 1881). Alternately praised and taunted by the Wagners, Rubinstein's awkward position was typical of many Jewish Wagnerians. Cosima remarked that Rubinstein "in the way of Jews has copied all sorts of things from my father, much to his own advantage" (CWD 7 June 1874). He made accomplished PIANO TRANSCRIPTIONS of Wagner's work, including the SIEGFRIED IDYLL, which apparently "pleased" Wagner (CWD 14 December 1874), though the Meister was occasionally "vexed by the 'capers' of J. Rubinstein, who starts off playing like a virtuoso" (CWD 10 June 1874). Soon after Wagner's death, Rubinstein committed suicide. Twelve years earlier, Cosima had complained specifically in reference to Rubinstein that "these young people are a great problem, the way they do not know what to do with themselves" (CWD 22 August 1872).   DAVID HUCKVALE

Russia. Wagner's music was first performed in Russia, as far as is known, on 15 March 1856, when the ST. PETERSBURG Philharmonic Society played a concert including the TANNHÄUSER Overture. Wagner's most enthusiastic Russian supporter was the composer and critic Alexander SEROV, who became familiar with Wagner's ideas through OPER UND DRAMA (Opera and Drama) and Das KUNSTWERK DER ZUKUNFT (The Artwork of the Future) in the early 1850s. Serov also translated Wagner into Russian and influenced the first complete opera performances in the late 1860s. His plan was to get *Tannhäuser* staged at the Mariinski Theater (St. Petersburg), but the Board of Directors chose LOHENGRIN instead, performed in 1868. However, it must be remembered that, in the nineteenth century, Finland, Estonia, Courland, and Livonia were all part of the Russian Empire, and *Tannhäuser* had already been performed in Helsinki, Tallinn, and RIGA in the 1850s. Riga, with its strong German minority, became the most influential Wagner center on the shores of the Baltic Sea.

Despite Serov's efforts, there were anti-Wagnerian sentiments among Russian composers. Alexander Dargomyzhsky became acquainted with Wagner after he borrowed a piano transcription of *Tannhäuser* from Serov, but became hostile towards Wagner, fearing perhaps that "the music of the future" had negative influences on the emerging New Russian Nationalist School – known later as "The Five." Instead of seeing Wagner as a threat, the composers of the younger generation, including Mili Balakirev, César Cui, Modest Mussorgsky, Alexander Borodin, and Nicolai Rimsky-Korsakov, seemed rather uninterested.

Wagner recognized the importance of the Russian musical scene. Between February and April 1863, he made a promotional tour to St. Petersburg and Moscow. Given his participation in the DRESDEN UPRISING (1849), Wagner was regarded as a revolutionary. Throughout his visit, he was kept under surveillance by the secret police. An eight-page memorandum concerning

Wagner's movements has been preserved in the Russian State Archives in Moscow. On 12 February, the police stated that Wagner, despite his participation in the uprisings of 1848 (sic), seemed to have settled down.

The Grand Duchess Elena Pavlovna was Wagner's most significant acquaintance in Russia, and she promised to support his projects with annual donations. The Russian tour was so successful that, at the beginning of 1864, Wagner intended to return to Russia. This did not materialize, however, as he suddenly received an invitation to MUNICH from King LUDWIG II. Later, Russian aristocrats, and artists too, were a visible part of the festival audience in Bayreuth.

Wagner's influence on Russian MODERNISM was distinctive in the late nineteenth and early twentieth centuries. He inspired both symbolists, such as Vyacheslav Ivanov (1866–1949) and Alexander Blok (1880–1921), and theater theorists and practitioners, such as Sergei Diaghilev (1872–1929), Vsevolod Meyerhold (1874–1940), and Sergei Eisenstein (1898–1948). In the Soviet Union, Wagner aroused strong interest before World War II, which culminated in Eisenstein's production of *Die WALKÜRE* at the Bolshoi Theater in 1940. The postwar period saw a clear decline in interest, but, during *glasnost* and since, Wagner has been rediscovered.   HANNU SALMI

See also WAGNER IN THE VISUAL ARTS

Rosamund Bartlett, *Wagner and Russia* (Cambridge University Press, 1995).

Sachs, Hans (b. Nuremberg, 5 Nov. 1494; d. Nuremberg, 19 Jan. 1576). Married to Künigunde Creutzer from 1519 until her death in March 1560; some eighteen months later, he wed the young widow Barbara Endres (née Harscher), forty years his junior.

Sachs was the most prolific German author of the sixteenth century. He learned the art of *Meistersang* in 1509–11 while apprenticing as a shoemaker, and eventually produced over 4,000 mastersongs, largely on biblical themes. He is also responsible for the *Schulzettel* of 1540, a compilation of local statutes that became a model for mastersinging guilds elsewhere, as well as for the *Gemerkbüchlein*, the earliest surviving minutes of the Nuremberg MASTERSINGERS' competitions from 1555 to 1561. Nonetheless, Sachs is better known today as an author of humorous carnival plays (*Fastnachtspiele*), often didactic portrayals of squabbling couples, and four Reformation dialogues, which belong to the best prose works of the period. His most successful work in support of the Reformation was *Die WITTEMBERGISCHE NACHTIGALL* of 1523. GLENN EHRSTINE

See also HANS SACHS; *MEISTERSINGER VON NÜRNBERG*, Die; NUREMBERG

Saga of the Volsungs, the. See *Völsunga Saga*

St. Petersburg, in Wagner's day the capital of the Russian Empire. Site of the probable first performance of Wagner's music in RUSSIA: 15 March 1856, *TANNHÄUSER* Overture. Real interest in Wagner started seven years later, when he visited both St. Petersburg and Moscow with the support of Alexander SEROV. Wagner arrived on 12 February 1863 (Julian calendar). Regarded both as a celebrity and as a dangerous revolutionary, he was followed by the secret police. He gave concerts but also lectured on his plans for the RING. On 15 April, he returned to Germany. Later, St. Petersburg became the host of the first performance of a Wagner opera in Russia, when *Lohengrin* was staged at the Mariinski Theater (14 October 1868). In Finland, there was a persistent rumor that, during his stay in St. Petersburg, Wagner had also visited the famous Imatra rapids (Finland). This never happened, but the rumor also reached Wagner's ears through Serov in 1869 (CWD 11 July 1869). HANNU SALMI

Sämtliche Werke. Founded in 1968 by Carl DAHLHAUS and still in progress, *Richard Wagner: Sämtliche Werke* (SW) aims to provide the first collected edition of Richard Wagner's musical works. SW is published by Schott Music, and funded by the Gesellschaft zur Förderung der Richard Wagner-Gesamtausgabe in Mainz under the auspices of the Academy of Sciences and Literature (Mainz) and the Bavarian Academy of Fine Arts (Munich), making it the first critical edition of Wagner's works to be supported by an academic body. The edition, led by Dr. Egon Voss, is based in MUNICH and has employed Wagner specialists from Germany and the UK. Planned in sixty-nine volumes, it is divided into two series. Series (Reihe) A consists of fifty-seven volumes of musical scores complete with critical commentary (*Notenteil*). Series B has twelve volumes of literary sources and documentation relating to each of the works (*Dokumententeil*).

As of 2011, fifty-one volumes of Series A and eight of Series B have been published. Apart from one volume (31) devoted to drafts of, and contextual documentation about, incomplete or fragmentary works (see STAGE WORKS, INCOMPLETE), Series B comprises excerpts from CORRESPONDENCE, diaries, and autobiographies relevant to the completed stage works and their conception, genesis, performance(s), and subsequent interpretation(s) by the composer himself. These volumes are therefore not intended as mere append-ages, but are meant to shed light on Wagner's concept of the stage work as a continually evolving entity subject to constant reinterpretation. This explains the essentially literary nature of the enterprise (music sketches are limited to those notated in the margins of prose and verse drafts, or in letters), which does not place exclusive emphasis merely on the genesis of the works. The voluminous extant musical sketches and drafts prior to the completion of the scores are for the most part still unpublished.

Prepared in conjunction with the definitive catalogue WAGNER-WERK-VERZEICHNIS (WWV), SW incorporates minor or "lesser" works (e.g., juven-ilia, songs, instrumental works, and occasional works, see WORKS, LESSER MUSICAL), many of which have not previously been published. Furthermore, the edition includes not only marginal or incomplete works, but also multiple versions of well-known works. (*Der FLIEGENDE HOLLÄNDER*, for example, has been published in SW for the first time in its original instrumentation and Scottish setting.)

Plans for a collected edition can be traced to Wagner himself. On 26 August 1871 Wagner wrote to the publisher Hermann Müller that he was considering a "complete edition of the scores" of his operas, implying some degree of interpretation in the search for definitive versions of his works. In the absence of such clear-cut solutions, SW recognizes the need for critical evaluation of source material as a means of de-mythologizing Wagner as well as offering a more complex picture of his intentions.

The first significant collected edition of Wagner's works was attempted by the violist and conductor Michael Balling, who brought out the first volume with BREITKOPF & HÄRTEL in 1912. Balling introduced cosmetic changes in dynamics, phrasing, and articulation, in effect prioritizing the need for so-called "performing" editions over any rigorous philological criticism. Ten volumes were published over a period of approximately twenty years, and the project was aborted soon after Balling's death in 1925. The edition was reissued abridged in seven volumes by Da Capo Press, New York, in 1971. The fact that Balling had access to the manuscripts later in HITLER'S possession, and now missing, means that certain of his editions (e.g., *Die FEEN* and *Das LIEBESVERBOT*) preserve faint traces of important and irrecoverable evidence. (Suffice it to say that the absence of these scores has greatly aggravated the task of producing authoritative editions.) The Bayreuth archivist Otto STROBEL planned a collected edition under the aegis of the Wagner research institute (Richard-Wagner-Forschungsstätte) founded on Hitler's orders in 1938 and intended it as a continuation of Balling's. What might have been a more scholarly piece of work in the end never materialized.

JEREMY COLEMAN

John Deathridge, Martin Geck, and Egon Voss, eds., *Wagner-Werk-Verzeichnis: Verzeichnis der musikalischen Werke Richard Wagners und ihrer Quellen* (Mainz: Schott, 1986).
Egon Voss, *Wagner und kein Ende: Betrachtungen und Studien* (Zurich: Atlantis, 1996).

Sayn-Wittgenstein, Carolyne Iwanowska zu (b. Woronince [Ukraine], 8 Feb. 1819; d. Rome, 9 March 1887), Roman Catholic essayist, estranged wife of Prince Nicholas zu Sayn-Wittgenstein-Ludwigsburg, and long-term mistress of Franz LISZT. She met Liszt in 1847, moving to Weimar in 1848, where during numerous social gatherings at the Altenburg she encountered BERLIOZ, who dedicated *Les Troyens* to her, and WAGNER, whose music she passionately admired at first, but whose religious stage projects (especially *Jesus von Nazareth*) she cautioned against. Despite protracted negotiations, she and Liszt were unable to marry in Rome because of political opposition to an annulment of her first marriage. While she had supported Liszt's performances of *TANNHÄUSER* and *LOHENGRIN* in Weimar (and most likely ghost-wrote minor portions of his propagandistic essays on the same), by 1872 she came increasingly to resent Wagner's hold over Liszt, urging the latter to sever all ties with Wagner and COSIMA, whose Protestant marriage (along with Cosima's Protestant divorce and subsequent conversion) aggravated her own Catholic devotion.

DAVID TRIPPETT

Scaria, Emil (b. Graz, 18 Sep. 1838; d. Blasewitz, 22 July 1886), Austrian bass engaged at VIENNA (1873–86), where he sang WOTAN in the first production there of *Die WALKÜRE* (1875). His portrayal of GURNEMANZ (Bayreuth, 1882–4) was extravagantly admired, and he assumed duties as stage director for *PARSIFAL* at the first festival following Wagner's death. He also sang Wotan at the first performances of the *RING* in Berlin (1881) and London (1882).

DAVID BRECKBILL

Schelling, Friedrich Wilhelm Joseph (b. Leonberg [near Stuttgart], 27 Jan. 1775; d. Bad Ragaz, 20 Aug. 1854), German idealist philosopher, whose restless career spanned a bewildering array of positions. A child prodigy, Schelling studied together with HEGEL and the poet Friedrich Hölderlin at the Tübingen theological seminary. Teaching in Jena between 1798 and 1803, he enjoyed GOETHE's support and became famous as the charismatic visionary of the early ROMANTIC circle. During this period, he developed complementary theories of the subject and of nature, as well as an aesthetic philosophy that exalted art as the highest manifestation of the absolute (see *KUNSTRELIGION*). Between 1801 and 1809 Schelling elaborated his so-called "identity philosophy," in opposition to which Schelling's erstwhile ally Hegel soon began to outline his rival brand of idealism.

As Hegel's star kept rising, Schelling lapsed into obscurity, with no works published after 1812. Few took notice of the bold move beyond idealism in his speculations about the emergence of freedom and sense from the dark ground of divine being (1809–27). In his last decades, Schelling inquired into mythology and religion to formulate a "positive philosophy" that acknowledged the primacy of being before thought. Eliciting European-wide curiosity, in 1841 Schelling was called to teach in Berlin to counter the spread of Hegelianism. His lectures perplexed audiences and interest in him quickly subsided. Long eclipsed by Hegel, in recent years Schelling has received considerable attention as a forerunner of such thinkers as SCHOPENHAUER, Marx, Kierkegaard, Freud, and Heidegger.

Although GLASENAPP suggests that the young Wagner was a Schellingian, Wagner's references to Schelling are rare and dismissive. His friend Gustav Schlesier tried to make him read Schelling's *System of Transcendental Idealism* (1800), with little success. Yet the young Wagner was undoubtedly exposed to Schelling's later ideas through his uncle ADOLF, who had studied with Schelling, as well as through the Schellingian scholars Johann Arnold Kanne and Christian Hermann Weiße. Wagner likely read, or was indirectly influenced by, the transcripts of Schelling's lectures that were in circulation from the 1830s onwards. In November 1880 Constantin Frantz published a three-volume book on Schelling dedicated to Wagner. Immersing himself in the book for several weeks, Wagner vented his outrage over Schelling's philosophy of religion to COSIMA.

Not unlike Schopenhauer's own invectives against Schelling, Wagner's scornful comments may be intended to disguise Schelling's subterranean influence. Joachim Köhler has drawn attention to echoes of Schelling's 1809 *Philosophical Investigations into the Essence of Human Freedom* in Wagner's theory of MUSIC DRAMA as well as in the cosmology of the RING, and suggestive parallels obtain between Schelling's meditations on freedom and the terms in which Wagner's tetralogy unfolds the problem of the "free hero." Manfred Frank has proposed that the *Ring* shows the influence of the later Schelling's understanding of MYTH as a baleful nexus of delusion which is fated to destroy itself through a hero's redemptive death.   MÁRTON DORNBACH

Manfred Frank, *Mythendämmerung: Richard Wagner im frühromantischen Kontext* (Munich: Fink, 2008).
Joachim Köhler, *The Last of the Titans* (see bibliography).

Schemann, (Karl) Ludwig (b. Cologne, 16 Oct. 1852; d. Freiburg im Breisgau, 13 Feb. 1938), racial theorist, studied classical philology and history in Heidelberg and Berlin. He attended the first BAYREUTH FESTIVAL and thereafter was active in promoting the Wagnerian cause, although he declined Wagner's invitation to settle permanently in BAYREUTH. He was dismissive of sycophantic WAGNERISM and always maintained a degree of intellectual distance between himself and Wagner's less discriminating acolytes such as WOLZOGEN and GLASENAPP.

Schemann was an important figure in the development of racial thinking. He translated GOBINEAU's essay "On the Inequality of the Races" into German, and wrote a biography of Gobineau that drew attention to the points of contact between Wagner's thought and Gobineau's racial theories. He was an admirer of the influential *völkische* thinker Paul Lagarde and thus an important link between the esoteric world of Bayreuth and the wider constituency of organized ANTI-SEMITISM. On Schemann's 85th birthday in 1937, HITLER personally awarded him the GOETHE medal in recognition of his contribution to racial science.   ROGER ALLEN

See also BAYREUTH CIRCLE; CHAMBERLAIN, HOUSTON STEWART

Ludwig Schemann, *Meine Erinnerungen an Richard Wagner* (Stuttgart: Frommann, 1902).

Schiller, Friedrich (b. Marbach, 10 Nov. 1759; d. Weimar, 9 May 1805), German poet and dramatist. Wagner once remarked to COSIMA: "If you discount SHAKESPEARE then Schiller is the greatest dramatist" (CWD 3 March 1879). Schiller was a central figure in Wagner's aesthetic world. Conversations with Cosima are evidence of an almost uninterrupted lifelong interest in Schiller's work, particularly his poetry and dramas. Even Schiller's birthday was commemorated every year in TRIBSCHEN and at WAHNFRIED with a small ceremony. This affinity for Schiller became a point of contention for NIETZSCHE after his break with Wagner, prompting the essay from 1888: *Das Schillersche an Wagner* (The Schiller Element in Wagner, published posthumously).

In particular, it is the musical element of Schiller's dramas that attracted Wagner. From Wagner's art historical perspective, it is comparable to BEETHOVEN's music in that both are at the threshold of MUSIC DRAMA, specifically, the addition of Schiller's *Ode to Joy* to the last movement of Beethoven's Ninth Symphony crosses the boundary from ABSOLUTE MUSIC into drama. In the same way, Schiller's plays cross from "literary dramas" (to use the terminology from *OPER UND DRAMA* [Opera and Drama, 1851]) to music. In the preface to his tragedy *The Bride of Messina*, "Concerning the Use of the Chorus in Tragedy," Schiller specifically develops a concept of tragedy as music-dramatic total work of art (*GESAMTKUNSTWERK*): "But the tragic work of art first becomes a whole in theatrical performance: the poet only provides the words; music and dance must be added to bring life to them." This idea influenced Wagner's theory about the Greek chorus and its replacement with the modern orchestra. As early as 1830 Wagner composed a now lost overture for Schiller's tragic drama. Wagner rightly believed that the tendency toward musical tragedy was already palpable in *The Maiden of Orleans*. When Wagner and Cosima re-read Schiller's "romantic tragedy," Cosima noted that after reading the "Prologue," Wagner remarked: "Yes, it all begs for music, though that is not to say it fails as a work of art" (CWD 29 May 1870). It would only be missing something if it were not in itself supreme poetry. Cosima continues: "As, in tears, we come to the end of the first act, R. says: 'Goethe touches us through his objectivity, Schiller touches us through his subjectivity.'" Wagner explained this point a year later in his lecture *Über die Bestimmung der Oper* (The Destiny of Opera), where he included Schiller as one of "our . . . pioneers of opera" (PW 5:131). In particular, he referred to a letter dated 29 December 1797 where Schiller expressed to GOETHE his hope for a "suppression of the common imitation of nature in art" through opera: "I always had a certain faith in opera that, out of it as out of the choruses of the ancient festival of Bacchus, tragedy would develop into a nobler form. In opera one really does drop those servile imitations of nature . . . Opera, by means of the power of music and a freer fascination of the senses by harmony, places the mind in a finer state of susceptibility; here we actually have a freer play even in the pathos itself, inasmuch as it is accompanied by music." Earlier in the letter, Schiller had added: "The ideal [of opera] might in this manner steal its way on to the stage," which has been suppressed by the fashionable bourgeois drama. Wagner clearly had Schiller's "opera letter" in mind during a conversation with Cosima where he talks about a "true pathos" in reference to music with which Goethe and Schiller wanted to free the German theater from "vulgar realism" (CWD 29 May 1870).

When Wagner talks about Goethe's objectivity and Schiller's subjectivity, he draws on the ideal-typical juxtaposition, which Schiller himself thematized in his aesthetic discussions with Goethe, a difference that lies at the conceptual heart of his treatise *Über naive und sentimentalische Dichtung* (On Naïve and Sentimental Poetry, 1795). Schiller distinguishes between the more "plastic" naïve and the sentimental poet, considering the latter the "musical poet," because he is concerned more with producing a "state of mind" than with imitating a "thing." Thus the (sentimental) subjectivity that Wagner ascribes to Schiller's poetry is directly connected to its musicality. Wagner sees this as one of the most important insights in the area of music aesthetics before Schopenhauer, which is evidenced in a letter to Mathilde Wesendonck (December 1858).

In Wagner's opinion, Schiller's most significant work was the *Wallenstein*-trilogy, which, according to Cosima's diary from 13 May 1870, he hoped to someday put on a Bayreuth stage. However, none of Schiller's plays left such a deep impression as *The Maiden of Orleans*. In a letter to Mathilde Wesendonck, Wagner emphasized the play's musicality: "Yesterday I read *The Maiden* and was so musically disposed that I could fill Joan's silence – when she is publicly accused – most wonderfully with tones: her guilt – the wonder" (29 October 1859). The situation he describes is reminiscent of the accused ELSA's silence in both Acts I and III of *LOHENGRIN*. Beyond the dramaturgic affinity, there are also concrete contextual similarities between *The Maiden of Orleans* and Wagner's music dramas. Along with her resemblance to the accused Elsa, who is inspired by dreamy visions, its title character also has similarities to BRÜNNHILDE – who like Joan is condemned by divine order – and ISOLDE. In Act III, Scene 10 of *The Maiden*, Joan fights with Lionel and, just as she is about to deal the deadly blow, "she looks him in the face and she is gripped by the sight of him. She stands motionless and slowly lets her arm drop." The similarity between this episode and the mercy Isolde shows Tristan is impossible to overlook, particularly because of the Glance motive: "[Isolde:] From his bed / he looked here / not at the sword / not at my hand / he looked me in the eyes. / His misery / grieved me; / the sword – I let it fall" (Act I). Wagner himself compared both scenes in a conversation with Cosima on 17 November 1873 and, on 12 June 1878, he further connected *The Maiden* to *Parsifal*, telling Cosima that both "are forever deprived of sensual urges." These connections between Schiller's and Wagner's dramas are merely illustrative of the countless references to Schiller's theoretical and poetic writings that permeate Wagner's writings, letters, and conversations.   DIETER BORCHMEYER

TRANS. HOLLY WERMTER

Dieter Borchmeyer, *Richard Wagner: Ahasvers Wandlungen* (see bibliography).

Schladebach, Julius (1810–72), a Dresden physician, music critic, and one of Wagner's *bêtes noires*. He authored his own memoir of the May 1849 uprisings, and began a *Universal Lexicon of Music* in 1854, later completed by others.

Schladebach's antipathy for Wagner was immediate and longstanding. A sometime choral conductor, Schladebach was particularly upset by Wagner's appointment as director of the *Liedertafel* in 1843, feeling that he and others of the local musical community had been shunted aside for the newcomer.

Schladebach's opposition to Wagner's 1846 Palm Sunday benefit concert shows the critic at his most aggrieved. In criticizing the proposed programming of BEETHOVEN's Ninth Symphony, a piece deemed to be too difficult and unpopular with DRESDEN audiences, Schladebach was supported in his concerns by the Court Theater's director LÜTTICHAU. In the end, however, Wagner was proved right; the concert was a resounding success. Schladebach's caustic review apparently also cost him his job at the *Abend-Zeitung*.   MARGARET ELEANOR MENNINGER

Julius Schladebach, *Dresdens Barrikanden-Kampf: Tatsächliche Darstellung der Erignisse vom 3. bis 9. Mai* (Dresden, 1849).

Schleinitz-Wolkenstein, Countess Marie ("Mimi") von (b. Rome, 22 Jan. 1842; d. Berlin, 18 May 1912), a wealthy, liberal *salonnière*, and a firm supporter and friend of Wagner. An influential Berlin socialite, she advocated for Wagner's music at the Prussian court, establishing in 1871 the PATRONS' ASSOCIATION (with her former piano teacher Carl TAUSIG), and persuading Emperor Wilhelm I to attend the first BAYREUTH FESTIVAL in 1876.   DAVID TRIPPETT

Nicolaus Steenken, "Die Erfindung des Fundraising: Private Förderung der Bayreuther Festspiele," *Almanach 2010 der Gesellschaft der Freunde von Bayreuth* (Bayreuth: Gesellschaft der Freunde von Bayreuth, 2010): 144–51; 178–81.

Schlesinger, Maurice [Born: Schlesinger, Moritz (initially Mora) Abraham Adolf?] (b. Berlin, 30 Oct. 1798; d. Baden-Baden, 25 Feb. 1871), son of the Berlin music publisher Adolph Martin Schlesinger (1769–1838). Maurice Schlesinger settled in PARIS in 1819, initially working at the library *Bossange père*. His first publications are traceable from July 1821. Schlesinger quickly came into contact with French contemporary composers and eventually edited the large-scale operas of his era, such as Giacomo MEYERBEER's *Robert le diable* (1831), or Jacques-Fromental HALÉVY's *La Juive* (1835). Schlesinger's influence in French musical life was considerable, among other things through his main journal REVUE ET GAZETTE MUSICALE DE PARIS (1834–80). In 1846, at the peak of its circulation and influence, Schlesinger sold his stock to Louis Brandus and retired to Vernon, later to Baden-Baden, where he died in 1871. He was eternalized in Flaubert's novel *L'Éducation sentimentale*, whose heroine Madame Arnoux is modeled after Schlesinger's wife Élisa Foucault, while Schlesinger's character is hidden behind the art dealer Jacques Arnoux.

On Meyerbeer's recommendation, Wagner contacted Schlesinger upon arrival in Paris in 1839. Even if the publisher did not appreciate Wagner's music, he gave the German composer editorial tasks such as the creation of piano reductions, for example Donizetti's *La Favorite*, or Halévy's *La Reine de Chypre* and *Le Guitarrero*. Furthermore, Wagner wrote essays for Schlesinger's *Revue et gazette musicale de Paris*, publishing ten pieces between 1840 and 1842. The only composition by Wagner published by Schlesinger was the *Lied* "Les Deux Grenadiers" (1840) – based on a poem by Heinrich HEINE. Wagner paid his own costs (50 francs) and the work was later republished by Schott in 1843. Schlesinger also intervened to have Wagner's *Columbus* Overture performed, which was given, without success, in the concert series of the *Revue et gazette musicale de Paris* on 4 February 1841. When Wagner writes about him, it is not with particular sympathy. Indeed, his expressions of ANTI-SEMITISM, already evident during this first Paris stay, ten years before the publication of *Das JUDENTUM IN DER MUSIK* (Jewishness in Music, 1850), might in part have been fueled by his acquaintance with Schlesinger. Later, Wagner wrote how Meyerbeer left him to the "fate of this monstrous acquaintance" (ML 184). On the whole, Schlesinger did not approve of or understand Wagner's music, but Wagner did benefit from Schlesinger's assignments since they constituted the most important source of income during his first Paris stay.

HERMANN GRAMPP

Schoenberg, Arnold (b. Vienna, 13 Sep. 1874; d. Los Angeles, 13 July 1951), one of the most prominent and controversial figures in modern music, during and after his lifetime. Largely self-taught, he became a celebrated teacher, with Alban Berg, Hanns Eisler, and Roberto Gerhard among his pupils. His compositional style evolved from an intensely expressive late-romanticism owing something to STRAUSS and MAHLER (*Verklärte Nacht*, 1899), by way of a concentrated post-tonal expressionism (*Pierrot lunaire*, 1912), to an intricately polyphonic idiom rooted in the twelve-tone method which often used classical forms but was entirely of its own time in emotional force and technical sophistication. Important works of the years after 1930, during which he left Europe and settled in America, include the opera *Moses und Aron* (1930–2), concertos for violin (1936) and piano (1942), and *A Survivor from Warsaw* (1947).

In his *Theory of Harmony* (*Harmonielehre*, 1922), Schoenberg wrote of Wagner as "starting wholly from within the bounds of what everyone of his time understood music to be . . . But without his noticing it, traits that point toward his future insinuate themselves" (400). Schoenberg revered Wagner as a leading pioneer of what he termed "extended tonality," an approach to harmony in which "remote transformations and successions of harmony were understood as remaining within the tonality" (*Structural Functions of Harmony* 76). By juxtaposing an analysis of the first sixteen bars of TRISTAN UND ISOLDE with an extract from Strauss's *Salome*, Schoenberg underlined a continuity which, without any arrogant self-promotion, he saw as validating his own creative initiatives – above all, the kind of harmonic thinking which he insisted should be called "floating" or even "suspended" tonality, but never "atonality."

Schoenberg believed that extended tonality in nineteenth-century music was most commonly the result of "extra-musical influences" – that is, of the composer's desire to respond to poetic or pictorial imagery. However, as a composer himself, he could not limit Wagner's importance to such associations. In his essay "National Music" (1931), he listed those composers who were, as he put it, "my teachers: . . . primarily, BACH and MOZART; and secondarily BEETHOVEN, BRAHMS, and Wagner." Of the three debts he associates with Wagner, the first – "the way it is possible to manipulate themes for expressive purposes and the art of formulating them in the way that will serve this end" – still has an element of the "extra-musical" about it. But the other two debts, "relatedness of tones and chords," and "the possibility of regarding themes and motives as if they were complex ornaments, so that they can be used against harmonies in a dissonant way" (Schoenberg, *Style and Idea*, 173–4) – allude to Wagner as supremely progressive in his use of tonality and texture. Wagner is seen as anticipating not only Schoenbergian "suspended tonality" but the "emancipation of the dissonance" that went with it, and which was perhaps the most significant feature in the evolution of MODERN MUSIC during the twentieth century's first decade, setting composition on the pluralistically progressive path it has followed ever since.

ARNOLD WHITTALL

See also TRISTAN CHORD

Arnold Schoenberg, *Structural Functions of Harmony*, trans. L. Stein (London: Norton, 1969).
Style and Idea (see bibliography).
Theory of Harmony, trans. Roy E. Carter (London: Faber, 1978).

Schön, Friedrich Wilhelm (b. Worms, 22 Dec. 1849; d. Berchtesgaden, 9 Sep. 1941). A noted leather manufacturer and patron of the arts in Worms, Schön was an early supporter of Wagner's festival idea. He was a particularly generous member of the Worms Society of Patrons and, in 1879, approached Wagner about helping finance his dream of founding a special music school in Bayreuth. In 1880, Wagner charged Schön to set up what became the Wagner Scholarship Foundation, which he directed during 1882–92 and again in 1907–14.　　　　ANTHONY J. STEINHOFF
See also SCHULE FÜR STYL UND TRADITION

Schopenhauer, Arthur (b. Danzig [Gdańsk], 22 Feb. 1788; d. Frankfurt am Main, 21 Sep. 1860), German philosopher.
1. Schopenhauer's philosophy
2. Wagner and Schopenhauer
3. Schopenhauer in Wagner's later works

1. Schopenhauer's philosophy

Schopenhauer wrote one major work, *The World as Will and Representation* (1818). It is divided into four books. Following Kant, Book One argues that "the world is my representation": the manifest world of space and time is mere "appearance" or "phenomenon." Metaphysically considered, it is but a "dream" (1:11). In Book Two, we learn that the underlying and unifying feature of this world is "will": whether we are talking about human or animal action or even the "battle" between centrifugal and centripetal forces, the driving force underlying the play of visible phenomena is a universal *striving*, at the most basic level "for life." This turns out to be the basis of Schopenhauer's "pessimism":

to live is, overwhelmingly, to suffer because, given the scarcity of resources, striving entails strife which entails suffering. Animal must feed on animal in order to survive; human beings, even in conditions of material plenty, must compete with each other for social status and sexual partners. With us, moreover, even if we find all our desires satisfied, so that striving for a moment ceases, there is a terrible penalty – boredom. Hence human life "swings like a pendulum to and fro between pain and boredom" (1:312).

Book Three discusses art, which is principally important as a pointer towards "REDEMPTION" – escape from this world of will and pain. While absorbed in an artwork, we momentarily forget our individuality and thereby our unhappy will, thereby receiving an intimation of "how blessed must be the life of a man whose will is silenced not for a few moments, as in the enjoyment of the beautiful, but for ever" (1:390).

Music stands outside Schopenhauer's general account of art: whereas all the other arts represent objects and events in the visible world of "appearance," music self-evidently does not. What it represents, rather, is the inner reality that underlies the visible surface of things, the "will." Music is the "secret history of the will" (1:260). It follows that music is the highest of the arts: whereas the others represent the physical surface of things, music discloses the metaphysical: it is "an unconscious exercise in metaphysics in which the mind does not know it is philosophizing" (1:264).

An implication of the supremacy of music is that when it combines with words in an artwork, its own requirements should always take priority. What, however, makes the combination legitimate is that, while music expresses emotion, it expresses it without an object. Sad music expresses sadness but does not tell us what the sadness is about. Hence there is a natural impulse to set words to music that stand to it "in the relation of an example." Even purely instrumental music invites us to "clothe it, in the imagination, with flesh and bone, to see in it all the different scenes of life and nature" (1:263; 2:449); hence the "Moonlight" Sonata and the "Sunrise" Quartet.

Book Four concerns ethics and redemption. Since – as the Buddha saw – life is suffering, the proper ethical stance is that of compassion towards all living things. The importance of compassion, however, is not that it improves the condition of the world. Human action can make no ultimate difference to that condition for "the ceaseless effort to banish suffering achieves at most a change in its form" (1:315). Compassion is important, rather, because it is a path to insight: through identifying with the suffering of others (the saint identifies with the suffering of all living things) we come to realize the *universality* of suffering and hence the *futility* of the works of LOVE. This brings about a "transition from virtue to asceticism" (1:380), from the life of compassionate willing to the "denial of the will," the cessation of all willing. The final consequence of this is, of course, death. Redemption, the enlightened person realizes, can consist only in death. Enlightenment thus becomes, in NIETZSCHE'S phrase, the "will to death."

Why should death be redemptive? Space and time, Schopenhauer observes, are the *principium individuationis*. We can only make sense of the idea of a plurality of individuals in terms of their occupying different parts of space and/or time. But space and time pertain, we know, merely to appearance. It follows that the "thing in itself," that ultimate reality which lies beyond both the world "as representation" and the world "as will," is in a certain sense "One." Apart from that, we can say nothing about it: to reason and literal language it is "nothing." Yet the remarkable unanimity with which the mystics report absorption into a divine totality – they speak, metaphorically, of "union with God" or "entry into *nirvana*" – gives us a certain assurance that it is a beatific "nothing" (1:411–12).

2. Wagner and Schopenhauer

Wagner discovered Schopenhauer's masterwork in December 1854, read and immediately re-read the work, experiencing something like a religious conversion. It produced five major changes in his PHILOSOPHY, changes that would remain with him the remainder of his life. First, the commonsense naturalism of his earlier outlook is replaced by Kantian-Schopenhauerian idealism: the natural world, he now asserts, is a mere "dream," a world of "semblance," "illusion," "fancy" (*WAHN*). Second, the reality beyond the world of appearance is "above all bounds of individuality," and in that – Schopenhauerian – sense "One" (PW 5:72). Third, the "optimism" (Wagner to RÖCKEL, 23 August 1856) of his earlier, anarchist version of utopian "communism" (PW 1:78) which inspired his part in the attempted revolution of 1848–9, now gives way to Schopenhauerian "pessimism." Though "world improvers" such as the 1848 revolutionaries had "great hearts and spacious minds" they were "victims of a fundamental error." Since human efforts "can never have the slightest influence on the lasting shape of things" world-improvers "demand from the world a thing it cannot give" (PW 4:9–10). Fourth, since pessimism is true, "redemption" is now transposed from a this-worldly anarchist paradise into an other-worldly "nothingness" (4:34). "The only ultimate redemption," he writes Liszt, consists in "total unconsciousness, complete annihilation, the end of all dreams" (16? December 1854). Hence Nietzsche's description of later Wagner's fundamental impulse as, like Schopenhauer's, the "will to death."

Schopenhauer's final major impact on Wagner's philosophic outlook concerns the internal economy of the MUSIC DRAMA, the relation between music and words. In his pre-Schopenhauerian OPER UND DRAMA (Opera and Drama, 1851), Wagner asserted the priority of words. What was disastrous about nineteenth-century opera was that "the means (music)" had become the "end," while the "end (the drama)" had (in the ridiculous plots of ROSSINI, above all) become the means (PW 2:17). After 1854, however, Wagner reverses himself and accepts Schopenhauer's thesis of the primacy of music over words. Whereas early Wagner had viewed the bursting of symphony into words in BEETHOVEN's Ninth Symphony as a "world-historical" necessity (PW 1:127, 130), a redemption of "ABSOLUTE MUSIC" from triviality, he now points out that the famous melody of the last movement is "first unrolled in its breadth . . . as an entity per se, entrusted to the instruments alone" (PW 5:102) and further suggests that Beethoven's adoption of SCHILLER's optimistic words about world-brotherhood was Beethoven the man of somewhat shallow rationality obscuring the much deeper insights of the "intuitive artist." This might make one wonder why Wagner continued to write opera after 1854 (he did, in fact, plan, after *Parsifal*, to write only symphonies) but in fact he legitimizes opera in, essentially, Schopenhauer's manner. Absolute music, he says, "contains the drama in itself" (is the "secret history of the will"), a drama which "towers above the bounds of poetry as music towers above those of every other art." Hence, in proper operatic writing, the music provides the "a priori" basis on which the dramatist constructs a narrative of individuals and events in this "world of semblance" (PW 5:106–7).

3. Schopenhauer in Wagner's later works

Schopenhauer is a major presence in all Wagner's later operas. On the RING (the 1854 conversion occurred after the completion of Die WALKÜRE thus neatly bisecting the cycle) the most obvious impact was the replacement of the world-affirming "FEUERBACH ending" by the world-denying "Schopenhauer ending." Whereas, in 1852, BRÜNNHILDE's final peroration had foreseen the arrival of the anarchist-communist utopia in which "troubled treaties," "wealth," and "overbearing pomp" would all be overthrown by that "rapture in joy and sorrow [that] comes from love alone," by 1856 her vision of redemption now consists in "depart[ing] the home of desire . . . redeemed from incarnation." With the relief of waking from a bad dream she sees "the world end" (see SSD 6:254–6 including author footnote). Though neither ending is used in the final version of the libretto, Wagner explains in a footnote that the second ending is the correct one but that its meaning is better expressed by the music alone.

TRISTAN UND ISOLDE was the first opera to be composed in its entirety after 1854. Act II contains virtually a lecture on Schopenhauer's philosophy. Redemption, TRISTAN explains to ISOLDE, can only be achieved through absorption into the unity of ultimate reality. Only when the illusion of individuality – the "and" that appears to separate them – has been abolished can they "live in love." And Isolde's final words as she sinks in transfiguring death onto Tristan's lifeless body: "In the surging swell, / in the ringing sound, / in the world-breath / in the waves of the All / to drown / to sink down – / unconscious – / supreme bliss" are surely a rendition of the mystical "nothingness" towards which Schopenhauer points at the end of his philosophy.

Die MEISTERSINGER VON NÜRNBERG represents a momentary return of something of the earlier optimism. Provided tradition bends to innovation, worldly existence is presented as desirable. Even here, however, in HANS SACHS's "Wahn [delusion] monologue," Schopenhauer's presence is felt. "Driven into flight [man] believes he is hunting, and does not hear his own cry of pain: when he tears into his own flesh, he imagines he is giving himself pleasure" is a close paraphrase of a passage in which Schopenhauer compares the world's will to the Australian bulldog ant whose sharp-tooth head and stinging tail fight to the death (Schopenhauer 1:147).

PARSIFAL is Wagner's final and, I think, most completely Schopenhauerian opera. Though Schopenhauerian in its conception of redemption, Tristan was distinctly non-Schopenhauerian in its eroticism. Whereas for Schopenhauer the path to redemption is "denial of the will," above all of the sexual will, Tristan presents erotic but star-crossed union as at least one path to redemption. Wagner knew of his heterodoxy and in December 1858 sketched out a defense in an (unfinished) letter to Schopenhauer. In it, Wagner reflects on the regularly recurring phenomenon of "the joint suicide of two people who were in love but were prevented from marrying by external circumstances," and claims that "the natural tendency to sexual love represents a way to redemption, to self-knowledge and to self-negation of the will" (SSD 12:189).

In *Parsifal*, Wagner sets out to correct his heterodoxy. Though love is still the key to redemption, it is love as Schopenhauerian compassion – and Christian *agape* – that enables PARSIFAL to heal AMFORTAS and restore the community of the Grail. Love as *Eros* is explicitly rejected. KUNDRY, attempting to seduce the resisting Parsifal, makes, effectively, a direct reference to *Tristan*: "If you are a redeemer what evil stops you from uniting with me for my redemption?" a question to which Tristan would surely have answered "None." Parsifal's victory over her, however, consists in succeeding where Amfortas had failed in resisting her advances. Of Amfortas, he states with disgust "her mouth kissed away the redemption of his soul."

Parsifal ends with the chorus singing "redemption for the redeemer." The significance of these words is quite opaque until one recalls that, for Schopenhauer, compassion is ultimately important, not for the sake of its effect, but because of the world-denying insight that is achieved through it. Having completed the works of compassion, the words tell us, Parsifal now understands the path to his own redemption – through death.

In all the libretti written after 1854, it is possible to see Schopenhauer's thesis of the priority of music over words at work. Traditional libretti had favored the use of "end-rhyme" because rhymes at the end of a line correspond to breathing pauses, and because the short, easy-to-remember, musical phrases generated by end-rhyme add up to the traditional "tune." Yet because we never speak in end-rhyme, and because its metrical straitjacket placed accents in semantically absurd places, as well as destroying dramatic continuity, *Oper und Drama* banned the use of end-rhyme in accordance with early Wagner's thesis of the priority of words over music, preferring STABREIM, alliteration, as a means of poetic elevation and musical fertility.

In the libretti he wrote after 1854, however, and in accordance with his return to the thesis of the priority of music over words, end-rhyme reappears in many places. To cite but one of innumerable examples, the final words of the LIEBESTOD, quoted earlier in translation, read, in German,

> *In dem wogenden Schwall,*
> *in dem tönenden Schall,*
> *in des Weltatems*
> *wehendem All, –*
> *ertrinken,*
> *versinken, –*
> *unbewusst, –*
> *höchste Lust!*

Thomas Mann no doubt had the thesis of musical priority in mind when he claimed that it was Schopenhauer who "freed Wagner's music from bondage [to words] and gave it courage to be itself" (330). It is possible to believe, however, that the earlier thesis of the priority of words (as manifested in the relative musical austerity of *Das* RHEINGOLD) provides the basis for opera as a more serious art-form than that allowed for by the thesis of musical priority.

Early Wagner's project had been the "rebirth of Greek tragedy"; the rebirth of an artwork that would be "collective" (a *GESAMTKUNSTWERK*) partly in the sense of collecting the individual arts but more importantly in the sense of gathering the community, following the purpose of Greek tragedy to collect the community into a clarifying affirmation of fundamental ethical commitments (see also PHILOSOPHY). Since one can only engage with ethos in words, *that* project would seem to *demand* the priority of words over music.

JULIAN YOUNG

See also AESTHETICS

Thomas Mann, *Essays of Three Decades*, trans. H. T. Lowe-Porter (London: Secker & Warburg, 1947).
Arthur Schopenhauer, *The World as Will and Representation*, trans. E. F. J. Payne (New York: Dover 1969).

Schott's Söhne. See PUBLISHERS

Schröder-Devrient, Wilhelmine (b. Hamburg, 6 Dec. 1804; d. Coburg, 26 Jan. 1860), in the heyday of her career, from the mid-1820s to the mid-1840s, probably the most famous and popular soprano in Germany. Contemporaries praised the extraordinary passion and realism of her acting, but often criticized her vocal deficiencies. Wagner's early experiences of Schröder-Devrient's performances (particularly her portrayal of Romeo in Bellini's *I Capuletti ed i Montecchi* in 1834 and her depictions of Leonore in *Fidelio*) were revelatory. During the 1840s, she was employed at the DRESDEN opera, where she created the roles of Adriano, SENTA, and VENUS, the latter two under Wagner's baton. Wagner's descriptions of Schröder-Devrient in *MEIN LEBEN* (My Life, 1865–81) give insight not only into his relationship with the singer, but also into the ideal fusion of acting and singing that she represented for him. Wagner's extended discussion of Schröder-Devrient in *ÜBER SCHAUSPIELER UND SÄNGER* (Actors and Singers, 1872), which is dedicated to her, testifies to the powerful effect that she had on his creative development.

STEPHEN MEYER

Stephen Meyer, "*Das wilde Herz*: Interpreting Wilhelmine Schröder-Devrient," *The Opera Quarterly* 14 (1997/8): 23–40.
Henry Pleasants, *The Great Singers*, 2nd edn. (New York: Simon & Schuster, 1981).

Schule für Styl und Tradition (School for Style and Tradition). Wagner's program for reforming German opera rested on three elements: new scores, a new stage, and a music school that could properly cultivate a German performance style and, thereby, found a truly German tradition of musical practice. Only this third piece remained unrealized upon the composer's death in 1883, although not for lack of effort. Wagner first proposed establishing such a school in MUNICH in a report to LUDWIG II, dated 31 March 1865. Initially dismissed as being too expensive, this project was definitively tabled when Wagner was forced to quit Munich at the end of the year. After the first BAYREUTH FESTIVAL had finished, he decided to try again. In September 1877, he published (as an addendum to the statutes for the PATRONS' ASSOCIATIONS, SSD 12: 324–32) a prospectus for a music school at Bayreuth, whose activities were to begin in January 1878. But this plan foundered due to lack of funds. So, Wagner hit upon the idea of using the Festival itself, beginning with the productions of PARSIFAL, as a sort of school for singers, musicians, and designers. In 1880, he asked Friedrich SCHÖN to organize a scholarship fund to enable a number of talented young artists to attend the Bayreuth Festival each year. This project evolved into the Wagner Scholarship Foundation (*Stipendienstiftung*). Officially founded in 1882, it has been maintained by contributions from the local Richard Wagner Society chapters since 1909. In 2010, 250 grants were awarded to fellows from thirty-four countries.

ANTHONY J. STEINHOFF

Schumann, Robert (b. Zwickau, 8 June 1810; d. Endenich [near Bonn], 29 July 1856), composer, born only three years apart from Wagner, in Protestant Saxony. Both worked as conductors and were prolific writers about music: Schumann edited the LEIPZIG-based journal *NEUE ZEITSCHRIFT FÜR MUSIK* from 1835 to 1843; Wagner was a contributor. Although they shared some common ground artistically and politically, in temperament Schumann and Wagner were very different. In the increasingly polarized German music scene of the 1850s they came to represent contrasting schools.

Today, Schumann is best known as a composer of solo piano music and *Lieder*. His great ambition, though, was to reinvigorate German opera. He followed Wagner's career with interest; despite criticizing technical aspects of *TANNHÄUSER*'s score, he conceded that it worked well on stage. Schumann considered similar mythical sources for libretti to Wagner: from Karl Leberecht Immermann's *Tristan und Isolde* (suggested by Felix MENDELSSOHN) to the *Nibelungenlied*. Like Wagner, Schumann wrote his own text for his one completed opera, *Genoveva*, which premiered in Leipzig the same year as *LOHENGRIN*, 1850.

The plots of *Genoveva* and *Lohengrin* are strikingly similar. Each is set in chivalric Brabant and centers on a German hero who questions female virtue because of a witch's machinations. That *Lohengrin* remained in the repertoire while *Genoveva* quickly faded from view has been put down to weaknesses in the latter's libretto and its lack of theatrical flair (Wagner had found Schumann unresponsive to his advice about *Genoveva*, describing him in *MEIN LEBEN* [My Life, 1865–81] as "stubborn" and "prickly" [ML/E 320]). Yet on a musical level Wagner and Schumann were not so far apart. As several critics noted of *Genoveva* and other large-scale choral works by Schumann, such as the *Szenen aus Goethe's Faust*, the two composers favored a declamatory vocal style and used a similar harmonic vocabulary.

Schumann's successor as editor of the *Neue Zeitschrift* was Franz BRENDEL, who turned the journal into a mouthpiece for the NEW GERMAN SCHOOL. Schumann and his followers were perceived as being in opposition to Wagner and Franz LISZT; some, such as critic Richard POHL, publicly switched allegiances between sides. Schumann's promotion of the young Johannes BRAHMS (in his famous article *Neue Bahnen* [1853]) deepened the divide. After Schumann's death in 1856, his influence was felt most strongly among composers of instrumental music and *Lieder*. The "Schumann'sche," according to its detractors, represented the small-scale and small-minded (Rubinstein).

Outside of Germany, Schumann and Wagner were more often considered together. In Britain, in the second half of the nineteenth century they were viewed as twin peaks of the AVANT GARDE, while *fin-de-siècle* French

WAGNERITES were often also Schumannians. Since the late twentieth century, there has been renewed interest in Schumann's large-scale choral and dramatic works, which bear closest resemblance to Wagner's music. It is thus becoming clearer that, although never allies, in creative terms Schumann and Wagner should not be seen as diametrically opposed. LAURA TUNBRIDGE

Ulrich Konrad, "Robert Schumann und Richard Wagner: Studien und Dokumente," *Augsburger Jahrbuch für Musikwissenschaft* 4 (1987): 211–320.

Peter Ramroth, *Robert Schumann und Richard Wagner im geschichtsphilosophischen Urteil von Franz Brendel* (Frankfurt am Main: Peter Lang, 1991).

Joseph Rubinstein, "Über die Schumann'sche Musik," *Bayreuther Blätter* 8 (1879): 217–29.

Laura Tunbridge, "Weber's Ghost: *Euryanthe, Genoveva, Lohengrin,*" in *Music, Theatre and Politics in Germany: 1848 to the Third Reich*, ed. Nikolaus Bacht (Aldershot: Ashgate, 2006): 9–29.

Schuré, Édouard (b. Strasbourg, 21 Jan. 1841; d. Paris, 7 April 1929), French music critic, *homme de lettres*, and ardent Germanophile. His early nonfiction works include *Histoire du lied, ou la chanson populaire en Allemagne* (1868) and the two-volume *Le Drame musical: Richard Wagner, son oeuvre et son idée* (1875), the latter of which generated significant interest in Wagner's works in France. Schuré was personally acquainted with both Wagner and NIETZSCHE in the 1860s and 1870s. His initial enthusiasm for the MUSIC DRAMA remained largely unaffected by the FRANCO-PRUSSIAN WAR (1870–1), and he traveled to Germany to hear the 1876 premiere of the complete RING cycle. Schuré turned to mysticism and the occult in the 1880s, largely abandoning music criticism for esoteric philosophy. In this vein, his best-known text is *Les Grands Initiés* (The Great Initiates, 1889), which attempted to synthesize and explain the teachings of Jesus, Plato, Orpheus, Krisha, Moses, and so on.

WILLIAM GIBBONS

Seidl, Anton (b. Pest, 7 May 1850; d. New York, 28 March 1898), Wagner's central missionary in the UNITED STATES for a dozen years; exerted an influence on opera in America greater than that of any other conductor. His first, decisive encounter with Wagner was in 1872 when, with his mentor Hans RICHTER, he heard Wagner conduct BEETHOVEN's Ninth Symphony at BAYREUTH as part of the ceremony laying the FESTIVAL THEATER's foundation stone. Resolving "at any cost to get near to Wagner," he lived with the Wagner family as Wagner's amanuensis for the next six years, becoming a member of the so-called NIBELUNG CHANCELLERY, serving also as a coach and staging assistant for the first RING cycle (1876). In 1879, at Wagner's suggestion, he became chief conductor of Angelo NEUMANN's Neues Theater. With Neumann, he toured the *Ring* throughout Europe with a polished orchestra and ensemble.

Beginning in 1885, Seidl's career was based in New York. As principal conductor (and de facto artistic director) at the Metropolitan Opera, he began with *LOHENGRIN* – and discovered 180 errors in the parts previously used. Presiding over six German seasons (1885–91), he led the American premieres of *Das RHEINGOLD, SIEGFRIED, GÖTTERDÄMMERUNG, TRISTAN UND ISOLDE*, and *Die MEISTERSINGER*. The ensemble included such singing actors as Lilli LEHMANN, Marianne Brandt, Albert NIEMANN, and Emil Fischer. Seidl superintended the integration of stage and pit. New York's seasoned Wagnerite critics favorably compared the results to standards abroad, including Bayreuth. After 1891, the Met evolved into a multi-lingual house, and Seidl conducted less frequently. His casts now included Lillian Nordica, and Édouard and Jean de Rezske, all mentored in Wagner by Seidl. Of 473 performances Seidl conducted at the Met, 295 were of Wagner operas.

Seidl also led the New York Philharmonic (1891–8). As conductor of Brooklyn's Seidl Society, he led winter concerts at the Brooklyn Academy of Music and summer concerts at Coney Island's Brighton Beach; Wagner was by far the composer most performed. He also toured widely in the USA, both with the Met and with his own orchestras. He returned to Europe in 1897 to conduct Wagner at Covent Garden and at Bayreuth. At the time of his death, a Seidl Orchestra was in formation; it would have become both the pit orchestra for the Met and New York's leading concert ensemble, with Eugène Ysaÿe as concertmaster. Seidl was also newly in demand abroad.

As a conductor, Seidl embodied a new Wagnerian style. His BACH and MOZART were formidably Romantic. The former he played in his own transcriptions for modern orchestra. Of Mozart, he gravitated to *Don Giovanni*, which he rendered with tragic weight, slighting the humor. In the *Eroica* Symphony, Seidl's plasticity of pulse in the outer movements was considered an innovation; like Wagner (in *Über das Dirigiren* [On Conducting], 1869) he read both with maximum expressive variety. In the finale to BEETHOVEN's Seventh Symphony, he adhered to Wagner's advice that "it is . . . impossible to take [this movement] too quickly"; the critic Henry Krehbiel recorded the metronome marking for Seidl's performance as 92 per half note, versus Beethoven's 72. In Wagner, Seidl was considered a master of the calibrated climax.   JOSEPH HOROWITZ

Arthur Farwell, "America's Gain from a Bayreuth Romance: The Mystery of Anton Seidl," *Musical Quarterly* 30.4 (1944): 448–57.

Joseph Horowitz, *Classical Music in America: A History of Its Rise and Fall* (New York: Norton, 2005).

Wagner Nights: An American History (see bibliography).

Seidl, Arthur (b. Munich, 8 June 1863; d. Dessau, 11 April 1928), German writer on topics in music history and aesthetics, and active as a music critic in the decades around 1900, advocating the cause of new music, above all Richard STRAUSS. He also wrote about modern poetry, drama, painting, and stage production. He studied at the universities of Munich, Tübingen (where he founded a local "Academic WAGNER SOCIETY"), Berlin, and Leipzig, and was influenced above all by NIETZSCHE's colleague Erwin Rohde and by the Wagnerian disciple Heinrich von Stein (former tutor of SIEGFRIED WAGNER). Seidl's doctoral thesis was published in abridged form in 1887 as *Vom Musikalisch-Erhabenen* (On the Musically Sublime). The study follows up the suggestion of Wagner's 1870 essay BEETHOVEN that an aesthetics of the "musically beautiful" (that is, Eduard HANSLICK's theory of ABSOLUTE MUSIC) raises the question of the role of the "musically sublime" in modern music since BEETHOVEN and, by implication, in Wagnerian MUSIC DRAMA. The book is mainly a scholarly study of the idea of the "sublime" as a musical category since the time of SCHILLER, Kant, Burke, and HERDER. The final third of the book takes up Wagner's ideas about the "musically sublime" in

Beethoven, and grounds them in a discussion of musical style and technique (the only example from Wagner's own music is the opening of the PRELUDE to *Das RHEINGOLD*). Of the three volumes of essays and journalism published under the collective title *Wagneriana* (1901–2), only the first (subtitled *Richard Wagner Credo*) concerns the composer directly; the second (*Von Palestrina zu Wagner*) consists of assorted music-historical essays written from a "Wagnerian" standpoint, and the third (*Die Wagner-Nachfolge im Musikdrama*) examines the legacy of "music drama" up to the end of the nineteenth century. An 1892 monograph already posed the question whether Wagner had created a "school" of composition (*Hat Richard Wagner eine Schule hinterlassen?*), and four lectures published in 1901 as *Moderner Geist in der deutschen Tonkunst* consider Wagner's contribution to the "modern" elements in music of Richard Strauss, Hugo WOLF, and other German composers at the turn of the century.

THOMAS S. GREY

Self-promotion. See PUBLICITY

Semper, Gottfried (b. Hamburg-Altona, 29 Nov. 1803; d. Rome, 15 May 1879), one of nineteenth-century Europe's leading architects and theorists of art. His theater designs were widely admired and adopted, most consequentially by Richard Wagner. He wrote extensively on the arts and their relationship to cultural-historical conditions, and he tried to realize his ideas about the interactions of the arts in the ancient world in his practical work as an architect. Along with Friedrich NIETZSCHE, he was Wagner's most important interlocutor on the relevance of the ancient Greeks to the renovation of art and society in the modern age. For Semper, the basic human impulse to create had found its highest expression in the combined arts of theater and temple in ANCIENT GREECE; art, he believed, made possible spiritual freedom through its capacity to mask and thus transcend the materiality of its production. In the estimation of Wilhelm Dilthey writing in 1892, "AESTHETICS in our century owes more to him than to anyone" (Dilthey 204).

Semper was born in Altona and studied mathematics and architecture at German universities, and then moved to PARIS to gain practical experience. He soon travelled to Greece and southern Italy to investigate for himself whether ancient buildings had been painted (a burning question in his time). The result of his three-year scramble among the ruins was a publication that won him the post of Professor of Architecture at the Royal Academy of Fine Arts in DRESDEN. Dresden became the city most associated with Semper's architectural achievement, largely because of his design of the Court Theater in 1838–41. It burned down in 1869, and he was commissioned to rebuild it. His design of the new theater incorporated his innovative ideas about interior spaces for opera, especially the double proscenium masking the orchestra.

Dresden was where his lifelong, contentious friendship with Richard Wagner began. The two met when Wagner moved there in 1842 for the premiere of *RIENZI* and, ultimately, took up the post of *Kapellmeister*. Their shared political radicalism led them to participate in the wave of REVOLUTIONS when it reached Dresden in 1849. Both men fled into exile when Prussian troops suppressed the DRESDEN UPRISING. Semper went to Paris and then London, where he wrote two of his most important theoretical works, *Four Elements of Architecture* (1851) and *Science, Industry and Art* (1852). In 1855, their paths again converged, partially due to Wagner's influence, when Semper joined the faculty at ZURICH's new Polytechnic Institute; there he wrote the first two of a projected three-volume study, *Style in the Practical and Tectonic Arts or, Practical Aesthetics* (1860). During his Zurich years, he expended enormous effort in working with Wagner to design a FESTIVAL THEATER for MUNICH that would meet Wagner's requirements for the *RING* cycle, and realize both men's ideas about theater's role in social change. The project came to nothing and left considerable ill-feeling between them. Both the FESTIVAL THEATER in BAYREUTH and the second Dresden Court Theater embodied the innovative aspects of Semper's design for Munich. Semper subsequently moved to Vienna in 1871 where he played a leading role in the Ringstrasse project, which transformed the Vienna cityscape.

CELIA APPLEGATE

Wilhelm Dilthey, "Three Epochs of Modern Aesthetics and its Present Task," in *Selected Works*, vol. 5, *Poetry and Experience*, ed. R. A. Makkreel and F. Rodi, trans. M. Neville (Princeton University Press, 1985).

Senta (soprano; leading role in *Der FLIEGENDE HOLLÄNDER*; it is also the only substantial woman's role, since the contralto part of her nurse, Mary, is just a small comprimario role). The part of Senta was created at the Dresden premiere by the dramatic soprano Wilhelmine SCHRÖDER-DEVRIENT, a singer who herself assumes a nearly mythological role in Wagner's biography. The character is based on the unnamed daughter of the "Scottish merchant" in Heinrich HEINE's "Fable of the Flying Dutchman," who served as the model, in turn, for Wagner's DALAND. Senta otherwise has no direct precedent in the versions of the Flying Dutchman story current in Wagner's day. The ballad she performs tells the story of the Dutchman's curse: how he incurred the ire of heaven by boasting that he would sail "until the Day of Judgement," if necessary, rather than give up his intention of rounding the Cape of Good Hope. The Dutchman can only be saved from his maritime wanderings by a woman "who will remain true unto death." The story and an alleged portrait of the "lost" captain have become a point of obsessive identification for Senta. Now, as she finishes the ballad, she announces that she herself is the woman who will save him. In uttering this promise, she seems to conjure the Dutchman from the realm of legend into a real presence: shortly afterwards he is standing before her in the same room.

Where the Dutchman longs to be free from his endless, aimless voyages around the seven seas, Senta yearns to escape the confines of her small northern fishing village and the narrow, repetitive existence to which its women are condemned. Senta's monomaniacal attitude towards the Dutchman's portrait and his legend invokes elements of contemporary (and GENDER-based) psychological theory. When Erik relates to her the dream-image he has had of her elopement with the fantastical Dutchman she falls into what Wagner indicates as a "magnetic slumber," or a hypnotic trance. Her behavior, including that of her vocal role as such, is easily connected with later nineteenth-century notions of female hysteria. Because she is forced to subordinate her own dreams of personal freedom to the redemptive needs of the

529

Dutchman, Senta's supposedly transfiguring act of self-sacrifice at the conclusion of the opera is often interpreted in critical, even cynical terms in modern productions, where the promise of a heavenly union with the Dutchman no longer seems viable.

Few singers became noted for the role before Emmy Destinn sang it in BAYREUTH in 1901, five years before creating the title role of Strauss's Salome (Destinn was otherwise known especially for dramatic soprano roles in VERDI and Puccini). During the interwar years Maria Müller was a major exponent of the part, as well as of SIEGLINDE in *Die WALKÜRE*. A great Senta of the decades following World War II was Leonie Rysanek (like Müller, also much admired for her Sieglinde as well as Salome), along with Astrid Varnay at Bayreuth. Swedish soprano Nina Stemme has made a specialty of the role in recent years, combining like her predecessors qualities of the Italian *spinto* and German dramatic soprano ideals.   THOMAS. S. GREY

See also SLEEP / DREAM

Serov, Alexander Nikolayevich (b. St. Petersburg, 23 Jan. 1820; d. St. Petersburg, 1 Feb. 1871), Russian music critic, composer, and ardent advocate of Wagner. During his visit to DRESDEN in 1858, he listened to *TANNHÄUSER*, "the best foreign modern opera," six times in a row. He wrote: "Wagner's work has put me into naïve astonishment, as though I had never known what theater, drama, or opera were!" (quoted in Martynow 60). Serov became an important contact in ST. PETERSBURG and acted as Wagner's adviser during his Russian tour in 1863. Serov translated the libretti of *Tannhäuser* (1862) and *LOHENGRIN* (1868), and worked actively to arrange Russian performances of Wagner at the Mariinski Theater. Serov was also a productive opera composer whose works include *Judith* (1861–3), *Rogneda* (1863–5), and *The Power of the Fiend* (1867–71). Alexander Serov and his wife Valentina (1846–1927) were close friends of the Wagners and are also mentioned in COSIMA WAGNER'S DIARIES.   HANNU SALMI

Sergej Martynow, "Richard Wagner in Russland: Zum 100. Todestag des Musikdramatikers," *Sowjetunion Heute* 2 (1983): 60.

Servants / domestic staff The fully staffed households at TRIBSCHEN and WAHNFRIED late in Wagner's life were a far cry from his early years. Throughout most of his first marriage, MINNA undertook the cooking and housekeeping, in PARIS from 1840 being reduced to menial tasks such as cleaning the grates and even blacking the lodger's boots. In DRESDEN, ZURICH, and subsequently Paris, they had no permanent servants, just occasionally hiring domestic help.

Wagner's first servants as valet and housekeeper thus entered the scene only after his final separation from Minna. Bohemian-born Franz Mrazék (died 1874) with his wife Anna (*c.* 1834–1914) served the composer in Penzing (VIENNA) from 1863, at Starnberg, and in MUNICH. Subsequently Franz worked at the Munich Music School. (It was the elderly Anna Mrazék's court testimony in 1914 that helped prevent ISOLDE BEIDLER legally being declared Wagner's child.)

Verena ("Vreneli") Weidmann (1832–1906) first encountered Wagner at the Hotel Schweizerhof, Lucerne, where she waited on him as chambermaid in the months during 1859 when he completed TRISTAN UND ISOLDE. He was much taken with her and attempted to engage her as his housekeeper in Vienna, but she was contracted elsewhere. He re-engaged her at Munich in 1864, and she stayed with him until the end of the Tribschen period. In January 1867 she married Jakob Stocker (1827–1909), only on condition that he too would join Wagner's service. The Tribschen household thus consisted of a housekeeper, manservant, two stable lads, a parlor maid, a French cook, a nanny, and a governess for the children, who of course by 1869 numbered five (two by Bülow and three by Wagner). The hypothesis that Vreneli bore Wagner three children (and that COSIMA knew of this) is unproved but not incredible. Earlier he seems to have enjoyed intimacy with a servant, Marie Völkl, while at Penzing (see SEXUALITY AND EROTICISM).

Conscious of having risen from what was the servant class (court officials, actors, musicians) Wagner's personal relations with his domestic staff were friendly (occasionally it seems over-friendly) and he was much liked as an employer. Cosima's attitude stemmed from a very different social background. She was more distant and consequently respected but less liked.

At Wahnfried, the staff included Wagner's valet Georg, also responsible for minor household expenses, a lady's maid, a cook, a gardener, a caretaker/ groom, a chambermaid, and other staff hired to cater for the many visitors and the receptions held during preparations for the first two Bayreuth festivals. Governesses and tutors were not regarded as servants; the four girls had a succession of the former (one of whom, Susanne Weinert, kept a diary, 1875–6, acquired by Mary BURRELL for her collection); Heinrich von Stein and Paul JOUKOWSKY were from time to time the young SIEGFRIED's resident tutors.

The splendidly named Bernhard Schnappauf (1840–1904) was Wagner's trusted Bayreuth barber and general factotum. Once more there is a Beaumarchais-like distinction between resident domestic staff and useful local artisan. Schnappauf had his shop in Ochsengasse (today Kirchengasse), the discreet address for perfumes and pomades sent by Judith GAUTIER from PARIS for the Master's use. He would help out too at social functions, run errands, and as surgeon attend to minor ailments, administer medicines, injections, leeches, and so forth to the ailing composer. Cosima retained him in her service after Wagner's death. He had in 1877 accompanied the family to ITALY. En route in Munich, Cosima's neckerchief and hair caught alight at table in the Hotel Vier Jahreszeiten. Schnappauf extinguished the blaze.   DEREK WATSON

Eva Rieger, *Richard Wagner's Women* (see bibliography).
Stewart Spencer, *Wagner Remembered* (see bibliography).

Sexuality and eroticism Sexuality and the erotic are crucial to Wagner's biography, writings, compositions, and AESTHETICS. His sexual desires determined his decision-making at important junctures; the erotic is a prime determinant in the actions of the characters he created for the stage; he utilized sexual metaphors to illuminate his aesthetic theories; and he was one of the first composers to offer a depiction of the sexual act itself in music.

Little is known of Wagner's first sexual experiences, though he seems early on to have been untroubled by contemporary morality. His family's proximity to the theater meant access to a world where sexual license was unexceptional and he was also aware that he might be the product of an extramarital relationship between his mother and Ludwig GEYER. When his relationship began with the actress MINNA Planer in 1834, he was attracted by the "free love" propagated by the YOUNG GERMANY movement and suggested to his friend Theodor APEL that they share her. Wagner's jealousy – a lifelong trait – soon led him to abandon notions of sexual freedom for his female partners, though he retained a relaxed attitude to infidelity on his own part. His later actions even suggest a predilection for women who were already committed to others. In her reminiscences of the ZURICH Wagner festival of 1853, Bertha Roner-Lipka wrote of his predatory sexual attitude towards young women in general, and also noted his love of scents and velvets. The latter trait became a fetish that involved an element of cross-dressing, as witnessed by his CORRESPONDENCE with Bertha Goldwag, and later also found dramatic expression in PARSIFAL's frilly, fragrant Flower Maidens. Wagner's repeated use of enemas might also be deemed latently fetishistic. They featured large in his efforts to improve his intestinal HEALTH (thus in late 1851 he took a cure that involved colonic irrigation four times daily for nine weeks), though his repeated use of them over the ensuing decades means that "medical" necessity might have masked personal proclivity.

Wagner's affair with Mathilde WESENDONCK apparently remained uncon-summated. The sources suggest that, by mutual agreement, they both also refrained from sexual relations with their respective spouses (though a letter from Minna to her friend Mathilde Schiffner of 1860 implies that this would have been liberation to her, not a burden). Thus while TRISTAN UND ISOLDE idealizes both erotic love and adultery, it was conceived at a time of self-enforced celibacy. The repeated inability of the "TRISTAN CHORD" to achieve resolution, like the interrupted cadence at the climax of the love scene, reflect on a harmonic and structural level the inability of the protagonists (and, by inference, Wagner and Mathilde) to achieve erotic fulfillment. The opera's closing scene, the so-called LIEBESTOD, features what was perhaps the first graphic depiction of sexual climax in music, though it is undeniably autoerotic in character as it is sung by Isolde alone, after Tristan's death. Tellingly, it was composed after Wagner's increasingly proprietary attitude towards Mathilde had finally led to open scandal and their permanent separation.

After leaving Zurich, Minna, and Mathilde, Wagner's undimmed libido, coupled with his belief in the detrimental physical and mental effects of masturbation, led him to engage in a number of primarily sexual relationships. His partners in the late 1850s and 1860s probably included his long-time maid, Verena Weidemann (whose children he might well have fathered; see SERVANTS / DOMESTIC STAFF). The intensity of his physical needs becomes particularly evident during his hunt for a new female partner in 1862–3. In letters to Mathilde MAIER he railed against "bourgeois bigotry" and complained (without irony) of the "gaping hole" he felt when without a woman. When his relationship began with COSIMA von Bülow in late 1863 she was just one of several women who were the object of his attention.

In his letters of this time he clearly linked the satisfaction of his sexual needs with his creative potency.

Within less than a decade, COSIMA WAGNER'S DIARY (11 November 1870) implies that her interest in sex had waned, while Wagner's had not. At the time of the first BAYREUTH FESTIVAL, Wagner embarked on an affair with Judith GAUTIER. It is unclear whether it was consummated, though his feelings seem to have been subsumed into a fetishistic pleasure in the perfumes and textiles that she procured for him.

Sexual METAPHORS are especially common in Wagner's writings during his Zurich exile. His 1853 note for the LOHENGRIN Prelude, written ostensibly for the public but implicitly for Mathilde Wesendonck, offers "shudderings of blissful pain," "swelling . . . seeds of love," and "intoxicatingly sweet scents gushing forth," from the midst ("Schoss," also "womb") of angels, and only its pseudo-religious context of a descending Holy Grail lets Wagner avoid by a whisker what would otherwise verge on smut. In OPER UND DRAMA (Opera and Drama, 1851) the text as "male seed" fertilizes (female) music in the "most heated moment of love's arousal," while his preferred term for the "unified artwork" was "vereinigtes Kunstwerk," derived from the word "Vereinigung" (union) that he used elsewhere (as in his correspondence with Minna and Mathilde) to imply sexual congress. Wagner's attitudes to the erotic are also reflected in his libretti from the very start of his career. Thus the libertine notions expressed in his letters to Apel find their way into Das LIEBESVERBOT. His frustrations with Minna find compensation in the heroines of Der FLIEGENDE HOLLÄNDER and TANNHÄUSER, whose urge to serve and save their men is all-consuming. In Zurich, Wagner's continuing marital strife and his passion for Mathilde Wesendonck found a correlation in the bickering couple of WOTAN/FRICKA in Die WALKÜRE on the one hand, and in the glorification of the "forbidden" love of SIEGMUND/SIEGLINDE and TRISTAN/ISOLDE on the other. Wagner himself referred openly to such generalized comparisons between his love life and his operatic creations. His rejection by Mathilde seems to have prompted him to turn the tables in Die MEISTERSINGER VON NÜRNBERG by having his alter ego (HANS SACHS) turn down hers (EVA), while in Parsifal female sexuality becomes destructive, with man now assigned the task of REDEMPTION. This finds a reflection in Wagner's late "REGENERATION essays," which tend to misogyny and are concerned with the quasi-religious function both of the work of art and of the (male) artist himself.

Wagner's unfettered approach to his own sexuality seems to have left him largely free of conventional moral qualms regarding the orientation of others. He implicitly accepted the sexual component of the hero-worship offered by young male acolytes such as Karl RITTER and NIETZSCHE, though he did accuse both of "onanism." Wagner regarded the latter as a sign of effeminacy (for which he often used the noun "Weichheit") and allied to homosexuality, though his correspondence with Nietzsche's doctor makes evident that he regarded all such practices as a medical condition, not a matter for mere moral censure (COSIMA WAGNER'S DIARIES incidentally record their repeated fears of "Weichheit" in their son SIEGFRIED: e.g., CWD 24 June 1878; 1 January and 15 July 1882). Wagner seems to have been keenly attuned to any "otherness" in those around him and adapted his language and conduct accordingly when it furthered his own interests. Thus his efforts to acquire the patronage of Otto Wesendonck centered (successfully) on a private performance of the first act of *Die Walküre*, perhaps because Wagner sensed in him a latently incestuous trait (Otto had re-named his wife "Mathilde" after his deceased elder sister and deceased first wife). Wagner's effusive correspondence with LUDWIG II of Bavaria verges on the homoerotic, in mimicry of the King's own prose.

Since the last quarter of the twentieth century, scholars have focused increasingly on evaluating the impact of sexuality and the erotic on Wagner's works, their genesis, context, and reception. CHRIS WALTON

See also GENDER; LOVE

Laurence Dreyfus, *Wagner and the Erotic Impulse* (see bibliography).
Lawrence Kramer, *Opera and Modern Culture: Wagner and Strauss* (Berkeley: University of California Press, 2004).
Jean-Jacques Nattiez, *Wagner Androgyne* (see bibliography).
Eva Rieger, *Richard Wagner's Women* (see bibliography).
Roger Scruton, *Death-Devoted Heart: Sex and the Sacred in Wagner's "Tristan und Isolde"* (see bibliography).
Chris Walton, *Richard Wagner's Zurich* (see bibliography).

Shakespeare, William (1564–1616). Even though, late in life, Wagner referred to Shakespeare as "my only spiritual friend" (CWD 27 May 1882), the influence of Shakespeare's dramaturgy on the composition of his MUSIC DRAMAS is minor. The earliest of Wagner's juvenilia, the dramatic fragment *Leubald*, is compiled from situations taken from *Hamlet*, *Macbeth*, *King Lear*, and *Henry IV Part 1* (STAGE WORKS, INCOMPLETE), while his second opera, *Das LIEBESVERBOT*, is loosely based on the plot of *Measure for Measure*. In contrast to Shakespeare's darkly ironic work, however, Wagner's comedy is predominantly light and festive. Among the mature works, only *Die MEISTERSINGER VON NÜRNBERG* might be considered Shakespearean, not because it shares source material with the English playwright, but because the employment of a comic subplot, the contrast of romantic and satirical material, the panoramic view of NUREMBERG society, and a lyrical atmosphere, which recalls *A Midsummer Night's Dream*, provide a particularly "Shakespearean" milieu. Although *Romeo and Juliet* is occasionally mentioned alongside *TRISTAN UND ISOLDE*, as if the works are companion pieces, they are so different in theme and action that no meaningful comparison can be made between them. Wagner's music dramas are constructed according to very different dramaturgical principles from the ones employed by Shakespeare.

Nevertheless, Wagner never ceased to idolize Shakespeare, whom he considered, along with BEETHOVEN, to be the chief inspiration behind all his creative work. Shakespeare's plays were probably read with greater frequency by Wagner and COSIMA during their evenings at TRIBSCHEN and WAHNFRIED than the works of any other writer. Although Wagner never wrote an essay or extended commentary on Shakespeare, observations in his essays and occasional comments in COSIMA WAGNER'S DIARIES give some indication as to why he considered Shakespeare to be "the mightiest" poet of all (PW 1:140).

First, there was a completeness in Shakespeare's work that Wagner, always exercised by the ideal of totality in art, could be swept away by. At his most adulatory, he would refer to Shakespeare as a "second Creator [who] has opened for us the endless realm of human nature" (PW 1:46). The art that Shakespeare employed was never apparent, so that one was unaware of any artifice and gathered from his work an extraordinary sense of concrete engagement with the world. Shakespeare, Wagner claimed, was the "unmatched master" at revealing the "actuality of life" (PW 2:168). So complete was this impression that the revelation itself was the justification for the work. "In Shakespeare," Wagner claimed, "there is neither mood nor purpose, a veil is torn aside, and we see things as they are" (CWD 14 September 1880). Shakespeare depicted "everything as it is, without explanation or solution" (CWD 4 March 1869). He considered Shakespeare's vision to be unfailingly "truthful"; he was incapable of misrepresenting life. Furthermore, he never used the play as a means of displaying personal feelings; these, Wagner insisted, were totally absent in his work. The all-encompassing quality of Shakespeare's works was apparent not only from reading, but from the stage as well. When he was still young, Wagner witnessed the mesmerizing influence on the audience of Ludwig Devrient's celebrated performance as Lear in Berlin. From this time on he always claimed that Shakespeare could only be fully understood through the medium of the actor.

Wagner, whose knowledge of English was limited and who read Shakespeare mainly in translation, was less impressed by Shakespeare's language. On comparing the original English with the Schlegel-Tieck translations, he even considered the German to be an improvement. However, he greatly admired Shakespeare's grasp of character, which was economical, concrete, and constantly informed by his knowledge of the contradictory nature of being human. Shakespeare's characters which, he pointed out, were always written with specific actors in mind, were to his plays what Beethoven's melodies were to his musical works. Both served a structural function within their respective works and yet each character, and each Beethovenian melody, was alive, well-rounded, and individual. In Shakespeare and Beethoven the symbolic was consistently fused with the individual, so that one was unaware of a rupture between the two.

Shakespeare also provided Wagner with a model for the Theater of the VOLK. He stood, Wagner claimed, at "a culminating point in civilization" (CWD 21 January 1877), which he did not expand upon, though elsewhere he referred to Shakespeare as the "triumph of the resurgence of the oppressed Anglo-Saxon spirit" (CWD 21 July 1871). He recognized the origins of Shakespeare's work in the mixed theatrical genres of the MIDDLE AGES and prized it above all for the way in which, from these origins, Shakespeare had devised a means of expressing epic and heroic experience in the idiom of the common people: "the boorish figure of the homely Folk's comedian takes on the bearing of a hero, the raucous clang of daily speech becomes the sounding music of the soul, the rude scaffolding of carpet-hung boards becomes a world-stage with all its wealth of scene" (PW 1:140). Although there was clearly a continuity between medieval theater and Shakespeare, it was not an antiquated or nostalgic drama. On the contrary, Wagner considered

Shakespeare's drama to be "the only true product of the newer European spirit, the only thing that escaped all influence of the antiquising Renaissance" (PW 5:192)

Wagner was aware that the theater, for which Shakespeare wrote, was different from the realistic theater in which he was obliged to stage his own music dramas, and he understood that the freedom provided by the sparsely decorated, flexible space of the Elizabethan theater was unattainable in the nineteenth century. This may well have been one of the principal reasons why Shakespeare had so little impact upon his own stage work; the styles and stage milieu of the two ages were so far apart that a revival of Shakespearean dramaturgy would only lead to unsatisfactory compromise. Nevertheless, Shakespeare, who Wagner always claimed could not have thrived in the narrow confines of the nineteenth century, represented an ideal of theater to which he aspired, in full knowledge that he could not achieve it.

SIMON WILLIAMS

See also READING

Yvonne Nilges, *Richard Wagners Shakespeare* (Würzburg: Königshausen & Neumann, 2007).

Shaw, George Bernard (b. Dublin, 26 July 1856; d. Hertfordshire, 2 Nov. 1950). Arguably the most famous anglophone playwright after Shakespeare, Shaw was also a prolific novelist, journalist, and public gadfly whose opinions on matters ranging from politics to education to medicine to the arts defy catalogue. Born into a genteel but economically declining Protestant family, Shaw left for London at age 20. He soon found work as a music and drama critic, and began writing for the theater in 1892. He was awarded the Nobel Prize for Literature in 1925, and many of his plays remain staples of the international repertoire.

The Perfect Wagnerite is the centerpiece of Shaw's Wagner criticism. First published in 1898 and revised three times thereafter (1901, 1913, and 1922), the book-length essay interprets the RING cycle as an allegory of capitalism, with ALBERICH read as predatory capitalist, Nibelheim his dark satanic mill, and the gods simply as "the intellectual, moral, talented people who devise and administer States and Churches" (29). SIEGFRIED emerges as a revolutionary hero whose pursuit of freedom leads him to overthrow the whole tyrannical order, a figure Shaw believed to have been modeled on BAKUNIN.

While the interpretation resonates strongly with the Wagner of the DRESDEN UPRISING, it must struggle to make sense of the apparently pessimistic, or at least cyclical, ending of the tetralogy. In response to this, Shaw suggested that GÖTTERDÄMMERUNG was an aesthetic retreat for Wagner, a regression from MUSIC DRAMA back to the sentimental conventions of GRAND OPERA. In the 1898 edition, Shaw explained this relapse by arguing that Wagner wrote the libretto of *Götterdämmerung* early in the development of the cycle and never sufficiently revised it to cohere with the whole. A different rationale appears in the 1913 edition, where Shaw interpreted *Götterdämmerung* as Wagner's response to the collapse of the revolutions of 1848–9. Simply put, "Siegfried did not arrive but BISMARCK did" (87) – and the catastrophe of Wagner's ending signals his resulting despair.

Shaw was also a frequent visitor to BAYREUTH, first attending the FESTIVAL in 1889 and publishing his impressions in *The Hawk* (13 August) and *The*

English Illustrated Magazine (October). While taking obvious pleasure in the rapid rise of Wagner's reputation, Shaw nevertheless turned a critical eye on some of the practices at the FESTIVAL THEATER. The singing he found "competent" but "terribly dry," the acting style antiquated, and the orchestra generally inferior to ones in London (quoted in Hartford 142–3). More troublingly, COSIMA's Bayreuth exhibited features of a death-cult. "[T]he Master's widow, it is said, sits in the wing as the jealous guardian of the traditions of his own personal direction, there is already a perceptible numbness – the symptom of paralysis" (Hartford 144). Against such mummification, Shaw urged that every new Wagner production "should be an original artistic creation, and not an imitation of the last one" (145). Many of these criticisms would only sharpen over subsequent visits. Both the successes and failures of Bayreuth suggested to Shaw that England should build its own Wagner Theater and develop its own practices of Wagner production. MATTHEW WILSON SMITH

Robert Hartford, ed., *Bayreuth: The Early Years* (Cambridge University Press, 1980).

Christopher Innes, "The (Im)perfect Wagnerite: Bernard Shaw and Richard Wagner," *Text and Presentation* 33 (2009): 22–31.

George Bernard Shaw, *The Perfect Wagnerite* (New York: Dover, 1967).

Siegfried (WWV 86c), "Second Day" (*Zweiter Tag*), in three acts, and third part of Wagner's *Der RING DES NIBELUNGEN*. Premiered as part of the first performance of the complete *Ring* cycle, 16 August 1876, at the Bayreuth FESTIVAL THEATER.

1. Genesis, sources, and development
2. Composition
3. Plot summary
4. Musical structure
5. Critical reception and problems of interpretation

(Note: For issues applicable to the entire cycle – including publication, first staging, and significant performances – please consult the entry for *Der Ring des Nibelungen*.)

1. Genesis, sources, and development

Siegfried, the *Ring* cycle's "second day," was sequentially the second opera to be conceived. Wagner put his drafts of *Siegfrieds Tod* (Siegfried's Death, which later became *GÖTTERDÄMMERUNG*) aside during the tumultuous events of 1849, but returned to the project in the summer of 1850, when he began to compose music for the text that he had written in 1848. But then, after sketching only part of the first scene, he abandoned it again. He did not return to the SIEGFRIED material until May of 1851, when he suddenly had the idea of composing a comic "prequel" to the tragic *Siegfrieds Tod*. He named the opera *Der junge Siegfried* (Young Siegfried), and he wrote the libretto in just a few weeks.

Rather than drawing from the *VÖLSUNGA SAGA* (NORDIC MYTHOLOGY) or the *Nibelungenlied*, Wagner took the main plot dynamic (Siegfried's quest to learn what fear is) from a Brothers Grimm fairy tale, although Siegfried's sheltered existence in Mime's forest owes a clear debt to WOLFRAM VON ESCHENBACH's *Parzival* as well. While *Siegfried* resembles the drafts for *Der junge Siegfried* much less than the eventual *Götterdämmerung* resembles *Siegfrieds Tod*, the opera preserves a noticeable difference in tone, literary style, and musical execution when compared to the rest of the cycle.

2. Composition

Siegfried has the most complicated compositional history of the four operas of the *Ring* – indeed, of any of Wagner's operas, and probably of any opera in the nineteenth century, save Mussorgsky's *Boris Godunov*. It is the opera in which Wagner, frustrated at the possibility of securing a performance of his cycle, and finding himself in a compositional cul-de-sac as well, decided to break off his work after he completed the first draft of Act II at the end of July 1857, and to begin work on TRISTAN UND ISOLDE. He came back to *Siegfried* briefly, after his rescue by LUDWIG II in the summer of 1864, since the king's first request was to see and hear the *Ring*. But at that time he only orchestrated Act II of the opera – his political troubles in MUNICH derailed his plans for finishing the cycle. He only returned to the project in 1869, after he had written and premiered *Tristan und Isolde* (1857–9) and Die MEISTERSINGER VON NÜRNBERG (1861–7).

Also essential to an understanding of the work is the complexity of the evolution of the libretto. It was *Siegfried* – or, in May of 1851, when Wagner first conceived it, *Der junge Siegfried* – that embodied his initial decision to make his drama on the Siegfried story a two-part work: to precede the tragic *Siegfrieds Tod*, the libretto of which he had already composed in 1848, with a comic opera. In 1851, he was energized by this idea: not only would the comedy/tragedy pairing be attractive to audiences, but the comic opera would play out on stage some of the material that would have had to be recounted in long narratives in *Siegfrieds Tod*. Wagner composed the libretto of *Der junge Siegfried* quickly – a short prose draft in a week in early May, and the full libretto in a three-week period in June; these two months were surely the most optimistic and happy months in all of his years of work on the *Ring*. But, not long thereafter, he decided to precede these two dramas with two more (*Das* RHEINGOLD and Die WALKÜRE), and after these were completed in the fall of 1852 he had to return to his original two libretti and make substantial changes in order to render them consistent with the two new works. What this meant for *Der junge Siegfried* was that, whereas the first version of the libretto concentrated on the exploits of young Siegfried and allotted to WOTAN a relatively minor part (his appearance in the opera was necessary, though, for tying the story of Siegfried to that of the gods), the version of late 1852 reflected a turn in Wagner himself: from an interest in, and identification with, Siegfried, to more of an interest in and identification with Wotan. Indeed, as numerous Wagner scholars have pointed out, over the twenty-six years of his compositional work on the *Ring*, Wagner turned from his political utopianism of the 1840s and early 1850s to a philosophy of resignation and Schopenhauerian denial of the self. The *Ring* thus transforms itself, over the course of its four operas, from a story of the striving toward a new world order based on love, as it unfolds in the relationships of SIEGMUND, SIEGLINDE, BRÜNNHILDE, and SIEGFRIED, to an abandonment of will, as represented by Wotan's rising "to the tragic grandeur of willing his own destruction," as Wagner put it in a letter of 1854. The tension between these two contradictory points of view is especially evident in the drama and music of *Siegfried*.

3. Plot summary

The *Ring* cycle's "second day" opens approximately two decades after the end of *Die Walküre*. After giving birth to her brother Siegmund's child, a dying Sieglinde has entrusted her infant to a lonely dwarf she encounters in the woods – MIME, Alberich's brother. Mime has raised the boy as his own son in perfect ignorance of his legendary provenance. As the opera opens, Siegfried, a callow and moody youngster, has begun openly questioning Mime's authority, and by extension, his own paternity. Under Siegfried's persistent questioning, and threats of violence, Mime finally reveals what he knows of the boy's origins, and sets his plan in motion: He hopes to arm Siegfried with the sword "Nothung" and have him slay Fafner, now a dragon thanks to the power of the Ring, who guards his hoard near Mime's hut. While Siegfried is off in the forest, Wotan appears, disguised as a wanderer, and challenges Mime to a series of riddles – in them, Mime forfeits his life, though Wotan declines (for now) to collect on the debt. Siegfried returns only after his grandfather has left. The dwarf tells him of Nothung and Fafner, and promises that slaying the dragon might yet teach him a feeling of which the boy has heard from his cowardly guardian, but which he has never experienced for himself: fear. The act ends with Siegfried himself heroically re-forging Nothung.

Act II opens on Fafner's lair, where the three creatures vying for the Ring encounter each other. The Wanderer confronts Alberich, but informs the irascible dwarf that he does not plan to interfere. At Wotan's suggestion Alberich rouses Fafner from his slumbers and warns him of Siegfried's coming. Siegfried and Mime appear. Siegfried encounters a forest bird (*Waldvogel*), and is disappointed that the flute he has fashioned from a reed is unable to speak to the creature. He then plays his horn. This rouses the dragon, whom Siegfried kills after a brief fight. Upon tasting the dead dragon's blood, Siegfried can suddenly understand the bird, who instructs him to take Ring and *Tarnhelm* from Fafner's lair, and warns Siegfried of Mime's intentions. While Siegfried is inside, Mime and Alberich bicker over who now has rights to the treasure. Alberich disappears into the woods when Siegfried reemerges from the cave. Mime now seeks to poison Siegfried, but the youth can now hear Mime's true thoughts – outraged at Mime's deceit, he slays the dwarf. After Siegfried has sealed Fafner's cave, the forest bird tells him of a beautiful woman asleep on a rock – Siegfried, thinking that she might teach him fear, decides to awaken her.

Act III takes place "at the foot of a rocky mountain" (Brünnhilde's rock), where Wotan summons ERDA, only to inform her that he no longer fears the end of the gods that she forecast in *Das Rheingold* – Siegfried will now be his legacy. After Erda has returned into the depths of the earth, Siegfried appears – after a brief quarrel with his grandfather (whom the youth does not recognize), Siegfried shatters Wotan's spear with Nothung. Wotan disappears, taking the shards of the spear with him. Siegfried passes Wotan's magic fire without fear and finds Brünnhilde on her rock. Siegfried removes Brünnhilde's armor, thinking she is a man (only dimly aware that there are humanoid women). Upon realizing that "this is no man," he finally learns the meaning of fear. He kisses Brünnhilde awake, who, after initial confusion and hesitation, reciprocates his love. The curtain falls as the two sing a paean to the fiery love that unites their blood.

4. Musical structure

Wagner faced a number of challenges when he set about composing the music for *Siegfried* in the summer of 1856. One challenge was simply to provide effective musical elaboration of the principal, comic story line, which takes Siegfried from a raucous uneducated youth to the hero who shatters Wotan's symbol of power and awakens Brünnhilde from her eternal sleep (see plot summary). Another challenge was to portray Wotan, who by 1856 was for Wagner the central hero of the *Ring* cycle, in a way that would preserve his musical grandeur, as established in the two preceding operas, and dignify his tragic renunciation of power in Act III, even in what was essentially a comic role. Another was to write music for Mime that would depict him as a comic blocking figure, while at the same time making his murderous intentions, and the evil behind them, musically clear. A final challenge was to keep fresh and compelling the musical material – LEITMOTIVE, harmony, tonal relations – with which he had been working for three years and across two operas.

Siegfried is Wagner's response to all these challenges. The music for Siegfried himself tracks his growth and upward trajectory: initially crude and perhaps even deliberately ugly (the crass repetitions of his horn motive on his initial entrance with the bear, or his anger motive), it becomes heroic in his two Forging Songs, reflective in his imagining of his father and mother, brash and arrogant in his killing of Fafner, naïve as he listens to the forest bird, and jubilant as he rejoices with Brünnhilde. The wanderer's (Wotan's) music is sturdy and dignified, never more so than in his calling up Erda in Act III, Scene 1 – the first scene Wagner composed in 1869 after a twelve-year break from the *Ring* – courageously to announce and accept his own demise. Mime is given some of the most distinctive music in the opera – his brooding over how to gain the Ring in his opening "Zwangvolle Plage"; his Starling Song ("Ein zullendes Kind," Act I, Scene 1), with its crocodile tears; and the augmented triads of his terror as he waits for Siegfried's return after the Wanderer departs at the end of Act I, Scene 2. It was perhaps in part through such chromaticism – a chromaticism strongly influenced by LISZT, whose symphonic poems Wagner was becoming acquainted with at the time – that he was trying to keep the *Ring* fresh and vibrant. As it turned out, in the summer of 1857, Wagner began to have musical ideas that were better suited to his new project on *Tristan* than to *Siegfried*, and it was especially from composing this new opera that he gained the security with chromatic harmony that so characterizes the music of the *Ring* once he returned to it in 1869.

Formally *Siegfried* is essentially a series of dialogues. Never are more than two characters on stage at the same time, and only very occasionally is there just one. Act I sandwiches Wotan's and Mime's Riddle Game (Scene 2) between two tense Siegfried/Mime tiffs; Act II offers a dialogue between Wotan and Alberich in Scene 1, followed by six short segments, three each in Scenes 2 and 3 – Mime/Siegfried, Siegfried alone, Siegfried/Fafner, Mime/

Alberich, Mime/Siegfried, and Siegfried/forest bird; and Act III features the great confrontations of Wotan and Erda (Scene 1), and Wotan and Siegfried (Scene 2), leading up to Siegfried's awakening of Brünnhilde (Scene 3). The cramping together of so many short dialogues into the brief space of the final two scenes of Act II accentuates the broader, more expansive pace that soon becomes evident early in Act III. Indeed, in addition to its more chromatic harmonic language, Act III differs from Act II and all the earlier parts of the *Ring* in that its musical sweep seems to take place on a grander scale, with longer musical divisions, and fewer subdivisions within an act. This is a change that Wagner made gradually over the course of his composition of *Tristan* and *Meistersinger*, and it will make itself felt also throughout *Götterdämmerung* and PARSIFAL.

5. Critical reception and problems of interpretation

Siegfried has long enjoyed a questionable reputation among both general audiences and scholars. Unlike the psychologically nuanced final act of *Die Walküre* and the apocalyptic immensity of *Götterdämmerung*, the vestiges of *Siegfried*'s long genesis have often been considered defects: the awkwardness with which fairy tale and wider MYTHOS are grafted onto each other, the sometimes questionable attempts at comedy, and the overstuffed plot have combined to consign *Siegfried* to relative neglect among Wagner scholars.

Those who do analyze *Siegfried* seem to be drawn in precisely by its slightly unwieldy and unfinished aspects: A lot of *Siegfried* is taken up by characters narrating events to each other that the opera-goer has witnessed first hand – especially Mime's and Wotan's guessing game simply rehearses events the listeners understands well. Given that Wagner expanded his initial double-opera project into the *Ring* in order to turn background narration into dramatic presentation (Wagner to UHLIG, 12 November 1851), these remainders are problematic and the opera seems aware that they are. Having to narrate, to explain, and to justify belongs in Mime's and Alberich's domain, and they are what a callow Siegfried wants from his ward; the forest bird, Wotan, and above all Brünnhilde embody a kind of communication that does without much explaining or justifying.

When it comes to the *Ring*'s philosophical program, the shattering of Wotan's spear may well constitute the cycle's central episode. However, there is considerable ambiguity about how it is to be read. It is clear that Wagner's initial plans for the Siegfried story understood this moment as heroic, but in the finalized *Ring*-cycle the opera-goer is much more familiar with the order that Siegfried shatters in that moment, and is led to sympathize with it. Moreover, given that the Mime-episodes with which Wagner chooses to introduce Siegfried make the youth appear not just boisterous, but downright idiotic, if not sadistic, the completed cycle makes painfully clear that, in transvaluing Wotan's order, Siegfried simply has nothing to put in its place.

Because it starts with a hero who recognizes that he does not much resemble a vastly inferior character (Mime), and ends with the same hero recognizing his kinship with a woman of similarly high birth, *Siegfried* is also a *locus classicus* for investigations into Wagnerian racism (Weiner). While attempts to locate specific Wagnerian prejudices in Siegfried's trajectory have not found universal assent among scholars, few deny that there is a peculiar attention paid in the poem to how one espies one's relatives and equals, how one manages to discover that another is inferior, and that the music (in particular Mime's square, plaintive sing-song, or Alberich's hysterical invectives in Act II) seems determined to help the audience apply categories of degeneracy and aristocracy to the characters.

ADRIAN DAUB AND PATRICK MCCRELESS

Marc A. Weiner, *Wagner and the Anti-Semitic Imagination* (see bibliography).

Siegfried (HELDENTENOR; character in *Der RING DES NIBELUNGEN*, with appearances in *SIEGFRIED* and *GÖTTERDÄMMERUNG*), son of SIEGMUND and SIEGLINDE; raised by MIME; wedded to BRÜNNHILDE (biologically his aunt by WOTAN). While the story of Siegfried was at the core of Wagner's intentions for the *Ring* from the first, the character changed considerably as the initial drafts for *Siegfrieds Tod* slowly expanded into the final tetralogy. However, even as early as the *Nibelungen-Mythus* Wagner drafted in DRESDEN, it was clear that Wagner's conception of the Germanic hero would depart significantly from the character of the *Nibelungenlied*. Siegfried was conceived as a revolutionary, Promethean figure, whose death would indict and end the corrupt rule of the gods. While the Siegfried of the *Nibelungenlied* is more independent of social codes than Gunther, Siegfried's Promethean dimensions, and his alignment with nature and naturalness, are Wagner's additions.

A character named Sigurd appears in the *VÖLSUNGA SAGA* and the *Poetic EDDA*, but no such character appears in the *Lay of Atli*, one of the oldest parts of the *Poetic Edda* and the blueprint for the second part of the *Nibelungenlied*. Where, in the *Nibelungenlied*, Atli/Etzel is motivated in his slaughter of the Burgundians by Kriemhild's desire to avenge the dead Siegfried, the *Lay of Atli* tells the same story without Siegfried and his murder as a plot point. In expanding the *Ring* cycle beyond *Siegfrieds Tod*, Wagner thus began embedding the story of Siegfried in a set of texts that predate Siegfried's appearance in NORDIC MYTHOLOGY. As a result, only *Götterdämmerung* follows either the Germanic or the Nordic sources in describing Siegfried's actions; wherever Wagner presents the genesis of his hero (mostly *Die WALKÜRE* and *Siegfried*), he departs from the Germanic or Nordic stories of Siegfried/Sigurd, and presents an entirely new character.

The musical role of Siegfried is part Heldentenor, part *komischer Bursche*. In the end, looking over his massive role in *Siegfried* and *Götterdämmerung*, one is easily persuaded that it is the comic element that ultimately wins out. That he is a comic character (albeit a rough-hewn and violent one) in the low comedy of *Siegfried* is clear enough, both dramatically and musically. Certainly, the heroic, Heldentenor element comes out strongly in his two Forging Songs and in (especially the latter parts of) his love duet with the newly awakened Brünnhilde, in Act III, Scene 3. But most of his music is that of the exuberant strapling that Wagner imagined when he conceived of the light-hearted comedy *Der junge Siegfried* in 1851. Proceeding on to *Götterdämmerung*, one is hard-pressed to claim that his character, or the character of his music, changes significantly, even in this plodding, grim drama, weighted down as it is with the motives, keys, and emotions of the three operas preceding it.

In Siegfried's scene with Brünnhilde in the prologue, the heroic element again surfaces, as it did in the final scene of *Siegfried*, but once he arrives in the Hall of the Gibichungs, he is again the churlish, though now fully grown, boy, barely able to articulate a phrase as long as four measures in the entire act.

Similarly, in Act II, his energetic and jolly demeanor shows that he is oblivious to the horror unfolding around him. Of course, HAGEN'S potion has erased his memory of Brünnhilde, so he comes by his behavior honestly. Still, amnesia is hardly conducive to great music; throughout Act II, and indeed through his scene with the Rhinemaidens in Act III, Scene I, his vocal lines are generic, and the leitmotivic references accompanying him detached and distant – a striking contrast to the music of Brünnhilde and Hagen. Only after Hagen delivers his fatal blow does Siegfried recapture a sense of the heroic – or, better, here at the end of the cycle, the *rein menschliches* (the purely human) that Wagner so cherished and sought in the early years of his work on the *Ring*, and with which he so wished to imbue "his Siegfried" on the stage.

As the crucible of the *Ring* cycle and Wagner's intentions for it, interpretations of Siegfried were those of the *Ring* as a whole. For Wagner's more traditional-minded listeners, Siegfried constituted the moral center of the *Ring*, a transvaluer of values in NIETZSCHE's sense. Others, such as George Bernard SHAW, emphasized the revolutionary element in Siegfried's transvaluation, the fact that the world he dooms by shattering Wotan's spear looks a lot like that of aristocracy and bourgeoisie. Especially after the Nazis adjusted Wagner to their purposes, Siegfried's obtuseness and cruelty were often understood as those of the *Ring* as such: Adorno, for instance, singles out Siegfried's treatment of his foster father Mime, and thus Siegfried's "comedic" side, as symptomatic for the *Ring*'s more general treatment of otherness and weakness.   ADRIAN DAUB AND PATRICK MCCRELESS

Siegfried Idyll (WWV 103), Wagner's best-known work of instrumental music. It was composed between unspecified dates in late November and December 1870 and, as is well known, was first performed in a purely domestic situation early on Christmas Day 1870 on the staircase at TRIBSCHEN as a tribute to COSIMA for her 33rd birthday (CWD 25 December 1870). The overall character of the music reflects the state of domestic harmony prevailing in the household following the birth of Wagner and Cosima's son SIEGFRIED on 6 June 1869 and the legalizing of their union through marriage on 25 August 1870.

The *Idyll* is scored for small ensemble, although Cosima later noted Wagner's stated intention to arrange the work for large orchestra (CWD 14 January 1874). The autograph score is inscribed "Tribschen Idyll with Fidi – Birdsong and orange Sunrise, presented as a symphonic birthday greeting to his Cosima by her Richard, 1870." The title *Siegfried Idyll* appears to date from a performance in Meiningen on 10 March 1877 (Millington 312).

The primary thematic material (m. 1) also occurs towards the close of SIEGFRIED Act III, which Wagner had completed in draft on 14 June 1869; the lullaby "Schlaf, Kindchen, schlafe," as noted in Wagner's *BRAUNES BUCH* on New Year's Eve 1868–9 (BB/E 170–1), provides contrasting episodic material (mm. 91ff.). The music is prefaced by a poem of two stanzas in which Wagner expresses his gratitude for the birth of their son: "Ein Sohn ist da! – der musste Siegfried heissen." (A son is here! – He simply had to be named Siegfried.)

The *Siegfried Idyll* is far more than just a serendipitous shaving from the workbench on which the *Ring* was being brought to completion. Its wider significance beyond its beguiling domestic context is twofold. First, in generic terms it stands midway between the symphonic poems of LISZT and the tone poems of Richard STRAUSS as a significant example of the evolving instrumental form in which poetic ideas are expressed through non-texted music. Secondly, the *Idyll* shows a command of musical structure which challenges the assumption that Wagner was incapable of expressing himself in instrumental forms (see Voss). The balance achieved between form and content in this work is masterly. It is best described as cast in an extended rounded binary structure: statement (mm. 1–115); expanded counter-statement with episodes containing new material working towards a climax (mm. 295–350); coda (mm. 351 to the end). It is misleading to see the work as conforming to a modified sonata paradigm. There is no goal-directed movement towards a point of tonal resolution; rather, the music follows a process of continuous motivic expansion and the creation of symmetries. This can be seen in the treatment of the material in the opening paragraph, where the principal theme is continuously expanded through a process of what SCHOENBERG was later to call "developing variation."

The *Idyll* fits Wagner's inscription in that it is indeed symphonic in conception. A statement of Wagner's symphonic ambition, it is a precursor of how he might have developed had he lived to fulfill his stated ambition to compose symphonies (CWD 13 August 1881). ROGER ALLEN

John Deathridge, "Unfinished Symphonies," in *Wagner Beyond Good and Evil* (see bibliography).
Barry Millington, ed., *The Wagner Compendium* (see bibliography): 311–12.
Arnold Schoenberg, "Brahms the Progressive," in *Style and Idea* (see bibliography): 398–441.
Egon Voss, *Richard Wagner und die Instrumentalmusik: Wagners symphonischer Ehrgeiz* (Wilhelmshaven: Heinrichshofen, 1977).

Siegmund (tenor) **and Sieglinde** (soprano; characters in Der RING DES NIBEL-UNGEN, appearing only in Die WALKÜRE), the *Nibelungenlied* identifies SIEGFRIED's parents as Siegmund and Sieglinde. The two neither appear as characters in the epic, nor do they conform to Wagner's characters of the same name: they are not blood relations, they are very much alive, and are king and queen in Xanthen. Wagner characteristically grafted onto these side characters of the *Nibelungenlied* a pair of siblings from the VÖLSUNGA SAGA, Signy and Sigmund, and draws much of the story of the first act of Die Walküre from the NORDIC sagas.

In the *Völsunga Saga*, the woman Signy is married to the king of Gautland, a man named Siggeir. At their wedding, Sigmund, one of Signy's ten brothers, humiliates Siggeir by pointing out his inability to pull the sword Gram from the tree Barnstokkr. Siggeir is furious, and eventually slays Sigmund's father Völse and imprisons Sigmund and his brothers. His sister manages to help him escape, and together they plot to avenge their father. To that end, Signy tricks Sigmund into incest: hoping to give birth to a champion who could help in their quest for revenge, Signy disguises herself by magic and sneaks into her twin brother's bed. Her son, Sinfjötli, indeed helps Sigmund slay Siggeir and restore the honor of the Volsungs. Only after Siggeir is dead does Signy confess her ruse, following her little-loved husband into the fire of his hall.

In adapting this story into the triangular configuration of Siegmund, Sieglinde, and HUNDING, Wagner makes several important changes. Most decisively, neither of the twins is in any way deceived by the other; the incest is, at least for the twins themselves, not means to an end, but an end in itself. Wagner emphasizes the implicit erotic rivalry between brother and husband. The fact that Siegmund can do what Hunding cannot (pull Nothung from the ash tree) means that he is the right mate for her, and that Hunding's claim to her is essentially illegitimate. Since nature smiles on their union ("Winterstürme wichen dem Wonnemond"), the siblings believe their incest licensed by a higher authority than the laws of man. The Signy of the *VÖLSUNGA SAGA*, on the other hand, turns to incest out of necessity, and understands that she is committing an atrocity, albeit a necessary one.

At the same time, Wagner does maintain some of the sense that incest may be the means to a dynastic end – it's just WOTAN's end, not the twins'. After all, the second scene of *Die Walküre* Act II finds Wotan in a suspiciously forgiving mood, and FRICKA seems to suspect that the twins' incest is somehow part of Wotan's design. While Wagner's earlier drafts were more explicit in justifying Siegmund and Sieglinde's incestuous union as part of Wotan's plan (in the final version of Act II of *Die Walküre* he is very much on the defensive when challenged by Fricka, the guardian of bourgeois morality), there are plenty of hints in the libretto that Wotan wanted the siblings to reunite from the very beginning. For instance, Wagner takes the idea of a sword stuck in a tree from the *VÖLSUNGA SAGA*, but adds the detail that Wotan thrust the sword into the ash tree on the day Sieglinde wedded Hunding. Given that the sword in the *VÖLSUNGA SAGA* constitutes a rather unsubtle jab at Siggeir's manhood, it seems as though Wotan declares Hunding's and Sieglinde's marriage illegitimate *ab ovo*.

Siegmund's music in Act I of *Die Walküre* moves from the barest recitative in the pantomime that portrays the beginning of his relationship with Sieglinde, to the more extended declamation of his narrative to Sieglinde and Hunding, to the rich lyricism of his "Winterstürme wichen dem Wonnemond" (Lenzeslied), and his heroic seizing of the sword and triumphant declaration of love to Sieglinde near the end of the act. His music in Act II, Scenes 3–5, also covers a wide expressive range, the climax of his role here being the *Todesverkündigung* (Scene 4), BRÜNNHILDE's announcing to him his fated death in battle, one of the great dialogues in the *Ring*. Here he cuts a commanding dramatic and musical figure. His defiance of Brünnhilde because of his love of Sieglinde ("So grüße mir Walhall, / grüße mir Wotan, / grüße mir Wälse / und alle Helden – grüß auch die holden / Wünsches-Mädchen: / – zu ihnen folg' ich dir nicht") constitutes a central moment in the *Ring*, not only for its intrinsic poetic and musical power, but also for what it teaches Brünnhilde. What she learns from this moment affects her thoughts and actions, and their musical representation, through the rest of the cycle.

Sieglinde's music in Act I of *Die Walküre*, like Siegmund's, progresses from a pantomime, with its short, recitative-like interjections as she queries Siegmund early in the act, to her narrative to Siegmund early in Scene 3, which grows more and more lyrical and expansive as it progresses, to the triumphant love duet at the end of the act. Her most extensive passage of music in Act II portrays the nightmare that she has, as Siegmund protects her in the forest (Scene 3); this scene constitutes the center of the act, with Wotan's Monologue (Scene 2) on one side, the *Todesverkündigung* (Scene 4) on the other. She awakens from her nightmare at the beginning of Scene 5, just before the duel between Siegmund and Hunding.

Her most significant musical moment, however, is the motive she sings to Brünnhilde ("O hehrstes Wunder! Herrliches Maid!" see Appendix 4: *Leitmotive in Der Ring des Nibelungen*; CWE 14) as Brünnhilde rescues her in her one brief appearance in Act III (end of Scene 1). The motive appears again only at the very end of the cycle, in Act III of *Götterdämmerung*: first, during the final surging moments of Brünnhilde's Immolation Monologue, and then, with utter serenity, following the breath-taking pause at the end of the cataclysmic orchestral postlude. This sublime reappearance has generated hundreds of pages of interpretive commentary. For decades the motive was most commonly designated as "Redemption by Love" – a name that entails its own interpretation of the meaning of the *Ring* cycle. We now know that Wagner himself called the motive "the Glorification of Brünnhilde," a designation that makes no definitive claim as to what the cycle means.

ADRIAN DAUB AND PATRICK MCCRELESS

See also LOVE; SEXUALITY AND EROTICISM

Singers, Wagner's relationship with/to. Whatever else he may have been, Wagner was a man of the theater. Nowhere is this reality more apparent than in his relationship with singers, both individually and as a breed. He seems genuinely to have reveled in the camaraderie, high spirits, energy, and outlook of singers, often preferring their company to that of the other sorts of people with whom he came into contact. At some times, Wagner was sorely tried by the situations in which he was landed by uncooperative and high-strung singers; at others, it seems that he found some of his greatest satisfactions in helping singers to achieve and realize his artistic aims. More broadly, his connection to singers is apparent through his discourse (whether to or about singers, but also in general), which was often modeled on the sort of effusive theater-speak which gushes praise and affection in a person's presence while indulging in catty and spiteful outbursts concerning the same person in other settings. Unraveling Wagner's feelings about the personalities and artistry of specific singers thus requires constant awareness of the context and purpose of each of his pronouncements, since it is all too possible for this double-edged perspective to be misleading – as, one suspects, it was often designed to be.

The leading singers with whom Wagner worked during his tenure in DRESDEN (1842–9) provided initial examples of types he would encounter through his career. Wilhelmine SCHRÖDER-DEVRIENT was *sui generis*: given Wagner's passionate admiration for her artistry from earlier years, he began his work with her while mired in star-struck respect, and thus was somewhat nonplused, even disillusioned, to find that she had difficulty in learning new roles, and that there was sometimes little connection between her uplifting stage personae and the petty, jealous, and moody traits she possessed behind the scenes. Joseph TICHATSCHEK, with whom Wagner got along splendidly on the personal level, was the prototypical singer with a beautiful, thrilling voice and little dramatic aptitude or interest, while Wagner's niece Johanna Jachmann-Wagner possessed enough talent that her uncle wished she could distance herself more decisively from traditional operatic practice than she was willing to do. By contrast, the baritone Anton Mitterwurzer (1818–76) was the first singer Wagner encountered who sensed both Wagner's dramatic aims and his own inability to achieve them via the means he had so far developed; eventually he succeeded in transforming his style so that it encompassed Wagner's more dramatic than operatic demands.

Wagner's attempts to find and develop singers who could effectively meet the unprecedented difficulties of his heroic tenor (HELDENTENOR) roles produced extremes in both reward and frustration. Albert NIEMANN possessed the vocal qualifications and was a galvanizing performer but did not care for Wagner the man, and resisted adopting Wagner's suggestions. The composer's famous and revealing letter of 21 February 1861 to Niemann, written when the tenor had threatened to abandon the PARIS TANNHÄUSER production if Wagner would not permit a cut that he had authorized for Tichatschek, gives a bleak picture of the relationship between the two men and implies an unbridgeable artistic gap. Despite Niemann's perpetually frosty attitude toward the composer, however, Wagner seems to have been deeply moved by Niemann's SIEGMUND (BAYREUTH, 1876), and the many reports of the tenor's overwhelming performances in Wagner roles suggest that Wagner's objections to Niemann's interpretations represented a clash of strong artistic wills rather than fundamental shortcomings on Niemann's part. With Ludwig Schnorr von CAROLSFELD, Wagner finally encountered a singer who was extremely gifted, intelligent, malleable, and devoted both to Wagner and to his works, but Schnorr's sudden death at age 29 – a month after the first four performances of TRISTAN UND ISOLDE – turned him into a Wagnerian martyr rather than allowing him to develop and demonstrate over an extended period of time the singing and performance style at which Wagner aimed. The relationship between Heinrich VOGL and Wagner got off on the wrong foot – the composer perceived a snub in the process of arranging their first encounter, when Vogl was a mere stripling of 20 – and did not improve when the tenor took leading roles in the MUNICH performances Wagner did not authorize (*Tristan* and *Das RHEINGOLD* in 1869, *Die WALKÜRE* in 1870). Despite his standing as one of the leading Wagner tenors of his time, and the existence of several reasonable-sounding letters from Wagner to Vogl, Wagner's comments about Vogl in other contexts are invariably colored by a personal animus that prevented him from either valuing or dispassionately assessing Vogl's artistic nature and achievements. In the case of both Georg UNGER (SIEGFRIED in the first Bayreuth *Ring*) and Ferdinand Jäger (one of three PARSIFALS alongside Hermann WINKELMANN and Heinrich Gudehus at Bayreuth in 1882), Wagner seems to have micro-managed (and thus infected with a lack of confidence) singers whose vocal endowment and/or training was not substantial enough to benefit from his advice. Despite these less than successful examples, when COSIMA Wagner took the reins of the BAYREUTH FESTIVAL, her preference for untried but malleable talent had "authentic" roots in Wagner's own hopes and practice.

For the two Bayreuth Festivals he supervised, Wagner found leading and gifted singers who were both cooperative (Amalie MATERNA, Eugen Gura, Karl Hill) and difficult (Niemann and Franz BETZ – the two of whom Wagner called "matadors" in looking ahead to life without them after the first RING), some who were a mixture of both (Emil SCARIA), and a number of enthusiastic younger singers (Lilli LEHMANN chief among them). Wagner was extremely loyal to singers who demonstrated aptitude for his requirements or were personally well disposed toward him – Mitterwurzer was called upon to create KURWENAL two decades after becoming the first to perform WOLFRAM VON ESCHINBACH; Tichatschek was allowed to appear in a Munich LOHENGRIN of 1867 even though Wagner correctly suspected that his visual appearance would not please LUDWIG II; Marianne Brandt was awarded some performances as KUNDRY in 1882 because of her kindness in substituting as Waltraute for the indisposed Luise Jaide in the second GÖTTERDÄMMERUNG of 1876; and so on. In dealing with singers, Wagner's artistic idealism could manifest a warmly personal dimension.

DAVID BRECKBILL

Hans Hey, ed., *Richard Wagner als Vortragsmeister, 1864–1876: Erinnerungen von Julius Hey* (Leipzig: Breitkopf & Härtel, 1911).

Erich Kloss, ed., *Richard Wagner an seine Künstler: Zweiter Band der "Bayreuther Briefe" (1872–1883)* (Berlin: Schuster & Loeffler, 1908).

Lilli Lehmann, *Mein Weg* (Leipzig: Hirzel, 1913), trans. *My Path Through Life* (New York: Putnam, 1914; repr. New York: Arno, 1977).

Einhard Luther, *Biographie eines Stimmfaches* (see bibliography): esp. vol. 1.

Angelo Neumann, *Erinnerungen an Richard Wagner* (see bibliography).

Richard Wagner, "Meine Erinnerungen an Ludwig Schnorr von Carolsfeld," *Neue Zeitschrift für Musik*, 5 and 12 June 1868.

Sixtus Beckmesser (baritone; character in *Die MEISTERSINGER VON NÜRNBERG*), one of the most controversial figures in Wagner's oeuvre. He is officially the NUREMBERG town clerk and a leading member of the Mastersinger guild (in his elected post of marker, he evaluates the correctness of mastersongs), but Beckmesser is also portrayed as a narrow-minded pedant, unable to see beyond his guild's codified rules. The nemesis of not only HANS SACHS and WALTHER VON STOLZING but also, the opera would have us believe, of artistic integrity itself, Beckmesser is repeatedly subjected to ridicule and humiliation. For modern audiences, the overriding question – one that has come to serve as a referendum on the opera itself, and indeed the entire Wagnerian project – is whether Wagner's treatment of Beckmesser is not merely cruel but ANTI-SEMITIC.

Starting at least with MAHLER, scattered critics, including Theodor W. ADORNO, have charged in passing that Beckmesser's characterization amounted to an anti-Semitic stereotype. But the first sustained indictment came with Barry Millington's 1991 article, which made its case in fairly straightforward terms by lining up Beckmesser's characterization with the playbook of nineteenth-century anti-Semitic stereotypes: a scheming pedant with a persecution complex, a lack of natural artistic intuition, and a high-lying tessitura that Wagner hoped would make the singer's voice crack (an effect he believed would be humorous). Millington also linked Beckmesser's garbled prize song of Act III to contemporary parodies of cantorial singing, as well as to the Grimm brothers' explicitly anti-Semitic "The Jew in the Thorn Bush." A complementary treatment by Marc Weiner (1995) amplified and extended Millington's critique by situating Beckmesser within the context of other potentially anti-Semitic characterizations in Wagner's oeuvre (MIME, ALBERICH) as well as the terms of Wagner's own anti-Semitism. Even before these studies, it was known that an early version of the Beckmesser character was named Hanslich, a not particularly subtle reference to one of Wagner's prominent and presumably Jewish critics, Eduard HANSLICK.

Responses to Millington and Weiner have taken a number of forms. David Levin has suggested that *Meistersinger*'s anti-Semitism operates more on the level of aesthetic practice and dramaturgical function than outright stereotype alone. Conversely, some prominent Wagnerians, led by Dieter Borchmeyer, rejected Millington's thesis, arguing that Wagner would have had to specific-ally designate his characters as being Jewish for such a charge to be valid. Such critics, who also insist on a divide between Wagner's POLITICS and his art, tend to ignore the argument that Wagner himself would have avoided the very kind of literalism Borchmeyer demands. On the other hand, historians such as Thomas Grey and David Dennis have noted that neither Wagner's own anti-Semitism nor its potential outlet in the figure of Beckmesser seems to have been acknowledged by Wagner's anti-Semitic and German nationalist supporters – precisely the group for whom, one imagines, it would matter most.

Parallel to the academic treatment of Beckmesser has been the dramatur-gical one. Most explicitly, stagings such as Christoph Nel's in Frankfurt and Hans Neuenfels's in Stuttgart (both from the mid-1990s), have more than hinted that the opera's treatment of Beckmesser is an anticipation of twentieth-century violence towards Jews. And yet, well before Millington or Weiner – and perhaps just as relevant, well before the *Regietheater* of the 1990s – postwar German productions of *Meistersinger* seem intuitively to have grasped that the opera's stance towards Beckmesser demanded some extra attention, even if that attention was unwilling or unable to invoke the specter of Wagner's anti-Semitism *per se*. Joachim Herz's staging for Leipzig (1960) was explicitly sympathetic towards Beckmesser, down to assigning him sup-porters among the onstage crowds, and Götz Friedrich's early productions – Stockholm (1977) and Deutsche Oper Berlin (1979) – were also notably concili-atory towards Beckmesser. Perhaps most famously, WOLFGANG WAGNER's 1984 production for Bayreuth attempted to defuse the tension by inserting Wolfgang himself into the final scene to join Sachs's and Beckmesser's hands. August Everding's Munich staging (1979) also acknowledged the problem, although, instead of trying to solve it, Everding highlighted it by denying Beckmesser a curtain call until the last possible moment. Thus while the postwar Wagnerian establishment has officially resisted acknowledg-ing a connection between Beckmesser's characterization and Wagner's anti-Semitism, it has also felt compelled – long before any academics forced the issue – to intervene on Beckmesser's behalf, without ever saying exactly why.

Yet if *Meistersinger*'s sheer nastiness towards Beckmesser is undeniable, and at least arguably related to Wagner's anti-Semitism, it is also the case that the opera can be staged effectively without focusing on that specific characterization. Most recently, Andreas Homoki's 2011 production for the Komische Oper Berlin presented Beckmesser as an awkward but loveable fop – equal parts Franz Liszt, André Rieu, and Mr. Bean – as if to suggest that Beckmesser need only be shown as *an* outsized caricature, not necessarily an anti-Semitic one. (Although Homoki's characterization was new, even shocking, there is ample literary precedent for a foppish Beckmesser: not only the old lover in *commedia dell'arte*, but more directly the character of Eoban, Beckmesser's aristocratic equivalent in the Lortzing/Deinhardstein opera *Hans Sachs*, which Wagner knew.) It is also possible to remove Beckmesser from caricature entirely by presenting his prize song in Act III not as a comical mistake but as a principled artistic statement: Ernst Bloch called the moment a kind of Dadaism *avant la lettre* and the 2007 Bayreuth production by KATHARINA WAGNER and dramaturge Robert Sollich used the Act II brawl as a pivot point from which Beckmesser emerged as an avatar of the AVANT-GARDE, heroically juxtaposed against a demagogic Sachs and a spineless, pandering Walther.

The specifically vocal qualities of Beckmesser's role also play a large part in how the character is perceived. If the part is sung lyrically, without the sediment of parody and caricature – more WOLFRAM than Mime – an actual, even sympathetic, person can emerge beneath the role's ideological function within the opera. It was partially for this reason – beautifully sustained BEL CANTO singing – that both Michael Volle and Adrian Eröd as Beckmesser in the Wagner/Sollich Bayreuth production proved to be so compelling. And even in the absence of careful dramaturgy, careful singing can rescue Beckmesser from caricature; Thomas Allen turned the role into a signature showpiece of his vocal talents (and Beckmesser's humanity) almost regardless of the production. Ultimately, however, one might argue that a human Beckmesser serves more to indict the opera than to vindicate it.   RYAN MINOR

Ernst Bloch, "On the Text of Beckmesser's Prize Song," in *Literary Essays*, trans. Andrew Joron et al. (Stanford University Press, 1998): 178–83.

Dieter Borchmeyer, "Nuremberg as an Aesthetic State: *Die Meistersinger*, an Image and Counterimage of History," *Drama and the World of Richard Wagner* (see bibliography): 180–211.

David Dennis, "'The Most German of all German Operas': *Die Meistersinger* Through the Lens of the Third Reich," in *Wagner's "Meistersinger": Performance, History, Representation*, ed. Nicholas Vazsonyi (University of Rochester Press, 2003): 98–119.

Thomas S. Grey, "Wagner's *Die Meistersinger* as National Opera (1868–1945)," in Celia Applegate and Pamela Potter, eds., *Music and German National Identity* (University of Chicago Press, 2002): 78–104.

David J. Levin, "Reading Beckmesser Reading: Anti-Semitism and Aesthetic Practice in *The Mastersingers of Nuremberg*," New German Critique 69 (1996): 127–46.

Barry Millington, "Nuremberg Trial: Is There Anti-Semitism in *Die Meistersinger?*" Cambridge Opera Journal 3.3 (1991): 247–60.

Marc A. Weiner, "Reading the Ideal," New German Critique 69 (1996): 53–83.

Richard Wagner and the Anti-Semitic Imagination (see bibliography).

Sleep / dream

1. Dream as a primal state
2. Sleep as a meta-principle

1. Dream as a primal state

SIEGFRIED, Act III, Scene I: high mountains, thunder, night – one of the most radical sequences of the entire RING. To gain counsel on how things are to continue with the world, the Wanderer awakens the all-knowing primal mother from the dream that had previously ensured the continuation of the world order. WOTAN mercilessly forces ERDA out of her cave into the daylight. But she cannot help the Wanderer, for her awakening results in the opposite of what help *per se* might have been: "My sleep is dreaming," sings Wagner's "wise one of the primeval world" (*Urweltweise*), "my dreaming musing, / my musing the working of knowledge." This means that her dream is identical to the primeval state of creation – genesis in permanence. It is the matrix of all life nature. Being awake, on the other hand, connotes confusion, deception, despotism, violence, betrayal, and downfall.

In this sense, the confrontation between the Wanderer and the *völva* is prototypical of Wagner's oeuvre. In all his MUSIC DRAMAS, the rule of the actionists and "slaves of day" (*Tagesknechte*), is contrasted with the gentle brigades of the "nightbound" (*Nacht-Geweihte*) and their subversive web of metaphysical connections. Often the dramaturgical tension in Wagner's works is virtually built up from the flip side, as paradoxical as this might initially seem. But a completely visible world no longer holds any surprises, and Wagner understood that night does not necessarily have to be a negating principle. Instead, it is stylized to become the antidote for day. Wagner was in search of new plot potential for the ARTWORK OF THE FUTURE and found it in these counter-worlds. His works are so overflowing with anxious characters that have chimerical, introspective, timeless or time-transcending missions: dreamers and visionaries, somnambulists and hallucinators, emigrants from the sphere of conscious life who impede and redirect the external plot – to which they themselves belong – inwards as it tumbles forwards, in order to continue it on a parallel level under new, more elastic laws. In this manner, one finds outsiders at the center of all Wagner's music dramas and, aside from such significant exceptions as the tireless hero SIEGFRIED, whose restlessness and dreamlessness lead directly into the catastrophe of GÖTTERDÄMMERUNG, Wagner's protagonists are assigned major dream passages, some of which display a revolutionary driving force. LOHENGRIN develops almost directly from ELSA's dream narrative. In Der FLIEGENDE HOLLÄNDER, the Ahasver of the sea only finds salvation thanks to SENTA's visionary fits. The fable of TANNHÄUSER, who would otherwise have remained in the kingdom of Venus, is initialized by a claustrophobic dream from which he must awaken. TRISTAN's feverish delirium in Act III can be read as a narcoleptic phantasmagoria. In Die MEISTERSINGER VON NÜRNBERG, STOLZING's dream account provides the foundation for a new poetics. And let us not forget HAGEN's auto-hypnosis in Act II of *Götterdämmerung*, whose conspiratorial energy reminds us that night also spawns evil. The penchant for compaction and floating connections transpires as a decisive motive. Moments of hindsight and foresight, which are both possible in dreams, develop plot reservoirs that point beyond the acute present of the figures and open up Wagner's works structurally to a meandering dramaturgy.

This dramaturgy finds a broad theoretical foundation in Wagner's programmatic and AESTHETIC writings, and journal entries. Music itself, for example, is revealed as a "direct dream image" (BB/E 177). In his essay BEETHOVEN (1870), Wagner draws on SCHOPENHAUER and also presents his thesis of the "innermost" and "allegorical dream" (SSD 9:94; Wagner/ Dannreuther 26), which reads like a metaphysics of the creative act: as dreams generate wish-fulfillment; the process of sociopolitical exhaustion can be overcome through a utopian form of artistic production that manifests itself as "true dream interpretation" (*Wahrtraumdeuterei*; *Meistersinger* Act III, Scene 2). Analogously, the "true dream shapes" (*Wahrtraumgestalten*, SSD 10:227; PW 6:172) of the music drama come into being on Wagner's stage as emanations of collective inspiration: on the one hand that of the festival audience, which learns to mobilize the "image of the inner imagination taken out into reality" (Porges 8) in the darkened BAYREUTH auditorium, and on the other hand that of the prototypical artist, who – called to be an awakener – must dream in order to awaken for all.

The combination of epistemological, methodical, and practical scenic examinations of semi-conscious or unconscious areas of life in Wagner has, admittedly, led to him being named the first depth psychologist in opera history. Placing his oeuvre in the milieu of Freudian dream interpretation is nonetheless problematic. In addition, Wagner's own life is rich in dream material. Since the publication of COSIMA WAGNER'S DIARIES in 1976 at the latest, enough documents have been available showing that Wagner suffered from a neurasthenic disposition which intensified his private dream experiences to a sometimes unbearable degree, and there is probably no other historical personality who left behind as many shorthand dream notes as Wagner. This has, however, tempted researchers to submit not only the man, but also his works, too hastily to psychoanalytical interpretation, in part because dreams have become a fashionable topic, which makes it all the more surprising that a systematic concordance of all Wagner's recorded dreams was not produced until 2007 (Dombois, "complicirte Ruhe," 235–52). With reference to the works, a comparable basis for discussion would be that Wagner's cast of characters consists of artificial figures who act as their own mouthpieces, and are thus insufficient for the dialogic constellation of classical psychoanalysis. Dreams and their interpretation become artistically one. In this sense, Wagner's dreams are always poetic rather than intimately real psychological material, and a discourse based on practical theatrical and media-aesthetic concerns would come closest to meeting the demands of this genuinely dreamlike oeuvre. Aside from this, the topic "dream in Wagner" seems increasingly old-fashioned precisely because of contemporary attempts to bring it up to date. Under the pressure of research, the object of examination has lost its tension. Yet, by the same token, dream also gives us access to a subject that, under normal circumstances, is its prerequisite.

2. Sleep as a meta-principle

The topos in question is that of sleep, which may initially seem empty because it does not reveal itself immediately. *Die WALKÜRE*, Act III, Scene 3: Wotan sends Brünnhilde into a sleep in which she will remain – crossing over into *Siegfried* – for around 15 years until the boyish awakener is old enough to rouse her with a kiss. The enigma of this sequence lies in the fact that not a single dream is composed into the sleep of the most beautiful sleeper in the *Ring*, even though Wagner can otherwise be considered a garrulous arranger. In his magnum opus, however, there is not one scene that does not draw on the realm of sleep in some way – including those appearances in which individual figures consciously seek to resist the pull of somnolence. Certainly many characters are temporarily fed paranoid, hallucinogenic, or visionary dream images during sleep; but Wagner's oeuvre demonstrates that dreams cannot exist without sleep, whereas sleep certainly can exist without dreams. In light of this enormous "sleep mass" and the many self-negating, covetous urges of Wagner's sleepers that are connected to it, one must wonder how any plot can flourish in the music dramas.

The extent of the absurdity becomes clear as soon as one recalls the laws of practical theater work. Sleepers are not only choreographically disobedient; they are simply not fit for the stage. For the audience scarcely distinguishable from the dead, they form part of the action, yet cannot contribute to it – at most, one can speak of an *agitatio ex negativo*. It is characteristic that this is also mirrored in the research, which has been rather silent on the issue. Until recently, there had been no comprehensive investigation of *sleep* as a dramaturgical motif which, unlike *dream*, has clearly not been considered sufficiently sensational or rewarding. The only reflections on the subject are limited to a few pages, and on the whole constitute either quantifications of sleep scenes or presentations of well-known Romanticisms and psychopathologies, none of which takes the practical side of theater into account (see Dombois, "Das Auge," note 24).

Examined more closely, however, sleep is a portal, and thus provides an opening for expanded insights. It maintains the connection between the close and the distant, between experience of the present and of the horizon, between life and the hereafter, and makes them mutually permeable. Even if it is a gap, it is precisely this that enables the music drama to achieve its great moments of structural autonomy: through a sleep sequence, the scenic continuum is halted and the visible world blocked out. In the darkness, a crack opens. Acoustic expectations are stimulated. And finally, with the music, reflexive elements flow into this crack, parable-like memory and future images, usually tied to sonic, lighting, and gestural shifts, all of which successively cause represented time to be "written over" by narrative time.

The dream-filled sleep of the *völva* provides a vivid example of this in compositional terms: the Magic sleep motive here appears as a chromatically descending succession of dysfunctional three- and four-note chords that produce an aura that is simultaneously static and weightless (see Appendix 4: *Leitmotive* in *Der Ring des Nibelungen*, music example CWE 18). Ernst Bloch referred to this passage as a "unique expressive advance" (Bloch 1067). It not only combines such LEITMOTIVIC phenomena as representations of becoming or of Valhalla, fortress of the gods, or the Ring motive. The semantic nub lies in the fact that the same musical figure which had accompanied Brünnhilde's descent into sleep is also used when it is time to awaken Erda, the eternally sleeping mother. It transpires, then, that the sleep of Wagner's figures allows the rupturing power of the music to enter the drama, along with various forms of subtext and meta-text that foil the old Aristotelian unities and destabilize the narrative center in favor of a widely frayed, multi-perspectival network. "Wagner appears to have realized the profound necessity of allowing the music drama to 'stop,' to breathe and to reflect upon itself," Adorno noted in a similar context (19:401). In other words, the Magic sleep motive stands as a sign for the rupturing of time. Its catalytic potential ultimately marks Wagner's work as a medial occurrence, providing a model for the new and newest interactive and non-linear media technologies in the field of stage work.

Wagner himself was responsible for outstanding architectural and technical innovations in the theater. Thus the dream factory of the Bayreuth FESTIVAL THEATER was consciously conceived into a dreamlike biosphere in the manner of ancient sleep temples – music and musical experience are thus brought into contact with healing methods via the nexus of sleep. For the dramaturgy of the program, Wagner envisaged a stepwise process of "unlighting" (*Entleuchtung*; Lindau 13) – from the onset of twilight at the start of the performance to the dimming of the lighting in the auditorium, whose "mysterious half-darkness" (Glasenapp 5:268) is really the precondition for that creative slumber of the audience from which the collective dream image of the stage is intended to rise. The mechanism of the "Wagner curtain," an invention of Wagner's still used in theaters, was in fact based on the alternately opening and closing reflex of an eye (see Dombois, "Das Auge").

Sleep imagery plays an equally significant part in the story of Wagner's life. Along with a psychosomatically based inclination towards the aura of dimly lit living quarters and venues, Wagner's lifelong predilection for lavish materials and dressing-gowns, satin divan covers, and padded leisure suits has acquired a degree of dubious renown in the reception of his work and life. The theory that this was simply the indulgence of an exaggerated desire for luxury, however, is untenable. From a costume-historical perspective, one finds that, in their materials and design, the forms of clothing preferred by Wagner presented a remake of traditional patriotic German dress on the one hand, but also the fashion of the French Revolution. It is not a matter of fetishism, but rather stimulation. Wagner's costume is the sublimation of a dreamed revolt, and can thus be integrated retrospectively into work-constitutive contexts (Dombois, "complicirte Ruhe," 25–79).

It belongs to the constructive potential of the motif that biographical and work-immanent aspects of sleep also combine quite concretely on numerous occasions to keep mythological opening or ending scenarios elastic for the stage; sleep enables a beginning without birthing pains and an end without death. The famous opening bars of *Das RHEINGOLD*, where the gold itself is asleep on the river bed, guarded by the Rhinemaidens' lullaby, were evolved from the "somnambulant state" (ML 511; ML/E 505) of the one who produced them. This also applies to the aforementioned scene between the Wanderer and the *völva*, which heralded Wagner's resumption of work on the *Ring* after its twelve-year interruption, and thus also constituted a reawakening of the creator to his own creation. Sleep asserts itself not only as a connecting point between apparatus and myth, theater practice and music philosophy, but also between product and production, form and content. The forgotten motif becomes a "pre-liminary" catalyst of Wagner's art.   JOHANNA DOMBOIS

TRANSLATION: WIELAND HOBAN

Theodor Adorno, *Gesammelte Schriften* (see bibliography).

Ernst Bloch, *The Principle of Hope*, trans. Neville Plaice, Stephen Plaice, and Paul Knight (Cambridge, MA: The MIT Press, 1996).

Johanna Dombois, "Das Auge, das sich wechselnd öffnet und schließt: Zur Szenographie des Wagner-Vorhangs," *wagnerspectrum* 4.2 (2008): 209–35.

"Die 'complicirte Ruhe.' Richard Wagner und der Schlaf: Biographie – Musikästhetik – Festspieldramaturgie," Ph.D. thesis, Technische Universität Berlin, microfiche (2007), www.jhnndmbs.net/de/projekte/2007/03/pdf.php (accessed on 19 March 2013).

"Schlaf als Struktur in Wagners Theater," in *Richard Wagner und seine Medien: Für eine kritische Praxis des Musiktheaters*, Dombois and Richard Klein (Stuttgart: Klett-Cotta, 2012).

Ralf Eisinger, "Richard Wagner: Idee und Dramaturgie des allegorischen Traumbildes," Ph.D. dissertation, Ludwig-Maximilians-Universität Munich (Munich, 1987).

Carl Friedrich Glasenapp, *Das Leben Richard Wagners* (see bibliography).

Paul Lindau, *Nüchterne Briefe aus Bayreuth* (Breslau: Schottlaender, 1877).

Heinrich Porges, *Das Bühnenfestspiel zu Bayreuth* (see bibliography).

Richard Wagner, *On Conducting*, trans. Edward Dannreuther (London: William Reeves, 1887).

Society of Patrons. See PATRONS' ASSOCIATION

Solti, Sir Georg (b. Budapest, 21 Oct. 1912; d. Antibes, 5 Sep. 1997), Hungarian conductor. Solti studied at the Liszt Academy in Budapest and, after World War II, became Director of the Bavarian State opera in MUNICH; later appointments included Music Director of the Royal Opera House, Covent Garden (1961–71) and the Chicago Symphony Orchestra (1969–91). Solti made acclaimed commercial recordings of all ten canonical Wagner operas, including the famed first ever studio recording of the complete *RING* cycle (1958–65) with the Vienna Philharmonic.   ROGER ALLEN

See also PERFORMANCE, CONDUCTORS; PERFORMANCE, RECORDING

John Culshaw, *Ring Resounding* (London: Secker & Warburg, 1967).

Souvenirs. See MEMORABILIA

Spohr, Louis (Ludwig) (b. Brunswick, 5 April 1784; d. Kassel, 22 Oct. 1859), German violinist, conductor, and opera composer. Spohr's contact with Wagner's life and works comes principally through his opera *Jessonda* (1823), the first German opera in which dialogue was completely replaced by recitatives. During the nineteenth century, Spohr's opera had a secure place in the repertoire, particularly in German houses. In his *Aufruf an deutsche Componisten* (1823), Spohr anticipated some aspects of Wagner's critique of contemporary styles; *Jessonda* may partly be understood as Spohr's implementation of these ideas. Despite (or perhaps because of) the theoretical and practical connections between *Jessonda* and Wagner's works, however, Wagner is largely critical. In his early essay *Die deutsche Oper* (On German Opera, 1834), Wagner dismisses Spohr's style, and even in later essays such as *Über eine*

Opernaufführung in Leipzig (1874), Wagner criticizes the text declamation in *Jessonda*. In his *Nachruf an L. Spohr und Chordirektor W. Fischer* (Homage to L. Spohr and Chorus-Master W. Fischer, 1859), on the other hand, Wagner celebrates Spohr as a noble champion of German art. STEPHEN MEYER

Clive Brown, *Louis Spohr: A Critical Biography* (Cambridge University Press, 1984).

Stabreim, customarily translated as "alliteration." This is unfortunate given that, strictly speaking, alliteration refers to the repetition of the initial sound (usually a consonant) in a string of words, as in a tongue-twister. But *Stabreim* includes assonance and the full play of consonants and vowels. Certainly it stands as an alternative to end-rhymes, but it also covers all other sound patterns a poet might use. Here, for instance, is SIEGFRIED in Act II of the eponymous *RING* drama, when the spitting phonetic effects alone make his loathing of Mime palpable: "Grade so garstig, griesig und grau, / klein und krumm, höckrig und hinkend, / mit hängenden Ohren, triefigen Augen. . ." And here he is in Act III, the long vowels expressing his wonderment on Brünnhilde's rock: "Selige Öde auf sonniger Höh! / Was ruht dort schlummernd im schattigen Tann?"

In producing his libretti (and we must remember he saw them as poems), Wagner on occasion writes as though *Stabreim* were the key structural unit; a linguistic parallel to the *LEITMOTIV* in the music. But, as with the latter, this is an exaggeration and a simplification. In fact, the more lyrical Wagner becomes, the more end-rhymes dominate as a poetic device; something which is palpable in the Act II love duet in *TRISTAN UND ISOLDE*, and in the so-called *LIEBESTOD*.

Nonetheless, aside from its practical function, Wagner has an ideological role for *Stabreim*. It, too, establishes the spiritual essence of the German people. First, in being "the very oldest attribute of all poetic speech" (PW 2:227), it is a way into a deep encounter with culture and race. For instance, in *Eine MITTEILUNG AN MEINE FREUNDE* (A Communication to my Friends, 1851) we learn that in the "Siegfried-man" Wagner found the perfect mode of utterance, namely: "that *Stabreim* which the *Volk* itself once sang, when *it* was still both Poet and Myth-Maker" (PW 1:376). Nor is he alone in foregrounding *Stabreim* in the anthropological context. HERDER, perhaps the most influential figure in the revival of native *VOLK* art and in the related rejection of French influence in Germany, also sees alliteration (including vowel sounds) as lying at the root of the German spirit. But while Herder's comprehensive celebration of *Volk* cultures is critically important, Wagner goes further and emphasizes the absolute superiority of what is quintessentially German over French (*welsch*) alternatives. He already did so in fanciful pseudo-historical terms in *Die WIBELUNGEN* (1848–50). But in *OPER UND DRAMA* (Opera and Drama, 1851) he returns to the dialectic interaction of *Stabreim* and music and, finding an analogy in male/female coupling, "explains" the uniquely lofty genius of German art. It is this dialectic that is put on the stage in *Die MEISTERSINGER VON NÜRNBERG* where a song/child is "begat." Ironically, though, that song/child is shaped by end-rhymes.

A further ideological function of *Stabreim* should also be viewed with skepticism. Allegedly speech has precedence – in every sense. The young

Wagner goes so far as to claim that setting his libretti was relatively straightforward as the music was naturally born of the poem. No doubt there is some truth to this, but as a hard and fast methodological rule it is bogus.

BARRY EMSLIE

See also WAGNER AS COMPOSER; WAGNER AS LIBRETTIST

Stage consecration festival play. See *BÜHNENWEIHFESTSPIEL*

Stage design. Wagner wrote his MUSIC DRAMAS for a theater in which the aesthetic of scenic design and the technology by which it was realized had changed relatively little over the previous two to three centuries. The romantic-realistic scenery of the mid-nineteenth-century European theater provided historical, natural, urban, or domestic settings of a beautified and idealized kind, against which most drama, sung or spoken, was performed. The employment of wings arranged in perspective with shutters or a backdrop at the back, all of which could be changed in the course of performance, was essentially the same as had been employed in the baroque period. Toward the end of Wagner's lifetime, the means of lighting the set changed from gas to electricity.

1. Wagner's lifetime
2. Tradition and experimentation after 1883
3. New Bayreuth and the postwar period
4. Current and future directions

1. Wagner's lifetime

All of Wagner's music dramas were composed with this romantic-realist scenery in mind and, for many decades after their first performance, they continued to be produced on such settings. Wagner was not, however, happy either with the style of scenery or with scenic practices. When his early music dramas were staged in the 1840s, almost all works in the repertory were staged against stock scenery and little care was generally taken by theater and stage managers to select sets that complemented and expressed the dramatic action. In those writings in which he theorized the *GESAMTKUNSTWERK*, Wagner elucidated the relationship between action and setting which, as with all elements of the theater, he regarded as equal and complementary to other elements. Later, especially in the *BEETHOVEN* essay (1870), he devised a hierarchy of theatrical elements, and placed the visual below the musical in importance, but above the verbal. His main criticism of the scenic practices of his time was that they did not provide audiences with access to the inner action of the drama and, all too frequently, designers were concerned purely to provide virtuosic displays of their talents, not to interpret the drama.

While Wagner was a perceptive critic of the contemporary theater, the "model" production of his music dramas that he staged in MUNICH in the 1860s and his productions of the *RING* and *PARSIFAL* at BAYREUTH provided little evidence that he could do much to change current scenic practices. For a start, he had to depend upon designers such as Heinrich Döll, Angelo II Quaglio, and Christian Jank, who, while highly skilled at their craft, worked entirely within the aesthetic parameters of contemporary scenic design. But Wagner had difficulty in visualizing an alternative to nineteenth-century stage practices and even though the sets he used at Bayreuth attempted to complement the mythological ambience of the drama, it was not easy from the designs for the production of the *Ring* to divine the symbolic meaning of the action. Furthermore, the literalistic character of romantic-realistic scenery tended to inhibit the audience's imaginative response to the music rather than encourage it.

2. Tradition and experimentation after 1883

It was in the cause of releasing the imagination to respond fully to the demands of Wagner's music that Adolphe APPIA was initially drawn to the problematics of scenic design. In a series of publications, the most germane of which are *La Mise en scène wagnérien* (Wagnerian Production; Paris, 1891) and *La Musique et la mise en scène* (Music and Production; Paris, 1897), Appia sustained the idea of the seamless union of all theatrical elements, which was the key concept of the *Gesamtkunstwerk*, but advocated the erasure of almost all realistic detail from the scenery, and the employment of changing light – "the paint of the stage" – as the primary means of reflecting the dynamic emotions of the characters. On Appia's stage, not only would the natural dimensions of the human form be seen more clearly, but the abstract space which constituted so much of his sets provided the audience with the opportunity to respond imaginatively to Wagner's music, a freedom that was previously denied by the romantic-realistic style. With Appia, the drama ultimately took place less before the audience's eyes, more within their minds.

Appia's ideas were decisively rejected by COSIMA WAGNER, who insisted that productions in Bayreuth should follow the models established by her husband. However, even though Appia himself was not employed at Bayreuth, the tendency toward greater abstraction and stylization on stage which, under the name of symbolism, was widespread in the European theater as a whole, could not be resisted. Wagner himself had advocated, but not achieved, a stripping down of the stage to the barest essentials, and even Cosima, as she revived the entire Wagnerian canon, found herself trimming the physical aspects of the productions. By the 1920s and early 1930s, the spare approach advocated by Appia could be seen in the sets of Emil PREETORIUS for the *Ring*. Elsewhere, the influence of Appiaesque symbolism could be seen in the sets designed by Alfred ROLLER for the celebrated production of *TRISTAN UND ISOLDE* at the Vienna Opera in 1903, and on the stages of German regional theater in the work of such designers of Hans Wildermann, Ludwig Sievert, and Leo Pasetti. Jürgen Fehling's famous production of *Der FLIEGENDE HOLLÄNDER* at the KROLL OPER in Berlin (1929) employed cubistic style sets by Eduard Dahlberg, which also suggested rather than stated the background, though the rigorously naturalistic production deprived the abstract spaces of any mystery.

3. New Bayreuth and the postwar period

It was not until after World War II that Appia's theories were fully embraced by Wagnerian directors and designers. When WIELAND WAGNER took over the directorship of the BAYREUTH FESTIVAL in 1951, he made a virtue of economic and political necessity. The Festival could not afford elaborate sets in the romantic-realistic style, and he and his brother WOLFGANG also wished to downplay the political reverberations of Wagner's music drama, so during the 1950s all the music dramas including, controversially, *Die MEISTERSINGER VON NÜRNBERG*, were performed against severely minimalistic sets, designed by Wieland and Wolfgang themselves. These designs, which were either centered upon a single scenic feature that gained powerful symbolic meaning, or were virtually featureless, provided the setting for productions that either probed the psychic life of the characters or drew attention to the "timeless" mythical aspects of the action. No reference was made to the traditional modes of designing Wagner. As the popularity of opera grew in the postwar decades, and more and more opera houses assayed the production of Wagner, Bayreuth minimalism became so widely imitated that by the mid-1960s it had became the new norm for Wagnerian stage design.

Although since the 1970s Wagnerian stage design has become marked by eclecticism, minimalist approaches to designing and staging the music dramas are still quite common, notably in the widely seen work of Robert Wilson – *Parsifal* (Hamburg, 1991), *LOHENGRIN* (Metropolitan Opera, New York, 1998), *Ring* (Zurich, 1999) – which is characterized by intense and constantly changing colors projected onto a cyclorama, sharply etched and often puzzling symbolic figures, and hieratically clad actors who move with extreme slowness, so creating an atmosphere on stage of a quasi-religious ritual. Minimalist approaches to design can be seen today in Stéphane Braunschweig's severe sets for his own production of the *Ring* (Aix-en-Provence, 2005–9) and in the mobile, concentric rings designed by Jens Kilian for Vera Namirova's *Ring* (Frankfurt, 2010 ongoing).

Wagner's music dramas have invited such a wide range of interpretation that, since the 1970s, almost every artistic style has been utilized to find meanings for today's audiences. So-called "traditional" designs, such as Gunther Schneider-Siemssen's romantic settings for the New York Met *Ring* (1987–2009), employ visual themes from nineteenth-century realism and symbolism, while the "natural" *Ring* at the Seattle Opera, in which designer Thomas Lynch was inspired by the scenery of the Pacific Northwest, did not so much revert to nineteenth-century tradition as highlight, often quite effectively, themes of nature and REGENERATION. But these productions have bucked the general trend in contemporary Wagnerian stage design. While they offer an ameliorative vision of Wagner's work, the energies and interests of contemporary designers and directors strive toward realizing the darker and more disruptive aspects of the music dramas, to interrogating Wagner himself and to challenging the entire notion of the *Gesamtkunstwerk*, whose ethos of total harmony does not sit well with postwar generations.

The pivotal event in this sea-change in Wagnerian stage design was Patrice CHÉREAU's centenary production of the *Ring* in Bayreuth (1976–81), in which Richard Peduzzi's sets evoked the industrial history of Europe and the USA from the Enlightenment through to the twentieth century, and placed Wagner's tragic themes in an unfamiliar perspective, though this was not the first political and industrial *Ring*; Joachim Herz's pioneering production, designed by Rudolf and Reinhard Heinrich, in Leipzig (1973–6) had prepared the way. Even earlier, Wieland Wagner's Brechtian-inspired second production of *Die Meistersinger* at Bayreuth (1963), in a setting reminiscent of London's Globe Theatre, had highlighted the social and political tensions of Wagner's comedy. But the Chéreau/Peduzzi *Ring* served as the impetus to steer Wagnerian design away from Wieland's minimalism into an eclectic postmodernism in which there are no overriding thematic approaches. Certainly the blending of politics and industrialism continues to be a major theme, as in Robert Carsen's production of the *Ring*, designed by Patrick Kinmonth (Cologne, 2001–3), and in Francesca Zambello's *Ring* (Washington and San Francisco, 2006–11), where Michael Yeargan's sets suggested an industrialized America which, along with Jan Hartley's massive video projections, told a story of the potential destruction of the human race by its own pollution.

4. Current and future directions

Although industry is far from the sole subject for stage designers, the theme has introduced a new realism into Wagnerian production as a whole, so that even works such as *Tristan und Isolde* and *Parsifal*, which inhabit numinous and incorporeal realms, have been staged in the most specific, even domestic contexts. For example, Christian Schmidt set *Tristan* in the WESENDONCK household for Claus Guth's production (Zurich, 2008), while Heike Schiele provided Villa WAHNFRIED as the background for Stefan Herheim's *Parsifal* (Bayreuth, 2008), in a production that, among other things, meditated on the historical fortune of Wagner's work.

But the most arresting developments in contemporary stage design are less dependent on theme, more upon experimental approaches to space. The production of the *Ring* by the Amsterdam company, Het Muziektheater (1999), directed by Pierre Audi and designed by George Tsypin, dispensed with any attempt to create a realistic illusion, placing the orchestra in the middle of the stage and surrounding it with sweeping ramps, skeletal tubular structures, and other scenic features that suggested both the past world of epic and a futuristic utopia. The limits of the stage are being challenged, even perhaps to the point of dissolving, by the advent of video. The barrage of video monitors, amidst which the Fura dels Baus production of the *Ring* in Valencia (2009) took place, provided a seemingly endless stream of visual responses to Wagner's music and was therefore the antithesis of Appiaesque symbolism in which the response lies always within the audience's imagination. Technology will perhaps even become the point of the production, as seemed to be the case with Robert Lepage's 2010 staging of the *Ring* at the Met, which was dominated by a massive tentacular machine, where the focus was upon the operations of the machine itself, so the complexity of Wagner's action disappeared. Perhaps the most radical experimentation with space and design in the USA occurred with the controversial production of the *Ring* at the Los Angeles Opera (2009–10), directed and designed by Achim Freyer, on a steeply raked stage, in which the icons and staging principles of European theatre from the Middle Ages through to the baroque were employed in conjunction with popular modern art styles. Among the most remarkable aspects of this production was its use of design to establish visual LEITMOTIVE that complemented those played by the orchestra. Such an approach to designing Wagner offers great promise for future experimentation. SIMON WILLIAMS

Oswald Georg Bauer, *Richard Wagner: The Stage Designs and Productions from the Premieres to the Present* (New York: Rizzoli, 1983).
Patrick Carnegy, *Wagner and the Art of the Theatre* (see bibliography).

Stage works, incomplete. The works featured herein correspond to SÄMTLICHE WERKE, Vol. 31: *Dokumente und Texte zu unvollendeten Bühnenwerken* – with one exception: *Die Schäferoper* (WWV 6), which counts as a LOST WORK. Wagner left fourteen incomplete stage works spanning his creative life. It was typical of him to have several works in progress simultaneously, but many of them were aborted owing as much to Wagner's capacity for self-criticism as to financial and institutional circumstances. While Wagner probably intended many of these to be set to music, few of them were developed beyond the stage of prose draft: Wagner versified only *Leubald* (WWV 1), *Die Hochzeit* (WWV 31), *Die hohe Braut* (WWV 40), *Männerlist größer als Frauenlist* (WWV 48), and *Eine Kapitulation* (WWV 102), while *Die Hochzeit* is the sole work for which musical settings of individual numbers are extant.

Wagner's earliest work is a five-act tragedy *Leubald*, drafted between 1826 and 1828. Wagner had probably intended to compose incidental music for the play in the manner of BEETHOVEN's music to *Egmont*. From October 1832 to February 1833 Wagner worked on his first opera, *Die Hochzeit*. Borchmeyer identifies "pre-echoes" of TRISTAN UND ISOLDE in this chivalrous tale of a knight who is mortally wounded after falling from his lover's balcony. Although the poetic text is lost (allegedly because Wagner destroyed it in reaction to his sister Rosalie's criticism of the poem), Wagner completed three musical numbers which are extant: an orchestral introduction, a chorus, and a septet, first performed in 1933 at the Stadttheater Rostock. In July 1836, while he was trying to secure a post in Königsberg, Wagner drafted the libretto of a grand opera *Die hohe Braut*, intended as a "revolutionary" work for Paris along the lines of AUBER's *La Muette de Portici*. A revised version of the libretto was subsequently set to music by Johann Friedrich Kittl and first performed on 19 February 1848 in Prague, but in view of the compromises made in the revision, Wagner requested that his name be removed from the playbill. Wagner's *Männerlist größer als Frauenlist* of summer 1838 has been described as a comic counterpart to the tragic *Die hohe Braut*, as it contains spoken dialogue in the style of German *Spieloper* of the Biedermeier period (Zegowitz).

Drafted towards the end of his early "PARIS" period, *Die Sarazenin* (WWV 66) and *Die Bergwerke zu Falun* (WWV 67) were intended as GRAND OPERAS for the Paris OPÉRA, and Wagner aborted *Die Bergwerke* only after the work was officially rejected. Whereas *Die Bergwerke* is adapted from E. T. A. HOFFMANN's darkly romantic novel of the same name, *Die Sarazenin* concerns the medieval Hohenstaufen dynasty, in particular Friedrich II, his son Manfred, and daughter Fatima. Wagner resumed and developed this historical subject matter in a prose sketch finished on 31 October 1846, *Friedrich I* (WWV 76), a grand opera about the twelfth-century emperor Friedrich Barbarossa. In winter 1848–9, *Friedrich I* was revised and expanded into a complex essay *Die WIBELUNGEN: Weltgeschichte aus der Sage*, by which point work on *Siegfrieds Tod*, begun in autumn 1848, was already under way (see RING DES NIBELUNGEN, Der). However, in *MEIN LEBEN* (My Life, 1865–81) and in the second edition of his collected writings, Wagner reversed the chronology of *Siegfrieds Tod* and *Die*

Wibelungen, "to make it seem that his interest in history was a mere foil to his more meaningful preoccupation with MYTH" (Deathridge and Dahlhaus 33). In fact, it is clear that the historical subject of *Friedrich I*, if not its potential for operatic treatment, continued to preoccupy Wagner well into the period in which *Siegfrieds Tod* was conceived and developed.

Other works for which Wagner made prose drafts at this time were *Jesus von Nazareth* (WWV 80), *Achilleus* (WWV 81) – both begun around spring 1849 – and *Wieland der Schmied* (WWV 82) – begun in December 1849 and discontinued in March 1850. Given that these works were written in the aftermath of the DRESDEN UPRISING, it is unsurprising that each in its own way is shot through with social revolutionary POLITICS. Working earnestly on all of these projects simultaneously, Wagner would not settle on *Siegfrieds Tod* until 1851. That these projects (including *Friedrich I*) were originally planned as operas is made sufficiently clear by Wagner's contemporary correspondence; in later years, however, he referred to them as pure spoken dramas. This falsification was arguably *not* in order to portray himself as a playwright on his own merit, but rather to obscure the fact that many of these works were conceived along the lines of "historical" grand opera: Wagner entertained notions of staging both *Jesus von Nazareth* and *Wieland* at the Paris Opéra (the former is in five acts), while the prose draft of *Friedrich I* (also in five acts) bears striking resemblance to that of Wagner's only successful grand opera, his earlier RIENZI.

In May 1865, Wagner began work on a Buddhist music drama *Die Sieger*, which explores several SCHOPENHAUERIAN themes such as metempsychosis, later to be incorporated in PARSIFAL. *Die Sieger* is one of the only incomplete stage works for which a musical sketch has been identified (the other is *Jesus von Nazareth*); however, Wagner later considered making a play of *Die Sieger* instead (CWD 27 June 1869). In August 1868, Wagner worked on the stage works *Luthers Hochzeit* (WWV 99) and *Ein Lustspiel in 1 Akt* (WWV 100), for which only a prose sketch and a prose draft respectively were completed. As COSIMA WAGNER'S DIARIES indicate, Wagner often referred to the latter two works in the same breath as some of his projected stage works based on historical and/or comic subject matter (see PROJECTS). Wagner's last stage work to remain unfinished was *Eine Kapitulation*, a heavy-handed farce on the "capitulation" of FRANCE in the FRANCO-PRUSSIAN WAR, drafted in the first half of November 1870. Hans RICHTER composed the music between 21 November and mid-December, but the score is now lost, Richter presumably having destroyed it himself. Although Wagner was eager to stage the work, *Eine Kapitulation* was met with flat disapproval even from Wagner's closest allies. Perhaps for the first time, the factor determining the completion or abortion of a work was less Wagner's self-criticism than the criticism he received from others. JEREMY COLEMAN

See also PROJECTS; WORKS, LOST; *WAGNER WERK-VERZEICHNIS*

Dieter Borchmeyer, *Drama and the World of Richard Wagner* (see bibliography).
John Deathridge and Carl Dahlhaus, *The New Grove Wagner* (see bibliography).
Richard Wagner, *Sämtliche Werke* vol. 31: *Dokumente und Texte zu unvollendeten Bühnenwerken* (see bibliography).
Bernd Zegowitz, *Richard Wagners unvertonte Opern* (Frankfurt am Main: Lang, 2000).

Stahr, Adolf Wilhelm Theodor (b. Prenzlau, 22 Oct. 1805; d. Wiesbaden, 3 Oct. 1876), well-known literary historian, particularly of the classical period; writer with strong political ties to liberalism both before and after the 1848–9 revolutions. He became important to Wagner because of an essay on the fifth performance of LOHENGRIN in Weimar (11 May 1851), which was published in the morning editions of the *National Zeitung* (Berlin) on 27 and 28 May 1851. His thesis that LOHENGRIN, not ELSA, is responsible for the unfortunate outcome is still significant. At the time, it turned the internal relationships of the opera upside down and triggered a dispute between Wagner and LISZT. Wagner, who was initially excited by the unexpected attention from such a famous contemporary, later agreed with Liszt, who disagreed with Stahr's de-mythologized interpretation. Thanks to Franz BRENDEL, the essay was widely distributed and became one of many catalysts for Wagner's RECEP-TION after 1850.   HELMUT KIRCHMEYER

TRANS. HOLLY WERMTER

Standhartner, Josef (b. Troppau [now Opava, Czech Republic], 4 Feb. 1818; d. Vienna, 29 Aug. 1892), leading Austrian physician and one of Wagner's closest friends in VIENNA, whom Wagner met shortly after hearing LOHENGRIN performed there in spring 1861. In addition to becoming Wagner's personal physician, Standhartner provided material support, and the two socialized regularly throughout Wagner's stay in the city. Among their most famous exploits was Wagner's public reading of the libretto to *Die MEISTERSINGER VON NÜRNBERG* at the Standhartners' home in 1862, to which Standhartner had invited Eduard HANSLICK, the city's leading music critic. Wagner later recalled this event as the beginning of Hanslick's famous animosity towards him; supposedly, Hanslick understood the character of SIXTUS BECKMESSER as Wagner's parody of Hanslick himself. In his memoirs, however, Hanslick recalled the reading favorably, and he praised the *Meistersinger* libretto (ML/E 703–4; Hanslick 2:7–8). In 1864, when Wagner ran into trouble with creditors and fled Vienna for MUNICH, Standhartner once again provided both logistical and financial support.   KEVIN C. KARNES

See also HEALTH

Eduard Hanslick, *Aus meinem Leben* (see bibliography).

Stassen, Franz (b. Hanau, 12 Feb. 1869; d. Berlin, 18 April 1949), in his day one of the most popular graphic artists in Germany. A leading practitioner of the *art nouveau* style, Stassen illustrated nearly the entire Wagnerian oeuvre. His most significant works are large-scale portfolios of *TRISTAN UND ISOLDE* (1899) and *PARSIFAL* (1902). Images from these works (especially from the *Parsifal* portfolio) employ music notation in highly ornate and inventive ways. Stassen was closely connected to the BAYREUTH CIRCLE (he was a personal friend of Wagner's son SIEGFRIED), and his images were a central part of Wagnerian ICONOGRAPHY during the late nineteenth and early twentieth centuries. Stassen's association with *völkisch* ideologies and eventually with NAZI cultural policies may help account for the neglect into which his work fell during the postwar period, and he remains largely unknown today.   STEPHEN MEYER

David Huckvale, "Kitsch and Curiosities," *Wagner* 13 (1992): 3–11.

Stephen Meyer, "Illustrating Transcendence: *Parsifal*, Franz Stassen, and the *Leitmotive*," *The Musical Quarterly* 92 (2009): 9–32.

Stern, Adolf (born Adolf Ernst) (b. Leipzig, 14 June 1835; d. Dresden, 14 April 1907), professor of literary history at the Dresden Polytechnic and poet. Stern also contributed regularly to the NEUE ZEITSCHRIFT FÜR MUSIK and, in 1867, joined the board of the Allgemeiner deutscher Musikverein. A committed Wagnerian, Stern penned the "Appeal for Subscriptions" that the delegates from the PATRONS' ASSOCIATION endorsed in 1873 over a text (*Mahnruf*) proposed by Friedrich NIETZSCHE. Stern's text was circulated to numerous book and music shops, along with a petition sent to some seventy-eight theaters suggesting benefit performances for BAYREUTH. Later on, Stern served as the first chair of DRESDEN's chapter of the Wagner Scholarship Foundation (Wagner-Stipendien-Stiftung).   ANTHONY J. STEINHOFF

Stollen. See CANZONA

Strauss, Richard (b. Munich, 11 June 1864; d. Garmisch, 8 Sep. 1949), composer and conductor. Dubbed "Richard III" by Hans von BÜLOW (because there could be no Richard II), Strauss justified his mentor's prediction over a seven-decade career. As the son of Franz Strauss, principal hornist of the MUNICH Court Opera and chief local antagonist of Wagner, the young composer overheard complaints of "immeasurable megalomania" but was permitted to attend early performances of *Das RHEINGOLD* and *Die WALKÜRE* and even to tag along to BAYREUTH for the premiere of *PARSIFAL* (1882). These mixed signals were the norm; at age 6, Strauss participated in a children's arrangement of *TANNHÄUSER*, a work even Franz admired, but at 16 he aroused hell's fury for sneaking a midnight peek at *TRISTAN UND ISOLDE*. The father's ambivalence became the teenager's, especially in correspondence with boyhood confidant Ludwig Thuille, whom Strauss regaled with parodies of *Stabreim* (to his later embarrassment) and tellingly detailed commentary on the aural wonders of the *Ring*.

When in 1885 Strauss moved to Meiningen as Bülow's assistant, he found a new mentor: the Wagnerian partisan Alexander Ritter, a violinist in the famed orchestra and husband of Wagner's niece. Ritter inspired an apparent "conversion" to the "cause"; this period saw the early tone poems as well as the outwardly epigonic first opera *Guntram* (1893). But a swerve from SCHOPENHAUER to NIETZSCHE, begun in the ill-fated stage work and trumpeted in *Also sprach Zarathustra* (1896), dashed the hopes of COSIMA, who had entrusted *Tannhäuser* to Strauss at the 1894 festival but would issue no further invitations. As colleague of and then successor to Hermann LEVI in Munich (1886–9, 1894–8), Strauss would lead an important competitor of Bayreuth, always maintaining the highest respect for Wagner's intentions, an ideal he adopted from Bülow and never renounced.

In the creative sphere, Strauss faced Wagner "by making a detour around him," or so he told Stefan Zweig. The works themselves blend homage with open confrontation. The medieval fairy tale *Feuersnot* (1901) chastises Munich for its treatment of Wagner – the autobiographically marked magician-protagonist, Kunrad, laments the expulsion of his teacher Meister Reichardt, a wheelwright (*Wagner*) – even as the music's unruly pastiche leaves Wagnerian gravity far behind. *Salome* (1905) culminates in a grotesque inversion of the LIEBESTOD, a graphically sexualized *Erlösung* rudely undercutting the metaphysical pretensions of its model. Under the influence of Hofmannsthal, Strauss deployed a sensationalized Wagnerian extravagance in a different kind of GESAMTKUNSTWERK in *Elektra* (1908), with deeper emphasis on non-musical elements, especially gesture. Yet, structurally, that work relies on the same pre-Wagnerian tonal orientation heard on the surface of *Der Rosenkavalier* (1910), a work that invokes *Die* MEISTERSINGER VON NÜRNBERG (HANS SACHS/Marschallin, EVA/Octavian) within a temporally confused world of eighteenth-century manners and Johann Strauss waltzes.

While Wagner would never be entirely absent from Strauss's subsequent stage works, he would return most decisively in the late "wrist exercises," especially *Metamorphosen* and the last songs. In the former, Strauss recasts the chromatic counterpoint of *Tristan* as hopelessness and obliteration; the songs strike a final note of optimism, however, with a distinctly Straussian lyricism that complements the orchestral Wagnerisms without being subsumed by them – as one might say of Strauss's oeuvre as a whole.

CHARLES YOUMANS

Street-Klindworth, Agnes (b. Bremen, 19 Oct. 1825; d. Paris, 25 Dec. 1906), a student and lover of Franz LISZT. Cousin to Karl KLINDWORTH, and daughter to Georg Klindworth (Metternich's master spy), she arrived in Weimar in 1853 ostensibly as a piano student, but more likely as part of her father's intelligence-gathering network. Her secret affair with Liszt (1854–61) was discovered by Carolyne zu SAYN-WITTGENSTEIN in 1858, and by Liszt biographer Marie Lipsius in 1894. Richard Wagner reports spending an evening with Agnes and her father in 1860, and receiving a letter of introduction from him to Metternich.

DAVID TRIPPETT

Strobel, Gertrud (née Degenhardt) (b. Nordhausen [Harz], 20 Mar. 1898; d. Bayreuth, 11 June 1979). In 1953, Gertrud Strobel succeeded her husband, Otto STROBEL, as the Wagner family archivist, a position she held until 1976 when the Richard-Wagner-Archiv was incorporated into the Richard-Wagner-Stiftung (RICHARD WAGNER FOUNDATION). From 1938 to 1945, she assisted her husband with the Richard-Wagner Forschungsstätte, for which she received remuneration from the Reichskanzlei. The Strobels joined the NAZI party together on 1 December 1931.

Although stories abound about her close control of access to the archive, Strobel made an important contribution to Wagner studies by initiating a complete edition of Wagner's CORRESPONDENCE, in collaboration with Werner Wolf (*Sämtliche Briefe*, 9 vols., Leipzig, 1967–2000; later reconceptualized and relaunched by Werner Breig in 1999). A close confidante of WINIFRED WAGNER, Strobel appeared as an alto in the Festspiel chorus (1930, 1931, 1933). Her diary, now in the Richard-Wagner-Archiv, is a valuable source of information on daily life in Bayreuth in the 1930s and 1940s.

STEPHEN MCCLATCHIE

Strobel, Otto (b. Munich, 30 Aug. 1895; d. Bayreuth, 23 Feb. 1953), Wagner scholar and the Wagner family archivist from 1932 until his death. From 1938 to 1945 he was director of the Richard-Wagner-Forschungsstätte, a research institute established by edict of HITLER on 22 May 1938. Strobel's published and unpublished work with primary source material provided the basis for modern Wagner research, yet his career was irreparably tainted by his NATIONAL SOCIALIST convictions.

After publishing a dissertation on Wagner's creative process (*Richard Wagner über sein Schaffen: Ein Beitrag zur "Künstlerästhetik,"* 1924), Strobel contracted with the Wagner family to edit and publish Wagner's sketches and drafts for the text of Der RING DES NIBELUNGEN (*Richard Wagner: Skizzen und Entwürfe zur Ring-Dichtung. Mit der Dichtung "Der Junge Siegfried,"* 1930) and was hired by WINIFRED WAGNER on 1 June 1932 as the family archivist. From November 1933, he was also employed by the town of BAYREUTH as town librarian. From 1939, editor of the *Bayreuther Festspielführer*, Strobel published numerous articles on Wagner's sketches and drafts while working on an internal catalogue of these materials that laid the foundation for the later WAGNER WERK-VERZEICHNIS. His five-volume critical edition of Wagner's correspondence with LUDWIG II (*König Ludwig II. und Richard Wagner: Briefwechsel*) was unexpurgated and marks a new rigor in Wagner scholarship, which angered many of the old guard by showing Wagner in a less-than-flattering light. (COSIMA WAGNER'S DIARIES were embargoed by Eva Wagner CHAMBERLAIN to ensure that Strobel would never get his hands on them.)

Strobel joined the Nazi Party on 1 December 1931 (Pg. [membership number] 171 464) and was involved in a number of other Nazi organizations. At Winifred Wagner's instigation, Strobel drew up plans for what became the Richard-Wagner-Forschungsstätte (RWF), overseen directly by the Reich Chancellery. Its plans and activities reflected the tension within Strobel himself between scholarship and ideology. In addition to collecting copies of primary documents and publishing a scholarly journal, NEUE WAGNER-FORSCHUNGEN, the RWF was to oversee critical editions of Wagner's works and writings, as well as a comprehensive biography based on authentic source materials. Central among these would be documents to establish Wagner's Aryan ancestry. A completed manuscript, *Die Abstammung Richard Wagners: Legende und Wirklichkeit*, survives in eighteen binders in Strobel's *Nachlaß* in the Richard-Wagner-MUSEUM mit Nationalarchiv der Richard-Wagner-Stiftung, Bayreuth. The "chronology" (*Richard Wagner: Leben und Schaffen: Eine Zeittafel*) published in 1952 was also intended as preliminary work for this biography. In 1943, Winifred Wagner and Strobel approached Heinrich Himmler to obtain a ban on all publications about Wagner not issued in cooperation with the RWF; after some debate amongst the top Nazis, including Hitler, it was refused.

Strobel was dismissed by the Military Government on 18 June 1945 and imprisoned until sometime late in 1946. Although judged only a *Mitläufer* (fellow traveler; category IV) at his denazification tribunal, as one who joined the Nazi Party before 1933, Strobel was unable to return to his position in the town civil service. He continued to work for the Wagner family until his death from a stroke. His wife, Gertrud STROBEL, continued in this capacity until the establishment of the RICHARD WAGNER FOUNDATION (Richard-Wagner-Stiftung) by the state in 1973.　　　STEPHEN MCCLATCHIE

Stephen McClatchie, "Wagner Research as 'Service to the People': The *Richard-Wagner-Forschungsstätte, 1938–1945*," in *Music and Nazism: Art under Tyranny, 1933–1945*, ed. Michael H. Kater and Albrecht Riethmüller (Laaber Verlag, 2003): 150–69.

Sulzer, (Johann) Jakob (b. Winterthur, 23 Dec. 1821; d. Winterthur, 27 June 1897), leading Swiss liberal politician, City President of Winterthur 1858–73. Studied in ZURICH, Bonn, and Berlin. As Zurich Cantonal Secretary, he met Wagner upon his arrival in May 1849 and provided him with a passport for his journey on to PARIS. Sulzer was later a signatory to the financial guarantee necessary for Wagner to take up residence in Zurich. He became a member of Wagner's inner circle, introduced him to Gottfried Keller, and in the mid-1850s acted as his financial manager at the behest of Otto WESENDONCK. Sulzer remained close to Wagner and, later, to COSIMA too. He travelled to BAYREUTH for both FESTIVAL performances and family occasions, and published a report of *PARSIFAL* in the Swiss press. CHRIS WALTON

Chris Walton, *Richard Wagner's Zurich* (see bibliography).

Switzerland. The state emerged out of the Holy Roman Empire as a loose confederation of tiny states (today's "cantons"), mostly German though partly French, Italian, and Romansh speaking, and with the post-Reformation religious split occurring independently of linguistic divisions. The Congress of Vienna of 1814–15 affirmed its independent, neutral status. The absence of an aristocracy and of a centralized state meant that the music scene remained fragmented. Even the first Swiss Music Society, founded in 1807 to give more or less annual festivals around the country, remained amateur.

Increasing polarization between the liberal, Protestant cantons and the conservative, Catholic cantons led in 1847 to a brief civil war, the *Sonderbundskrieg*, won by the former. Switzerland now became a federal state with a democratic constitution, making it attractive to political exiles when the rest of Europe succumbed to a conservative backlash after the revolutions of 1848–9. Wagner arrived in Switzerland in 1849, basing himself in ZURICH from where he took cures for his HEALTH and went on extensive HIKING tours through the Alps, whose natural beauty and breathtakingly dramatic landscapes clearly served as a source of inspiration. In part because of his enduring passion for Mathilde WESENDONCK, and perhaps because of his intense creativity in these years, Switzerland remained for him a preferred place of refuge. He took up residence in Lucerne in April 1859 in order to complete *TRISTAN UND ISOLDE*, and when he left MUNICH in late 1866 he went to Geneva before settling in TRIBSCHEN near Lucerne in April 1867, staying until 1872. When Wagner first arrived in Switzerland he traveled by boat and stagecoach, and its population was 2.4 million; by the time he came to Tribschen he could travel almost everywhere by train and the country's population had expanded to 2.7 million. CHRIS WALTON

Chris Walton, *Richard Wagner's Zurich* (see bibliography).

Syberberg, Hans-Jürgen (b. Nossendorf, 8 Dec. 1935), German film director. Several of Syberberg's best-known films have dealt with Wagner and his role within German culture, beginning with *Ludwig: Requiem for a Virgin King* (1972), an AVANT-GARDE portrait of Wagner's royal patron, LUDWIG II. *Winifred Wagner* *und die Geschichte des Hauses Wahnfried von 1914–1975* (The Confessions of Winifred Wagner, 1975) was based around a lengthy interview with WINIFRED. Wagner figured prominently in both soundtrack and script of Syberberg's controversial *Hitler: A Film from Germany* (1977), a 7-hour-long cinematic meditation on the causes and legacy of HITLER. Like *Hitler* and *Ludwig*, *Parsifal* (1982) was filmed in a highly stylized and presentational manner, surrounded by visual allusions to art, history, and Wagner's life. Syberberg and others have aptly described his style as a fusion between the traditions of Wagnerian MUSIC DRAMA and the "alienation effects" of Bertolt Brecht's epic theater that are integral to the films of the so-called New German Cinema.   HILAN WARSHAW

See also Appendix 9: Documentaries and films

Roger Hillman, "A Wagnerian German Requiem: Syberberg's *Hitler* (1977)," in Hillman, *Unsettling Scores: German Film, Music, and Ideology* (Bloomington: Indiana University Press, 2005).

Solveig Olsen, *Hans Jürgen Syberberg and His Film of Wagner's "Parsifal"* (New York: University Press of America, 2006).

Hans-Jürgen Syberberg, *Hitler: A Film from Germany*, preface by Susan Sontag, trans. Joachim Neugroschl (New York: Farrar, Straus, and Giroux, 1982).

Symphony in C major (WWV 29), Wagner's only completed symphony. Composed in April–June 1832, LEIPZIG, it was rehearsed in November 1832, Prague, conducted by Dionys Weber, and received its first public performance on 15 December at the Musikgesellschaft Euterpe in Leipzig under Wagner's first composition teacher Christian Gottlieb MÜLLER. Clearly proud of it as a worthy successor to BEETHOVEN, Wagner sent the autograph score "as a present" to MENDELSSOHN on 11 April 1836, who apparently lost it (Deathridge). The original orchestral parts were discovered by Wilhelm TAPPERT in Dresden and used by Anton SEIDL to reconstruct the work in March–April 1878. Wagner revised it and led a private performance on 24 December 1882 at La Fenice in VENICE as a surprise for COSIMA's birthday. It was the last time he conducted, and his death in 1883 thwarted immediate publication. The firm of Max BROCKHAUS in Leipzig brought out a first edition in 1911.   JEREMY COLEMAN

John Deathridge, "Mendelssohn and the Strange Case of the (Lost) Symphony in C," in *Wagner Beyond Good and Evil* (see bibliography): 178–88.

T

Tannhäuser und der Sängerkrieg auf Wartburg (Tannhäuser and the Singers' Contest on the Wartburg, WWV 70), grand romantic opera in three acts, text and music by Richard Wagner. First performance: DRESDEN, Royal Saxon Court Theater, 19 October 1845. Cond. Richard Wagner; TANNHÄUSER: Joseph TICHATSCHEK; Venus: Wilhelmine SCHRÖDER-DEVRIENT; ELISABETH: Johanna Wagner (Wagner's niece); WOLFRAM: Anton Mitterwurzer. Revised ("Paris") version, French translation by Charles NUITTER: Paris, Académie imperiale de musique ("Opéra," Salle Peletier), 13 March 1861. Revised version with German text (Wagner's last version or *Fassung letzter Hand*): Vienna, Court Theater, 22 November 1875.

1. Sources, genesis of libretto, and composition
2. Revisions to score and libretto, publication
3. The drama
4. The music
5. Premiere, performance history, interpretation

1. Sources, genesis of libretto, and composition

The idea for an opera on the subject of the legendary troubadour or *Minnesänger* Tannhäuser goes back to Wagner's stay in PARIS at the beginning of the 1840s, the matrix for so much of his consciously "GERMAN" IDENTITY as an individual and as creative artist. During the final months in Paris in the winter and early spring of 1842, after RIENZI had been accepted for production in DRESDEN and plans were set for his return to Germany, Wagner says he happened upon a chapbook (*Volksbuch*) of the Tannhäuser legend which, in his present mood of longing for the German *Heimat*, seized his imagination in a particularly vivid way. The precise identity of this source is unclear: the Bibliothèque nationale did hold an early sixteenth-century pamphlet on the subject, but a more likely source would be Ludwig Bechstein's 1835 collection of stories about the medieval Wartburg (*Die Sagen von Eisenach und der Wartburg, dem Hörseelberg und Reinhardsbrunn*). The principal autobiographical accounts in *Eine Mitteilung an meine Freunde* (A Communication to my Friends, 1851) and *MEIN LEBEN* (My Life, 1865–81; relevant portions dictated in 1866–7) insist on a tendentious contrast between traditional, popular, "authentic" versions of the material, on one hand, and modern literary treatments by Ludwig Tieck, E. T. A. HOFFMANN, Friedrich de la Motte Fouqué, and Heinrich HEINE, on the other hand. Wagner's philologist friend and fellow expatriate in Paris, Samuel LEHRS, showed him the edition of the medieval poem *Der Wartburgkrieg* with commentary by the scholar C. T. L. Lucas (*Ueber den Krieg von Wartburg,*

Königsberg, 1838), if not also the first modern edition of 1818. Wagner himself places great emphasis on the importance of Jacob and Wilhelm Grimm's *Deutsche Mythologie* and *Deutsche Sagen* for his overall initiation into the atmosphere of Germanic MYTH and legend, though his discovery of these occurred only in between his completion of the *Tannhäuser* libretto and his attempts to begin its composition. Lucas's commentaries on the medieval poem supported Wagner's identification of the Tannhäuser figure with Heinrich von Ofterdingen, the antagonist of the other historical *Minnesänger* (WOLFRAM VON ESCHENBACH, WALTHER VON DER VOGELWEIDE, et al.) in these sources, and hence the combination of the "Contest of Song" with the story of Tannhäuser's transgressive dalliance with the pagan goddess Venus in the Hörselberg (Venusberg) in his opera. Still, the psychosexual dimension of Tannhäuser's conflict in Wagner's opera certainly owes much to Heine's modern satirical variation of the *Tannhäuserlied* (originally a ballad from 1515) in his *Elementargeister* (*Der Salon*, vol. 3, 1837), while Hoffmann's story "Der Kampf der Sänger" (The Singers' Contest) in *Die Serapionsbrüder* (vol. 2, 1819) anticipates the dramaturgy of Wagner's song contest in many details and even invokes the "Venusburg" legend as the subject of Heinrich von Ofterdingen's profane challenge to the courtly love songs of his fellow *Minnesänger* at the court of Landgraf Hermann.

During the first summer he spent back in Germany, in 1842, Wagner conceived the scenario for the opera while on holiday in the Bohemian countryside near Dresden (28 June–6 July), eventually completing the verse libretto on his birthday, 22 May 1843. The underlying conception of the material is succinctly outlined in a letter of 30 January 1844 to an early critical advocate, the Berlin-based Karl Gaillard. While climbing the "Wostrai" one day, he claims to have heard a shepherd piping a "merry tune" that chimed perfectly with his idea for the scene of the pilgrims and shepherd in Act I, though afterwards he was not able to recall the tune as such and had eventually to invent his own. (The anecdote linking a scene of "natural" music in his opera to a lived experience is highly characteristic of Wagner's accounts of his creative process, from *Der* FLIEGENDE HOLLÄNDER onward.)

Previewing, on a smaller scale, the situation he would experience in approaching the *Ring* cycle, Wagner found himself forced to wait a considerable time after the conception and execution of the dramatic text before he was able to get started on the composition. When he finally did begin, it was in a state of feverish excitement, and the process of drafting and then orchestrating the score moved rapidly. The music for Act I was completed at the beginning of 1844, Act II between early September and 15 October. The draft of Act III was completed on 29 December 1844. He quickly proceeded to produce the full orchestral score (completed April 1845). This was carried out in such a way that the publisher, C. F. Meser, could produce lithographic copies directly from Wagner's manuscript (with the result, however, that the manuscript itself did not survive the production of the first 100 copies).

2. Revisions to score and libretto, publication

"I still owe the world a *Tannhäuser*," Wagner remarked to his wife COSIMA (CWD 23 January 1883) only a few weeks before his death. He was alluding to the unusually complicated and ultimately unresolved history of this work's text, both the libretto and, above all, the score. The WAGNER WERK-VERZEICHNIS divides the large array of manuscript and printed materials into four general "stages," representing (1) the materials as they developed up to the premiere in Dresden (19 October 1845); (2) the variety of revisions to text and music made by Wagner in the course of performances in Dresden and up to the time of the first engraved full score (C. F. Meser, Dresden, 1860); (3) the version prepared with French text for the Paris Opéra performances of 13, 18, and 24 March 1861 (loosely represented by the piano-vocal score issue by Flaxland in 1861); and (4) the lightly revised version of the "Paris" score with German text performed under Wagner's direction in Vienna in 1875 (published by Adolf Fürstner, Berlin, 1888). The changes in stage 2 concerned above all Act III. Already before the second performance in Dresden, Wagner prepared a much shorter version of the Act III Prelude (45 measures) originally conceived as a detailed instrumental *précis* of Tannhäuser's penitential journey to Rome (155 measures); a compromise of 92 measures was effected by the end of 1845 and retained in later versions. Above all, Wagner intensified the climactic scene in which Wolfram attempts to prevent Tannhäuser from returning to the Venusberg. In addition to expanding quotations from the opening "Venusberg" scene, Wagner now had Venus herself reappear and address Tannhäuser directly. The Pilgrims and the other *Minnesänger* reprise the familiar music of the "Pilgrims' Chorus" to the distinctive string figuration from the overture. A still fuller variant of the final scene prepared in 1851 combined the earlier versions in one.

The most radical of any revisions to his scores was of course the overhaul of the Tannhäuser-Venus scene and the preceding "Bacchanal" undertaken for the famous attempt to revive *Tannhäuser* in French translation at the Paris Opéra in 1861. In place of the traditional, full-length ballet divertissement expected with most large-scale productions at the Opéra, Wagner decided to develop his original Venusberg Bacchanal into a frenzied, ultra-modern "tone-poem" several times the length of the original, with amplified orchestra (and much percussion), seething chromatic sequences, and a longer, more lush phase of final quiescence. While most of Tannhäuser's music in the following scene (Act I, scene 2) remained the same, Venus's entreaties to her wayward guest became much extended in text and composition alike, with tones from BRANGÄNE's "Watch Song" and the Act II love duet in TRISTAN UND ISOLDE employed to intensify the erotic allure of her pleas. Only in the Viennese production of 1875 (stage 4) did Wagner manage to realize his Parisian plan to elide the overture directly with the new Bacchanal. Otherwise, the 1875 production retained the Paris revisions and paired them (where necessary) with new German text prepared between 1861 and the time of two Munich productions in 1867 and 1869. The "Vienna" score should have been definitive, but Wagner himself soon came to have doubts about the overextension of the Venusberg scene and the stylistic heterogeneity it introduced into the score (see CWD 6 November 1877). Cosima opted for this *Fassung letzter Hand* when she finally staged the opera at BAYREUTH in the 1890s. Since the mid-twentieth century the standard "Dresden" and "Paris" scores (essentially, stages 2 and 4) have both continued to be produced regularly.

3. The drama

Act I

Scene 1. Inside the "Venusberg" (or "Hörselberg"), the legendary abode of the exiled pagan goddess of love, the knight Tannhäuser is being entertained by a Bacchanal of nymphs and satyrs emblematic of the realm of endless sensual pleasure in which he has been tarrying. As the Bacchanal subsides, a languorous chorus of "sirens" beckons the listener to this perpetual garden of earthly delights.

Scene 2. Tannhäuser, in the lap of Venus, suddenly starts up as from a DREAM. He explains that he has dreamed of the outside world he left behind. Venus asks him to sing her once more his songs in praise of love. To the accompaniment of his harp (with orchestral enhancements), Tannhäuser begins his song to Venus, previewed in the overture, though each of the three strophes is interrupted in the middle with a new rhetorical turn, each attempting to explain why Tannhäuser now seeks to return to the world above. After the second strophe Venus tries to seduce him back into complacency; Tannhäuser assures her in a third strophe that he will be her emissary on earth (that is, in the world of medieval Christian courts and their culture of "courtly love"), and that only there can he actively serve her cause. This time Venus responds with threats and admonitions: he will find above only a barren, loveless world and will afterwards yearn in vain to return to her fond embrace – the outside world will never forgive him when it learns of his secret dalliance below. As Tannhäuser invokes the power of the Holy Virgin ("My salvation lies in Mary!") Venus and her magical grotto disappear amidst a great crash.

Scene 3. Tannhäuser finds himself in a beautiful sylvan glade close to the Wartburg fortress. A shepherd boy alternately sings and plays a chalumeau or reed-pipe, welcoming the arrival of springtime. A band of pilgrims is heard approaching from the direction of the Wartburg; their chants mingle with the music of the young shepherd. Tannhäuser greets the whole spectacle as a miraculous sign of divine intervention and repeats the penitential verses of the pilgrims' song. To the sound of church bells the pilgrims disappear in the other direction.

Scene 4. Echoing horns off stage announce the hunting party of Landgraf Hermann of Thuringia accompanied by the *Minnesänger* (Tannhäuser's former comrades) Wolfram von Eschinbach, Walther von der Vogelweide, Heinrich der Schreiber, Reinmar von Zweter, and Biterolf. They greet the prodigal Tannhäuser with jubilation, but he at first resists their entreaties to return to the Landgraf's court. When Wolfram recalls to him the Landgraf's pure and fair niece, Elisabeth, Tannhäuser is seized as by a sudden inspiration; he joins the knights in an ebullient ensemble as they ride up to the Wartburg.

Act II

Scene 1. The Hall of Song in the Wartburg. Alone, Elisabeth enters the hall and greets it for the first time since Tannhäuser left the Landgraf's court. News of his return has reanimated the hall for her, along with her own hopes and dreams.

Scene 2. Wolfram quietly leads Tannhäuser into her vicinity and steps aside. Gradually overcoming her natural modesty, she admits to him the feelings his songs had awoken in her before, and admonishes him for having left the court. They express their mutual joy at this reunion, while Wolfram quietly laments it, aside.

Scene 3. Landgraf Hermann discovers Elisabeth. Pleased by the change in her demeanor, he informs her of a great feast to which he has summoned all the nobles of the land, and over which she will preside as queen.

Scene 4. Trumpets announce the arrival of the noble guests who are led into the hall by pages. The guests enter in solemn procession, praising the Hall of Song and its master, Landgraf Hermann; he, in turn, praises the contributions of his courtiers to the culture of his court. Hermann announces the theme of the contest: who can most effectively identify the true nature of love? Elisabeth will crown the singer who answers this question most perfectly. Wolfram goes first and sings the praises of the assembled company, both the men and the women. Among the latter there is one whose beauty and virtue have shown him the fount of "pure" love. Tannhäuser replies that he too knows this fount; but without the thirst of desire, he insists, no one can know the "true" meaning of love. Walther von der Vogelweide intervenes, defending Wolfram and insisting that "virtue" is the spring in question, and one must approach it only ideally, through the heart, not with the lips. Tannhäuser decries Walther's courtly ideals, and Biterolf challenges Tannhäuser with arms, rather than song, in defense of courtly love. (The idea of a "singers' battle," the *Sängerkampf* or *-krieg* invoked in the traditional sources, is thus concretely realized.) Again, Tannhäuser mocks the impoverished notions of love expressed by the *Minnesänger* and their refusal to acknowledge the dimension of sensual pleasure. Wolfram attempts to intercede, singing praises of "noble love" (and implicitly, Elisabeth). Tannhäuser breaks in and sings a new verse of his song in praise of "the goddess of love," as he had promised Venus. The final lines of this verse exhort the listeners to "enter the Venusberg" to learn the side of love they all ignore, arousing universal shock and dismay. The women all flee the hall, except Elisabeth. The men threaten Tannhäuser with their swords. Elisabeth intercedes. No one has been more gravely wounded by this outburst than she, and she begs them to consider the means of his salvation. All present join in a large ensemble: Tannhäuser expresses his deep regret and desire to atone for his transgressions, the knights praise Elisabeth's noble intercession on his behalf. Landgraf Hermann reminds them that the younger band of pilgrims is poised to follow the older group on their journey to Rome: Tannhäuser shall join them and seek absolution from the pope. All agree to this plan, though Tannhäuser wonders if he can still be saved. The departing pilgrims are heard from the Wartburg valley, and Tannhäuser is sent to meet them.

Act III

Scene 1. The valley of the Wartburg, as in Act I, scene 3. It is now fall, and the pilgrims are due back from their journey. Wolfram espies Elisabeth sunk in fervent prayer before a statue of the Virgin, where she has come "day and night" during Tannhäuser's absence to pray for his absolution. The older band of pilgrims is heard approaching. She watches in nervous anticipation as they appear in the valley. Tannhäuser is not among them. Despondent, Elisabeth addresses a final prayer to the Virgin, begging forgiveness if she has ever failed to mortify any trace of earthly passion, and asks to be received in heaven, there to plead once more for Tannhäuser's salvation. Wolfram gently approaches her, but she responds in silent pantomime: her path leads to heaven now, and she must proceed alone. She does so, slowly returning to the Wartburg.

Scene 2. Left alone in the darkening valley, Wolfram addresses a song to the evening star (i.e., Venus, as a distant celestial body). The friendly light of this star has guided him time and again out of the valley; let it now greet her (Elisabeth's) soul as it rises above the valley to join the angels in heaven.

Scene 3. Darkness has fallen; Tannhäuser appears – pale, faltering, and in rags. Wolfram asks if he has received the pardon. Tannhäuser replies that he seeks only the secret path he found once before, to the Venusberg. Horrified, Wolfram begs to know what happened on his pilgrimage. Tannhäuser narrates the journey to Rome, his severely penitential conduct along the way, and his confession to the pope. "If you have tarried amidst the hellish fires of the Venusberg," he was told, "you are eternally damned; you will no sooner find pardon than the staff in my hand will sprout again green leaves." All have received pardon but him, and Tannhäuser can do nothing but return to the arms of Venus. A rosy mist and faint light appear, then Venus and her nymphs. She is ready to welcome the lost prodigal. Wolfram entreats him to desist: the angelic soul who pleaded for him before (Elisabeth) will soon do so in heaven. Her name has the same effect as before, recalling as well Tannhäuser's invocation of the Virgin that freed him from the realm of Venus. As dawn approaches, so does a funeral cortège from the direction of the Wartburg. Tannhäuser collapses on the bier of the deceased Elisabeth, and dies. At that same moment, the younger pilgrims approach the valley singing a new song: a miracle has occurred during the night, and the "priest's" (i.e., the pope's) staff has sprung green leaves; the sinner has been redeemed from the lustful fires of hell. Elisabeth's prayers for Tannhäuser's salvation have been answered.

4. The music

Wagner's earlier operas are typically assessed as milestones along the inexorable path to MUSIC DRAMA. While the three "Romantic operas" from the Dresden years are in many ways susceptible to this familiar interpretation, *Tannhäuser* can also be understood in a more contextual, less teleological way, as a dialectical synthesis of the French GRAND OPERA model cultivated in *Rienzi* and the German Romantic "antithesis" to that stylistic "thesis" represented by *Der fliegende Holländer*. Another dialectic, one that remains unresolved, grew from the revisions Wagner made to the Venusberg scenes for Paris in 1860–1. In these the composer consciously applied the musical discoveries of *Tristan und Isolde* to evoke the sensual abandon of Venus's secret grotto and the exquisite flux of sensual longing and satisfaction she offers Tannhäuser. The contrast to the formal processions and faux-archaic minstrelsy of Landgraf Hermann's court, to the decorous "operatic" tone of Tannhäuser's courtship of Elisabeth and of her elegiac prayers, or to the sacred chorales of the pilgrims is a calculated one, magnifying an element of contrast Wagner had clearly sought to implant in the original score. But opinions differ (including Wagner's own) as to whether the somewhat lopsided infusion of "new music" in the revised score might not ultimately undermine the equilibrium of the more conventional musical dramaturgy that still dominates the opera overall.

The grand operatic model informs Act II almost from start to finish, while the flanking acts can be seen as leaning toward a "German Romantic" idiom in the role granted there to freer, less structured musical discourse (e.g., the Bacchanal and Tannhäuser-Venus dialogue in Act I, or Tannhäuser's "Rome narrative" and the renewed temptation of Venus in Act III), as well as the preponderance of characteristic topical references such as chorale and chorale-prelude, the shepherd's neo-folklike piping and singing, the hunting calls of the Landgraf's retinue, Elisabeth's devout prayer, or the Biedermeier cantilena of Wolfram's "Song to the Evening Star."

Act II moves systematically though the accustomed paces of a grand operatic middle act. Following its expansive orchestral ritornello, Elizabeth's "Dich, teure Halle" is an unapologetically formal aria of a simple ternary shape (though smuggling in some proto-leitmotivic recollections of themes from Act I). As in many French and Italian operas of the era, the solo number yields to a more complexly structured duet scene, culminating in a vigorous cabaletta movement ("Gepriesen sei die Stunde"). Its melodic language, however, is redolent of the deliberately "Germanic" MELOS, rather square and flat-footed, found in some of Wagner's earliest works. The entry and chorus of Thuringian nobles likewise infuses a staple of grand operatic spectacle (the choral march or procession) with a solidly German cadence, sonorous brass fanfares, and moments of poetic introspection. The "Contest of Song" that provides the occasion for the whole act now allows Wagner to execute a classic grand opera finale on the largest scale. A formal public event, the song contest, is catastrophically interrupted when Tannhäuser bursts out with his reprise of the song in praise of Venus from Act I ("Dir, Göttin der Liebe, soll mein Lied ertönen"). Typical of Wagner's pre-*Ring* operas is the complex, rhythmically staggered choral writing aiming at a sort of stylized realism in depicting the "voice" of the energized or agitated crowd (an effect that would find its apotheosis in Act II of Die MEISTERSINGER VON NÜRNBERG). In place of the up-tempo stretta that would normally unite all the disparate voices at the end, Wagner introduces the chorale-prelude of the marching pilgrims from Act I. Their hymn theme, however, is gradually subjected to stretta-like acceleration and amplification, thus linking the grand opera idiom of Act II with the German Romantic topoi characteristic of the outer acts.

Stylistically, Tannhäuser's song in praise of Venus in Act I already places him at odds with the licentious chaos of the Venusberg. The melody is simple, rough-cut, even stolid, and entirely devoid of the harmonic or textural sophistications that characterize Venus even in the first version (Example 17).

17. Theme of Tannhäuser's song to Venus

As early as the overture, this melody is placed in symbolic contrast to the seething chromatic sequences which spell erotic desire, and whose musical ingredients the Wagner of *Tristan* and the Paris *Tannhäuser* revisions would exploit to ever-increasing levels of intensity. In both the overture and the Tannhäuser-Venus dialogue of Act I, scene 2, the sturdy theme of Tannhäuser's song is pitted against Venus's chromatic blandishments ("Geliebter, komm'! Sieh' dort die Grotte") and the music of the Bacchanal staged in his honor. The placement of this contrasting music on the far sharp side of the tonal spectrum (F♯ major, C♯ major) in Act I, scene 2 plays into a tonal contrast consciously exploited across the whole opera, in which the key of E major (four sharps) represents the sensual love celebrated in the Venusberg while the key of E♭ major (three flats) represents the sacred, spiritual love embodied by Elisabeth. It was of course the alluring chromaticism of Venus's realm that Wagner was at pains to develop in the Paris revisions of the Bacchanal and the Venus-Tannhäuser dialogue. The most prominent new motive introduced in the revised Bacchanal suggests a deliberate allusion to the so-called "desire" motive of the *Tristan* Prelude (Example 18). As if to confirm the allusion, Wagner re-writes the recitative of Venus's first response to Tannhäuser's protestations as a languid arioso accompanied by the famous *Tristan* chord itself (on its original pitches), resolved here to a V⁹ of F♯ major (Example 19).

The loose dialogic structure of the Venusberg scene in Act I is matched by the extended narrative monologue of Tannhäuser in Act III, which leads directly into Tannhäuser's renewed temptation by Venus and her music at the climax of the drama. Tannhäuser's "Rome narrative" represents Wagner's

18. New motive in "Paris" Bacchanal (1861)

19. *Tristan* chord in Venus's response to Tannhäuser, Act I, Scene 2 (1861 revision)

20. Theme of Pilgrims' Chorus (mm. 1–8 of overture)

closest approach to the through-composed, motivically grounded discursive idiom of the later "music dramas" in the original score of the opera. A kind of musical synthesis of the themes of sacred and profane love is achieved when the melody of the so-called "Pilgrims' Chorus," played in the overture in the "profane" key of E major (Example 20), is introduced with text in Act III ("Beglückt darf nun dich, O Heimat, ich schau'n") and reprised in the final measures of the opera in the "sacred" key of E♭ major.

In the original overture, Wagner had underlined the idea of synthesis by having the chromatic-diminished whirrings of the Venusberg music transform almost imperceptibly into the diatonic "halo" of pulsing violin figuration that crowns the reprise of the "Pilgrims' Chorus" theme there. In the Paris-Vienna revision, this reprise is suppressed in favor of a direct segue to the new Bacchanal scene. But the sense of this vigorous string figuration as an expression of renewed, pulsing, "organic" life (and not merely an imagined celestial light) is still suggested by its role in accompanying the miracle of the Pope's dry staff sprouting new green leaves, as announced by the chorus of younger pilgrims at the opera's end.

5. Premiere, performance history, interpretation

Despite the considerable pains taken by Wagner to ensure a strong premiere of *Tannhäuser* in Dresden, the first performance left him dissatisfied with the quality of the production no less than with the audience's seeming incomprehension of his work. The sets had been produced in part by expert Parisian designers Édouard Desplechin and Jules Diéterle, but the Wartburg Hall had not arrived in time. Wagner's youthful idol, Wilhelmine SCHRÖDER-DEVRIENT, created the role of Venus; it was well suited to her theatrical and real-life personae, but her vocal powers were no longer at their peak. The able Heldentenor Josef Tichatschek had little feeling for the inner life of the title character, though he sang the notes well enough. Only the Wolfram of the company, baritone Anton Mitterwurzer (later Wagner's first KURWENAL in *Tristan*), commanded the full respect of composer and audience. By the third performance, Wagner felt confident that at least a coterie of more sophisticated listeners had come to appreciate the achievement of this first opera composed after his return to Germany. By the end of the first run, the initially skeptical Robert SCHUMANN had come around, and the 1846 revival was reviewed enthusiastically and at great length by none other than the young Eduard HANSLICK. Wagner continued to tinker with the text, music, and scoring of the final chorus. For the last Dresden revival during his Kapellmeister years (beginning August 1847) and performances in the early 1850s he made a point of visibly representing Venus's last "temptation" of Tannhäuser and subsequently the papal staff "adorned with new green leaves" amidst the chorus of pilgrims, now giving the theme of the earlier $\frac{3}{4}$ "Pilgrims' Chorus" to the voices as well as the orchestra.

Beginning with Franz LISZT's production at the Weimar Court Theater in February 1849, *Tannhäuser* became the first of Wagner's Dresden-period operas to be produced throughout Germany. Between 1852 and 1856 the opera was produced in Schwerin, Wiesbaden, LEIPZIG, Kassel, Posen, Hanover, Karlsruhe, MUNICH, and Berlin. The "unofficial" Viennese premiere mounted by the small suburban Thalia Theater prompted an elaborate PARODY by the comedian Johann Nepomuk Nestroy, and by April 1859 the opera had already reached New York. Immediately upon finishing the score of *Tristan und Isolde* in the summer of 1859, Wagner followed up plans for a belated conquest of the Paris Opéra with a French redaction of *Tannhäuser*. Apart from the contested issue of a mid-opera ballet divertissement, in lieu of which Wagner would only offer an amplified Bacchanal at the opening of Act I, the plan was by no means unreasonable: here was something recognizable as "grand opera," if with a German accent, with no shortage of medieval courtly panoply and romantic *couleur locale*, now to be updated with small doses of Wagner's latest AVANT-GARDE experimentation. A mixture of politics and aesthetics, both real and notional, undermined the laborious preparations for the Paris production and ended in the celebrated and catastrophic Paris TANNHÄUSER SCANDAL of 13 March 1861. The Dresden version was staged during Wagner's Munich years (5 March 1865) with Ludwig Schnorr von CAROLSFELD, followed by the first German performances of the "Paris" score in 1867. A carefully supervised revival in Vienna (22 November 1875) with future Bayreuth participants Amalie MATERNA and Emil SCARIA was the last time Wagner personally involved himself with the work, but he clearly expressed to Cosima toward the end of his life his hopes that *Tannhäuser* would be produced at the FESTIVAL THEATER in Bayreuth someday.

When Cosima did carry out her late husband's wishes in 1891, she lavished an exceptional degree of care on the enterprise. Photographs attest to her meticulous realization of the elaborate scenario of the "Paris-Vienna" Bacchanal, complete with visionary tableaux of "The Rape of Europa" and "Leda and the Swan" and multidimensional views of the Wartburg. Richard STRAUSS conducted the 1894 revival, and Isadora DUNCAN choreographed a new Bacchanal in 1904. (Despite Duncan's personal reputation as a barefoot rebel, her conception of the scene was derided as incongruously chaste and ethereal.) The Bacchanal remained a defining focus of many subsequent productions, as a proving ground for changing conceptions of the psychosexual symbolism of the Venusberg and directorial responses to the "avant-garde" component of the revised score. Later twentieth-century productions, whether provocative (Götz Friedrich, Bayreuth 1972–8) or programmatically traditional (Otto Schenk and Günther Schneider-Siemssen, Metropolitan Opera, 1977–82), routinely offer quantities of simulated copulation and post-coital languor, for which the Paris score offers ample encouragement. The seeds of a postwar "New Bayreuth" could already be detected in Rudolf von Laban's spare neoclassical Bacchanal for SIEGFRIED WAGNER's *Tannhäuser* production in the 1920s, conducted by Arturo

TOSCANINI. When WIELAND WAGNER applied his stripped-down, anti-representational approach to the opera (Bayreuth, 1954–64) the choreographer Maurice Béjart favored a more macabre tone, with "desperate couplings reminiscent of Bosch or Dante" (Carnegy 302). A similar vision of the Venusberg as a repository of nightmare-archetypes from the collective cultural unconscious was developed in a Munich production (1994) directed by David Alden in which creatures out of Hieronymous Bosch crawl around the oblivious protagonist, who is more benumbed than aroused by the surreal vision of his erotic imagination.

The roles of the main characters are relatively unambiguous as scripted and composed by Wagner. TANNHÄUSER seeks a Faustian knowledge and experience outside the pale of his native society (the Wartburg court), vouchsafed by diabolical agents (Venus and her grotto) but at the expense of his "Christian" soul and of the pure, redemptive love embodied in the "eternal feminine" ideal (Elisabeth). The true, self-sacrificing friend (Wolfram) is also a rival, in the realm of art as well as love; but he willingly yields Elisabeth to Tannhäuser in hopes of thus securing his salvation. Wagner imbues these seemingly fixed positions with dramatic and psychological interest by representing the protagonist's distrust of the two extremes offered to him: Venus's endless carnival of sensual pleasures and the chaste, courtly, Christian notion of woman as pure, untouchable ideal. Above all, Wagner's depiction of Tannhäuser as an apostate from the code of idealized courtly love provides a basis for interpretations of the character as a Romantic rebel, an artistic outlaw at odds with a bourgeois status quo.

While the scenario of REDEMPTION played out in the opera's final scene seems to validate a conventional victory of pure, spiritual love over sexual indulgence, Wagner makes a point of suggesting that Elisabeth has been fascinated by Tannhäuser's passionate, sensual nature from the beginning – something that makes him, to her, the better artist and the better lover than his rival Wolfram. It is not difficult to see Wagner coming to terms with his own conflicting allegiances to "New German" moral rebellion and sensualism, on one hand, and to intellectual traditions of German ROMANTICISM and idealism, on the other, that had influenced his first decade of creative activity, up to the time of *Tannhäuser* (see Borchmeyer). Charles BAUDELAIRE, one of the earliest and most trenchant readers of the opera, drew attention to the multiple levels at which the opera and its music play out its overriding dynamic of "the struggle between the two principles that have chosen the human heart for their chief battlefield; in other words, the struggle between flesh and spirit, Heaven and Hell, Satan and God" (Baudelaire 126). Baudelaire was fascinated above all by the "Satanic" majesty of Wagner's Venus, "the absolute ideal of sensual love." Her importance is underlined by a recent study of eroticism in Wagner's oeuvre which recalls the composer's original intention to call his opera *Der Venusberg* despite the disproportionate relation of that title to the action of the drama as a whole (Dreyfus 77). The revisions of 1860–1 certainly increased the prominence of the Venusberg vis-à-vis the Wartburg. In this regard they serve to amplify the underlying dynamic of the piece and thus to provoke directors, critics, and listeners to engage more actively with the problems of its resolution, reminding us of the centrality of this dynamic to Wagner's creative vision throughout his career.   THOMAS S. GREY

See also TANNHÄUSER, PARIS SCANDAL OF 1861

Charles Baudelaire, *The Painter of Modern Life and other Essays*, trans. and ed. Jonathan Mayne (London: Phaidon, 1964): 111–46.
"Richard Wagner and *Tannhäuser* in Paris," *Revue européenne*, 1 April 1861.
Dieter Borchmeyer, "Venus in Exile: *Tannhäuser* between Romanticism and Young Germany," in *Drama and the World of Richard Wagner*, trans. Daphne Ellis (Princeton University Press, 2003): 101–46.
Patrick Carnegy, *Wagner and the Art of the Theatre* (see bibliography).
Mary Cicora, *From History to Myth: Wagner's "Tannhäuser" and its Literary Sources* (Bern: Peter Lang, 1992).
Attila Csampai and Dietmar Holland, *Richard Wagner, "Tannhäuser": Texte, Materialen, Kommentare* (Reinbek bei Hamburg: Rowohlt, 1986).
Laurence Dreyfus, *Wagner and the Erotic Impulse* (see bibliography): especially chapter 4.
Eduard Hanslick, "Richard Wagner: *Tannhäuser*" (review, 1846), *Vienna's Golden Years of Music 1850–1900: Eduard Hanslick*, trans. and ed. Henry Pleasants III (New York: Simon & Schuster, 1950): 21–36.
Nicholas Johns, ed., *Tannhäuser*, English National Opera Guide Series 39 (London: John Calder and New York: Riverrun Press, 1988).

Tannhäuser (tenor; the title role in *TANNHÄUSER*). Created by the principal tenor of the Dresden Court Theater, Josef TICHATSCHEK, the first Wagnerian HELDENTENOR. The part is demanding even by Wagnerian standards, dominating all three acts of the opera.

The historical prototype of the character is a Middle High German poet (*c*. 1200–67), apparently from the Franconian town of Tannhausen. He may have been a member of the lesser nobility. "Der Tannhûser" or "Der Tanhusære" is believed to have participated in the Crusades between 1228 and 1233, later serving at the court of Frederick II of Babenberg. Sixteen poems are attributed to him in the Manesse (Heidelberg) Codex, which also includes portrait-illustrations of him and several other of Wagner's historical *Minnesänger* (WOLFRAM VON ESCHENBACH, WALTHER VON DER VOGELWEIDE, Reinmar von Zweter). The evocations of sensual pleasures and the critical attitude toward the tradition of idealized courtly love poetry expressed in some of his poems have suggested biographical links with the legendary variation of the character as it developed some centuries later, said to have tarried with the pagan goddess of love in the "Venusberg" (originally associated with the Monte della Sibilla in the central Italian Apennines) and afterwards to have sought absolution from Pope Urban IV for this sinful episode. The principal written source for this story is a broadsheet ballad, "Das Lied von dem Danheüser," printed in Nuremberg (1515). This poem also includes the motif of the pope's refusal to grant absolution ("no sooner than the dry staff in his hands should sprout new green leaves").

Following some hints in his contemporary sources (Ludwig Bechstein, *Die Sagen von Eisenach und der Wartburg*, 1835, and C. T. L. Lucas, *Über den Krieg von Wartburg*, 1838), Wagner conflated the legendary Tannhäuser with the figure of Heinrich von Ofterdingen, a non-noble *Minnesänger* who figures as a rebellious outsider in league with the Hungarian sorcerer KLINGSOR (Klinsor, Klingsohr) and at odds with the other poet-singers patronized by the Landgraf Hermann of Thuringia at the Wartburg. Wagner's characterization of his

Tannhäuser as a social, sexual, and artistic rebel also draws on portrayals both of the legendary Tannhäuser and of Heinrich von Ofterdingen in a number of Romantic literary works.

Musically, Wagner's Tannhäuser does not strongly distinguish himself from his fellow *Minnesänger* in his song praising Venus, which differs from theirs only in key and in a somewhat more active rhythmic accompaniment. (It is rather the role of Venus, above all as revised for Paris in 1860–1, that embodies a radical stylistic contrast to the operatic-musical norms of the Wartburg.) Only in his tormented "Rome narrative" in Act III does Tannhäuser explore a distinctly new musical-discursive idiom, anticipating the musical-dramatic monologues of figures such as WOTAN (*Die WALKÜRE*), HANS SACHS, or GURNEMANZ (though the genealogy could also be traced back to the DUTCHMAN's opening monologue in Act I of *Der FLIEGENDE HOLLÄNDER*).

Albert NIEMANN created the French-language Tannhäuser for the ill-fated Paris production of 1861. While Niemann sung the role as early as 1854, Wagner was not happy with the Parisian performance (though of course Niemann went on to become one of the leading Wagner tenors of the day, singing the first SIEGMUND at BAYREUTH). A leading Tannhäuser of the next generation was Leo Slezak (1873–1946), who performed the role at the Metropolitan Opera. The role also served as the Metropolitan Opera debut of Lauritz MELCHIOR in 1926. While most well-known Wagnerian Heldentenors have performed the role, some of the most successful have been those also noted for performances of Siegmund and TRISTAN: Niemann, in Wagner's day, Melchior, Wolfgang WINDGASSEN in postwar Bayreuth, René Kollo, and (in studio recordings) Placido Domingo. In recent years German tenor Peter Seiffert has been one of the most frequent interpreters of the part.

THOMAS. S. GREY

Reinhold Brinkmann, "Tannhäuser's Lied," in *Das Drama Richard Wagners als musikalisches Kunstwerk*, ed. Carl Dahlhaus (Regensburg: Bosse, 1970): 199–211.

Tannhäuser, Paris scandal of 1861. Like the equally notorious Paris premiere of Stravinsky's *Rite of Spring* some fifty years later, the performance of *TANNHÄUSER* (painstakingly revised for the occasion) at the Paris Opéra on 13 March 1861 is famous in part for scarcely having been heard. As the story is usually told, the members of the aristocratic "Jockey Club," devotees of horse-racing and the female corps de ballet, protested the lack of a conventional opera ballet in the middle act by interrupting every scene with jeering, catcalls, and dog whistles. In point of fact, much of the first performance proceeded without disturbance, at least until the third act. According to the diary of composer Heinrich MARSCHNER, who was in Paris at the time, a few moments in the first act occasioned mischievous laughter, such as the shepherd's piping and the appearance of a brace of dogs with Landgraf Hermann's hunting party. The set designs, the "Entry of the Guests" tableau in Act II, the singing of Marie Sass [Sax] as ELISABETH and that of Ferdinand Morelli as WOLFRAM (in his "Song to the Evening Star") all elicited general applause. At the end of Act II, however, the applause competed with hisses and whistling from other quarters. With the exception of Wolfram's song, the third act

581

devolved into a genuine fiasco due to ever-increasing outbursts of calculated laughter. For the second performance on 18 March 1861, much of Wagner's adventurously revised music for the Venus-Tannhäuser scene was omitted, as was Venus's reappearance in Act III (which had been added to the score in 1847) along with the offending piping of the shepherd in Act I and the hunting party with its dogs. All the same, this performance met with similar demonstrations of public resistance, abetted by the distribution of whistles to the public on the part of Jockey Club members beforehand, according to some sources. The fiasco of the Paris *Tannhäuser* reached its full proportions only with the third performance (24 March), despite the precaution of moving this to a Sunday, outside of the regular subscription schedule. The composer did not attend, and his request to withdraw the opera from further performances was granted.

Wagner himself influenced most accounts of this debacle by emphasizing, in *MEIN LEBEN* (My Life, 1865–81) and in an account written at the end of March 1861 ("Report on the Production of *Tannhäuser* in Paris," SSD 7:138–49; PW 3:347–60), the role of the Jockey Club and their disgruntlement over the ballet affair. He consistently represents a pitched battle between a curious, enthusiastic public and a small organized opposition. In the 1861 "Report," Wagner claimed it was a clique of journalists who had staged the laughter, according to premeditated cues, at the first performance, and that "Jockeys" began their campaign only upon arriving at the middle of the second. It could be argued that the "ballet" Wagner *did* provide for Paris, the new Venusberg Bacchanal, had in its way much more sex in it that anything the Opéra audience was used to seeing, although this was more implicit in the score and scenario than visible in the choreography. The placement immediately after the overture was by any measure unconventional. Wagner's novel concept was met with little understanding by ballet master Lucien Petipa, and he had, he claimed, to make do with diminished resources.

Other factors likely also played a role. The production had been made possible by the advocacy of Princess Pauline METTERNICH, wife of the Austrian ambassador, who persuaded the emperor Louis-Napoléon to issue a formal command for it. Princess Metternich was the object of visible protests during the performances (Austrian interests had been defeated by French-Italian alliances in the battle of Solferino in June 1859), and the Jockey Club constituency may have seen this as an opportunity to manifest its well-known disapproval of imperial government. Above all, the overweening and distinctly "Germanic" aesthetic posturing of Wagner had become well known to the Parisian public, more so than his music. As the reviews testify, they were more than ready to find fault with the alleged musical-dramatic reforms of this foreign composer. The extended musical dialogue of Tannhäuser and Venus in Act I, the drawn-out attempt at imagining an idiom for medieval *Minnesang* in Act II, and the succession of slow, introverted musical scenes in Act III all tried the patience of Parisian opera audiences. (For his part, Wagner also blamed the conducting of Pierre-Louis DIETSCH, the former chorus-master who had, ironically, been commissioned to write an opera on Wagner's own "Flying Dutchman" subject almost twenty years earlier.)

The Paris *Tannhäuser* affair is characteristic of Wagner's relationship to Paris and the French: apparent professional failure and public antagonism are offset by cultural publicity at a higher, more enduring level. Despite all Wagner's loud protests against it, French culture played an enormous role in his creative and psychological biography, just as the "case of Wagner" did in the annals of cultural modernity in France, in turn.   THOMAS S. GREY

See also BAUDELAIRE, CHARLES

Annegret Fauser and Thomas S. Grey, eds. and trans., "Debâcle at the Paris Opera: *Tannhäuser* and the French Critics, 1861," *Wagner and His World*, ed. Thomas S. Grey (see bibliography): 347–71.

Paul Lindau, "Der *Tannhäuser*-Skandal. März 1861," in *Nur Erinnerungen* (Stuttgart, 1916): 70–90; "The *Tannhäuser* Scandal in March 1861," trans. Daphne Ellis, *Wagner* 24.1 (September 2003): 3–22.

Tappert, Wilhelm (b. Ober-Thomaswaldau [Silesia], 19 Feb. 1830; d. Berlin, 27 Oct. 1907). German musical scholar and writer, best remembered in the Wagner literature for his "dictionary" of critical abuse leveled at Wagner in the press during the later nineteenth century, *Ein Wagner-Lexikon* (1877). After training as a schoolteacher, Tappert decided to pursue a career as musical pedagogue, scholar, and critic, studying harmony and piano at the conservatory in Berlin. From 1878 to 1881 he was editor of the *Allgemeine deutsche Musikzeitung*, and he also contributed numerous articles about Wagner to the *Musikalisches Wochenblatt* in the 1870s and 1880s. He headed the Berlin branch of the Bayreuth PATRONS' ASSOCIATION (*Patronatverein*). In the essays collected as *Musikalische Studien* (1868), Tappert claimed to apply popularized notions of Darwininan evolutionary theory to modern culture and music, in particular an "evolutionary history of harmony." The essay on "altered chords" in this collection contains perhaps the first identification of the now so-called TRISTAN CHORD as a phenomenon of music-theoretical significance. Aside from his critical support for Wagner and "new music," Tappert was also a noted scholar of Renaissance lute tablature, eventually donating his significant collection of early manuscript and print materials to the Prussian Royal Library in Berlin.   THOMAS S. GREY

Wilhelm Tappert, *Ein Wagner-Lexikon* (see bibliography).

Tausig, Carl (b. Warsaw, 4 Nov. 1841; d. Leipzig, 17 July 1871), German-Jewish pianist. A prodigiously gifted student of Franz LISZT and devoted Wagner supporter, he (along with his student Marie von SCHLEINITZ) helped to establish the BAYREUTH *Patronatverein* (PATRONS' ASSOCIATION).

1. Career
2. Relations with Wagner

1. Career

The son of a respected piano teacher and composer (Aloys Tausig, pupil of Sigismond Thalberg), Carl performed Chopin's Op. 53 Polonaise to Liszt aged 14, and was immediately accepted as his pupil, studying with him between 1855 and 1859. During this time, he produced piano transcriptions of six of Liszt's symphonic poems. Living at the Altenburg exposed him to the artistically rich environment of Liszt's circle. His intellectual curiosity led him to study the natural sciences and mathematics as well as French philosophy. Hans von BÜLOW reports that Tausig also began composing at this time, producing a piano concerto, a concert polonaise (with orchestra), and several symphonic poems, though no manuscripts survive. Tausig's musical ascendency was rapid despite mixed reactions to his technically unrestrained execution. His Berlin debut (under Bülow) in 1858, was followed by solo recitals across Germany, including Dresden (1859–60), which became his base, and where he conversed with BRAHMS over piano technique, stimulating the young composer to finish two books of the Paganini studies. In 1862, Tausig relocated to Vienna, where he established and conducted a loss-making concert series of NEW GERMAN music.

While visiting Pressburg in July 1864, he met the pianist Szerafina von Vrabély (1841–1931), a student of Dreyschock; in November they were married, but would divorce within a few years. On resuming his career as a virtuoso in the Prussian capital in 1865, Tausig was appointed Royal Court Pianist, and in 1866 he opened the Akademie für das höhere Klavierspiel (school of advanced piano instruction), which he ran together with Louis Ehlert until 1870. At this time, Tausig developed his *Tägliche Studien*, studies designed to maintain the technique of advanced pianists. Tausig's numerous arrangements and editions from this period include transcriptions of Beethoven's string quartets; selections from J. S. BACH, Chopin, Clementi, Scarlatti, Schubert, SCHUMANN, Weber, and paraphrases of Wagner's *Tristan*, Siegmund's *Liebesgesang*, and *KAISERMARSCH*.

After closing his *Akademie* in 1870, Tausig embarked on a tour of Russia and Eastern Europe, returning to Weimar for the Beethoven celebrations on 29 May, performing the "Emperor" concerto under Liszt, in what would be their final encounter.

Judging from reviews and surviving descriptions, Tausig must have had a phenomenal technique as a pianist. Critics and friends (including Wagner) openly likened his pianistic aptitude to Liszt's, who regarded Tausig as "infallible" with "fingers of steel." HANSLICK spoke contrariwise of a "cold aesthetic" in his interpretations, indicating the differing attitudes within Vienna and Germany proper.

His correspondence reveals that his health was never robust, and he suffered from fatigue. He was particularly ill for several months during 1863 and even had an operation, though the details remain unknown. He died unexpectedly of typhoid, aged 29.

2. Relations with Wagner

In May 1858, Liszt introduced Tausig to Wagner, who would exert an increasingly powerful influence over the young pianist during the 1860s. At this time Tausig lived next to TRIBSCHEN, and his Berlin colleague, Ehlert, later rued that "Tausig joined with heart and soul the partisanship [over Wagner] that was soon established" (18). Wagner viewed Tausig almost paternally, describing him as "amusing" and "cheeky," but quickly came to admire his intelligence and exceptional musical talent (Wagner to Liszt, 2 July 1858).

As part of the preparations for the planned production of *TRISTAN UND ISOLDE* in VIENNA in 1862, Tausig was enlisted (along with Peter

CORNELIUS, Wendelin WEISSHEIMER, and Brahms) to copy out sections of his operas for concert performance, essentially to advertise the upcoming premiere. (Tausig would later produce a piano score of *Die MEISTERSINGER*.) Convivial musical gatherings in Wagner's hotel were frequent; Wagner described one such where "the musical temperature soon ran high" as Tausig played from Bülow's piano score of *Tristan* (ML/E 645). As the two became closer, Wagner obliquely solicited Tausig's help in raising funds against the expenses he was incurring (Wagner to Tausig, 8 June 1861) and Tausig – obliging – became liable for some of Wagner's debts. Eduard Liszt, Liszt's uncle, a lawyer and manager of Liszt's estate, had to resolve the situation, not before Wagner's glib remark to Cornelius: "If all turns out well, perhaps [Tausig] will succeed in being nailed to the cross for my sake" (Wagner to Eduard Liszt, 25 March 1864; Wagner to Peter Cornelius, Vienna, 8 April 1864).

Wagner also performed with Tausig, on occasion, conducting a notable concert with him in Vienna's Redoutensaal on 27 December 1863. Furthermore, their correspondence over the revised republication of *Das JUDENTUM IN DER MUSIK* (Jewishness in Music) in 1869 is revealing – Tausig was a devoted JEWISH Wagnerite – in that it clarifies certain aspects of Wagner's position.

In 1871, to raise funds for the first BAYREUTH FESTIVAL, Tausig originated the model of the *Patronatverein* (Patrons' Association) together with Marie von SCHLEINITZ. The plan was simple: society members would purchase a total of 1,000 *Patronatscheine* (PATRON CERTIFICATES), each costing 300 thalers, to raise the estimated 300,000 thalers needed to build the theater and inaugurate the festival. One certificate would guarantee a seat for the three planned *Ring* cycles at the festival, and certificates could be divided among members. Indeed, it was precisely through Emil HECKEL's concept of splitting the cost of a certificate that the notion of a WAGNER SOCIETY arose.

Three months before Tausig's death, Wagner appointed him manager of the planned Bayreuth Festival. Cosima and Wagner immediately eyed the practical difficulties that his passing presented: "in Tausig we have certainly lost a great pillar of our enterprise." Wagner reportedly "shrugs his shoulders over the stupidity of Fate, snatching Tausig away at the moment when a great new activity would have brought inner joy and satisfaction" (CWD 20 July 1871).

On 7 September 1872, Wagner penned an epitaph for Tausig's gravestone – still extant – in the Friedhof der Jerusalems- und der Neuen Kirchengemeinde in Berlin:

To be mature for death,	Reif sein zum Sterben
life's slowly thriving fruit,	des Lebens zögernd spriessende Frucht,
to win it early ripe	früh reif sie erweben
in sudden blossoming of spring –	in Lenzes jäh eblühender Flucht, –
that was your fate, and that your daring, –	war es Dein Loos, war es Dein Wagen, –
your fate we must lament, so too your	Wir müssen Dein Loos wie Dein Wagen
daring	beklagen

DAVID TRIPPETT

Louis Ehlert, *From the Tone World: A Series of Essays*, trans. Helen D. Tretbar (New York: Tretbar, 1885).

Theater in Zürich, Ein (A Theater in Zurich). Brochure – written after OPER UND DRAMA (Opera and Drama, 1851) and before the MITTEILUNG AN MEINE FREUNDE (Communication to My Friends) – published in April 1851. It was one of several texts Wagner wrote in an attempt to convince the ZURICH political authorities and potential local patrons to reorganize the theater and concert life in their city, and renew their means of funding. The Zurich theater (opened only in 1834) had to be rented by its director, whose finances thus depended on his immediate takings. Wagner criticizes the resultant, inevitable vicious circle of repeated near-bankruptcies, short-term planning, and rapid change of personnel. He also pillories those who think theater in Germany must mimic the fashions of Paris. He proposes close links between the Zurich theater and the local education authorities. Money should be raised among theater lovers in the region in order to allow adequate, intensive rehearsals at the beginning of the season. In order to raise standards, young actors and singers should be engaged (better, he says, to use limited funds to hire a few good people than many mediocrities). The repertoire should be chosen according to the possibilities of the ensemble, and the number of performances reduced (with a corresponding increase in the number of orchestral concerts per season). Wagner postulates a point in the future when these measures would result in a self-sustaining ensemble of high-class local talent.

Wagner's aim with this brochure was primarily practical, to "show [the people here] what they should do if they want something proper" (letter to Ferdinand HEINE, 26 April 1851). Although he would have profited from an implementation of his proposals (see letter to Julie RITTER, 30 April 1851), he concentrates here largely on the putative general benefits, and tempers his social utopianism with much common sense. But his tortuous prose, his ill-founded belief in the deepness of Zurich pockets, and his sideswipes at Charlotte Birch-Pfeiffer (the popular, hitherto only successful director in the short history of the Zurich theater) made it inevitable that his ideas would be ignored, as indeed they were. CHRIS WALTON

Eva Martina Hanke, *Wagner in Zürich* (see bibliography).
Chris Walton, *Richard Wagner's Zurich* (see bibliography).

Thielemann, Christian (b. Berlin, 1 April 1959), conductor. He worked as Herbert von KARAJAN's assistant and was appointed Generalmusikdirektor successively in NUREMBERG, at the Deutsche Oper Berlin, and with the MUNICH Philharmonic. His interpretations of Wagner and STRAUSS have won particular praise. In the decade after his BAYREUTH debut with *Die MEISTERSINGER VON NÜRNBERG* in 2000, he conducted over 100 festival performances. Since 2010, he has been music advisor to the festival directors. CHRIS WALTON

Thode, Henry (b. Dresden, 13 Jan. 1857; d. Copenhagen, 19 Nov, 1920), art historian. He became a member of the so-called BAYREUTH CIRCLE around COSIMA in 1886, on his marriage to her eldest daughter, Daniela von Bülow. His personal intimacy with WAHNFRIED ended with his divorce in 1914, but his loyalty to Wagner the artist remained undiminished.

Thode's devotion to Wagner affected his work as an art historian. He believed Wagner's work analogous to the art of the Middle Ages, and that Wagner was the spiritual heir to Albrecht Dürer. He argued that Wagner's work would engender a revival of the medieval mysticism which had nourished the art of the Renaissance. Thode was critical of what he regarded as DECADENCE in the art of his time, especially the vogue amongst some German critics for the French Impressionists. He thus identified by association Wagner's work with the anti-modernist movement in German culture, without acknowledging its radical elements. His philosophy of art was influential in the development of the Nazi concept of "degenerate art."   ROGER ALLEN

See also CHAMBERLAIN, HOUSTON STEWART

Tichatschek, Josef Aloys (b. Ober-Weckelsdorf, 11 July 1807; d. Dresden, 18 Jan. 1886), Bohemian tenor. Engaged at DRESDEN (1838–61), with appearances in England in the 1840s, he was considered by many observers to be the greatest German tenor of his day. He was the first to sing the title roles in *RIENZI* (1842) and *TANNHÄUSER* (1845), and eventually added LOHENGRIN to his repertory. Wagner admired his brilliant voice and musicality, and appreciated Tichatschek's cheerfulness and infectious enthusiasm for his music, but deeply regretted the singer's blithe inability to grasp the dramatic nature of his roles. Wagner nevertheless continued to promote and stand by his old friend – in 1867, the composer called him the best tenor available for the *Lohengrin* production King LUDWIG II wished to mount in MUNICH, and had Tichatschek appear in the dress rehearsal. Unfortunately, the king could not recognize his image of the Grail Knight in the sixty-year-old Tichatschek's physical appearance, and had him replaced by the young Heinrich VOGL for the first public performance.   DAVID BRECKBILL

Einhard Luther, *Biographie eines Stimmfaches* (see bibliography): 1:20–31.

Tietjen, Heinz (b. Tangier, 24 July 1881; d. Baden-Baden, 30 Nov. 1967), theater director and conductor. Son of a German diplomat and English mother. Tietjen studied in Wiesbaden and in LEIPZIG with the conductor Arthur Nikisch and, in 1925, was appointed Director (Intendant) of the State Opera Unter den Linden and the KROLL OPER, both in Berlin. He was unable to prevent the downfall of the Kroll Oper. In 1929, SIEGFRIED WAGNER saw Tietjen's *LOHENGRIN* production (Wilhelm FURTWÄNGLER conducting, set design Emil PREETORIUS) and advised his wife WINIFRED to choose Tietjen as his successor after his death. Siegfried died in August 1930; Winifred contacted Tietjen that same month, and he accepted.

Tietjen's association with BAYREUTH coincided with HITLER's rise to power and the establishment of the Third Reich, so questions persist on the degree of his complicity with the Nazi regime. Although Hitler had substantial influence on the FESTIVAL, Tietjen, who possessed diplomatic skill, always stressed that he was never put under any pressure by him. He was protected in Berlin by Hermann Goering (the most important Nazi official after Hitler) and in Bayreuth by Winifred Wagner, who assured Hitler that the Festival could not function without him. He faced problems when a large group of Wagner fans (mostly from the WAGNER SOCIETIES) wanted to keep the repertory as originally conceived by Cosima, while others clamored against the romantic naturalism which Adolphe APPIA and Gordon Craig had already criticized and undermined. But he managed to cope, combining his technical and managerial abilities with artistic professionalism. Together with Emil Preetorius as stage designer, with whom he began to work in 1931, Tietjen created a legendary *Lohengrin* in 1936 with Furtwängler conducting. That same year, he became principal conductor because Furtwängler would not accept Winifred's leadership. In 1940, WOLFGANG worked at the Berlin State Opera as a trainee under Tietjen's supervision.

Until 1945, Tietjen was General Director of all Prussian State theaters as well as Bayreuth. He managed to raise the musical and production quality in Bayreuth to hitherto unsurpassed heights, assisted by the finest soloists available and with Hugo Rüdel as choir director. In the 1940s, there was a serious rift between Tietjen and WIELAND WAGNER, who was convinced that Tietjen was preventing him from taking over the Festival. After the war, Winifred suggested that Tietjen should continue to direct the Festival, an idea Wieland and Wolfgang successfully resisted. Tietjen underwent a process of denazification, which ended with his complete exoneration in 1947. His declaration that he had supported a Nazi resistance group could not be verified by historians. In 1954, he was appointed Director of the State Opera in Hamburg; in 1959 he conducted *Lohengrin* performances in Bayreuth which Wieland Wagner directed. He is today regarded as a producer and manager of excellent quality, but politically as an opportunist who managed to adjust to every regime. EVA RIEGER

Hannes Heer and Boris von Haken, "Der Überläufer Heinz Tietjen: Der Generalintendant der Preußischen Staatstheater im Dritten Reich," *Zeitschrift für Geschichtswissenschaft* 58.1 (2010): 28–53.

Toscanini, Arturo (b. Parma, 25 March 1867; d. New York, 16 Jan. 1957), conductor. He began his musical career as a cellist before establishing himself as a conductor at the Teatro Regio, Turin (1895) and La Scala, Milan (1898). He soon became known as a notable Wagnerian, and Wagner's operas featured strongly during his early seasons at La Scala. In 1930, Toscanini became the first non-German to conduct at BAYREUTH, when he was invited by SIEGFRIED WAGNER for *TRISTAN UND ISOLDE* and *TANNHÄUSER*. He returned in 1931 but, as a committed anti-fascist, he declined the invitation to conduct at the 1933 Festival. Like WEINGARTNER and MUCK, Toscanini was an exponent of the style of conducting that advocated fidelity to the score. On hearing him conduct *Tristan* at Bayreuth, Ernest NEWMAN wrote, "I was amazed to find, here and there, a passage coming on me like a dagger stroke. Then I found that all, or practically all, he had done was to play the notes just as Wagner directs them to be played" (Schonberg 257). ROGER ALLEN
See also PERFORMANCE, CONDUCTORS

Harold C. Schonberg, *The Great Conductors* (London: Victor Gollancz, 1968).

Tribschen (sometimes incorrectly spelled "Triebschen"), a small promontory on the banks of Lake Lucerne (Vierwaldstättersee), just 2 kilometers from the Lucerne train station. The merchant family Meyer von Schauensee acquired it in 1623, erecting a villa in 1627 that was rebuilt in 1800 after being acquired by the Amrhyn family (also "Am Rhyn"). The career soldier Walter Amrhyn, a member of the Swiss general staff, rented the fully furnished villa to Wagner for 3,000 francs a year. Wagner moved in on 15 April 1866, followed by COSIMA's first visit on 12 May. Wagner had his own furniture delivered and in 1867 had extensive renovations made, with the kitchen moved into an annex to make way for his new bedroom and his composing room. Besides the attic and a cellar, there are three main floors with roughly half a dozen rooms each, which afforded Wagner enough space to accommodate the many guests who visited, from LUDWIG II to Friedrich NIETZSCHE and Hans RICHTER. The villa stands in a park, atop a small hill just a few steps from the lake, and to the east has splendid views of the Rigi mountain (it was the "orange" sunrise over the Rigi to which Wagner's original title of the SIEGFRIED IDYLL referred). Wagner's SERVANTS, including Vreneli Weidmann, lived on the estate in a nearby house (demolished in 1933).

Cosima's salon was on the first upper floor, just off the landing where Wagner on 25 December 1870 conducted his musicians in the *Siegfried Idyll*. The door to her bedroom was at the far end of her salon. Wagner seems to have conceived the *Idyll* with this in mind, for while the acoustic in the staircase itself is dreadful, the sound of the ensemble when heard from behind closed doors in Cosima's bedroom is perfectly blended.

Relations with the Amrhyns, who lived with their children nearby and with whom social visits were exchanged, were sometimes fraught. Wagner did not always pay the rent on time, while COSIMA WAGNER'S DIARIES record disputes over a toboggan carriage, a horse, and finally frustration at bills for expenses sent by Amrhyn after their move to BAYREUTH (see, e.g., CWD 17 February and 11 March 1873). Wagner left Tribschen for good on 22 April 1872; Cosima left with the children on 29 April.

The house is currently the site of the Richard Wagner Museum Lucerne.

CHRIS WALTON

See also MUSEUMS AND ARCHIVES; Appendix 12: Archives and museums

Max Fehr, *Richard Wagners Schweizer Zeit*, vol. 2 (Aarau: Sauerländer, 1953).

Tristan (HELDENTENOR; title role in *TRISTAN UND ISOLDE*). The variants of the name Tristan over history practically equal the number of people, functions, moods, and actions that have been attached to it. Whether Droston, Drust, *Drūstanos*, Drystan, Tristam, Trystan, Tristram, Tristran, or Tristan, it runs the gamut of ancient legend from the worlds of King Arthur and Pictish Kings in the sixth century to the more sophisticated continental courtly literature of the thirteenth. In the legends the name has a wealth of reference (not all of it exactly free from moral black-spots) including the powerful swineherd, loyal servant, chief huntsman, subjugator of enemies, dragon-slayer, invincible swordsman, adulterous lover, ingenious deceiver, master of disguise, and, last but not least, the master musician, who can charm whole courts with his singing and playing of the harp.

Many opinions have been put forward about who invented Tristan. Celtic monasticism and lonely monks in the North of Britain steeped in Greek and Roman texts (especially Virgil and Plutarch's life of Theseus) have entered the fray, as has the idea that there existed at some point in the twelfth century an "unknown prime-poet" (Ernest NEWMAN), who was the author of a lost master text from which all later versions of the story derive. Wagner was absolutely clear that his hero had to assume both the name used in GOTTFRIED VON STRASSBURG's thirteenth-century romance *Tristan* and significant traits of the character exploited by its author in a special way.

Most MEDIEVAL texts agree that Tristan was a child born to a degree of suffering beyond the scale of most mortals. The name bestowed on him by his mother Blanchefleur, who died in childbirth after she had heard news of the death of Tristan's father Rivalin, could be no other. Tristan came into the world *par tristesse*, out of melancholy, a state of mind encapsulated concisely in the third act of Wagner's drama by the hero's own devastating observation: "As he [my father] conceived me and died, she [my mother] died as she gave birth to me" (*Da er mich zeugt' und starb, sie sterbend mich gebar*). Leaving aside Wagner's trenchant gloom, the double death of Tristan's parents in Gottfried's narrative is actually part of a simpler, essentially positive message that joy in love is inconceivable without suffering. That the story of Tristan could never comfort so many had he not endured profound grief is therefore central to his exquisite, tormented, and ultimately fated passion for "the queen of his heart."

The quaint liturgy of Tristan's sorrow in Gottfried's text had a profound effect on Wagner despite the fact that, with several variations inspired by SCHOPENHAUER, he basically turned it upside down. The hero's devastating wounds in Gottfried, for example, become in Wagner a single wound on a pathway to "oblivion" (*Urvergessenheit*). Wagner also turns the word play on the name Tristan in the medieval source into an ominous reference. Gottfried's Tristan divides his name into two and reverses its halves to create an undercover alias – Tantris – to gain illicit access to the Court of Ireland. Ernest Newman drily noted the laughable transparency of the ruse, rather as if Winston Churchill were to try to gain entry to Hitler's War Cabinet as Chinston Wurchill. Only a patch of dry musical analysis, however, can explain why Wagner entered into the spirit of the game. In Tristan Act I, Scene 3, Isolde sings "Tantris" to the notes a♭' and e♭" and a few seconds later "Tristan" to their inversion e♮" and a♮' half a tone higher. The two musical letters in Tristan's name are not coincidentally "s" (in German "es" = E♭) and "a" (a = A♮), the two pivotal pitches of this tiny musical structure. Moreover, the two chords A♭ and A major outlined by the first two pitches and then their transposed inversion are not only the exact ones underpinning the opening of one of the opera's most striking motives (the "death-devoted head" / *Tod geweihtes Haupt* motive first heard near the start of Act I, Scene 2) but also a conundrum: they are spatially intimate, at a distance of only half a tone, yet at the same time – in terms of key relations in the tonal system – worlds apart (Example 21).

Wagner's musical game with Tantris/Tristan encapsulates a larger vision about deceitfulness that actually dominates *Tristan und Isolde* despite the high Romanticism the work is often mistakenly taken to represent. Tristan's reputation as a master of disguise in the medieval sources, in other words, became in Wagner's hands a cipher for the idea that love is essentially a delusion, moreover an "utterly and completely devastating" one, as he wrote in a letter to

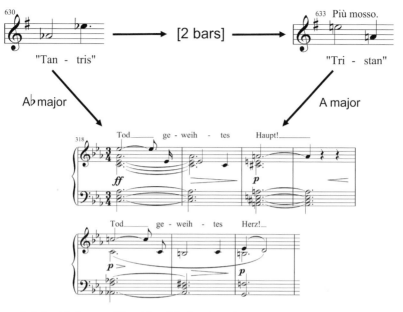

21. Relationship between "Tantris" and "Tristan" motives.

August RÖCKEL (23 August 1856) just before he started serious work on the opera. Indeed, in a startling moment of clarity at the very end of Act I, it is no less a person than Tristan himself who puts it best: "happiness in thrall to deceit" (*truggeweihtes Glücke*).

Tristan is one of the toughest roles in the operatic repertoire and performances that do it justice are rare. Its first creator, Ludwig Schnorr von CAROLSFELD, had the necessary intellect and a "full, soft, and brilliant" voice ideally suited to the part, according to Wagner's reminiscences of the singer (1868). The 1930s and 1940s witnessed outstanding performances from Max LORENZ (BAYREUTH, VIENNA, Milan, New York) and Lauritz MELCHIOR, who – in mostly mediocre productions – sang the role 223 times (Bayreuth, LONDON, PARIS, and mainly New York). Later Tristan voices did not quite achieve the same shining brilliance and were also unlucky in having to work with unimaginative directors. Indeed, interpretations by Jon Vickers and Siegfried Jerusalem in the 1960s and beyond only stay in the memory for the intelligence and intense feeling the singers themselves brought to the task. Despite WIELAND WAGNER'S overrated 1962 Bayreuth production (albeit with Wolfgang WINDGASSEN as Tristan at the top of his form) and its quasi-Jungian ambitions, it was not until Götz Friedrich's controversial experiments with the role sung by Pekka Nuotio in Amsterdam in 1974 (the critic Stefan Jaeger referred to it as "choreographed psychoanalysis") and Harry Kupfer's still more radical view – "more psychopath than rebel" – in Mannheim in 1982 (sung by Wolfgang Neumann) that this most subjectively complex of roles began to influence productions of *Tristan* as a whole.

JOHN DEATHRIDGE

Tristan chord. Art music of what might be termed a "late-Romantic" style (stretching from the second half of the nineteenth century well into the twentieth) bore witness to the rise of the iconic sonority – a moment in musical time whose harmonic content and musico-dramatic context capture the essence of an entire work. One thinks of examples such as Scriabin's "Mystic" chord, Richard STRAUSS's "Till" chord, and Stravinsky's "Petroushka" chord, all emblematic of, and uniquely identified with, the harmonic/dramatic *esprit de corps* of the works they inhabit. Among such iconic sonorities, though, the greatest is certainly Richard Wagner's "Tristan" chord.

While it may be striking to imagine that one sonority is capable of summing up the sensuous ambiguity that sits at the heart of Wagner's TRISTAN UND ISOLDE, it is undeniable that this musical object is one whose content and context have been treated as such by commentators and scholars since the premiere of the work. The following is a two-part exploration of the reasons for the lasting fascination with the chord, considering, first, its abstract harmonic content and, second, the various contexts it occupies.

The "Tristan" chord is the first sonority in Wagner's MUSIC DRAMA *Tristan und Isolde* to include more than one pitch simultaneously (Example 22). Its primacy, however, is salient largely because its harmonic content renders it ambiguous.

In fact, the jury remains out on whether the "Tristan" chord is a chord at all, or whether its uppermost pitch – G♯ – is rather a decorative tone. In recent years, opinion has shifted in favor of treating the G♯ as part of the sonority, for both motivic and harmonic reasons to be discussed shortly. Nevertheless, one must concede that its harmonic status remains in doubt and has contributed significantly to the chord's notoriety.

The chord comprises four distinct pitches – F, B, D♯, and G♯. Taken out of context, it sounds like a harmonic object many analysts term a half-diminished seventh chord (that is, a diminished triad – F, A♭, C♭ – plus a minor seventh above the root F – E♭), though such an interpretation requires respelling three of the notes – G♯, B, and D♯ – as their enharmonic equivalents: A♭, C♭, and E♭. (Such enharmonic spellings are common in Romantic-era music, where a high premium is placed on abstruse harmonic functionality.) The half-diminished seventh sonority was often used in the late-Romantic period because of its great functional flexibility and potential for ambiguity.

In order to understand the power of the "Tristan" chord as emblematic of an entire music drama, it is necessary to comprehend it also as a motivic object. Not only does the sonority arise and recur at moments of both formal

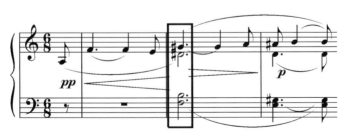

22. *Tristan* chord

and dramatic salience throughout *Tristan und Isolde*, but it often returns at the same pitch level and with a characteristic ORCHESTRATION that features double reeds. Many commentators consider the chord to be part of a *LEITMOTIV* – a musico-dramatic object that develops across the drama and recurs to recall in the mind of the listener the musical and emotional residue of earlier scenes. The specific label given to the *Leitmotiv* containing the "Tristan" chord differs from source to source, but a common name is "the glance." In any case, the *Leitmotiv* symbolizes the unrequited longing between the opera's title characters.

The chord's motivic status as a singularity is established in the opening measures of the opera's *Vorspiel* ("Prelude"). The first three phrases of the *Vorspiel* each lead to an arrival on a "Tristan" chord, and each subsequently resolves to what sounds like a dominant seventh chord of A, C, and E, respectively. This creates an implied arpeggiation of an A minor triad, ostensibly the key of the *Vorspiel*, though said key, like the "Tristan" chord itself, remains ambiguous and hotly debated. These three opening statements are often erroneously referred to as transpositions of one another. In fact, the second is a near transposition of the first (the opening melodic lines differing by a semitone), but the third is not even close. Its "Tristan" chord seems specially engineered by Wagner not only to fit the aforementioned arpeggiation of dominant seventh chords, but also to retain the chromatically rising melodic line evident from the opening of the *Vorspiel*, the falling bass semitone that leads into each statement of the "Tristan" chord, and the motivic, half-diminished sound of the sonority itself.

It is also important to consider the chord within its larger harmonic context. While it is always treated as a dissonance, the "Tristan" chord enjoys a flexible manner of resolution. In the *Vorspiel*, for instance, it functions not only as a special type of pre-dominant sonority in A minor that theorists refer to as a chord of the augmented sixth, but also, near the end of the *Vorspiel*, as a supertonic seventh chord that resolves to a dominant in E♭ minor, a key far distant from the opening implication of A. Its usage at the opera's opening is balanced by its appearance at the end, as a plagal resolution to the tonic symbolizing the spiritual apotheosis achieved in the work's closing moments.

In addition to the reams of commentary and music that *Tristan* and its iconic sonority have inspired, we might also note the work's lasting influence in the many parodies that the "Tristan" chord has provoked. Among them are statements in Debussy's piano piece, "Golliwogg's Cakewalk" from the suite for piano entitled *Children's Corner*; Benjamin Britten's opera, *Albert Herring*; Richard STRAUSS's symphonic poem *Till Eulenspiegels lustige Streiche*; and Peter Schikele's bassoon quartet *Last Tango in Bayreuth*.

MATTHEW BRIBITZER-STULL

See also MODERN MUSIC

Tristan und Isolde (Tristan and Isolde, WWV 90), *Handlung* (literally: action) in three acts. Final text written in ZURICH between August and September 1857; music composed in Zurich, VENICE, Lucerne, and PARIS between December 1856 and August 1859; first published by BREITKOPF & HÄRTEL, Leipzig, on 13 January 1860; first performed at the Königliches Hof- und National-Theater,

Munich, 10 June 1865. Cond. Hans von BÜLOW. For cast information, see Appendix 10: Stage productions.

Soon after the world premiere of *Tristan und Isolde*, Wagner wrote to LUDWIG II of Bavaria that "this wondrous Tristan is – complete. You know that everyone else who has written a Tristan has left it incomplete – starting with GOTTFRIED VON STRASSBURG. The old misfortune almost seemed to want to dog my work too, for it was only complete when as drama it fully and physically came to life in front of us and spoke directly to our hearts and senses" (13 June 1865). The process of creating and performing *Tristan und Isolde* was indeed unusual. Unlike nearly all Wagner's other major works it had no roots in the creative plans he made during the 1840s and early 1850s: no hints in letters or diaries, no drafts, no musical sketches. And yet the time between his decision in the mid-1850s to compose it and the appearance of the engraved full score in January 1860 was a record. No other work by Wagner was imagined and published so fast. Acknowledging that it had erupted like a volcano in his life, he wrote in September 1859 to Eduard DEVRIENT, Director of the Court Theatre in Karlsruhe, that it was "the *most musical* score" he had "ever written and was ever likely to write" with "the most vivid dramatic allusions totally at one with the dynamic of its musical texture" (Wagner's emphasis). In a single sentence he gave two reasons for *Tristan und Isolde*'s future seismic influence on Western culture. Not only was it one of the most daring musical adventures in harmony and form ever attempted by any composer anywhere, its fusion of advanced musical techniques with ideas about sex, death, adultery, heroism, sickness, burgeoning insanity, to name but a few, also opened an entirely new world to many at the cutting edge of a rapidly emerging MODERNITY. By the beginning of the twentieth century, no one seriously interested in theater, literature, the visual arts, psychoanalysis, cultural politics, and film could afford to ignore it.

1. Nineteenth-century adaptations of the Tristan legend
2. Wagner's conception
3. Perfumed gardens; or how *Tristan* changed music
4. Synopsis
5. First performances
6. Reception

1. Nineteenth-century adaptations of the Tristan legend

Wagner and Ludwig II were both acquainted with the work of German scholars, who in the first part of the nineteenth century had drawn the attention of the public to French and German medieval versions of the Tristan legend. Gottfried von Strassburg himself said that his romance *Tristan* – Wagner's main medieval source – was based on Thomas of Britain's earlier twelfth-century version of the legend of *Tristan and Iseult*. Gottfried's text was unfinished at his death (*c.* 1210) and Thomas's text only partially survived, ironically with precisely those episodes of the story Gottfried omitted. (However, 154 previously unknown lines of Thomas's version discovered in Britain in the early 1990s in the Cumbrian Record Office in Carlisle tend to support Gottfried's claim.) Wagner knew the remains of Thomas's version, and he was well acquainted with the completion of Gottfried's text by two later Middle

High German poets, Ulrich von Türheim and Heinrich von Freiberg. He also purchased another edition of Gottfried's text in the 1840s, this time completed by a modern scholar, Hermann Kurtz. Any creative interest he may have had in Tristan at this time has not been recorded.

Wagner's initial reticence and the collision of the Tristan legend with nineteenth-century sexual ethics are perhaps not coincidental. A fine literary specimen such as Gottfried's *Tristan* that also happened to be about a celebration of adultery was always going to be difficult to reconcile with bourgeois propriety. Most poets simply changed the story. Julius Mosen, for instance, made Isolde openly confess her guilt as soon as she reaches Marke's court, leaving plenty of time for her due punishment (1841). Robert Reinick's scenario for Robert Schumann of a projected five-act opera *Tristan und Isolde* (*c.* 1846) presents the lovers as charming figures accidentally caught up in bizarrely episodic adventures.

Wagner's friend Karl RITTER showed him a presumably not dissimilar adaptation in 1854, which has not survived, though Wagner's astute comments in his autobiography have: "[My young friend] had confined himself to the boisterous episodes of the romance, while I had been immediately attracted to its profound tragedy, sensing that everything inessential to its main trajectory had to be cut away. Returning from a walk one day I jotted down for myself the contents of three acts in concentrated form to be worked on in detail at some future date" (ML/E 511, translation modified).

2. Wagner's conception

Wagner's "jotted down" three-act scenario does not exist. Indeed, it is still not entirely clear why he began *Tristan* at all, given that he was at a crucial stage in composing the *Ring*. His "affair" with Mathilde WESENDONCK, the wife of wealthy silk merchant Otto Wesendonck, easily his most generous patron after Ludwig II, is usually described as a major factor. There is good reason to be skeptical about this. From what remains of their correspondence it is clear that Mathilde was an intelligent woman who recognized the huge importance of *Tristan* and became a sounding board for Wagner's ideas about it. In his imagination he was smitten, it is true, but no evidence exists that she felt the same way.

The most likely stimulus for the start of serious work on *Tristan* was the onset of the composition of *SIEGFRIED* in December 1856. Finding the music for this work seems to have sparked off a chain of associations in Wagner's mind about birth, death, motherless heroes, and above all about the repeal of violence with acts of self-sacrifice and healing that led him to abandon the idea (first mentioned in a letter of 16 December 1854 to Franz Liszt) of using the Tristan legend to erect a "monument to love." Under the influence of a more complex understanding of SCHOPENHAUER's major philosophical writings he decided to create a drama of greater existential complexity, drawn from medieval and modern sources, about the "torment of love" (a phrase to be found in Gottfried von Strassburg) and the escape from that torment into the realm of night and death.

In the first prose sketches from late 1856 and 1857, PARSIFAL visits the wounded Tristan on his sickbed. It was the "starting-point for the atmosphere of the entire project," according to Wagner's *Annals* (February 1868), and indeed it opened a veritable can of psychoanalytical worms. Tristan announces that his "mother died as she gave birth to me" (*Meine Mutter starb als sie mich gebar*), echoing SIEGFRIED's similar words in *Siegfried* Act I, and "now I'm living, I'm dying of having been born. Why?" (*nun ich lebe, sterbe ich daran, geboren worden zu sein: warum das?*) He is answered by "Parsifal's refrain." Three conspicuously motherless heroes were thus linked in Wagner's imagination, all destined to appease the badness of the world with their death or self-denial. The intertextual links were deliberate; but even for Wagner the virtual meeting of three heroes in the same work was too much. The reference to Siegfried was dropped and Parsifal's response to Tristan turned into *Parsifal*, a work he had still to write. The gaping painful wound of AMFORTAS in this work, Wagner confidently predicted in a letter to Mathilde Wesendonck (30 May 1859), would be "an unimaginable intensification of my Tristan in Act III."

3. Perfumed gardens; or how *Tristan* changed music

When Wagner told Eduard Devrient in September 1859 that *Tristan und Isolde* was "the *most musical* score" he had ever written, he had in mind both music at one with the idea of METAPHOR and a celebration of instrumental music for its own sake. The paradox explains why *Tristan* can have the texture and mood of a German *Lied* at one moment and a much broader symphonic ambition at another, a subtle movement between two kinds of music that expresses the fraught tension between the private and the public at the core of the drama. Wagner wrote five songs to texts by Mathilde Wesendonck (the WESENDONCK LIEDER, WWV 91) in the early stages of composing *Tristan*, describing two of them as "studies" for the larger work – "Träume" (Dreams) and "Im Treibhaus" (In the Greenhouse). And, indeed, on the broader canvas of *Tristan* in the love duet of the second act ("O sink' hernieder") and at the opening of the third, the music of the songs seems not only more intimately allied to specific feeling but also independent of exterior meaning the more it expands into Wagner's symphonic universe. The texts of the songs allude to the evocative powers of dreams and the "sweet perfume" of high-arching vegetal growth. Potent reference points were Schopenhauer's work on dreams (and earlier studies on dreams and SLEEP consulted by Schopenhauer and Wagner) and the "inseparable embrace" of ivy and vine over Tristan and Isolde's graves the medieval sources vividly describe.

But even these powerful references seem to wilt in *Tristan*'s white-hot musical environment. Music as organic vegetal growth is a metaphor Wagner consciously exploited in *Tristan* to create development with inwardly tense harmonies and rapidly expanding melodic strands that constantly verge on the idea of music for its own sake (see also ABSOLUTE MUSIC). The metaphor dominates the score and its dramatic *raison d'être*; moreover, it made an indelible impression on later musicians and artists willing to blend the vegetal and the musical in the same radical spirit. Arnold SCHOENBERG's *Herzgewächse* (Foliage of the Heart), Op. 20, a vertiginous setting of Maurice Maeterlinck's poem of the same name for coloratura soprano, celesta, harmonium, and harp, is – to cite just one example – still one of the most original and striking compositions of the early twentieth century.

Wagner's unusual adaptation of the Tristan sources also had a profoundly musical purpose from the start. Events are never episodes stacked together as literal presence in a ramshackle woodpile of epic adventure as they are in most other nineteenth-century adaptations. Rather they are gradually revealed as bitter memory and delirious recollection on the borders of sanity. At a stroke, extraneous detail is removed so that a drama can emerge relying for its power not on picaresque action, but on an increasingly anguished reaction to situations that exist only in the recesses of the characters' remembrance of them.

At first the method seems akin to mid-nineteenth-century analytic drama (e.g., Friedrich Hebbel) where events precipitating the crisis pre-date the beginning of the drama and are only revealed as the action nears its climax. But the resemblance is superficial. In *Tristan* the tragic import of fatal recollection goes far deeper entirely because of Wagner's clear-sighted view of music and the role it had to play. The subjective response to past events – the fleeting vividness of doomed memory, the final flush of exhausted vitality – is carried by a continuum of wildly proliferating harmonies, melodic tendrils, and a sense of permanently open-ended musical growth, the seeds of which are planted in the mind of the spectator at the very start. In *Ecce homo* (1888) NIETZSCHE called it, accurately, "sweet and shuddery infinity," almost as if he were entering a perfumed garden of the human soul. Just as accurately, Wagner wrote in his autobiography that *Tristan und Isolde* was "the most audacious and original work of my life" (ML/E 588). After it, music would never be the same again.

4. Synopsis

Act I. An awning on board TRISTAN's ship during a crossing from Ireland to Cornwall. ISOLDE is being taken by Tristan to Cornwall against her will to marry King Marke. She bids her confidante BRANGÄNE to fetch Tristan in order to confront him. KURWENAL, Tristan's trusted companion, sings mockingly about Morold, a famously powerful knight of Ireland killed by Tristan. Isolde furiously confides to Brangäne that Morold was her fiancé, who in his last battle seriously wounded Tristan. Tristan returned to Ireland sick and dying. Isolde found him, but while curing him noticed a notch in his sword perfectly matching a splinter extracted from Morold's body. She raised a sword to kill Tristan, but as he looked longingly into her eyes, she let it fall. Now in return he is forcing her into a loveless marriage. Brangäne reminds her of the elixir of love, given to Isolde by her mother to arouse passion in her ageing husband-to-be. But Isolde wants only the elixir of death. Tristan approaches. Isolde demands vengeance for the death of Morold and offers a drink of atonement. Sensing the potion's ominous purpose, Tristan drinks to Isolde; she wrenches the cup from his hand and drains it. Expecting to die, they feel passionate love instead, oblivious to outside cries of jubilation as the ship prepares to land. Brangäne senses that her well-intended deceit of surreptitiously substituting the elixir of love for the elixir of death will lead to tragedy. Tristan sings agonizingly of "bliss dedicated to deceit" (*Trug-geweihtes Glücke*), his voice quickly giving way to general rejoicing at the arrival of the new queen.

Act II. A garden in front of Isolde's apartment in King Marke's royal fortress in Cornwall. It is a summer night and the king's hunting party can be heard setting out. The torch burning by the door is to be extinguished by Brangäne as a pre-arranged signal giving Tristan the all clear to be with Isolde. But Melot, Tristan's ambitious rival, has arranged the hunt at this unusual time, Brangäne insists, to lure the lovers into a trap. Isolde is scornful and impatiently extinguishes the torch herself, ordering Brangäne to stand watch in the tower. Tristan enters and the lovers fall passionately into each other's arms. They curse their worst enemy, "the spiteful day" (*dem tückischen Tage*), and sing a hymn to a night of love. Brangäne's suspicions prove to be correct. The lovers' ecstatic duet is brutally interrupted at its climax as Kurwenal bursts in to protect his master from King Marke, Melot, and several people of the court entering urgently to discover the truth of Tristan's betrayal. But Melot's priggish triumph in unmasking the lovers' deceit has an unexpected effect: instead of meting out punishment, the king enters into a heart-searching monologue. Where is honor in the world if even his most trusted knight betrays him? Tristan's response is both compassionate and critical. The king can never experience what he, Tristan, is going through: humanity's essential futility – death's unforgiving truth – is beyond his grasp. Tristan invites Isolde to follow him to a land where the sun does not shine. She acquiesces. Tristan suddenly attacks Melot, deliberately dropping his sword when Melot retaliates. He falls wounded into Kurwenal's arms.

Act III. Tristan's fortress in Brittany. The opening music conveys the profound loneliness of the wounded Tristan as he lies on the Breton coast. A melancholy tune played by an old shepherd awakens him from a deep coma. Overjoyed, Kurwenal tells how he brought Tristan back to his homeland; he has sent a ship for Isolde, the only one who can heal Tristan's wound. The shepherd will play a joyful new melody when the ship is sighted. But for now, and long into the scene, only "the old melody" (*die alte Weise*) is heard intermittently from the shepherd as Tristan subjects himself to a lacerating self-examination about his past and his longing for death. In demented excitement, he lays a "curse on the terrible drink" (*verflucht sei, furchtbarer Trank*), the elixir of love at the root of his burgeoning insanity. He imagines he sees the ship approaching with Isolde transfigured and full of grace, when suddenly the shepherd sounds the new, joyful melody marking her actual arrival. Tristan rips the bandages off his wound and leaps from his sickbed to meet Isolde, only to die in her arms with her name on his lips. A second ship arrives, and King Marke, Melot, and their retinue pour into the castle. Kurwenal kills Melot, only to collapse fatally wounded at the feet of the dead Tristan. Brangäne tells Isolde that the king has come to Brittany to forgive Tristan. Isolde is deaf to her words. She sees Tristan awakened to new life in eternal death and falls gently, as if transfigured, into Brangäne's arms.

5. First performances

For Wagner no work was complete before it had been performed – a down-to-earth principle that accounts in part for the swift genesis of *Tristan und Isolde*. In a letter to Liszt in December 1856, he proposed interrupting work on the *Ring* to write "a simple piece – like *Tristan*" which would give him "the advantage of getting opera houses to produce it quickly." He even made an agreement with Breitkopf & Härtel to speed up the publishing of the score by delivering his manuscript an act at a time so that they could start printing it before he had finished composing it.

Ironically, when the score appeared in 1860 it was generally declared to be "unperformable." Having written it quickly in under three years, Wagner was forced to take another six, more than double the time, to overcome prejudice about its viability. Vain hope, nervous letters, frantic rehearsal – but also oases of good will – all contributed to the dizzying rollercoaster ride. Strasbourg, Karlsruhe, PARIS, Rio de Janeiro, DRESDEN, Hanover, Stuttgart, Prague, and VIENNA: in the end none of these opera houses would touch it.

Wagner conducted the Prelude in three ORCHESTRAL CONCERTS in Paris in January and February 1860. But it was in Vienna in the following year that he first heard vocal parts of *Tristan* with orchestra. For a free Saturday morning in late October, he invited the instrumentalists of the Court Opera to participate voluntarily in a two-hour run-through of the Prelude, the introduction and love duet of the second act, and the final scene (twice each). Luise MEYER-DUSTMANN (Isolde) and Marie Destinn (Brangäne) sang their roles brilliantly from memory. Vienna's most famous tenor Alois Anders (Tristan) was present, but failed to utter a sound. The composer Peter CORNELIUS described the occasion as "two beautiful hours."

Trying to cope with Anders's inadequacy (including concessions about drastic cuts) ultimately doomed the Vienna enterprise. In July 1862 Wagner met Ludwig and Malvina Schnorr von CAROLSFELD, two married singers who proved they could master the leading roles. Less than two years later Ludwig II unexpectedly acceded to the Bavarian throne and immediately invited Wagner to MUNICH. The young king had already heard Wagner's by now favorite tenor sing the title role of *LOHENGRIN* in Munich and readily agreed to the participation of the Schnorrs in a production of *Tristan*. Wagner also encountered little resistance in arranging for his protégé Hans von BÜLOW to come from Berlin to rehearse and conduct the work.

After nearly twenty-five orchestral rehearsals and many delays, the premiere conducted by Bülow finally took place (without cuts) in the Royal Court Theater in Munich on 10 June 1865. Wagner supervised the entire production from first to last.

Tragedy struck three weeks after the last of four successful performances when Ludwig Schnorr von Carolsfeld died of typhus on 21 July. Discontent in some quarters about the supposed indecency of *Tristan und Isolde* now spiraled into the perception that the dangerous work had "killed" its lead singer. Wagner tried to allay fears with some dignified reminiscences of the great artist (1868) that played down the actual circumstances of his death. Two more performances eventually took place in 1869 with Heinrich and Therese VOGL in the title roles; these marked the end of Bülow's four-year sojourn in Munich, a time he described as a "nightmare."

Other productions in the composer's lifetime took place in Weimar (1874), Berlin (1876, the only other one supervised by Wagner), KÖNIGSBERG (1881), LEIPZIG, and Hamburg (1882). The British premiere in LONDON conducted by Hans RICHTER at the Theatre Royal, Drury Lane on 20 June 1882 was the first performance outside Germany.

6. Reception

Reactions to *Tristan und Isolde* were not confined to the history of music and opera, especially in the two decades after Wagner's death when its reputation as the *ne plus ultra* of European artistic achievement gradually took hold. It touched spoken theater, literature, philosophy, film, and not least psychoanalytic theory. The adjective "Tristanesque" even suggests a separation of the work from its composer: as Elliot Zuckerman once observed, very few works of art live a verbal life of their own.

The critical fact about *Tristan* is that once the hullabaloo about Wagner's chicanery (and most of his heirs) fades away, this astonishing work still stands head and shoulders above anything comparable. That large swathes of the nineteenth century supposedly found the work "repugnant" (Clara Schumann's word for it) is a myth far outweighed by the near euphoric testimony of scores of witnesses. Peter Cornelius was already calling it the "greatest piece of music since Beethoven" (1861) before it was even performed. Nietzsche was still affected by it after turning against Wagner. Indeed, so powerful was its impact that even devotees saw fit to temper their ardor. The French author Romain Rolland spoke surprisingly of its "sober" drama and restraint "almost carried to excess" (1915). Jon Vickers, one of the greatest tenors ever to sing Tristan, said in a Radio-Canada broadcast introducing one of his own performances that Wagner's "idea that the highest love can only be fulfilled in death is a thesis that I reject completely" (1976). Rolland's almost perverse sobriety and the firm conviction of Vickers's singing of the role together with his equally firm rational rejection of its *raison d'être* are conflicted in the same Nietzschean spirit that has always been a significant element in the reception of *Tristan*.

Its influence on literature and theater was most potent during the twenty years preceding World War I. From Gabriele D'Annunzio's novel *The Triumph of Death* (1894) to Thomas MANN's novella *Death in Venice* (1912) many tried their hand at literary configurations, inspired by *Tristan*, of eroticism, disease, and death. And it is not hard to see Wagner's masterpiece at the centre of Adolphe APPIA's influential rethinking of the relation between lighting and performance space in his *Musique et mise en scène* (1897), published two years later in German and soon leaving its mark on productions of *Tristan* conducted by Arturo TOSCANINI at La Scala, Milan (1900), and Gustav MAHLER in Vienna (1903).

If the impact of *Tristan* was colossal during the late nineteenth and early twentieth centuries, however, its later influence was more sporadic; and it met with more hostility than before. Resisting *Tristan* in the twentieth century in any case had more creative significance than simply succumbing to its seductive power. The deliberate musical understatement of Claude Debussy's opera *Pelléas et Mélisande* (1902) set in train a tantalizing I-love-it / I-don't-love-it syndrome decisive for all conscientious modernists. Even Schoenberg's notorious serial method in the early 1920s, after two decades of allegiance to *Tristan*'s seductive chromatic labyrinths, can be seen as a final escape from the gravitational pull it exerted, and continued to exert, on Richard STRAUSS, Franz Schreker, and Erich Wolfgang Korngold, to name only a few. The most below-the-belt instance of anti-*Tristan* sentiment is Hanns Eisler's setting of the famous opening chords of the *Tristan* Prelude (see TRISTAN CHORD) in Bertolt Brecht's epic parable *Round Heads and Pointed Heads* (1934–6) to the words: "cash makes you randy."

But any demeaning of *Tristan*, frivolous or not, did not banish it from the AVANT-GARDE entirely, especially in FRANCE. Olivier Messiaen's *Tristan* trilogy, *Harawi* (1945), *Cinq rechants* (1948), and the perfumed excesses of the ten-movement symphony *Turangalîla* (1946–8), revived interest among young composers, though not without skepticism. Messiaen's own pupil Pierre BOULEZ was a stalwart critic of his teacher's attempt in *Turangalîla* to surpass the ecstatic verve of *Tristan*; yet the sensuousness and open-ended form of Wagner's music left palpable traces too in his ambitious settings of Stéphane Mallarmé's poetry in *Pli selon pli* (1957–62). Boulez also accepted an invitation from Wagner's grandson WIELAND WAGNER to conduct the latter's production of *Tristan* at the Osaka Festival (1967) with Birgit NILSSON (Isolde), Wolfgang WINDGASSEN (Tristan), and Hans HOTTER (King Marke). It was filmed in black and white and survives as the only complete video of a Wieland Wagner production.

Distinguished recordings of *Tristan und Isolde* are perhaps the most lasting remnants of its impact on modern culture. They include two conducted respectively by Carlos Kleiber (1980) and Anthony Pappano (2005) with brilliant singers – Margaret Price as Isolde (Kleiber) and Placido Domingo as Tristan (Pappano) – who never performed their roles in the theater. Indeed, other legendary studio productions led by Wilhelm FURTWÄNGLER (1952) and Herbert von KARAJAN (1972) seem just as utopian now in their ambition to capture the "liberal and splendid in passions about art" that Wagner – as he put it in a letter to Liszt (13 September 1860) – saw as a non-negotiable condition for any outstanding performance of the work. The conditions of modern opera houses are still not wholly commensurate with this ideal. And fabulous support for studio opera production in the recording industry has relentlessly declined in the twenty-first century. Still, as Wagner himself observed, nothing can replace *Tristan und Isolde* fully and physically coming to life in front of an audience, speaking directly to its hearts and senses. Superb studio recordings made without regard to the day-to-day encumbrances of actual theater practice, however, may well be – promises held out by twenty-first-century new media notwithstanding – the only meaningful relic of Wagner's most daring challenge to theater and music we have left.

JOHN DEATHRIDGE

Robert Bailey, ed., *Prelude and Transfiguration from "Tristan und Isolde,"* Norton Critical Score (New York: Norton, 1985).

Eric Chafe, *The Tragic and the Ecstatic: The Musical Revolution of Wagner's "Tristan und Isolde"* (New York: Oxford University Press, 2005).

John Deathridge, *Wagner Beyond Good and Evil* (see bibliography).

Arthur Groos, ed., *Richard Wagner: "Tristan und Isolde,"* Cambridge Opera Handbook (Cambridge University Press, 2011).

Jean-Jacques Nattiez, *Wagner Androgyne: A Study in Interpretation*, trans. S. Spencer (Princeton University Press, 1997).

Roger Scruton, *Death-Devoted Heart: Sex and the Sacred in Wagner's "Tristan und Isolde"* (New York: Oxford University Press, 2004).

Elliot Zuckerman, *The First Hundred Years of Wagner's "Tristan"* (New York: Columbia University Press, 1964).

Über die Anwendung der Musik auf das Drama (On the Application of Music to Drama).
Wagner's essay appeared in the BAYREUTHER BLÄTTER in November 1879.
Wagner describes it as a follow-up to *Über das Opern-Dichten und Komponieren im Besondern* (On Opera Libretti and Composition in Particular), which had
appeared two months earlier, and as a response to his conviction that there
was more to be said about the similarities and differences between symphonic
and dramatic composition. Discussing the symphonies of Haydn and
BEETHOVEN (the first movement of the *Eroica* in particular) Wagner returned
to an idea first outlined many years before in *Das KUNSTWERK DER
ZUKUNFT* (The Artwork of the Future, 1849/50): the basis of the symphony
is "the dance melody" (PW 6:176). Moreover, in symphonic music "you never
have two themes of totally opposite character set against one another in one
movement" (PW 6:176).

Wagner argues that symphonic composition should always have the aim of
establishing and sustaining a "unity which maintains our interest and keeps
the work's overall effect before us" (PW 6:176–7). In the "program music" of
BERLIOZ, WEBER, and LISZT – and even when, as with Weber's Overture
to *Der Freischütz*, sonata form governs the design – there was evidence of
"an unconventional and passionate character such as purely symphonic
music seemed destined to avoid entirely" (PW 6:179). Nevertheless, Wagner
claims that

> the new form of dramatic music, if it is to continue to constitute a work of
> art, must maintain the same unity as a sonata movement: and to achieve this
> form it must integrate the whole drama from beginning to end. This unity is
> underpinned by a basic web of themes threaded through the fabric of the
> whole work. As in a symphonic movement, these themes are contrasted,
> correlated, re-formed, separated and linked together again: the difference is
> that it is the dramatic action on the stage which determines the separations
> and reconnections, which in the symphony were dependent originally on the
> motions of the dance.
>
> (PW 6:183)

After a brief reproof to Hans von WOLZOGEN for discussing LEITMOTIVE
more for their dramatic effect than "as elements of the musical structure" (PW
6:184), Wagner ends the essay with a discussion of short extracts from
Das RHEINGOLD, *GÖTTERDÄMMERUNG*, and *LOHENGRIN* which provides
the most explicit defense of his belief that his dramatic music could still be
symphonically unified as long as the strong contrasts of "rhetorical dialectics"
were dramatically convincing. For his final example of "transformation and

23. Elsa's Dream (*Lohengrin*, Act I)

use of motives such as the drama demands but the symphony cannot permit" (PW 6:189), he cites the theme which appears in Act I of *Lohengrin* "at the end of ELSA's first arioso when she is lost to the world in narration of her DREAM." This short phrase extends its basic A♭ tonality with a sequence of progressions dividing the octave by minor thirds – from A♭ to C♭, D, F, and back to A♭ (Example 23).

It therefore provides "a web of distant progressions" of a kind which is "not imaginable for the basic subject of a symphonic movement" (PW 6:189). Wagner then wraps up his argument in typically combative style, declaring that the less said about recent symphonies the better.   ARNOLD WHITTALL

Über die Benennung "Musikdrama" (On the Term "Music Drama"). Wagner's short essay was published in the *Musikalisches Wochenblatt* for 8 November 1872. With the RING still unfinished, but with the foundation stone for the Bayreuth FESTIVAL THEATER laid in May of that year and plans for its inauguration taking shape, Wagner offered a few skeptical thoughts about the difficulty and (he also seemed to suggest) the irrelevance of seeking a fixed and immutable label for the genre to which his later works belonged. Twenty years after he had called his major essay on the subject OPER UND DRAMA (Opera and Drama, 1851), and not *Oper und Musikdrama*, Wagner's conviction that "opera" could never fulfill the social, political, and even religious functions of that Greek drama on which he modeled his own principles was as strong as ever. No less powerful was his awareness that the public remained reluctant to call his own works anything but operas.

If, as he argued, the ancient Athenians were content to leave the incomparable works of their greatest dramatists generically nameless, he too was content to offer his admirers "nameless works of art" – or "nameless artistic deeds" (PW 5:304). The most resonant descriptive phrase in this essay comes when Wagner declares with a paradoxical rhetorical flourish that he would like to regard his dramas as "deeds of music made visible" (PW 5:303). This occurs on the way to a sardonic celebration of the fact that in Act II of *TRISTAN UND ISOLDE*, already notorious for its radicalism, "little or nothing happens except music," and "there is practically nothing to see" (PW 5:303–4).

At the beginning of the essay, Wagner rehearses the growing tendency to use the term *music drama* despite the logical difficulties of thinking of a drama "for the purpose of music" as anything other than a libretto to be set to music. If, as he argues, the important thing is for music to function as the "womb" giving birth to true drama, then it might be difficult to imagine why opera, to which music is so fundamental, cannot also be drama. However, if what is most apparent to opera audiences is not dramatic *music* but virtuoso *singers*, it is clear that the personalities of performers are preventing that magically intense and immediate interaction between what the dramatist has created and what the attending acolytes perceive, which was Wagner's social and cultural ideal for his own artistic productions.

After 1872, the experience of bringing the *Ring* and *PARSIFAL* to audiences at BAYREUTH might have made Wagner rather less idealistic about the "nameless" character of the events that he had devised. Yet – apart from choosing a work-specific term avoiding "drama" for *Parsifal* (*BÜHNENWEIHFESTSPIEL*) – he did not return to the topic of generic naming in his writings. As a result, and given that it was never a practical proposition to leave Wagner's most richly constructed and inspiring compositions generically nameless, the term *music drama* remains a convenient label, even if it is thought of more as a subgenre of opera than as something fundamentally un-operatic. ARNOLD WHITTALL

Über die "Goethe-Stiftung." Brief an F. Liszt (Concerning the Goethe-Foundation, 1851), Wagner's response to Liszt's writing and activities on behalf of a GOETHE Foundation in Weimar. In the summer of 1849, in connection with the Goethe centenary jubilee, a group of Berlin intellectual luminaries proposed the creation of a benevolent, art-centered Goethe Foundation, a concept that found strong support in Weimar. Liszt picked up the idea and developed it into a regular competition for the arts in the sense of the Greek Olympic Games, which he expressed in a memorandum to Duke Carl Alexander entitled *De la Fondation-Goethe à Weimar*. This document served as the basis for Liszt's eponymous book of early 1851, which BROCKHAUS issued in LEIPZIG (in French). The published version retained the core concept of a recurring competition in Weimar for new artistic creations, both to honor Goethe's legacy and to elevate standards for the arts. Liszt's plan envisioned a national subscription in order to raise the needed funds – the foundation would rely upon nationally recognized experts for the adjudication itself.

Liszt sent the book to Wagner, who responded with an extended letter dated 8 May 1851. Wagner criticized the proposal, because it participated in the fragmentation of art and amounted to an "artistic lottery of the Goethe corporation" (SSD 5:6–7). He declared that only "true" poets and musicians who dedicate themselves to "scenic drama" should qualify for support. For him, the highest goal of such a foundation would be the establishment of an "original theater" in Weimar, for the creation of the "dramatic art work" (SSD 5:16). In this letter, Wagner refers to his pamphlet *Ein THEATER IN ZÜRICH*

(A Theater in Zurich, 1851), which had just appeared in print and spelled out his conditions for the needed theater (this passage is omitted in the published version).

Liszt replied to Wagner with the suggestion that the letter be reprinted in a periodical; Wagner initially gave Liszt carte blanche, but he ultimately did make some minor editorial changes to the text, which appeared in the NEUE ZEITSCHRIFT FÜR MUSIK on 5 March 1852, as "Ein Brief an Franz Liszt über die Goethe-Stiftung." Liszt's reasons for delaying the publication are not clear; however, since May of 1851, Wagner had made considerable progress in his plans for the RING tetralogy. Although Liszt had Wagner and his works in mind as part of his plans for Weimar, the composer's political difficulties were a liability for the realization of that intention. And despite the serious efforts of Liszt and others in Weimar, the Goethe Foundation never became a reality.

JAMES DEAVILLE

D. Altenburg and B. Schilling-Wang, eds., "Die Goethe-Stiftung," *Franz Liszt: Sämtliche Schriften*, vol. 3 (Wiesbaden: Breitkopf & Härtel, 1997).

Über Franz Liszts symphonische Dichtungen (On Franz Liszt's Symphonic Poems; open letter to Marie Wittgenstein, 1857). Essay in the form of an "open letter" to the young daughter, Marie, of Franz LISZT's consort during his years as music director for the Weimar court, the Ukrainian-Polish Princess Carolyne von SAYN-WITTGENSTEIN. Liszt turned from his legendary career as a virtuoso pianist to focus on "serious" composition exploring new forms, styles, and genres under the aegis of the Grand Duke of Weimar at the same time Wagner was driven into political exile in Switzerland. On top of his many other creative activities, Liszt took up the cause of promoting Wagner's operas through productions, TRANSCRIPTIONS, journalism, and, not least, direct financial support of his fellow composer. Liszt began to publish and perform his own series of "symphonic poems" in the mid-1850s, generating considerable resistance from early audiences and critics. Wagner had occasion to learn something of these new works in the course of several visits from Liszt between 1853 and 1856, and in early 1857 he decided to return the favor of Liszt's advocacy with a published appreciation of his friend's controversial experiments in symphonic program music.

The "letter" to Marie von Wittgenstein was completed on 17 February 1857 and published in the NEUE ZEITSCHRIFT FÜR MUSIK on 10 April 1857. Wagner first addresses skeptics of Liszt's new-found calling as a composer of original, large-scale orchestral works by praising the scope of Liszt's innate musicality and highlighting the "creative" dimension of his performances of such challenging works as BEETHOVEN's "Hammerklavier" Sonata, Op. 106, or the C minor Sonata, Op. 111. He then moves, somewhat obliquely, to address critical concerns about the form (or "formlessness") of the symphonic poems, surely in the awareness that these same criticisms were increasingly being directed at his own scores. Wagner notes the genealogy of Liszt's works in operatic and concert overtures, citing in particular Beethoven's *Leonore* Overture No. 3. The challenge facing the composer of a dramatic or "poetic- ally" motivated OVERTURE, he explains, is how far the seemingly self-evident, internally justified designs of "ABSOLUTE MUSIC" (such as a slow introduction followed by a sonata-allegro form) may be modified for the purposes of dramatic, characteristic, or expressive signification. Beethoven, he argues, went not far enough, whereas BERLIOZ, in the Adagio from *Roméo et Juliette*, went too far. Liszt's success lies in the all-important capacity to frame his "poetic object" in relatively generalized terms susceptible to expression through intelligible musical designs. But where DANCE-based instrumental forms had traditionally relied on a simple principle of alternating thematic units (*Wechsel*), new poetically motivated forms such as the symphonic poem (or, implicitly, the Wagnerian MUSIC DRAMA) can and should implement a principle of development or evolution (*Entwicklung*). The discussion of instrumental or "absolute" music in the essay probably reflects Wagner's reading of SCHOPENHAUER's chapters on music in *The World as Will and Representation*, which he had discovered in 1854. It can also be read as a covert response to aspects of Eduard HANSLICK's *Vom Musikalisch-Schönen* (On the Musically Beautiful), likewise from 1854.   THOMAS S. GREY

Versions of the text:

- SSD 5:182–98 (reproduces the first published text: *Neue Zeitschrift für Musik* 46:15 [10 April 1857]).
- SB 8:265–82 (Wagner's original manuscript, including material deleted from or altered in the first printed text).
- PW 3:235–54 (translation of SSD 5).
- "Wagner's Open Letter to Marie Wittgenstein on Liszt's Symphonic Poems," trans., ed., and intro. by Thomas S. Grey, *The Wagner Journal* 5:1 (March 2011): 65–81 (translation based on the original text from SB 8 with annotations concerning principal differences between this and the original published text).

Über Schauspieler und Sänger (Actors and Singers, 1872). This essay, first published by Fritzsch in LEIPZIG, constitutes one of Wagner's important attempts to articulate the nature of artistic performance and experience. "Art ceases ... to be art from the moment it presents itself as art to our reflecting consciousness," he claims, but alas, "our whole modern theater ... is based on affectation" (PW 5:162, 190). Wagner develops an historical overview in which he describes and rejects French models of theater and Italian models of opera, and in which he commends some features of SHAKESPEARE, before identifying performers as the foundation from which genuine artistic experience arises in theatrical and operatic contexts. After describing successful efforts in teaching singers to perform his music with understanding and correct style, Wagner hymns a paean to the artistry of Wilhelmine SCHRÖDER-DEVRIENT (to whose memory the essay is dedicated), and offers a neglected key to understanding the origin and nature of his works: "she had the gift of teaching a composer how to compose, to be worth the pains of such a woman's 'singing'" (PW 5:219).   DAVID BRECKBILL

Über Staat und Religion (On State and Religion). Written in July 1864 in MUNICH, this essay was intended as a private response to questioning from a "highly loved young friend," LUDWIG II (SSD 8:3).

Ludwig wished to know whether and how Wagner's views on state and religion had changed since his writings of the period 1849–51, meaning the early years of his ZURICH exile following the DRESDEN UPRISING. First published in 1873, the essay was not entirely unknown before then; NIETZSCHE read the manuscript in 1869 during a hike outside TRIBSCHEN. The strategy resembles that of the contemporary MEIN LEBEN (My Life, 1865–81). Not least on account of the works' common – royal – addressee, Wagner presents himself as a revolutionary primarily for the sake of (his) art. Such an attitude would eventually also characterize the BAYREUTH CIRCLE; some may even have believed that. Nevertheless, the strong relationship between POLITICS and AESTHETICS endures. Wagner claims political interest to be a reflection and product of artistic concerns; ensuing discussion of his aesthetics immediately renders the relationship dialectical, just as when he had tilted the scales towards politics earlier. Moreover, Wagner does not disavow but revisits and sometimes reiterates certain key socialist themes from DRESDEN and Zurich, for instance abolition of the state and overcoming the constrictions of modern labor. He distances himself from a form of "newer socialist" distribution to which he had never subscribed in the first place (SSD 8:5). The word is killed that the spirit might live.

SCHOPENHAUER is the principal agent of intellectual as opposed to circumstantial transformation, though the distinction is not always clear. The blind striving of Schopenhauer's Will paints humanity less optimistically: egoistic individualism requires societal stability (Stabilität), which individuals have for their own protection invested in the state. Schopenhauer's WAHN (illusion) bids individual hopes express themselves in patriotism, embodied in the monarch. (This need not entail a nation-state; Bavarian particularism would be just as well served here.) Monarchical independence furthers a number of related purposes, including restraint of the base commercial imperatives of the press – Wagner would soon be in need of that – and inspiration to redeem life by rising above it. Monarchy appears a political and metaphysical necessity. No REVOLUTION – Wagner cannot quite bring himself to use the word – has ever failed to result in restoration of that ideal representation of the state.

In a new twist upon his idea of republican monarchy as adumbrated in the 1849 speech to the Dresden Vaterlandsverein, the king, as self-sacrificing "saint" – in the vein of Schopenhauerian renunciation – dispenses "grace" (Gnade), rising above any particular interest, his own or others'. State power is mitigated and ultimately negated by two higher, ascending forms of Wahn: RELIGION (avowedly not theology: FEUERBACH's distinction still holds) and art. Art's superiority over religion as announced in the opening of Religion und Kunst – no one believes art must be "true" – is foreshadowed. Reading between the lines, artistic patronage would seem a good practical example of how Wahn might be harnessed, HANS SACHS–like, to public good as well as princely salvation. Ludwig's response seems to have been of that ilk.   MARK BERRY

Uhlig, Theodor (b. Wurzen, 15 Feb. 1822; d. Dresden, 3 Jan. 1853): MUSIC CRITIC. Despite his short life, Uhlig played a major role in publicizing Wagner's music and ideas in the NEUE ZEITSCHRIFT FÜR MUSIK from 1849 to 1852. He played violin under Wagner's direction in Dresden's Königliche Kapelle, which he had joined in 1841 after musical training in Dessau. Initially Uhlig opposed Wagner's music, but after 1847 dedicated himself wholly to Wagner's cause. Uhlig attributed his change of attitude to the time when Wagner prepared the BEETHOVEN symphonies with the orchestra and revealed Beethoven's artistic greatness, especially with his PROGRAM NOTES to the Ninth Symphony.

Uhlig's first piece as a music critic appeared in January 1849. The editor of the *Neue Zeitschrift*, Franz BRENDEL, claimed that it was SCHUMANN who recommended Uhlig as a contributor, which is certainly ironic, since Uhlig virtually single-handedly transformed the journal into a publicity and propaganda outlet for Wagner. In the aftermath of the failed REVOLUTIONS of 1848–9, Brendel had been leaning toward Schumann as the most promising composer of the future, but allowed Uhlig to convince him otherwise. At first, Uhlig expounded on two of Wagner's main obsessions of the time: MEYERBEER and Beethoven. The occasion of the much-anticipated premiere of Meyerbeer's *Le Prophète* in 1849 caused Uhlig to attack Meyerbeer with such extreme ANTI-SEMITISM that another journal, the newly founded *Rheinische Musikzeitung*, objected. This was the beginning of a long polemic carried on between Uhlig and the journal, and also the beginning of the anti-Semitic rhetoric in the *Neue Zeitschrift* that culminated in Wagner's *Das JUDENTUM IN DER MUSIK* (Jewishness in Music) in September of 1850.

Uhlig's articles on Beethoven's symphonies explored the limitations of instrumental music and argued that the symphonies should be seen as a transition to Wagnerian MUSIC DRAMA. These essays were followed by a lengthy account of the premiere of *LOHENGRIN* in Weimar, which he had attended. Then he began a long series of summaries of Wagner's AESTHETIC writings that were appearing from ZURICH, all the while keeping up quarrels with other journals and even with other contributors to the *Neue Zeitschrift*.

Uhlig carried on a voluminous CORRESPONDENCE with Wagner, and read the manuscript of *OPER UND DRAMA* (Opera and Drama, 1851) before it was published. Several commentators have speculated that Uhlig had some influence in the forming of Wagner's ideas. Uhlig made the only extended trip of his life to visit Wagner in SWITZERLAND in July of 1851. Wagner recalled their time together fondly in *MEIN LEBEN* (My Life, 1865–81), where he described their ambitious mountain HIKES, interests in water cures, and the possibility that the blond, blue-eyed Uhlig was the illegitimate son of King Friedrich August of Sachsen.

In 1852, Uhlig continued his series on Wagner's writings, which are often more cogent than the originals. He also engaged in polemics with Eduard Krüger, a long-time contributor to the *Neue Zeitschrift*, and with J. C. Lobe, whose *Musikalische Briefe eines Wohlbekannten* took an extremely skeptical view towards Wagner. Uhlig's prolific contributions ended abruptly when he died, presumably of tuberculosis, at age 31. The long obituary in the *Neue Zeitschrift* is the basis for Frankenstein's biographical introduction to the collection of Uhlig's writings.   SANNA PEDERSON

Sanna Pederson, "Enlightened and Romantic German Music Criticism, 1800–1850," Ph.D. dissertation, University of Pennsylvania, 1995.

J. Rühlmann, "Theodor Uhlig," *Neue Zeitschrift für Musik* 38 (1853): 33–7.

Theodor Uhlig, *Musikalische Schriften*, ed. Ludwig Frankenstein (Regensburg: Bosse, n.d.).

Unger, Georg (b. Leipzig, 6 March 1837; d. Leipzig, 2 Feb. 1887), tenor. Unger undertook the role of SIEGFRIED in the premiere of the RING (BAYREUTH, 1876) after special study for many months with Wagner and the vocal pedagogue Julius Hey (1831–1909). Unger also appeared in the Ring tour with Angelo NEUMANN's company (1882–3). His heavy voice was unreliable, and after painful experiences with Unger at concerts in LONDON (1877), Wagner broke with him.   DAVID BRECKBILL

Einhard Luther, Biographie eines Stimmfaches (see bibliography): 1:296–307.

United States of America. As in Europe, WAGNERISM peaked in the USA in the late nineteenth century. But Wagnerism in America did not connect, as abroad, with socialism, decadence, or proto-MODERNISM. Rather, its distinctive keynote was uplift. American readings of the Wagner operas were wholesome. Henry Krehbiel – who as "dean" of New York's music critics was Wagnerism's major American chronicler – called the ending of the RING "a stupendous deed of morality" (148). Of SIEGFRIED, Krehbiel wrote: "There is something peculiarly sympathetic to our people in the character of the chief personages of the drama ... In their rude forcefulness and freedom from restrictive conventions they might be said to be representative of the American people. They are so full of that vital energy which made us a nation ... Siegfried is a prototype, too, of the American people in being an unspoiled nature. He looks at the world through glowing eyes that have not grown accustomed to the false and meretricious" (New York Tribune, 22 February 1888). As America's leading authority on culture and race, Krehbiel liberally championed the music of African-Americans, Native Americans, and JEWS. Concomitantly, Wagner the man was sanitized. In his influential two-volume Wagner biography (1893), Henry Finck called Wagner's "JEWISHNESS IN MUSIC" essay "deplorable," yet more exonerated than blamed its author. ANTI-SEMITISM did not inflect American Wagnerism.

The vast majority of American Wagnerites were women. A SENTA or BRÜNNHILDE could subversively inspire suppressed and corseted Gilded Age housewives. Willa Cather's short story "A Wagner Matinee" (1904) furnishes a classic account of Wagner awakening dormant feeling; its main character is an aged Nebraska farm wife who returns to Boston to collect a small inheritance, and there attends a Wagner concert. Cather was herself notably a Wagnerite (an element of her creative personality slighted by Cather scholars). Her novel A Song of the Lark (1915) is partly based on her acquaintance with the soprano Olive Fremstad, whose peerless KUNDRY was unforgettably described by Cather in McClure's Magazine (December 1913).

The first complete Wagner performance given in the USA was of TANNHÄUSER, conducted by Carl Bergmann at the New York Stadttheater (4 April 1859). He also gave the first known American Wagner performance (1852) and the first all-Wagner concert in the USA (1853). Theodore Thomas, as conductor of the New York Philharmonic (1877–8, 1879–81) and the Chicago Orchestra (1891–1905), was a world-class executant for whom Wagner and Beethoven were twin repertoire "pillars." But Thomas rarely led staged performances; late in life, he opined that TRISTAN UND ISOLDE would never become popular. Thomas was displaced as New York's leading conductor by Anton SEIDL, who arrived in 1885 to become principal conductor (and de facto music director) of the Metropolitan Opera. A season before, under Leopold Damrosch, the Met had turned into a German house, stressing German repertoire and performing even non-German operas in German. With Damrosch's death, Seidl presided over six additional German seasons. Of 599 staged performances during the Met's seven German seasons, including 155 on tour, 320 were of works by Wagner.

A Wagner protégé, Seidl was galvanizing and charismatic; he became Wagner's central American missionary. A singular Seidl outpost was Brooklyn (an independent city before it was absorbed by New York in 1898), where a women's Seidl Society, led by Laura LANGFORD, sought to create an American BAYREUTH. Wagner was by far the most popular composer at the Seidl Society's summertime concerts, given fourteen times weekly at Coney Island's Brighton Beach. Neither Seidl nor Langford wished to challenge COSIMA WAGNER's ban on PARSIFAL stagings outside Bayreuth. Instead, the Seidl Society presented an elaborate but truncated concert performance at the Brooklyn Academy of Music: the "Parsifal Entertainment" (31 March 1890).

The somber pageantry of Seidl's funeral (31 March 1898) demonstrated the magnitude of the American Wagner movement. The cortege, down Fifth Avenue, was mobbed by bystanders. Funeral services, at the Metropolitan Opera House, attracted an overflow audience. Women outnumbered men twenty to one in the downstairs seats; standees were packed five and six rows deep. Krehbiel read a eulogy by Robert Ingersoll, the renowned orator and atheist, who (on another occasion) said of Wagner: "the man who understands that music can love better and with greater intensity than he ever did before" (Smith 381).

The scope of American Wagnerism can hardly be exaggerated. Wagner topics were a dominant motif in general intellectual discourse. The Met toured Wagner widely, as did Seidl and Walter Damrosch (Leopold's son). Albert Pinkham Ryder attended GÖTTERDÄMMERUNG at the Met in 1888, then returned home and worked for two days without sleep or food on his "Siegfried and the Rhine Maidens." "One could hardly listen to the Götterdämmerung in New York among throngs of intense young enthusiasts, without paroxysms of nervous excitement," reported Henry Adams (404–5). Mark Twain's favorite opera was Tannhäuser. John Philip Sousa's favorite composer was Wagner; his huge repertoire of Wagner band transcriptions did not exclude such weighty fare as the Parsifal Prelude. Upton Sinclair's novel Prince Hagen: A Phantasy (1903) used Der Ring des Nibelungen to critique Wall Street. The bohémiennes Mabel Dodge Luhan and Isabella Stewart Gardner were Wagnerites. So was M. Carey Thomas, the founding dean and second president of Bryn Mawr College, who in a letter (3 March 1891) wrote of Tristan at the Met: "I never in a public place came so near to losing my self control."

At the post-Seidl Met, Gustav MAHLER and Arturo TOSCANINI were potent Wagner advocates. But as a cultural movement powered by the meliorist energies of the late Gilded Age, Wagnerism expired after World War I, undone by Germanophobia and modernism. Beginning in 1935, Wagner in America was mainly identified not with a state of being but with a singer: Kirsten FLAGSTAD. Artur Bodanzky, who headed the Met's German wing

(1915–39), is by comparison today far too little remembered. Met Wagner broadcasts of the 1930s document febrile Wagner conducting of maximum fire and drive. In particular, *Siegfried* (30 January 1937), with Bodanzky, Flagstad, Lauritz MELCHOIR, and Friedrich SCHORR, is arguably the most satisfying performance of this opera ever preserved on record. The directorship of Rudolf Bing (1950–72) marked the nadir of Wagner at the Met. With the arrival of James LEVINE in 1971, Wagner returned in abundance. Under Levine, the Met has remained a conservative Wagner house, spurning European *Regietheater*. The most adventurous American Wagner house in the USA has long been the Seattle Opera, whose 1986 *Ring*, directed by François Rochaix, was remarkable for its dramaturgical acuity and intellectual panache.

JOSEPH HOROWITZ

Henry Adams, *The Education of Henry Adams* (New York, 1907).

John Dizikes, *Opera in America: A Cultural History* (New Haven, CT: Yale University Press, 1993).

Henry Finck, *Wagner and His Works*, 2 vols. (New York, 1893).

Joseph Horowitz, *Moral Fire: Portraits from America's Fin-de-Siecle* (Berkeley: University of California Press, 2012).

   Wagner Nights: An American History (see bibliography).

Henry Krehbiel, *Studies in the Wagnerian Drama* (New York: Harper, 1891).

Joseph Mussulman, *Music in the Cultured Generation: A Social History of Music in America 1870–1900* (Evanston, IL: Northwestern University Press, 1971).

Frank Smith, *Robert G. Ingersoll: A Life* (Buffalo, NY: Prometheus, 1990).

Vegetarianism in Germany was closely tied throughout the 1860s to republicanism, utopian socialism, and naturopathy. Gustav Struve (1805–70), who helped lead the Badenese revolution in 1848, became a vegetarian in 1832 after reading Jean-Jacques Rousseau's *Émile*. He later published *Mandaras Wanderungen* (1845) and *Pflanzenkost* (1869), where he portrayed vegetarianism as promoting republican virtues such as moderation and military manhood. Wilhelm Zimmermann (1819–82) lived for a time at Alcott House, an English utopian socialist settlement, where he wrote *Der Weg zum Paradies* (1846), an important synthesis and translation of English-language vegetarian literature. Theodor Hahn (1824–83) made vegetarianism central to cures at his naturopathic sanatorium Auf der Waid (St. Gallen, Switzerland) and published several books, including *Die naturgemäße Diät, die Diät der Zukunft* (1859). This text precipitated the conversion of Eduard Baltzer (1814–87), a prominent republican and dissenting Protestant, whose four-volume *Die natürliche Lebensweise* (1867–72) framed vegetarianism as an antidote to the dire material situation of German workers, and as a tool for teaching the republican virtues of sobriety and self-governance. In 1867, Baltzer launched a movement by founding Germany's first vegetarian club, the Verein für natürliche Lebensweise, and establishing the nation's first vegetarian periodical, the *Vereinsblatt für Freunde der natürlichen Lebensweise*.

The cultural and political resonance of vegetarianism became more diverse in the 1870s. Richard Wagner became interested in the vegetable diet late in the decade, after reading a translation of the vegetarian classic *Thalysie* by the French utopian socialist Jean-Antoine Gleïzès (1773–1843). In several essays published in BAYREUTHER BLÄTTER between 1879 and 1881, Wagner linked meat-eating to JEWS, race mixing, and animal VIVISECTION. Although never able to practice the diet himself, he advocated vegetarianism as a tool of German REGENERATION. The writer Robert Springer (1816–85), physician Richard Nagel (1823–95), and animal rights activist Otto Rabe also published important articles on these topics in the *Bayreuther Blätter*. Even Baltzer, who did not share Wagner's ANTI-SEMITIC German NATIONALISM, contributed an essay on Pythagoras.

Wagner's advocacy for vegetarianism continued to have wide influence long after his death. Bernhard Förster (1843–89), an enthusiastic follower, helped solidify the links between vegetarianism and radical anti-Semitism in numerous publications. Perhaps most famous is the case of Adolf HITLER, who idolized Wagner and embraced a vegetarian diet via the influence of the Austrian radical Georg von Schönerer (1842–1921). Although closely tied to anti-Semitic German nationalism in the late nineteenth and early twentieth centuries, vegetarianism also continued to attract support across the political spectrum, including socialists, who edited *Vegetarischer Vorwärts*, and cultural radicals such as Magnus Schwantje (1877–1959), who mixed praise for Wagner with lifelong pacifism.   CORINNA TREITEL

See also RELIGION

Richard Wagner, *Religion und Kunst* (see Appendix 5: Prose works).

Venice. See ITALY, WAGNER'S TRAVELS TO

Verdi, Giuseppe (b. Roncole [near Busseto], 9/10 Oct. 1813; d. Milan, 27 Jan. 1901), the foremost composer of opera in Italy during Wagner's lifetime. Like Wagner, Verdi played a significant role in shaping the cultural identity of his country. The two men never met, but each heard the works of the other.

It seems that Verdi first encountered the music of Wagner in PARIS when he heard the Concerts Populaires perform the OVERTURE to *TANNHÄUSER* in 1865: the experience prompted Verdi to label Wagner a madman ("E matto!"). In November 1871, Verdi heard the first Wagner opera to be performed in ITALY: *LOHENGRIN* at the Teatro Comunale in Bologna. And he did so with score in hand. Comments scattered throughout his copy of the piano-vocal score convey his impressions of the performance and, of greater importance, of the work: "Beautiful music, when it is clear and when there is thought [behind it]. The action moves as slowly as the words. Thus, boredom. Beautiful instrumental effects. Excess of sustained notes, and it becomes heavy." Verdi also heard a performance of *Tannhäuser* (in Vienna) in 1875, but there is no certainty that he heard other, later works of Wagner.

Verdi's personal library contains piano-vocal scores of several of Wagner's operas, including *Tannhäuser*, *Die WALKÜRE*, *Die MEISTERSINGER VON NÜRNBERG*, and *TRISTAN UND ISOLDE*, which he acquired later in his career. Verdi also owned a copy of Wagner's *Quatre poèmes d'opéra traduits en prose française, précedés d'une lettre sur la musique* (Ger. *Zukunftsmusik* 1860/1; see Appendix 5: Prose works) and was presumably, at least to some extent, acquainted with Wagner's ideas about "ZUKUNFTSMUSIK" through this publication (although in Verdi's copy of the text several pages remain uncut). Verdi may have come to know Wagner's works also through the composer and librettist Arrigo Boito. Verdi's collaborator on the revised version of *Simon Boccanegra*, as well as for *Otello* and *Falstaff*, Boito was involved in the 1871 Bologna *Lohengrin* production and was an avid and vociferous admirer of the German composer.

Verdi railed against Wagner's influence in Italy. Troubled by foreign, specifically Teutonic (Wagnerian), influences that he believed had caused Italians to renounce their own artistic tradition, Verdi called "Germanism" an "illness" that had "infected" Italian composers. And one of the composer's confidants once referred to the "music of the future" as the "delirium of the crazed or excuse of the impotent." It was inevitable that commentators would compare Verdi and Wagner, a practice upon which Verdi frowned. He especially took offense at being called an "imitator" of his German contemporary. And when given the opportunity to offer advice to young composers, Verdi postulated that they should not be seduced by new trends in the "music from beyond the Alps," but should remain true to their own national traditions.

Despite his concerns over the influence of Wagnerian ideas, later in life Verdi came to admire what the German artist had attempted to do. He lamented the death of Wagner, "a name that leaves a very strong impression on the history of the Art."

Verdi's thoughts may perhaps best be summed up in his words to his close Milanese friend the Countess Clara Maffei: "Wagner is not a ferocious beast as the purists think, nor is he a prophet as his apostles believe. He is a man of great talent who is pleased by difficult paths, because he does not know how to find easy and direct ones" (31 July 1863).   ROBERTA MONTEMORRA MARVIN

Marcello Conati, "Appendix (Verdi and *Tannhäuser*)," trans. Roberta M. Marvin, *Verdi Forum* 28–9 (2001–2): 42–4.

"Verdi vs. Wagner," trans. Francesco Izzo and Linda B. Fairtile, *Verdi Forum* 26–7 (1999–2000): 4–16.

Peter Conrad, *Verdi and/or Wagner: Two Men, Two Worlds, Two Centuries* (London: Thames & Hudson, 2011).

Roberta Montemorra Marvin, "Verdi's 'Music of the Future'," in *Music in Print and Beyond: Hildegard von Bingen to The Beatles*, ed. Craig Monson and Roberta Montemorra Marvin (University of Rochester Press, 2013).

Wolfgang Osthoff, "Verdi e Wagner," *Giuseppe Verdi: L'uomo, l'opera, il mito* (Milan: Ricordi, 2000): 115–23.

Video recordings. Below is a selective discussion of some notable productions of Wagner's "mature" dramas released on video, arranged by title in chronological order of the works' composition. For a more complete listing, see Appendix 8: Selected video recordings.

Der fliegende Holländer

Joachim Herz's striking 1964 feature film version, adapted from his influential LEIPZIG stage production, has previously been released on VHS and laser disc; a DVD release is certainly overdue. Václav Kašlík's studio production from 1975 features excellent vocal performances from Donald McIntyre and Catarina Ligendza, although the film suffers from potentially distracting video production flaws, including poor lip-syncing. Other releases include Harry Kupfer's seminal Bayreuth production (1985), and a 2010 modern-dress production from the Netherlands, staged with an eye to contemporary issues of asylum and immigration.

Tannhäuser

The 1978 video of Götz Friedrich's production was the first complete opera film released from BAYREUTH. Friedrich's psychologically detailed directing is well served by the power of the close-up; even the guests arriving in Act II appear to be fully individuated characters. Otto Schenk's production for the Metropolitan Opera (1982) is unrivaled for its sumptuous Romanticism, as with other Wagner productions from this house. More recent directorial approaches include David Alden's surreal, politically inflected production from Munich (1994); Nikolaus Lehnhoff's sleekly abstract staging in Baden-Baden (2008); and Kasper Holten's Copenhagen production, depicting TANN-HÄUSER as a conflicted modern artist (2009).

Lohengrin

Peter Hofmann was a charismatic LOHENGRIN in two contrasting although essentially conservative productions: a musically and visually lustrous staging from the Met (1986), and Götz Friedrich's darker, more militaristic rendering for Bayreuth (1982). In a subsequent Bayreuth production (1990), Werner Herzog's cinematic sensibility is evident in his subtle use of lighting and composition – expertly framed on video by the cameras of producer Brian Large. The Vienna State Opera's production (1990) features Plácido Domingo as Lohengrin, Domingo's only complete Wagnerian performance on DVD to date. Two important productions probe the political dimensions of *Lohengrin*'s themes of faith and authority: Peter Konwitschny's "schoolroom *Lohengrin*" (filmed in Barcelona in 2006, originally staged in Hamburg), and Richard Jones's controversial production in MUNICH, featuring Jonas Kaufmann in the title role (2009).

Tristan und Isolde

A wealth of *Tristan*s have been released on DVD, beginning chronologically with a historic Birgit NILSSON/Jon Vickers performance from 1973, conducted by Karl Böhm. In Jean-Pierre Ponnelle's Bayreuth production (1983), René Kollo and Johanna Meier brought not only great vocal agility but uncommon physical passion to their roles. This production marked the Bayreuth debut of Daniel BARENBOIM; Barenboim also led subsequent releases from Bayreuth (featuring Waltraud Meier and Siegfried Jerusalem, 1995), and La Scala (featuring Meier and Ian Storey, 2007). Among the many distinguished releases are Nikolaus Lehnhoff's Glyndebourne production (2007), with Robert Gambill and Nina Stemme; Ben Heppner and Jane Eaglen in a spare, affecting production from the Met (2001); and Peter Konwitschny's production from Munich (1998), which dispenses with the typical visual gloom and stages the work as a fundamentally optimistic tale.

Die Meistersinger von Nürnberg

The Hamburg State Opera's 1970 studio production brings the viewer into the midst of the story with impressively mobile camerawork. Notable stage productions include WOLFGANG WAGNER's two productions for Bayreuth (1984 and 1999), and Götz Friedrich's production from Berlin (1995). Two DVDs of similar productions by Otto Schenk – from the Metropolitan Opera (2005) and Vienna State Opera (2008) – achieve very different effects, largely due to the stylistic contrasts between the conductors (James Levine and Christian Thielemann, respectively) and the individuality of several key performances; the Vienna performance is particularly noteworthy for Adrian Eröd's elegant, sympathetic SIXTUS BECKMESSER. KATHARINA WAGNER's iconoclastic production became the first Bayreuth video release filmed in performance before a live audience (2008).

Der Ring des Nibelungen

Nearly forty years after its Bayreuth premiere, Patrice Chéreau's centennial production (filmed in 1980) remains as remarkable for its dramatically perceptive acting as for its Industrial Age concept, radical in its time. The second cycle to appear on video, the Metropolitan Opera's scrupulously Romantic production (1990), provided an ideal counterweight to Chéreau's modernized rendering; to date, it is the only *Ring* on video to attempt a faithful realization of Wagner's original vision. For the DVD release of Harry Kupfer's Bayreuth cycle (1991), the videos were restored to their original widescreen format – befitting the bleak expanses of Kupfer's set, as well as the physically energetic performances from the young cast. Pierre Audi's Amsterdam *Ring* (1999) reconstructed the stage to put the orchestra in the midst of the action; the DVDs are visually spectacular, although they attest to the acoustical difficulties arising from the unusual configurations.

Also available are two benchmark interpretations from the school often referred to as *Regietheater* (director's theater): the Stuttgart Opera's *Ring* staged by four different production teams (2002–3), and Kasper Holten's version from Copenhagen (2006). For the Copenhagen DVDs, the producers have intensified the performance footage with point-of-view camera angles and rapid editing, sometimes suggesting the aesthetic of a feature film rather than that of a live performance. Dichotomies between stage and film are, however, largely irrelevant in the multimedia *Ring* staged in Valencia, Spain by the theatrical group La Fura dels Baus, under the baton of Zubin Mehta (2010). This visually stunning cycle is so saturated with high-definition video projections that the DVDs occasionally seem like the film of a film. Leaving behind both traditional Wagnerian aesthetics and the interpretive controversies of the later twentieth century, the production restores the *Ring*'s mythic aura in an idiom instantly recognizable from science fiction and fantasy cinema.

Parsifal

Wolfgang Wagner's 1998 Bayreuth production – often reminiscent of WIELAND WAGNER in its deployment of lighting effects – represented a stylistic departure from Wolfgang's more visually conservative 1981 staging (also on DVD). Hans-Jürgen SYBERBERG's feature film (1982) is an ambitious exploration of *Parsifal*'s legacy, staging the work against a shifting web of visual allusions to German culture and history. The Metropolitan Opera's 1993 DVD vividly captures the body-and-soul commitment of James Levine and a cast anchored by Waltraud Meier's riveting KUNDRY. Meier returns in Nikolaus Lehnhoff's production from Baden-Baden (2004), opposite Christopher Ventris's PARSIFAL. Lehnhoff's final image – Parsifal and Kundry walking down a railroad towards a distant light, followed by several Grail Knights – is a fitting emblem for a production that eschews the work's original setting and religious message, while transmitting the full emotional force of Wagner's drama.   HILAN WARSHAW

Vienna
1. Wagner in Vienna
2. Reception, remembrance, and legacy

1. Wagner in Vienna

Wagner's first visits to Vienna took place in 1832 and 1848 – the former with his friend Vincenz Tyszkiéwitcz to sample the city's musical life, and the latter to sample traces of the revolutionary upheavals that rocked the city in the spring of that year, though Wagner later denied that purpose (ML/E 61–3 and 366–9). An enduring relationship with Vienna and its institutions began in May 1861, when Wagner visited looking for singers for his planned premiere of TRISTAN UND ISOLDE in Karlsruhe. Welcomed by Heinrich Esser, conductor of the Vienna Hofoper, Wagner attended a dress rehearsal of LOHENGRIN on 11 May. It was the first time he had heard the work played, and he was so overcome by the performance and the greeting that he quickly scrapped his Karlsruhe plans and determined that Tristan should have its premiere in the Habsburg capital instead. As he wrote to MINNA of assurances he had received from the opera's ministerial director, "He has placed his theater at my disposal for each and every one of my operas: and I am told that he is not joking ... here, where *everything*, but *everything* that I need is ready to hand, with a large and enthusiastic public to back me up" (13 May 1861).

By the fall of that year, Wagner's plans had already begun to falter, but he did not give up hope just yet. After a period of extensive travels and communications (and a decisive split from his wife), Wagner returned to Vienna in November 1862, accompanied by the actress Friederike MEYER. Then, his troubles deepened. His soprano, Luise MEYER-DUSTMANN, resented Wagner's involvement with her estranged sister Friederike. And the declining health of his tenor, Aloys Ander, had taken a serious toll on the singer's voice. Within weeks, Wagner's plans became hopelessly mired, and he turned his attention instead to a trio of ORCHESTRAL CONCERTS to be staged at Vienna's Theater an der Wien. The first on 26 December 1862 featured excerpts from the unfinished Die MEISTERSINGER VON NÜRNBERG and Der RING DES NIBELUNGEN tetralogy. After a rocky start, the concert series wrapped up with a performance on 11 January 1863 before an ecstatic, overflowing crowd. Once again, the reception that his work received prompted Wagner to gush with praise for the Viennese public, and to proclaim confidently his vision of sustained successes in the city. As he exclaimed in a letter to Mathilde MAIER after the disappointing second concert (1 January 1863) of the run, "In spite of my concerts, in spite of Tristan – I now know that I need look no further than *Vienna* as the focus of my activities. Everything is possible here; the ground is extremely fertile; I am held in high regard here: there is wealth in plenty. I need only to *will* things to happen" (4 January 1863).

After a trip to RUSSIA in early 1863, Wagner settled in the Vienna suburb of Penzing, not far from the imperial Schönbrunn Palace (see Appendix 3: Wagner's addresses). Over the course of his ensuing ten-month residency, his plans for a Tristan premiere were dashed by Ander's worsening health. His work on Die Meistersinger was halted by anxiety over his mounting troubles with creditors, and he increasingly felt neglected and unappreciated by the Hofoper and its imperial directors. "I was and continued to be ignored in high places," he later recalled (ML/E 732). By early 1864 he realized that he had no hopes of repaying his debts, and he began to fear for his freedom. With the help of friends, he fled Vienna and its creditors on 23 March. Thereafter, he visited only briefly and occasionally, to rehearse or conduct his works.

2. Reception, remembrance, and legacy

Although Wagner wrote excitedly of the rapturous enthusiasm with which the city greeted his work in 1861–3, Eduard HANSLICK wrote of the tremendous obstacles that had stood in the way of programming Wagner's music in the 1850s and 1860s on account of the composer's revolutionary associations. He recalled that when *TANNHÄUSER* was finally granted a premiere at the Hofoper in 1859, the imperial censor had insisted on suppressing every appearance of the word *Rome* in the libretto, since the monarchy's ties to the Vatican had been a rallying point for protesters in 1848 (Hanslick, *Aus meinem Leben* 2:4). Indeed, writing in 1869, Hanslick remarked on the striking *lateness* that had characterized the widespread acceptance of Wagner's work in the Habsburg capital, a situation Hanslick lamented as exemplary of "the characteristically ponderous and indolent manner with which our musical institutions greet new, sensational happenings," and of the generally "'belated' character' of musical Vienna" as a whole (Hanslick, *Geschichte* 430).

In fact, it was not the city's imperial institutions but its vibrant youth culture that transformed Wagner's writings and music dramas into vital cultural phenomena in the 1870s. In November 1872, a group of university and conservatory students founded the Viennese Academic WAGNER SOCIETY, organizing concerts of Wagner's music, publishing on Wagner's art, and raising funds to support the BAYREUTH FESTIVAL. As the movement grew, rifts emerged between those attracted chiefly by Wagner's artistic legacy and those animated by his politics. In March 1883, Wagner's memorial wake, promoted by student organizers as a celebration of Wagner's artistic achievements, dissolved into a pan-German rally unforeseen by authorities and ended only by police intercession. When its pan-German faction embraced the rise of political ANTI-SEMITISM in the later 1880s, the student movement split decisively.

By the turn of the twentieth century, the founding members of the Academic Wagner Society had come of age, and some had assumed for themselves leading positions in hallowed imperial institutions, such as Gustav MAHLER, appointed director of the Hofoper in 1897, and Guido Adler, appointed to the chair in musicology at the University of Vienna in 1898. These appointments – and the appointees' continued engagement with Wagner's work as creative artists, performers, and scholars – marked the completion of a gradual revolution in imperial attitudes toward the composer. Wagner was no longer an outsider to be resisted; indeed, his work and ideas had penetrated to the core of the imperial establishment.   KEVIN C. KARNES

Eduard Hanslick, *Aus meinem Leben* (see bibliography).
  Geschichte des Concertwesens in Wien, 2 vols. (Vienna: Wilhelm Braumüller, 1869–70).
Kevin C. Karnes, *Music, Criticism, and the Challenge of History: Shaping Modern Musical Thought in Late Nineteenth-Century Vienna* (Oxford University Press, 2008).

Virtuos und der Künstler, Der (The Virtuoso and the Artist). This essay by Wagner was published in the *REVUE ET GAZETTE MUSICALE DE PARIS* as "Du métier de virtuose et de l'indépendance des compositeurs: Fantaisie esthétique d'un musicien" (18 October 1840), and substantially revised for the *Gesammelte Schriften* (1871). Written during Wagner's first stay in PARIS (1839–42), the piece begins with an allegorical tale of a jewel hidden deep in the earth, a symbol for the ancient magic of music. Among moderns, only two "miners" – one from Salzburg, the other from Bonn (references to MOZART and BEETHOVEN respectively) – have managed to glimpse the jewel. Pondering the virtuoso's role in penetrating music's depths, Wagner stipulates that performers should strive to faithfully transmit the composer's intentions. Yet he also recognizes that performers make an essential contribution to the musical art. The article closes with a discussion (much expanded in the 1871 version) of Italian singing practices, French tastes, and a production of Mozart's *Don Giovanni* mounted by the Théâtre-Italien. HOLLY WATKINS

Vivisection. Animal experimentation was emotionally debated in Wagner's household, and COSIMA noted Wagner's repugnance for such "senseless crimes" (CWD 11 October 1878). On 31 July 1879 (CWD), he received *The Torture Chambers of Science* by Ernst von Weber (*Die Folterkammern der Wissenschaft: Eine Sammlung von Thatsachen für das Laienpublikum,* 1879). Weber, a wealthy landowner, was organizing the German anti-experimentalist movement. His seventy-seven tendentious pages about practices, called "vivisections" whether or not living bodies were cut open, shocked the Wagners. In August 1879, Richard wrote to Weber, became a member of his International Society for the Prevention of Scientific Torture of Animals, and underlined his commitment with a generous donation. Weber invited himself to WAHNFRIED for 12 September and brought anti-vivisectionist literature along (CWD 12 September 1879 through 9 October 1879), which in turn prompted Wagner to write his *Open Letter to Ernst von Weber . . . on Vivisection,* which preoccupied him from 20 September until 9 October, and interrupted his work on the score of PARSIFAL. It was published in the BAYREUTHER BLÄTTER with an additional two thousand off-prints placed at Weber's disposal at Wagner's expense.

The *Open Letter* agreed with the philosophical argument current among German anti-vivisectionists: The future of medicine lay "neither . . . in an increase of diagnostic wisdom nor in the discovery and testing of new remedies, but in hygiene" (Iatros 62). Wagner denigrated those who experimented as being interested in illnesses which the affluent brought down on themselves through their unnatural way of life. Since the true causes of illness-related suffering were sociocultural – an old idea of his – experiments (even on humans), would never grasp them; they made no sense. Moreover it was morally irresponsible to use poor hospital patients as guinea pigs; such patients "make themselves useful to the rich even as they lie dying" (SSD 10:204–5). Wagner held that a doctor whose expertise was based on physiology could only be "a man entirely incapable of compassion, even a bungler in his profession" (SSD 10:200), in which he ought to empathize with patients rather than "pursue abstract findings intended to enhance his own reputation" (SSD 10:199). Compassion should direct doctors rather than the "anxiety about their own ignorance" which made them climb "on the tree of knowledge like apes" (SSD 10:207).

Wagner's condemnation of scientific experiments on animals was tainted with socialist ideas and (privately) with ANTI-SEMITISM. It originated in his inclination to deplore the contemporary intellectual, moral, and artistic state of

Germany, from his concern for animals and from his equally longstanding interpretation of human relationships and man's attitude to nature, typified as fellow-suffering (*Mitleiden*). In sharp contrast to this cosmology of compassion – with its link to *Parsifal* – Wagner saw medicine in his "despiritualized age" beset by an unfeeling, technologically orientated utilitarianism in the service of a state increasingly addicted to militaristic expansionism, evident in his original thought that the "specter of science . . . has worked up its way from the dissecting table to the firearms factory" (SSD 10:194; PW 6:195; CWD 18 September 1879).

Writing in axioms, Wagner failed to see that actions, not only theoretical value systems, conditioned civilization. So he ignored the potentially serious consequences of the proposed ban on animal experimentation, given their importance in the rapidly ongoing development of operative surgery and vaccinations which benefited the whole population and not just the affluent as Wagner claimed. But then, though he suffered from chronic digestive problems, he had limited contact with the medical world. Neither Cosima nor his children fell seriously ill. What prompted him to act was "a vague feeling of the necessity to inquire into the character of artistic influence in an area apparently remote of aesthetic interest" (SSD 10:194). This study failed, yet Wagner served as figurehead in the nineteenth-century anti-vivisection movement.   ULRICH TRÖHLER

See also HEALTH; VEGETARIANISM

Iatros (alias of E. G. F. Grysanowski), *Die Vivisektion, ihr wissenschaftlicher Wert und ihre ethische Berechtigung* (Leipzig: Barth, 1877).

Joachim Thiery and Ulrich Tröhler, "Doubt about Progress, but Trust in Compassion. Wagner the Anti-Vivisectionist: His Motives and his Contemporaries' Reactions," *Programmhefte der Bayreuther Festspiele: "Parsifal"* (Bayreuth: Festspielverlag, 1987): 65–101.

"Wagner, Animals and Modern Scientific Medicine," in *The Wagner Compendium*, ed. Barry Millington (see bibliography): 174–7.

Ulrich Tröhler and Holger-Andreas Maehle, "Anti-Vivisection in Nineteenth-Century Germany and Switzerland: Motives and Methods," in *Vivisection in Historical Perspective*, ed. Nicolaas Rupke (London: Routledge, 1990).

Ernst von Weber, ed., *Bisher ungedruckte Briefe von Richard Wagner an Ernst von Weber* (Dresden: Internationaler Verein zur Bekämpfung der wissenschaftlichen Thierfolter, 1883).

Vogl, Heinrich (b. Munich, 15 Jan. 1845; d. Munich, 21 April 1900), German tenor and a mainstay of the Munich Hofoper (1865–1900). His wide-ranging repertory included all the leading Wagner tenor roles. He created LOGE (1869) and SIEGMUND (1870) in the MUNICH premieres of *Das RHEINGOLD* and *Die WALKÜRE*, and was Loge in the BAYREUTH premiere of the *RING* (1876) and in its first revival (1896–7). In 1869, Vogl and his wife Therese Vogl (née Thoma) (1845–1921) were the first to appear in the title roles of *TRISTAN UND ISOLDE* after the tragic death of Ludwig Schnorr von CAROLSFELD four years earlier. Until the mid-1880s they were by far the most frequent portrayers of these roles throughout Germany, and Heinrich Vogl was Bayreuth's first Tristan (1886).   DAVID BRECKBILL

Einhard Luther, *Biographie eines Stimmfaches* (see bibliography).

Rolf Wünnenberg, *Das Sängerehepaar Heinrich und Therese Vogl* (Tutzing: Hans Schneider, 1982).

Volk. A German word with a richer set of meanings than any one of the English words commonly used to translate it: "people," "folk," or "nation." In medieval and early modern German, the word was used to denote the people of God (*Gottesvolk*), the "peoples" of the ancient world, or armies (in Luther's translation of the Bible, literally *Kriegsvolk*). By the end of the seventeenth century, the word had come to refer, pejoratively, to the lower strata of society, made up of poor and uneducated people. Over the course of the eighteenth century, these *Volk* came increasingly into enlightened discourse as the object of efforts to improve them, a development that continued to inform nineteenth-century uses of the word. The pejorative connotations of *Volk* gradually fell away (its place of disrepute taken over by words like "masses" or "mob"), but the defining distinction between the ill-educated majority and the more educated, gifted, and empowered minority remained. Wagner sometimes referred to the *Volk* in this connotative context, as in his treatise OPER UND DRAMA (Opera and Drama, 1851), where he rebukes artists and social elites – referred to sarcastically as "we privileged persons, we elect of God, we plutocrats and we geniuses" – for having "fed off the *Volk*," "robbing their fruits with bare-faced impudence" (PW 2:58).

But this passage, with its rhetorical exploitation of the old distinction between the privileged and the people, also reveals the late eighteenth-century "Copernican turn" in *Volk*'s meaning. The decisive shift, from a word denoting a social group within the larger collectivity to one denoting the collectivity itself, represents an unusual etymological phenomenon, insofar as it resulted from the work of one person, in this case the philosopher-scholar Johann Gottfried HERDER (*Geschichtliche Grundbegriffe* 7:283). Wagner, like most other German nationalists of the nineteenth century, conceived of the *Volk* in Herderian terms. Herder's treatises on language and history effected a deepening and broadening of the word. In his writings, the *Volk* represented a collectivity with a mind of its own (a *Seele*, a spirit, soul, or essence), and its expression could be found not in politics and wars but in language and poetry, as well as all distinctive phenomena of the world – customs, tastes, arts (including music), beliefs. In *Volks-poesie*, one found "the epitome of the faults and the achievements of a nation, a mirror of its attitudes, the expression of the highest toward which it strives" (*Geschichtliche Grundbegriffe* 7:317). Of language Herder wrote: "He who is brought up in a language, who pours his heart into it and learns to express his spirit in it, this person belongs to the *Volk* ... and by means of this language will the Nation mature and be educated" (*Geschichtliche Grundbegriffe* 7:317).

The influence of Herder was also responsible for the increasing convergence of *Volk* and *Nation*, to the point where the two became essentially interchangeable in nineteenth-century usage. Along with his contemporaries, the liberal nationalists of the 1848–9 Frankfurt Parliament, Wagner shared a way of speaking about the *Volk* as constitutive of the nation, just as the nation constituted the boundaries within which the distinctive language, customs, and beliefs of the *Volk* existed. The coming-together of *Volk* and nation in contemporary discourse, before the political unification of the German-speaking states in 1871, finds expression in the final minutes of

Der MEISTERSINGER VON NÜRNBERG, when HANS SACHS urges the people (*Volk*) of Nuremberg to "honor their masters." Singing in full Herderian mode, he proclaims them the protectors of that which is "German and true," through good times and bad: it is "not your coat-of-arms, spear, or sword," he says to the aristocratic WALTHER VON STOLZING, that has made you one of the *Volk*, but poetry alone.

The problems for the *Volk* came, as Wagner suggests in *Meistersinger*, from enemies both external and internal. Herder himself had been profoundly opposed to the idea that one *Volk* was necessarily opposed to another: "No nationality has been solely designated by God as the chosen people of the earth; hence no nationality of Europe may separate itself sharply, and foolishly say, 'With us alone, with us dwells *all* wisdom'" (*Geschichtliche Grundbegriffe* 7:318–19). But his successors, including Wagner, combined Herder's notions of *Volk* with an older German self-consciousness as beleaguered by outsiders and conquerors, the French chief among them – the "foreign princes and foreign ways" Hans Sachs warns against in his final speech. Wagner's own references to the *Volk* invariably come in the context of their vulnerability and decline. He finds betrayal among the German princes, corruption and decadence among the French masters of European cultural life, greed, ambition, and parasitism among the JEWS, and weakness to all this among the Germans themselves.

In *Oper und Drama*, the *Volksseele* can barely find any sort of authentic expression. On the one hand are the French-bewitched masses, seduced by mere imitations of German art, a hymn-like song here, a folk-like melody there: as Wagner wrote later in *WAS IST DEUTSCH?* (What is German?, 1865/78), French-imitating "democratic speculators" fill the shops with "every so-called *Volks*-this or that, vulgar, utterly vapid dummies ... to decoy the easygoing crowd" (PW 4:166). On the other hand, there were ultimately barren searches through the past for expressions of the *Volk* that might be revived – more "restoration" than "revolution," at best "ringing the changes" on "our old friend the *Volkslied*" (PW 2:48, 310). In the immediate wake of the failed political revolution in Germany, Wagner looked not to the past, as had Herder, but to some retrieval of the *Volk* through a new burst of authentic, uncorrupted creation in the future.

By the end of his life, Wagner showed signs of moving beyond Herderian culturalist definitions of the *Volk* to racialist ones that anticipated the harsher ideology of *völkisch* NATIONALISM. In *Erkenne dich selbst* (Know Thyself, 1881), he had come to express the threat to the *Volk* in terms of racial mixing and party-political strife. Yet, even so, the echoes of Herder sound in Wagner's claim to sense "something higher" than "a purely racial instinct" in a *Volk* "full of delusions" (*wahnvoll*), something "of far nobler origin and loftier aim," which might be called "the spirit of the purely Human" (PW 6:272).

CELIA APPLEGATE

See also GERMANNESS; GERMAN HISTORY; GERMAN UNIFICATION; NATIONALISM; WAHN

"Volk, Nation," in *Geschichtliche Grundbegriffe: Historisches Lexikon zur politisch-sozialen Sprache in Deutschland*, vol. 7, ed. Otto Brunner, Werner Conze, and Reinhart Koselleck (Stuttgart: Klett-Cotta, 1992).

Völsunga Saga (The Saga of the Volsungs). This is the long prose version of the tragic tale of three great heroic families, the Volsungs, Gjukungs, and Budlungs, well known and popular in texts, and wood and stone carvings in Nordic tradition from the Viking Age to the late MIDDLE AGES. Written by an anonymous author and dated in its original prose conception to the mid-thirteenth century, the saga is preserved in a single vellum manuscript dated to around 1400 and housed in the Royal Library in Copenhagen, Denmark. In addition there are twenty-one paper manuscripts containing the saga from the seventeenth century or later. Because the first page of the vellum manuscript is now so faded and damaged as to be illegible, we do not know the original title of the work or even if there was a title. However, we have a reference to a work entitled *Völsunga Saga* in a collection of sagas in the inventory of an Icelandic monastery from 1461–1510.

The plot of *Völsunga Saga* is structured chronologically, and follows five generations of the male line of the legendary family known as the Volsungs, beginning with King Volsung's grandfather, who is descended from the god Odin, and ending with his grandson Sigurd the Dragon-Slayer, whose heroic adventures constitute the subject matter for the saga's longest episode. Here is related the story of the origin of the great treasure and the cursed ring, Sigurd's slaying of the great dragon Fafnir and acquisition of the treasure and ring, and his encounter with Brynhild, whom he awakens from her magic sleep on a mountain, vows to marry, and then betrays because a magic potion has caused him to forget her. This betrayal leads to his death. After the slaying of Sigurd, the narrative turns to follow the fortunes of his wife Gudrun and her brothers, the children of King Gjuki, known as the Gjukungs. A third family, the Budlungs, becomes embroiled through the main character Brynhild and her tragic connection with Sigurd and through Gudrun's marriage to Brynhild's brother Atli. When the story finally comes to its conclusion, nearly all the members of these great families have perished, and the saga ends on an apocalyptic note.

The saga's subject matter is concerned with a world of legendary history, of the beginnings and endings of heroic dynasties and of a heroic age. We know that the author composed the saga using earlier cycles of heroic poems that recounted the adventures and destinies of these characters, because the prose text includes a number of poetic stanzas from the heroic poems we have preserved in the thirteenth-century collection known as the *Poetic* EDDA.

The *Völsunga Saga* was the main source of Wagner's plot for *Der* RING DES NIBELUNGEN; he is known to have used a translation by Friedrich Heinrich von der Hagen, *Volsunga saga oder Sigurd der Fafnirtödter und die Niflungen*, Breslau, 1815 (Cooke 112).   KAAREN GRIMSTAD

See also NORDIC MYTHOLOGY

Deryck Cooke, *I Saw the World End* (see bibliography).
Kaaren Grimstad, ed. and trans., *Völsunga Saga: The Saga of the Volsungs* (Saarbrücken: A-Q, 2000).

Vorspiel. See OVERTURE

Vorwort zur Herausgabe der Dichtung des Bühnenfestspiels "Der Ring des Nibelungen" (Preface to the Publication of the Poem of the Stage Festival Play *The Ring of the Nibelung*). The Preface was written in 1863, at a time when the text of the four operas that constitute the *Ring* cycle had taken on its final shape (with minor variation). At this point, Wagner sought to publicize his *Ring* plans to a wider audience than the friends with whom he had previously shared it. While the publication of the "poems" to *Das* RHEINGOLD, *Die* WALKÜRE, SIEGFRIED, and GÖTTERDÄMMERUNG gave his readers an idea of the content of the *Ring* cycle, the "Preface" emerged as perhaps Wagner's most influential manifesto in part because it summarizes in clear terms the kernel of his new ideas of GESAMTKUNSTWERK and its ideal performance.

Throughout, Wagner invokes a line from GOETHE's *Faust*, where the eponymous hero reformulates the opening of the Gospel of John: "In the beginning was the deed." Accordingly, Wagner insists that only the kind of staging and presentation he envisions can effectively bring to life the words and music of the *Ring*. He explains why he decided to sidestep the existing opera houses of Germany, as well as the idea of a stable ensemble of full-time singers. Most of the ideas laid out in the "Vorwort" were realized, including his plan for a makeshift "amphitheater-like" wooden structure with invisible orchestra, and the selection every spring of top-notch musicians from the best opera houses of Germany to prepare and perform the full cycle during the summer.

While Wagner's "Preface" is rather unphilosophical, and argues almost entirely along pragmatic lines, there lurks behind his program a metaphysics of unification. Opera as it is practiced in his day, as well as the character of the German nation and of MODERNITY more generally, tends toward particularization, and requires periodic "reunification." Wagner understands his vision as a corrective for the mercantile undercurrents he detects in German opera houses. He is horrified by the idea that his singers would have to sing their way through the operatic canon, rather than being able to concentrate on his cycle, at least for a time. Similarly, he thinks that the "FESTIVAL" character of the proceedings would transform the kind of audience found in his amphitheater: an audience that has come to the opera not as a distraction after a hard day of work, but rather to witness in almost religious devotion ("Andacht," as Wagner puts it) a "genuine art experience."

Wagner assumes that his operas will serve to educate the taste of the Festival audience in ways that opera houses which alternate Wagner-operas with light Italian fare supposedly cannot. At the same time, Wagner envisions his operas having an altogether different effect on his audiences than that other fare. The more limited repertoire of his theater would allow for more dynamic and complex stage design and machinery. Most famously perhaps, Wagner insists that his vision of an "amphitheater" with a hidden orchestra would hide from the viewer the "technological evolutions" of aesthetic effects that in traditional opera serve to undercut the immediacy of the experience. When nineteenth-century aestheticians of synesthesia turned to Wagner (including French *wagnérisme*), when twentieth-century critics from Bertholt Brecht to Theodor W. ADORNO criticize Wagnerian aesthetics, Wagner's ideas in the "Preface" are their points of departure.   ADRIAN DAUB

See also KUNSTRELIGION

Wagenseil, Johann Christoph (b. Nuremberg, 26 Nov. 1633; d. Altdorf, 9 Oct. 1705), German polymath. Held the Chair of History and Oriental Studies at the newly founded University of NUREMBERG in Altdorf. He was best known for his knowledge of Judaeica and for his work on Jewish-Christian relations. Author of a book about the MASTERSINGER tradition, especially in Nuremberg, Wagenseil became a source amongst German Romantic authors, including E. T. A. HOFFMANN, Ludwig Tieck, and Heinrich HEINE. Wagner used Wagenseil's book extensively for *Die MEISTERSINGER VON NÜRNBERG*, including the rules of the Tabulatur, specific names of the Mastersingers, such as Veit Pogner and SIXTUS BECKMESSER, and the melody for the guild motive. COSIMA notes Wagner re-reading Wagenseil aloud and remarks on the degree to which he was able to extract its "essence" for his opera (CWD 6 January 1873). NICHOLAS VAZSONYI

Johann Christoph Wagenseil, *Buch von der Meister-Singer Holdseligen Kunst* (in *de civitate Noribergensi commentatio* [Altdorf, 1697]), ed. Horst Brunner. Facsimile repr. (Göppingen: Kümmerle, 1975): 436–576.

Wagner, periodical (ISSN 0963-3332) published quarterly by the Wagner Society of London between 1980 and 2005. From 1984 onwards, the same society also published *Wagner News* (ISSN 0261-3468) as an organizational newsletter. *Wagner* featured often highly specialized articles on numerous issues concerning Wagner's life, work, and thought, and was edited by Stewart Spencer and Barry Millington, who also contributed frequently. The journal also published English translations of Wagner's essays, as well as detailed reviews of books and recordings. MICHAEL SAFFLE

Wagner, (Gottlob Heinrich) Adolf (b. Leipzig, 15 Nov. 1774; d. Großstädteln, 1 Aug. 1835), uncle of Richard Wagner, literary scholar, playwright, translator. Adolf studied at the Thomasschule in LEIPZIG, and went on to study theology and philosophy at Leipzig University. He had met SCHILLER and was on friendly terms with E. T. A. HOFFMANN. With a noted talent for languages, Adolf translated the works of Byron, and edited the works of Giordano Bruno. He was a father-figure and in many ways an inspiration to Richard, who lived with Adolf in Leipzig for a short period in 1822, while his mother was still in DRESDEN. In *MEIN LEBEN* (My Life, 1865–81), Wagner describes the magnificent old house overlooking the Leipzig market and the great room in which he slept, which induced fantastic dreams (ML 14–16). NICHOLAS VAZSONYI

Wagner, Albert (b. [Leipzig?] 2 March 1799; d. Berlin, 31 Oct. 1874), Wagner's older brother and adoptive father of the mezzo-soprano Johanna (Jachmann-) Wagner. Albert worked as an actor and singer then later as a stage manager and director, ultimately employed at the Berlin Court Theater. He used his theatrical connections to advance Richard Wagner's early career.

LYDIA MAYNE

Wagner-Briefe-Verzeichnis **[WBV].** A catalog of Wagner's CORRESPONDENCE compiled by Werner Breig, Martin Dürrer, and Andreas Mielke, and published by BREITKOPF & HÄRTEL (Wiesbaden, 1998). Subtitled "Chronologisches Verzeichnis der Briefe von Richard Wagner," this important reference work identifies 9,030 dated and undated letters written by Wagner; it also identifies an additional 694 documents by year and, insofar as possible, by month and date of composition. Each entry is numbered and provides the addressee's name (if known), the location(s) of drafts, holographs, and/or copies (if known), and publication information (if relevant). The WBV also includes an English-language foreword (pp. 17–26), an index of recipients (pp. 747–74), and an alphabetical list of incipits of letter texts (pp. 775–835) rather than of dates or salutations. Its cover displays a facsimile of a letter addressed by Wagner on 6 April 1870 to Breitkopf & Härtel, his own publisher.

Among its other appendices, WBV contains a concordance (pp. 836–45) of its contents with Wilhelm Altmann's *Richard Wagners Briefe nach Zeitfolge und Inhalt* (Leipzig: Breitkopf & Härtel, 1905; reprinted 1971), an earlier attempt at cataloging Wagner's letters. Launched in the 1960s, *Richard Wagner: Sämtliche Briefe*, a comprehensive chronological edition of the composer's correspondence – published initially by the VEB Deutscher Verlag für Musik (Leipzig, 1967–91); and, after the collapse of East Germany as an independent nation, by Breitkopf & Härtel (Wiesbaden, 2000–) – had by 2008 reached only 1866 (i.e., Vol. 18). The WBV is, in effect, a guide to the contents of *Sämtliche Briefe* volumes both published and not yet published. To the extent that it contains information otherwise unavailable or incorrectly presented in Altmann's catalog and the incomplete *Briefe* collected edition, it represents the best survey of Wagner's letters available at the present time. MICHAEL SAFFLE

See also CORRESPONDENCE, EDITIONS OF

Ulrich Konrad, Review, *Die Musikforschung* 54.1 (January–March 2001): 89–90.

Wagner, Carl Friedrich Wilhelm. See WAGNER, RICHARD

Wagner as composer. In the stage works of Richard Wagner, elements of German Romantic opera stemming especially from MOZART's *Die Zauberflöte* and WEBER's *Der Freischütz* were developed into a highly original artistic synthesis often described as MUSIC DRAMA, although that term was disowned by Wagner himself. The influence of Wagner has been immense, extending beyond opera and drama into AESTHETIC theory, literature, POLITICS, and PERFORMANCE PRACTICE. A prolific writer, Wagner composed the texts as well as the music of his works, adapting material from medieval epics such as the *Nibelungenlied*, the *EDDA*, GOTTFRIED VON STRASSBURG's *Tristan*, and WOLFRAM VON ESCHENBACH's *Parzival*. Wagner's music shows major innovations in its form, ORCHESTRATION, and harmonic language. In the works of his most advanced style, beginning with TRISTAN UND ISOLDE, an expanded tonal practice based on the twelve chromatic modes, a richly allusive, polyphonic motivic texture, and a formal control over vast temporal spans all contribute to an artistic synthesis in which the music assumes a central role. In order to promote his goals, Wagner founded a center for performance of his works at BAYREUTH, Germany, where a theater was constructed according to the composer's specifications, and festivals have continued since 1876.

Wagner's first three operas – Die FEEN, Das LIEBESVERBOT, and RIENZI – have never been performed at Bayreuth, and have remained much less familiar than the ten works from Der FLIEGENDE HOLLÄNDER to PARSIFAL on which his reputation mainly rests. Especially unfamiliar is Die Feen (The Fairies), an ambitious opera completed by Wagner in 1834 at the age of twenty that did not reach performance during his lifetime.

Following his failure to bring Die Feen to the stage, Wagner turned to Italian and French operatic models for his next two works: Das Liebesverbot (1836) and Rienzi (1840). In Liebesverbot, a two-act work based on SHAKESPEARE's Measure for Measure, with a shift of the action to Sicily, Wagner followed an eclectic blend of models, including the BEL CANTO melodic style of BELLINI's I Capuleti e I Montecchi, and works by Hérold and AUBER. Some aspects of Liebesverbot, with its crowd scenes and striking orchestral effects, recall French GRAND OPERA, a dominant new development of the 1830s. Wagner's next work and first major professional success, Rienzi, owes much to the grand opera of Spontini, HALÉVY, and MEYERBEER. Wagner later polemicized vigorously against "opera," but some features of grand opera style neverthe-less reemerge in certain of his ripest works, such as Die MEISTERSINGER VON NÜRNBERG and GÖTTERDÄMMERUNG.

It was in the first of his German romantic operas, Der fliegende Holländer (1843), that Wagner successfully developed material from legend centered on his favorite theme of REDEMPTION. In this context, he returned to the three-act structure and dualistic dramatic framework of Die Feen. Der fliegende Holländer and the succeeding works from the 1840s show notable musical innovations. Wagner goes beyond the strict sectional divisions and stereo-typed conventions of opera in his treatment of SENTA's ballad, with its powerful evocation of the chromatic music in the minor associated with the DUTCHMAN, with whom she is obsessed. That music, in turn, is first heard at the beginning of the overture, where its open fifths in D minor, projected in the string tremolo and ghostly horn call, recall the opening of BEETHOVEN's Ninth Symphony. In the two following operas written while he was Kapellmeister at DRESDEN, TANNHÄUSER and especially LOHEN-GRIN, Wagner tended to blur or eliminate divisions between successive set-numbers, and merge the functions of recitative and aria into an arioso-like Sprechgesang or "speech song," while imposing a unity of tone on the whole, in part through the resourceful use of recurring motives in the orchestra. Especially in Lohengrin, not only themes and motives but also keys assume consistent dramatic associations: the A major of the Prelude, for instance, is linked with LOHENGRIN and the Grail, A♭ major with ELSA of Brabant, and F♯ minor with ORTRUD.

24. Elsa's entrance (*Lohengrin*, Act I)

An example of Wagner's musical resourcefulness is provided by Elsa's initial entrance in Act I of *Lohengrin*. She remains mute in response to the King's questions, yet, as the composer put it in his 1879 essay *ÜBER DIE ANWENDUNG DER MUSIK AUF DAS DRAMA* (On the Application of Music to Drama, 1879), "a single gaze at her passionately transfigured demeanor conveys to us what lives in her." The music conveying "what lives in her" involves a shift from the G♭ major chord in A♭ major to an F♯ minor triad leading with a crescendo to the A major sonority which forms the peak of this melodic gesture (Example 24).

The double-dotted rhythms and orchestration featuring woodwinds are features associated with Elsa, yet the special expressive quality of the passage depends largely on the harmonic and melodic treatment. A key to understanding Elsa's inward vision is the modulation that carries the music beyond her own tonality of A♭ to the A major of the Grail, the sound-space of Lohengrin's music. The melody of the second two measures of this excerpt – with its falling fourth A–E followed by the falling second F♯–E – is identical to the so-called Grail motive first heard near the outset of the Prelude. Hence this gestural passage – often labeled the "Unschulds-Motiv" (Innocence Motive) – is not an independent idea, but embodies the *connection* between Elsa and Lohengrin as Grail Knight. Only at the actual appearance of Lohengrin does the distinctive modulation to A major return, in conjunction with the words and dramatic action that realize its full implications. What remained latent in this earlier instrumental passage and in Elsa's ensuing DREAM vision anticipates the dramatic turning-point of the entire act: the astonishing arrival of the Grail Knight.

The music at Lohengrin's arrival transforms a premonition into an action. At Elsa's words "Lass mich ihn seh'n wie ich ihn sah, wie ich ihn sah, sei er mir nah'!" (Let me see him as I saw him, as I saw him, let him be close to me!), the earlier progression returns with Elsa's voice carrying the melody, reaching the peak of its crescendo at the high A set to "sah" before Lohengrin's music unfolds in A major in a lively tempo (Example 25).

What had been merely an inward dream-vision here asserts its force in a public space, stirring the chorus to their astonished response: "Welch' ein seltsam Wunder!" (What a strange miracle!). "As I saw him, let him be close to me!": this formula, with its shift from past to present tense, is tangibly embodied in the music. Passionately recapturing the memory of her inward vision, Elsa moves beyond it by seemingly conjuring up Lohengrin as a *presence*. The narrative significance of Wagner's procedure is important, showing how

25. Lohengrin's entrance ("Lass mich ihn seh'n")

music can convey the difference between past and present tenses, as past-oriented reminiscence yields to fresh enactment in the present.

Wagner's involvement with the unsuccessful DRESDEN UPRISING (1849) led to his exile in Switzerland, where he spent several years occupied not with musical composition but with prose writings and the poem of his gigantic cycle *Der RING DES NIBELUNGEN*. For the music of this vast cycle, he devised a large number of motives and themes that have often been labeled as LEITMOTIVE or "leading motives." The term *Leitmotiv* does not stem from Wagner, however, and the familiar labels have little meaning in themselves and can easily mislead, by giving the false impression of a fixed and constant symbolic association. Actually, Wagner's motives tend to evolve in their dramatic associations as well as their intervallic configuration, so their significance is usually dependent on the larger context.

A central innovation of Wagner's *Ring* and later works is his abolition of set-numbers as such, and his equation of the development of music with the development of the entire drama. The slow pacing and enormous time-scale of Wagner's music make possible this identification, whereby, in Wagner's words from his aforementioned essay *Über die Anwendung der Musik auf das Drama*, "the music spreads itself over the entire drama, and not just over small, isolated, arbitrarily separated parts of the whole." One is reminded of Beethoven's imposition of a tighter musical and dramatic interconnection between the successive movements of pieces such as the Fifth and Ninth Symphonies. Wagner could claim with some justification to be Beethoven's heir in this respect.

The constant recall of short motives and more extended themes – however important – would not always suffice to articulate the events of the drama on such a massive time-scale, and Wagner also relies on extended, varied musical recapitulation. In the *Ring*, these recapitulatory elements are especially prominent in *Götterdämmerung*, which begins and ends with references to the beginning of the cycle, and culminates in a great recapitulation from the preceding drama leading to a new outcome. The opening of its Prelude, for example, recalls not only the chords from BRÜNNHILDE's awakening in *SIEGFRIED*, but also the rising motivic arpeggiations from the outset of *Das RHEINGOLD*. The very first vocal theme of the cycle, the Rhinemaidens' "Weia! Waga! Woge, du Welle, walle zur Wiege!" (an extreme example of the alliteration [*STABREIM*] which replaces end-rhyme in the *Ring* poem) recurs for the last time near the close of *Götterdämmerung*, where Flosshilde's music at the recovery of the ring corresponds closely, even in its pitch level, to the initial appearance of this theme from the prologue in *Das Rheingold*; the theme is then transposed, and combined and juxtaposed with other motives as the Rhinemaidens swim into the depths with their prize. The setting of Siegfried's final narrative, death, and funeral procession earlier in the last act of *Götterdämmerung*, on the other hand, involves a massive varied recapitulation of material drawn from both Acts II and III of the preceding drama, *Siegfried*, which is even grouped into a modulatory structure passing from E to C that recalls and transforms the tonal progression from Brünnhilde's awakening in *Siegfried*. Such modulatory structures often assume importance in the later works, but, as Robert Bailey has shown, Wagner had determined an overall framework of tonalities with dramatic associations already at a formative stage in the composition of the *Ring*.

Other innovations of the *Ring* include the use of so-called WAGNER TUBAS – baritone horns specifically designed for this work – and the curtailment of ensemble singing in those portions of the cycle composed up to 1857, namely *Das Rheingold*, *Die WALKÜRE*, and the first two acts of *Siegfried*. The music of the later portions of the *Ring* was composed only in 1869–74, following a twelve-year hiatus during which Wagner wrote *Tristan und Isolde* and *Die Meistersinger von Nürnberg*. There is consequently a noticeable stylistic shift within the *Ring* to a more advanced and polyphonic musical style in the last act of *Siegfried* and in *Götterdämmerung*, whose text is nevertheless the oldest and in part the most conventionally operatic. A somewhat analogous stylistic discontinuity was introduced into the final version of *Tannhäuser* written for

Paris in 1861, when Wagner added chromatic music in a Tristanesque style to the Venusberg scene, in contrast to the rest of the score.

As a culminating monument to ROMANTICISM and a starting-point of MODERN MUSIC, *Tristan und Isolde* assumes a pivotal position in MUSIC HISTORY. The famous chromatic music of the Prelude embodies the unfulfilled yearning of the lovers not only through its use of the harmonically ambiguous TRISTAN CHORD (a minor triad with added sixth), rising semitonal motion, and the melodic intensity and rich contrapuntal texture of its "ENDLESS MELODY" – to use Wagner's term – but also through its tonal context: a tonal center of A minor is implied, yet its actual triad is withheld. In the structural unit comprising the first seventeen measures, the music outlines a chromatic ascent through the octave from G♯ to G♯ an octave higher – leading tones of the implied tonic – while the chords at the phrase endings sound the dominant-seventh chords of the triadic degrees of A minor. Here, as elsewhere, the cadence at the end of the progression is deceptive, with the bass moving to the sixth degree, since a resolution to the implied tonic would break the tension and disrupt the musical continuity, and would be dramatically unmotivated. This example shows how Wagner's dramatic effects can be embedded in the larger musical structure, and not only reflected in referential motives. His later music, while more autonomous and less dependent on the text in specific details, often becomes thereby an ever greater and more generalized dimension of the drama.

Wagner restates this entire progression at several important dramatic junctures (at the drinking of the love potion in Act I, at Tristan's confrontation with King Marke in Act II, and at Tristan's death in the final act). Most consequential for the drama as a whole, however, is Wagner's transformation of the structural basis for the passage at the climax of the love-duet in Act II, and again in the closing moments of Isolde's transfiguration in Act III (often described as her *LIEBESTOD* or "Love-Death," though his label *Verklärung* or "transfiguration" is more fitting). In these passages, the idea of the chromatic ascent through the octave from G♯ is altered through the substitution of one pitch – F natural for F♯ – purging thereby the mysterious ambiguity of the "Tristan" chord (Example 26).

The resulting appoggiatura chord then becomes the stable tonic of B major, but only at the conclusion of Isolde's transfiguration is the cadence, with its accompanying large-scale rhythmic resolution, supplied. Isolde's text in this section is allied solely with the inward, metaphysical action, since she finds

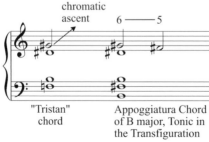

26. "Resolution" of *Tristan* chord

Tristan "awake" and describes the "ringing sound" – that is, the music – that envelops her. The great cadence, treated as the culmination of a large-scale recapitulatory gesture, is Wagner's means of symbolizing Isolde's ascent into Night, and the all-encompassing nature of the resolution is underlined by his recall of the "Tristan" chord in the final moments. The revolutionary chromaticism of *Tristan* still depends crucially on the diatonic background of this resolution, which signals the dramatic breakthrough as the lovers disappear, as it were, from the level of the visible action.

Die Meistersinger, Wagner's major work of the 1860s and the only comic opera of his maturity, centers on the relation between art and society. The predominant diatonicism of *Die Meistersinger* – with social roots in its chorales, marches, and dances – is rendered fragile through a juxtaposition with chromaticism throughout, but nowhere more evident than in the scenes for EVA and HANS SACHS in Act III, that culminates in an explicit quotation from *Tristan*.

After the completion of the *Ring* and its first performance at Bayreuth (1876), Wagner succeeded in finishing one remaining work, the BÜHNENWEIHFESTSPIEL (stage consecration festival play) PARSIFAL. *Parsifal* is the only one of Wagner's major works composed at and for Bayreuth, and its subtleties take full advantage of the sunken orchestra pit and superb acoustics of the Bayreuth FESTIVAL THEATER.

The documentation of Wagner's compositional process for *Parsifal* is unusually detailed, and includes a large number of individual musical sketches in addition to the two complete drafts Wagner typically made while composing his works. The first of these documents, the composition draft (*Kompositionsskizze*) is mainly written in pencil on oblong pages that could be easily substituted if needed; a more developed version, the orchestral draft (*Orchesterskizze*), is written in ink on gatherings of paper with more staves and includes some indications of the orchestration. While composing the music of his most mature works, Wagner worked back and forth between this pair of drafts, sometimes making separate sketches for challenging passages. Only after completing both drafts would he begin to write out the autograph full score (*Partitur*), a labor that he regarded as relatively undemanding, since most of the creative decisions had already been made. Wagner's patterns of compositional work on *Parsifal* are clarified as well by entries in COSIMA WAGNER'S DIARIES, which correspond closely to the manuscript sources. Study of these sources reveals surprises: for instance, the last music conceived for *Parsifal* was the second half of the Transformation Music in Act I, which Wagner composed in March 1881 after realizing that this transitional musical passage was too short for the purposes of the staging. Wagner was angered about the need to compose additional music, but the expansion is effective, and the work benefited from his inconvenience. The expanded Transformation Music proved still too short for purposes of the staging in 1882, and Engelbert HUMPERDINCK arranged a loop-like repetition to achieve the necessary length.

The theme of redemption takes on a more radical, collective character in *Parsifal*, as aspects of Christianity are assimilated into Wagner's temple of art. Thus the "transfiguration" of the central protagonist(s) does not occur as an end point to the action, as in *Der fliegende Holländer* or *Tristan*, but begins as early as Act II, as PARSIFAL recoils from KUNDRY's seduction attempt, with its musical embodiment in the contaminating chromaticism of her music. Parsifal's denial of the temptation of the senses is connected to his capacity for compassion; Agapē overcomes Eros. Musically, there is no resolution of chromaticism into diatonicism here, as in *Tristan und Isolde*, but rather a purification *from* chromaticism of the diatonic themes and motives of the Grail, which are integrated and combined for the first time in the closing recapitulatory synthesis at the end of Act III, when Parsifal appears as redeemer and reveals the Grail. Wagner's attempts to express the inexpressible, or at least the extraordinary, were carried to their limits in *Parsifal*, and, not surprisingly, it proved difficult if not impossible for subsequent composers of opera to build further on this line of approach. In recognition of its exhaustive character, DEBUSSY once described Wagner's legacy as "a beautiful sunset that was mistaken for a dawn."   WILLIAM KINDERMAN

Robert Bailey, "The Structure of the *Ring* and Its Evolution," *19th Century Music* 1 (1977): 48–61; repr. *National Traditions in Nineteenth-Century Opera*, vol. 2, ed. Michael C. Tusa (Surrey: Ashgate, 2010): 143–56.

William Kinderman, "Dramatic Recapitulation and Tonal Pairing in Wagner's *Tristan und Isolde* and *Parsifal*," in *The Second Practice of Nineteenth-Century Tonality*, ed. William Kinderman and Harald Krebs (Lincoln: University of Nebraska Press, 1996): 178–214.

"The Genesis of the Music," in *A Companion to Wagner's "Parsifal,"* ed. William Kinderman and Katherine Syer (Rochester: Camden House, 2005): 133–75.

Klaus Kropfinger, *Wagner and Beethoven* (see bibliography).

Wagner as conductor. Wagner's art of conducting was the prime influence on his successors in the German tradition, from his student Hans von BÜLOW to Gustav MAHLER, Richard STRAUSS, Arthur Nikisch, Wilhelm FURTWÄNGLER, and beyond. The impact of his 1869 tract *Über das Dirigieren* (On Conducting) has proven of even longer-lasting significance.

As a conductor Wagner was essentially self-taught, learning as he worked his way up the hierarchy of provincial German theaters. His reminiscences of conductors he admired, primarily François-Antoine Habeneck and Gaspare Spontini, nevertheless show him to have been a keen observer of the practices of others. He made his conducting debut in MAGDEBURG in the summer of 1834 with MOZART's *Don Giovanni* and thereafter cut his teeth on the standard operatic works of the day, from AUBER to BELLINI, ROSSINI, WEBER, and so on. The opera orchestras of Magdeburg, KÖNIGSBERG, and RIGA were small and poorly staffed, and they afforded limited rehearsal time for a high turnover of repertoire. Wagner's later uncompromising insistence on sufficient, well-organized rehearsals was perhaps a logical reaction to the experiences of these galley years. Only when appointed Kapellmeister in DRESDEN in 1843 did he begin to work with a high-class ensemble in a properly equipped opera house. He also now began conducting in concerts, most notably the Palm Sunday performance of BEETHOVEN's Ninth Symphony on 5 April 1846 for which he placed the chorus in a semicircle behind the orchestra – a decision at the time revolutionary, but which later became the norm.

Dresden was Wagner's last full-time post, though conducting long remained his prime source of income. In ZURICH he became de facto the musical director of the local orchestra from 1850 to 1855, soon earning as much per concert as had his predecessor Franz Abt for the whole season. He also conducted in the local theater. Zurich concerts had hitherto comprised a potpourri of vocal and instrumental items, but Wagner made Beethoven's symphonies the core of the repertoire and introduced the new concept of having an overture followed by a concerto, then a symphony after the interval.

Wagner conducted the Philharmonic Society in LONDON in 1855, with mixed success. He continued giving guest performances at home and abroad until his London concerts of 1877, though he now focused on promoting his own works. He still occasionally performed Beethoven's symphonies, such as the Ninth on 22 May 1872 in celebration of the laying of the cornerstone of the FESTIVAL THEATER in BAYREUTH.

Wagner delegated conducting the *RING* in 1876 to Hans RICHTER, and *PARSIFAL* in 1882 to Hermann LEVI. His last appearances on the podium were for the latter half of the final performance of *Parsifal* in August 1882 and for a private performance of his early SYMPHONY IN C with the orchestra of the Liceo Benedetto Marcello in VENICE in December 1882.

Wagner's many moves meant that he was unable to build up a library of marked-up scores that might let us deduce his interpretations of the classics. And since he gave few performances in later years when others were at hand to record his thoughts and actions, we have but sparse descriptions of his conducting style. We know that the mature Wagner did not beat time in the manner to which many orchestral players were accustomed. The critic of *The Times* on 14 March 1855 called his beat "perplexing" and criticized the "confusion between the 'up' and 'down' beat, which he appears to employ indiscriminately." The critic further disliked both Wagner's conducting from memory and his "changes perpetual and finicky," but at least admitted his "unabated energy and fire." This energy was remarked upon by numerous others, from his Zurich friend Wilhelm BAUMGARTNER in the early 1850s ("He knew how to rule and inspire the orchestra like a military leader, full of life, spirit, clarity and fire" [Widmer 131]) to his Bayreuth doctor Carl Landgraf ("[Wagner's] spirit went into the [musicians] like an electric battery," quoted in CWD 1 January 1879).

Numerous orchestral parts used by Wagner have nevertheless survived in Zurich. Together with letters, concert programs, and receipts these allow a partial reconstruction of his working methods there. Besides insisting on full attendance for the statutory three rehearsals per concert, he sometimes worked individually with players. He also had expression marks and rehearsal letters added to the orchestral parts in advance.

In *Über das Dirigieren*, Wagner codified some of his practices, though it offers little hands-on advice after the manner of Berlioz's treatise. Wagner discusses general matters of tempo and expression with specific reference to works by Beethoven, Mozart, and GLUCK. He adopts the terminology of SCHILLER, stating that sharp differences between loud and soft were characteristic of the older, "naïve" style of composition (for us "classical"), whereas the symphonies of Beethoven from the *Eroica* onwards represented the newer, "sentimental" (for us "Romantic") style. He justifies inserting more differentiated dynamics into the last symphonies of Mozart by claiming that these works had already crossed the boundary into Romanticism, though the composer himself had remained unaware of it. Indeed, Wagner's extant marked-up parts in Zurich for Mozart's Symphony No. 41 and Haydn's No. 104 comprise mostly *crescendi* and *decrescendi* to lessen the impact of sudden *piani* and *forti*. On the one hand, Wagner insists on fidelity to the composer's intentions: thus he criticizes the tendency to play the *Tempo di menuetto* movement of Beethoven's Eighth Symphony as if it were a fast scherzo, and recalls how he had replaced a *piano* inserted by Carl REISSIGER in the last movement of Beethoven's Ninth with the composer's original *forte*. But on the other hand, as in the abovementioned works by Mozart and Haydn, he also allows the performer the freedom to decide what he believes the composer's intentions to have been. His article on performing Beethoven's Ninth, *Zum Vortrag der neunten Symphonie Beethoven's* (April 1873), also states clearly that developments in instrument-building since Beethoven's day make necessary certain slight modifications to the musical text.

Above all, Wagner says, it is the "MELOS," the melodic essence of a work, that must be found and that will give the right tempo (a belief upheld by conductors as diverse as John Barbirolli and Daniel BARENBOIM). Furthermore, just as the *crescendo* was an innovation in Mozart's day, he says, so does the use of *rubato* belong to the interpretation of music from the Romantic works of Beethoven onwards. Beethoven's motivic technique imparted fluidity to the thematic content of his music, but "the tempo ... [should] not be any less fluid than the thematic web." According to Heinrich Sczadrowsky in the NEUE ZEITSCHRIFT FÜR MUSIK of 26 June 1857 (46.26: 276–7), Wagner's tempo fluctuations were already a matter of debate in Germany. *Über das Dirigieren* nevertheless offers Wagner's first codification of this so-called *espressivo* conducting style that was adopted by successors in the German tradition, as we can hear in the recordings of Arthur Nikisch and Wilhelm Furtwängler.

Wagner further approves of taking the second subject in a sonata movement at a different tempo from the first (something that raised the ire of the *Times* critic in London in May 1855 when done in the first movement of Mozart's Symphony No. 39). Wagner's "ART OF TRANSITION" thus extended beyond his composing into his style of interpretation, both in dynamics and in tempi. For his own works, the few extant sources – such as Wagner's statement in *Über das Dirigieren* that his TANNHÄUSER overture should take just 12 minutes, the metronome measurements recorded by Edward DANNREUTHER at the first BAYREUTH FESTIVAL, or recordings made by his son SIEGFRIED in the 1920s of works such as the SIEGFRIED IDYLL – suggest that Wagner preferred generally faster tempi than are the norm today. CHRIS WALTON

Michael Allis, "Richter's Wagner: A New Source for Tempi in *Das Rheingold*," *Cambridge Opera Journal* 20.2 (2008): 117–48.

Norbert Heinel, *Richard Wagner als Dirigent* (Vienna: Praesens Verlag, 2006).

Raymond Holden, *The Virtuoso Conductors* (see bibliography).

Chris Walton, *Richard Wagner's Zurich* (see bibliography).

"Upstairs, Downstairs: Acoustics and Tempi in Wagner's 'Träume' and *Siegfried Idyll*," *The Musical Times* 153.1918 (spring 2012): 7–18.

C. Widmer, *Wilhelm Baumgartner: Ein Lebensbild* (Zurich: David Bürkli, 1868).

Wagner, Cosima (b. Bellagio, 24 Dec. 1837; d. Bayreuth, 1 Apr. 1930), born Francesca Gaetana Cosima, illegitimate offspring of the connection between Franz LISZT and Countess Marie D'AGOULT, was brought up together with her sister Blandine and her brother Daniel by an austere Russian governess (Madame Patersi) in PARIS. She was an excellent pianist, but her father forbade her from becoming a professional artist. She married the conductor and composer Hans von BÜLOW in 1857. Their honeymoon led them to ZURICH, where Richard Wagner and his wife MINNA were living in the so-called "Asyl(um)" next to the villa of Otto and Mathilde WESENDONCK. Cosima was fascinated by Wagner's music, but in a letter to Emma Herwegh (9 April 1858) joked over his intense love for Mathilde. Various meetings ensued, and, as Wagner writes in his autobiography, on 28 November 1863 he and Cosima swore in Berlin to belong to each other (ML 4:745–6). (At the time he was engaged in a love affair with his maid Maria Völkl in Austria.) When, at Wagner's instigation, Hans and Cosima moved to MUNICH, Wagner and Cosima began their relationship. Hans was aware of the liaison, but he remained tolerant of it. Whereas Jessie LAUSSOT feared the scandal of elopement, and Mathilde Wesendonck was inclined to put her family first, and both she and Mathilde MAIER were too conservative to live in an unmarried state, Cosima ignored all moral attacks on her behavior and bore Wagner three children (ISOLDE, EVA, and SIEGFRIED). Her illegitimate relationship with Richard meant a double life. In November 1868, she moved to TRIBSCHEN near Lucerne and stayed by his side from then on. In July 1870, Hans von Bülow agreed to a divorce and the new couple married a month later. Cosima was not only Wagner's lover, friend, and mother of his children, but also his secretary, copying his scores and dealing with correspondence (extensively, for instance, with LUDWIG II) and visitors. From 1 January 1869 until Wagner's death on 13 February 1883, she kept diaries, describing in detail their conversations on politics, philosophy, art, the books they read, the music they studied, and so on (see COSIMA WAGNER'S DIARIES). They demonstrate her profound literary and musical knowledge as well as her broad cultural and musical education, and they remain important research sources on Wagner. Judging from her statements, Cosima was a German nationalist and anti-Semite, though she often cautioned Wagner to keep his sentiments to himself, and even urged him not to re-publish Das JUDENTUM IN DER MUSIK (Jewishness in Music, 1850) in 1869. After her husband's death, a group of ideological extremists (known at the BAYREUTH CIRCLE) formed around her, including Hans von WOLZOGEN and Houston Stewart CHAMBERLAIN.

Since Wagner left no will, Cosima temporarily took charge of the organization of the BAYREUTH FESTIVAL, having been his closest assistant during the composition of his late works, and also during the first production of the RING cycle (1876). After two seasons, she accepted the role as responsible director, feeling compelled to present his operas according to his intentions, without however striving to copy his productions exactly. In the ensuing years, she enlarged the number of productions from PARSIFAL to the Ring cycle, and gained renown for her TRISTAN production in 1886, for which she designed the stage set and gave written instructions for props, lighting, colors, and costumes. She studied all of Wagner's theoretical writings and insisted on predetermining gestures and movements on the stage, including even the position of hands, cueing characteristic gestures to specific passages in the score. She gave the singers detailed instructions and passed short but precise messages to the conductors, while sitting in a partitioned area which had been especially constructed for her. When she directed *Die MEISTERSINGER* in 1888, the figure of SIXTUS BECKMESSER was shown not as an exaggerated caricature but as someone possessing a tragic dimension. She produced *Parsifal* in 1888, and her 1891 *TANNHÄUSER* was prepared by conscientious study and assembling a competent production team. She accentuated the plot by pitting a Dionysian Venus from antiquity against an ELISABETH who symbolized the pure and simple (German) MIDDLE AGES. Her *LOHENGRIN* (1894) was followed by her last new production in 1901, *Der FLIEGENDE HOLLÄNDER*, set in seventeenth-century Norway. In 1906, she presented an altered version of her old *Tristan* production. Although she claimed authenticity, she had an individual style in her productions: "Theater history knows of no other woman who brought forth anything comparable to this and who exerted such an enormous influence" (Mack 15). She worked hard for twenty-three years to make the Festival an event of world renown, but she hardly made a mark on performance history as it was generally believed that her staging was solely an act of reverence to the Master. Seeing herself as executor of his will, she refused to have her name mentioned in the programs. In 1906, she suffered a heart attack and sometime shortly thereafter withdrew from running of the Festival, passing it on to her son Siegfried.

In 1913, Isolde, biologically Richard's daughter, but legally claimed by Bülow, decided to take her mother to court in order to prove her true heredity. Isolde was married to the conductor Franz BEIDLER, and their son would have been heir to the Bayreuth festival as long as Siegfried had no children. Cosima remained adamant in her denial and, after a scandalous trial, the court ruled against Isolde. The outbreak of World War I in 1914 forced the Festival into a decade-long hiatus.

Cosima created the basis for the Richard Wagner ARCHIVE in Bayreuth by collecting documents, scores, letters, and so on. However, she was also responsible for destroying materials (e.g., letters to Minna, to Mathilde Wesendonck, and from NIETZSCHE to herself) for the sake of constructing and preserving Wagner's image. She died in 1930 at the age of 92, a few months before her beloved son passed away. There are 4,500 letters written by her that still exist. EVA RIEGER

Franz Wilhelm Beidler, *Cosima Wagner-Liszt: Der Weg zum Wagner-Mythos*, ed. Dieter Borchmeyer (Bielefeld: Pendragon, 1997).

Dietrich Mack, ed., *Cosima Wagner. Das zweite Leben. Briefe und Aufzeichnungen 1883–1930* (Munich: Piper, 1980).

Wagner as essayist. The composer Richard Wagner was a writer. He wrote around ten thousand letters; newspaper articles; polemical pamphlets; treatises on technical matters such as conducting and how to run an opera house; major theoretical texts (book length in the case of *OPER UND DRAMA* [Opera and Drama, 1851]); a substantial autobiography (*MEIN LEBEN* [My Life, 1865–81]); and, by-the-by, the libretti of his own MUSIC DRAMAS. Excluding the letters and *Mein Leben*, but including the libretti, all this occupies thirteen of the sixteen volumes of the "complete" Edition (*Sämtliche Schriften und Dichtungen*; SSD). In short, Wagner was a devoted and serious writer, and he would not be happy to see the degree to which this has been marginalized.

In particular, he would not be pleased to see his essays ignored. And, despite (or even because of) their occasional follies and offensive character, he would have been right. For, taken as a whole, they reveal him to have been intellectually bold, bent on synthesizing material over a massive eclectic terrain. They also show him working opportunistically within conventional scholarly parameters in order to explode them. Moreover, while it could be correctly argued that the essays form a body of vital theoretical and ideological commentary on the music dramas, they can also be seen as valid in their own terms. Wagner certainly did. Writing to MINNA on 16 April 1850 he laments: "you detested my writings, in spite of the fact that I tried to make clear to you that they were now more necessary to me than all my useless attempts to write operas."

It might seem self-evidently impossible to find in this plethora an interpretative approach that could make sense of the whole without throwing out a good many babies with the bathwater. But the essays show a common interest in metaphysics, meaning Wagner consistently foregrounds a form of anti-materialism which he employs to understand his favored notions of VOLK, history, anthropology, AESTHETICS, and RELIGION.

Wagner was probably predisposed to metaphysical thinking by two factors, one biographical and the other cultural. He was born into a family of artists; writers, composers, actors, and singers shaped his domestic milieu. It would have been odd indeed if Thomas Mann's *Buddenbrooks* had been reversed and he had turned out a merchant. Meanwhile, the contemporary cultural climate was heavily weighted in favor of anti-materialist philosophy. German thinking was innately idealist – at least before Marx became a Marxist. Kant and HEGEL dominated, and Wagner studied both, in particular struggling with the latter. Then, in his early forties, he adopted SCHOPENHAUER who developed the Kantian agenda, taking a grim and dismissive attitude to our material lives in the here and now. Important is the role of AESTHETICS. In his Third Critique (On Judgment), Kant suggests that aesthetics gives us special knowledge of the world and underpins ethical judgments as a result. Therefore it is hardly surprising if nineteenth-century German thinkers often claim art has a unique epistemological status. Nor was this an exclusively philosophical business. Poets and dramatists such as GOETHE and SCHILLER were well versed in philosophy (often personally acquainted with the philosophers), and artistic activity was interwoven with the intellectual life of the academy. Thus in Wagner's world, whether personal or cultural, metaphysics was dominant, and art was seen as a particularly apposite field in which to tackle – to take a central Wagnerian example – REDEMPTION.

If we are to appreciate why, and how, Wagner became arguably the key artist-intellect of German idealism, two other factors (again one specific and one general) need to be added to the mix. The specific is WOMEN as the paradigmatic site of moral salvation. Wagner turned several times in his writings to Goethe's "eternal feminine." It clearly inspires his notion of the redeeming woman. The general is the *Volk*. When Wagner was a boy, the German cultural revival was under way. It had been intellectually under-pinned by the philosophers Fichte (like Wagner, a passionate nationalist and ANTI-SEMITE) and HERDER, whose path-breaking work in anthropology and linguistics established the theoretical basis on which indigenous culture could be celebrated in its own terms. Both lacerated the contemporary passion for all things French, something emphatically reflected in Wagner's *Deutsche Kunst und deutsche Politik* (German Art and German Policy, 1867). Indeed, Wagner could not have been more predisposed to a folk-oriented cultural polemic, and duly folded it within his broader metaphysical agenda.

As a result, Wagner's metaphysics are profoundly German. Abstract theor-izing and all its lofty connotations have a rooted and racial place for him. And although that rooted place is also fancifully explained (above all in his invent-ive anthropology), it is incontestable. Therefore in *Die WIBELUNGEN* (1848), we find the most extravagant claims designed to establish the special status of the German tribe. The Germans are, unlike the other European peoples who emigrated from the Central Asian Highlands, "echt" (genuine) in that they have not prostituted their language (which also means their *Volk* music) and they have not corrupted their blood strain. This celebration of the *Volk* satur-ates the late 1840s and is present in the Nibelungen essay (1848), the work on Frederick Barbarossa, and the libretto for *Siegfrieds Tod*. But one way and another it is pursued, in increasingly abstract terms, through to the final essays that make up *RELIGION UND KUNST*.

Behind all of this is a wide-ranging and, from an epistemological point of view, particularly interesting claim. Privileging the *Volk*, and with it *völkisch* music and language, and so on, necessitates a rejection of standard historical probity. MYTH takes precedence. The result is a massive degree of freedom, allowing Wagner to claim whatever he wants as soon as he puts it in the context of mystical *Volk* knowledge. He has, in short, given himself the perfect rationalization for his polemical essays. True, every now and again he will toss in a dash of conventional history, but it is only to underpin his metaphysical agenda. Paradoxically this allows him to appeal to empiricism as long as it is grounded in "instinct." So, in the upfront racist essay *Das JUDENTUM IN DER MUSIK* (Jewishness in Music, 1850), he simply tells us that "we" non-JEWS feel an instinctive revulsion towards everything Jewish, and it is pretty clear that if a German gentile were to say he didn't feel that, he would be accused of either idiocy or mendacity. In all cases, hostile arguments are ruled out by means that Wagner thinks are entirely kosher and which – should one accept his premises – probably are. The problem, of course, is the premises.

Nor is this a superficial business, as the premises, with respect to both what is vilified as alien and decadent, and what is celebrated as innately *echt* and spiritual, go to the very root of the argument. Wagner's agenda is elevated (he imagines) even when addressing seemingly minor matters (e.g., rhyming systems) precisely because truth is a matter of essence. The quintessential values of race and culture transcend prosaic reality. Just like the redeemed heroes and heroines, they exist in a lofty state that, *finally*, has nothing to do with the everyday world. In this context, to mount a critique of the essays on the basis of conventional academic probity would make one, in Wagner's eyes, axiomatically guilty of a solecism. And so his theories on rhyme are rooted in the essential nature of the *Ur-Volk* (see PW 2:227–8).

Wagner also plays fast and loose in other ways. Just as he has recourse to facts and empirical research when it suits him, so he moves the goalposts when it comes to style. Interestingly, as in his music, he is a master of style, something all the understandable talk about his occasionally turbid prose too often obscures. His early newspaper articles from Paris are perfectly suited to his German readership, just as *Mein Leben* is a continual source of pleasure. The letters, in particular, are intellectually stimulating and often peppered with word play and entertaining doggerel. And even when he is writing upfront, and relatively brief, polemical stuff he can be no less approachable. Anyone can (unfortunately) understand *Das Judentum in der Musik*; its argument is clearly laid out. Nor are the late essays that make up RELIGION UND KUNST unreadable. Ironically, however, when he produces heavy-going prose, he seems to believe it is necessary to establish the academic credentials he otherwise mocks. In *Oper und Drama* he drapes himself in the mantle of a stringent scholar, declares his premises and clearly defines his terms. As it happens, the terminology slips, but the style remains abstruse. Behind this is an admiration for a philosopher famous for difficult syntax. He says in *Mein Leben* that he was led to see in Hegel's "incomprehensible" and "speculative" writings the cornerstone of all philosophical knowledge (ML 442; ML/E 429–30). Here again Wagner is having it both ways. He is right to insist on his status as an artist but he is being inconsistent when soon after finishing *Oper und Drama* he declares in Eine MITTEILUNG AN MEINE FREUNDE (A Communication to my Friends, 1851) that: "thus did I become an *artist*, and not a carping man of letters" (PW 1:306). Well, he may not have wanted to carp (although he often did), but there were certainly times when he wants the status of a man of letters.

While it didn't do Wagner's prose any harm to ditch Hegel for SCHOPENHAUER after 1854, it did not lead to a complete abandonment of Hegelian ideas. Most notably "Aufhebung" remains important to his thinking. A famous/notorious three-way German pun, it is often translated into English as "synthesis" (or in some academic texts "sublation"). In the philosophical context it indicates an enhanced state which comes about from the merger of the best aspects of the two conflicting states that precede it. This process is driven by something called a dialectic, whereby each state is bent on producing its negation or opposite. As such it is a crucial component in Wagner's metaphysical thinking and is prominent in the essays. Unfortunately, it disappears in the standard and inelegant ELLIS translations, where, for instance, in *Jesus von Nazareth* you find it and its derivatives translated, not very helpfully, as "upheaval," "abrogation," "repeal," and "abolished."

One common function of *Aufhebung* (notably in *Das KUNSTWERK DER ZUKUNFT* [The Artwork of the Future, 1849/50]) concerns the dialectical tension between the individual and the *Volk*. In this case the synthesis is engineered when the individual enriches his personality by giving himself over to the greater category of the *Volk*. This proves an adept shift, as it enhances Wagner's 1840s enthusiasm for communism without undermining his essentially sentimental notion of the Germans – after all, he was never going to develop into a dialectical *materialist*. A further pay-off is appropriately contradictory. While the dialectical synthesis seems to privilege the *Volk*, this does not mean Wagner has to downgrade the individual as the unit where the *Aufhebung* becomes active, indeed dramatic, in narrative terms. For stage works are invariably narratives centered on individuals. Paradoxically this causes a further dialectical contradiction as the Wagner hero becomes the privileged site of everything. This does not come about because of any disillusionment with the German *Volk*. Certainly, that does happen later, where it leads to yet more anti-materialist theorizing, notably fusing religion with art. It also leads Wagner to tell Nietzsche (letter, 24 October 1872) that "Germanness" is wholly metaphysical in nature. However, earlier there is a dialectical progress whereby the ego is initially denied in the interests of the *Volk* only to be subsequently celebrated (in the appropriate *Aufhebung*) once S I E G F R I E D struts the boards.

Nevertheless, spotlighting the hero is misleading, for he only realizes his destiny – becomes sublimely *himself* – by his union with a woman equal to this mighty task. Now, while the notion of the redemptive woman was always the kernel for Wagner, it reaches its onstage apotheosis post-Schopenhauer when the sexual character of the privileged pair is paramount. Whereupon we uncover a further contradiction. Sex smuggles into the essays a materialist category (the body), although Wagner can disguise this by packaging it as the royal road to the highest (idealized) form of love. More important, however, is a related problem. For, while Schopenhauer encourages the development of Wagner's metaphysical thinking, he would never have swallowed either the special constellation of the pair or the transfiguring role of sex. And Wagner knew it, as both his correspondence with Mathilde W E S E N D O N C K and his aborted letter to Schopenhauer (both 1858) make clear. This, however, only convinced him that he was right; that he could "improve" on Schopenhauer. Above all in the late essays, he writes as though the Will (for Schopenhauer a blind, arbitrary drive) can be raised through sex to a lofty category. This privileging of sex is common in Wagner's writings, where it also functions as an explanation of the creative activity itself. Indeed, he writes of impregnation or fertilization, and so on, in a manner that goes far beyond mere analogy. It is as though he is revealing the DNA of culture. Furthermore, it is an indication of how central these metaphysical struggles are, that they can be found as early as *Oper und Drama* – that is, before he read Schopenhauer.

Here, too, *Aufhebung* continues to be relevant, for what is Wagner's notion of sex if not an enriching, dialectical, synthesis? Through *Aufhebung*, sex intellectually infiltrates the essays on religion. Christ on the Cross is now the privileged icon, just as he is by implication in the last music drama, but this is not a category change; rather, it is the conclusion of a theme that takes us back to, at least, *Jesus von Nazareth* and Siegfried, the Ur-Christ of *Die Wibelungen*. But there is a potent shift in tone. The atmosphere becomes pacific; killing dragons is no longer on the agenda, though we should not forget that, according to *Die Wibelungen*, the Nibelung/Dragon's Hoard becomes the Grail; in other words, the vessel in which the supreme miracle of transubstantiation occurs. Blood was always vital to Wagner's theorizing, but now it reaches an apotheosis in Christ's blood: the gentle blood of the lamb, unambiguously opposed to "corrosive" Jewish blood (CWD 7 April 1873). Furthermore in *Religion und Kunst* it is the Jewish God who is painted as a Lord of War (PW 6:233–4), while in *WAS IST DEUTSCH?* (What is German?, 1865/78) the increasingly metaphysical status of the German *Volk* is established by conjuring up opportunistically the contrasting stereotype of the grasping Jew. Meanwhile the intellectual freedom which is inscribed into the Hegelian dialectic duly does the business again, Wagner arguing, in obscure language, that the Will-less Savior (will-less-ness being a Schopenhauerian ideal) somehow dialectically embodies a transcendent expression of the Will. This time *Aufhebung* is translated by Ellis as a "cancelling" (PW 6:244–5).

For the highly contradictory manner in which sex is transfigured in order to be fit for all this metaphysical theorizing, one has to go to the related music drama. PARSIFAL wins enlightenment through a sexual encounter with the paradigmatic – that is, both sinful and sacred – woman, and thereby attains the identity of an ersatz Christ; a Christ awash with all the blood-significance found in the late essays. Nonetheless, Wagner was not finished with polemical work on sex, the feminine, and race. On the day he died he was writing *Über das Weibliche im Menschlichen* (On the Womanly in the Human Race) where he once again tries to get anthropology to work for him. The female remains both morally paradigmatic (in her identity as the Mother) and sexual, being the object of the "ideal love" of the male. Wagner, as always, wants to hold onto male sexual freedom, yet seems forced to insist on monogamy. After all, he argues, its alternative (polygamy) leads to racial degeneracy. Thus race and sexuality remain vital and contradictory ingredients in Wagner's metaphysical worldview.

Wagner's essays require an open mind. They are thematically multifarious, willful, at times remarkably insightful and at others foolish. They can on occasion be both frustratingly difficult to read and offensive. They are also fascinating, novel; an astonishing quarry of ideas and commentary. In Wagner studies there is no better indicator of intellectual cowardice and shallowness than the advice (gratuitously given by some) to ignore them. The contrary is the case. Anyone who wants to come to terms with Wagner (writer and composer) needs them.   BARRY EMSLIE

See also GENDER; SEXUALITY AND EROTICISM; *STABREIM*

Wagner, Eva. See CHAMBERLAIN, EVA

Wagner, Friedelind (nickname: "Maus"; b. Bayreuth, 29 Mar. 1918; d. Herdecke, 8 May 1991), second child of SIEGFRIED and WINIFRED. Left Germany in 1939 out of protest against the National Socialist regime and the friendship between Adolf HITLER and her family.

In England, she published newspaper articles criticizing BAYREUTH's Nazi connection. Interned in Great Britain in 1940, her release to Argentina (1941) was obtained with Arturo TOSCANINI's help. They met in Buenos Aires, where he was on tour. Afterwards, he took her to New York. She obtained US citizenship, worked as a secretary and waitress, gave lectures all over the USA, studied stage production at Columbia University and, in 1945, published *Heritage of Fire*, the story of her early life, including the political involvement of the Festival (the book was released in the UK as *The Royal Family of Bayreuth*). In

1946, she founded the "Friedelind Wagner Opera Company," to tour the United States with a group of singers, but gave up the project for financial reasons.

She refused to reply to offers from the Mayor of Bayreuth to direct the Festival in 1947, as she believed it was too soon after the war to restart the Festival. Though Siegfried had bequeathed the Festival to all four children, a crafty legal arrangement allowed Winifred to delegate management of the Festival to her sons, keeping Friedelind out. From 1959 to 1967, she organized and directed master classes in Bayreuth for hand-picked young musicians, theater architects, and stage directors, but efforts to organize master classes in Great Britain were unsuccessful. She devoted the rest of her life to promoting her father's music, and arranged a concert of his music in London (1975). She never succeeded in shedding her status as an exile and spent her final years in Lucerne, not far from TRIBSCHEN. EVA RIEGER

Eva Rieger, *Friedelind Wagner: Die rebellische Enkelin Richard Wagners* (Munich: Piper, 2012). Friedelind Wagner, *Heritage of Fire* (see bibliography).

Wagner, Gottfried Helferich (b. Bayreuth, 13 April 1947), multimedia director, musicologist, writer; son of WOLFGANG WAGNER and great-grandson of Richard Wagner. He studied musicology, philosophy, and German philology, and received his Ph.D. from the University of Vienna in 1977 with a dissertation on Kurt Weill and Bertolt Brecht. Upon discovering his family's connections with HITLER and the Nazi party, he distanced himself from the Festival and became a staunch critic of Richard Wagner's legacy, making him a pariah within the Wagner clan. In his autobiography, *Wer nicht mit dem Wolf heult* (1977), he emphasizes his family's involvement with the Nazi party. Along with Abraham Peck, he founded the "Post-Holocaust Dialogue Group" in 1992. He has directed opera, written and produced radio programs, and written and lectured extensively on humanitarian issues, anti-Semitism, German culture, and politics. He is featured in a documentary film, *The Wagner Family* (2011) by Tony Palmer. ALEXIS LUKO

Gottfried Wagner, *Du sollst keine anderen Götter haben neben mir: Richard Wagner – Ein Minenfeld* (Munich: Propyläen, 2013).
Twilight of the Wagners: The Unveiling of a Family's Legacy, trans. Della Couling (New York: Picador, 1999).
Wer nicht mit dem Wolf heult, foreword Ralph Giordano (Cologne: Kiepenheuer & Witsch, 1997).

Wagner, Gudrun (née Armann) (b. Allenstein, East Prussia [now Olsztyn, Poland] 15 June 1944; d. Bayreuth, 28 Nov. 2007). Because of the war, she was taken aged four weeks to Bavaria, and grew up near Regensburg. Trained there as a translator and secretary, she joined the press department of the BAYREUTH FESTIVAL in 1965, working initially for WIELAND WAGNER. In 1970, she married the scholar Dietrich Mack, from whom she was later divorced. Secretary to WOLFGANG WAGNER in 1976, she married him later that year. Their only child, KATHARINA, was born in 1978.

"Personal advisor" to Wolfgang from 1985, she gained intimate knowledge of the workings of the festival. Her diplomacy, organizational flair, and skill managing artists led her husband to propose her as his successor in 2001 – an idea rejected by the RICHARD WAGNER FOUNDATION. From then, however, she increasingly shared Wolfgang's workload. Her death while recovering from surgery in hospital was totally unexpected. DEREK WATSON

Wagner, Isolde. See BEIDLER, ISOLDE

Wagner, Johanna Rosine (Geyer, née Pätz) (b. Weissenfels, 19 Sep. 1774; d. Leipzig, 9 Jan. 1848), Richard Wagner's mother. Sixth child of Johann Gottlob Pätz (a baker) and Dorothea Erdmuthe, Johanna was the mistress of Prince Constantin of Saxe-Weimar-Eisenach, who, until his death in 1793, provided her with lodging and an education in LEIPZIG. She married Carl Friedrich Wagner in 1798 and had nine children, among whom Albert and Richard stand out, the former as father of noted singer Johanna (Jachmann-)Wagner. After Carl Friedrich's death, Johanna married Ludwig GEYER (28 August 1814) and gave birth to a daughter, Cäcilie, half a year later. Johanna spoke fondly of all the arts with the exception of the theater, which she dissuaded Wagner from joining (ML/E 12). In *MEIN LEBEN* (My Life, 1865–81), Wagner describes his mother as distant, lacking in maternal tenderness, and secretive with regards to her family background and early life. ALEXIS LUKO

Wagner Journal, The (March 2007–), periodical (ISSN 1755–0173), published three times each year in English, originally edited by Barry Millington and Stewart Spencer, after the first year exclusively by the former. The Editorial Board includes Roger Allen, Mike Ashman, Tim Blanning, Werner Breig, John Deathridge, and Laurence Dreyfus, among others. *The Wagner Journal* seeks to examine Wagner and his works from a variety of perspectives – musicological, historical, literary, philosophical, and political. The journal's main thrust concerns the theory and practice of staging and performing, although it offers a wide range of articles written by both scholars and artists. In addition to feature articles and reviews of live performances, books, CDs, and DVDs, *The Wagner Journal* periodically offers new translations of Wagner's prose works. MICHAEL SAFFLE

www.thewagnerjournal.co.uk: website sponsored by the Wagner Society of Washington, DC.

Wagner, Katharina (b. Bayreuth, 21 May 1978), German opera stage-director. Daughter of WOLFGANG WAGNER and his second wife GUDRUN, she staged Der *FLIEGENDE HOLLÄNDER* in Würzburg and *LOHENGRIN* in Budapest before debuting at the 2007 BAYREUTH FESTIVAL with a production of Die *MEISTERSINGER VON NÜRNBERG* conceived with her dramaturge Robert Sollich. She was appointed co-director of the Bayreuth Festival together with her half-sister EVA WAGNER-PASQUIER on 1 September 2008; their contract expires in 2015. Although they are nominally co-directors, by all appearances Katharina is in charge. She instituted many updates to the festival, including open-air public viewing of select performances on a large screen in Bayreuth sponsored by Siemens, specially adapted versions of the operas for performance to children, and an interactive web presence, including the opportunity to watch web simulcasts of Bayreuth performances for a fee. She has come under intense criticism for her selection of stage directors, especially for the 2013 bicentennial production of the *RING* and for the new production of *PARSIFAL* in 2016.

NICHOLAS VAZSONYI

Wagner as librettist

1. The (German) libretto in Wagner's time
2. The young Wagner as librettist
3. Wagner as librettist in his Romantic operas
4. Wagner as librettist in the *Ring* cycle
5. Wagner as librettist in his post-*Ring* operas
6. The (German) libretto after Wagner

1. The (German) libretto in Wagner's time

At the beginning of the nineteenth century, the genre of the libretto was dominated by manifold Italian and French influences, as was the opera business *in toto*. Significantly, neither at this point nor later did the German libretto arrive at a standardization of types comparable to both Italian and French libretti. The German libretto was as multiform as it was incidental given the lack of operatic mass production and the lack of professional librettists (such as Eugène Scribe, 1791–1861, who founded the Romantic libretto type of the GRAND OPERA). German librettists, be they men of letters, involved in the theater, or dilettantes, did not pursue a trade. Rather, they were casual librettists, experimenters, and imitators who depended on Italian and French models, and it is characteristic that Wagner as librettist began his career experimenting and imitating too. His dual role as both librettist and composer was anomalous, but not unique: precedents can be traced back to the seventeenth century (cf. the Venetian Benedetto Ferrari, *c.* 1603–81). Nevertheless, the particular claims Wagner made in reference to the libretto in his later years were indeed a case *sui generis* and remain unparalleled. They evolved as a result of his practical experiences as both librettist and composer.

2. The young Wagner as librettist

In a letter to Karl Gaillard (30 January 1844), Wagner admits that his being a librettist had originally been a mishap. "[Ich] gestehe, daß ich nur aus Nothdurft, weil mir keine guten Texte geboten wurden, dazu griff, mir diese selbst zu dichten. Jetzt aber würde mir es ganz unmöglich sein, ein fremdes Opernbuch zu componiren." (I confess that I but acted from necessity writing the libretti myself, because I was not offered any good ones. Meanwhile, however, it would be completely impossible for me to compose an operatic text other than my own.) It was not until Der *FLIEGENDE HOLLÄNDER* (1843), when Wagner began modeling his libretti on folk tales, legends, and – subsequently – MYTH, that he accorded specific attention to its texture. Der *fliegende Holländer* marks a caesura: not only Wagner's music, but also his libretti underwent a fundamental change. From then on, they began to form a union that became increasingly tighter.

Wagner's early libretti – Die *FEEN* (1834), Das *LIEBESVERBOT* (1836), *RIENZI* (1840), as well as his first piece of writing, the libretto of *Leubald* (not set to music, 1826) – all illustrate the degree to which experimentation as well as imitation predominated. Demands for "dramatic truth" are scattered in Wagner's early prose writings (e.g., *Die deutsche Oper* [On German Opera, 1834]) and for a unity of poetry and song (e.g., *Pasticcio von Canto Spianato*, 1834), but these demands remain vague, which is in line with the young Wagner's tentative approach to his own libretti.

These take a heterogeneous form. The choice of topic, the number of acts, the meter, the use of rhymes, and so on, are highly mutable, and Wagner alters the original texts considerably, often adding completely different sources to his primary ones. In *Die Feen*, for instance, whose libretto is based on Carlo Gozzi's *La donna serpente* (1762), there are reminiscences of Emanuel Schikaneder's *The Magic Flute* (1791) as well as Friedrich SCHILLER's *Jungfrau von Orleans* (1801) and Heinrich von Kleist's *Das Käthchen von Heilbronn* (1810). In his autobiography, Wagner recalls his early years as librettist as follows: "ich war wirklich 'Musiker' und 'Komponist' geworden und wollte mir einen gehörigen 'Operntext' machen" (ML 81) (I had truly become a "musician" and "composer" and wanted to provide myself with a proper "libretto"). The libretto, therefore, was but a means to an ambitious end. In his first work *Leubald*, Wagner had enthusiastically compiled plots and characters of no fewer than nine SHAKESPEARE plays, whereas *Das Liebesverbot*, based on Shakespeare's *Measure for Measure* (1604), transforms both the plot and imagery of the original in accordance with Wagner's own preoccupation with POLITICS, hedonism, and the German political restoration of the time. In *Rienzi*, the young Wagner, still in search of what would work best, adapted Edward BULWER-LYTTON's novel *Rienzi* (1835) in the manner of Scribe's grand opera. The years that Wagner spent in PARIS (1839–42), where he aspired in vain to make his mark, eventually resulted not only in resentment against more successful composers such as MEYERBEER, but also in bitterness about the ubiquitous Scribe. Wagner was struggling to carve out his own niche. When, after *Rienzi*, he turned away from historical subjects, his intentions as librettist became more precise.

3. Wagner as librettist in his Romantic operas

In *Eine MITTEILUNG AN MEINE FREUNDE* (A Communication to My Friends, 1851), Wagner comments on his significant shift by anticipating his later preference for mythic plots: he interprets *Der fliegende Holländer* as a future-oriented version of Ulysses – and SENTA as "das Weib der Zukunft" (the woman of the future), who longs to redeem the beloved man. This is not only a substantial recurrent motif from then on for Wagner's libretti, it also goes to the heart of Wagner's later aesthetic writings and his notion of the GESAMTKUNSTWERK – in other words, in this respect to the unity of the libretto and the music. We shall return to this below. This was the decisive moment, when Wagner decided to concentrate on folk tales and legends in his stage works (see *VOLK*), for "das war das erste *Volksgedicht*, das mir tief in das Herz drang, und mich als künstlerischen Menschen zu seiner Deutung und Gestaltung im Kunstwerke mahnte. Von hier an beginnt meine Laufbahn als *Dichter*, mit der ich die des [bloßen] Verfertigers von Operntexten verließ" (SSD 4:266). ([*Der fliegende Holländer*] was the first *folk tale* that captured my heart, urging me as an artist to explain and frame it in the artwork. That marks the beginning of my career as a *poet*, with which I left the one as a [mere] librettist.)

Thus Wagner's self-conception as librettist was transformed from that of functional practitioner to the more sophisticated role of poet. It is no coincidence, also in terms of the libretti, that popular acquaintance with Wagner starts with his Romantic operas, where he began to devote himself to folk tales and expressive legends, and that following the somewhat lengthy libretto of *Rienzi*, the text of *Der fliegende Holländer* was remarkably short. Here, Wagner began to strive for poetic compression and a more distinct interrelation between words and their musical realization: what would become his focus in later years. Even if Wagner was not completely done with historical themes, the primary structure of Wagner's libretti would from now on always consist of three acts (except *Das* RHEINGOLD). In terms of meter, Wagner showed a preference for iambic pentameter, which dominates both *Tannhäuser* (1845) and *Lohengrin* (1850). But the latter already suggests Wagner's later use of STABREIM (alliterative verse): for example, when Telramund accuses ELSA: "Du hörst die Klage! König, richte recht!" Although both *Tannhäuser* and *Lohengrin* still contain traces of the number opera (e.g., "Dich, teure Halle," "O du, mein holder Abendstern," and "Einsam in trüben Tagen," "In fernem Land," respectively), the libretti increasingly foreshadow Wagner's mature operas in that they approach the MUSIC DRAMA: Wagner creates a comprehensive, floating continuity that goes along with his musical development and style of composition.

4. Wagner as librettist in the *Ring* cycle

Wagner's notion of the *Gesamtkunstwerk*, the total work of art, is derived from a circumstantial theory set down during the years that the exiled Wagner spent in ZURICH. The artwork of the future, which is to combine music, poetry, and DANCE, is – in consideration of the role of the libretto – elucidated in Wagner's major aesthetic treatise OPER UND DRAMA (Opera and Drama, 1851). Here, Wagner describes in theory what he illustrates with the *Ring* cycle in practice (the four libretti were finished in 1853). The mature Wagner is convinced that dramatic truth and historical subject matters are mutually exclusive. Instead, MYTH conveys all universally valid human messages in the most compact, distinct, and symbolically charged form. The libretto and the music (as well as the staging) must serve this one "reinmenschlich" (purely human) purpose to create clarity and represent truth. The libretto thus lends itself to archaisms, neologisms, and, most prominently, to the alliterative verse that Wagner adopts from Old High German poetry. The *Stabreim*, to Wagner, is the most archetypal choice of diction as it denotes primal density and perspicuity. The goal is to compress the wording (which, for Wagner, is "logical" and thus the "male" principle) in such a way that it expresses easily accessible emotion. This is the true merit of *Stabreim*. However, this is what music transmits anyway. In Wagner's GENDERED use of METAPHOR, music, guided by feeling, is "female." Music drama represents a form of sexual union between poet-librettist and composer. Both are mutually dependent. While the music "gives birth" to the drama, only the libretto is able to "beget." Thus the two coalesce and become indissoluble. This, however, also implies that the poet-librettist, in his "male" quality, is in need of "REDEMPTION" through the beloved "female" music – just as Wagner's heroes are through the woman of the future (SSD 4:146). Consequently, Wagner's artwork of the future is an all-embracing synthesis. The libretto and the music, in Wagner's metaphorical language, make sacrifices for one another, enriching and completing each other out of LOVE. The alliterative verse does what it can to achieve a full expression of emotion. Music, in turn, becomes almost verbal by means of LEITMOTIVE. It is a reciprocal relationship that must work in order for the potential of music drama to be fulfilled.

5. Wagner as librettist in his post-*Ring* operas

The exclusive emphasis on *Stabreim* is only evident in Wagner's *Ring* cycle, however. In *TRISTAN UND ISOLDE* (1865), alliterative verse is just one of various possibilities, and the iamb becomes more common again. Yet the symbolic concentration of the plot remains distinctive: for instance the reduced significance Wagner attaches to the role of the love potion as compared to his medieval sources. *Die MEISTERSINGER VON NÜRNBERG* (1868), by contrast, is dominated by rhyme, and Wagner's libretto deliberately adheres to an early modern diction modeled on Martin Luther, Hans SACHS, and GOETHE's poem "Hans Sachsens poetische Sendung" (1776). But even here, Wagner's credo applies: "Mich dünkt, 's sollt' passen Ton und Wort" (*Meistersinger* Act II, Scene 6). In the libretto of Wagner's last opera *PARSIFAL* (completed 1877), the meter is flexible and smooth, and again the most conspicuous feature is the degree to which the wording and the melody essentially flow together.

6. The (German) libretto after Wagner

Wagner's influence as librettist was significant. Because of the increased attention and the raised expectations Wagner accorded to operatic texts, composers of the nineteenth and twentieth centuries, both German and foreign, had the ambition to write their own libretti too. In Germany, a remarkable number of Wagner epigones emerged, who adopted Wagnerian qualities such as Nordic subject matters, metaphysical tendencies, solemn diction, and alliterative verse, though many shifted from sophisticated myth to the more modest fairy tale (e.g., Wagner's son, SIEGFRIED). Other artists assuming the dual role of librettist and composer focused on Wagner's aesthetic innovations, devoting their dramatically intense works to a close interplay between libretto and music (e.g., Arrigo Boito and Franz Schreker). In the fourth of his *Untimely Meditations*, "Richard Wagner in Bayreuth" (1876), Friedrich NIETZSCHE summarized Wagner's legacy as librettist thus: "verwegene Gedrängtheit, Gewalt und rhythmische Vielartigkeit, ein merkwürdiger Reichtum an starken und bedeutenden Wörtern, Vereinfachung der Satzgliederung, eine fast einzige Erfindsamkeit in der Sprache des wogenden Gefühls und der [psychologischen] Ahnung" (1:487). ([B]old compendiousness, force and rhythmic diversity, a remarkable abundance of expressive and meaningful words, simplification of syntax, an almost one-of-a-kind ingeniousness in the language of surging emotion and of [psychological] anticipation.)   YVONNE NILGES

See also STAGE WORKS, INCOMPLETE

Dieter Borchmeyer, *Richard Wagner: Theory and Theatre* (Oxford University Press, 1991).

Friedrich Nietzsche, *Sämtliche Werke: Kritische Studienausgabe in 15 Bänden*, ed. Giorgio Colli and Mazzino Montinari (Munich: dtv, 1999).

Yvonne Nilges, *Richard Wagners Shakespeare* (Würzburg: Königshausen & Neumann, 2007).

"Tradition and the Individual Talent in Wagner's Juvenilia," in *Wagner Outside the "Ring": Essays on the Operas, Their Performance and Their Connections With Other Arts*, ed. John L. DiGaetani (Jefferson, NC: McFarland, 2009): 9–22.

Wagner in literature. Wagner's impact on literature is an immensely broad subject. It is, at least notionally, a never-ending one. As Raymond Furness rightly remarks: "That a *musician* should have had such an overwhelming effect on *literature* is . . . remarkable, but the age was ready for a shift towards music in the arts, and it was Wagner who provided a unique and almost mystical stimulus. It was he more than any other artist who was able to fructify and enrich imaginative writing: it may safely be claimed that without Wagner the literature of at least a century would be immeasurably impoverished, as regards topics as well as structures" (p. x). Wagner's influence on literature was, however, above all a major phenomenon of European (early) MODERNISM. It could be systematized in a variety of ways: with reference to biographical allusions (Wagner as an historical figure) and to thematic adaptations (Wagnerian plots), or though textural treatments (the musicalization of literature, such as the literary reworking of Wagner's mnemonic LEITMOTIVE, or the interior monologue and stream of consciousness techniques as literary equivalents of Wagner's ENDLESS MELODY). Within this categorization, in turn, the following sub-aspects stand out: Wagner's aesthetic principles (lending themselves to PARODIES in particular); Wagner as the epitome of intoxication, narcotization, and morbidity (as depicted, above all, in the DECADENT movement of *fin-de-siècle* writers); Wagner as the exemplary shaper of MYTH; and, finally, Wagner against the backdrop of political and ideological literary treatments.

1. Wagner in French literature
2. Wagner in British, Irish, and American literature
3. Wagner in Italian literature
4. Wagner in German and Austrian literature
5. Wagner in Scandinavian and Slavic literature

1. Wagner in French literature

The earliest Wagnerians are to be found in FRANCE, and the earliest French poet of importance who indulged in Wagner was Charles BAUDELAIRE. French symbolism and French decadence were highly susceptible to Wagner's art, with Wagner himself becoming a veritable cult figure. Significant French poets of the late nineteenth century were – at least temporarily – influenced by Wagner, emphasizing the musicality of poetic language, synesthesia, stylization, and intoxication, neuropathy, eroticism, decay, and death, respectively (both literary movements, symbolism and decadence, thus renouncing naturalism). Wagner was an integral part of French AVANT-GARDE literature and, indeed, at its peak omnipresent. His reception was also a prime example of surrogate religion (*KUNSTRELIGION*) at a time of increasing secularization.

In 1885, Édouard Dujardin (1861–1949) founded the REVUE WAGNÉRIENNE which, despite its short-lived existence (until 1887), published contributions of numerous intellectuals and high-ranking poets of the time: Stéphane Mallarmé, for instance (1842–1898, "Richard Wagner: Rêverie d'un poète français," 1885; "Hommage à Richard Wagner," 1886); Paul Verlaine (1844–1896, "Parsifal," 1886; also, e.g., his poem "Saint Graal," 1888); Joris-Karl Huysmans (1848–1907, "L'Ouverture de Tannhäuser," 1885; also cf. his decadent novel A rebours, 1884); and others. The Revue wagnérienne included writers such as Auguste de Villiers de L'Isle-Adam (1838–1889) who, as a passionate Wagnerian, dedicated several of his works to Wagner, and Catulle MENDÈS, whose first wife was Judith GAUTIER, and whose novels adopt Wagnerian plots as well as biographical information (see, above all, his roman à clef on Wagner and LUDWIG II: Le Roi vierge, 1881). Similar characteristics apply to the decadent works of Maurice Barrès (1862–1923, La Mort de Venise, 1903) and Elémir Bourges (1852–1925, Le Crépuscule des dieux, 1884: a novel where Wagner appears ficti-tiously). Édouard Dujardin endeavored to adopt Wagner's style of composition (e.g., the "monologue intérieur" in his novel Les Lauriers sont coupés, 1887), which foreshadowed further modern psychological developments of the twentieth-century novel (Proust and Joyce).

Even writers who did not favor Wagner's art had no choice but to take notice of the distinct WAGNERISM of the time. The naturalist writer Émile Zola (1840–1902), for instance, turned against the idea of the total work of art in his novel L'Œuvre (1886), which deals with a painter's fruitless adoration of Wagner. When, in 1900, Joseph Bédier (1864–1938) published a novel based on the French – not Wagner's – medieval sources of Tristan and Isolde (Le Roman de Tristan et Iseut), he involuntarily incorporated Wagnerian traces into his plot which, again, attests to the vast influence Wagner had at that time.

Other notable works include Romain Rolland's (1866–1944) artist's novel Jean-Christophe (1904–1912) and, most prominently, Marcel Proust's (1871–1922) À la recherche du temps perdu (1913–1927) – one of the longest novels in world literature, whose Wagnerian stimuli are as manifold as they are existen-tial (the usage of literary Leitmotive, involuntary memory, etc.). Throughout the twentieth century, Wagner continued to preoccupy French intellectuals in a variety of ways, as can be seen with regards to Paul Claudel (1868–1955), for instance – albeit anti-Wagnerian (e.g., "Le Poison wagnérien," 1938) – or Claude Lévi-Strauss (1908–2009), whose structural anthropology by his own admission was indebted to Wagner's analysis of myth. Jean-Paul Sartre (1905–80) was inspired by Wagner's relationship to NIETZSCHE (e.g., his early fragment Une défaite, c. 1927). More distinct literary influences can be seen in writers such as Georges Duhamel (1884–1966, Le Jardin des bêtes sauvages, 1934; Le Desert de Bièvres, 1937) and Julien Gracq (1910–2007, Au château d'Argol, 1938; Le Roi pêcheur, 1948; "Un balcon au forêt," 1958, all of which engage with Wagner's Parsifal).

2. Wagner in British, Irish, and American literature

The reception of Wagner in ENGLAND was, at the end of the nineteenth century, intense. Here too, a Wagner journal was founded following the

French example (*THE MEISTER*, London 1888–95), though it was not as vanguard and sophisticated as the *Revue wagnérienne*. Algernon Charles Swinburne's (1837–1909) poem "The Death of Richard Wagner" appeared in translation in the French journal. It is not certain, however, if Swinburne was already familiar with Wagner's *Tannhäuser* when he wrote his earlier poem, "Laus veneris" (1866).

Numerous artists of the time were fascinated by the decadent movement and affected by the French treatment of the matter (see, above all, Aubrey BEARDSLEY's illustrated novel *Venus and Tannhäuser*, 1907). Decadence is also at the center of Oscar Wilde's *The Picture of Dorian Gray* (1891), which treats Wagner's *Tannhäuser* as exemplary mind-altering music, and George Moore's (1852–1933) artist's novel *Evelyn Innes* (1898), which, in turn, revolves around a young Wagner singer identifying herself with Wagner's heroines (also see the sequel to that novel, *Sister Theresa*, 1901). Yet the decadent influence did not dominate the British Isles: George Bernard SHAW presented a socialist interpretation of the *Ring* cycle in *The Perfect Wagnerite* (1898), and mythical reverberations accompany several of Joseph Conrad's (1857–1924) novels (*Almayer's Folly*, 1895; *Nostromo*, 1904; *Chance*, 1914; *Victory*, 1915). *The Trespasser* (1912), an early novel from D. H. Lawrence (1885–1930), alludes to Wagnerian patterns too (it was originally called *The Saga of Siegmund*), as does his later novel *Women in Love* (1920). Most important in this mythical respect, but also in terms of the *Leitmotiv* and, finally, the stream of consciousness technique, is the modernist novelist James Joyce (1882–1941). Joyce employs Wagnerian references in *A Portrait of the Artist as a Young Man* (1916); in his "never-ending" text comparable to Wagner's *Ring*, *Ulysses* (1922); and in *Finnegans Wake* (1939). Joyce directly quotes from Wagner, as does T. S. Eliot (1888–1965) in his disjointed poem "The Waste Land" (1922). The most significant impact that Wagner had on British and Irish literature can therefore be seen in the psychological structures of modernism: also see Virginia WOOLF's (1882–1941) novel *The Waves* (1931) in this respect (Woolf, as early as 1909, had written an article for *The Times* on her "Impressions at Bayreuth"), as well as the novels by E. M. Forster (1879–1970; *Howards End*, 1910; *A Passage to India*, 1924; *Maurice*, 1971).

As for Wagner's reception in the UNITED STATES OF AMERICA, his impact on American literature initially coincided with the "Gilded Age." For that reason, the Wagner cult there was different. Most Wagnerians were women, and there was no decadent movement or avant-garde literature engaging with Wagner. Rather, Wagnerism became part of the genteel tradition and remained somewhat parochial. In the USA, Wagner's female characters were at the center of attention and regarded as models of exalted purity or of oppression. There is a degree of sentimentalism or proto-feminism in American Wagner literature at the turn of the century, above all, Kate Chopin's (1850–1904) *The Awakening* (1899) and Willa Cather's (1873–1947) short story "A Wagner Matinee" (1904). Within this context, Upton Sinclair's (1878–1968) play *Prince Hagen* (1901) is not typical.

3. Wagner in Italian literature

ITALY also had a Wagner journal (*CRONACA WAGNERIANA*, 1893–95), despite the fact that the Italian reception of Wagner was by comparison not pronounced. Apart from occasional traces to be found in Italian literature at the end of the nineteenth century, it is only Gabriele D'Annunzio (1863–1938) whose literary engagement with Wagner was intense: his decadent novels *Il trionfo della morte* (1894) and *Il fuoco* (1900) stand out in that the former is based on Wagner's *Tristan und Isolde* (the protagonist maintains an exalted love relationship, finally forcing his beloved into a mutual LIEBESTOD), while the latter is set against the last days of Wagner's life in Venice.

4. Wagner in German and Austrian literature

In the German-speaking countries, Wagner's art provoked many authors to be dismissive – and to PARODY. The Viennese playwright Johann Nestroy (1801–62) parodied two Wagner operas (*Tannhäuser*, 1857, and *Lohengrin*, 1859); in 1879, Friedrich Theodor Vischer (1807–87) parodied Wagner's *Rheingold* (*Auch Einer*). Paul Heyse (1830–1914), in *Kinder der Welt* (1873), denounced Wagner's art as "eine musikalische Haschisch-Benebelung" (a musical hashish-fog), while the Viennese journalist Daniel Spitzer (1835–93) – a colleague of Eduard HANSLICK – mocked "Verliebte Wagnerianer" (Wagner-ians in love) in a novella of that name (1878). Early literary criticism focused, above all, on Wagner's AESTHETICS and was mostly adduced by authors of minor importance.

The first serious engagement with Wagner was Theodor Fontane's (1819–98) social novel *L'Adultera* (1880), which elevates Wagner's *Tristan* to literary significance in a work of poetic realism. Apart from that, however, Wagner in German (and Austrian) literature remained strangely diffuse, and it is certainly true that Wagner in literature achieved greater heights elsewhere in Europe – particularly France – than in Germany. Wagner and the decadent movement remained alien to many German-speaking authors as well as to German intellectuals; the – most relevant – exceptions to that rule were all drawn to French literature and culture.

Friedrich NIETZSCHE's philosophy, for instance, consistently engages with Wagner; his elucidations on the Apollonian and Dionysian principles, Wagner as decadent, and so on proved to be crucial for Thomas MANN's literary works. Mann is the only world-class German author who intensely reworked Wagnerian themes and structures throughout his entire oeuvre (abundant motifs of decadence, countless direct and indirect allusions in his texts, the literary *Leitmotiv* technique, myth, and archetypal patterns of narration).

Although there were also naturalistic approaches to Wagner, such as Elsa Bernstein's (1866–1949) play *Dämmerung* (1893), a majority of Wagner adapta-tions in German literature of the time were patriotic and nationalistic. After the formation of the Second Reich (1871) and then especially under the influence of COSIMA, the BAYREUTH CIRCLE, and the *BAYREUTHER BLÄTTER*, once again lesser authors began to discover Wagner, this time developing a new Wagner cult that was considered to be particularly "German." This phenom-enon persisted and intensified until the end of the Third Reich; Thomas Mann's brother, Heinrich Mann (1871–1950), unmasked the pettiness of nationalistic Wagnerism in his novel *Der Untertan* (1918).

In 1913 and 1914, Gerhart Hauptmann (1862–1946) published two fantasias dealing with the Grail (*Lohengrin* and *Parsival*). In 1924, Franz Werfel's

(1890–1945) novel *VERDI* played Wagner off against the other great composer of the nineteenth century. Bertolt Brecht (1898–1956) framed his conception of epic theater as a reaction against Wagner, although in practice the two seemingly divergent aesthetics share some basic principles.

The case of the largely unknown Austrian Wagnerian Egon Wayrer-Fauland (1917–2004) is a curiosity. Wayrer-Fauland wrote a libretto, *Erda* (1977/8), to fill the gap between Wagner's *Rheingold* and *Die Walküre*; he also considered the pre-history of KUNDRY leading up to PARSIFAL (*Die Höllenrose*, 1985). In the same year, 1985, Thomas Mann's grandson Frido Mann (b. 1940) published an autobiographical novel entitled *Professor Parsifal*.

5. Wagner in Scandinavian and Slavic literature

In the preface to his play *Fröken Julie* (1888), the Swedish author August Strindberg (1849–1912) calls for a hidden orchestra, a claim obviously inspired by Wagner's FESTIVAL THEATER at Bayreuth. Strindberg engaged with Wagner and his art particularly closely.

The reception of Wagner in the Slavic countries manifests itself, above all, in the literature of the Russian symbolists (Vyacheslav Ivanov, 1866–1949; Alexander Blok, 1880–1921). Leo Tolstoy (1828–1910) was a determined anti-Wagnerian (i.e., his essay "What is Art?," 1898). YVONNE NILGES

Raymond Furness, *Wagner and Literature* (University of Manchester Press, 1982).

Joseph Horowitz, *Wagner Nights: An American History* (Berkeley: University of California Press, 1994).

Erwin Koppen, *Dekadenter Wagnerismus: Studien zur europäischen Literatur des Fin de siècle* (Berlin: De Gruyter, 1973).

Stoddard Martin, *Wagner to "The Waste Land": A Study of the Relationship of Wagner to English Literature* (London: Macmillan, 1982).

Hans-Martin Pleßke (ed.), *Richard Wagner in der Dichtung: Bibliographie deutschsprachiger Veröffentlichungen* (Bayreuth: Edition Musica, 1971).

Wagner, Christine Wilhelmine "Minna" (née Planer) (b. Oederan, 5 Sep. 1809; d. Dresden, 25 Jan. 1866), actress, who performed in various theaters such as Dessau and MAGDEBURG. For some time she was better known in the theater world than Wagner, whom she met in Magdeburg in 1834, where he was director of the theater society. They married on 24 November 1836. With the exception of PARSIFAL, all his operas have their origins in his years with Minna. The couple lived in RIGA and PARIS without Richard achieving much success as a composer. In DRESDEN he received great acclaim for his opera *RIENZI* and was offered the post as conductor (Kapellmeister) of the Dresden court. After the failure of the DRESDEN UPRISING (May 1849), in which he had actively participated, he fled the country to escape an arrest warrant and a possible death sentence. Losing his prestigious job shocked Minna, as they had experienced phases of near starvation in Paris. After a period of hesitation, she joined him in ZURICH, where Richard was again unable to earn a regular income. In Zurich, he insisted on moving six times, which was an arduous burden for her.

Shortly thereafter, Richard fell in love with Jessie LAUSSOT in Bordeaux and, when Minna found out, she travelled alone to Paris, where Richard hid from her. She nevertheless accepted his return when Laussot rejected him. In

1858, a new rift occurred on account of Wagner's love for Mathilde WESEN-DONCK. Many authors wrongly blame Minna for the scandal that ensued in Zurich, when she found out about the affair. On the advice of her friend Emma HERWEGH, she only spoke with Mathilde, but Mathilde had revealed the relationship to her husband Otto, and it was he who insisted that Richard leave the "Asyl."

Afterwards, Wagner moved to VENICE and Minna travelled to Dresden, where she remained until her death. They spent time together from 1859 to 1861, when Richard prepared a *Tannhäuser* production for Paris. In 1862, they met once again in Biebrich near Wiesbaden, where Richard was working on his *Meistersinger* opera, but they quarreled and decided to separate for good. She hoped in vain that he would return to her in Dresden, but Richard never even visited her grave.

Minna is often criticized for not having fully understood her husband's musical development from *Rienzi* to *Tristan*. She was convinced that operas have a limited period of success and judged them by the money they earned. She was not alone in this opinion; his earlier friends such as Ferdinand HEINE, Wilhelm Fischer, Joseph TICHATSCHEK, and Anton PUSINELLI, and Wagner's sisters would also have preferred for him to continue composing operas like *Rienzi* or *Tannhäuser*.   EVA RIEGER

Eva Rieger, *Minna und Richard Wagner: Stationen einer Liebe* (Dusseldorf: Patmos, 2003).
Sibylle Zehle, *Minna Wagner: Eine Spurensuche* (Hamburg: Hoffmann und Campe, 2004).

Wagner and new media. Similar to how Richard Wagner's work has often been seen, celebrated, and denigrated as that of a classical Hollywood filmmaker *avant la lettre*, his understanding of future opera as a total work of art (*GESAMTKUNSTWERK*) has come to play a significant role in more recent debates about new media practice and art. For Randall Packer and Ken Jordan, Wagner's thoughts about the immersive qualities of future art foreshadow the simulated worlds and ubiquitous interfaces that digital culture offers to twenty-first-century computer users. In the eyes of Matthew Wilson Smith, not only do cyberspace artists such as Roy Ascott (*Aspects of Gaia*, 1989) and Char Davies (*Osmose*, 1995) continue Wagner's dream of organic totality and sensory integration, they also – like Wagner's BAYREUTH – rely on advanced technologies to obscure what enables the viewer's immersive experience in the first place. In the works of installation artists such as the Russian collaborative AES+F (Tatiana Arzamasova, Lev Vzovich, Evgeny Svyatsky, and Vladimir Fridkes), or of video artists such as Bill Viola, the link between Wagner's yearning for REDEMPTION and the absorptive effects of new media is taken for granted, whether it results in fantasies of apocalyptic doom as in AES+F's 2007 *Last Riot*, or in images of spiritual transcendence as in Viola's contribution to the so-called *Tristan Project* (2004–7) in Paris and Los Angeles.

Energized by the power of advanced computing, new media and screen culture today indeed seem to offer impressive resources to address a viewer's entire sensorium and hence operate as a twenty-first-century version of Wagner's dream of reunifying the different channels of sensory perception. But just as Wagner's hope for synthesizing different art forms exceeded a mere wish of transforming stage and auditorium into a perfect tool of emotional involvement, what we have come to call new media is not simply all about the staging of virtual realities, overwhelming simulations, and self-effacing interfaces. Though Wagner hardly ever used the term himself, his notion of the *Gesamtkunstwerk* (total work of art) relied as much on an argument about the structural logic of different artistic forms as it desired to reshape the viewer's senses and thereby overcome the fragmenting power of modern culture. Reunifying the separated sisters of DANCE, music, and poetry, future MUSIC DRAMA was intended as the redemption of individual art forms from their historical isolation, yet in order to do so it had to recuperate what in each art form inherently pointed toward the other. The visual and rhythmic aspects of dance called for sound and music; the harmonic and melodic qualities of music required words to achieve highest fulfillment; and the poetic word showed all the others what art at its best was all about, namely to invent something from nothing, to present – rather than represent – aesthetic material within the self-contained universe of the dramatic stage, and thus to bring forth the totality and freedom of unbridled creativity. No matter what Bayreuth may have done to it, total art in Wagner's original sense wasn't merely meant to provide a multitude of individual stimulations so as to absorb the viewer's senses most effectively. Total art, instead, was to result from the actualization of different structural or ontological features embedded in each and every art form – a process Wagner himself extravagantly described as a process of loving entwinement in whose context all three sister arts "tight-clasped, breast on breast, and limb to limb, melt with the fervor of love-kisses into one only, living shape of beauty" (PW 1:96).

The concept of new media today is at least as elusive as Wagner's rhapsodic notion of the *Gesamtkunstwerk*. In historical terms, it hints at the paths that, on the one hand, have led from nineteenth-century technologies of image capture, manipulation, and dissemination to the advent of a computer's graphical human interface in the course of the 1980s; and that, on the other, resulted in our ever more advanced ability to break down, store, and transmit any information whatsoever in the form of digital code. In a more systematic perspective, as theorist Lev Manovich has argued, new media combine five different principles, some of them already prefigured in earlier machines of mediation, yet all of them necessary to define the newness of what we call new media today: numerical representation (each distinct element of data can be encoded in mathematical form); modularity (discrete elements can be articulated in open-ended and variable structures); automation (machines take over some of the principal tasks of recording, processing, modifying, and displaying data); variability (users can use their machines in order to infinitely change the objects produced by other users' machines); and transcoding (code is shared across perceptual or representational modalities; a sound file can be played as image file, etc.).

Though not immune to critical challenge, Manovich's five principles are useful to complicate the often presumed continuity between Wagner's *Gesamtkunstwerk* and new media's ability to reorganize the entire landscape of what we can know and sense, remember and anticipate. First, though Wagner was of course quite critical of the logic of modern rationalization, his concept of drama as a unifying umbrella of various artistic enterprises resembles the role of numerical representation in digital culture as a catalyst of integrating different channels of representation. Second, we may think of the role of modular elements in contemporary computing as similar to what Wagner pursued with the use of the *LEITMOTIV*, understood as an attempt to repeat set elements with a difference so as to develop a complex language of anticipation, memory, psychological depth, and authorial commentary. Third, Manovich's stress on processes of automation may have its equivalent in how Wagner associated certain linguistic properties with musical valences as much as in the at once unbound and seemingly self-contained flow of Wagner's ENDLESS MELODIES. Fourth, familiar traces of what Manovich calls the productive variability of new media might be detected in Wagner's polemical valorization of the folkish over the academic – that is, his stress on the ongoing creativity of popular appropriation as compared with the lifeless and ultimately reifying effects of highbrow analysis.

While it might be possible to identify in Wagner's compositional technique early components of the first four principles of what defines new media as new, new media's fifth and perhaps most decisive feature – transcoding – resists easy translation. To be sure, Wagner's vision of total art as a loving entwinement of dance, music, and poetry relies on the assumption that all three sister arts share some structural elements in common whose successful (re-)actualization would allow future artists to overcome the painful fragmentation of the modern institutions of art. However, the total work of art, in Wagner's understanding, essentially synthesizes different registers of artistic representation, not by denying or erasing their differences, but on the contrary by exploring their particularity and nurturing what each has to contribute to a more comprehensive notion of art. New media's logic of transcoding, on the other hand, refers to a regime of sameness undergirding each and every mode of artistic representation; in other words, digital culture's relentless logic of breaking information into discrete sets of os and 1s such that one and the same pattern of data can potentially be transmitted as a static image, a sequence of sound, or a motion picture. New media, in other words, proceed from sameness to difference, whereas Wagner's concept of the total work of art envisioned future forms of art able to integrate differences into some kind of organic unity.

What is new about new media, it has been argued by critics such as David Bolter and Robert Grusin, is their ability to absorb, incorporate, assimilate, pillage, rework, or simply overwrite the content and formal logic of other older media. The newness of new media resides in nothing more and nothing less than their capacity to erase any clear-cut differentiation between old and new and thus define the present as a simultaneity of asynchronous practices, meanings, pleasures, and possibilities. The formal exigencies of new media should thus make us question any kind of linear narrative directly tracing the origins of cyberspace to Wagner's vision of total art, or seeing in Bayreuth an early precursor of how computers today change the way we think about and sense the world. The critical point for future artists and critics, therefore, is not to seek direct historical or causal continuities between the formal properties of new media and Wagner's techniques of composing and staging music drama. Rather, what is at stake is to ask what we can learn from the one in order to better understand the make-up and historical unfolding of the other; and how both encourage us to think about artistic media, not as finished products and fixed containers of meaning, but as ongoing processes and open resources of aesthetic experience.

LUTZ KOEPNICK

David Bolter and Richard Grusin, *Remediation: Understanding New Media* (Cambridge, MA: The MIT Press, 2000).
Jeongwon Joe and Sander Gilman, eds., *Wagner and Cinema* (see bibliography).
Lev Manovich, *The Language of New Media* (Cambridge, MA: The MIT Press, 2001).
Randall Packer and Ken Jordan, *Multimedia: From Wagner to Virtual Reality* (New York: Norton, 2001).
Matthew W. Smith, *The Total Work of Art* (see bibliography).

Wagner, Nike (b. Überlingen, 9 June 1945), great-granddaughter of Richard Wagner, and third child of WIELAND WAGNER and Gertrud REISSINGER. She grew up in WAHNFRIED and, between 1963 and 1965, appeared on the FESTIVAL THEATER stage as a dancer in her father's productions of TANN-HÄUSER, PARSIFAL, and *Die* MEISTERSINGER VON NÜRNBERG. Nike Wagner is a distinguished cultural critic and scholar of the *fin de siècle*. Her doctoral thesis, written under the supervision of the notable humanist Erich Heller, was a study of the Austrian satirist and poet Karl Kraus (1874–1936); she has published widely on related subjects and her work is highly regarded for its critical perception and historical detachment. She is also the author of an important study of Wagner's canonical operas in relation to the history of the Wagner family. In 2004, Nike Wagner became Artistic Director of the "Pèlerinage" Kunstfest Weimar, an art festival in honor of her great-great-grandfather, Franz LISZT.

ROGER ALLEN

Erich Heller, *The Disinherited Mind* (Cambridge: Bowes and Bowes, 1952).
Nike Wagner, *The Wagners: The Dramas of a Musical Dynasty* (London: Weidenfeld & Nicolson, 2000).

Wagner Notes. A newsletter (OCLC 40826354) published bi-monthly by the Wagner Society of New York as the house organ, and for the benefit of its membership almost since the Society's founding in 1977. *Wagner Notes* contains reviews of Wagner performances and productions around the globe, as well as reviews of books and recordings. An earlier but shorter-lived periodical, *The Richard Wagner Quarterly* (1937–8), was also published in New York City by the Wagner Society of America.

MICHAEL SAFFLE

Wagner and popular culture

1. Contexts, themes, and motifs
2. Parodies
3. Adaptations
4. Mixed forms

1. Contexts, themes, and motifs

Though forever marked by his experiences as a young unsuccessful musician in the fully commercialized Parisian music scene of the 1830s and 1840s,

Wagner also came to understand that a wide audience could be reached not as a virtuoso or solely as a composer-conductor, but rather as a musician-writer, not unlike Hector BERLIOZ and Robert SCHUMANN. A decade later, Wagner found himself hard pressed to capitalize on his burgeoning career as a composer, following his exile in 1849 and his politically suspect reputation as a revolutionary. However, making his works known to a wider public, especially in Germany, was offset by the lure of the forbidden that also made Wagner attractive for some, a status enhanced by his programmatic writings (and polemics) on AESTHETICS, culture, and POLITICS, which increased in quantity around that same time. Beyond this, and despite some miscalculations (like the LONDON concerts), Wagner was skilled at the new art of commercialization and SELF-PROMOTION, his organization of the BAYREUTH FESTIVAL being the clearest example of his work as a forerunner of the modern-day concert manager and theatrical entrepreneur. Wagner also successfully branded himself and his works, evident already during his residence in Munich (c. 1865) when metal and porcelain *LOHENGRIN* swans were used for interior decoration, not unlike the merchandizing of branded tie-in products today.

The study of Wagner's influence on and reception through popular culture can be framed in three ways: first, his image as a personality; second, the performance of his works; third, the ideas and themes he took up and developed. Theodor W. ADORNO has argued that Wagner is a key figure in the development of the "culture industry," mass and popular culture, because his manipulative aesthetics and calculated effects were aimed at a public that functions as a mass consumerist target. It is certainly clear that the consumption of Wagner has from the start been bound up with complex issues of culture and ideology. Wagner actively and directly appealed to the Germans, as a people, and this is certainly a factor in the posthumous propagandistic efforts to appropriate his works during the period of NATIONAL SOCIALISM. This is especially the case with *Die MEISTERSINGER VON NÜRNBERG*, for instance during a performance at the City Opera of Berlin on 17 November 1935 where HANS SACHS's closing monologue even made it to the *Deutsche Wochenschau*. Less ideologically pernicious constellations are also prevalent, such as the programming of *Die Meistersinger* during trade fairs (e.g., in postwar Germany) or the (often unknowing) use of the bridal chorus from *Lohengrin* at weddings around the globe.

Since Wagner made full use of the storehouse of German sagas, it is difficult to ascertain whether the popular adaptation of a particular story can be directly attributed to Wagnerian influence rather than simply being based on the same original source. The Nibelungen story had in any case swept German-speaking areas well before Wagner's tetralogy was premiered, for example Friedrich Hebbel's play *Die Nibelungen* (1861). Decades later, famous allusions to the Nibelung saga, such as the operetta *Die lustigen Nibelungen* by Oscar Straus (1904), or the collector cards made by the food company "Liebigs Fleischextrakt," are more closely oriented to the original medieval *Nibelungenlied* than to Wagner's work, though Liebig also had a popular *Meistersinger* series. Fritz Lang's filmic adaptation of *Die Nibelungen* is also closer to the medieval epos, although the original music by Gottfried Huppertz with its simplified LEITMOTIV technique seems more informed by Wagner's aesthetics, and so demonstrates the relationship between Wagner and the cinema. Similarly, Howard Shore's musical soundtrack for Peter Jackson's Lord of the Rings film trilogy has suggested deeper connections between it and Wagner's Ring than J. R. R. Tolkien's novels may actually justify. Certainly, the simplified Leitmotiv technique of the film score can also be found in a number of other films, musicals, and in the design of musical pop culture's "concept album."

2. Parodies

The popularity of Wagner's work from the beginning of its reception until well into the twentieth century is apparent in caricatures, parodies, and pastiches, explicitly aimed at him. Johann Nestroy's 1857 farce Tannhäuser und die Keilerei auf der Wartburg (based on a literary model written by Hermann Wollheim) is an example of how, within the Vienna folk theater tradition, Wagner's works were already being subjected to comical as well as critical treatment during his lifetime. Interestingly, Wagner publicly announced his bemusement at the parody, yet another example of his skill at remaining the focus of attention even when he was the object of ridicule. Such treatment also befell the term Zukunftsmusik, as well as the public debate around the second edition of Das JUDENTUM IN DER MUSIK (Jewishness in Music, 1869) (e.g., by Franz Bittong, Fritz Mauthner, or Richard Schmidt-Cabanis).

3. Adaptations

Franz LISZT was at the forefront of early attempts around 1850 to popularize Wagner's work, not only as a conductor, but also as an arranger of PIANO TRANSCRIPTIONS. During Wagner's lifetime, unwanted adaptations were often bothersome because nineteenth-century copyright legislation meant that the original author had little or no legal recourse. For instance, in a letter from 19 October 1871 to his publisher Ernst Wilhelm FRITZSCH, Wagner complains about the unauthorized distribution of a concert version of the "Ride of the Valkyries." Still, chamber adaptations for salons, and orchestral adaptations for performance in spa towns and resorts played an important role in making Wagner's works known to a wider audience. Mechanical instruments such as barrel organs also increased the popularity of Wagner's music outside the theater, a phenomenon Wagner found amusing (see Wagner mécanique below).

4. Mixed forms

Beyond musical and dramatic forms of Wagner popularization, visual artists such as Aubrey BEARDSLEY and Arthur RACKHAM developed distinctive depictions that had a tremendous impact. Rackham's pictures for the Ring des Nibelungen (1909) focus on the fairy-tale and fantastical elements of the drama, whereas Beardsley's Under the Hill (1899), in line with his provocative aestheticism, extends the erotic implications of the Tannhäuser theme by presenting blatant imagery. The narrative and its illustration remained a fragment, but its partial publication in a magazine marked Wagner's transition into the world of comics and cartoons. This continued into the twentieth century, though mostly in the form of quotations and associations, for instance the *Merrie Melodies* cartoon *What's Opera, Doc?* (1957), where "Kill the wabbit" is sung to the melody of the "Ride of the Valkyries."

Wagner was also taken up by the parodistic and satirical cabaret tradition, for instance in the Viennese skit written by Gerhard Bronner and Peter Wehle titled *Der volkseigene Wagner* (1959), which pokes fun at East German (GDR) attempts to appropriate Wagner's works to conform with socialism, along with textual changes: for example, a song praising the sublimity and sweetness of the "Soviet star" rather than the "evening star" (*Abendstern*). This skit is an unusual example from the twentieth century of sociopolitical critique using Wagner's oeuvre.

It contrasts with more mainstream attempts to popularize Wagner through humor, such as Anna Russell's or Victor Borge's shows in English, or the German-speaking parodies, such a "Oper auf Bayrisch." The fact that Wagner has reached quite a large cross-section of the public via popular culture (when compared with the average audience of serious music) is evident in the work of the well-known German presenter, comedian, and cartoonist Loriot (Vicco von Bülow, 1923–2011), who achieved enormous success with a recording of *Ring* highlights connected by humorous texts. His *Der Ring an einem Abend* (1992) became a popular vehicle for big as well as small theaters and concert promoters in Germany to present Wagner's tetralogy as a potpourri, but in its original orchestration.

More recently, cross-over projects like those by Ben Lierhouse or Stefan Kaminski have presented Wagner's music and dramatic text in new and innovative ways, making use of technological advances in media and sound reproduction. Similarly, the Bayreuth Festival under the new leadership of KATHARINA WAGNER has experimented with popular means of diffusion: since 2008, an annual so-called "public viewing" of a live performance from the Bayreuth stage broadcast on large video screens and, since 2009, abridged productions for children making Wagner available and accessible for future audiences.

SEBASTIAN STAUSS

TRANS. ULRIKE LELICKENS

Jürgen Kolbe, ed., *Wagners Welten (exhibition catalogue)* (Wolfratshausen: Minerva, 2003).
Andrea Schneider, *Die parodierten Musikdramen Richard Wagners: Geschichte und Dokumentation Wagnerscher Opernparodien im deutschsprachigen Raum von der Mitte des 19. Jahrhunderts bis zum Ende des Weltkrieges* (Anif and Salzburg: Müller-Speiser, 1996).
Wagner mécanique, Oehms Classics in coproduction with Bayerischer Rundfunk, 2003.

Wagner, (Wilhelm) Richard (b. Leipzig, 22 May 1813; d. Venice, 13 Feb. 1883).

1. Family and childhood, 1813–1827
2. Early works and career, 1828–1839
3. Paris and Dresden, 1839–1849
4. Exile, 1849–1863
5. Royal patronage, 1864–1871
6. Bayreuth, 1872–1883

1. Family and childhood, 1813–1827

The composer was born on 22 May 1813 in the House of the Red and White Lion in the Brühl, LEIPZIG; ninth child of the marriage of Carl Friedrich Wilhelm Wagner (b. 18 June 1770), a police registrar, and JOHANNA Rosine née Pätz

(b. 19 September 1774), daughter of a baker in Weissenfels. Of their children (two died in infancy), ALBERT, the eldest, became a tenor and stage producer, and Julius a goldsmith. Richard was closest to his female siblings: ROSALIE and Luisa, both actresses; Klara, a singer; and Ottilie, who married into the BROCKHAUS family of philologists and publishers (as did Luisa). Their father complemented his actuarial training with enthusiasm for the theater and amateur acting. His own father was an assistant excise officer and his forebears in turn were for some generations village schoolmasters, thus probably also church organists. There is no other record of musical talent in Richard's ancestry. He had no memory of his father, who died on 22 November 1813 of "hospital fever" (i.e., typhus), a direct consequence of wartime conditions. The kingdom of Saxony (allied to France) was then the nucleus of the Napoleonic wars, the French occupying Leipzig and DRESDEN. The decisive change in Napoleon's fortunes came with the three-day "Battle of the Nations" at Leipzig (16–19 October 1813) during which the Saxons deserted to the victorious allies.

In July of that turbulent summer, Johanna Wagner travelled to Teplitz in Bohemia, 150 miles from Leipzig, probably taking her newly born son along on this hazardous journey through a volatile, unstable war zone. As Teplitz can have been no safer than Leipzig, historians have puzzled over the purpose of her visit. Her certain goal was to meet Ludwig GEYER, an actor friend of the family, appearing there with a theater troupe. When she returned to Leipzig, Richard was baptized in the Thomaskirche on 16 August. Again, the delay of three months between birth and christening has intrigued scholars. Geyer was descended from a line of Protestant church musicians. Friendly with the Wagners since his student days in the late 1790s, when acting in Leipzig he usually lodged with them. Following her husband's death, Johanna wed Geyer (as soon as the ten months required by Saxon law for a widow to re-marry had elapsed) on 28 August 1814. By that date she was expecting his child: a daughter, Cäcilie (AVENARIUS), born 26 February 1815.

These facts have led some to conjecture that Geyer was Richard Wagner's biological father. The composer too may have believed this, but Johanna carried the truth to her grave. Another secret taken there was her affair with Prince Constantin of Saxe-Weimar-Eisenach, who kept her in Leipzig as one of his many mistresses until his death in 1793. Stifling or manipulation of facts, which is endemic to Wagnerian historiography, thus began in his family prior even to his birth.

The family settled in Dresden late in 1814. Geyer was now a "court actor," and it was the theatrical milieu that most excited Richard and came to dominate his imagination. Schooling began in 1820, when he was lodged with Pastor Christian Wetzel in Possendorf and received some piano lessons. A year later (September 1821) he was summoned home to find Geyer on his deathbed from tuberculosis. Geyer's younger brother Karl eased Johanna's burden by taking Richard into his care at Eisleben, his education continuing locally. Then he was sent for a time to an uncle in Leipzig: ADOLF WAGNER (Carl Friedrich's brother). Afterwards, he rejoined his mother in Dresden, where, in December 1822, he enrolled at the Kreuzschule under the name Richard Geyer, developing an interest in Greek (mythology more than language). The greatest musical impression was WEBER's new *Der Freischütz*, at first mainly on account of its spooky plot. Indeed, spooks, hallucinations, and nightmares were constant companions. He was an extremely sensitive child; his autobiography *MEIN LEBEN* (My Life, 1865–81) tellingly recalls that he scarcely ever was comforted or caressed by his mother.

Late in 1826, the family moved to Prague leaving Richard behind, boarded out with a school friend. A winter visit to Prague brought first acquaintance with Count Pachta's illegitimate daughters Jenny and Auguste, whose beauty awakened new emotions in Richard, prompting a walking trip there the following spring. Part of the summer was spent appreciating Uncle Adolf's books in Leipzig, and when his mother and sisters returned to that city he settled there in December 1827, enrolling at the Nikolaischule under the name Richard Wagner.

2. Early works and career, 1828–1839

Musical education took place in Leipzig, and was literally impelled by his drama *Leubald* – a heroically juvenile five-act distillation of the gorier episodes from SHAKESPEARE, GOETHE's *Götz von Berlichingen*, and much else. Despite family disapprobation, he resolved to provide music for his tragedy in the manner of Beethoven's *Egmont* (see STAGE WORKS, INCOMPLETE). To this end he borrowed a copy of *Logier's Thorough-Bass*, but was soon obliged to have tuition in harmony and counterpoint from a Gewandhaus orchestra player, Christian Gottlieb MÜLLER. These produced results, including two piano sonatas, a string quartet, vocal items, and four orchestral overtures by the close of 1830.

At Easter 1830 he left the Nikolaischule to enroll at the Thomasschule, where his neglect hitherto of basic schoolwork saw him downgraded a class. Theater, books, and music were his stimuli: above all BEETHOVEN, especially the Ninth Symphony. He copied out the full score and arranged the symphony for piano solo. An Overture in B♭ major (WWV 10) was his first publicly performed work, conducted by Heinrich DORN at Leipzig's Hoftheater on Christmas Day 1830: a naïve timpani crash every fifth bar produced an uproarious effect. More significant were *Seven Compositions for Goethe's "Faust"* (WWV 15) early the next year.

In the wake of the Paris July Revolution, Leipzig encountered its share of unrest, Wagner enthusiastically joining in the disorder. He subsequently viewed his engagement with the mob (on this occasion and during other student escapades) with horrified distaste. Such experiences gained him a realization of dark, unpredictable forces that motivate human behavior and are the inchoate elements of what he would classify as "WAHN." The contemporary yearning for greater personal liberty and political emancipation was given unsentimental voice with the "YOUNG GERMANY" movement, whose notable spokesman Heinrich LAUBE moved to Leipzig and was befriended by Wagner's family.

For some time Wagner's envious eye had been fixed on the Leipzig University student fraternity with their clubs, colors, and roistering *Kameradschaft*. Unable to matriculate formally without school qualifications, he simply enrolled himself as a *studiosus musicae* in February 1831 and gloried for a while in dueling and gambling. Six months of serious study began in the autumn with Thomaskantor Theodor WEINLIG, fruits of which are two piano works: a Sonata in B♭ major (WWV 21, his first published work) and a Fantasia in F♯ minor (WWV 22).

After completing a SYMPHONY IN C MAJOR by midsummer 1832 he spent some weeks in Vienna, encountering the ubiquitous Johann Strauss I, GLUCK's *Iphigenia in Tauris*, and Hérold's *Zampa*. Prague beckoned next, where he wrote the text for an opera, *Die Hochzeit* (WWV 31). Music for this was abandoned after the first scene, as were any hopes of romance with one of the Pachta daughters. In January 1833, Wagner began the libretto of *Die* FEEN before joining his brother Albert in WÜRZBURG, where he became chorus master for three months. The season ended on 30 April but Wagner remained in Würzburg until January 1834 to complete *Die Feen*, incidentally enjoying a couple of short-lived love affairs.

He returned to Leipzig hoping in vain for a production of *Die Feen* (it was never performed in his lifetime). Among the most profound experiences of his life were performances in Leipzig by the dramatic soprano Wilhelmine SCHRÖDER-DEVRIENT in many roles including Leonore and Norma. Her BELLINI indelibly impressed Wagner with the expressive power of BEL CANTO. Praise of Bellini, and contrasted observations on the failings of German opera, are the essentials of Wagner's early articles on musical aesthetics, and he embraced the Italian style in his next opera *Das* LIEBESVERBOT, a dramaturgical and musical motif that Wagner pursued until PARSIFAL.

From July 1834, he became musical director of Heinrich Bethmann's touring theater troupe, based in MAGDEBURG, making his debut as CON-DUCTOR with MOZART's *Don Giovanni* at Bad Läuchstadt. He fell in love with the attractive actress MINNA PLANER who, after stormy months of courtship and occasional separation, would become his first wife. After a disastrous single performance of *Das Liebesverbot* and the dissolution of Bethmann's company, Wagner travelled to Berlin attempting to arouse interest in his new opera, meanwhile enjoying the splendors of SPONTINI's *Fernand Cortez*, which, along with HALÉVY's *La Juive*, would fertilize his next operatic project. Minna took an engagement in KÖNIGSBERG, where Wagner followed her in July. They wed in nearby Tragheim on 24 November 1836. Wagner thus became stepfather to Natalie, actually Minna's illegitimate daughter, the result of her seduction by an army captain when only 15, but raised as her "younger sister." The truth was confided to Wagner at an early stage and he never disclosed it. Tension between mother and daughter, Natalie's resentment at demands from an "elder sister," the several male admirers paying court to Minna, Wagner's resultant rages, and persistent household penury, meant the new ménage was not altogether a happy one. That a strong physical attraction existed between the couple cannot however be doubted. Creative work in Königsberg included two overtures, *Polonia* and *Rule Britannia*, plus a scenario for a grand opera, *Die hohe Braut*, which he sent to Scribe in Paris. Appointed musical director in Königsberg only on 1 April 1837, his miserable sojourn there culminated with the theater's imminent bankruptcy and Minna running off with a rich admirer on 31 May. He pursued her and for some days they lodged together in Blasewitz near Dresden, where he read BULWER-LYTTON's novel RIENZI, discovering ideal material for a grand opera. When Minna again decamped Wagner contemplated suing for divorce.

Securing a contract as musical director in RIGA, he sailed there in August. Minna rejoined him in October. In two seasons he conducted twenty-six operas and mounted six orchestral concerts. When a *Singspiel*, *Männerlist grösser als Frauenlist* (WWV 48), was abandoned after two numbers, his energies turned to the libretto of *Rienzi*, beginning the music in early August 1838. Hostility between Wagner and the Riga theater director, ever-mounting debts, and the loss of his contract in March 1839 led to crisis, flight, and a perilous journey, with PARIS as his goal. With Minna and their Newfoundland dog, but without passports, his creditors were eluded, armed Russian border guards evaded, and East Prussia attained on 10 July. En route, a vehicle accident may have caused Minna to miscarry and prohibited future child-bearing. A terrible sea voyage ensued from Pillau on the Baltic to LONDON. Battered by successive storms their vessel took refuge on the Norwegian coast (events which the composer claimed inspired *Der FLIEGENDE HOLLÄNDER*), reaching London eventually on 12 August, before they crossed to Boulogne. There, unexpectedly, Wagner found MEYERBEER in residence, played him the completed first two acts of *Rienzi*, and received letters of introduction for Paris, where they arrived on 17 September 1839.

3. Paris and Dresden, 1839–1849

Hopes of achieving success in the Parisian musical world were slowly and decisively demolished during the ensuing thirty months, which reduced the couple to hitherto unknown depths of misery. Paradoxically, Paris also brought great riches: experiencing BEETHOVEN symphonies under Habeneck and BERLIOZ's new *Roméo et Juliette*; the company of fellow Germans including Hallé, Heller, HEINE, the painter Ernst Benedikt KIETZ, librarian Gottfried ANDERS, and philologist Samuel LEHRS. Helped by the last two, Wagner immersed himself in Norse, Arthurian, and Teutonic mythology. Intellectually, Paris transformed him.

His hand-to-mouth existence was modestly helped by the publisher Moritz SCHLESINGER, who commissioned vocal scores and myriad arrangements, mainly DONIZETTI and HALÉVY. For Schlesinger's *REVUE ET GAZETTE MUSICALE* Wagner wrote reviews of Paris concerts, some pointedly autobiographical short stories (e.g., *Eine PILGERFAHRT ZU BEETHOVEN* [A Pilgrimage to Beethoven, 1840]) and essays on musical AESTHETICS. These pieces (including some sent to the Dresden *Abend-Zeitung* and other German periodicals) rank among his most enjoyable prose.

The winter of 1839–40 saw the first movement for a symphony on Goethe's *Faust* (revised as *Eine FAUST-OUVERTÜRE*) and completion of Act III of *Rienzi*. He also penned a number of *mélodies* in the hope of making a quicker reputation. The five acts of *Rienzi* were complete in November 1840. In April 1841, Richard and Minna moved to Meudon, outside Paris. There he wrote his text for *Der fliegende Holländer* (drawing partly on a story by Heine) and completed the score in November. With this opera, Wagner believed he had truly found himself as a composer. Meanwhile, Meyerbeer had persuaded the Intendant of the Dresden

Court Opera, Freiherr von LÜTTICHAU, to stage *Rienzi*. After spending the winter sketching further potential opera projects he grew impatient with the seeming procrastination over *Rienzi*, and left Paris with Minna for Dresden in April 1842. Assured that the opera would launch the next season, they visited Teplitz where he drafted a scenario for *TANNHÄUSER*.

Wagner's first triumph was the premiere of *Rienzi*, 20 October 1842. The premiere of *Der fliegende Holländer* under his own baton on 2 January 1843 met with less enthusiasm, but exactly a month later he was appointed Royal Saxon Kapellmeister (alongside Carl REISSIGER). February brought publication of his *AUTOBIOGRAPHISCHE SKIZZE* (Autobiographical Sketch, 1842/3) and a notable visitor – Berlioz. Wagner helped prepare concerts containing a rich selection of the Frenchman's music, and Berlioz attended *Holländer* and the second part of *Rienzi*. They must have discussed a mutual enthusiasm for Gluck, as in March Wagner conducted a new production of *Armida*, a success leading to further Gluck performances, notably *Iphigénie en Aulide* in his own version (February 1847, WWV 77). Wagner's new "biblical scene" for male chorus and orchestra *Das Liebesmahl der Apostel* (WWV 69) was given in the Frauenkirche, 6 July 1843, after which composition of *Tannhäuser* was commenced at Teplitz and his vacation reading of Jacob Grimm's *German Mythology* opened up a whole new world (ML/E 260). Moving to a larger apartment on 1 October encouraged Wagner to amass his own book collection, (the so-called DRESDEN LIBRARY), consisting of classical and medieval literature and works on mythology. Lost to him permanently on his flight from Dresden six years later, this library was fortunately preserved (now in Bayreuth); it proves he possessed virtually the entire source material for all his future works by this time. In 1847, his READING embraced Hegel, Gibbon, and Aeschylus.

Seeds of financial instability (see MONEY) were sown early on Wagner's path through life, but with the decision to self-publish his scores with the local firm of C. F. Meser (*Rienzi*, *Der fliegende Holländer*, and soon *Tannhäuser*) catastrophe loomed. Nor were his hopes raised by any sign of interest in his works outside Dresden. Riga and Kassel mounted *Der fliegende Holländer* in 1843, and Wagner conducted its first performance in Berlin in January 1844, followed by *Rienzi* in Hamburg in March. Their lack of success and slow progress (*Rienzi* seen only in Königsberg in 1845 and in Berlin only by 1847) was the depressing pattern of the 1840s. Yet Wagner's indomitable faith in himself, his irrepressible energy and enthusiasms allowed no surrender to despair. He invited Spontini to Dresden to supervise *La vestale* in November 1844 (with Albert Wagner's daughter Johanna in the cast) and helped arrange the return of WEBER's remains from London and their re-interment at Dresden in December, composing two works for the occasion. He completed the full score of *Tannhäuser* (13 April 1845) and spent a stimulating summer at MARIENBAD with dog, parrot, and wife, immersing himself not in the curative waters, but in the legends of PARSIFAL and LOHENGRIN, and writing prose drafts for *Die MEISTERSINGER VON NÜRNBERG* and *LOHEN-GRIN*. For the traditional Palm Sunday concert in April 1846, Wagner overcame strong opposition to conduct Beethoven's Ninth with much PUBLICITY and success (repeated in 1847 and 1849). He conducted the first *Tannhäuser* at the Hofoper on 19 October 1845, but it was not well received. So began a series of revisions. Of all his oeuvre, *Tannhäuser* was the most often revised. *Rienzi* was ripe for cuts as early as its first rehearsals; the scoring of *Der fliegende Holländer* was endlessly tinkered with; but a perfect final form for *Tannhäuser* was to elude him. *Lohengrin* was different. Once the score was complete (24 April 1848) he made no alterations to it (save cutting a second verse to Lohengrin's Narration "In fernem Land" prior to the premiere).

The year of REVOLUTIONS, 1848, began with the death of Wagner's mother on 9 January. Wagner had observed social unrest across Europe growing to bursting point. He concluded that art, especially opera, could lead the way in transforming society. For art to flourish effectively, however, conditions for it must be perfect. In March 1846, he had submitted a plan for reform of the court orchestra; it was rejected a year later. In May 1848, he followed with *Entwurf zur Organisation eines deutschen Nationaltheaters für das Königreich Sachsen* (Plan for the Organization of a German National Theater for the Kingdom of Saxony), including suggestions for a conservatory of music, reform of Dresden's church music, the creation of a union of composers and musicians to elect the Kapellmeister, determine the repertory, and so on. By that time Wagner the reformer was becoming Wagner the revolutionary: it was the authorities' failure to enact any of his proposals that drove him to revolution. To quell rumblings of insurrection in Saxony, Friedrich August II reformed his cabinet along more liberal lines in March 1848. He and Lüttichau held Kapellmeister Wagner in high esteem and at first displayed remarkable forbearance. Understandably their regard for him diminished as his involvement in POLITICS increased. The uprisings throughout Europe stimulated him greatly: a poem signed by him (published in Vienna, 1 June), *Gruß aus Sachsen an die Wiener* (Greeting from Saxony to the Viennese, 1848), praises the Austrians for having "drawn the sword" in an insurrection that saw their Emperor flee his capital. On 15 June Wagner addressed a gathering of over 3,000 members of the Dresden Vaterlandsverein; next day his speech was published (without signature) as *Wie verhalten sich republikanische Bestrebungen dem Königthume gegnüber?* (How Do Republican Aspirations Stand in Relation to the Monarchy?, 1848). July found him in Vienna itself. Ironically his reputation was known there only through some admiring articles on *Tannhäuser* (November–December 1846) by Eduard HANSLICK (later his sharpest critical enemy). In 1848, Hanslick observed that Wagner was "all politics: the victory of the revolution, he was sure, would bring a complete rebirth of art, society and religion." An increasingly radical tone is traceable in Wagner's three articles for August RÖCKEL's *Volksblätter* in Dresden. The royal employee had moved from utopian socialism to an openly seditious and anarchistic stance. The court's failure to produce *Lohengrin* further spurred his rebelliousness.

Röckel was Wagner's assistant conductor. Another colleague who had latterly become a close friend and shared Wagner's reformist zeal was Theodor UHLIG, a violinist in the court orchestra. Others encountered in the Dresden period who were to play important roles in his life included the wealthy widow Julie RITTER and her sons KARL and Alexander (the last married Albert Wagner's daughter Franziska; later he was mentor to Richard STRAUSS); their houseguest Jessie Taylor (soon to marry Eugène

LAUSSOT); and their friend Hans von BÜLOW. The most significant
FRIENDSHIP to develop was that with Franz LISZT. They first met in Paris
in 1841 when Wagner was wary and disapproving of the virtuoso's lifestyle.
After Liszt heard *Rienzi* in 1844 his interest in its composer waxed considerably. By summer 1848, Liszt was settled in Weimar as Kapellmeister and
now in a position to help Wagner with his purse, pen, piano, conductor's
podium, and his international influence. He conducted the first *Tannhäuser*
production outside Dresden in Weimar (February 1849), made PIANO
TRANSCRIPTIONS from the score, and subsequently wrote about the
opera, advocating its performance wherever he could. His inestimable service
to Wagner included extricating him from the calamitous consequences of the
revolution.

On 30 April 1849 the Saxon king dissolved parliament and revoked the
constitution. Fuelled by rumor that he had summoned Prussian troops, the
DRESDEN UPRISING began in earnest, and the king fled on 4 May. Wagner
actively participated with the leaders of the provisional government who
included Röckel and Mikhail BAKUNIN. After four days of fighting the
insurgents were in retreat. Wagner fled, was separated from other rebel
leaders at Freiberg and thus escaped arrest and imprisonment. (Röckel,
initially condemned to death, actually served thirteen years.) Proceeding to
Weimar, he saw a rehearsal of *Tannhäuser* under Liszt on 14 May, was received
by Grand Duchess Maria Pawlowna at Eisenach, and visited the Wartburg.
Returning to Weimar he learned that a warrant for his arrest had been issued
and he was no longer safe in any German state. Liszt provided funds and a
passport with a false identity, and Wagner left for Switzerland, arriving in
ZURICH on 28 May.

4. Exile, 1849–1863

In September 1849, Minna joined Wagner in Zurich. Her world was shattered:
his revolutionary folly was devastating, his new plans incomprehensible.
His world, he realized, had to be reshaped entirely: revolution had failed
in practicality, but artistic revolution was still pre-eminent in his thinking.
The seeds of a creative enterprise on a cosmic scale had been sown in the
months before the Dresden debacle: the libretto of *Siegfrieds Tod* (later
GÖTTERDÄMMERUNG) was read to friends late in 1848. That winter he toyed
with ideas connecting Friedrich Barbarossa, the Nibelung Hoard, and the
Grail, also sketching a drama, *Jesus von Nazareth*. His recent discovery of
FEUERBACH greatly influenced his thinking at this time. In Zurich, the
Nibelung/Siegfried threads were gradually woven into a cycle: a *Vorabend* and
a trio of three-act dramas: *Der RING DES NIBELUNGEN*. Before creative work
on the *Ring* could advance he grappled with the whole subject of art and
society in a series of prose works, including his longest book, *OPER UND
DRAMA* (Opera and Drama, 1851). ANCIENT GREEK drama had gloriously
embraced an entire civilization, uniting the mimetic, poetic, and musical arts.
The artwork of the future (*Das KUNSTWERK DER ZUKUNFT*, 1849/50) was to
be a GESAMTKUNSTWERK (total work of art) transcending even the splendid
Greek model. *Die KUNST UND DIE REVOLUTION* (Art and Revolution, 1849)
declares that "the art-work of the future is intended to express the spirit of free

people irrespective of all national boundaries" (PW 1:53–4, translation amended). Wagner echoes Enlightenment and Romantic writers (Lessing, GOETHE, SCHELLING, Proudhon, HEGEL, and his recent discovery of Feuerbach), but he is the first composer consciously to apply such ideas to opera. The autobiographical *Eine MITTEILUNG AN MEINE FREUNDE* (Communication to My Friends, 1851) contains the essence of these aesthetic writings plus highly personalized interpretations of *Der fliegende Holländer*, *Tannhäuser*, and *Lohengrin*, seen in terms of the artist (i.e., Wagner) as outsider in (an imperfect) society, and adducing classical roots for each of these operas. Wagner's own thinking is revealed in his voluminous CORRESPONDENCE from exile to friends in Germany, notably Röckel, Liszt, and Uhlig.

Encouraged by Liszt, Wagner again tried his luck in Paris early in 1850 with a prose sketch for *Wieland der Schmied*. He subsequently visited Jessie Laussot and her wine merchant spouse in Bordeaux and began an affair with her. Husband Eugène frustrated a planned elopement, and by 3 July Wagner was back with Minna in Zurich. To his delight Liszt conducted the premiere of *Lohengrin* (Weimar, 28 August): above all, this encouraged the dissemination of his operas all over Germany.

The banished composer, unable to attend any of these, wrote essays on how to present *Tannhäuser* and *Lohengrin*. The latter was published in full score and piano score (arranged by Uhlig) by BREITKOPF & HÄRTEL. Wagner's conducting of concerts with the Allgemeine Musikgesellschaft Orchestra of Zurich from 1850 to 1855 had considerable and lasting impact on musical life there. He also conducted seventeen performances of operas at the city theater. He had for years suffered from erysipelas, and attempted to alleviate this with lengthy and rigorous hydropathic treatments (see HEALTH). Long and frequent HIKING tours in the spectacular Swiss Alps were among his greatest delights. Vivid impressions of this dramatic landscape are reflected in the stage directions of the *Ring*.

Zurich had become a haven for political exiles of the 1848–9 events. The poet Georg HERWEGH became a firm friend and introduced the composer to François and Eliza WILLE, soon dedicated supporters. Wagner's circle included the architect Gottfried SEMPER (a Dresden fugitive), the Swiss writer Gottfried Keller, the Cantonal secretary Jacob SULZER, and local composers such as Wilhelm BAUMGARTNER and Johann Carl Eschmann. There were also deepening friendships with men who at this time were akin to surrogate sons: Bülow and Karl Ritter. Karl's mother Julie provided Wagner with a substantial allowance from 1851 to 1859. Early in 1852 Wagner met a wealthy silk merchant Otto WESENDONCK and his 23-year-old wife Mathilde, lately settled in Zurich. Soon he would be numbered among Wagner's most generous patrons and she among the great loves of his life.

In May and June of 1851, the text of *Der junge Siegfried* was written and by the end of the following year the whole tetralogy was completed with the poems of *Die WALKÜRE* and *Das RHEINGOLD*. Fifty copies of the entire *Ring* text were privately published and read to an invited audience at the Zurich Hotel Baur au Lac in February 1853. With money from Wesendonck, Wagner travelled to Italy where, at LA SPEZIA, *Mein Leben* tells us, he experienced the musical sounds of the Prelude to *Rheingold* in a fevered SLEEP. He and Liszt were together again in October and visited Paris, where he met Liszt's daughters Blandine and COSIMA. On 1 November he at last began the music of *Rheingold* and proceeded rapidly: the composition draft was finished in two and a half months. During 1854, Wagner also became acquainted with the work of SCHOPENHAUER. The following year, Wagner spent four months in London, where he had accepted an engagement to conduct eight concerts for the Philharmonic Society (March–June 1855). The visit was a bitter failure artistically and financially, but he was received cordially by Queen Victoria and Prince Albert, and saw more of Berlioz, who was also conducting concerts there.

By the close of 1856, musical ideas for an opera on *Tristan und Isolde* were beginning to mingle with the music of *Siegfried*. On 28 April 1857 the Wagners moved into the "Asyl," a small house adjoining the Wesendonck villa. Here composition of *Siegfried* continued to the end of Act II until, on 9 August, he laid the score aside and began to draft the poem of *Tristan*. Among many visitors, Bülow and his wife Cosima came to the Asyl for their honeymoon in September. The poem complete, Wagner then read it to an audience of his wife, his beloved, his wife-to-be, and both their husbands. The music of Act I was sketched by the last day of the year. Five settings of poems by Mathilde were composed at this time: they contain musical material developed in *Tristan*.

Richard's passion for Mathilde fatally exacerbated tensions in his marriage. Minna had suffered from heart disease for some years, attempted several cures, and was increasingly dependent on drugs to alleviate her condition and relieve insomnia. Now she lived with a man whose art was beyond her understanding and who shared its intimate secrets with the younger woman next door. Town gossip about her husband's obvious infatuation with his benefactor's wife was common. Nevertheless, he completed Act I of *Tristan* in orchestral score (3 April). Four days later Minna intercepted a letter of his to Mathilde, known as the "Morning Confession." She read it, interpreted it as a love letter, and confronted her husband and then Mathilde, who told Otto. The impossible situation could only worsen. Minna spent most of the following three months at a water cure sanatorium in Brestenberg in the Aargau, while Wagner wrote the composition draft of *Tristan* Act II. Minna's return in mid-July proved disastrous, the pair relapsing into series of dreadful rows. A month later Wagner left the Asyl forever. He travelled alone to Geneva, then arrived in Venice at the end of August accompanied by Karl Ritter, took an apartment in the Palazzo Giustiniani on the Grand Canal, and set to work orchestrating the central act of *Tristan*. Minna returned to Dresden.

Propriety decreed that Mathilde and Richard did not correspond while he was in Italy. Instead he poured out his feelings and ideas in a so-called "Venice Diary" to be read by her later. This is of great interest for its revelation of a mind imbued with Buddhism and Schopenhauer, meditations on the role of suffering, cruelty to animals, fellow-suffering (*Mitleid*), the uncompassionate rich, renunciation, and REDEMPTION. He tells Mathilde that one day the meaning of all this will become clear in the Good Friday scene of *Parsifal*. Wagner's physical sufferings at that time slowed progress with *Tristan*: dysentery and a leg ulcer. As a political fugitive he was also harassed by the Austrian police. He forsook Venice for Lucerne, where he completed *Tristan und Isolde* on 6 August 1859.

The specter of poverty haunted him always. He had arrived in Venice with virtually nothing. Breitkopf had pleased him by agreeing to publish *Tristan* and sending him an advance of 200 louis d'or (one third of what he had requested). Hopes of that firm taking a risk with the *Ring* scores were disappointed. Hopes of more MONEY from Liszt in Weimar were also dashed by a foolishly worded and ill-timed letter Wagner sent (31 December 1858) to which Liszt took offence. Things were patched up but the friendship never again recaptured the ardor and enthusiasm of earlier years. Julie Ritter made a last payment to Wagner in 1859 and he received royalties from performances in Germany: Munich gave *Lohengrin* in February 1858; Vienna followed in August. In September 1859 he revisited the Wesendoncks in Zurich and concluded a business arrangement with Otto, who would purchase the copyright of Wagner's *Ring* scores.

Paris was again Wagner's goal in September 1859: his hope was to mount model performances of *Tannhäuser*, *Lohengrin*, and *Tristan*, and to complete *Siegfried*. A successful Paris premiere of *Tristan* with German singers would, he believed, open up German theaters for his *Ring* operas. This second attempted siege of Paris failed on all counts. The greatest failure was the one opera actually produced: *Tannhäuser* at the Opéra, by Imperial command. Paradoxically this very debacle stirred Germany's awareness of Wagner's importance, and immensely increased his reputation among artists and intellectuals across Europe. In October he found a quiet house in the rue Newton at a rent of 4,000 francs per year, at the landlord's insistence paying 2 years' installments in advance. He had the dilapidated house restored and redecorated at considerable expense. Here Minna, dog, and parrot joined him on 17 November: the final attempt to restore domestic harmony. He lost everything he had expended on the rue Newton property when he discovered that the street was to be swept away as part of the municipal construction by Baron Haussmann. The cost of removal (October 1860), rent in advance for a smaller apartment in rue d'Aumale, and the expense of futile legal action to recover his original outgoings added grievously to his many burdens.

Early in 1860 he conducted three concerts of extracts from his works, including the *Tristan* Prelude. Financially a disaster, these evenings awoke enthusiasm for Wagner's music among a new generation of admirers including BAUDELAIRE, CHAMPFLEURY, Gounod, and Saint-Saëns. Wagner met ROSSINI for the one and only time in March 1860. The efforts of Princess Pauline METTERNICH, wife of the Austrian ambassador, persuaded Napoleon III to commission *Tannhäuser* for the Opéra. A French translation was commenced, a new ballet and Venusberg scene composed, and an unprecedented 164 rehearsals occurred before the infamous fiasco of March 1861. The work was withdrawn after three disrupted performances. On the credit side Wagner's imperial patronage brought amnesty (July 1860) in all German states, except Saxony, which followed in March 1862.

Some unsettled years, with many changes of address, ensued, dictated by protracted, ill-fated hopes for a performance of *Tristan* either in Karlsruhe or in Vienna, and by his need for a creative retreat to compose *Die MEISTERSINGER VON NÜRNBERG*, for which he wrote a new prose sketch and libretto in the winter of 1861–2. He settled in Biebrich, near his publisher Schott in Mainz. When Minna arrived there, the ten atrocious days that followed caused them to separate permanently. They met for the last time in Dresden in November 1862, and she died there in January 1866. Slow progress with *Meistersinger* and Schott's refusal to part with further payment led again to money worries. He hoped a series of concerts in Vienna of EXCERPTS from the completed sections of the *Ring* and *Meistersinger* would bring him income and stimulate interest in them. Among the copyists of the orchestral parts were BRAHMS, Carl TAUSIG, and two composers close to Wagner at this time, Peter CORNELIUS and Wendelin WEISSHEIMER. The concerts (December 1862–January 1863) won the public, were damned by the critics, and lost money (Wagner's costs were met by rich admirers). He next embarked on concerts of further extracts, alongside Beethoven symphonies, in RUSSIA (February–April). These proved enormously successful, bringing handsome rewards artistically and financially. There was some opposition to him on account of his controversial "theories," but in Alexander SEROV, whom he already knew, he found a trusty champion. Later, Wagner's art and writings would have seminal influence on Russian MODERNISM, as on the symbolist movement generally. At one ST. PETERSBURG concert the later familiar coupling of the *Tristan* Prelude and Isolde's *Verklärung* (the so-called *LIEBESTOD*) was first heard. With proceeds from his Russian adventure he took an apartment in a villa at Penzing in the Viennese suburbs (May 1863) furnishing it in luxurious style and dispensing hospitality on a lavish scale. Unsurprisingly, the threat of insolvency reemerged and he was compelled to give further concerts in Pest, Prague, Karlsruhe, Löwenberg, Breslau, and again Vienna. Never could he understand how the world could make things so hard for him when he had such beauties to give it.

5. Royal patronage, 1864–1871

Early in 1864, Wagner's finances were out of control and he faced arrest for debt. He fled his Vienna creditors on 23 March, stayed for a month with Eliza WILLE at Mariafeld (outside Zurich), but was made less welcome by her husband. Proceeding to Stuttgart he was surprised there on 3 May by the appearance of the private secretary to the king of Bavaria, Franz von PFISTER-MEISTER. LUDWIG II had succeeded to the throne on 10 March, aged 18, and had already conceived a passion for Wagner's work. One of his first acts was to seek out the composer. Pfistermeister presented the astounded Wagner with a ring and a photograph of the king, and next day in Munich Wagner had a first audience of his royal benefactor. Ludwig promised to pay off his debts and remove all future care from him. He lent him Villa Pellet on Lake Starnberg, where Wagner stayed until October. He composed a *HULDIGUNGSMARSCH* for the king and, at Ludwig's request, an essay *Über Staat und Religion* (On State and Religion, 1864) to clarify developments in his thinking since the writings of 1849–51. This was followed over the next year or so with *Deutsche Kunst und deutsche Politik* (German Art and German Politics, 1867) and *Was ist deutsch?* (What is German?, 1865/78). Cosima von Bülow arrived at Villa Pellet on 29 June. Hans followed her eight days later. In the interim, she consummated her union with Wagner: their daughter ISOLDE was born on 10 April 1865.

Wagner moved to a Munich home acquired by the king in October and at once decked it out in sumptuous style, with silks and satins sent by his Viennese seamstress Bertha Goldwag. The Bülows with their daughters Daniela and Blandine arrived in Munich in November, Wagner having secured Hans a court appointment (thus effectively ousting Franz Lachner, who had introduced Wagner's works to Munich). By the end of the year Wagner had resumed the full orchestral score of *Siegfried* Act II and Ludwig approved plans for a FESTIVAL THEATER in Munich to be designed by Semper for performances of the *Ring*. In March 1865, Wagner submitted a report on a school of music to be founded in Munich. To Munich's citizens these plans seemed mad. Why should one man have his own theater? Why should this man oust all the city's fine music teachers to replace them with his own? He was an outsider, as was his hated, haughty, "Prussian" assistant Bülow. Wagner was an easy target for calumny: a dangerous demagogue, adulterer, wild spender, incorrigible borrower, a drain on the state's resources, and an unwelcome influence on the young monarch. He quickly made political enemies. They awaited their moment to topple him.

Tristan und Isolde went into rehearsal, the musical direction in Bülow's most capable hands. The title roles in an unprecedented style of daunting difficulty were allotted to Ludwig Schnorr von CAROLSFELD and his wife Malwina. On the morning of the planned premiere (15 May) bailiffs arrived to seize Wagner's furniture. Then Schnorr arrived with calamitous news: Malwina was hoarse. The postponed "model performance" took place on 19 June and was given three more times. On 17 July, at the king's request, Wagner began to dictate *MEIN LEBEN* (My Life, 1865–81) to Cosima, aided by a diary, the "Red Book," he had kept since 1835. Nevertheless, attacks on Wagner for undue political interference led the Bavarian Minister-President to ask the king "to choose between the love and honor of his loyal subjects and the friendship of Richard Wagner." Reluctantly Ludwig requested him to leave Bavaria on 10 December.

His second Swiss "exile" began in Geneva where he completed orchestration of *Die Meistersinger* Act I (March 1866). With Cosima he discovered a home, TRIBSCHEN, in a breathtaking setting on Lake Lucerne (Vierwaldstättersee). The king visited Tribschen secretly for Wagner's birthday that year. Unaware of the true relations of Cosima and his friend he was persuaded by Wagner and the Bülows to sign a letter affirming her innocence and condemning perpetrators of gossip about the now-notorious "love triangle." Ludwig was thus shamefully deceived. When the truth of the adultery was made known to him, anguish of betrayal was added to the misery of enforced separation from Wagner. On 17 February, Cosima's second daughter by Wagner, EVA, was born at Tribschen. *Die Meistersinger* was finished on 24 October and premiered in Munich on 21 June 1868 under Bülow. Ludwig allowed Wagner to acknowledge the tumultuous ovation from the royal box. They did not meet again for eight years.

Liszt was also estranged from Wagner. They had an emotional confrontation the previous October about the "triangle." Cosima asked Bülow for a divorce in 1868. Her father was fundamentally opposed to this, and Bülow at first refused. She and her four daughters moved in permanently with Wagner at Tribschen in November. Soon after this she began writing her diary, one of the most important primary sources for Wagner's later years (see COSIMA WAGNER'S DIARIES). Her third illegitimate child was a boy, SIEGFRIED, born 6 June 1869. Bülow now agreed to a separation and resigned his post in Munich. He and Wagner never met again. Bülow agreed to divorce only in July 1870, and Cosima married Wagner in the Protestant church of Lucerne on 25 August, date of the king's twenty-fifth birthday. Relations with Ludwig, who remained faithful to Wagner's art, were soured by the king's insistence on staging *Das Rheingold* (1869) and *Die Walküre* (1870) in Munich, against the composer's wish. Hans RICHTER had emerged as Wagner's conductor-acolyte in Bülow's wake, and was entrusted with the first of these and then ordered by Wagner to pull out. Both premieres were finally conducted by Franz Wüllner. To prevent Ludwig staging *Siegfried*, Wagner deliberately delayed completion of the score of Act III. Composition of *Götterdämmerung* began in October 1869. Other writing of this time included the sketch for a play about Luther (1869), and the essays *Über das Dirigiren* (On Conducting, 1869) and *BEETHOVEN* (1870).

Of visitors to Tribschen besides Richter, the most frequent and significant was Friedrich NIETZSCHE, professor of philology at Basel. At that time Wagner was the adored Master for Nietzsche, and the Tribschen years coincided with his book *The Birth of Tragedy*. He was also witness to the first performance of what posterity calls the *SIEGFRIED IDYLL* to celebrate Cosima's birthday at Christmas 1870. Other callers included a group of French admirers: Henri Duparc, Judith GAUTIER, Catulle MENDÈS, Saint-Saëns, and Villiers de l'Isle-Adam. Embarrassingly this group found itself with Wagner when the Franco-Prussian War broke out (July 1870). Although Wagner later would declare his detestation of Bismarck and Prussian militarism, at that time his patriotic fervor and Francophobia knew no bounds, and resulted in *Eine Kapitulation*, a farce which gloated over the misery of the defeated French, and a nationalistic poem *An das deutsche Heer vor Paris* (To the German Army before Paris, January 1871). *Über die Bestimmung der Oper* (On the Destiny of Opera, his installation address upon election to the Berlin Royal Academy of Arts, April 1871) adds further thoughts to the *Beethoven* essay about "musically conceived drama." In Berlin, he met Bismarck and conducted a concert at the opera before Wilhelm I, including his recent *KAISERMARSCH* (5 May). That spring the Wagners visited the Upper Franconian town of BAYREUTH and he decided, with encouragement from the civic authorities, to build his FESTIVAL THEATER there. In Berlin, he sounded out an architect and enlisted practical support, Tausig joining the fundraising plan until his untimely death that summer.

6. Bayreuth, 1872–1883

Ludwig's reaction to the Bayreuth scheme was characteristically altruistic. Despite the resolution of the Cosima affair, he knew Wagner would never return to Munich: the idea of the Semper theater was dead and the spiritual bond forged so lovingly between them in 1864 broken asunder. Bayreuth was within his domains and although skeptical as to how quickly or practically Wagner's ambitions might be realized, he provided funds for land on which the composer built a residence. Both the site for Haus WAHNFRIED and the *Festspielhaus* (purchased by the town) were chosen early in 1872, anticipating a first festival in 1873, at an estimated cost for construction and an initial festival of 300,000 thalers. A society of patrons would be formed and 1,000 PATRON CERTIFICATES (*Patronatscheine*) at 300 thalers each issued. WAGNER SOCIETIES were founded in many cities. The Wagners, with the five children, left Tribschen for Bayreuth in April 1872, occupying temporary accommodation for two years until Wahnfried was completed. The *Festspielhaus* foundation stone was laid on his fifty-ninth birthday (Nietzsche attended), and he also conducted Beethoven's Ninth that evening. Wagner invited Liszt to Bayreuth and from this time their former affinity was rekindled; Liszt's glowing admiration for Wagner's art never dimmed. Despite several generous supporters, income for the festival plan was tardy. Thus the festival was postponed until 1876, and only made feasible by a loan from Ludwig of 100,000 thalers. The composer's energies were consumed by completing the score of *Götterdämmerung* (November 1874), the constant cares of his ambitious plan, lengthy tours of opera houses in search of casts, and busy periods of coaching and rehearsing.

For the first festival, 13–30 August 1876, three cycles of the *Ring* were given, before an illustrious gathering, Richter conducting. Ludwig attended the dress rehearsals. The festival made a loss of 148,000 marks. September to December saw the first of several family visits to ITALY. In an attempt to reduce the Bayreuth debt Wagner again mounted the podium, including a series of concerts with Richter at London's Royal Albert Hall in May 1877, although this netted a derisory sum. The exceptional energies expended in the preparation of the first festival, and his anxious striving to solve the problem of its deficit, weakened Wagner's physical health. Although not diagnosed as heart disease until shortly before his death, he experienced increasing chest pains over the coming years.

The text of PARSIFAL was completed during April and composition began in September 1877, occupying him until April 1879 (end of the second complete draft). The full score took steady shape (August 1879–January 1882), much of it during extended Italian sojourns. Meanwhile, he wrote articles for the newly founded *BAYREUTHER BLÄTTER*, which became the organ for Wagnerian propaganda under the editorship of Hans von WOLZOGEN. Wagner's later essays are less concerned with music, rather art and aesthetics in general relation to life, theories about race, socialism, VIVISECTION, VEGETARIANISM, and so on. The most substantial piece, *Religion und Kunst* (Religion and Art), with its various supplements, is greatly indebted to Schopenhauer, and echoes the racial theories of his new friend Joseph-Arthur GOBINEAU. Others new to his circle included Siegfried's tutor Heinrich von Stein, the painter Paul von JOUKOWSKY, pianist and arranger Joseph RUBINSTEIN, and musical assistant Engelbert HUMPERDINCK. In 1878, Wagner agreed that the *Ring* could be toured by the impresario Angelo NEUMANN. Another important agreement of that year was with Ludwig: the festival deficit was cleared in exchange for Munich's right to perform all Wagner's works without fee save a 10 percent royalty set against the Bayreuth debt. Also the personnel of the Munich opera would perform *Parsifal* under Hofkapellmeister Herman LEVI.

675

At the end of 1880, a year spent mostly in Italy (where the gardens at Ravello and Siena cathedral inspired images for *Parsifal*), Wagner met Ludwig in Munich for the last time: there was a private performance of *Lohengrin*, and he conducted the *Parsifal* Prelude for the king. In May 1881, the Wagners attended the Neumann production of the *Ring* in Berlin. Palermo was their home for the winter of 1881–2; there he finished *Parsifal*, and RENOIR sketched him two days later. During 1882, as his health slowly worsened, he immersed himself in preparations for the production of his last opera. At Bayreuth he set up a stipendiary fund (*Stipendienstiftung*) to enable those of little means to attend future festivals. This was an important thread from his original idea of allowing free admission to all, and still exists (administered by the Richard-Wagner-Verband International) to enable students to attend without charge.

At the second Bayreuth Festival *Parsifal* was premiered (26 July 1882), and there were fifteen further performances. During the last, 29 August, Wagner took the baton from Levi during the final transformation scene and conducted to the end. After the festival, the family settled in Venice, occupying the mezzanine floor of the Palazzo Vendramin-Calergi on the Grand Canal. Liszt joined them from mid-November to 13 January. The celebration of Cosima's birthday on Christmas Eve each year – a tradition from Tribschen times – took the form in 1882 of a private performance of his early C major Symphony in the Teatro la Fenice.

On 13 February 1883, while working at an essay *Über das Weibliche im Menschlichen* (On the Womanly in the Human Race), Wagner suffered a fatal heart attack and died in Cosima's arms in the mid-afternoon. A funeral gondola took his body to the railway station, whence it journeyed to Bayreuth and was buried at a private ceremony in the garden of Wahnfried on 18 February. The pallbearers were Friedrich FEUSTEL; Adolf GROSS; Franz MUNCKER (representing Bayreuth); Wolzogen; the conductors and assistants Levi, Richter, Anton SEIDL, Joukowsky, and Heinrich PORGES; the violinist WILHELMJ; the tenor Albert NIEMANN; and the physician Joseph STANDHARTNER.   DEREK WATSON

William Ashton Ellis, *Life of Richard Wagner* (see bibliography).
Carl Friedrich Glasenapp, *Das Leben Richard Wagners* (see bibliography).
Joachim Köhler, *Richard Wagner: The Last of the Titans* (see bibliography).
Barry Millington, *Wagner. Master Musicians Series* (see bibliography).
Ernest Newman, *The Life of Richard Wagner* (see bibliography).
Stewart Spencer, *Wagner Remembered* (see bibliography).
Derek Watson, *Richard Wagner: A Biography* (see bibliography).

Wagner, Rosalie (b. Leipzig, 4 March 1803; d. Leipzig, 12 Oct. 1837), Wagner's older sister. Singer and actress married to university professor Oswald Marbach; died in childbirth. Financially supported the family after Ludwig GEYER's death. Like Wilhelmine SCHRÖDER-DEVRIENT, she had a weak voice but compensated with diction and acting. Introduced Wagner to BEETHOVEN's heroine Leonore and to impassioned singing and eloquent acting. Perhaps Wagner's first ideal of the self-sacrificing, female redeemer.   LYDIA MAYNE

Wagner, Siegfried (Helferich Richard), (b. Tribschen, 6 June 1869; d. Bayreuth, 4 Aug. 1930), composer, conductor, opera producer, artistic director at Bayreuth; son of Richard Wagner and COSIMA von Bülow, (later Wagner). According to a journal entry written in Wagner's hand, Cosima's portrait was transfigured by the rays of sunlight entering their bedroom on the morning of Siegfried's birth. The work *SIEGFRIED IDYLL* (1870) was composed retrospectively to honor that occasion. In his early twenties, Siegfried studied architecture at the Technical University in Charlottenburg (Berlin), and musical composition with Engelbert HUMPERDINCK. He later moved to Karlsruhe to continue his architectural education and to study composition with the Baden Court Kapellmeister Felix MOTTL. Evidence from letters and diary entries suggests that it was at this time that Siegfried began to explore his sexuality with his friend and lover, English composer and pianist Clement Harris. After a sailing trip with Harris to India, Siegfried returned to BAYREUTH in 1892 and decided to pursue a career in music.

Siegfried served as both conductor at Bayreuth (first conducting the *RING* in 1896) and assistant director (producing *Der FLIEGENDE HOLLÄNDER* in 1901). After Cosima's retirement following the 1906 season, he took over as artistic director of the Festival, holding the position until his death in 1930 – outliving his mother by only four months. For Siegfried, Cosima's presence was always felt from the sidelines (she remained in WAHNFRIED), perhaps prompting him to maintain a conservative staging style, though he did break free from some nineteenth-century traditions with his 1908 production of *LOHENGRIN*, which he referred to as "a production for gourmets." When the festival reopened in 1924, after a nine-year hiatus occasioned by World War I, he continued to introduce certain innovations (inspired by Adolphe APPIA) such as solid three-dimensional sets and less literal visual imagery. Notable among these were structures for the *Ring* that included Gibichung Hall, rocky landscapes for the Valkyries, and creative use of electric lighting. Here, drafting and architectural skills he had acquired in earlier years proved helpful at Bayreuth when communicating with stage designers Max Brückner and Kurt Söhnlein.

With the success of his first stage work, *Der Bärenhäuter* (premiered in 1899), followed by *Herzog Wildfang*, *Der Kobold*, *Bruder Lustig*, *Sternengebot*, and *Banadietrich*, Siegfried (clearly influenced by Humperdinck) became recognized as a composer of fairy-tale operas. After initial successes, his popularity with audiences declined. Many of his works were rejected by critics who disparaged his talents, detecting a naïve reliance on his father's musical language.

Given contemporaneous attitudes and laws that prohibited homosexual acts, Siegfried was forced to hide his relationships with other men, and faced several scandals involving individuals, including his sister Isolde BEIDLER, who threatened to "out" him to the public. He finally succumbed to his mother's wishes at age 46 when he married an 18-year-old Englishwoman named WINIFRED (née Williams) on 22 September 1915. Together they had four children: WIELAND (1917–66), FRIEDELIND (1918–91), WOLFGANG (1919–2010), and VERENA (b. 1920).

Siegfried adopted the anti-Semitic attitudes of the Wagner household and, along with Winifred, seems to have been an early supporter of Adolf HITLER, who was a guest at Wahnfried in 1923. Hitler later wrote to Siegfried praising Bayreuth as the "city where first the Master [i.e., Wagner] and then CHAMBERLAIN forged the spiritual sword with which we fight today" (Hitler to Siegfried Wagner, 5 May 1924). ALEXIS LUKO

Siegfried Wagner, *Erinnerungen* (Stuttgart: 1923, repr. Frankfurt am Main: Lang, 2005).

Wagner societies
1. Original concept and societies
2. International Association of Richard Wagner Societies / Richard-Wagner-Verband International

1. Original concept and societies

On 12 May 1871, Wagner announced the plan to found a PATRONS' ASSOCI-ATION that would sell PATRON CERTIFICATES each priced at 300 thaler to fund the construction of the Bayreuth FESTIVAL THEATER. Certificate owners would receive tickets to all three performances of the *Ring* cycle. On 15 May, Emil HECKEL, a Mannheim publisher and instrument dealer, responded to the plan in a letter to Wagner. Concerned that those with modest financial resources would unable to participate in the venture and thus have no chance to experience the festival, he subsequently proposed the formation of "societies" (*Vereine*) allowing potentially unlimited numbers of members to share in the cost of a certificate. Attendance at the festival would then be decided by lot.

On 1 June 1871, Heckel and a group of fellow enthusiasts in MANNHEIM founded the first "Wagner Society," officially called a "Society in Support of the Great National Undertaking" (*Verein zur Förderung des grossen nationalen Unternehmens*). Membership was restricted to "Friends and supporters of Wagner's artistic endeavors," who committed to pay a contribution in 1871, 1872, and 1873. The Mannheim statutes set the standard for all future Wagner societies. On 16 July, COSIMA wrote to Heckel, encouraging him to "get in touch with various cities and spread the Wagner society throughout Germany." Within five months of the Mannheim founding, Wagner societies were formed in MUNICH, LEIPZIG, and VIENNA. The following year (1872) saw explosive growth: DRESDEN, BAYREUTH, Weimar, NUREMBERG, Darmstadt, Mainz, Göttingen, Cologne, and two in Berlin, including an Academic Richard Wagner Society. The same year, Wagner societies were founded outside the German-speaking world in Pest (Buda and Pest merged in 1873), LONDON, and New York. By the 1876 opening of the Bayreuth festival, there were additional Wagner societies in Prague, Basel, ZURICH, RIGA, PARIS, Florence, Milan, Boston, Cairo, Warsaw, Amsterdam, Stockholm, and Copenhagen.

The initial growth of the Wagner societies was unprecedented for a living artist and, in the realm of "serious" (as opposed to popular) art, remains unmatched. While pleased with the existence of the societies, Wagner maintained a certain distance. Nevertheless, in his *Mitteilung an die deutschen Wagner-Vereine* (Communication to the German Wagner Societies) published on Christmas Day 1871, Wagner proposed a centrally organized "Allgemeiner deutscher Wagner-Verein" that would consolidate the individual societies.

By early 1872, Wagner had moved the central administration from Mannheim to Bayreuth.

Despite the exponential growth of the Wagner society network, the effort to raise the necessary 300,000 thalers failed. After one and a half years, only 340 certificates were sold. Wagner ultimately had to rely on LUDWIG II to finance the completion and first festival with a loan of 100,000 thalers, which the Wagner family paid back in full by 1906.

The fiscal failure of the first festival prompted a lengthy appeal on 1 January 1877 in which Wagner among other things suggested a newly formed "Patrons' Association" to be funded out of the coffers of the individual Wagner societies. This new central body would be different from the organization for the first festival because it was designed to ensure a recurring festival. At the meeting of delegates on 2 April 1877 in Leipzig, the "General Patrons Association for the Maintenance and Preservation of the Stage Festivals in Bayreuth" (Allgemeiner Patronat-Verein zur Pflege und Erhaltung der Bühnenfestspiele zu Bayreuth) was formed. Wagner sent out an appeal on 15 January 1878 asking local Wagner societies to become branches (*Zweigverein*) of the Central Society and to send their annual dues directly to Bayreuth. If they preferred not to do so, he asked that they at least send a certain percentage or surplus of the funds they raised to contribute to the cash reserves of the Society (SSD 16:162–3).

2. International Association of Richard Wagner Societies / Richard-Wagner-Verband International

On 13 February 1909, Anna Held founded the Richard Wagner Verband deutscher Frauen (RWVdF; Richard Wagner Association of German Women) in Leipzig with the goal of raising one million marks for the festival bursary fund. By 1913, this was achieved but, after World War I and the devastating inflation of 1923, fundraising had to begin anew.

After World War II, the Richard Wagner Verband was re-founded on 9 October 1947 in Hanover; the suffix "of German Women" was dropped from the name in 1949. Meanwhile, Richard Wagner associations were being re-founded outside of Germany, in Paris and London. Both Wagner societies regarded the German national association as their umbrella organization. However, they had no voting rights at the national conferences and were not able to obtain any Bayreuth bursaries.

The internationalization of the hitherto German association followed slowly, reaching consensus at an extraordinary general meeting in Wiesbaden in January 1991, followed in May that year with the declaration in Lyon of the International Association of Richard Wagner Societies. With the fall of the Berlin Wall in 1989/90, the founding of RWV associations in the former East quickly followed: Moscow and Budapest, cities in former East Germany, followed by St. Petersburg and the Baltic States, Sofia and Zagreb. More recently, associations have been formed in the Far and Middle East and, in 2010, there is even a Wagner Society in Jerusalem. Currently, there are 130 societies spread over every continent. The Wagner society with the largest membership is in WÜRZBURG.   NICHOLAS VAZSONYI

Karl Heckel, *Die Bühnenfestspiele in Bayreuth: Authentischer Beitrag zur Geschichte ihrer Entstehung und Entwicklung* (Leipzig: Fritzsch, 1891).

Wagner as stage director. During the course of the nineteenth century, improvements in STAGE DESIGN, technology, and scenic painting, and the installation of electric lighting enabled theater practitioners to devise elaborate spectacles. Wagner fully exploited these advances, especially in the production of the RING at Bayreuth in 1876, but it was not until after his death that the stage director, who would coordinate the increasingly complex machinery of theatrical production, would be acknowledged as the prime creative artist in the theater. Nevertheless, Wagner, who was consistently involved in the staging of his MUSIC DRAMAS, did much to prepare the ground for this figure.

When Wagner's first works were staged in the 1840s, most productions of new as well as established operas were put on with scenery and costumes that were drawn from stock, so that the physical production rarely articulated with any specificity the action of the drama. No single individual was responsible for integrating all elements of the production. Wagner quickly understood that such lack of coordination meant that audiences had difficulty in understanding his work. In several of the essays written in the late 1840s and early 1850s, he theorized a concept of integrated production. His inquiries ranged from a proposed reorganization of the administrative structure of the theater in a plan designed for the Saxon National Theatre in Dresden (1849), through major writings such as Die KUNST UND DIE REVOLUTION (Art and Revolution, 1849) and OPER UND DRAMA (Opera and Drama, 1851) in which he envisioned his concept of the GESAMTKUNSTWERK or total work of art, to specific analyses (1852) in which he showed how it was only through careful attention to staging in coordination with the singers' acting that TANNHÄUSER and Der FLIEGENDE HOLLÄNDER could be made fully intelligible to audiences. Wagner's lack of contact with theaters during the 1850s meant that he had no opportunity to try out his ideas in practice. When he did have the opportunity to stage *Tannhäuser*, at the Paris OPÉRA in March 1861, the resistance of some performers and a hostile reception from nationalist segments of the audience meant that his stage direction made little impact.

The patronage of LUDWIG II enabled Wagner to stage what have come to be regarded as "model" productions of his work at the Hof- und National Theater in MUNICH during the 1860s. Here, on sets designed by Heinrich Döll and Angelo II Quaglio, Wagner staged revivals of *Der fliegende Holländer* (1864), *Lohengrin* (1867), and *Tannhäuser* (1867), which represented an extension of the historicist production style of the 1840s and 1850s, but the successful premieres of TRISTAN UND ISOLDE (1865) and Die MEISTERSINGER VON NÜRNBERG (1868) suggested a major shift in Wagner's concept of stage production. Even though Quaglio and Döll's sets for *Tristan* reflected the dominant Romantic-realistic tastes of the time, evidence suggests that under Wagner's direction the emotional world of the lovers was palpably realized on stage, while *Meistersinger* was remarkable less for picturesque and purportedly historically "accurate" settings, and more for the abundant movement, cogent blocking, detailed motivation, and effective ensemble of the production.

Wagner's theory of the total work of art as worked out in the early 1850s depended upon the theoretical equality of different elements of performance, but during the Munich years he came to reject this concept and, in the major essay, BEETHOVEN (1870), he asserted the superiority of music as the prime expressive means of the drama. This implied a reappraisal of the function of the stage director, who should be less concerned with the realistic and detailed realization of human behavior on stage, more with creating an illusion of total harmony, in which nothing disrupts the audience's absorption in the music and the action it expresses. The achievement of such an illusion was the prime purpose of the Bayreuth FESTIVAL THEATER, which opened with the first complete production of the *Ring* in 1876.

Although Wagner served as stage director for this production, he was far from satisfied with the result. In part this was because the Romantic-realistic settings by Josef HOFFMANN and, especially, the costumes by Carl Emil DOEPLER, were too realistic and weakened the imaginative perspectives opened up by the music. But Wagner himself was to blame as well. According to his assistant Richard FRICKE, Wagner was extraordinarily inventive in his direction of the actors, but changed his blocking from day to day. As he also claimed that the actors were free to improvise, something virtually unheard of in operatic production at that time, there were difficulties in arriving at a coherent stage interpretation of the action. Furthermore, while Fricke understood that suggestion was more effective on the operatic stage than literal representation, Wagner did not and so the production still bore many of the hallmarks of the historicist, Romantic-realistic style that Wagner had hoped to leave behind. Had he been able to revive the *Ring* at Bayreuth, he claimed that he would have done everything differently when it came to staging.

The premiere of *PARSIFAL* in 1882 was, along with the *Meistersinger* premiere of 1868, the high point of Wagner's work as a stage director. There is much evidence that not only did he realize how suggestion on stage can support and even strengthen the capacity of music to express the action, he was beginning to find ways to realize this. Although to the eyes of later generations, the sets of the Bayreuth *Parsifal* look lush and over-detailed, Wagner's instructions to the designer indicate that he had some ideas as to how scenery could suggest rather than completely realize space, and a report he wrote after the production shows that he understood how a half-realized gesture by the actors could have greater power than a completed one. Audiences were moved by his intensely atmospheric staging of *Parsifal*, which might be grounds to speculate that he would have been open to the more abstract approaches to staging his music dramas that were developed, above all by APPIA, in the years following his death. COSIMA WAGNER insisted, however, that the "model" productions of his work from the 1860s and 1870s should be the basis for all productions at Bayreuth until well into the twentieth century.   SIMON WILLIAMS

Richard Fricke, *Wagner in Rehearsal* (see bibliography).

Wagner statues. Unlike many painted, drawn, engraved, or sculpted portraits of famous composers, full-size statues are almost always posthumous memorials (also known as *Denkmäler*). This is true of Wagner, whose likeness has graced a thousand concert programs, souvenir postcards, scholarly monographs, advertising campaigns, and music-student prize-givings, but who "survives" in just four important, life-size or larger-than-life, full-figure statues: the Richard-Wagner-Denkmal in Berlin's Tiergarten; the Richard-Wagner-Denkmal in Pirna (originally Graupa), Saxony; the Richard Wagner memorial in MUNICH; and the Richard Wagner memorial in Cleveland, Ohio. Designed in 1903 by Gustav Eberlein, the Berlin memorial features a seated Wagner (thus the German term *Sitzdenkmal*) accompanied by two additional figures standing or sitting beneath his throne: WOLFRAM VON ESCHENBACH holding a lyre and handing the composer a laurel wreath, and TANNHÄUSER lost in thought. Also a *Sitzdenkmal*, the Munich Wagner memorial was dedicated in 1913 and stands today close to the Prinzregententheater. The statue in Cleveland's Edgewater Park was designed by German-American enthusiast Herman Matzen and dedicated in 1911. The Pirna memorial, designed by Richard Guhr and dedicated in 1933, commemorates Nazi-era Germany's admiration for the composer and purported anti-Semite. Plans for a similar monument in 1930s–50s LEIPZIG never came to fruition. Today, however, a bust of Wagner stands on a plinth behind the Opera House completed in 1960. Large memorial busts of Wagner are also located today in BAYREUTH; in Baltimore's Druid Hill Park; in the Giardini Pubblici, Venice (Castello), Italy; and in Graupa, Saxony. The unveiling of the 1903 Berlin memorial itself inspired a painting completed in 1908 by Anton von Werner; the Berlin and unfinished Leipzig memorials have been discussed in some detail by Günter Metken.

MICHAEL SAFFLE

See also ICONOGRAPHY

Grit Hartmann, *Richard Wagner gefpändet: Ein Leipziger Denkmal in Dokumenten, 1931–1955* (Leipzig: Forum, 2003).

Günter Metken, "Denkmale, wo keine sind: Richard Wagner in der plastischen Erinnerung," *Laut-Malereien: Grenzgänge zwischen Kunst und Musik* (Frankfurt am Main: Campus, 1995): 63–83.

Wagner tuba, brass instrument in the tenor-baritone range. The tuba was conceived by Wagner in 1853/4 for Scene 2 of *Das* RHEINGOLD, and utilized throughout the RING. Military-band bugle horns (by Sax, Cerveny, and others) served as stopgaps before former hornist Hans RICHTER and MUNICH craftsman Georg Ottensteiner produced the first quartet of oval-shaped instruments, termed "tenor" in B♭ and "bass" in F, to be played with horn mouthpieces by hornists 5–8. These debuted in VIENNA in 1875, and BAYREUTH in 1876. Their conical, wide bore gave a dark but diffuse sound that excelled in measured, solemn passages. Subsequent years brought new makers (C. W. Moritz, Gebr. Alexander, Kruspe, Uhlmann) and employment by BRUCKNER, DRAESEKE, Richard STRAUSS, SCHOENBERG, and Stravinsky. Composer interest in the instrument quickened in the later twentieth century, including wide use in film scores.

WILLIAM MELTON

William Melton, *The Wagner Tuba: A History* (Aachen: Ebenos, 2008).

Wagner, Verena. See LAFFERENTZ, VERENA

Wagner in the visual arts. The visual arts played a relatively peripheral part in Wagner's life, writings, and aesthetic theories, but an immense one in the contemporary and posthumous RECEPTION of his work. Underexplored in criticism to date, Wagner's influence on the visual arts was undoubtedly as extensive as that on literature, politics, or theater. This is apparent in the work and writings of canonical artists from Germany to the UNITED STATES OF AMERICA, and RUSSIA; in aesthetic theories, innovations, and movements that were internationally influential; in the number and diversity of genres and styles influenced by his work; and in the range of media shaped by Wagnerian subject matter or AESTHETICS. As with many other aspects of WAGNERISM, this influence extended into high art, popular forms, quotidian culture, PARODY, and kitsch: academic oils, lithographs, drawings, and watercolors coexisted with, and were outnumbered by, illustrated scores and books, ephemera such as postcards, *ex libris* plates, stamps, cartoons, and posters, and applied and decorative arts including stained glass, murals, and décor. The plastic arts and architecture too, though beyond the scope of this entry, record his influence. This diversity persists: cinema, television (from epics to *Bugs Bunny*), advertising, and, most recently, graphic novels all demonstrate Wagner's enduring significance. The following offers an introduction to this enormous topic, hopeful that it and other preliminary work may encourage further study. Organized chronologically and thematically, it attempts to indicate some of the aesthetic, cultural, and political factors shaping Wagnerian art internationally.

1. Wagner on the visual arts: life and work
2. Wagner in the visual arts: nineteenth-century Wagnerism
3. Wagner in the visual arts: the twentieth century and beyond

1. Wagner on the visual arts: life and work

Biographical details alone indicate the limited but suggestive significance of the visual arts in Wagner's life and work. *MEIN LEBEN* (My Life, 1865–81) states that Wagner's stepfather, the actor and painter Ludwig GEYER, encouraged him to study painting, and Wagner notes his childhood enthusiasm, dampened by an uncongenial teacher. Painters including Julius Schnorr von Carolsfeld and Friedrich PECHT were among friends to whom he read the libretto of *LOHENGRIN* in DRESDEN in 1845; Pecht and Ernst KIETZ were frequent companions during the 1850s. Gustave Doré regularly attended Wagner's salon in PARIS in 1860 and, following his public success, Wagner's contact with prominent artists of the *Gründerzeit* increased: the fashionable portraitist Franz-Seraph von Lenbach painted him, and Adolf Menzel drew him at Bayreuth. In 1882, Wagner met RENOIR in Palermo: sketches and a portrait resulted. Several of Wagner's closest adult friendships were with conservative, naturalistic painters: Kietz (whom Wagner offered to adopt in 1858) and Paul von JOUKOWSKY. Such friendships did not necessarily reflect his own tastes, however, nor display either aesthetic consistency or interest in the AVANT-GARDE: Wagner rejected historicism in painting, criticizing the images of the dramas that LUDWIG II had commissioned from Wilhelm von Kaulbach, Ferdinand Piloty, Bonaventura Genelli, and Michael Echter on these grounds. He advocated, instead, art that was more "ideal," "purely human," and "generally valid" (letter to Ludwig II, 21–22 July 1865), admiring Anselm Feuerbach and Genelli's late classicism and use of mythology. His admiration for Leonardo's *Last Supper*, which he found "absolutely inimitable" (ML/E: 584–5, translation amended), suggests Wagner's regard for the evocativeness and mellifluence of old masters over design, aesthetic theories, or characterization.

683

Wagner's collaborations with visual artists on productions of the dramas also suggest that pragmatism overruled aesthetics (see WAGNER AS STAGE DIRECTOR). Latterly Wagner employed the prominent Hans MAKART as a set designer and approached, unsuccessfully, the distinguished Swiss symbolist Arnold Böcklin to produce the designs for the *RING* and *PARSIFAL*. Wagner also skillfully employed (new) visual media for the purposes of PUBLICITY and self-promotion, collaborating in the production of numerous engravings, lithographs, and photographs. His direction of and reflections on these works in CORRESPONDENCE and elsewhere document his awareness of the convergence of the aesthetic and commercial domains.

Mein Leben records several instances of the visual arts' influence on Wagner's creative life. The conception of *Das KUNSTWERK DER ZUKUNFT* (The Artwork of the Future, 1849/50) is attributed to the influence of Genelli's watercolour *Dionysus and the Muses of Apollo* (via classical motifs on the wallpaper of a Paris café), and Titian's *Assumption of the Virgin* identified as the catalyst for the composition of *Die MEISTERSINGER VON NÜRNBERG*. Furthermore, pictorialism and intermedial similes suffuse Wagner's writings on music here and in the essays: he compares *PARSIFAL*'s orchestration to Titian's use of paint, for example (see METAPHOR). The *BAYREUTHER BLÄTTER*'s publication of essays on the relationship between Wagner's aesthetics and visual art also suggests endorsement of intermedial parallels. The Spanish painter Rogelio de Egusquiza, for example, friend of Wagner and FORTUNY, whose work dealt principally with Wagnerian themes and whose last request was to be buried with Titurel's sword made to his own design, wrote an open letter to the editor in 1885 on Wagnerian innovations in (theatrical) lighting.

Despite his lifelong friendships with artists and the acknowledged influence of specific works and artists on his oeuvre, however, the visual arts have a subsidiary role in Wagner's aesthetic theories. *Das Kunstwerk der Zukunft* identifies music, poetry, and DANCE as the three "purely human arts," ascribing a secondary role to painting, sculpture, and architecture, intended only to support drama. Landscape painting, he proposed, should provide a natural backdrop as stage scenery, whilst sculpture's role was to assist architecture in proving appropriate stage-sets for the drama. Later revisions to this aesthetic hierarchy (e.g., *BEETHOVEN*, 1870) awarded music an increasingly dominant role, the visual arts remaining secondary. Wagner's adult interest in, and aesthetic theories of, visual art were thus primarily utilitarian, even dilettantish, driven not by attention to the arts in themselves but by their potential to support his own work.

2. Wagner in the visual arts: nineteenth-century Wagnerism

Wagner's impact on the visual arts in the nineteenth century was largely shaped by the music and subjects of the dramas, and by the theory and practice of the *GESAMTKUNSTWERK*. Visual representations of the subject matter of the dramas predominated, as did works that responded in different ways to the intermedial aspects of Wagnerian MUSIC DRAMA or his aesthetic theories. Such responses peaked in the *fin de siècle*, particularly in FRANCE, and included paintings that alluded to or evoked music through their titles, or that attempted through color or line to convey qualities of, or emotions evoked by, Wagner's music. Innovations in interior design promoted unified décor in which the component parts constituted a *Gesamtkunstwerk*. Few artists had a technical understanding of music; rather, their interests in the *Gesamtkunstwerk*, and in synesthesia, abstraction, and symbolism, were inspired by the intermediality of the dramas and theory, and by Wagner's evocation of emotions and pictorial effect through an apparently abstract medium.

Even during his lifetime, there were numerous critical analyses, literary responses, and polemics on the relationship between Wagner's works and visual art. LISZT's 1849 essay on *Tannhäuser* compared the need for more "realistic drawing, coloring, and perspective in art" with that for "more dramatic qualities and more firmly constructed libretti in opera." During the 1850s, the association was reiterated in France: Wagner was attacked as the "Courbet of music," his dramas and aesthetics characterized as sharing the realist iconoclasm of Gustave Courbet's work for the 1850–1 Salon. BAUDELAIRE's essay on the 1846 Salon proposed the inherent musicality of color, and pictorialism pervaded his landmark essay "Richard Wagner et *Tannhäuser* à Paris" (1861) in which his theory of "correspondences" is articulated through a theory of musical affect, specifically a comparison between the visual images evoked by the music. Here, he famously and influentially proposed: "the only really surprising thing would be that sound could not suggest color, that colors could not give the idea of melody" (14). As such early examples suggest, it was the intermediality of Wagner's work that was to prove especially fruitful, but Wagnerian art was amplified by diverse aesthetic and cultural trends too.

Representations of the music dramas converged with many facets of ROMANTICISM. FANTIN-LATOUR's numerous Wagnerian works indicate the pull of the fantastic, of imagination, and of what he called the "féerique" (elfin; fairylike). The composer and his protagonists were also frequently depicted heroically, as types of the outcast artist and, more broadly, the individualist hostile to bourgeois culture. (Modern echoes appear in Gil Kane's comic-book *Ring* [1989–90], where Wagnerism meets *Marvel Comic* superheroes, and in P. Craig Russell's 2002 graphic novel of the *Ring*.) Romanticism shaped the depiction of landscape too, Wagnerian subjects combining with the sublime: examples include the Swedish Knut Eckwall's *Ring* engravings for the *Illustrirte Zeitung* (1876), Hugo Knorr's series of fifteen *Ring* designs (*c.* 1887), and the American Albert Pinkham Ryder's Wagnerian paintings of the 1880s: *The Flying Dutchman, Siegfried and the Rhine Maidens*, and *Götterdämmerung*. The Belgian James Ensor also produced epic landscapes influenced by Wagner, and a gouache *Ride of the Valkyries* (1883). Works such as Ryder's are, in their attention to the sublime and atmospheric, arguably more indebted to Wagner's music than to the dramatic texts. The influence persists in, for instance, the *Dutchman* and *Ring* oils (both 1990s) of the Catalan Ferrán Roca Bon.

Wagnerian (landscape) art was also shaped by contemporary valorizations of both Nordic and southern culture and aesthetics. In contrast to the Italianate pastoral scenes in some of Fantin-Latour's Wagnerian works, or Böcklin's

Parsifal-inspired *Sieh! es lacht die Aue* (1887), Nordicism was also a fruitful strand of Wagnerian art. Its influence was apparent not only in landscape but also in stylistic homages and intertextual allusions to Germanic and other Northern European artists and subjects: Aubrey BEARDSLEY's evocations of Dürer in *Venus* (1898), for instance, and his German contemporary Johannes Gehrts's illustrations of subjects from Teutonic and Norse mythology. Aleksandr Benois's designs for *Götterdämmerung* in St. Petersburg (1903) eschewed what he termed the "false romantic monumentalism" of most Wagner productions, drawing instead on contemporary Finnish landscape painting and a pared-down aesthetic of simplicity. Arthur RACKHAM's illustrated books of the *Ring* (1910–11) continued the Nordic trend.

Wagnerian art was shaped, then, not only by discourses about northern and southern European identity, but also by many strands of nineteenth-century historicism. From oils to pastels, postcards to illustrated books, Wagnerism interpenetrated with the revival of MEDIEVAL visual motifs and subject matter, of which Wagner's dramas and their stagings at the time were themselves examples. This was apparent in details such as the use of Gothic type or imitation of black and white woodcuts and, alternatively, the bright colors of heraldry, pageantry, and pseudo-historical costume. The German Hans Thoma, for example, whose style was influenced by German Renaissance masters, especially Cranach and Altdorfer, painted murals on the *Ring* for a Frankfurt doctor in 1877–80, and designed costumes for the tetralogy. Hans Makart, who dominated Viennese artistic and society life in the last quarter of the nineteenth century with his decorative, lushly colored historic paintings, expressed his Wagnerism not only through the costume ball thrown for COSIMA and Wagner in 1875, but also through designs for a ceiling fresco on subjects from the *Ring* (1870–2) and for a room decoration comprising eight large *Ring* scenes (1883). *Die Versenkung des Nibelungenhortes in den Rhein* (1882–3) also demonstrates the convergence of Wagnerian subjects, monumentalism, and historicism in his work. Three prolific German illustrators of the *fin de siècle* – Franz STASSEN, Hugo Braune, and Ferdinand Leeke – who together produced dozens of lithographs, paintings, watercolors, book illustrations, and postcards illustrating the music dramas, variously drew on woodcuts, German MYTH, and medieval motifs in their work. Wagnerism in nineteenth-century visual art thus intersected with contemporary interest in the MIDDLE AGES, and in historical literature, myth, and visual art, particularly pre-Raphaelitism, Arthurian legend, and French, Nordic, and Teutonic mythology.

Another strand of historicist Wagnerian art was the neoclassical, evident in Beardsley's six *Rhinegold* drawings (1896) and in innumerable illustrated books, scores, libretti, programs, *ex libris* plates, and postcards. Many included images (imitating medals) of the composer himself, and employed details such as classical architectural motifs, roundels, laurel wreaths, allegorical elements, and Orphic emblems. These stock conventions, routinely applied to artists of all types, may have been encouraged by Wagner's acknowledged debts to classical art and drama.

Wagnerian art pervaded seminal aesthetic movements as well as cultural trends of the later nineteenth century. As Zola's *L'Œuvre* (1886) records, many of the painters and critics who met at the Café Guerbois in Paris in the 1860s were Wagnerians and exponents of Impressionism. Fantin-Latour's dance-scene *Venusberg*, shown at the 1864 Salon, for example, was conceived in response to the hostile reception of the opera (see TANNHÄUSER, PARIS SCANDAL OF 1861), and in around 1869 Cézanne painted *L'Ouverture de "Tannhäuser,"* an early version of *Jeune fille au piano*. Wagnerism coincided with and in some cases directly informed attempts to invoke music through the titles and coloration of individual works, such as Whistler's *Harmony in White* (1862) and Monet's *Harmonie verte* (1872). Wagner discussed Impressionism (possibly its first application to musical techniques) with Renoir when they met in 1882, and, in his 1883 article on Impressionism, the poet and critic Jules Laforgue compared Wagner's music to Impressionist techniques. The German Impressionist Max Slevogt decorated the music room of his country house in the 1920s with scenes from MOZART's operas and the *Ring*.

Aestheticism, too, drew on Wagnerism, which shaped the *fin-de-siècle* revolt against realism, positivism, and utilitarianism in the visual arts. Whistler's work, for example, does not directly invoke Wagner, but its resistance to didactic, utilitarian art and bourgeois aesthetics is encapsulated in the use of musical titles; other prominent examples include the work of the Ballets Russes, and Mariano Fortuny's numerous works on Wagnerian subjects and experiments in pictorial and theatrical lighting. Such principles continued in DECADENT Wagnerian art, frequently combined with provocative GENDER, NATIONALIST, and class POLITICS. Beardsley's black-and-white Wagnerian drawings, for example, combine subjects from the music dramas with EROTICISM, *femmes fatales*, stylistic elements from popular genres such as poster art, and Francophilia. Similarly, in *À rebours* (1884), Des Esseintes's decadent tastes are denoted partly through his admiration of Redon, Moreau, and Wagner, and augment his "effeminate" enervation, his contempt for the bourgeois and his celebration of artifice. The influence of French Wagnerism on *fin-de-siècle* Austro-German artists was considerable: Gustav Klimt produced a small oil, *Bewegtes Wasser* (1898), suggesting the Rhinemaidens and anticipating his frescoes for Vienna University, rejected for their eroticism and enervation. In the late twentieth century, similar subjects and stylistic elements suffused the stage designs and paintings of the Austrian Ernst Fuchs.

Wagner's influence on symbolist art was also substantial, evident in the use of iconography and color, and the commitment to emotional expression. Synesthesia and "correspondences" were embraced by the REVUE WAGNÉRI-ENNE, exercising a substantial influence on symbolism and decadence in the 1880s and 1890s. In an 1886 article, co-editor Théodore de Wyzewa praised Odilon Redon and Gustave Moreau, and Fantin-Latour, for their "Wagnerian" qualities: they depicted "not a direct vision of things but – as a consequence of age-old associations between images and feelings – a world of living, blissful emotion." Redon and Moreau's works for the 1885 Salon were reviewed as "peinture symphonique" and "peinture wagnérienne," and Redon's first Wagnerian lithograph, *Brünnhilde*, was published in the *Revue* in 1885. Redon's *Parsifal* (1892) is representative of symbolists' responses not to Wagnerian mythology or performance, but to the symbolic and mystical aspects of Wagner's characters. In Britain, the journal of the Wagner Society, THE

MEISTER (1888–95), published essays and allegorical images combining elements of symbolism, orientalism, Theosophy, and the occult. Belgian symbolists including Jean Delville (*Tristan and Parsifal*, 1890), Fernand Khnopff (*Isolde*, 1905), and Henri de Groux (*Lohengrin*, 1908) were also drawn to the mysticism, enervation, and eroticism they found in Wagner's protagonists – the *LIEBESTOD* loomed large. Such themes contributed to symbolists' and decadents' contempt for the bourgeoisie – an attitude exemplified in Ensor's satirical, carnivalesque oil *Au conservatoire* (1902), depicting Wagner flinching during a performance of *Die WALKÜRE*.

Orientalism and eroticism also shaped art-nouveau Wagnerian works, such as the English Charles Robinson's black-and-white *Ring* illustrations (1898). The Hungarian Willy Pogany produced numerous book illustrations on Wagnerian themes, including designs for verse versions of *Tannhäuser* (1911), *Parsifal* (1912), and *Lohengrin* (1913). The influence persisted in Charles Ricketts's stage designs for the *Ring*, *Parsifal*, and *Tristan* of the 1910s–20s, and the Catalan Marti Teixidor's series of art-nouveau–style drawings on Wagnerian subjects in the 1980s.

3. Wagner in the visual arts: the twentieth century and beyond

In the twentieth century, Wagner's influence was more fragmented and that of the operatic subject matter less overt. When Wagnerian subjects were addressed, it was often from Oedipal or psychoanalytic perspectives, but Wagner's influence on expressionist and abstract art was also immense. Such moves were prefigured in the multifarious responses to the *Gesamtkunstwerk* at the turn of the century. Across Europe, innovations in interior design and exhibition practice reflected its accretive intermedial principles. From 1897, for example, Diaghilev organized art exhibitions in which the paintings, selected and arranged to create mood, were accompanied by music and original décor. Such experiments, intended to convey a unity of impression, were continued by the journal *Zolotoe runo* (Golden Fleece, 1906–9) in 1907–9. Similarly, the exhibition of the Vienna Secession in 1902 was conceived as a *Gesamtkunstwerk* on the subject of BEETHOVEN (mediated by Wagner): attended by over 50,000, it became a manifesto for internationalism, the heroism of the artist and emancipation from bourgeois values.

Despite the importance of synesthesia to *fin-de-siècle* French art, there were few attempts to produce intermedial works; in RUSSIA, however, this was a significant trend. The influence of the *Gesamtkunstwerk* on the aesthetics and creative practice of the Ballets Russes, and on the seminal Russian journal *Mir iskusstva* (World of Art, 1898–1904), edited by Diaghilev, was immeasurable. The latter was founded by several painters, including Benois, who recalled that, in the 1890s, "we were all Wagnerians," describing the *Gesamtkunstwerk* as "the idea for which our circle was ready to give its soul" (*Memoirs* II, 78; *Reminiscences* 370–1). The journal and the company fostered discourse and collaboration between musicians and distinguished artists including Léon Bakst, Konstantin Korovin, Valentin A. SEROV, and Sergei Maliutin, many of whom designed sets, costumes, and props for the Ballets Russes. The set designs were conceived as parts of a holistic "multimedia" aesthetic – Korovin and Aleksandr Golovin describing their fusions of painting, music, costumes, and theme as "music for the eyes" (207). Combining folk elements, primitivism, the Dionysian, and – particularly in Bakst's case – orientalism, the designs had an enduring international influence, anticipating many of the characteristics of Wagnerian visual art in the later twentieth century. Benois and Bakst, like Roger Fry and Clive Bell, valorized line as a visual equivalent to musical rhythm; consequently, Wagnerism fuelled a move towards abstraction.

Post-Impressionists' interest in color and abstraction was also partly shaped by Wagner. This was prefigured as early as 1888, when Van Gogh recorded his rapturous responses to the dramas: "I made a vain attempt to learn music, so much did I already feel the relation between our color and Wagner's music" (letter to Theo Van Gogh, *c.* 17 September 1888). Gauguin's "Texte Wagner" (a collection of quotations by and about the composer, *c.* 1889) records Wagner's influence on his conception of "l'union féconde de tous les arts" (the fertile union of all the arts; 215–17) as he formulated a theory of non-representational art. The pension he shared with the Nabis in Le Pouldu, Brittany, in 1889–90 was decorated with Wagnerian quotations. The artist and critic Émile Bernard, friend of Van Gogh and Cézanne, produced a portrait of Wagner in 1925 and his monumental late series of figure paintings, the *Human Cycle* (1922–5), evokes Wagnerian myth.

The Russian Wassily Kandinsky suggests Wagner's influence not only on post-Impressionism but also on abstract art: again, the apparently intermedial qualities of color were central. In *Reminiscences* (1913), he identified a performance of *Lohengrin* as a formative experience; unlike the French synesthetes, he saw it as a challenge to his medium, believing that the dramas conveyed visual experience more powerfully than any painting. From 1908 to 1912 he experimented with combinations of dance, drama, and music (a *Bühnengesamtkunstwerk*); Wagner remained a significant influence until his *Blauer Reiter* period, and his later abstraction was influenced by Baudelaire's Wagnerian "correspondences." Paul Klee's figure drawing of TANNHÄUSER (1924) is comic in tone, belying Wagner's significance (and that of music more widely) to his writings on color theory and rhythm, and to non-representational works including *Fugue in Red* (1921) and *Ancient Sound* (1925). Expressionism, too, suggests Wagnerian influence: the great Swedish dramatist August Strindberg, friend of Munch and Gauguin, produced tumultuous, expressionist landscapes in the period around 1890–1910 that appeared to his wife reminiscent of the dramas. Kokoschka's expressionist self-portrait with his lover Alma Mahler in a boat in a turbulent seascape (*Die Windsbraut*, 1914) was, as he acknowledged in correspondence, shaped by *Tristan* and the LIEBESTOD, and Jackson Pollock's early *Seascape* (1934) is arguably indebted to Ryder's Wagnerian works, suggesting the possible influence of Romantic Wagnerian landscapes on abstract expressionism.

Surrealists, however, responded more typically to the subject matter than the formal qualities of the music dramas. Dalí's Wagnerian works included costume design for *Mad Tristan* (1934–6), an oil *Mad Tristan* (*c.* 1938), the set design and libretto for *Bacchanale* (1939, a ballet based on the Venusberg scenes and set to *Tannhäuser*), designs for the ballet *Mad Tristan* (1944), and a series of *Tristan* drawings. Wagnerism informed his numerous explorations of the subconscious, of tortured love, and of psychoanalysis. His castle at Púbol, Girona, included a grotto next to the swimming pool incorporating multiple ceramic busts of Wagner. Surrealist elements linger in the Italian Ul de Rico's 1980 graphic novel of the *Ring*.

A notable strand of twentieth-century Wagnerian art has also addressed the relationship between mythology (myth in the dramas, and Wagner's role in national myth) and political history. Hermann HENDRICH's numerous Wagnerian paintings continued symbolist and orientalist motifs but also contextualized Wagner within German myth, particularly in his twelve *Ring* paintings for the Nibelungenhalle, Drachenfels (1913) and his *Parsifal* series for the Halle Deutscher Sagenring (1926). Since 1945, German artists have been slow to reclaim Wagnerian subjects or aesthetics but notable exceptions include Anselm Kiefer's series of reflections on German mythology and history, such as *Parsifal*, *Nothung*, and *Deutschlands Geisteshelden* (1973), *Brünnhilde's Death* (1976), and *Nuremberg and the Mastersingers* (1981–2). In these large-scale works, whose size and materials suggest the theater, he reflects on heroism, NATIONAL IDENTITY, and history, in the last eerily evoking spaces including the meadow of the Festspielhaus, the NUREMBERG rallies, and the trials. Alfred Hredlicka's 1985 series *Adalbert Stifter. . .* also uses Wagnerian allusions to critique heroism and nationalism. Satire has, unsurprisingly, been fruitful, as in the work of Johannes Grützke and Paul Flora. Wagner remains, then, a protean, far-reaching presence in later twentieth-century and contemporary art.

EMMA SUTTON

Charles Baudelaire, *Richard Wagner et "Tannhäuser" à Paris* (Paris: E. Dentu, 1861).
Alexsandr Benois, *Memoirs*, 2 vols. (London: Chatto & Windus, 1964).
    Reminiscences of the Russian Ballet (London: Putnam, 1941).
Paul Gaugin, 'Texte Wagner', in *Diverses choses 1896–8* (Musée du Louvre, RF7259).
Martin Geck, *Die Bildnisse Richard Wagners* (Munich: Prestel, 1970).
Michael Hall, "Wagner's Impact on the Visual Arts," in *The Wagner Compendium*, ed. Barry Millington (see bibliography): 398–401.
David C. Large and William Weber, eds., *Wagnerism in European Culture and Politics* (see bibliography).
Franz Liszt, "Le Tannhaueser," *Journal des débats*, 18 May 1849.
Günter Metken, "Wagner and the Visual Arts," in *The Wagner Handbook*, ed. Ulrich Müller and Peter Wapnewski, trans. John Deathridge (see bibliography): 354–72.
Jordi Mota and María Infiesta, eds., *Pintores Wagnerianos* (Barcelona: Nou Art Thor, 1988).
    Das Werk Richard Wagners im Spiegel der Kunst (Tübingen: Graebert, 1995).
Bernice Glatzer Rosenthal, "Wagner and Wagnerian Ideas in Russia," in *Wagnerism in European Culture and Politics*, ed. David C. Large and William Weber (see bibliography): 198–245.
Jack M. Stein, *Richard Wagner and the Synthesis of the Arts* (Detroit, MI: Wayne State University Press, 1960; repr. Westport, CT: Greenwood, 1973).
André Tubeuf, *Wagner: L'Opera des images* (Paris: Chêne, 1993).
Solveig Weber, *Das Bild Richard Wagners*, 2 vols. (Mainz: Schott, 1993).
Théodore de Wyzewa, "Notes sur la peinture wagnérienne et le Salon de 1886," *La Revue wagnérienne* 1886.

Wagner weltweit, periodical (ISSN 1618-3886) published twice a year by the Richard-Wagner-Verband International (Freiburg im Breisgau, 1989 [1993]–2008) at the initiative of then president Josef Lienhart. Publication was suspended when its usefulness was superseded by information available more readily on the internet. Issues document the annual congresses of the International Association of the Wagner Societies, often with lavish color photos, and provide current data on and annual reports from all WAGNER SOCIETIES, including contact information and membership figures. In addition, issues feature assorted articles on singers, performances, and productions as well as obituaries of noted Wagnerians. Original archival materials on the history of Wagner societies and related documents are also reproduced.

NICHOLAS VAZSONYI

***Wagner Werk-Verzeichnis* [WWV].** A comprehensive thematic catalog of Wagner's musical compositions and arrangements compiled by John Deathridge, Martin Geck, and Egon Voss; published by B. Schott's Sons (Mainz, 1986). Subtitled "Verzeichnis der musikalischen Werke Richard Wagners und ihrer Quellen," and prepared in cooperation with the *Richard Wagner-Gesamtausgabe*, this invaluable reference work embodies lengthy and careful planning on the part of its editors, especially Deathridge. The catalog itself identifies all of Wagner's known compositions – finished or unfinished, extant or lost – first by title and WWV number in chronological order of composition, then in terms of performing forces, principal themes or incipit(s), date(s) of first performances, descriptions of manuscript source(s), published editions, references in autobiographical documents and reminiscences, appropriate secondary sources of information, and so on. Appendices also identify doubtful and lost works, the names of Wagner's copyists, dedicatees of individual compositions, and so on. An introductory essay appears both in German (9–18) and in English (19–25). It is also the first *Werkverzeichnis* to have an essay attached to each entry (*Erläuterungen*) commenting on the sources and various matters of publication, as well as clarifying some of Wagner's myth-making tendencies. In 1875, Wagner corrected two pages from a draft catalog subsequently published by Wilhelm TAPPERT; these pages are reproduced in WWV, 111–12. Reviewed enthusiastically and at length by several scholars – including David Breckbill (719), who observes succinctly that the WWV "brings together an unprecedented range of pertinent information on the sources of Wagner's musical works."

MICHAEL SAFFLE

See also Appendix 6: Musical works

David Breckbill, Review, *Notes: Quarterly Journal of the Music Library Association* 47.3 (March 1991): 718–22.
John Deathridge, "Cataloguing Wagner," *The Musical Times* 124 (1983): 92–6.
Wilhelm Tappert, "Chronologisches Verzeichniss der musikalisch-dramatischen Werke Richard Wagner's," *Richard Wagner: Sein Leben und seine Werk* (Elberfeld: S. Lucas, 1883): 98–100.

Wagner, Wieland (nickname: "Huschele"; b. Bayreuth, 5 Jan. 1917; d. Munich, 17 Oct. 1966), first child of SIEGFRIED and WINIFRED WAGNER, was brought up in WAHNFRIED together with his siblings FRIEDELIND, WOLFGANG, and VERENA. He studied painting and photography and was much influenced by the Viennese stage designer Alfred ROLLER, who came to BAYREUTH (1934) to prepare new sets for *PARSIFAL*. In 1936, Heinz TIETJEN used scenery based on a painting by Wieland for the Good Friday meadow in *Parsifal*. Although Siegfried had passed the leadership of the Festival on to all four children, the "Führer" saw in him the legitimate successor, and Wieland was exempted from the army in 1937 at Hitler's orders. From 1940 to 1951, Wieland worked with the composer and conductor Kurt Overhoff, minutely studying Wagner's scores. His career as a producer began in Altenburg and Nuremberg. In 1943, he created the stage design for the Bayreuth war production of *Die MEISTER-SINGER VON NÜRNBERG*. Later on, he acknowledged the influence of the stage designers Gordon Craig and Adolphe APPIA. In the 1940s, he accused Heinz Tietjen (appointed director of the Festival by Winifred) of preventing him from directing in Bayreuth. His attempt to persuade Hitler to expel Tietjen failed, however. In 1944, he met Hitler for the last time when he traveled to Berlin and unsuccessfully attempted to get original Wagner scores returned. From 1944 onwards, Wieland worked near Bayreuth at a satellite branch of the concentration camp Flossenbürg, headed by his brother-in-law Bodo LAFFERENTZ.

After the war, Winifred was barred from working in the Festival management on account of her Nazi past, so she rented out the FESTIVAL THEATER and Wahnfried to her two sons, thus circumventing Siegfried's will and preventing the two sisters from involvement. By tacit agreement, Wieland was responsible for the artistic side and his brother for the management, so Wieland had a free hand at producing.

When the Festival reopened in 1951, Wieland astonished the world by creating a new style. In his staging of *Parsifal*, he avoided geographic and period references, stripping the opera of all romantic remains. This reduced style had already been introduced at the Berlin KROLL OPER in the 1920s, but he developed it further with special lighting effects, used to underline the psychological meaning. He did away with the traditional Bayreuth style and its correspondence of music, acting, and stage design, and thus became an antipode to Walter Felsenstein, who, at the Comic Opera in East Berlin, represented a more realistic approach. In the 1960s, Wieland entered a symbolic phase, beginning with Verdi's *Aida* in Berlin (1961). He produced operas by GLUCK, BEETHOVEN, VERDI, Bizet, STRAUSS, Berg, and Orff in many cities and countries. His daughter, NIKE WAGNER, interprets the various productions as an attempt to escape from the stifling atmosphere of Bayreuth. Perhaps this aesthetic revolution was his method of coping with his past, when Hitler was a frequent visitor to the Festival Theater.

Wieland's sudden and early death of cancer was a shock to the theater world. In the 1970s much of his theater scenery was burnt and no complete video tapes exist.   EVA RIEGER

Ingrid Kapsamer, *Wieland Wagner: Wegbereiter und Weltwirkung* (Vienna: Styria, 2010).
Geoffrey Skelton, *Wieland Wagner: The Positive Sceptic* (London: Gollancz, 1971).

Wagner, Winifred Marjorie (née Williams-Klindworth) (b. Hastings [England], 23 June 1897; d. Überlingen, 5 March 1980), wife of SIEGFRIED Wagner, daughter of John Williams (writer) and Emily Florence Karop (actress). At the age of 3, after the death of her parents (father – liver disease; mother – typhus), she was sent to an orphanage in Sussex. In 1907, she was sent to live with Karl and Henriette KLINDWORTH, a couple in their seventies, who resided in a country house near Berlin. Henriette was a distant relative of Winifred's mother, and Karl was a pianist who had studied piano with LISZT. The Klindworths eventually adopted Winifred, moved to Berlin, and provided her with a well-rounded education that included musical studies in piano. Karl, an old friend of Wagner and a regular guest at BAYREUTH, brought along 17-year-old Winifred in 1914, who, as an avid Wagnerite (sometimes signing her name "SENTA"), was keen to see her first production.

Ulterior motives may have been at work as, for some time, 45-year-old Siegfried Wagner, son of Richard Wagner and Cosima von Bülow, had been under considerable pressure to marry. His mother and his sister Eva felt that it was vital that Siegfried continue the Wagner family line, and there were fears that public scandals might expose his homosexual affairs. Siegfried did not waste any time proposing to Winifred, and the two were married on 22 September 1915. The birth of their first child, WIELAND, on 5 January 1917 was cause for great celebration at WAHNFRIED, prompting Cosima to sit down at the piano (apparently for the first time since Wagner's death) to play an excerpt from the SIEGFRIED IDYLL. After Wieland, three more children followed: FRIEDELIND (1918–91), WOLFGANG (1919–2010), and VERENA (b. 1920).

Winifred depicted her daily routine at WAHNFRIED as one that revolved around the needs of both Cosima and Siegfried. She read to Cosima in French and helped with daily letter-writing duties. She tended to Siegfried's correspondence and organized his trips. In a landmark film interview by Hans-Jürgen SYBERBERG, Winifred says that she acted as Siegfried's secretary: "Everything that he found disagreeable – receiving people whom he didn't want to see and whom he may not have liked – that was where I came in." Over the years, there has been much speculation about the details of their marriage arrangement, especially in light of Siegfried's homosexuality.

As a staunch German nationalist and anti-Semite, Winifred was drawn very early to Adolf HITLER, himself a longtime admirer of Wagner's music. Hitler was a guest at Wahnfried already in 1923 and, when in November later that year the putsch in Munich failed, Winifred collected clothing and money for the families of jailed Nazis, sought signatures for a petition, and even sent supplies including writing paper to Hitler in prison, fueling speculation that he may have used this stationery for early drafts of *Mein Kampf*. As Siegfried infamously noted at the time: "My wife is fighting like a lion for Hitler! Magnificent!" (letter from Siegfried Wagner to Rosa Eidam, Christmas 1923; quoted in Hamann 94). After his release, Hitler became a frequent guest at Wahnfried and very close friend to the Wagner family, a friendship that involved secret meetings with Winifred after Siegfried's death in 1930. The exact nature of these meetings is unknown, but has fueled much speculation about the extent of the relationship between Winifred and Hitler.

Siegfried's death also meant that Winifred inherited the entire Wagner estate including the FESTIVAL THEATER and Wahnfried. She appointed Wilhelm FURTWÄNGLER as music director, Heinz TIETJEN as artistic director, and Emil PREETORIUS as scenic designer. Her leadership signified a break with the reverence that had previously marked directorship under Cosima and Siegfried. With less concern for adherence to Wagner's presumed aesthetic intentions, she and her artistic team explored further the new approaches to lighting and scenery tentatively made by Siegfried. After Hitler came to power in 1933, the Bayreuth Festival became closely associated with

Hitler's regime. This ultimately led to an estrangement with Winifred's daughter Friedelind, who went into exile and published an autobiography (*Heritage of Fire*) that caused much embarrassment both for the regime and for Winifred with its frank revelations about the private life of Hitler. Unlike during World War I, Hitler also ensured that the festival would continue running, despite wartime conditions and shortages of supplies and manpower.

After World War II, Winifred faced a denazification tribunal that began on 25 June 1947, where she was accused of being one of Hitler's "most fanatical and loyal supporters." In her defense, she claimed that she had only met with Hitler in the early years of the war, that she had helped Jewish people, and that Nazi funds had never been used for personal gain. She appealed the court's verdict that classified her as a category-two "activist" (*Belastete*) and managed to get reclassified in 1948 as a category-three "lesser offender" (*Minderbelastete*). Nevertheless, Festival assets were frozen until 1949, when Winifred agreed to relinquish control to her two sons Wieland and Wolfgang, thus also shutting out her daughters, Verena and, most of all, Friedelind.

In 1973, after extensive wrangling, Winifred participated in establishing the RICHARD WAGNER FOUNDATION (Richard-Wagner-Stiftung Bayreuth), which resolved the inheritance of an ever-growing, increasingly fractious Wagner family, and settled legal ownership of the Festival Theater.

In 1975, film director Hans-Jürgen SYBERBERG shot a documentary interview entitled *Winifred Wagner und die Geschichte des Hauses Wahnfried 1914–1975* (Winifred Wagner and the History of Wahnfried 1914–1975). GOTTFRIED WAGNER, grandson of Winifred, had met with Syberberg and helped make arrangements prior to the film shoot. In his autobiography, he claims that Syberberg showed him and his father Wolfgang a version of the film that bore little resemblance to the finished product, and furthermore that Syberberg had left the recorder running during breaks thus catching Winifred's unguarded remarks. Nevertheless, in the film, Winifred is unabashed about her closeness with Hitler, explaining that she called him "Wolf" while he called her "Winnie." She steadfastly claimed that she separated politics from her private relationship with him. According to her, they never discussed politics as she was a totally apolitical person.

The release of Syberberg's film was met with so much controversy that, amidst preparations for the 1976 centenary celebrations at Bayreuth, Wolfgang publically distanced himself from his mother and banned her from the Festival Theater for two years until the media storm subsided. Winifred died shortly thereafter on 5 March 1980 at the age of 82, and is buried in Bayreuth's municipal cemetery. ALEXIS LUKO

See also BAYREUTH FESTIVAL, HISTORY OF THE

Brigitte Hamann, *Winifred Wagner oder Hitlers Bayreuth* (see bibliography).
Hans Jürgen Syberberg, *Winifred Wagner und die Geschichte des Hauses Wahnfried 1914–1975*, interview with Winifred Wagner released by Alexander Verlag in 1975.

Wagner, (Manfred) Wolfgang (Martin) (b. Bayreuth, 30 Aug. 1919; d. Bayreuth, 21 March 2010), grandson of Richard Wagner, the third child and second son of SIEGFRIED and WINIFRED WAGNER. Educated at local schools. Conscripted into the Wehrmacht in November 1938, he was wounded during the invasion of Poland (September 1939) and discharged in June 1940. First practical theater experience came as basic trainee for that year's BAYREUTH FESTIVAL. He then became an assistant to Heinz TIETJEN, director at the Staatsoper, Berlin, learning music theory, stage management, production skills, and acquiring knowledge of the administrative and financial aspects of a large opera company. In April 1943 he married a dancer there, Ellen DREXEL, and they had two children: EVA (b. 1945) and GOTTFRIED (b. 1947).

He assisted on Tietjen's 1943 Bayreuth production of *Die MEISTERSINGER VON NÜRNBERG* which was designed by his elder brother WIELAND. His own first production was Siegfried Wagner's *Bruder Lustig [Andreasnacht]*, Berlin Staatsoper, 7 June 1944. From 1949, Wolfgang and Wieland prepared for their joint direction of the Bayreuth Festivals, which resumed in 1951. Wolfgang excelled in administration, and was gifted with financial and political acumen. His Bayreuth debut as director and designer was in 1953, beginning a production history of 50 years:

LOHENGRIN	1953–4
DER FLIEGENDER HOLLÄNDER	1955–6
TRISTAN UND ISOLDE	1957–9
Der *RING DES NIBELUNGEN*	1960–4
Lohengrin	1967–72
Die Meistersinger von Nürnberg	1968–75
Der Ring des Nibelungen	1970–5
PARSIFAL	1975–81
Die Meistersinger von Nürnberg	1981–8
TANNHÄUSER	1985–95
Parsifal	1989–2001
Die Meistersinger von Nürnberg	1996–2002

He occasionally directed Wagner operas outside Bayreuth. Critics inevitably compared his work with that of his more innovative brother, some finding it too conservative, even derivative. His *Lohengrin* in 1967, second *Ring* cycle, 1975 *Parsifal*, and three *Meistersinger* stagings (especially that of 1981) were most highly praised. Like Wieland, he was an acknowledged master of lighting effects, possessed technical skill second to none, and singers appreciated his human, person-to-person style of direction.

With Wieland's death in 1966, the Bayreuth enterprise fell to his sole care, until his retirement in 2008 following the sudden death of his second wife, GUDRUN. He maintained the highest standards of casting, conducting, and orchestral performance. Commissioning an impressive series of international directors, he ensured Bayreuth remained at the forefront of contemporary production. The "French" *Ring* for the centenary year 1976, directed by CHÉREAU, designed by Peduzzi, and conducted by BOULEZ, provoked initial outrage and subsequent glowing approbation. (It was also the first *Ring* to reach a world audience through film and television.) Directors he invited to Bayreuth were Philippe Arlaud, Dieter Dorn, Tankred Dorst, August Everding, Jürgen Flimm, Götz Friedrich, Claus Guth, Peter Hall, Werner Herzog, Alfred Kirchner, Harry Kupfer, Christoph Marthaler, Heiner Müller, Jean-Pierre Ponnelle, Christoph Schlingensief, and Keith Warner. The last new productions during Wolfgang's long term of office were a provocatively unconventional *Meistersinger* (2007) from his daughter KATHARINA, and Stefan Herheim's *Parsifal* (2008).

The legacy entrusted to Wolfgang enshrined the physical structure of the FESTIVAL THEATER itself. Initially undertaking long overdue repairs and lighting replacement in 1953, he continued to oversee upgrading of technical resources, expansion of scene docks, rehearsal facilities and catering areas, installation of the latest theater machinery, and so on, while simultaneously preserving the historical monument at the center: his grandfather's theater.

Wolfgang and Winifred were deeply involved in long, difficult negotiations which in 1973 established the RICHARD WAGNER FOUNDATION (RWF; Richard-Wagner-Stiftung Bayreuth). Wolfgang also took active interest in the GESELLSCHAFT DER FREUNDE VON BAYREUTH, the "Internationales Festspieltreffen" (making his festival accessible to young people, including those from communist countries), and WAGNER SOCIETIES, including the Richard-Wagner-Verband International.

In 1976 Wolfgang and Ellen were divorced and he wed his secretary Gudrun Mack; the one child of this marriage was Katharina, born 1978. The vital question of Wolfgang's successor at Bayreuth began to loom large. In 2001, he proposed Gudrun, as her knowledge of every aspect of the festival was next only to his own. This plan was rejected by the RWF in 2001, their preferred candidate being Eva Wagner-Pasquier. Wolfgang in turn rejected this idea: he had become bitterly estranged from the children of his first marriage. The unexpected death of Gudrun in 2007, together with his increasingly frail health, led to a crisis. In 2008 the RWF, with his agreement, appointed Katharina and Eva as joint directors from 2009. Wolfgang died at his home next to the *Festspielhaus* on 21 March 2010.   DEREK WATSON

See also BAYREUTH FESTIVAL, HISTORY OF THE

Laurence B. Lueck, ed., *Wolfgang Wagner: An Appreciation* (Honolulu: Hawaii Opera Publications Group, 2003).

Wolfgang Wagner, *Lebens-Akte* (Munich: Knaus, 1994); trans. *Acts: The Autobiography of Wolfgang Wagner*, trans. John Brownjohn (London: Weidenfeld & Nicolson, 1994).

Wagnerism (Wagnerians, Wagnerites), of or relating to the political and aesthetic ideas or the musical works of Wagner. Wagner's works and ideas spread across late nineteenth-century Europe and America, becoming an "-ism" during the composer's lifetime. His supporters had been already identified as such ("Wagnerianer") by the *Signale für die musikalische Welt* in 1847. Composers of opera confronted his musical works and his aesthetic and dramaturgical ideas directly, but his influence was also felt in instrumental music, LITERATURE, VISUAL ARTS, and POLITICS. Wagner's aesthetic ideas first began to be discussed in Europe in the 1850s, and Wagnerism, as a driving force in artistic and political circles, gained steady momentum over the next fifty years – peaking around the turn of the century. Wagnerism was influenced by "musical idealism," a movement formed in reaction to the commercialization that took place in music in the latter half of the eighteenth century, but more broadly against the effects of industrialization and MODERNITY.

Musical idealists were wary of passing fashions, empty virtuosity, and dilettantism. Such ideas were also central to Wagner's new form of opera, which in part, explains his enormous appeal to idealists in both artistic and political circles across Europe.

Wagnerism is notoriously difficult to define, as Wagner published copiously and on a wide range of topics. Individuals or groups who felt influenced by him and who have called themselves "Wagnerians" or "Wagnerites" varied in their interpretation of his life and work. One example would be Wagner's intense following in French AVANT-GARDE circles of the late nineteenth century, which required ignoring Wagner's strong German NATIONALISM and occasionally vehement anti-French sentiments.

Wagnerism in the 1850s and 1860s engaged more with his prose works than his operas, which were not yet widely performed. At this time, Wagnerism was restricted to a small circle of supporters and enthusiasts, including Franz BRENDEL, Franz LISZT, and Theodor UHLIG. Two decades later the effort to finance the Bayreuth FESTIVAL THEATER led to the creation of WAGNER SOCIETIES, which represented the first organized appearance of Wagnerites. Wagnerism gained strength after Wagner's death in 1883, though the dissemination of ideological Wagnerism had already begun in 1878 with the publication of the *BAYREUTHER BLÄTTER*. Bayreuth henceforth became the center of German Wagnerism and a place of pilgrimage for Wagnerians worldwide, with COSIMA WAGNER presiding over what came to be known as the BAYREUTH CIRCLE.

Wagner's writings circulated in FRANCE at mid-century bringing him under the scrutiny of the musicologist François-Joseph Fétis and the music critic Pierre Scudo, both of whom felt Wagner favored poetry at the expense of the music. They were also critical of a composer who wrote so much prose – great composers should have no need of voluminous theoretical writings. The Paris premiere of *TANNHÄUSER* (1861) was a fiasco for both aesthetic and political reasons. Two weeks later, Charles BAUDELAIRE published an article in staunch support of Wagner. Both Paul Cézanne and Henri FANTIN-LATOUR painted pieces inspired by *Tannhäuser*. Théodore de Banville saw a unity of expression in the works of Wagner, while Auguste de Gasperini and Léon Leroy were drawn to the idea of a free and sincere art that would be accessible to all. Jules Étienne PASDELOUP drew huge crowds to his Wagner concerts at the Cirque Napoléon. The decadents found a multisensory delight in Wagner's works and spiritual and mystical quests. The *REVUE WAGNÉRIENNE* was founded to promote Wagnerism Later taken over by Stéphane Mallarmé and his circle during its run from 1885 to 1888, it was used as the mouthpiece of the symbolist movement. Wagnerism had a significant impact on French opera as well, inspiring a shift from historical topics to MYTH and French medieval legend. Composers followed Wagner's lead in looking to literary models, and this contributed to the formation of the genre of *Literaturoper* (e.g., *Salome* and *Wozzeck*). Massenet, Reyer, and Saint-Saëns incorporated Wagnerian elements of ORCHESTRATION, *LEITMOTIV*, and chromatic harmony into French opera while Chabrier, Chausson, d'Indy, and DEBUSSY contended with the MUSIC DRAMA as a whole.

In ITALY, the political revolutionary Giussepe Mazzini published his *Filoso-fia della musica* (1836). In it he argued that a politically unified ITALY could only be achieved through cultural and spiritual unity. For Mazzini, the state of Italian music reflected the state of Italian society – a conglomeration of clashing parts that lacked coherence. He wished for a worthy artist who could realize his aesthetic goals. When Arrigo Boito and Franco Faccio, both part of the group of bohemian artists and writers called the *scapigliati* (tousled or disheveled ones), rejected the complacency of bourgeois society and embraced the aesthetic and political ideas of Mazzini, they were charged with being Wagnerians when, in fact, they were adopting a wholly native tradition. The two aspiring composers were labeled as pro-Wagner (and therefore anti-VERDI) when, in fact, they embraced both composers.

The premiere of *LOHENGRIN* in Bologna was well received but subsequent performances there and in Milan and Turin were known to echo with calls of "Viva Rossini!," "Viva Verdi!," and "Death to Wagner!" Ruggero Leoncavallo's music was thought to be quite Wagnerian but the composer rejected the idea of ENDLESS MELODY. Pietro Mascagni's *Cavalleria rusticana* ushered in *verismo* opera, which was a rejection of the mythical world of Wagner, while Puccini adopted Wagnerian techniques such as *Leitmotiv*, a dramaturgical orchestra, and declamatory musical prose.

In RUSSIA all members of the Five (also known as the Mighty Handful) rejected Wagner. The *RING* was premiered by a touring company from Prague; before that only *Tannhäuser* and *Lohengrin* had been performed. The German-born Empress Alexandra loved Wagner's works, and the Mariinsky Theater produced *TRISTAN UND ISOLDE* and the *Ring* between 1899 and 1905. Ardent Wagnerians Aleksandr Benois and Sergei Diaghilev, frustrated with the traditions of the Imperial Theater, formed the Ballets Russes, which expressed the russification of the *GESAMTKUNSTWERK*. Russian artists and intellectuals responded strongly to what they saw as the mysticism and symbolism in Wagner's works and ideas. The poet Vyacheslav Ivanov embraced first NIETZSCHE then Wagner and became a proponent of *KUNSTRELIGION*. Ivanov, along with Georgi Chulkov, thought that art as religion would provide a spiritual unity of society that was necessary to bring about "mystical anarchy." There would be no audience at Ivanov's and Chulkov's temple-theatre as all would participate in the drama as a Dionysian ritual. Aleksandr Skryabin's *Mysterium* took the concept of the *Gesamtkunstwerk* and combined it with Russian mysticism; the piece was meant to trigger the apocalypse and thus bring about the ultimate unity of man and cosmos. The poet Aleksandr Blok wrote an essay entitled *Art and Revolution* as a commentary on Wagner's text of the same name (Die *KUNST UND DIE REVOLUTION*), and Andrei Bely's pamphlet *Revolution and Culture* was in a similar vein. They saw the Bolshevik revolution as a *GÖTTERDÄMMERUNG* that would bring about a revolution of the spirit. Anatoly Lunacharsky, first Soviet minister for art and culture, and Sergei EISENSTEIN, film director and theorist, were also influenced by the idea of the temple of art and its fusion of art and politics.

Wagner visited LONDON three times but never the UNITED STATES OF AMERICA, although he dreamt of building a festival theater among the German immigrants in MINNESOTA. The resident German population played a role in the promotion and reception of his works in both countries. *Der FLIEGENDE HOLLÄNDER* introduced Wagner to London in 1870 and, by 1888, the city had seen *Tristan, Die MEISTERSINGER VON NÜRNBERG*, and the *Ring*. Between 1884 and 1891, the Metropolitan Opera in New York premiered the *Ring, Tristan*, and *Meistersinger*. The London Wagner Society was founded in 1873 and, in 1888, began publication of *The MEISTER*, edited by William Ashton ELLIS. The magazine promoted not only the works of Wagner but also his greatness as a philosopher.

Playwright George Bernard SHAW was an ardent Wagnerian and viewed the *Ring* as a socialist allegory that depicted the evils of unrestrained capitalism in the nineteenth century. Rutland Boughton, inspired by the concept of the *Ring*, wrote an opera on a text by Reginald Buckley based on Arthurian legend. Boughton and Buckley embraced the idea of *Kunstreligion* and envisioned a theater surrounded by a farm – a place where artists and laborers could enrich the work of one other. Christian commentators such as Peter Taylor Forsyth and Washington Gladden interpreted the *Ring* and *PARSIFAL* in ethical and religious terms. In 1903, the Met performed *Parsifal* in violation of the copyright claimed by the Wagner family. The public was divided as to whether the work was sacrilegious or spiritually edifying, but, by the time of the premiere, *Parsifal* was a great success. Wagnerism was taken up not only by Christians but also by occultists such as William Butler Yeats, Vasily Kandinsky, Skryabin, Cyril Scott, and William Ashton Ellis, who translated all of Wagner's prose works into English. Wagnerism also had an impact on the work of D. H. Lawrence, Virginia WOOLF, T. S. Eliot, James Joyce, and Willa Cather.

LYDIA MAYNE

See also WAGNER IN LITERATURE; WAGNER IN THE VISUAL ARTS

Hermann Danuser and Herfried Münkler, eds., *Zukunftsbilder: Richard Wagners Revolution und ihre Folgen in Kunst und Politik* (Schliengen: Argus, 2002).

Annegret Fauser, "'Wagnerism': Responses to Wagner in Music and the Arts," in *The Cambridge Companion to Wagner*, ed. Thomas S. Grey (see bibliography): 221–34.

David C. Large and William Weber, eds., *Wagnerism in European Culture and Politics* (see bibliography).

Wagner-Pasquier, Eva (b. Oberwarmensteinach, 14 April 1945), opera manager; daughter of WOLFGANG WAGNER and Ellen DREXEL, and married to the French film producer Yves Pasquier. Eva Wagner-Pasquier worked as a personal assistant to her father from 1967 to 1975, when he took over as sole director of the Bayreuth Festival after the death of his brother WIELAND. Concurrently, she worked in opera production at the Vienna State Opera and the Royal Opera House Covent Garden. As an executive at Unitel Films, she oversaw opera and concert productions until 1984. Following that, she was an opera director at Covent Garden for three years, and then director of programming at Opera Bastille from 1987 to 1993. Since then, she has been an artistic consultant at the Houston Grand Opera, the Théâtre du Châtelet in Paris, and Teatro Real in Madrid. On 1 September 2008, Wagner-Pasquier and her half-sister KATHARINA WAGNER were named as joint directors of the Bayreuth Festival in a compromise move that would satisfy both then director Wolfgang Wagner and the RICHARD WAGNER FOUNDATION.

NICHOLAS VAZSONYI

wagnerspectrum, (2005–), periodical (ISSN 1614-9459), published twice a year by Königshausen & Neumann (Würzburg); originally in German and English, but switched exclusively to German after the first issues. Abstracts in English. Editorial Board includes Udo Bermbach, Dieter Borchmeyer, Hans-Joachim Hinrichsen, Sven Friedrich, Arne Stollberg, and Nicholas Vazsonyi. All issues have a central theme with additional articles and reviews of recent books and recordings. Intended as an interdisciplinary forum on all aspects of Wagner, his life, work, and thought. Themes have included "Wagner und Buddhismus," Vol. 3.2 (2007); "Wagner und Fantasy/Hollywood," Vol. 4.2 (2008); "Wagner und seine Dirigenten," Vol. 5.1 (2009); and "Bayreuther Theologie," Vol. 5.2 (2009). MICHAEL SAFFLE

Stefan Breuer, Review [of vol. 5.2], *Musik & Ästhetik* 14.54 (April 2010): 111–14. www.wagnerspectrum.de/index.html.

Wahn. The root meanings of the word include illusion, hallucination, error, folly, and madness (the latter more commonly as *Wahnsinn*). The elusive and multivalent Wagnerian concept is expounded as the key to HANS SACHS's philosophy of art in his so-called *Wahn* monologue in Act III of *Die MEISTERSINGER VON NÜRNBERG*. Sachs interprets the nocturnal riot his own singing had accidentally unleashed the previous evening as a figure for "poetic frenzy," the outward manifestation of a rapturous dream-state that initiates the creative process. The motive force behind this "frenzy" may be difficult to determine, as the source of inspiration is necessarily mysterious: "A glow-worm failed to find his mate; / he started all this strife. – / The lilac bush: – Midsummer's eve" (*Meistersinger*, Act III, Scene 1). The poet's work is to direct these inchoate, Dionysian drives into clear Apollonian forms in the conscious light of day. WALTHER VON STOLZING duly appears, suffused with the recollection of a poetic DREAM, and Sachs helps him craft from this a "master-song" in the requisite *Bar* form of two matching stanzas (*STOLLEN*) and an "after-song" (*ABGESANG*).

Between completing the libretto of *Die Meistersinger* and composing the score, Wagner wrote an essay *ÜBER STAAT UND RELIGION* (On State and Religion, 1864) advising his new patron, LUDWIG II, on the nature of kingship. Here, *Wahn* is construed as a sociopolitical analogue to the instinct that drives lower life forms to sacrifice their immediate wants to behaviors that will benefit the preservation of the group or species. In human societies this self-sacrificing drive is manifested as patriotism, and the king provides a humanly embodied symbol for the social ends of this patriotic "instinct." The ideal (Wagnerian) artwork provides, in turn, an edifying, life-sustaining illusion (*Wahngebild, Wahnspiel* – an image or play of *Wahn*) to inspire the king himself in the performance of his symbolic office. Both Wagner's essay and Sachs's monologue acknowledge the potentially violent, disturbing social implications of *Wahn* as well as an idealized view of the king's and/or the artist's role in "channeling" *Wahn* to productive political and creative ends ("jetzt schaun wir, wie Hans Sachs es macht, / daß er den Wahn fein lenken mag / kann"). Wagner alluded to the concept in the name he gave to his villa in Bayreuth: WAHNFRIED ("peace from illusion" or "folly").

THOMAS S. GREY

See also SCHOPENHAUER

John Warrack, "*Wahn*, Words and Music," *Richard Wagner: "Die Meistersinger von Nürnberg"* (Cambridge University Press, 1994): 111–34.

Wahnfried. In a letter to the King LUDWIG II's Cabinet Secretary, Lorenz von DÜFFLIPP, dated 20 April 1871 (quoted in Habel 325), Richard Wagner announced that he was so impressed with Bayreuth and its surroundings that he wished to establish a domicile and his festival project there. Three years later, on 28 April 1874, this first desire was fulfilled when the composer and his family moved into the villa they had built for them on a parcel adjoining the former court gardens. The villa itself was a realization of Wagner's yearnings for a home and the solidly bourgeois status such a dwelling represented. Wagner hit upon the name "Wahnfried" for the house (CWD 4 May and 7 May 1874), explaining it in a simple verse: "Hier, wo mein Wähnen Frieden fand – Wahnfried sei dieses Haus von mir benannt" (Here, where my delusions found peace – Wahnfried shall this house be named) (see also Wagner to Ludwig II, 25 May 1874).

Work on the two-story house had begun in 1872. The BAYREUTH-based master bricklayer Carl Wölffel drafted the final plans (with considerable input from Wagner) and supervised the actual construction. Ever the generous patron, Ludwig II financed most of the building with a gift of 25,000 thaler (roughly $1,875 at the time). The villa's ground floor was the house's public face, with its two-story central hall, great room, dining room, guest bedroom, and the Lilac Room, which served as COSIMA Wagner's parlor. The upper story contained the family's private rooms: bedrooms for Richard and Cosima, their daughters, and oldest son, SIEGFRIED; Richard's study; Cosima's private living room; and a large nursery. Wagner finished GÖTTERDÄMMERUNG and wrote PARSIFAL at Wahnfried. He and Cosima also entertained numerous guests there: friends, admirers, and important visitors to Bayreuth. When the composer died in Venice on 13 February 1883, his body was returned to Wahnfried for burial in a grave located in the garden. Cosima was buried there upon her death in 1930.

As long as Cosima lived, few physical changes were made to Wahnfried. In 1896, though, Siegfried had a separate structure erected to the east of the villa, which served as his own residence. After his death in 1930, his wife, WINIFRED, used the Siegfried Wagner House to host guests, including such luminaries as Arturo TOSCANINI, Richard STRAUSS, and Adolf HITLER. Then came the final month of World War II. On 5 April 1945, a bomb from a British plane landed on Wahnfried, destroying the garden and most of the villa facing it. American troops took possession of the estate nine days later, returning Wahnfried to the Wagner family in 1949 (but the Siegfried Wagner House only in 1957). Although Winifred lived in the Siegfried Wagner House until her death in 1980, Wahnfried ceased being a family residence upon Wieland Wagner's passing in 1966. In 1973, the Wagner family gave the entire property to the city of Bayreuth, which promptly undertook a complete renovation. It reopened to the public in 1976 in the dual capacity of "Richard Wagner MUSEUM" and "National Archive of the Richard Wagner Foundation." ANTHONY J. STEINHOFF

Heinrich Habel, *Festspielhaus und Wahnfried* (Munich: Prestel, 1985).

Walking. See HIKING AND WALKING

Walküre, Die (WWV 86b), "First Day" (*Erster Tag*), in three acts, and second part of Wagner's *Der RING DES NIBELUNGEN*. At the insistence of King LUDWIG II and over Wagner's objections, first performed separately in the Munich Nationaltheater on 26 June 1870, cond. Franz Wüllner; first performance as part of the complete *Ring* cycle on 14 August 1876 at the Bayreuth FESTIVAL THEATER.

1. Genesis, sources, and development
2. Composition
3. Plot summary
4. Musical structure

(Note: For issues applicable to the entire cycle – including publication, first staging, and significant performances – please also consult the entry for *Der Ring des Nibelungen*.)

1. Genesis, sources, and development

Die Walküre emerged from what was initially conceived as the first part of a trilogy, which was to present the backstory to *Der junge Siegfried*, but became an opera of its own when Wagner decided to open his cycle with the *Vorabend* of *Das RHEINGOLD*. Consequently, he wrote the texts for both operas simultaneously in late 1851 and early 1852. In the process, he heightened the difference between the world of the gods and the world of humans: He had originally planned to have WOTAN appear in HUNDING's hut (the way he would in MIME's in *Siegfried*), but instead decided to have the Volsungs' incestuous love affair play out in the human world, and chart its repercussions among the gods only in the second act.

In drafting the plot of *Die Walküre*, Wagner drew on NORDIC MYTHOLOGY (both the VÖLSUNGA SAGA and the *Poetic EDDA*), but connected those elements in altogether new ways. The romance of SIEGMUND and SIEGLINDE and the conflict with Hunding is a very pared-down version of a conflict in the *Völsunga Saga*, which similarly ends with Odin's (Wotan's) intervention. While various Valkyries make appearances in the *Poetic Edda*, the Valkyries as we meet them in the *Ring* and their relationship to Odin/Wotan are probably drawn mostly from the *Prose Edda* of Snorri Sturluson.

2. Composition

Die Walküre is much longer than *Das RHEINGOLD*, and it took Wagner much more time to compose than was the case there. Although he had produced a draft of *Rheingold* in eleven weeks, it took him six months to compose that of *Walküre* – from 28 June 1854 to 27 December 1854. Furthermore, a four-month trip to LONDON in 1855 lengthened the time between the completion and the orchestration of the draft. Complaining that he sometimes lost the thread of his draft when he returned to orchestrate it, he took more time than expected and did not complete the full score until 23 March 1856, so that the total time of composition was twenty-one months, as opposed to seven months for *Rheingold*. (See also *Der Ring des Nibelungen*.)

3. Plot summary

The opera opens on a storm-battered house in the forest. A stranger, Siegmund, staggers in, fleeing from nameless pursuers, exhausted and desperate. Surprised, the lady of the house, SIEGLINDE, offers him shelter and tends to him. The two are the twin children of Wotan, but have been separated as children, and do not immediately recognize one another – he calls himself Wehwalt (Man of Woe), and recounts the litany of misfortune that has led him to adopt this name. When Sieglinde's husband Hunding returns, he reveals himself as one of Siegmund's pursuers, eager to finish the job. Since his wife has already offered the stranger his home as a shelter for the night, he decides that the law of hospitality dictates he oblige Siegmund, but tells him the two will have to duel in the morning.

Sieglinde, who begins to realize who it is that has staggered into her home, mixes a sleeping potion for the unloved Hunding and returns to the stranger in her hall once Hunding is asleep. Sieglinde tells Siegmund of the sword Nothung, which a wanderer (Wotan) thrust into the ash tree around which Hunding's house is built, and which no one can pull from its trunk. Siegmund manages to pull the sword out of the tree, the two realize that they are siblings, children of Wälse (Wotan) and an anonymous mother. They lie down in an ecstatic burst of passion and, after the curtain falls, sire Siegfried to the sounds of a graphic musical surge and climax.

Act II opens in Valhalla, where the joyous reunion of Wotan's spawn upsets his marriage's fragile balance. Wotan seeks the counsel of his daughter (by the Earth goddess ERDA), the Valkyrie BRÜNNHILDE, who guides the souls of dead heroes to Wotan's fortress, which they will defend in case ALBERICH attacks. Wotan's wife FRICKA is incensed at the incestuous Volsung brood and the mockery they have made of the sacrament of marriage. Angrily she reminds Wotan that he is the master of promises and contracts, and demands action – specifically, Wotan is to take Hunding's side in the coming duel. Wotan relents, recognizing that he has already meddled too much in Siegmund's fate (by providing the sword Nothung) to make good on his "grosser Gedanke" (great idea) of the end of *Rheingold*. A crestfallen Wotan swears that he won't support his son in battle.

Wotan summons Brünnhilde and informs her of his decision to tilt the fortunes in Hunding's favor. Brünnhilde is devastated, and when she has to inform Siegmund of his impending doom, his devotion to his sister and mate inspires her to contravene her own orders and save Siegmund. During the duel, Wotan intervenes, shattering Nothung with his spear. Siegmund is killed. Wotan tells Hunding to inform Fricka that he has kept his promise, then kills him unceremoniously to send him to Valhalla. Finally he thunders that Brünnhilde will pay dearly for her disobedience.

Act III opens on the rocky gathering place of the Valkyries. Brünnhilde's sisters, collecting dead heroes after a battle, are shocked when Brünnhilde arrives carrying a very much alive Sieglinde. As they fearfully refuse her pleas for help, Brünnhilde sends Sieglinde into the forest for safety and prepares to face Wotan's wrath alone. In parting, she reveals to Sieglinde that the Volsungs' tryst has spawned a child, and that the child Sieglinde is carrying should be named Siegfried. When Wotan arrives, he condemns Brünnhilde to mortality; what is worse, she will be imprisoned asleep on a mountaintop, to become the prey and prize of any man who happens upon her. Brünnhilde pleads for mercy, and claims that her insubordination only realized Wotan's secret desire. Somewhat mollified, Wotan changes her punishment slightly: the mountaintop will be safeguarded by a magical circle of flames, which should deter unworthy suitors. Wotan kisses his daughter and she falls asleep on the rock; he then summons LOGE, who forms a magic circle of fire around the sleeping Valkyrie. Wotan resolves that whoever "fears the point of my spear" shall never pass the circle and awaken the god's favorite daughter.

4. Musical structure

(Note: music examples [CWE #] can be found in Appendix 4: *Leitmotive* in *Der Ring des Nibelungen*.)

As the first "Day" of the *Ring*'s "Three Days and a Preliminary Evening," *Die Walküre* greatly exceeds the scope of *Das Rheingold*. Its performance time is well over an hour longer; and, with intermissions between the acts, the "First Day" turns out to be about twice as long as the "Preliminary Evening." This broader conception repays a close look at its overall structure. The work is symmetrically disposed around Act II, with Acts I and III both having three scenes, and Act II five. Act II itself reveals a similar symmetry, with the great Scenes 2 and 4 – Wotan's Monologue and the *Todesverkündigung* (Brünnhilde's announcing to Siegmund his impending death) – bearing more weight than Scenes 1, 3, and 5 (the confrontation of Fricka and Wotan, Siegmund and Sieglinde in the forest, and Hunding's killing Siegmund). Even the disposition of characters across the acts exhibits a clear symmetry. The story of Siegmund, Sieglinde, and Hunding essentially plays out over Acts I and II, that of Wotan and Brünnhilde over Acts II and III, so that Act II is the one act that involves all the major characters.

Large-scale tonal relations play an important role as well. As Robert Bailey has pointed out, the move from the world of the gods in *Rheingold* into the human world of *Walküre* is articulated by the tonal move from the D♭ of Valhalla up a semitone to D minor. Act I begins in this key with the storm and Siegmund's arrival at Hunding's hut; and Act II ends in it with Siegmund's and Hunding's deaths, so that D minor in essence encapsulates all the narrative involving these characters, except for Sieglinde's pregnancy and rescue. Act III then moves to a different tonal world, from the B minor of the Valkyries at the beginning of the act to the E major of Wotan's kissing Brünnhilde to sleep at the end. Nor are the initial and final keys of the opera without broad ramifications for the future. In Act I of *Siegfried*, the D minor of Siegmund/Sieglinde returns as Siegfried begins to reclaim their heritage by reforging his father's sword: the first of his two Forging Songs is in D minor and, once he has forged it, he triumphantly departs from Mime's cave into the forest in D major. Similarly, just as Brünnhilde was put to sleep at the top of the mountain in E major at the end of *Walküre* Act III, so is the first sonority that accompanies her, when Siegfried wakes her with a kiss, an E (minor) triad.

However useful a knowledge of these broad symmetries and tonal relations may be in developing a synoptic, structural view of the opera, they are far from our moment-to-moment experience of it in the opera house. There, within a few minutes, we know that we are in an entirely different world from that of *Das Rheingold*. To be sure, *Rheingold* ends with a storm and *Walküre* begins with one. But the storms could hardly be more different: we experience the former from the point of view of the gods who conjure up storms, the latter from the point of view of the human beings who must try to survive them. Siegmund and Sieglinde are such human beings, and it is quickly evident that Wagner the musician is now working on compositionally more secure and expressively more nuanced ground, as befits the "purely human" (*rein menschliche*) figures that he wants his characters to be. Now the vocal lines are perfectly calibrated to both the declamation and the psychological resonance of each line, even each word. The vestiges of conventional recitative that were evident in Scenes 2 and 4 of *Rheingold* have disappeared, and the lines are supple and emotionally focused. Generally the music eschews foursquare phrasing, although it appears occasionally, in places where it might be expected: Siegmund's lyrical "Winterstürme" love song in Act I, and the Valkyries' sturdy music in Act III. Within the individual acts, *Die Walküre* exhibits a level of continuity, and ambiguity of formal closure, that makes it seem less sectional. Whereas Warren Darcy's division of *Das Rheingold* into twenty episodes is reasonably clear and entirely plausible, a similar parsing of *Die Walküre* would encounter grave problems long before the end of Act I.

Die Walküre gives us some of the first great narratives, monologues, and confrontational dialogues in the *Ring*. *Rheingold* offers Loge's monologue in Scene 2 and the electric confrontation of Wotan and Erda in Scene 4, but neither of these has the scope and breadth that characterize comparable scenes in *Walküre*: Siegmund's and Sieglinde's narratives in Act I, Scenes 2 and 3; Wotan's massive monologue in Act II, Scene 2; and the confrontations of Wotan and Fricka in Act II, Scene 1, Brünnhilde and Siegmund in Act II, Scene 4, and Brünnhilde and Wotan in Act III, Scenes 2 and 3. What makes these scenes so powerful is not only the rich humanity of the characters – Siegmund's courage and his love for Sieglinde, her initial care for and love of him, the way Siegmund's devotion to Sieglinde softens the stern Valkyrie Brünnhilde, and the way her understanding of and compassion for the twins in turn softens Wotan – but also the way the actions, thoughts, and emotions of these archetypal figures are clothed musically.

A critical player here is again the LEITMOTIV. Certain crucial *Leitmotive* from *Rheingold* sound out and play upon our memory, enriching our experience of the moments in *Walküre* when we hear them, and accumulating still deeper associations yet to be experienced: Valhalla (see Appendix 4; CWE 4), the Sword (CWE 12), Wotan's Spear and Treaties (CWE 5), Loge/Fire (CWE 6), the Curse (CWE 9), and Erda (CWE 10). In addition, new motives whose usage is essentially limited to *Walküre* are introduced – motives for the opening storm, various motives associated with the growing love of Siegmund and Sieglinde in Act I, a motive for Hunding (CWE 13), and local motives for Wotan's confrontation with Fricka, and for his long monologue.

By the end of the opera, the *Leitmotiv* has become so malleable in Wagner's hands, and so powerful, that it is almost as though he himself has been surprised by its utility. It is not without justification that Barry Millington has suggested that in Acts II and III of *Die Walküre* we get a sense that Wagner is relaxing his stricture in OPER UND DRAMA (Opera and Drama, 1851) about word over tone, drama over music, and letting music soar on its own – as his reading of Schopenhauer in late 1854, right as he was working on the first draft of the opera, might have been subliminally encouraging him to do.

In the past century or more, *Die Walküre* has, among the four operas of the *Ring*, been the one most frequently produced separately, or given in concert version. Surely this popularity rests on the sheer brilliance of its music, the pathos of its human relations and their representation in music, and the grandeur and power of its large-scale musical and dramatic conception.

ADRIAN DAUB AND PATRICK MCCRELESS

Robert Bailey, "The Structure of the *Ring* and Its Evolution" (see bibliography).

Walther von der Vogelweide (*c.* 1170–*c.* 1230), one of the few medieval German writers for whom we have historical documentation: in the accounts of Bishop Wolfger of Passau, Walther is given the gift of a fur coat on 12 November 1203. Walther is the most highly regarded and anthologized German lyric poet of his era. His poetry encompasses a wide range of courtly love lyrics as well as songs critical of that genre. He is also known for his sharp political poetry, in which he directs his criticism toward both the pope and the emperor. His poems describing the political chaos in the Empire at the beginning of the thirteenth century are particularly intense, as are his poignant musings on the transience of life and on the impossibility of living up to the conflicting ideals propounded by spiritual and secular authorities. RAY M. WAKEFIELD

Walther von Stolzing (tenor; character in *Die MEISTERSINGER VON NÜRNBERG*). Walther's part in the drama is simple enough: he needs to win the song contest in order to win EVA POGNER, and he must do so in a way that both supersedes and pays homage to the MASTERSINGERS' art. Yet as straightforward as the role may be, it is also heavily overladen with the charge of promoting the Wagnerian project – a less than subtle duty whose paper-thin metaphor NIETZSCHE was the first to ridicule in his famous summary of the opera's message: "beautiful maidens most like to be seduced by a knight who is a Wagnerian" (*The Case of Wagner* §3).

But given that Walther's singing also garners the immediate approval from the VOLK, it is clear that his intended appeal is as much artistic and political as it is romantic. And it should be noted that in none of the sources Wagner drew on for the opera is there any correlate to Walther's character; there, it was HANS SACHS who won the song contest and the woman's heart. Yet presumably because Wagner sought to present a parable about youth and outsiders reinvigorating communities and communal art, he added Walther's character, for transparently functional reasons. Indeed, Walther's utility can be traced in the evolution of the opera's libretto: initially he comes to NUREMBERG specifically to learn from the mastersingers, and to perfect pre-existing songs. It is only as the libretto progressed that Walther was posed in such opposition to the mastersingers, and that his songs (now newly composed) acquired the status of AVANT-GARDE – yet intuitively popular – reimaginings of inherited forms.

The burden placed on Walther – he must obtain instant popularity with the *Volk* while simultaneously articulating a new way forward for "advanced" composition – is perhaps felt most obviously (and, often, painfully) in the ungainly vocal demands Wagner places on the character. Walther's music is notoriously difficult, its relentlessly high tessitura paired with a robust ORCHESTRATION requesting the services of a SIEGFRIED or TRISTAN. Yet the honey-toned, almost Schlager-like sweetness of the Prize Song – not to mention that of the Act III quintet – requires a much lighter voice. And if audiences have generally come to accept a heavier instrument in the Prize Song as a necessity for simply getting through the material, the quintet often suffers immensely, with Walther reduced to barking or braying (and occasionally an unholy combination of the two) in the attempt to scale the music's upper reaches.

Klaus Florian Vogt, in BAYREUTH's recent KATHARINA WAGNER / Robert Sollich staging, has shown that the vocal demands are not insurmountable – even if that production's depiction of Walther as a reactionary tool significantly complicates the appeal of Vogt's lyricism. Typically, however, Walther is portrayed as a genial if headstrong young artist, and with a weightier voice than Vogt's; accordingly, the Walther of Siegfried Jerusalem and Ben Heppner has been a step towards Tristan in terms of both their own careers as well as their characterization of the role. RYAN MINOR

Was ist deutsch? (What is German?). This essay had a genesis and publication history that was far from straightforward. Wagner began it in late 1865, jotting down ideas about the relations between art and POLITICS in a journal intended for the instruction of his protégé, LUDWIG II of Bavaria. He expanded on some aspects of the essay, particularly its quasi-historical musings about the role of the princes and the JEWS, in the 1867 essay *Deutsche Kunst und deutsche Politik* (German Art and German Politics). Thirteen years after his first jottings, with the premieres of his most "German" operas (*Die MEISTERSINGER VON NÜRNBERG* and the *RING* cycle) behind him and the political unification of the German states achieved, he revisited his thoughts on the "German spirit" and published them in the *BAYREUTHER BLÄTTER* (1878).

The essay takes the form of an attempt to "gain a clear idea of what is really to be understood by the expression '*deutsch*' [German]" (PW 4:151). Wagner tries to answer his question first etymologically and then historically, dashing through GERMAN HISTORY from the barbarian invasions to his own times. Although the first task is inconclusive and the second is unwieldy, the essay nevertheless comes back repeatedly to a notion Wagner found in the word *deutsch* itself, having to do with "what is homelike [*heimatlich*] to ourselves" (PW 4:152). He develops many variations on this basic theme of the home-centered, home-seeking Germans, finding it the essential element in everything from the Germans' phlegmatic willingness to "abide beneath a foreign scepter," if only their speech and customs are not under attack, to their capacity to express the universal truths (the "purely human") in Christianity and classical antiquity (PW 4:154, 155). The German can "strip the foreign of its accidental, its external, of all that to him is unintelligible," and by the same token assimilate foreign influences so successfully that they become German, in other words, homelike, intelligible (PW 4:160).

Further elaborations of this theme provided Wagner with the soapbox he needed to exhort Germans to put up more resistance to "French maxims" wrapped in German clothing (e.g., democracy and REVOLUTION) and to Jewish influence in German life (PW 4:165). If the effect of the former was to make fools of the Germans, the effect of the latter was to alienate them from their essence. In contrast to the alleged Jewish desire to make a profit out of everything great and noble, to be German meant to do something for its own sake and "the very joy of doing it" (PW 4:158, 163). At the same time, Wagner emphasized the need for the German princes to cultivate a spiritual bond with their people, to give up their infatuation with foreign ways and their dependence on Jewish money and to cultivate German art. A postscript to the 1865 jottings, written for the 1878 publication, made clear his disappointment with the new German Empire, only lightly disguised as his continuing confusion about what is, in fact, German. Despite the magnificence of the victory over France in 1871, a mere *Liedertafel* drinking song ("Die Wacht am Rhein") celebrated the triumph (PW 4:168). The truly German remained inaudible.

CELIA APPLEGATE

See also ANTI-SEMITISM; FRANCO-PRUSSIAN WAR (1870–1); GERMAN UNIFICATION

Weber, Carl Maria von (b. Eutin [Holstein], 18/19 Nov. 1786; d. London, 4/5 June 1826), frequently described as the most important German operatic composer between MOZART and Wagner, he was Wagner's predecessor as the leader of the German opera in DRESDEN. He is most famous as the composer of *Der Freischütz* (1821), but during the so-called *Vormärz* period two of his other works – the through-composed *Euryanthe* (1823) and the fairy-tale opera *Oberon* (1826) – were also an important part of the repertoire in German theaters. His influence on Wagner may be traced as two distinct yet overlapping trajectories. Wagner was quite familiar with Weber's music, and many elements in Wagner's works (especially in *Der FLIEGENDE HOLLÄNDER, TANNHÄUSER*, and *LOHENGRIN*) show clear affinities with Weber's style. But Weber was also a central figure in the nationalistic discourse surrounding German opera in the early nineteenth century. In Wagner's theoretical writings and other prose works, Weber thus appears as an emblematic figure, symbolizing both the virtues and the inadequacies of early nineteenth-century German opera.

If we are to believe the *AUTOBIOGRAPHISCHE SKIZZE* (Autobiographical Sketch, 1842/3) and the personal reminiscences in *MEIN LEBEN* (My Life, 1865–81), this emblematic position that Weber held for Wagner may be traced back to the latter's childhood experiences in Dresden. In these and other works, Wagner describes his youthful infatuation with *Der Freischütz*, and he clearly retained a deep affection for Weber's 1821 work for his entire life. *Der Freischütz* is the subject of two substantial review essays that Wagner wrote in 1841 on the occasion of a performance in which the original dialogues were replaced by recitatives (supplied by BERLIOZ). Wagner is critical of these additions, which (in his view) undermine the sense of organic unity that informs Weber's score. Wagner links this sense of organic unity to a cluster of other characteristics – freshness and authenticity, a deep feeling for nature, a particular sense of good and evil – that make *Der Freischütz* the epitome of GERMANNESS. A similar kind of aestheticized NATIONALISM informs the speech and subsequent report that Wagner gave on the occasion of the reinterment of Weber's mortal remains in Dresden late in 1844. Wagner's narration of this event is notable not only for the encomiums that he lavishes on Weber, but also for the description of an "out-of-body experience" that Wagner apparently had at the beginning of his speech. From this and other accounts, it is clear that the figure of Weber and especially the music of *Der Freischütz* had a deeply personal and almost talismanic significance for Wagner.

Wagner's attitude towards Weber's *Euryanthe*, on the other hand, was highly ambivalent. This work – Weber's only through-composed opera – met with only moderate success. Wagner himself describes the opera dismissively in his early essay *Die deutsche Oper* (On German Opera, 1834), where he criticizes Weber's text declamation (a topic to which he returned in his *Über das Opern-Dichten und Komponieren im Besonderen* [On Opera Libretti and Composition in Particular, 1879]) and his excessively learned style. In his more extensive discussion of Weber's style in OPER UND DRAMA (Opera and Drama, 1851: Chapter 6, Part One), Wagner is more charitable towards *Euryanthe*, ascribing the relative failure of the work to the weakness of its libretto. Wagner's ambivalent attitude towards *Euryanthe* may partly be explained by his *historical* understanding of his own relationship to Weber. As is clear from his late essay ÜBER SCHAUSPIELER UND SÄNGER (Actors and Singers, 1872), Wagner understood himself as Weber's artistic successor, who was at last able to solve the central problem of Weber's style: namely, his inability to create authentic and compelling German-language recitative. Wagner's critique of *Euryanthe* thus centered on precisely that aspect of the work (i.e., text declamation) in which he felt his own contribution to be most profound.

Wagner's ambivalence towards *Euryanthe* is especially interesting in light of the many similarities between Weber's work and Wagner's own operas, similarities that in some cases suggest direct stylistic influence. In assessing this issue, one must draw a distinction between those general characteristics that were common to the musical dramaturgy of nineteenth-century opera, and those more specific instances in which we might posit a direct connection between the works of the two men. The association between diminished tonalities and evil or deeply troubled characters, for example, may be found in a wide variety of different operas, and is unique neither to Samiel (from *Der Freischütz*) nor to the DUTCHMAN. The fundamental idea of the LEITMOTIV, which some earlier scholars treated as part of Wagner's inheritance from Weber, is likewise part of a much broader tradition of musical signification. Of a different order are the specific links between *Euryanthe* and *Lohengrin*. Both operas feature a villain pair, who conspire against the hero and heroine in a monumental duet placed near the beginning of the second act. The female villains in both operas (Eglantine and ORTRUD) feign friendship with the heroine in order to substantiate false claims of moral or social impropriety. The musical strategies that Wagner and Weber use to depict these dramatic situations are similar, and it seems probable that – at least in these instances – Wagner was directly influenced by his predecessor's work. A similar correspondence may be hypothesized with regard to *Der Freischütz* and *Der FLIEGENDE HOLLÄNDER*. In each of these works, the beginning of the second act represents a "retreat" into the world of feminine domesticity, a world that is then complicated by the intrusion of the supernatural. Here – as with *Euryanthe* – it is more appropriate to speak of subconscious influence rather than direct borrowing. In this sense, Weber's music was simply one component (albeit a particularly important one) in the complex of operatic and non-operatic sources from which Wagner drew his ideas. Ultimately, the question of Weber's stylistic influence on Wagner cannot be separated from a consideration of historical understanding of opera itself, an understanding in which Weber played a complex and vital role.   STEPHEN MEYER

Stephen Meyer, *Carl Maria von Weber and the Search for a German Opera* (Bloomington: Indiana University Press, 2003).

Michael C. Tusa, "Richard Wagner and Weber's Euryanthe," *19th-Century Music* 9.3 (1986): 206–21.

Weingartner, Paul Felix von (b. Zara [Dalmatia], 2 June 1863; d. Winterthur, 7 May 1942), highly influential European conductor, composer, and critic, and one of LISZT's later pupils. As a student, he visited the 1882 BAYREUTH FESTIVAL, where he attended early performances of *PARSIFAL* and was fleetingly introduced to Wagner (Hartford 134). His subsequent association with Bayreuth was less happy: he was engaged as a musical assistant for the 1886 Festival, which included the Bayreuth premiere of *TRISTAN*, but was openly critical of COSIMA's direction and was not invited to return. He later voiced his criticisms in a pamphlet, *Bayreuth 1876–1896*, which warned of the adverse effect that Cosima's rigid approach would have on Wagner's artistic legacy. Weingartner was an early exponent of advocating fidelity to the printed score. His essay *On Conducting* (1895) was clearly intended as a response to Wagner; the revised third edition (1905) contains a detailed critique of Hans von BÜLOW's heavily inflected style, and is an important primary source in the understanding of late nineteenth-century PERFORMANCE PRACTICE.

ROGER ALLEN

See also PERFORMANCE, CONDUCTORS

Robert Hartford, ed., *Bayreuth: The Early Years* (Cambridge University Press, 1980).

Felix Weingartner, "Bayreuth (1876–1896)," trans. and ed. Stewart Spencer, *Wagner* 14.1: 38–48 and 14.2: 70–93.

Weingartner on Music and Conducting (New York: Dover, 1969).

Weinlig, Christian Theodor (b. Dresden, 25 July 1780; d. Leipzig, 7 March 1842), composer, teacher, choirmaster; studied in DRESDEN and Bologna. Returning home, he served as Cantor of the Kreuzkirche from 1814 to 1817. He then became Cantor of the Thomaskirche (LEIPZIG) in 1823 and remained there until his death. In addition to his duties for the church, Weinlig taught composition. Other than Wagner, his most famous student was Clara Schumann.

According to Wagner's memoirs, where Weinlig features sympathetically (if inaccurately; the name is spelled Weinlich), Wagner studied with him for only six months, concentrating on counterpoint at Weinlig's insistence. However, manuscript evidence shows that Wagner wrote other material simultaneously with his studies with the Cantor in particular the piano Fantasia in F♯ minor (WWV 22) and the Overture in D minor (WWV 20), both completed in November 1831. Wagner dedicated the 1832 Piano Sonata in B♭ major (WWV 21) to Weinlig, who had recommended its publication to BREITKOPF & HÄRTEL.   MARGARET ELEANOR MENNINGER

Weissheimer, Wendelin (b. Osthofen [Alsace], 26 Feb. 1838; d. Nuremberg, 16 June 1910), German conductor, composer, and writer on music. He studied at the LEIPZIG conservatory (1856–8), and later under Franz LISZT in Weimar (1859–61), who introduced him to Wagner in ZURICH (1858). Weissheimer's career as Kapellmeister took him from post to post, including Mainz, Augsburg, WÜRZBURG, Zurich, Strasbourg, Baden-Baden, and Milan. In 1893, he relocated to Freiburg, finally settling in NUREMBERG in 1900. As a NEW GERMAN acolyte, Weissheimer serialized a fifteen-part analytical appreciation of *TRISTAN UND ISOLDE* in the *NEUE ZEITSCHRIFT FÜR MUSIK* (September 1860–May 1861), in which he predicted *Tristan* would endure as "a pinnacle in the genre of music drama." This article functioned as a preview based on Hans von BÜLOW's piano score (the opera would appear four years later) though was billed as a review.

Weissheimer became closely acquainted with Wagner after the inaugural festival of the Allgemeiner Deutscher Musikverein in Weimar (1861), where Wagner praised his new cantata *Das Grab im Busento* and was subsequently impressed by Weissheimer's conducting of Offenbach's *Orpheus* in Mainz; thereafter the two became closer in Biebrich (today: Wiesbaden), discussing everything from gambling to AESTHETICS on their regular walks during 1862. Wagner's letters to Weissheimer have a confessional character ("I am tired of life" [Wagner to Weissheimer, 10 July 1863]); he even borrowed money from Weissheimer on occasion, and was prevailed upon – reluctantly – to persuade the boy's father that his son had a promising career in music.

The first cracks in their relationship appeared at a concert (1 November 1862) Weissheimer was arranging for his own compositions alongside those of Wagner and Liszt at the Leipzig Gewandhaus. Five of Weissheimer's large-scale works (including the premiere of his Schillerian symphonic poem *Der Ritter Toggenburg*) were performed alongside Wagner's *MEISTERSINGER* Prelude and *TANNHÄUSER* Overture, with Bülow also playing Liszt's Second Piano Concerto. (It was in a letter to Weissheimer about this concert, furthermore, that Wagner envisaged the "cut" from Prelude to "transfiguration" [*LIEBESTOD*] in *Tristan*, though ultimately this was not performed.) The public boycotted the event, however, leaving Weissheimer in considerable debt. Wagner reflects in *MEIN LEBEN* (My Life, 1865–81): "My friend Weissheimer, who had really exhausted everybody's patience in the most irresponsible way, gradually developed a feeling of resentment toward me dating from this period: he felt entitled to contend that he would have done better not to have included my brilliant orchestral works but rather to have offered solely his own compositions to the public at reduced prices" (ML/E 699).

Stemming from this disappointment, the major break between the two men occurred in 1868, when Wagner refused to hear Weissheimer's first opera

Theodor Körner in order possibly to recommend it for performance in Munich. Hans von Bülow – as Munich's Royal Kapellmeister – obliged, but Weissheimer reports that, as they were playing and singing through the score at around 11am, Wagner (in whose Villa Bülow was currently staying) sent a note via the maid that they should stop as he was "trying to sleep" (Weissheimer 392–3). DAVID TRIPPETT

Wendelin Weissheimer, *Erlebnisse mit Richard Wagner, Franz Liszt und vielen anderen Zeitgenossen nebst deren Briefen*, 3rd edn. (Stuttgart: Deutsche Verlags-Anstalt, 1898).

Wesendonck, Mathilde (née Agnes Luckemeyer) (b. Elberfeld [Germany], 23 Dec. 1828; d. Traunblick [Austria], 31 Aug. 1902), German poet, and married to **Otto** (also "Wesendonk"; b. Elberfeld, 16 March 1815; d. Berlin, 18 Nov. 1896), German silk merchant. Otto Wesendonck's father ran a silk-dying business, his uncle a silk factory. Otto's mother died in 1824, his elder sister Mathilde in 1837. Otto was sent to New York in around 1833 to help run the silk-importing firm Loeschigk, Wesendonck, & Co. and, as its European representative, commuted regularly back to that continent. In 1844, he married Mathilde Eckhard from Frankfurt am Main, who died on their honeymoon. In 1847, again in Europe, he met Agnes Luckemeyer, whom he married on 19 May 1848. Otto asked her to adopt the name "Mathilde"; some sources maintain that Agnes knew nothing of her predecessor. Otto's brother Hugo was a member of the Frankfurt parliament of 1848 and upon its dissolution fled to New York a wanted man. Otto and Mathilde followed in 1850; Otto later helped Hugo to found the insurance company known today as *Guardian Life*. But Mathilde disliked the USA, so she and Otto returned in late 1850. While Hugo was a leftist, Mathilde's father was a prominent conservative. So their decision to settle in ZURICH, outside Germany, might have been intended to avoid family strife. Otto and Mathilde arrived in March 1851, living at first in hotels.

Otto collected paintings, Mathilde had literary interests, but they both liked music. They attended Wagner's concert of 17 February 1852 and soon afterwards met him at the home of a mutual acquaintance. Wagner's correspondence with Theodor UHLIG proves that he straightaway coveted Wesendonck's wealth and had noticed Mathilde's interest in him. He also knew of Hugo's fate and seems to have played on his own status as a political exile to elicit Otto's sympathy. Otto's first major act was to help fund the Zurich "Wagner festival" in May 1853. Wagner was by now in love with Mathilde, as he admitted (though without naming her directly) in a letter to LISZT (30 May 1853). He wrote her a one-movement Piano Sonata in A♭ major (WWV 85) in June 1853, his first substantial work for five years. He apparently gave her some lessons in music theory and encouraged her to write poetry, and after his discovery of Arthur SCHOPENHAUER in late 1854, he made sure that she shared his enthusiasm. In autumn 1854, Otto cleared Wagner's debts, gave him a stipend of 2,000 francs a year, and appointed Jakob SULZER to manage his finances. While sources are scant, it seems that Mathilde became an important conversation partner when the death of Uhlig in January 1853 deprived Wagner of a sounding board for his opinions.

In early 1855, Wagner dedicated the new version of his FAUST-OUVERTÜRE (Faust Overture) to "S[einer] l[ieben] F[reundin]," (To his dear [girl]friend: i.e., Mathilde). The sketch of the first act of Die WALKÜRE, given to her in about 1855, was covered with similarly cryptic abbreviations (e.g., "I.l.d.g.!": "Ich liebe dich grenzenlos," I love you boundlessly). We do not know if Wagner was aware of the potentially incestuous nature of Otto's obsession with "Mathilde" (the name of his dead sister and both his wives), but it was after the private performance on 26 April 1856 of Walküre Act I, with its conflation of sister and wife, that Otto gave Wagner a sudden increase in salary of 50 percent. Wagner's passion for Mathilde was now obvious, not least on account of his extreme irascibility whenever she denied him her undivided attention in the company of others. Nevertheless, when Otto built a new villa on the edge of Zurich, he bought the next-door house and allowed Wagner to move there in April 1857 (this became his "Asyl").

In autumn 1857, Wagner began TRISTAN UND ISOLDE as a monument to his love for Mathilde. He later claimed that he and Mathilde had sworn themselves to chastity in order to keep themselves pure for each other. Thus Tristan was conceived amidst a domestic drama in which sexual relations existed only in the imaginings of its participants (see SEXUALITY). In late 1857 and early 1858, he also set five of her poems to music (the WESENDONCK LIEDER). When Otto was on urgent business in the USA in December 1857, Wagner began dictating the day-to-day running of the Wesendonck household and organized an early-morning serenade on Mathilde's birthday that included his chamber arrangement of "Träume" from the Wesendonck Lieder. Otto tried to reassert his authority upon his return, and, in compensation for Mathilde's birthday serenade, Wagner conducted a house concert in Otto's honor on 30 March 1858.

In late 1857, Mathilde had begun Italian lessons with Francesco De Sanctis (1817–83), a professor at the Federal Institute of Technology ETH. He was handsome, brilliant, and a man of action who had escaped from captivity after participating in the Italian uprisings. He was also an object of much female attention in Zurich society. So when Mathilde invited him and Wagner to a joint lunch in February 1858, we must assume her intention was to make Wagner jealous. It did, as is clear from his "Morgenbeichte," written to her on 7 April 1858, in which he disputed De Sanctis's interpretation of GOETHE. This letter was intercepted by Wagner's wife MINNA, who took its effusive tone as proof of infidelity. She confronted Mathilde, who in turn informed Otto. Minna's dogged, self-destructive persistence in the matter led to an open scandal. In July 1858, Wagner tried to convince Mathilde to elope with him. He failed, and so left Zurich alone on 19 August. He confided his thoughts to a diary written for her, and then began corresponding with her again. She sent him her poems and he continued to hope for a return to the Asyl. When Wagner and the Wesendoncks finally met again in autumn 1861 in VENICE, Mathilde was pregnant. Wagner only now acknowledged his rejection.

In 1862, Mathilde began publishing her literary works, many of which have Wagnerian resonances and use STABREIM (she too wrote a Siegfried, though one in which the hero finds not Brünnhilde, but Sleeping Beauty). Polite contact between the households was maintained, and Wagner claimed to have modeled Veit Pogner in *Die MEISTERSINGER VON NÜRNBERG* on Otto. Mathilde and Otto helped to found the Zurich Tonhalle Orchestra in 1868, and later also attended the BAYREUTH FESTIVAL. In the 1860s, Mathilde turned her attention to other artists. She inspired passionate love letters from Theodor Kirchner (the accompanist of the private *Walküre* premiere in 1856), but her attempts to entice Johannes BRAHMS to the Asyl were unsuccessful. Other composers did set her texts, including Otto Lessmann and Heinrich Schulz-Beuthen. The latter's opera *Der Zauberschlaf* (now lost) to a libretto by Mathilde was performed in Zurich in 1879 and must count as one of the first German fairy-tale operas.

The Wesendoncks fled Zurich in 1871 when an angry Francophile mob marched on their villa in protest at Otto having organized a public celebration of Germany's victory in the FRANCO-PRUSSIAN WAR. They moved to DRESDEN, then to Berlin, where SIEGFRIED WAGNER was a regular guest when a student. COSIMA WAGNER'S DIARIES show her to have harbored an intense jealousy of Mathilde, culminating in her efforts to destroy the Wagner-Wesendonck CORRESPONDENCE. Mathilde thwarted her by keeping copies of Wagner's letters and planning for their publication after her death. But the absence of her "voice" in the published sources served to underline Mathilde's own portrayal of herself as purely passive. The testimony of Wagner's stepdaughter Natalie PLANER – that Mathilde was a "cold snake ... [a] flirtatious, heartless creature ... so deliberate and cunning" – was long disregarded on account of its excessive vitriol, but deserves attention. Wagner's extant letters, Mathilde's writings, and her copious correspondence with other men of letters suggest that her self-proclaimed naïve innocence was rather a stratagem by which to circumvent the gender-based power hierarchies of her day. Far from being a "white sheet of paper," as she claimed, she was in fact a woman possessed of a keen intelligence and a steely determination to be treated seriously by the men around her.   CHRIS WALTON

See also MONEY

Max Fehr, *Richard Wagners Schweizer Zeit*, 2 vols. (Aarau: Sauerländer, 1934 and 1953).

Wolfgang Golther, ed., *Briefe Richard Wagners an Otto Wesendonk, 1852–1870*. Neue, vollständige Ausgabe (Berlin: Duncker, 1905).

ed., *Richard Wagner an Mathilde Wesendonck: Tagebuchblätter und Briefe, 1853–1871* (Berlin: Duncker, 1904).

Albert Heintz, "Richard Wagner in Zürich," *Allgemeine Musikzeitung* 23.7 (1896): 91–4.

Axel Langer and Chris Walton, eds., *Minne, Muse und Mäzen: Otto und Mathilde Wesendonck und ihr Zürcher Künstlerzirkel* (Zurich: Museum Rietberg, 2002).

Francesco de Sanctis, *Epistolario (1856–1858)*, eds. Giovanni Ferretti and Muzio Mazzocchi Alemanni (Turin: Einaudi, 1965).

Chris Walton, *Richard Wagner's Zurich* (see bibliography)

Wesendonck Lieder (WWV 91). The *Lied*, so the story goes, has little influenced the commanding and public genres of symphony and opera. Yet as the finale of BEETHOVEN's Ninth, MAHLER's *Wunderhorn* symphonies, and Wagner's *TRISTAN UND ISOLDE* affirm, such thinking obscures more than it reveals. The Ninth Symphony's *Freude* tune begins thirty years earlier in Beethoven's *Gegenliebe* (Mutual Love), while Mahler's Second through Fourth Symphonies draw on melodies or complete songs whose texts derive from Achim von Arnim and Clemens Brentano's folk anthology *Des Knaben Wunderhorn* (The

Youth's Magic Horn). Alongside Wagner's *Wesendonck Lieder* and *Tristan und Isolde*, these works make clear that while the nineteenth century valued musical monumentality, diminutive, private song was its frequent confederate.

The stimulus of the five Wesendonck songs on *Tristan* constitutes a singular event in Wagner's career, for he interrupted the larger composition to take up a repertory he had shown no interest in since the handful of French settings he (wrongly) had hoped would impress early 1840s PARIS. Eighteen years later, the stakes were higher. Much like the ancient Ouroboros symbol, in which a serpent continually consumes its tail thereby engaging in perpetual renewal, *Tristan* engendered the songs just as they sparked the opera. On 18 September 1857, Wagner presented the MUSIC DRAMA's Act III libretto to Mathilde WESENDONCK, wife of his generous Swiss patron Otto Wesendonck (only LUDWIG II would surpass his munificence). Wagner started the Act I compositional sketch soon thereafter; completing this, he again made Mathilde a gift. Under the *Tristan* spell she responded with a number of poems, five of which Wagner set to music. In order of composition they are: 1. "Der Engel" (Angel), 30 November 1857; 2. "Träume" (Dreams) 4–5 December 1857; 3. "Schmerzen" (Anguish), 17 December 1857; 4. "Stehe still!" (Stand Still), 22 February 1858; and 5. "Im Treibhaus" (In the Greenhouse), 1 May 1858. Amending their order twice, Wagner adopted a final sequence for publication in 1862 (1, 4, 5, 3, 2). Deathridge cites this to support the contention the composer did not conceive "the lieder as a cycle." The nineteenth century understood the concept *Liederzyklus* more flexibly than we do nowadays, thus it is best not to discard the idea out of hand.

Do these songs, like *Tristan*, underscore an adulterous affair between Wagner and Mathilde? Answers rival the number of words expended on Wagner himself. Schott's 1862 publication mentions no poet; Mathilde was not so identified until after her death. One is on firmer ground in observing that Wagner described two of the songs as "studies for *Tristan und Isolde*": "Im Treibhaus" forecasts the Act III Prelude, while "Träume" is used almost unchanged in the Act II duet. *Tristan*'s harmonic idiom was born in song's laboratory. Although the songs are invariably heard as orchestral *Lieder*, Wagner conceived them for female voice and piano. He orchestrated only "Träume," and this for violin (not voice) and small orchestra. Under Wagner's supervision, Felix MOTTL scored all five. In 1976, Hans Werner Henze supplied another version for alto and chamber orchestra.   JAMES PARSONS

John Deathridge, *Wagner Beyond Good and Evil* (see bibliography).

Westernhagen, Curt von (b. Riga, 9 June 1893; d. Preetz/Holstein, 3 Sep. 1982), German writer on music. Westernhagen, a practicing dental surgeon by profession, was a prolific amateur Wagner scholar whose work was widely read and long regarded as authoritative. He was also a politically active NATIONAL SOCIALIST, a racist, and an anti-Semite. Mentored by GLASENAPP in RIGA from a tender age, Westernhagen wrote his first essay on Wagner in 1928 before joining the National Socialist party in January 1930. Throughout the Third Reich he published numerous essays and books on Wagner and related subjects that conformed to party ideology, though there were disagreements in the party hierarchy about his all-too-negative view of NIETZSCHE

(Curt von Westernhagen, *Nietzsche*). Westernhagen was spared denazification after 1945, but nonetheless sought to cover up his past. From 1952 almost until his death, he wrote for Bayreuth upon the express invitation of WIELAND WAGNER (Dörte von Westernhagen, *"Und was haben Sie"*). In his postwar writings, Westernhagen soft-pedaled Wagner's anti-Semitism and his revolutionary credentials by suppressing evidence, in effect offering a tendentious version of Wagner no less problematical than the openly racist readings of Wagner he had propagated during the Third Reich (see comparative citations in Deathridge, "Review"). For more mundane reasons, Westernhagen's book on the sketches of the *Ring* also presents problems (Deathridge, "Wagner's Sketches"), though his two postwar biographies of Wagner have endured popular success, thanks to their uncompromising hagiographical portrait of the composer.   JEREMY COLEMAN

John Deathridge, "Review," *19th-Century Music*, 5.1 (Summer 1981): 81–9.
"Wagner's Sketches for the 'Ring': Some Recent Studies," *The Musical Times*, 118.1611 (May 1977): 383–9.
Curt von Westernhagen, *Nietzsche, Juden, Antijuden* (Weimar: Duncker, 1936).
Richard Wagner: Sein Werk, sein Wesen, seine Welt (Zurich: Atlantis, 1956).
Wagner (Zurich: Atlantis, 1968); trans. Mary Whittall, *Wagner: A Biography* (Cambridge University Press, 1981).
Dörte von Westernhagen, *"Und was haben Sie vor 1945 gemacht? Der Wagner-Forscher Curt von Westernhagen," wagnerspectrum* 7.1 (2011): 83–99.

Wibelungen, Die (subtitled "World History Drawn from Saga"), one of Wagner's most fantastic and important essays. Probably written in 1848 around the time of *Siegfrieds Tod*, it initially appeared in pamphlet form in late 1849 (published by WIGAND of LEIPZIG). There has been some debate as to chronology, but today it is common for scholars to place the essay first (see Wilberg). The link between *Die Wibelungen* and the *Nibelung* epic is unmistakable. For instance Wagner's prose sketch for a "Nibelung drama," also called a saga, goes (Wibelungen-like) much further back in time than the plot ideas found in *Siegfrieds Tod* (*GÖTTERDÄMMERUNG*). Also roughly contemporaneous is a planned "drama" on the Holy Roman Emperor Frederick Barbarossa – a figure central to *Die Wibelungen*. In *MEIN LEBEN* (My Life, 1865–81) Wagner claims he put that drama aside when he saw the "resemblance" between it and the Nibelung and Siegfried "myths," although it is likely that he continued work on it after *Siegfrieds Tod* (Millington 35). In this nexus of Nibelung-related work, all inspired to one degree or another by the epic poem *Das Nibelungenlied* (*c.* 1200), the boldest intellectually and the most fundamental to Wagner's worldview is *Die Wibelungen*. Indeed, its influence can be traced right through to *PARSIFAL*.

Die Wibelungen purports to tell the history of the German people in the general context of the Eurasian world. Upon leaving the Central Asian Highlands after a great flood recedes, the German tribes were able to hold onto their "essential" spiritual character in their new European homelands. In this they differ from the lesser peoples who surround them. Therefore their status was – and potentially still is – both singular and superior.

Into this fable, Wagner interweaves the struggles between kaiser and pope, the development of Christianity, and much else besides, peppering the tale with historical facts. Yet the gestures toward scholarly probity are bogus. What is explicitly asserted is the priority of MYTH, of beliefs that exist in the common *völkisch* mind. It does not matter that myths are contradicted by facts, for *völkisch* myths are the royal road to deeper truths. The conventional historian is simply wrong when he turns his back on these things; he is shutting his eyes to the essential nature of nation and race. And so we learn that the Nibelung Hoard initially expressed the status of the first king (the Stem Father and manifestation of the Godhead: WOTAN), and that the young hero or Sun God (SIEGFRIED as an Ur-Christ) is a further representative of the metaphysical and loving nature of the German people. Subsequently, the Nibelung Hoard transforms into the Grail, which is then brought from the East to the Occident. Ultimately, the quintessential message of *Die Wibelungen* is better expressed in *Parsifal* than in the Nibelung epic.

In all of this, "essence" is of the essence. Wagner asserts a metaphysical identity for the German people which he dialectically opposes to materialism. So while the pope turns into a worldly prince, the greatest German kaisers still embody the "bloom" of the primal spirituality. Frederick Barbarossa looks longingly east whence it (now the Grail) came and where it is still present in Eastern religions. And this is the same spiritual quality apostrophized at the end of *Die MEISTERSINGER VON NÜRNBERG*. What counts is not the Holy Roman Empire as a worldly power, but holy German art.

If one turns to the *Nibelung* epic expecting an adequate dramatization of all this, one will be disappointed. In the essay, Siegfried as the bringer of light (the dragon is the bringer of darkness) is clearly kernel, but his stage manifestation is innocent, all instinct, axiomatically denied deep understanding. He has not read *Die Wibelungen*. Nor does he connect to the German VOLK. Wagner attempts to get around this by folding the Hero into Nature, itself packaged as a spiritual entity. And certainly in the essay the German *Volk* has a special relation to Nature. For instance, when the awakening BRÜNNHILDE hails "the sun, the light, the day" she is quoting *Die Wibelungen*. But finding a theatrical expression for the fundamental idealist agenda is beyond Wagner at this time. Nonetheless, his problems force him back to the mythic narrative itself. And in, above all, *Die WALKÜRE*, the pay-offs of foregoing the Sun-God/ Christ figure for the Stem Father and his struggles are surely considerable.

BARRY EMSLIE

See also *KUNSTRELIGION*

Barry Millington, *Wagner* (see bibliography).
Petra-Hildegard Wilberg, *Richard Wagners mythische Welt: Versuche wider den Historismus* (Freiburg: Rombach, 1996).

Wigand, Otto Friedrich (b. Göttingen, 10 Aug. 1795; d. Leipzig, 1 Sep. 1870), publisher and supporter of democratic and revolutionary causes, worked as a bookseller in the Habsburg Empire, first in Pressburg (Bratislava) and then in Pest. Along with his brother and fellow publisher Georg, he supported Hungarian nationalism, a position which eventually forced his departure to LEIPZIG, where he set up shop in 1833. Georg arrived the following year and set up partnership with Johann Jakob Weber (1803–80). Both Wigands remained staunch proponents of Hungary's literature, and Otto's firm was among those in Leipzig (along with BROCKHAUS) which supported and published translated works. Wigand's political engagement on behalf of Hungarians (and also Poles) as well as German democratic causes was consistent and fervent. In partial retaliation, his company was searched by the police fifteen times between 1833 and 1849. He was active in calling for press freedoms during the Gutenberg festival of 1840 and was a central figure in Leipzig's 1848 revolutions. In response to his radical politics and his calls for the abolition of serfdom, Austria-Hungary accused Wigand of treason and banned his books. It also successfully pressured Saxony to force Wigand to cease publication about Hungary. Unsurprisingly, such external interference strengthened his political energies. Even into the 1850s, Wigand continued to be brought up on charges, although all sentences involving jail time were commuted to fines. The government of Saxony refused him a passport, and in 1859 his election to the Leipzig city council was overturned. Wigand retired in 1864.

A great sponsor of the so-called Hegelian Left (*Herbergsvater der Hegelschen Linken*), Wigand published many works associated with both the Young Hegelians and the YOUNG GERMANS as well as Friedrich Engels's *The Condition of the Working Class in England* (1845). He also helped sponsor a visit to Leipzig by Karl Marx in 1843, and helped to prepare the first edition of *Das Kapital*.

Wigand's most important author was Ludwig FEUERBACH, publishing his complete works. Wagner's interest in Feuerbach led him to submit his manuscript *Die KUNST UND DIE REVOLUTION* (Art and Revolution) to Wigand in August of 1849. Wigand published it, paying Wagner 10 louis d'or. The composer also sent Wigand a manuscript copy of *Die WIBELUNGEN*, which was not accepted for publication. Wagner soon became disenchanted with Wigand, complaining that the latter's correspondence went astray. Moreover, Wagner wrote to others, Wigand had sent neither his fee nor author copies promptly after he had published *Die Kunst und die Revolution*. By 1850, Wagner was considering other Leipzig publishing firms for future manuscripts, including J. J. Weber, who numbered Eduard DEVRIENT and Heinrich LAUBE among his authors. MARGARET ELEANOR MENNINGER

Wilhelmj, August (b. Usingen, 21 Sep. 1845; d. London, 22 Jan. 1908), one of the great virtuoso violinists of the late nineteenth century. Wilhelmj was the concertmaster at the first BAYREUTH FESTIVAL (1876), and of the orchestra he helped to assemble for the concerts in LONDON the following year, conducted jointly by Wagner and Hans RICHTER. Wilhelmj became a friend of Wagner in the process and served as a pallbearer at the composer's funeral.

DAVID BRECKBILL

Wille, Eliza (née Sloman) (b. Itzehoe [Germany], 9 March 1804; d. Mariafeld [Switzerland], 23 Dec. 1893), a novelist, married to **François** (b. Hamburg, 20 Jan. 1811; d. Mariafeld, 8 Jan. 1896), journalist, and member of the Frankfurt Parliament of 1848. Eliza's first brief acquaintance with Wagner was in DRESDEN (1843). In late 1851, the Willes moved to Mariafeld outside ZURICH, where their home became a focal point for intellectuals and artists. Georg HERWEGH brought Wagner to Mariafeld in 1852, after which he became a regular visitor and there gave the first readings of his texts for *Der*

RING DES NIBELUNGEN. François joined Wagner on HIKING trips. Eliza was Wagner's confidante during the WESENDONCK crisis, though François thwarted his efforts to use her as an intimate go-between with Mathilde. In 1863, Wagner contemplated marriage with Eliza's sister, Henriette von Bissing. He sought long-term refuge with the Willes in March 1864, but left after five weeks and was instructed not to return. They remained on friendly terms, though contact dwindled after his second marriage.   CHRIS WALTON

Chris Walton, *Richard Wagner's Zurich* (see bibliography).
Eliza Wille, *Erinnerungen an Richard Wagner: Mit 15 Briefen Richard Wagners* (Zurich: Atlantis, 1982).

Windgassen, Wolfgang (b. Annemasse, 26 June 1914; d. Stuttgart, 8 Sep. 1974), German tenor, and the leading Wagner tenor of the 1950s–60s. Although Windgassen appeared at Covent Garden, the Metropolitan Opera, La Scala, and throughout the German-speaking orbit, BAYREUTH was his artistic home from 1951 to 1970, where at one time or another he sang the leading tenor roles in all ten canonical Wagner operas.   DAVID BRECKBILL

Winkelmann, Hermann (b. Braunschweig, 8 March 1849; d. Vienna, 18 Jan. 1912), German tenor. After establishing himself as a leading tenor in Hamburg (beginning in 1878), Winkelmann appeared in the LONDON (1882) and VIENNA (1883) premieres of *TRISTAN UND ISOLDE*, and was the first PARSIFAL (BAYREUTH, 1882). He became the leading HELDENTENOR in Vienna (1883–1906), where his plangent voice contributed to his great acclaim.   DAVID BRECKBILL

Einhard Luther, *Biographie eines Stimmfaches* (see bibliography), vols. 1–2.

Wittembergische Nachtigall, Die. Pro-Lutheran *Spruchgedicht* (sententious poem) by Hans SACHS. Following a three-year pause in literary production, during which he seems to have immersed himself in the writings of Martin Luther, Sachs created a lasting monument to the reformer with the publication of this 702-line poem in 1523, two years before the city of NUREMBERG officially introduced Protestant worship. The work portrays the spread of the new religion allegorically: Luther is the "Wittenberg Nightingale," who announces the dawn of the gospel to the Christian flock of sheep who have been led astray by the "lion" (Pope Leo X) and allied beasts, all signifying prominent Catholic opponents of Luther. It is written in the common verse of the period, rhymed couplets of iambic quadrameter, otherwise known as *Knittelvers*. The *Nachtigall* was hugely successful, appearing within a year in seven editions and making Sachs known throughout German-speaking Europe. In Act III of *Die MEISTERSINGER VON NÜRNBERG*, the first lines of the poem ("Wach auf. . .") are sung by the *VOLK* on the festival meadow, as a tribute to HANS SACHS.
          GLENN EHRSTINE

Wolf, Hugo (b. Windischgraz, Styria [Slovenjgradec, Slovenia], 13 March 1860; d. Vienna, 22 Feb. 1903), German composer of *Lieder*. Writing about Hugo Wolf nowadays is altogether more challenging than it was a century ago. Then he was the "Wagner of the Lied" (according to Eduard HANSLICK, who by no means intended to praise), a master of "de-cla-ma-tion" (in Gustav MAHLER's doubled-edged yet ultimately censorious quip), and an imaginatively expert yet subservient acolyte to the writers he set to music. While many a stereotypical view of Wolf has been challenged, above all the belief that he uncritically followed the lead of his poets, in an entry on Wolf for a Wagner encyclopedia the matter comes down to this: how completely did he take up a Wagnerian influence, with all of the MUSIC DRAMA's ambition and ethos, and translate such in terms of the infinitely more circumscribed *Lied*? Beyond this, is it correct to assume that just because a late nineteenth-century composer took up a chromatically enriched harmonic vocabulary, the influence flows always from *TRISTAN UND ISOLDE*?

As his letters tell us, Wolf's youthful infatuation with Wagner was extreme. When Wagner visited VIENNA in 1875, Wolf ran after his coach wherever it went and stood in the lobby of Wagner's hotel in the hopes of a meeting, so that he could show the master some of his compositions (see Glauert 15). However, beyond this, Wolf's music and writings require a more nuanced framing of these questions. Disdainful of contemporaneous poets, he revered early nineteenth-century writers such as GOETHE, Eichendorff, and Mörike, masters all of German lyric poetry. In a letter (22 December 1890) Wolf asserts that Schubert's settings of Goethe's "Prometheus" and "Ganymed" were lacking because such "magnificent poems" were "reserved for a time after Wagner," a remark underscoring a concomitant commitment to tradition and innovation. The phrase "after Wagner" ought not to be taken too far, for Wolf learned as much from LISZT, SCHUMANN, and, despite his dig, Schubert.

Whether one describes Wolf's musical style – above all his harmonic language – as Wagnerian, post-Wagnerian, post-Romantic, proto-modern, or simply Wolfian, there is no disputing, to quote the first work of his *Italienisches Liederbuch* (completed 1896), his gift for making "small things . . . enchant us." That enthralling small thing of course is song itself, in which the medium's contained resources of solo voice and keyboard, of music and words, pivot on the paradox of bounded boundlessness. Wolf's strategies are many, including in his *Mir ward gesagt* (*Italienisches Liederbuch*, 2) conflicting vocal and piano phrasing, competing contrapuntal lines in the voice and piano's bass line, and an A A' formal design in which the song's second half moves up a whole step. Amatory rupture seldom has been more searchingly probed!

A hundred years after Wolf's death one hears, as the composer noted in the self-appraisal "Wölferl's own howl," a union of music and verse owing allegiance to no single composer, instead building on many, yet in the end his own. While Wolf does not always howl, he can move one intensely as the best of his some three hundred *Lieder* consistently prove.   JAMES PARSONS

Amanda Glauert, *Hugo Wolf and the Wagnerian Inheritance* (Cambridge University Press, 1999).

Wolfram von Eschenbach (*c.* 1170–*c.* 1220) is among the most read authors of medieval German literature, and is considered the best among the narrative writers in the medieval German tradition. We know very little about his life. His language indicates a home in northern Bavaria, and his own references reveal that his patron was the famous nobleman Hermann, Landgrave of Thuringia. In another famous reference in *Parzival*, Wolfram seems to claim that he is illiterate. This statement has occasioned various interpretations: for example, that Wolfram is telling his audience he does not read Latin. Whatever he may have intended, we do know from his writings that Wolfram was remarkably erudite; he knew and included the latest discourses on medicine, theology, and astronomy. It is difficult to imagine his being illiterate and still having access to such a broad knowledge base.

We have eight or nine complex and beautifully crafted lyric poems, which are assumed to have been written early in Wolfram's career; most of these belong to the genre of the "alba" or dawn song. Wolfram is best known, however, for his narrative poems, and *Parzival* is one of the greatest masterpieces in the tradition of medieval verse romances. This work depicts the voyage of self-discovery on which a knight travels from foolish innocence through numerous challenging adventures to the ultimate realization of his unique secular and spiritual blood lineage. Richard Wagner adapted this romance for his opera PARSIFAL, which has brought increased attention in modernity to Wolfram's medieval narrative. We have two other narratives by Wolfram: *Willehalm*, which is unfinished, and *Titurel*, which survives in two fragments. *Titurel* deals with the earlier tragic love story of two characters who appear in *Parzival*: Schianatulander and Sigune. In *Parzival*, Schianatulander is already dead when he first appears. Sigune is holding his embalmed body and grieving for her friend who, she tells Parzival, died in combat for her sake. It is uncertain whether *Titurel* was written before or after *Parzival*. We have nine books of Wolfram's *Willehalm*, which is based on a historical figure, Count William of Toulouse. Count William is known to us from Carolingian times as a hero in the battle against the Saracens who eventually retires to a monastery. *Willehalm* was clearly the last of Wolfram's projects, undertaken after the completion of *Parzival*.   RAY M. WAKEFIELD

James F. Poag, *Wolfram von Eschenbach* (New York: Twayne, 1972).
Wolfram von Eschenbach, *Parzival and Titurel*, trans. Cyril Edwards (Oxford University Press, 2009).

Wolfram von Eschinbach (baritone; character in TANNHÄUSER). Wolfram's role as a dramatic character in Wagner's opera derives ultimately from the anonymous Middle High German poem "Der Wartburgkrieg," written around 1250, which casts a number of historical *Minnesänger* as contestants in a "war of song" at the court of Landgrave Hermann of Thuringia in 1207. The historical poet-singers, including Wolfram, WALTHER VON DER VOGELWEIDE, Reinmar von Zweter, and Biterolf, are challenged by an outsider figure, the fictional Heinrich von Ofterdingen, whom Wagner replaced with the character of TANNHÄUSER so as to conflate the "contest of song" legend with that of the Venusberg. The medieval poem (which Wagner learned through the work of scholars E. T. L. Lucas and Ludwig Bechstein published in the 1830s), like E. T. A. HOFFMANN's Romantic narrative based on it ("Der Kampf der Sänger," 1818), portrays Wolfram as the particular rival of Ofterdingen. In Hoffmann, the two are respectful artistic rivals, otherwise close friends, but they also become rivals for the affection of the Landgräfin Mathilde. This dynamic is adapted by Wagner to his triangle of Tannhäuser, Wolfram, and ELISABETH. Wolfram's role in Act III of the opera, when he tries to prevent

Tannhäuser from returning to the Venusberg in despair over failing to win the pope's absolution, is based on the figure of the *getreue Eckart* (the faithful Eckart), who guards the entrance to the Venusberg and warns off travelers tempted to enter it.

Wolfram is the second principal male role in the opera, after Tannhäuser. In the final scene of Act I, it is Wolfram who recognizes the truant singer as he is sunk in prayer, and who selflessly persuades him to return to the Wartburg by invoking the name of Elisabeth ("Bleib bei Elisabeth!" [Stay with Elisabeth]), after which he inaugurates the closing lyrical ensemble ("War's Zauber, war es reine Macht" [Was it magic, was it pure power]). In Act II he takes the leading role in the "contest of song," setting the courtly, dignified tone that Tannhäuser will reject, and attempting to mediate between his rebellious friend and the other singers as long as possible. However it is Wolfram's song ("Dir, hohe Liebe, töne begeistert mein Gesang" [To you, mighty Love, shall my song enthusiastically sound]) that Tannhäuser interrupts with his blasphemous praise of Venus. His compact solo scene in Act III, the recitative and "song to the evening star" ("O du mein holder Abendstern"), was one of Wagner's last concessions to the practice of wholly excerptable lyrical numbers, and it quickly succeeded in becoming one of his best-known, if not most characteristic, compositions.

Wagner's first Wolfram, the baritone Anton Mitterwurzer, was one of the most successful members of the cast in the composer's view and that of others in the first audience (twenty years later he created the role of Kurwenal in *Tristan und Isolde*). The role is somewhat higher and, of course, more consistently lyrical than principal bass-baritone roles of Wagnerian oeuvre such as the DUTCHMAN, WOTAN, HANS SACHS, or AMFORTAS, although some singers have sung both types of role, notably Dietrich Fischer-Dieskau, as well as Eberhard Wächter and Bernd Weikl. More typically the role is taken by lighter lyric baritones who also specialize in *Lied* repertoire, such as Hermann Prey (or, more recently, Thomas Hampson). Theodor Reichmann, Wagner's original Amfortas, sang the first Wolfram at Bayreuth in COSIMA WAGNER's production of 1891, and Herbert Janssen in SIEGFRIED WAGNER's 1930 revival, conducted by TOSCANINI. THOMAS S. GREY

Wolzogen, Baron Hans Paul von (b. Potsdam, 13 Nov. 1848; d. Bayreuth, 2 June 1938), one of the most influential WAGNERITES. He was the grandson of Karl Friedrich Schinkel, the famous architect who designed almost all the most prestigious buildings in Berlin during the first half of the nineteenth century. Wolzogen's mother died when he was just 2 years old, and for that reason he grew up in the Schinkel family house, which was filled with the spirit of classical antiquity. This had a substantial impact on him: the age he lived in seemed inferior by comparison. In 1863, he moved to Breslau to live with his father. From 1868 until 1879 he studied comparative linguistics, history, and philosophy at Berlin University. In 1872, he married the daughter of a Prussian general and moved to his family's estate in Thuringia, where he worked as a freelance writer. As early as 1866, he saw a performance of *TANNHÄUSER*, which moved him deeply. He began to read the writings of Wagner and SCHOPENHAUER, and in 1872 he traveled to BAYREUTH for the first time.

Prompted by the deep impression made by his studies of Wagner's work, he sought out and met the "master" for the first time in 1875. Wagner was pleased by the young man's enthusiasm, and encouraged him to move to Bayreuth, which Wolzogen did in 1877. He later built his own house on Wahnfriedstraße and, until his death, remained a neighbor of WAHNFRIED, treated like a member of the family. His house was destroyed during an airstrike shortly before the end of the war in April 1945.

In 1876, Wolzogen published *Der Nibelungenmythos in Sage und Literatur* (The Nibelung Myth in Saga and Literature), and made a name for himself because of its success. For the world premiere of the complete RING in 1876, he published *Thematischer Leitfaden durch die Musik zu Richard Wagner's Festspiel "Der Ring des Nibelungen"* (A Guide through Richard Wagner's *The Ring of the Nibelung*). This book was an instant bestseller and had the effect of establishing once and for all the identification and labeling of the musical motives as the path of choice in the analysis and discussion of Wagner's works (see also LEITMOTIV for discussion of the term's development). His literary success and his ability to explain Wagner's works to the general public prompted the composer to return to an old idea of having his own newsletter, now with Wolzogen as editor and publisher. In the first issue of the BAYREUTHER BLÄTTER (1878), Wolzogen opened with an article explaining that the aim of the newsletter was the "purification and re-establishment of the true German culture." For the next sixty years, until his death, he remained the sole editor. Starting in 1884, the chair of the General Richard Wagner Society (Allgemeiner Richard Wagner-Verein) acted formally as the editor. Wolzogen decided on the topics and authors, and in this way shaped the profile of the newsletter, which had a fluctuating monthly circulation of 700, then 1,700, and later 500 conservative middle-class homes.

Wolzogen not only wrote a large number of the articles, but also reviews and obituaries. Most of the unsigned articles were written by him. Together with COSIMA and especially Houston Stewart CHAMBERLAIN, who was his intellectual superior, Wolzogen became a leading figure of the BAYREUTH CIRCLE and is partly responsible for the problematic reception of Wagner's work today. Wagner sometimes expressed his own reservations about Wolzogen, but continued to stand by him.

In Bayreuth, Wolzogen blossomed as a writer and journalist. He wrote poems and fairy tales, drafted essays on mythology and theology, art and music. He also wrote treatises on aesthetics and contemporary criticism, and composed libretti for opera composers, including Eugen d'Albert. In addition, he translated the EDDA and published Germanic sagas. In the *Bayreuther Blätter*, he ranted about the supposed decay of the German language due to foreign influence. He warned of the threat and the decline of German culture. He praised German classicism, condemned the literature and art of his time, and rejected the notion of the then popular naturalistic theater. He was also opposed to modern economic liberalism and favored a self-sufficient German agriculture and industry. He was against forced industrialization, modern party pluralism, and a parliamentary democracy. Most of all, he railed against the press, which he claimed was dominated by the JEWS. He was particularly interested in theological questions, and in turn the link between RELIGION and (Wagner's) art. He argued the case for a fundamental reform of German Protestantism, which he wanted to reduce to a few articles of faith, and he believed that Christianity corresponded perfectly to the Germanic character of the Germans. However, he thought it must first evolve into a "true" Christianity, by which he meant adapted to the racial character of the Germans. Therefore, his primary goal was the "Germanization" of Christianity – in other words, the removal of all Jewish elements from the Old Testament, and the establishment of an "Aryan Jesus." This was to be achieved through German art. In his opinion, its pinnacle was to be found in the work of Richard Wagner, who united religion and art, and formed a new worldview that he hoped would lead to a fundamental social and cultural REGENERATION through its connection to the obscured ethnic roots of the German people (*VOLK*).

Wolzogen was an effective and tenacious, though in person somewhat modest, propagandist of the Bayreuth AESTHETICS and MUSIC DRAMAS. Like Chamberlain, he also interpreted Wagner's ideas and works in the sense of an ethnic-nationalist ethos and, thus, effaced all memory of Wagner's revolutionary, anarchistic, and radical democratic past that was central to his participation in YOUNG GERMANY and the REVOLUTIONS of 1848/9. On the other hand, he should be credited for convincing Cosima to continue hosting the festivals after Wagner's death.

In May 1922, both he and Chamberlain were made honorary citizens of Bayreuth. Before and after World War I, he belonged to various nationalist organizations, including the radical right-wing "Werdandi" Association. In 1928, he was one of the first members of the ANTI-SEMITIC "Kampfbund für deutsche Kultur" (Fighting League for German Culture) founded by Alfred Rosenberg. Long before 1933, he had supported the ideas of NATIONAL SOCIALISM in the *Bayreuther Blätter*, and he had celebrated HITLER as the embodiment of the German spirit. After his death, the *Bayreuther Blätter* ceased publication, and he was lauded by ideologically kindred spirits as the "guardian" of Bayreuth.

See also *LEITMOTIV* GUIDES

Udo Bermbach, *Richard Wagner in Deutschland: Rezeption – Verfälschungen* (Stuttgart: Metzler, 2011).

Annette Hein, *"Es ist viel 'Hitler' in Wagner": Rassismus und antisemitische Deutschtumsideologie in den Bayreuther Blättern (1878–1938)* (Tübingen: Niemeyer, 1996).

Hans von Wolzogen, *Wagner und seine Werke: Ausgewählte Aufsätze* (Regensburg, 1924).

　Wagneriana: Gesammelte Aufsätze über R. Wagner's Werke vom "Ring" bis zum Gral (Leipzig, 1888).

　Zum deutschen Glauben: Die Religion des Mitleids und dreizehn andere Vorträge (Leipzig, 1913).

Women. "In the mingling of races the blood of the nobler males is ruined by the baser female element: the masculine element suffers, character founders, whilst the women gain as much as to take the men's place," wrote Wagner (BB/E 23 October 1881), thus combining racism with anti-feminism. COSIMA WAGNER'S DIARY entries, in which she jotted down Richard's remarks, contain many disparaging comments about educated women ("bluestockings"), although she herself was highly educated. He saw the relationship between the sexes as biologically fixed, similar to his opinion of the JEWS as biologically deficient. Yet he could not exist without an EROTIC relationship. A compassionate woman or an erotic attraction would stimulate his mood and enable him to compose; Mathilde WESENDONCK was such a stimulus. He fell in LOVE with her in 1852 and her admiration and compassion inspired him in the composition of TRISTAN UND ISOLDE two years later. In his first version of the opera, he saw the protagonists as a classical love couple. Around 1856, he felt thwarted in his love for Mathilde, and changed this version, placing anguish over unfulfilled desire into the center of his concept. His first draft of the love scene between SIEGMUND and SIEGLINDE in Act I of Die WALKÜRE contains a number of abbreviated messages to her (e.g., "I.l.d.i.m" = "Ich liebe dich immer mehr" [I love you more and more]). After his departure from ZURICH, he saw himself in the role of HANS SACHS in Die MEISTERSINGER VON NÜRNBERG, where Sachs renounces his love for EVA.

In his operas, he repeatedly depicts erotic attraction as being inescapable. By attributing a strong power of love to women, he places the erotic element above ethical standards: breaking the rules of convention (e.g., incest) is permitted, as LOVE overrides all man-made laws. Perhaps Wagner wanted to legitimize his own transgressions; after all, he fathered three children with a married woman (COSIMA von Bülow), strove to seduce married women (Jessie LAUSSOT, Mathilde Wesendonck), and bade an unmarried young woman (Mathilde MAIER) live with him, though still married to MINNA. Although he often conveyed male-dominated, bourgeois attitudes of his times and was convinced that women were inferior to men, he created remarkable female characters such as Sieglinde (RING cycle), who has the guts to leave her violent and aggressive husband, HUNDING, a character portrayed negatively. Wagner openly sympathizes with individuals who truly love one another and disobey convention. This was a courageous step at the time. BRÜNNHILDE, the most complex and dynamic character of all women roles, defies her father and is later raped: an act of violence that bears no trace of voyeurism and is not in the least sexual, but is composed with sympathy for her.

Nevertheless, for Wagner, women are sexual by nature. Thus he created the ambivalence of the "good" woman who was desirous of man (even TANNHÄUSER's ELISABETH mentions her erotic desire) but could also create fear and aggression. The musical description of sexuality, which Wagner conveys convincingly in Tannhäuser and in Tristan und Isolde (ISOLDE's "LIEBESTOD" with its musically orgasmic climax), was taboo in the nineteenth century, similar to incest. From a feminist perspective, this erotic power which Wagner gives women can be interpreted as a positive force. On the other hand, he stripped women of independence and autonomy by idealizing pure women who defer to men and bring them salvation. Contrary to Siegfried, who builds his identity as hero and never suffers throughout the Ring, Brünnhilde is burdened with conflicts, loses her identity as a Valkyrie, and must begin a new life. Wagner often describes women as helpless creatures, possessing no power (ERDA, the Rhinemaidens, and the Norns of the Ring cycle are all a part of nature and therefore can only warn others, having no power to decide for themselves). EVA in Die Meistersinger von Nürnberg functions as WALTHER VON STOLZING's muse. ORTRUD's evil character is marked by diminished sevenths, string tremolos, stark dissonances, stopped brass timbre, tritones, large intervals, and the use of deep instruments. The Flower Maidens in the magic garden (PARSIFAL) resemble the nymphs and sirens of Venus's underworld (*Tannhäuser*) and are characterized by serpentine-like chromaticism. These examples show how Wagner adhered to the normative code of the nineteenth-century male-dominated society, while at the same time transgressing the moral rules of his time. This might explain why contemporary women such as Clara Schumann, Elisabeth von Herzogenberg, and Luise Büchner found his figures indecent and indiscreet or, like Minna Wagner, criticized his opera *Tristan and Isolde*, while others like Marie Lipsius were thrilled.

In his last opera, *Parsifal*, KUNDRY is shown as a sexually empowered person, who endangers the messianic PARSIFAL, and in Act III she is condemned to silence and can only worship him contritely. The religious society of men symbolizes spirituality, from which she is expelled. It seems that Wagner, who – contrary to composers like BEETHOVEN or BRAHMS – was dependent on women all his life, now wanted to punish them for his obsession. Kundry's death, symbolizing the demise of female sexuality, can be seen as a warning to all women who try to force men into dependency. In the same vein, Ortrud's downfall is her punishment for dominating her husband.

EVA RIEGER

See also GENDER

Woolf, (Adeline) Virginia (née Stephen) (b. London, 25 Jan. 1882; d. Rodmell [Sussex], 28 March 1941), English novelist and prose writer. Woolf attended numerous performances of Wagner's work in LONDON between 1898 and the 1920s, recalling she had spent her "youth" in Covent Garden; from 1925, she listened to recorded music almost daily. In 1909, she heard *PARSIFAL* twice at BAYREUTH and published the essays "The Opera" and "Impressions at Bayreuth." Her novels allude to a wide variety of music and composers, including Wagner; his dramas also shaped some of her numerous formal developments – such as her use of narrative perspective – characteristic of literary MODERNISM. Ethel Smyth was a close friend from the 1930s. Woolf's Hogarth Press published musical criticism and memoirs, and she stated in 1940, "I always think of my books as music before I write them." Explicit references to Wagner are more frequent in the earlier novels (*The Voyage Out* [1915], *Jacob's Room* [1922], and *Mrs Dalloway* [1925]), where they inform her sociopolitical vision, particularly her representations of GENDER, national and class politics, ANTI-SEMITISM, and war. Arguably, the plot, language, and formal characteristics of *The Voyage Out* are also pervasively indebted to *TRISTAN UND ISOLDE*, which the novel critiques. Revulsion from the *RING* in 1913 marks an apparent break, but the late novels are also formally indebted to Wagner, as the *LEITMOTIVE* and poetic prose of *The Waves* (1931) exemplify. Overt allusions, such as those in *The Years* (1937), which associate Wagner with fascism and anti-Semitism, did become more barbed. Many contemporaries noted the "musical" characteristics of her prose. EMMA SUTTON

See also WAGNER IN LITERATURE

John Louis DiGaetani, *Richard Wagner and the Modern British Novel* (Rutherford, NJ: Fairleigh Dickinson University Press, 1978).

Raymond Furness, *Wagner and Literature* (New York: St. Martin's Press, 1982).

Emma Sutton, *Virginia Woolf and Classical Music* (Edinburgh University Press, 2013).

Works, lesser musical. Wagner was happy to admit to the less-than-stellar parts of his musical output. He insisted that even his monumental choral work *Das Liebesmahl der Apostel* (WWV 69) should be placed "in the category of occasional works" (ML/E 258). And he doubtless saw other large-scale pieces such as the *KAISERMARSCH* (WWV 104) the same way. When he received the generous commission from the publisher C. F. Peters to write it in celebration of the German victory in the FRANCO-PRUSSIAN WAR (1870–1), COSIMA remarked in her diaries "it's only a pity that Richard absolutely cannot write to order" (CWD 30 December 1870). And on composing the *Grosser Festmarsch* (WWV 110), written for the one hundredth anniversary of the Declaration of Independence in the UNITED STATES OF AMERICA in 1876, Wagner told Cosima he could "think of nothing but the 5,000 dollars" he had demanded for it (CWD 14 February 1876).

Wagner wrote two other marches not "to order" for occasions closer to his heart that are by no means entirely trivial: the solemn music for the final stage of the transport of Carl Maria von WEBER's ashes from LONDON to DRESDEN in 1844 (*Trauermusik* WWV 73) and the march of homage to the young King LUDWIG II after the momentous invitation to MUNICH in 1864 (*HULDIGUNGSMARSCH* WWV 97). Not all Wagner's minor music took the form of a heavy-hearted concession to circumstances. Nor is that music usually less than professionally made (the charge of dilettantism leveled against Wagner by NIETZSCHE and others has always seemed unjust) or indeed as unoriginal as some of his critics have gleefully maintained.

Still, try as the well-disposed critic might to highlight striking moments in the early *Columbus* Overture (WWV 37), for example, or the Sonata in A♭ major for piano (WWV 85) he wrote for Mathilde WESENDONCK in 1853, there is no getting around the fact that for the most part Wagner was not an outstanding writer of purely instrumental music. The wonderfully evocative *SIEGFRIED IDYLL* (WWV 103) is the famous exception that proves the rule. But not even Wagner's next best instrumental work, *Eine FAUST-OUVERTÜRE* (WWV 59), has found as robust a place in the repertoire. From another five (early) piano sonatas (WWV 2, 5, 16, 21, 26) and ten more OVERTURES (WWV 10, 11, 12, 14, 17, 20, 24, 27, 39, 42), some of which are no longer extant, a picture quickly emerges of an assiduous worker wanting desperately to be an instrumental composer on a par with BEETHOVEN. The young Wagner even attempted a string quartet (WWV 4, no longer extant); and there still exist two early symphonies in C major (WWV 29) and E major (WWV 35, unfinished), as well as complete and somewhat underwhelming solo piano transcriptions of Joseph Haydn's Symphony No. 103 in E♭ major (WWV 18) and Beethoven's Ninth Symphony (WWV 9) to underscore the point.

The striking fissure in Wagner's musical output between its "lesser" and truly great components, however, is not just an issue of frustrated ambition. Selmar Bagge, the editor of the *Deutsche Musik-Zeitung* in Vienna, printed bits of the early piano sonata in B♭ major (WWV 21) anonymously in 1862 and invited his readers to solve the "riddle" of who had written them. Wagner had every reason to be annoyed when in the next issue it was revealed that the author of the work – a robustly ingenious imitation of Beethoven he had written at the age of 19, but an imitation nonetheless – was none other than the composer of

TRISTAN UND ISOLDE. At the time in rehearsal in Vienna, *Tristan* was already causing controversy among traditionalists, including Bagge, who with his "riddle" backhandedly reinforced the view that Wagner was no second Beethoven, nor even a competent composer. The concerted critical attack on the composer of *Tristan*, indeed, was one reason why, after more than seventy rehearsals, its projected premiere never took place.

Using the "lesser" works to bludgeon Wagner has always been a blood sport among conservative critics, who prompted him in his lifetime on more than one occasion to rewrite history in response. In the aftermath of Bagge's critical prank, the B♭ major piano sonata suddenly became a "feeble" exercise demanded by his teacher modeled on a "child-like" sonata by Ignaz Pleyel (ML/E 56). But no sonata by Pleyel even remotely resembles it. Not only did the 19-year-old Wagner proudly call it his "Op. 1," it was also deemed a good enough sonata in the post-Beethoven tradition in 1832 for BREITKOPF & HÄRTEL to publish it. The first of Wagner's works to appear in print, it found little resonance and the publishers eventually destroyed the plates. But thirty years later, after the appearance of Bagge's articles, they decided without consulting Wagner to print an entirely new edition to meet – ironically – a sudden rush of interest.

The problem of his "other" composing self made prematurely public was if anything still more acute in the case of the smaller vocal music pieces he wrote in the first part of his career. Up to and including his first PARIS sojourn (1839–42) there are nineteen arias and *Lieder*, or sets of *Lieder*, to French, Italian, and German texts (WWV 3, 7, 8, 15, 28, 30, 43, 45, 50–58, 60, 61), as well as arrangements and complete vocal scores of, among other things, Donizetti's opera *La Favorite* and HALÉVY's *La Reine du Chypre*. All of it is competent, some of it charming, and some of it was immediately published, making it not quite so easy to interpret as a necessary sacrifice to corrupt practice, one of the key strategies of Wagner's autobiographical writings. In truth, the works show a composer enthusiastic about many different kinds of music, including the chorus "Descendons gaiment la courtille" he wrote for a Parisian vaudeville (WWV 65). For the mature composer, however, a work like this stood on the side of a philosophical divide that belonged to a time when music was formally constrained by regressive social interests, particularly in France. Surviving it was a rite of passage leading to a new age of bold expression, in which music could no longer remain the way it was. The "lesser" works were not just about competence, failed ambition, or even quality for Wagner, but also about what could never really belong to this other side of the divide.   JOHN DEATHRIDGE

Works, lesser prose. Wagner published so many words about himself – more than any composer in the history of music – that it is hard at first to distinguish his lesser prose works from his major ones. The task is made slightly easier, perhaps, if we start with an overview.

In the most complete edition in sixteen volumes (*Sämtliche Schriften und Dichtungen*, 1912–14) the prose writings encompass about 4,000 printed pages (not including the texts of the stage works) and belong to journalistic and literary genres ranging from brief press statements to full-length books. At the latest count, including texts with pseudonyms (Wagner preferred either the quasi-liberal or pugilistic varieties such as "K. Freigedank" [K. Freethought] or "Wilhelm Drach" [William Dragon]) and a few still in need of further investigation that may or may not be authentic, there are 229 items in all. Setting aside issues of origin, it can safely be said that roughly a third are major theoretical or autobiographical texts, while the rest consist of small essays, novellas, commentaries in journals, speeches, open letters, reviews, reports, PROGRAM NOTES, advertisements, forewords, brief and not-so-brief personal statements, elucidations of issues of public interest, fragments, aphorisms, and writings by others authorized or commissioned by Wagner.

It would be nice to think that the main purpose of the prose writings is principally exegetical and theoretical. They raise substantive issues about the relation of music and theater to PHILOSOPHY, POLITICS, MYTH, and society-at-large. But they are far from being a systematic examination of cultural problems and their solution, even though at times – in the so-called ZURICH writings, for instance (1849–57) – the major and lesser writings seem to exude a missionary zeal devoted to the utopian prospect of root-and-branch reform in about equal measure. In this sense, there is little difference between a major theoretical work such as OPER UND DRAMA (Opera and Drama, 1851) that posits a utopian future for music theater over many pages in copious detail and the two-page plea *Über die musikalische Direktion der Züricher Oper* (On the Musical Direction of the [Zurich] Opera, 1850) published in a Swiss newspaper asking the public to support Wagner's recommendation of his protégé Hans von BÜLOW as the new musical director of the Zurich Aktientheater. In their different ways, the one was just as important to Wagner as the other.

The impression given by the "lesser" prose work in particular is that they came into being in a refreshingly unsystematic way. In her diaries, Cosima reports Wagner's opinion that "he had never been a writer in the literal sense of the word" (24 October 1869), suggesting that he saw his prose writings as a means to an end rather than a body of work with its own intrinsic value. Everything was geared towards "a record of the life's work of an artist" whose life was the "*true music*" (foreword to *Gesammelte Schriften und Dichtungen*, 1871–83, emphasis RW) during which the artist had grasped any opportunity that had come his way to express his thoughts in print about art, RELIGION, philosophy, politics, and whatever else that happened to suit the occasion at hand. The point was that even minor statements like KUNST UND KLIMA (Art and Climate, 1850), in which – absurdly – he blamed the ills of modernity on the indifference of "civilization" to the weather, were intended to enhance his stage works rather than be read for their own sake. This explains why Wagner insisted on introducing the libretti of his operas and dramas into his collected writings when these were already easily available elsewhere. And it also points to the (for some unpalatable) truth that everything he wrote, the nondescript and the reactionary, as well as the brilliant and insightful, was meant to be in the cause of his art.

To see Wagner only as an "occasional" author, however, is to do him an injustice. This is especially true of the best of the so-called lesser writings that are normally without the groaning theoretical structures in the German idealist tradition that often lend the "major" prose works a sense of the unintentionally grotesque. On a smaller scale, Wagner galvanized his first-rate critical instincts into more coherent – and precise – narratives that still count as beacons of light in nineteenth-century writings about music. *Über die Ouvertüre* (On the Overture) first published in French in 1841 and *ÜBER DIE ANWENDUNG DER MUSIK AUF DAS DRAMA* (On the Application of Music to Drama, 1879), for instance, are early and late essays of modest dimensions that raise pertinent theoretical questions about instrumental music and its relation to dramatic structures that not only preoccupied Wagner for most of his life, but also relate to issues about the role of symphonic music and its relation to drama and media in the twenty-first century.

The smaller writings are also a goldmine of insights into nineteenth-century PERFORMANCE PRACTICE. Starting with a trenchant review of BELLINI's *Norma* (1837) discovered by Friedrich Lippmann in 1973, Wagner began a series of remarkable critical accounts of singing, acting, production, conducting, and the general management of theaters in Germany, Austria, and France that are still salutary reminders of the perennial difficulties facing the financing and social role of live music theater. Examples include an incisive forty-page analysis of theater reform that not surprisingly fell on deaf ears in Saxony immediately prior to the DRESDEN UPRISING (*Entwurf zur Organisation eines deutschen Nationaltheaters für das Königreich Sachsen* [Plan for the Organization of a German National Theater for the Kingdom of Saxony, 1848]) and another of more than twenty pages directed at the authorities in Vienna (*Das Wiener Hofoperntheater* [The Vienna Court Theater, 1863]) after he had signally failed in that city to secure the world premiere of *TRISTAN UND ISOLDE*.

Wagner's most critical comments about production standards were written after travelling through Germany to visit selected theaters in search of singers for his BAYREUTH project (*Ein Einblick in das heutige deutsche Opernwesen* [A Look at German Opera Today, 1872, pub. 1873]). After reading this gloomy diagnosis, it is easy to understand why he took so much trouble to write detailed essays about the performance of his own works, one of the most illuminating of which is *Über die Aufführung des "Tannhaüser"* (On performing *Tannhäuser*, 1852). Here one can sense Wagner in action doing the thing he liked best, which was to create and produce opera at the most exacting level possible (see WAGNER AS STAGE DIRECTOR). NIETZSCHE once observed that Wagner wrote as he spoke. Indeed, the shorter prose works often resemble the best moments in his letters – among the most spontaneous and lucid documents he ever penned – where he is strikingly eloquent and persuasive in explaining the reasons for his bold actions. The disconcerting unevenness of Wagner's major writings has often been in dispute. In the finest of his smaller prose works, however, the sensitive reader will always have the feeling that less is more.

JOHN DEATHRIDGE

See also Appendix 5: Prose works

Works, lost. As many as twenty-three lost works by Wagner are recorded in writings, diaries, and letters, of which sixteen were written while he was still a teenager. Wagner mentions four lost works dating to 1829: Sonata in D minor for piano (WWV 2), Aria (WWV 3), String Quartet in D major (WWV 4), and Sonata in

F minor for piano (WWV 5). The existence of the "aria" is doubtful, given that the work is absent from his early diary *Die rote Brieftasche*, appearing only in the later, more "literary" autobiographical writings AUTOBIOGRAPHISCHE SKIZZE (Autobiographical Sketch, 1842/3) and MEIN LEBEN (My Life, 1865–81). Wagner may have been at pains to obscure the fact that his earliest studies in composition were limited to instrumental genres, preferring to see himself as a fully fledged music-dramatist from the start. In spring 1830, Wagner sketched his first opera *Die Schäferoper* (WWV 6), conceived as a prelude to GOETHE's *Die Laune des Verliebten*. In *Mein Leben*, Wagner writes that he composed "a scene for three female voices" with a closing "aria for tenor," though his claim that he wrote these "without the least knowledge of instrumental writing" is probably exaggerated. He also mentions one Aria for Soprano and Orchestra (WWV 8), written shortly after he had acquired and studied a score of MOZART's *Don Giovanni*. Whether this "aria" belonged to *Schäferoper*, or was an independent work, is unclear.

From summer 1830 to spring 1831, Wagner wrote various orchestral works which are now lost, if they were ever completed – Overture in B♭, "Paukenschlag" (WWV 10); Political Overture (WWV 11); Overture in C (in ⁶⁄₈ time) (WWV 14); Overture in E♭ (WWV 17) – as well as a Sonata in B♭ for piano, four hands (WWV 16). His incidental music to the plays *König Enzio* (WWV 24B) and Theodore APEL's historical drama *Columbus* (WWV 37B) – written in winters 1831–2 and 1834–5 respectively – do not survive, although the overtures to both are extant. With these two exceptions, Wagner's lost works from summer 1831 onwards are less original works in their own right than arrangements of other composers' works, or "occasional" pieces. These arrangements include: Haydn's Symphony in E♭ No. 103 for two-hand piano (WWV 18), a cavatina from BELLINI's opera *Il pirata* (WWV 34), a reorchestration of Spontini's *La Vestale* (WWV 74), operatic numbers for *cornet à pistons* produced in autumn 1840 for publisher Maurice SCHLESINGER (WWV 62A), and an arrangement made in early November 1850 of *Don Giovanni* for performance in ZURICH (WWV 83). Examples of Wagner's lost "occasional" pieces are *Gesang am Grabe* (WWV 51) and various substitute or inserted numbers intended for a particular performance, such as Wagner's bass aria (prayer) for Joseph Weigl's lyric opera *Die Schweizerfamilie* (WWV 45).

The speculative identification of "lost" works has been a contentious issue. Gerald Abraham's thesis that the Scene and Aria for Soprano and Orchestra (WWV 28) was the first version of the Ada aria "Ich sollte ihm entsagen" from Act II of *Die FEEN* cannot be proven (Deathridge); yet, as Egon Voss has argued, Wagner's "lost" Overture to SCHILLER's *Die Braut von Messina* (WWV 12) may be identical with the fragmentary Orchestral work in E minor (WWV 13). Of all Wagner's lost works, the one he valued most was *Glockentöne* (WWV 30), a song for voice and piano setting words by Theodore Apel in the manner of BEETHOVEN's *An die ferne Geliebte*, Op. 98.

JEREMY COLEMAN

See also WAGNER AS COMPOSER; *WAGNER WERK-VERZEICHNIS*; Appendix 6: Musical works

Gerald Abraham, "A Lost Wagner Aria," *The Musical Times* 110.1519 (1969): 927–9.

John Deathridge, "Eine verschollene Wagner-Arie?," *Melos / Neue Zeitschrift für Musik* 4 (1978): 208–14.

Egon Voss, "Wagners fragmentarisches Orchesterwerk in e-Moll: Die früheste erhaltene Komposition?," *Die Musikforschung* 23 (1970): 50–4.

Wotan (bass-baritone; character in *Der RING DES NIBELUNGEN*, with appearances in *Das RHEINGOLD*, *Die WALKÜRE*, and *SIEGFRIED*. King/father of the gods; husband of FRICKA; father of SIEGMUND, SIEGLINDE, and, via ERDA, the Valkyries [including BRÜNNHILDE]; Grandfather of SIEGFRIED). Of all the *Ring*'s vast cast of characters, Wotan and his daughter Brünnhilde have perhaps the most minutely charted and most psychologically dynamic trajectories. But where Brünnhilde's trajectory makes her unique, Wotan has invited interpretation in terms of certain (and often peculiarly modern) types: *paterfamilias*, bankrupt entrepreneur, resigned politician. He is the proud man of action who transforms into a melancholic thinker; the guardian of treaties who gradually comes to understand the limits of the order he has created; the bourgeois patriarch who seeks to cure all his problems through procreation and acquisition, but arrives at a deep pessimism. More recent interpretations tend to pick up on the profound ambivalence of Wagner's characterization, over older conceptions of Wotan as a heroic "Germanic" god.

Just how significant the meaning of Wotan's transformation must have been to Wagner becomes visible when one considers how much time is allotted to plumbing its depths: when Wotan spends much of *Die Walküre* Act II in thought, when he awakens Erda in *Siegfried* just to inform her that he no longer fears the downfall of the gods. While the original conception of the *Ring* belonged to Siegfried, the cycle as it grew became increasingly Wotan's story. Given Wagner's own transformation following the events of 1849 and his encounter with the philosophy of SCHOPENHAUER, it is impossible not to read Wotan's sentimental education in the course of the *Ring* as an at once self-aggrandizing and chillingly detached self-portrait.

That is not to say that Wagner invented either Wotan or his trajectory out of whole cloth. But the idea that his Wotan would not just perish in *Ragnarök* (*Götterdämmerung*), but would actually precipitate the event by his own short-sightedness, was part of Wagner's design from at least the draft entitled *Der Nibelungen-Mythus* (1848). It speaks to the change in Wagner's conception of Wotan over time that initially Wotan's end was to come in *Ragnarök* as one casualty among many. In the cycle as it stands today, Wagner has him set his own palace on fire – Wotan is the author of his own demise. His resignation and fear when faced with *Götterdämmerung*, not the event itself, undoes him. Wotan's story, the more integral it became to the plot of the *Ring*, no longer depended on outside antagonists, and turned them into mere catalysts for the god's complex psychology.

Even though divergences from the source material were early and significant, Wagner nevertheless drew on NORDIC MYTHOLOGY for a host of details. From them Wagner took the idea of Wotan's sacrifice of an eye, as well as the idea that Wotan appears to mortals as a wanderer. Wotan's plan to fend off Alberich's assault by gathering fallen heroes in Valhalla is taken from Snorri Sturluson's *Prose EDDA*, where Wotan gathers his forces in this way in preparation for *Ragnarök*. The Norse sagas also inspired Wotan's use of ravens and wolves as messengers.

Most centrally, the origin of his dominion, outlined by the three Norns in the prologue to *Götterdämmerung*, is a more philosophically nuanced version of accounts presented in the Nordic sagas: The spear fashioned from the *Weltesche*, carved with a record of all contracts, comes to represent Wotan's powerful yet ultimately tenuous hold over forces more primordial than he (embodied particularly by the goddess Erda), and the internally contradictory sources of his power. At the same time, Wagner's Wotan owes a pronounced debt to another father of gods, Zeus. Especially the Wotan of *Die Walküre*, hectored by his wife for compulsively siring children out of wedlock, seems closer to the legends of Greek antiquity than to Norse mythology.

Wotan is introduced into the *Ring* through the majestic Valhalla music (see Appendix 4: *Leitmotive* in *Der Ring des Nibelungen*; CWE 4) at the beginning of Scene 2 of *Rheingold* – the eight new WAGNER TUBAS and the other brass instruments opening up the visual spectacle of Valhalla with an orchestral sound that, at the *Ring*'s premiere in 1876, had never been heard before. The music is appropriate for this first appearance, because his role requires a rich baritone voice of rare power and a commanding dramatic and musical presence. Although he has no *Leitmotiv* of his own, many motives are associated with him throughout the *Ring*: the Valhalla motive (CWE 4) soon comes to represent Wotan himself, as well as his castle; and the descending scale in the bass register associated with his treaties and contracts (CWE 5) is ubiquitous. Another central motive in this regard is the trumpet melody that appears near the end of *Das Rheingold* (Scene 4, mm. 3779–80, CWE 12), precisely at the moment when Wotan suddenly seems to have an idea of how to right his wrongs. How that is to happen is left unstated in *Das Rheingold*, but in *Die Walküre* it becomes clear that he hopes to do so through Siegmund and Sieglinde – and implicitly, given the disaster that befalls these twins, through Siegfried. His hopes are symbolized by the Sword, which is dramatically foregrounded when Siegmund discovers it in his hour of need in *Die Walküre*, Act 1, Scene 3 (mm. 849–52). The trumpet *Leitmotiv* of the "grand idea" from the end of *Rheingold* resurfaces again, for the first time, at precisely this moment, and for the remainder of the cycle it is associated with the Sword Nothung, and, more broadly, with Wotan's plans to redeem the world.

More than any character in the *Ring* except Brünnhilde, Wotan gains in musical depth as the cycle proceeds. His musical growth goes hand in hand with his dramatic growth across the cycle. In *Rheingold*, his music is stately and noble, but this quality ensues in part from the fact that he does little but sing arpeggios, albeit arpeggios of extraordinary majesty. But by Act 11, Scene 2 of *Die Walküre*, he is a tragic figure capable of the longest and most wrenching monologue in the entire *Ring*. Then, in *Siegfried*, still with great nobility, he sings himself out of the drama, "rising to the tragic heights of willing his own destruction" (letter to RÖCKEL 25/26 January 1854).

ADRIAN DAUB AND PATRICK MCCRELESS

Würzburg, city in Franconia (northern Bavaria), on the Main river. The seat of an independent prince-bishopric until the end of the Holy Roman Empire, later seat of the Bavarian regional government of lower Franconia. Wagner obtained here his first official (or semi-official) position as répétiteur of the chorus for the town theater, for which his older brother ALBERT had been serving as stage director, actor, and leading tenor for about three years when Richard arrived at the beginning of 1833. He received the modest salary of 10 gulden a month for the duration of the short season. Wagner stayed in Würzburg for almost one year, returning to his home town LEIPZIG on 15 January 1834, having completed the composition of his first opera, *Die Feen,* just one week earlier. (The libretto and composition of *Die Feen* were all undertaken during this sojourn in Würzburg.)

The small theater was ambitious (not to say reckless) in its programming, characteristic of the era, and the repertoire Wagner was involved with included AUBER's *Fra Diavolo,* BEETHOVEN's *Fidelio,* Cherubini's *Les Deux Journées* (as *Der Wasserträger*), Hérold's *Zampa,* Paër's *Camilla,* WEBER's *Der Freischütz,* and even MEYERBEER's recent debut grand opera, *Robert le diable.* During the second season, Wagner also assisted with new productions of Marschner's *Der Vampyr* and *Hans Heiling,* both of which left a mark on the composition of his own Romantic magic-opera, *Die Feen.* The only surviving fragment of his first attempted opera, *Die Hochzeit,* owes its survival to materials prepared for a performance by the local musical society in March 1833. A trio and Ada's grand scene and aria from Act II of *Die Feen* – also previewed by local forces on 12 December 1833 – would be the only music from his first completed opera that Wagner ever had a chance to hear performed (apart from the overture, which he conducted later in MAGDEBURG).

During his time in Würzburg the theater also produced J. L. Deinhardstein's then relatively popular play *Hans Sachs* (adapted as an opera by Lortzing in the 1840s). Ironically, on the day Wagner left town, the theater was putting on a comedy entitled *Richard's Wanderleben,* whose title character went by the incognito "Richard Wanderer" – an "enthusiastic young actor and member of a pathetic travelling troupe," whose parts consisted mostly of quotations from his roles in plays by SHAKESPEARE, SCHILLER, and Kotzebue (Bauer 148–9). Wagner's own life among the theater folk included an affair with a certain Frederike Galvani, a singer with the company, following an earlier liaison with Therese Ringelmann, the daughter of a local grave-digger. Upon leaving Würzburg he would, indeed, continue his own "journeyman" period, moving between Berlin, KÖNIGSBERG, MAGDEBURG, RIGA, and finally PARIS within the space of five years.   THOMAS S. GREY

Oswald Georg Bauer, *Richard Wagner in Würzburg: Der Beginn einer Theatralischer Sendung* (Petersberg: Michael Imhof, 2004).

Young Germany. A group of German writers during the pre-1848 period. Reacted strongly against perceived apolitical and reactionary tendencies in German ROMANTICISM. Several, including Heinrich LAUBE, Karl GUTZKOW, Heinrich HEINE, and Georg HERWEGH, were known personally to Wagner; others include Ludwig Börne, Theodor Mundt, Ludolf Wienbarg, and Georg Büchner. In 1835, the German Confederation proscribed many such writings as injurious to the Christian RELIGION and MORALITY; Laube's subsequent imprisonment made a great impression upon Wagner. According to Heine (*Die romantische Schule*), Young Germans, unlike GOETHE and the Romantics, treated life and literature as one; as for Wagner, this signaled revival of the Hellenic spirit following Christian aberration. Wagner published articles in Laube's LEIPZIG-based *Zeitung für die elegante Welt*, including his *AUTOBIOGRAPHISCHE SKIZZE* (Autobiographical Sketch, 1842/3), where Wagner likens *Das LIEBESVERBOT* to Laube's *Young Europe* in their "victory of free sensualism over puritanical hypocrisy." Young German influence may be traced throughout Wagner's dramatic oeuvre, especially *TANNHÄUSER*.   MARK BERRY

Zukunftsmusik (Music of the Future). Title of essay by Wagner, and pejorative term from the second half of the nineteenth century for the music and the aesthetic movement associated with the compositional innovations of Wagner and LISZT. The first use of the concept as an unfavorable epithet for progressive music has been traditionally ascribed to an 1847 dismissal of BERLIOZ by Berlin music critic Karl GAILLARD ("Musik der Zukunft"). Wagner's 1850 publication *Das KUNSTWERK DER ZUKUNFT* (The Artwork of the Future) invited the neologism in application to his new concepts (see ML 480; ML/E 467–8). In 1852, J. C. Lobe's *Musikalische Briefe* applied the term *Zukunftsmusik* to the new direction in music. As a designation for music that would only find its audience in the future, the term found quick dissemination among conservative music critics before 1855, most notably Ludwig Bischoff in the *Niederrheinische Musik-Zeitung*. Most members of the NEW GERMAN SCHOOL avoided using the term, given that pejorative interpretation. Wagner himself took up the designation in his 1860 essay "Zukunftsmusik," which recapitulates his earlier thoughts (in light of his autobiography and with a new emphasis on BEETHOVEN) and sees their fulfillment in the MUSIC DRAMA and the BAYREUTH FESTIVAL.   JAMES DEAVILLE

Francis Hueffer, *Richard Wagner and the Music of the Future: History and Aesthetics* (London: Chapman and Hall, 1874).

Zumpe, Hermann (b. Taubenheim, 9 April 1850; d. Munich, 4 Sep. 1903), composer and conductor. Zumpe began his career as a schoolmaster before joining Wagner in BAYREUTH in 1873 as a member of the so-called NIBELUNGEN CHANCELLERY. He subsequently enjoyed considerable success as a conductor of Wagner's works, and held a number of important appointments. In 1891, he became Court Kapellmeister in Stuttgart and, in 1898, visited LONDON to direct Wagner performances at Covent Garden. In 1900, Zumpe achieved the high point of his career with his appointment as Court Kapellmeister in MUNICH, where he directed a notable series of Wagner performances at the Prinzregententheater that had been modeled on the Bayreuth FESTIVAL THEATER. His stage works include operas and operettas, which enjoyed some success in his lifetime.   ROGER ALLEN

Zurich. A customs post in Roman times, later an important religious and trading center on Europe's north-south axis, its population in 1850 was 17,000 (including nearly 2,000 foreigners) with a further 33,000 (including 1,300 foreigners) living in the greater conurbation outside the old city boundaries.

After the Reformation its music life shifted into private societies that in 1812 merged into one, the Allgemeine Musikgesellschaft (AMG), with responsibility for the city's orchestral concerts. The first dominant figure of Zurich's music scene was the pedagogue and publisher Hans Georg Nägeli (1773–1836). A concert hall opened in 1806, but theater was banned for religious reasons until the privately run city theater opened in 1834 (Wagner was reputedly offered the post of music director but was denied permission to travel by the Leipzig authorities [letter to ROSALIE on 11 December 1833]). Zurich's liberal politicians played a major role in setting up the new Swiss federal state in 1848, foremost among them Alfred Escher (1819–82), Zurich city president, venture capitalist, and friend of Jakob SULZER.

On the run after the failed DRESDEN UPRISING, Wagner arrived in Zurich on 28 May 1849, having traveled by boat from Lindau (Germany) to Rorschach (Switzerland) and thence by coach via St. Gallen and Winterthur. He sought out Alexander Müller, a friend from his WÜRZBURG days, who brought him together with the Cantonal Secretaries Jakob Sulzer and Franz Hagenbuch. They issued him a passport to allow him to continue to PARIS. He returned to Zurich in July and was joined in September by his wife, MINNA, stepdaughter Natalie PLANER, and their PETS. They moved into an apartment on the Zeltweg owned by Clementine Stockar-Escher (Alfred Escher's sister), who later painted portraits of Wagner and Minna. His Zurich circle of friends centered on the "Trinity" of Wilhelm BAUMGARTNER, Sulzer, and the newspaper editor Bernhard Spyri (husband of Johanna, later the author of *Heidi*).

Over the next two years Wagner wrote several of his most important tracts, *Die KUNST UND DIE REVOLUTION* (Art and Revolution, 1849), *Das KUNSTWERK DER ZUKUNFT* (The Artwork of the Future, 1849/50), *Das JUDENTUM IN DER MUSIK* (Jewishness in Music, 1850), *Eine MITTEILUNG AN MEINE FREUNDE* (A Communication to My Friends, 1851), and *OPER UND DRAMA* (Opera and Drama, 1851). At LISZT's prompting, he began CONDUCTING the orchestra of the AMG in January 1850 and, over the next five years, he expanded its forces, introduced rigorous rehearsal planning, wrote regular PROGRAM NOTES for advance publication in Spyri's *Eidgenössische Zeitung*, made BEETHOVEN'S music the core repertoire, and essentially paved the way for the ensemble's transformation into the professional Zurich Tonhalle Orchestra a decade after he left (see WAGNER AS CONDUCTOR). Wagner also conducted as a guest in the local theater from autumn 1850 onwards and arranged for Hans von BÜLOW and Karl RITTER to be appointed to their first conducting posts. Beginning with *Ein THEATER IN ZÜRICH* (A Theater in Zurich, 1851) he made a series of proposals to improve the city's artistic life.

As the biggest city in neutral, democratic Switzerland, Zurich was a place of refuge for foreign intellectuals. Here, Wagner mixed with other emigrants such as the architect Gottfried SEMPER, the poet Georg HERWEGH, the aesthetician Friedrich Theodor Vischer, and the literary historian Francesco De Sanctis, as well as with prominent locals such as the writer Gottfried Keller. Zurich's proximity to assorted spas and to the HIKING trails of the Alps also made it attractive. Wagner's decision to settle there was consolidated by the prospect of more permanent financial support after his acquaintance with the

WESENDONCKS in early 1852. Friends from Germany also visited him, such as Franz Liszt and Theodor UHLIG.

Stimulated in part by conversations with the local Old Norse expert Ludwig Ettmüller, Wagner wrote the libretti for Der RING DES NIBELUNGEN in 1850–1, published them at the beginning of 1853, and gave public readings of them in the Hotel Baur au Lac in February 1853. Emboldened by his success and with financial guarantees from Otto Wesendonck and others, Wagner now organized a festival of operatic excerpts from RIENZI to LOHENGRIN in the city theater the following May. He engaged musicians from all over Switzerland and southern Germany, wrote program notes, designed an acoustic shell for the stage, organized the publicity, and introduced "patronage certificates" to raise money. This was in effect a pre-run of what he would later do in BAYREUTH. Some two hundred musicians and singers took part, and the sell-out concert was given three times: on 18, 20, and 22 May 1853. However, this immense success served to mark the limit of Zurich's musical ambitions, not (as Wagner had hoped) the beginning of them. His latest proposals to overhaul the city's music scene were rejected by the AMG in September 1853. He continued to conduct in Zurich for another two years – most notably a production of TANNHÄUSER in 1855 – but his increasing frustration with the local scene now coincided with a refocusing of his attention on composition. He began the music for the Ring in November 1853, completing Das RHEIN-GOLD in 1854 and Die WALKÜRE in March 1856. He gave a private performance of the first act of the latter for the Wesendoncks on 26 April 1856, singing both HUNDING and SIEGMUND. Emilie HEIM sang SIEGLINDE, and they were accompanied by Theodor Kirchner. A repeat performance took place in the Hotel Baur au Lac on 22 October 1856, Liszt's birthday, accompanied by Liszt himself. In April 1857 Wagner moved into the Asyl next to the Wesendonck Villa, where he soon after made his first prose sketch for PARSIFAL. That summer he halted work on SIEGFRIED in order to write TRISTAN UND ISOLDE. He gave the first reading of Tristan's libretto on 18 September 1857 to an audience of his wife, the Wesendoncks, and the visiting honeymooners Hans and COSIMA von Bülow. Wagner's passion for Mathilde Wesendonck led to open conflict with their spouses in April 1858. The ensuing public scandal made Wagner's departure from Zurich inevitable: he left on 19 August 1858. But Wagner maintained contact with his Zurich friends for many years and was planning a visit there on his return from VENICE when he died in early 1883.

It was in Zurich that Wagner wrote his most important theoretical works, where he completed or conceived most of his later operas from Rheingold onwards, where he held the first festival devoted to his works, and first contemplated the erection of his own theater. For the first time he had patrons to pay his debts and no compulsion to take on a full-time job. Most importantly, being cut off from mainstream musical life and from the constraints of institutional infrastructure seems to have unfettered Wagner's imagination and propelled him to conceive his newest works on a vast, near-utopian scale. CHRIS WALTON

Gordon A. Craig, The Triumph of Liberalism: Zürich in the Golden Age, 1830–1869 (New York: Collier, 1990).
Chris Walton, Richard Wagner's Zurich (see bibliography).

Appendix 1 Wagner family tree

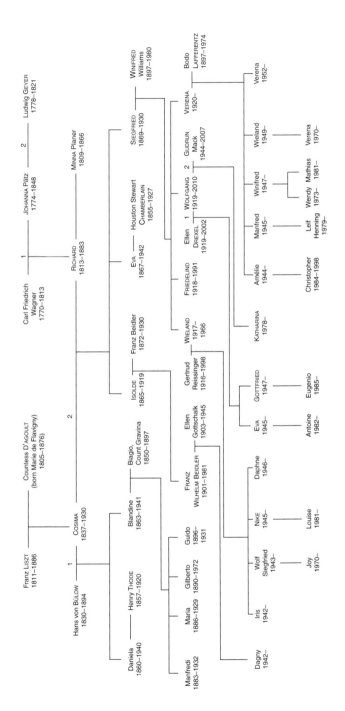

Appendix 2   Chronology

Compiled by Nicholas Vazsonyi

Research assistant: Leigh Buches

For more detail about Wagner's biography, consult the extended entry WAGNER, (WILHELM) RICHARD. For more extensive details on the chronology of "works," consult Appendix 6: Musical works or the entry on the work itself, if applicable. Items in SMALL CAPS denote individual entries in this volume.

Year	Day/month	Life events	Works
1813	22 May	Born in the Brühl, LEIPZIG.	
	16 August	Baptized in the Thomaskirche, Leipzig.	
	22 November	Richard's father, Carl Friedrich, dies.	
1814	February	Wagner's mother, Johanna, visits Ludwig GEYER in DRESDEN; they become engaged.	
	28 August	Johanna marries Ludwig Geyer.	
1820		Enters care of Pastor Christian Wetzel at Possendorf, near Dresden; has some piano lessons.	
1821	30 September	Ludwig Geyer dies.	
1822	December	Enters Dresden Kreuzschule as Richard Geyer.	
1826	December	Family moves to Prague, where sister Rosalie has a post at theater. Wagner stays in Dresden, with the family of some	*Leubald* probably also begun at this time.

(cont.)

Year	Day/month	Life events	Works
		schoolfriends, to continue studies at the Kreuzschule.	
1827	8 April	Confirmation in Kreuzkirche, Dresden.	
	Summer	School trip to Leipzig; stimulated by uncle ADOLF WAGNER.	
	December	Moves to Leipzig, where most of family has now returned.	
1828	21 January	Enters Nicolaischule in Leipzig, now under the name Richard Wagner.	
	Summer	Studies J. B. Logier's *Thorough-Bass*.	Finishes *Leubald*.
	Fall	Begins harmony lessons with Christian Gottlieb MÜLLER.	
1829	Summer		Sonatas in D minor and F minor. Quartet in D major (all LOST).
1830	Easter	Leaves Nicolaischule.	Overtures in B♭ major and C major, and to SCHILLER'S *Braut von Messina* (all LOST).
	16 June	Enrolls at Thomasschule, Leipzig.	
	6 October		Offers piano transcription of Beethoven's Ninth Symphony to Schott PUBLISHERS.
	25 December		B major "Drum-beat Overture" performed in Leipzig under Heinrich DORN.
1831	Early 1831		Composes seven pieces for GOETHE'S *Faust* (voice and piano) and Piano Sonata in B♭ major for four hands. Overture in E♭ (LOST and probably incomplete).

(*cont.*)

Year	Day/month	Life events	Works
	23 February	Matriculates at Leipzig University.	
	Autumn	Studies with new teacher, Christian Theodor WEINLIG.	
1832		Wagner travels to Vienna and Prague.	Overture to Raupach's *König Enzio*.
	April–June		Composes SYMPHONY IN C MAJOR (WWV 29, performed in Prague in November).
	September–October	Brief infatuation with daughter of Count Pachta, on whose estate at Pravonin, near Prague, he stays.	Conceives opera, *Die Hochzeit* (WWV 31), while at Pravonin.
1833	End January/ February	Moves to WÜRZBURG to take up post of chorus master.	Writes text for *Die* FEEN (WWV 32).
1834	6 January		Music completed for *Die Feen*.
	21 January	Returns to Leipzig, where he comes under the influence of Heinrich LAUBE and YOUNG GERMANY.	*Dichtung der Oper "Das Liebesverbot"*; *Pasticcio*.
	March	Wilhelmine SCHRÖDER-DEVRIENT makes guest appearance in Leipzig as Romeo in Bellini's *I Capuleti ed i Montecchi*.	Essay on aesthetics of opera, *Die deutsche Oper*, published in Laube's journal.
	10 June		Inspiration for *Das* LIEBESVERBOT.
	June–July	Holiday in Bohemia with Theodor APEL.	
	End July	Becomes musical director of Heinrich Bethmann's travelling theater company, based in MAGDEBURG.	
	2 August	Debut as opera conductor with *Don Giovanni* in Bad Lauchstädt. Meets MINNA PLANER (later Wagner).	

(cont.)

Year	Day/month	Life events	Works
1835	January		Overture to Apel's *Columbus*.
	April	Wilhelmine Schröder-Devrient arrives in Magdeburg for series of performances under Wagner.	
	Summer	Tours Bohemia and south Germany in search of vocal talent. Bavarian town of BAYREUTH makes favourable impression; witnesses street brawl in NUREMBERG (later to be recalled in *Die* MEISTERSINGER VON NÜRNBERG).	
	August		Begins notes in Red Pocketbook for future autobiography.
	November	Minna leaves to take up engagement at Königstadt Theatre in Berlin; stream of letters from Wagner obliges her to return.	
1836	29 March		Premiere of *Das Liebesverbot* in Magdeburg.
	April	Bethmann company collapses.	
	May	Travels to Berlin in vain bid to secure performance of *Das Liebesverbot*; impressed by Spontini's grand opera *Fernand Cortez*.	
	July		Composes *Polonia* Overture.
	7 July	Follows Minna to KÖNIGSBERG, where she has been offered another engagement.	Sketches prose scenario for *Die hohe Braut*.

(cont.)

Year	Day/month	Life events	Works
	24 November	Marries Minna in the little church at Königsberg-Tragheim.	
1837	March		Composes *Rule Britannia* Overture (WWV 42).
	1 April	Appointed musical director at Königsberg Theatre.	
	31 May	Minna leaves him for another man. He pursues her and they stay for a time in lodgings at Blasewitz, near Dresden. There he reads Bulwer-Lytton's novel *Rienzi*.	Sketches opera on Rienzi subject.
	June	Appointed musical director at theater in RIGA.	
	1 September	First conducting engagement in Riga.	
	24 December	COSIMA Liszt born at Como.	
1838	Summer		Completes poem of *RIENZI*; begins music.
1839	March	Contract not renewed in Riga. Leaves Riga clandestinely (to elude creditors).	
	July	Minna suffers miscarriage. Stormy sea crossing.	
	12 August	Arrives in LONDON.	
	20 August	Travel to FRANCE; received by MEYERBEER at Boulogne.	
	17 September	Arrives in Paris.	
	December		Drafts for first movement of a *Faust* Symphony (to become the *FAUST-OUVERTÜRE* WWW 59).
1840	6 May		Prose sketch of *Der FLIEGENDE HOLLÄNDER*.

(*cont.*)

Year	Day/month	Life events	Works
	May–July		Music of the *Holländer* begun.
	12 July		Publication of Wagner's first essay for SCHLESINGER's *REVUE ET GAZETTE MUSICALE*.
	October/ November	Extreme financial problems.	
	19 November		Completes *Rienzi*.
1841	March		Begins to file reports for the Dresden *Abend-Zeitung*.
	18–28 May		Poem of the *Holländer* written.
	November		Score of the *Holländer* completed.
1842	7 April	Wagner and Minna leave Paris for Dresden.	
	June–July	Holiday in Teplitz.	Sketches for *Tannhäuser*.
	20 October		Dresden premiere of *Rienzi*; immense success.
1843	2 January		Premiere in Dresden of *Holländer*, under Wagner.
	1 and 8 February		*AUTOBIOGRAPHISCHE SKIZZE* appears in Laube's *Zeitung für die elegante Welt*.
	2 February	Appointed Kapellmeister (with REISSIGER) at Royal Court of Saxony in Dresden.	
	April		Completes composition of *Tannhäuser*.
	6 July		Conducts *Das Liebesmahl der Apostel* in Frauenkirche, Dresden.
	Summer		Begins composition of *Tannhäuser*.
	1 October	Moves to relatively expensive apartment in the Ostra-Allee and starts building a book collection (DRESDEN LIBRARY).	

(*cont.*)

Year	Day/month	Life events	Works
1844	7 January		Conducts first Berlin performance of the *Holländer.*
	14 December	Ceremony for transfer of WEBER's remains from London to Dresden.	*An Webers Grab* (WWV 72) performed.
	15 December	Delivers oration at Weber's graveside.	
1845	13 April		Completes score of *Tannhäuser.*
	3 July	Summer in MARIENBAD for water cure; readings of Parzival and Lohengrin legends.	
	16 July		Prose drafts for *Die Meistersinger* completed.
	3 August		Prose drafts for LOHENGRIN completed.
	19 October		Premiere of *Tannhäuser* under Wagner in Dresden.
1846	2 March	Submits report about reorganization of royal orchestra.	
	5 April	Conducts Beethoven's Ninth Symphony at traditional Palm Sunday concert.	
	30 July		Finishes first complete draft of *Lohengrin.*
	October		Prose sketch for a five-act work on the Friedrich Barbarossa legend.
1847	22 February	Conducts his own version of Gluck's *Iphigenie en Aulide.*	
	August	Reads Greek authors in translation, including Aeschylus (the *Oresteia*).	Finishes second complete draft of *Lohengrin.*
1848	28 April		Completes score of *Lohengrin.*

(cont.)

Year	Day/month	Life events	Works
	May		Wagner submits his *Entwurf zur Organisation eines deutschen Nationaltheaters für das Königreich Sachsen*.
	14 June	Delivers address to the republican Vaterlands-verein, published as *Wie verhalten sich republikanische Bestrebungen dem Königthume gegenüber?*	
	4 October		Original prose resume for the RING: *Der Nibelungen-Mythus*.
	Autumn		Above turned into libretto, called *Siegfrieds Tod*.
	Winter		Further sketch (for second act) of *Friedrich I*.
1849	January–April		Scenario for five-act drama (opera), *Jesus von Nazareth* (WWV 80).
	Mid-February		DIE WIBELUNGEN.
	April–May	Active in revolutionary struggle, possibly involved in manufacture of hand-grenades.	
	5 May	Climbs tower of Kreuzkirche to report on troop movements.	
	9 May	Retreat of insurrectionists begins.	
	16 May	Warrant for Wagner's arrest issued (published in *Dresdner Anzeiger* on 19 May).	
	24–28 May	Flees to Switzerland with Liszt's help. Travels on to Paris.	
	2 June	Settles down in Zurich.	
	July		Writes *Die KUNST UND DIE REVOLUTION*.
	4 November		Completes *Das KUNSTWERK DER ZUKUNFT*.

(cont.)

Year	Day/month	Life events	Works
	December		Begins prose draft for *Wieland der Schmied*.
1850	January	Julie RITTER and Jessie LAUSSOT propose annual allowance of 3,000 francs (see MONEY).	
	14 March	Visits Jessie and Eugène Laussot in Bordeaux.	
	March–May	Affair with Jessie Laussot; plan to elope to Greece or Asia Minor thwarted by Jessie's husband.	
	3 July	Returns to Zurich and Minna.	
	Summer		Preliminary musical sketches for *Siegfrieds Tod*.
	28 August		Premiere of *Lohengrin* in Weimar, under Liszt.
	September		*Das JUDENTUM IN DER MUSIK* published.
	Winter		Writes OPER UND DRAMA (completed 10 January 1851).
1851	May–June		Sketches *Der junge Siegfried*, then writes poem.
	July–August		Writes *Eine MITTEILUNG AN MEINE FREUNDE*.
	15 September	Water cure in Albisbrunn, near Zurich (see HEALTH).	
	Autumn	Receives allowance from Julie Ritter (continued until 1859; see MONEY).	Prose sketches for *Das RHEINGOLD* and *Die WALKÜRE*.
1852	February	Meets Otto and Mathilde WESENDONCK, and subsequently Georg HERWEGH and François and Eliza WILLE.	
	1 July		Verse draft of *Walküre* completed.

(cont.)

Year	Day/month	Life events	Works
	November–December		Revisions of texts for *Der junge Siegfried* and *Siegfrieds Tod*.
1853	February		Publishes fifty copies of complete *Ring* poem, and reads it to an invited audience at the Hotel Baur au Lac in Zurich.
	15 April	Moves with Minna into larger apartment on the second floor of 13 Zeltweg (Zurich).	
	18, 20, and 22 May	Mini Wagner Festival in Zurich, with three concerts of music from his works.	
	May–June		Writes piano sonata for Mathilde Wesendonck.
	July	Liszt visits and impresses Wagner with his *Faust* Symphony and symphonic poems.	
	August–September		Holiday in Italy, during which inspiration for opening music of *Rheingold* supposedly occurs in a dream experience in a hotel room in LA SPEZIA.
	10 October	Meets the 15-year-old Cosima Liszt and her sister Blandine while dining with Liszt in Paris.	
	1 November		Begins complete draft of *Rheingold*.
1854	January–June	Minna's heart condition deteriorates, as does the Wagners' marriage.	
	28 June		Begins complete draft of *Walküre*.

(cont.)

Year	Day/month	Life events	Works
	September	Wagner's debts settled by Otto Wesendonck, who provides regular allowance (see MONEY). Minna addresses a petition for clemency to King of Saxony, which is rejected.	
	September/ October	Herwegh introduces him to philosophy of SCHOPENHAUER.	Conceives *Tristan*.
1855	March–June	In England, conducting series of eight concerts for the Philharmonic Society.	
	Fall	Frequent attacks of erysipelas (see HEALTH).	
1856	23 March		Finishes fair copy of full score of *Walküre*.
	16 May		Prose sketch for projected Buddhist opera *Die Sieger* (WWV 89).
	Summer		New Schopenhauer-inspired ending for the *Ring*; later rejected.
	September		Begins composition of *Siegfried*.
	19 December		First dated musical sketches for *Tristan*.
1857	28 April	Moves into "Asyl," adjoining the Wesendoncks' villa.	Conceives *Parsifal*.
	9 August		Breaks off composition of *Siegfried* at the end of Act II.
	September	Hans von BÜLOW and his bride Cosima stay with the Wagners on their honeymoon.	Works on *Tristan*, and sets five of Mathilde Wesendonck's poems to music.
1858	7 April	Minna intercepts "Morning Confession" letter to Mathilde.	

(cont.)

Year	Day/month	Life events	Works
	17 August	Wagner vacates the Asyl.	
	29 August	Arrives in Venice with Karl RITTER; stays in apartment in Palazzo Giustiniani on Grand Canal.	Continues to work on Act II of *Tristan*.
1859	Early 1859	Continues stay in Venice.	
	24 March	Leaves Venice for Lucerne.	Completes Act III of *Tristan*.
	6 August		Completes full score of *Tristan*.
	September	Revisits Wesendoncks in Zurich; Otto buys copyright to four *Ring* scores (see MONEY).	
	10 September	Settles in Paris (where he remains until July 1861) in the hope of bringing about performances of *Tannhäuser*, *Lohengrin*, and *Tristan*.	
	17 November	Minna arrives with dog and parrot; some attempt made to salvage marriage.	
1860	Winter	Schott negotiates for rights in Wagner's music; is offered *Rheingold* for 10,000 francs.	
	January–February		Conducts three concerts of his music in Paris.
	12 August	Partial amnesty allows him to return to Germany, but not yet Saxony.	
	24 September		Rehearsals begin for *Tannhäuser* at Paris Opéra.
1861	March		*TANNHÄUSER* SCANDAL at Opéra. Withdrawn after three performances.
	April–May		Plans for *Tristan* in Karlsruhe.

(cont.)

Year	Day/month	Life events	Works
	November		Starts *Die* *MEISTERSINGER VON* *NÜRNBERG*.
1862	25 January		Poem of *Die Meistersinger* completed.
	5 February		Public reading of *Die Meistersinger* poem at Schott's house in Mainz.
	15 February	Takes lodgings in Biebrich, across Rhine from Mainz.	Works on *Die Meistersinger*.
	21 February	Minna arrives uninvited; described by Wagner as "ten days in hell."	
	28 March	Full amnesty allows RW to reenter Saxony. Encounters with Mathilde MAIER and Friederike MEYER (see SEXUALITY and WOMEN).	
	July	Hans and Cosima von Bülow visit him in Biebrich. Coaches Ludwig Schnorr von CAROLSFELD and his wife Malvina in the roles of TRISTAN and ISOLDE, with Bülow at the piano.	
	November	Last meeting with Minna in Dresden.	
	23 November		Reading of *Die Meistersinger* at Dr. STANDHARTNER's house in Vienna, at which the critic HANSLICK was present.
1863	January–April	Travels to Prague, ST. PETERSBURG, and Moscow to give concerts of his music.	
	12 May	Moves to new apartment in Penzing, near Vienna;	

(cont.)

Year	Day/month	Life events	Works
		Viennese seamstress Bertha Goldwag furnishes it luxuriously.	
	July–December	Further concerts in Budapest, Prague, Karlsruhe, Breslau, and Vienna.	
	28 November	Wagner and Cosima von Bülow commit themselves to each other in Berlin.	
1864	10 March	Eighteen-year-old Wagner enthusiast becomes King LUDWIG II of Bavaria.	
	26 March	Mounting debts force Wagner to leave Vienna to escape arrest; takes refuge with Eliza WILLE at Mariafeld.	
	May–June	Ludwig II summons Wagner, pays off his debts, and houses him near the royal castle Schloss Berg, overlooking Lake Starnberg, near Munich. Cosima arrives at Starnberg with two daughters; union with Wagner consummated.	
	12 October	Moves into spacious house at 21 Briennerstrasse in Munich, provided by king, who also authorizes generous annual stipend.	
1865	10 April	RW's and Cosima's first child, ISOLDE, born.	
	10 June		Premiere of *Tristan und Isolde* in Munich under Bülow.
	17 July	Begins to dictate autobiography *MEIN*	

(cont.)

Year	Day/month	Life events	Works
		LEBEN to Cosima, using notes from the Red Pocketbook.	
	August	Hostility to Wagner in Munich mounts.	
	October	Campaign to have Wagner banished from Munich finally successful.	
	10 December	Wagner leaves Munich.	Prose draft for *Parsifal*.
1866	25 January	Minna dies in Dresden.	
	8 March	Cosima joins Wagner in Geneva.	
	15 April	They move into TRIBSCHEN on Lake Lucerne.	
	22 May	Receives secret birthday visit from King Ludwig.	
	June	Public scandal over the liaison with Cosima.	
1867	17 February	Birth of second daughter, EVA.	
	March–June	Visits to Munich.	
	April	Bülow appointed court Kapellmeister to Ludwig and director of proposed music school.	
	24 October		Full score of *Die Meistersinger* finished.
	23 December	Returns to Munich and stays there until 9 February 1868.	
1868	21 June		Premiere of *Die Meistersinger* in Munich under Bülow.
	September–October	Travels to Italy with Cosima.	
	8 November	Meets NIETZSCHE in Leipzig.	
	16 November	Cosima officially moves into Tribschen with Isolde and Eva.	
1869	1 March		Resumes work on the *Ring* with composition of *Siegfried* Act III.

(*cont.*)

Year	Day/month	Life events	Works
	Spring		*Das JUDENTUM IN DER MUSIK* reprinted with new preface.
	6 June	Birth of son, SIEGFRIED; Nietzsche present at Tribschen and visits frequently thereafter.	
	July	Visited by three French admirers: Judith GAUTIER, her husband Catulle MENDÈS, and Villiers de l'Isle-Adam.	
	22 September		Over Wagner's objections, *Rheingold* performed in Munich under Franz Wüllner.
	Christmas		Reads *Parsifal* sketch to Nietzsche.
1870	March	Bayreuth considered as venue for festival.	
	26 June		Premiere of *Walküre* in Munich under Wüllner.
	18 July	The Bülows' marriage legally dissolved.	
	25 August	Marriage of Wagner and Cosima in the Protestant church in Lucerne.	
	7 September		Completes essay *BEETHOVEN* in celebration of composer's centenary.
	November		Text for *Eine Kapitulation* written.
	25 December		*SIEGFRIED IDYLL* performed on the staircase at Tribschen in honor of Cosima's birthday.
1871	5 February		Work on *Siegfried* completed.
	14 April		First performance of *KAISERMARSCH* in Berlin.

(cont.)

Year	Day/month	Life events	Works
	April	Wagners visit Bayreuth. They decide against the MARKGRÄFLICHES OPERNHAUS and that a new theater will have to be built.	
	12 May	Wagner announces that the first BAYREUTH FESTIVAL will be held in 1873, and forms the PATRONS' ASSOCIATION.	
	13 May	In Darmstadt, Wagner discusses the technical direction of the Festival with Carl BRANDT.	
	22 May		Writes the foreword for the edition of his collected writings (*Gesammelte Schriften und Dichtungen*).
	1 June	Emil HECKEL founds first WAGNER SOCIETY in Mannheim.	
	November	RW informs Friedrich FEUSTEL of his decision to hold the Festival in Bayreuth.	
1872	February	Acquires site adjoining the palace gardens in Bayreuth for his future home, WAHNFRIED. "Green Hill" of Bürgerreuth chosen for the theater.	
	22 May	Laying of foundation stone of new theater, followed by speeches and performance of Beethoven's Ninth Symphony.	
	September		Writes essay *ÜBER SCHAUSPIELER UND SÄNGER*.

(cont.)

Year	Day/month	Life events	Works
	21 September	The Wagners move into a temporary home in Bayreuth: Dammallee 7.	
1873	January–February (also April)	Further tours to scout for artists for the Festival; Wagner also conducts fundraising concerts.	
	May		Begins full score of GÖTTERDÄMMERUNG.
	24 June	Sends Bismarck his report on the laying of the foundation stone of the *Festspielhaus*, including his nationalistic speech.	
	30 August	Announces that the Festival must be postponed until 1875.	
	November	Given financial shortfall, Wagner asks King Ludwig for help to fund the Festival.	
1874	January	King Ludwig initially refuses, but subsequently extends loan.	
	28 April	Wagners move into WAHNFRIED.	
	June–September		Rehearsals for *Ring* with conductor Hans RICHTER and singers.
	21 November		Finishes score of *Götterdämmerung*.
1875	February–May	Concert tours in Vienna, Budapest, and Berlin; travels also to Leipzig, Hanover, and Brunswick.	
	July–August		Rehearsals for the *Ring* with soloists and orchestra. All energies directed toward realization of Festival the following year.

(cont.)

Year	Day/month	Life events	Works
1876	February–March		Composes *Grosser Festmarsch* for a commission to celebrate the hundreth anniversary of the American Declaration of Independence.
	3 June		Rehearsals for *Ring* begin.
	13–30 August	First Bayreuth Festival: three complete cycles of the *Ring*.	
	5 November	Last meeting between Wagner and Nietzsche in Sorrento.	
1877	23 February		Second prose draft of *Parsifal* completed.
	19 April		*Parsifal* text completed.
	7–29 May	Series of eight concerts given in the recently opened Royal Albert Hall in London.	
	September		Begins composition of *Parsifal*.
	October	Hans von WOLZOGEN invited to edit the newly founded BAYREUTHER BLÄTTER.	
1878	January		First issue of *Bayreuther Blätter* published.
	12 March		Finishes *Modern*, the first of the series of so-called "regeneration essays."
	31 March	Question of Bayreuth deficit settled by agreement with King Ludwig.	
1879	April		Finishes drafts of music for *Parsifal*.
	July	Anti-vivisectionists appeal to him to lend his voice to their campaign.	
	31 December	Advised by his doctor to seek a milder climate, Wagner leaves Bayreuth with his family for Italy.	

(cont.)

Year	Day/month	Life events	Works
1880	4 January	The family takes up residence in the Villa d'Angri, overlooking the Bay of Naples, and remains there until 8 August. Joined there by Paul von JOUKOWSKY, the future stage designer for *Parsifal*.	
	21 August	Returns to Bayreuth.	
	12 November		Wagner conducts private performance for King Ludwig of *Parsifal* Prelude in the Court Theatre in Munich. Last meeting with the king.
1881	5–9 May		First complete performance of the *Ring* in Berlin, given in the presence of the composer by Angelo NEUMANN's company.
	11 May	The French writer Count GOBINEAU comes to Bayreuth, where he spends several weeks.	
	25–29 May	The Wagners, with Gobineau and Joukowsky, attend the fourth cycle of the *Ring* in Berlin.	
	August–September		Writes essay *Heldentum und Christentum*.
	5 November	The family arrives in Palermo, where they stay at Hotel des Palmes until 2 February 1882.	
	December	Suffers chest spasms, which his doctor fails to diagnose as a heart condition.	
1882	13 January		Finishes score of *Parsifal*.
	15 January	Portrait sketched by Renoir.	

(*cont.*)

Year	Day/month	Life events	Works
	End March	First major heart attack, after continuing chest spasms.	
	May	Gobineau visits Wagner in Bayreuth. Bayreuth scholarship fund set up.	
	26 July		Premiere of *Parsifal* in Bayreuth under Hermann Levi.
	14 September	Departure from Bayreuth for Venice.	
	18 September	Family and entourage take up residence on the mezzanine floor of the Palazzo Vendramin.	
	25 December		Conducts his youthful Symphony in C major (WWV 29) at La Fenice in celebration of Cosima's birthday.
1883	11 February		Begins essay entitled *Über das Weibliche im Menschlichen* (uncompleted).
	13 February	Wagner suffers fatal heart attack and dies some time after 3 o'clock in Cosima's arms.	
	18 February	Private burial in the garden of Wahnfried.	

ADDITIONAL SOURCES

Barry Millington, ed., *Wagner Compendium* (see bibliography): 12–19.

Appendix 3   Wagner's addresses

Compiled by Nicholas Vazsonyi
Research assistant: Leigh Buches
Additional contributions by John W. Barker,
Barry Millington, and Chris Walton

This is by no means an exhaustive listing of places where Wagner lived. In many cases, street names and house numbers have changed since Wagner's residence. When relevant, the original address is given with the current version in parentheses. If the location no longer exists, this is also noted.

   Residences have been grouped alphabetically by city or location name and, within those, arranged chronologically. Hotels are listed only if they are still in business, or otherwise significant.

BAYREUTH AND ENVIRONS

Hotel Fantaisie Bamberger Strasse 5 95488 Eckersdorf-Donndorf	27 April–21 September 1872
Dammallee 7 95444 Bayreuth	21 September 1872–28 April 1874
Haus Wahnfried Richard-Wagner-Strasse 48 95444 Bayreuth	28 April 1874 (main residence until death)

BIEBRICH (TODAY WIESBADEN)

@ Architekt Frickhöfer Rheingaustrasse 137 65203 Wiesbaden (Biebrich)	15 February–13 November 1862

BORDEAUX

@ Eugene and Jessie Laussot 26 cours du 30 Juillet 33000 Bordeaux	14 March–3 April 1850

DRESDEN AND ENVIRONS (GRAUPA)

During childhood:
Moritzstrasse 15
Neumarkt

Waisenhaus-Strasse 24
Dresden

Töpfergasse 7 (Frauenkirche 5) Dresden	April–June 1842
Waisenhaus-Strasse 5 (destroyed)	July–August 1842 (?)
Marienstrasse 9 Dresden	August(?) 1842–October 1843
Ostra-Allee 6 (would now be Ostra-Allee 13) Dresden (house destroyed in WWII)	1 October 1843–April 1847
"Lohengrinhaus" (Richard-Wagner-Strasse 6) 01796 Graupa	May–July 1846
Palais Marcolini (Friedrichsstrasse 41) Dresden	April 1847–8 May 1849

LEIPZIG

"Haus zum roten und weissen Löwe" Brühl 3 (demolished 1886; plaque) 04109 Leipzig	Birth–November 1813
"Im Pichhof vor dem Hallischen Thore" (approximate location of Richard-Wagner-Strasse) 04109 Leipzig	1827–January 1833

LONDON

King's Arms 7 Old Compton Street London WID 5JE	August 1839
22 Portland Terrace (demolished 1905)	March–June 1855

[Upon arrival, stayed briefly with Ferdinand PRAEGER at 31 Milton Street
(today 65 Balcombe Street).]

12 Orme Square London W2 4RS (home of Edward DANNREUTHER)	1 May–4 June 1877

LUCERNE AND ENVIRONS (TRIBSCHEN)

Gasthaus "Zum Schwanen" (Restaurant Schwanen) Schwanenplatz 4 6004 Luzern	28 August 1850 (during *Lohengrin* premiere)
Hotel Schweizerhof Schweizerhofquai 6004 Luzern	28 March–7 September 1859
Landhaus Tribschen (Richard-Wagner-Weg 27) 6005 Luzern	15 April 1866–April 1872 (rented 4 April, moved in 15 April)

MAGDEBURG

Margaretenstrasse 2 (destroyed) Magdeburg	October 1834–17 May 1836

MUNICH AND ENVIRONS

Hotel Bayerischer Hof Promenadeplatz 2–6 80333 München	4–14 May 1864
Landhaus Pellet (plaque) Münchener Strasse 49–61 82335 Berg	14 May–3 October 1864
(today a boarding school) Brienner Strasse 21 (today 37?) 80333 München (villa destroyed in WWII; plaque)	12 October 1864–10 December 1865

NAPLES AND ENVIRONS (SORRENTO)

Grand Hotel Vittoria Piazza Tasso 34 80067 Sorrento	6 October–7 November 1876
Villa Doria d'Angri Via Francesco Petrarca 80 / Via Posilippo 408 80122 Napoli	4 January–8 August 1880

PALERMO

Grand Hotel delle Palme Via Roma 398 90139 Palermo	5 November 1881–2 February 1882
Palazzo Valguarnera-Gangi Piazza dei Porazzi Palermo	2 February–19 March 1882

PARIS AND ENVIRONS

3 rue de la Tonnellerie (today: 31, Rue du Pont-Neuf) 75001 Paris	17 September 1839–15 April 1840
25 rue du Helder 75009 Paris	15 April 1840–29 April 1841
3 avenue de Meudon (plaque) (27 avenue du château) 92190 Meudon	29 April–30 October 1841
14 rue Jacob (plaque) 75006 Paris	30 October 1841–7 April 1842
59 rue de Provence 75009 Paris	Early February–14 March 1850
4 rue Matignon 75008 Paris	15 September–7 October 1859
16 rue Newton 75116 Paris	7 October 1859–October 1860
3 rue d'Aumale (plaque) 75009 Paris	mid-October 1860–early July 1861
78 rue de Lille Legation de Prusse 75007 Paris	8(?)–30 July 1861
Hôtel du Quai Voltaire (plaque) 19 Quai Voltaire 75007 Paris	3 December 1861–1 February 1862 (with interruptions)

STUTTGART

Hotel Marquardt (Marquardtbau; Hotel ceased operation in 1938) Corner Bolzstrasse and Königsstrasse 70173 Stuttgart	Early May 1864

VENICE

Palazzo Giustiniani Canal Grande 30123 Venezia	30 August 1858–24 March 1859
Hotel Europa (The Westin Europa & Regina?) San Marco 2159 30124 Venezia	20–27 September 1876
Hotel Danieli Riva degli Schiavoni 4196 30122 Venezia	4–6 October 1880
Palazzo Contarini delle Figure Canal Grande 3327 Venezia	6–30 October 1880

Palazzo Vendramin-Calergi
  (mezzanine)
Cannaregio 2079
30121 Venezia
	18 September 1882–13 February
	  1883
	(death)

VIENNA AND ENVIRONS

Hotel Kaiserin Elisabeth Weihburggasse 3 1010 Wien	mid-September–1 December 1861 mid-November 1862–mid-February 1863 28 April–12 May 1863
Landhaus des Barons Rachowin Wienstrasse 221 Penzing bei Wien (today: Richard Wagner Villa Hadikgasse 72 [plaque] 1140 Wien)	12 May 1863–23 March 1864

WÜRZBURG

Kapuzinerstrasse 40 97070 Würzburg	January 1833–January 1834

ZURICH AND ENVIRONS

@ Dr. Alexander Müller Rennweg 55 8001 Zürich	May–September 1849
"Akazie" Oetenbachgasse 7 8001 Zürich	September 1849
Steinwiesstrasse 3/ Zeltweg 8032 Zürich	17 September 1849–29 January 1850

"Zum Abendstern"
Sterngasse 22, Enge
    (Sternenstrasse,
    demolished)
8002 Zürich
	July 1850–September 1851

Zeltweg 11 8032 Zürich	mid-September 1851–April 1853
Zeltweg 13 8032 Zürich	April 1853–28 April 1857
"Asyl" (Villa Schönberg, demolished) Wesendonck Estate (Museum Rietberg) Gablerstrasse 14 8002 Zürich	28 April 1857–17 August 1858
@ François and Eliza WILLE "Mariafeld" bei Meilen General Wille-Strasse 165 8706 Meilen	26 March 1864–30 April 1864

ADDITIONAL SOURCES

Bernhard Hangartner, Eva Martina Hanke, and Laurenz Lütteken, eds., *Durch Richard Wagners Zürich: Ein Stadtrundgang* (Zurich: Stroemfeld, 2012).

Michael von Soden, *Richard Wagner: Ein Reiseführer* (Dortmund: Harenberg, 1991). [contains some factual errors]

Stewart Spencer, "Wagner's Addresses in London," *Wagner* 26 (2005): 33–51.

Appendix 4   *Leitmotive* in *Der Ring des Nibelungen*

Compiled by Patrick McCreless

The following list of LEITMOTIVE is solely intended to accompany and illustrate the discussion of the works in the group of entries associated with *Der RING DES NIBELUNGEN*. It is thus not at all complete – indeed, given the similarity of some motives to others, the density of their occurrence, and the flexibility with which Wagner uses them, the very notion of a "complete" list is in itself problematic. Nonetheless, readers interested in a more thorough listing of motives may consult the following works:

Deryck Cooke, *An Introduction to "Der Ring des Nibelungen," Being an Explanation and Analysis of Wagner's System of Leitmotive . . . with 193 Musical Examples*. Compact discs (set of 2) (London: Decca, 1995 [1968]).

Stewart Spencer and Barry Millington, *Wagner's "Ring of the Nibelung": A Companion* (New York: Thames and Hudson, 1993).

Leitmotive listed herein are ordered chronologically according to when they first occur in the *Ring*. Each is given a number (CWE #) for ease of cross-reference between the text and Appendix. Each is also given a name or label. Although some scholars and commentators oppose naming the motives at all, we take the position that the longstanding convention of so designating them, along with their frequent occurrence and their absolutely central role in the musical unfolding of the drama, argues for their inclusion. Those motives whose appearance is strongly associated with a musical key are given with that key. Finally, since all the motives but one also appear in the useful and more extensive Spencer/Millington list, we supply their numbers as well. (The one motive here that does not appear in other lists is No. 17, "Siegfried's Death/ Murder," which seems to deserve an explicit referential name, although it is not one of the traditionally cited *Leitmotive*.) A full understanding of the dramatic and musical meaning of *Leitmotive*, of course, must go beyond the simple attribution of names; too rigid an adherence to *Leitmotiv* labels can easily lead to misunderstanding and misinterpretation.

CWE #	Name/tag	Associative key	Spencer/ Millington #
1	Rhine	E♭ major	S/M 1a and 1b
2a/2b	Ring	E major/minor	S/M 6
3	Renunciation of love	C minor	S/M 7
4	Valhalla	D♭ major	S/M 8
5	Wotan's spear/treaties	—	S/M 9
6a	Loge (Magic Fire)	—	S/M 14b

(cont.)

CWE #	Name/tag	Associative key	Spencer/ Millington #

6b   Loge   —   S/M 14a

7   Nibelheim/forging   Bb minor   S/M 15

8   Tarnhelm   B minor   S/M 16

9   Curse   B minor   S/M 19

10   Erda   C# minor   S/M 20 [cf. CWE 1]

11   Twilight of the gods   —   S/M 21

(cont.)

CWE #	Name/tag	Associative key	Spencer/ Millington #
12	Wotan's idea→Sword	C major	S/M 23
13	Hunding	C minor	S/M 28
14	Glorification of Brünnhilde	—	S/M 36
15	Hagen	—	S/M 59
16	Gutrune	G major	S/M 61

(cont.)

CWE #	Name/tag	Associative key	Spencer/ Millington #

| 17 | Siegfried's Death/Murder | D♭→c over F♯ | |

| 18 | Magic sleep | — | S/M 38 |

Appendix 5 Prose works

Compiled by Nicholas Vazsonyi
With the assistance of Leigh Buches and
Kyle W. Miller

To date, there is still no complete and authoritative listing of all Wagner's prose writings, nor is there what scholars call a (historical-)critical edition of these works. Given the significance of Richard Wagner and the enduring impact of his often hastily written writings, this is a lacuna that urgently needs to be addressed. The following list does not break new ground but is simply an edited compilation of existing sources, listed at the end. English titles are taken from PW (and occasionally edited); other English translations of titles (not from PW) are given for the reader's benefit in square brackets. English translations listed frequently in abbreviated form are given full bibliographic treatment at the end of the Appendix.

Title/date (German)	First edition	SSD	Title (English)	PW	Other translation / notes
Die deutsche Oper, 1834	*Zeitung für die elegante Welt*, 10 June 1834	xii	On German Opera	viii	
Pasticcio, 1834	*Neue Zeitschrift für Musik*, 6 and 10 November 1834	xii	Pasticcio	viii	
Die rote Brieftasche (begun August 1835)	*Allgemeine Musik-Zeitung*, 63 (1936): 196		The Red Pocketbook		Also in: SB 1:81–4
Eine Kritik aus Magdeburg, 1835	*Magdeburgische Zeitung*, 7 November 1835	xvi	A review from Magdeburg		On *Der Freischütz*
Aus Magdeburg, 1836	*Neue Zeitschrift für Musik*, 3 May 1836	xii	From Magdeburg		
Berliner Kunstchronik von Wilhelm Drach, 1836			Chronicle of Berlin's artistic life by Wilhelm Drach		
"*Das LIEBESVERBOT*": *Bericht über eine erste Opernaufführung*, 1836	First published in 1871	i	*Das Liebesverbot*: Account of a first Operatic Performance	vii	
Bellinis Norma, 1837 [review of performance in Magdeburg first published in F. Lippmann, "Ein neu entdecktes Autograph Richard Wagners," *Musicae scientiae collectanea: Festschrift Karl Gustav Fellerer* (Cologne: Volk, 1973)]			Bellini's *Norma*		*The Wagner Journal* 1.1 (March 2007): 33–40

(cont.)

Title/date (German)	First edition	SSD	Title (English)	PW	Other translation / notes
Zwei Zeitungs-Anzeigen aus Riga [i, Theateranzeige; ii, Konzertanzeige], 1837, 1839	Der Zuschauer, 8 December 1837 and 8 March 1839	xvi	[Two Newspaper Notices from Riga: i, Theater Notice; ii, Concert Notice]		
Der dramatische Gesang, 1837 [?]	Musik Zeitung 15, 1888	xii	[Dramatic Singing]		
Bellini. Ein Wort zu seiner Zeit, 1837	Der Zuschauer, 7–19 December 1837	xii	Bellini: A Word in Season	viii	
Konzertanzeige	Der Zuschauer, 8 March 1839		Concert Announcement		
Über Meyerbeers "Hugenotten," written 1837 or 1840		xii	On Meyerbeer's Les Huguenots		Grey, ed., Richard Wagner and his World: 335–46
Ein Tagebuch aus Paris, 1840	RICHARD WAGNER-JAHRBUCH, 1886	xvi	A Paris Diary		
Eine PILGERFAHRT ZU BEETHOVEN, novella, 1840	"Une visite à Beethoven, épisode de la vie d'un musicien allemande," Revue et gazette musicale de Paris, 19, 22, 29 November and 3 December 1840	i	A Pilgrimage to Beethoven, novella	vii	Art, Life and Theories of Richard Wagner, ed. Edward L. Burlingame (New York: Holt, 1904) Wagner Writes from Paris, ed. Jacobs and Skelton Wagner: Stories and Essays, trans. Osborne: 56–79
Über deutsche Musik, 1840	Revue et gazette musicale de Paris, 12 July 1840	i	On German Music	vii	

					Wagner: Stories and Essays, trans. Osborne: 136–49
Der VIRTUOS UND DER KÜNSTLER, 1840	i	*Revue et gazette musicale de Paris,* 18 October 1840 (in French); republished revised 1871 (in German)	The Virtuoso and the Artist	vii	
"Stabat mater" de Pergolese par *Lvoff,* 1840	xii	*Revue et gazette musicale de Paris,* 11 October 1840	Pergolesi's *Stabat Mater*	vii	
Über die Ouvertüre, 1840–1	i	*Revue et gazette musicale de Paris,* 10, 14, 17 January 1841	On the Overture	vii	
Pariser Amüsements, 1841	xii	*Europa* (Stuttgart), spring issue, April 1841	Parisian Amusements	viii	
Pariser Fatalitäten für Deutsche, 1841	xii	*Europa* (Stuttgart), summer issue, 1841	Parisian Fatalities for the German	viii	
"*Der Freischütz*": an das Pariser Publikum, 1841	i	*Revue et gazette musicale de Paris,* 23 and 30 May 1841	*Der Freischütz:* To the Paris Public	vii	
"*Le Freischütz*" in Paris: Bericht nach Deutschland, 1841	i	*Abend-Zeitung* (Dresden), 16–21 July 1841	*Le Freischütz:* Report to Germany	vii	
Rossini's "Stabat mater," 1841	i	*Neue Zeitschrift für Musik,* 28 December 1841	Rossini's *Stabat Mater*	vii	
Der Künstler und die Öffentlichkeit, 1841	i	*Revue et gazette musicale de Paris,* 1 April 1841	The Artist and Publicity	vii	
9 Paris Berichte für die "Dresdener Abend-Zeitung," 1841	xii	*Abend-Zeitung* (Dresden), 1841: 19–22 March (i), 24–28 May (ii), 14–16 June (iii), 2–4 August (iv), 23 August (v), 1–2 October (vi), 4–8 December (vii), 25 December (viii), and in 1842 on 10–11 January (ix)	9 Paris reports for the *Dresdener Abend-Zeitung*	viii	

(cont.)

Title/date (German)	First edition	SSD	Title (English)	PW	Other translation / notes
Ein ENDE IN PARIS, novella, 1841	"Un musicien étranger à Paris," *Revue et gazette musicale de Paris*, 31 January, and 7 and 11 February 1841	i	An End in Paris, novella	vii	*Wagner: Stories and Essays*, trans. Osborne: 92–112
Ein glücklicher Abend, novella, 1841	*Revue et gazette musicale de Paris*, 24 October and 7 November 1841	i	A Happy Evening, novella	vii	*Wagner: Stories and Essays*, trans. Osborne: 80–91
HALÉVY und die französische Oper, 1842	1871	xii	Halévy and French Opera		
"La Reine de Chypre" d'Halévy, 1842	*Revue et gazette musicale de Paris*, 27 February, 13 March, 24 April, 1 May 1842	xii	Halévy and *La Reine de Chypre*	viii	
Bericht über eine neue Oper [Halévy: *La Reine de Chypre*], 1842	*Abend-Zeitung* (Dresden), 26–29 January 1842	i	Report on a New Opera [Halévy: *La Reine de Chypre*]	vii	
AUTOBIOGRAPHISCHE SKIZZE, 1842–3	*Zeitung für die elegante Welt*, 1 and 8 February 1843	i	Autobiographical Sketch	i	*The Wagner Journal* 2:1 (March 2008): 42–58
Ein Pariser Bericht für Robert SCHUMANNS "Neue Zeitschrift für Musik," 1842	*Neue Zeitschrift für Musik*, 22 February 1842	xvi	A Parisian Report for Robert Schumann's *Neue Zeitschrift für Musik*	viii	
Das Oratorium "Paulus" von Mendelssohn Bartholdy, 1843	*Bayreuther Blätter* 20 (1899): 4	xii	The Oratorio St Paul by Mendelssohn Bartholdy		

(cont.)

Title/date (German)	First edition	SSD	Title (English)	PW	Other translation / notes
Bericht über die Aufführung der neunten Symphonie von Beethoven im Jahre 1846 in Dresden, 1846		ii	Report on the Performance of Beethoven's Ninth Symphony in Dresden in the year 1846, Together with a Program	vii	
Künstler und Kritiker, mit Bezug auf einen besonderen Fall, 1846	Dresdener Anzeiger, 14 August 1846	xii	Artist and Critic	viii	
Eine Rede auf Friedrich Schneider, 1846	Der Merker, 15 October 1913	xvi	A Speech on Friedrich Schneider		
Programm zur 9. Symphonie von Beethoven, 1846	Program for a concert on 5 April 1846	ii	Program of Beethoven's Ninth Symphony	vii	Grey, ed., Richard Wagner and his World: 480–90
Wie verhalten sich republikanische Bestrebungen dem Königthume gegenüber?, 1848	Dresdener Anzeiger, 16 June 1848	xii	How Do Republican Aspirations Stand in Relation to the Monarchy?	iv	
Trinkspruch am Gedenktage des 300jährigen Bestehens der königlichen musikalischen Kapelle in Dresden, 1848		ii	Toast on the Tercentenary of the Royal Kapelle at Dresden	vii	
Deutschland und seine Fürsten, 1848	Volksblätter, 15 October 1848	xii	Germany and her Princes		
Der Nibelungen-Mythus: Als Entwurf zu einem Drama, 1848		ii	The Nibelungen Myth: As Sketch for a Drama	vii	

Entwurf zur Organisation eines deutschen Nationaltheaters für das Königreich Sachsen, 1848	Dated: 11 May 1848	ii	Plan of Organization of a German National Theatre for the Kingdom of Saxony	vii	*Richard Wagner: Stories and Essays*, trans. Osborne: 150–87
Zwei Schreiben aus dem Jahre 1848 [i, an Franz Wigand; ii, an Lüttichau], 1848		1. xvi, 2. xii	Two letters from the year 1848 [i, to Franz Wigand; ii, to Lüttichau]	2. iv	
Vier Zeitungs-Erklärungen [i and ii, *Dresdener Anzeige*; iii, *Europa artiste*, Paris; iv, *Ostdeutsche Post*], 1848–61	20 June 1848 (i), 22 June 1848 (ii), November 1859 (iii), November 1861 (iv)	xvi	[Four Explanations in Newspapers]		
Die WIBELUNGEN: Weltgeschichte aus der Sage, date uncertain: *c*. 1848–50 (see entry)	Leipzig, early 1850	ii	The Wibelungen: World History as told in Saga	vii	
Über Eduard DEVRIENT's "Geschichte der deutschen Schauspielkunst," 1849	*Der junge Wagner*, 1910	xii	On Eduard Devrient's *History of German Acting*	viii	
Theater-Reform, 1849	*Dresdener Anzeiger*, 16 January 1849	xii	Theater Reform	viii	
Nochmals Theater-Reform, 1849	*Dresdener Anzeiger*, 18 January 1849	xii	[More on Theater Reform]		
Der Mensch und die bestehende Gesellschaft, 1849	*Volksblätter*, 10 February 1849	xii	Man and Established Society	viii	
Die Revolution, 1849 (authorship uncertain)	*Volksblätter*, 8 April 1849	xii	The Revolution	viii	
Die KUNST UND DIE REVOLUTION, 1849	Leipzig: Wigand, 1849	iii	Art and Revolution	i	

Title/date (German)	First edition	SSD	Title (English)	PW	Other translation / notes
Das KUNSTWERK DER ZUKUNFT, 1849	Leipzig: Wigand, 1850	iii	The Artwork of the Future	i	
Zu "Die Kunst und die Revolution," 1849	Entwürfe, Gedanken, Fragmente aus nachgelassenen Papieren zusammengestellt, 1885	xii	On Art and Revolution	viii	
Flüchtige Aufzeichnung einzelner Gedanken zu einem größeren Aufsatze: "Das Künstlertum der Zukunft"	Entwürfe, Gedanken, Fragmente aus nachgelassenen Papieren zusammengestellt, 1885	xii	Artistry of the Future [diverse notes for a projected essay]	viii	
Entwürfe, Gedanken und Fragmente aus der Zeit der großen Kunstschriften, 1849–51		xii	[Drafts, Ideas and Fragments from the Period of the Major Aesthetic Treatises, 1849–51]	viii	
KUNST UND KLIMA, 1850	Deutsche Monatsschrift für Politik Wissenschaft, Kunst und Leben, April 1850	iii	Art and Climate	i	
Das JUDENTUM IN DER MUSIK, 1850, revised 1869	Neue Zeitschrift für Musik 33.19 (3 September 1850): 101–7 and 33.20 (6 September 1850): 109–12	v	Judaism in Music (also translated Jewishness in Music)	iii	Judaism in Music: Being the Original Essay Together with the Later Supplement, trans. Edwin Evans (London: William Reeves, 1910) Trans. S. Spencer, Wagner 9.1 (January 1988): 20–33 Wagner: Stories and Essays, trans. Osborne: 23–39

Title/date (German)	First edition	SSD	Title (English)	PW	Other translation / notes
Eine *MITTEILUNG AN MEINE FREUNDE*, 1851	Leipzig, 1851	iv	A Communication to my Friends	i	
Nachruf an Spontini, 1851	*Eidgenössische Zeitung*, 25 January 1851	v	Obituary of Spontini	iii	
Über die musikalische Berichterstattung in der "Eidegenössischen Zeitung," 1851	7 February 1851	xvi	[On Music Reporting in the *Eidegenössische Zeitung*, 1851]		
Zur Empfehlung Gottfried Sempers, 1851	*Eidgenössische Zeitung*, 6 February 1851	xvi	In Recommendation of Gottfried Semper		
Über musikalische Kritik: Brief an den Herausgeber der "Neuen Zeitschrift für Musik," 25 January 1852	*Neue Zeitschrift für Musik*, 6 February 1852	v	On Musical Criticism: A Letter to the Editor of the *Neuen Zeitschrift für Musik*	iii	
Über die Aufführung des "Tannhäuser": eine Mitteilung an die Dirigenten und Darsteller dieser Oper, 1852	Completed 23 August 1852; published privately	v	On the Performing of *Tannhäuser*: An Address to the Directors and Performers of this Opera	iii	
Bemerkungen zur Aufführung der Oper "Der fliegende Holländer," 1852		v	Remarks on Performing the Opera *The Flying Dutchman*	iii	Thomas S. Grey, ed., *Richard Wagner: "Der fliegende Holländer"* (see bibliography): 193–200

Title/date (German)	First edition	SSD	Title (English)	PW	Other translation / notes
ii: Tannhäusers Romfahrt, 1853			Rome [explanatory program]		
Vorspiel zu "Lohengrin," 1853	For the concerts on 18, 20, and 22 May 1853	v	Prelude to Lohengrin [explanatory program]	iii	Grey, ed., Richard Wagner and his World: 499–501
Lohengrin, i: Männerszene und Brautzug; ii: Hochzeitmusik und Brautlied, 1853	For the concerts on 18, 20, and 22 May 1853	xvi	i: Men's Chorus and Bridal Procession; ii: Wedding Music and Bridal Chorus [explanatory program]		Grey, ed., Richard Wagner and his World: 504
Ouvertüre zum "Fliegenden Holländer," 1853	For a concert in Zurich, 25 April 1853	v	Overture to Der fliegende Holländer [explanatory program]	iii	Grey, ed., Richard Wagner and his World: 498–9
Über die programmatischen Erklärungen zu den Konzerten im Mai 1853, 1853		xvi	On the programmatical explanations for the concerts in May 1853		
Vorwort zum ersten Druck des "Ring des Nibelungen," 1853	Zurich 1853	xii	Foreword to the first publication of the Ring des Nibelungen		
Beethovens Cis moll Quartett, 1854	Program note for concert on 12 December 1854; also: Entwürfe, Gedanken, Fragmente aus nachgelassenen Papieren zusammengestellt, 1885	xii	Beethoven's C♯ minor Quartet [explanatory program]	viii	Grey, ed., Richard Wagner and his World: 504–5

Gluck's Ouvertüre zu "Iphigenie in Aulis," 1854	Neue Zeitschrift für Musik, 1 July 1854	v	Gluck's Overture to Iphigenie in Aulis, 1854	iii	
Empfehlung einer Streichquartett-Vereinigung, 1854	Eidgenössische Zeitung, 3 October 1853	xvi	Recommendation of a String Quartet Organization		
Bemerkung zu einer angeblichen Äusserung Rossinis	Entwürfe, Gedanken, Fragmente aus nachgelassenen Papieren zusammengestellt, 1885		Comment on an Alleged Remark of Rossini's		
Dante-Schopenhauer [letter to Liszt], 1855		xvi	Dante-Schopenhauer, 1855		
Über die Leitung einer Mozart-Feier, 1856	Eidgenössische Zeitung, 15 February 1856	xvi	On the Administration of a Mozart Festival	iii	
ÜBER FRANZ LISZTS SYMPHONISCHE DICHTUNGEN: Brief an M[arie zu Sayn] W[ittgenstein], 1857	Completed 15 February 1857; Neue Zeitschrift für Musik, 10 April 1857	v	On Liszt's Symphonic Poems: A Letter to M[arie zu Sayn] W[ittgenstein], 1857	iii	"Wagner's Open Letter to Marie Wittgenstein on Liszt's Symphonic Poems," trans. Thomas Grey, The Wagner Journal 5:1 (March 2011): 65–81
Entwurf eines Amnestiegesuches an den Sächsischen Justizminister Behr, 1858		xvi	[Draft of an Appeal for Amnesty from the Minister of Justice of Saxony Behr, 1858]		
Metaphysik der Geschlechtsliebe, 1858		xii	The Metaphysics of Sexual Love, 1858		

Title/date (German)	First edition	SSD	Title (English)	PW	Other translation / notes
Nachruf an L. Spohr und Chordirektor W. Fischer: brieflich an einen älteren Freund in Dresden, 1860	*Neue Zeitschrift für Musik*, 2 December 1859	v	Homage to L. Spohr and Chorus-Master W. Fischer: A Letter to an Old Dresden Friend, 1860	iii	
"Tristan und Isolde": Vorspiel, 1859	For a concert in Paris on 25 January 1860; *Entwürfe, Gedanken, Fragmente aus nachgelassenen Papieren zusammengestellt*, 1885	xii	*Tristan und Isolde*: Prelude, 1859 [explanatory program]	viii	Grey, ed., *Richard Wagner and his World*: 505–7
Ein Brief an Hector Berlioz, 1860	*Journal des débats*, 22 February 1860	vii	A Letter to Hector Berlioz	iii	
"ZUKUNFTSMUSIK": an einen französischen Freund (F. Villot) als Vorwort zu einer Prosa-Übersetzung meiner Operndichtungen, September 1860	Leipzig 1861	vii	"Music of the Future": to a French Friend (F. Villot) as Preface to a Prose-Translation of my Opera-Poems	iii	*Three Wagner Essays*, trans. Jacobs: 13–44
Bericht über die Aufführung des "Tannhäuser" in Paris [letter 27 March 1861]	*Deutsche Allgemeine Zeitung*, 7 April 1861	vii	A Report on the Production of *Tannhäuser* in Paris	iii	
Vom Wiener Hofoperntheater, 1861	*Österreichische Zeitung*, 8 October 1861	xii	On the Vienna Court Opera		

Vorwort zur Herausgabe der Dichtung des Bühnen festspieles "Der Ring des Nibelungen," 1862	Leipzig, 1863	vi	Preface to an edition of the poem of *Der Ring des Nibelungen*	iii	
Richard Wagner über die ungarische Musik [letter of 8 August 1863 to Abrányi]	*Pesther Lloyd* 188 and *Niederrheinische Musik-Zeitung*, 29 August 1863		[Richard Wagner on Hungarian Music]		
Drei Schreiben an die Direktion der Philharmonischen Gesellschaft in St. Petersburg, 1862–6	12 December 1862 (i), 30 March 1863 (ii), 8 November 1866 (iii)	xvi	Three Letters to the Board of the St. Petersburg Philharmonic Society		
Das Wiener Hofoperntheater, 1863	*Der Wiener Botschafter*, October 1863	vii	The Vienna Court Opera	iii	
"Die Meistersinger von Nürnberg": Vorspiel, 1863	Program note for a concert 2 December 1863; also *Bayreuther Blätter* 25 (1902): 168	xii	*Die Meistersinger von Nürnberg:* Prelude [explanatory program]		Grey, ed., *Richard Wagner and his World:* 507–9
"Tristan und Isolde": Vorspiel und Schlussatz, 1863	Program note for a concert in Vienna, 27 December 1863; also *Bayreuther Blätter* 25 (1902): 167	xii	*Tristan und Isolde:* Prelude and Final Section [explanatory program]		Grey, ed., *Richard Wagner and his World:* 507
Über Staat und Religion, 1864	Completed 16 July 1864	viii	On State and Religion	iv	
Buddha-Luther, 1864	*Entwürfe, Gedanken, Fragmente aus nachgelassenen Papieren zusammengestellt*, 1885	xii		viii	
Zur Erwiderung des Aufsatzes "Richard Wagner und die öffentliche Meinung" [by O. von Redwitz], 1865	*Allgemeine Zeitung* (Augsburg), 22 February 1865	xii	By way of a reply to the article *Richard Wagner and Public Opinion*		

(cont.)

Title/date (German)	First edition	SSD	Title (English)	PW	Other translation / notes
Bericht an Seine Majestät den König Ludwig II. von Bayern über eine in München zu errichtende deutsche Musikschule, 1865	Completed 23 March 1865; published Munich 1865	viii	Report to His Majesty, King Ludwig II of Bavaria, on a German Music School to Be Founded in Munich	iv	
Einladung zur ersten Aufführung von "Tristan und Isolde," 18 April 1865	*Der Botschafter,* 21 April 1865	xvi	Invitation to the First Production of *Tristan und Isolde* in Munich [letter of 18 April 1865]	viii	
Ansprache an das Hoforchester in München vor der Hauptprobe zu "Tristan" am Vormittag des 11. Mai 1865	*Bayrische Zeitung,* 15 May 1865	xvi	Address to the court orchestra in Munich before the dress rehearsal of *Tristan* on the morning of 11 May 1865.		
Dankschreiben an das Münchener Hoforchester, 19 Juli 1865		xvi	Letter of Thanks to the Munich Court Orchestra		
Ein Artikel der Münchener "Neuesten Nachrichten" vom 29 November 1865	*Neueste Nachrichten,* 29 November 1865	xvi	An Article in the Munich *Neuesten Nachrichten* on 29 November 1865		
WAS IST DEUTSCH?, 1865	Written 14–27 September 1865; *Bayreuther Blätter,* February 1878; *König Ludwig II. und Richard Wagner: Briefwechesel*	x	What is German?	iv	*Wagner: Stories and Essays,* trans. Osborne: 40–55

(cont.)

Title/date (German)	First edition	SSD	Title (English)	PW	Other translation / notes
Über das Dirigieren, 1869	Begun 31 October 1869; Leipzig, 1869	viii	On Conducting	iv	*On Conducting*, trans. Edward Dannreuther (London: William Reeves, 1887); *Three Wagner Essays*, trans. Jacobs: 47–93
Censuren IV: "E. Devrient: Meine Erinnerungen an Felix Mendelssohn Bartholdy," 1869	Munich 1869	viii	Review: "E. Devrient: My Recollections of Felix Mendelssohn Bartholdy"	iv	
Censuren V: Aufklärungen über "Das Judentum in der Musik": an Frau Marie Muchanoff, geb. Gräfin Nesselrode, 1869	Leipzig 1869	viii	Review: Some explanations concerning *Judaism in Music* [*Jewishness in Music*]: to Frau Marie Muchanoff, née Countess Nesselrode	iii	*Judaism in Music: Being the Original Essay Together with the Later Supplement*, trans. Edwin Evans (London: William Reeves, 1910)
Persönliches: warum ich den zahllosen Angriffen auf mich und meine Kunstansichten nichts erwidere, 1869	*Entwürfe, Gedanken, Fragmente aus nachgelassenen Papieren zusammengestellt*, 1885	xii	Why I Do Not Reply to the Countless Attacks on Me and My Artistic Views	viii	
"Die Meistersinger von Nürnberg": Vorspiel zum 3. Akt, 1869		xii	*Die Meistersinger von Nürnberg*: Prelude to the 3rd Act [explanatory program]	viii	Grey, ed., *Richard Wagner and his World*: 507–9
Fragment eines Aufsatzes über Hector Berlioz, c. 11 March 1869	*Entwürfe, Gedanken, Fragmente aus nachgelassenen Papieren zusammengestellt*, 1885	xii	Fragment of an Essay on Hector Berlioz	viii	

Title/date (German)	First edition	SSD	Title (English)	PW	Other translation / notes
Ein nicht veröffentlichter Schluss der Schrift "Beethoven," 1870		xvi	[An Unpublished Ending of the Essay *Beethoven*, 1870]		
Offener Brief an Dr. phil. Friedrich Stade, 31 December 1870	*Musikalisches Wochenblatt,* 13 January 1871	xvi	Open Letter to Dr. phil. Friedrich Stade		
Über die Bestimmung der Oper, 1871	Leipzig, 1871	ix	The Destiny of Opera	v	
Ansprache an das Orchester in der Singakademie, 1871	Manuscript		Address to the Orchestra at the Singakademie on 30 April 1871		
Über die Aufführung des Bühnenfestspieles: "Der Ring des Nibelungen" und Memorandum über Aufführung des "Ring" im markgräflichen Opernhaus Bayreuth, 1871			On the Performance of the Stage Festival Drama *Der Ring des Nibelungen* and Memorandum on the Performance of the *Ring* in the Margravial Opera House, Bayreuth		
Vorwort zur Gesamtherausgabe, 1871	Dated 22 May 1871	i	Foreword to *Gesammelte Schriften und Dichtungen*	i	
Erinnerungen an Auber, 1871	*Musikalisches Wochenblatt,* 10, 17, and 24 November 1871	ix	Reminiscences of Auber	v	
Epilogischer Bericht über die Umstände und Schicksale, welche die Ausführung des	Leipzig, 1872	vi, iii	Report to the German Wagner Union on Circumstances and fates	iii, v	

(cont.)

Title/date (German)	First edition	SSD	Title (English)	PW	Other translation / notes
Vorwort zu GS 3/4, 1871		iii	Foreword to GS 3/4	vii	
Censuren: Vorbericht, 1872	*Musikalisches Wochenblatt*, 19 April 1872	viii	Reviews: Preliminary Report	iv	
Ankündigung für den 22. Mai 1872	Dated 1 February 1872; *Bayreuther Blätter* 9 (1886): 9	xvi	Announcement for 22 May 1872 [laying of foundation-stone in Bayreuth]	v	
Ankündigung der Aufführung der 9. Symphonie für den 22. Mai 1872	Dated 16 March 1872; *Bayreuther Blätter* 9 (1886): 10–11	xvi	Announcement of Performance of Ninth Symphony for 22 May 1872	v	
An Friedrich Nietzsche, 12 June 1872	*Norddeutsche Allgemeine Zeitung*, 23 June 1872	ix	(Letter) To Friedrich Nietzsche	v	
Über Schauspieler und Sänger, 1872	Completed 14 September 1872; Leipzig, 1872	ix	On Actors and Singers	v	
Schreiben an den Bürgermeister von Bologna, 1872	*Musikalisches Wochenblatt*, 11 October 1872	ix	A Letter to the Mayor of Bologna	v	
Brief über das Schauspielerwesen an einen Schauspieler, 9 November 1872	*Almanach der Bühnengenossenschaft*, 1873	ix	Letter [on Being an Actor Addressed] to an Actor	v	
Unter Gott sucht sich der Mensch	*Entwürfe, Gedanken, Fragmente aus nachgelassenen Papieren zusammengestellt*, 1885	xii	Man Seeks Himself in God	viii	
Ein Einblick in das heutige deutsche Opernwesen, 1872	*Musikalisches Wochenblatt*, 3, 10, and 17 January 1873	ix	A Glance at the German Operatic Stage of Today	v	

Title/date (German)	First edition	SSD	Title (English)	PW	Other translation / notes
Zwei Reden gehalten anläßlich eines Banketts auf der Brühlschen Terrasse in Dresden am 14. Januar 1873	Manuscript		Two Speeches Given at a Banquet on the Brühl Terrace in Dresden on 14 January 1873		
Einleitung zu einer Vorlesung der "Götterdämmerung" vor einem auserwählten Zuhörer in Berlin, 17 January 1873	Musikalisches Wochenblatt, 7 March 1873	ix	Introduction to a Reading of Götterdämmerung Before a Select Audience in Berlin	v	
Zum Vortrag der neunten Symphonie Beethovens, 1873	Musikalisches Wochenblatt, 11 April 1873	ix	On Performing Beethoven's Ninth Symphony	v	Three Wagner Essays, trans. Jacobs: 97–127
Schlussbericht über die Umstände und Schicksale, welche die Ausführung des Bühnenfestspieles "Der Ring des Nibelungen" bis zur Gründung von Wagner-Vereinen begleiteten, 1873		ix	[Final Report on the Fates and Circumstances that Attended the Execution of the Stage Festival Play Der Ring des Nibelungen and the Founding of Wagner Societies]	v	
Das Bühnenfestspielhaus zu Bayreuth: nebst einem Bericht über die Grundsteinlegung desselben, 1873	Dated 1 May 1873 and 22 May 1873; Leipzig 1873	ix	The Festival Theater in Bayreuth, with an Account of the Laying of its Foundation-Stone	v	
An die Patrone der Bühnenfestspiele in Bayreuth, 15 September 1873	Bayreuther Blätter 9 (1886): 18	xii	To the Patrons of the Bayreuth Festival		

MEIN LEBEN, vols. I–III, 1865–75 (published privately, 1870–5), IV, 1879–80 (published privately, 1881)	Vols. I–IV, abridged (Munich, 1911) suppressed passages first published in *Die Musik* 22 (1929–30): 725 First complete edition, ed. M. Gregor-Dellin (Munich 1963)	xiii–xv	My Life		Trans. A. Gray, ed. Mary Whittall (Cambridge University Press, 1983)
Über eine Opernaufführung in Leipzig: Brief an den Herausgeber des "Musikalischen Wochenblattes," 1874	*Musikalisches Wochenblatt,* 8 January 1875	x	On an Opera Performance in Leipzig: Letter to the Editor of the *Musikalisches Wochenblatt*	vi	
Notgedrungene Erklärung, 16 February 1874	*Bayreuther Blätter* 9 (1886): 21–2	xii	Necessary declaration		
Die "Presse" zu den "Proben," 1875	*Bayreuther Blätter* 9 (1886): 26	xii	The "Press" on "Rehearsals"		Grey, ed., *Richard Wagner and his World*: 509–13
Götterdämmerung, i: Vorspiel; ii: Hagens Wacht; iii: Siegfrieds Tod; iv: Schluss des letzten Aktes, 1875	Program notes for a concert in Vienna on 1 March 1875	xvi	*Götterdämmerung,* i: Prelude; ii: Hagen's Watch; iii: Siegfried's Death; iv: Finale of the Last Act		
Einladungsschreiben an die Sänger für Proben und Aufführungen des Bühnenfestspiels "Der Ring des Nibelungen," 14/15 January 1875	*Bayreuther Blätter* 9 (1886): 22–4	xvi	Invitation to the Singers for Rehearsals and Performances of the Stage Festival Drama *Der Ring des Nibelungen*		
Ankündigung der Festspiele für 1876, letter, 28 August 1875	*Bayreuther Blätter* 9 (1886): 26–7	xvi	Announcement of the Festival for 1876		

Title/date (German)	First edition	SSD	Title (English)	PW	Other translation / notes
Über Bewerbungen zu den Festspielen, 4 Okt. 1876	*Musikalisches Wochenblatt,* 8 October 1875	xvi	On Applications for the Festival, 4 October 1876		
An die Künstler (zum ersten Festspiel), 1 November 1875	*Bayreuther Blätter* 9 (1886): 28	xvi	To the Artists (for the first festival)		
Austeilung der Rollen, 1876	Manuscript		Distribution of Roles		
Voranschlag der "Entschädigungen," 1876	Manuscript		Estimate of "Compensation"		
Skizzierung der Proben und Aufführungen, 1876	Manuscript		Draft Schedule of Rehearsals and Performances		
An die Orchestermitglieder (zum ersten Festspiel), 6 April 1876	*Bayreuther Blätter* 9 (1886): 29	xvi	To the Members of the Orchestra (for the first festival)		
An die Sänger (Einladung), 9 April 1876	*Bayreuther Blätter* 9 (1886): 29–30	xvi	To the Singers (Invitation)		
Für die Patrone, 18 April 1876	*Bayreuther Blätter* 9 (1886): 30	xvi	To the Patrons		
Circular, die "Costümproben auf der beleuchteten Bühne betreffend," 22 July 1876	Manuscript		Circular Relating to Dress Rehearsals on the Lit Stage		
Verzeichnis der Ehrenpatrone und Freikarten-Empfänger, 1876	Manuscript		List of Honorary Patrons and Those in Receipt of Complimentary Tickets		

(cont.)

Title/date (German)	First edition	SSD	Title (English)	PW	Other translation / notes
An die geehrten Vorstände der Richard Wagnervereine, 1 January 1877	Printed privately	x	To the Honorable Presidents of the Richard Wagner Societies	vi	
Entwurf, veröffentlicht mit den Statuten des Patronat-vereines, 15 September 1877		x	Prospectus Published with the Statutes of the Patrons' Association	vi	Re: Proposed Bayreuth "School"
Ansprache an die Abgesandten des Bayreuther Patronats, 15 September 1877	RICHARD WAGNER-JAHRBUCH, ed. Kürschner (Stuttgart, 1886)	xii	Address to the Delegates of the Bayreuth Patronage Scheme	vi	
Ankündigung der Aufführung des "Parsifal," 8 December 1877	*Bayreuther Blätter* 1 (1878): 15–17	xii	Announcement of the performance of *Parsifal*	vi	
Zur Einführung, 8 January 1878	*Bayreuther Blätter* 1 (1878): 1–5	x	Introduction [to the first number of the *Bayreuther Blätter*]	vi	
An die geehrten Vorstände der noch bestehenden lokalen Wagner-Vereine, 15 January 1878	*Bayreuther Blätter* 1 (1878): 23–4	xvi	To the Honored Presidents of such Local Wagner Societies as Still Exist	vi	
Modern, 1878	*Bayreuther Blätter* 1 (1878): 59–63	x	Modern	vi	
Erläuterung des "Siegfried-Idylls" für S. M. den König, 1878			Note on *Siegfried Idyll* for His Majesty the King		
Publikum und Popularität, 1878	*Bayreuther Blätter* 1 (1878): 85–92, 171–7, 213–22	x	Public and Popularity	vi	

(cont.)

Title/date (German)	First edition	SSD	Title (English)	PW	Other translation / notes
Zur Einführung in das Jahr 1880, written December 1879	Bayreuther Blätter 3 (1880): 1–5	x	Introduction to the Year 1880	vi	
Religion und Kunst, completed 19 July 1880	Bayreuther Blätter 3 (1880): 269–300	x	Religion and Art, 1880	vi	
"Was nützt diese Erkenntnis?": ein Nachtrag zu "Religion und Kunst," completed 25 October 1880	Bayreuther Blätter 3 (1880): 333–41	x	"What Use is this Knowledge?": A Supplement to Religion and Art	vi	
Zur Mitteilung an die geehrten Patrone der Bühnenfestspiele in Bayreuth, letter of 1 December 1880	Privately printed	x	To the Honoured Patrons of the Stage-Festivals at Bayreuth	vi	
Gedanken zur Fortführung der Festspiele, 1880	Manuscript		Thoughts on Continuing the Festival		
"Parsifal: Vorspiel." An König Ludwig II. über die Aufführung des "Parsifal," 1880	Program note for performance on 12 November 1880	xii	"Parsifal: Prelude." To King Ludwig II on the Performance of Parsifal		Grey, ed., Richard Wagner and his World: 515–16
Zur Einführung der Arbeit des Grafen Gobineau "Ein Urteil über die jetzige Weltlage," 25 April 1881	Bayreuther Blätter 4 (1881): 249–58	x	Introduction to the Work of Count Gobineau's: A Critique of the Present State of the World	vi	
Ausführungen zu "Religion und Kunst": "Erkenne dich	Bayreuther Blätter 4 (1881): 33–41 and 249–58	x	Continuation of Religion and Art: "Know Thyself";	vi	

German Title	Source			English Title	Notes
"selbst" February 1881; "Heldentum u. Christentum," 4 September 1881				"Heroism and Christianity"	
Einladung der Sänger, 1882	Manuscript			Invitation to the Singers	
Austheilung der Partien, 1882	Manuscript			Distribution of Roles	
Begleitschreiben zur "Austheilung" der Partien sowie Plan der Proben und Aufführungen, 1882	Manuscript			Letter Accompanying Distribution of Roles and Timetables of Rehearsals and Performances	
Proben-Plan. Entwurf, 1882	Manuscript			Rehearsal Schedule. Draft	
Brief an H. v. Wolzogen, 13 March 1882	*Bayreuther Blätter*, 5 (1882): 97–100	x	vi	A Letter to H. v. Wolzogen, 13 March 1882	
Offenes Schreiben an Herrn Friedrich Schön in Worms, 16 June 1882	*Bayreuther Blätter* 5 (1882): 193–7	x	vi	Open Letter to Herr Friedrich Schön in Worms, 16 June 1882	Re: The Stipendary Fund
Rede, gehalten in Wahnfried anläßlich der Hochzeit Blandine von Bülows, 25 August 1882	Manuscript			Speech Given in Wahnfried on the Occasion of Blandine von Bülow's wedding	Accuracy of manuscript in doubt
Das Bühnenweihfestspiel in Bayreuth 1882, completed 1 November 1882	*Bayreuther Blätter* 5 (1882): 321–9	x	vi	[The Stage Consecration Festival Drama] "Parsifal" at Bayreuth 1882	
Bericht über die Wieder-aufführung eines Jugend-werkes. An den Herausgeber des "Musikalischen	*Musikalisches Wochenblatt*, 11 January 1883	x	vi	Report on the Revival of an Early Work: To the Editor	

Title/date (German)	First edition	SSD	Title (English)	PW	Other translation / notes
Wochen-blattes," letter of 31 December 1882			of the *Musikalisches Wochenblatt*		
Danksagung an die Bayreuther Bürgerschaft, letter of 3 September 1882	*Bayreuther Tagblatt,* 5 September 1882	xvi	Letter of Thanks to the Bayreuth Citizenry		
Brief an H. v. Stein, 31 January 1883	*Bayreuther Blätter* 6 (1883): 5–10	x	A Letter to H. v. Stein	vi	
Über das Weibliche im Menschlichen, written 11–13 Feb. 1883, unfinished.	*Entwürfe, Gedanken, Fragmente aus nachgelassenen Papieren zusammengestellt,* 1885	xii	On the Womanly in the Human Race	vi, viii	
Metaphysik. Kunst und Religion. Moral. Christentum [aphorisms]	*Entwürfe, Gedanken, Fragmente aus nachgelassenen Papieren zusammengestellt,* 1885	xii	Metaphysics. Art and Religion. Morality. Christianity	viii	

TRANSLATIONS CITED

Thomas S. Grey, ed., *Richard Wagner and His World* (Princeton University Press, 2009).

Richard Wagner: Stories and Essays, trans. Charles Osborne (New York: Library Press, 1973).

Three Wagner Essays, trans. Robert L. Jacobs (Eulenberg: London, 1979).

Wagner Writes from Paris: Stories, Essays and Articles by the Young Composer, ed. Robert Jacobs and Geoffrey Skelton (New York: Day, 1973).

SOURCES CONSULTED

John Deathridge and Carl Dahlhaus, *The New Grove Wagner* (see bibliography): 188–93.

Jürgen Kühmel, "The Prose Writings," in *Wagner Handbook*, ed. U. Müller and P. Wapnewski, trans. and ed. J. Deathridge (see bibliography): 638–51.

Barry Millington, ed., *Wagner Compendium* (see bibliography): 326–32.

Jean-Jacques Nattiez, "Catalog of Wagner's Writings," in *Wagner Androgyne* (see bibliography): 303–22.

Appendix 6 Musical works

Compiled by Nicholas Vazsonyi and
Ulrich Drüner
With the assistance of Leigh Buches

The following is a concise rendition of selected information from the WAGNER WERK-VERZEICHNIS (WWV). Works and persons in SMALL CAPS have separate entries. Please consult those for further information. Most details relating to development, composition, and publication have been omitted, so reference to this chart in no way replaces careful consultation of the WWV itself. In most cases, the information under "publication" is simply the critical edition in *Sämtliche Werke* (SW). However, some details of the first publication are also listed when this occurred as part of the work's composition and first performance. For stage works, publication refers to the complete score only, and not to various stages of libretto, piano reduction, etc. For items marked LOST or INCOMPLETE, please consult the entry under WORKS, LOST and WORKS, INCOMPLETE, respectively. For current status of the SW project and detailed contents of each volume, see: www.adwmainz.de/index. php?id=381.

WWV	Title	First performance	Publication	Remarks
1	Leubald (Trauerspiel in fünf Aufzügen)		Extracts from Act v: Leipzig, 1908; SSD 16; SW 31	Written 1826–8; no music survives
2	Piano Sonata, D minor, LOST			1829; Wagner's "first sonata" (ML)
3	Arie, LOST	Circumstances of first performance in "Kintschy's Schweizer-hütte" (ML) are doubtful		1829
4	String Quartet, D major, LOST			1829; mentioned in ML
5	Piano Sonata, F minor, LOST			1829; mentioned in Red Pocketbook
6	Schäferoper (fragment; after Goethe's *Die Laune des Verliebten*), LOST			1830
7	Songs (unidentified), fragment		SW 21	1828–30
8	Arie for soprano and orchestra, LOST			1830; mention in ML
9	Beethoven: Symphony No. 9, piano reduction for two hands		SW 20.1	1830–1; offered to Schott for publication
10	Overture in B♭ major, "Drumbeat" (*Paukenschlag*), LOST	25 December 1830; Leipzig, Königlich Sächsisches Hoftheater; Cond. DORN		Summer 1830

(cont.)

WWV	Title	First performance	Publication	Remarks
11	Political Overture, LOST			Possibly September 1830
12	Overture to Schiller's *Die Braut von Messina*, LOST			Possibly identical with WWV 13
13	Orchestral piece, E minor, fragment		SW 18.1	
14	Overture, C major, LOST			Late 1830; according to CWD (15 December 1878) in $\frac{6}{8}$
15	Seven Compositions for Goethe's *Faust*: 1. Lied der Soldaten; 2. Bauer unter der Linde; 3. Branders Lied; 4. Lied des Mephistopheles: "Es war einmal ein König"; 5. Lied des Mephistopheles: "Was machst du mir vor Liebchens Tür"; 6. Gretchen am Spinnrade; 7. Melodram (Gretchen, spoken text)		SW 17	Early 1831
16	Piano Sonata, B♭ major, four hands, LOST			Early 1831; mentioned in ML
17	Overture, E♭ major, probably fragment; LOST			Early 1831; not identical with WWV 11

No.	Work	SW / Publication	Premiere	Notes
18	Haydn: Symphony No. 103, piano reduction for two hands, LOST			Mentioned in undated letter to BREITKOPF & HÄRTEL (letter received 14 August 1831)
19a	Four-Part Fugue: "Dein ist das Reich"	SW 16		Fall/winter 1831–2
19b	Four-Part Double Fugue in C major	SW 21		Early 1832
20	Overture, D minor (Concert Overture No. 1)	SW 18.1 (both versions)	25 December 1831; Leipzig Königlich Sächsisches Hoftheater; Cond. prob. DORN	Summer 1831; two versions
21	Piano Sonata, B♭ major, Op. 1	Breitkopf & Härtel 1832; SW 19		Fall 1831; dedicated to C. T. WEINLIG; mentioned as "Op. 1" in letter to sister Ottilie, 3 March 1832
22	Fantasie (Fantasia) for Piano, F♯ minor	SW 19		Fall 1831
23a	Polonaise for Piano, D major	SW 21		Late 1831/early 1832
23b	Polonaise for Piano four hands, D major, Op. 2	Breitkopf & Härtel 1832; SW 19		"Op. 2" added later by Breitkopf & Härtel
24	Overture, E minor, and stage music to Ernst Raupach's *König Enzio* (Trauerspiel in 5 Akten)	SW 18.1	17 February 1832, Leipzig Königlich Sächsisches Hoftheater; cond. DORN	
25	Entreactes tragiques No. 1, D major No. 2, C minor	SW 18.1		Early 1832; nowhere mentioned by Wagner

WWV	Title	First performance	Publication	Remarks
26	Grosse Sonata für Klavier, A major, Op. 4		SW 19	Early 1832; "Op. 4" on title-page of autograph manuscript
27	Concert Overture No. 2, C major	Presumably end March 1832; Leipzig, Musikverein Euterpe; cond. Wagner	SW 18.1	March 1832; mentioned in ML and letter to Ottilie 3 March 1832
28	Szene und Arie for Soprano and Orchestra, LOST	22 April 1832, Leipzig, Königlich Sächsisches Hoftheater, cond. DORN		
29	SYMPHONY, C major	November 1832, Prague, Ständisches Konservatorium, cond. Dionys Weber	SW 18.1	April–June; revised for private performance Venice, La Fenice, 25 December 1882
30	Glockentöne; *Lied* for voice and piano (to a text by T. APEL), LOST			Entitled "Abendglocken" (letter to Apel, 12 October 1832) and "Glockentöne" (ML); text probably identical with Apel's poem "Der Entfernten"
31	Die Hochzeit (Opera, adapted from J. Büsching, *Ritterzeit und Ritterwesen*), INCOMPLETE	13 February 1933, Rostock, Stadttheater	SW 15	Text: October/November 1832; Music: December 1832– February 1833
32	Die FEEN (Grosse romantische Oper in 3 Akten, after C. Gozzi, *La donna serpente*)	Overture only: 10 January 1835, Magdeburg, cond. Wagner; Complete: 29 June 1888, Munich, Königliches Hof- und Nationaltheater, cond. Fischer	SW 1	Text: January–February 1833/ summer 1834; Music: February 1833–January 1834

No.	Work	Performance	SW	Date/notes
33	New ending (Allegro) to Aria No. 15 (Aubry) from H. Marschner's *Der Vampyr*	29 September 1833, Würzburg, Stadttheater; Aubry: Albert Wagner	SW 15	September 1833
34	Instrumentation for a Cavatine from Bellini's *Il pirata*, LOST			November–December 1833; mentioned and wrongly dated in ML
35	Symphony, E major, fragment			August–September 1834
36	Music for W. Schmale's *Beim Antritt des neuen Jahres 1835*	1 January 1835, Magdeburg, Stadttheater, cond. Wagner; Cornelius version: 22 May 1873, Bayreuth, Markgräfliches Opernhaus	SW 16	December 1834; with new text written by P. CORNELIUS for Wagner's 60th birthday entitled "Künstler-Weihe"
37	Overture, E♭ major and stage music for T. Apel's Drama, *Columbus*	16 February 1835, Magdeburg, Stadttheater, cond. Wagner	SW 18.2	December 1834–January 1835; Overture WWV 37a; Stage Music WWV 37b, LOST (see notes in WWV)
38	Das LIEBESVERBOT oder Die Novize von Palermo (Grosse komische Oper in zwei Akten, after Shakespeare's *Measure for Measure*)	29 March 1836, Magdeburg, Stadttheater, cond. Wagner	SW 22	
39	Overture in C major, *Polonia*	Possibly: winter 1836–7, Königsberg, Stadttheater, cond. Wagner; 2 January 1905, London, Queen's Hall, cond. Henry Wood	SW 18.2	18 May–7 July 1836 (ML)

(cont.)

WWV	Title	First performance	Publication	Remarks
40	Die hohe Braut (Grosse Oper in fünf Akten, after eponymous novel by Heinrich Koenig)		SW 31	July 1836; August 1842; Wagner wrote the text but no music has been found, nor does Wagner mention any
41	Stage music to J. Singer's *Die letzte Heidenverschwörung in Preussen oder Der Deutsche Ritterorden in Königsberg*	Presumably 17 February 1837 Königsberg, Stadttheater	SW 15	February 1837
42	Overture in D major, *Rule Britannia*	Probably 19 March 1838, Riga, Schwarzhäuptersaal, cond. Wagner	SW 18.2	March 1837
43	Aria in G major for bass (insert for Max) "Sanfte Wehmut will sich regen," for Carl Blum: *Mary, Max und Michel*	1 September 1837, Riga, Stadttheater, cond. Wagner	SW 15	August 1837
44	Volks-Hymne in G major, *Nicolay*	21 November 1837, Riga, Stadttheater, cond. probably Wagner	SW 16	
45	Aria for Bass as insert for J. Weigl's *Die Schweizerfamilie*, LOST	Probably Riga, Stadttheater, 22 December 1837; B solo: F. W. Scheibler		Mentioned in Red Pocketbook and *Mein Leben*
46	Opera Reworkings for Riga			

46a	BELLINI: *Norma*, additions and changes to orchestration	Probably 11 December 1837, Riga, Stadttheater, cond. Wagner	SW 20.2	
46b	MEYERBEER: *Robert le diable*, Cavatina, "Robert, toi que j'aime" transcription of harp part	Probably 30 November 1838, Riga, Stadttheater, cond. Wagner	SW 20.2	
46c	WEBER: *Euryanthe*, reinstrumentation of Hunting Chorus	Probably 17 January 1839, Riga, Schwarzhäupter-Saal, cond. Wagner	SW 20.2	
47	ROSSINI: *Les Soirées musicales* reinstrumentation of duet "Die Seemänner"	Probably 19 March 1838, Riga, Schwarzhäupter-Saal, cond. Wagner	SW 20.2	
48	*Männerlist grösser als Frauenlist oder Die glückliche Bärenfamilie* (Komische Oper in zwei Akten, after 1001 Nights)		SW 31 (text in SSD 11)	Music LOST
49	*RIENZI, DER LETZTE DER TRIBUNEN* (Grosse tragische Oper in fünf Akten, after E. BULWER-LYTTON: *Rienzi: the Last of the Roman Tribunes*)	20 October 1842, Dresden, Königlich Sächsisches Hoftheater, cond. REISSIGER	Dresden, 1842; SW 23	Text written 1837–40; music, 1838–40
50	Der Tannenbaum, *Lied* for voice and piano in E♭ minor (text by G. Scheurlin)		*Europa*, 1839, vol. IV; SW 17	Composed Riga, 1838, not earlier in Königsberg as in ML

WWV	Title	First performance	Publication	Remarks
51	Gesang am Grabe (text by H. von Brackel), LOST	4 January 1839, Riga, Jakobi-Kirchhof		Written 29 December 1838–4 January 1839
52	Bellini: *Norma*, bass aria "Norma il predisse" as insert		SW 15	Written for L. Lablache who, according to Wagner's letter to G. E. Anders (13 October 1839), refused to sing it
53	Dors mon enfant (author unknown); *Lied* for voice and piano in F major		*Europa*, 1841, vol. III; SW 17	
54	Extase (text by V. Hugo), *Lied* for voice and piano in D major		SW 17	Fall 1839
55	Attente (text by V. Hugo), *Lied* for voice and piano in G major		*Europa*, 1842, vol. I; SW 17	Fall 1839
56	La tombe dit à la rose (text by V. Hugo), *Lied* for voice and piano in E minor		*Europa*, 1843, vol. II; SW 17	Fall 1839
57	Mignonne (text by P. de Ronsard), *Lied* for voice and piano in E major		*Europa*, 1843, vol. II; SW 17	Fall 1839
58	Tout n'est qu'images fugitives (Soupir) (text by J. Reboul) *Lied* for voice and piano in B♭ major		SW 17	Fall 1839

No.	Title			
59	Eine Faust-Ouvertüre, D minor	Version 1: 22 July 1844 Dresden, Palais des Königlichen Grossen Gartens, cond. Wagner; version 2: 23 January 1855, Zurich, Casino, cond. Wagner	Version 1: SW 18.2. Version 2: Breitkopf & Härtel (1855); SW 18.3	December 1839–January 1840; January 1855 (originally first movement of projected Faust Symphony)
60	Les Deux Grenadiers (text by H. Heine, trans. F. A. Loeve-Veimar) *Lied* for voice [baritone] and piano in A minor		*Revue et gazette musicale*, 1840; SW 17	December 1839–early 1840; dedicated to Heinrich HEINE
61	Adieux de Marie Stuart (text by P. J. de Beranger) *Lied* for voice [soprano] and piano in E♭ major		SW 17	March 1840
62	Paris arrangements		SW 20.2	
62a	Suites for cornets à pistons (potpourris) LOST			
62b	DONIZETTI: *La favorite*, arrangements	Possibly 2 December 1840	*Revue et gazette musicale*, 1841	
62c	H. Herz: *Grande fantaisie sur La romanesca*, piano four hands			
62d	HALÉVY: *Le guitarrero*, arrangements	Presumably 21 January 1841		
62e	Halévy: *La Reine de Chypre*, arrangements	Presumably 22 December 1841		
62f	AUBER: *Zanetta, ou Jouer avec le feu*, arr., string quartet			

WWV	Title	First performance	Publication	Remarks
63	Der FLIEGENDE HOLLÄNDER (Romantische Oper in drei Aufzügen, after H. HEINE: Aus den Memoiren des Herrn von Schnabelewopski)	2 January 1843, Dresden, Königlich Sächsisches Hoftheater, cond. Wagner	Self-published; SW 4	Overture completed 5 November 1841; dedicated to Ida von Lüttichau (née von Knobelsdorf); original version in one act
64	Work for Piano in E major; Albumblatt für E. B. KIETZ "Lied ohne Worte"		SW 19	
65	Chorus in B♭ major: "Descendons gaiment la courtille" as insert for Vaudeville Ballett	Possibly 20 January 1841, Paris, Théâtre des Variétés,	SW 15	
66	Die Sarazenin (Oper in fünf Akten), scenario		SW 31	Wagner never set the text to music
67	Die Bergwerke zu Falun (Oper in drei Akten after a work by E. T. A. HOFFMANN), scenario		SW 31	Wagner never set the text to music
68	Festgesang "Der Tag erscheint" (text by C. C. Hohlfeld)	7 June 1843, Dresden, cond. Wagner	SW 16	May 1843; commissioned by King Frederick August II for statue unveiling
69	Das Liebesmahl der Apostel: eine biblische Szene	6 July 1843, Dresden, Frauenkirche, cond. Wagner	Breitkopf & Härtel (1845); SW 16	April to June 1843; dedicated to Charlotte Emilie Weinlig

70	TANNHÄUSER und der Sängerkrieg auf Wartburg (Grosse romantische Oper in drei Akten) (1859–60: Handlung in drei Aufzügen)	Stage 1: 19 October 1845, Dresden, Königlich Sächsisches Hoftheater, cond. Wagner; stage 3: 13 March 1861, Paris, OPÉRA, cond. DIETSCH	Stage 1: SW 5 / Stage 2: SW 5 / Stage 3: SW 6 / Stage 4: SW 6	Continuous process of reworking and revision right up to Wagner's death; see WWV for detailed account
71a	Gruss seiner Treuen an Friedich August den Geliebten bei seiner Zurückkunft aus England den 9. August 1844, "Im treuen Sachsenland," male chorus and wind band in B♭ major	12 August 1844, Pillnitz, near Dresden; cond. Reissiger	SW 16	
71b	71a for Voice and Piano in G major		SW 17	
72	An Webers Grabe, in D♭ major; male chorus	15 December 1844, Dresden-Friedrichstadt, Catholic Cemetery, cond. Wagner	SW 16	Written for the reinterment of Weber's remains
73	Trauermusik (On motives from Weber's Euryanthe)	14 December 1844, Dresden, during procession transfering Weber's remains from the Elbe to the Catholic Cemetery, cond. Wagner	SW 18.2	
74	Spontini: La vestale, instrumental additions, LOST	29 November 1844, Dresden, Königlich Sächsisches Hoftheater, cond. Spontini		Mentioned in ML
75	LOHENGRIN (Romantische Oper in drei Akten)	28 August 1850, Weimar, Grossherzogliches Hof-Theater, cond. Liszt;	Breitkopf & Härtel (1852); SW 7	Text July–November 1845; music early 1846–April 1848. Dedicated to F. Liszt

WWV	Title	First performance	Publication	Remarks
76	Friedrich I ([? Oper] in fünf Akten), fragment, scenario	Act I finale (in concert): 22 September 1848, Dresden, Königlich Sächsisches Hoftheater, cond. Wagner	SSD 11; SW 31	Originally planned as an opera, not a play without music, as Wagner later claimed
77	Gluck: *Iphigenie en Aulide*, arrangement	24 February 1847, Dresden, Königlich Sächsisches Hoftheater, cond. Wagner	SW 20.4	
78	Symphonies			1846–7, see WWV
79	Palestrina: *Stabat mater*, arrangement	8 March 1848, Dresden, Königlich Sächsisches Hoftheater, cond. Wagner	SW 20.2	
80	Jesus von Nazareth ([? Oper] in fünf Akten), scenario		SSD 11; SW 31	Early 1849; Entitled "Tragödie" and "Drama" in ML
81	Achilleus ([? Oper] in drei Akten)			Projected work
82	Wieland der Schmied (Heldenoper in drei Akten), scenario		SSD 3; SW 31	
83	Mozart: *Don Giovanni*, arrangement, LOST	8 November 1850, Zurich, Stadt-Theater, cond. Wagner		

84	[Polka] in G major for Piano		SW 19	
85	Sonate for Piano in A♭ major		SW 19	May 1853 "Sonate für Mathilde WESENDONCK" (autograph MS)
86	Der RING DES NIBELUNGEN (Ein Bühnenfestspiel für drei Tage und einen Vorabend)	As a cycle: Bayreuth, Festspielhaus, 13, 14, 16, 17 August 1876; cond. Richter		
86a	Vorabend: Das RHEINGOLD	22 September 1869, Munich, Königliches Hof- und Nationaltheater, cond. Wüllner	Schott (1873); SW 10	See SW for chronology of extracts: "Ride of the Valkyries," "Winterstürme," etc.
86b	Erster Tag: Die WALKÜRE (in drei Aufzügen)	26 June 1870, Munich, Königliches Hof- und Nationaltheater, cond. Wüllner	Schott (1874); SW 11	See SW for details on performances of extracts prior to Bayreuth premiere
86c	Zweiter Tag: SIEGFRIED (in drei Aufzügen)	16 August 1876, Bayreuth, Festspielhaus, cond. Richter	Schott (1875); SW 12	See SW for details on performances of extracts prior to Bayreuth premiere
86d	Dritter Tag: GÖTTERDÄMMERUNG (Vorspiel und drei Aufzügen)	17 August 1876, Bayreuth, Festspielhaus, cond. Richter	Schott (1876); SW 13	
87	Concert ending to overture for Gluck: *Iphigenie en Aulis*	7 March 1854, Zurich, Casino, cond. Wagner	NZfM (1854); SW 20.4	
88	Züricher Vielliebchen-Walzer for Piano in E♭ major		SW 19	May 1854
89	Die Sieger ([? Oper in drei Akten]), projected		SSD 11; SW 31	See CWD 11 January and 20 July 1878; also RELIGION

(cont.)

WWV	Title	First performance	Publication	Remarks
90	TRISTAN UND ISOLDE (Handlung in drei Aufzügen)	10 June 1865, Munich, Königliches Hof- und Nationaltheater, cond. BÜLOW	Breitkopf & Härtel (1860); SW 8	Practice of ending Prelude with conclusion of Act III introduced by Wagner, 26 February 1863, St. Petersburg
91a	Fünf Gedichte für eine Frauenstimme with piano accompaniment (texts by M. Wesendonck):	30 July 1862, Villa Schott near Mainz	Schott (1862); SW 17 (all versions)	"WESENDONCK LIEDER"
	1. Der Engel		Schott (1862); SW 17 (all versions)	
	2. Träume		Schott (1862); SW 17 (all versions)	Also version for solo violin, chamber orch; Wagner added "Studie zu Tristan und Isolde"
	3. Schmerzen		Schott (1862); SW 17 (all versions)	
	4. Stehe still!		Schott (1862); SW 17 (all versions)	
	5. Im Treibhaus		Schott (1862); SW 17 (all versions)	Wagner added "Studie zu Tristan und Isolde"
91b	Träume, version for solo violin and orchestra in A♭ major	23 December 1857, Zurich, Villa Wesendonck, cond. Wagner	Schott (1878); SW 18.3	

No.	Work		Publication	Notes
92	Es ist bestimmt in Gottes Rat, *Lied* for voice and piano (text by E. Freiherr von Feuchtersleben), draft		SW 21	
93	[Theme] in A♭ major		SW 21	Wrongly known as "Porazzi" theme. See WWV 107
94	In das Album der Fürstin M[etternich], Albumblatt in C major for piano		SW 19	June 1861
95	Ankunft bei den schwarzen Schwänen, Albumblatt in A♭ major for piano		SW 19	
96	Die MEISTERSINGER VON NÜRNBURG (in drei Aufzügen)	21 June 1868, Munich, Königliches Hof- und Nationaltheater, cond. Bülow	B. Schott's Söhne (1868); SW 9	
97	HULDIGUNGSMARSCH, E♭ major	(Band version) 5 October 1864, Munich, Hof der Residenz, cond. Siebenkäs; (orchestral version) 12 November 1871, Vienna, Gesellschaft der Musikfreunde, cond. Dessoff	SW 18.3	Dedicated to Ludwig II, King of Bavaria; version for large orchestra by J. J. RAFF (Mainz, 1871)
98	Romeo und Julie, sketches		SW 21	
99	Luthers Hochzeit ([? Oper]), projected		SW 31	
100	Ein Lustspiel in ein Akt, scenario		SW 31	

(cont.)

WWV	Title	First performance	Publication	Remarks
101	Wahlspruch für die deutsche Feuerwehr, *Lied* for male chorus in G major		SW 16	
102	Eine Kapitulation (Lustspiel in antiker Manier in ein Akt)		SSD 9; SW 31	Written in response to the FRANCO-PRUSSIAN WAR, 1870–1
103	SIEGFRIED IDYLL, E major, small orchestra	25 December 1870, TRIBSCHEN, cond. Wagner	B. Schott's Söhne (1878); SW 18.3	Dedicated: Cosima "Tribschener Idyll… als Symphonischer Geburtstagsgruss Seiner Cosima dargestellt von ihrem Richard" (sfs); originally entitled "Symphonie"
104	KAISERMARSCH, B♭ major	14 April 1871, Berlin, Konzerthaus, cond. Bilse	C. F. Peters (1871); SW 18.3	
105	Der Worte viele sind gemacht, *Lied* for voice in F major		SW 21	Song for Louis Kraft, Hotel manager in Leipzig
106a	Kinder-Kathechismus, for children's chorus and piano	25 December 1873, Bayreuth, Haus Wahnfried	SW 21	
106b	Kinder-Kathechismus, for children's chorus and orchestra	25 December 1874, Bayreuth, Haus Wahnfried	SW 21	
107	Plans for Overtures and Symphonies, 1874–83		SW 21	See WWV for details. Also called "Porazzi-Theme"
108	Albumblatt in E♭ major for piano		B. Schott's Söhne (1876); SW 19	Dedicated to Frau Betty Schott

109	J. Strauss: Wein, Weib und Gesang, Waltz, Op. 333, arrangement	SW 20.2	Possibly 22 May 1875, Bayreuth, Haus Wahnfried	
110	Grosser Festmarsch zur Eröffnung der hundert-jährigen Gedenkfeier der Unabhängigkeitserklärung der Vereinigten Staaten von Nordamerika, in G major	B. Schott's Söhne (1876); SW 18.3	10 May 1876, Philadelphia, Opening Ceremony of the World Fair, cond. Thomas	Dedicated to the Women's Centennial Committees (for centenary of the declaration of independence of USA)
111	PARSIFAL (Ein BÜHNENWEIHFESTSPIEL in drei Aufzügen)	B. Schott's Söhne (1883); SW 14	26 July 1882, Bayreuth, Festspielhaus, cond. Levi	
112	"Wilkommen in Wahnfried, du heil'ger Christ," in C major for children's voices	SW 21	24 December 1877, Bayreuth, Haus Wahnfried	SW 21; title in MS in Cosima's hand
113	"Ihr Kinder, geschwinde, geschwinde," Lied for three children in G major	SW 21	25 December 1880, Bayreuth, Haus Wahnfried	

Appendix 7   Selected sound recordings

Compiled by David Breckbill

The following list is highly selective, and – apart from offering a general historical overview of Wagner recordings – is intended merely (1) to suggest a few standard, outstanding, and/or influential recordings of Wagner's most important works, (2) to identify recordings that present alternative textual versions of Wagner's scores, and (3) to represent some of the most important Wagner performers or impersonations (even if certain relevant names do not appear in these abbreviated listings). There is a bias toward complete or large-scale recordings – any systematic attempt to account for the innumerable important recordings of Wagner EXCERPTS by leading singers and conductors would expand this list far beyond manageable proportions, while any abbreviated attempt to do so would only make it seem even more arbitrary and selective than it already is. Release dates for commercially made recordings are provided only if they followed the recording date by more than a year or two, and are included in order to clarify the era in which such recordings first came to public awareness.

SYMBOLS AND ABBREVIATIONS

CG	Royal Opera House, Covent Garden
DG	Deutsche Grammophon
DHM	Deutsche Harmonia Mundi
ENO	English National Opera
FM	Funeral Music
L	*LIEBESTOD*
M&A	Music & Arts
Met	Metropolitan Opera
O	Orchestra
Ov	Overture
P1	Prelude to Act I
P2	Prelude to Act II
P3	Prelude to Act III
PO	Philharmonic [Orchestra]

RSO	Radio Symphony Orchestra
SO	Symphony Orchestra
SRJ	Siegfried's Rhine Journey
StOpO	State Opera Orchestra
★	Recording not marketed by those who made it (e.g., radio broadcast, unpublished commercial recording); this recording may be available on numerous labels, and was usually in circulation long before it was taken up by the label listed here.
+	Recording issued in audio-only format, but which also serves as soundtrack of a video recording.
#	Made at least in part at a public performance.

1. EARLY RECORDINGS

A. *Commercially made recordings*

1. From Bayreuth

1904, G&T	Excerpts from *Ring*, *Tannhäuser*, and non-Wagner works. Festival singers and others (piano accompaniment). Most of the surviving 1904 Bayreuth G&Ts are included in *Richard Wagner: 100 Jahre Bayreuth auf Schallplatte. Die frühen Festspielsänger 1876–1906. Recordings 1900–1930*. Gebhardt JGCD 0062–12 (12 CDs, rel. 2004), an invaluable collection of more than 300 recordings by 93 singers who performed at Bayreuth up to the end of Cosima Wagner's tenure as festival director.
1927, Columbia	Excerpts from *Ring* and *Parsifal*. MUCK, S. Wagner, and von Hoeßlin, conductors; F. Wolff, Kipnis, et al.
1928, Columbia	*Tristan und Isolde* (abridged). ELMENDORFF; Larsen-Todsen, Helm, Graarud, Bockelmann, Andresen
1930, Columbia	*Tannhäuser* (abridged). Elmendorff; Müller, Jost-Arden, Pilinsky, Janssen, Andresen
1936, Telefunken	Excerpts from *Walküre*, *Siegfried*, and *Lohengrin*. TIETJEN; Müller, Völker, M. LORENZ, etc.

2. Significant large-scale recordings of operas, acts, or scenes involving largely stable personnel

1909, Odeon	*Tannhäuser*, Act II. Künneke/O; Krull, Vogelstrom, Weil, Rains
1913, Gramophone	*Parsifal* (over twenty excerpts, some in multiple casting). Singers include Denera/Kurt, Jörn/Jadlowker,

	Breitenfeld, Knüpfer/J. Müller; orchestra-only recordings led by Alfred Hertz
1923–4, HMV	*Meistersinger* (abridged, in English). Coates/O; Austral, Davies, Radford (Sachs and Pogner), Michael
1928, HMV	*Parsifal*, Act III (P, then complete from Parsifal's entrance on). Muck/Berlin StOpO; Pistor, Bronsgeest, L. Hofmann
1935, HMV	*Walküre*, Act I. Walter/Vienna PO; Lotte Lehmann, Melchior, List
1938, Electrola	*Meistersinger*, Act III. Böhm/Saxon StO; Teschemacher, Ralf, Nissen, E. Fuchs
1945, Columbia	*Walküre*, Act III. Rodzinski/New York PO; Traubel, Janssen

One of the most substantial Wagner recordings of the interwar period was HMV's series of volumes that assembled, into one continuous sequence, numerous extensive excerpts from the *Ring*, performed by a variety of conductors, orchestras, and singers. These composite performances remain valuable because they contain outstanding work by LEIDER, MELCHIOR, Schorr, and others, and have been recompiled in *Wagner: Der Ring des Nibelungen. The 1927–32 HMV 'Potted' RING cycle.* Pearl GEMM CDS 9137 (7 CDs, rel. 1994).

B. *Live recordings*

1900–3	Excerpts from seven of the ten canonical Wagner operas (plus much other material). The Mapleson cylinders, recorded during performances at the Metropolitan Opera by Lionel Mapleson, include brief excerpts from about forty Wagner performances, featuring such singers as J. de Reszke, Ternina, Gadski, Nordica, van Rooy, Anthes, Bispham, Reuss-Belce, etc. Complete edition on Rodgers & Hammerstein R&H-100 (6 LPs, rel. 1985).
1928, HMV	*Meistersinger* (excerpts). Blech/Berlin StOpO; Marherr, Hutt, Schorr, List, Schützendorf.
1933–44	Excerpts, many extensive, from seventy-five live performances of *Rienzi* and the ten canonical Wagner operas, recorded during performances at the Vienna State Opera by Hermann May. Published by Koch/Schwann in 1994–5 as *Wiener Staatsoper/Vienna State Opera Live* on 24 two-CD sets (only five of which do not include any Wagner).
1936, Columbia	*Meistersinger, Götterdämmerung* (brief excerpts). Beecham/Covent Garden; Lemnitz, Ralf, L. Weber, et al. Numerous unpublished Covent Garden Wagner performances recorded by HMV in 1936–8 have more recently circulated on private labels (see 1936 *Tristan* below).

2. RECORDINGS OF COMPLETE OPERAS

Die FEEN

1983, Orfeo#	Sawallisch/Bavarian RSO; Gray, Moll, etc.

Das LIEBESVERBOT

1983 (1995), Orfeo#	Sawallisch/Bavarian StOpO; Haas, Coburn, Schunk, Prey, etc.

RIENZI

1974–6, EMI	Hollreiser/Staatskapelle Dresden; Wennberg, Martin, Kollo. The most textually comprehensive recording of Wagner's now little-performed grand opera.

Der FLIEGENDE HOLLÄNDER (Senta, Dutchman, Daland)

1960, Decca	Dorati/CG; Rysanek, London, Tozzi
1968, EMI	Klemperer/New Philharmonia O; Silja, Adam, Talvela (with breaks between acts)
1985, Philips+	Nelsson/Bayreuth; Balslev, Estes, Salminen
2004, DHM	Weil/Cappella Coloniensis; A. Weber, Stensvold, Selig (1841 Paris version)

TANNHÄUSER (Elisabeth, Venus, Tannhäuser, Wolfram, Landgraf)

1942, M&A*#	Szell/Met; Traubel, Thorborg, Melchior, Janssen, Kipnis
1970, Decca	Solti/Vienna PO; Dernesch, Ludwig, Kollo, Braun, Sotin ("Paris" version)
1985, EMI	Haitink/Bavarian RSO; Popp, W. Meier, König, Weikl, Moll ("Dresden" version)

LOHENGRIN (Elsa, Ortrud, Lohengrin, Telramund, König Heinrich)

1962–3, EMI	Kempe/Vienna PO; Grümmer, Ludwig, Thomas, Fischer-Dieskau, Frick
1998, Teldec	Barenboim/Staatskapelle Berlin; Magee, Polaski, Seiffert, Struckmann, Pape (includes fuller version of Lohengrin's narration, as do 1965 RCA recording, cond. Leinsdorf, and 1936 Bayreuth excerpts, cond. Tietjen)

Der RING DES NIBELUNGEN (Brünnhilde, Sieglinde, Siegmund, Siegfried, Wotan, Alberich, Hagen)

1953, Orfeo*#	Krauss/Bayreuth; Varnay, Resnik, Vinay, Windgassen, Hotter, Neidlinger, Greindl
1958–65, Decca	Solti/Vienna PO; Nilsson, Crespin, King, Windgassen, London/Hotter, Neidlinger, Frick
1966–70, DG	Karajan/Berlin PO; Crespin/Dernesch, Janowitz, Vickers, Thomas/Brilioth, Fischer-Dieskau/Stewart, Kelemen, Ridderbusch

| 1973–7, EMI # | (Now Chandos) Goodall/ENO; Hunter, Curphey, Remedios, Remedios, Bailey, Hammond-Stroud, Haugland (in Andrew Porter's English translation) |
| 1987–9, DG | Levine/Met; Behrens, Norman, Lakes, Goldberg, Morris, Wlaschiha, Salminen |

TRISTAN UND ISOLDE (Isolde, Brangäne, Tristan, Kurwenal, König Marke)

1936, Naxos*#	Reiner/CG; Flagstad, Kalter, Melchior, Janssen, List
1952, HMV/EMI	Furtwängler/Philharmonia O; Flagstad, Thebom, Suthaus, Fischer-Dieskau, Greindl
1966, DG#	Böhm/Bayreuth; Nilsson, Ludwig, Windgassen, Waechter, Talvela
1980–2, DG	C. Kleiber/Dresden Staatskapelle; M. Price, Fassbaender, Kollo, Fischer-Dieskau, Moll
2004–5, EMI	Pappano/CG; Stemme, Fujimura, Domingo, Bär, Pape

Die MEISTERSINGER VON NÜRNBERG (Eva, Walter von Stolzing, Hans Sachs, Veit Pogner, Sixtus Beckmesser)

1949, Myto*#	Jochum/Bavarian StOpO; Kupper, Treptow, Hotter, Proebstl, Kusche
1956, EMI	Kempe/Berlin PO; Grümmer, Schock, Frantz, Frick, Kusche
1967 (1992), DG*	(Myto, now Arts Archives) Kubelik/Bavarian RSO; Janowitz, Kónya, Stewart, Crass, Hemsley
1993, EMI	Sawallisch/Bavarian StOpO; Studer, Heppner, Weikl, Moll, S. Lorenz

PARSIFAL (Kundry, Parsifal, Amfortas, Gurnemanz)

1951, Decca#	Knappertsbusch/Bayreuth; Mödl, Windgassen, London, L. Weber
1962, Philips#	Knappertsbusch/Bayreuth; Dalis, Thomas, London, Hotter
1979–80, DG	Karajan/Berlin PO; Vejzovic, P. Hofmann, van Dam, Moll
1989–90, Teldec	Barenboim/Berlin PO; W. Meier, Jerusalem, van Dam, Hölle
2005, DG#	Thielemann/Vienna StOpO; W. Meier, Domingo, Struckmann, Selig

3. ORCHESTRAL MUSIC AND EXCERPTS

| 1927–8, HMV | Muck/Berlin StOpO. *Siegfried Idyll*, *Dutchman* (Ov), *Tannhäuser* (Ov), *Tristan* (P1, with Wagner's concert ending), *Meistersinger* (P1), *Götterdämmerung* (SRJ, FM), *Parsifal* (P1) |
| 1928, Polydor | R. Strauss/Berlin PO. *Dutchman* (Ov), *Tristan* (P1, with Wagner's concert ending) |

1972, EMI	Janowski/London SO. *Kaisermarsch, Faust-Ouvertüre, Huldigungsmarsch, American Centennial March, Feen* (Ov), *Liebesverbot* (Ov)
1983, Naxos	Kojian, Hong Kong PO. *Polonia* Overture, *Rule Britannia* Overture, *American Centennial March, Kaisermarsch*
1988[a] and 1994, EMI	Norrington/London Classical Players. *Dutchman* (Ov)[a], *Siegfried Idyll, Rienzi* (Ov), *Lohengrin* (P3), *Tristan* (P1&L [Eaglen]), *Meistersinger* (P1), *Parsifal* (P1). Perhaps the most noted among ostensibly "historically informed performance" recordings of Wagner works
1992, Denon	Wakasugi/Tokyo Metropolitan SO. Symphony in C; Symphony in E (unfinished)

4. MISCELLANEOUS WORKS

Wesendonck Lieder

1948, HMV/EMI	Flagstad; Moore (piano)
1963, EMI	Ludwig; Klemperer/Philharmonia O (orchestration by Mottl/Wagner)
1995, EMI	Lipovšek; Sawallisch/Philadelphia O (orchestration by H. W. Henze)

Other vocal/choral music

1975, Sony	Boulez/Westminster Choir, New York PO; *Das Liebesmahl der Apostel*
1993, Orfeo	Rickenbacker/Bamberg Symphony and Chorus; *Beim Antritt des neuen Jahres 1835, Nicolay, Descendons gaiement la courtille, Der Tag erscheint, An Webers Grabe*
1993, EMI	Hampson, Parsons (six songs)
1999, Fermate#	M. Bach (soprano), Laske (baritone), Hadulla (piano), Heidelberger Madrigalchor. *Sieben Kompositionen zu Goethes "Faust"*

Piano music

1996, Kontrapunkt	Kavtaradze (complete)

Appendix 8 Selected video recordings

Compiled by Hilan Warshaw

The list below provides information about commercially released audiovisual recordings of Wagner's stage works. As such, it does not encompass recorded performances that have not been made commercially available. The list is arranged by work in chronological order. Each recording is listed in the following format: opera company name, year of video release, stage director, conductor, selected vocal cast members (listed according to the selection of roles as presented in the title header), available media format. For studio productions in which the vocal cast differs from the on-camera cast, members of both casts are listed consecutively, in order of role.

RIENZI

(Rienzi, Adriana, Irene)
Deutsche Oper Berlin, 2010. Philipp Stölzl; Sebastian Lang-Lessing. Torsten Kerl, Kate Aldrich, Camilla Nylund. (DVD/Blu-ray)

Der FLIEGENDE HOLLÄNDER

(HOLLÄNDER, SENTA, DALAND)
DEFA, 1964 (feature film). Joachim Herz; Rolf Reuter. Rainer Lüdecke, Gerda Hannemann, Hans Krämer (vocal cast); Fred Düren, Anna Prucnal, Gerd Ehlers (on-camera cast). (Laserdisc/VHS)
Bayerische Staatsoper/Bavaria Studios, 1975 (studio production). Václav Kašlík; Wolfgang Sawallisch. Donald McIntyre, Catarina Ligendza, Bengt Rundgren. (DVD)
Bayreuther Festspiele, 1985. Harry Kupfer; Woldemar Nelsson. Simon Estes, Lisbeth Balslev, Matti Salminen. (DVD)
Savonlinna Opera Festival, 1988. Ilkka Bäckmann; Leif Segerstam. Franz Grundheber, Hildegard Behrens, Matti Salminen. (DVD)
De Nederlandse Opera, 2010. Martin Kušej; Hartmut Haenchen. Juha Uusitalo, Catherine Naglestad, Robert Lloyd. (DVD/Blu-ray)

TANNHÄUSER

(TANNHÄUSER, VENUS, ELISABETH)
Bayreuther Festspiele, 1978. Götz Friedrich; Colin Davis. Spas Wenkoff,
  Gwyneth Jones. (DVD)
Metropolitan Opera, 1982. Otto Schenk; James Levine. Richard Cassilly,
  Tatiana Troyanos, Eva Marton. (DVD)
Teatro di San Carlo, Naples, 1984. Werner Herzog; Gustav Kuhn. Alan
  Woodrow, Marianna Pentcheva, Gertrud Ottenthal. (DVD)
Bayreuther Festspiele, 1989. Wolfgang Wagner; Giuseppe Sinopoli. Richard
  Versalle, Ruthild Engert-Ely, Cheryl Studer. (DVD)
Bayerische Staatsoper, 1994. David Alden; Zubin Mehta. René Kollo, Waltraud
  Meier, Nadine Secunde. (DVD)
Zürich Opera, 2003. Jens-Daniel Herzog; Franz Welser-Möst. Peter Seiffert,
  Solveig Kringelborn, Isabelle Kabatu. (DVD)
Festspiele Baden-Baden, 2008. Nikolaus Lehnhoff; Phillippe Jordan. Robert
  Gambill, Waltraud Meier, Camilla Nylund. (DVD/Blu-ray)
Gran Teatre del Liceu, Barcelona, 2008. Robert Carsen; Sebastian Weigle.
  Peter Seiffert, Béatrice Uria-Monzon, Petra Maria Schnitzer. (DVD/Blu-ray)
Royal Danish Opera, 2009. Kaspar Holten; Friedemann Layer. Stig Andersen,
  Susanne Resmark, Tina Kiberg. (DVD)

LOHENGRIN

(LOHENGRIN, ELSA, ORTRUD)
Bayreuther Festspiele, 1982. Götz Friedrich; Woldemar Nelsson. Peter
  Hofmann, Karan Armstrong, Elizabeth Connell. (DVD)
Metropolitan Opera, 1986. August Everding; James Levine. Peter Hofmann,
  Eva Marton, Leonie Rysanek. (DVD)
Bayreuther Festspiele, 1990. Werner Herzog; Peter Schneider. Paul Frey,
  Cheryl Studer, Gabriele Schnaut. (DVD)
Wiener Staatsoper, 1990. Wolfgang Weber; Claudio Abbado. Plácido
  Domingo, Cheryl Studer, Dunja Vejzovic. (DVD)
Festspiele Baden-Baden, 2006. Nikolaus Lehnhoff; Kent Nagano. Klaus
  Florian Vogt, Solveig Kringelborn, Waltraud Meier. (DVD/Blu-ray)
Gran Teatre del Liceu, 2006. Peter Konwitschny; Sebastian Weigle. John
  Treleaven, Emily Magee, Luana DeVol. (DVD)
Bayerische Staatsoper, 2009. Richard Jones; Kent Nagano. Jonas Kaufmann,
  Anja Harteros, Michaela Schuster. (DVD/Blu-ray)
Bayreuther Festspiele, 2011. Hans Neuenfels, Andris Nelsons. Klaus Florian
  Vogt, Annette Dash, Petra Lang. (DVD/Blu-ray)

TRISTAN UND ISOLDE

(TRISTAN, ISOLDE)
Théâtre Antique d'Orange, 1973. Pierre Jourdan; Karl Böhm. Jon Vickers, Birgit Nilsson. (DVD)
Bayreuther Festspiele, 1983. Jean-Pierre Ponnelle; Daniel Barenboim. René Kollo, Johanna Meier. (DVD)
Deutsches Oper Berlin, 1993. Götz Friedrich; Jiří Kout. René Kollo, Gwyneth Jones. (DVD)
Bayreuther Festspiele, 1995. Heiner Müller; Daniel Barenboim. Siegfried Jerusalem, Waltraud Meier. (DVD)
Bayerische Staatsoper, 1998. Peter Konwitschny; Zubin Mehta. Jon Fredric West, Waltraud Meier. (DVD)
Metropolitan Opera, 2001. Dieter Dorn; James Levine. Ben Heppner, Jane Eaglen. (DVD)
Gran Teatre del Liceu, 2005. Alfred Kirchner; Bertrand de Billy. John Treleaven, Deborah Polaski. (DVD)
Grand Théâtre de Genève, 2006. Olivier Py; Armin Jordan. Clifton Forbis, Jeanne-Michèle Charbonnet. (DVD)
Tyrolean Festival Erl, 2006 (recorded during rehearsals). Gustav Kuhn; Gustav Kuhn. Alan Woodrow, Michela Sburlati. (DVD)
Anhaltisches Theater, Dessau, 2007. Johannes Felsenstein; Golo Berg. Richard Decker, Iordanka Derilova. (DVD)
Glyndebourne Festival, 2007. Nikolaus Lehnhoff; Jiří Bělohlávek. Robert Gambill, Nina Stemme. (DVD/Blu-ray)
Teatro alla Scala, 2007. Patrice Chéreau; Daniel Barenboim. Ian Storey, Waltraud Meier. (DVD)
Bayreuther Festspiele, 2009. Christoph Marthaler; Peter Schneider. Robert Dean Smith, Iréne Theorin. (DVD/Blu-ray)

Die MEISTERSINGER VON NÜRNBERG

(HANS SACHS, SIXTUS BECKMESSER, WALTHER, EVA)
Hamburg State Opera, 1970 (studio production). Joachim Hess; Leopold Ludwig. Giorgio Tozzi, Toni Blankenheim, Richard Cassilly, Arlene Saunders. (DVD)
Bayreuther Festspiele, 1984. Wolfgang Wagner; Horst Stein. Bernd Weikl, Hermann Prey, Siegfried Jerusalem, Mari Anne Häggander. (DVD)
Opera Australia, 1988. Michael Hampe; Charles Mackerras. Donald McIntyre, John Pringle. Paul Frey, Helena Döse. (DVD)
Deutsche Oper Berlin, 1995. Götz Friedrich; Rafael Frühbeck de Burgos. Wolfgang Brendel, Eike Wilm Schulte, Gösta Winbergh, Eva Johansson. (DVD)

Bayreuther Festspiele, 1999. Wolfgang Wagner; Daniel Barenboim. Robert Holl, Andreas Schmidt, Peter Seiffert, Emily Magee. (DVD)

Zürich Opera, 2003. Nikolaus Lehnhoff; Franz Welser-Möst. José van Dam, Michael Volle, Michael Volle, Petra-Maria Schnitzer. (DVD)

Metropolitan Opera, 2005. Otto Schenk; James Levine. James Morris, Thomas Allen, Ben Heppner, Karita Mattila. (DVD)

Bayreuther Festspiele, 2008. Katharina Wagner; Sebastian Weigle. Franz Hawlata, Michael Volle, Klaus Florian Vogt, Michaela Kaune. (DVD/Blu-ray)

Wiener Staatsoper, 2008. Otto Schenk; Christian Thielemann. Falk Struckmann, Adrian Eröd, Johan Botha, Ricarda Merbeth. (DVD)

Glyndebourne Festival, 2011. David McVicar, Vladimir Jurowski. Gerald Finley, Johannes Martin Kränzle, Marco Jentzsch, Anna Gabler. (DVD/Blu-ray)

Staatstheater Nürnberg Chorus & Staatsphilharmonie Nürnberg, 2012. David Mouchtar-Samorai; Marcos Bosch. Albert Pesendorf, Jochen Kupfer, Michael Putsch, Michaela Maria Mayer. (DVD)

Der RING DES NIBELUNGEN (COMPLETE)

(WOTAN/The Wanderer, ALBERICH, HAGEN, SIEGMUND, SIEGLINDE, SIEGFRIED, BRÜNNHILDE)

Bayreuther Festspiele, 1980. Patrice Chéreau; Pierre Boulez. Donald McIntyre, Hermann Becht, Fritz Hübner, Peter Hofmann, Jeannine Altmeyer, Manfred Jung, Gwyneth Jones. (DVD)

Metropolitan Opera, 1990. Otto Schenk; James Levine. James Morris, Ekkehard Wlaschiha, Matti Salminen, Gary Lakes, Jessye Norman, Siegfried Jerusalem, Hildegard Behrens. (DVD)

Bayreuther Festspiele, 1991. Harry Kupfer; Daniel Barenboim. John Tomlinson, Günter von Kannen, Philip Kang, Poul Elming, Nadine Secunde, Siegfried Jerusalem, Anne Evans. (DVD)

De Nederlandse Opera, 1999. Pierre Audi; Hartmut Haenchen. John Bröcheler, Henk Smit, Kurt Rydl, John Keyes, Nadine Secunde, Heinz Kruse, Jeannine Altmeyer. (DVD)

Staatsoper Stuttgart, 2002–3. Joachim Schlömer (*Das Rheingold*), Christof Nel (*Die Walküre*), Jossi Wieler/Sergio Morabita (*Siegfried*), Peter Konwitschny (*Götterdämmerung*); Lothar Zagrosek. Wolfgang Probst *(R)* / Jan-Hendrik Rootering *(W)* / Wolfgang Schöne *(S)*, Esa Ruuttunen *(R)* / Björn Waag *(S)* / Franz-Josef Kapellmann *(G)*, Roland Bracht, Robert Gambill, Angela Denoke, Jon Fredric West *(S)* / Albert Bonnema *(G)*, Renate Behle *(W)* / Lisa Gasteen *(S)* / Luana DeVol *(G)*. (DVD)

Gran Teatre del Liceu, 2003–4. Harry Kupfer; Bertrand de Billy. Falk Struckmann, Günter von Kannen, Matti Salminen, Richard Berkeley-Steele, Linda Watson, John Treleaven, Deborah Polaski. (DVD)

Royal Danish Opera, 2006. Kasper Holten; Michael Schønwandt. Johan
Reuter, Sten Byriel, Peter Klaveness, Stig Fogh Andersen, Gitta-Maria
Sjöberg, Stig Fogh Andersen, Iréne Theorin. (DVD)
Deutsches Nationaltheater & Staatskapelle Weimar, 2008. Michael Schulz;
Carl St. Clair. Mario Hoff, Tomas Möwes, Renatus Mészár, Erin Caves,
Kirsten Blanck, Johnny van Hall, Catherine Foster. (DVD/Blu-ray)
Palau de les Arts Reina Sofía, València, 2008–10. La Fura dels Baus, Carlus
Padrissa, director; Zubin Mehta. Juha Uusitalo, Franz Josef Kapellmann,
Matti Salminen, Peter Seiffert, Petra Maria Schnitzer, Lance Ryan, Jennifer
Wilson. (DVD/Blu-ray)
Philharmonisches Orchester der Hansestadt Lübeck, 2011. Roman
Brogli-Sacher; Anthony Pilavachi. Stefan Heidemann, Antonio Yang, Gary
Jankowski, Andrew Sritheran, Marion Ammann, Jürgen Müller *(S)* /
Richard Decker *(G)*, Rebecca Teem. (DVD)
Metropolitan Opera, 2012. Robert Lepage; James Levine/Fabio Luisi. Bryn
Terfel, Eric Owens, Hans-Peter König, Jonas Kaufmann, Eva-Maria
Westbroek, Jay Hunter Morris, Deborah Voigt. (DVD/Blu-ray)

Der Ring des Nibelungen (individual parts)

Das Rheingold (Wotan, Alberich)
Salzburg Festival/Metropolitan Opera, 1978 (studio production). Herbert von
Karajan; Herbert von Karajan. Thomas Stewart, Zoltán Kelemen. (DVD)
Die Walküre (Wotan, Siegmund, Sieglinde, Brünnhilde)
Festival d'Aix-en-Provence, 2008. Stéphane Braunschweig; Simon Rattle.
Willard White, Robert Gambill, Eva-Maria Westbroek, Eva Johansson.
(DVD/Blu-ray)
Bayreuther Festspiele, 2010. Tankred Dorst; Christian Thielemann. Albert
Dohmen, Johan Botha, Edith Haller, Linda Watson. (DVD/Blu-ray)
Götterdämmerung (Siegfried, Brunnhilde, Hagen)
Bayreuther Festspiele, 1997. Alfred Kirchner; James Levine. Wolfgang
Schmidt, Deborah Polaski, Eric Halfvarson. (DVD)

Parsifal

(Parsifal, Kundry, Amfortas, Gurnemanz)
Bayreuther Festspiele, 1981. Wolfgang Wagner; Horst Stein. Siegfried
Jerusalem, Eva Randova, Bernd Weikl, Hans Sotin. (DVD)
TMS Film GmbH/Gaumont, 1982 (feature film). Hans-Jürgen Syberberg;
Armin Jordan. Reiner Goldberg, Yvonne Minton, Wolfgang Schöne,

Robert Lloyd (vocal cast); Michael Kutter / Karen Krick, Edith Clever, Armin Jordan, Robert Lloyd (on-camera cast). (DVD)
Bayreuther Festspiele, 1992. Harry Kupfer; Daniel Barenboim. Poul Elming, Waltraud Meier, Falk Struckmann, John Tomlinson. (DVD)
Metropolitan Opera, 1993. Otto Schenk; James Levine. Siegfried Jerusalem, Waltraud Meier, Bernd Weikl, Kurt Moll. (DVD)
Bayreuther Festspiele, 1998. Wolfgang Wagner; Giuseppe Sinopoli. Poul Elming, Linda Watson, Falk Struckmann, Hans Sotin. (DVD)
Festspiele Baden-Baden, 2004. Nikolaus Lehnhoff; Kent Nagano. Christopher Ventris, Waltraud Meier, Thomas Hampson, Matti Salminen. (DVD/Blu-ray)
Teatro la Fenice di Venezia, 2006. Denis Krief; Gabor Ötvös. Richard Decker, Doris Soffel, Wolfgang Schöne, Matthias Hölle. (DVD)
Tyrolean Festival Erl, 2006 (recorded during rehearsals). Gustav Kuhn; Gustav Kuhn. Michael Baba, Emanuela Barazia / Martina Tomcic, Thomas Gazheli, Manfred Hemm. (DVD)
Zürich Opera, 2007. Hans Hollmann; Bernard Haitink. Christopher Ventris, Yvonne Naef, Michael Volle, Matti Salminen. (DVD)

See also VIDEO RECORDINGS

Appendix 9   Documentaries and films

Compiled by Hilan Warshaw

Below is a chronologically organized list of documentaries about Wagner and his works, as well as narrative FILMS about Wagner, and films adapted from Wagner's music dramas. The latter category does not include video recordings of stage productions, which are listed in Appendix 8: Selected video recordings.

Many of these titles are commercially available on DVD, as indicated below. Some others may be found in private and institutional archives or the catalogues of online dealers in opera video, or viewed as streaming video on the internet.

DOCUMENTARIES

Biographical and historical

Richard Wagner (USA, 1925, short film, prod. James A. FitzPatrick)

Winifred Wagner und die Geschichte des Hauses Wahnfried von 1914–1975 (West Germany, 1975, dir. Hans-Jürgen SYBERBERG; released in the USA as *The Confessions of Winifred Wagner*) (DVD)

Wagner and Venice (Italy/Czechoslovakia, 1982, television, dir. Petr Ruttner; narrated by Orson Welles)

Wagner's Women (UK, 1995, television, dir. Steve Ruggi)

Famous Composers: Richard Wagner (USA, 1996, short film, dir. Malcolm Hossick) (DVD)

Great Composers: Richard Wagner (UK, 1997, television, dir. Kriss Rusmanis) (DVD)

Parsifal: The Search for the Grail (UK, 1998, television, dir. Tony Palmer) (DVD)

Wagner (France, 1999, dir. Marie-Dominique Blanc-Hermeline and Philippe Orreindy)

Art That Shook the World: Richard Wagner: The "Ring" Cycle (UK, 2002, television, dir. Michael Waldman)

We Want the Light (UK, 2003, television, dir. Christopher Nupen) (DVD)

Parsifal: Indiana Jones und Richard Wagner (Austria, 2004, television, dir. Werner Boote)

Das Familientheater der Wagners: Leuchtende Liebe – Lachender Tod (Germany, 2005, television, dir. Oliver Becker)

Richard Wagner und die Frauen (Germany, 2005, television, dir. Andreas Morell) (DVD)

Hitler and the Wagner Clan: Twilight of the Gods in Bayreuth (UK, 2007, television, dir. Michael Kloft)

Wagners Meistersänger, Hitlers Siegfried (Germany, 2008, television, dir. Eric Schulz and Claus Wischmann); documentary about Max LORENZ (DVD)

Mythos Ring (Austria, 2009, television, dir. Werner Boote)

Stephen Fry on Wagner (UK, 2010, television, dir. Patrick McGrady), subsequently expanded to a feature-length version, *Stephen Fry: Wagner and Me* (DVD)

The Wagner Family (UK, 2010, television, dir. Tony Palmer) (DVD)

Wagner's Jews (USA/Germany, 2013, television, dir. Hilan Warshaw)

Documentaries about Wagner productions and performance

The Golden Ring (UK, 1965, television, dir. Humphrey Burton), about Decca's recording of the *Ring* (DVD)

The Making of "Der Ring des Nibelungen" (UK, 1983, television, dir. Peter Weinberg), about Patrice CHÉREAU's 1976 Bayreuth production (included with the production DVDs; also released as an independent DVD)

A to Z of Wagner (UK, 1995, television, dir. Peter Webber), about David Alden's Munich production of *Tannhäuser*

Die Verwandlung der Welt in Musik: Bayreuth vor der Premiere (Germany, 1996, television, dir. Werner Herzog), about Herzog's Bayreuth production of *Lohengrin*

Rosalie: The Way to the Green Hill (1998, Germany, dir. Dieter Schickling), about Alfred Kirchner's Bayreuth *Ring* cycle, with stage designs by Rosalie

The Forging of the Ring (Netherlands, 1999, dir. Roeland Hazendonk), about Pierre Audi's Amsterdam *Ring* cycle (included with the production DVDs)

Roger Norrington: Wagner's Overtures (Germany, 1999, television, dir. Dieter Schickling)

Sing Faster: The Stagehands' Ring Cycle (USA, 1999, dir. Jon Else), filmed at the San Francisco Opera (DVD)

Lieben Sie Wagner? Ein Sommer in Bayreuth (Germany, 2003, television, dir. Michael Strauven)

Never Shalt Thou Ask of Me (Germany, 2006, dir. Reiner Moritz), about Nikolaus Lehnhoff's *Lohengrin* in Baden-Baden (included with the production DVDs)

Baptism of Fire: Katharina Wagners Feuertaufe (Germany, 2007, dir. Dagmar Krauss), about KATHARINA WAGNER's Bayreuth production of *Die Meistersinger von Nürnberg* (DVD)

Tannhäuser the Revolutionary (Germany, 2009, dir. Rainer Moritz), about Nikolaus Lehnhoff's *Tannhäuser* in Baden-Baden (included with the production DVDs)

Wagner's Dream (USA, 2012, dir. Susan Froemke), about Robert Lepage's production of the *Ring* at the Metropolitan Opera (DVD/Blu-ray; also included with the production DVDs/Blu-rays)

NARRATIVE FILMS

Fregoli, the Protean Artiste (UK, 1898, short film, prod. Robert W. Paul)

Maestri di musica (Italy, 1898, short film, dir. Leopoldo Fregoli)

L'Homme Protée (France, 1899, short film, directed by George Méliès)

The Life and Works of Richard Wagner (Germany, 1913, dir. Carl Froelich; released on DVD as *Silent Wagner*, 2011)

Der Taktstock Richard Wagners (Germany, 1918, dir. Robert Leffler)

Ludwig II (Germany, 1922, dir. Otto Kreisler)

Ludwig II: Glanz und Ende eines Königs (West Germany, 1955, dir. Helmut Käutner)

Magic Fire (USA, 1955, dir. William Dieterle)

Die Barrikade: Richard Wagner und Michael Bakunin – eine Begegnung (West Germany, 1970, television, dir. Carlheinz Caspari)

Ludwig (Italy/France/West Germany, 1972, dir. Luchino Visconti) (DVD)

Ludwig: Requiem for a Virgin King (West Germany, 1972, dir. Hans-Jürgen Syberberg) (DVD)

Auf den Spuren von Richard Wagners Tristan und Isolde (West Germany, 1973, television, dir. Václav Kaslik)

Lisztomania (UK, 1975, dir. Ken Russell) (DVD)

La Mort du Titan (France, 1975, television, dir. Josée Dayan)

Hitler, a Film from Germany (West Germany/France/UK, 1977, dir. Hans-Jürgen Syberberg) (DVD)

Wagner (UK/Austria/Hungary, 1983, dir. Tony Palmer) (DVD)

Wahnfried (France/West Germany, 1986, dir. Peter Patzak; released in France as *Richard et Cosima*)

Celles qui aimaient Richard Wagner (France, 2011, dir. Jean-Louis Guillermou)

FILM ADAPTATIONS

Lohengrin (USA, 1902, short film, distributed by S. Lubin)

Parsifal (USA, 1904, short film, dir. Edwin S. Porter)

Siegfried: Schmiedelied (Germany, 1905, short film, dir. Oskar Messter)

Lohengrin (Germany, 1907, short film, dir. Franz Porten)

Lohengrin (Germany, 1910, short film, dir. Franz Porten)

Tristan et Yseult (France, 1911, short film, dir. Albert Capellani)

Tristano e Isolda (Italy, 1911, short film, dir. Ugo Falena)

Parsifal (Italy, 1912, short film, dir. Mario Caserini)

Sigfrido (Italy, 1912, short film, dir. Mario Caserini)

Tannhäuser (USA, 1913, short film, dir. Lucius J. Henderson)

Der fliegende Holländer (Germany, 1918, short film, dir. Hans Neumann)

Parzifal: Ein Kinoweihfestfilm (Germany, 1921, short film, dir. Max Reinhardt)

Die Nibelungen (Part I: *Siegfried*; Part II, *Kriemhilds Rache*) (Germany, 1924, dir. Fritz Lang), Lang's epic based on the medieval *Nibelungenlied*. The film studio's original intention to use Wagner's *Ring* music was abandoned when Wagner's heirs withheld their permission; excerpts from the original Wagner score were subsequently introduced for the US premiere of *Siegfried* (1925) and the soundtrack for the re-edited German version of *Siegfried* (released as *Siegfrieds Tod*, 1933). (DVD)

Ride of the Valkyries (USA, 1941, short animation, Walt Disney Pictures), developed for inclusion in future sequels to Disney's *Fantasia* (1940). While the episode was not completed, an edited assembly of the original sketches is included in the DVD set *The Fantasia Anthology* (Walt Disney Video, 2000).

Parsifal (Spain, 1951; dir. Daniel Mangrané and Carlos Serrano de Osma; released in the USA as *The Evil Forest*), a dramatic adaptation filmed in Montserrat and Barcelona, with a soundtrack of excerpts from *Parsifal*.

What's Opera, Doc? (USA, 1957, short animation, dir. Chuck Jones), featuring music from the *Ring*, *Tannhäuser*, and *Der fliegender Holländer* (DVD)

Der fliegende Holländer (East Germany, 1964, dir. Joachim Herz) (Laserdisc/VHS)

Parsifal (France/West Germany, 1983, dir. Hans-Jürgen Syberberg) (DVD)

Liebestod (UK, 1987, short film, dir. Frank Roddam), a cinematic interpretation of the climax of *Tristan und Isolde*, included in the anthology film *Aria* (DVD)

Das Rheingold (UK, 1996, short animation, dir. Graham Ralph), a 27-minute adaptation included in *Operavox*, a BBC series of animated opera adaptations (DVD)

The Tristan Project (USA, 2004, dir. Bill Viola), originated as the visual component of the Los Angeles Philharmonic's "The Tristan Project," in collaboration with stage director Peter Sellars. Viola's work was subsequently screened without musical accompaniment at international galleries.

Appendix 10 Stage productions

Compiled by Katherine Syer

The number of productions of Wagner's operas has grown substantially since the early 1980s, particularly of Der *RING DES NIBELUNGEN*. For much of the twentieth century, Wagner's mature stage works were mounted mainly in major theaters in urban centers. However, mid-sized and smaller theaters have increasingly become part of the picture, which has simultaneously become more internationally diversified. What follows is a skeletal overview of Wagner productions that can be regarded as influential; staging and design strategies have been prioritized (many outstanding vocal casts of yesteryear and important, much-admired productions could not be included).

Wagner's stage works are listed in chronological order, and information for the world premiere launches each section. Following the production location and theater, each entry is presented in the following format: conductor / stage director / set designer. The vocal cast members are subsequently listed according to the selection of roles as presented in the title header. Nominal cast information has been included due to the high degree of variability across the lifespan of a production; every effort has been made to include cast information for the premieres (or premiere runs) but cast details are not easy to trace for all early productions. Those that are available commercially in an audiovisual format have been marked by an * at the end of the entry and can be located in Appendix 8: Selected video recordings.

Die *FEEN*

(Arindal, Ada)

1888   MUNICH: Königliches Hof- und Nationaltheater, 29 June. Franz Fischer / Karl Brulliot / Carlo Brioschi, Hermann Burghart, Karl Lautenschläger. Max Mikorey, Lili Dressler.

2009   PARIS, Théâtre du Chatelet. Marc Minkowski / Emilio Sagi / Daniel Bianco. William Joyner / David Curry, Christiane Libor / Deborah Mayer.

2013   Oper LEIPZIG. Ulf Schirmer / Renaud Doucet / André Barbe. Arnold Bezuyen, Christian Libor.

Das LIEBESVERBOT

(Isabella, Claudio, Friedrich, Luzio)

1836 MAGDEBURG, Stadttheater, 29 March. Richard Wagner. Caroline Pollert, Herr Schreiber, Herr Gräfe, Herr Freimüller.

1983 MUNICH, Bayerische Staatsoper. Wolfgang Sawallisch / Jean-Pierre Ponnelle / Jean-Pierre Ponnelle. Sabine Hass, Robert Schunk, Hermann Prey, Wolfgang Fassler.

2008 Cooperstown, NY, Glimmerglass Opera. Corrado Rovaris / Nicholas Muni / John Conklin. Claudia Waite, Richard Cox, Mark Schnaible, Ryan MacPherson.

RIENZI

(Rienzi, Irene, Adriano)

1842 DRESDEN, Königlich Sächsisches Hoftheater, 20 October. Carl Gottlieb REISSIGER / Ferdinand HEINE, Wilhelm Fischer / inhouse sets. Josef Aloys TICHATSCHEK, Henriette Wüst, Wilhelmine SCHRÖDER-DEVRIENT.

1957 Stuttgart, Staatsoper. Lovro von Matačić / WIELAND WAGNER / Wieland Wagner. Wolfgang WINDGASSEN, Paula Brivkalne, Josef Traxel.

1979 Wiesbaden, Hessisches Staatstheater. Siegfried Köhler / Hans Peter Lehmann / Ekkehard Grübler. Gerd Brenneis, Jeannine Altmeyer, Glenys Linos.

1983 LONDON, English National Opera. Herbert Esser / Nicholas Hytner / David Fielding. Kenneth Woollam, Kathryn Harries, Felicity Palmer.

1997 Vienna, Staatoper. Zubin Mehta / David Pountney / Robert Israel. Siegfried Jerusalem, Nancy Gustafson, Violeta Urmana.

2010 Berlin, Deutsche Oper. Sebastian Lang-Lessing / Philipp Stölzl, Mara Kurotschka / Ulrike Siegrist, Philipp Stölzl. Torsten Kerl, Camilla Nylund, Kate Aldrich.*

Der FLIEGENDE HOLLÄNDER

(DUTCHMAN, SENTA)

1843 DRESDEN, Königlich Sächsisches Hoftheater, 2 January. Richard Wagner / Wilhelm Fischer / Ferdinand HEINE. Johann Michael Wächter, Wilhemine SCHRÖDER-DEVRIENT.

1864   MUNICH, Königliches Hof- und Nationaltheater. Franz Lachner / Richard Wagner / Heinrich DÖLL, Angelo II Quaglio. August Kindermann, Sophie Stehle.

1901   BAYREUTH FESTPIELHAUS. Felix MOTTL / SIEGFRIED WAGNER / Max BRÜCKNER. Anton von Rooey / Theodor Bertram, Emily Destinn.

1929   Berlin, KROLL OPER. Otto Klemperer / Jürgen Fehling / Ewald Dühlberg. Fritz Krenn, Moje Forbach.

1939   Bayreuth, Festspielhaus. Karl ELMENDORFF / Heinz TIETJEN / Emil PREETORIUS. Rudolf Bockelmann / Jaro Prohaska, Maria Müller.

1955   Bayreuth, Festspielhaus. Hans KNAPPERTSBUSCH / Joseph Keilberth / WOLFGANG WAGNER / Wolfgang Wagner. Hermann Uhde / Hans Hotter, Astrid Varnay.

1959   Bayreuth, Festspielhaus. Wolfgang Sawallisch / WIELAND WAGNER / Wieland Wagner. George London / Otto Wiener, Leonie Rysanek / Astrid Varnay.

1962   Oper LEIPZIG, Rolf Reuter / Joachim Herz / Reinhardt Zimmermann. Wilhelm Klemm, Hannelore Kuhse.

1975   San Francisco, War Memorial Opera House. Kenneth Schermerhorn / Jean-Pierre Ponnelle / Jean-Pierre Ponnelle. Theo Adam, Marita Napier.

1976   Kassel, Staatstheater. James Lockhart / Ulrich Melchinger / Thomas Richter-Forgách. Edgar Keenon, Janet Hardy.

1978   Bayreuth, Festspielhaus. Dennis Russell Davies / Harry Kupfer / Peter Sykora. Simon Estes, Lisbeth Balslev.

1981   Munich, Bayerische Staatsoper. Wolfgang Sawallisch / Herbert Wernicke / Herbert Wernicke. Franz Ferdinand Nentwig, Catarina Ligendza.

1989   Bregenz, Seebühne. Ulf Schirmer, Wolfgang Rot / David Pountney / Stefanos Lazaridis. Robert Hale / Philipp Joll / Monte Pederson / Wicus Slabbert / Hartmut Welker, Rebecca Blankenship / Luana Devol / Linda Plech.

1990   Bayreuth, Festspielhaus. Giuseppe Sinopoli / Dieter Dorn / Jürgen Rose. Bernd Weikl, Elizabeth Connell.

2003   Bayreuth, Festspielhaus. Marc Albrecht / Claus Guth / Christian Schmidt. John Tomlinson, Adrienne Dugger.

TANNHÄUSER

(TANNHÄUSER, Venus, ELISABETH)

1845   DRESDEN, Königlich Sächsisches Hoftheater, 19 October. Richard Wagner / Ferdinand HEINE, Wilhelm Fischer / Edouard-Désiré-Joseph Despléchin. Joseph TICHATSCHEK, Wilhelmine SCHRÖDER-DEVRIENT, Johanna Wagner.

1861   PARIS, Théâtre Impérial de l'Opéra / Salle Peletier (in French). Pierre-Louis-Philippe DIETSCH / house stage direction / Edouard-Désiré-Joseph Despléchin. Albert NIEMANN, Fortunata Tedesco, Marie Sasse (see also TANNHÄUSER, PARIS SCANDAL OF 1861).

1884   New York, Metropolitan Opera. Leopold Damrosch / Wilhelm Hock / Charles Fox (Jr.). Anton Schott, Anna Slach, Auguste Seidl-Kraus.

1891   Bayreuth, Festspielhaus. Felix MOTTL / COSIMA WAGNER / Max BRÜCKNER.

1913   Amsterdam, Stadsschouwburg. Henri Viotta / Anton Fuchs / Hermann Burghart. Walther Kirchhof, Borghild Langaard, Maude Fay.

1928   Berlin-Charlottenburg, Deutsche Oper. Bruno Walter / Ernst Lert / Max Reinhardt.

1961   Bayreuth, Festspielhaus. Wolfgang Sawallisch / WIELAND WAGNER / Wieland Wagner. Wolfgang WINDGASSEN / Hans Beirer, Grace Bumbry, Victoria de los Angeles.

1972   Bayreuth, Festspielhaus. Erich Leinsdorf, Horst Stein / Götz Friedrich / Jürgen Rose. Hugh Beresford / Hermin Esser, Gwyneth Jones, Gwyneth Jones.*

1977   New York, Metropolitan Opera. James LEVINE / Otto Schenk / Günther Schneider-Siemssen. James McCracken, Grace Bumbry, Leonie Rysanek.*

1994   Munich, Bayerische Staatsoper. Zubin Mehta / David Alden / Roni Toren.* René Kollo, Nadine Secunde, Waltraud Meier.

2004   Bayreuth, Festspielhaus. Christian Thielemann / Philippe Arlaud / Philippe Arlaud. Stephen Gould, Judit Nemeth, Ricarda Merberth.

2007   Paris, Opéra Bastille. Seiji Ozawa / Robert Carsen / Paul Steinberg. Stephen Gould, Béatrice Uria-Monz, Eva-Maria Westbroek.*

2009   Copenhagen, Det Kongelige Teater. Friedemann Layer / Kasper Bech Holten / Mia Stensgaard. Stig Fogh Andersen, Susanne Resmark, Tina Kiberg.

LOHENGRIN

ELSA, LOHENGRIN, ORTRUD

1850   Weimar, Hoftheater, 28 August. Franz LISZT / Eduard Genast / Karl Wilhelm Holdermann. Rosa von Milde-Agthe, Carl Beck, Josephine Fastlinger.

1871   Bologna, Teatro Comunale di Bologna (in Italian). Bianca Blume, Angelo Mariani / Ernst Frank / Carlo Ferrario, Maria Löwe Destin (see also ITALY; VERDI, GIUSEPPE).

1871   New York, Stadt Theater. Adolf Neuendorff. Luise Garay-Lichtmay, Theodor Habelmann, Marie Frederici.

1908	Bayreuth, Festspielhaus. SIEGFRIED WAGNER / Siegfried Wagner / Max BRÜCKNER. Emmy Destinn, Charles Dalmorès, Edyth Walker.
1958	Bayreuth, Festspielhaus (travelled to New York, Stuttgart and Vienna). André Cluytens / WIELAND WAGNER / Wieland Wagner. Leonie Rysanek, Sándor Kónya, Astrid Varnay.
1987	Bayreuth, Festspielhaus. Peter Schneider / Werner Herzog / Henning von Gierke. Nadine Secunde, Paul Frey, Gabriele Schnaut.*
1998	Hamburg, Staatsoper. Ingo Metzmacher / Peter Konwitschny / Helmut Brade. Inga Nielsen / Thomas Moser / Eva Marton.*
2006	Baden-Baden, Festspielhaus. Kent Nagano / Nikolaus Lehnhoff / Stephan Braunfels. Solveig Kringelborn, Klaus Florian Vogt, Waltraud Meier.*
2009	Berlin, Staatsoper. Daniel Barenboim / Stefan Herheim / Heike Scheele. Dorothea Röschmann, Klaus Florian Vogt, Michaela Schuster.
2010	Bayreuth, Festspielhaus. Andris Nelsons / Hans Neuenfels / Reinhard von der Tannen. Annette Dash, Jonas Kaufmann / Klaus Florian Vogt, Evelyn Herlizius.

TRISTAN UND ISOLDE

TRISTAN, ISOLDE

1865	MUNICH, Königliches Hof- und Nationaltheater, 10 June. Hans von BÜLOW / Richard Wagner / Angelo II Quaglio, Heinrich DÖLL. Ludwig and Malvina Schnorr von CAROLSFELD.
1886	Bayreuth, Festspielhaus. Felix MOTTL / COSIMA WAGNER / Cosima Wagner, Max and Gotthold BRÜCKNER. Heinrich VOGL, Rosa Sucher.
1886	New York, Metropolitan Opera. Anton SEIDL / Mr. Van Hell / Henry E. Hoyt. Albert NIEMANN, Lilli LEHMANN.
1903	Vienna, Hofoper. Gustav MAHLER / Gustav Mahler / Alfred ROLLER. Erik Schmedes, Anna Bahr-Mildenburg.
1923	Milan, Teatro alla Scala. Arturo TOSCANINI / Adolphe APPIA / Adolphe Appia.
1952	Bayreuth, Festspielhaus. Herbert von KARAJAN / WIELAND WAGNER / Wieland Wagner. Ramon Vinay, Martha Mödl / Astrid Varnay.
1962	Bayreuth, Festspielhaus. Karl BÖHM / Wieland Wagner / Wieland Wagner. Wolfgang WINDGASSEN, Birgit NILSSON.*
1975	Staatsoper Dresden. Marek Janowski / Harry Kupfer / Peter Sykora. Spas Wenkoff, Ingeborg Zobel.
1981	Bayreuth, Festspielhaus. Daniel Barenboim / Jean-Pierre Ponnelle / Jean-Pierre Ponnelle. René Kollo / Hermin Esser, Johanna Meier.*

1987   Los Angeles, Dorothy Chandler Pavilion. Zubin Mehta / John Cox / David Hockney. William Johns, Jeannine Altmeyer.

1993   Bayreuth, Festspielhaus. Daniel Barenboim / Heiner Müller / Erich Wonder. Siegfried Jerusalem / Waltraud Meier.*

1995   Munich, Bayerische Staatsoper. Zubin Mehta / Peter Konwitschny / Johannes Leiacker. Siegfried Jerusalem, Waltraud Meier.*

2003   Glyndebourne Festival Theatre. Jiří Bělohlávek / Nikolaus Lehnhoff / Roland Aeschlimann. Robert Gambill, Nina Stemme.*

2005   Paris, Opéra Bastille. Esa-Pekka Salonen / Peter Sellars / Bill Viola (initially conceived as the "Tristan Project" in Los Angeles and also mounted at the Brooklyn Academy of Music; full production format revived in Los Angeles and Toronto). Ben Heppner, Waltraud Meier.

2007   Milan, Teatro alla Scala. Daniel Barenboim / Patrice Chéreau / Richard Peduzzi. Ian Story / Waltraud Meier.*

Die MEISTERSINGER VON NÜRNBERG

(HANS SACHS, SIXTUS BECKMESSER, WALTHER, EVA)

1868   MUNICH, Königliches Hof- und Nationaltheater, 21 June. Hans von BÜLOW / Richard Wagner, Reinhard Hallwachs / Angelo II Quaglio, Heinrich DÖLL, Christian Jank. Franz BETZ, Gustav Hölzel, Franz Nachbaur, Mathilde Mallinger.

1932   Berlin, Staatsoper. Wilhelm FURTWÄNGLER / Heinz TIETJEN / Otto Pankok.

1956   Bayreuth, Festspielhaus. André Cluytens / WIELAND WAGNER / Wieland Wagner. Hans HOTTER, Karl Schmitt-Walter, Wolfgang WINDGASSEN, Gré Brouwenstijn.

1962   New York, Metropolitan Opera. Joseph Rosenstock / Nathaniel Merrill / Robert O'Hearn. Otto Wiener, Karl Dönch, Sándor Kónya, Ingrid Bjoner.

1963   Bayreuth, Festspielhaus. Thomas Schippers / WIELAND WAGNER / Wieland Wagner. Otto Wiener / Josef Greindl, Carlos Alexander, Jess Thomas / Wolfgang WINDGASSEN, Anja Silja.

1967   Stockholm, Kungliga Operan. Berislav Klobucar / Götz Friedrich / Günther Schneider-Siemssen. Leif Roar, Erik Saedén, Sven-Olof Eliasson, Helena Döse.

1981   Bayreuth, Festspielhaus. Mark Elder / WOLFGANG WAGNER / Wolfgang Wagner. Bernd Weikl, Hermann Prey, Siegfried Jerusalem, Mari-Anne Häggander.*

1993   New York, Metropolitan Opera. James Levine / Otto Schenk / Günther Schneider-Siemssen. Donald McIntyre, Hermann Prey, Francisco Araiza, Karita Mattila.*

2002 Hamburg, Staatsoper. Ingo Metzmacher / Peter Konwitschny / Johannes Leiacker. Wolfgang Schöne, Hans-Joachim Ketelsen, John Treleaven, Anja Harteros.

2008 Bayreuth, Festspielhaus. Sebastian Weigle / KATHARINA WAGNER / Tilo Steffens. Franz Hawlata, Michael Volle, Klaus Florian Vogt, Amanda Mace.*

2011 Glyndebourne Festival Theatre. Vladimir Jurowski / David McVicar / Vicki Mortimer. Gerald Finley, Johannes Martin Kranzle, Topi Lehtipuu, Anna Gabler.

2012 Zurich, Staatsoper. Daniele Gatti / Harry Kupfer / Hans Schavernoch. Michael Volle, Martin Gantner, Roberto Saccà, Juliane Banse.

Der RING DES NIBELUNGEN

WOTAN/The Wanderer, ALBERICH, HAGEN, SIEGMUND, SIEGLINDE, SIEGFRIED, BRÜNNHILDE
The Ring cycle has been produced hundreds of times around the world. In this highly selective overview, a few complete productions are listed below, including some early productions and a sampling from the years following World War II. Cast details, where provided, represent premieres of the individual works. For productions that have been recorded in an audiovisual format, only information about the production team has been provided here. (Note: recordings are typically made after the premiere.)

1876 BAYREUTH, Festspielhaus, 13–17 August. Hans RICHTER / Richard Wagner, Richard FRICKE / Josef HOFFMANN, Max and Gotthold BRÜCKNER. Franz BETZ, Carl Hill, Gustav Siehr, Albert NIEMANN, Josefine Scheffzky, Georg UNGER, Amalie MATERNA. (Das RHEINGOLD and Die WALKÜRE premiered individually in Munich, in 1869 and 1870 respectively.)

1878 Oper LEIPZIG, Josef Sucher / Angelo NEUMANN / Atelier Lütkemeyer.

1878 MUNICH, Königliches Hof- und Nationaltheater. Hermann LEVI / Karl Brulliot / Henrich DÖLL, Christian Jank.

1896 Bayreuth, Festspielhaus. Hans RICHTER / COSIMA WAGNER / Max Brückner.

1951 Bayreuth, Festspielhaus. Hans KNAPPERTSBUSCH / WIELAND WAGNER / Wieland Wagner. Sigurd Björling, Heinrich Pfanzl, Ludwig Weber, Günther Treptow, Leonie Rysanek, Bernd Aldenhoff, Astrid Varnay.

1970–4 Kassel, Staatstheater. Gerd Albrecht / Ulrich Melchinger / Thomas Richter-Forgách.

1971–3	London, English National Opera (in English). Reginald GOODALL / Glen Byam Shaw, John Blatchley / Ralph Koltai.
1973–6	Oper Leipzig. Gert Bahner / Joachim Herz / Rudolf Heinrich.
1976	Bayreuth, Festspielhaus. Pierre BOULEZ / Patrice CHÉREAU / Richard Peduzzi.*
1977	Stuttgart, Staatstheater. Silvio Varviso / Jean-Pierre Ponnelle / Jean-Pierre Ponnelle.
1984–5	Berlin, Deutsche Oper. Jesús López-Cobos / Götz Friedrich / Peter Sykora.
1985–6	Seattle, Manuel Rosenthal / François Rochaix / Robert Israel.
1985–7	Oper Frankfurt. Michael Gielen / Ruth Berghaus / Axel Manthey.
1987	Munich, Bayerische Staatsoper. Wolfgang Sawallisch / Nikolaus Lehnhoff / Erich Wonder.
1988	Bayreuth, Festspielhaus. Daniel Barenboim / Harry Kupfer / Hans Schavernoch.*
1989	New York, Metropolitan Opera. James LEVINE / Otto Schenk / Gunther Schneider-Siemssen.*
1991	Brussels, Théâtre de la Monnaie. Sylvain Cambreling / Herbert Wernicke / Herbert Wernicke.
1997–8	Amsterdam, Het Muziktheater. Hartmut Haenchen / Pierre Audi / George Tsypin.*
1999– 2000	Stuttgart, Staatsoper. Lothar Zagrosek conducted the entire cycle. Production teams varied by work: Das RHEINGOLD: Joachim Schlömer / Jens Kilian; Die WALKÜRE: Christof Nel / Karl Kneidl; SIEGFRIED: Jossi Wieler, Sergio Morobito / Anna Viebrock; GÖTTERDÄMMERUNG: Peter Konwitschny / Bert Neumann.*
2004	Adelaide, Festival Theater. Asher Fisch / Elke Neidhardt / Michael Scott-Mitchell. John Bröcheler, John Wegener, Duccio dal Monte, Stuart Skelton, Deborah Reidel, Timothy Massard, Lisa Gasteen.
2004–5	London, The Royal Opera, Covent Garden. Antonio Pappano / Keith Warner / Stefanos Lazaridis. Bryn Terfel, Günter von Kannen, John Tomlinson, Jorma Silvasti / Plácido Domingo, Katarina Dalayman, John Treleaven, Lisa Gasteen.
2005–6	Copenhagen, Det Kongelige Teater. Michael Schønwandt / Kasper Bech Holten / Marie í Dali, Steffen Aarfing.*
2007	Toronto, Canadian Opera Company. Richard Bradshaw conducted the cycle, which was designed throughout by Michael Levine. Directors varied by opera, in order: Michael Levine, Atom Egoyan, François Girard, Tim Albery. Pavlo Hunka, Richard Paul Fink, Mats Almgren, Clifton Forbis, Adrianne Pieczonka, Christian Franz, Susan Bullock / Frances Ginzer.

2007–8	Vienna, Staatsoper. Franz-Welser Möst / Sven-Eric Bechtolf / Marianne and Rolf Glittenberg. Juha Uusitalo, Tomasz Konieczny, Eric Halfvarson, Johan Botha, Nina Stemme, Stephen Gould, Nina Stemme / Eva Johansson.
2010–12	New York, Metropolitan Opera. James Levine / Robert Lepage / Carl Fillion. Bryn Terfel, Eric Owens, Hans-Peter König, Jonas Kaufmann, Eva-Maria Westbroek / Margaret Jane Wray, Jay Hunter Morris, Deborah Voigt.
2011	San Francisco, War Memorial Opera House. Donald Runnicles / Francesca Zambello / Michael Yeargen (the production was launched at Washington National Opera but first reached completion in San Francisco.) Mark Delavan, Gordon Hawkins, Andrea Silvestrelli, Brandon Jovanovich, Anje Kampe, Jay Hunter Morris, Nina Stemme.
2011–12	Munich, Bayerische Staatsoper. Kent Nagano / Andreas Kriegenburg / Harald B. Thor. Johan Reuter / Thomas J. Mayer, Johannes Martin Kränzle / Wolfgang Koch, Eric Halfvarson, Klaus Florian Vogt, Anja Kampe, Lance Ryan / Stephen Gould, Nina Stemme.

PARSIFAL

(Parsifal, Kundry, Amfortas, Gurnemanz)

1882	Bayreuth, Festspielhaus. Hermann Levi, Franz Fischer / Richard Wagner / Paul von Joukowsky, Max and Gotthold Brückner. Ferdinand Jäger / Hermann Winkelmann / Heinrich Gudehus, Amalie Materna / Marianne Brandt / Therese Malten, Theodor Reichmann, Emil Scaria / Gustav Siehr.
1903	New York, Metropolitan Opera. Alfred Hertz/Anton Fuchs/ Hermann Burghart. Alois Burgstaller, Milka Ternina, Anton von Rooy, Robert Blass.
1905	Amsterdam, Stadsschouwburg. Henri Viotta / Emil Valdek / Burghart Weenen. Ejnar Forchhammer, Felia Litvinne, Richard Breitenfeld, Robert Blass.
1920	New York, Metropolitan Opera. Artur Bodanzky / Samuel Thewman / Joseph Urban. Orville Harrold, Margarete Matzenauer, Clarence Whitehill, Léon Rothier.
1951	Bayreuth, Festspielhaus. Hans Knappertsbusch / Wieland Wagner / Wieland Wagner. Wolfgang Windgassen, Martha Mödl, George London, Ludwig Weber.
1975	Bayreuth, Festspielhaus. Horst Stein, Hans Zender / Wolfgang Wagner / Wolfgang Wagner. René Kollo, Eva Randová / Ursula Schröder-Feinen, Bernd Weikl, Hans Sotin.
1982	Bayreuth, Festspielhaus. James Levine / Götz Friedrich / Andreas Reinhardt. Peter Hofmann, Leonie Rysanek, Simon Estes, Hans Sotin.

848

1991 Hamburg, Staatsoper (co-production with Houston Grand Opera, revived in Los Angeles). Gerd Albrecht / Robert Wilson / Robert Wilson. Siegfried Jerusalem, Dunja Vejzovic, Franz Grundheber, Kurt Moll.

1991 New York, Metropolitan Opera. James Levine / Otto Schenk / Günther Schneider-Siemssen. Plácido Domingo, Jessye Norman, Ekkehard Wlaschiha, Robert Lloyd.

1999 London, English National Opera (also mounted in San Francisco, Chicago, and Baden-Baden). Mark Elder / Nicholas Lehnhoff / Raimund Bauer. Kim Begley, Kathryn Harris, Jonathan Summers, Gwynne Howell.

2008 Bayreuth, Festspielhaus. Daniele Gatti / Stefan Herheim / Heike Scheele. Christopher Ventris, Mihoko Fojimura, Detlef Roth, Kwangchul Youn.

SOURCES

Complete Bayreuth production information (and cast lists, for all performances since 1951) is available at:

www.bayreuther-festspiele.de/statistiken/auffuehrungen_sortiert_nach_inszenierungen_309.html

Appendix II   Websites

Compiled by Nicholas Vazsonyi

There are dozens of websites, blogs, and groups on Facebook devoted to Richard Wagner. The following is only a listing of a few websites to get the interested reader started. Most of these have links to additional sites, and so on.

GENERAL INFORMATION

www.richard-wagner-web.de	German site with a wealth of information and data about Wagner's works and life.
www.wagneropera.net	Site maintained in Norway (in English) by Per-Erik Skramstad and Erling Guldbrandsen with a wealth of information about the operas, current productions, new releases of books, recordings, DVDs, and so on.
www.archivowagner.com	"Archivo Richard Wagner." Site maintained in Spanish, containing loads of information, including a remarkably complete listing of all Wagner's prose works, their first appearance, and their publication in SSD and PW. Also ample links to other Wagner sites globally.
http://users.belgacom.net/ wagnerlibrary	Site maintained in Belgium by Patrick Swinkels. Contains, among other texts, pdf versions of the complete edition of William Ashton Ellis's English translation of Wagner's prose works. Also contains e-versions of significant chunks of the piano-vocal scores for the major operas.

www.rwagner.net/e-frame.html	Site devoted to the operas, including plot synopses and list of *Leitmotive* with score extracts brought to life by synthesized audio examples.
www.ehow.com/ info_7865420_worldwide-wagner-music-festivals.html	Site devoted to all the Wagner festivals, including Wels, Budapest, Ravello.
http://opera.stanford.edu/main.html	"Opera Glass" project run out of Stanford University. Wealth of information on all opera (not just Wagner), including libretti, data on performance history, and so on.
www.wagnermuseum.de	Wagner Museum in Bayreuth.
www.adwmainz.de/index.php?id=381	Site for the *Richard Wagner, SÄMTLICHE WERKE* (SW), including contents for all the volumes.

BAYREUTH FESTIVAL

www.bayreuther-festspiele.de	Official website of the Bayreuth Festival.
http://taffbayreuth.org/deutsch/home_3.html	TAFF = Team Aktiver Festspielförderer. Organization formed to support the initiatives of the current Festival directors, Katharina Wagner and Eva Wagner-Pasquier.
www.freunde-bayreuth.org	Site of the Society of Friends of Bayreuth, financial supporters of the Bayreuth Festival since 1949.

WAGNER SOCIETIES AND ORGANIZATIONS

www.richard-wagner-verband.de	Website of the International Association of Wagner Societies, which unites the 135 regional Wagner societies around the world.
www.wagnersocietyny.org	Wagner Society of New York (USA).
www.wagnersociety.org	Wagner Society of London.

Appendix 12   Archives and Museums

Compiled by Nicholas Vazsonyi

Wahnfried and Richard Wagner Museum
with National Archives and Research Institute of the Richard Wagner
    Foundation
Richard-Wagner-Strasse 48
95444 Bayreuth / Germany
Tel.: +49 (0)921 - 757 28 - 0
Fax: +49 (0)921 - 757 28 - 22
Open: Monday to Thursday 10am–12 noon and 2–4pm; Friday 10am–12 noon;
    and by arrangement.
Researchers wishing to use the archives must generally announce themselves
    ahead of time, explain the nature of their research, ensure that the
    requested materials are available, and obtain permission to view them.
    Application forms are available on the website (www.wagnermuseum.de).

EISENACH

Reuter-Wagner-Museum
im Thüringer Museum
Reuterweg 2
99817 Eisenach / Germany
Tel.: +49 (0) 36 91 – 74 32 93
Fax: +49 (0) 36 91 – 74 32 94
Open: Tuesday through Sunday, 11am–5pm.
The Reuter Villa is home to the Reuter Wagner Museum, after Bayreuth the
    most comprehensive collection relating to Richard Wagner. The collection
    originated with Nikolaus OESTERLEIN, who assembled a collection of
    images, busts, letters, and writings, theater playbills, and a library of around
    5,000 volumes during the composer's lifetime. Oesterlein opened a private
    museum in Vienna in 1887, but was soon obliged to put the collection of
    around 20,000 items on the market. Josef Kürschner, a respected publisher
    of dictionaries and literary catalogs, encouraged the Eisenach Council to
    purchase the collection. The acquisition was made in 1895. The Oesterlein
    Collection was placed in Fritz Reuter's villa and presented to the public in
    1897 as the Reuter Wagner Museum. The Oesterlein Wagner Collection was
    redesigned in 1997.

GRAUPA

Lohengrinhaus / Richard-Wagner-Museum Graupa
Richard-Wagner-Straße 6
01796 Pirna, OT Graupa / Germany
Tel.: +49 (0) 35 01 – 54 82 29
Fax: +49 (0) 35 01 – 54 82 29
wagnermuseum@pirna.de
Open: Tuesday through Sunday and holidays, 10am–4pm

LUCERNE / TRIBSCHEN

Richard Wagner Museum
Richard Wagner Weg 27
CH-6005 Lucerne / Switzerland
Tel.: +41 (0) 41 – 360 23 70
Fax: +41 (0) 41 – 360 23 79
info@richard-wagner-museum.ch
The exhibition on the life and work of Richard Wagner can be viewed on the
  ground level of the villa. Historic photographs and paintings are on display
  in five rooms on this level, together with a collection of original
  manuscripts (letters and musical scores), several items of Wagner's
  clothing, and pieces of furniture from his stay.

VENICE

Wagner Museum Ca' Vendramin Calergi
For information, contact:
Associazione Richard Wagner – Venezia
Cannaregio 2040
Venice / Italy
Tel. +39 (0) 41 – 276 04 07
Offers guided tours of the Wagner rooms in Ca' Vendramin Calergi on
  Tuesday and Saturday morning and Thursday afternoon. Reservations
  required.
e-mail: arwv@libero.it
www.casinovenezia.it/en/museo_wagner.jsp

Select bibliography

Apart from the first two sections, this bibliography is merely a list of the works cited frequently in the encyclopedia: nothing more. Additional references are listed at the end of specific entries relating to the subject matter of that entry alone. Works cited in several entries are generally given there in abbreviated form and below with full details.

There is no complete Wagner bibliography and, with the advent of the web, there likely will never be one. An excellent resource, however, is Michael Saffle's *Richard Wagner: A Research and Information Guide* (London: Routledge, 2010).

PRIMARY SOURCES AND CRITICAL EDITIONS (SELECTIONS)

König Ludwig II. und Richard Wagner. Briefwechsel. Mit vielen anderen Urkunden. 5 vols. Ed. Otto Strobel. Karlsruhe: Braun, 1936–9.

Richard Wagner an Mathilde Wesendonk: Tagebuchblätter und Briefe 1853–1871. Berlin: Alexander Duncker, 1910.

Selected Letters of Richard Wagner. Trans. and ed. Stewart Spencer and Barry Millington. New York and London: Norton, 1987.

Wagner, Cosima. *Die Tagebücher.* Ed. Martin Gregor-Dellin and Dietrich Mack. 2 vols. Munich: Piper, 1976–7. Trans. and annotated Geoffrey Skelton, *Cosima Wagner's Diaries.* 2 vols. New York: Harcourt Brace Jovanovich, 1978–80. Abbrev. CWD.

Wagner, Richard. *The Diary of Richard Wagner 1865–1882: The Brown Book.* Ed. Joachim Bergfeld, trans. George Bird. Cambridge University Press, 1980. Abbrev. BB/E.

Mein Leben. Ed. Martin Gregor-Dellin. Munich: List, 1963. Abbrev. ML.

My Life. Trans. Andrew Gray, ed. Mary Whittall. New York: Da Capo Press, 1992. Abbrev. ML/E.

Prose Works. Trans. William Ashton Ellis. 8 vols. London: Kegan Paul, Trench, Trübner, 1892–9. Paperback reprint, Lincoln: University of Nebraska Press, 1995. Abbrev. PW.

Sämtliche Briefe. Ed. Gertrud Strobel, Werner Wolf, et al. Leipzig: Deutscher Verlag für Musik, 1967–2000; Wiesbaden: Breitkopf & Härtel, 1999–. Abbrev. SB.

Sämtliche Schriften und Dichtungen: Volksausgabe. 16 vols. Leipzig: Breitkopf & Härtel, n.d. [1911]. Abbrev. SSD.

Sämtliche Werke. Ed. Egon Voss. Gesellschaft zur Förderung der Richard
Wagner-Gesamtausgabe and the Bayerische Akademie der Schönen
Künste, München. Mainz: Schott, 1970–. Abbrev. SW.

REFERENCE WORKS, LEXIKA, AND COMPANIONS (SELECTIONS,
IN CHRONOLOGICAL ORDER, LISTED BY TITLE)

1882   Nikolaus Oesterlein, *Katalog einer Richard-Wagner-Bibliothek: Nach den
        vorliegenden Originalien systematisch-chronologisch geordnetes und mit
        Citaten und Anmerkungen versehenes authentisches Nachschlagebuch durch
        die gesammte Wagner-Litteratur.* 4 vols. Leipzig: Breitkopf & Härtel,
        1882–95.

1883   *Wagner-lexicon: Hauptbegriffe der Kunst- und Weltanschauung Richard
        Wagner's.* Ed. Carl Friedrich Glasenapp and Heinrich von Stein.
        Stuttgart: J. G. Cotta, 1883.

1891   *Wagner-Encyklopädie: Haupterscheinungen der Kunst- und Kulturgeschichte
        im Lichte der Anschauung Richard Wagners.* Ed. Carl Glasenapp. 2 vols.
        Leipzig: Fritsch, 1891.

1939   *A Richard Wagner Dictionary,* Edward M. Terry. New York: Wilson, 1939.

1979   *The Wagner Companion.* Ed. Peter Burbidge and Richard Sutton.
        Cambridge University Press, 1979.

1983   *Richard Wagner: Leben – Werk – Wirkung,* Hermes Hand Lexikon. Ed.
        Martin Gregor-Dellin and Michael von Soden. Düsseldorf: Econ,
        1983.

1984   *The New Grove Wagner.* Carl Dahlhaus and John Deathridge.
        Macmillan: London, 1984.

1984   *Who's Who in Wagner: An A–Z Look at his Life and Work.* Phillip Hodson.
        New York: Macmillan, 1984.

1986   *Richard-Wagner-Handbuch.* Ed. Ulrich Müller and Peter Wapnewski.
        Stuttgart: Kröner, 1986. English trans. *The Wagner Handbook.* Ed.
        John Deathridge (Cambridge, MA: Harvard University Press, 1992).

1986   *Wagner Werk-Verzeichnis (WWV). Verzeichnis der musikalischen Werke Rich-
        ard Wagners und ihrer Quellen, erarbeitet im Rahmen der Richard Wagner-
        Gesamtausgabe.* Ed. John Deathridge, Martin Geck, and Egon Voss.
        Mainz: Schott, 1986.

1992   *The Wagner Compendium: A Guide to Wagner's Life and Music.* Ed. Barry
        Millington. New York: Shirmer, 1992.

1992   *The Wagner Handbook* (see 1986).

1998   *Richard Wagner Lexikon.* Ed. Hans-Joachim Bauer. Bergisch-
        Gladbach: Gustav Lübbe, 1998.

1998   *Chronologisches Verzeichnis der Briefe von Richard Wagner: Wagner Briefe-
        Verzeichnis (WBV).* Ed. Werner Breig, Martin Dürrer, and Andreas
        Mielke. Wiesbaden: Breitkopf & Härtel, 1998.

2006   *The New Grove Guide to Wagner and His Operas.* Barry Millington.
        Oxford University Press, 2006.

2008   *The Cambridge Companion to Wagner.* Ed. Thomas S. Grey. Cambridge
        University Press, 2008.

2010   *Dictionnaire encyclopédique Wagner*. Ed. Timothée Picard. Arles: Actes Sud, 2010.

2012   *Wagner-Handbuch*. Ed. Laurenz Lütteken. Stuttgart: Metzler, 2012.

2012   *Das Wagner-Lexikon*. Ed. Daniel Brandenburg, Rainer Franke, and Anno Mungen under the auspices of the Forschungsinstitut für Musiktheater Thurnau. Laaber Verlag, 2012.

FREQUENTLY CITED WORKS

Abbate, Carolyn. *Unsung Voices: Opera and Musical Narrative in the Nineteenth Century*. Princeton University Press, 1991.

Adorno, Theodor W. *Essays on Music*. Ed. Richard Leppert. Berkeley: University of California Press, 2002.

    Gesammelte Schriften in 20 Bänden. Ed. Rolf Tiedemann. Frankfurt: Suhrkamp, 1970–80.

    In Search of Wagner. Trans. Rodney Livingstone. London: Verso, 1991.

Ambros, August Wilhelm. *Culturhistorische Bilder aus dem Musikleben der Gegenwart*. Leipzig, 1860.

Bailey, Robert, ed. *Prelude and Transfiguration from "Tristan und Isolde."* Norton Critical Score. New York: Norton, 1985.

    "The Structure of the Ring and Its Evolution," *19th-Century Music* 1.1 (1977): 48–61.

Barker, John W. *Wagner and Venice*. University of Rochester Press, 2008.

Bauer, Oswald Georg. *Richard Wagner: The Stage Designs and Productions from the Premieres to the Present*. New York: Rizzoli, 1983.

Baumann, Carl-Friedrich. *Bühnentechnik im Festspielhaus Bayreuth*. Munich: Prestel, 1980.

Berlioz, Hector. *The Memoirs of Hector Berlioz*. Trans. David Cairns. London: Cardinal, 1990.

Bermbach, Udo. *Der Wahn des Gesamtkunstwerks: Richard Wagners politisch-ästhetische Utopie*. Frankfurt: Fischer, 1994. 2nd edn. Stuttgart: Metzler, 2004.

Berry, Mark. *Treacherous Bonds and Laughing Fire: Politics and Religion in Wagner's "Ring."* Aldershot: Ashgate, 2006.

Borchmeyer, Dieter. *Richard Wagner: Ahasvers Wandlung*. Frankfurt am Main: Insel, 2002. Trans. Daphne Ellis, *Drama and the World of Richard Wagner*. Princeton University Press, 2002.

    Das Theater Richard Wagners: Idee – Dichtung – Wirkung. Stuttgart: Reclam, 1982. Trans. Stewart Spencer, *Richard Wagner: Theory and Theatre*. Oxford: Clarendon, 1991.

Borchmeyer, Dieter, Ami Maayani, and Susanne Vill, eds. *Richard Wagner und die Juden*. Stuttgart: Metzler, 2000.

Carnegy, Patrick. *Wagner and the Art of the Theatre*. New Haven, CT: Yale University Press, 2006.

Carr, Jonathan. *The Wagner Clan*. New York: Atlantic Monthly, 2007.

Chafe, Eric. *The Tragic and the Ecstatic: The Musical Revolution of Wagner's "Tristan und Isolde."* New York: Oxford University Press, 2005.

Chamberlain, H. S. *Richard Wagner an Ferdinand Praeger*, 2nd edn. Leipzig, 1908.

Cooke, Deryck. *I Saw the World End: A Study of Wagner's "Ring."* London: Oxford University Press, 1979.

Csampai, Attila and Dietmar Holland, eds. *Richard Wagner, "Lohengrin": Texte, Materialien, Kommentare.* Reinbek bei Hamburg: Rowohlt, 1989.

eds. *Richard Wagner, "Der fliegende Holländer": Texte, Materialen, Kommentare.* Reinbek bei Hamburg: Rowohlt, 1982.

Culshaw, John. *Ring Resounding.* London: Secker & Warburg / New York: Viking Press, 1967.

Dahlhaus, Carl. *Wagners Konzeption des musikalischen Dramas.* Regensburg: Bosse, 1971. Trans. Mary Whittall. *Richard Wagner's Music Dramas.* Cambridge University Press, 1979.

Dahlhaus, Carl and Egon Voss, eds. *Wagnerliteratur: Wagnerforschung.* Mainz: Schott, 1985.

Danuser, Hermann and Herfried Münkler, eds. *Zukunftsbilder. Richard Wagners Revolution und ihre Folgen in Kunst und Politik.* Schliengen: Argus, 2002.

Darcy, Warren. "The Ursatz in Wagner: or, Was Wagner a Background Composer After All?," *Intégral* 4 (1990): 1–35.

Wagner's "Das Rheingold." New York: Oxford University Press, 1993.

Deathridge, John. *Wagner Beyond Good and Evil.* Berkeley: University of California Press, 2008.

Wagner's "Rienzi": A Reappraisal Based on a Study of the Sketches and Drafts. Oxford: Clarendon, 1977.

Donington, Robert. *Wagner's Ring and its Symbols: The Music and the Myth.* London: Faber & Faber, 1963.

Dreyfus, Laurence. *Wagner and the Erotic Impulse.* Cambridge, MA: Harvard University Press, 2010.

du Moulin Eckhart, Richard Graf. *Cosima Wagner, ein Lebens- und Charakterbild,* 2 vols. Berlin: Drei Masken, 1929.

Ellis, William Ashton, *Life of Richard Wagner: Being an Authorised English Version of C. F. Glasenapp's "Das Leben Richard Wagner's,"* 6 vols. (London: Kegan Paul, Trench, Trübner, 1900–8).

Ewans, Michael. *Wagner and Aeschylus: The Ring and the Oresteia.* Cambridge University Press, 1983.

Fischer, Jens Malte. *Richard Wagners "Das Judentum in der Musik": Eine kritische Dokumentation als Beitrag zur Geschichte des Antisemitismus.* Frankfurt am Main: Insel Verlag, 2000.

Franke, Rainer. *Richard Wagners Zürcher Kunstschriften: Politische und Ästhetische Entwürfe auf seinem Weg zum "Ring der Nibelungen."* Hamburger Beiträge zur Musikwissenschaft, vol. 26. Hamburg: Verlag der Musikalienhandlung K. D. Wagner, 1983.

Fricke, Richard. *Richard Wagner auf der Probe: Das Bayreuther Tagebuch des Ballettmeisters und Hilfsregisseurs Richard Fricke.* Stuttgart: Akademischer Verlag H.-D. Heinz, 1983. Trans. and ed. George Fricke, James Deaville, and Evan Baker. *Wagner in Rehearsal, 1875–1876.* Stuyvesant, NY: Pendragon, 1998.

Friedländer, Saul and Jörn Rüsen, eds. *Richard Wagner im Dritten Reich.* Munich: Beck, 2000.

Gautier, Judith. *Wagner at Home.* New York: John Lane, 1911.

Geck, Martin. *Die Bildnisse Richard Wagners.* Munich: Prestel, 1970.

Glasenapp, Carl Friedrich. *Das Leben Richard Wagners in sechs Büchern.* Leipzig: Breitkopf & Härtel, 1912.

    Richard Wagner's Leben und Wirken, 2 vols. (Cassel and Leipzig: Carl Maurer's Verlags-Buchhandlung, 1876–7).

Gregor-Dellin, Martin. *Richard Wagner: Sein Leben, sein Werk, sein Jahrhundert.* Munich: Piper, 1980. Trans. J. Maxwell Brownjohn, *Richard Wagner: His Life, His Work, His Century.* San Diego, CA: Harcourt Brace Jovanovich, 1983.

Grey, Thomas S., ed. *Richard Wagner: "Der fliegende Holländer"* (Cambridge Opera Handbook). Cambridge University Press, 2000.

    ed. *Richard Wagner and His World.* Princeton University Press, 2009.

    Wagner's Musical Prose: Texts and Contexts. Cambridge University Press, 1995.

    "...*wie ein roter Faden*: On the Origins of the 'leitmotif' as Critical Construct and Musical Practice," in *Music Theory in the Age of Romanticism.* Ed. Ian Bent. Cambridge University Press, 1996. 187–210.

Großmann-Vendrey, Susanna. *Bayreuth in der deutschen Presse: Beiträge zur Rezeptionsgeschichte Richard Wagners und seiner Festspiele,* 3 vols. Regensburg: Bosse, 1977–83.

Gutman, Robert W. *Richard Wagner: The Man, His Mind, and His Music.* New York: Harcourt, Brace, & World, 1968.

Habel, Heinrich. *Festspielhaus und Wahnfried.* Munich: Prestel, 1985.

Hamann, Brigitte. *Winifred Wagner oder Hitlers Bayreuth.* Munich: Piper, 2002. Trans. Alan Bance. *Winifred Wagner: A Life at the Heart of Hitler's Germany.* London: Houghton Mifflin, 2006.

Hanke, Eva Martina. *Wagner in Zürich: Individuum und Lebenswelt.* Kassel: Bärenreiter, 2007.

Hanslick, Eduard. *Aus meinem Leben,* 2 vols. Berlin: Allgemeiner Verein für Deutsche Litteratur, 1894.

Hein, Annette. *"Es ist viel 'Hitler' in Wagner": Rassismus und antisemitische Deutschtumsideologie in den "Bayreuther Blättern" (1878–1938).* Tübingen: Niemeyer, 1996.

Hilmes, Oliver. *Cosima Wagner: The Lady of Bayreuth.* Trans. Stewart Spencer. New Haven, CT: Yale University Press, 2010.

Holden, Raymond. *The Virtuoso Conductors: The Central European Tradition from Wagner to Karajan.* New Haven, CT: Yale University Press, 2005.

Horowitz, Joseph. *Wagner Nights: An American History.* Berkeley: University of California Press, 1994.

Jacobs, Robert L., trans. *Three Wagner Essays.* Eulenberg: London, 1979.

    "Wagner and Judith Gautier," *Music & Letters* 8 (1937): 134–49.

Joe, Jeongwon and Sander Gilman, eds. *Wagner and Cinema.* Bloomington: Indiana University Press, 2010.

Kaiser, Hermann. *Der Bühnenmeister Carl Brandt und Richard Wagner. Kunst der Szene in Darmstadt und Bayreuth.* Darmstadt: Roether, 1968.

Karbaum, Michael. *Studien zur Geschichte der Bayreuther Festspiele: (1876–1976).* Regensburg: Bosse, 1976.

Katz, Jacob. *The Darker Side of Genius: Richard Wagner's Anti-Semitism.* Hanover: Brandeis University Press, 1986.

Kinderman, William and Katherine Syer, eds. *A Companion to Wagner's "Parsifal."* Rochester, NY: Camden House, 2005.

Kirchmeyer, Helmut. *Situationsgeschichte der Musikkritik und des musikalischen Pressewesens in Deutschland. Vol. IV: Das zeitgenössische Wagner-Bild.* Regensburg: Bosse, 1968–85.

Köhler, Joachim. *Richard Wagner: The Last of the Titans.* Trans. Stewart Spencer. New Haven, CT: Yale University Press, 2004.

Wagner's Hitler. Trans. Ronald Taylor. Cambridge University Press, 2000.

Kropfinger, Karl. *Wagner and Beethoven: Richard Wagner's Reception of Beethoven.* Trans. P. Palmer. Cambridge University Press, 1991.

Large, David C. and William Weber, eds., in collaboration with Anne Dzamba Sessa. *Wagnerism in European Culture and Politics.* Ithaca, NY: Cornell University Press, 1984.

Liszt, Franz. *Correspondence of Wagner and Liszt (vols. 1 & 2).* Trans. Francis Hueffer. Cirencester: Echo, 2005.

Lorenz, Alfred. *Das Geheimnis der Form bei Richard Wagner. Vol. I: Der musikalische Aufbau des Bühnenfestspieles Der Ring des Nibelungen; Vol. II: Der musikalische Aufbau von Richard Wagners Tristan und Isolde; Vol. III: Der musikalische Aufbau von Richard Wagners Die Meistersinger von Nürnberg; Vol. IV: Der musikalische Aufbau von Richard Wagners Parsifal.* Berlin: Max Hesse, 1924–33. Repr. Tutzing: Hans Schneider, 1966.

Luther, Einhard. *Helden an geweihtem Ort: Biographie eines Stimmfaches. Vol. II: Wagnertenöre in Bayreuth, 1884–1914.* Trossingen and Berlin: Edition Omega Wolfgang Layer, 2002.

"So singe, Held!" Biographie eines Stimmfaches. Vol. I: Wagnertenöre der Wagnerzeit, 1842–1883. Trossingen and Berlin: Edition Omega Wolfgang Layer, 1998.

"So viel der Helden." Biographie eines Stimmfaches. Vol. III: Wagnertenöre der Kaiserzeit, 1871–1918. Berlin: Pro Business, 2006.

McCreless, Patrick. *Wagner's "Siegfried": Its Drama, History, and its Music.* Ann Arbor: University of Michigan Press, 1982.

Millington, Barry. *Wagner.* Master Musicians Series. London: Dent, 1984.

Wagner. Oxford University Press, 2000.

Mösch, Stephan. *Weihe, Werkstatt, Wirklichkeit: Wagners "Parsifal" in Bayreuth, 1882–1933.* Kassel: Bärenreiter / Stuttgart and Weimar: J. B. Metzler, 2009.

Nattiez, Jean-Jacques. *Wagner Androgyne: A Study in Interpretation.* Trans. S. Spencer. Princeton University Press, 1997.

Neumann, Angelo. *Erinnerungen an Richard Wagner.* Leipzig: Staackmann, 1907; Trans. Edith Livermore. *Personal Recollections of Wagner.* London: Schirmer, 1908.

Newman, Ernest. *The Life of Richard Wagner,* 4 vols. First edn. 1933–47. London: Cassell, 1976.

Nietzsche, Friedrich. *"The Case of Wagner": Basic Writings of Nietzsche.* Trans. Walter Kaufmann. New York: Modern Library, 2000.

Selected Letters of Friedrich Nietzsche. Ed. and trans. Christopher Middleton. University of Chicago Press, 1969.

Oesterlein, Nikolaus. *Bayreuth: Eine Erinnerungsskizze.* Vienna: privately published, 1877.

Entwurf zu einem Richard Wagner-Museum. Vienna: A. J. Gutmann, 1884.

Katalog einer Richard Wagner-Bibliothek, 4 vols. Leipzig: Breitkopf & Härtel, 1882–95; repr. Wiesbaden: 1970.

Petzet, Detta and Michael Petzet. *Die Richard Wagner-Bühne König Ludwigs II.* Munich: Prestel, 1970.

Porges, Heinrich. *Das Bühnenfestspiel zu Bayreuth: Eine Studie über Richard Wagners Ring des Nibelungen.* Munich: Merhoff, 1877.

Die Bühnenproben zu den Bayreuther Festspielen des Jahres 1876, 4 vols. Chemnitz: Schmeitzner, 1881/2 / Leipzig: Siegismund & Volkening, 1896. Trans. Robert L. Jacobs. *Wagner Rehearsing the "Ring": An Eyewitness Account of the Stage Rehearsals of the First Bayreuth Festival.* Cambridge University Press, 1983.

Praeger, Ferdinand. *Wagner as I Knew Him.* London, 1892.

Rieger, Eva. *Leuchtende Liebe, lachender Tod.* Düsseldorf: Artemis, 2009. Trans. Chris Walton. *Richard Wagner's Women.* Woodbridge: Boydell, 2011.

Salmi, Hannu. *Die schriftstellerische und politische Tätigkeit Richard Wagners als Gestalter nationaler Identität während der staatlichen Vereinigung Deutschlands.* Turku: Turun Yliopisto, 1993.

Wagner and Wagnerism in Nineteenth-Century Sweden, Finland, and the Baltic Provinces. Rochester University Press, 2005.

Schoenberg, Arnold. *Style and Idea: Selected Writings.* Ed. Leonard Stein, trans. Leo Black. London: Faber & Faber, 1975.

Schüler, Winfried. *Der Bayreuther Kreis von seiner Entstehung bis zum Ausgang der Wilhelminischen Ära: Wagnerkult und Kulturreform im Geiste Völkischer Weltanschauung.* Münster: Aschendorff, 1971.

Scruton, Roger. *Death-Devoted Heart: Sex and the Sacred in Wagner's "Tristan und Isolde."* New York: Oxford University Press, 2004.

Shaw, George Bernard. *The Perfect Wagnerite: A Commentary on the Niblung's Ring.* 4th edn. London: Constable, 1923.

Sheffi, Na'ama. *The Ring of Myths: The Israelis, Wagner and the Nazis.* Trans. Martha Grenzeback. Brighton: Sussex Academic Press, 2001.

Smith, Matthew Wilson. *The Total Work of Art: From Bayreuth to Cyberspace.* New York: Routledge, 2007.

Sollich, Robert and Clemens Risi, et al., eds. *Angst vor der Zerstörung: Der Meister Künste zwischen Archiv und Erneuerung.* Berlin: Theater der Zeit, 2008.

Spencer, Stewart. *Wagner Remembered.* London: Faber & Faber, 2000.

Spotts, Frederic. *Bayreuth: A History of the Wagner Festival.* New Haven, CT: Yale University Press, 1994.

Stein, Jack. *Richard Wagner and the Synthesis of the Arts.* Detroit, MI: Wayne State University Press, 1960.

Tanner, Michael. *Wagner.* London: HarperCollins, 1996.

Tappert, Wilhelm. *Richard Wagner: Sein Leben und seine Werk.* Elberfeld: S. Lucas, 1883.

Ein Wagner-Lexikon: Wörterbuch der Unhöflichkeit [etc.] (Leipzig, 1877; revised and enlarged 1903 as *Richard Wagner im Spiegel der Kritik: Wörterbuch der Unhöflichkeit* [etc.], 1915).

Thorau, Christian. *Semantisierte Sinnlichkeit: Studien zu Rezeption und Zeichenstruktur der Leitmotivtechnik Richard Wagners.* Stuttgart: Franz Steiner, 2003.

Treadwell, James. *Interpreting Wagner.* New Haven, CT: Yale University Press, 2003.

Vazsonyi, Nicholas. *Richard Wagner: Self-Promotion and the Making of a Brand.* Cambridge University Press, 2010.

ed. *Wagner's "Meistersinger": Performance, History, Representation.* University of Rochester Press, 2003.

Voss, Egon. *Die Dirigenten der Bayreuther Festspiele.* Regensburg: Bosse, 1976.

Wagner, Friedelind, with Page Cooper. *Heritage of Fire: The Story of Richard Wagner's Granddaughter.* New York: Harper, 1945. UK edition, *The Royal Family of Bayreuth.* London: Eyre & Spottiswoode, 1948.

Wagner, Gottfried. *Wer nicht mit dem Wolf heult: Autobiographische Aufzeichnungen eines Wagner-Urenkels.* Cologne: Kiepenheuer & Witsch, 2010.

Wagner, Richard. *Richard Wagner Stories and Essays.* Ed. and intro. Charles Osborne. London: Peter Owen, 1973.

Three Wagner Essays. Trans. Robert L. Jacobs. Eulenberg: London, 1979.

Wagner Writes from Paris. Ed. and trans. Robert Jacobs and Geoffrey Skelton. London: Allen & Unwin, 1973.

Walton, Chris. *Richard Wagner's Zurich: The Muse of Place.* Rochester, NY: Camden House, 2007.

Warrack, John Hamilton. *Richard Wagner: "Die Meistersinger von Nürnberg."* Cambridge Opera Handbooks. Cambridge University Press, 1994.

Watson, Derek. *Richard Wagner: A Biography.* New York: Schirmer, 1981.

Weiner, Marc A. *Richard Wagner and the Anti-Semitic Imagination.* Lincoln: University of Nebraska Press, 1997.

Wolzogen, Hans von. *Thematischer Leitfaden durch die Musik zu Richard Wagner's Festspiel "Der Ring des Nibelungen."* Second revised edn. Leipzig: Edwin Schloemp, 1876.

Zelinsky, Hartmut. *Richard Wagner – ein deutsches Thema: Eine Dokumentation zur Wirkungsgeschichte Richard Wagners 1876–1976.* Third edn. Berlin: Medusa, 1983.

Index